AF732082

Land and Privilege in Byzantium

A pronoia was a type of conditional grant from the emperor, often to soldiers, of various properties and privileges. In large measure the institution of pronoia characterized social and economic relations in later Byzantium, and its study is the study of later Byzantium. Filling the need for a comprehensive study of the institution, this book examines the origin, evolution, and characteristics of pronoia, focusing particularly on the later thirteenth and fourteenth centuries. But the book is much more than a study of a single institution. With a broad chronological scope extending from the mid-tenth to the mid-fifteenth century, it incorporates the latest understanding of Byzantine agrarian relations, taxation, administration, and the economy, as it deals with relations between the emperor, monastic and lay landholders, including soldiers and peasants. Particular attention is paid to the relation between the pronoia and western European, Slavic, and Middle Eastern institutions, especially the Ottoman *timar.*

MARK C. BARTUSIS is Professor of History at Northern State University. He is an expert in later Byzantine political, social, and military history and author of *The Late Byzantine Army: Arms and Society, 1204–1453.*

Land and Privilege in Byzantium

The Institution of Pronoia

MARK C. BARTUSIS

CAMBRIDGE
UNIVERSITY PRESS

21 MAY 2013

333.16
BAR

CAMBRIDGE UNIVERSITY PRESS
Cambridge, New York, Melbourne, Madrid, Cape Town,
Singapore, São Paulo, Delhi, Mexico City

Cambridge University Press
The Edinburgh Building, Cambridge CB2 8RU, UK

Published in the United States of America by Cambridge University Press, New York

www.cambridge.org
Information on this title: www.cambridge.org/9781107009622

© Mark C. Bartusis 2012

This publication is in copyright. Subject to statutory exception
and to the provisions of relevant collective licensing agreements,
no reproduction of any part may take place without the written
permission of Cambridge University Press.

First published 2012

Printed and bound in the United Kingdom by the MPG Books Group

A catalogue record for this publication is available from the British Library

Library of Congress Cataloguing in Publication data
Bartusis, Mark C.
Land and privilege in Byzantium : the institution of pronoia / Mark C. Bartusis.
pages cm
Includes bibliographical references and index.
ISBN 978-1-107-00962-2
1. Byzantine Empire – Charters, grants, privileges. 2. Land grants – Byzantine Empire. 3. Land tenure – Byzantine Empire. 4. Social structure – Byzantine Empire. I. Title.
DF632.B37 2012
333.1′6 – dc23 2012010628
3364732

ISBN 978-1-107-00962-2 Hardback

Cambridge University Press has no responsibility for the persistence or
accuracy of URLs for external or third-party internet websites referred to
in this publication and does not guarantee that any content on such
websites is, or will remain, accurate or appropriate.

To Lyn

Contents

Maps

Figures

Tables

List of major sources

Because most of the documents and literary passages used in this book are referred to in more than one section, I have adopted a rudimentary cross-referencing system. In order to avoid duplication of explanations and citations, each major source (a document or literary passage) is described fully with complete citations in one primary location. Then, in other sections of the book where the source is discussed, a reference number in brackets refers the reader to the primary section dealing with the source.

[8.67] Chrysobull of Stefan Uroš II Milutin for the monastery of St. George near Skopje (1299/1300)
[8.68] Chrysobull of Michael IX Palaiologos for the monastery of Hilandar, and Chrysobull of Andronikos II Palaiologos for the monastery of Hilandar, mentioning the village of Banjane (both 1299–1300)
[8.69] Falsified act involving the monastery of Lavra's property on Lemnos (mid-fifteenth century)
[8.70] Chrysobull of Andronikos II Palaiologos for the monastery of Vrontochiou at Mistra (February 1320)
[8.71] *Periorismoi* of Demetrios Apelmene for the monastery of Lavra (1300), and *Periorismoi* of Constantine Pergamenos and George Pharisaios for the monastery of Lavra (1321)
[8.72] Slavic translation of a praktikon for the monastery of Hilandar (1300)
[8.73] Act of the *apographeus* Nikephoros Choumnos for the monastery of Zographou involving Gazes, a soldier from the Thessalonian *mega allagion* (1286)
[8.74] *Prostagma* of Andronikos III for the benefit of the monastery of Asomatoi near Zichna involving an *epiteleia* paid to Preakotzelos (1333)
[8.75] Chrysobull of Andronikos II Palaiologos for the monastery of St. John Prodromos (September 1317), *Prostagma* of Andronikos II Palaiologos to a fiscal official (April 1325), *Prostagma* of Andronikos II Palaiologos to a fiscal official (November 1325), and *Orismos* of Andronikos III Palaiologos to a fiscal official (1327), regarding the *agridion* of Monospeton
[8.76] Chrysobull of Andronikos III Palaiologos for the monastery of Zographou regarding the oikonomia of the *sevastos* Devlitzenos (1328)
[8.77] Greek chrysobull of Symeon Uroš for the monastery of St. George in Zavlantia (1359)
[8.78] Chrysobull of John V Palaiologos for the *stratopedarches* of the *monokavalloi* John Choumnos (1344)
[9.1] *Prostagma* of Manuel II Palaiologos for the monasteries of Mount Athos (1408)
[9.2] *Prostagma* of Manuel II Palaiologos for two Thessalonian monasteries (1415)
[9.3] Act of Paul Gazes and George Prinkips for the monastery of Docheiariou (1409)

Acknowledgments

With numerous interruptions, the research and writing of this book were conducted over a twenty-year period during which time I was the recipient of material support from several institutions and organizations. An Andrew W. Mellon Faculty Fellowship at Harvard University, a National Endowment for the Humanities Fellowship at the American School of Classical Studies at Athens, a Dumbarton Oaks Summer Fellowship, and a National Endowment for the Humanities Fellowship for College Teachers and Independent Scholars afforded me access to library materials and respite from my teaching responsibilities. A Faculty Development Grant, a Nora Staael Evert Summer Research Grant, and a Faculty Travel Grant, all from Northern State University, along with sabbatical leave, were appreciated. As always, the librarians of Northern State University were most helpful in facilitating my work. And finally, to the friends and colleagues and family who offered advice or a sympathetic ear, thanks much, really.

A note on transliteration, pronunciation, and dates

Byzantine Greek is a challenge to transliterate. In the interest of standardization, I have transliterated most Greek (as well as Slavic and Turkish) technical terms and names of people and places according to the form in which they appear in the *Oxford Dictionary of Byzantium* (1991), the editors of which have adopted a system for Greek that uses a modified letter-for-letter approach ("a" for *alpha*, "b" for *beta*) but employs common English forms wherever they are well established ("Constantine" rather than "Konstantinos"). I depart from the *ODB* when I transliterate the letter *beta*. In the period this book deals with (the eleventh through the fifteenth centuries), *beta* was generally pronounced like a "v." Thus, throughout the book, I have opted for the transliteration that better represents the sound of medieval Greek. And so, "Glavas" rather than the *ODB*'s "Glabas," and "Vryennios" rather than "Bryennios," and in technical terms "*sevastos*" rather than "*sebastos*." There are a handful of exceptions, such as "Bosporos," "Bulgaria," "Botaneiates," and of course "Byzantium."

Even though Byzantine Greek sounded much like modern Greek, scholars sometimes pronounce it as if it were ancient Greek or some mixture of ancient and modern. The *ODB* system of transliteration, while it has the virtue of simplicity and is rather faithful to the spelling of Greek, is quite misleading in regard to pronunciation (for which it offers no assistance). Consequently, and with no claim to be doing justice to the complexities of the medieval Greek language, I provide a few general rules here to help the reader approximate the later Byzantine pronunciations of the strange names and terms that appear in this book.

o is always long as in *low*

ei, *i*, *oi*, *y*, and the final *e* are all pronounced as *ee* in *tree* (thus, two of the most commonly used words in this book, *pronoia* and *oikonomia*, are pronounced "PRO-nee-ah" and "ee-ko-no-MEE-ah")

-es at the end of words (Metochites, *vestiarites*) is pronounced as *eece* in *Greece*, except in plural forms (*praktores*, *posotetes*), where it is pronounced as *ess* in *less*

au and *eu* are respectively pronounced "af" and "ef" before a consonant and "av" and "ev" before another vowel
ch is pronounced as in the Scottish *loch* or German *nach*
d is pronounced as *th* in *then*
g between two vowels is pronounced as the *y* in *mayor*
h at the beginning of a word is silent
rh is pronounced as *r*

In Slavic words, *c* is pronounced "ts," *č* and *ć* are pronounced "ch," *dj* is pronounced as the *j* in *judge*, *j* is pronounced as the *y* in *yellow*, *š* is pronounced "sh," and *ž* is pronounced "zh" as in *measure* and *vision*. For the handful of Turkish words that appear in these pages, it is perhaps worth noting that *c* is pronounced as the *j* in *judge*, *ç* is pronounced "ch,"and *ş* is pronounced "sh."

Dates

The Byzantine year began on September 1. A few dates are cited in the form "1267/8," which signifies the period from September 1, 1267, to August 31, 1268.

Abbreviations

Ahrweiler, *Byzance et la mer*	Hélène Ahrweiler, *Byzance et la mer: la marine de guerre, la politique et les institutions maritimes de Byzance aux* VII*ᵉ*–XV*ᵉ* *siècles*. Paris: Presses Universitaires de France, 1966.
Ahrweiler, "La concession des droits incorporels"	Hélène Glykatzi-Ahrweiler, "La concession des droits incorporels, Donations conditionelles." *Actes du* XII*ᵉ* *Congrès international d'études byzantines, Ohrid 1961*, II, 103–14. Belgrade, 1964. Repr. in H. Ahrweiler, *Études sur les structures*, no. I
Ahrweiler, "La 'pronoia' à Byzance"	Hélène Ahrweiler, "La 'pronoia' à Byzance," 681–89. In *Structures féodales et féodalisme dans l'occident méditerranéen (*X*ᵉ*–XIII*ᵉ* *s.)*. Collection de l'école française de Rome 44. Rome: École française de Rome, 1980
Ahrweiler, "Smyrne"	H. Ahrweiler, "L'histoire et la géographie de la région de Smyrne entre les deux occupations turques (1081–1317) particulièrement au XIIIᵉ siècle." *TM* 1 (1965), 1–204. Repr. in Ahrweiler, *Byzance: les pays et les territoires*. London: Variorum Reprints, 1976, no. IV
Alexiad ed. Leib	*Anne Comnène, Alexiade. Règne de l'empereur Alexis I Comnène 1081–1118*. Ed. Bernard Leib. 3 vols. Paris: Société d'édition "Les Belles Lettres," 1937–45
Alexiad ed. Reinsch	*Annae Comnenae Alexias*. Part 1: Prolegomena and Text. Ed. Diether R. Reinsch and Athanasios Kambylis. CFHB 40/1. Berlin and New York: W. de Gruyter, 2001

Bartusis, *Late Byzantine Army*	Mark Bartusis, *The Late Byzantine Army: Arms and Society, 1204–1453.* Philadelphia: University of Pennsylvania Press, 1992
Bartusis, "Smallholding Soldiers"	Mark Bartusis, "On the Problem of Smallholding Soldiers in Late Byzantium." *Dumbarton Oaks Papers* 44 (1990), 1–26.
Byz	*Byzantion.* Brussels, 1924–
BZ	*Byzantinische Zeitschrift.* Leipzig, Munich, 1892ff.
CFHB	Corpus Fontium Historiae Byzantinae
Charanis, "Monastic Properties"	Peter Charanis, "The Monastic Properties and the State in the Byzantine Empire." *Dumbarton Oaks Papers* 4 (1948), 51–118. Repr. in Charanis, *Social, Economic and Political Life in the Byzantine Empire,* no. I
Charanis, "Social Structure"	Peter Charanis, "On the Social Structure and Economic Organization of the Byzantine Empire in the Thirteenth Century and Later." *Byzantinoslavica* 12 (1951), 94–153. Repr. in Charanis, *Social, Economic and Political Life in the Byzantine Empire,* no. IV
Chilandar ed. Petit	*Actes de Chilandar, I. Actes grecs* ed. Louis Petit. *VizVrem* 17 (1911), suppl. 1. Repr. Amsterdam: Hakkert, 1975
Chilandar ed. Živojinović	*Actes de Chilandar I: des origines à 1319* ed. Mirjana Živojinović, Vasiliki Kravari, Christophe Giros. Archives de l'Athos XX. Paris: Éditions du CNRS and P. Lethielleux, 1998
Choniates, Bonn edn.	Choniates, Niketas, *Nicetae Choniatae Historia.* Ed. I. Bekker. CSHB. Bonn, 1835
Choniates, ed. van Dieten	Choniates, Niketas, *Nicetae Choniatae Historia.* Ed. Jan L. van Dieten. CFHB. Berlin: W. de Gruyter, 1975
CSHB	Corpus Scriptorum Historiae Byzantinae, 50 vols. Bonn, 1828–97
Dionysiou	*Actes de Dionysiou,* ed. Nicolas Oikonomides. Archives de l'Athos IV. Paris: P. Lethielleux, 1968

Docheiariou	*Actes de Docheiariou*, ed. Nicolas Oikonomides. Archives de l'Athos XIII. Paris: P. Lethielleux, 1984
Dölger, *Beiträge*	Franz Dölger, *Beiträge zur Geschichte des byzantinischen Finanzverwaltung besonders des 10. und 11. Jahrhunderts*. Byzantinisches Archiv 9. Leipzig and Berlin: Teubner, 1927; repr. Hildesheim: G. Olms, 1960
Dölger, *Regesten*	*Regesten der Kaiserurkunden des oströmischen Reiches von 565–1453*. Corpus der griechischen Urkunden des Mittelalters und der neueren Zeit, Reihe A, Abt. I: Regesten der Kaiserurkunden des Oströmischen Reiches. 1. Teil: *Regesten von 565–1025*, 2nd edn., ed. F. Dölger and Andreas E. Müller; 2. Teil: *Regesten von 1025–1204*, 2nd edn. and 3. Teil: *Regesten von 1204–1282*, 2nd edn., ed. F. Dölger and Peter Wirth; 4. Teil: *Regesten von 1282–1341*, and 5. Teil: *Regesten von 1341–1453*, ed. F. Dölger. Munich: C. H. Beck, 2009, 1995, 1977, 1960, 1965
EHB	*The Economic History of Byzantium, from the Seventh through the Fifteenth Century*, ed. Angeliki E. Laiou. 3 vols. Dumbarton Oaks Studies XXXIX. Washington, D.C.: Dumbarton Oaks, 2002
Esphigménou	*Actes d'Esphigménou* ed. Jacques Lefort. Archives de l'Athos VI. Paris: P. Lethielleux, 1973
Gregoras	*Nicephori Gregorae Byzantina Historia*, ed. L. Schopen. 3 vols. CSHB. Bonn, 1829, 1830, 1855
Hohlweg, "Zur Frage der Pronoia"	Armin Hohlweg, "Zur Frage der Pronoia in Byzanz." *BZ* 60 (1967), 288–308
Hvostova, *Osobennosti*	Ksenia V. Hvostova, *Osobennosti agrarnopravovyh otnošenij v pozdnej Vizantii XIV–XV vv*. Moscow: Akademija nauk, 1968
IRAIK	*Izvestija Russkogo arheologičeskago instituta v Konstantinopole*

Iviron	*Actes d'Iviron* I–IV, ed. Jacques Lefort, Nicolas Oikonomides, Denise Papachryssanthou, Vassiliki Kravari, Hélène Métrévéli. Archives de l'Athos XIV, XVI, XVIII, XIX. Paris: P. Lethielleux, 1985, 1990, 1994, 1995
JÖB	*Jahrbuch der Österreichischen Byzantinistik (byzantinischen Gesellschaft)*. Vienna, 1951–
Kantakouzenos	*Ioannis Cantacuzeni eximperatoris historiarum libri IV*. 3 vols. Vol. 1, ed. L. Schopen; vols. 2, 3, ed. B. Niehbuhr. CSHB. Bonn, 1828, 1831, 1832
Kazhdan, *Agrarnye otnošenija*	A. P. Kazhdan, *Agrarnye otnošenija v Vizantii, XIII–XIV vv*. Moscow: Akademija nauk, 1952
Kazhdan, *Derevnja i gorod*	A. P. Kazhdan, *Derevnja i gorod v Vizantii IX–X vv*. Moscow, 1960
Kazhdan, "Formen"	A. P. Kazhdan, "Formen des bedingten Eigentums in Byzanz während des x.–XII. Jahrhunderts." *Byzantinisch-Neugriechische Jahrbücher* 19 (1966), 217–24 = "Formy uslovnoj sobstvennosti v Vizantii v X–XII vv." *XXV. Meždunarodnyj kongress vostokovedov, Doklady delegacii SSSR* (Moscow, 1960)
Kutlumus	*Actes de Kutlumus*, ed. Paul Lemerle. Archives de l'Athos II, 2d edn. Paris: P. Lethielleux, 1988.
Lavra	*Actes de Lavra* I–IV, ed. Paul Lemerle, André Guillou, Nicolas Svoronos, Denise Papachryssanthou, Sima Ćirković. Archives de l'Athos V, VIII, X, XI. Paris: P. Lethielleux, 1970–82
Lefort, *Villages de Macédoine*	Jacques Lefort, *Villages de Macédoine. Notices historiques et topographiques sur la Macédoine orientale au Moyen Age: 1. La Chalcidique occidentale.* Travaux et Mémoires du Centre de Recherche d'Histoire et Civilisation de Byzance, Monographies 1. Paris: Diffusion de Boccard, 1982

Lemerle, *Agrarian History*	Paul Lemerle, *The Agrarian History of Byzantium from the Origins to the Twelfth Century: The Sources and Problems.* Galway: Galway University Press, 1979
Lemerle, *Cinq études*	Paul Lemerle, *Cinq études sur le* xie *siècle byzantin.* Paris: Centre National de la Recherche Scientifique, 1977
Migne, *PG*	J.-P. Migne. *Patrologiae cursus completus. Series graeca,* 161 vols. Paris, 1857–66
MM	Franz Miklosich and J. Müller, *Acta et diplomata Graeca medii aevi sacra et profana.* 6 vols. Vienna, 1860–90
Mutafčiev, "Vojniški zemi"	Petar Mutafčiev, "Vojniški zemi i vojnici v Vizantija prez xiii–xiv v." *Spisanie na Bŭlgarskata Akademija na naukite,* Kniga 27, Klon istoriko-filologičen i filosofsko obščestven 15 (Sofia, 1923), 1–113; repr. in P. Mutafčiev, *Izbrani proizvedenija,* i (Sofia, 1973), 518–652
Oikonomides, *Fiscalité*	Nicolas Oikonomides, *Fiscalité et exemption fiscale à Byzance (*ixe*–*xie *s.).* Fondation Nationale de la Recherche Scientifique, Institut de Recherches Byzantines. Monographies 2. Athens, 1996
Oikonomides, "A propos des armées"	N. Oikonomides, "A propos des armées des premiers Palèologues et des compagnies de soldats." *TM* 8 (1981), 353–71. Repr. in Oikonomides, *Society, Culture and Politics in Byzantium,* no. xvi
ODB	*The Oxford Dictionary of Byzantium,* ed. A. P. Kazhdan et al. 3 vols. New York: Oxford University Press, 1991
Ostrogorsky, *Féodalité*	G. Ostrogorsky, *Pour l'histoire de la féodalité byzantine.* Corpus bruxellense historiae byzantinae, Subsidia i. Brussels: Institut de philologie et d'histoire orientales et slaves, 1954
Ostrogorsky, "Die Pronoia unter den Komnenen"	G. Ostrogorsky, "Die Pronoia unter den Komnenen." *ZRVI* 12 (1970), 41–54

Pachymeres, ed. Failler	*Georges Pachymérès, Relations historiques*, CFHB 24. Vols. 1–2, ed. Albert Failler, French trans. Vitalien Laurent. Paris: Société d'édition "Les Belles Lettres," 1984. Vols. 3–4, ed. and trans. Albert Failler. Paris: Institut Français d'Études Byzantines, 1999. Vol. 5: Index, ed. Albert Failler. Paris: Institut Français d'Études Byzantines, 2000
Pachymeres, Bonn edn.	*Georgii Pachymeris de Michaele et Andronico Palaeologis*, ed. I. Bekker. 2 vols. CSHB. Bonn, 1835
Pantéléèmôn	*Actes de Saint-Pantéléèmôn*, ed. Paul Lemerle, Gilbert Dagron, Sima Ćirković. Archives de l'Athos XII. Paris: P. Lethielleux, 1982
Patmos, I	Era Vranouse, *Βυζαντινὰ ἔγγραφα τῆς μονῆς Πάτμου*, I: *Αὐτοκρατορικά*. Athens: Ethnika Idryma Ereunon, 1980
Patmos, II	Maria Nystazopoulou-Pelekidou, *Βυζαντινὰ ἔγγραφα τῆς μονῆς Πάτμου*, II: *Δημοσίων λειτουργιῶν*. Athens: Ethnika Idryma Ereunon, 1980
PLP	Erich Trapp, Rainer Walther, Hans-Veit Beyer, *Prosopographisches Lexikon der Palaiologenzeit*. Vienna: Österreichische Akademie der Wissenschaften, 1976–96. CD-ROM version, 2001
Prodrome	*Les archives de Saint-Jean-Prodrome sur le mont Ménécée*, ed. André Guillou. Paris: Presses Universitaires de France, 1955
Prodrome B	*Le codex B du monastère Saint-Jean-Prodrome (Serrès)*. 2 volumes. *A: XIIIe–XVe siècles*, ed. Lisa Bénou. *B: XVe–XIXe siècles* ed. Paolo Odorico. Textes, Documents, Études sur le Monde Byzantin, Néohellénique et Balkanique. Paris: Association Pierre Belon, 1998
Prôtaton	*Actes du Prôtaton*, ed. Denise Papachryssanthou. Archives de l'Athos VII. Paris: P. Lethielleux, 1975
REB	*Revue des Études Byzantines*. Paris, 1949–

SAN(U)	Srpska Akademija Nauka (i Umetnosti)
SnM	Vladimir Mošin, Lidija Slaveva, et al. *Spomenici za srednovekovnata i ponovata istorija na Makedonija*, i–iii. Skopje: Arhiv na Makedonija, 1975–80. Vol. iv. Skopje: Institut za istražuvanje na staroslovenskata kultura, 1981. Vol. v. Prilep: Institut za istražuvanje na staroslovenskata kultura, 1988
Solovjev–Mošin, *Grčke povelje*	Aleksandar Solovjev and Vladimir Mošin, *Grčke povelje srpskih vladara.* Srpska Kraljevska Akademija, Zbornik za istoriju, jezik i književnost srpskog naroda, treće odeljenje, knjiga 7. Belgrade, 1936; repr. London: Variorum Reprints, 1974
TLG	*Thesaurus Linguae Graecae.* University of California, Irvine, 1985–. CD-ROM "E" and online database: <www.tlg.uci.edu>
TM	*Travaux et Mémoires du Centre de Recherche d'Histoire et Civilisation de Byzance.* Paris, 1965–
Uspenskij, "Značenie"	Fedor I. Uspenskij, "Značenie vizantijskoj i južnoslavjanskoj pronii." *Sbornik statej po slavjanovedeniju, sostavlennyj i izdannyj učenikami V. I. Lamanskogo*, 1–32. St. Petersburg, 1883
Vatopédi	*Actes de Vatopédi i–ii*, ed. Jacques Bompaire, Jacques Lefort, Vassiliki Kravari, Christophe Giros, Kostis Smyrlis. Archives de l'Athos xxi–xxii. Paris: P. Lethielleux, 2001, 2006
VizVrem	*Vizantijskij Vremennik.* St. Petersburg, 1894–1927. New series, Moscow and Leningrad, 1947–
Xénophon	*Actes de Xénophon*, ed. Denise Papachryssanthou. Archives de l'Athos xv. Paris: P. Lethielleux, 1986
Xéropotamou	*Actes de Xéropotamou*, ed. Jacques Bompaire. Archives de l'Athos iii. Paris: P. Lethielleux, 1964

Zachariä, *Jus*	C. E. Zachariä von Lingenthal, *Jus Greco-romanum*, 4 vols. Leipzig, 1856–84
Zepos, *JGR*	J. and P. Zepos, *Jus graecoromanum*. 8 vols. Athens: G. Fexis, 1931; repr. Aalen: Scientia, 1962
Zographou	*Actes de Zographou, I. Actes grecs*, ed. W. Regel, E. Kurtz, and B. Korablev. *VizVrem* 13 (1907), suppl. 1. Repr. Amsterdam: Hakkert, 1969
ZRVI	*Zbornik radova Vizantološkog instituta*. Belgrade, 1952ff.
ŽMNP	*Žurnal Ministerstva narodnogo prosveščenija*. St. Petersburg, 1834–1917

Glossary

For terms not listed here, see the Index.

anagrapheus (before 1204), *apographeus* (after 1204)	fiscal assessor
archon	a general term for a member of the ruling class broadly conceived, including the leading citizens of a town
charistike	a grant of a religious foundation, usually a monastery, by any number of persons (emperor, patriarch, bishop, state official, founder of the institution) to a laymen for life or two or three generations, by which the recipient agreed to manage the finances of the foundation in return for which he was permitted to draw an income
choraphion	a general term for a field
chrysovoullaton	an adjective denoting something, usually property
chrysobull	the most formal imperial document, so named because of the gold seal (*chryse voulla*) attached to it
despot (*despotes*)	a title second in precedence only to that of emperor, usually held by sons or brothers of the emperor; also held by the semi-independent rulers of the Byzantine Morea and applied to other rulers in the southern Balkans; for most of the late period, with slight variations over time, the first twelve court titles after that of emperor were despot, *sevastokrator*, caesar, *panhypersevastos*, *protovestiarios*, *megas doux*, *megas domestikos*,

	protostrator, *megas logothetes*, *megas stratopedarches*, *megas primmikerios*, and *megas konostaulos*
dioiketes	originally a fiscal official, a title encountered only rarely after the eleventh century
domestikos of the *scholai*	originally commander of a bodyguard, by the eleventh century a commander-in-chief of the army, and by the fourteenth century a somewhat elevated honorary title
domestikos of the themes	a humble court title originally connected with theme finances
doux	originally a military commander, in the twelfth and thirteenth centuries often held by provincial fiscal officials
eparchos	a somewhat elevated court title with no fixed function
episkepsis	imperial estate
hyperpyron, pl. hyperpyra	the name for the basic late Byzantine gold coin, equivalent to the *nomisma*; as with the Roman *solidus* there were seventy-two to the pound, although, due to frequent debasement, its value steadily declined
hegoumenos	the superior of a monastery
hetaireiarches	originally denoting the head of the *hetaireia*, an imperial bodyguard, by the fourteenth century it was a lowly court title
hypostasis	(see *stasis*)
indiction	a year in a fifteen-year cycle, originally established by Constantine I, for the collection of a special tax levied for a limited number of years; eventually the term acquired merely a chronological sense as a means by which to date documents, i.e., every Byzantine year (September 1 to August 31) corresponded to a number between 1 and 15
judge of the army	a middling court title with no fixed function
kaisar (caesar)	in the twelfth century, a high title often granted to foreigners

kastron, pl. *kastra*	the most common designation for a fortified town. The word could also be applied to almost any fortification including the walls of Constantinople
kastrophylax	"castle-guard," the official responsible for the upkeep of a town's fortifications and for organizing the watch
katepanikion	a provincial unit usually consisting of a *kastron* and its environs
kavallarios	from the Latin *caballarius*, "knight," a semi-official title applied to certain western Europeans in imperial service, to certain native Byzantine warriors, and also, from the late fourteenth century, to certain high-ranking Byzantine assistants to the emperor
klasma, pl. *klasmata*	through the twelfth century, rural property that, after time, reverted to the fisc through non-payment of taxes
kommerkion	the basic tax on merchandise
kyr	an unofficial title of respect corresponding to "Mister" (for women, *kyra*)
logariastes	any of a variety financial officials serving the state, monasteries, or private persons
logariastes of the court	in the fourteenth century, a courtly title of modest rank
mega allagion, pl. *megala allagia*	a provincial military unit
megale doukaina	wife of a *megas doux*
megaloallagites	a member of a *mega allagion*
megalodoxotatos	"exceedingly most glorious," an unofficial epithet
megas	"grand"
megas adnoumiastes	a court title of middling status with no fixed function, ostensibly connected with the muster lists of the army
megas chartoularios	a rather high-ranking title with no fixed function

megas dioiketes	a court title of middling status with no fixed function, ostensibly connected with fiscal matters
megas domestikos	a high-ranking court title, often held by the commander-in-chief of the army
megas doux	"grand duke," a high-ranking court title, held during the twelfth and thirteenth centuries by the commander of the navy, but later often denoting no fixed function, frequently granted as an honorary title to important foreigners
megas konostaulos	"grand constable," a high-ranking court title which first appears in the mid-thirteenth century, often held by military leaders
megas logothetes	a high-ranking court title, sometimes held by the first minister of the empire
megas papias	a somewhat elevated court title with no fixed function
megas primmikerios (or *primikerios*)	a high-ranking title with no fixed function
megas stratopedarches	a high-ranking title, created in the mid-thirteenth century, with no fixed function; *stratopedarchai* were originally military commanders
metochion	a usually small, dependent monastic establishment subordinate to a larger monastery
modios	the standard Byzantine unit of area, equivalent to about one-quarter of an acre or 1,000 m^2; also a unit of capacity
nomisma, pl. nomismata	the earlier name for the hyperpyron
oikeios	"familiar, kin," an appellation indicating a personal relationship to someone, especially the emperor. An individual who signed a document as "*doulos* (slave) of the emperor" was usually addressed by the emperor as "*oikeios* of my Majesty"
orismos	a type of imperial document usually issuing a command; equivalent to a *prostagma*

panhypersevastos	in the fourteenth century, a very high court title
pansevastos	literally, "all-august," an honorary epithet
parakoimomenos	lit. "sleeping at the side," i.e., of the emperor; a high office in the tenth and eleventh centuries, often held by eunuchs
parakoimomenos of the *megale sphendone*	a court title of high status, attested from the reign of Michael VIII Palaiologos onward, ostensibly held by an official entrusted with the "great seal" for making wax sealings
periorismos	a detailed description of the borders of a property, sometimes with measurements
pinkernes	"cup-bearer," a relatively elevated title in the thirteenth and fourteenth centuries
praktikon	the primary form of tax records in late Byzantium, an inventory listing the taxes, property, and peasant households held by an individual or religious institution
proasteion	lit. "suburb," but from the tenth century a rural estate; some properties called *proasteia* are later referred to as villages (*choria*)
pronoiar	holder of a pronoia, a modern term derived from the relatively rare Byzantine term *pronoiarios*
proskathemenos	lit. "settlers," a category of peasant
prostagma, prostaxis	(see *orismos*)
protasekretis	a somewhat elevated court title with no fixed function, originally denoting the first of the imperial secretaries
protokynegos	literally "first huntsman," a court title of middling status with no fixed function
protonovelissimos	lit. "first most noble," a rather uncommon dignity of very modest status
proedros, protoproedros	titles of rank, granted rather frequently in the eleventh century
protos	the elected head of the monastic community on Mount Athos

protosevastos	a high-ranking court title
protostrator	originally the head of the imperial guard called the *stratores*; by the twelfth century a high official, and in the fourteenth century a high-ranking court title often held by military commanders
protovestiarios	a very high court title
protovestiarites	lit. "first of the *vestiaritai*," a high-ranking court title first appearing in the thirteenth century
protovestiaritissa	wife of a *protovestiarites*
senate (*synkletos*)	a general term for the aristocracy, especially in Constantinople
sevastokrator	a very high title, created by Alexios I Komnenos, subordinate in precedence only to that of despot and emperor, held by close relatives of the emperor and also, in the fourteenth century, by the rulers of Thessaly
sevastos	"august," an honorary epithet
skouterios	literally "shield-bearer," a court title of middling status, attested during the thirteenth and fourteenth centuries, and sometimes held by military leaders
stasis or *stasion* (pl. *staseis*, *stasia*)	the taxable property of a property owner, usually a peasant, upon which the *telos* was based
stratopedarches of the *allagia*, *stratopedarches* of the *monokavalloi*	court titles of modest status, ostensibly military commanders
syr	the Greek transliteration of "Sir," occasionally found preceding or attached to (e.g., Syrgares) the names of certain western Europeans in Byzantine service
telos	the basic tax on agricultural land including the *staseis* of peasants
theme	the technical term for a large provincial administrative unit
typikon	the foundation charter of a monastery

tzaousios	a military officer often associated with the *megala allagia*
universal judges	a supreme judicial tribunal created by Andronikos II Palaiologos
vasilissa	a title applied to the wives of rulers, especially the despots in Epiros and in the Morea
vestiarites	a court title of modest rank
world year	year since Creation; by the tenth century, the year of Creation had been fixed at 5508 BC
zeugelateion	a rural estate

List of rulers

Rulers not mentioned in the text are omitted.

Byzantine emperors

920–44	Romanos I Lekapenos
945–59	Constantine VII Porphyrogennetos
959–63	Romanos II
963–69	Nikephoros II Phokas (co-emperor)
969–76	John I Tzimiskes
976–1025	Basil II
1028–34	Romanos III Argyros
1034–41	Michael IV Paphlagon
1042–55	Constantine IX Monomachos
1057–59	Isaac I Komnenos
1059–67	Constantine X Doukas
1068–71	Romanos IV Diogenes
1071–78	Michael VII Doukas
1078–81	Nikephoros III Botaneiates
1081–1118	Alexios I Komnenos
1118–43	John II Komnenos
1143–80	Manuel I Komnenos
1180–83	Alexios II Komnenos
1183–85	Andronikos I Komnenos
1185–95	Isaac II Angelos
1195–1203	Alexios III Angelos
1203–04	Isaac II Angelos (again) and Alexios IV Angelos
1205–21	Theodore I Laskaris
1221–54	John III Vatatzes
1254–58	Theodore II Laskaris
1258–61	John IV Laskaris

1259–82	Michael VIII Palaiologos
1282–1328	Andronikos II Palaiologos
1294/5–1320	Michael IX Palaiologos (co-emperor)
1328–41	Andronikos III Palaiologos
1341–91	John V Palaiologos
1347–54	John VI Kantakouzenos
1353–57	Matthew Kantakouzenos (co-emperor)
1376–79	Andronikos IV Palaiologos
1390	John VII Palaiologos
1391–1425	Manuel II Palaiologos
1425–48	John VIII Palaiologos
1449–53	Constantine XI Palaiologos

Rulers in Epiros

ca. 1215–30	Theodore Komnenos Doukas, emperor in Thessaloniki from 1224/5
ca. 1230–67/8	Michael II Komnenos Doukas, despot from ca. 1250
1323–36/7	John II Orsini, despot
1356–58 or 59	Nikephoros II, despot
1358 or 1359–after 1369	Symeon Uroš, despot

Rulers in Thessaloniki

1224/5–1230	Theodore Komnenos Doukas, emperor
1230–ca. 1237	Manuel Angelos, despot and emperor

Despots in the Morea

1349–80	Manuel Kantakouzenos
1380–83	Matthew Kantakouzenos
1407–43	Theodore II Palaiologos
1428–49	Constantine Palaiologos
1428–60	Thomas Palaiologos
1449–60	Demetrios Palaiologos

Emperors of Trebizond

1332–40	Basil I Komnenos
1349–90	Alexios III Komnenos

Rulers of Serbia

1282–21	Stefan Uroš II Milutin
1321–31	Stefan Uroš III Dečanski
1331–55	Stefan Dušan, emperor from 1345
1355–71	Stefan Uros V
(1365–71	King Vukašin)
1371–89	Prince Lazar
1389–1427	Stefan Lazarević, despot from 1402
1427–56	George Branković, despot from 1429

Tsars of Bulgaria

1279–80	John Asen III

Ottoman Turkish Rulers

1288–1326	Osman
1326–62	Orhan
1362–89	Murad I
1389–1402	Bayezid I
1402–21	Mehmed I
1402–11	Süleyman Çelebi
1421–51	Murad II
1451–81	Mehmed II the Conqueror

Map 1 The Byzantine Empire at the death of Basil II

Map 2 Greece and Macedonia

Map 3 Asia Minor and Thrace

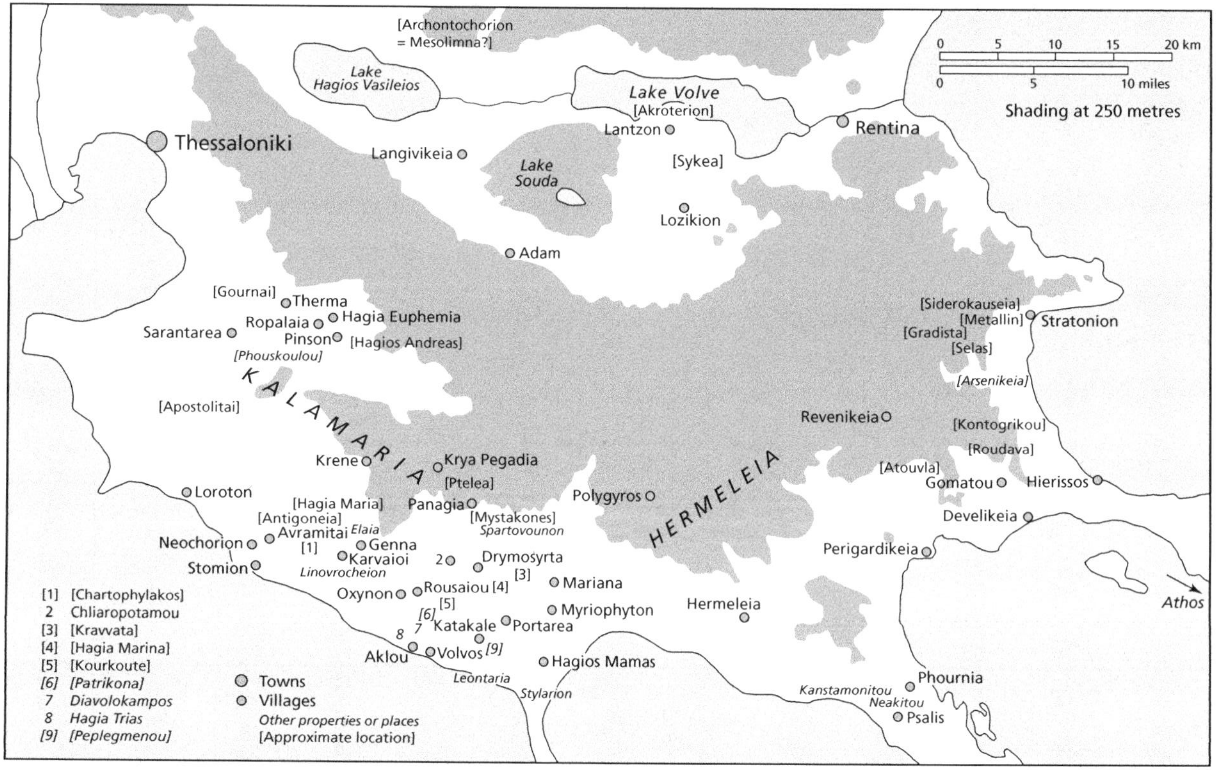

Map 4 The Chalkidike

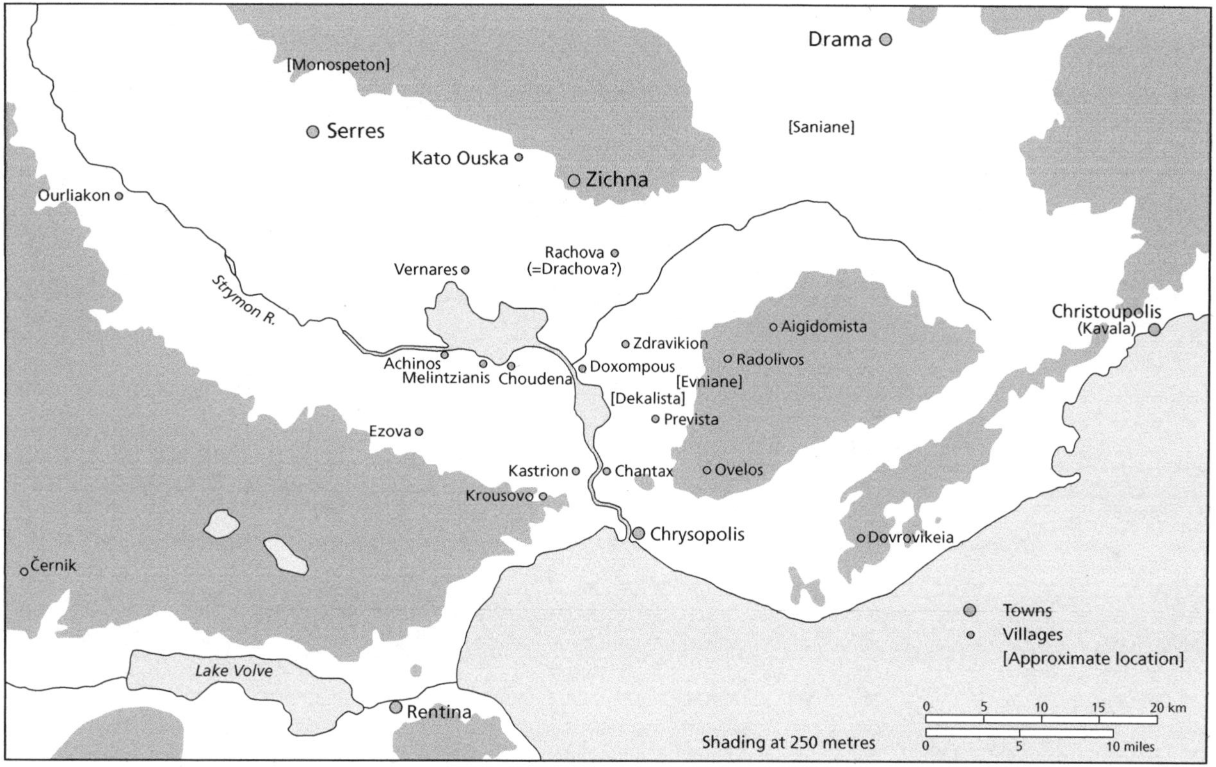

Map 5 The Strymon valley

Introduction

This is a book about the Byzantine institution of pronoia: what it was, how it originated, how it changed over time, and the effect it had on society. A pronoia was a type of grant, conferred by the Byzantine emperor from the twelfth century through the end of the empire in the fifteenth century. The term itself – *pronoia* (πρόνοια, pronounced *PRO-nee-ah*) – is a relatively common Greek word that usually means "care," "providence," "foresight." However, in certain contexts it denotes something much more specific. A few examples from the documentary sources illustrate this use of the word *pronoia*:

- In 1234 a group of monks complained to the emperor about being forced to pay taxes on a fish pond to a certain Constantine Kalegopoulos because "all the fish ponds there pay taxes to Kalegopoulos, since he holds in pronoia the rights of the river" *[5.7]*.
- A document from 1251, notes that, in order to resolve a property dispute, a soldier had convened an assembly of "all the head men of his pronoia" *[5.9]*.
- An early fourteenth-century book of mathematical problems includes one about four soldiers who had "an imperial pronoia of 600" gold coins *[8.8]*.
- In a document from 1314 two men donate some fields they held "pronoiastically" to a monastery. They state that the donation was to be valid "as long as our pronoia is held by us" *[8.55]*.[1]
- An act from 1228 describes the killing of a peasant by a man whom he had insulted. The man said he was astonished "that a peasant spoke with such impudence, shooting forth bold words toward me his *pronoiarios*" *[5.16]*.

The narrative sources also use *pronoia* in this sense:

- In the later thirteenth century the historian Theodore Skoutariotes, addressing the policies of the emperors around the middle of the

[1] Because much of the source material useful to this study is cited more than once, as a way of facilitating cross-referencing I have given some sources a number *[in brackets]* indicating the chapter and position within the chapter in which the source is presented most fully.

century, wrote, "And from this all of the taxpayers became wealthy, and those of the military lists and the magnates had many times larger revenues from the pronoiai and properties and many times the incomes supplied to them for sustenance" *[5.13]*.

- In the early fourteenth century the historian George Pachymeres writes that, after coming to the throne, Emperor Michael VIII Palaiologos (1259–82) allowed soldiers to transmit their pronoiai to their children, even if they were as yet unborn: "Loving the soldiery exceedingly, he established the pronoiai of these, should they fall in battle and die, as patrimonial property to the children, even if, for some, the mothers should have the fetus in the womb" *[6.10]*.
- In another passage Pachymeres explains that Emperor Andronikos II Palaiologos, in order to finance a military campaign in 1283, had levied a special 10 percent tax: "This was the tenth of the pronoia of those having pronoiai. While it was collected ostensibly from the rights of the lords, the peasants of the powerful paid everything" *[8.34]*.
- In a letter to the emperor Patriarch Athanasios I (1289–93, 1303–09) complained about bishops who had abandoned their sees for life in Constantinople: "pronoiai and residences have been granted to any bishop who wishes as an allotment, and they make merry in the capital with impunity, and seek their livelihood here" *[7.1]*.

Collating the information provided by this handful of diverse sources, we may infer, at least on the face of things, that a pronoia was a kind of grant from the emperor to soldiers, "lords," the "powerful," and bishops. The holder of a pronoia could be called a "*pronoiarios*" (*pro-nee-AH-ree-os*). Pronoia grants seem to have produced revenues that could be quantified by a cash amount and that were derived from land, the rights to a river, and the labors of peasants who were attached to the pronoiai. Further, pronoiai evidently could be taxed, shared by individuals, donated to a monastery, and inherited.

It is from sources like these that scholars have sought to define the institution associated with this word *pronoia*. It has not been easy. Few source references are any more explicit than these, and most are far less specific. Almost all assume that the intended reader knew exactly what a "pronoia" was.

The historiography of pronoia

Serious interest in the study of pronoia began, not with the study of such Byzantine sources, but with the examination of the appearance of the word in Serbian, Bosnian, and Venetian sources. In 1860 the Russian scholar A. A. Majkov published an article entitled "On Landed Property in Medieval Serbia." There he examined the clauses dealing with property found in the Law Code (*Zakonik*) of the Serbian ruler Stefan Dušan (1331–55). Toward the end of the article Majkov wrote, "In concluding this investigation of various forms of landed property in Serbia, I direct attention to an aspect of landed property designated in the *Zakonik* by the foreign name *pronija*," the Slavic transliteration of *pronoia*. What he viewed as the precarious nature of the possession of *pronija* led him to differentiate it from patrimonial property (called *baština*). He hypothesized that it indicated a form of "incomplete possession, possibly contingent on a state obligation," and he pondered, "Was it not imperial land, placed in the power of lords and cultivated by them?"[2]

Eight years later he published another article, "What is *Pronija* in Medieval Serbia?" Basing his research on a single document, an act from 1458 of the king of Bosnia Stefan Tomašević, he concluded that *pronija* was a temporary possession, analogous to the Muscovite institutions of *kormlenie* and *pomestie*, and that it "represents subsistence land [*kormežnuju zemlju*], an estate [*pomestie*] allotted by the decision of a sovereign power to someone personally, given without right of perpetual use, so that the sovereign could either take it back and give it to another or effect an exchange."[3]

Majkov's research was born amid the Balkan and agrarian questions, as well as the Slavophilism, of nineteenth-century Russia. The Crimean War had ended in 1856 and Russia's serfs were formally emancipated five years later. Another product of Slavic nationalism was the edition of Dušan's *Zakonik* that Majkov had used. It had been edited by the Pole Andrzej Kucharski, and translated into German by the Slovak Paul Šafařík and published in 1838. While Šafařík translated the *Zakonik*'s *pronijar* as simply "Grundherr" and its *pronijarska zemlja* as "grundherrliches Land," he ventured an etymology for *pronija* that Majkov echoed. Šafařík suggested that the word was Germanic in origin, equivalent to the modern *Frone* "compulsory service," from the Old High German *frô* "lord," which derived ultimately from the Gothic *frao* and *fraujana*.[4]

[2] A. Majkov, "O zemel'noj sobstvennosti v drevnej Serbii," *Čtenija v Imperatorskom obščestve istorii i drevnostej rossijskih* (1860), kniga 1, 1–30, esp. 28–29. Ostrogorsky, *Féodalité*, 2. On pronoia in the *Zakonik*, see M. Bartusis, "Serbian Pronoia and Pronoia in Serbia: The Diffusion of an Institution," *ZRVI* 48 (2011), 190–93, as well as pp. 607–08 below.

[3] A. Majkov, "Čto takoe pronija v drevnej Serbii?" *Čtenija v Imperatorskom obščestve istorii i drevnostej rossijskih* (1868), kniga 1, 227–32, esp. 231. Uspenskij, "Značenie," 1. Ostrogorsky, *Féodalité*, 2. On this document, see Bartusis, "Serbian Pronoia," 207, 210.

[4] A. Kucharski, *Najdawniejsze pomniki prawodawstwa słowiańskiego* (Warsaw, 1838), 183–84, 217 note 54. The title page of the work is trilingual: Polish, Russian, and Latin. Šafařík repeated this

Nevertheless, the origin of the Slavic word *pronija* is not Germanic, but Greek, a fact first recognized by the Serb Djura Daničić in his dictionary of old Serbian published in 1863. Independently of Majkov, but still on the evidence of Dušan's *Zakonik*, Daničić defined *pronija* as "*fundus ad usumfructum datus*" ("estate given in usufruct").[5]

After Majkov, work on Serbian pronoia was continued by Vikentij Makušev in "On Pronija in Medieval Serbia," published in 1874. While Makušev recognized the Byzantine origin of the term, he, like Majkov, focused on the appearance of the term in fifteenth-century Venetian and Dalmatian acts, concluding that pronoia in these documents was a form of precarious and conditional possession which the Venetian government granted on a broad scale to aristocrats, in compliance with Albanian customs ("*secundum consuetudinem Albaniae*"), for life and on condition of paying a certain sum and bearing mounted military service. Pronoia was inalienable and could be confiscated for the good of the treasury.[6]

In articles published in 1878 and 1879 V. G. Vasil'evskij turned the attention of Russian scholars to the Byzantine sources for the study of this phenomenon called "pronoia." He provided references to "where one meets Greek pronoia, corresponding to the Serbian," and pointed out that "pronoia must be studied on the basis of Byzantine sources, because here we encounter its earliest mention."[7]

But indeed the Byzantine use of the word *pronoia* had not gone unnoticed by earlier scholars. Prior to Daničić, philologists of Byzantine Greek had occasionally noted strange usages of the word *pronoia.* In the commentary to his 1845 edition of the fifteenth-century *Chronicle of Ioannina [7.4]* the Greek Andreas Moustoxydes wrote that *pronoiai* meant "the yearly collections of incomes which the founders leave to the church."[8] And even as early as the late seventeenth century the French scholar Charles Du Cange,

etymology in his *Geschichte der südslawischen Literatur* (Prague, 1864–65), III, 162. Ostrogorsky, *Féodalité*, 2.

5 Dj. Daničić, *Rječnik iz književnih starina srpskih*, 3 vols. (1863–64; repr. Belgrade, 1975), II, 458. Ostrogorsky, *Féodalité*, 3.

6 V. Makušev, "O pronii v drevnej Serbii," *ŽMNP* 175 (Sept. 1874), 1–20. Uspenskij, "Značenie," 1–2. Kazhdan, *Agrarnye otnošenija*, 202. Ostrogorsky, *Féodalité*, 3. In Serbia research on pronoia remained restricted to its manifestations in Serbian sources: Stojan Novaković, "Pronijari i baštinici (spahije i čitluk sahibije). Prilog k istoriji nepokretne imovine u Srbiji XIII do XIX v.," *Glas* 1 (1887), 1–102, and *Stara Srpska vojska* (Belgrade, 1893), esp. 72–77.

7 V. G. Vasil'evskij, "Zakonodatel'stvo ikonoborcev," *ŽMNP* 200 (1878), 127, 129 (= *Trudy*, IV [Leningrad, 1930], 232, 235), and "Materialy dlja vnutrennej istorii Vizantijskogo gosudarstva," *ŽMNP* 202 (April 1879), 415. Uspenskij, "Značenie," 2. Kazhdan, *Agrarnye otnošenija*, 202.

8 A. Moustoxydes, *Ἑλληνομνήμων ἢ Συμμικτὰ ἑλληνικά, φυλλάδια* [parts] 1–12 (1843–53; repr. Athens, 1965), 531 note 88.

in his dictionary of medieval Greek, had translated *pronoia* as "*provisiones, pensiones annuae*" ("provisions, yearly payments").[9]

The turning point came with the publication in 1883 of Fedor I. Uspenskij's article, "The Significance of Byzantine and South Slav Pronoia." Uspenskij definitively established the Byzantine origin of pronoia, and set the tone of future research by defining pronoia as "a grant to state servants of land and other income producing property in reward for service and on condition of future service" . . . "especially," he added, "as a reward for military service and on condition to continue to undertake military service."[10]

The understanding of pronoia was becoming more sophisticated, but the veil of historicism lay heavy on Russian scholarship. The following year, 1884, Nikolaj Skabalanovič in a book entitled *The Byzantine State and Church in the Eleventh Century* wrote the following:

> The system of pronoia represented the greatest danger for the liberty and prosperity of the peasantry. The granting in pronoia of community lands directly menaced the rural community . . . the political significance of the community to the state was weakened, free peasants fell into dependence to pronoiars to whom they had to pay taxes and furnish corvées; from every point of view . . . their situation doubtlessly worsened . . . pronoia was dangerous for the peasant community and for the peasants because it increased the social power of the nobles.[11]

Russian scholars continued work along these lines up until the Bolshevik takeover of Russia in 1917. After that serious scholarship was stifled, and the pre-revolution generation passed away. Four of the more prominent Russian Byzantinists in the early years of the twentieth century, Konstantin Uspenskij, Boris Pančenko, Petr Jakovenko, and Pavel Bezobrazov, died between 1917 and 1920, at the ages of 43, 48, 50, and 59.

Throughout the 1920s and 1930s, scholarship, like many things, suffered in the Soviet Union. What little scholarship there was became derivative and doctrinaire. And the center of gravity of the study of pronoia, as well as of Byzantine studies as a whole, moved westward.

[9] C. du Fresne Du Cange, *Glossarium ad scriptores mediae et infimae graecitatis*, 2 vols. (Paris, 1688; repr. Graz, 1958), col. 1246. He cited a letter of Patriarch Michael II Oxeites from 1143, now in G. Rhalles and M. Potles, *Σύνταγμα τῶν θείων καὶ ἱερῶν κανόνων* (Athens, 1852–59), V, 89: καὶ τῆς ἐνδεχομένης προνοίας ἀπὸ τῆς δηλωθείσης μονῆς χάριν ψυχικῆς σωτηρίας τοῦ ἀοιδίμου κτίτορος αὐτῆς ἀξιούμενον ("And worthy of appropriate pronoia from the said monastery for the sake of the spiritual salvation of its founder of blessed memory").

[10] Uspenskij, "Značenie." Also, F. Uspenskij, "Sledy piscovyh knig v Vizantii," *ŽMNP* 231 (Feb. 1884), 315.

[11] N. Skabalanovič, *Vizantijskoe gosudarstvo i cerkov v xi v.* (Saint Petersburg, 1884), 266.

In 1923 Peter Mutafčiev published a monograph, in Bulgarian, on the Byzantine army in the thirteenth and fourteenth centuries. This contained a long chapter on pronoia with an extensive analysis of the sources.[12] Despite the often seriously flawed aspects of Mutafčiev's work, a new chapter in the study of pronoia was opened, for the book came into the hands of the great German Byzantinist Franz Dölger, who was able to read Bulgarian. During the 1930s, as Dölger edited texts and wrote commentaries, the subject of pronoia became known to western European and American scholars.[13] This was fortified by the work of Russian expatriates – Alexander Vasiliev in the United States, and Alexander Solovjev and George Ostrogorsky in Yugoslavia – who kept alive the tradition of Russian Byzantine scholarship and exported it westward.[14]

After World War II, a new generation of western Byzantinists, such as Peter Charanis in the United States, emerged who began to take up the issue of Byzantine agrarian relations and pronoia. At the same time a slightly more relaxed climate in the Soviet Union produced a new and better caliber of Byzantine scholar, of whom the sterling example was Alexander Kazhdan, who raised an unending string of questions about all matters Byzantine.[15]

But this was all prelude to what was to come. In 1951 the Russian George Ostrogorsky, director of the newly established Byzantine Institute in Belgrade, published, in Serbian, a monograph entitled *Pronoia: A Contribution to the History of Feudalism in Byzantium and in the South Slavic Lands.*[16] Ostrogorsky was a brilliant, first-rate scholar. But while conditions in eastern

[12] P. Mutafčiev, "Vojniški zemi i vojnici v Vizantija prez xiii–xiv v.," *Spisanie na Bŭlgarskata Akademija na naukite* 27 (1923), 1–113, repr. in P. Mutafčiev, *Izbrani proizvedenija*, i (Sofia, 1973), 518–652; the chapter on pronoia: pp. 37–61 (pp. 561–89 in the reprint). This chapter on pronoia appeared as an article: "Pronijata v Vizantija i otnošenieto u kjum voennata služba," *Izvestija na istoričeskoto druž̌estvo v Sofija* 6 (1924), 1–30.

[13] E.g., Dölger, *Beiträge*, 65, and "Die Frage des Grundeigentums in Byzanz," in Dölger, *Byzanz und die europäische Staatenwelt* (Ettal, 1953; repr. Darmstadt, 1964), 14.

[14] E.g., A. A. Vasiliev, "On the Question of Byzantine Feudalism," *Byz* 8 (1933), 584–604; Solovjev–Mošin, *Grčke povelje*, 486; P. Lemerle and A. Solovjev, "Trois chartes des souverains serbes conservées au monastère de Kutlumus," in Lemerle, *Le monde de Byzance* (London, 1978), no. xix; and G. Ostrogorsky, "Agrarian Conditions in the Byzantine Empire in the Middle Ages," *The Cambridge Economic History of Europe*, 2nd edn., ed. M. Postan, i (Cambridge, 1966), 226–28, and "Vizantijskie piscovye knigi," *Byzantinoslavica* 9 (1948), 286.

[15] P. Charanis, "The Aristocracy of Byzantium in the Thirteenth Century," in *Studies in Roman Economic and Social History in Honor of Allan Chester Johnson*, ed. P. R. Coleman-Norton (Princeton, 1951), 336–55; "Monastic Properties"; and "Social Structure." Kazhdan, *Agrarnye otnošenija*; *Derevnja i gorod*; and "Formen."

[16] G. Ostrogorski, *Pronija, prilog istoriji feudalizma u Vizantiji i u južnoslovenskim zemljama* (Belgrade, 1951). He introduced his work on the subject three years earlier: G. Ostrogorsky, "Le système de la pronoia à Byzance et en Serbie médiévale," *Actes du VIe Congrès international d'études byzantines, Paris 1948* (Paris, 1950–51), i, 181–89.

Europe after World War II were far less hostile to independent scholarship than those in the Soviet Union since the Bolshevik coup, he nevertheless had to be comfortable with arriving at conclusions in accord with Marxist doctrine. Thus, he argued that the function of the institution of pronoia, which first appeared in the middle of the eleventh century, was to raise a feudal army and its effect was to create a feudal aristocracy that exploited a subject, dependent peasantry. A pronoia was, more or less, a fief, and the existence of pronoia therefore was further proof of the ubiquity of the feudal mode of production during the Middle Ages.

Had Ostrogorsky's book remained in a Serbian edition it would have had no more influence than Peter Mutafčiev's Bulgarian monograph on the Byzantine army thirty years earlier. But in 1954 the work was translated into French by Henri Grégoire and published in Brussels, together with a translation of another of Ostrogorsky's works, as *Pour l'histoire de la féodalité byzantine.*[17] Western scholars and students now had, more or less, direct access to a century of Slavic research on Byzantine agrarian relations. Even today George Ostrogorsky is the first scholar that Byzantinists think of when the subject is pronoia. His emphasis on the military role of pronoia has left a profound imprint on all later research.

And much research there was. From the late 1950s on, agrarian relations became a popular topic among western European and American Byzantinists as researchers became more interested in social and economic questions. The same social conditions that gave rise and prominence in the 1960s to the *Annales* school and to the New Social History made the institution of pronoia a staple topic in modern Byzantine historical studies.

Numerous works have been written which deal with agrarian relations in Byzantium which, even if their focus was not the institution of pronoia *per se*, have illuminated the social and economic context in which pronoia operated. Particular mention should be made of the work of Paul Lemerle, Hélène Ahrweiler, Nicolas Oikonomides, Jacques Lefort, Ksenia Hvostova, Angeliki Laiou, and David Jacoby. This is not the place to discuss the historiography on pronoia since the 1950s. There are good treatments of this elsewhere, and I will be evaluating this scholarship in detail in the course of this study.[18]

[17] G. Ostrogorskij, *Pour l'histoire de la féodalité byzantine*, trans. Henri Grégoire, with Paul Lemerle (Brussels, 1954). The translation of *Pronija* (pp. 1–257) is followed by "Les praktika byzantin" (pp. 259–368), a translation by M. C. de Grünwald, reviewed by P. Lemerle, and reviewed and revised by Ostrogorsky himself, of "Vizantijskie piscovye knigi."

[18] For the publications of these scholars, see the Bibliography of Works Cited. For extended treatments of the history of the study of pronoia since the 1950s, see G. R. Ross, "A Survey

The approach

That much said, do we know what a pronoia was?

The study of pronoia began with Russians studying the Serbian sources, then moving on to Venetian and Dalmatian sources, and only after that settling in with the Byzantine sources. But no matter what the Byzantine sources had to say about pronoia, the evolving understanding of the institution would be colored by the non-Byzantine sources, even if this had no bearing on the Byzantine institution. I'll cite two important examples: the standard question of how pronoia fit into the distinction between hereditary or patrimonial property and conditional holdings is a legacy from Slavic historiography. Nineteenth-century Russian scholars were fascinated by the question of how, during the rise of Muscovy, patrimonial landholdings (or *votchina* in Russian) were gradually transformed into conditionally held estates (*pomestie*, or "service estates" as they are often called in English). And so when nineteenth-century Russian scholars saw that the Serbian sources made a distinction between *pronija* and patrimony (*baština* in Serbian), they concluded that pronoia was a parallel to the *pomestie* and they linked it to the creation of a dependent peasantry. Thus, the questions that emerged were, first, how is pronoia to be distinguished from hereditary property, and, second, how bad did the peasants have it under the sway of pronoia?

In similar fashion, the Venetian sources that mention pronoia led scholars into the world of feudalism, a dangerous place. Now the questions were: To what extent was a pronoia a fief? Did administrative and judicial rights follow the granting of seigneurial rights? And to what extent did the granting of pronoiai lead to the feudalization and political fragmentation of the Byzantine Empire?

The non-Byzantine sources from areas and cultures that experienced the diffusion of pronoia (as both term and institution) – Serbia, Bosnia, the Venetian Levant, the Frankish Morea – provide interesting information, but in the end, with the important exception of the Serbian sources, they tell us little about the original institution and usually just confuse things.

of Pronoia in the Historiography of Byzantium," *The New Review: A Journal of East-European History* 10 (1970), 1–29; A. Kazhdan, "*Pronoia*: The History of a Scholarly Discussion," in *Intercultural Contacts in the Medieval Mediterranean*, ed. B. Arbel (London and Portland, Or., 1996), 133–63, originally published in *Mediterranean Historical Review* 10, no. 1–2 (1995); and I. Karayannopoulos, "Ein Beitrag zur Militärpronoia der Palaiologenzeit," in *Geschichte und Kultur der Palaiologenzeit*, ed. W. Seibt (Vienna, 1996), 71–89. It is unfortunate that T. Maniati-Kokkini, *Ο Βυζαντινός θεσμός της πρόνοιας: συμβολή στή μελέτη του χαρακτήρα του*, Diss. Aristotle University of Thessaloniki, 1990, has not been polished and published as a monograph.

By analogy, one might think of the law codes of the Crusaders, from the Holy Land, as well as from the Frankish Morea, which define the meanings of feudal concepts so much more clearly than they were ever applied back home in western Europe, the land of their origin.

If the word *pronoia* was unusual or appeared only in particular contexts, it would be rather easy to study its meaning. But it is neither unusual nor is its use restricted to particular contexts. Or if we could at least restrict ourselves to this word alone, its uses and meanings for the Byzantines, the following study would be quite brief. We would gather all the references to this word, arrange them in categories, and draw conclusions. Unfortunately, the concepts that the word *pronoia* involves extend beyond the word itself. They embrace a number of other words and phrases which themselves have a variety of simple and more complex meanings.

Further, throughout this investigation it is necessary to hold to several principles. (a) Because no society is static, attention must be paid to chronology as reflected in institutional changes as well as in the changing fashions of literary expression. Technical senses of words, or even general meanings, may change over time, perhaps decades, certainly centuries. (b) Attention must also be paid to the cultural milieu that produced each historical source. The institutions and terminology appropriated by men who lived within Serbian, Venetian, Bosnian, Frankish, or Turkish cultural spheres may reflect but dimly their Byzantine antecedents. (c) Attention must also be paid not only to the differences between the major categories of sources (documentary, narrative, epistolary, etc.), but to the differences in the uses of terminology even within each genre. I am thinking, for example, of the distinctions between the language of George Pachymeres' history and John Kantakouzenos' memoirs, and of the sometimes significant differences in the terminology of documents issued by an emperor and those issued by provincial officials. (d) Finally, as a kind of palliative to the foregoing and to keep us grounded in the real world of human beings, it is important not to force distinctions and seek precision where these may not have existed. While acknowledging, for example, that the documentary sources tend to display more of a regularity than the literary sources, it should never be assumed that the authors of documents possessed the same concern for legal precision as do legal scholars of our or any age.

And there is one further consideration. As the foregoing discussion has already made clear, the institution of pronoia comes to us with a lot of baggage. For well over a century scholars have been studying the institution in earnest, identifying source material dealing with pronoiai and forming conclusions about the institution based on this material. At times they arrived at conclusions that, I think, have to be revised, and at times they formed conclusions based on source material that, I think, has nothing to do with the institution of pronoia. Some might say I ought to ignore such baggage, turn a corner, and start fresh. Certainly, omitting discussion of interpretations other than my own and omitting all reference to source material that I think has nothing to do with pronoia despite the views of earlier scholars would make the book a lot shorter. But then, knowledgeable readers would be left wondering how I would respond to earlier interpretations or even whether I was aware of them, and those same readers might wonder why I had ignored or even whether I was aware of evidence that earlier scholars thought important.

Years ago, Alexander Kazhdan told me there was good reason why no one had written a monograph on the subject since George Ostrogorsky. A new book on the subject, he said, would have to be much longer than Ostrogorsky's book on pronoia because, not only would it have to reexamine every piece of evidence that Ostrogorsky examined, but it also would have to take into account all the source material, as well as all the scholarly interpretations, published since then. In this book I have tried to incorporate every piece of evidence ever cited by anyone as a reference to the Byzantine institution of pronoia, either to use it to increase our understanding of the institution, or to dismiss it as irrelevant or too ambiguous to be of much use. It is the latter cases that the reader might find unsatisfying, to read a page or two discussing a passage from a document which ultimately I conclude has no connection to the institution of pronoia. But there's no way around this.

Thus, I approach this subject in several stages. First, I consider the word *pronoia*, offering a survey (as a historian with no pretensions of being a skilled philologist) of the various meanings that the word *pronoia* had in the Byzantine era. I feel obliged to apologize in advance for delaying the jump into the actual subject matter of this book, but this preliminary chapter is essential. It is absolutely necessary, to the extent possible, to distinguish "technical" uses of the word *pronoia* from simple "non-technical" uses, and to exclude the latter from further consideration. At times this distinction can appear arbitrary, but, in order to develop a group of data, the basic principle I follow is that, unless there is some strong reason to think the contrary, any passage in which a single English word, such as "care," "foresight," or "provision," can reasonably be substituted for "pronoia" should not be considered a technical use of the word. Once non-technical or uncertain uses are excluded, we are left with the technical uses from which we may draw out the characteristics of the institution.

After this I will present the information we have about the institution of pronoia as it existed during the twelfth century, in its earliest manifestation. Ordinarily, one might begin the study of any institution with a chapter on origins, but that would presuppose we knew the approximate nature of what we were studying. Past research on pronoia provides many definitions and explanations of the characteristics of the institution, but these are often at odds with one another and rarely is much attention paid to chronology and the evolution of the institution. And so I will let the sources speak for themselves and create the first definition of the institution. After that I will turn to the matter of origins, a messy business because no source mentions the creation of the institution. It simply appeared following the fiscal crises of the second half of the eleventh century. All that can be done is to look for what needs the institution satisfied and what institutions may have served as its inspiration.

Following this we return to a chronological treatment, describing pronoia as it existed in the first half of the thirteenth century through the dramatic changes implemented by Michael VIII Palaiologos. By the late thirteenth century pronoia had reached its "mature" stage, in the sense that nearly all its variations and characteristics had manifested themselves by then in one form or another, and almost all of the terminology that would be used to describe pronoia grants had appeared in one source or another. This, then, is the place for a chapter on how the sources refer to pronoia grants. It is important to be meticulous as I pick my way through the other words and phrases used to refer to the grant, because this will provide us with our collection of historical material with which to describe the fully developed fourteenth-century institution. Perhaps this chapter, more than any other, will illustrate why no one has published a monograph on pronoia since George Ostrogorsky.

The chapter that follows was envisioned as a kind of handbook on pronoia during the late thirteenth and fourteenth centuries. The material is organized around the process of receiving, holding, and eventually relinquishing the pronoia grant. If it does not answer every question about pronoia in its most developed state, then at least it poses the questions: the characteristics of a pronoia grant and how can it be distinguished from other kinds of grants and from private property; the kind of people who received grants of pronoiai, their social status and how holding such a grant affected their social status; the kinds of property, revenues, and rights a pronoia consisted of; the economic benefit the holder of a pronoia received from the grant; the obligations and terms connected with the grant; the nature of the pronoia holder's possession of the pronoia grant including the extent to which pronoiai were alienated through donation, sale, and bequeathal; the status of the peasants who were associated with the grant; the administration of the grants, and so on. This chapter includes larger issues as well, such as how prevalent were pronoia grants within the empire, the economic impact of pronoiai and the role they played in military organization, the percentage of the army made up of the holders of pronoia grants, and the extent to which pronoia grants were a fundamental feature of Byzantium. Because I have dealt with the military aspects of pronoia in my book on the late Byzantine army and other articles, matters such as military organization and the relation between pronoia soldiers and other soldiers are dealt with only in passing.

From there, the book examines the few manifestations of pronoia in the fifteenth century. This is followed by two comparative chapters: one dealing primarily with the appropriation of the institution of pronoia by the Serbs, and the other a comparison of the pronoia and the Ottoman *timar*, examining the possibility of influence in one direction or the other. Serbian pronoiai and Ottoman *timars* are worth examining because they shed light on Byzantine pronoiai. This is much less the case with the appropriation of the institution of pronoia by the Venetians in their Levantine possessions. Further, because the Venetian source material is quite substantial and deserves a monograph in its own right, I will say little about Venetian "pronoia" in these pages. In addition, I say almost nothing about feudalism and I make very few comparisons between the pronoia and the western European fief, primarily because the former seems to be avoided by even historians of the western Middle Ages and because the latter, to me, seems to be completely unrelated to pronoia. Nevertheless, the question I ask of pronoia are the kind of questions that scholars ask – or used to ask – about the fief, and so specialists in affairs western European will have no difficulty deciding how the Byzantine pronoia compares to whatever conception they have of fiefs.

The Greek sources for studying pronoia are primarily documentary. The overwhelming majority of these are found in the archives of the monasteries of Mount Athos. Most of the rest are found (or were once found) in the archives of a handful of other monasteries: the cartulary of the monastery of the Lemviotissa outside Smyrna (Izmir), the monastery of St. John Prodromos outside Serres in Greek Macedonia, and the monastery of St. John Theologos on the island of Patmos. The Greek documents are supplemented by the narrative histories, some letters, a few treatises, an occasional chronicle, and a handful of other odds and ends. The Slavic sources used are mainly documents issued by Serbian rulers, plus the *Law Code* of Stefan Dušan. In addition, a few western European documents and chronicles were useful. With one exception, all of the sources I have consulted are published materials.

1 | The non-technical senses of the word *pronoia*

The word *pronoia* (πρόνοια) is derived from the adjective *pronoos* (πρόνοος) "thinking beforehand, wary, discreet" which is formed from the prepositional prefix *pro* (πρό) "before, forward" and the noun *noos* (νόος) with its simple meaning "the mind, a thought." Thus, in its simplest sense *pronoia* means "a seeing or perceiving beforehand, foresight, forethought, forecast." From Plato downwards the word also acquired a sense of "providence" (paralleling the Latin *provideo*), especially "divine providence."

The word was used throughout the Byzantine era in a number of senses. The following survey begins with the use of the word in its simple meaning "care" or "solicitude," and the special cases of divine and imperial solicitude. From there we follow the philological development of the word as its meaning forked into the sense of a concrete manifestation of such solicitude – "reward" or "benefaction," as well as "maintenance" – and into a practical, almost bureaucratic sense involving "administration" or "management." Along the way we will also be dealing with a number of idiomatic expressions that use the word.

This overview has two purposes. The first is to demonstrate the polysemy of the word in the Byzantine era. In this I make no claim to comprehensiveness. To treat or even discern every nuance of the word would require its own monograph. I am merely establishing a few general categories. The second purpose of this overview is to demonstrate, as we seek to establish certain technical uses of the word, how some specific passages interpreted by previous scholars as a technical use of the word need not have had any technical sense whatsoever. Because it is important to establish that most of the senses of the word existed contemporaneously, the examples I cite tend to fall chronologically within the later centuries of Byzantium.

Simple "care" or "solicitude"

Often *pronoia* means simply "care" or "solicitude." In 1312 the *protos* (head of the governing council) of Mount Athos wrote that a certain property dispute was "worthy of our pronoia and attention and correcting." In a chrysobull of John VI Kantakouzenos from 1349 we encounter the clause, ". . . it is always necessary for the emperor to have pronoia for the useful things" in regard to the laws of the empire, and we have the phrase "pronoia toward the poor" in a letter of Patriarch Athanasios I.[1] In a passage from the *typikon* (foundation charter) for the monastery of Hilandar which deals with the treatment of the ill within the monastery, the monks are ordered "to entrust to the will of the leader everything of their [i.e., the sick brothers'] pronoia." The Slavic version of the *typikon* for the Studenica monastery in Serbia substitutes *promyšljenije*, literally "forethought," for pronoia in the parallel passage. This sense of "care" could merge with the sense of "providence," as is seen in a passage from the history of George Pachymeres dealing with the insecure position of the nine-year-old John IV Laskaris after his father's death: "He had absolutely a need of pronoia so as not to suffer from anything unforeseen, as there were many intrigues."[2]

The word *pronoia* also appears in a number of idiomatic expressions with the meaning "care" or "solicitude." The most common of these constructions is ποιεῖσθαι (τὴν) πρόνοιάν τινος, meaning "to have forethought for" or simply "to take care of something." Thus, the Continuator of Skylitzes (late eleventh century) writes about the need "to have taken care of [or to make provision for] victuals by transporting grain via grain ships." In the eleventh century Kekaumenos recommended that generals receive enemy deserters with joy, "show [them] kindness and take good and liberal care of them [lit. 'make the pronoia of them good and liberal'], but keep an eye on them." Since *pronoia* here naturally would have included the daily maintenance of these deserters, Paul Lemerle wrote that this passage offers

[1] *Docheiariou*, no. 12.1: ἀξία . . . προνοίας καὶ τῆς παρ' ἡμῶν ἐπιμελείας καὶ διορθώσεως, and similarly, line 10. *Vatopédi*, II, no. 102.10: τῶν συμφερόντων ἀεὶ τὸν βασιλέα δεῖ πρόνοιαν ἔχειν. The idiom ἔχειν τινος πρόνοιαν "to have thought for something" is recorded in the lexica, but it appears much more rarely than the other idiomatic expressions discussed below. We may also note that the phrase πρόνοια τοῦ συμφέροντος appears, in various forms, several times in the letters of Emperor Theodore I Laskaris. For example, he wrote to George Akropolites, "I am astonished at your solicitude toward my well-being" (Θαυμάζω σου τὴν πρὸς ἐμὲ πρόνοιαν τοῦ συμφέροντος): *Theodori Ducae Lascaris Epistulae CCXVII*, ed. N. Festa (Florence, 1898), no. 54.1. *The Correspondence of Athanasius I Patriarch of Constantinople*, ed. and trans. A.-M. Talbot (Washington, D.C., 1975), no. 78.39: ἡ πρὸς τοὺς πένητας πρόνοια, and Ad App. 1.

[2] V. Ćorović, *Spisi sv. Save* (Belgrade, 1928), 142.16–18, and 139.9. Similarly, P. Gautier, "Le typikon du Christ Sauveur Pantokrator," *REB* 32 (1974), 1–145, line 1171. Other examples of *pronoia* as "solicitude" or "care": (10th c.) *Three Byzantine Military Treatises*, ed. G. Dennis (Washington, 1985), 200.10; (12th c.) P. Gautier, "Réquisitoire du patriarche Jean d'Antioche contre le charisticariat," *REB* 33 (1975), 125.502; and (14th c.) *Nikephoros Gregoras, Antirrhetika I*, ed. H.-V. Beyer (Vienna, 1976), 91. Pachymeres, ed. Failler, I, 63.18: προνοίας ἔδει πάντως τοῦ μή τι παθεῖν ἀπροόπτως, and cf. 31.25–26 for a similar usage.

a new and interesting example of the word's semantic development. But there really was nothing new about *pronoia* implying subsistence. In the *Strategikon* of Maurice (ca. 600) the word is linked to animal feed: "it is necessary to take care of the feeding of the horses [lit. 'make provision for the feeding of the horses']."[3]

In his memoirs John Kantakouzenos uses this idiom frequently. For example, in the space of some forty lines of printed text he employs the idiom three times in regard to Alexios Apokaukos, governor of Constantinople and Kantakouzenos' enemy during the early 1340s. Apokaukos, he writes, "always took care to be near the walls" so that he could escape easily from the capital in the event of a popular revolt against him. He also "took much care for the guard around him," and whenever he entered the prison of the Great Palace, "he took great care of himself," surrounded as he was with bodyguards.[4]

Even more common is Kantakouzenos' use of the idiom ἀξίῶ τινα προνοίας. This expression appears in a novel (law) of Justin II from 570: "and worthy of such pronoia from our majesty" (καὶ τοσαύτης ἠξιωμένον παρὰ τοῦ ἡμετέρου κράτους προνοίας); in a writing of John Oxeites, patriarch of Antioch, from the late eleventh century: "those worthy of a certain pronoia" (μερικῆς τινος προνοίας ἀξιουμένους); and in a letter of Patriarch Gregory II Kyprios from 1284: a man claiming to be a relative of the patriarch "thought himself worthy of a certain pronoia" (καὶ τινος ἀξιωθῆναι προνοίας αὐτόν). In the later fourteenth century Patriarch Philotheos used this expression to refer to imperial benefactions: "these [children] were

[3] Skylitzes Continuatus, ed. E. Tsolakes, *Ἡ συνέχεια τῆς Χρονογραφίας τοῦ Ἰωάννου Σκυλίτση* (Thessaloniki, 1968), 171.5–6: πρόνοιαν γοῦν τροφῶν καὶ διὰ μετακομιδῆς γεννημάτων διὰ σιτηγῶν πλοίων ποιήσασθαι. Kekaumenos, *Sovety i rasskazy Kekavmena, sočinenie vizantijskogo polkovodca XI veka*, ed. G. Litavrin (Moscow, 1972), 138.7–9: καὶ εὐεργέτει καὶ τὴν πρόνοιαν αὐτῶν ποίει ἀγαθὴν καὶ δαψιλῆ, ἔχε δὲ αὐτοὺς εὐόπτους. Lemerle, *Agrarian History*, 222. Maurikios, *Das Strategikon des Maurikios*, ed. G. Dennis, trans. E. Gamillscheg (Vienna, 1981), XI.2.106: δέον πρόνοιαν . . . ποιεῖσθαι τῆς ἀποτροφῆς τῶν ἀλόγων. Other examples of this idiom: Romans 13:14; (6th c.) *Three Byzantine Military Treatises*, 82.(chap. 26)9; (7th c.) *Das Strategikon des Maurikios*, XII, B Pr.5: καὶ ὁπλίσεως καὶ ἐσθῆτος ἐποιησάμεθα πρόνοιαν; (10th c.) *Lavra*, I, no. 8.1; (11th c.) the *typikon* of Constantine Monomachos from 1045 for the monks of Athos: *Prôtaton*, no. 8.6; the *Peira* (38, 11): Zepos, *JGR*, IV, 153–54 = Zacharia, *Jus*, I, 168, cited by Uspenskij, "Značenie," 3–4; (12th c.) P. Gautier, "Le typikon de la Théotokos Kécharitoménè," *REB* 43 (1985), 1–165, line 674; Gautier, "Le typikon du Christ Sauveur Pantokrator," line 984: πρὸς τὸ ποιεῖν ἀνελλιπῆ τὴν πρόνοιαν ἁπάντων; *Docheiariou*, no. 4.15; (13th c.) *The Correspondence of Athanasius I*, no. 102.12; *Iviron*, III, no. 58.77; and (14th c.) *Docheiariou*, no. 48.11, and *Kutlumus*, no. 11.1–2.

[4] Kantakouzenos, II, 541.13: ἀεὶ γὰρ ἐποιεῖτο πρόνοιαν ἐγγὺς εἶναι τῶν τειχῶν, 542.6–7: τῆς . . . φρουρᾶς περὶ ἑαυτὸν πολλὴν ἐποιεῖτο πρόνοιαν, 542.21–22: πολλὴν πρόνοιαν αὐτοῦ ποιούμενος, and cf. 536.12–14.

worthy of all other pronoia – I speak of all kinds of outlays and provisions from the imperial treasury and of money, of which those enjoying imperial favor partake."[5]

While the construction (a form of ἀξίω with προνοίας) appears just over 200 times in the online *TLG*, with all but a handful of instances from the Christian era, the writings of John Kantakouzenos account for about 14 percent of the total instances. For example, he writes that at the time of the Zealot revolt in Thessaloniki the leaders of the revolt refused to allow Gregory Palamas to assume his see. Thereupon, "he returned to Lemnos and lived there, and he was deemed worthy of appropriate pronoia by the emperor." Alexander Kazhdan interpreted *pronoia* in this passage in a technical sense and wrote that Palamas had received a pronoia grant from the emperor. On the other hand, Timothy Miller translated the key phrase with the simple sense "the emperor cared for him as was fitting." While it is certainly possible that Kantakouzenos was using *pronoia* in a technical sense, this conclusion is far from secure.[6]

In another instance Kantakouzenos reports that in 1342, during a period of civil war, Alexios Apokaukos wrote to Manuel Asan, the commander of Didymoteichon, and Asan's sister Irene, Kantakouzenos' wife. Seeking to win them over to the side of the young John V Palaiologos, Apokaukos attempted to buy their defection: "Asan and his sister and her children, when I arrive in Didymoteichon, are worthy of pronoia, which should appear sufficient to them under the present circumstances." Was Kantakouzenos suggesting that Apokaukos, in the name of John V, intended to grant pronoiai to Asan and his family? John Kantakouzenos was quite familiar with the technical meaning of "pronoia" as an imperial grant; and he indeed employs the word in his history in that sense *[8.26]*. To what extent then was his use of the idiom in passages such as this a play on words?[7]

[5] Zacharia, *Jus*, II, 18.34–35. Gautier, "Réquisitoire du patriarche Jean d'Antioche," 125.502. Gregory II Kyprios, ed. S. Eustratiades, "Τοῦ σοφωτάτου καὶ λογιωτάτου καὶ οἰκουμενικοῦ πατριάρχου κύρου Γρηγορίου τοῦ Κυπρίου Ἐπιστολαί," *Ἐκκλησιαστικὸς Φάρος* 4 (1909), 23 (no. 136). D. Angelov, *Imperial Ideology and Political Thought in Byzantium, 1204–1330* (Cambridge and New York, 2007), 144, considers the passage from Gregory II a request for a real pronoia grant. Migne, *PG* 151, col. 559C: ὡς ἀξιῶσαι μὲν αὐτοὺς καὶ τῆς ἄλλης πάσης προνοίας.

[6] Kantakouzenos, III, 105.12: καὶ προνοίας παρὰ βασιλέως τῆς δεούσης ἠξιοῦτο. Kazhdan, *Agrarnye otnošenija*, 218. *The History of John Cantacuzenus (Book IV): Text, Translation and Commentary*, ed. T. Miller, diss. Catholic Univ. (Ann Arbor, 1975), 236.

[7] Kantakouzenos, II, 278.5–8: Ἀσάνην δὲ καὶ τὴν ἀδελφὴν καὶ παιδία τὰ ἐκείνης... προνοίας ἀξιώσειν, ἥτις καὶ αὐτοῖς ἂν δόξειεν ἀρκοῦσα ὡς τοῖς παροῦσαν. Kazhdan, *Agrarnye otnošenija*, 218, linked this passage to the institution of pronoia. For the correct identification of Manuel Komnenos Raoul Asanes, see *PLP*, no. 1506.

In one case, the idiom seems to be simply an idiom. Kantakouzenos writes about how his supporters had been mistreated by those who opposed his usurpation in 1342. One such supporter was a monk named Savas who remained loyal to Kantakouzenos despite being confined to a monastery by his enemies. Even though the latter wished "to honor [the monk] with much pronoia [βουλομένων δὲ καὶ προνοίας ἀξιοῦν πολλῆς], he did not accept [it], saying that it was not right to take something from those who enjoy bloodshed and murder." Kazhdan thought that this was a technical reference to a pronoia grant. However, this is unlikely. Just prior to this passage Kantakouzenos writes that these same enemies condemned another monk, the head of a monastery, "to remain in seclusion," but nevertheless, "depriving [him] of no pronoia fitting to the body."[8]

Less common is the idiom τίθεσθαι πρόνοιάν τινος, as in the phrase "to take care of the wounded" (τῶν τραυματίων τίθεσθαι πρόνοιαν) or "to make provision for the future" (τινα καὶ τοῦ μέλλοντος τίθεσθαι πρόνοιαν).[9] Zonaras (mid-twelfth century) writes that an emperor "did not deem those of the senate worthy of honor which was fitting nor provided for them [lit. 'took care of them'] in due measure [οὔτε πρόνοιαν αὐτῶν ἐτίθετο κατὰ τὸ ἀνάλογον]; rather, he hastened to humble them." In the early tenth century Patriarch Nicholas Mystikos granted the administration of a monastery to a bishop with the command that he "show care. . . for the improvement of [its] condition" (θοῦ πρόνοιαν . . . εἰς ἐπίδοσιν καταστάσεως).[10]

I think we must be careful not to read too much into these idiomatic constructions. While we should obviously expect the phrase "to take care of someone" often to include providing one with sustenance, it is imprudent in these cases to conclude that the word *pronoia* must therefore signify "one's

[8] Kantakouzenos, II, 213.11–12, 213.6–7: προνοίας τῆς εἰς τὸ σῶμα προσηκούσης οὐδεμιᾶς ἀποστερήσαντες. A. Kazhdan, "The Fate of the Intellectual in Byzantium A Propos of *Society and Intellectual Life in Late Byzantium* by Ihor Ševčenko," *The Greek Orthodox Theological Review* 27/1 (1982), 87.

[9] *Das Strategikon des Maurikios*, VIII.2.126, VIII.2.160, and cf. VIII.2.154.

[10] Zonaras, *Ioannis Zonarae Epitomae Historiarum libri XVIII*, ed. M. Pinder (Bonn, 1841–97), III, 766.17–19. *Nicholas I Patriarch of Constantinople, Letters*, ed. R. Jenkins and L. Westerink (Washington, 1973), no. 123.26. In this case, the claims of J. Thomas, *Private Religious Foundations in the Byzantine Empire* (Washington, 1987), 146–47, 156–57, for a technical significance for *epidosis* may be overstated. Other examples of this idiom: (6th c.) a novel of Justin II from 569: Zacharia, *Jus*, II, 12; and (10th c.) from a novel of Constantine VII: Zepos, *JGR*, I, 222.9. Even less common is the idiom γίνεσθαι πρόνοιαν: N. Svoronos, *Les Novelles des empereurs Macédoniens concernant la terre et les stratiotes* (Athens, 1994), no. 9A.37–38 (and cf. no. 9B.23–24) = Zepos, *JGR*, I, 248.19–20. Also, cf. Zacharia, *Jus*, II, 18.5. The expression is also found in the form πρόνοια γίνεταί τινος: *Docheiariou*, no. 3.20.

livelihood." In a passage from the Continuator of Skylitzes, the author writes of how Nikephoros III Botaneiates dealt with Eudokia Makremvolitissa, the mother of the deposed emperor Michael VII, and two defeated rivals to the throne, Nikephoros Vryennios and Nikephoros Vasilakios. "He deemed the former empress Eudokia and her son worthy of great pronoia and honor, and made her mistress of three government bureaus [*sekreta*]. But he did not deem Vryennios and Vasilakios worthy of fitting pronoia." While our first inclination is to conclude with confidence that *pronoia* meant some kind of concrete grant in this passage, another manuscript of this text reads, for the first occurrence of "pronoia," *kedemonia* (κηδεμονίας), simply "solicitude."[11]

Divine and imperial "solicitude"

"Divine pronoia" (θεία πρόνοια, πρόνοια Θεοῦ) was a very special form of pronoia usually rendered in English as "Providence." In a chrysobull of Nikephoros Botaneiates for Iviron from 1079 we read, "everything of the monastery would have been threatened with deadly danger if pronoia had not shone on them from above." Theodore I Laskaris writes, "Should not one say that this deed is of pronoia and of divine dispensation and entirely of God?" This is one of the most common uses of the word *pronoia*.[12]

There is also imperial pronoia (βασιλικὴ πρόνοια), "solicitude," flowing as a benefaction from the imperial office. Thus, in a novel of Basil II from 996 the emperor refers to oratories that were receiving yearly cash allowances from the emperor "since earlier they were worthy of imperial pronoia." And much later, we read in a silver bull of Despot Demetrios Palaiologos

11 Skylitzes Continuatus, 184.22–25: Ἠξίωσε δὲ ὁ βασιλεὺς καὶ τὴν πρὸ τοῦ αὐγοῦσταν Εὐδοκίαν καὶ τοὺς παῖδας αὐτῆς προνοίας τε μεγάλης καὶ τιμῆς, . . . οὐ μὴν ἀλλὰ καὶ τὸν Βρυέννιον καὶ τὸν Βασιλάκιον προνοίας ἐνδεχομένης ἠξίωσεν.

12 *Iviron*, II, no. 41.19–20: εἰ μή τις ἄνωθεν αὐτοῖς ἐπέλαμψε πρόνοια. *Theodori Ducae Lascaris Epistulae CCXVII*, no. 95.25: ἆρ᾽ οὖν οὐ προνοίας εἴποι τις εἶναι τὸ ἔργον τοῦτο καὶ θείας οἰκονομίας καὶ ὅλως ὅλον Θεοῦ;, and cf. no. 39.54: ἡ ἡμετέρα μετὰ Θεὸν πρόνοια. Other examples: (ca. 600) *Das Strategikon des Maurikios*, XII D.9; (10th c.) *Three Byzantine Military Treatises*, 210.135, 224.28; (12th c.) a chrysobull of Manuel Komnenos in Zepos, *JGR*, I, 389.16ff, cited by H. Hunger, *Prooimion, Elemente der byzantinischen Kaiseridee in der Arengen der Urkunden* (Vienna, 1964), 85; (13th c.) *Theodori Ducae Lascaris Epistulae CCXVII*, no. 39.54, and cf. Appendix III, no. VII.1–3; *The Correspondence of Athanasius I*, no. 17.95, no. 83.19; (14th c.) Gregory Palamas in Migne, *PG*, 150, 1185C, cited by Hunger, *Prooimion*, 84, also citing Gennadios II Scholarios and Nicholas of Methone; an act of Despot John Uglješa: Solovjev–Mošin, *Grčke povelje*, no. 35.63; a chrysobull of John V: *Pantéléèmôn*, no. 11.4; *Nikephoros Gregoras, Antirrhetika I*, 167.12, 229.18, 235.15; *The Letters of Manuel II Palaeologus*, ed. G. Dennis (Washington, 1977), no. 67.87.

for the city of Monemvasia from 1450: "For my majesty wishes and orders that this city of Monemvasia enjoy pronoia and care in its constitution and amelioration, since this is one of the most valuable cities subject to my majesty." *Pronoia* here is simply imperial "solicitude," "favor," or even "kindness," a purely abstract concept.[13]

The historian Pachymeres speaks of such imperial pronoia when discussing John III Vatatzes' scrupulous attention to provincial defenses:

> For at this time John had forethought for everything, so that, showing the [things] called *zeugelateia* a special solicitude of [his] imperial authority, he established villages on these around each *kastron* and fort, where from their fruits and income they could provision the local fort, and hence the ruler could open to many or even to all the floodgates of kindness.

Zeugelateia were imperial estates, and the emperor's plan here was to reinforce the self-sufficiency of provincial forts. While this "special concern" (ἰδίαν πρόνοιαν) could be viewed as simply a use of *pronoia* in its most elementary sense as care, its association with "the imperial authority" lends a further nuance.[14]

To enjoy imperial solicitude was also to enjoy the effects of this solicitude, which could be something as abstract as a grant of imperial attention or as concrete as a grant of money, titles, or property. We can see this in a chrysobull of Romanos I Lekapenos from 934, which confirms an act of Leo VI from 908. Romanos' act first makes a reference to "imperial pronoia and sagacity" (βασιλικῆς . . . προνοίας καὶ ἀγχινοίας), and then repeats a phrase of Leo's from the earlier act: "the monastery founded by John Kolovos is to enjoy such pronoia and to hold the region of Hierissos." In other words, one might say that because the monastery enjoyed imperial "solicitude" (*pronoia*), it held the region of Hierissos.[15]

[13] Svoronos, *Les Novelles des empereurs Macédoniens*, no. 14A.127–28 = Zepos, *JGR*, ɪ, 268.29–30; Thomas, *Private Religious Foundations*, 160–61. MM, v, 171.6–9: προνοίας ἀπολαύειν καὶ ἐπιμελείας τὴν τοιαύτην πόλιν τῆς Μονεμβασίας εἰς τὸ συνίστασθαι καὶ βελτιοῦσθαι αὐτήν. Other examples: a novel of Constantine VII from around 947 (Svoronos, *Les Novelles des empereurs Macédoniens*, no. 5.51–52 = Zepos, *JGR*, ɪ, 224.1–2); an act of Patriarch Niphon from 1312 (*Prôtaton*, no. 11.50); and *The Letters of Manuel II Palaeologus*, no. 13.5: προνοίας καὶ εὐμενείας βασιλικῆς.

[14] Pachymeres, ed. Failler, ɪ, 99.6–11 (Bonn edn., I, 69.5–10): ἰδίαν πρόνοιαν τῆς βασιλικῆς ἐξουσίας, cited by Ostrogorsky, *Féodalité*, 64, who considered the arrangement described here as a possible, though certainly oblique reference to the institution of pronoia.

[15] *Prôtaton*, no. 3.3–4 (Romanos' act). *Prôtaton*, no. 2.7 (Leo's act) = no. 3.9–10: καὶ τὴν παρὰ τοῦ Κολοβοῦ Ἰωάννου νεουργηθεῖσαν μονὴν τῆς τοιαύτης προνοίας καταπολαύειν καὶ κατέχειν τὴν ἐνορίαν τοῦ Ἐρισοῦ καὶ μόνον. The difficulties involved in interpreting the meaning of *pronoia* in a given passage are illustrated by A. Kazhdan's interpretation of Leo's act (Kazhdan, *Agrarnye otnošenija*, 210, and *Derevnja i gorod*, 107), written before the act of Romanos was

"Maintenance"

In the above examples, by enjoying the emperor's solicitude (*pronoia*), a monastery might also enjoy property, yearly allowances, or other material benefits. *Pronoia* therefore could be not only the abstract solicitous regard of an emperor toward a subject, but the concrete benefactions bestowed because of this regard. In a letter of Patriarch Michael Oxeites from 1143 the patriarch writes that a particular man was "worthy of the appropriate pronoia" from a monastery for the sake of the salvation of its deceased founder. In his lexicon Du Cange rendered *pronoia* here as "*provisiones, pensiones annuae.*" Thus *pronoia* could denote "maintenance," another non-technical meaning of the word. Similarly, in 1465 Cardinal Bessarion wrote a letter about the children of the deceased despot Thomas Palaiologos. Their father had been receiving 300 ducats a month from the pope and Bessarion addresses the need for "the restoration of the pronoia of the ruler's children."[16] *Pronoia* is used here in the sense of a pension. Further, in the second half of the eleventh century Eustathios Voïlas bequeathed some property to a church he founded, λόγου προνοίας τῶν ἐκδουλευόντων ἐν αὐτῇ κληρικῶν. This phrase can be translated any number of ways: "out of concern for the clergy serving in it," "in order to care for the clergy," "for the maintenance of the clergy," and so on. The idea of "concern" attached to property leads to the more concrete use of the word *pronoia* as "maintenance."[17]

published. Since the opening lines of Leo's act are mutilated, the connection between the "pronoia" the monastery enjoyed and imperial solicitude can be made only on the basis of Romanos' act. But since Kazhdan had access only to the act of Leo, he constructed a very different interpretation of the phrase in question and concluded that Leo used the word *pronoia* to signify the power of an outsider or monastery (in this case John Kolovos) over a spiritual institution; in fact, he later claimed that "pronoia" in Leo's act meant *charistike* (the temporary grant of the administration of a monastery to a layman) and that John Kolovos was a *charistikarios* (the *charistike* is discussed below, in Chapter 4, "Grants for life").

16 G. Rhalles and M. Potles, *Σύνταγμα τῶν θείων καὶ ἱερῶν κανόνων* (Athens, 1852–59), v, 89: καὶ τῆς ἐνδεχομένης προνοίας ἀπὸ τῆς δηλωθείσης μονῆς χάριν ψυχικῆς σωτηρίας τοῦ ἀοιδίμου κτίτορος αὐτῆς ἀξιούμενον. C. du Fresne Du Cange, *Glossarium ad scriptores mediae et infimae graecitatis* (Paris, 1688; repr. Graz, 1958), col. 1246. For another example of this expression: Thomas Magistros in Migne, *PG* 145, col. 545; A. S. Lampros, *Παλαιολόγεια καὶ Πελοποννησιακά* (Athens, 1912–30), iv, 284.3–4 = S. Lampros, "Τρεῖς ἐπιστολαὶ τοῦ καρδιναλίου Βησσαρίωνος ἐν τῇ δημώδει γλώσσῃ," *Νέος Ἑλληνομνήμων* 5 (1908), 21.1–2: τις ἀποκατάστασις τῆς τῶν αὐθεντοπούλων προνοίας, cited by Ahrweiler, "La concession des droits incorporels," 104 note 10. In the apparatus a variant refers to "some restoration for the pronoia [εἰς τὴν πρόνοιαν] of the ruler's children."

17 Lemerle, *Cinq études*, 23.101–02. The last rendering is that of S. Vryonis, "The Will of a Provincial Magnate, Eustathios Boïlas (1059)," *Dumbarton Oaks Papers* 11 (1957), 267. Also, cf. *Three Byzantine Military Treatises*, 220.65–66.

[1.1] Anna Komnene on her father's orphanage (ca. 1150)

This is how Anna Komnene uses the word in the often-cited description of her father's state-run orphanage (*orphanotropheion*). She first employs *pronoia* in its simple sense of "care" or "solicitude," by asking rhetorically "who could possibly number those who eat there daily or the expenses each day and the pronoia devoted to each?" but then adds that Alexios "set aside the pronoiai for them from land and sea." George Ostrogorsky regarded this as a play on words proving the existence of the institution of pronoia grants under Alexios I, but on the face of things Anna is simply telling us that her father had furnished his endowment with incomes from the land economy and from fisheries or the sea trade.[18] In fact Fedor Uspenskij had already noted that a few lines later she uses the verb προνοῶ in the more elementary sense of "to administer," referring to the "accounts of those administering the properties of the poor" (καὶ λογοπραγίαι τῶν προνοουμένων τὰ τῶν πενήτων κτήματα). Nevertheless, Paul Lemerle rightly observed that *pronoia* "in the sense of solicitude for a certain category of beneficiaries, passes to that of resources for whom this solicitude is exercised," demonstrating its evolution toward a technical sense.[19]

"Administration" or "management"

Just as the meaning of *pronoia* could expand from simple "solicitude" to the object of that solicitude, so a parallel extension of the word's meaning occurred that embraced the idea of administration and management. Thus, according to the historian John Zonaras, Nikephoros III Botaneiates entrusted to John, metropolitan of Sidon, "the pronoia of the public matters." This sense of "administration" or "management" – in effect the kind of care exercised by someone in authority – is encountered frequently in sources from the tenth and eleventh centuries.[20]

[18] *Alexiad*, xv.vii.7: ed. Reinsch, 483.79–484.82 = ed. Leib, iii, 216.27–31: ἀλλὰ τίς ἐξαριθμῆσαι δυνήσαιτο τοὺς καθημέραν ἐσθίοντας ἢ τὴν καθεκάστην δαπάνην καὶ τὴν γινομένην εἰς ἕκαστον πρόνοιαν, and ἐκεῖνος γὰρ ἀφωρίσατο τὰς ἀπὸ γῆς καὶ θαλάττης αὐτοῖς προνοίας. Ostrogorsky, *Féodalité*, 27–28, and also A. Hohlweg, *Beiträge zur Verwaltungsgeschichte des oströmischen Reiches unter den Komnenen* (Munich, 1965), 84. But cf. Hohlweg, "Zur Frage der Pronoia," 298; Kazhdan, *Agrarnye otnošenija*, 204, 211; Kazhdan, "Formen," 220; and D. Constantelos, *Byzantine Philanthropy and Social Welfare* (New Brunswick, N.J., 1968), 129.

[19] *Alexiad*, xv.vii.7: ed. Reinsch, 484.88–89 = ed. Leib, iii, 217.7–9. Uspenskij, "Značenie," 6. Lemerle, *Cinq études*, 283, 311 note 122.

[20] Zonaras, Bonn ed., iii, 725.4: τὴν τῶν κοινῶν ἀνέθετο πρόνοιαν. Evidently, the Armenian word *hog* ("care," solicitude") was used in the eleventh century in this sense as well: K. Juzbašjan, "'Varjagi' i 'pronija' v sočinenii Aristakesa Lastivertci," *VizVrem* 16 (1959), 21–24.

One could be given the "pronoia" of a theme (military district),[21] and the emperor could entrust someone with the "pronoia" of church and imperial property.[22] It is this latter sense that we find expressed in one of the best-known examples of the use of the word *pronoia*. After the deposition and death of Patriarch Michael Keroularios in 1059, Constantine Leichoudes, a man who had risen to the office of *mesazon* (first minister and the emperor's chief confidant) under Constantine Monomachos (1042–55), was chosen as patriarch. According to Skylitzes Continuatus (written not long after 1079), Monomachos had appointed Leichoudes to be "guardian of the pronoia and of the property titles of the Mangana" (καὶ τῆς τῶν Μαγγάνων προνοίας καὶ τῶν δικαιωμάτων φύλαξ). John Zonaras, who composed his chronicle after 1118 and who was familiar with Skylitzes Continuatus, wrote, "Monomachos assigned [to Leichoudes] the pronoia of the Mangana and entrusted [to him] the documents concerning its freedom" (ὁ Μονομάχος καὶ τὴν τῶν Μαγγάνων ἀνέθετο πρόνοιαν καὶ τὰ περὶ τῆς ἐλευθερίας αὐτῶν ἐνεπίστευσεν ἔγγραφα). Upon nominating him to be patriarch, Isaac I Komnenos thought the moment propitious to set himself in possession of these documents. Isaac halted his consecration as patriarch until Leichoudes gave way and returned the documents of the Mangana. His elevation to the patriarchate then proceeded smoothly.[23]

It seems that Nikolaj Skabalanovič was the first to suggest that in these passages we should see the first mention of the institution of pronoia. This opinion was later adopted by George Ostrogorsky, repeated by Armin Hohlweg, and became what Paul Lemerle called a "legend."[24] However, while the notion that Leichoudes was the "first *pronoiarios*" still appears

[21] *Three Byzantine Military Treatises*, 150.4–5: τοὺς τῶν μεγάλων ἀκριτικῶν θεμάτων τὴν πρόνοιαν ἀναδεχομένους. *Theophanes Continuatus, Ioannes Cameniata, Symeon Magister, Georgius Monachus*, ed. I. Bekker (Bonn, 1838), 6.14–16: τῶν πέντε θεμάτων τῶν κατὰ τὴν Ἀνατολὴν τὴν ἐφορείαν καὶ πρόνοιαν διοικούμενον, and H. Delehaye, "Vita S. Pauli iunioris in monte Latro," *Analecta Bollandiana* 11 (1892), 64.1–2, both cited by Kazhdan, *Agrarnye otnošenija*, 212. Nikephoros II Phokas' *taktikon*, *Le traité sur la guérilla (De velitatione) de l'empereur Nicéphore Phocas*, ed. G. Dagron and H. Mihaescu (Paris, 1986), I.3 (cited by Uspenskij, "Značenie," 3), as well as XVI.7 and XX.53.

[22] Skylitzes Continuatus, 103.13: ἐπὶ τῆς οἰκονομίας . . . ἐπὶ τῆς τῶν ἱερῶν κειμηλίων προνοίας καὶ προστασίας, and Delehaye, "Vita S. Pauli iunioris in monte Latro," 138.17ff.: ἡ τῶν βασιλικῶν κτημάτων ἐγκεχείριστο πρόνοια (both cited by Kazhdan, *Agrarnye otnošenija*, 209, 211).

[23] Attaleiates, *Miguel Ataliates, Historia*, ed. and trans. I. Pérez Martín (Madrid, 2002), 51.1–6 = *Michaelis Attaliotae Historia*, ed. W. Brunet de Presle (Bonn, 1853), 66.12–19. Skylitzes Continuatus, 106.8–9. Zonaras, XVIII.5.9–13: Bonn edn., III, 670.7–9.

[24] N. Skabalanovič, *Vizantijskoe gosudarstvo i cerkov v XI v.* (St. Petersburg, 1884), 264. Ostrogorsky, *Féodalité*, 22, and *History of the Byzantine State*, rev. ed. (New Brunswick, N.J., 1969), 331 note 1. Hohlweg, *Beiträge zur Verwaltungsgeschichte*, 84. Lemerle, *Cinq études*, 281.

from time to time in historical writing,[25] for the most part this view has been abandoned. Rather, beginning with Hélène Ahrweiler, most scholars have argued that Leichoudes actually received a *charistike*.[26] As for what "the Mangana" was, initially scholars tended to identify it as the monastery of the Mangana in Constantinople,[27] but scholars now generally connect it to the government bureau (*sekreton*) of the Mangana which administered extensive properties belonging to the imperial domain. For example, Nicolas Oikonomides suggested that the grant to Leichoudes was neither a pronoia nor a *charistike*, but a special arrangement in which Leichoudes was granted a lifetime appointment as head of the *sekreton* of the Mangana.[28]

The Leichoudes–Mangana affair can safely be omitted from any discussion of pronoia as an institution. That "pronoia" in the Zonaras passage has no technical sense, but simply meant "administration," is confirmed by the other passage from Zonaras cited above in which he writes that Nikephoros Botaneiates entrusted to John, metropolitan of Sidon, "the pronoia of public affairs," which in fact parallels Michael Attaleiates' statement that John of Sidon was "governor of public matters" (τῶν κοινῶν πραγμάτων διοικητής) under Michael VII. Similarly, it is clear that Skylitzes Continuatus did not use the word *pronoia* in a technical sense either. Several lines after stating that Leichoudes received the "pronoia of the Mangana," he juxtaposes the adjective *pronoetikos* with the noun *pronoia*, and writes that Patriarch Leichoudes "was generous [δωρηματικός] and solicitous [προνοητικός] not only of those of the Church, but simply of all, so

25 K. Varzos, *Ἡ γενεαλογία τῶν Κομνηνῶν*, 2 vols. (Thessaloniki, 1984), II, 10, and D. Geanakoplos, *Byzantium: Church, Society, and Civilization Seen through Contemporary Eyes* (Chicago, 1984), 68–69. With some subtlety, G. Litavrin, *Vizantijskoe obščestvo i gosudarstvo v X–XI vv.* (Moscow, 1977), 108, argued that, inasmuch as Leichoudes' pronoia was a grant of an incorporeal right, in a broad sense it could be called a pronoia.

26 Ahrweiler, "La concession des droits incorporels," 108, and H. Ahrweiler, "Charisticariat et autres formes d'attribution de donations pieuses aux Xᵉ–XIᵉ siècles," *ZRVI* 10 (1967), 10, 25. Ostrogorsky, "Die Pronoia unter den Komnenen," 42; Hohlweg, "Zur Frage der Pronoia," 294; Lemerle, *Agrarian History*, 222, *Cinq études*, 280–81 and note 70, and "Un aspect du rôle des monastères à Byzance,"in Lemerle, *Le monde de Byzance* (London, 1978), no. XV, 24 note 3; N. Svoronos, "'Ἡ «Χαριστικὴ δωρεά»," in *Ἱστορία τοῦ Ἑλληνικοῦ Ἔθνους*, vol. 9 (Athens, 1980), 70; and S. Varnalides, *Ὁ θεσμὸς τῆς Χαριστικῆς (Δωρεᾶς) τῶν μοναστηρίων εἰς τοὺς Βυζαντινούς* (Thessaloniki, 1985), 138–39.

27 Mutafčiev, "Vojniški zemi," 42. Dölger, *Regesten*, II, no. 925. Hohlweg, "Zur Frage der Pronoia," 292. Ostrogorsky, "Die Pronoia unter den Komnenen," 42.

28 Kazhdan, *Agrarnye otnošenija*, 212–13. Ahrweiler, "La concession des droits incorporels," 108, and "Charisticariat et autres formes d'attribution," 10 and 25. Lemerle, *Cinq études*, 280–81. N. Oikonomides, "St. George of Mangana, Maria Skleraina, and the 'Maly Sion' of Novgorod," in Oikonomides, *Byzantium from the Ninth Century to the Fourth Crusade* (London, 1992), no. XVI, 245.

that no one remained without a measure of his pronoia and did not profit from his hand."[29]

Rights to administer something (to be entrusted with its pronoia) were not conferred by the emperor alone, nor did they consist only of state properties. In 1071 the metropolitan of Kyzikos asked whether "it is not just for the archpriest of an area to have the pronoia of monastic matters . . . if otherwise at the time the means are insufficient?" And the *typikon* of the empress Irene for the Kecharitomene monastery in Constantinople (1118) refers to people who were "appointed to the pronoia of the properties of the monastery" that she founded. This is evidently a reference to *charistike*, but as in other cases, one need not see an equivalence between pronoia and the latter institution; rather, a formal institution was being alluded to in a non-technical manner.[30]

In Michael Attaleiates' *Diataxis* (1077), the instructions for the administration of his religious and charitable foundations after his death, the word *pronoia* appears numerous times. Several times he writes of God's pronoia, and once the word is used simply to mean "care,"[31] but most often the word *pronoia* appears as a component of the responsibilities of the secular administrator, stipulated by Attaleiates to be a relative, who after his death would succeed him in the management of his monastic and religious foundations. Thus, we read that if any successor to Attaleiates did not hold to the rules of the founder, he was "to be expelled from its overseeing and lordship and pronoia." Everyone should be subordinate to Attaleiates' heir, "who is lord of the pronoia and management of everything." If one of his relatives shamed the monks and their monastery, "he shall be removed from their overseeing and lordship and pronoia." If there is no relative left to replace a bad one, he who holds the "lordship" (*kyriotes*) and "overseeing"

[29] Zonaras, Bonn edn., III, 725.4, and Attaleiates, ed. Pérez Martín, 133.6 = Bonn ed., 180, cited by Lemerle, *Cinq études*, 281 note 71 and 262 note 25. Skylitzes Continuatus, 106.19–22. Hohlweg, "Zur Frage der Pronoia," 290, 292.

[30] F. Uspenskij, "Mnenija i postanovlenija," *IRAIK* 5 (1900), 23.12: τὴν πρόνοιαν τῶν μοναχικῶν πραγμάτων, cited by Kazhdan, *Agrarnye otnošenija*, 209. Gautier, "Le typikon de la Théotokos Kécharitoménè," line 1064: ἀποστελλόμενοι εἰς τὴν τῶν κτημάτων τῆς μονῆς πρόνοιαν. Kazhdan, *Agrarnye otnošenija*, 209, viewed a passage from the 1093 will of Christodoulos, founder of the Patmos monastery, as evidence of the word *pronoia* being used to indicate a *charistike*. Christodoulos ordered that, once the bishop George Strovelitzes entered his monastery, he should be treated by future *charistikarioi* (lay administrators) of the monastery no differently than the other monks: "his [Strovelitzes'] pronoia shall be without hindrance" (καὶ γένηται ἡ πρόνοια αὐτοῦ . . . ἀκωλύτως): MM, VI, 84.27–33. Strovelitzes' "pronoia" was, broadly conceived, the solicitude directed toward him, manifested concretely in the maintenance or sustenance he was to receive. The passage makes no connection between pronoia and *charistike*.

[31] P. Gautier, ed., *La diataxis de Michel Attaleiate* (Paris, 1981), 19.25, 85.1123, 117.1619, and 31.241.

(*ephoreia*) should abandon the "management" (*dioikesis*) and "pronoia" of the monastery, and the monks "should manage things for themselves, and take thought for and govern everything according to my instruction."[32]

In these passages there is a close association between the words *kyriotes*, *ephoreia*, *dioikesis*, and *pronoia*, but by no means should this suggest that the words were synonyms. Rather, they reflected aspects of the authority of Attaleiates' successor: lordship, overseeing, management, and administration. Similar juxtapositions are found in the *typikon* of the monastery of St. Mamas from 1158: "pronoia and management [*dioikesis*]" of the monastery, and in the 1136 *typikon* for the Pantokrator monastery in Constantinople: "the care [*kedemonia*] and pronoia and management [*dioikesis*]" of the monastery. Indeed as early as the sixth century, when a man transferred a religious foundation to his brother, he referred to its "holy governance [*dioikesis*], management [*epimeleia*], and pronoia." In all of these passages *pronoia* means "administration" or a type of formal "care."[33]

This sense of *pronoia* also appears in the idiomatic constructions discussed earlier. In the eleventh century Kekaumenos uses the idiomatic phrase ποιεῖσθαι πρόνοιάν τινος in regard to the administration of a *kastron*: "the one taking care of the *kastron*" (ὁ τοῦ κάστρου τὴν πρόνοιαν ποιούμενος). This idiom is also found in the *typikon* of Gregory Pakourianos, where he writes of "the *hegoumenoi* and the rest of the brothers taking care [of the monastery] along with me."[34] The construction with γίγνομαι is found in a document which notes that Romanos I Lekapenos (920–44) and his co-emperors granted a yearly allowance to a monastery on the condition that the monks take care of a spring, literally "the pronoia of this [spring] shall be by the monks."[35]

[32] Gautier, *Diataxis*, 37.318–19: ἐκδιωχθήσεται τῆς ἐφορείας καὶ κυριότητος καὶ προνοίας αὐτοῦ, 57.653–54: ὡς κύριον τῆς τῶν ὅλων προνοίας καὶ διοικήσεως, 71.896–97: ὁ τοιοῦτος ἀποκινῆται τῆς ἐφορείας καὶ κυριότητος καὶ προνοίας αὐτῶν, 73.908–13: διοικῶσι τὰ ἐπ' αὐτοῖς καὶ προνοῶται καὶ διανέμωσι πάντα κατὰ τὴν παροῦσάν μου διάταξιν.

[33] S. Eustratiades, "Τυπικὸν τῆς ἐν Κωνσταντινουπόλει Μονῆς τοῦ Ἁγίου μεγαλομάρτυρος Μάμαντος," *Ἑλληνικά* 1 (1928), 256–314, prologue, line 122. Gautier, "Le typikon du Christ Sauveur Pantokrator," line 42, and also lines 691, 1406. Thomas, *Private Religious Foundations*, 68.

[34] *Sovety i rasskazy Kekavmena*, ed. Litavrin, 178.7–8, and cf. 296.30. P. Gautier, "Le typikon du sébaste Grégoire Pakourianos," *REB* 42 (1984), 119.1656–57: τοὺς μετ' ἐμὲ τὴν πρόνοιαν ποιουμένους καθηγουμένους τε καὶ λοιποὺς ἀδελφούς (cited by Kazhdan, *Agrarnye otnošenija*, 209). For another example, MM, VI, 72.4–6.

[35] *Synaxarium ecclesiae Constantinopolitanae*, ed. H. Delehaye (Brussels, 1902), 937.17–18: ἐφ' ᾧ γίνεσθαι τὴν τούτου πρόνοιαν παρὰ τῶν μοναχῶν τῆς τοιαύτης μονῆς (cited by Kazhdan, *Derevnja i gorod*, 108, and *Agrarnye otnošenija*, 210, who tried to read a more technical sense into the word *pronoia* here). The idiomatic construction with τίθημι is found in a document from 1094: MM, VI, 91.7–12, cited by Kazhdan, *Agrarnye otnošenija*, 209.

The verb προνοῶ

Related to the noun *pronoia* are the verb προνοῶ and the noun προνοητής. The ancient verb προνοῶ (πρό and νοῶ from νόος), as well as its middle form προνοοῦμαι meant "to perceive beforehand," "to act cautiously (providently)," "to provide" something, and with an object in the genitive, "to provide for" or "to look after" something. In the Byzantine era the latter senses are the most common. In the thirteenth century Theodore II Laskaris wrote: "I shall take care of my affairs as Christ governs me" (προνοήσω μου τοῦ συμφέροντος ὡς πρυτανεύσει μοι ὁ Χριστός). The preface of a chrysobull of Michael VIII Palaiologos from 1258/9 states that, since the emperor provides for soldiers, it would be wrong not "to provide for and to reward [monks] with costly gifts and to devise means of provisions." And a document from 1353 refers to inhabitants of the area of Karyes on Mount Athos who, from their tower, were "providing for [their] safety and freedom from danger from" the attacks of Turks (τὸ ἀσφαλὲς ἐκ τούτου καὶ ἀκίνδυνον . . . προνοούμενοι).[36]

As a man can provide for his affairs, the emperor can provide for monks, and people can provide for their own safety, so God provides for His people. In the late eleventh century, John Oxeites, patriarch of Antioch, prayed for God to "watch over us and direct our life in mercy and compassion" (ἡμῶν καὶ προνοεῖς καὶ διοικεῖς ἐν ἐλέει καὶ οἰκτιρμοῖς τὴν ζωὴν ἡμῶν). In these examples, προνοεῖν and the middle προνοεῖσθαι both mean "to have pronoia," and are equivalent to ἔχειν πρόνοιαν.[37]

Just as pronoia, when exercised by people in authority, took on the sense of administration or management, so προνοεῖν and προνοεῖσθαι could take on the sense of "to administer or manage," or, literally, "to undertake the

[36] *Theodori Ducae Lascaris Epistulae* CCXVII, no. 61.38, and also, no. 48.15. *Esphigménou*, no. 6.16: προνοεῖσθαι καὶ δωρεαῖς ἀνταμείβειν πολυτελέσι καὶ σιτηρεσίων ἐπινοεῖν ἀφορμάς, and cf. *Esphigménou*, no. 23.9. V. Mošin and A. Sovre, *Supplementa ad acta graeca Chilandarii* (Ljubljana, 1948), no. 7.29, and cf. *Iviron*, III, no. 72.6. Also, in an act from southern Italy from 1130: "and to confirm and to provide for the security [of certain properties] in every way" (κυροῦν καὶ τὸ ἀσφαλὲς αὐτοῖς πάντοθεν προνοεῖν): F. Trinchera, *Syllabus graecarum membranarum* (Naples, 1865), no. 106, p. 139.2–3, cited by Kazhdan, *Agrarnye otnošenija*, 221, who thought the verb was used here in the sense of "to grant, or to entrust."

[37] Gautier, "Réquisitoire du patriarche Jean d'Antioche," 129.52. Similarly, *Theodori Ducae Lascaris Epistulae* CCXVII, 100.9, and 130.18: προνοησαμένης μοι τοῦτ' αὐτὸ τῆς δυνάμεως τοῦ Χριστοῦ. Other examples of the use of these verbs: (6th c.) a novel of Justin II from 570: Zacharia, *Jus*, II, 18.28; (7th c.) *Das Strategikon des Maurikios*, VIII.2.224; (10th c.) *Le traité sur la guérilla (De velitatione) de l'empereur Nicéphore Phocas*, XVI.1 (p. 91); *typikon* from ca. 970: P. Meyer, *Die Haupturkunden für die Geschichte der Athosklöster* (Leipzig, 1894), 115.22: ποιμαίνεσθαί τε καὶ προνοεῖσθαι.

pronoia of something." Nikephoros II Phokas (963–69), in his treatise on warfare, speaks of "the generals administering the borders at the time" (παρὰ τῶν τότε τῆς ἄκρας προνοουμένων στρατηγῶν). This parallels a passage from the tenth-century treatise on skirmishing which mentions those commanders "undertaking the pronoia of the large border themes."[38]

The verb is used frequently in regard to financial officials. Thus, an act of Tiberios Constantine (578–82) refers to "the *kouratores* . . . of the divine houses administered by them" (τοὺς . . . κουράτωρας . . . τῶν παρ' αὐτῶν προνοουμένων θείων οἴκων), and in a novel of Basil II from 996: "the *epoptai* [fiscal assessors] and those otherwise managing the fisc" (οἱ ἐπόπται καὶ οἱ ἄλλως προνοούμενοι τοῦ δημοσίου). The use of the verb in this sense has already been cited in a passage from Anna Komnene which refers to "accounts of those administering the properties of the poor" *[1.1]*.[39]

This sense of "to administer" was by no means a technical formulation, for it could be applied to people with no real official (public) responsibilities. In the late eleventh century John Oxeites complained that an "impious" *charistikarios* would often circumvent the normal administrative structure of the monastery with which he was entrusted by sending his orders not to the *hegoumenos*, but "to his man who was appointed to manage the [affairs] of the monastery" (πρὸς ὃν ἐπέστησε τὰ τῆς μονῆς προνοεῖσθαι ἄνθρωπον αὐτοῦ). In this case a private arrangement led to the exercise of pronoia.[40]

Pronoetes

The word *pronoetes* (προνοητής), via the verb προνοῶ, is, like *pronoia*, ultimately derived from πρό and νόος. It denotes someone who exercises pronoia, who administers or manages or cares for things. Manuel II

[38] *Le traité sur la guérilla (De velitatione) de l'empereur Nicéphore Phocas*, III.6 (p. 45). *Three Byzantine Military Treatises*, 150.4–5, and also 200.6.

[39] Zacharia, *Jus*, II, 26.30–31. For other examples of the use of the verb in the sixth and seventh centuries in regard to an imperial *oikos*, and for the construction προνοούμενος ὑπό, see L. Jalabert and R. Mouterde, *Inscriptions grecques et latines de la Syrie*, II (Paris, 1939), 290, no. 528, cited by Lemerle, *Cinq études*, 280 note 69. Zepos, *JGR*, I, 270.4–5 = Zacharia, *Jus*, III, 316.9, cited by Kazhdan, *Agrarnye otnošenija*, 211.

[40] Gautier, "Réquisitoire du patriarche Jean d'Antioche," 121.452. The verb is connected as well to the institution of *ephoreia* (similar to the *charistike*): John Apokaukos, ed. S. Pétridès, "Jean Apokaukos, lettres et autres documents inédits," *IRAIK* 14 (1909), 7, no. 5.5–6.

Palaiologos (1391–1425) once referred to God as "the maker of all, the *pronoetes* of all, overseeing all."[41]

Sometimes a *pronoetes* was a government official.[42] An act of Nikephoros III Botaneiates from 1080 freed a monastery from the "incursions" of "*kastrophylakes* [commanders of fortresses], *episkeptitai* [administrators of imperial domains], *pronoetai*, and everyone else," and in 1085 Alexios I Komnenos ordered that a monastery's properties be troubled "neither by *strategoi* [provincial military governors] nor *kastrophylakes* nor *pronoetai* nor by any others." This meaning is based on the verb προνοῶ in its sense "to provide for" or "to administer," and the connection is seen clearly in a passage from a chrysobull of Alexios I that refers to "the *epoptai* and those otherwise administering [*pronooumenoi*] the fisc."[43]

Specifically, a *pronoetes* could also be the administrator of an imperial property, such as an *episkepsis*, a usage that dates back at least to the sixth century.[44] Other *pronoetai* appear to have had even more important responsibilities. In the tenth century the *vestarches* Michael Antipapas was a *pronoetes* of Athens, and the *protoproedros* Xiphilinos was a *pronoetes* of Lakedaimonia, while in 1089 the *patrikios* Eustathios Charsianites was "*strategos* and *pronoetes* of Samos."[45] Lead seals mention an official called the "*pronoetes* of Bulgaria," and in Kekaumenos' *Strategikon* the military commander Basil Monachos is called "*pronoetes* of the Bulgarians" (προνοητὴς Βουλγάρων). While there is disagreement whether the "*pronoetes* of Bulgaria" was the Byzantine governor of Bulgaria, or simply the military commander of the forces stationed in the newly conquered region, the charge clearly had no direct connection to land tenure or any kind of imperial grant.[46]

41 *Manuel II. Palaiologos, Dialoge mit einem "Perser,"* ed. E. Trapp (Vienna, 1966), 122.27, and cf. 264.3. And cf. *Letters of Gregory Akindynos*, ed. and trans. A. Hero (Washington, 1983), no. 66.69–70, 16–17.

42 Hohlweg, "Zur Frage der Pronoia," 294 and note 34. G. Stadtmüller, *Michael Choniates, Metropolit von Athen* (Rome, 1934), 25.

43 *Vatopédi*, I, no. 10.55. L. Petit, "Le monastère de Notre-Dame de Pitié," *IRAIK* 6 (1900), 26.22–23. Zepos, *JGR*, I, 270.4–5, and cf. Zacharia, *Jus*, III, 429.

44 E.g., *Iviron*, II, no. 50.70, G. Schlumberger, *Sigillographie de l'empire byzantine* (Paris, 1884), 151. Zacharia, *Jus*, II, 26.9, 28.34. Kazhdan, *Agrarnye otnošenija*, 213. H. Glykatzi-Ahrweiler, "Recherches sur l'administration de l'empire byzantin aux IXe–XIe siècles," in Ahrweiler, *Études sur les structures administratives et sociales de Byzance* (London, 1971), no. VIII, 50 note 4. N. Banescu, "La signification des titres de Πραίτωρ et de Προνοητής à Byzance aux XIe et XIIe siècles," *Miscellanea Giovanni Mercati, III = Studi e Testi* 123 (Vatican, 1946), 396, incorrectly argued that *pronoetai* were *only* financial officials and administrators of imperial domains.

45 Schlumberger, *Sigillographie*, 170. Kazhdan, *Agrarnye otnošenija*, 212. *Patmos*, II, no. 52.3–4,42,129,183, and also no. 53.186. Banescu, "La signification des titres," 396.

46 C. Sathas, *Μνημεῖα Ἑλληνικῆς Ἱστορίας, Documents inédits relatifs à l'histoire de la Grèce au moyen âge* (Paris, 1880–90), II, p. iv note 3, and Schlumberger, *Sigillographie*, 239–41, 575.

In a related sense, a *pronoetes* could be a kind of servant or steward who was employed by the beneficiary of an imperial grant. For example, a 1092 act of Alexios I ordered that a *metochion* of Lavra in the area of Thessaloniki enjoy a tax exemption and not be bothered by "the *pronoetai* of the properties" of his brother the *sevastokrator* Isaac.[47] That the *pronoetes* was in these cases a subordinate to a private individual is clear from the *typikon* of Gregory Pakourianos *[4.2]*. Among the properties listed in the *typikon* are several buildings purchased "by our man Vardanes, who became *pronoetes* from our decision." Monasteries also had *pronoetai* to manage their properties. In a document from 1103 a monk is identified as both "the one taking care of [or administering]" (ὁ τοῦ χωρίου . . . προνοούμενος) a village held by a monastery, as well as the *pronoetes* of this village. Thus, we can at times translate the word simply as "manager" or even "caretaker."[48]

As early as the fourth century in Egypt, there were also lay *pronoetai* of monasteries. Some were appointed by the founder, while others were appointed and supervised by clerical authorities for the management of the religious institution. In this same sense holders of *charistikai* sometimes employed *pronoetai* to manage the monasteries they held. A document from 1049 mentions a monk who was *pronoetes* of a monastery.[49] This, and the fact that, on rare occasions, the word *pronoetes* appears as a synonym for *charistikarios*,[50] have led some scholars to the conclusion that *pronoetes* and *charistikarios* meant essentially the same thing.[51]

Uspenskij, "Značenie," 3. *Sovety i rasskazy Kekavmena*, ed. Litavrin, 164.20–21. T. Wasilewski, "Les titres de duc, de catépan et de pronoétès dans l'empire byzantin du IXᵉ jusqu'au XIIᵉ siècle," *Actes du XIIᵉ Congrès international d'études byzantines* (Belgrade, 1964), II, 236–37. Banescu, "La signification des titres," 396 note 22, 398, denied that the *pronoetes* could be governor of a theme and calls the reference "l'effet d'une inadvertence."

47 *Lavra*, I, no. 51.13–14. Other examples of this: L. Petit, "Typikon du monastère de la Kosmosotira près d'Aenos," *IRAIK* 13 (1908), 71.15 = G. Papazoglou, *Τυπικὸν Ἰσαακίου Ἀλεξίου Κομνηνοῦ τῆς Μονῆς Θεοτόκου τῆς Κοσμοσωτείρας (1151/52)* (Komotini, 1994), lines 2043–44; *Xéropotamou*, no. 7.25; and *Iviron*, II, no. 45.24.

48 Gautier, "Le typikon du sébaste Grégoire Pakourianos," 37.292–95. Banescu, "La signification des titres," 397. Kazhdan, *Agrarnye otnošenija*, 211. Lemerle, *Cinq études*, 135. *Iviron*, II, no. 51.96,105, and cf. line 129.

49 Thomas, *Private Religious Foundations*, 66–69, 190. MM, IV, 315.17–18. Skabalanovič, *Vizantijskoe gosudarstvo i cerkov*, 264. Uspenskij, "Značenie," 3. Cf. the phrase in the *Peira* IX.10, cited by Kazhdan, *Derevnja i gorod*, 105: προνοοῦντες τῆς μονῆς.

50 E.g., Uspenskij, "Mnenija," 19.12–13, 20.4. Varnalides, *Ὁ θεσμὸς τῆς Χαριστικῆς*, 41. Kazhdan, *Agrarnye otnošenija*, 209. Thomas, *Private Religious Foundations*, 169.

51 W. Nissen, *Die Diataxis des Michael Attaleiates* (Jena, 1894), 53, and Hohlweg, "Zur Frage der Pronoia," 291.

In his *Diataxis*, Michael Attaleiates often writes of *pronoetai*, and perhaps he saw little distinction between *charistikarios* and *pronoetes* when he ordered the monks not "to install some other *charistikarios* or *pronoetes* aside from those I mention." However, it seems that when *pronoetes* is encountered in relation to *charistikai*, it is not really synonymous with *charistikarios*, but merely reflects one aspect of the *charistikarios* (*pronooumenos*, "he who takes care" of a monastery), or is a general term denoting someone who administers a monastery regardless of his status (founder, *charistikarios*, *ephoros*, etc.). As George Ostrogorsky wrote, a *charistikarios* could be called a *pronoetes*. But the word *pronoetes*, even when it appears in the context of religious foundations, need not mean *charistikarios*.[52]

Peter Charanis believed that the word *pronoetes* was connected to the word *pronoia* in its technical sense, that a *pronoetes* was someone who "held a pronoia." The preceding discussion shows that this view cannot be maintained. *Pronoetes* was a multipurpose word that was applied to many types of occupations. Even when it appears as a title, that is, with a technical sense, it should be translated as "caretaker" or "administrator." This technical sense predates the technical sense of *pronoia*, and in fact, one does not find the words *pronoia* and *pronoetes* in proximity in any source.[53]

As this survey of the general senses of the word *pronoia* comes to a close, it is necessary to repeat that some of the passages cited in this chapter may indeed have at their core a more technical meaning of pronoia. Here and throughout this study I have chosen to err on the side of caution and exclude references which, after careful examination, remain ambiguous. When seeking to characterize the nature of an institution, it is my belief that to include a single bad reference that in reality had nothing to do with the institution can cause much more mischief than to dismiss accidentally a few legitimate references. With that said, let us look at the first references to the institution of pronoia.

[52] Gautier, *Diataxis*, 33.251–52. Other uses of the word: 25.133, 35.280, 49.528, 51.556–59. Lemerle, *Cinq études*, 79–80. Varnalides, *Ὁ θεσμὸς τῆς Χαριστικῆς*, 41 note 24. Ostrogorsky, *Féodalité*, 18.

[53] Charanis, "Monastic Properties," 87. Alexander Kazhdan, *Agrarnye otnošenija*, 213, went a step further than Charanis, arguing that the various applications of the word *pronoetes* showed that the term *pronoia* signified a variety of institutions that had in common the right to extract income in various forms, at times from monasteries, at times from taxes and so on. However, it seems to me that the collection of revenues was essentially only incidental to the functions of most of the *pronoetai* described above.

2 | Pronoia during the twelfth century

The early development of the institution of pronoia is obscure. The first use of *pronoia* in a technical sense appears in a handful of twelfth-century sources.

Ta pronoiatika

[2.1] The *Zavorda Treatise*

One of the earliest references to the institution of pronoia is found in a brief passage from an anonymous treatise on taxation published in 1966 by Ioannes Karayannopulos. The manuscript, of which only a rather long fragment exists, was discovered in the monastery of Zavorda, founded in the sixteenth century by Hosios Nikanor and located on the Aliakmon river about twenty miles east–southeast of Grevena on the border between Greek Macedonia and Thessaly. In a question-and-answer format, the text presents technical information for guiding a tax assessor in his duties. The passage of interest to us reads, "What *pronoiatika* are. The [things] granted by the emperor for the lifetime of the man."[1]

The portion of the treatise still extant bears no chronological indications. Therefore its date can be discovered only through indirect evidence. The treatise employs a vocabulary of fiscal terms (e.g., *klasma*, *sympatheia*, *kouphismos*) characteristic of the fiscal system involving the village community. Since these terms generally are not encountered after 1204, we may at least say that the treatise dates to a period no later than the twelfth century (or more accurately, it deals with the fiscal system as it existed before the thirteenth century). A terminus post quem is more difficult to establish. On the basis of his examination of the palaeographical style of the manuscript containing the treatise, Karayannopulos suggested that the manuscript itself

[1] J. Karayannopulos, "Fragmente aus dem Vademecum eines byzantinischen Finanzbeamten," in *Polychronion, Festschrift Franz Dölger zum 75. Geburtstag* (Heidelberg, 1966), 322.56–57: Τίνα εἰσὶ τὰ προνοιατικά. Τὰ ἐφ' ὅρω τῆς τοῦ ἀνθρώπου ζωῆς δωρούμενα παρὰ τοῦ βασιλέως. Cf. the trans. of C. Brand, "Two Byzantine Treatises on Taxation," *Traditio* 25 (1969), 59.

was probably written in the eleventh century. An eleventh-century date is supported by a few other scholars, but their arguments tend to be circular, based as they are on the very phrase with which we are dealing: that is, because *pronoiatika* must refer to the institution of pronoia, and because, according to the old thesis of George Ostrogorsky, the institution of pronoia did not appear until the middle of the eleventh century, the treatise must date to the middle or late eleventh century.[2]

The content of the *Zavorda Treatise* parallels that of a better known and much more lengthy treatise on taxation, sometimes called the *Marcian Treatise*. Since the *Zavorda Treatise* mentions *pronoiatika* and the more detailed *Marcian Treatise* does not, it would seem to post-date the *Marcian Treatise*. However, the *Marcian Treatise* itself has proven difficult to date. Because of a reference within it to Emperor Leo VI (886–912) as deceased, we have a terminus post quem of 912, and the date of the manuscript containing the treatise – the twelfth century – provides a terminus ante quem. Beyond this, Franz Dölger, who produced a critical edition and analysis of the text in 1927, favored a tenth-century date, as did George Ostrogorsky, who published a monograph on the work that same year. For decades this was the working hypothesis more or less accepted by most scholars.[3]

However, more recently Nicolas Oikonomides argued for much later dates for the two treatises: the first half of the twelfth century for the *Marcian Treatise* and the middle of the twelfth century or perhaps even later for the *Zavorda Treatise*. His reasoning is rather persuasive: both treatises state that the charges called the *synetheia* and the *elatikon* earlier had been received directly by the tax collector and his entourage for their expenses, but now both charges went directly to the fisc. These charges are last attested as direct payments to the tax collector and his suite in 1079; by 1095 they were going to the fisc to the account of the tax collector and by 1098 to the fisc as a regular tax. Therefore, the terminus post quem for both treatises is 1079 or, more likely, 1095. For our purposes, then, I will treat the *Zavorda Treatise* as a twelfth-century work.[4] A twelfth-century date would

[2] Karayannopulos, "Fragmente," 320. K. Osipova, "K voprosu o roli gosudarstva v utverždenii feodalizma v Vizantii," in *XVI. Internationaler Byzantinistenkongress, Résumés des Kurzbeiträge* (Vienna 1981), section 4.1. Brand, "Two Byzantine Treatises," 36–37.

[3] Dölger, *Beiträge*, 4. G. Ostrogorsky, "Die ländliche Steuergemeinde des byzantinischen Reiches im x. Jahrhundert," *Vierteljahreschrift für Sozial- und Wirtschaftsgeschichte 20* (Stuttgart, 1927), 4, and reprinted separately (Amsterdam, 1969).

[4] Oikonomides, *Fiscalité*, 44–46, 78–79. *Lavra*, I, no. 39 (1079). *Esphigménou*, no. 5 (1095). *Iviron*, II, no. 48 (1098). L. Neville, "The Marcian Treatise on Taxation and the Nature of Bureaucracy

also explain why neither treatise makes any mention of several tenth-century fiscal institutions, such as the middle Byzantine military lands (*stratiotika ktemata*) and *exkoussatoi*.

The passage is dealing with some kind of imperial grant conferred for the lifetime of the grantee. The key to the passage is of course the word *pronoiatika*, the plural neuter form of the adjective *pronoiatikos* (προνοιατικός), which is formed directly from the word *pronoia*. It is quite rare, appearing to my knowledge in only one other source *[2.6]*. More common, though still relatively rare, is the similar adjective *pronoiastikos* (προνοιαστικός), also directly derived from *pronoia*, and its adverb προνοιαστικῶς, which together appear in about seventeen Greek documents from 1258 *[5.2]* to the mid-fifteenth century *[8.69]*.

Much more common is the ancient form *pronoetikos* (προνοητικός) and its adverb προνοητικῶς, ultimately derived, like *pronoia*, from πρό and νόος, but via the verb προνοῶ. These adjectival and adverbial forms were used throughout the Byzantine era. In the later eleventh century there is an occasional, yet nevertheless noteworthy association of the word *pronoia* and this adjective. In his essay against the institution of *charistike* John Oxeites, patriarch of Antioch, deplored the fact that pious foundations were given by emperors to archons "by, I suppose, a reason showing solicitousness" (ἐξ αἰτίας δῆθεν προνοητικῆς). Also, Skylitzes Continuatus juxtaposes the adjective *pronoetikos* with the noun *pronoia* when writing of how "generous [*dorematikos*] and solicitous [*pronoetikos*]" Patriarch Constantine Leichoudes was to those of the Church and others only a few lines after referring to Leichoudes receiving the "pronoia of the Mangana."[5]

After 1204 the forms προνοητικός and προνοητικῶς are used almost exclusively in relation to theological matters. For example, in one of his letters Emperor Theodore II Laskaris writes of "the solicitousness of God" (τοῦ θείου τὸ προνοητικόν), and in another he uses the phrase καὶ δίκαιον προνοητικῶς λογικῶς τε, which can be translated as something like "providentially and rationally just." Nikephoros Gregoras writes of God's "providential powers," as does Manuel II Palaiologos when he compares "the

in Byzantium," *Byzantinische Forschungen* 26 (2000), 58 note 1, favored a late eleventh- or twelfth-century date for the *Marcian Treatise*, but in light of A. Kazhdan's skepticism toward Oikonomides' argument (review of Oikonomides, *Fiscalité*, in *BZ* 91 [1998], 175 and note 1), revised this in her *Authority in Byzantine Provincial Society, 950–1100* (Cambridge, 2004), 177, to "an eleventh-century context."

[5] P. Gautier, "Réquisitoire du patriarche Jean d'Antioche contre le charisticariat," *REB* 33 (1975), 107.254. Lemerle, *Cinq études*, 280. Hohlweg, "Zur Frage der Pronoia," 294 note 31. *Ἡ συνέχεια τῆς Χρονογραφίας τοῦ Ἰωάννου Σκυλίτση*, ed. E. Tsolakes (Thessaloniki, 1968), 106.19–22.

providential powers" of a father (τὰς προνοητικὰς . . . δυνάμεις) to those of God.[6]

Returning to the *Zavorda Treatise*, given that the word *pronoiatika* is rare, what kind of institution does it describe? Were *pronoiatika* "properties" or "revenues," that is, did the author of the treatise conceive of a pronoia as fundamentally a grant of properties or of revenues? Ksenia Hvostova concluded that the *pronoiatika* were actual properties, basing this conclusion on a comparison of the passage with fourteenth-century documents which refer to "*pronoiastika* rights" (*dikaia*). But this assumes too much. We must be careful not to read into the passage the characteristics of the institution of pronoia found in later sources. Hélène Ahrweiler, on the other hand, assumed that *ta pronoiatika* were tax revenues from land, but she made no argument to support this view.[7]

The passage about *pronoiatika* has little in common with the rest of the fragment. The fragment itself is repetitive and poorly organized (several passages discuss *klasmata* before the term is defined). All of the other sixteen rubrics deal with the taxation of land before or after it became *klasma* (a property that devolved to the fisc through non-payment of taxes). The *pronoiatika* passage appears in the middle of the text, sandwiched after the definitions of "unassigned" and "omitted" properties (τὰ ἀνέκδοτα and τὰ ἐαθέντα), and before a discussion of how sales of *klasmata* were annulled and the definition of a *kouphismos* (a temporary tax alleviation). The only relevance I can see for including a definition of *pronoiatika* in this fragmentary section of the treatise is that one of the ways that *klasmata* could be dealt with, aside from being sold, was by being granted as pronoiai. As such, I tend to think that the author viewed *pronoiatika* as real properties.

We do learn that *pronoiatika* were the component parts of an imperial lifetime grant, "granted by the emperor for the lifetime of the man." Ostensibly when the recipient died, they returned to the emperor. Ahrweiler pointed out that since the passage states the grant was "for life," it would seem that the treatise's author felt that a pronoia could be granted only to an individual, not to an institution such as a monastery.[8]

[6] *Theodori Ducae Lascaris Epistulae* CCXVII, ed. N. Festa (Florence, 1898), no. 198.11, no. 95.19. *Nikephoros Gregoras, Antirrhetika I*, ed. H.-V. Beyer (Vienna, 1976), 225.15. *Manuel II. Palaiologos, Dialoge mit einem "Perser,"* ed. E. Trapp (Vienna, 1966), 203.39, and cf. 39.23.

[7] Ks. Hvostova, "Pronija: social'no-ekonomičeskie i pravovye problemy," *VizVrem* 49 (1988), 15–17. Ahrweiler, "La 'pronoia' à Byzance," 682–83.

[8] Ahrweiler, "La 'pronoia' à Byzance," 684.

The treatise may represent the first indication of the use of the word *pronoia* in a technical sense. On the one hand, this is quite peculiar, because whatever sense *pronoiatika* had must derive from the technical sense of *pronoia* and the appearance of a new adjectival form of *pronoia* would suggest that by the time of the treatise the technical sense of the word was well established. Indeed, the first securely dated technical reference to pronoia dates to 1136, and in the whole of the twelfth century, only four documents (and no other sources aside from the *Zavorda Treatise*) use *pronoia* in a technical sense. There may well be good reason to push the *Zavorda Treatise* into the second half of the twelfth century, but, on the other hand, the twelfth century is less well documented by monastic archival material than the eleventh and, certainly, the thirteenth and later centuries. If the *Zavorda Treatise* does date from the early days of the establishment of *pronoia* as a technical term, it may mean merely that the practice which the word *pronoia* describes was established quickly and relatively broadly.

The pronoia of the deceased Synadenos

[2.2] Typikon for the Pantokrator monastery mentioning the pronoia of Synadenos (1136)

The first firmly dated use of the word *pronoia* in a technical fiscal sense is found in the 1136 *typikon* for the Pantokrator monastery in Constantinople. In it *pronoia* is used to designate a particular property and the passage provides some confirmation for the information from the *Zavorda Treatise.* Among the properties given to the monastery by John II Komnenos (1118–43) was "the pronoia of the deceased Synadenos by Hexamilion in the market of Vrachionion." Hexamilion was at the site of ancient Lysimachia, toward the northern end of the Gallipoli peninsula. The simplest hypothetical reconstruction of the events behind this passage is that someone named Synadenos had been granted this "pronoia" by the emperor (John II, or perhaps his father Alexios I), and that after Synadenos died, it reverted to the emperor ("granted by the emperor for the lifetime of the man") who then made a gift of it to the monastery. We have no idea who this Synadenos was, nor do we know what this "pronoia" consisted of (though it is listed among the real properties granted to the monastery: villages, *proasteia*, *hypostaseis*, and so forth), nor the circumstances or conditions under which Synadenos held it or the emperor acquired it. In any event, this passage allows us to date the genesis of the use of the word *pronoia* in a technical sense, as George Ostrogorsky observed, to no later than the reign of John II.[9]

Pankratios Anemas

[2.3] Act of the *doux* of Thessaloniki John Kontostephanos for the monastery of Lavra (1162)

Our knowledge of the early technical use of the word *pronoia* is enlarged dramatically by a document from 1162 involving a dispute between the monastery of the Great Lavra on Mount Athos and a man named Pankratios Anemas.[10] This is a complicated document. Barlaam, the *hegoumenos* of Lavra, had complained to the emperor that someone named Koskinas "took away eight paroikoi of the monastery and simply tried to depopulate" (line 1) an estate (*proasteion*) of Lavra. He requested that the emperor restore to the monastery the eight paroikoi which had been taken from it by Koskinas, and not to allow to him to keep the piece of land given by Lavra "to the soldier before him," but to confer this property upon the monastery because Koskinas had violated the agreement between them (lines 8–10). In March 1162 Manuel I Komnenos ordered his nephew the *doux* of Thessaloniki John Kontostephanos to conduct an inquiry.

Part of the dispute concerned paroikoi, a term denoting a category of peasant that occupies a central role in Byzantine agrarian relations in general and the institution of pronoia in particular. In the tenth through twelfth centuries paroikoi were often peasants with very little property of their own who made their living through leasing the land of others. Emperors "granted" such paroikoi to monasteries and other privileged landholders (including those holding pronoiai) as a benefaction. The characteristics of paroikoi, including what it meant to be "granted" to a monastery or other landholder, along with the evolution of the institution will be developed in the course of these pages (see, for example, *[4.5]*). For now, suffice it

[9] P. Gautier, "Le typikon du Christ Sauveur Pantokrator," *REB* 32 (1974), 117.1473–74: ἡ κατὰ τὸ Ἑξαμίλιον ἐν τῷ ἐμπορίῳ τοῦ Βραχιονίου πρόνοια τοῦ ἀποιχομένου Συναδηνοῦ. Without further elucidation, Ahrweiler, *Byzance et la mer*, 220, proposed that Synadenos was Basil Synadenos, successively *doux* of Epidamnos (Dyrrachion), Niš, Cyprus, and Trebizond. Ostrogorsky, "Die Pronoia unter den Komnenen," 51. Lemerle, *Agrarian History*, 223. Kazhdan, *Agrarnye otnošenija*, 211, made the unlikely suggestion that the pronoia consisted of the market itself.

[10] *Lavra*, I, no. 64.

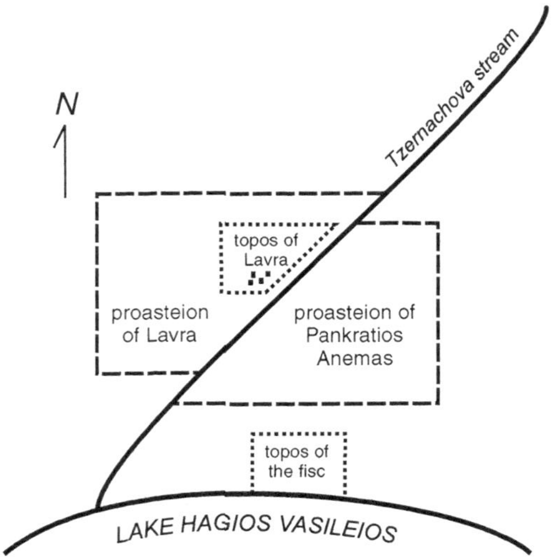

Figure 2.1 Schematic diagram of Archontochorion.

to say that landholders quarreled over who was to enjoy the services of these peasants. In the present document, the monks were claiming that a number of paroikoi belonging to the Lavra monastery had been unjustly "taken away" by a private individual named Koskinas and they wanted the emperor to return them to their monastery. Further, they desired that a parcel of land given to a soldier "before Koskinas" be granted to the monastery.

First Kontostephanos examined the relevant description of the borders of the property included within an act (*praxis*) of the *logariastes* Constantine bearing the date "November, indiction 7, 6597" (line 23) and determined that the disputed property was within the property (*ktema*) of Lavra called Archontochorion. Then Kontostephanos went to the place in dispute, that is, "the *kathedra* of those held in pronoia [*eis pronoian*] by the said *kyr* Pankratios Anemas" (lines 26–27), reviewed the property description of Lavra's *proasteion* of Archontochorion, and confirmed that the disputed place (*topos*), "at which are found the houses of the paroikoi of *kyr* Pankratios" (lines 40–41), was within the *proasteion* of Archontochorion because the houses were to the west of a stream called Tzernachova. This stream formed the eastern border of the monastery's *proasteion* (see Figure 2.1) and separated the monastery's *proasteion* (called Archontochorion) "from the *proasteion* held in pronoia by *kyr* Pankratios" (also called Archontochorion) which was located to the east of the stream (lines 41–44).[11]

[11] The toponym "Tzernachova" was preserved in a village called Černik (today Areti) between and to the north of lakes Hagios Vasileios (today Koroneia) and Volve, to the east of Thessaloniki: see

However, Pankratios asserted that "the houses of his paroikoi" were built during the time of "the deceased Loukites" who "was holding the said *proasteion* in pronoia before him" (lines 45–47). The monks acknowledged this, adding that the disputed *topos* was given by the monastery "to the soldiers having [it] in pronoia before *kyr* Pankratios, the deceased Romanos Rentinos and the brothers Theotimos and Leo Loukites."[12] But, the monks noted, because the monastery stipulated that "the paroikoi of the soldiers" (lines 50–51) should use the land only for cultivation and not live on it (since it eventually would be returned to the monastery), the soldiers had violated this condition, and so the *topos* should return to Lavra. Further, this condition aside, the monastery had not given the *topos* to the soldiers "so that [it] should pass to those after them who should hold in pronoia the *proasteion* called Archontochorion, but to them alone" (lines 55–57). And because these soldiers were dead, the *topos* ought to return to the monastery.

The monks then presented to Kontostephanos an act (*praxis*) of the deceased Xiphilinos, *logariastes* of the old *doux* and *praktor* of the theme of Voleron, Strymon, and Thessaloniki Constantine Doukas, established in "December indiction 13" of the world year "6627," which related earlier conflicts between Lavra and the soldiers "Andreas Romanos Rentinos and the brothers Theotimos and Leo Loukites" (lines 61–64). As a result of this act, these soldiers were granted "a *topos* of the fisc" located on the left bank of the lake of Hagios Vasileios (today Koroneia) "as a *kathedra* for their paroikoi" (lines 66–67), and further, at the request of the soldiers the monks themselves gave them a *topos* from their own *proasteion*, located on the west bank of the stream, on the condition that this *topos* be used only for cultivation and not for houses or threshing floors.

Having examined the evidence Kontostephanos decided for Lavra and returned the *topos* on the west bank of the Tzernachova stream to the monks. "The homes of the paroikoi of *kyr* Pankratios" (lines 88–89) were removed and transported across the stream to the eastern side.

Finally, Kontostephanos seems to return to the original complaint of Barlaam. He explains that eight paroikoi, who had been transferred

P. Bellier et al., *Paysages de Macédoine* (Paris, 1986), 253 (Tserniki, Çernovo, Černak). And less than two miles to the north is a peak that was called Čereniki: Vojnogeografski institut (Belgrade), topographical map, 1:200000, sheet 63, "Solun" (1966). The *proasteia* called Archontochorion were to the southeast, probably near the modern village of Analypsi.

12 *Lavra*, I, no. 64.47–49: τοῖς πρὸ τοῦ κυροῦ Παγκρατίου εἰς πρόνοιαν ἔχουσι, τοῖς στρατιώταις, τῶ τε Ῥεντινῶ ἐκείνω Ῥωμανῶ καὶ τοῖς ἀυταδέλφοις τοῖς Λουκίταις τῶ τε Θεοτίμω καὶ τῶ Λέοντι. Oddly, the preserved copy of the document provides no direct object for the participle ἔχουσι. Was this an inadvertence of the early nineteenth-century copyist, or does the omission have some significance? In any event, in the four other passages mentioning the word *pronoia*, the object that was "held in pronoia" is the *proasteion*.

(evidently recently) from the *proasteion* of Pankratios to the *proasteion* of the monastery, were questioned at the time by "Heliopolos, the brother of Constantine, the man of our master the *doux*," who had visited the *proasteion*. The paroikoi were asked whose paroikoi they first were and why they had been transplanted earlier from the *proasteion* of the monastery to that of Pankratios. They responded that they were first paroikoi of the monastery and that later they left the monastery's *proasteion* and after some time installed themselves where the paroikoi of Pankratios were settled. Consequently, Kontostephanos reports, Heliopolos ordered their return. And with this the document concludes.

An analysis of this act must begin by noting several problems. First, the original act is lost; the text is known only through a copy made by Theodoretos, *hegoumenos* of Lavra at the beginning of the nineteenth century. Second, since Theodoretos did not transcribe the beginning of the act, evidently because it was missing or illegible, it is impossible to determine the circumstances that led to the creation of this document in 1162, and, further, it is difficult to determine the relation between the Koskinas mentioned at the beginning of the preserved portion of the act and Pankratios Anemas. Koskinas had taken eight paroikoi from the monastery; toward the end of the document we learn that so had Pankratios (more or less). Some property had been given to a soldier before Koskinas, and now the monastery wanted it back because an agreement was broken; the same (more or less) applied to Pankratios. The coincidence between the situations of Koskinas and Pankratios led George Ostrogorsky to conclude that they were probably the same person; the modern editors of the document came to the same conclusion, but add that Koskinas may have been a representative of Pankratios.[13]

Moreover, there are problems in reconciling the world years with the indictions given for the other documents cited by the act. In Kontostephanos' act, the *praxis* of the *logariastes* Constantine is dated "November, indiction 7, 6597," but November 6597 (=1088) corresponds to indiction 12. The modern editors of the document have proposed that Theodoretos misread "7" for "2" in the world year, and that this act actually was issued in November 6592 (=1083).

More important for our purposes is the *praxis* of the *logariastes* Xiphilinos. While the summary of this act as found in Kontostephanos' act makes no mention of pronoia, it does establish the principals – the soldiers Rentinos and the Loukites brothers – as property holders at an earlier date in

[13] Ostrogorsky, *Féodalité*, 32. *Lavra*, I, p. 329.

the same location at which Kontostephanos states they held property "in pronoia." But how much earlier is the problem. While Kontostephanos' act notes that this *praxis* was composed in December, indiction 13, of the year 6627 (κατὰ τὸν Δεκέμβριον μῆνα τῆς τρίτης καὶ δεκάτης ἰνδικτιῶνος τοῦ ,ϛχκζʹ ἔτους), December 6627 (=1118) corresponds to indiction 12. G. Ostrogorsky argued that since the indiction number is written out in longhand, the error must lie in the world year. Thus, the *praxis* should be dated to December 1119 (the year 6628, indiction 13), rather than December 1118 (6627, indiction 12). Because he simply assumed that the principals held their properties "in pronoia" at the time of Xiphilinos' act, he concluded that grants "in pronoia" were being made to soldiers before 1119, that is, during the reign of Alexios I Komnenos.[14]

On the other hand, Paul Lemerle suggested that Xiphilinos' *praxis* could date to the reign of John II or even as late as the reign of Manuel I. As Ostrogorsky pointed out, if we accept "13" as the indiction year of Xiphilinos' *praxis*, the only possible years we could replace 1118 (,ϛχκζʹ or 6627) with, beside 1119 (,ϛχκηʹ or 6628), are 1134 (,ϛχμγʹ or 6643, during John II's reign) and 1149 (,ϛχνηʹ or 6658, Manuel I's reign), both of which would require an error or misreading in two digits of the world year. Moreover, a date of 1149 would mean that all the men mentioned in Xiphilinos' *praxis* (Rentinos, the Loukites brothers, and Xiphilinos himself) had died within a relatively short period of thirteen years.[15]

All things considered, it is difficult to present any convincing argument against Ostrogorsky's dating. It is the most persuasive simply because it requires the least alteration of the preserved text. The second most likely redating, I think, is to read ,ϛχμγʹ (6643=1134) for ,ϛχκζʹ (6627=1118), because *kappa* and *mu*, in the paleography of the documents, could easily be confused. As for Ostrogorsky's assumption that the principals held their property "in pronoia" at the time of Xiphilinos' *praxis*, while some caution is in order, this too is a reasonable conclusion. Indeed, the document offers no hint as to what other reason the principals may have had for holding property in that area. In sum, I think we can say that it is quite likely (though by no means indisputable) that at least some soldiers were holding property "in pronoia" during the reign of Alexios I.[16]

[14] Ostrogorsky, *Féodalité*, 34, and "Die Pronoia unter den Komnenen," 49.

[15] Lemerle, *Agrarian History*, 223, 239 and note 1. Ostrogorsky, "Die Pronoia unter den Komnenen," 50.

[16] Charanis, "Monastic Properties," 91, wrote incorrectly that this document "explicitly" states that Alexios I gave pronoiai to soldiers. Hohlweg, "Zur Frage der Pronoia," 306, cautioned that

The document mentions three properties held by Pankratios and the three soldiers: (i) the *proasteion* called Archontochorion, (ii) the *topos* "from those of the fisc" (ἀπὸ τῶν τοῦ δημοσίου) given to the soldiers by the *logariastes* Xiphilinos as a dwelling place for their paroikoi, and (iii) the *topos* situated within the monastery's *proasteion* of Archontochorion. The soldiers' *proasteion* is explicitly "held in pronoia"; the *topos* given by Xiphilinos may have become part of the property they held in pronoia, though nothing is said of this; but the *topos* within Lavra's *proasteion* was clearly not held in pronoia by any of these men. This last *topos* was given by the monastery to the soldiers so that "the paroikoi of the soldiers should use [κεχρῆσθαι] it" for cultivation (line 50). Perhaps one could distinguish the *usus* of these paroikoi from the *possessio* of the soldiers, but this would posit legal distinctions that may not have inhered within the words employed. (When this phrase is repeated in line 71, it is not clear syntactically whether it was the paroikoi or the soldiers who were to κεχρῆσθαι the *topos.*) Rightly, Ostrogorsky noted that while the land had been ceded to the paroikoi to cultivate, all the issues are framed as if it was the land of the pronoia holders. When the latter died, the agreement with the monastery was to end, even though the paroikoi were still around.[17]

The matter of the order and terms of the succession to the *proasteion* is far from clear. While Pankratios held the *proasteion* in pronoia by himself in 1162, we cannot be sure who held the *proasteion* immediately before him. Pankratios himself told Kontostephanos that a man named Loukites held the *proasteion* in pronoia before him.[18] However, the monks told Kontostephanos that the *topos* in dispute was given by the monastery to those who held the *proasteion* in pronoia "before *kyr* Pankratios, to soldiers, to the deceased Romanos Rentinos and to the Loukites brothers Theotimos and Leo," so that "the paroikoi of the soldiers should use it for cultivation." Further, they added that "the said *topos* was not given by the monastery to the said soldiers so that [it] should pass to those after them who should hold in pronoia the *proasteion*. . . , but to them alone." This suggests that all three soldiers were holding the *proasteion* in pronoia at the same time, and that the *topos* they received from the monastery was for the use of all of their paroikoi. Similarly, the summary of the act of Xiphilinos states that to resolve conflicts between Lavra and the soldiers "Andreas Romanos

since the document might be referring to an isolated case, it does not allow us to conclude that Alexios I created an extensive class of pronoia-holding soldiers.

17 Ostrogorsky, *Féodalité*, 36.

18 *Lavra*, I, no. 64.46: τοῦ πρὸ αὐτοῦ κατέχοντος εἰς πρόνοιαν τὸ εἰρημένον προάστειον ἤγουν τοῦ Λουκίτου ἐκείνου, and cf. line 9 which speaks of a πρὸ αὐτοῦ στρατιώτης.

Rentinos and the brothers Theotimos and Leo Loukites," the monastery gave them a *topos* from their own property and Xiphilinos gave them a *topos* from state land "as a dwelling place for their paroikoi." This seems to confirm that all three soldiers were in the disputed area at the same time. Finally, the monks repeat that since the *topos* was given only to the soldiers mentioned "and not to their successors" (line 79: *diadochoi*), it should not pass "to the successors of the Loukitai, that is, to *kyr* Pankratios" (lines 80–81), and Kontostephanos agreed that it was given "only to the Loukitai" (line 86), adding that the houses on the *topos* were built before Pankratios' time "by the deceased Loukitai before him" (lines 83–84). This suggests that Pankratios' immediate predecessors were at least two men named Loukites.

It is quite possible that the copy of the document as it has been preserved includes some inaccuracies, confusions of singular and plural names, or other imprecisions. The original could have included these as well. But if we accept what the document states at face value, the only way to reconcile the above passages is to suggest the following sequence of events: (i) The soldiers Andreas Romanos Rentinos, Leo Loukites, and Theotimos Loukites held a *proasteion* in pronoia. (ii) To resolve a dispute, Lavra gave all three men a piece of land from its own property, and a state official gave them another property for habitation by their paroikoi. (iii) Rentinos (I am assuming, for simplicity's sake, that Romanos Rentinos was the same person as Andreas Romanos Rentinos) died (naturally, we must bear in mind that there are other possible reasons why a man might lose possession of property), and the *proasteion* continued to be held in pronoia by the Loukites brothers. (iv) One of the Loukites brothers died; his brother continued to hold the *proasteion*. (v) Finally, the last Loukites brother died, and the *proasteion* was transferred to Pankratios Anemas.

This reconstruction accords with the preserved text. All we need to assume is that Rentinos died (or otherwise passed from the scene) first, and that both Loukites brothers did not die (or whatever) at the same time. If so, it would be equally true to say that Pankratios had as predecessors "Rentinos and the Loukites brothers," "the Loukitai," "a Loukites," and, to take into consideration the mysterious early phrases in the document, a "soldier." And this is what we read in the text.

Ostrogorsky wrote matter-of-factly that Romanos Rentinos and the brothers Loukites together possessed this property in pronoia which then later Pankratios held alone (though he noted that since Pankratios cites only the Loukites brothers as his predecessors, it is possible that Rentinos held a different property). But Armin Hohlweg preferred to think that the four men held the *proasteion* successively because he had difficulty imagining a pronoia held by two or three persons.[19] And yet there are certain elements in the story that lead to this conclusion. In Xiphilinos' act, there are three soldiers, but only one *proasteion*; Xiphilinos gave all three soldiers a single *topos* from state property; the paroikoi of the three soldiers cultivated the land together and, at least at one point, the paroikoi lived together. There is a real possibility that the *proasteion* was held in pronoia *jointly* by Rentinos and the Loukites brothers, a phenomenon for which there is evidence from the thirteenth and fourteenth centuries (see *[8.1]*, etc).

How did Pankratios come into possession of the *proasteion*? George Ostrogorsky assumed that Pankratios did not receive the *proasteion* by virtue of any familial relation to the Loukites brothers, thus demonstrating that at the time pronoia was a lifetime grant only and not hereditary property. He based this on the monks' insistence that Pankratios, even though he was the *diadochos* (διάδοχος "successor") of the Loukitai, nevertheless had no right to what the earlier soldiers had, proving that there was no familial and legal tie between Pankratios as *kleronomos* (κληρονόμος "heir") and the others.[20] But this line of argument cannot be sustained for two reasons. First, the monks were only concerned about their *topos*, not the *proasteion* held in pronoia. Their point was that, even if Pankratios had the right to succeed to the *proasteion* (for whatever reasons), he had no right to succeed to the *topos*, because the soldiers' possession of the *topos* was a private agreement not directly connected to their holding of the *proasteion* in pronoia.

Second, as Alexander Kazhdan pointed out, *diadochoi* can mean heirs no less than *kleronomoi*. Since the document does not suggest that the *proasteion* went back to the state after the death of the Loukites brothers, Pankratios could just as well have been related to the predecessors, or he could even have purchased the land.[21] Ultimately, we do not know how Pankratios acquired the *proasteion*, and consequently the document neither supports nor contradicts the evidence of the *Zavorda Treatise* that a pronoia (or a grant in pronoia) was a lifetime grant and not inheritable.

In the *Zavorda Treatise [2.1]* and in the *typikon* from 1136 *[2.2] ta pronoiatika* and *he pronoia*, respectively, both seem to refer to a type of real property. This meaning will not suffice for Kontostephanos' act. Here

[19] Ostrogorsky, *Féodalité*, 35. Hohlweg, "Zur Frage der Pronoia," 305–06.

[20] Ostrogorsky, *Féodalité*, 35. Also, Lemerle, *Agrarian History*, 239.

[21] Kazhdan, "Formen," 220, citing acts from Hilandar's archives: *Chilandar*, ed. Živojinović, I, no. 16.8–9: ἅπαν τὸ μέρος, τοὺς κληρονόμους δηλαδὴ πάντας καὶ διαδόχους σου, and similar phrases in *Chilandar*, ed. Živojinović, I, no. 22.27–28, and *Chilandar*, ed. Petit, no. 23.26–27 and no. 127.4–5.

pronoia appears five times, always in some form of the expression "to hold something in pronoia" (ἔχειν or κατέχειν τι εἰς πρόνοιαν: cf. lines 27, 43, 46, 48, 56). I know of no earlier appearance of this expression in any source.[22] What did it mean to hold a *proasteion* or paroikoi *eis pronoian* (εἰς πρόνοιαν)? More generally, what did the phrase *eis pronoian* mean?

I have been translating *eis pronoian* with the literal but relatively meaningless phrase "in pronoia," as if it paralleled such English expressions as "in possession," "in conditional tenure" or "in leasehold," much like the Latin would employ *in* or the French *en* (French scholars usually translate the phrase as "en pronoia"). But this is misleading. *Eis* is not a preposition of agency ("by means of"), but rather of place, of time, of number, or of purpose, consequence or reference. Only the latter set of functions can apply to the phrase in question. Accordingly, *eis* translates as "for the purpose of, or for the end of" or "for the result of" (as "in" is used in the English phrases "to send in reply" and "to do in honor of"), or, more vaguely, as "in regard to," "as regards" or "regarding" (as "in" is used in the English phrase "to be first in beauty"). Thus, we can translate more precisely the phrase κατέχειν τι εἰς πρόνοιαν as "to hold something for the purpose of pronoia," "to hold something in which the consequence, or result, was pronoia," or "to hold something in regard to pronoia." All of these phrases can be summed up neatly in the phrase "for pronoia."

What sense of the word *pronoia* was used in the phrase *eis pronoian*? As discussed in the previous chapter, the elementary senses of *pronoia* embraced care/solicitude, divine and imperial solicitude, reward/benefaction, maintenance, and administration/management. From the start the meanings involving divine or imperial solicitude may be excluded. One could hold a property or a paroikos "out of" or "because of" divine or imperial solicitude, but it is difficult to imagine how one could hold a property or a paroikos "for the purpose of" or "in regard to" divine or imperial solicitude. The meanings we are left with divide themselves into two categories. To one side, we have reward, benefaction, and maintenance (in the sense of livelihood), and to the other we have administration and management. "Care" and "solicitude" can be placed in either category depending on the object of pronoia: the person who received the property or paroikoi, or the property or paroikoi themselves. And here lies the problem. It is difficult to say who or what was receiving the pronoia in the phrase. Did *eis pronoian*

[22] While the noun *pronoia* in one of its conjugated forms appears more than 12,000 times in the online *TLG*, the phrase *eis pronoian* appears a mere thirty-six times in twenty-nine distinct works. Of these thirty-six occurrences of the phrase, fourteen (in eight distinct works) refer to pronoia in its technical sense.

mean that a property or paroikoi were held "for the purpose of administration (of the property and paroikoi)" or "for the purpose of (the recipient's personal) care or maintenance"? To hold a property "for administration" is quite different from holding a property "for maintenance." One emphasizes an administrative function as the purpose of the grant (the things granted are themselves the object of pronoia); the other emphasizes the grant as a means to maintain the recipient (the recipient is the object of pronoia).

Scholars have taken both points of view. For Ostrogorsky, the technical sense of *pronoia* came from the emperor granting people properties "to administer." Thus, the phrase *eis pronoian* meant a grant "for administration" ("*na upravu*" in Ostrogorsky's original Serbian), and the property itself was called elliptically a "pronoia." On the other hand, Armin Hohlweg relied on the meaning of *pronoia* as "maintenance" when he surmised that *eis pronoian* meant "for support" ("*zum Unterhalt*").[23]

This distinction is important because it involves the fundamental purpose of the grant. Were these grants made, primarily, to effect the administration of property, or were they made, primarily, to provide a livelihood for their recipients? Kontostephanos' act suggests an answer to this question. In the document at least three of the men involved (Rentinos and the Loukites brothers) are called soldiers (*stratiotai*). If the main purpose of the grant was to administer the property involved, it is unlikely that soldiers, who had other responsibilities, would have been chosen for this task. On the other hand, if the purpose was to provide a livelihood, then soldiers would have been ideal candidates to receive such a grant. This does not mean there was necessarily a connection between the pronoia grant and their occupation as soldiers; they may have held the properties involved for some other reason. But it does mean that they held the properties to derive benefit from them, not to manage them on behalf of the state.

Let us now return to the question of what it meant "to hold something *eis pronoian*." Pankratios and the soldiers held the *proasteion* in pronoia. The *Marcian Treatise* explains that, for various reasons, agricultural land was often located at some distance from the inhabited center (*kathedra*) of a village, causing some inhabitants to move their dwellings to areas more accessible to their work. At times, however, well-to-do members of the village community continued to live in the village proper while they sent hired workers or slaves to live at the distant place of work itself. This new

[23] Ostrogorsky, *Féodalité*, 9, and *Pronija* (Belgrade, 1951), 7, and accepted by H. Hunger, *Prooimion: Elemente der byzantinischen Kaiseridee in der Arengen der Urkunden* (Vienna, 1964), 91–92. Hohlweg, "Zur Frage der Pronoia," 308.

dwelling place, with its agricultural land, was called a *proasteion*.[24] With the passage of time these *proasteia* were often acquired by large landowners, including monasteries, and became independent land holdings, separated from the village community. Both *proasteia* called Archontochorion (that of Lavra and that of the soldiers) were probably once a single *proasteion* which most likely had such an origin. By the second half of the eleventh century some *proasteia* were large estates worked by peasant tenants, and during the thirteenth century the term was commonly applied to monastic estates, large or small, worked by paroikoi.

Paroikoi were a basic part of the *proasteion*, and indeed Pankratios also held paroikoi in pronoia. On the disputed *topos* one found "the *kathedra* of those held in pronoia" by Pankratios (lines 26–27), "the houses [*oikiai*] of the paroikoi" of Pankratios" (lines 40–41 and 88–89), "the houses of his paroikoi" (line 45), or "the *kathedrai*" of Pankratios' paroikoi (lines 82–83). In these passages *kathedra* (in both singular and plural) and *oikiai* all refer to the houses of the paroikoi. *Kathedra* (in the singular) has broadened its meaning from that found in the *Marcian Treatise* to signify any area with dwellings. After these houses were transported to Pankratios' *proasteion* on Kontostephanos' order, Kontostephanos ordered that these "paroikoi of *kyr* Pankratios" (line 105) not return to the monastery's *proasteion*.

Pankratios also had other paroikoi, though the document does not state explicitly that these were held by him in pronoia. Among these were the eight paroikoi who had moved from Lavra's *proasteion* to live "where the paroikoi of *kyr* Pankratios are settled" (lines 97–98), and which were returned to Lavra.

Similarly, the document cites "the paroikoi of the soldiers" (lines 50–51), "neither the said soldiers nor their paroikoi" (lines 72–73), and "such soldiers and their paroikoi" (line 75). The arrangement between the monastery and the soldiers stipulated that these paroikoi were not to live on the *topos* of the monastery but rather on the "*topos* of the fisc" which had been granted by Xiphilinos "as a *kathedra*" for the soldiers' paroikoi (lines 66–67).

Thus, the soldiers held a *proasteion* in pronoia and paroikoi in pronoia, and an official gave the soldiers a place for the paroikoi to live. Pankratios also held a *proasteion* and paroikoi in pronoia. Some of his paroikoi lived on the property of the monastery, others elsewhere.

What benefit did the soldiers and Pankratios derive from holding the *proasteion* and the paroikoi in pronoia? George Ostrogorsky wrote that

[24] Dölger, *Beiträge*, 115.21ff.

> the document of John Kontostephanos shows in unmistakable terms that the pronoiarioi mentioned were the actual possessors of the lands granted to them as pronoia and lords of the accompanying paroikoi. This must be emphasized, because the view has been held that the bestowal of pronoia – originally at least – meant only a conferral of tax revenues, but not an actual assignment of the corresponding property as well.[25]

In this passage Ostrogorsky distinguished the right to possess a property and the right to direct supervision of a group of peasants from the right to receive taxes from a property and from peasants. We can restate Ostrogorsky's conclusions: (i) Pankratios and the soldiers were the actual possessors of the *proasteion* of Archontochorion because they received not only the tax revenues but the actual assignment of the property from which the revenues were derived, and (ii) they were lords of the paroikoi found on the property. Are these points defensible? To consider the second point first, the document refers to the paroikoi of Pankratios and of the soldiers, as well as "the paroikoi of the monastery" (lines 96–97, 99). Because toward the end of the document we read that eight particular paroikoi had first been paroikoi of the monastery but later settled among the paroikoi of Pankratios, there is a clear parallel between the monastery's relationship to its paroikoi and Pankratios' and the soldiers' relationship to their paroikoi which they held in pronoia. To the extent that a monastery was "lord" of its paroikoi, then a pronoia holder was "lord" of his paroikoi. Thus we can say that Pankratios and the others were "lords" of the paroikoi on their *proasteion*. But the document offers absolutely nothing specific regarding what it meant to be a "lord" of paroikoi. Other documents tell us that the benefits from holding paroikoi included taxes and fiscal charges, as well as labor services (see Chapter 3). Since Pankratios and the soldiers held paroikoi, they, like any monastery or other landowner who held paroikoi, enjoyed whatever taxes and charges were assessed on the households and property of the paroikoi and had the right to demand the labor services that were traditionally owed the state. If the paroikoi had no property (such people were called *eleutheroi*, "free"), the soldiers could demand only their labor services. Thus it is certain that, at the very least, the soldiers and Pankratios benefitted from the labor services of their paroikoi.

The situation is more complicated with regard to property. The benefits from holding property could fall into several categories: taxes, rents in kind

[25] Ostrogorsky, "Die Pronoia unter den Komnenen," 47. Hohlweg, "Zur Frage der Pronoia," 305, with perhaps too much caution, concluded that the document does not tell us whether the *proasteion* was the actual possession of Pankratios and the soldiers.

or in specie, and agricultural produce, depending on how the property was held. An individual or monastery who held property could cultivate it directly, have others cultivate it, or, in some cases, receive from the actual owner of the property the taxes burdening the property. The last case can probably be excluded here since the document says nothing about any other individuals who had a legal interest in the property. Thus Pankratios and the soldiers either cultivated the *proasteion* themselves or arranged for others to work it. Since the document is concerned with illegally-held paroikoi and other paroikoi improperly inhabiting a monastery's property, the latter case is probably the situation. Pankratios' and the other soldiers' paroikoi worked the *proasteion* and from this the men derived two kinds of benefit. First, to the extent that the paroikoi owed labor services, Pankratios and the soldiers received the agricultural produce (or its equivalent in specie) raised by their paroikoi. Second, if the labor services owed by their paroikoi were insufficient to ensure the cultivation of the entire *proasteion*, they, like most landholders, leased part of the *proasteion* either to their own paroikoi and perhaps to other unspecified peasants, and derived in benefit a simple rent. In my view Pankratios and the other soldiers were the lords but not the masters of their paroikoi. They were merely owed certain obligations from their paroikoi.

The reconstruction I have suggested above accords with the information provided by Kontostephanos' act and with what we know about paroikoi and landholders from other sources. Nevertheless, some questions cannot be answered. We do not know, for example, whether Pankratios and the soldiers lived on their *proasteion*, or what role, if any, they played in organizing or controlling the economic production of the *proasteion*. Nor do we know how holding a property or paroikoi "in pronoia" differed from, say, a monastery holding a property and paroikoi. Perhaps the only difference was that the holding of property and paroikoi in pronoia was limited, as the *Zavorda Treatise* states, to "the lifetime of a man."

In any event Kontostephanos' act is the first source that tells us anything explicit about the kind of people who held property in pronoia. George Ostrogorsky used the fact that three of the men involved are called soldiers to support his view that the character of pronoia was fundamentally military, that pronoia holders were called "soldiers," and that this military character had its origins during the reign of Alexios I.[26] "The pronoiarioi whom we meet," he wrote, "were therefore warriors, and that leads to the natural conclusion that they held their pronoia grants under the obligation of

[26] Ostrogorsky, *Féodalité*, 36–37.

military service, something stressed more frequently and more explicitly in later documents." And even though the document itself provides no evidence that these three soldiers and Pankratios held their property in pronoia because they were soldiers, Ostrogorsky argued that one naturally cannot expect this kind of document to address military obligations and their connection to the pronoia. He further claimed that the document shows that the men belonged to the lesser nobility since all bore family names and Pankratios himself is addressed with the unofficial title of respect *kyr*.[27]

A connection between the pronoia of these soldiers and their military service, while certainly not established by this document, is reasonable. Further, we can say that in the twelfth century, some people who held property in pronoia were soldiers. Nevertheless, we can hardly conclude, on the basis of this document, that all pronoia holders were soldiers. The social status of these soldiers is difficult to judge. That they bore family names is not particularly remarkable. Even peasants at times bore family names in the twelfth century. Moreover, we observe that only Pankratios, the one man *not* identified explicitly as a soldier, bore the common title of respect *kyr*.[28]

In the end this interesting document raises more questions than it answers. If we wish to be extremely cautious, all it tells us for certain is that at some time before 1162 some soldiers held a *proasteion* and paroikoi "in pronoia."

The Cumans of Moglena

[2.4] Praktikon of Andronikos Vatatzes for the monastery of Lavra regarding the Cumans of Moglena (1181)

A praktikon of Andronikos Vatatzes from August 1181 introduces us to a group of Cumans who held pronoiai in Moglena, the region to the north of Vodena. The document begins with a transcription of a *prostagma* of Alexios II Komnenos from April of the same year, dealing with a *proasteion* called Chostianes which had been donated to Lavra by the Kephalas family (see *[4.6]*). We read there that certain paroikoi of this *proasteion* had

[27] Ostrogorsky, "Die Pronoia unter den Komnenen," 47 and note 28, 49. Cf. Hohlweg, "Zur Frage der Pronoia," 306.

[28] G. Litavrin, *Bolgarija i Vizantija v XI–XII vv.* (Moscow, 1960), 150, mistakenly claimed that Pankratios is called a soldier in the document.

been attributed to Cumans by "those making the conferrals of the Cuman pronoiai of the theme of Moglena," a phrase that perhaps appears in two other thoroughly mutilated passages.[29] The emperor ordered Vatatzes to restore the sixty-two paroikoi to Lavra.

This part of the document makes the distinction between the *despoteia* (δεσποτεία "ownership") of the paroikoi of Lavra held by the Cumans, which ought to return immediately to Lavra, and the *chresis kai nome* (χρῆσις καὶ νομή, "use and usufruct") which appears to remain for the lifetime of the Cumans: "those [paroikoi] held by the Cumans and inscribed in their praktika . . . [are] to be set apart toward the monastery so that while this monastery holds their *despoteia* henceforth, their *chresis* and *nome* remain with the Cumans for life and at the time of their death the *chresis* and *nome* return to the monastery absolutely."[30]

In lines 39–51 we have the second *prostagma* of the same month. While the emperor ordered Vatatzes to fulfill what the previous *prostagma* decreed, there apparently was a modification of orders. Even though the state of the document does not allow us to restore the meaning of the text with complete certainty, it seems that the emperor had changed his mind. As the earlier *prostagma* decreed, Lavra, which maintained the "ownership" of the paroikoi held in pronoia by the Cumans, was to receive them back after the death of the Cumans.[31] But now the emperor ordered Vatatzes to give Lavra "the *nome* and *chresis* [of these] paroikoi along with the *despoteia* [. . .] and to confer [upon] the Cumans holding these *kata* [*pro*]*noian* other paroikoi [. . . from other villages] belonging to the fisc."[32] Further, the

29 *Lavra*, I, no. 65.7: οἱ τὰς παραδ[όσεις] τῶν κομανικῶν προ[ν]οιῶν τοῦ θέματος Μογλ[έ]νων ποιού[μενοι], and cf. lines 12–13 and 39. Chostianes (today Archangelos) is about 22 miles north-northeast of Vodena (mod. Edessa). See V. Kravari, *Villes et villages de Macédoine occidentale* (Paris, 1989), 71–72 and map 10. It appears as Ošin on Vojnogeografski institut (Belgrade), topographical map, 1:200000, sheet 62, "Voden" (1963), and as both Ošin and Hošan on Österreichisch-Ungarischen Monarchie, die dritte militärische Aufnahme, topographical map, 1:200000, sheet "40° 41° Vodena" (1904) (http://lazarus.elte.hu/hun/digkonyv/topo/200e/40–41.jpg).

30 *Lavra*, I, no. 65.25–27: παρὰ τῶν Κομάνων κατεχό[μεν]οι καὶ τοῖς πρακ[τικοῖς αὐτῶν] ἐγκαταγεγραμ[μένοι.....] αὐτοὺς ἀφ[ορισθῆ]ναι πρὸς τὴν μονὴν ὥστε τὴν μὲν δεσποτείαν αὐτῶν ἀπεντεῦθεν τὴν τοιαύτην ἔχειν μονήν, τὴν δὲ χρῆσιν αὐτῶν καὶ νομὴν παραμένειν τοῖς Κομάνοις μέχ[ρι] αὐτῆς ζωῆς καὶ ἅμα τῇ τελευτῇ αὐτῶν [ἐπ]ανατρέχειν καὶ τὴν χρῆσιν καὶ τὴν νομὴν εἰς τὴν μονὴν αὐθεντικῶς.

31 *Lavra*, I, no. 65.41–42: προσκαθισάντων παροίκων [...ca. 18 characters...] πρόνοιαν κατεχομένων.

32 *Lavra*, I, no. 65.43–45: σὺν τῇ δεσποτείᾳ καὶ τὴν νομὴν καὶ τὴν χρῆσιν [τῶν τοιούτων] παροί[κων ...ca. 16 characters... τοῖς] δὲ κατὰ [πρό]νοιαν κατέχουσι τούτους Κομάνοις παραδοῦναι ἑτέρους παροίκους [...ca. 35 characters... χωρίοις τῷ] δημοσίῳ διαφέρουσι.

emperor ordered Vatatzes to remove whatever the Cumans built, including pasturage enclosures, on Lavra's land (line 45–46).

Finally, we have the actual text of Vatatzes' praktikon. It begins with a mutilated passage referring to "the sixteen soldiers settled in it" (line 52), obviously a reference to Chostianes. A badly mutilated list of names follows. Nevertheless, the appearance of the family name "Komanopoulos" three times, along with clearly non-Greek given names such as "Valtzantares," "Taptoukos," and the fragmentary "Masout . . . ," indicates that these men are the Cumans to which the document is referring.

Vatatzes then notes that he earlier ordered "these soldiers to move from the village of Chostianes and to settle in other villages," and to remove "their houses and all pasturage enclosures from such *proasteion* Chostianes" according to the imperial order (lines 55–56). He then confirms Lavra's possession of the paroikoi: [we confer] "those held by various soldiers *kata logon pronoias* and [settled] in these *pr[oasteia]* there" upon Lavra. Apparently he had already compensated the soldiers with the same number of paroikoi from other villages: "earlier having given in return for other paroikoi in other fiscal villages." A list of sixty-two *zeugaratoi* paroikoi follows. The praktikon concludes with the order that Lavra is to own and hold these paroikoi "so that neither military persons nor neighbors in any part of this village of Chostianes" harass them.[33]

The poor state of this document makes it impossible to work out fully the dispute and its resolution. In particular there is the confusion over the "*proasteion* of Chostianes" (owned by Lavra) and the "village of Chostianes." At first one might think these were different properties, but that raises the question of why the Cumans were ordered to leave the village of Chostianes.

Where in fact did the Cumans live? A fragmentary passage refers to the Cumans "settled on this land," which suggests, though does not prove, that they had been living on the land of Lavra.[34] However, the phrase ordering the removal of "their houses and all pasturage enclosures from such *proasteion* Chostianes" must be referring to the houses and enclosures of the Cumans. It cannot be referring to the paroikoi improperly given to the Cumans, because these paroikoi were to remain on the *proasteion* of Chostianes. Thus, the Cumans were given not only all or part of the paroikoi of Chostianes, but they were given all or part of the land as well. Did they actually work these

[33] *Lavra*, I, no. 65.58: τοὺς παρὰ διαφόρων στρατιωτῶν κατεχομένους κατὰ λόγον προνοίας καὶ ἐν τοῖς προσοῦσιν αὐτοῖς πρ[οαστείοις], line 60: πρότερον παραδεδωκότες ἀνθετέρους παροίκους ἐν ἑτέροις δημοσίοις χωρίοις, and lines 79–80: μήτε ἢ στρατιωτικὰ πρόσω[πα ...ca. 20 characters...] ἢ ἀν[α]κοινοῦσιν.

[34] *Lavra*, I, no. 65.31: ἐπὶ τοῖς Κομάνοις τοῖς προσκαθημένοις ἐν τῇ το[ι]αύτῃ γῇ.

pasturage enclosures or did their paroikoi? While this question is important for estimating the social status of the Cumans, it cannot be answered.

George Ostrogorsky felt that the Cumans were rich and powerful pronoia holders.[35] Yet three of the Cumans found in the list of sixteen names are identified through patronyms, "(son) of Tartzes," "(son) of Komp. . . . ," and "(son) of Isa . . . ." By the second half of the twelfth century, one would expect rich and powerful men to bear family names. Further, one should not lose sight of the fact that these Cumans were forced to relocate. Evidently they were less powerful than the monastery.

As for the paroikoi, the sixty-two households are listed by the name of a male head of household (to the extent that their names can be read) and all are described as *zeugaratoi*, that is, relatively well-off peasant households which owned a yoke of oxen (*zeugarion*) and paid a corresponding hearth tax. From the document itself, it is not clear what benefit the Cumans would have derived from these paroikoi, whether their taxes, their labor services, or both. But typically, paroikoi rendered both their taxes (personal and secondary charges) and labor services to those who were granted them. One wonders what benefit Lavra may have retained, according to the initial resolution of the dispute, through holding the *despoteia* of these paroikoi, while the Cumans had their "use and usufruct." But what is clear is that sixty-two paroikos households divided by sixteen Cuman families gives a little less than four paroikos families per Cuman household, which would hardly have made the Cumans major landlords. Since we are told that the Cumans were to move and receive replacement paroikoi elsewhere, it seems that they were holding no more than these sixty-two paroikoi. On the whole, I think these sixteen Cumans, though soldiers and holders of pronoia grants, were herdsmen.

The document neither confirms nor contradicts the evidence of the *Zavorda Treatise* that a pronoia was a lifetime grant. George Ostrogorsky concluded that the Cumans had been permitted to hold these paroikoi only for their lifetime specifically because they were pronoia holders.[36] This need not have been the case. Once the imperial officials realized the monastery's paroikoi had been mistakenly assigned to the Cumans, apparently an initial compromise solution was suggested, that the Cumans should continue to hold the paroikoi for life. The clause that the monastery retained the

[35] Ostrogorsky, *Féodalité*, 49, 52. D. Anastasijević and G. Ostrogorsky, "Les Koumanes pronoïaires," *Annuaire de l'Institut de philologie et d'histoire orientale et slave* 11 (1951) = *Mélanges H. Grégoire III*, 28.

[36] G. Ostrogorski, "Još jednom o proniarima Kumanima," in *Zbornik Vladimira Mošina*, ed. D. Dogdanović et al. (Belgrade, 1977), 69.

despoteia of these paroikoi would ensure that the Cumans' heirs could not inherit the paroikoi. No doubt pressure from Lavra caused this arrangement to be scrapped. Indeed the act of Kontostephanos from 1162 shows how difficult it was to reclaim property that had been "temporarily" removed from the control of a monastery, and the memory of that incident may have still been in the minds of the monks of Lavra.

On the other hand, the document does lead to a few conclusions. The phrase "the conferrals of the Cuman pronoiai of the theme of Moglena" suggests a more or less substantial government policy with regard to the Cumans. Evidently there was no need to explain what "Cuman pronoiai" were because the phenomenon, at least in that area, was widespread. George Ostrogorsky interpreted this, correctly I think, as evidence of a significant extension of pronoia, particularly to foreigners, during the reign of Manuel I Komnenos.[37]

The Cumans were a nomadic Turkic people who frequently made incursions into Byzantium from the north from the eleventh to the thirteenth century. Anna Komnene, for example, writes in some detail of her father's campaigns against the Cumans in the late eleventh century in which many prisoners were taken. Presumably many of these were recruited into the army. Indeed the presence of a Cuman contingent in the Byzantine army, and in particular their deployment in Thrace and Macedonia, is attested during the later eleventh, twelfth, and later centuries.[38]

Gennadij Litavrin wrote that the Cumans of Moglena had received the right to enjoy state land on condition of military service, and Ostrogorsky viewed the military nature of the Cumans as lending further support to his thesis that holders of pronoiai tended to be soldiers.[39] The connection between the Cumans' military service and their pronoiai is not established by the document, but it is quite likely. That the holders of pronoia grants tended to be soldiers cannot be concluded on the basis of this document, though this act plus the Kontostephanos act and another document from the twelfth century *[2.5]* makes this a reasonable conclusion as well.

The document also provides us with the first known instances of a number of expressions using the word *pronoia* in this technical sense. The phrase "the conferrals of Cuman pronoiai of the theme of Moglena" (line 7) is

[37] Ostrogorsky, *Féodalité*, 53.

[38] C. Asdracha, *La région des Rhodopes aux XIIIe et XIVe siècles* (Athens, 1976), 80–82. *Alexiad*, X.2.3–4.11: ed. Reinsch, 285–95, esp. 293.95–96: 3,000 prisoners, and 295.47 = ed. B. Leib, II, 191–204, esp. 202.26–28, and 204.22.

[39] Litavrin, *Bolgarija i Vizantija v XI–XII vv.*, 148. Ostrogorski, "Još jednom o proniarima Kumanima," 66–67.

quite interesting. Despite several lacunae the restorations are sure. The passage gives us the word *pronoia* in the plural (ostensibly equivalent to *ta pronoiatika* of the *Zavorda Treatise*), the expressions "conferrals (*paradoseis*) of pronoiai" and "Cuman pronoiai," as well as the concept of "pronoia of a theme."

In lines 44–45, if the restoration is correct, we encounter the phrase "to those Cumans holding these [paroikoi] according to pronoia" ([τοῖς] δὲ κατὰ [πρό]νοιαν κατέχουσι τούτους Κομάνοις), which gives us the construction "to hold someone according to pronoia" (κατέχειν τι κατὰ πρόνοιαν). *Kata pronoian* would seem to be roughly equivalent then to *eis pronoian*, as found in the Kontostephanos act.[40] Further, in line 58 the expression "paroikoi held by reason of pronoia" (πάροικοι κατεχομένοι κατὰ λόγον προνοίας) yields the construction κατέχειν τι κατὰ λόγον προνοίας. This has a parallel in the passage from the testament of Eustathios Voïlas: he left land to a church he founded "for the maintenance of the clergy serving in it" (λόγου προνοίας τῶν ἐκδουλευόντων ἐν αὐτῇ κληρικῶν).[41] Thus, *eis pronoian*, *kata pronoian*, and *kata logon pronoias* would seem to be synonymous.

[2.5] Prostaxis of Andronikos I Komnenos for the monastery of Lavra regarding the Cumans of Moglena (1184)

The monastery of Lavra's problems with Cumans living in the Moglena area continued. Three years after Andronikos Vatatzes' praktikon a *prostaxis* was issued by Andronikos I Komnenos which deals with another dispute between Lavra and some Cumans. The monks complained to the emperor that "the Cumans living [*oikountes*] in Moglena" had entered a mountain belonging to the monastery and built some livestock enclosures (*mandria*) there without agreeing to pay Lavra the "*dekateia* of their animals," that is, the rental charge for the use of pasturage. The emperor ordered his tax collectors (*praktores*) to force the Cumans to pay this *dekateia* and everything else owed, and to prevent them from appropriating the Vlachs or Bulgars held by others. Evidently some of these were paroikoi of the monastery.

[40] It is possible to complete the critical lacuna in line 45 without any reference to pronoia at all. Nevertheless, the phrase κατὰ πρόνοιαν is not uncommon. It appears 231 times in the online *TLG* with a non-technical sense (about one-third of these instances with the verb γίγνομαι). However, the construction with any verb derived from ἔχω appears only about seven times in a non-technical sense.

[41] Lemerle, *Cinq études*, 23.101–02. The incomplete phrase πρόνοιαν κατεχομένων in line 42 does not permit us to establish any new phrases; it might have been preceded by εἰς or κατὰ λόγον.

Further, the emperor decreed that if the Cumans continued to withhold what they owed "or to exempt [*exkousseuein*] Vlachs or Bulgars, according to the bad custom prevailing until now by them," they should be expelled from the mountain, by force if necessary.[42] This is an unusual context for the verb *exkousseuo* (ἐξκουσσεύω), which normally is used with regard to fiscal exemptions granted by the state, particularly to peasants. In the twelfth century, the paroikoi held by a privileged landowner were often "excused" from the corvées and secondary charges and taxes owed to the state and, instead, furnished these burdens to the landowner. However, here it seems to mean that the Cumans were "exempting" the peasants of the charges owed to others, including the monastery, that is, they themselves were collecting the charges owed by the peasants.

Perhaps one of these charges was a fee for pasturing animals, because the emperor further ordered that the Vlachs belonging to the monastery should be permitted to pasture their animals freely within the borders of the theme of Moglena without paying any fee and that "they not be hindered or kept away by anyone of those there, either tax collectors [*praktores*], or soldiers or thematic [officials] or the Cumans themselves" (line 10).

The same document also treats another problem faced by the monks. Certain "paroikoi workers" (*douleutai* or *paroikoi douleutai*) had settled outside the monastery of St. John Prodromos, a dependency of Lavra located within the village of Chostianes. Since these workers had not been conferred through praktikon on the monastery, the official charged with making the conferrals (*paradoseis*) of the district (*petiton*) of the theme of Moglena harassed them "as unconferred" (line 20: ὡς ἀπαραδότους), that is, they were rendering their taxes and labor obligations neither to the fisc nor to any landholder. And so "he conferred two of them in pronoia upon Cumans."[43] The emperor countermanded this decision and donated these people to the monastery while the Cumans themselves were to be compensated with other paroikoi (line 23). It is impossible to know whether these were the same sixteen Cuman soldiers referred to in the previous document *[2.4]* who had been ordered to move from the area of Chostianes. If they were, the order to move was not carried out; if they were not, there seems to have been quite a few Cumans in the area of Chostianes.

This document offers a new phrase: "to confer paroikoi in pronoia" (εἰς πρόνοιαν παροίκους παραδοῦναι). More significant is how the 1162 Kontostephanos act *[2.3]* differs from this act and the previous act from

[42] *Lavra*, I, no. 66.1–2, and lines 5–6.

[43] *Lavra*, I, no. 66.20: καὶ δύο ἀπ᾽ αὐτῶν εἰς πρόνοιαν παραδέδωκε Κομάνοις.

1181 *[2.4]*, both dealing with the Cumans of Moglena, in regard to who lived and worked in the areas in question. Kontostephanos' act mentions "the houses of the paroikoi" held by the pronoia holders and gives no indication that the pronoia-holding soldiers and Pankratios Anemas themselves had a physical presence in the area of Archontochorion. On the other hand, the act from 1181 notes that the Cumans lived in the area of Chostianes and refers to "their houses and pasturage enclosures," and in the current act the Cumans "living in Moglena" had trespassed on the monastery's property and "built some livestock enclosures for their animals." The references to the Cumans' livestock enclosures is understandable in light of the pastoral traditions of these people. Yet it would seem that they had a closer relation to the economic sources of production than the soldiers in Kontostephanos' act. Nevertheless, the Cumans of both acts held paroikoi, and, on the parallel with monasteries holding paroikoi, they would have benefitted from receipt of the taxes and labor services of the paroikoi.

One final document concerning Moglena should be mentioned here, a two-part act containing both a request of the monks of Lavra and a decision (*lysis*) of Alexios III Angelos, both from October 1196. The monks petitioned the emperor regarding a village they owned in the theme of Verrhoia, which had been granted to the monastery by the uncle of the emperor. The document does not provide the name of the village, but it was not near Chostianes. Lavra had been leasing (*ekdidei*) some plots of land (*topia*) within this village "to some soldiers of the theme of Moglena and to paroikoi of the bishop of Moglena for the sake of a *dekateia*." But "some of them in the summertime did not prudently pay their *dekateia* to our monastery." Lavra asked the emperor to order the tax collectors of Verrhoia and of Moglena to force the recalcitrants to pay double the rental payment (*dekateia*). The emperor ruled that if the parcels in question were truly within Lavra's borders, local officials should enforce the rights of Lavra regarding the property it was renting out and not permit those leasing these properties to withhold the *dekateia* owed.[44]

George Ostrogorsky and Dragutin Anastasijević concluded that the soldiers mentioned in the act appear to have been pronoia holders, and Paul Lemerle thought the soldiers were "no doubt Cumans."[45] While there seems to have been a strong presence of Cuman soldiers who were pronoia holders in the area of Moglena, we cannot assume that every reference to soldiers in

[44] *Lavra*, I, no. 69.7–9,17–18, and p. 72.

[45] Ostrogorsky, *Féodalité*, 46, and Anastasijević and Ostrogorsky, "Les Koumanes pronoïaires," 21–22, who based their analysis of this document on the earlier edition of Rouillard and Collomp. Lemerle, *Agrarian History*, 240.

the area was connected to them. We observe that the document juxtaposes these soldiers with episcopal paroikoi, which opens the possibility that they were of rather low status. Further, we know from the history of Zonaras, written after 1118 and probably around the middle of the twelfth century, that a group of Pechenegs, who had entered the empire for plunder, were settled as soldiers in Moglena after being defeated by Alexios I Komnenos in 1091. The emperor "settled them with wives and children in the theme of the Moglena and organized them as a 'most separate corps.' They remain up to now through hereditary succession and are called Pechenegs Moglenitai [Πατζινάκοι Μογλενῖται], having as an epithet the place in which they were settled."[46] Based on the passage from the *Zavorda Treatise*, these Pechenegs could not have been pronoia holders because their lands were hereditary, and so they must have been smallholding soldiers.[47] This does not mean that the soldiers in the 1196 *lysis* were Pechenegs, but it does mean that we cannot conclude that they were either Cumans or pronoia holders.

The Skordiles family of Crete

[2.6] Act of the *doux* of Crete Constantine Doukas for the Skordiles family (1183 or 1192)

Outside of the *Zavorda Treatise* the only appearance of the adjective *pronoiatikos* is in one variant of an odd document from 1183 or 1192 in which the *doux* of Crete Constantine Doukas confirmed the property possessions of the Skordiles family. The document exists only in three late- or post-Byzantine versions, two Greek and one Italian, all of which have clearly been emended and modified to suit later historical circumstances. In the introduction to the document, in what apparently is a formulaic passage, Doukas explains that he was ordered to allocate to each person his proper property. In the three versions of the document the phrase of interest to us appears as follows. Doukas writes that he had been ordered by the emperor

46 Zonaras, XVIII.23: *Ioannis Zonarae Epitomae Historiarum libri XVIII*, ed. M. Pinder (Bonn, 1841–97), III, 740–41: εἰς τὸ τῶν Μογλένων θέμα τούτους... κατῴκισε καὶ τάγμα τούτους κατέστησεν ἰδιαίτατον. Cf. Anna Komnene's account which claims the complete annihilation of the Pechenegs: *Alexiad*, VIII.5.8: ed. Reinsch, 248 = ed. Leib, II, 142–43, and Asdracha, *La région des Rhodopes*, 83. *ODB*, s.v. "Lebounion, Mount."

47 Lemerle, *Agrarian History*, 230, and Ahrweiler, *Byzance et la mer*, 220 note 3, neither of whom were familiar with the *Zavorda Treatise*, came to the same conclusion. Ahrweiler erroneously wrote of "'Manichaioi' Pechenegs," conflating two passages in Zonaras. On smallholding soldiers, see Bartusis, "Smallholding Soldiers," esp. 22–23.

(i) "to arrange... each in his patrimonial *eparchia* and land given through providential grant of the... emperors" (ἀποκαθιστᾶν... ἑνὶ ἑκάστῳ εἰς τὴν γονικὴν ἐπαρχίαν καὶ γῆν αὐτοῦ, καὶ διὰ προνοιατικῆς δωρεᾶς τῶν... βασιλέων... διδομένην);

(ii) "to distribute the old patrimonial soil to each, given through providential grant of the... emperors" (νὰ διανέμωμεν τὸ παλαιὸν πατρικὸν ἔδαφος εἰς τὸν καθένα, διὰ προνοητικῆς δωρεᾶς τῶν... αὐτοκρατόρων... δοθείσης); and

(iii) "to arrange... to each his paternal diocese and land, given through the due providence of the... emperors" (*accomodar... cadauno nella paternal diocese et terra sua, et per providentia dovuta alli... imperatori... dato*).[48]

On the basis of the first version of the passage some scholars have seen a distinction between hereditary property (τὴν γονικὴν ἐπαρχίαν) and pronoia (γῆν... διὰ προνοιατικῆς δωρεᾶς... διδομένην). Ostrogorsky wrote that Doukas was ordered "to put each of the nobles and faithful archons in possession of their patrimonial lands as well as lands which had been allotted to them in pronoia."[49] But there are many problems with this interpretation. First, the second Greek variant of the document notes that it was simply "the old patrimonial soil" (τὸ παλαιὸν πατρικὸν ἔδαφος, not a Byzantine expression at all) that had been given "through providential grant" (διὰ προνοητικῆς δωρεᾶς), with no distinction between hereditary property and pronoia. Second, the phrase τὴν γονικὴν ἐπαρχίαν ("patrimonial *eparchia*") is unknown in Byzantine documents. Even the word *eparchia* is quite rare in the documentary sources; a perusal of the indices of the published acts of the monasteries of Mount Athos, the Patmos monastery, and the Prodromos monastery near Serres yields a mere three appearances of the

48 E. Gerland, *Histoire de la noblesse crétoise au moyen âge* (Paris, 1907), 91 A, B, and C. The first of these is found also in MM, III, 235.12–16, and was reedited by S. Xanthoudides, "Τὸ δίπλωμα (προβελέγιον) τῶν Σκορδιλῶν Κρήτης," *Ἐρετηρὶς Ἑταιρείας Κρητικῶν Σπουδῶν* 2 (1939), 299–312. On the date of the original document and its authenticity, see Dölger, *Regesten*, II, no. 1561; Ostrogorsky, *Féodalité*, 43–44; and C. Brand, *Byzantium Confronts the West, 1180–1204* (Cambridge, Mass., 1968), 107–09, 344–45 notes 72–78. On the problematic identity of this Constantine Doukas, see D. Polemis, *The Doukai* (London, 1968), 191–92.

49 Uspenskij, "Značenie," 4. Ostrogorsky, *Féodalité*, 45. M. Sjuzjumov, "Vnutrennjaja politika Andronika Komnina i razgrom prigorodov Konstantinopolja v 1187 godu," *VizVrem* 12 (1957), 65. B. Gorjanov, *Pozdnevizantijskij feodalizm* (Moscow, 1962), 130–31. N. Oikonomides, "Ἡ διανομὴ τῶν βασιλικῶν «ἐπισκέψεων» τῆς Κρήτης (1170–1171) καὶ ἡ δημοσιονομικὴ πολιτικὴ τοῦ Μανουὴλ Α΄ Κομνηνοῦ," in Oikonomides, *Documents et études sur les institutions de Byzance* (London, 1976), no. XVII, 199–200. D. Jacoby, "Les états latins en Romanie: phénomènes sociaux et économiques (1204–1350 environ)," in Jacoby, *Recherches sur la Méditerranée orientale*, no. I, pp. 7–8.

word, each time with the unambiguous and simple meaning "province."[50] Further, the Greek variant of the document that contains the word *eparchia* in the phrase in question employs this same word four other times, while the other Greek variant does not use this word at all. In its place it consistently utilizes *dioikesis* (διοίκησις "diocese"). The Italian version reads *provincia* in three of these instances and *territorio* in the fourth (Gerland, 91–94). On the other hand, we may observe that neither of the Greek variants of the document employs either *ktemata* (κτήματα) or *dikaia* (δίκαια), the words that Byzantine documents employ habitually to denote properties and the rights to properties.

It would seem that the word that originally appeared in place of *eparchia* and *dioikesis* was *dikaia*. Indeed in the preface to a late- or post-Byzantine version of another act of Constantine Doukas, originally dating to 1182, 1185, or 1192, and which confirms the property possessions of twelve Cretan families, one variant reads αἱ ἐπαρχίαι καὶ γονικὰ for another variant's τὰ δικαιώματα καὶ κτήματα (Gerland, 99 A and B). In the text itself, one variant's τὸ . . . δικαίωμα parallels another's τῶν ἐπαρχιῶν (Gerland, 101 B and C), and τὰ κτήματα καὶ πατρικὰ δικαιώματα parallels τῶν πατρῴων ἐπαρχιῶν (Gerland, 103 B and C). *Ta dikaiomata* (τὰ δικαιώματα) is the modern Greek equivalent of the Byzantine *ta dikaia* (τὰ δίκαια), meaning rights to properties or simply the properties themselves.

Apparently, as suggested by Nicolas Oikonomides, the Greek versions of the document from 1183 or 1192 were based on the Italian version. This would explain why the Byzantine emperor is referred to in the Greek versions, not as emperor "of the Romans," but as emperor "of Constantinople." This phrase is unheard of in official Greek documents, but makes sense in an Italian version intended for a western audience. It would seem then that the original Greek text of Doukas' document read *dikaia* rather than *eparchia* or *dioikesis*, and that the Italian version's *diocese* may be a mistranslation of *dikaia*, to which the later Greek variants correctly responded with *eparchia* and *dioikesis*.[51]

But the most serious problem with seeing a distinction between hereditary property and pronoia in the act from 1183 or 1192, indeed with seeing any reference to the pronoia in a technical sense at all in this document, is that

[50] *Iviron*, I, no. 9.17 (from 995). *Lavra*, I, no. 31.72 (1052). *Prôtaton*, App. Ia.3 (1084 or 1109).

[51] Oikonomides, "Ἡ διανομὴ τῶν βασιλικῶν «ἐπισκέψεων»," 199. Alternatively, one wonders whether τὴν γονικὴν ἐπαρχίαν and τὸ παλαιὸν πατρικὸν ἔδαφος in the two Greek versions of Constantine Doukas' act are the post-Byzantine renderings, via a mangled Italian translation, of an original τὰ παλαιγενῆ δικαιώματα, "old documents," a common phrase in documents dealing with fiscal matters.

the terminology, vocabulary, and syntax of the preserved Greek variants reflect late Byzantine or (in my view) post-Byzantine demoticism. Even the most clever interpretations of the strange terminology in the Greek and Italian versions of the document can do little to illuminate the Byzantine reality hidden under the post-Byzantine vocabulary.[52]

Thus, there is insufficient reason to conclude that the phrases διὰ προνοιατικῆς δωρεᾶς, διὰ προνοητικῆς δωρεᾶς, and *per providentia dovuta* were intended to indicate pronoia in the technical sense. It is quite possible that the meaning of the phrase in the original document was simply that the ownership of the lands of the people of Crete had been "solicitously bestowed," or even merely "solicitously confirmed" by earlier emperors.[53] Further, the nature of the manuscript tradition of these documents does not permit us to conclude that either of the Greek phrases actually appeared in the original document, and so the document provides no reliable information about the use of the adjectives *pronoetikos* and *pronoiatikos* during the Byzantine period. At best, the documents suggest that imperial grants of property were given to members of the Skordiles family in the later twelfth century, but the nature of these grants is unknown.

Observations

The terminology encountered so far can be summarized. "The pronoia" (*he pronoia*) of the 1136 *typikon* seems to be an example of *ta pronoiatika* of the *Zavorda Treatise.*

The 1162 Kontostephanos act has the construction "to hold something (a *proasteion* or paroikoi) in pronoia" (ἔχειν or κατέχειν τι εἰς πρόνοιαν). It appears that "something held in pronoia" is "a pronoia," and "in pronoia" seems to mean "for maintenance (of the recipient of the grant)."

In the 1181 praktikon of Andronikos Vatatzes we find *pronoia* in the plural, evidently meaning multiple grants in pronoia, in the phrase "conferrals of pronoiai" (τὰς παραδόσεις τῶν . . . προνοιῶν), which ought to be synonymous with "conferrals in pronoia." This same document refers

52 For example, Kazhdan, *Agrarnye otnošenija*, 204, and "Formen," 220, tried to read "a hereditary office in the administration of provinces" into τῆς γονικὴν ἐπαρχίαν and a general "feudal administrative right to a territory" into *eparchia* itself. And cf. Oikonomides, "Ἡ διανομὴ τῶν βασιλικῶν «ἐπισκέψεων»," 200.

53 With a bit too much certainty, Kazhdan, *Agrarnye otnošenija*, 205, and "Formen," 220, nevertheless concluded that the phrases meant merely that the lands in question had been "carefully bestowed" or "transferred solicitously."

to a particular kind of grant in pronoia, "Cuman pronoiai" (*komanikai pronoiai*). Further, we encounter the construction "to hold someone according to pronoia" (κατέχειν τι κατὰ [πρό]νοιαν) as well as the construction κατέχειν τι κατὰ λόγον προνοίας, indicating that the phrases *eis pronoian*, *kata pronoian*, and *kata logon pronoias* were synonymous.

The 1184 *prostaxis* of Andronikos I offers the phrase "to confer paroikoi in pronoia" (εἰς πρόνοιαν παροίκους παραδοῦναι), indicating that the act of "conferring something in pronoia" was equivalent to "a conferral in pronoia."

What can we conclude about the institution of pronoia in the twelfth century? According to the *Zavorda Treatise*, *ta pronoiatika*, as "the [things] granted by the emperor for the lifetime of the man," were the component parts of a grant of (i) something, (ii) from the emperor (iii) for life. Further, (iv) the treatise's author evidently thought that a pronoia could be granted only to an individual.

As for point (i), the documents involving Synadenos, Pankratios Anemas, and the Cumans *[2.2–2.3] [2.5]* all indicate that the pronoia or the objects held in pronoia could include property. The 1162 Kontostephanos act adds that the objects that could be held in pronoia included not only property (a *proasteion*), but paroikoi as well; in the 1181 and 1184 documents involving the Cumans of Moglena the only objects specifically noted as held in pronoia were paroikoi. Both of these documents suggest that the paroikoi within pronoia grants were fungible in that exchanges or substitutions of the paroikoi were easily made. Real property and paroikoi could be held in pronoia.

The information supplied by the four documents is consistent with (ii): the granting of the pronoia of a deceased man to a monastery in the 1136 *typikon* by John II implicitly indicates that the emperor had the right to arrange the distribution of pronoiai; the 1162 Kontostephanos act, while saying nothing directly regarding how the soldiers and Pankratios first came to hold their *proasteion* and paroikoi, does say that these soldiers were granted "a *topos* of the fisc" as a place for their paroikoi to settle, indicating the state was involved in the arrangements of their livelihood; the 1181 praktikon of Andronikos Vatatzes explicitly says that paroikoi had been attributed to Cumans by "those making the conferrals of the Cuman pronoiai of the theme of Moglena"; and the 1184 *prostaxis* of Andronikos I explicitly notes that a fiscal official had conferred two paroikoi "in pronoia on Cumans." Pronoiai, therefore, were conferred upon imperial officials, directly or indirectly at the behest of the emperor.

As for point (iii), that such grants were for life, we might conclude that the reason the pronoia in the 1136 *typikon* was in the possession of John II was because its original recipient had died. The Kontostephanos act is unclear about whether a pronoia could be inherited, and the two acts dealing with the Cumans of Moglena add nothing to our knowledge of such matters.

Regarding point (iv), that a pronoia could be granted only to an individual, one could say that the 1136 *typikon* suggests otherwise, since a monastery was now granted the pronoia of a deceased individual. Yet it is not necessary to conclude that the monastery would hold this property under the same conditions as the deceased Synadenos.

What kind of individuals held pronoiai? We do not know who Synadenos was in the 1136 *typikon [2.2]*, and we are not told very much about Pankratios Anemas in the Kontostephanos act *[2.3]*. But all of the other pronoia holders in the Kontostephanos act and the praktikon of Vatatzes *[2.4]* were soldiers, as were, probably, the Cumans in the *prostaxis* of Andronikos I *[2.5]*. One of the functions of pronoia grants, then, appears to be as a means of financing soldiers.

Where did the holders of pronoiai live? The 1136 *typikon* and the Kontostephanos act provide no information on this, but both documents involving the Cumans indicate that the pronoia holders lived very near the site of their grant. Therefore, we can say that pronoia holders sometimes had close physical proximity to the property they held in pronoia.

Both the *Zavorda Treatise* and the 1136 *typikon* suggest that a pronoia grant consisted of real property, and the other documents specifically mention a *proasteion [2.3]* and paroikoi *[2.3–2.5]*. But as for the actual concrete benefits of holding such things, none of these sources tells us very much. The normal benefit of holding land (such as the *proasteion* in the Kontostephanos act) was to receive some combination of rents and the harvest, and the normal benefit of holding paroikoi *[2.3–2.5]* was to receive some combination of taxes, other fiscal charges, and labor services. But none of these sources allows us to determine which of these the pronoia holders were receiving. In the *prostaxis* of Andronikos I *[2.5]* it seems that the Cumans were appropriating fiscal charges of peasants, but this was deemed illegal, not a part of any pronoia grant. Nevertheless, the manner in which pronoia holders held their property and the conflicts they had with other landholders, specifically a monastery *[2.3–2.5]*, suggests that there was a fundamental similarity between various forms of landholding.

3 | Choniates' "gifts of paroikoi"

[3.1] Choniates on "gifts of paroikoi" (early thirteenth century)

The historian Niketas Choniates, writing in the early thirteenth century, describes a change in the manner by which Manuel I Komnenos financed the military. Even though Choniates does not employ the word *pronoia* in the passage, nearly every scholar who has ever written about it has interpreted this passage as a reference to the institution of pronoia.[1] In the course of praising the efforts of Manuel I Komnenos to limit the wealth of monasteries in land, Choniates condemns his measures concerning the army. This well-known text is of such importance that I present it here, in translation, in its entirety:

There is a custom among the Romans, prevailing I think among the barbarians also, to provide a wage [*opsonia*] to the soldiers, to inspect them frequently, whether they were well-armed, whether they took care of their horses, as well as to examine the recruits, whether they were able-bodied, whether they were skilled in the bow, whether they were experienced in brandishing a lance. Only then were they inscribed in the rolls. But this emperor [Manuel I] poured into the treasury, like water into a cistern, the wages [*siteresia*] given to the soldiers, and quenched the thirst of the troops with what are called "gifts of paroikoi," abusing a practice devised by previous emperors though seldom performed for those who often thrashed the enemy.

[1] For example: F. Chalandon, *Les Comnènes*, II (Paris, 1912), 614. Mutafčiev, "Vojniški zemi," 48/574, 51/577. E. Darkó, "La militarizzazione dell'Impero Bizantino," *Atti del V Congresso internazionale bizantini* (Rome 1936), I = *Studi bizantini e neoellenici* 5 (1939), 97. A. Hohlweg, *Beiträge zur Verwaltungsgeschichte des oströmischen Reiches unter den Komnenen* (Munich, 1965), 84, 86, and "Zur Frage der Pronoia," 303. Ahrweiler, "La concession des droits incorporels," 110, 112, and "La 'pronoia' à Byzance," 681–82, 687, 688. Ostrogorsky, "Die Pronoia unter den Komnenen," 46. M. Sjuzjumov, "Vnutrennjaja politika Andronika Komnina i razgrom prigorodov Konstantinopolja v 1187 godu," *VizVrem* 12 (1957), 60–61, and "Suvernitet, nalog i zemelnaja renta v Vizantii," *Antičnaja drevnost' i srednie veka* 9 (1973), 62. To my knowledge, Alexander Kazhdan was the only scholar who ever seriously questioned that Choniates was describing pronoia grants, primarily because Choniates did not use the word *pronoia*. Until we ascertain the characteristics of the pronoia grant, he reasoned, "we could apply the term *pronoia* to almost any Byzantine institution of this time": Kazhdan, "Formen," 220 (quotation), 223, and *Derevnja i gorod*, 176–77.

It passed unnoticed that he was thus making the military more slack, pouring enormous sums of money into idle bellies and mistreating the Roman provinces. For the good soldiers lost their eagerness for danger, no longer spurred to displays of bravery as before, but all set out to become wealthy. The inhabitants of the provinces, who formerly had the fisc as master, suffered most lamentably from the insatiable desire of the military. They were deprived not only of silver and obols, but were stripped of their last tunic, and sometimes they were torn away from their loved ones.

Because of this everyone wanted to enlist in the army, and many bade farewell to their needles with which they said they eked out with difficulty their livelihoods; others, spurning the grooming of horses and washing off the mud from the brick works, and still others wiping away the soot of the smithies, presented themselves to the recruiters. Handing over a Persian horse or by laying down a little gold they were registered among the military troops with no questions asked, and immediately were provided with imperial diplomas assigning them acres of dewy and grain-bearing land and Roman taxpayers [πλέθρα γῆς δροσερὰ καὶ ἀρούρας σιτοφόρους καὶ Ῥωμαίους ὑποφόρους] in order to serve in the manner of slaves. And sometimes a Roman of proud bearing had to pay his taxes to a half-barbarian runt who was completely ignorant of the order of battle even though the Roman was more familiar with warlike matters and superior to he who had become his tax collector [τοῦ φορολογοῦντος], and seemed like an Achilles next to him or like a man armed with two hands compared to one who lifted not even one due to infirmity.

The Roman provinces fared as one might expect from this disarray of the army. While some were stripped before our eyes by foreigners and were brought under their domination, others were destroyed and ravaged by our own people as if they were foreign lands.

How long, O Lord, will you forget your posterity, and turning your face from us give free course to your wrath?[2]

According to Choniates, Manuel I discontinued the pay that soldiers traditionally received in cash (*opsonion* or *siteresion*) and substituted for it "gifts of paroikoi." The phrase he uses – ταῖς λεγομέναις τῶν παροίκων δωρεαῖς – which can be translated literally as "the gifts called 'of paroikoi'" or "the so-called gifts of paroikoi," suggests a technical expression. George Ostrogorsky wrote that Choniates, a classicizing writer, preferred to use the phrase "gifts of paroikoi" rather than *pronoia*, but that both were technical terms.[3]

Was "gifts of paroikoi" a technical term, and did it signify pronoiai?

[2] Choniates, ed. van Dieten, 208.16–209.55. Translation adapted in part from those of Lemerle, *Agrarian History*, 231–32; H. Magoulias, *O City of Byzantium, Annals of Niketas Choniatēs* (Detroit, 1984), 118–19 (where the key sentence involving "gifts of paroikoi" is mistranslated); and Ostrogorsky, *Féodalité*, 28–29 (partial). For references to other translations, see Ostrogorsky, "Die Pronoia unter den Komnenen," 44 note 19.

[3] Ostrogorsky, "Die Pronoia unter den Komnenen," 44. For the meaning of *siteresion*, see *[6.11]*.

"Gifts of paroikoi" in other sources and its meaning

Aside from the single passage from Choniates' history, the phrase "gift(s) of paroikoi" appears in five documents from the second half of the eleventh through the early thirteenth century and, evidently, nowhere else.[4] Three of the documents provide some confirmation of Choniates by providing a link between Manuel I Komnenos and "gifts of paroikoi," and two of the documents permit us to determine what a "gift of paroikoi" was. Of the documents that link Manuel I to "gifts of paroikoi" two were issued by Manuel himself. One is a chrysobull for the Great Church from 1148 in which Manuel notes that the Church, across the empire, was holding land without proper documentation, and he specifies what should be done to rectify the situation. In one passage he refers to one of the irregular ways bishoprics held property: "perhaps there may have been an unquantified gift to them of paroikoi or measures of land."[5]

Another chrysobull of Manuel I, from 1158, refers to all the various benefactions showered upon the Patmos monastery by Alexios I, John II, and himself, including fiscal exemptions referred to as *exkousseiai*. The monastery benefitted "by dispositions of grain, of nomismata, by *exkousseiai* of boats, by gifts of paroikoi, by all manner of *exkousseiai* of those serving in the monastery."[6] The third document connecting Manuel I to "gifts of paroikoi" is a chrysobull from 1228 of the ruler of Epiros Theodore Doukas (ca. 1215–1230). Theodore lists a number of grants that Manuel I had made to the church of Kerkyra around 1148–49: (i) "a gift of 80 paroikoi and 40 households of *klerikoi*" (δωρεὰ παροίκων ὀγδοήκοντα καὶ οἰκίαι κληρικῶν τεσσαράκοντα); (ii) "another gift of 30 *hagiodouloi*" (δωρεὰ ἁγιοδούλων τριάκοντα); (iii) "another similar gift of 30 *hagiodouloi* [δωρεὰ . . . ἁγιοδούλων τριάκοντα], in which there is mention of an earlier gift of 120 paroikoi [δωρεὰ ἑκατὸν εἴκοσι παροίκων] given to the church at various times"; (iv) "another gift of 24 households of *exkoussateutoi* [δωρεὰ . . . εἴκοσι τεσσάρων οἰκιῶν ἐξκουσσατεύτων] in the *kastron* of Kerkyra and 50 outside"; and (v) a document "giving [διδόν] 20 paroikoi *eleutheroi* and *ateleis*." Here, *klerikoi* probably were those who worked in

[4] A proximity search with the online *TLG* for any form of *dorea* and any form of *paroikos* yields no other results.

[5] Zepos, *JGR*, I, 377.26–27: ἐὰν τυχὸν δωρεὰ αὐτοῖς παροίκων ἄποσος εἴη ἢ μέτρων γῆς. This may be connected to the prohibition in Roman law of making gifts without specifying their size.

[6] *Patmos*, I, no. 20.15: τυπώσεσι σίτου, νομισμάτων, ἐξκουσίαις πλοίων, δωρεαῖς παροίκων, ἐξκουσσείαις παντοίαις τῶν ἐκδουλευόντων ἐν τῇ μονῇ. On "those serving in the monastery," perhaps a reference to hired workers, see *Patmos*, I, pp. *40–*42.

lowly positions in the office of the bishop. I do not know what an *hagiodoulos* (lit. "holy slave or servant") was. *Exkoussateutos* is probably equivalent to *exkoussatos*, the recipient of an *exkousseia*. "*Eleutheroi* and *ateleis*" literally means "free and untaxed," terms commonly found in connection with these grants of paroikoi. They are discussed in detail later in this chapter.[7]

The other two documents that mention "gifts of paroikoi" permit us to ascertain the meaning of the phrase. One is an act of the *anagrapheus* Leo from 1059 (or possibly 1074) which uses the phrase a number of times to refer to privileges granted to monasteries by Constantine VII in 945/6 and in 957/8, and by Romanos II in 959/60,[8] and the other is a chrysobull of Nikephoros III Botaneiates for the monastery of Lavra from 1079 which mentions an earlier "gift by chrysobull of 100 *ateleis* paroikoi and *douloparoikoi*." *Douloparoikoi* were an obscure category of peasant, known from only a handful of sources. They were most likely either agricultural slaves or some type of propertyless peasant.[9]

A comparison of the manner in which some of these grants are described in other documents permits us to ascertain what a "gift of paroikoi" was. According to Leo's act a chrysobull of Romanos II granted the monastery of Kolovou "a gift of forty *ateleis* paroikoi." This same grant is mentioned in an act of an official named Theodore Kladon from 975. Here the "gift of forty *ateleis* paroikoi" is referred to simply as "the forty paroikoi given" to the monastery by Romanos.[10] Thus, to make a "gift of paroikoi" was to "give paroikoi."

Another grant mentioned in Leo's act was conferred by a chrysobull of Constantine VII from 945/6. The monastery of Leontia (which was later absorbed by Iviron) was given "an *exkousseia* to it and to the *proasteia* under it and to the unquantified number of paroikoi and *douloparoikoi* settled in them, and further, furnishing a gift of thirty-six *ateleis* paroikoi not subject

[7] MM, v, 15. Dölger, *Regesten*, ii, nos. 1371a–1371e. N. Svoronos, "Les privilèges de l'église à l'époque des Comnènes," in Svoronos, *Études sur l'organisation intérieure, la société et l'économie de l'empire byzantin* (London, 1973), no. vii, 361–63.

[8] *Iviron*, ii, no. 32.6, 9, 11–12. A fourth passage (line 23) refers more generally to chrysobulls, κτημάτων τινῶν δωρεάς τε καὶ ἐξκουσατίωνας περιποιούμενα ταύτῃ καὶ παροίκων. This phrase can be translated two ways, only one of which links "gift" to "paroikos": "furnishing this [monastery] with both gifts and *exkoussationai* [i.e., exemptions] of certain properties and of paroikoi" or "furnishing this [monastery] with both gifts of certain properties and *exkoussationai* of paroikoi."

[9] *Lavra*, i, no. 38.22–24: τῆ . . . χρυσοβούλλῳ δωρεᾶ τῶν ἑκατὸν ἀτελῶν παροίκων καὶ δουλοπαροίκων. *ODB*, s.v. "douloparoikos."

[10] *Iviron*, ii, no. 32.11–12: παροίκων ἀτελῶν τεσσαράκοντα δωρεάν. *Iviron*, i, no. 2.11: τοὺς . . . τεσσαράκοντα παροίκους τοὺς δοθέντας.

to any taxes of the state or imperial services but released from all liability."[11] According to the 975 act of Theodore Kladon the chrysobull of Constantine VII for Leontia contained

> the exempting of the monastery itself and the *proasteia* belonging to it and the *ateleis* paroikoi and *douloparoikoi* settled in them from every *epereia* [i.e., secondary charge] and corvée of the fisc . . . and in addition the dedicating to this monastery of *exkoussatoi* households [*oikoi*], thirty-six in number, in the theme of Thessaloniki, and keeping these unharmed from every attack and imposition.[12]

And so, through comparison of the two passages, "the exempting of paroikoi from every *epereia* and corvée" was equivalent to an "*exkousseia* of paroikoi," and "the dedicating of *exkoussatoi oikoi*" was equivalent to "a gift of *ateleis* paroikoi."

Finally, the earlier "gift by chrysobull of 100 *ateleis* paroikoi and *douloparoikoi*" mentioned in the 1079 chrysobull of Nikephoros III Botaneiates is also mentioned in a chrysobull of Constantine X Doukas from 1060. The act of 1060 explains that Constantine VII had issued a chrysobull for the monastery of St. Andreas near Thessaloniki "furnishing an *exkousseia* of 100 *ateleis* paroikoi and *douloparoikoi* for all the *proasteia* belonging to these monks."[13] Under Nikephoros II Phokas (963–69) Lavra absorbed St. Andreas and the grant passed to Lavra. Thus, by comparing the passages, "a gift of 100 *ateleis* paroikoi and *douloparoikoi*" was equivalent to "an *exkousseia* of 100 *ateleis* paroikoi and *douloparoikoi*."

When all this is put together, we see that a number of phrases are more or less synonymous:

to make a gift of paroikoi = to give paroikoi
the exempting of paroikoi from every *epereia* and corvée = an *exkousseia* of paroikoi
the dedicating of *exkoussatoi* households = a gift of *ateleis* paroikoi
a gift of *ateleis* paroikoi and *douloparoikoi* = an *exkousseia* of *ateleis* paroikoi and *douloparoikoi*

[11] *Iviron*, II, no. 32.5–7: ἐξκουσείαν αὐτῇ καὶ τοῖς ὑπ' αὐτὴν προαστείοις καὶ τοῖς ἐν αὐτοῖς προσκαθεζομένοις παροίκοις καὶ δουλοπαροίκοις ἀπόσοις, ἔτι γε μὴν καὶ δωρεὰν παροίκων ἀτελῶν τριακονταὲξ μή τισι τοῦ δημοσίου τελέσμασιν ἢ βασιλικοῖς λειτουργήμασι καθυποβεβλημένων ἀλλὰ πάσης ἐνοχῆς ἀπηλλαγμένων παρεχόμενος.

[12] *Iviron*, I, no. 2.17–23: περιέχον τοῦ ἐξκουσσεύεσθαι αὐτὴν τὲ τὴν μονὴν καὶ τὰ διαφέροντα αὐτῇ προάστεια καὶ τοὺς ἐν αὐτοῖς προσκαθεζομένους ἀτελεῖς, παροίκους καὶ δουλοπαροίκους, ἀπὸ πάσης ἐπηρείας καὶ ἀγγαρείας τοῦ δημοσίου . . . πρὸς τούτοις ἀνακεῖσθαι τῇ τοιαύτῃ μονῇ καὶ ἐξκουσάτους οἴκους τὸν ἀριθμὸν τριακαονταὲξ κατὰ τὸ θέμα Θεσσαλονίκης καὶ διατηρεῖσθαι αὐτοὺς ἀπὸ πάσης ἐπαγωγῆς καὶ ἐπιθέσεως ἀβλαβεῖς.

[13] *Lavra*, I, no.33.31–34: ἐξκουσσείαν παρεχόμενον ἐν πᾶσι τοῖς διαφέρουσι τοῖς αὐτοῖς μοναχοῖς προαστείοις παροίκων ἀτελῶν καὶ δουλοπαροίκων ἑκατόν.

Therefore, a "gift of paroikoi" was an *exkousseia* of paroikoi. The earliest examples known to us of this kind of exemption date from the reign of Constantine VII (945–59) when they were not called "gifts of paroikoi," but "*exkousseiai* of paroikoi." At this time such grants appear to have been part of a well-established process, and so their origin dates back considerably further.

Why should there be two phrases for the same phenomenon? Chronology provides the answer. All of the known references to "*exkoussatoi oikoi*" date from 975 to 1061, and the known references to "*exkousseiai* of paroikoi" date from 995 through the reign of Alexios I Komnenos (d. 1118).[14] On the other hand, the known references to "gifts of paroikoi" fall within the period from 1059 or 1074 and 1228, spanning Manuel I's reign as well as the era in which Choniates wrote his history. After the reign of Alexios I Komnenos, there are no more references to "*exkousseiai* of paroikoi." Thus, there appears to have been a shift in terminology from "*exkousseiai*" of paroikoi to "gifts" of paroikoi. I think this phrase was replaced with "gifts of paroikoi" because the term *exkousseia* no longer adequately represented what was being granted. To understand why, it is necessary to consider the tax system.

Byzantine taxation in the eleventh and twelfth centuries

An *exkousseia* was a type of tax exemption that affected a specific category of taxes. Agrarian fiscal burdens (as distinguished from urban and commercial taxes which are not germane here) can be divided into four major categories: (i) the property tax on land and other immovable property; (ii) taxes on cultivators and their animals; (iii) a small number of supplemental taxes; and (iv) a large number of secondary charges and corvées.

(i) The *demosia* (literally "state things") consisted of the *demosios kanon* and the surtaxes. The *demosios kanon*, or base tax (*telos*), was the fundamental tax on land. Accompanying the *demosios kanon* as part of the *demosia* were the surtaxes collectively called *parakolouthemata* (literally, "things following closely") which were based roughly proportionately upon the *telos*. Most of these were intended to support or compensate the fiscal officials who assessed or collected the taxes. Oikonomides estimated that the surtaxes added about 20 percent to the base *demosion*; Dölger estimated they comprised about one-quarter of the total tax burden. During the course of

[14] *Iviron*, I, no. 2, and II, no. 33. *Iviron*, I, no. 8 (995), and P. Gautier, "Le typikon de la Théotokos Evergétis," *REB* 40 (1982), 93 (1098–1118).

the tenth and eleventh centuries there was a tendency for these surtaxes to be redirected from provincial officials to the central treasury. By the year 1100 all of them were sent to Constantinople, and so they became just another part of the *telos*.[15]

(ii) The second category involved taxes on cultivators and their animals. The personal taxes on cultivators (peasants) was based, generally speaking, on the number of oxen owned. From the eighth century, all peasant households paid the hearth tax (*kapnikon*). In addition, those with one or more oxen paid a tax called the *synone*. Originally, the *synone* was the adaeration (replacement of a charge in kind with one in cash) of a grain demand at a fixed price for the state, but by the tenth century it was a simple tax varying with the number of oxen owned. On the other animals owned by peasants (above all sheep, but including over the course of time other livestock) a charge was levied called the *ennomion* or *dekateia*, which, originally at least, was a charge for the right to pasture animals on state land.[16]

(iii) The supplemental taxes are poorly understood. They included the *aerikon*, which in the tenth through twelfth century seems to have been a charge levied collectively on the livestock of the entire village community, and the *paroikiatikon*, *aktemonitikon*, and *zeugaratikion*, which were levies on paroikoi in general or specific types of paroikoi (*aktemones*, *zeugaratoi*), and which first appear in the eleventh century.[17]

(iv) The last category of fiscal burdens were the secondary charges and corvées. These, depending on their particular nature, were levied either irregularly on both people and privately held property, or only on certain categories of people. In the sources they are frequently referred to by such terms as *kakosis* (literally "damage"), *zemia* ("injury"), and, especially, *epereia* ("abuse," "contumely"), a clear acknowledgment of their onerous nature. Their amount was not fixed and therefore they had the potential of being imposed arbitrarily. Scholars often refer to them as the "extraordinary charges," a phrase I will avoid, because they were "extraordinary" in the sense of being "special" and often excessive, but they were hardly unusual. As Oikonomides noted, the secondary charges, together with the corvées, probably comprised the largest part of the obligations of the peasantry.[18] One group of these secondary charges was for the benefit of officials, such as the *kaniskion*, a gift of food for fiscal officials. Further, there were quite

[15] Oikonomides, *Fiscalité*, 76–79.
[16] Oikonomides, *Fiscalité*, 42–76.
[17] Oikonomides, *Fiscalité*, 80–84.
[18] Oikonomides, *Fiscalité*, 85.

a few varieties of demands to furnish lodging, food, and fodder to high officials and soldiers passing through one's area of domicile. Those most commonly mentioned in the sources are the *mitaton*, the requisition by soldiers of part of one's home for an extended period, and the *aplekton*, an obligation to furnish campground and provisions for an army or officials in transit. In addition there were various kinds of requisitions for food, fodder, grain, and horses. There were also a couple of varieties of forced sales.[19]

Among the more onerous burdens were corvées, uncompensated labor services, sometimes referred to by the terms *leitourgia* or *leitourgema* (both literally "public service"), or *douleia* ("service"), but most commonly by a term of ancient Persian origin, *angareia*. In addition there were more specific burdens such as *kastroktisia*, a corvée to build fortifications, and others to build boats and ships.[20]

Last, there were military and paramilitary obligations, some of which could be imposed on anyone, others only on certain legally defined categories of people. Of the former there were charges paid to support certain types of soldiers, such as garrisons and the armed men who accompanied high officials in their provincial duties; demands for weapons; and forced conscriptions of various types of soldiers. The obligations that affected only certain people were, first and foremost, *strateia*, originally an obligation to serve in the army burdening those who held *stratiotika ktemata*, or military lands. By the twelfth century, it had been almost completely fiscalized, converted into a tax payment. In this category we also may place *enoche tou dromou* (lit. "liability of the post"), an obligation on peasants called *exkoussatoi tou dromou* who were obligated to assist with the imperial mail.[21]

Exempting and reducing taxes

There were numerous ways that taxes and other fiscal charges could be exempted or lessened, either temporarily or permanently. Some of these had no direct connection to imperial benefactions but were administrative procedures authorized by fiscal assessors (*epoptai*) and were intended to maintain the fiscal integrity of the village community. The best known of these procedures were several forms of tax reduction and relief called

[19] Oikonomides, *Fiscalité*, 86–105.

[20] Oikonomides, *Fiscalité*, 105–12.

[21] Oikonomides, *Fiscalité*, 112–21.

kouphismos, *sympatheia*, and *klasma*. They came into play when a property had suffered from a natural disaster or enemy incursion, or when the owner of a property simply disappeared, either temporarily or permanently. In these cases it was either impossible for the owner to pay his taxes or no owner was present to pay them. The state always had the right to confiscate such land, but this meant the permanent separation of the land from its original fiscal unit (the village community). In the tenth and eleventh centuries the state preferred not to do this for a number of reasons related, primarily, to administrative efficiency. In cases where the owner was simply absent, the state could transfer the tax burden collectively to the other property owners within the village community, but here it ran the risk of inducing other members of the community to abandon their lands as well.

Consequently, the fisc developed several alternative procedures. A *kouphismos* (lit. "relief, alleviation") was employed when the property owner had abandoned his property but the tax inspector expected that the owner would eventually return. Because it was feared that other members of the village community would abandon their own properties if required to shoulder the full tax burden of the member who fled, the inspector temporarily reduced the tax burden on the abandoned property until the original owner returned, at which time the property's full tax liability was restored.[22]

Alternatively, if it was not expected that the owner would return, or if the owner was present but the property had suffered from natural or man-made depredations, the tax inspector could grant the property a *sympatheia* (lit. "sympathy"), a complete tax remission. If the owner or his heirs reclaimed the property within a thirty-year period, the full tax liability was gradually restored through a process called *orthosis* ("righting"). If the thirty years passed without *orthosis* taking place, the land became *klasma* (lit. a "fragment"), was fiscally separated from the village community, and was disposed of permanently as the state saw fit (sale, donation, lease, etc.). A *klasma* that had been leased to cultivators while under *sympatheia* was sold at its normal price and the new owner henceforth paid the tax on the property at $\frac{1}{12}$ the normal assessment; *klasmata* which were located in depopulated areas or which needed to be re-cleared before cultivation were sold at a reduced price and taxed at $\frac{1}{24}$ the normal assessment for fifteen years, and then raised to

22 *ODB*, s.v. "kouphismos" and "epoptes." In the narrative sources, *kouphismos* could refer to any kind of tax alleviation: e.g., Strabo, *Geographica*, x.5.3.16–19; *Georgii monachi chronicon*, ed. C. de Boor (Leipzig, 1904, repr. Stuttgart, 1978), II, 774.3–9; and Migne, *PG*, 110, col. 973.46. Gregoras, I, 300.4, uses the word to refer to the tax relief promised to the inhabitants of Thrace by Andronikos III in the 1320s.

$\frac{1}{12}$. Presumably, the eventual goal was to restore the normal tax burden on such properties.[23]

As described here, *kouphismoi* and *sympatheiai* were administrative procedures, granted by fiscal officials, to reduce or entirely remit the base tax, surtaxes, and supplementary taxes burdening the owner of a property. Normally these procedures were not intended to be rewards, or compensation, or gifts. And so for these reasons, they were not imperial grants. But there are always exceptions. When Emperor Constantine Monomachos granted the monastery of Nea Mone the *klasma* of Kalothekia in 1044, he noted that the fiscal burden of the property was to remain "unrestored" (ἀνόρθωτον). Therefore, the monastery effectively received a tax exemption of the *demosion* (*telos*).[24]

The simple *logisimon* and the *logisimon autourgion solemnion*

Normally, however, when the emperor himself wished to remit taxes permanently, he used different techniques. These were called the *logisimon* and the *exkousseia*. As a rule, when the emperor wished to exempt the property tax with its surtaxes, he granted a *logisimon*. When he wished to exempt any of the other categories of taxes (the personal property and hearth tax, the supplemental taxes, and the secondary charges and corvées, as well as commercial taxes), he granted an *exkousseia*.

According to the *Marcian Treatise* there were several types of *logisima*. A "simple" *logisimon* (ἁπλῶς λογίσιμον or δι' ἁπλότητα λογίσιμον) occurred when the emperor granted a property owner an exemption of the *demosios kanon* on his property; technically, as the verb *logizein* implies, the taxes owed were not so much suppressed as "reckoned to the account" of the beneficiary.

To my knowledge there is no documented case of a simple *logisimon* until the 1070s.[25] Nevertheless, prior to treating the simple *logisimon* the

23 *ODB*, s.v. "sympatheia," "tax alleviation," "orthosis," "klasma." As with *kouphismos*, *sympatheia* too could refer to any kind of tax alleviation in the narrative sources: e.g., *Alexiad*, III.6.7: ed. Reinsch, 102.84–85 = ed. Leib, I, 122. All of these procedures described above disappeared after the twelfth century, and new procedures, using some of the same terminology, arose. Thus, a thirteenth-century notarial form describes village priests presenting a chrysobull "for a *sympatheia* of priests" to the tax collector in order to receive a *sympatheia*: K. Sathas, *Μεσαιωνική Βιβλιοθήκη* (repr. Athens, 1972), VI, 627–28, esp. 627.21–22.

24 Zepos, *JGR*, I, 616. Oikonomides, *Fiscalité*, 202.

25 R. Morris, "Monastic Exemptions in Tenth- and Eleventh-Century Byzantium," in *Property and Power in the Early Middle Ages*, ed. W. Davies and P. Fouracre (Cambridge, 1995), 210–11, believed she found an earlier example in the 1044 act of Constantine IX Monomachos for

Marcian Treatise discusses something called *prokatespasmena logisima* which were granted by "long deceased emperors up to the emperor called Leo the Wise [886–912]" whereby an emperor ordered that the taxes on properties "belonging to this or that hostel or old people's home or monastery or church or something else, should not be collected, but remitted and reckoned eternally as an imperial gift."[26] Thus, the treatise asserts that at least one type of *logisimon* – a tax exemption given to the property of a religious foundation as a gift – had been granted before the tenth century.[27] Perhaps the lack of specific references to *logisima* in the documents before the later eleventh century is easy to explain. Most extant documents from this period deal with properties later held by the monasteries of Mount Athos. During the tenth century the area of Macedonia was recovering from Arab and Bulgarian incursions, evidenced by the number of sales of *klasmata* in the area. Thus, laymen or monasteries seeking tax benefits acquired *klasmata* (with their greatly reduced tax burden) rather than *logisima*. Certainly the state itself benefitted from granting tax reductions in order to restore the productivity of land. Ordinarily *logisima* did not benefit the state in this way.

Nea Mone mentioned above (Zepos, *JGR*, I, 616). However, far from the emperor granting a *sympatheia* on the small village in question (as Morris contends, and which would not have been a *logisimon* anyway), the emperor states that the village he was granting to the monastery, which had *earlier* received a *sympatheia*, was, unlike the *klasma* he granted at the same time, now restored to full tax liability through the process of *orthosis*. As a result, rather than receiving any kind of exemption of the base property tax on the property, Nea Mone had to pay the full *demosion* of $7\frac{1}{2}$ nomismata (not 6 as Morris wrote) for the newly granted property.

26 *Prokatespasmenos* (προσκατεσπασμένος) is a difficult word to translate. Charles Brand, in his English translation of the treatise (cited below), renders the word as both "favor-granted" and "given as previous favors." Dölger, *Beiträge*, 117: τῷδε ἢ τῷδε τῷ ξενῶνι ἢ τῷ γηροκομείῳ ἢ τῷ μοναστηρίῳ ἢ τῇ ἐκκλησίᾳ ἢ ἑτέρῳ τινί. Numerous scholars interpret ἢ ἑτέρῳ τινι in the passage as "or some*one* else," and conclude that *prokatespasmena logisima* were given to laymen as well: e.g., Dölger, *Beiträge*, 105, 145, and Morris, "Monastic Exemptions," 205, and this is how C. Brand, "Two Byzantine Treatises on Taxation," *Traditio* 25 (1969), 50, translates it. However, given that the list of recipients offered by the author of the treatise includes nothing but religious foundations, and given that the phrase ἑτέρῳ τινί is *either* masculine or neuter, there is little reason to think that the treatise's author had laymen in mind. Indeed, in the entire section of the treatise dealing with *logisima* and *solemnia* (the latter being simple gifts in cash or in kind to religious institutions), laymen are mentioned only in regard to simple *logisima* (by the use of the word *prosopon*); in the author's treatment of all the other *logisima* and *solemnia*, when he mentions recipients, the subject is exclusively religious foundations (*euageis oikoi*).

27 Morris, "Monastic Exemptions," 204, cites, as a possible early example of a *prokatespasmenon logisimon*, a 688 grant of Justinian II of salt pans near Thessaloniki to the church of St. Demetrios in the city: H. Grégoire, "Un édit de l'empereur Justinien II," *Byz* 17 (1944–45), 119–25. However, the numerous lacunae in the document render it not at all certain that a full or even a partial tax exemption was being granted.

The earliest known examples of simple *logisima* were those granted to the general Gregory Pakourianos. In his 1083 *typikon [4.2]* he writes of "the properties given to us through pious chrysobulls by reason of hereditary possession, in inalienable and complete ownership and true authority, which becoming *logisima* were confirmed by pious chrysobulls." Later in the *typikon* he mentions a document concerning the *logisimon* of all his properties and another for the properties he owned in Mosynopolis. While the *typikon* dates to 1083, it is likely that he received some of these *logisima* in the 1070s, because among the scores of imperial documents that he lists as having received over the years, there are numerous documents from emperors as early as Michael VII (1071–1078). Pakourianos' *logisima*, which seem to have followed the initial property grants ("becoming" *logisima*), could date to the early 1070s.[28]

Closely related to the simple *logisimon* was the *logisimon autourgion solemnion*. A *solemnion* was a simple gift in cash or kind from the emperor to a religious foundation. According to the *Marcian Treatise*, religious foundations could receive a *solemnion*, not in the form of a direct grant, but through a tax exemption of the property tax on their own property. Such an *autourgion* (lit. "self-working") *logisimon* (or *autourgion solemnion*, as it is referred to earlier in the treatise) was both a *logisimon* and a *solemnion*. Yet, the only difference between it and a simple *logisimon* is that it was specifically intended to replace a simple *solemnion* granted to a religious foundation.[29] We have only one example of this variety of *logisimon solemnion*. In February 1082 Alexios I conferred as a *logisimon* the *telos* of two of the monastery of Vatopedi's properties in exchange for the monastery renouncing a *solemnion* it had been granted many years earlier.[30]

[28] A simpler technique called *ekkope* (ἐκκοπή, literally, "cutting off" or "striking out," sc. from the tax books) was often utilized when a property was granted to a beneficiary and exempted of its property tax at the same time. In this case, because the property had been state property, it was not registered in the ordinary tax rolls (*kodikes*) and therefore there was no need to employ the *logisimon* process. Rather, the tax was simply "struck out" (ἐκκόπτειν). This is probably what happened when Nikephoros Botaneiates granted the monk Christodoulos and his disciples two small properties (*topia*) on Kos in March 1080: *Patmos*, I, no. 4.11–17 = MM, VI, 24.9–22. The emperor freed the properties of the *telos* of ¼ nomisma that was levied on the one and of the rent (*pakton*) of ¼ nomisma levied on the other. Later in the relevant document the exempted charges for both properties are called "their *pakton*, that is, ½ nomisma," illustrating that when state land was rented to private individuals, the rental payment in specie (*pakton*) was at times simply viewed as a property tax (*telos*). Oikonomides, *Fiscalité*, 180, 205.

[29] Dölger, *Beiträge*, 118.3–7. L. Neville, "The Marcian Treatise on Taxation and the Nature of Bureaucracy in Byzantium," *Byzantinische Forschungen* 26 (2000), 53, translates *autourgion* as "automatic," which accommodates the sense of the word as it is used here, but renders the word meaningless in other contexts. See *ODB*, s.v. "autourgion," "solemnion."

[30] *Vatopédi*, I, no. 11, and I, p. 11. Oikonomides, *Fiscalité*, 209, 244–45.

The *exkousseia*

While *logisima* generally exempted the property tax (*telos*), an *exkousseia* was an exemption of any tax or charge aside from the basic property tax.[31] That an *exkousseia* did not mean an exemption of the basic property tax is proved by a pair of documents issued for Vatopedi. In January 1080 Nikephoros Botaneiates granted an *exkousseia* to five of its properties (*ktemata*), which probably was all that the monastery owned then, and in 1082, Alexios I Komnenos exempted – through a *logisimon* – the property tax on two of them.[32]

Exkousseiai on property seem to have been more common than *logisima*. The earliest known exemption of secondary charges on property dates to the ninth century. A chrysobull of Romanos I Lekapenos, issued in August 934, ordered, among other things, that a small monastic settlement near Hierissos was to remain "unvexed from every *epereia* and *angareia* and injury as should arise from bishops and archons and everyone else, as it was from the beginning."[33] Because this settlement was described in a document from 908 as "ancient" (*archaia*), the original exemption certainly dates to the ninth century.[34] Whoever was there, perhaps no more than a small group of monks, had been thus exempted from secondary charges (*epereiai*) and corvées (*angareiai*).

In the tenth century, examples of the exemption of the secondary charges on property are quite rare. In 945/6 Constantine VII granted the monastery of Prodromos at Leontia in Thessaloniki an *exkousseia* for the monastery and its *proasteia* as well, and another chrysobull of Constantine VII, from 957/8, granted the monastery *tou Athonos* on Mount Athos "exemption and relief" (ἐξκουσείαν καὶ περίθαλψιν) for its *proasteia* on the Kassandra peninsula. In both of these cases the monasteries probably continued to pay the property tax (*telos*) on their *proasteia*, but were freed of secondary charges and corvées.[35]

31 Oikonomides, *Fiscalité*, 156. Movable property also benefitted from *exkousseiai*. Between 976 and 984 Basil II granted to Lavra an exemption of the fiscal charges for a boat of 6,000 modioi. The vessel is referred to as an "excused ship" (τὸ ἐξκουσεῦον πλοῖον), which probably refers to an exemption of the *kommerkion*: *Lavra*, I, p. 61, and *Iviron*, I, no. 6.21–37. An 1197 chrysobull of Alexios III, granting an *exkousseia* for the boats belonging to the Patmos monastery, notes that "the . . . *exkousseia* shall not exempt forbidden goods," implying a tax not on the ships themselves but on the cargo (*Patmos*, I, no. 11.52–53).

32 *Vatopédi*, I, no. 10.27–30, no. 11.19.

33 *Prôtaton*, no. 3.12–15, and pp. 111–14. Two earlier acts–*Prôtaton*, no. 1 (from 883) and 2 (from 908)–free the monks of Athos from being "vexed," but the phrases are much too vague to conclude that any exemption of fiscal charges was involved. See Oikonomides, *Fiscalité*, 162–63.

34 *Prôtaton*, no. 2.17.

35 *Iviron*, II, no. 32.5, and no. 32.8–9. On the monastery τοῦ Ἄθωνος or τοῦ Ἄθω, see *Prôtaton*, pp. 61–64.

After this I do not know of any examples of *exkousseiai* of the secondary charges on property until the reign of Constantine Monomachos. Beginning with his reign, and through the rest of the eleventh century, they become quite common. During this period a number of monasteries received a full *exkousseia* of all secondary charges and corvées on all of their properties: Nea Mone on Chios in 1044, Amalfitains in 1057–59, Lavra perhaps as early as 1060 but no later than 1074, Iviron in 1079, Strovilos and Skenoure on Kos in 1079, and Eleousa near Strumica in 1085.[36] Laymen also received *exkousseia* for their properties during this period. The first known example is that of the imperial estate newly granted to Andronikos Doukas in 1073 *[4.1]*. The following year Michael Attaleiates received from Michael VII an *exkousseia* for all of his hereditary property (MM, V, 136).

Logisima and *exkousseiai* for the benefit of a third party

Up to this point all of the tax exemptions I have been dealing with were granted to property owned by an individual or religious foundation for the benefit of that individual or religious foundation. But there were also two varieties of tax exemption that individuals and religious foundations benefitted from indirectly. One involved the granting of *logisima* to a group of taxpayers in order to provide a *solemnion* to a religious foundation. The second involved granting an *exkousseia*, that is, an exemption of secondary charges and corvées, to a group of taxpayers for the benefit of a layman or religious foundation.

The first of these is described in the *Marcian Treatise* as follows:

> A *logisimon* is a *solemnion* when the emperor, instead of giving the *solemnion* to this or that pious house, orders, at the request of the superiors, or the officers, or the monks in the pious house, that the amount itself [of the *solemnion*] be reckoned from the public tax [*demosios kanon*] of some villages not subject to the pious house itself, so that the reckoned nomismata are furnished by the villagers instead of the tax collector for the pious house for the sake of the earlier *solemnion*.[37]

Thus, certain villagers were ordered to give their taxes directly to a religious foundation, bypassing both the provincial and central administration. From the point of view of the fisc, this was regarded as a *logisimon* for the villagers and a *solemnion* for the religious foundation.

[36] Oikonomides, *Fiscalité*, 198, 201, 205, 207, 237, 239, 242–43.

[37] Dölger, *Beiträge*, 117.38–118.3. Kazhdan, *Agrarnye otnošenija*, 215–16. Lemerle, *Agrarian History*, 84. The passage is ambiguous as to what this type of *logisimon* should be called, whether a *logisimon solemnion* or a *logisimon anti solemnion* ("a *logisimon* instead of a *solemnion*").

I know of no explicit example of such a *logisimon solemnion*, that is, there is no source that states that certain taxpayers explicitly received a *logisimon* in order to provide a monastery explicitly with a *solemnion*. Rather, what we do encounter is a de facto grant of property tax to a monastery as well as a *logisimon* granted to taxpayers for the benefit of a layman. An appendix to the *typikon* for the Kecharitomene monastery from the early twelfth century lists a dozen vineyard parcels along with their owners, their sizes, and their tax which was received by the monastery.[38] There is also the case of Adrian Komnenos, Alexios I's younger brother, who received a *logisimon* for the tax revenues of the Kassandra peninsula on the Chalkidike (discussed below *[4.5]*).

Taxes other than the basic property tax were exempted for the benefit of a third party as well. Ahrweiler noted this kind of grant, and, as an example, she cited the *typikon* for the Constantinopolitan monastery of the Pantokrator *[2.2]* which lists, among the monastery's endowment, "all the *hevraïke* on the Chersonesos in the market of Koila and the *dekateia* [commercial tax] of the wine merchants." Whether the *hevraïke* was a reference to a Jewish quarter within the market or (as Ahrweiler believed) a tax on Jews, the effect was to transfer taxes from Jews and from wine merchants to the monastery. This type of grant had similarities to a *logisimon solemnion*, but it differed in that the sum given was not fixed and, more importantly, in that the tax revenues granted were not part of the *telos*, as the *Marcian Treatise* describes, but secondary charges. Properly speaking, the Jews and the wine merchants who paid their taxes to the monastery received an *exkousseia*, not a *logisimon*.[39]

The *exkousseia* of paroikoi

Exkousseiai granted for the benefit of a third party were most commonly granted to peasants as a way to grant privileges to large landowners. Ordinarily, every peasant in the tenth and first half of the eleventh centuries was a member of a peasant household and every peasant household was a member of a village community. Each peasant household owned a collection of dwellings, livestock, and arable land, from which it derived its livelihood. The state levied taxes and charges upon each household, based

[38] P. Gautier, "Le typikon de la Théotokos Kécharitoménè," *REB* 43 (1985), 148–49. The tax was levied at a fairly consistent rate of one nomisma per three modioi.

[39] Ahrweiler, "La concession des droits incorporels," 106–07. P. Gautier, "Le typikon du Christ Sauveur Pantokrator," *REB* 32 (1974), 120. R. Jordan in *Byzantine Monastic Foundation Documents*, ed. J. Thomas and A. Hero (Washington, D.C., 2000), II, 770, translates *hevraïke* as "Jewish quarter." *ODB*, s.v. "tithe."

partly on the amount of property each household owned (*ad valorem*) and based partly on the size of the household (*ad capitatum*). A small number of obligations, such as the responsibility of paying the taxes on land abandoned by its owner, burdened the entire village collectively. Most of the cultivated areas of the countryside were composed of such villages and such peasants. As a rule, the state wished to keep things this way.

But there were exceptions. There were larger estates. Some of these were part of a village community; others (called *idiostata*) had been separated from any village community. In both cases, the owners of these estates needed labor for the cultivation of these larger properties. In the ninth and tenth centuries, as more land was brought under cultivation, private landowners and the state competed for the labor services of the peasantry. In the middle of the tenth century the first evidence appears that emperors were granting special favors to some monasteries, freeing specified numbers of the peasant-tenants working the land of the monasteries from the secondary charges (*epereiai* and corvées) owed to the state or permitting the monasteries to settle a specified number of peasant-tenants who were freed of secondary charges.

The number of paroikoi

The gift of paroikoi was usually quantified by an explicit statement of the number of paroikoi granted (e.g., a "gift of *X* paroikoi," "an *exkousseia* of *X* paroikoi," "we excuse paroikoi the number *X*"). Table 3.1 provides a more or less complete list of known grants of *exkousseiai* of specific numbers of households to monasteries and churches from the tenth through the twelfth centuries.[40]

There is something suspicious about the figures in these exemptions: 6, 12, 15, 16, 20, 24, 25, 30, 32, 36, 40, 50, 60, 70, 80, 100. All but three are multiples of 5 or 12, which suggests that the number did not correspond to the number of households working the monastery's or church's land

[40] Cf. the table of R. Morris, *Monks and Laymen in Byzantium, 843–1118* (Cambridge, 1995), 186–88. A. Kazhdan gave the name "arithmos" (ἀριθμός, "number") to the "gift of paroikoi" grant: Kazhdan, "Formen," 223, *Derevnja i gorod*, 176–77, and his review of H. Glykatzi-Ahrweiler, "La concession des droits incorporels," in *VizVrem* 27 (1967), 345–46. Ksenia Hvostova also uses this term: "Pronija: social'no-ekonomičeskie i pravovye problemy," *VizVrem* 49 (1988), 15. See *ODB*, s.v. "arithmos." However, while passages from the sources do indeed frequently use the word *arithmos* when referring to the specific number of paroikoi granted, I do not think the word *arithmos* is used in a technical sense. Further, since the Byzantine sources themselves provide two technical terms for this variety of grant ("gift of paroikoi" and "*exkousseia* of paroikoi"), it seems unnecessary to seek another.

Table 3.1 Grants of *exkousseiai* of specific numbers of paroikoi and households to monasteries and churches, 945–1203

	Date of grant	Monastery or church	Peasants involved (date of document mentioning the grant)	Reference and notes
	945/6	monastery of Leontia	36 new *exkoussatoi oikoi* (975) = 36 new *ateleis* paroikoi (1059 or 1074)	*Iviron*, I, no. 2; II, no. 32 mon. absorbed by Iviron
	945–59	mon. of Polygyros	20 new paroikoi (975)	*Iviron*, I, no. 2 mon. absorbed by Kolovou
(a)	945–59	mon. of St. Andreas	100 new *ateleis* paroikoi and *douloparoikoi* (1060)	*Lavra*, I, no. 33 mon. absorbed by Lavra
(b)	957/8	mon. tou Athonos	70 new *ateleis* paroikoi (1059 or 1074)	*Iviron*, II, no. 32 mon. absorbed by Iviron
	959/60	mon. of Kolovou	40 new paroikoi (975) = 40 *stichoi* (995) = 40 new *ateleis* paroikoi (1059 or 1074)	*Iviron*, I, no. 2, no. 8; II, no. 32 mon. absorbed by Iviron
(c)	959–63	mon. of Lavra	32 new (?) paroikoi – by name (974) "given," "to be excused"	*Lavra*, I, no. 6 may have been part of (a)
	976–979/80	mon. of Iviron	40 new *ateleis* paroikoi (1059 or 1074)	*Iviron*, II, no. 32
	979/80	mon. of Iviron	60 new *demosiarioi oikoi* / paroikoi *dedemosieumenoi* (1059 or 1074)	*Iviron*, II, no. 32
	979–84	mon. of Lavra	25 new *exkoussatoi oikoi* (984)	*Iviron*, I, no. 6
	bef. 1025	mon. of Xenophon	12 *proskathemenoi*	*Xénophon*, no. 1
	1020	church of Bulgaria	more than 700 paroikoi and more than 700 *klerikoi*; a new privilege for almost half of the bishoprics (1020)	H. Gelzer, in *BZ* 2 (1893), 42–46 12, 15, 30, or 40 of each per bishopric
(d)	1044	mon. of Nea Mone	24 new *ateleis* paroikoi (1044) = 24 existing *ateleis* paroikoi – by name (1050)	Zepos, *JGR*, I, 616–17, 635
	1049	mon. of Nea Mone	15 families of Jews (1049)	Zepos, *JGR*, I, 633

(e)	1079	mon. of Lavra	100 new *ateleis* paroikoi and *douloparoikoi* (1079)	*Lavra*, I, no. 38
(f)	1080	mon. of Vatopedi	50 paroikoi *ateleis zeugaratoi* (1080)	*Vatopédi*, I, no. 10
(g)	1099 or 1114	mon. of St. John on Patmos	12 *eleutheroi* and *ateleis* paroikoi (1099 or 1114)	*Patmos*, I, no. 18
	1101	mon. of Iviron	100 *eleutheroi* and *ateleis* paroikoi "granted" and "excused" of charges (1104)	*Iviron*, II, no. 52
(h)	1106	mon. of Eleousa	*exkousseia* of 12 *eleutheroi* and *ateleis* paroikoi (1106)	Petit, "Le monastère de Notre-Dame," no. 2
	bef. 1118	mon. of Evergetis	*exkousseia* of 12 and 16 *zeugaratoi* paroikoi (1098–1118)	P. Gautier, in *REB* 40 (1982), 93
(i)	1145	mon. of St. John on Patmos	12 existing paroikoi plus 6 new *zeugaratoi* paroikoi (1145)	*Patmos*, I, no. 19 extension of privilege in (g)
	ca. 1148–49	church of Kerkyra	80 paroikoi and 40 households of *klerikoi* 30 *hagiodouloi* 24 households of *exkoussateutoi* 50 households of *exkoussateutoi* 20 *eleutheroi* & *ateleis* paroikoi (1228)	MM, V, 15
(j)	1152	mon. of Eleousa	12 existing *zeugaratoi* paroikoi – by name (1152)	Petit, "Le monastère de Notre-Dame," no. 8 extension of privilege in (h)
	1195–1203	mon. of Theotokos on Cyprus	24 new paroikoi "granted" (1210)	I. Tsiknopoullos, *Κυπριακὰ Τυπικά* (Leukosia, 1969), 17

at the moment of the grant, but was an abstract figure either smaller or, most likely, larger than the number of peasants working the monastery's or church's property at the moment of the grant.

It would appear that the initial grant conceded an *exkousseia* over an abstract number of paroikoi. These were drawn from paroikoi already working the properties of the recipient or it was left to the initiative of the recipient to attract peasants from elsewhere. This seems to be in accord with the examples in the table. In case (d) twenty-four paroikoi were granted to the monastery in question, and then six years later the twenty-four paroikoi are listed by name. In case (h) the monastery was granted twelve paroikoi and forty-six years later (j) the twelve paroikoi (perhaps descendants of the original twelve) are listed by name. In case (c) thirty-two paroikoi are listed by name, based on an original grant of thirty-two paroikoi made by Romanos II (959–63), some dozen years earlier. It is possible that these thirty-two paroikoi were part of an initial grant of 100 paroikoi (a) that transferred to Lavra when it acquired the monastery of St. Andreas. The grant of 100 paroikoi granted in (a) seems more like a hypothetical privilege, that the monastery was granted *up to* 100 paroikoi.

Ateles and *eleutheros* status of the paroikoi

In the majority of cases the paroikoi that comprised a gift of paroikoi are referred to as *ateleis* paroikoi. The word *ateles* denotes a fiscal condition: "untaxed" or, more accurately, "not levied a tax." It was applied to peasants who paid no *telos* because they and whatever property they owned were not listed in any fiscal register. This situation arose either because inadvertently they had never been assessed (usually because they had no immovable property) or because the emperor had decided to grant them this status for the benefit of the party from whom the peasants were renting land. In both cases, *ateleis* peasants, as a rule, probably never owned immovable property. The *ateleis* paroikoi in case (b) in Table 3.1 are described as "having neither their own land nor subject to any state taxes or imperial services." Their landlessness would explain both why they had never been assessed and why emperors would grant them *ateles* status. They were a marginal and generally poorer type of peasant who were more difficult to keep track of than landowning peasants, and their tax burden, if normally levied, would have been much smaller than that of landowning peasants and thus easier for the state to forsake. But this did not mean that they owned no property at all. A chrysobull from 1080 granted Vatopedi "fifty *ateleis zeugaratoi* paroikoi," that is, peasants who owned no arable land (and hence were *ateleis*) but nevertheless owned yokes of oxen (*zeugaria*).[41]

While *ateles* meant "not levied a property tax," *eleutheros* meant completely exempt of all taxes and charges. An *eleutheros* paroikos was one who had no personal fiscal obligation either toward the state or toward a third party. As more and more privileged landholders were granted the right to settle peasants with *exkousseiai* (in other words, as more gifts of paroikoi were granted), the emperor and fiscal officials had to specify that the gift of paroikoi was to involve only peasants whose fiscal obligations had not been exempted for the benefit of another landholder. Merely noting that the peasants were to be *ateleis* became insufficient; it was felt necessary to add this term as well. For example, case (f) in Table 3.1, a chrysobull from 1080, refers to the fifty *ateleis* paroikoi, "neither subject to the fisc nor any *strateia* service, but being free [*eleutheroi*] completely." We see this also in case (g) in which the monks of the monastery of St. John on Patmos were permitted "to settle 4 *eleutheroi* and *ateleis* paroikoi, not having their own land, nor inscribed in fiscal documents, exempted from all and every *epereia* and *angareia* and from every state tax and charge," on each of the monastery's three properties on the island of Leros.[42]

The term *eleutheros* is often accompanied by a phrase noting that the paroikoi were not inscribed in the praktikon of any individual or of the state, were "unknown to the fisc," or, as here, "not inscribed in fiscal documents." Rather than signifying some new variation in the status of such paroikoi, I think the term and the phrases show how common this type of grant was becoming. Not only were beneficiaries not to acquire peasants who were working on state property or inhabiting villages of taxpaying peasants, but they were not to acquire these peasants from the properties of other privileged property owners, such as these monasteries. One would suppose that as time passed, fewer and fewer peasants would escape the bureaucracy of the fisc.[43]

The nature of the concession

The gift of paroikoi was an exemption of a fixed number of *ateleis* paroikoi. In one case – (e) in Table 3.1 – the emperor specified that the paroikoi were to come from those already working the recipient's land. In another

[41] *Iviron*, II, no. 32.9–10. *Vatopédi*, I, no. 10.29: τοὺς . . . παροίκους ἀτελεῖς, πεντήκοντα ζευγαράτους, and p. 12.

[42] *Vatopédi*, I, no. 10.25–26: μήτε δημοσίω ὑποκειμένους μήτε στρατεία λειτουργοῦντας τινί, ἀλλ' ἐλευθέρους πάντη τυγχάνοντας. *Patmos*, I, no. 18. Oikonomides, *Fiscalité*, 206.

[43] *ODB*, s.v. "eleutheros."

case (g) the recipient was permitted to seek such paroikoi from outside his property. In the 1044 chrysobull for Nea Mone (d), Constantine IX granted an *exkousseia* on "the paroikoi now settled" on a newly granted property of the monastery and additionally granted "an *exkousseia* of another 24 *ateleis* paroikoi."[44]

Despite the fact that the gift of paroikoi almost always involved peasants who owned no land of their own and therefore did not owe a tax on real property, the state was making a true concession to the recipient. It was foregoing its claim to the personal taxes and secondary charges that normally burdened even landless peasants.

It is important to emphasize that a complete *exkousseia* was an exemption of all state burdens except the basic property tax. Thus it included an exemption of all of the taxes on cultivators and their animals (e.g., *kapnikon, synone, ennomion*), of the supplemental taxes (e.g., *aerikon, paroikiatikon, aktemonitikon, zeugaratikion*), and of the secondary charges and corvées (e.g., all the *epereiai* and *angareiai*, including charges and burdens such as *kaniskion, mitaton, aplekton, kastroktisia, strateia*). Thus, a "gift of paroikoi" was a grant of an *exkousseia* to a third party of the taxes and charges (but not the property tax) that would ordinarily be levied on the persons and property of the paroikoi.

The paroikoi rented land from the monastery or worked the monastery's land. In case (i) in Table 3.1 the monastery had received an *exkousseia* of 12 *eleutheroi* and *ateleis* paroikoi so that the paroikoi could rent (*enoikisai*) the monastery's land. And Alexios I's 1106 chrysobull for the Eleousa monastery states that the 12 paroikoi were granted to the monastery so that they would work the land of the monastery and serve the monks, "not recognizing another master."[45] We may compare this to Choniates' description of those granted to soldiers: "the inhabitants of the provinces, who formerly had the fisc as master." The recipient of a "gift of paroikoi" replaced the state as the "lord" (*despotes*) of the peasants.

Why did monasteries desire "gifts of paroikoi"? Peasants might rent monastic land (and even live on monastic property) while rendering their secondary burdens to the fisc, but it was much more profitable to the monastery to hold peasants exempted of these secondary burdens. If exempted peasants were available to a monastery, the monastery could set aside a reserve of domain land that was not rented to peasants or worked

[44] *Lavra*, I, no. 38. *Patmos*, I, no. 18. Zepos, *JGR*, 616.49, 617.5.

[45] *Patmos*, I, no. 19.3–4. L. Petit, "Le monastère de Notre-Dame de Pitié en Macédoine," *IRAIK* 6 (1900), no. 2, p. 29.9–15.

by hired men, but cultivated through the labor services of the exempted paroikoi. In this way the monastery could enjoy the full profit from its domain land with no labor costs. Moreover, if there was a shortage of peasant labor, much monastic land may have gone uncultivated save for the labor services that could be demanded from these exempted peasants.

Changes in status and terminology: *aktemon* to *zeugaratos*, *exkousseiai* to "gifts of paroikoi"

In the case of the *ateleis* paroikoi that the Patmos monastery was permitted to settle with an *exkousseia* – (g) in Table 3.1 – a document from 1145 notes that while the monastery had been granted "an *exkousseia* of 12 *eleutheroi* and *ateleis* paroikoi," tax officials had been harassing the monks because the original grant did not denote these paroikoi as *zeugaratoi*, which evidently they had become over the course of time. At the monks' request Manuel I confirmed "the *exkousseia* of twelve paroikoi" and added an *exkousseia* of six additional *zeugaratoi* paroikoi: case (i).

Another change in status, also involving *zeugaratoi* paroikoi, is found in the dossier of the Eleousa monastery outside Strumica. First, in July 1085 Alexios I granted the newly founded monastery 500 modioi of land and an *exkousseia* to the monastery itself and "to the land granted to it with all those unspecified [ἀπροσδιορίστως] settled in it." Then, in August 1106 Alexios granted a complete fiscal exemption to the 500 modioi and added another 162 modioi as a gift for the site of the monastery itself. Further, he granted the monks "an *exkousseia* of twelve paroikoi, free [*eleutheroi*] and *ateleis*, not having their own *staseis* or earlier subject to state taxes, so that they should work the 500 modioi of land given earlier to the monastery."[46]

With the passage of time (forty-six years) the small monastery prospered. The twelve paroikoi acquired their own draft animals and this required further imperial intervention. A praktikon from July 1152 notes that while Alexios I had originally granted the monastery twelve paroikoi *aktemones* who did not have their own property holdings (*hypostaseis*), the fiscal official found that these *aktemones* were now *zeugaratoi*. *Aktemon* (ἀκτήμων, lit. "landless") was a fiscal designation for a peasant who possessed no draft animals and little or no real property (at most, perhaps, only small vineyards or garden plots), but who possessed other livestock (e.g., asses, sheep, goats, beehives). Manuel I now formally adjusted the status of the paroikoi: "from

[46] Petit, "Le monastère de Notre-Dame," no. 1, p. 27.17ff.; and no. 2, p. 29.9–15.

aktemones such [paroikoi] become *zeugaratoi*," and the monastery was to hold them "completely untaxed and uncharged."[47]

Here we have the reason for the change in terminology from "*exkousseiai* of paroikoi" to "gifts of paroikoi." Originally the peasants that comprised these grants were propertyless (*aktemones*) and so it was only the secondary charges, primarily corvées, that the state was conceding to the privileged recipient. However, as the number of recipients of *exkousseiai* of paroikoi grew and as the number of peasants so granted grew, perhaps even as the state became more efficient at categorizing and assessing peasants, it became increasingly difficult to ensure and it could no longer be assumed that the peasants within an "*exkousseia* of paroikoi" were propertyless. When the emperor granted peasants with property, however meager, to a monastery or any other privileged recipient, and did not demand the tax on this property, the state was entering territory it had long avoided. It was forsaking the basic property tax. For this reason, it was no longer appropriate to call such a grant a mere *exkousseia*, and so the more general phrase "gift of paroikoi" was adopted.

Laymen and gifts of paroikoi

Gifts of paroikoi to laymen are unknown until the 1070s, but from that point on, they are as common as grants of paroikoi to monasteries.

(i) In 1073 Michael VII Doukas granted the general Andronikos Doukas properties in full ownership and with tax exemption from an imperial domain outside the town of Miletos in Asia Minor. The emperor ordered that the properties and paroikoi settled on them were exempted from a long list of secondary charges and obligations. Thus, within the grant to Andronikos was a gift of paroikoi *[4.1]*.

(ii) Two men, Othon and Leo Vaasprakanites, were granted a *proasteion* near Thessaloniki by Nikephoros III Botaneiates (1078–1081). Later it passed to the general Leo Kephalas with "all the agricultural fruits in it and the oxen and paroikoi found in it." No doubt Othon and Vaasprakanites had been the previous recipients of this gift of paroikoi *[4.3]*.

[47] See *ODB*, s.v. "aktemon." Petit, "Le monastère de Notre-Dame," no. 8, p. 35: γεγόνασιν οἱ τοιοῦτοι ἀπὸ ἀκτημόνων ζευγαράτοι, and pp. 38–39.

(iii) Leo Kephalas received the village of Chostianes in the theme of Moglena from Alexios I in 1086. The grant included a small number of peasants who lived in the village *[4.6]*.

(iv) Another of Alexios' generals, Gregory Pakourianos, was also a recipient of a gift of paroikoi. Among the many properties and privileges Pakourianos received from emperors during the 1070s through Alexios I was a gift of a number of paroikoi who had received an *exkousseia* of secondary charges and corvées *[4.2]*.

(v) Sometime before 1098 Kale Vasilakaina was granted the taxes of the paroikoi on her land, among which was the village of Radolivos *[4.7]*.

The known grants of paroikoi to laymen differ from the known grants of paroikoi to monasteries in that the former tended to involve grants of state land as well. And that brings us back to the passage from Choniates. Ahrweiler thought that Choniates was employing the phrase "gifts of paroikoi" in a new sense, signifying a new form of grant, different from the "gifts of paroikoi" to monasteries.[48] Yet it is difficult to accept this view, for the phrase has a continuous history in the documents and has a consistent meaning through the early thirteenth century, that is, through the time Choniates wrote his history. The only evolution in the phrase was a tendency in the twelfth century for the grant to include peasants who were not completely propertyless, but owned livestock. But the grant implied by the phrase remained an indirect tax exemption for the benefit of a privileged landowner. The application of the term to laymen by Choniates was not new, for, as the examples above show, laymen received "gifts of paroikoi" as well, even if the sources do not use this phrase.

Analysis of the Choniates passage

[3.2] Marginal note to the History attributed to Skoutariotes (end of thirteenth century or later)

But was Choniates referring to pronoia grants in his passage? Certainly one Byzantine writer from around the turn of the fourteenth century thought so. The late thirteenth-century chronicle often attributed to Theodore Skoutariotes contains part of Choniates' text (the first two paragraphs of my translation at the beginning of this chapter) in a somewhat abbreviated form. It begins, "While there is a law among the Romans that wages be

[48] Ahrweiler, "La concession des droits incorporels," 106.

granted to the soldiers, the emperor himself cut off the wages granted to the soldiers and with gifts of paroikoi he arranged for the soldiers to have the things sufficient, abusing a practice effected by previous emperors for those who thrashed the enemies." This text adds nothing to what Choniates reports, but there is a marginal note, added by a copyist of the chronicle, which reads "On military pronoiai" (Περὶ Στρατιωτικῶν προνοιῶν). On the one hand, it is certain that the copyist of Skoutariotes thought that Choniates was referring to grants of pronoiai, but on the other, since this note cannot be dated earlier than the end of the thirteenth century, one could argue that the copyist's opinion has little significance for interpreting the meaning of Choniates. Nevertheless, it is not altogether without interest that the copyist himself believed that Choniates was referring to pronoia grants as the copyist understood them at the time he copied the work.[49]

Based on the characteristics we determined in Chapter 2, a pronoia grant during the twelfth century was a grant for life, conferred upon an individual by an imperial official at the behest of emperor, especially upon soldiers, and consisting of real property and of paroikoi who rendered to the pronoia holder the taxes and services they ordinarily would have rendered to the state. All of these elements – an imperial grant conferred by an official, upon soldiers, real property, paroikoi who pay taxes to the recipient – are mentioned explicitly in Choniates' description, with the exception of one, the lifetime element.

Were "gifts of paroikoi" pronoia grants? No, for, in fact, according to Choniates, Manuel I's grants to soldiers were not limited to paroikoi; the soldiers were also assigned "acres of dewy and grain-bearing land," and thus we are dealing with a compound grant involving both "gifts of paroikoi" and land. A "gift of paroikoi" was just one part of the pronoia grant.

But we are getting ahead of ourselves. Let us examine in detail what Choniates has to say about Manuel's policy to see what we can learn about it. First, who were the "earlier" emperors that Choniates claims had used this technique to reward soldiers? And does Choniates' reference to the actions of "earlier" emperors allow us to conclude anything about when emperors began to bestow "gifts of paroikoi" upon soldiers? Since Ostrogorsky regarded the word "practice" in Choniates' assertion that Manuel I "abused a practice devised by previous emperors though seldom performed for those who often thrashed the enemy" as a reference to the institution of pronoia, and since he viewed Alexios I as the originator of the institution,

[49] Sathas, *Μεσαιωνικὴ Βιβλιοθήκη*, VII, 301.14–27: τὰ τοῖς στρατιώταις διδόμενα σιτηρέσια περικόψας, δωρεαῖς παροίκων τοὺς στρατιώτας ἔχειν τὰ ἱκανὰ ᾠκονόμησεν. Ostrogorsky, "Die Pronoia unter den Komnenen," 46. Ahrweiler, "La concession des droits incorporels," 112. Hohlweg, "Zur Frage der Pronoia," 300 note 59. Cf. Lemerle, *Agrarian History*, 231.

he concluded that the "earlier" emperors were Alexios I and John II. On the other hand, Hohlweg questioned whether the scope of the word "earlier" (πρώην) should be so clearly limited to Manuel's father and grandfather. Perhaps, he wrote, Choniates was not specifically thinking of pronoia when he wrote the quoted phrase. Perhaps Choniates was merely thinking of the practice, perennial in Byzantium as well as in Rome, of granting soldiers property, either as a reward or on condition of continued service. Such grants of property, seen in Byzantium in the old military lands (*stratiotika ktemata*) and in the settling of foreign prisoners of war, and in Rome in the border soldiers called the *limitanei*, were no innovation of the Komnenian dynasty. Thus, even if the specific subject of Choniates' passage was pronoia (a specific type of conditional grant of imperial property), Choniates may be merely emphasizing that while previous emperors did give, in one form or another, grants of property to soldiers, Manuel was debasing the practice by conferring such grants upon unworthy soldiers. Therefore, Hohlweg's argument leads to the conclusions that (i) we cannot say who the earlier emperors were (and Choniates may not have had anyone particular in mind), and that (ii) the phrase in Choniates' passage about "earlier" emperors tells us nothing about when the institution of pronoia began. One could argue that grants of property to soldiers, particularly to defeated foreign ethnic groups, was never a "rare" practice, that it was rather common, even in the twelfth century. Ostrogorsky, who nevertheless thought that Choniates had pronoia grants in mind throughout, suggested, reasonably enough, that Choniates' claim that such grants were made only "seldom" was probably a deliberate underestimation on Choniates' part. In any event, the passage does not permit us to say when the practice of granting "gifts of paroikoi" to soldiers began, only that it predated Manuel.[50]

Who were these "paroikoi" who now paid their taxes to the soldiers? Choniates writes that they were "Roman taxpayers" (Ῥωμαίους ὑποφόρους), "inhabitants of the provinces, who formerly had the fisc as master" (τὸν δημόσιον πάλαι δεσπότην λαχόντες). Sometimes the paroikos was "a Roman of proud bearing." Lemerle wrote that they must have been paroikoi settled on state lands, as distinguished from both peasant proprietors and paroikoi who had already been allotted to a private landowner. Lefort agreed: they were paroikoi working estates of the fisc rather than peasant members of a village community. On the other hand, Ahrweiler thought that Choniates was using the word *paroikos* as a synonym for the taxpaying peasant.[51]

[50] Ostrogorsky, *Féodalité*, 30, and Ostrogorsky, "Die Pronoia unter den Komnenen," 47, 50. Hohlweg, "Zur Frage der Pronoia," 303.

[51] Lemerle, *Agrarian History*, 233. J. Lefort, "The Rural Economy, Seventh–Twelfth Centuries," *EHB*, I, 290. Ahrweiler, *Byzance et la mer*, 220.

Were they propertyless peasants renting state land or were they peasant proprietors? The question is difficult to answer but it is important because it defines the social hierarchy that such grants created. "Roman taxpayers" suggests peasant proprietors; those "who formerly had the fisc as master" could apply to either peasant proprietors or peasants renting state land; "a Roman of proud bearing" seems more likely to refer to peasant proprietors. In the middle of the twelfth century, and certainly by the time Choniates wrote his history, "paroikos" was applied to any peasant who paid his taxes or charges to someone other than the fisc. And yet, the reference to the granting of land as well as paroikoi suggests that the soldiers received agricultural land owned by the state, and this would have been cultivated by peasant tenants. Perhaps the difficulty in determining what sense of *paroikos* was intended by Choniates reflects the conflation of the two categories – propertyless peasant tenants and taxpaying peasant proprietors. In any event, while these peasants previously paid their taxes (or charges) to the government, now they rendered these to a soldier.

Why did their situation worsen? According to Choniates, "they were deprived not only of silver and obols, but were stripped of their last tunic," and some provinces of the empire "were destroyed and ravaged by our own people as if they were foreign lands." These "Romans" had to pay their taxes to a new "tax collector" (τοῦ φορολογοῦντος). All of this emphasizes the fiscal burden on these "paroikoi." But he also adds that "sometimes they were torn away from their loved ones." What does this mean? Ostrogorsky thought it meant they were obliged to join the army, though this is mere speculation. Hohlweg suggested that perhaps they were assigned to different pronoia holders. It is more likely that Choniates was simply using hyperbole, that the financial burden was so great that "families were torn apart." Hyperbole is in fact the best explanation for his assertion that these taxpayers were to serve the soldiers "in the manner of slaves" (ἐν σχήματι δούλων), a locution derived from the fact that the taxpayers were now beholden to a private individual rather than to the state. Because of their close relation to the taxpayers they were assigned, the soldiers, who now became in effect their tax collectors, had much more incentive than ordinary government officials to be as efficient and ruthless as possible in collecting every cent their taxpayers owed.[52]

Some of these grants were made to serving soldiers, while others were made to new recruits. Who were these recruits? Choniates claims that now "everyone wanted to enlist in the army" and that this included tailors,

[52] Ostrogorsky, *Féodalité*, 28. Hohlweg, "Zur Frage der Pronoia," 301, 305.

stableboys, brick makers, and blacksmiths. Are we to accept this literally, as Lemerle did, when he wrote that the recruits came from the lower classes of the urban population? For his part, Ostrogorsky claimed that the relevant part of Choniates' text (the third paragraph of my translation up through the phrase "no questions asked") had nothing to do with "gifts of paroikoi" or, more specifically, pronoia:

> To his fiery protest against the broad granting of pronoia undertaken by Manuel, Niketas [Choniates] adds an equally fiery protest against the indiscriminate enlistment of mercenaries, and in his polemical zeal he throws these two quite different things together. The tradesmen of whom Niketas speaks could have been at most enrolled as mercenaries. It is entirely certain that they could not have been pronoiarioi and holders of paroikoi, since it is also certain that properties granted in pronoia were not something given simply by recruiters, but were granted through imperial documents.

According to Ostrogorsky, only when Choniates refers to "imperial diplomas" does he return to the subject of "gifts of paroikoi." Ostrogorsky therefore concluded that "gifts of paroikoi" were not made to poor tradesmen.[53]

This interpretation could hardly be more strained. Only a reader who refused to admit the possibility that more or less common people could receive pronoiai would attempt to dissociate the people in Choniates' passage who "were registered among the military troops with no questions asked" from those who, in the very next phrase, "were provided with imperial diplomas." Yet I agree with Ostrogorsky to the extent that we cannot accept literally everything Choniates says in these passages. We should expect that there would be some exaggeration in a narrative that concludes by paraphrasing scriptural lamentations (Psalms 12:2, 77:50). It is doubtful, for example, that hordes of tailors were receiving land and gifts of paroikoi. Rather, we should simply conclude that Choniates felt unworthy people were receiving these grants and that Choniates did not approve of the social origins of these new soldiers.[54]

Indeed it is not necessary to believe that these grants were necessarily small and represented a "pronoia of the proletariat," to use Lemerle's phrase.[55]

53 Lemerle, *Agrarian History*, 233, and cf. E. Stanescu, "Les 'stratiotès': diffusion et survivance d'une institution byzantine dans le sud-est de l'Europe," *Actes du premier Congrès international des études balkaniques et sud-est européennes*, III (Sofia, 1969), 228. Ostrogorsky, "Die Pronoia unter den Komnenen," 45 note 21, 46.

54 Cf. Hohlweg, *Beiträge zur Verwaltungsgeschichte*, 86–87, and M. Angold, *The Byzantine Empire 1025–1204*, 2nd ed. (London and New York, 1997), 258.

55 Cf. Mutafčiev, "Vojniški zemi," 48/574, 51/577; Darkó, "La militarizzazione dell'Impero Bizantino," 97; Ahrweiler, *Byzance et la mer*, 221; and Lemerle, *Agrarian History*, 241.

Neither can we necessarily exclude the lower classes from the set of recipients nor can we state flatly that Choniates' soldiers were of a lower class than thirteenth-century pronoia soldiers.[56] All we can say is that Choniates did not like the class of men who were becoming soldiers.

This also explains Choniates' characterization of some of these new soldiers as "semi-barbarian runts" (to borrow Michael Angold's apt rendering of the Greek ἀνδραρίῳ μιξοβαρβάρῳ). Ostrogorsky, who felt that we should not accept everything Choniates says, nevertheless claimed that this phrase meant that non-Greeks, such as the Cumans of Moglena *[2.4–2.5]*, were among the recipients of Manuel's grants. But "semi-barbarian" never means "foreigner." It means "half-Greek" or, as an insult, "uncultured Greek." Since Choniates already pointed out that the new recruits came from within the empire, we should conclude that "semi-barbarian" merely related to his disapproval of their social origins. In fact he uses the expression in syntactical apposition to "a Roman of proud bearing," i.e., a "true Roman" now had to pay taxes to a "semi-Roman."[57]

How did the new recruits become soldiers? According to Choniates they "presented themselves to the recruiters. Handing over a Persian horse [*hippon Persaion*] or by laying down a little gold they were registered among the military troops with no questions asked, and immediately were provided with imperial diplomas assigning them acres of dewy and grain-bearing land and Roman taxpayers." Hohlweg wondered about the horse and the money, whether this horse belonged to the equipment of the new recruit or whether the money was an entrance fee into the lists, that is, the price of an imperial document. He opted for the former, and in it saw some kind of link (albeit tenuous) to middle Byzantine practices in which soldiers were usually required to maintain their own horses. On the other hand, Angold linked this passage to Manuel I's likely adoption of the western European lance and large triangular shield as replacements for the traditional inexpensive bow and arrow and small circular shield. He suggests that the meaning of the "Persian horse . . . and a little gold" passage is that the new soldiers themselves were responsible for the expense of their new equipment. He adds, with needless ingenuity, that the artisans the emperor was recruiting would have had the means, if not for themselves, then for their children. All in all, I think Choniates' use of the expression "with no questions asked" and the word "immediately" suggests that he felt there was something unethical

56 Cf. Hohlweg, "Zur Frage der Pronoia," 303.

57 Ostrogorsky, "Die Pronoia unter den Komnenen," 51, and D. Anastasijević and G. Ostrogorsky, "Les Koumanes pronoïaires," *Annuaire de l'Institut de philologie et d'histoire orientale et slave* 11 (1951), 19–20. Cf. Ahrweiler, "La 'pronoia' à Byzance," 688.

or inappropriate about this handing over of horse or money. The simplest explanation of the passage, as Lemerle has suggested, is that the hopeful recruits were probably bribing recruitment officials to enroll even if they did not have the proper martial qualities.[58]

And what about the "imperial diplomas" (*vasilika grammata*)? The *Zavorda Treatise* states explicitly that a pronoia grant came from the emperor, but Choniates' passage suggests that while "imperial" documents were issued, there was little personal involvement by the emperor in making these grants. Were these "imperial diplomas" a kind of form, presigned by the emperor, and negotiated in the provinces by imperial officials? This would accord with Choniates' suggestion that the recruits were of low social status.

Why were these grants so popular? In other words, what made men enlist so willingly? Obviously the terms they were offered as pronoia soldiers were perceived as superior to the benefits afforded them by their previous non-military occupations. If Manuel had had the means to hire mercenaries, they may have enlisted just as eagerly. Thus, we cannot say that the new recruits preferred to be pronoia soldiers rather than mercenaries.

As for why a man would prefer collecting taxes and rents from peasants to receiving a cash stipend from the imperial treasury, clearly many factors were involved. The advantages of holding a pronoia over receiving cash pay were that (i) the soldier was not dependent on state officials for obtaining his pay, (ii) with his "authority" over other taxpayers, he probably acquired more prestige and power, and (iii) he was afforded more general autonomy from the government. On the negative side, (i) the pronoia soldier now bore the "administrative" burden of collecting his pay and possibly of organizing the leasing of his land, and (ii) while he was not dependent on the government for this pay, he was dependent on the uncertainties of agrarian production. Under these circumstances, if the economic benefits of mercenary pay and pronoia were perceived as identical, we might conclude that most men would have preferred pronoiai. But if mercenary pay was commonly furnished irregularly or was not forthcoming at all, as was evidently the case, a pronoia grant was obviously preferable.[59]

[58] Hohlweg, "Zur Frage der Pronoia," 302. Angold, *Byzantine Empire*, 258. Lemerle, *Agrarian History*, 233. I am not familiar with Choniates' "Persian horse" expression. It could be a general allusion to tribute or, perhaps, to ancient Persian gift-giving customs (see, e.g., Thucydides, II, 97).

[59] On the unreliability of payments to mercenaries, see Bartusis, *Late Byzantine Army*, index, q.v. "salary, mercenary," albeit focusing on the period after 1204.

Granting that the local population who were now subjected to the demands of these soldiers would resent the policy and suffer because of it, why did Choniates think the effects of all this were bad for the army, weakening it so that provinces of the empire were overrun by enemies? We are told that Manuel's policy led to the "disarray of the army." It became "more slack" through "pouring enormous sums of money into idle bellies. For the good soldiers lost their eagerness for danger" and "all set out to become wealthy." All of this accords well with the general impression that the haste to recruit led to a lowering of standards. The economic rewards attracted men with no military vocation who were more interested in wealth than in fighting. The size of the army increased, but its morale, discipline, and effectiveness diminished. Naturally, we should bear in mind that since Choniates was viewing Manuel's reign from a post-1204 perspective, he stresses the dark side of his policies. We cannot be certain that this was not the best policy possible at the time.

Rather than identifying the morale problem as simply the resentment that good soldiers felt over the recruitment of men who became poor soldiers, Angold attempted to tie it directly to the institution of pronoia. He speculated that while previously "only a few élite units had enjoyed the privilege of pronoia," Manuel's decision "to extend grants of pronoia to most of the troops in the Byzantine army" undermined the morale of the elite troops. Assuming that pronoia soldiers before the implementation of Manuel's policy were not only numerically few but also elite troops, there is no reason to doubt this was the case. And yet it is also likely that other soldiers, aside from pronoia soldiers, such as the more distinguished mercenaries, whether or not they now received their own "gifts of paroikoi," would be disheartened by the recruitment of inferior soldiers, whatever the form of their remuneration.[60]

Evidently the main purpose of Manuel's policy was to raise more soldiers. But there were numerous ways to do this without resorting to grants of land and paroikoi. Lemerle suggested that another reason for Manuel's policy may have been to redress the imbalance between native and foreign troops. While this may have been one of Manuel's goals, it had little bearing on the form of remuneration chosen by Manuel. Hiring more native mercenaries would have had the same effect.[61]

From the point of view of the state, grants of pronoia to soldiers, as described by Choniates, had a number of advantages over mercenary pay.

[60] Angold, *Byzantine Empire*, 257–58.

[61] Lemerle, *Agrarian History*, 233. Hohlweg, *Beiträge zur Verwaltungsgeschichte*, 86.

(i) It relieved the government of the administrative burden of collecting taxes and distributing mercenary pay and, possibly, of organizing the leasing of state land. Further, (ii) out of self-interest the pronoia soldier might be more efficient in maximizing revenues than official state tax collectors. Thus, a smaller number of taxpayers could finance a larger number of soldiers. Also, (iii) grants of pronoiai could create more loyalty and commitment among soldiers by providing them with a stake in the empire not based merely on cash, perhaps even a stake in the fortunes of a particular locale. Among the disadvantages of pronoia was that (i) it led to a decentralization of administration. Amateurs, motivated primarily by self-interest, were now collecting taxes. This could lead to hostility within the taxpaying population toward the state. Further, (ii) since there was not the regular link between soldier and state (scheduled pay disbursements), pronoia diminished the state's control over its soldiers, and (iii) since pronoia grants were more complex, long-term commitments of state revenues than mercenary pay, they greatly limited the state's ability to hire and fire soldiers as needed.

From both a military and an administrative perspective, it is difficult to see why an emperor, given the choice, would prefer to give his soldiers pronoiai rather than cash. Ahrweiler viewed Manuel's policy as a way to restore the administrative machinery of the state after the invasions and incursions of the Seljuks, Normans, and Pechenegs. Initially the government hired mercenaries to restore the empire, then "after the reconquest of a part of the territory, it was necessary to reestablish the administrative machinery and to interest soldiers in its defense.... Thus one found the means to pay people directly, since the state treasury was empty, and to lighten the administrative machinery by suppressing the crowd of fiscal agents who previously traversed the empire." The key phrase in the previous sentence is "since the state treasury was empty." If there had been cash in the treasury, the imperial government would have financed its armed forces through cash. There were clearly adequate economic resources available to the imperial government from the countryside; otherwise pronoia could not have been used to finance soldiers. Thus the problem was getting the state's share of the resources of the countryside to the treasury, and this means there was no adequate, functioning fiscal administrative apparatus to bring cash to the treasury. Even though soldiers hardly make the best tax collectors, and men too concerned with collecting taxes do not make the best soldiers, the policy Choniates describes was an expedient born of necessity no less than the western European *beneficium*.[62]

[62] Ahrweiler, "La 'pronoia' à Byzance," 688–89. Also, Ahrweiler, *Byzance et la mer*, 218.

In summary Choniates' narrative allows us to conclude that current and newly recruited soldiers received, as a reward for service (current soldiers) and for services to be rendered (current and new recruits), imperial documents granting them arable land and the tax revenues of specific taxpayers. The status of the land is not specified, but evidently it belonged to the state. While no firm conclusions can be made regarding whether the soldiers farmed this land themselves or leased it to peasants, the latter, which would parallel their fiscal connection to the taxpayers, is more likely. While we are not told directly that the grants of land and paroikoi were conditional on military service, there would be little logic in the emperor bestowing this kind of grant upon a newly recruited soldier without stipulating that the continued enjoyment of the grant was so qualified.

From these observations, it is reasonable to conclude that Choniates was describing grants of pronoiai as the word was used in documents from the twelfth century: a lifetime imperial grant conferred by an official, especially upon soldiers, of real property and of the taxes and services owed by paroikoi. The only element not mentioned explicitly in Choniates' description is the lifetime character of the grant, but, by the same token, there is nothing in Choniates' passage that suggests that these were *not* grants for life.

It is legitimate to ask why Choniates does not use the word *pronoia*. In fact Choniates employs the word *pronoia* quite infrequently in his history: only eleven times (and no other form of the root, such as the verb *pronoo* or the noun *pronoetes*, appears at all). In ten of the instances the word means "divine providence"; in the remaining instance he uses the word to contrast "human forethought" with acts of God. On the basis of this, I would have to conclude that he was uncomfortable using the word *pronoia* in any but a religious context and that he consciously chose to use the word only in such a context.[63]

Choniates adds nothing to our knowledge of whether pronoia grants were given only to military people during the era of Manuel I, or of whether the soldiers lived near the properties and peasants they were granted, or of what geographical area these grants involved, whether frontier areas recently recovered or the more secure internal territories of the empire. Rather, Choniates is important because he suggests a change in the social level of recipients and in the number of grants during Manuel's reign. And since he points out that earlier emperors made similar grants, he points to a change in the purpose of the grant earlier than the reign of Manuel. This,

[63] Choniates, ed. van Dieten, 96.3, 143.17, 264.11, 278.16, 286.22, 308.2, 424.20, 426.22, 452.8, 490.21, 494.12 ("human forethought").

with the evidence of the *Zavorda Treatise*, also suggests an earlier change in the conditions of the grant (for life, as well as for service).

Conferring state property and state revenues upon individuals, thereby substituting the individual for the state, was not unheard of in the earlier centuries of Byzantium. But it had always been a rare thing, bestowed on a few privileged and socially connected individuals and monasteries. The novelty of Manuel's policy was in applying the practice widely and systematically to the army. Only when the grant was given to a soldier and when the grant was for life can we speak of a "pronoia" grant. In effect, Manuel created the *institution* of pronoia.

Evidence to support Choniates

Scholars have sought most earnestly evidence with which to confirm Choniates' assertion that Manuel implemented a widespread policy of granting pronoiai to soldiers. However, such supporting material is not abundant. From Choniates' history itself Paul Lemerle pointed out a passage which seems to refer to a parallel reform of the navy during John II's reign. John's minister John of Poutze directed that "the things collected from the naval *strateiai*, given of old to the navy," be "conveyed to the treasury." This meager evidence, while supporting Lemerle's notion of the "fiscalization" of the *strateia* (originally perhaps a service burden, but in this passage a fiscal charge) and suggesting an overall reworking of military policy, provides no direct link to the institution of pronoia.[64] Further, Choniates writes of how Isaac II Angelos (1185–95) returned properties that had been confiscated by Andronikos I (1183–85):

> All those who had suffered affliction in exile and those whom Andronikos had stripped bare of their properties . . . Isaac gathered together and rewarded with substantial benefactions, restoring whatever of their possessions had been kept hidden in the imperial treasury and had not disappeared or which, awarded by Andronikos to others, still survived. In addition he greeted them with a generous hand and provided large sums of money from the palace treasuries.

He notes that these measures and others gave Isaac many soldiers for his campaigns against the Normans. According to G. Litavrin and Michail Sjuzjumov this is a reference to the institution of pronoia. However, all

[64] Choniates, Bonn edn., 75 = ed. van Dieten, 55.7–9: τὰ . . . ἐκ τῶν πλευστικῶν ἐρανιζόμενα στρατειῶν. Lemerle, *Agrarian History*, 234–35.

we are told is that confiscated property was returned, even if it had been granted to others. The first group of men, who had lost their property, need not have been pronoia holders or recipients of any kind of imperial grant at all. It is the second group, those who were granted the confiscated property by Andronikos I, whom we can view as recipients of imperial grants. Nevertheless, we are told nothing about their social status or the terms under which they were granted these confiscated properties.[65]

[3.3] Choniates on the brothers Peter and Asen (early thirteenth century)

Scholars have also cited the case of the Balkan brothers Peter and Asen as support for Manuel's policy of granting pronoiai to soldiers. In Choniates' history we read that during the reign of Isaac II Angelos (1185–95) the pair petitioned the emperor, "asking to enlist among the Romans and to be awarded through an imperial letter a certain village producing a small income located near Mount Haimos." The emperor refused their request, and soon they led a revolt against the empire. A number of scholars have concluded that Peter and Asen had demanded a pronoia grant, while others have denied this. Petar Mutafčiev concluded that they wanted a military command in Danubian Bulgaria along with hereditary property in this region. Lemerle, who thought a pronoia grant required a specific service requirement, similarly viewed the requested grant as a commonplace kind without any necessary link to service, and wrote that inasmuch as the brothers' request was refused anyway, it would not be appropriate to speak of a pronoia here. Indeed certainty is not possible, but the notion of enlisting in the army and receiving "a certain village producing a small income" conferred through "an imperial letter" does parallel Choniates' passage about "gifts of paroikoi." All that is lacking is the lifetime element.[66]

[65] Choniates, ed. van Dieten, 355–56, trans. based on Magoulias, 197. G. Litavrin, *Bolgarija i Vizantija v XI–XII vv.* (Moscow, 1960), 156. Sjuzjumov, "Vnutrennjaja politika Andronika Komnina," 64 note 35.

[66] Choniates, Bonn edn., 482 = ed. van Dieten, 369.61–63: αἰτούμενοι συστρατολογηθῆναι Ῥωμαίοις καὶ διὰ βασιλείου γράμματος σφίσι βραβευθῆναι χωρίον τι βραχυπρόσοδον κατὰ τὸν Αἷμον κείμενον. Pronoia grant: V. Zlatarski, *Istorija na bŭlgarskata dŭržava prez srednite vekove*, II (Sofia, 1934; repr. 1972), 412, 435–37; Ostrogorsky, *Féodalité*, 53–54; Anastasijević and Ostrogorsky, "Les Koumanes pronoïaires," 20; C. Brand, *Byzantium Confronts the West, 1180–1204* (Cambridge, Mass., 1968), 89; and Litavrin, *Bolgarija i Vizantija*, 156. Uspenskij, "Značenie," 32 note 1, thought it might be dealing with the concept of a pronoia. Cf. Oikonomides, "A propos des armées," 369 note 101. P. Mutafčiev, *Istorija na bŭlgarskija narod*, II (Sofia, 1944), 34. Lemerle, *Agrarian History*, 240 note 1.

A couple of other passages from Choniates' history have been linked to pronoia. In 1197 or 1198 in an effort to deal with the depredations of the Genoese pirate Gafforio, Alexios III Angelos attempted to lull Gafforio into a false sense of security by offering him 600 pounds of gold "and to apportion Roman land sufficient to maintain his 700 kindred men-at-arms." Gerald Day considered this a "sizable pronoia." Sizable indeed; as Charles Brand observed, it would have been "a Byzantine province."[67] One last passage from Choniates that one might cite notes that Alexios III Angelos was inclined to furnish, to those who asked, "fruit-bearing lands and state taxes."[68]

Outside of Choniates' history, the evidence to support Manuel's pronoia policy is equally thin. Both Lemerle and Ahrweiler saw a connection between Choniates' passage and a passage in a discourse to Manuel I written around 1175 by Eustathios, the future archbishop of Thessaloniki. Eustathios praised the scope and intensity of the emperor's activities: "meetings everyday, embassies at all times, some sent out, others received, care to lawgiving, resolving disputes, recruiting of soldiers, battling of rumors . . . , rules of governance [οἰκονομιῶν τύποι], judgements of things to be done, masses of needs . . . " Ahrweiler rendered my "rules of governance" as "forms of grants" ("formes des concessions") and, with no real justification, directly connected these grants to the phrase "recruiting of soldiers." Since both of the words *oikonomia* and *typos* can mean so many things (*typos* is also applied to a specific type of imperial document), of which my translation of the phrase is merely one suggestion, it cannot be concluded that Eustathios had pronoia in mind.[69]

Aside from the twelfth-century documents discussed in the previous chapter, a number of twelfth-century documents that do not employ the word *pronoia* have been cited by scholars as possible evidence to support Choniates:

[67] Choniates, ed. van Dieten, 482.26–27: καὶ χώραν ἀποδάσασθαι οἱ Ῥωμαϊκὴν ἑπτακοσίους ἔχουσαν τρέφειν ὁμογενεῖς ἐκείνῳ ὁπλίτας. G. Day, *Genoa's Response to Byzantium, 1155–1204* (Urbana and Chicago, 1988), 32. Brand, *Byzantium Confronts the West*, 214. Adding more detail than Choniates provides, Angold, *Byzantine Empire*, 322, writes that Gafforio was offered "revenues from the coastal provinces."

[68] Choniates, ed. van Dieten, 454.18–19: γήδια καρποφόρα καὶ δημοσίους συνεισφοράς, cited by Oikonomides, *Fiscalité*, 187. Also worth noting here is a comment by Brand, *Byzantium Confronts the West*, 111. Discussing the rebellion of Isaac II Angelos' cousin, Constantine Angelos, in 1193, Brand writes that Constantine "secured the temporary allegiance of his officers and the local pronoiarioi," though Choniates' text (Choniates, ed. van Dieten, 435.56–57 = Bonn edn., 570–71) mentions only "local soldiers [*stratiotai*]."

[69] W. Regel and N. Novasadskij, *Fontes rerum byzantinarum*, I (St. Petersburg, 1892), 5.25–30. Lemerle, *Agrarian History*, 231. Ahrweiler, *Byzance et la mer*, 222.

An order of Manuel I from 1144 or 1159, known only from its rubric, ordered that the transfer of immovable imperial property in gift (δωρεὰς ἀκινήτων παρὰ βασιλέων) be limited to two categories of people: "those from the senate and from the military list." This order was later renewed by Manuel and abolished by Alexios II in 1183. As Uspenskij noted, Alexios II's repeal of the legislation was evidently motivated either by the desire to broaden the traffic in imperial property to people of less-privileged status or, conversely, by the desire to halt the distribution of imperial property to anyone regardless of their status. He opted for the latter interpretation, regarding Alexios' action as a probable reaction against the granting of pronoiai by Manuel and perhaps the earlier Komnenoi.[70]

While Manuel was obviously showing a preference for military people, linking them with the most distinguished people in Byzantine society, the question is what kind of grants and what kind of soldiers did Manuel have in mind or, rather, what were the qualifications under which these grants of imperial properties were made. Oikonomides approached the question by asking what the two groups of people had in common. His answer was that they were both groups of people who served the state. Consequently, he interpreted Manuel's legislation as motivated by the desire to keep state properties within the service of the state; therefore, only men who served the state should receive such grants. Could this have included soldiers who were not pronoia soldiers? For example, could the legislation be referring to the grants of land provided to groups of defeated foreigners, land upon which they were settled as soldiers and which they cultivated themselves? According to Oikonomides' interpretation, the answer is yes. Thus, while we may flinch at the notion of associating ethnic smallholding soldiers with the loftiest aristocrats, there is a reasonable interpretation of this legislation that does not involve pronoia. At best we can say, with Michael Angold, that "it is not impossible that this piece of legislation referred to pronoia."[71]

[70] Zepos, *JGR*, I, 387.20–21 = Zacharia, *Jus*, III, 457: εἰ μὴ εἰς πρόσωπα ἀπὸ τῆς συγκλήτου, ἢ ἀπὸ τοῦ στρατιωτικοῦ καταλόγου τυγχάνοντα. Zepos, *JGR*, I, 421.12–13 = Zacharia, *Jus*, III, 498 (1155 or 1170). Zepos, *JGR*, I, 429.15 = Zacharia, *Jus*, III, 507. Dölger, *Regesten*, II, nos. 1333, 1398, and 1553. Uspenskij, "Značenie," 6–7, 14. Litavrin, *Bolgarija i Vizantija*, 149, also relates this legislation to pronoia.

[71] N. Oikonomides, "'Η διανομὴ τῶν βασιλικῶν «ἐπισκέψεων» τῆς Κρήτης (1170–1171) καὶ ἡ δημοσιονομικὴ πολιτικὴ τοῦ Μανουὴλ Α' Κομνηνοῦ," in Oikonomides, *Documents et études sur les institutions de Byzance* (London, 1976), no. XVII, 198. Angold, *The Byzantine Empire, 1025–1204*, 1st ed. (London, 1984), 226 (the sentence does not appear in the second edition of the book).

Peter Charanis linked the ban on the creation of a certain kind of *solemnion* to Manuel's need to create pronoia grants. This was the *parechomenon* (παρεχόμενον, "furnished") or *cheirosdoton* (χειρόσδοτον, "hand-delivered") *solemnion*, according to which a provincial tax official bestowed the amount of the *solemnion* upon a religious establishment directly from the taxes he had collected in the area of his jurisdiction. Thus, it was "furnished" or "hand-delivered" by the provincial tax official himself. From the point of view of the fiscal official, this method of providing a *solemnion* involved a tax exemption (*logisimon*) because, in order for the tax official to set aside the amount of the *solemnion* (and thereby to reduce the amount of taxes he sent to the central treasury), a number of properties within his tax district had to receive a fictive exemption (*logisimon*) of their taxes. The properties so "exempted" still paid their taxes, but this accounting procedure produced balanced books.[72]

The earliest reference to this type of *solemnion* dates to 984, when a document mentions a *solemnion* of 244 nomismata, drawn from the tax receipts on Lemnos and granted to Lavra by John Tzimiskes (969–76).[73] These *solemnia* could also be granted in kind, as when Alexios I around 1093 granted the monastery of St. John on Patmos of 300 modioi of grain and 24 nomismata, drawn from the treasury of the *doux* of Crete. This solemnion was gradually enlarged by Alexios' successors, and as late as 1197 the monastery was still receiving a *solemnion* from the treasury of the *doux* of Crete.[74] Despite a couple of exceptions such as this, sometime before 1160 Manuel I ordered a general end to *parechomena solemnia* in cash.[75] Charanis reasoned that Manuel wanted to use these revenues for the creation of pronoia grants and that this was evidence of Manuel's pronoia policy. However, the argument falls apart because twelfth-century pronoia grants were not composed of tax revenues.

72 Charanis, "Monastic Properties," 84–85. Dölger, *Beiträge*, 118.7–12, 146.

73 *Iviron*, I, no. 6.14, and p. 43 note 156. Other examples: *Lavra*, I, App. II.6, and p. 61; *Patmos*, I, no. 3 (1079); and Oikonomides, *Fiscalité*, 205–06, 243.

74 *Patmos*, I, no. 8. MM, VI, 107.12, 117.30–118.2. *Patmos*, I, no. 22. Dölger, *Regesten*, II, nos. 1170, 1296, 1339, 1521a. *Patmos*, II, no. 57. Oikonomides, *Fiscalité*, 207.

75 N. Svoronos, "Les privilèges de l'église à l'époque des Comnènes: un rescrit inédit de Manuel Ier Comnène," in Svoronos, *Études sur l'organisation intérieure, la société et l'économie de l'empire byzantin* (London, 1973), no. VII, 377 and note 273, 379 note 284. *Patmos*, I, no. 22.13. Petit, "Le monastère de Notre-Dame de Pitié," 32. While there are no more references to *parechomena solemnia* in cash after 1200, the *solemnion* in kind that the Lemviotissa monastery was receiving in 1227 could be thought of as a *parechomenon solemnion* depending on whether it was drawn from a central or provincial account (MM, IV, 284).

[3.4] Accord between Venice and Boniface of Montferrat (1204)

Several months before Manuel I's death in 1180, his daughter Maria married Renier, the youngest son of William, marquess of Montferrat. He was given the title *kaisar* and, according to several western sources, he obtained some kind of rights over Thessaloniki which these sources describe as the "honor" or "kingdom" of Thessaloniki. Most notably, according to the terms of the accord concluded in 1204 between Venice and Boniface of Montferrat, leader of the Fourth Crusade and Renier's brother, Boniface himself abdicated his rights over the island of Crete which "was given or promised" to him by Alexios IV (1203–04), 100,000 hyperpyra that were "promised" to him, and the city of Thessaloniki which Manuel I gave to his brother Renier as a "fief": "the whole fief that the deceased former emperor Manuel gave to my brother." A number of scholars have considered this a pronoia.[76]

First of all, while Byzantine sources, including Niketas Choniates, discuss the marriage, sometimes in detail, they mention nothing about a grant of Thessaloniki. This makes it almost certain that, whether or not Thessaloniki had been promised to Renier, he derived little benefit from it. In fact Manuel's death and the intrigues that followed it could explain why the grant, even if consummated, was short-lived. But even if Renier never actually held Thessaloniki, what kind of a grant was envisioned? We cannot conclude that Renier actually received from the Byzantine emperor a fief in the classic western sense. Western European writers commonly fit things into feudal forms even when they were not feudal. At this time it was not unusual in western Europe for the term "fief" to be applied to almost any form of property tenure. Generally, the evidence of western European sources must be viewed with great caution.[77]

Should we consider Renier's grant, as described in the western sources, a pronoia? For his part, Ostrogorsky, while improperly finding significance in the fact that it was called a fief, denied that the grant could have constituted a true pronoia, because it was hereditary, though he suggested in a later article that Latins such as Boniface's brother may have been the "semi-barbarians" that Choniates mentioned when referring to his "gifts of

[76] Tafel and Thomas, *Urkunden zur älteren Handels- und Staatsgeschichte der Republik Venedig*, I, 513: *et de toto feudo, quod et Manuel quondam defunctus imperator dedit patri [sc. fratri] meo.* For bibliography, see Brand, *Byzantium Confronts the West*, 319 note 12, and D. Jacoby, "Les archontes grecs et la féodalité en Morée franque," in Jacoby, *Société et démographie à Byzance et en Romanie latine* (London, 1975), no. VI, 440. Uspenskij, "Značenie," 6; Charanis, "Monastic Properties," 91; A. Laiou, "A Byzantine Prince Latinized: Theodore Palaeologus, Marquis of Montferrat," *Byz* 38 (1968), 387.

[77] Jacoby, "Les archontes grecs," 440. M. Bloch, *Feudal Society* (Chicago, 1961), 188–89.

paroikoi." But, beyond this, we really do not know what kind of grant was envisioned. Was it to be a grant of lands in the region of Thessaloniki, a grant of fiscal revenues in the region of Thessaloniki, or even, perhaps, a grant of administrative rights over Thessaloniki? There is even a possibility that Manuel may have envisioned something unique, adapting Byzantine practices to create something that this Latin could understand.[78]

Another case involving a Latin and what some scholars regard as a pronoia grant is found in a Genoese document from 1201. The Genoese Baldovino Guercio, who had served a number of emperors beginning with John II, received "*casalem et possessionem in feudi beneficium*" from Manuel I. The Venetian–Genoese treaty of 1218 adds that the property was located outside Constantinople. Guercio lost this property when Alexios III confiscated Genoese property throughout the empire in retaliation for the Gafforio episode. The contents of the grant are unclear. Judith Herrin wrote that it was "a palace in Constantinople," and Charles Brand wrote that it was "a house and property." In any event, the fact that the Genoese government attempted to recover this property for the benefit of Guercio's heirs indicates that they regarded the grant as hereditary, which would mean it was not a pronoia.[79]

[3.5] Lysis of Alexios III Angelos for the monastery of St. John on Patmos (1196)

A quite peculiar case is found in a request attached to a document of Alexios III Angelos from 1196. For years the Patmos monastery had been receiving a grain supply from imperial estates (*episkepseis*) on Crete. Then Manuel I decided to confer these *episkepseis* upon local people (*entopioi*) and replace this grain supply with a cash *solemnion.* While these local people "paid a monetary payment" (τελουμένων . . . νομισματικῶν δόσεων) for the properties, this arrangement was only temporary, because later, Isaac II Angelos (1185–95) granted one of the properties within the *episkepseis* to a bishop

[78] Ostrogorsky, *Féodalité*, 31, and cf. Anastasijević and Ostrogorsky, "Les Koumanes pronoïaires," 19–20. See also, Hohlweg, "Zur Frage der Pronoia," 307; Lj. Maksimović, "Geneza i karakter apanaža u Vizantiji," *ZRVI* 14/15 (1973), 114–15; M. Hendy, *Studies in the Byzantine Monetary Economy c.300–1450* (Cambridge, Eng., 1985), 88.

[79] A. Sanguineti and G. Bertolotto, *Nuova serie di documenti sulle relazioni di Genova coll'Impero bizantino* (Genoa, 1898), 471. E. Ricotti, *Liber iurium rei publicae Genuensis, 1, col. 613B, vol. 7 of Historiae patriae monumenta* (Turin, 1854). J. Herrin, "The Collapse of the Byzantine Empire in the Twelfth Century," *University of Birmingham Historical Journal* 12 (1970), 195–96. Day, *Genoa's Response to Byzantium*, 43 note 59. Brand, *Byzantium Confronts the West*, 208–09, and *ODB*, s.v. "Guercio, Baldovino."

on Crete, releasing the property from its *telos* of forty-eight hyperpyra. The bishop built a monastery there. After his death a neighbor named Chortatzes received the monastery in *ephoreia* (a variation of *charistike*) from the *doux* of Crete. In 1196 Alexios III granted the property to the Patmos monastery.[80]

Oikonomides argued that the "local people" held the properties as pronoiai for which they paid a yearly tax. This would explain why the arrangement was temporary and why Isaac Angelos could later grant one of the properties to a bishop. Further, he explains that once a monastery was built on the property, the property could not be regranted as a pronoia, and this explains why Chortatzes held it in *ephoreia*.[81]

If Oikonomides' interpretation is correct, this case would be evidence not only for the existence of pronoia on Crete during the twelfth century, but for the taxation of pronoia grants at this time as well. However, there are complications. Oikonomides assumed that the phrase τελουμένων . . . νομισματικῶν δόσεων meant "paying a monetary tax," but this is not necessarily so. The verb *telo* is often connected to taxation, but it frequently has a more general sense of any payment to the fisc, including a rent (e.g., τοῦ νομίσματος πάκτον τελοῦν). Likewise the noun *dosis* can refer to any charge, including a rent (e.g., δόσεως πάκτου ἢ χωροπάκτου).[82] Thus, the passage could be referring to leasing out the *episkepseis* rather than conferring them as pronoiai. In fact the document is much less ambiguous when it refers to the forty-eight hyperpyra that the bishop no longer had to pay "for the sake of the state *telos*" (χάριν δημοσιακοῦ τέλους: line 7).

Oddly enough, it would be easier to view the bishop in this story as the pronoia holder. After all, he held the property as a personal lifetime imperial grant (the document specifically notes that it was "conferred upon him, not upon his church": line 6). However, it seems clear that the bishop, who held the property less than ten years before his death, received the property in the first place for the purpose of building a monastery there, and so we should probably connect the episode more to imperial participation in the founding of a monastery than to a pronoia grant.

Pronoia supposedly was detected in the 1152 *typikon* for the monastery of Kosmosoteira near Ainos in Thrace. Among the vast number of properties that the *sevastokrator* Isaac Komnenos, third son of Alexios I, was bequeathing to the monastery he was founding is a long list of fifteen

[80] *Patmos*, I, nos. 21 and 22.

[81] Oikonomides, "Ἡ διανομὴ τῶν βασιλικῶν «ἐπισκέψεων»," 196–201.

[82] *Patmos*, I, no. 4.16, a chrysobull from 1085, and no. 6.46–47, a chrysobull from 1088.

proasteia, thirteen villages, and other properties, "which passed to me from ancestral inheritance by both chrysobulls and commands."[83] The manner by which Isaac acquired these properties is not clear. Fundamentally, the phrase quoted is contradictory: "ancestral inheritance" implies one thing, a grant through the issuance of chrysobulls another. Yet individuals frequently requested chrysobulls confirming their ownership of patrimony, particularly with an eye to bequeathing it, and the terminology of hereditary ownership was at times a *titulus acquirendi* indicating present status rather than origin. But regardless of their origin, it is clear that he held them in hereditary tenure.

Two of the villages in the list are of interest: "the two *estrateumena* villages [τὰ ἐστρατευμένα δύο χωρία] of Dilianou and Dragavasta." Later in the document we learn that within these two villages

> there are certain soldiers who are taxpayers of mine [εἰσί τινες στρατιῶται ὑποτελεῖς ἡμῶν] and who are accustomed to behaving shamelessly toward their neighbors and the steward of my villages. They have to be forced to pay the taxes [τελέσματα] owed, presumptuous perhaps because of their military undertakings [θάρρει τάχα τῆς στρατιωτικῆς ἐγχειριάσεως]. It is necessary that the *kathegoumenos* [of the monastery] should receive them most cordially at his table after my death, and in every way treat them most graciously so that the beloved [monks] have allies, and especially so they have the strength to repel those from around my villages who wish, with grasping hands, to trample them insolently, as we see happening often. For these [soldiers] are sufficient and quite useful for protecting the monastery and for keeping away those who would harm it.[84]

In this vignette of the vicissitudes of provincial life we learn that these *estrateumena* villages were inhabited by real soldiers who were violent men and bad neighbors and who owed taxes to Isaac and, after Isaac's death, to the monastery. Presumably, before Isaac held these villages, the soldiers paid their taxes to the fisc. Therefore, Isaac, either through inheritance or through a grant from Alexios I (Isaac was in his mid-twenties at the time of his father's death) or his brother John II, was receiving the fiscal revenues of these villages, and probably the others listed in the *typikon*.

Ostrogorsky saw the possibility of pronoia being involved here, suggesting that the soldiers might have been pronoia holders and that this passage could be cited as evidence to corroborate Choniates' "gifts of paroikoi" passage.

83 G. Papazoglou, *Τυπικὸν Ἰσαακίου Ἀλεξίου Κομνηνοῦ τῆς Μονῆς Θεοτόκου τῆς Κοσμοσωτείρας (1151/52)* (Komotini, 1994), lines 1243–44: ἅπερ μοι περιήλθοσαν ἐκ γονικῆς κληροδοσίας χρυσοβούλλοις λόγοις τε καὶ κελεύσεσι.

84 Papazoglou, *Τυπικὸν*, lines 1265–66, 2009–18.

While admitting that the social class of these soldiers is hard to determine, he nevertheless concluded that they did not belong to the "poor" class like the old type of thematic soldier, and he suggested that they were probably "petty" pronoia holders. He made no attempt to explain why these soldiers, if they were pronoia holders, were rendering their taxes to the *sevastokrator* Isaac and would be rendering them to the monastery after his death.[85]

Lemerle also concluded that the passage involved pronoia, but in a much different (and more coherent) way. He posited that the rare term *estrateumena*, which appears only in this and one other twelfth-century document, was applied to villages and peasants who had been granted in pronoia. The other document is the *typikon* of the monastery of Pantokrator from 1136 which lists, among the twenty-six *proasteia* and twenty-two villages given to the monastery by the emperor John II Komnenos and his wife, the village of Thrymvakin which was donated "with its *estrateumenoi* settled there" (σὺν τοῖς προσκαθημένοις ἐκεῖσε ἐστρατευμένοις), and two other villages, Daphne and Damon, which are described as "*estrateumena* villages." According to Lemerle, these were villages "of which the lands and paroikoi have been allotted to soldiers, and which receive from this the designation *estrateumena*, the paroikoi being called *estrateumenoi*."[86]

By concluding that the villages in these documents were called *estrateumena* (from στρατεύω "to serve as a soldier, to enlist") because they were held in pronoia by soldiers, Lemerle overlooked an earlier argument he made regarding the 1089 act of a fiscal official which formally exchanged the lands of the monk Christodoulos on Kos for new lands on Patmos. The enclosed imperial order directed the fiscal official that "you release from *strateia* whoever earlier was subjected to *strateia* during the previous year's time on the island of Patmos, while subjecting to *strateia* those on the properties on Kos." The official then "releases from *strateia*" (ἀπεστρατεύσαμεν) a list of twelve peasant households on Patmos. Lemerle's interpretation (on which my translations are based) is that the peasants in question on Patmos were to be relieved of their fiscal obligations toward the state (*strateia*), but only to have them transferred to the new monastery, while those peasants on Kos would no longer render their *telos* and other burdens toward a private landowner (Christodoulos), but toward the state. He was trying to show that *strateia*, the usual term for the middle Byzantine military obligation, was becoming increasingly "fiscalized" in the eleventh and twelfth centuries, and that by the late eleventh century, the military verbs *strateuo* (στρατεύω,

[85] G. Ostrogorsky, "Observations on the Aristocracy in Byzantium," *Dumbarton Oaks Papers* 25 (1971), 15.

[86] Gautier, "Le typikon du Christ Sauveur Pantokrator," lines 1476, 1493–94. Lemerle, *Agrarian History*, 236–38.

"to enlist") and *apostrateuo* (ἀποστρατεύω, "to discharge") had acquired a purely fiscal sense.[87]

In light of this, *estrateumenoi* peasants were probably nothing more than those who had owed *strateia* (hence, the past participle ἐστρατευμένος rather than στρατευόμενος) before becoming paroikoi of the *sevastokrator* Isaac and John II. Thus, the terminology had nothing to do with pronoia but, rather, was merely the eleventh- and twelfth-century phase in the evolution of the institution of the middle Byzantine military lands. My interpretation receives some support from a 1061 act of a fiscal official for the monastery of Iviron. The monks of Iviron presented to the official in 1061 an act from the reign of John I Tzimiskes (969–76). In this earlier act the official states that he had been ordered to return certain taxpaying peasants (*demosiarioi*) to the "military villages" (τοῖς στρατιωτικοῖς χωρίοις). Since no one has ever suggested that we can look for evidence of the institution of pronoia in tenth-century acts, it is clear that these peasants had been trying to evade their military burdens (their *strateia*, real or fiscalized), and that the official's task was to ensure that the state would once again benefit from these burdens. The easy parallel between tenth-century *stratiotika* villages and twelfth-century *estrateumena* villages leads me to conclude that, in both of the twelfth-century *typika*, for the monastery of Kosmosoteira and for the monastery of Pantokrator, *estrateumena* villages and peasants were simply those subject to *strateia*. Since the peasants in the *typikon* of the monastery of the Virgin Kosmosoteira are identified as real soldiers, the burden evidently had not yet been fiscalized. If we need look for a pronoia holder in the *typikon* for Kosmosoteira monastery, we should start with Isaac Komnenos himself.[88]

My interpretation of these documents allows us quickly to dismiss another document cited by Lemerle as possible though certainly weak evidence for the existence of twelfth-century pronoia soldiers. Shortly before 1091 Christodoulos, abbot of the Patmos monastery, gave the following orders to his monks prior to his departure from the monastery for a long

[87] *Patmos*, II, no. 54.10–11: ἀποστρατεύσεις ὅσους ἂν ἔφθασας κατὰ τὸν πέρυσι καιρὸν ἐν τῇ νήσω τῇ Πάτμω στρατεῦσαι, στρατεύσης δὲ αὐτοὺς ἐν τοῖς κτήμασιν τοῖς ἐν τῇ Κῶ, and line 15. Lemerle, *Agrarian History*, 226–28.

[88] *Iviron*, II, no. 30.14–15 and see the notes. Ahrweiler, *Byzance et la mer*, 219, 220 note 3, in her brief reference to this document seems to regard Isaac as a pronoia holder. Cf. Kazhdan's cursory treatment of this document ("Formen," 219), which appears to misinterpret the evidence. The middle Byzantine institution of *strateia* continued to have faint echos into the late Byzantine period. For example, in a 1321 chrysobull for the church of Ioannina, Andronikos II ordered that the church again hold a particular village "along with the *astrateutoi* Vlachs in it" (μετὰ τῶν ἐν αὐτῷ ἀστρατεύτων Βλάχων): MM, v, 87.5. Since *astrateutos* would seem to mean *apostrateumenos*, I tend to think we should read *estrateutos* to parallel the twelfth-century *estrateumenos*.

absence: "Do not let the soldiers and the rest of the villagers move away each day after May, but they shall come and stay in the monastery for a guard: Fill all the ramparts with stones." Evidently the peasants wished to tend to their agricultural concerns. While the soldiers referred to were clearly peasants, there is no need to envision some kind of private militia. What Lemerle failed to emphasize is that the monastery was supposed to be guarded not only by these soldiers, but by the other villagers as well. I regard the "soldiers" as *estrateumenoi* peasants burdened with the obligation of *strateia*. The other villagers were peasants whose persons or properties, by origin, were not burdened with *strateia*, but by the normal charges burdening peasants. The obligations burdening both categories of peasants were owed at this time to the Patmos monastery.[89]

The reason that Lemerle and other scholars have looked to pronoia as the explanation for these kinds of passages is that there is a reticence to admit that elements of the middle Byzantine military lands could still exist at such a late date. There really is no reason for such reticence. Lemerle himself, when he wrote of a "fiscalized *strateia*" was admitting that elements of the old military system continued to exist long after the thematic armies were more or less moribund. There is some evidence suggesting that the old-style middle Byzantine thematic military lands had not completely disappeared by the twelfth century. Hohlweg pointed to an undated novel of Manuel I in which the military lands were protected and their minimum size was fixed corresponding to the known novel of Constantine VII. Ostrogorsky thought it was strange that Manuel I should renew this tenth-century legislation. Was it an archaism that accidentally found its way into the novel, or were there still some military lands?[90]

As Lemerle, Ahrweiler and others have noted, the usual terms denoting the middle Byzantine military lands, such as *stratiotikon ktema*, *topos*, *kleros*, and *ktesis*, rarely ever appear in the twelfth century. While we need to remember that one of the reasons for this is that we have relatively few documents for the twelfth century (after the reign of Alexios I), nevertheless this does show that the middle Byzantine institution was disappearing. With the gradual appearance of the institution of pronoia in the course of the twelfth century, terminology that had been applied to the old military lands was now transferred to pronoia. A possible example is found in a document from

[89] MM, VI, 147.23–27: τοὺς στρατιώτας καὶ τοὺς λοιποὺς χωρίτας. On this passage, see also *Patmos*, I, pp. 42*–43*. Lemerle, *Agrarian History*, 238 and note 1.

[90] Hohlweg, "Zur Frage der Pronoia," 302. Zepos, *JGR*, VI, 515 = Zacharia, *Jus*, II, 226 (Dölger, *Regesten*, II, no. 1535, and cf. I, no. 673). Ostrogorsky, *Féodalité*, 41.

1189 for the monastery of St. Paul on Mount Latros in which the fiscal assessor notes that he had made a fiscal survey "of the military, ecclesiastical, and monastic immovable properties" (τῶν ... στρατιωτικῶν, ἐκκλησιαστικῶν καὶ μοναστηριακῶν ἀκινήτων κτίσεων [sc. κτήσεων]) in the Anatolian theme of Mylasa and Melanoudion. Both Lemerle and Ahrweiler saw this reference to "military properties" as a probable reference to pronoia. Indeed, in this case it is hard to imagine that the phrase had any connection to the old thematic military lands. The formulaic phrase suggests that the "military properties" were privileged properties, like those of religious foundations, that were no longer part of the fiscal unity of a village. In the fourteenth century, similar formulaic expressions occur rather commonly, associating the properties of monasteries and the church and other privileged landholders with the properties held by military pronoia holders.[91]

Fundamentally, we do not know the extent to which the middle Byzantine military lands continued to exist in the twelfth century or whether they still had any military purpose. Ahrweiler, by writing that Manuel's "gifts of paroikoi" policy represented the end of the idea of a national army since the pronoia soldiers had no previous attachment to the area where their grants came from, was suggesting that the pronoia soldier replaced the middle Byzantine thematic soldier. Lemerle, on the other hand, who asserted that John II and Manuel Komnenos may have tried to rebuild a national army, on a certain scale at least, by attaching the army anew to the land, and that Manuel's pronoia policy perhaps strengthened the army's national character, took the opposing view that the pronoia soldier replaced the mercenary. I would argue that the pronoia soldier was introduced to replace the mercenary, while pronoia, as a fiscal institution, gradually replaced the *strateia*.[92]

Yet there was another type of soldier who existed in twelfth-century Byzantium, indeed throughout the Byzantine era. These were the smallholding soldiers who had no connection to the old thematic military system and who were settled in groups as the proprietors of specific territories. These men were usually foreigners and their settlement generally followed their defeat by the imperial army. These soldiers are difficult to identify because in some ways they are similar to the old thematic soldier. Ahrweiler,

[91] MM, IV, 319.8–9. Lemerle, *Agrarian History*, 223, 238. H. Glykatzi-Ahrweiler, "Recherches sur l'administration de l'empire byzantin aux IXe–XIe siècles," in Ahrweiler, *Études sur les structures administratives et sociales de Byzance* (London, 1971), no. VIII, 23 note 1. Cf. *Lavra*, II, App. VIII.3–4 (1316), and *Zographou*, no. 17.3–5 (1320).

[92] Ahrweiler, *Byzance et la mer*, 221. Lemerle, *Agrarian History*, 234, 241.

in fact, viewed the *estrateumenoi* mentioned in the two twelfth-century *typika* discussed above as examples of these smallholding soldiers.[93]

Most of the eleventh- and twelfth-century examples of defeated foreigners being settled within Byzantium and enrolled in the army are probably examples of such non-thematic smallholding soldiers. Yet the Byzantine historians who discuss them are so vague that modern scholars have interpreted the evidence relating to these settlements in one of three ways: (i) as the creation of new middle Byzantine military lands, (ii) as the creation of distinctive smallholding settlements of foreigners with no real connection to the middle Byzantine military lands, or (iii) as the creation of pronoia-holding soldiers. For example, Zonaras reports that after Alexios I's defeat of the Pechenegs in 1091 the emperor settled them with their wives and children in the theme of Moglena where they were formed into a "most distinct unit" (τάγμα . . . ἰδιαίτατον). Eugen Stanescu viewed this as the creation of new old-style military lands; Ahrweiler and Lemerle concluded they were smallholders forming distinctive ethnic enclaves; Hohlweg wrote that these Pechenegs were given either old-style military lands or pronoiai.[94]

There are other examples: the historian Kinnamos writes that after his victory over the Pechenegs in 1122 John II transformed the prisoners into soldiers. Choniates adds that some were settled along the western borders of the empire, while others entered the army. Kinnamos also writes that as a result of his campaigns in Anatolia John II defeated "barbarians," converted many to Orthodoxy, and made them join the army. In both of these cases, Ostrogorsky saw the old-style military lands, while in the first example, Ahrweiler saw the possibility of pronoia being involved. Lemerle, while rightly reminding us that we are not told that these prisoners of war received land, nevertheless thought it likely that these men formed settled ethnic enclaves.[95]

Further, Choniates reports that after defeating the Serbs John II deported the prisoners to the province of Nikomedeia and assigned them land, and he notes that some became soldiers, others taxpayers. While Ostrogorsky concluded this referred to the old-style military land, an opinion that Hohlweg also felt we should not reject out of hand, Lemerle once again thought that

93 Ahrweiler, *Byzance et la mer*, 220 note 3.

94 Zonaras, *Ioannis Zonarae Epitomae Historiarum libri xviii*, ed. M. Pinder (Bonn, 1841–97), iii, 740–41. Stanescu, "Les 'stratiotès'," 228. Ahrweiler, *Byzance et la mer*, 220 note 3. Lemerle, *Agrarian History*, 230. Hohlweg, *Beiträge zur Verwaltungsgeschichte*, 87.

95 Kinnamos, *Ioannis Cinnami epitome*, ed. A. Meineke (Bonn, 1836), 8.20–22, and Choniates, Bonn edn., 22 = ed. van Dieten, 16.6–10. Kinnamos, 9.5–6. Ostrogorsky, *Féodalité*, 40–41. Hohlweg, "Zur Frage der Pronoia," 302. Ahrweiler, *Byzance et la mer*, 219. Lemerle, *Agrarian History*, 230.

this was simply another example of the creation of special ethnic military units, connected to smallholdings, but which had nothing to do with the old thematic military organization.[96]

It is quite likely that most of the cited examples involved neither military lands nor pronoia; rather, with these settlements emperors were pursuing political and military goals. The foreigners were given means of subsistence, that is, land, with service in arms sometimes imposed on them. The institution was perennial in Byzantium and lasted into the fourteenth century. It is always necessary to distinguish these men, who were proprietors of the lands on which they were settled from military pronoia holders, who did not necessarily own or even possess the properties from which their fiscal revenues and rents were derived.[97]

In truth there is little evidence from the sources with which to confirm Choniates' view that there was a dramatic increase in the number of pronoia soldiers during the second half of the twelfth century. We do have the evidence of the documents in Chapter 2: the 1162 act of Kontostephanos *[2.3]*, and, especially, the later twelfth-century documents dealing with the Cumans of Moglena *[2.4–2.5]*.

Nevertheless, the importance of the evidence that Choniates provides should not be minimized. While it would be difficult to conclude that pronoia soldiers were a major element in Byzantine armies during the second half of the twelfth century, Choniates' view that there was a change in the social level of the recipients of imperial grants and a change, specifically an administrative regularization and formalization, in the process by which the grants were made does find support in other sources. Varieties of imperial grants that had been ad hoc, exceptional acts of imperial beneficence to friends and relatives in the later eleventh century became, without completely losing their original nature and form, also a regular means of financing soldiers in the twelfth century. In this way an occasional practice became an institution. The next chapter deals with this transition.

96 Choniates, ed. Bonn 23 = van Dieten, 16.23–24. Ostrogorsky, *Féodalité*, 40. Hohlweg, "Zur Frage der Pronoia," 302, and cf. Hohlweg, *Beiträge zur Verwaltungsgeschichte*, 88. Lemerle, *Agrarian History*, 230. Kinnamos does not tell us whether prisoners of war "imported" by Manuel I into the empire, for example the Serbian population of Galitza (Kinnamos, 102–03) settled around Sardis and other areas were solely to be agricultural workers or sometimes soldiers: Lemerle, *Agrarian History*, 230, and cf. Ostrogorsky, *Féodalité*, 41.

97 Lemerle, *Agrarian History*, 229–30. Ahrweiler, *Byzance et la mer*, 220 note 3. Hohlweg, "Zur Frage der Pronoia," 302. Bartusis, "Smallholding Soldiers."

4 | Origins

The evidence from the twelfth century shows that, at that time, a pronoia was a lifetime grant to a layman of state land and the fiscal obligations of peasants. The earliest known pronoia grant appears to date to the last years of Alexios I Komnenos' reign. Its holder was a soldier of a not particularly exalted status. Alexios' grandson Manuel I seems to have expanded the scope of these grants to a much larger set of common soldiers. There is no evidence that religious institutions held pronoiai during the twelfth century.

The sources provide us with no direct information about how or why Alexios I implemented his (evidently infrequent) grants of pronoiai. All we can do to seek the origins of pronoia is to turn to Alexios' reign and to the reigns of his predecessors during the eleventh century and follow two avenues of investigation: how pronoia fit into Alexios' policies and other developments during the eleventh century, and the extent to which the characteristics of the pronoia grant were influenced by and reflected in other varieties of imperial grants during this period.

The individual characteristics of the twelfth-century pronoia grant – (i) the gift of paroikoi, (ii) the grant of state immovable property, (iii) the lifetime element, (iv) the attachment of soldiers to the land – had institutional antecedents in earlier Byzantine practices. This is to say that what made the institution of pronoia unique was not the aspects of the grant but the combination of these aspects. The question: how could the conjunction of these four elements have been viewed by Alexios I as part of the solution to the fiscal and military problems he faced?

Problems after the death of Basil II

At the death of Basil II in 1025 the Byzantine state was in better condition than it had been in for centuries. Its borders extended in the north from the Danube and Cherson in the Crimea to Crete and Cyprus in the south, and from southern Italy in the west to the upper Euphrates in the east. Basil left a sizable surplus in the treasury and an effective army. Yet within half a century all this had changed, and the empire found itself battling for survival.

A number of factors were involved in this turn of events. The death of Basil II left a vacuum in the power structure. His failure to arrange for a competent successor led to factional struggles as political power shifted from the emperor to the aristocracy. Many within this aristocracy thought that Byzantium had entered a new golden age, that it was time to reduce the size of the army and to take advantage of the "peace dividend." It was a gradual process.

For a time military successes continued. In the first couple of decades following Basil's death there were a few conquests: Edessa in northern Syria in 1031, a small part of Sicily in 1038–42, and the province around Ani in 1045. No doubt this lulled contemporaries into a false sense of continuity with the preceding era. But these conquests were relatively minor, and without continued expansion imperial finances would suffer. After the seizure of Ani, there were no more conquests.[1]

More significant were losses. At first these took the form of raids, some of them major, into imperial territory by Arabs and Hungarians and by new enemies, the Normans to the west, the Pechenegs, Uzes, and Cumans to the north, and the Seljuk Turks to the east. By 1060 Byzantine Italy was reduced to the area around Bari. Ani was captured by the Seljuks in 1064. Bari itself fell in 1071, and that same year, much of Asia Minor was abandoned following the battle of Mantzikert, as a number of generals scurried westward to stake their claim to the imperial purple, to the further detriment of the empire's tax base.[2]

Exacerbating the loss of revenues due to territorial losses were the spending policies of Basil's successors. Nearly all of the emperors from 1025 through 1081 were known for their lavish gifts to curry favor with the powerful men who lived and worked at their side. Even in the most straitened of circumstances these emperors continued to grant gifts to courtiers. Aside from direct gifts of cash, there were other ways to please the aristocracy. Romanos III Argyros (1028–34) forgave debts, tolerated embezzlement, and revoked Basil's legislation regarding the *allelengyon*, which had required the powerful (*dynatoi*) in the provinces to pay the tax arrears for their poorer neighbors. A particularly important way of purchasing the loyalty of subordinates was through the granting of imperial *rogai*, the salaries

[1] W. Treadgold, *A History of the Byzantine State and Society* (Stanford, 1997), 585, 587–88. *ODB*, s.v. "Sicily," "Ani."

[2] Treadgold, *History*, 600. *ODB*, s.v. "Ani."

attached to honorary offices or titles within the court hierarchy. Traditionally courtiers paid a lump sum for the right to a title and its corresponding yearly *roga*. The *roga*, then, from the point of view of the recipient was a kind of annuity and, from the point of view of the government, it served the same function as government bonds and could be used by frugal emperors as an important source of revenue. However, a number of spendthrift emperors, beginning with Constantine IX and ending with Nikephoros III Botaneiates, by lowering or eliminating the initial cost of the *roga*, created a financial burden on the state which, once implemented, was difficult to countermand.[3]

The aristocracy and other laymen were not the only beneficiaries of favors from Basil II's successors. Romanos III built churches, Constantine IX spent on culture, and Nikephoros III granted fiscal privileges to monasteries.[4] Historians often speak of how these emperors "squandered" state resources through "wasteful" spending, but this is a matter of perspective. Lavish gifts to churches and monasteries preserved an emperor's soul, while lavish gifts to favorites, supporters, and potential rivals preserved his throne. The problem was really the rapid turnover in emperors during this period. We should not underestimate the financial cost of accession, particularly for rather weak men, who had little natural ability to win the loyalty of an entrenched religious and lay aristocracy.

The ill effects of the spending policies of the successors of Basil II were rather slow in coming, and this may explain why there was not a concerted effort to restrain government expenditures. Rather, most of the emperors from Michael IV through Nikephoros III (with the important exception of Isaac I) display an erratic pattern of spending and conserving, sometimes at different times during their reigns, sometimes at the same time. For example, while Constantine IX freely distributed titular offices with *rogai*, built lavish monasteries, and granted numerous privileges to monasteries, he instituted a modest debasement of the coinage, converted the military obligation (*strateia*) of peasants in the theme of Iveria into a tax, and, toward the end of his reign, attempted to restrict the revenues of the church, nullifying privileges to which it had no right.[5]

And yet it would be wrong to paint a picture of an imperial government in penury. Unlike the emperors in the middle of the fourteenth century who were indeed forced to melt down the palace dinnerware, the

[3] Treadgold, *History*, 583, 584, 591, 600, 607. *ODB*, s.v. "allelengyon."

[4] Treadgold, *History*, 585 593. Oikonomides, *Fiscalité*, 144.

[5] Attaleiates, *Miguel Ataliates, Historia*, ed. and trans. I. Pérez Martín (Madrid, 2002), 38 = *Michaelis Attaliotae Historia*, ed. W. Brunet de Presle (Bonn, 1853), 51.

eleventh-century Byzantine government was still relatively wealthy. The problem was not a lack of resources but a reordering of resources and a reorganization of budgetary priorities to immediate rather than long-term ends. Ultimately, the best evidence for the fiscal crisis the imperial government faced are the numerous measures emperors took to raise revenues.

Solutions

To maintain a high or expanded level of expenditure in light of a shrinking revenue base once there were no more new lands to be conquered or at least plundered, alternative means to balance the books had to be found, which either restrained spending, raised revenues, or sought alternative means of paying or rewarding people in lieu of cash. Few emperors attempted any serious cutting of expenses. Until Alexios I entirely abolished the traditional payment of *rogai* to officeholders, the only emperor who seems to have tried in earnest to curb spending was his uncle Isaac I. He demoted some civil servants which would have lowered their *rogai* and probably halted the *roga* payments to honorary officials.[6]

Among the various methods employed by Basil II's successors to increase government income were a variety of manipulations of the fiscal system (restoring old taxes, creating new taxes, raising tax rates on existing taxes, greater diligence in collecting taxes, rescinding privileges), as well as debasing coinage, confiscations, and selling titles. Almost all of the emperors, beginning with Michael IV attempted to employ greater efficiency, or ruthlessness, in tax collection. This was usually accompanied by a greater emphasis on secondary charges.[7]

Basil's successors implemented and sustained fiscal policies designed to foster more efficiency in tax collection. Beginning with Michael IV, they increased tax rates, imposed new taxes, and at times implemented more creative solutions. Michael IV demanded that the Bulgarians, whom Basil II had permitted to pay their taxes in kind, henceforth pay their taxes in cash, and Constantine IX replaced the obligation of those who owed military service in the theme of Iveria with a simple tax, an example of the fiscalization of the *strateia*. On occasion these measures led to rebellions and

6 Treadgold, *History*, 599. P. Magdalino, "The Byzantine Army and the Land: From Stratiotikon Ktema to Military Pronoia," in *Τὸ Ἐμπόλεμο Βυζάντιο (9ος-12ος αι.)* (Athens, 1997), 30, attributes the end of *roga* payments to office holders to Constantine X.

7 Treadgold, *History*, 588. Oikonomides, *Fiscalité*, 143–44.

revolts, which on occasion forced them to be abandoned. Other emperors rescinded fiscal privileges.[8]

Another traditional method of raising additional revenues was through the debasement of the coinage. The gold nomisma, which had been about 94 percent fine since the reign of Constantine VII, was reduced to 90 percent fine under Michael IV, and 87 percent under Constantine IX. Whether or not this relatively minor debasement was a sign of fiscal crisis or, as has been argued, merely an attempt to expand the currency supply in a growing economy, the debasements undertaken beginning with Romanos IV were clearly a sign of crisis. Under Romanos IV the nomisma contained an average of 70 percent gold, falling to 58 percent under Michael VII, and to less than 36 percent under Nikephoros III. In the first decade of his reign Alexios I was issuing nomismata on average less than 11 percent fine, which did not have the appearance of gold coins at all. The monetary crisis that worsened during Romanos IV's reign is seen with silver coinage as well. Romanos reduced the silver content in these coins from about 91 percent to 71 percent, and under Nikephoros III silver coins had a mere 45 percent silver.[9]

Alternatives to cash

When still more resources were needed than could be acquired through these techniques of raising cash, alternative means of paying or rewarding servants were employed which did not entail direct cash disbursements. These included grants of honorary titles, government bureaus (*sekreta*), *charistikai*, movable and immovable property, and tax exemptions. Throughout all, a spirit of innovation is less evident than the industriousness of the imperial administration in expanding techniques of raising revenues.

The granting of honorary titles and offices, while of no particular relevance for this study, was employed by numerous emperors. It had the advantage that it entailed no direct costs to the state and could be used selectively, incrementally conferring a title or honorary office that suited the degree to which the emperor wished to reward or flatter someone. Its disadvantage was that it devalued titles that had been granted earlier, leading to discontent among other office and title holders. Also of little relevance for us is the practice of granting movable property, as simple gifts,

[8] Oikonomides, *Fiscalité*, 142–45, 187, 209. *Iviron*, II, p. 131.

[9] C. Morrisson, "Byzantine Money: Its Production and Circulation," in *EHB*, III, 931–32.

to imperial subjects. All emperors did this, and Alexios I continued the practice.[10]

The granting of *sekreta*, or government bureaus, occurred at least several times during the eleventh century. The idea was to allow an important person to manage the *sekreton* and draw a profit. These were granted to people with very special relationships to the emperor. Generally, they were held at the emperor's pleasure though, in practice, they were held for life, either until the recipient or the emperor who made the grant died. Between 1042 and 1045 the *sekreton* of the Tropaiophoron was created by Constantine IX Monomachos for his mistress Maria Skleraina.[11] Upon his accession Nikephoros Botaneiates showered Eudokia Makremvolitissa, the former empress and mother of his predecessor Michael VII, with kindnesses, including three *sekreta*, and Alexios I gave his mother Anna Dalassene, among many other things, the *sekreton* of the Myrelaion.[12] The benefit of such grants was that they were temporary, and usually could be rescinded as needed. Yet, because of their size, they were limited in number and could be granted only to persons of the most lofty status.

Numerous emperors conferred *charistikai*, the right – usually for life – to administer monasteries and to profit from the efficient management of the foundation, upon privileged persons. *Charistikai* were granted by bishops, by the patriarch, and, when it was a question of an imperial monastery, by the emperor. For example, Michael VII granted the imperial monastery of the Hevdomon to his advisor Nikephoritzes, and after Nikephoritzes' murder it was conferred upon Michael VII's widow.[13] Because the revenues generated from imperial religious foundations were ordinarily difficult to transfer to other state purposes, the *charistike* had the advantage of causing no real loss to state revenues. However, such grants were limited in number, and some prominent members of the clergy complained bitterly about the practice, which they realized often had little connection to the well-being of the monastery involved.

The granting of tax exemptions, either directly for the beneficiary himself or indirectly, as a gift of paroikoi, was an effective way to reward or

10 P. Gautier, "Le typikon du sébaste Grégoire Pakourianos," *REB* 42 (1984), 43.403–06. *Iviron*, II, no. 44.10–11.

11 N. Oikonomides, "St. George of Mangana, Maria Skleraina, and the 'Maly Sion' of Novgorod," in Oikonomides, *Byzantium from the Ninth Century to the Fourth Crusade* (London, 1992), no. XVI, 240–43.

12 Attaleiates, ed. Pérez Martín, 217.19–23 = Bonn edn., 304.11–15. Skylitzes Continuatus, *Ἡ συνέχεια τῆς Χρονογραφίας τοῦ Ἰωάννου Σκυλίτση*, ed. E. Tsolakes (Thessaloniki, 1968), 184.22–25. *Patmos*, I, no. 5.

13 *ODB*, s.v. "Hebdomon."

compensate landholders without resorting to immediate disbursements of cash. Their value could be carefully regulated and they could be rescinded. As discussed in the previous chapter, there were two categories of taxes and thus two categories of exemption: *logisima*, which was the exemption of the basic property tax and which was quite rare (at least until the later eleventh century), and the *exkousseia*, the exemption of secondary taxes and charges, which was rather common in the tenth and later centuries.

Grants of property and grants of tax exemption were often combined, such that the beneficiary might receive a property plus some kind of tax exemption connected to that property. The tax exemption could follow at a later time, as an added benefit. Since there were many types of taxes, this afforded the emperor a great deal of latitude in incrementally increasing the value of the benefit as needed.

Grants of immovable property

The alienation through gift of income-producing immovable state property was a versatile method to reward and compensate imperial servants. Unlike grants of *sekreta* and *charistikai*, small grants were possible. On the other hand, such gifts tended to be permanent alienations, effectively "giving away the endowment."

Through the twelfth century there were two broad categories of state property: imperial estates which belonged to the emperor *ex officio* (usually called *kouratoreiai* or *episkepseis*) and property that belonged to the fisc. Imperial estates were acquired through confiscation from the church and private persons, through purchase, through conquest, and perhaps even through gift.[14] Fiscal property was acquired usually by more mundane administrative processes, such as escheat through *klasma*. *Klasmata* were parcels of land that had devolved to the fisc through abandonment by their taxpaying owners. Until the later tenth century it was common for the fisc to sell *klasmata*. Imperial and fiscal property were administered by different officials who had different concerns: the administrators of imperial land sought to maximize the rents that could be derived from imperial estates; their counterparts who administered fiscal land traditionally sought taxpayers who would assume the tax burden on the property. But for our purposes the two types of property were quite similar. In practice the emperor could dispose of either, and so either could form all or part of an imperial grant.

[14] Oikonomides, *Fiscalité*, 187. *Iviron*, II, pp. 27–31. Treadgold, *History*, 521, 599, 615–16.

During the middle Byzantine period the two basic categories of immovable property that could be alienated by the state in favor of private persons or religious foundations were imperial estates and *klasmata*. The grant to Andronikos Doukas was part of an *episkepsis [4.1]*; the land granted to Leo Kephalas in the village of Tadrinou was a *klasma [4.4]*. While grants of imperial land and escheat each required different paperwork, the nature of the elements within each type of grant and the terms under which the grant was held could be identical. Consequently, unless some documentation has been preserved, the original status of the property granted is difficult or impossible to determine. So I will distinguish "imperial" property from "fiscal" property when necessary, but "state" property will embrace both collectively.[15]

Byzantine territorial losses during the seventh and eighth centuries, combined with the decision to grant land to soldiers for the creation of the so-called thematic armies in the seventh century, depleted the quantity of land held by the fisc and the emperor. By the end of the eighth century there were almost no imperial estates.[16] Beginning with the reign of Basil I (867–86) the empire began a period of conquest that enabled the increase of imperial lands.

In 934, during the reign of Romanos I Lekapenos (920–44), there is the first clear evidence that emperors were adopting a policy of building up imperial estates. In that year Melitene was taken and Romanos appropriated the property of the emir and the lands of those Muslims who left the area rather than convert, and created a *kouratoreia*. This was followed by the establishment of *kouratoreiai* in numerous areas conquered in the following decades, a policy probably designed to keep the magnates of eastern and central Anatolia out of the area. Indeed, the first legislation attempting to limit the acquisition of peasant lands by the so-called "powerful" had been issued by Romanos I.[17]

Traditionally, the Byzantine state preferred land to be in private hands with the fisc collecting taxes. While direct exploitation of the land as imperial domain could produce significantly more revenue for the state than the

[15] N. Oikonomides, "The Role of the Byzantine State in the Economy," in *EHB*, III, 1006, and "L'évolution de l'organisation administrative de l'Empire byzantin au XIe siècle (1025–1118)," in Oikonomides, *Byzantium from the Ninth Century to the Fourth Crusade* (London, 1992), no. X, 136 note 66, 141. Lemerle, *Agrarian History*, 119 note 2.

[16] Treadgold, *History*, 381, 385.

[17] J. Howard-Johnston,"Crown Lands and the Defence of Imperial Authority in the Tenth and Eleventh Centuries," in *Bosphorus: Essays in Honour of Cyril Mango*, ed. S. Efthymiadis et al. (Amsterdam, 1995), 86, 89–90, 92, and Treadgold, *History*, 481. *ODB*, s.v. "Romanos I Lekapenos."

collection of taxes from the same land when privately owned, direct and indirect management costs made direct exploitation unattractive. However, the problem for tenth-century emperors was that much land was passing to wealthy landowners (the *dynatoi*, or "powerful," as they were called), either lay or religious, who were better able to elude their tax responsibilities than were poorer landowners (the *aporoi*, or "weak"). At the same time wealthy lay landowners were perceived as a political threat to the crown and limiting their landholdings was a means to limit their political power. The growth of the landholdings of religious institutions was regarded as undesirable as well. This would explain Nikephoros II's prohibition against gifts of new land to the church and the foundation of new religious institutions.[18]

Consequently, during the tenth century, there was a change in the state's preferred methods of land exploitation. With private landowners divided into two loose groups, the weak and the powerful, the order of preferred exploitation became, first, by the "weak" (i.e., peasants), and then by the state, with exploitation by the "powerful" a distant third. This did not mean that emperors ceased the age-old practice of granting property to favored individuals, merely that the decision was made more carefully. One sign of this change of emphasis was a new policy with regard to *klasma*. Because the buyers of such *klasmata* tended to be the "powerful," it appears that Basil II ended, or at least severely curtailed, the old practice of selling *klasmata*, preferring that these parcels be exploited directly by the fisc.[19]

Grants of state property had always existed in Byzantium, but they had always been rare, either to laymen or to monasteries. Contrary to the image of generous emperors bestowing lavish grants of lands on monasteries, there is relatively little evidence of grants of land to monasteries during the tenth and eleventh centuries (or earlier for that matter), and what little evidence there is indicates a real disinclination to make outright grants of imperial land. As usual, most of our documents come from the archives of Mount Athos, and at the time in Macedonia, land was relatively abundant, but people to work the land relatively rare. The monasteries of Athos seem to have acquired land in substantial quantity through the purchase of *klasmata* and through donation.[20]

[18] J. Lefort, "The Rural Economy, Seventh–Twelfth Centuries," in *EHB*, I, 304, table 2. Treadgold, *History*, 500.

[19] Examples of sales of *klasmata* in Macedonia: *Lavra*, I, no. 2 (941) and no. 3 (941), and no. 11 (994; sale in 972/3); *Vatopédi*, I, no. 1 (959?). Oikonomides, *Fiscalité*, 91. Oikonomides, "L'évolution de l'organisation administrative," 137.

[20] *Iviron*, I, p. 31.

When property grants to monasteries appear, there is usually some kind of qualifying element in the grant suggesting that the state was forsaking relatively little in the concession. The story of the endowment of the monastery of St. John Theologos on Patmos illustrates this nicely. In 1080, during the preliminary stages in the foundation of that monastery, Nikephoros Botaneiates granted to the monk Christodoulos and his disciples as a gift (*dorea*) the ownership of two small properties on Kos which had belonged to the *sekreton* of the pious house of the Hevdomon. Then, in 1087 Alexios I donated to Christodoulos' monastery on Kos several properties plus exemption of their *telos* (ἀτελῶς καὶ ἀβαρῶς), taken from the *sekreton* of the pious house of Myrelaion: the uninhabited isle of Leipso and, on the island of Leros, two *proasteia* and the upper fortress of Pantelion, all equally uninhabited. The gift can be explained as a means of resettling uncultivated land. Lastly, in 1088 Alexios I granted Christodoulos the abandoned island of Patmos in return for everything he and his monks owned on Kos. Again the state was sacrificing little for the end of bringing abandoned areas into cultivation.[21]

In some cases the properties granted to monasteries seem to have been small, as when, sometime before 959, perhaps as early as the reign of Basil I, the monastery of Kolovou near Hierissos on the Chalkidike was granted some small properties (*topia*).[22] Sometimes the lands granted were escheat: in 1044 Constantine IX granted Nea Mone the *klasma* of Kalothekia, and sometime before 1081, perhaps during the reign of Isaac Komnenos (1057–1059) the monastery of Amalfitains was granted ownership of some escheated *staseis*.[23] Because monasteries seem to have frequently purchased *klasmata* from the fisc, according to the normal practice, it is sometimes difficult to know if the acquisition of a *klasma* was through purchase or an imperial grant.[24] Ironically, the first substantial grant of land that we hear of, Alexios I's gift (τὴν τελευταίαν δωρεάν) of 5,000 modioi to Iviron at Leontaria shortly before 1104, consisted of property that the emperor had confiscated from the monastery about fifteen years earlier.[25]

21 *Patmos*, I, no. 4.11–17, no. 5, and no. 6. Oikonomides, *Fiscalité*, 205–06, 248–50.

22 *Iviron*, I, no. 32.11–13. For other evidence, quite weak to be sure, for the grant of property to Kolovou during the time of Basil I, see *Prôtaton*, no. 2.4–8, and cf. *Prôtaton*, no. 1.

23 Zepos, *JGR*, I, 615–16. Oikonomides, *Fiscalité*, 202, 234. *Lavra*, I, no. 43.10: τὰ τῶν ἐξηλειμμένων στάσεων τόπια. Also, *Lavra*, I, pp. 60–61, and note p. 153.

24 N. Oikonomides, "La fiscalité byzantine et la communauté villageoise au XIe s.," in *Septième Congrès International d'Études du Sud-Est Européen. Rapports* (Athens, 1994), 94, and *Iviron*, I, pp. 41 and 45.

25 *Iviron*, II, no. 52.23–24,92–93, and p. 27.

While evidence of grants of property to monasteries through the middle of the eleventh century is quite rare, evidence of grants of property to laymen is not much more common. Most of the evidence for grants of any kind of state land to laymen during the tenth and early eleventh centuries tends to fall into two categories: grants made to the lofty individuals in connection with diplomacy and foreign policy, and grants made to groups of foreign soldiers. For example, of the former, (i) around the year 900 Leo VI "gave imperial land at Trebizond" to two Armenian nobles.[26] (ii) In 966, after the Byzantine annexation of Taron, land was granted to the Taronite princes, the brothers Gregory and Bagrat.[27] (iii) In 1022 when Senachereim, the Armenian ruler of Vaspurakan, submitted to Basil II and surrendered his territory, the emperor granted him the title of patrikios, made him strategos of Cappadocia, and gave him "as possessions there the cities of Sevasteia, Larissa, Avara, and many other possessions."[28] (iv) Around 1054 Constantine IX granted his mistress, the Alan princess, the *episkepsis* of Helos.[29]

In all of these cases the precise nature of the grant is unclear: were these simple grants of estates, or did they include the concession of tax revenues or even administrative authority? What is clear is that such grants were made to individuals at the highest level of society, quite different from the early pronoia grant.

[26] Constantine VII Porphyrogenitus, *De administrando imperio*, ed. Gy. Moravcsik (Washington, D.C., 1967), ch. 50.124–25 (p. 238): ἐν Τραπεζοῦντι δέδωκεν γῆν βασιλικήν. Warren Treadgold provided me with this reference.

[27] Howard-Johnston, "Crown Lands," 96. *ODB*, s.v. "Taron."

[28] Skylitzes, *Ioannis Scylitzae synopsis historiarum*, ed. J. Thurn (Berlin and New York, 1973), 355. Oikonomides, *Fiscalité*, 221.

[29] Zepos, *JGR*, I, 637. Another possible case involves the *parakoimomenos* Basil Lekapenos who ruled the empire during Basil II's minority (up to 965). According to Treadgold, *History*, 521, Basil II "voided all grants of imperial estates made by Basil Lecapenus, unless they had received the emperor's explicit approval." Similarly, E. McGeer, *The Land Legislation of the Macedonian Emperors* (Toronto, 2000), 129 note 20, writes of Basil Lekapenos' "involvement in the wrongful alienation of crown lands (whence the emperor's complaints [in his novel of 996] of fraudulent land deeds and his insistence on validating imperial documents)." However, the novel in question (N. Svoronos, *Les Novelles des empereurs Macédoniens concernant la terre et les stratiotes* [Athens, 1994], no. 14, pp. 214.198–211, 215.234–47) makes no mention of land grants or land deeds; Basil II merely announced that "chrysobulls" issued by Lekapenos were invalid unless explicitly validated by the emperor himself. Psellos (*Chronographia*, I.20.7–8) writes that Basil II upheld the measures of Lekapenos which served the state, while rescinding those which dealt with "kindnesses and honors" (εἰς εὐεργετημάτων καὶ ἀξιωμάτων): *Chronographie ou Histoire d'un siècle de Byzance (976–1077)*, ed. É. Renauld (Paris, 1926–28), I, 12. Lekapenos' chrysobulls may have involved grants of land, but they may have included other varieties of benefaction as well, perhaps tax exemption, perhaps merely stipends and titles.

Grants of land to ethnic soldiers settled in colonies were not uncommon. Constantine IX Monomachos settled defeated Pechenegs near Serdica, and Constantine X Doukas settled Uzes in Thrace. In both cases the settlers were to be soldiers. A couple of other examples are known from documents. Not long before 996 a certain Basil, "*tourmarches* of the Bulgarians," was given an *episkepsis* on the Kassandra peninsula for reasons unknown. At about the same time, land near Myriophyton (today, Nea Olinthos), north of the entrance to the Kassandra peninsula, was "given to the Armenians." Both of these examples may well have involved grants of land to ethnic soldier colonies, a subject less connected to the grant of imperial privileges or rewards than to military exigencies.[30]

The 1070s

Beginning in the 1070s, or more precisely, with the reign of Michael VII Doukas (1071–78), there was, in comparison to the earlier decades of the eleventh century, a modest explosion of imperial grants to laymen, and this continued through the first half of the reign of Alexios I. From 1071 to 1081, during the reigns of Michael VII and Nikephoros III Botaneiates, preserved documents refer to imperial grants involving property to seven laymen. Let me present these in chronological order:

[4.1] Chrysobull of Michael VII Doukas for Andronikos Doukas (1073), and Praktikon of the official Adam for Andronikos Doukas (1073)

(i) The first of these is a grant to the *protoproedros* and *protovestiarios* Andronikos Doukas, who was *domestikos* of the *scholai* of the east (that is, commander of the army in Asia Minor) and a cousin of Michael VII Doukas. In February 1073 Michael VII Doukas granted his cousin properties from the imperial domain (*episkepsis*) of Alopekai, which was located outside the town of Miletos in Asia Minor, in full ownership and with tax exemption. Andronikos was granted hereditary rights as well as the right to alienate the property. Further, the emperor ordered that properties (*proasteia*) and the paroikoi settled on them were exempted from a long list of

[30] Treadgold, *History*, 593, 600. *Iviron*, I, no. 10.59, and p. 31.

fiscal charges and obligations.[31] Thus, Andronikos was granted a gift of paroikoi.

A praktikon issued four months later provides the details of the grant. Andronikos received "all the incomes of these *proasteia*," and this was substantial: from several *proasteia* totaling over 5,000 modioi of land and containing 48 paroikoi, revenues of over 300 nomismata were handed over to Doukas. This included a combination of rents (*pakta*), which the state had received as a property owner, as well as fiscal charges (*synetheia*). These paroikoi had been paying their rents and taxes to the fisc; these payments now were enjoyed by Andronikos Doukas. In its totality, the grant was much more than a gift of paroikoi.[32]

The case of Andronikos Doukas explains why the early pronoia grant included an *exkousseia* of paroikoi as well as a grant of land. The *proasteia* within the *episkepsis* that Andronikos was granted already had peasants living and working on them. These peasants not only paid a rent on the land they leased, but rendered their normal labor services and secondary charges to the state. In making the grant the emperor simply transferred everything to Andronikos. To grant Andronikos only the land of the *episkepsis* would have required a new fiscal census to separate the peasants from the *episkepsis*. Moreover, land without workers was of little value. Thus it was easiest, and certainly in Andronikos' interest, to grant Andronikos an *exkousseia* on the paroikoi, which kept the *episkepsis* and peasants together. Such was the situation with the early pronoia grant as well.

(ii) In October 1074 the historian and jurist Michael Attaleiates received from Michael VII an *exkousseia* for all of his hereditary property situated at Constantinople and at Rhaidestos. In April 1079 Nikephoros III Botaneiates (1078–81) confirmed this *exkousseia* for these properties, which Attaleiates used to found a monastery and almshouse. Botaneiates added a *solemnion* of twelve nomismata for Attaleiates' monastery. The exemption covered only the secondary charges and corvées, not the *telos* (which was perhaps 300–450 nomismata per year).[33]

31 *Patmos*, I, no. 1.37ff.: ἐξκουσσευθήσονται γὰρ τὰ δειλωθέντα προάστια καὶ οἱ ἐν αὐτοῖς πρὸσκαθήμενοι [sic] πάροικοι ἀπό τε συνωνεῖς [sic], καπνικοῦ, μιτάτου, ἀπλίκτου, κτλ. On Andronikos: D. Polemis, *The Doukai* (London, 1968), 55–59.

32 *Patmos*, II, no. 50.73–74,311. Oikonomides, *Fiscalité*, 237–39. By 1077 Andronikos was dead. Not long afterward the properties passed to the Turks before being restored to Byzantine authority in 1097–98. They were then given to the new monastery of Panachrantos in Constantinople, probably by the Doukas family: Oikonomides, *Fiscalité*, 188.

33 MM, V, 135–38, 138–45. Oikonomides, *Fiscalité*, 189, 240–41.

[4.2] Typikon of Gregory Pakourianos for the monastery of Petritzos-Bačkovo near Stenimachos (1083)

(iii) Another of Alexios' generals, the *megas domestikos* of the west Gregory Pakourianos, received privileges from a series of emperors, which included hereditary grants of income-producing property, *exkousseiai*, *logisima*, and gifts of paroikoi. Pakourianos was a Georgian who had served faithfully a series of emperors. According to the *typikon* he composed for the monastery of Petritzos-Bačkovo near Stenimachos which he founded, the majority of his properties originated as imperial grants. He explicitly states that the village in which the monastery was located had been given to him "by . . . chrysobull . . . , in recompense for my many and great struggles and exertions in blood . . . in defense of the Roman Empire."[34] Probably there was also present the element of compensation for properties abandoned in Anatolia. Pakourianos had held property there (lines 1769ff.), and the *typikon* specifically mentions a village in the theme of Thessaloniki which Pakourianos' brother Apasios "had received by chrysobull in exchange for the properties that [Apasisos] had abandoned at Antioch." At his brother's death Gregory inherited this and other properties which had been granted to Apasios "through pious chrysobull."[35]

Pakourianos does not mention which specific emperors gave him grants. But among the scores of imperial documents which the *typikon* lists that Pakourianos received, the only ones that mention an emperor by name as the issuing authority are three chrysobulls of Michael VII for Pakourianos' property at Mosynopolis (line 1775), a document of Michael VII concerning the metropolis of Philippopolis, and an act of Nikephoros Botaneiates for his property at Philippopolis (line 1788). Thus, Pakourianos received his property at Mosynopolis from Michael VII and those at Philippopolis most likely from the same emperor. A mention of "two *livelloi*" for villages in the theme of Mosynopolis among the documents indicates that at least some of the property he had received was *klasma*, for which Pakourianos initially paid what was called the *livellikon demosion*, calculated at $\frac{1}{12}$ of the normal tax. As time passed he received a series of additional benefits on these properties: *exkousseiai*, complete exemption of the *telos* (*logisima*), the

[34] P. Gautier, "Le typikon du sébaste Grégoire Pakourianos," *REB* 42 (1984), 33.232–36. All subsequent line numbers are from this edition.

[35] Gautier, "Le typikon du sébaste Grégoire Pakourianos," 39.314–23, 39.349–40.350. Cf. the will of Eustathios Voïlas from 1059 who also abandoned property in Cappadocia and received an uncultivated property elsewhere in Anatolia, evidently from a high local official: Lemerle, *Cinq études*, p. 22 line 50, and pp. 30, 58–59.

right to improve the properties with no additional tax assessment, and the right to transmit the properties to his heirs. Therefore, he did not receive the complete tax exemption, as well, perhaps, as hereditary rights, all at once. Since the snapshot we have of his holdings was taken in 1083, it is not possible to detail the chronology of his acquisitions of properties and privileges. Given his faithful service to Alexios I, the existence of many other, unattributed imperial documents among his personal papers (lines 1767ff.), and the fact that he notes clothing given to him by Alexios I (lines 403f.), it is likely that he received property from this emperor as well. But it is clear that the bulk of his fortune came from Michael VII and Nikephoros Botaneiates.

Pakourianos was absolved from paying the basic tax on land through a simple *logisimon*. He donated to his monastery "the properties given to us through pious chrysobulls in the manner of hereditary possession, in inalienable and complete ownership and true authority, which becoming *logisima* were confirmed by pious chrysobulls" (lines 259ff.: κτή-ματα . . . ἅτινα καὶ λογίσιμα γεγονότα). This meant that the basic tax on the properties went to Pakourianos and not the state, or rather, since he owned the properties, he simply did not pay the tax. Later in the *typikon* he mentions an imperial act (*pittakion*) concerning the *logisimon* of all his properties (line 1820) and another for the properties he owned in Mosyn-opolis (line 1840).[36] The number of properties which he received through chrysobull and for which he received *logisima* was extensive (lines 259–304): *kastra* and their surrounding villages, other villages, *proasteia*, the monastery of St. George with its land and a *metochion*, and other properties.

As Lemerle has pointed out, the properties which had become the patrimony of Pakourianos remained theoretically taxable, but the state renounced these taxes for the benefit of Pakourianos, who became the beneficiary of this fiscal income by the procedure of *logisimon* based on the original value of the property when acquired. If the property's value increased, the fisc could demand taxes on the added value. This explains why Pakourianos had to get chrysobulls to get exemption for the improve-ments he made on his properties (lines 1796f.).[37]

What was the status of Pakourianos' paroikoi? Did they rent land from Pakourianos or did they own their own parcels? In other words, were they paroikoi-tenants or paroikoi-taxpayers? The only clue is found in a passage from the *typikon* which forbade the *hegoumenos* of the monastery from giv-ing to any monk any of the monastery's property: "neither *paroikotopion*,

[36] Lemerle, *Cinq études*, 135, 155–56. Dölger, *Beiträge*, 105, 145.

[37] Lemerle, *Cinq études*, 182.

nor other land, nor garden or vines, nor any such thing belonging to the monastery" (lines 1643–44). Because Pakourianos considered a *paroikotopion*, literally "paroikos plot," to be something a monastery might be tempted to give away, in the context of the passage *paroikotopion* would seem to mean land the monastery owned and the peasant rented. Property that a peasant owned was referred to usually as a *stasis* or *hypostasis*.

At least some of Pakourianos' paroikoi owed him service, and after his death this obligation passed to the benefit of the monastery. In the *typikon* he orders that on the anniversary of his death, there should be a distribution to the poor including "those who are in the service of the monastery, salaried and paroikoi" (line 1336: μισθίοις τε καὶ παροίκοις). Paroikoi in the service of the monastery had been in the service of Pakourianos. How did they acquire this status? There was only one way: through the transfer of the usual state service obligations that burdened all peasants – whether they owned their own land or were tenant-farmers – from the state to a private landowner. In other words, like the many monasteries in the previous chapter, Pakourianos had received a gift of a number of paroikoi who had received an *exkousseia* of secondary charges and corvées.

Evidently everyone in at least one village – Stenimachos, one of the properties Pakourianos received from the emperor – owed these secondary charges to Pakourianos. This, along with further elucidation regarding the "salaried" workers mentioned above, is seen in the passages relating to the staffing of three guest lodgings that Pakourianos built. In one of them, he writes, there should be one paroikos from Stenimachos "free of every charge and service to which the whole village is subject, and subject only to the service of such guest lodging," and for this he should receive the salary (*roga*) of a monk of the third class (lines 1539–42, 1547f.). For each of the other two guest lodgings, in other locations, a paroikos was to be allotted who was exempt of charges (line 1567: ἐλευθερωθήτω πάροικος). These passages help us to understand another passage where Pakourianos proudly states that he constructed the monastery at his own expense without recourse to unjust actions, "or by corvées and requisitions and abusive demands of my paroikoi, forcing them to suffer in the construction of the holy churches or of the said monastery near them, but by my just and personal labors and exertions" (lines 252–57). Rather than implying he never required labor services of his paroikoi, he was asserting nothing more than that he was not a tyrannical landlord.

The impression we receive is that Pakourianos' paroikoi were included with whatever property he owned; they worked the property before he received it, and they would continue to work it after his death. He describes the various contents of the properties that would pass to the monastery (lines 389–96):

> *despotika* yokes [i.e., the oxen owned directly by Pakourianos himself], paroikoi, and all the animals belonging to them, all the land both in the mountains and the plains, mountain pasturages, pasture land, arable land, vineyards, all the fruit and other trees, water and animal mills, ponds and the fallow land around them, *kastra* and all the buildings in them, and all the items and incomes of movable and immovable property inside and outside them.

The concept of ownership displayed here is interesting. The paroikoi owned animals, distinct from Pakourianos' animals, but all belonged to Pakourianos.

Further, Pakourianos forbade the monastery from alienating in any way anything belonging to the monastery, "except only the paroikoi customarily serving" the monastery (lines 1649f.: τῶν παροίκων τῶν δουλευόντων συνήθως αὐτῇ). Again, the paroikoi are regarded as a type of property, although a special type. The fact that their separation from the monastery was permitted is, I think, less a sign of how inhumanely they were regarded than an acknowledgment that ultimately the paroikoi were free to leave the lands of the monastery. While it is possible that some of Pakourianos' paroikoi might have rented his land as well as own parcels of their own, it would seem that the vast majority were tenant-farmers not subject to the basic land tax (*ateleis*, in the terminology of the documents) but most definitely subject to service obligations. Further, it appears that all the property from which Pakourianos derived any benefit was owned by him.[38]

[4.3] Chrysobull of Alexios I Komnenos for Leo Kephalas regarding Mesolimna (1084)

(iv) In 1084 Alexios I granted his general Leo Kephalas a *proasteion* at a place called Mesolimna near Thessaloniki. It had earlier belonged, under unknown circumstances, to a certain Stephen Maleïnos before Nikephoros III Botaneiates gave it "by way of a gift" (τρόπω δὲ δωρεᾶς) to "the Frank Otos" (Othon) and one Leo Vaasprakanites. It had then been confiscated when these two took part in a revolt. Under Alexios I, it passed to Kephalas

[38] Ahrweiler, *Byzance et la mer*, 213, interpreted the presence of tax receipts from the theme of Smolenes among the personal papers of Pakourianos (lines 1834f.) as evidence that he had received a grant of fiscal revenues from properties he himself did not own. This is possible, but as Lemerle, *Cinq études*, 156 note 90, observed, since Pakourianos had been governor of the theme of Smolenes, these papers may have been left over from the time of his official responsibilities.

and his future heirs, who were "to be masters" (*despozein*) of the property (*ktema*) with "all the agricultural fruits in it and the oxen and paroikoi found in it." There would be no reason to mention the paroikoi on the property unless the emperor was making a gift of these as well to Kephalas. No doubt Othon and Vaasprakanites had been the previous recipients of this gift of paroikoi. The document mentions nothing about taxes or tax exemption. On the basis of this, we may infer that Kephalas and the earlier grantees had to pay the normal taxes on the *proasteion*. Evidently, then, this was a simple grant of income-producing property and a gift of paroikoi.[39]

[4.4] Chrysobull of Alexios I Komnenos for Leo Kephalas regarding Tadrinou (1082)

(v) The general Leo Kephalas also benefitted from Nikephoros III Botaneiates' beneficence. Toward the end of his reign Botaneiates granted him 334 modioi of *klasma* in the village of Tadrinou, in the region of Derkos, about 35 miles northwest of Constantinople. After the accession of Alexios I Komnenos, Kephalas received a praktikon for the property, and in 1082 Alexios issued a chrysobull confirming the grant and noting that Kephalas "owns it completely and without harassment, exempted from every demand and burden, except to pay the *fisc* $^{7}/_{12}$ nomismata." As *klasma*, this land had been abandoned by its previous taxpayer and, after some years, was confiscated. Because Alexios I granted an exemption from all the secondary charges (an *exkousseia*) on this property in 1082, but the *telos* was maintained, Kephalas was initially granted only the ownership of this *klasma* by Botaneiates.[40]

Andronikos Doukas, Michael Attaleiates, Gregory and Apasios Pakourianos, Leo Vaasprakanites and Othon, and Leo Kephalas. Overall the relative lack of documents from the tenth century as compared to the eleventh century might be attributable to the vicissitudes of time. However, this cannot

[39] *Lavra*, I, no. 45.13–14,16–18: καὶ τῶν ἐν τούτω γεωργηθέντων παντοίων καρπῶν καὶ τῶν ἐν ἀυτῶ ἑυρεθέντων ζευγῶν καὶ παροίκων. J. Herrin, "The Collapse of the Byzantine Empire in the Twelfth Century," *University of Birmingham Historical Journal* 12 (1970), 195, characterized this as a pronoia grant. On the revolt, J.-C. Cheynet, *Pouvoir et contestations à Byzance (963–1210)* (Paris, 1990), 363.

[40] *Lavra*, I, no. 44.19–20: ὥστε δεσπόζειν ταύτης ἀυτὸν τελείως καὶ ἀναφαιρέτως· ἐξκουσσεύεσθαι δὲ καὶ ἀπὸ πάσης καὶ παντοίας ἐπηρείας τὲ καὶ κακώσεως, καὶ μόνον τελεῖν τὸ δημόσιον τὰ τέσσαρα ἥμισυ καὶ δωδέκατον νομίσματα. For what little we know of the career of Kephalas, see the older work of G. Rouillard, "Un grand bénéficiaire sous Alexis Comnène: Léon Képhalas," *BZ* 30 (1930), 444–50. Oikonomides, *Fiscalité*, 192, 246.

explain the numerous references in documents to imperial grants to laymen during the decade from 1071 to 1081, and the utter lack of these in the decades prior to this. The increase cannot be attributed solely, or even significantly, to better documentation.

Some support for the novelty of the frequency of these grants can be found in the history of Attaleiates. He writes that Nikephoritzes, the favorite and chief minister of Michael VII Doukas (1071–78), had become quite wealthy and was given great power, "entrusted by the emperor with public matters, freely granting ranks and pronoiai to those whom he wished for not insignificant intakes of money," that is, through sale. Attaleiates then writes that Nikephoritzes received the monastery of the Hevdomon as a gift from the emperor. Noteworthy is the use of *pronoia*. Its appearance in the plural makes it difficult to translate the word as mere "solicitude." Indeed, Fedor Uspenskij, who first drew attention to this passage, viewed this as the earliest mention of the institution of pronoia. At almost the same time Nikolaj Skabalanovič wrote as well that this was an early example of the institution of pronoia, though, for him, in the eleventh century a pronoia was any grant of immovable property from the emperor to his ministers. Charanis and Ostrogorsky also viewed this passage as a reference to the institution of pronoia. If so, it would confirm that the authority Michael Doukas granted Nikephoritzes was great indeed.[41]

On the other hand, Lemerle and Hohlweg wrote that the use of the verb *charizomai* (χαρίζομαι) in the passage suggests, if anything, the institution of *charistike* (a view that Ostrogorsky later adopted, with some reservation), though Hohlweg added that Nikephoritzes' "pronoiai" should not be thought of as formal *charistikai* because there is no reason to think they involved exclusively grants of church properties. Finally, A. Kazhdan wrote that we are merely viewing the word *pronoia* used in the sense of "reward." The vagueness of the passage makes it difficult to attach any technical sense to *pronoia* in the passage at all. *Pronoiai* were simply benefactions, "tokens of solicitude." We are still at the point where *pronoia* has no technical sense, but can be used to denote, not only "solicitude," but any kind of grant or reward. In fact the usage is identical to Anna Komnene's description of the

[41] Attaleiates, ed. Pérez Martín, 147.25–148.2 = Bonn edn., 200.21ff.: καὶ τὰς τιμὰς καὶ προνοίας οἷς ἐβούλετο χαριζόμενος διὰ λημμάτων οὐχὶ μικρῶν. Uspenskij, "Značenie," 5. N. Skabalanovič, *Vizantijskoe gosudarstvo i cerkov v XI v.* (Saint Petersburg, 1884), 264. Charanis, "Monastic Properties," 69. Ostrogorsky, *Féodalité*, 22–23. Ahrweiler, "La concession des droits incorporels," 104 note 10, cited the passage to support her idea that the word *pronoia* designated the ensemble of pay, annual salary, or remuneration received by officials or persons in state service, corresponding to the charge or function they exercised.

manner by which Alexios I provided for the people at his orphanage: the emperor "set aside the pronoiai for them from land and sea" *[1.1]*.[42]

Attaleiates also notes that Nikephoros III Botaneiates distributed resources of the state and accorded exemptions in his populist politics which ended by ruining the empire. He granted "100-pound gifts of immovable properties," "all manner of offices," "illustrious ranks," "silver and gold," and "he banished *epereiai* for all who desired." Churches and monasteries were specially targeted for his beneficence. From the previous chapter we have seen how this emperor was indeed particularly solicitous of monasteries in granting *exkousseiai* to monasteries and to the paroikoi who worked on them.[43]

Aside from what appears to have been an undeniable increase in the frequency of grants to laymen during this period, was there anything special about the nature of the grants that made them different from earlier grants? The arrangements involved with most of these grants had precedents earlier in the eleventh century or even earlier. All of them for which any details are given (that is, all but the grant to Apasios Pakourianos, and to Othon and Vaasprakanites) involved an *exkousseia* of secondary charges. We look to the many *exkousseiai* accorded to monasteries for a parallel. The grants to Andronikos Doukas, Gregory Pakourianos, and to Leo Vaasprakanites and Othon involved a grant of a gift of paroikoi. All except the grant to Michael Attaleiates involved a gift of income-producing property, in one case explicitly part of an *episkepsis* (Andronikos Doukas) and in two others (Kephalas' grant in Tadrinou and part of Gregory Pakourianos' grant) explicitly *klasmata*. Here too we have earlier examples of the grant of state property to monasteries as well as to laymen, though, as pointed out earlier, grants of property were uncommon prior to this. Explicit *logisima* are just as uncommon here as in earlier periods. Only Gregory Pakourianos explicitly received them. Andronikos Doukas did not get a *logisimon* explicitly, because his revenues came from the rents of the paroikoi working the land drawn from an *episkepsis* which he received. Overall, his grant, it seems, was little different from the *episkepsis* of Helos that Constantine IX's mistress, the Alan princess, received around 1054.

Indeed, it is the *logisima* that Gregory Pakourianos received, and, further, what both Gregory and his brother received, that made their grants novelties.

42 Lemerle, *Cinq études*, 311 note 122, and Hohlweg, "Zur Frage der Pronoia," 295. Ostrogorsky, "Die Pronoia unter den Komnenen," 43, later questioned his earlier view and implied that Nikephoritzes' "pronoiai" seemed more closely linked to *charistikai*. Kazhdan, *Agrarnye otnošenija*, 204.

43 Attaleiates, ed. Pérez Martín, 197.7–13 = Bonn edn., 274.13–23. Oikonomides, *Fiscalité*, 187.

Gregory and Apasios received villages (*choria*). No document up to this time speaks of anyone, religious foundation or layman, receiving a village from the emperor. Did this reflect a new manner of grant, or did it reflect merely a change in terminology?

The reign of Alexios I Komnenos

Upon his accession, Alexios I Komnenos faced a great number of serious problems: invasions of Pechenegs, Turks, and Normans, the loss of land in Asia, and a lack of money. But before he could hope to solve the empire's problems he first needed to create a loyal administration by rewarding supporters and bringing rivals into his circle. He did this by creating a new aristocracy. The historian Zonaras writes of this. Alexios "did not deem those of the senate worthy of honor which was fitting nor took care of them in due measure; rather, he hastened to humble them." Instead, he "distributed among his relatives and some of his retinue cartfulls of money from the public treasury, provided them with ample yearly revenues [καὶ χορηγίας ἐκείνοις ἁδρὰς ἐτησίους ἀπένειμεν], so that their wealth became excessive; they acquired a suite [ὑπηρεσίαν] of a kind that is more appropriate to emperors than to private individuals."[44]

Since the cash was unavailable to provide all of the salaries and the simple gifts of money he may have wanted to distribute, he turned to the land. The tools at his disposal for distributing benefactions included many of the varieties of grants discussed in the previous two chapters: gifts of state property, the institution of *charistike*, grants of *sekreta* and other administrative posts, *logisima*, *exkousseiai*, and gifts of paroikoi. To acquire the property necessary, he resorted to confiscation. And, as Zonaras writes, tying all of this together were familial bonds. Because of the incursions of the Seljuk Turks the Komnenos family had been dispossessed of their ancestral estates in Asia Minor. As emperor, Alexios had the ability to compensate them royally.

We know of quite a few individuals who were beneficiaries of imperial grants during the first half of Alexios' reign. Again, I present these in chronological order:

(i) Nikephoros Melissenos (d. November 1104) was a brother-in-law of Alexios I. More importantly, he had been a rival claimant to the throne, and

[44] *Ioannis Zonarae Epitomae Historiarum libri XVIII*, ed. M. Pinder (Bonn, 1841–97), III, 766.17–19, 767.2–8. Ahrweiler, *Byzance et la mer*, 214.

after Alexios' accession he was granted the title *kaisar* (at the time, second only to the imperial dignity itself) and, according to Anna Komnene, "he was also to be given the great city of Thessaloniki." Zonaras writes only that he was granted "a wealth of money" (χορηγίαν χρημάτων), an ambiguous phrase that can be interpreted many ways, and notes that Melissenos went to live in Thessaloniki. A number of historians have construed this to mean that Melissenos was granted the tax revenues of Thessaloniki, and while we have no other direct evidence to link him to the city itself, a number of documents do suggest that he held significant wealth from property in the region of Thessaloniki.[45]

An act from 1085 hints at his power in the area. Melissenos had been asked to arbitrate a dispute between Iviron and the bishop of Ezova involving properties in the area of Ezova in the Strymon valley. He sent two of his "men" (*anthropoi*) to investigate the matter and they made a *periorismos* of a disputed property. In the view of the editors of the document, Melissenos' role can be explained by his rank and power in the area, that is, social rather than governmental authority, but one could also conclude that Melissenos had acquired quasi-governmental authority.[46]

He also held property in the Chalkidike, a *proasteion* at Hagia Marina, in 1104. Shortly earlier he had improperly held a property confiscated from Iviron at Chliaropotamou in the same area.[47] But even more important is an act from 1117 which notes that Samuel Vourtzes, whose family was related to Melissenos, had received the *proasteion* of Rousaiou as a gift (διὰ δωρεᾶς) from Melissenos. This grant was made before Melissenos' death in 1104, and probably before 1101, when another Vourtzes, Constantine, was holding property in the same area.[48] According to the act of 1117 Rousaiou had been part of an imperial *episkepsis*, evidently part of the property Melissenos received from Alexios I. Eventually Rousaiou passed from the Vourtzes family to the monastery of Docheiariou and a fragmentary document from the twelfth century gives its area as 6,111 modioi (*Docheiariou*, no. 5.13).

[45] *Iviron*, II, p. 225. *Alexiad*, II.8.3: ed. Reinsch, 76.56 = ed. Leib, I, 89.6–10. Zonaras, III, 732.9–14. Cf. also a vague passage in the history of Michael Glykas: *Michaelis Glycae Annales*, ed. I. Bekker (Bonn, 1886), 619. Ahrweiler, *Byzance et la mer*, 213. Lj. Maksimović, "Geneza i karakter apanaža u Vizantiji," *ZRVI* 14/15 (1973), 112–13. Treadgold, *History*, 613. *Iviron*, II, p. 28.

[46] *Iviron*, II, no. 43, and p. 144. On Ezova, see N. Zekos, "Εζεβαί· ένας βυζαντινός οικισμός στο κάτω τμήμα της κοιλάδας του Στρυμόνα," in *Μνήμη Μανόλη Ἀνδρόνικου* (Thessaloniki, 1997), 77–104.

[47] *Iviron*, II, no. 52.242,245,247,104–05,116. Lefort, *Villages de Macédoine*, 46, 53, 164.

[48] *Docheiariou*, no. 4.9–10, and pp. 76–77. Lefort, *Villages de Macédoine*, 138. *Iviron*, II, no. 52.101–02 (inserted act from 1101). As a side note, after Samuel Vourtzes' death, his son and daughter held the property; thus, evidence of hereditability.

In order for Melissenos to have made a gift of so large a property, his own holdings had to have been at least an order of magnitude larger.

[4.5] Chrysobull of Alexios I Komnenos for the monastery of the Lavra regarding Adrian Komnenos (1084)

(ii) One of the most interesting grants that Alexios I conferred was for the benefit of his brother, the *protosevastos* Adrian Komnenos (d. 1105). According to a chrysobull issued in August 1084 on behalf of the monastery of the Great Lavra, Alexios had granted the taxes of the Kassandra peninsula on the Chalkidike in Macedonia to Adrian, which made the monks, who owned property there, quite uncomfortable. The emperor explains that

> since my majesty granted all the things of that [peninsula] which belong in the treasury [ἐντὸς τῷ δημοσίῳ ἀνήκοντα] to . . . my brother Adrian, and reckoned yearly the sum of the state taxes [ἐτησίως τελούμενον τοῦ δημοσίου κανόνα] from the inhabitants of such peninsula to his person and party, so that these things be paid and rendered to him, the monks of the said monastery suspected somehow and feared lest they be reckoned as paroikoi of him to whom they rendered the taxes, as if they, by not having their own land, have been established as taxpayers and tributaries to another.

While the emperor assured them that they would hold their land forever as private property (δεσποτικῶς), they nevertheless would continue to pay yearly the state taxes (τὰ . . . δημόσια τελέσματα) for their properties on Kassandra. Tax collectors would not bother them because now all of their taxes went to Adrian. Further, he writes that Adrian's men would not impress the paroikoi of the monastery for labor services, but the paroikoi "shall bear only . . . the state taxes" belonging to Adrian.[49]

Adrian expressly received the *telos* of the properties on the peninsula that did not enjoy exemption from imperial taxation. Such was Lavra's land. And almost certainly he also had a claim to at least some of the usual secondary charges and corvées levied on property and people who had not been exempted from these, in part as a means of remunerating and accommodating his agents who collected the taxes. (But then, was Adrian given the right to conduct periodic fiscal revisions?) However, the paroikoi of Lavra had been exempted from these secondary charges, and so while they owed no secondary charges and corvées to Adrian, they did owe

[49] *Lavra*, I, no. 46.12–17: οἱ . . . μοναχοὶ ὑπώπτευόν που καὶ ἐδεδίεσαν μήποτε καὶ πάροικοι λογισθεῖεν τοῦ πρὸς ὃν καταβάλλονται τὰ δημόσια, ὡς τάχα τὴν γῆν ἰδίαν μὴ ἔχοντες ὑπὲρ ἧς ἑτέρῳ καθεστᾶσιν ὑποτελεῖς καὶ ὑπόφοροι, and lines 50–54.

state taxes. Unless the last phrase in the above quote was merely a blanket truism ("All owe taxes who owe taxes"), it suggests that at least some of Lavra's paroikoi owed taxes on property (movable or immovable) that they personally owned, these being distinguished from the taxes Lavra paid on its own land.

Thus, Lavra's paroikoi on Kassandra paid a rent to Lavra for the land belonging to the monastery that they worked as tenant-farmers. The usual secondary charges and corvée obligations were received by the monastery as well. The taxes on any property they owned personally went to Adrian.

This raises the issue of what it was to be a paroikos in the eleventh century. The traditional meaning is found in a decision of the tenth-century jurist Kosmas Magister and a passage from the eleventh-century legal compilation called the *Peira*. According to these, paroikoi were peasants who received land to cultivate based on an agreement with the proprietor. As long-term lessees, they enjoyed one important legal protection: while they could neither alienate the land, nor make any claim on it should they leave or should the proprietor ask them to leave, after thirty (or forty) years they could not be removed from the land as long as they paid their rent. They were essentially tenant-farmers who acquired a limited right of possession with the passage of a generation. Such paroikoi usually owned their own animals (cows, asses, pigs, sheep, etc.), often including draft animals (oxen) and sometimes including arable land, though the extent of the latter is difficult to determine. This traditional view of paroikoi says nothing about fiscal obligations because the fiscal obligations of a peasant did not change when he rented land; he still owed taxes and the customary service obligations and secondary charges to the fisc. Lavra's paroikoi on Kassandra differed to the extent that they rendered labor services to the monastery and not to the state.[50]

But what of the complaint of the monks themselves, that they feared being regarded as paroikoi of Adrian? According to the traditional definition of a paroikos, the monks may have felt that the taxes they paid to Adrian would appear to be a rent, and that would threaten their ownership of their properties. On the other hand, while the document suggests that at least some of the paroikoi on Lavra's properties evidently did not pay their taxes to the monastery, the monks of Lavra were familiar with the evolving conception of the paroikos which was connected with the granting

[50] G. Weiss, "Die Entscheidung des Kosmas Magistros über das Parökenrecht," *Byz* 48 (1978), 477–500. *Peira*, 15, 2–3: Zepos, *JGR*, IV, 48–49.

of fiscal revenues to a third party. Only five years earlier, in 1079, Nikephoros Botaneiates confirmed a gift of 100 *ateleis* paroikoi and *douloparoikoi* to Lavra dating from the time of Constantine VII and added another 100 *ateleis* paroikoi and *douloparoikoi* from among their descendants (*Lavra*, I, no. 38). In accord with the traditional status of paroikoi, these peasants were tenant-farmers on Lavra's property but, unlike traditional paroikoi, they no longer owed the usual secondary service or tax obligations toward the state; rather, the monastery was henceforth the recipient of these services and obligations.

Of course, what Botaneiates and Constantine VII had granted the monastery were the secondary taxes and burdens of these paroikoi, not their *telos*, for the peasants were too poor to be levied a *telos*, and so the parallel to the case of Adrian Komnenos is not complete. More relevant perhaps is Basil II's grant from 984 which granted Lavra 25 *exkoussatoi oikoi*. These "excused households" were exempted from paying taxes in the town of Chrysopolis (where they resided), only to have this tax burden (or some equivalent levy) transferred by chrysobull to Lavra. Here, as in the case of Adrian and unlike that of traditional paroikoi, the *telos* of these households was exempted and transferred from the fisc to a private party, specifically the monastery of Lavra itself. The monks of Lavra perhaps feared they were now in the same situation as these *exkoussatoi*.[51]

In any event the monks of Lavra were facing a new situation and they wanted clarification of the fiscal and juridical status of their property and of themselves. In effect the emperor assured them that they were not part of a gift of paroikoi, but, in reality, the definition of paroikos was evolving in the direction of meaning someone who did not render his taxes to an imperial tax collector but to a third party.

It must be emphasized that the grant given to Adrian Komnenos was perhaps not without precedent. Certainly it is possible that Nikephoros Melissenos had received tax revenues from Thessaloniki. But even earlier there is the case of Vardas Skleros, as reported in the Arabic history of Yahya ibn Said of Antioch. In 989 after the death of the rebel Vardas Phokas, the co-conspirator Vardas Skleros submitted to Basil II and the emperor granted him the title of *kouropalates* and "assigned him as a fief" two provinces "with their head tax and property tax in addition to his earlier possessions." In contrast, ibn Said adds that when Nikephoros Phokas, Vardas Phokas' son, submitted to the emperor at this same moment, the emperor merely "honored him with an important property." While we may express the usual caveats about accepting such information at face value, Skleros seems to have

[51] *Iviron*, I, no.6.23,32–33: οἶκοι εἰκοσιπέντε . . . ἐξκουσευόμενοι ἐν Χρυσοπόλει καὶ ἐν τῆ καθ' ἡμᾶς τελοῦντες Λαύρα.

been made some type of governor who benefitted from the tax receipts of the area conferred.[52] A similar example, cited above, is found in the history of Skylitzes. After submitting to Basil II, Senachereim, the ruler of Vaspurakan, was made strategos of Cappadocia and given "as possessions there" three cities and other possessions. If someone is given cities as "possessions," it is difficult to interpret it any way other than to conclude that he was given their tax revenues.[53]

Some scholars have considered Adrian's grant an early pronoia grant.[54] Yet the specific qualities of the grant to Adrian as inferred from the document have very few similarities to the twelfth-century pronoia grant. In Adrian's case an individual received a grant from the emperor that involved the taxes on property not owned by the grant recipient (a redirection of tax revenues at the source). According to the 1084 document, Adrian was granted the taxes of all the villages (and estates) of the Kassandra peninsula, and this is most similar to a *logisimon solemnion*. If the beneficiary of the grant had not been Adrian but a monastery, what little we know of the grant would fit the *Marcian Treatise*'s definition of a *logisimon solemnion* precisely.[55] It was essentially a "secular" *logisimon solemnion*, or simply, a *logisimon*: the tax revenues of Kassandra were "reckoned" to Adrian's account (lines 15–16: τῷ προσώπῳ τὲ καὶ τῷ μέρει αὐτοῦ ἐλογίσατο). Further, we do not know the formal conditions of the grant. Was it technically a grant for life? Or was it technically a hereditary grant (more like an "eternal" *solemnion*)? Or was it held simply at the emperor's pleasure? In reality, it was certainly a grant for as long as Adrian kept Alexios I's favor, which might be for as long as Alexios was emperor.

52 "Histoire de Yahya-ibn-Saïd d'Antioche," ed. and trans. I. Kratchkovsky and A. Vasiliev, in *Patrologia Orientalis* 23, fasc. 3 (Paris, 1932), 427, cited by Oikonomides, *Fiscalité*, 221. Psellos (1.29.2–3: ed. Renauld, I, 18) writes simply that after his submission Vardas Skleros "departed for the lands [*agroi*] assigned to him" and shortly thereafter died.

53 Skylitzes, ed. Thurn, 354.4–355.4, cited by Oikonomides, *Fiscalité*, 221.

54 F. Dölger, "Zur Textgestaltung der Lavra-Urkunden und zu ihrer geschichtlichen Auswertung," *BZ* 39 (1939), 59. Charanis, "Social Structure," 106, 152–53, and basically repeated in his "Monastic Properties," 88, and "The Aristocracy of Byzantium in the Thirteenth Century," in *Studies in Roman Economic and Social History in Honor of Allan Chester Johnson*, ed. P. R. Coleman-Norton (Princeton, 1951), 352. Ahrweiler, *Byzance et la mer*, 213, and "La concession des droits incorporels," 109, while in Ahrweiler, "La 'pronoia' à Byzance," 687–88, she backs away from this view and refers to Adrian's grant merely as a pronoia "in the large sense," that is, as a means of taking "care" of his brother. Hohlweg, "Zur Frage der Pronoia," 303–04. M. Angold, *The Byzantine Empire, 1025–1204*, 2nd ed. (London and New York, 1997), 149.

55 More or less, this was the view of Ostrogorsky, *Féodalité*, 72 note 1, and G. Litavrin, *Bolgarija i Vizantija v XI–XII vv.* (Moscow, 1960), 158. V. Vasil'evskij, "Materialy dlja vnutrennej istorii Vizantijskogo gosudarstva," *ŽMNP* 202 (April 1879), 415, hinted at this connection to a (*logisimon*) *solemnion*. Maksimović, "Geneza i karakter apanaža," 110–12, placed Adrian's grant within his definition of an "appanage" (see *ODB*, s.v. "appanage").

Only if we assume that other elements were present in the grant to Adrian does the similarity to the early pronoia grant increase. If there were state properties within Kassandra, such as *klasmata* or imperial *episkepseis*, it is possible that he received their incomes, in the form of rent. The document explains that Adrian was granted "all the things of that [peninsula] which belong in the treasury" (ἐντὸς τῷ δημοσίῳ ἀνήκοντα), which, technically, would include *klasma* but exclude imperial *episkepseis* which belonged to the emperor (*demosiaka* properties vs. *vasilika* properties). To the extent that *episkepseis* were involved then those elements would make Adrian's grant have similarities perhaps to the grants of *episkepseis* to Andronikos Doukas and to Constantine Monomachos' mistress.

Ultimately, Adrian may have held a unique and idiosyncratic package of benefits, one that may well have never been duplicated for anyone else. But we know quite little about Adrian's grant, and all that we do know for sure – that he received the *telos* of property owners on the Kassandra peninsula and that the monks of Lavra were unfamiliar with such a grant – bears no similarity whatsoever to the early pronoia grant.

(iii) An act from 1085 settled a dispute between the monastery of Xeropotamou and another monastery over a mill and its surrounding property at Develikeia, about five miles southwest of Hierissos. Xeropotamou was granted rights over the mill, on which it would continue to pay taxes. Of interest to us is the list of signatories to the act: seven witnesses including the bishop of Hierissos ("present and witnessing," according to the usual formula), the scribe who drew up the act, and, finally, "Niketas, the least monk . . . manager of the properties of the *megas doux*." Since Niketas was the only signatory, aside from the scribe, who did not sign the act as a witness, the editor of the act concluded that Niketas was the act's author and the authority who settled the dispute between the monasteries. Indeed, while a man like Niketas might be asked to decide an issue merely because he represented a powerful man who had interests in the area, in this case the bishop of Hierissos would have been as likely or more likely a candidate. Rather, it would appear that Niketas and the *megas doux* had more than a passing interest in the disputed properties, and the editor concluded that the reason for this is that the *megas doux* was the person who received the taxes on the property. This is a reasonable hypothesis and it has been adopted by a number of scholars.[56] Yet neither this document nor any other provides

[56] *Xéropotamou*, no. 7.14,25: προνοητὴς τῶν κτημάτων τοῦ μεγάλου δουκός, and p. 65. Ahrweiler, *Byzance et la mer*, 213; Angold, *Byzantine Empire*, 149; and M. Hendy, *Studies in the Byzantine Monetary Economy c.300–1450* (Cambridge, 1985), 88.

any direct evidence that property owners in the region of Hierissos paid their taxes directly to this *megas doux*. The possibility remains open that this *megas doux*, who cannot be securely identified, simply held significant property in the region of Hierissos with no connection to the property involved in this act.[57]

(iv) In addition to the *klasma* in the village of Tadrinou which he received from Nikephoros Botaneiates *[4.4]*, and the *proasteion* at a place called Mesolimna near Thessaloniki which he received from Alexios I *[4.3]*, the general Leo Kephalas received two other grants of property from Alexios, each with its own distinctive character: in May 1086, Alexios confirmed a gift to Kephalas of the village of Chostianes in the theme of Moglena. The emperor specifically ordered that Kephalas and his heirs enjoy the property, with its *voïdatoi* and *aktemones* peasants, exempt of all taxes and charges, for which he received a praktikon *[4.6]*. And sometime before 1089 Kephalas received a fourth property, the *proasteion* of Ano. In a chrysobull from 1089 Kephalas' children received confirmation of their father's rights over all of the properties he had received and of his right to bequeath them to his children. Tadrinou, Mesolimna, and Chostianes are mentioned, as well as Ano, which originally belonged to the *episkepsis* of Macedonia, and was given in full propriety and in perpetuity to Kephalas, with the right to alienate (ἐκποιεῖσθαι). There is no specific mention of taxes in the brief entry. In

57 The traditional view is that the title "*megas doux*" was created around 1092 for John Doukas, brother-in-law of Alexios I, who received it as a replacement for the title "*doux tou stolou*" ("of the fleet"): Polemis, *Doukai*, 67 note 6; *ODB*, s.v. "megas doux"; and Oikonomides, "L'évolution de l'organisation administrative," 147. This view must be modified: e.g., there is a lead seal of the Armenian Gagik II (d. ca. 1079/80) in which he refers to himself as "*megas doux*" of the theme of Charsianon: W. Seibt, "War Gagik II. von Grossarmenien ca. 1072–1073 Megas Doux Charsianou?," in *Tὸ Ἑλληνικόν. Studies in Honor of Speros Vryonis*, Jr., ed. J. S. Langdon et al. (New Rochelle, 1993), II, 159–68, esp. 163. It seems that the term *doux* was used at the time occasionally as a colloquial rendering of *droungarios* or *domestikos*. For example, John Komnenos, the brother of Isaac I Komnenos and father of Alexios I, was appointed "*domestikos* of the *scholai* of the West" by his brother Isaac in 1057, and before his death in 1067, he became "*megas domestikos*," the new title for the *domestikos* of the *scholai*: K. Varzos (Barzos), *Ἡ γενεαλογία τῶν Κομνηνῶν* (Thessaloniki, 1984), I, 49 and note 4. Yet, a document from 1062 mentions that John Komnenos had been "*megas doux* of all the West": *Iviron*, II, no. 35.36. If a *megas domestikos* or a *megas droungarios* could be referred to as a "*megas doux*," then there are two possibilities for the identity of the *megas doux* of this act: Alexios I's brother Adrian, the *megas domestikos* (*Alexiad*, VIII.4.4: ed. Reinsch, 244.65 = ed. Leib, II, 137.21.), and Nikephoros Komnenos, Alexios' youngest brother, who was *megas droungarios* of the fleet from 1081. Hendy, *Studies*, 88, and Angold, *Byzantine Empire*, 149, make the latter identification. On Nikephoros: Varzos, *Γενεαλογία*, I, 188. Ahrweiler, *Byzance et la mer*, 213, identified this *megas doux* as John Doukas, an *uncle* of Alexios I, but Alexios had but one uncle, the emperor Isaac I; Alexios' empress, Irene Doukaina, had one uncle as well, the *protostrator* Constantine Doukas: Polemis, *Doukai*, pp. 59–60, no. 22. Fortunately, the question of the identity of our *megas doux* has little bearing on our overall inquiry.

1115 all of these properties, except for Ano, were donated by Kephalas' son, the *proedros* Nikephoros, to Lavra. At the very least, Ano, like Mesolimna, was another simple gift of income-producing property.[58]

Tadrinou, originating as *klasma*, passed to Kephalas in full ownership, though he would pay the basic property tax on the property. Mesolimna had been confiscated before passing to Kephalas in full ownership, though he probably had to pay taxes on it. Ano had come from the *episkepsis* of Macedonia before passing in full ownership to Kephalas with the specific right to alienate; its tax status is unknown. Finally, there is the village of Chostianes, the earlier history of which is unknown. Kephalas received hereditary rights over the fiscal income of this village with the restriction that he could not alter the disposition of the village's peasants.

[4.6] Chrysobull of Alexios I Komnenos for Leo Kephalas regarding Chostianes (1086)

It is the grant of Chostianes that has rightly attracted the most attention of scholars over the years. While Mesolimna is called a *proasteion* and a *ktema*, Ano is called a *proasteion*, and Tadrinou is called a pasturage, Chostianes, like the subject of some of the grants to the Pakourianoi brothers, is called a village. Unlike the case of the Pakourianoi, we have one of the initial documents making the grant and this bears closer examination to determine its nature.

A chrysobull from May 1086 states that Kephalas was rewarded for his defense of Larissa by "having received the village of Chostianes located in the theme of Moglena, and carrying off a praktikon for its conferral . . . to show by name the [paroikoi of the area] of this village, the fewest number of *voïdatoi* and *aktemones*, and the signed *prostaxis* itself of our majesty for such gift."[59] In other words, sometime earlier Kephalas received the village via an imperial *prostaxis*, and a praktikon was issued detailing what was contained within the grant, including a small number of peasants, listed by name. Neither document is preserved. After that, Kephalas asked for a chrysobull confirming the grant, and the emperor acceded to the request. The chrysobull granted that Chostianes "remain with him and with all his party and with all his heirs and successors . . . , without hindrance and inseparably, forever untaxed and uncharged, neither he nor his party obliged

[58] *Lavra*, I, no. 49, no. 60, and p. 330.

[59] *Lavra*, I, no. 48.5–9. In 1181 Lavra held sixty-two paroikos families at Chostianes; twelve passed to Lavra when the village was donated by Leo's son Nikephoros in 1115: *Lavra*, I, no. 65.18.

to furnish anything at all to the fisc for the sake of any demand whatsoever" (lines 12–16). He would enjoy "the suppression of the entire taxes [*telesmata*] of this village" (line 19), and this *logisimon* would be recorded under his name in the provincial tax list.

The chrysobull specifies that "to his and to all his party's profit is reckoned [*logizesthai*] all the collected revenue [*prosodon*] from there" (lines 22–23). In regard to the paroikoi the party of Kephalas (lines 23–27)

> ought to maintain the arrangement and organization of the villagers, and not to expel them, nor to receive settlers of other villages, if they wish to keep valid the things of the grant to them. The said village along with the *proskathemenoi* in it is exempted [*exkousseuthesetai*] from the *mitaton* [and a long list of other secondary charges and corvées] and from every other *epereia* and hardship now and in the future.

The emphasis of the chrysobull is on the tax exemption (a *logisimon* and an *exkousseia*) from which Kephalas and his heirs were to benefit. The only physical "property" mentioned is the village itself. This is normal. The names of the peasants and any specific properties that Kephalas was given would have been listed in the praktikon, which is not preserved. But there are a few noteworthy things about the chrysobull. First, while Kephalas was given the right to transmit the grant to his heirs, nothing is said about any other right to alienate the village. We cannot conclude that he was free to dispose of the village as his personal property.

Further, the emperor shows an unusual solicitude toward the villagers of Chostianes, and this is nothing short of remarkable. The phrase that Kephalas should not introduce outsiders into the village could be interpreted as a directive against depriving other landowners or the state of their own peasant labor supply. But the phrase that Kephalas was not to dispossess the existing villagers and that, generally, he was to "maintain the arrangement and organization of the villagers" shows that the emperor wanted to preserve the status quo. And it is specifically noted that violation of these provisions would invalidate the grant. Thus, Kephalas' grant of Chostianes was *conditional* upon his proper treatment of the villagers.

This raises the question of the status of these villagers. Aside from this passage referring to "villagers" (*choritai*), the chrysobull mentions the people who lived in Chostianes in two other passages. First, it notes that the "[paroikoi of the area] of this village, a few *voïdatoi* and *aktemones*" were listed in Kephalas' praktikon. Here, *voïdatoi* would be peasants with one draft animal, and *aktemones* would be those with none. The words within the brackets are a translation of a restoration of a lacuna suggested by the editor of the document. It is possible that the word *paroikoi* did not appear in the document at all, although the parallel with documents for monasteries makes this restoration reasonable.

Second, Alexios' chrysobull states that the village and the "*proskathemenoi* in it" were exempted from a long series of secondary charges. This is a standard formula that appears frequently in documents for monasteries. *Proskathemenoi* means simply "those settled or living" in a particular place. By itself, it says nothing of the juridical or fiscal status of the people referred to. It is often found in this formula accompanied by the substantive *paroikoi*, but it also appears, for example, with *stratiotai* (with the literal meaning "soldiers") and *demosiarioi* (taxpaying peasants).[60]

And so we have "a few *voïdatoi* and *aktemones*" who may have been paroikoi, "villagers" who were to be respected and not expelled from the village, and "those settled" in the village. Were these all the same people? In other words, were the "*voïdatoi* and *aktemones*" identical with the "villagers" (*choritai*)?

There are two primary ways of interpreting the situation. One is that the "villagers" owned no land of their own, that they were the "*voïdatoi* and *aktemones*" mentioned earlier in the document, and that they had been living in the village long enough to establish the customary and legal right to remain in the village. The other interpretation is that Kephalas was given domain land within the village and a small number of paroikoi with which to work it. The "villagers," on the other hand, were a group of taxpaying peasants distinct from Kephalas' paroikoi. And "those settled" in the village were both groups. Since Kephalas was not permitted to settle new peasants (*epoikoi*) within the village, if he needed additional labor, it would have to come from the villagers.

Unfortunately, no matter how the matter is approached, it is impossible to make a confident choice between these two scenarios. If we begin by asking what kind of peasants normally could not be expelled from their place of residence, we get nowhere. Normally, the kind of peasants that could not be expelled were either paroikoi who had lived long enough on the land of a proprietor (usually thirty years) to establish a right to remain or peasants who owned their land.

We might focus on the terminology employed, particularly the distinction between how Kephalas was to hold the *proasteion* of Mesolimna and the village of Chostianes. He held the former with all its "agricultural fruits," while he held the latter with "all the income collected from there." This

[60] E.g., Zepos, *JGR*, I, 616, *Lavra*, I, no. 65.52, and *Iviron*, I, no. 33.14.

suggests that he collected taxes from the peasants living in Chostianes, but that does not prove that the peasants owned land in Chostianes, only that they paid taxes to Kephalas, which other passages in the document confirm. These taxes may have been only personal taxes such as the *kapnikon* which paroikoi (peasant-tenants) were liable for no less than peasant proprietors.

Or we can approach the matter by asking the question, why did the emperor envision that Kephalas might want to expel the villagers? The obvious possibility is that the villagers held land that Kephalas might wish to exploit with other, different peasants. This would make the most sense if the peasants owned their own land. But without straining the imagination one can think of other possibilities.

And then there is the odd way of describing the paroikoi Kephalas was granted: "the [paroikoi of the area] of such village, the fewest number of *voïdatoi* and *aktemones*" (τοὺς [παροίκους τῆς περιοχῆς τοῦ] τοιουτου χωρίου ὀλιγοστοὺς βοϊαδ[άτους] καὶ ἀκτήμονας). While this might suggest that there were only a handful of paroikoi-tenants, and that the rest of the inhabitants of the village were peasant proprietors, it could mean just that the village had very few inhabitants. (It would be quite desirable to have Kephalas' praktikon.)

Given that the passage dealing with the villagers has no parallel in any other document I know of, I think the emperor was aware that this was an unusual type of grant and he had to make clear to Kephalas that the peasants were not to be treated as simple tenants. While it seems somewhat more likely that some of the inhabitants of the village were peasant proprietors, we really do not know much about the composition of the village.

What exactly did Kephalas receive when he was granted Chostianes? What did it mean to be given a village? When one received a piece of land from the emperor, we assume the land was state property. Even if it had been confiscated from a private landowner, it passed through an intermediate stage in which it belonged to the state. If the emperor attached exemptions to the grant of a piece of land, then the grant of a piece of land could include, in addition to possession of the land, an exemption of the secondary charges that burdened the property (an *exkousseia*) and, less commonly, an exemption of the property tax on the land (a *logisimon*). It could also include an exemption of the secondary charges levied upon any peasant-tenants already working the land, or upon future peasant-tenants the beneficiary of the grant might install on the property (a gift of paroikoi). Always, the only things that the emperor could grant to someone were those things to which the emperor had a normal and customary right: state property and state taxes and charges.

A village, however, was more than a piece of land. It included permanently settled peasants, their homes, their gardens, their livestock, their personal possessions, perhaps a village chapel. And this was the case even if none of the inhabitants of the village owned arable land of their own. When Gregory Pakourianos was given a village or Leo Kephalas was given Chostianes, they did not acquire ownership of the homes and gardens of the peasants living there, or of the livestock of the peasants. And certainly they were not given ownership of the inhabitants themselves. Perhaps the emperor had this in mind, and perhaps this was why the grant to Kephalas was conditional upon Kephalas and his heirs treating the villagers properly.

So what did Kephalas get when he was granted the village of Chostianes? According to the document he received (i) a gift of a small number of *voïdatoi* and *aktemones*, (ii) a *logisimon* for the entire village, and (iii) an *exkousseia* of the secondary charges and corvées owed by the village's inhabitants and the village itself. Since Kephalas received paroikoi, it is reasonable to think that he also received a gift of arable land within the territory of the village. This was a kind of "seigneurial domain" which Kephalas exploited directly through his paroikoi-tenants (the "*voïdatoi* and *aktemones*"). Certainly if the inhabitants of the village did not own their own land, then Kephalas was granted all of the arable land of the village. In any event, because at least part of the village's land was granted to Kephalas himself, the *logisimon* technically must have included two parts: (a) a *logisimon solemnion* (or a "secular" *logisimon solemnion*) for Kephalas' benefit, of the personal taxes and any *telos* owed by the village's peasants, and (b) a simple *logisimon* for the land that was given directly as a gift to Kephalas. Nevertheless, the bookkeeping procedures of the fisc conflated the two; the village's taxes were simply suppressed for Kephalas' benefit. In practical economic terms, the grant gave Kephalas (i) a good share of the harvest of the land that was granted to him directly, (ii) labor services from the inhabitants of the village, and (iii) some portion of the personal taxes of the villagers and, if they owned their own land, the *telos* of this land.

Finally, according to the evidence of the *Zavorda Treatise*, we can state unequivocally that the grant of Chostianes to Kephalas, as well as the other properties granted to him, was not a pronoia grant. The salient feature of the early pronoia grant was that it was a lifetime grant. This was not the case with Kephalas' grants. Rather, the grant of Chostianes was a gift of income-producing property, combined with a *logisimon*, an *exkousseia*, and a gift of paroikoi. This was the same package of concessions that Gregory Pakourianos had received over the properties he had been granted. But

Pakourianos, unlike Kephalas, had received the entire package gradually. Kephalas received it at once.[61]

(v) The *kouropalates* Symbatios Pakourianos seems to have been another of those elevated imperial servants of Anatolian origin who was compensated with property in Europe for that which he had abandoned in the east. In his will from 1090, he bequeathed the *proasteion* of Soudaga in the theme of Macedonia (i.e., in Thrace) "which had been given to me by the holy emperor" to his wife Kale who in turn bequeathed it to a cousin.[62] Confirming Symbatios' status as an individual enjoying significant imperial favor is the reference in the document to a garment he had received from the emperor, this paralleling the similar gift Gregory Pakourianos, evidently a relative, had received from Alexios I.[63] Three other properties are mentioned in the will, including the *proasteion* of Radolivos in the Strymon valley, which he also bequeathed.[64] Their origin is not specified. Given the privileges enjoyed by his widow on the properties she owned (see below), it is likely that Symbatios received certain fiscal privileges on the property he received from the emperor.

[4.7] Testament of Kale Vasilakaina, the nun Maria (1098), and Extract of a fiscal register signed by Niketas Anzas regarding Radolivos (1098–1103)

(vi) Symbatios' wife, Kale Vasilakaina, the daughter of Nikephoros Vasilakes, the usurper who was blinded in 1078, also was the recipient of a grant from Alexios I. A widow since 1093, she took the monastic vow as the nun Maria, and in November 1098 bequeathed the property (*ktema*) of Radolivos to

61 Before the publication of the *Zavorda Treatise* it was possible to speak of the grant of Chostianes as a "hereditary pronoia": Dölger, "Zur Textgestaltung der Lavra-Urkunden," 59. A. Hohlweg, *Beiträge zur Verwaltungsgeschichte des oströmischen Reiches unter den Komnenen* (Munich, 1965), 86 note 4, and Hohlweg, "Zur Frage der Pronoia," 304. Also, with several factual errors, J. Herrin, "The Collapse of the Byzantine Empire in the Twelfth Century," *University of Birmingham Historical Journal* 12 (1970), 195. Based on his view of the development of the institution of pronoia, Ostrogorsky, *Féodalité*, 39 note 2, had always rejected the application of the term *pronoia* to this or any of the Kephalas grants precisely because they were hereditary.

62 *Iviron*, II, no. 44.7; no. 47.25–26. Soudaga is otherwise unknown. Cf. *Iviron*, II, no. 43.51–52, in which Symbatios and his half-brother Sergios witnessed in 1085 an act of the bishop of Ezova (in the Strymon valley).

63 *Iviron*, II, no. 44.10–11. Lemerle, *Cinq études*, 138.

64 Radolivos was state property in 1047. Therefore, between that time and 1090 it was granted (or possibly sold as *klasma*) to Symbatios Pakourianos or a relative: Oikonomides, "La fiscalité byzantine et la communauté villageoise au XIe s.," 100.

the monastery of Iviron. According to another document, a month later the emperor granted her all of the tax revenues of the *village* of Radolivos and the basic land tax as well as the surtaxes: "through chrysobull and *pittakion* of . . . Alexios Komnenos all the state tax of the present village of Radolivos along with the *dikeratoexafollon*, the *synetheia* and *elatikon* was reckoned [ἐλογίσθη] to the person of the nun Maria." This is the terminology of a *logisimon*, and the effect of the procedure was to allow Iviron, once it received Maria's bequest, to possess the entire village of Radolivos with a complete fiscal exemption for its land and its paroikoi.[65]

The tax status of Radolivos at this time is not stated explicitly, but from Maria's will it is clear that she, and perhaps she and her husband, already enjoyed a fiscal exemption of some sort on all of her properties. She writes that "I wish and order that, at the time of my death, the paroikoi of all my properties to be kept uncharged and untaxed from all their taxes [*telesmata*] paid by them today; I speak of the *oikomodion*, *zeugologion*, *dekata* of their animals, and all their other annual taxes," so that they would pray for her soul. The *oikomodion* is an obscure charge, probably a Bulgarian tax by origin that was appropriated by the Byzantine fisc after the conquest of Bulgaria in 1018. The *zeugologion* was levied only on the oxen (*zeugaria*) of people who did not own the land that they occupied. Such were Maria's paroikoi. And the *dekaton* was equivalent to the *ennomion*, a pasturage charge. These charges are often listed among the secondary charges and corvées, and so Maria was the beneficiary of an *exkousseia* on the paroikoi working her land. It should be noted that this kindness to her paroikoi would not leave her heirs in penury, because the paroikoi still owed their rents.[66]

The cases of Gregory Pakourianos, Apasios Pakourianos, Leo Kephalas, and the nun Maria Vasilakaina place us at a crossroads in Byzantine agrarian

[65] *Iviron*, II, no. 47.14 (1098). For the date of Symbatios' death, *Iviron*, II, no. 46 (1093). *Iviron*, II, no. 48.13–14 (1098–1103).

[66] *Iviron*, II, no. 47.49–50. Oikonomides, *Fiscalité*, 82–84. In his commentary to *Iviron*, II, no. 48 (p. 186) Jacques Lefort wrote that the *ktema* which the nun Maria inherited from her husband represented only a portion of the village of Radolivos. If so, when Maria was granted later the tax revenues of the entire village of Radolivos, she received the fiscal revenues owed by the *ktema* (in effect a simple *logisimon*) and the fiscal revenues of the portion of the village which was owned by a small number of peasant proprietors (a "secular" *logisimon solemnion*). However, Oikonomides, "La fiscalité byzantine et la communauté villageoise au XIe s.," 99–100, argued persuasively that, throughout the time Symbatios Pakourianos and his wife held Radolivos, there was no distinction between the *ktema* of Radolivos and the village of Radolivos. In other words, all of the inhabitants of Radolivos were paroikoi of Symbatios and his wife and none of the inhabitants owned their own land. Lefort, "The Rural Economy, Seventh–Twelfth Centuries," *EHB*, I, 288–89, appears to have adopted Oikonomides' view.

history. All were given what are called villages, and at least Leo and Maria, and probably Gregory, were granted all of the taxes of these villages. And even if none of the villages was inhabited by any peasants who owned their own land, it would take only one more step for the emperor to make such a grant. At that point the new concept of what it meant to be a paroikos – a peasant who paid his taxes, even the taxes on property he owned, to a third party – would be fully formed.

(vii) Major administrative appointments probably included property grants. For example, Anna Komnene writes that her father treated the sons of the former emperor Romanos Diogenes as if they were his own. To one of them, Nikephoros, "he entrusted the rule of the island of Crete for his personal dwelling place," which probably means he was appointed *doux* of Crete. This would have occurred in the early 1090s. In view of the policies of Alexios I toward other notable personages we may reasonably assume that Nikephoros was granted substantial property and privileges on Crete in addition to the administrative appointment.[67]

(viii) A brother-in-law of Alexios I, the *protosevastos* John Doukas, held property in the Strymon valley in the early 1090s.[68]

(ix) Perhaps the greatest beneficiary of Alexios I's grants was his older brother, the *sevastokrator* Isaac Komnenos. Aside from whatever else his brother had granted him throughout the empire, he held quite a few properties and privileges in the Chalkidike (Table 4.1). Of particular interest is the evidence that Isaac had been granted the taxes from certain areas.

In 1092 the emperor freed a *metochion* of Lavra called Hagios Andreas, located about fifteen miles southeast of Thessaloniki, along with its paroikoi, of secondary charges and labor services. He added that the managers (*pronoetai*) of the properties of Isaac Komnenos were forbidden to behave oppressively toward this *metochion* and its paroikoi, "but to receive only

[67] *Alexiad*, IX.6.3; ed. Reinsch, 271.24–25 = ed. Leib, II, 173.20–21: καὶ αὐτῷ δὴ τῷ Νικηφόρῳ τὴν τῆς νήσου Κρήτης ἀρχὴν ἀνέθετο εἰς ἐνδιαίτημα ἴδιον. E. Sewter's translation, *The Alexiad of Anna Comnena* (Baltimore, 1969), 281, erroneously states that Nikephoros received "Cyprus." 'Εις ἐνδιαίτημα ἴδιον is rendered by B. Leib as "en bien propre," by E. Dawes, *The Alexiad of the Princess Anna Comnena* (London, 1928), 225, as "as private property," and by E. Sewter as "which he could use as his own private property." (Both Dawes and Sewter often translate Leib's French translation rather than Anna's Greek.) But here, as elsewhere, Anna uses *endiaitema* to mean "dwelling": cf. V.viii.5.12 and XV.vii.4.10. D. Tsougarakis, *Byzantine Crete* (Athens, 1988), 77–78, concluded that Nikephoros held the position either from 1089 to 1090/1 or from 1092 to 1094. Since he was born around 1069, the latter set of dates seems more likely. Angold, *Byzantine Empire*, 149, linked this appointment to the type of grant Adrian Komnenos received and wrote that Diogenes was given not only the administration of Crete but the "revenues of the island." I do not agree.

[68] *Iviron*, II, no. 45.23–24.

Table 4.1 Known holdings and privileges of the *sevastokrator* Isaac Komnenos, primarily on the Chalkidike, with the date of the document mentioning the holding

1092	*telos* of a *metochion* of Lavra at Hagios Andreas		*Lavra*, I, no. 51.13–18
1089?	*proasteion* of the Kekaumenoi	taken from Xenophon which was compensated with other properties	*Xénophon*, no. 2.5–7
early 1090s	*proasteion* at Myriophyton	taken from Iviron	*Iviron*, II, no. 45.1,5,7, and pp. 29 and 159
early 1090s	a property	adjacent to the eastern side of Iviron's *proasteion* of Leontaria	*Iviron*, II, no. 45.82–83
early 1090s	*proasteion* of Volvos	belonged to the see of Thessaloniki in 1057; adjacent to the eastern side of Iviron's *proasteion* of Volvos	*Iviron*, II, no. 45.52; no. 52.409–10,415; I, no. 29.62.
1095	*proasteion* of Portarea	taken from Esphigmenou which was compensated	*Esphigménou*, no. 5.11–14
1101	taxes from the area of Hierissos?		*Iviron*, II, no. 50.67–70,72
1104	*proasteion* of Kravvata		*Iviron*, II, no. 52.247–48
1104	village of Kourkoute		*Iviron*, II, no. 52.407–08
1104	village of Aklou		*Iviron*, II, no. 52.450–51, 456–57

the appropriate taxes [ὡς μόνα τὰ ἀνήκοντα τέλη] owed by the monks and nothing more." So while this *metochion* and its paroikoi, like all the properties of Lavra at this time, had received an *exkousseia* from secondary charges and labor services, the monks were still required to pay the *telos* burdening the *metochion*, and to pay it to the *sevastokrator* Isaac.[69] If Alexios I's brother Adrian received the taxes from Kassandra and his brother Isaac received the taxes from a *metochion* not far from Thessaloniki, should we conclude that Isaac similarly received the taxes from a large area of which the *metochion* was a part? This would seem likely, but whatever the reality, it would have to accommodate Alexios' grant to his brother-in-law Nikephoros Melissenos who, according to Anna Komnene, was "to be given the great city of Thessaloniki" and who held a number of properties on the Chalkidike.

[69] *Lavra*, I, no. 51.13–18. Location: Lefort, *Villages de Macédoine*, 118. Bibliography: Ahrweiler, *Byzance et la mer*, 214; G. Ostrogorsky, "Observations on the Aristocracy in Byzantium," *Dumbarton Oaks Papers* 25 (1971), 10; Maksimović, "Geneza i karakter apanaža u Vizantiji," 110–12.

It is possible that Isaac was receiving the taxes from around Hierissos as well. A document from March 1101 issued by "Sgouros, *proedros* and *logariastes* of the properties of the . . . *sevastokrator*," lists the properties held by Iviron in the region of Hierissos, including a property of 3,200 modioi called Arsenikeia which had been taken from Iviron a short time earlier by Sgouros and given to the "*pronoetes* of the *episkepsis* of Aravenikeia [i.e., Revenikeia] and Hierissos." The document reports that the *sevastokrator* Isaac donated it back to Iviron, ostensibly out of piety.[70] We recall that the "*pronoetes* of the properties" of an anonymous *megas doux* resolved a dispute in 1085 in the region of Hierissos, and scholars have suggested this was because the *megas doux* was receiving the taxes from the properties in the area. If so, by the time of this act for Iviron, this privilege had passed to Isaac Komnenos. Further, this document provides clear evidence that Isaac and his servant Sgouros were acting as state officials. The praktikon from the early 1090s indicates as well that Isaac had been given some administrative authority, because in that document his *logariastes* (synonymous here with *pronoetes*) determined the border between the two properties, one of which Isaac held.[71]

Further, we need to bear in mind that we know of these properties, and those of the other laymen discussed here, only because the documents of Mount Athos have been preserved. Alexios' brothers, if not his brother-in-law and some of the others, almost certainly received grants involving properties in other locations within the empire.

(x) Quite a few of Isaac Komnenos' properties were granted from property confiscated from monasteries. It seems that shortly before February 1089 Alexios I initiated a revision of the tax code specifically designed to confiscate a great deal of land. The effects of this program were remarkable and provided Alexios I with another source of property for the grants he was bestowing. Jacques Lefort estimated that this program cost Iviron alone some 50,000 modioi of land (on the order of 20 square miles). And he estimates that Lavra lost some 43 percent of its land, some 20,000 modioi confiscated from a total of around 47,000 modioi. This program appears to have affected monasteries, churches, and laymen alike, providing Alexios I with vast quantities of land with which to make grants. Part of the property confiscated from Iviron was granted to the *protoproedros* Constantine Vourtzes, a member of a well-connected family.[72]

[70] *Iviron*, II, no. 50.67–70,72. [71] *Iviron*, II, no. 45.82–83.

[72] *Iviron*, II, pp. 27–31. Further, of the 23 properties the monastery of Iviron held in Macedonia in 1079, by 1104 it had lost 11 of them due to this confiscation and for other reasons (totaling in

What do we make of the grants to all of these individuals? All of them were made during the first half of Alexios' reign, that is, between 1081 and 1104, perhaps several years before 1104. I know of no such grants made by Alexios that can be securely dated to the period after 1104. It is not difficult to divine the emperor's motives for these grants. Obviously, he wanted to provide for his family, secure the loyalty of certain individuals, and reward others. The recipients were highly placed people within Alexios' administration or family members. Of the ten, two or perhaps three were brothers of the emperor; two were brothers-in-law of the emperor; one was the daughter of a usurper; one the son of a former emperor; one a general. At least four appear to have had administrative duties: perhaps two brothers, a brother-in-law, and the son of a former emperor. The size and nature of the grants received by these individuals seem to correspond to their position in relation to the emperor. There is much truth in the cliché that the empire became a family business under Alexios I.

The terms of their tenure are more difficult to estimate. Leo Kephalas held hereditary rights to all of the grants he received, as did Symbatios Pakourianos and his wife the nun Maria Vasilakaina, at least as far as we can tell. For the other individuals, the sources provide no clues, but common sense can be a guide. High-profile recipients such as the brothers and brothers-in-law of the emperor could expect to hold their grants as long as they remained on good terms with Alexios. After Alexios' death, continued tenure would depend on their personal relationship with the new emperor. Certainly the recipients hoped the benefits would pass to their heirs. And no doubt each of Alexios' relatives, to the most distant, was hoping that a premature death here, a falling from grace there, would improve his fortunes. Indeed Alexios had created an informal system of patronage with new titles and new types of grants to bestow on a (for the most part) new group of people. Cash grants were out, land and tax revenues were in. Everyone sought to become a landlord.

The grants show variety in their component parts and in the mix or "package" granted to each individual: gifts of income-producing property (initially *episkepseis*, but after 1089 increasingly confiscated land), *logisima* (simple *logisima*, "secular" *logisima solemnia*), *exkousseiai*, gifts of paroikoi (and we ought not to forget that Alexios was granting *charistikai* to people at the same time). All of these had been exploited before, in the 1070s if not

all some 75,000 modioi). *Iviron*, II, p. 29 notes 23 and 27. *Iviron*, II, no. 52.101–02, and p. 221. Lefort, *Villages de Macédoine*, 53.

earlier, but Alexios I brought all these elements together to create custom grant "packages."

The novelty of what Alexios did relates to how his government and his rule came to rely on these grants. Grants that had been uncommon earlier in Byzantine history became common in the 1070s and then became a natural part of how the state was run in the 1080s and 1090s.

What we do not see in any of these grants is an indication that the grant was restricted to the lifetime of the beneficiary nor do we see much of a connection to the kind of men who received pronoia grants in the twelfth century. None of the recipients discussed can be compared to the three soldiers, Romanos Rentinos and the brothers Theotimos and Leo Loukites, mentioned in the 1162 act of John Kontostephanos *[2.3]*, or, again, the Cumans of Moglena.[73]

The only evidence that Alexios I was making grants to soldiers (aside from that presented in Chapter 2 *[2.3]*) is found in a passage from Anna Komnene. Fearing an insurrection of the Paulicians living around Philippopolis, Alexios led an army into Thrace and arranged a parley at Mosynopolis. The chiefs of the Paulicians were brought into the city ten at a time and captured, and the rest followed and were captured as well. Alexios then sent an official to Philippopolis, and "Their property was confiscated and divided among the brave soldiers who had shared his privations in the battles and perils of the past." According to F. Chalandon, this occurred toward the end of 1083 or in the first few months of 1084. Anna adds that the official assigned to effect the distribution drove their wives from their homes.[74]

What kind of distribution was made? Taking Anna Komnene's testimony at face value, there were at least several hundred holdings available for redistribution. But were they all smallholdings or were there some estates (*proasteia*) in the mix? Were they all now empty, or were there some with paroikoi-tenants? Were they distributed to all the soldiers, or did they tend to pass to specific categories of soldiers? Anna mentions veterans, which

[73] To support the idea that Alexios I made large-scale systematic distributions of pronoiai, Ostrogorsky, *Féodalité*, 37–40, cited a passage from an 1104 chrysobull of Alexios I: *Lavra*, I, no. 56.7. However, since the pivotal phrase στρατιώτῃ τισί appears only in a modern and highly-suspect copy and has been relegated to the apparatus of the most recent edition of Lavra's acts, we need not devote any more attention to this passage. See Lemerle, *Agrarian History*, 239; Hohlweg, "Zur Frage der Pronoia," 306–07; and especially Ostrogorsky, "Die Pronoia unter den Komnenen," 51 note 39, where Ostrogorsky backed away from his earlier reliance on this document.

[74] *Alexiad*, VI.2.4: ed. Reinsch, 171.93–10 = ed. Leib, II, 45.8–14. Trans. adapted from E. Sewter. Hohlweg, *Beiträge zur Verwaltungsgeschichte*, 87, 89. F. Chalandon, *Les Comnènes*, I (Paris, 1900), 105 note.

suggests either mercenaries or those who had supported Alexios before and throughout his usurpation. Given that the episode occurred early in his reign, it would appear that Alexios was taking care of yet another constituency.

But how well-informed was Anna? Is it impossible that all the land was given to a handful of officers? Basically, we cannot say whether the institution of pronoia was involved here. It may have been, or Alexios may have simply granted hereditary smallholdings to a few hundred loyal soldiers, or a number of villages to a handful of officers. Whatever happened, it may well have been another example of Alexios' experimentation that was never repeated.

Grants for life

Grants of state property combined with gifts of paroikoi figure prominently in Alexios I's grants during the first half of his reign. What is lacking is the lifetime element. There is no evidence of this in any grant of property and paroikoi to Alexios I's relatives or to other privileged individuals. But other kinds of lifetime grants were well known during Alexios' time. These took several forms, and it is worthwhile listing them, to show how common they were, and how Alexios may have found inspiration for his early pronoia grants.

Alexander Kazhdan noted several examples of private grants that were limited to the lifetime of the recipient. For example, sometime before 1040/1 Eustratios, *hegoumenos* of the monastery *tes Galaiagres*, bequeathed a field to his nephew Theodore as property (δεσπόζειν) and stipulated that Theodore was to hold the field only for the duration of his life (τὸν ἅπαντα χρόνον τῆς ζωῆς μου), after which it was to pass to the monastery. In all of the known examples, the purpose of the lifetime element was, as in this case, to provide for the eventual transmission of the property to a monastery, or to ensure that monastic property would not permanently pass from a monastery's possession. The latter case is found in the 1162 act of John Kontostephanos *[2.3]*: Lavra had granted some soldiers possession of a piece of land on the condition that only the soldiers themselves were to hold the property, not their heirs. While Kazhdan thought that most likely anyone – monastery, private individuals, the state–could make such grants, they seem to have a rather narrow compass.[75]

[75] Kazhdan, "Formen," 218–19, 223. *Esphigménou*, no. 3.14. Other examples: *Pantéléèmôn*, no. 2; and S. Binon, *Les origines légendaires et l'histoire de Xéropotamou et de Saint-Paul de l'Athos* (Louvain, 1942), 284–86.

Another type of lifetime grant, also connected with monasteries, was the *adelphaton*. First attested in the eleventh century, an *adelphaton* was a living allowance in kind granted usually by a monastery to an individual for life in return for a donation of property or payment of a specific amount of money. Generally, the *adelphaton* amounted to an old-age pension or a lifetime annuity. It was a private arrangement, though in at least one case an emperor, Manuel I acting in his capacity as a patron of a monastery, granted someone an *adelphaton*. *Adelphata* became quite common in the fourteenth century, and there were occasionally attempts to make them hereditable.[76]

Yet another lifetime grant connected to monasteries is the *charistike*, and a great deal of attention has been paid to this institution in relation to the origin of pronoia grants. The word *charistike*, probably short for *charistike dorea* (literally, "gift of grace"), refers to the practice of giving monasteries or other religious foundations temporarily to laymen, or sometimes to institutions (though this is usually called an *epidosis*), on a conditional basis and for a restricted period, usually a lifetime, two, or three generations. While the origin of the *charistike* is unclear, two of the more recent students of the phenomenon date the genesis of the institution to the last third of the tenth century and connect it to the novel of Nikephoros Phokas (963–69) forbidding the creation of new monasteries and philanthropic institutions because so many old ones had fallen into disrepair.[77]

The main evidence for this type of grant comes from the eleventh and twelfth centuries. The original purpose of the *charistike* seems to have been the restoration of ruined or financially troubled ecclesiastical institutions, and in all likelihood the Church itself was the original force behind the *charistike*. Private individuals petitioned the emperor (in the case of imperial monasteries, which were owned by the emperor) or the patriarch, a metropolitan, or a bishop (depending on who issued a private foundation's foundation charter). The beneficiary was called a *charistikarios*, as well as a *pronoetes*, *prostates*, or *ephoros*, all terms emphasizing his function as supervisor and not as full proprietor. The beneficiary was supposed to wield administrative power over the monastic lands without interfering in religious affairs.[78]

In return the *charistikarios* enjoyed the usufruct of the religious foundation, drawing a profit from the monastic revenues. The historian and

[76] *ODB*, s.v. "adelphaton."

[77] On the *epidosis*, see P. Lemerle, "Un aspect du rôle des monastères à Byzance: les monastères donnés à des laïcs, les charisticaires," in Lemerle, *Le monde de Byzance* (London, 1978), no. xv, 16 note 2. *ODB*, s.v. "charistikion." J. Thomas, *Private Religious Foundations in the Byzantine Empire* (Washington, D.C., 1987), 58, 115, 150–51, 170. S. Varnalides, *῾Ο θεσμὸς τῆς Χαριστικῆς (Δωρεᾶς) τῶν μοναστηρίων εἰς τοὺς Βυζαντινούς* (Thessaloniki, 1985), 239–40.

[78] Varnalides, *῾Ο θεσμὸς τῆς Χαριστικῆς*, 239. Lemerle, "Un aspect du rôle des monastères à Byzance," 23. Thomas, *Private Religious Foundations*, 157.

scholar Michael Psellos, who had at least five *charistikai* in various areas of the empire, described the terms of his tenure of one *charistike*: "If I do for the monastery everything that is needed – buy meat, plant vineyards, change the course of a river, regulate the irrigation, set [matters] in motion on land and on sea – I shall obtain 100 measures of fish, twice that the best barley and as much olives as I wish."[79] It is easy to see that there was much room for abuse with such an institution. In 999 the governor of Byzantine Italy granted a monastery to a man as a reward for his service against the Arabs. The man was to hold the monastery for life; afterwards, it would pass to his son.[80]

From the late 990s through the eleventh century ecclesiastical objections were frequent. A series of patriarchs, bishops, and founders of monasteries condemned either abuses of the practice or the practice itself. The main complaint was that the system of giving monasteries to laymen led to the ruin of monasteries.[81] The most extensive of these attacks on the *charistike* was a treatise written sometime between 1085 and 1092 by John Oxeites, the patriarch of Antioch. He railed against the practice of emperors granting pious foundations to laymen. The purpose of such grants, he explained, was "by origin, I suppose, solicitous" (ἐξ αἰτίας δῆθεν προνοητικῆς), that is, for the benefit of the foundation, but by John's day nearly all monasteries, with the exception of recent foundations still in the hands of their founders, had come into the hands of *charistikarioi*, and the purpose of these grants was to enrich the layman at the expense of the monastery or other religious foundation so granted. He provides an example of the document issued pursuant to such a grant: "My Majesty, or our Mediocrity [if granted by the patriarch], grants to you *X* monastery *A* . . . with all its rights and privileges and the properties belonging to it, both immovable and its other incomes for the course of your life, or for two generations."[82]

[79] Trans. from M. Sjuzjumov, "Problemy ikonoborčestva v Vizantii," *Učenye zapiski Sverdlovskogo pedagogičeskogo instituta* 4 (1948), 90. Skabalanovič, *Vizantijskoe gosudarstvo*, 259.

[80] F. Trinchera, *Syllabus graecarum membranarum* (Naples, 1865), no. 10. Thomas, *Private Religious Foundations*, 159. Varnalides, *Ὁ θεσμὸς τῆς Χαριστικῆς*, 140, did not consider the 999 grant a *charistike* because it did not correspond to "the known canonical form" of the institution. But if a grant to a layman of a monastery was not a *charistike*, what was it?

[81] Thomas, *Private Religious Foundations*, 160, 168–69, 180. Kazhdan, *Agrarnye otnošenija*, 209, 211. F. Uspenskij, "Mnenija i postanovlenija," *IRAIK* 5 (1900), 16.13, 9.5. Skabalanovič, *Vizantijskoe gosudarstvo*, 422. P. Gautier, *La diataxis de Michel Attaleiate* (Paris, 1981), 33.250–52. Lemerle, *Cinq études*, 79. S. Eustratiades, "Τυπικὸν τῆς ἐν Κωνσταντινουπόλει Μονῆς τοῦ Ἁγίου μεγαλομάρτυρος Μάμαντος," *Ἑλληνικά* 1 (1928), 257.18–20.

[82] P. Gautier, "Réquisitoire du patriarche Jean d'Antioche contre le charisticariat," *REB* 33 (1975), 107.254; 109–10, lines 280–85: Ἡ βασιλεία μου, ἢ ἡ μετριότης ἡμῶν, δωρεῖταί σοι τῷ δεῖνι τὴν δεῖνα μονὴν . . . μετὰ πάντων τῶν δικαίων καὶ προνομίων αὐτῆς καὶ τῶν ὑπ' αὐτὴν

Many scholars view the institution of *charistike* as fundamentally a tool of political patronage, almost entirely divorced from any religious function. H. Ahrweiler simply linked the *charistike* with grants of *sekreta*, noting that both were gifts made to members of the imperial family, the close entourage of emperor, or very high officials. At the extreme end of the spectrum, Hohlweg considered the *charistike* as a kind of precursor to the institution of pronoia by which the economic resources of monasteries were transferred to relatives of the emperor or officials so that the state could rid itself of certain financial burdens.[83] This is like saying that, because many modern holders of public offices use their positions to enrich themselves, the purpose of public offices is to enrich the officeholder. Into this camp one places the many scholars who view the *charistike* as similar or analogous to the Carolingian *beneficium*, which, in the traditional sense of a grant of church lands to a vassal, was an institution which no one could argue was for the benefit of the religious foundation.[84]

In an attempt to rehabilitate the scholarly view of the institution Soterios Varnalides identified three forms of *charistikai* which developed over time. The aim of the first was the repair, conservation, and care of ruined and poor monasteries and their immovable property. Later, from around the second quarter of the eleventh century the emphasis shifted to safeguarding the religious character of monasteries by freeing the monks from concern about financial matters. Finally, in the second half of the eleventh century, beginning during the reign of Isaac I Komnenos, the *charistike* increasingly was the subject of abuse, as grants were made, especially by the emperor, to individuals for their own benefit, not for that of the monasteries. So desirous was Varnalides to differentiate the "genuine" canonical form of

κτημάτων, ἀκινήτων τε καὶ λοιπῶν προσόδων αὐτῆς ἐπὶ ὅρῳ ζωῆς σου, ἢ ἐπὶ δυσὶ προσώποις. Varnalides, *ʽΟ θεσμὸς τῆς Χαριστικῆς*, 199 note 500. Thomas, *Private Religious Foundations*, 167, 186–92. Lemerle, "Un aspect du rôle des monastères," 17.

83 Ahrweiler, "La concession des droits incorporels," 107–08. Varnalides, *ʽΟ θεσμὸς τῆς Χαριστικῆς*, 245. Hohlweg, *Beiträge zur Verwaltungsgeschichte*, 84. And see D. Xanalatos, *Beiträge zur Wirtschafts- und Sozialgeschichte Makedoniens im Mittelalter, hauptsächlich auf Grund der Briefe des Erzbischofs Theophylaktos von Achrida* (Speyer, 1937), 32–35.

84 F. Uspenskij, *Očerki po istorii Vizantijskoj obrazovannosti* (St. Petersburg, 1892), 258. A. Vasiliev, "On the Question of Byzantine Feudalism," *Byz* 8 (1933), 587. Charanis, "Monastic Properties," 72. F. Dölger, "Der Feudalismus in Byzanz," in *Studien zum mittelalterlichen Lehenswesen, Vorträge und Forschungen*, v (Lindau and Constance, 1960), 188. G. Ostrogorsky, "Agrarian Conditions in the Byzantine Empire in the Middle Ages," *The Cambridge Economic History of Europe*, 2nd edn., ed. M. Postan, I (Cambridge, 1966), 225. R. Boutruche, *Seigneurie et féodalité, II: L'apogée* (Paris, 1970), 356. For an opposing view, see Sjuzjumov, "Problemy ikonoborčestva v Vizantii," 90–91.

the *charistike* from these later abuses, that he refers to this third form as a "pseudo-*charistike*."[85]

John Thomas, on the other hand, emphasizes the distinction between benevolent and rapacious *charistikarioi*, regardless of the reason they received their *charistikai*. Thus, there were rapacious *charistikarioi* from the beginning. To some extent they are both right. No doubt there were always avaricious *charistikarioi*. But there is a true difference in degree once the state with its practical and moral authority supports the granting of *charistikai* for the purpose of benefitting the recipient rather than the religious foundation in question. Indeed, it is reasonable to think that Alexios I, as well as his immediate predecessors, when considering ways to reward and win the loyalty of supporters and other aristocrats without a direct outlay of gold, would view the *charistike* as a logical source of benefits to exploit.

Despite the criticism, the institution of *charistike* continued to exist. Theodore Valsamon, writing in the last quarter of the twelfth century, states that *charistikai* and *epidoseis* were still granted occasionally in his own day, and Eustathios of Thessaloniki (d. ca. 1194) defended the practice, arguing that the institution freed monks from temporal concerns.[86] After 1204 the term *charistike* disappears, but the system of *charistike* was preserved up until the fourteenth century. Around 1238 Nikephoros Vlemmydes owned (κέκτηται) a monastery "for his partial assistance by consequence of the *logos* [i.e., imperial order] to him."[87] In a letter from around 1300 Maximos Planoudes refers to a monastery in Bithynia which the bishop of Chalcedon "gave . . . to me to own for life." In 1302 Andronikos II granted a monk the right to possess for life a monastery in Linovrocheion. In a synodal decision of 1317/8 the metropolitan of Attaleia complained that in his metropolis some clerics and lay people, who had received properties from local monasteries "in order to reconstitute and improve these," transferred these properties by heredity and even gave them in dowry, with the result that the monasteries suffered.[88] And the teacher Theodore Hyrtakenos once

[85] Varnalides, *Ὁ θεσμὸς τῆς Χαριστικῆς*, 133–46, 240–41, 246. Cf. Ostrogorsky, "Le grand domaine dans l'Empire byzantin," *Recueils de la société Jean Bodin, IV, Le Domaine* (Wetteren, 1949), 46–47, and Hohlweg, *Beiträge zur Verwaltungsgeschichte*, 84.

[86] Thomas, *Private Religious Foundations*, 233. Varnalides, *Ὁ θεσμὸς τῆς Χαριστικῆς*, 242.

[87] *Theodori Ducae Lascaris Epistulae CCXVII*, ed. N. Festa (Florence, 1898), no. 107, p. 147.25–26: εἰς μερικὴν αὐτοῦ ἐξυπηρεσίαν διὰ τὸ περιὸν τοῦ ἐν αὐτῷ λόγου. Also referred to in *Nicephori Blemmydae Curriculum Vitae et Carmina*, ed. A. Heisenberg (Leipzig, 1896), 33.13–15. C. Constantinides, *Higher Education in Byzantium in the Thirteenth and Early Fourteenth Centuries (1204–ca.1310)* (Nicosia, 1982), 17, who cited both of these references, wrote of this as a pronoia grant.

[88] *Maximi monachi Planudis epistulae*, ed. M. Treu (Breslau, 1886–90; repr. Amsterdam, 1960), no. 24, p. 41.29–30: καὶ γὰρ δεσπόζειν αὐτοῦ διὰ βίου μοι παντὸς ὁ Χαλκηδόνος ἐξέδοτο,

asked Patriarch John Glykys to grant him a monastery (*monydrion*) near Kyzikos.[89]

The similarities between the *charistike* and the early pronoia grant cannot be denied. The *charistike* was a grant of limited, personal, temporary, precarious, conditional possession. An 1163 council of Constantinople declared that the grant of a *charistike* was not a gift but a loan: οὐ δωρεαστικῶς . . . ἀλλὰ μισθωτικῶς. Mihail Sjuzjumov considered both *charistike* and pronoia as forms of conditional possession (*possessio sub modo*) in which the beneficiary enjoyed the rights of usufruct (a *ius in re aliena*). And Varnalides asked whether his "pseudo-*charistike*" was a forerunner or a model or at least an inspiration for the institution of pronoia. Certainly, the rather vague definition of the *Zavorda Treatise*, "the things granted by the emperor for the lifetime of the man," fits the imperial *charistike*, even if the evidence of the other sources from the twelfth century does not.[90]

In particular, some scholars have focused on the area of terminology, suggesting that the word *pronoia* was used at times as a synonym for *charistike*.[91] The evidence for this is actually quite weak. Hohlweg, for example, claimed that Michael Attaleiates employs the word *pronoia* for the *charistike* in the *Diataxis* for the almshouse founded by him: "toward him who has the pronoia and ownership of the said pious houses organized by me" (πρὸς τῷ ἔχειν καὶ τὴν πρόνοιαν καὶ τὴν κυριότητα). First, I do not think that Attaleiates was referring to *charistike* in the passage, but rather, to the transfer of the founder's right to his successors. But even if Attaleiates did have *charistike* in mind here, anyone who wants to see *pronoia* as a synonym for

cited by Constantinides, *Higher Education*, 68, who considered it a pronoia grant. *Lavra*, II, no. 94, cited by A. Kazhdan, "The Fate of the Intellectual in Byzantium A Propos of *Society and Intellectual Life in Late Byzantium* by Ihor Ševčenko," *The Greek Orthodox Theological Review* 27/1 (1982), 88–89. H. Hunger and O. Kresten, *Das Register des Patriarchats von Konstantinopel*, I (Vienna, 1981), no. 53.8 = MM, I, 77.

89 F. J. G. La Porte-du Theil, "Notices et extraits d'un volume de la Bibliothèque Nationale, coté MCCIX parmi les manuscrits grecs, et contenant les opuscules et lettres anecdotes de Théodôre l'Hyrtacènien," *Notices et Extraits des Manuscrits de la Bibliothèque Nationale, et autres bibliothèques* 6 (1800), 29, no. 67. Constantinides, *Higher Education*, 95, considered this as a request for a pronoia. S. Kourouses, "Ὁ λόγιος οἰκουμενικὸς πατριάρχης Ἰωάννης ΙΓ΄ ὁ Γλυκύς," *ΕΕΒΣ* 41 (1974), 347–50, correctly links it to the *charistike*.

90 Uspenskij, "Mnenija," 34–35. M. Sjuzjumov, "Suvernitet, nalog i zemelnaja renta v Vizantii," *Antičnaja drevnost' i srednie veka* 9 (1973), 62. Varnalides, *Ὁ θεσμὸς τῆς Χαριστικῆς*, 164, 244. 246. Ostrogorsky, *Féodalité*, 18–19.

91 Vasiliev, "On the Question of Byzantine Feudalism," 589–90; Ostrogorsky, *Féodalité*, 18; Varnalides, *Ὁ θεσμὸς τῆς Χαριστικῆς*, 161; and Kazhdan, "Formen," 219, *Agrarnye otnošenija*, 209, and *Derevnja i gorod*, 105 and note 189.

charistike based on the passage must also conclude that "ownership" (*kyriotes*) was a synonym as well. Instead, care and ownership were simply aspects of the trusteeship of a religious foundation. The only times Attaleiates uses the word *charistikarios* (*charistike* does not appear) are when he writes about his and his son's rights as *charistikarioi* over certain foundations that evidently they themselves did not found, and when he specifically states that he wishes no *charistikarios* ever to control a particular foundation. These passages do not contain any reference to the word *pronoia* at all.[92]

Moreover, there were important differences between the *charistike* and the early pronoia grant. The *charistike*, as originally developed, was intended for the benefit of the thing granted, that is, the monastery or other foundation; the pronoia grant was for the benefit of the grantee and the grantor. *Charistikai* were granted by the emperor, but also by the clergy – patriarchs, metropolitans, and other bishops – while pronoiai were granted solely by the emperor. Consequently, pronoia grants could consist only of things that the emperor had direct control over (fiscal liabilities, imperial properties), while the *charistike* often involved religious foundations that were not under the control of the central government. Most early pronoia grants seem to have been connected with military service, an element completely lacking in the *charistike*. And, fundamentally, pronoia grants never involved granting someone the right to manage the property of a monastery, even a monastery owned by the emperor.[93]

Granting that *charistike* and pronoia were different, did the former serve as at least an inspiration for the latter? As I argued in Chapter 2, the phrase *eis pronoian*, commonly found in early pronoia grants, indicates that the grant was for the maintenance of the grantee. When eleventh-century writers linked the word *pronoia* with the *charistike*, the recipient of the "care" was the religious foundation involved. Thus, the equivalent of the religious foundation granted as a *charistike* was not the state land or tax revenues granted to the pronoia holder, but the pronoia holder himself. I think this disjuncture in terminology makes it difficult to posit a direct link, through terminology, between the two institutions, as well as a cognitive connection. Or, to view things from a slightly different angle, however one regards *charistikarioi* – as pious and devoted administrators or as avaricious

92 Gautier, *Diataxis*, 85.1112–13. Hohlweg, "Zur Frage der Pronoia," 295–96, and cf. Ostrogorsky, *Féodalité*, 22–23, and "Die Pronoia unter den Komnenen," 43. Gautier, *Diataxis*, 47.508–10,511–14, 33.250–52. And cf. the parallel of *charistikarios* and *pronoetes*, as discussed toward the end of Chapter 1 above.

93 Charanis, "Monastic Properties," 88. Varnalides, *῾Ο θεσμὸς τῆς Χαριστικῆς*, 164–66. Ahrweiler, "La 'pronoia' à Byzance," 684. Ostrogorsky, *Féodalité*, 19.

courtiers – is there any way to fit into this perception the Cumans of Moglena? On the whole, I think the only link between *charistike* and pronoia is found in three rather general elements: (i) the exploitation of new sources of revenue by the emperors, particularly Alexios I, (ii) the element of a lifetime grant, and (iii) the broad conception of caring implied by the word *pronoia*.

Related to the *charistike* was the so-called founder's right (*ktetoreia*), the collection of rights to which a layman who founded a religious foundation was entitled. This existed since the beginning of the empire and included the right to draw an income from the foundation, to administer it, and even to alienate it. Michael Attaleiates in his *Diataxis* mentions the right of his son and successor to two-thirds of the income of the almshouse founded by him in Rhaidestos. It is not really a type of grant (since there is no grantor), but an aspect of property law, enshrined by tradition and accommodated by church law. Nevertheless I mention it here for several reasons. First, just as with the *charistike*, the founder's right was at times limited to a certain number of generations. Second, the terminology of *charistike* and founder's right are quite similar. Indeed, the *charistike* can be viewed as a partial transfer of the founder's right to a third party, without the right to alienate the foundation. Third, references to the founder's right often use the word *pronoia*. Attaleiates calls the power of the founder "trusteeship, ownership, and pronoia [i.e., care]" (τῆς ἐφορείας, καὶ κυριότητος καὶ προνοίας). This, as we saw with the *charistike*, is an example of a series of words being used to define the sense of an institution.[94]

One of the very few references to lifetime grants that do *not* involve a monastery is found in a novel issued by Michael VII Doukas (1071–78). The novel itself is lost; only the rubric is preserved. It states that "anyone receiving *kastra*, howsoever they receive these, these are to be held for only one generation, and in such manner the grants should be enjoyed." While some scholars once regarded this as a reference to pronoiai, Oikonomides

[94] Thomas, *Private Religious Foundations*, 53–58. Gautier, *Diataxis*, 53.611. *ODB*, s.v. "ktetor." This similarity was alluded to by I. Sokolov, "Materialy po zemel'no-hozjajstvennomu bytu Vizantii," *Izvestija Akademii nauk SSSR, otdelenie obščestvennyh nauk* (1931), no. 6, 705–06. M. Sjuzjumov, "Vnutrennjaja politika Andronika Komnina i razgrom prigorodov Konstantinopolja v 1187 godu," *VizVrem* 12 (1957), 60 note 10, cites the founder's right as an example of how, under certain circumstances, the inalienable (church property) could be alienated. Gautier, *Diataxis*, 37.318–19. Kazhdan, *Agrarnye otnošenija*, 210, and *Derevnja i gorod*, 109–10. A further development was the institution of "honorary founders," encountered only in the fourteenth century: see Thomas, *Private Religious Foundations*, 252–53. On the institution of *ephoreia*, similar to the charistike, see *ODB*, s.v. "ephoros"; H. Ahrweiler, "Charisticariat et autres formes d'attribution de donations pieuses aux xe–xie siècles," *ZRVI* 10 (1967), 3–4; and Thomas, *Private Religious Foundations*, 218, 220, 258, 261.

has offered the most reasonable interpretation of the title, suggesting that it had nothing to do with pronoia, but rather the attribution of fortifications to persons able to hold them for the protection of territory and peasants.[95] Even though Oikonomides speculated that the new owner of the castle may have received certain taxes such as *kastroktisia*, it is important to note that the intent of such grants was not to provide direct economic benefit to its recipient (as was the case with *solemnia*, imperial *charistikai*, and, of course, pronoiai). It was primarily the right of physical possession of a defensive structure.[96] It was only because imperial policy dictated that these rights were to be held only for life, as a chrysobull of Alexios I from 1087 reiterates, that the grant was conditional.[97]

The novel suggests ("howsoever they receive these") that there were numerous ways to acquire a *kastron*. Ostensibly, a man could build one through his own means, acquire one through a private transaction (purchase, gift, etc.) or through an imperial grant, or take possession of an abandoned fortification. There is no evidence of this policy being enforced. In fact, both Gregory and Apasios Pakourianos donated *kastra* to the monastery founded by Gregory. This does raise the question whether the novel applied only to fortifications the emperor granted to someone and not to fortifications that one built oneself *[4.2]*.

Attaching soldiers to the land

The earliest known holders of pronoiai were probably the soldiers Andreas Romanos Rentinos and the brothers Theotimos and Leo Loukites who received their grant or grants sometime before 1119 *[2.3]*. One of the main uses of the early pronoia grant, according to Choniates and according to the documentary evidence, was to finance soldiers without relying on cash disbursements. To the degree that the early pronoia grant was a military institution, it had parallels in the institution of the military lands (*stratiotika*

95 Zepos, *JGR*, I, 282.7–9 = Zachariä, *Jus*, III, 330: Νεαρὰ τοῦ βασιλέως κυροῦ Μιχαὴλ τοῦ Δούκα θεσπίζουσα τοὺς κάστρα λαμβάνοντας οἱουσδήτινας κἂν ὅπως ταῦτα λάβωσιν, ἐφ' ἑνὶ προσώπῳ ταῦτα κεκτῆσθαι, καὶ οὕτω νοεῖσθαι τὰς δωρεάς. Dölger, *Regesten*, II, no. 1012. Uspenskij, "Značenie," 5, 14; Skabalanovič, *Vizantijskoe gosudarstvo*, 264; Ostrogorsky, *Féodalité*, 23–24; and cf. Hohlweg, "Zur Frage der Pronoia," 297. N. Oikonomides, "The Donation of Castles in the Last Quarter of the 11th Century," in Oikonomides, *Documents et études sur les institutions de Byzance* (London, 1976), no. XIV, 413–17. Ostrogorsky, "Die Pronoia unter den Komnenen," 43, and Lemerle, *Cinq études*, 311 note 122, accepted this interpretation.

96 For this reason, Ahrweiler's attempt ("La concession des droits incorporels," 106–07 and nn. 20, 22) to link the grant to a kind of *solemnion* is superfluous.

97 *Patmos*, I, no. 5.50–51: τὰς δωρεὰς τῶν κάστρων . . . ἐφ' ἑνὶ νοεῖσθαι καὶ μόνῳ προσώπῳ.

ktemata) and the practice of settling ethnic soldiers on smallholdings in colonies.

The system of military lands had certain similarities to the early pronoia grant. Obviously in both institutions soldiers were attached to land from which they derived their livelihoods. However, when compared to the early military lands there was an important difference. To borrow an image from Paul Magdalino, the soldier (*stratiotes*) of the thematic armies lived *on* the land; the pronoia soldier *off* the land.[98] The early military land system was more suited to financing infantry who could, possibly, work their own estates and hence live on the land.

The twelfth-century pronoia soldier, however, was not an infantryman. He was a cavalry soldier. There is no other way to explain why there was a need for numbers of paroikoi to support the soldier, to allow him to live *off* the land. In addition to maintaining a somewhat larger quantity of military equipment, the cavalryman required several horses (probably at least three per soldier), which were an enormous expense to acquire and maintain. Given that a horse requires about five or six times the caloric intake of a man, each cavalryman had to have the resources to support the equivalent of a good-sized peasant family for each horse he owned. If Manuel I's pronoia soldiers were intended to be heavy cavalry, they would have been outfitted at least as elaborately as later tenth-century heavy cavalry (*kataphraktoi*) after Nikephoros II Phokas' reform. As for the latter, Warren Treadgold estimates that the estates of these each required the labor of at least seven men.[99]

Thus, the better parallel to the twelfth-century pronoia grant is the military lands as reformed by Nikephoros Phokas, with an emphasis on cavalry. During his reign it became common for groups of peasants occupying military lands to support a single cavalryman, who essentially now lived *off* the land.

While we can say that the institution of military lands (*stratiotika ktemata*), in one form or another, was a precursor of the institution of pronoia, it is quite inconceivable that it was any kind of inspiration. A generation had passed since the thematic militias had played any significant role in the defense of the empire, and what was left of the thematic armies were standing salaried forces anyway. Alexios liked centralized control, and the armies generated by the military lands were decentralized.

98 Magdalino, "The Byzantine Army and the Land," 15.

99 W. Treadgold, *Byzantium and Its Army, 284–1081* (Stanford, Calif., 1995), 174. This explains why the Prosalentai (rowers) and Thelematarioi of the late thirteenth century were not generally pronoia holders but rather smallholding soldiers; they did not fight with horses: Bartusis, *Late Byzantine Army*, 158–59.

John Haldon describes how from the early tenth century an increase in the forces defending the capital and an increase in the recruitment of mercenaries, followed by a fiscalization of military service among households that owed service (*strateia*), led to the "increasing irrelevance" of the thematic militias. By the middle of the eleventh century there was a general fiscalization of the *strateia* as Constantine Monomachos commuted the service of the last remaining border militias for a cash payment.[100]

All of which leads me to conclude that Alexios I thought of the pronoia grant as a way to reward or compensate imperial servants rather than as a way to increase the size of the army. In other words, he conceived of it as a fiscal institution rather than a military institution. Given the limited extent of the institution during Alexios' reign, and given the fact that Alexios, despite a lack of cash, fielded armies composed primarily of mercenary forces, supplemented by some foreign smallholding soldiers, it seems he saw no great advantage in tying soldiers to the land. This probably also explains why the early pronoia grant was not hereditary. Perhaps some early grants to soldiers were hereditary; the possibility cannot be excluded. These might have carried a hereditary service obligation, or perhaps they might have been simply rewards to distinguished soldiers. But hereditary grants with hereditary service would have led down the road of the *stratiotika ktemata*, which in the eleventh century no longer proved to be an effective way to raise cavalry.

If anything, the smallholding ethnic soldiers were a greater inspiration than the thematic soldiers and their military lands. Alexios had utilized this concept successfully in regard to the Pechenegs. In fact the early twelfth-century pronoia grant was a kind of amalgam of the grant to Andronikos Doukas, the *charistike*, and the smallholding grant.

The possibility of external inspiration

There was a time, quite a long time really, when it was possible to suggest that the idea of the pronoia grant was inspired by western European feudalism and the fief in particular. Beginning with Fedor Uspenskij in 1883,

[100] J. Haldon, "Military Service, Military Lands, and the Status of Soldiers: Current Problems and Interpretations," in Haldon, *State, Army and Society in Byzantium* (Aldershot, 1995), no. VII, 49–52, 60. See as well, J. Haldon, "Approaches to an Alternative Military History of the Period ca. 1025–1071," in *Η Αυτοκρατορία σε Κρίση(;) Το βυζάντιο τον 11ο αιώνα (1025–1081)* (Athens, 2003), 45–74.

numerous scholars made this connection.[101] However, the evidence is purely circumstantial. Alexios I Komnenos was familiar with some western practices and at times adopted them. As is well known, he required the nobles of the First Crusade to swear oaths and become his "liege-men" (*lizioi*), and he adopted the couched lance for his cavalry. It would be surprising if Alexios I, through his contact in 1097 with the nobles of the First Crusade or earlier, during the 1080s, in his campaigns against the Normans, had not learned something about fiefs. Evidence of even greater western influence appears with Manuel I: the western triangular shield was adopted by the Byzantine cavalry, and the tournament appears at the Byzantine court. Many Latins were in Manuel's service; some received land grants from Manuel and they regarded them as fiefs.[102]

One might question why Byzantium in the later eleventh or early tweflth century would have looked to the "backward" medieval West as an inspiration for anything. Both Uspenskij and Hohlweg suggested that perhaps Manuel I was arranging the pay and service of his Latin soldiers in a manner that was familiar to them. And yet none of the known twelfth-century pronoia holders (Chapter 2) was a Latin.

But for the West to have inspired Byzantium in the creation of the pronoia, there would need to have been something that could have been the source of the inspiration. Did western Europe during the later eleventh and twelfth centuries have institutions that paralleled the twelfth-century pronoia grant? If we use the *Zavorda Treatise*'s definition, that "*pronoiatika*" were things given to someone by the emperor for life, the answer, as we currently understand matters western European, might well be no. In her influential book *Fiefs and Vassals*, Susan Reynolds argued that there is little evidence for a widespread practice involving kings or other laymen handing out temporary grants of property to free men, let alone to men who, on the basis of such a grant, were now obligated to perform military service. Temporary

101 Uspenskij, "Značenie," 5–6; Skabalanovič, *Vizantijskoe gosudarstvo*, 265–66 and 266 note 1; E. Darkó, "La militarizzazione dell'Impero Bizantino," *Atti del V Congresso internazionale bizantini*, Rome 1936, I = *Studi bizantini e neoellenici* 5 (1939), 96; F. Dölger, "Die Frage des Grundeigentums in Byzanz," in Dölger, *Byzanz und die europäische Staatenwelt* (Ettal, 1953), 228, and "Die mittelalterliche Kultur auf dem Balkan als byzantinisches Erbes," in *Byzanz und die europäische Staatenwelt*, 271; Hohlweg, "Zur Frage der Pronoia," 301; and Angold, *Byzantine Empire*, 149. On why there are no Marxists in this list, see M. Mladenovič, "Zur Frage der Pronoia und des Feudalismus im byzantinischen Reiche," *Südost-Forschungen* 15 (1956), 127.

102 *ODB*, s.v. "armor," "sports," "lizios." T. Kolias, *Byzantinische Waffen: ein Beitrag zur byzantinischen Waffenkunde von den Anfängen bis zur lateinischen Eroberung* (Vienna, 1988), 114–17, 121–22, 204–08. Angold, *Byzantine Empire*, 258. Bartusis, *Late Byzantine Army*, 326–27, 329.

grants are mostly found in regard to grants of church property by rulers or by the church, which is more reminiscent of *charistike*.[103]

Another possibility is that the pronoia was influenced by Arab or Persian institutions via the Seljuk Turks. The *iqta* – sometimes viewed as a grant of land, sometimes a grant of tax revenues – had many manifestations at different times in different Muslim societies. There is much uncertainty about the nature of the *iqta* among the Seljuks, particularly whether they were building on classical Islamic, Persian, or Mongol institutions. The current view tends to favor the conception of the Seljuk *iqta* as a fixed concession of fiscal revenues quantified by a monetary sum.[104] If this was the case, then it is not possible that the twelfth-century Byzantine pronoia derived from the Seljuk *iqta*. This is because the twelfth-century pronoia grant was a concession of exempt peasants and a quantity of state land, not a concession of fiscal revenue quantified by a monetary amount. (The monetary quantification of pronoia grants would not occur until the thirteenth century: see Chapter 6.) Thus, our present understanding of the institutions of Byzantium's neighbors affords little reason to see foreign influence in the origin of the pronoia grant.

Alexios I Komnenos displayed a great deal of creativity in his internal policies.

Numerous methods were used to provide a reward or an income to someone without resorting to a cash disbursement. He exploited every tool at his disposal and he had many ideas to draw upon. One point that must be emphasized is that these procedures were novel only in their combinations and in their scale. Somewhere in the midst of all these other varieties of grants was created a new variation of the grant of an *episkepsis*, distinguished by the lower social level of its recipients and by the specific limitation that it was to be held only for the lifetime of its recipient. The first characteristic – the lower social status of the recipients – was a natural and predictable consequence of the expansion of the procedure. The second characteristic – the lifetime element – is a bit more difficult to explain. Here we have to consider the difference in the nature of a grant from the emperor held by an aristocrat and such a grant held by a person of lesser status. Formally, grants to those of high status were held at the emperor's pleasure (as in the case of *sekreta*), or for life (such as with Constantine Leichoudes), or forever (as

[103] S. Reynolds, *Fiefs and Vassals, The Medieval Evidence Reinterpreted* (Oxford, 1994), e.g., 172–73, 254, 477, and index, s.v. "temporary grants."

[104] E.g., J. Barnes, *An Introduction to Religious Foundations in the Ottoman Empire* (Leiden and New York, 1987), 27, and B. McGowan, *Economic Life in Ottoman Europe: Taxation, Trade and the Struggle for Land, 1600–1800* (Cambridge, Eng., 1981), 49.

with Andronikos Doukas). However, in practice, the grant would be held until an emperor withdrew it (either the granting emperor or a successor). Political reasons came into play with such grants. Less so with the grants to less exalted individuals. For these, it was less likely for the emperor to wish to remove them from their grants.

It could be said that the development of pronoia was incremental, with no clear dividing line between the grants of *episkepseis* and *klasmata* to "important" people, and the grants of similar things, though on a much smaller scale, to much more humble recipients, including soldiers. What began as a series of special arrangements for the highest officials and generals and for the closest friends and relatives of the emperor gradually was applied to lower persons. In this sense the grants to Andronikos Doukas, to Leo Kephalas, perhaps even to Constantine IX's mistress, could be regarded as early examples, or antecedents of pronoiai, a kind of "proto-pronoia" perhaps. At certain undefinable points there were shifts from "special arrangement" to "frequent practice" to "institution." On the other hand, the moment the emperor made a grant of an *episkepsis* to a layman with the understanding that it was to be held only for life, a bridge was crossed.

The twelfth century after Alexios I

The early pronoia grant did not supplant any of the many Byzantine institutions described above. *Charistikai* were still granted, as were other lifetime and hereditary grants. Through the twelfth century the pronoia grant was simply one more type of grant, and it does not seem to have been a very important one. Curiously, during the second half of Alexios' reign through the reign of his son John II (1118–43), there are very few references to grants to laymen at all. Chapter 2 discussed "the pronoia of the deceased Synadenos" *[2.2]*, which had been granted by either Alexios I and John II, but other than this, during the whole of John II's twenty-five-year reign, there is no certain case of any kind of grant to a layman. This is surprising, if we assume that John would have continued Alexios' policies. The three non-pronoia grants we can link to John's reign are dubious, hypothetical, or not securely linkable to John: (i) Sometime before her death in 1144 Maria Tzousmene, daughter of John II and wife of the *kaisar* John Rogerios, donated property in the area of Hierissos to the monastery of Xeropotamou. Since John Rogerios outlived his wife, this property was almost certainly Maria's in her own right, and since Xeropotamou was obliged to pay a tax of five hyperpyra on this land, it is likely that Maria paid this as well.

Michael Hendy suggested that she be added to the list of important persons who received imperial grants under the Komnenoi. Yet we cannot say for sure that she received the property from her father or her brother Manuel I (immediately before her death); she may simply have purchased it. (ii) According to a vague passage in the history of Kinnamos, before death intervened John II had planned to grant Cilicia, Antioch, Attaleia, and Cyprus to his son Manuel. This is the first mention of the idea to grant an heir to the throne entire provinces. (iii) In the 1152 *typikon* for the monastery of Kosmosoteira near Ainos in Thrace we read of the vast number of properties that the *sevastokrator* Isaac Komnenos, third son of Alexios I, bequeathed to the monastery he was founding. Isaac, either through inheritance or through a grant from Alexios I (Isaac was in his mid-twenties at the time of his father's death) or his brother John II, was receiving the fiscal revenues of these villages, and probably the others listed in the praktikon.[105]

In some sense it is understandable that the number of grants to laymen should have diminished following the reign of Alexios I. All of the grants made by Alexios I for which we have any information were hereditary. Thus, Alexios created the fortunes of the various branches of the Komnenos family and his in-laws. There was less need for John II and Manuel I to fashion new grants. With the reign of Manuel I (1143–80), there is no great increase in the number of grants to "important" laymen.

(i) Manuel I made a number of grants to Alexios I's grandson Andronikos Komnenos, the future Andronikos I. First, the historian Kinnamos describes how Manuel I in 1153 treated him after his carelessness led to a Byzantine military defeat. While the emperor privately berated him, in public he honored Andronikos: "Indeed he then appointed [him] *doux* of Niš and Braničevo and also gave him Kastoria." Lj. Maksimović has remarked on the geographical distance between Niš–Braničevo and Kastoria, and on Kinnamos' distinction between Andronikos being "appointed" *doux* and being "given" Kastoria. While it is imprudent to make any firm conclusions regarding so brief a passage, it seems likely that Andronikos did not hold Kastoria in an administrative capacity. In fact what little information Kinnamos provides would be consistent with Manuel I granting his cousin the fiscal revenues in the area of Kastoria. More cannot be said.[106] Later,

[105] *Xéropotamou*, no. 8.13–14. Hendy, *Studies*, 86 note 60. Kinnamos, *Ioannis Cinnami epitome*, ed. A. Meineke (Bonn, 1836), 23.1–3. Ahrweiler, *Byzance et la mer*, 218 note 4. G. Papazoglou, *Τυπικὸν Ἰσαακίου Ἀλεξίου Κομνηνοῦ τῆς Μονῆς Θεοτόκου τῆς Κοσμοσωτείρας (1151/52)* (Komotini, 1994), lines 1248–76.

[106] Kinnamos, III.16: Bonn edn., 124.20–22: ἀμέλει καὶ τότε Ναϊσσοῦ τὲ καὶ Βρανιτζόβης προκεχείριστο δοῦκα προσέτι καὶ Καστορίαν αὐτοῦ ἔδοκεν. Maksimović, "Geneza i karakter

according to Kinnamos, Manuel I "granted that Cyprus be taxed by him," and Choniates states that he was "collecting the tribute of Cyprus, so that he could draw off expenses there." And finally, according to Eustathios of Thessaloniki, "he had been allotted the land of Paphlagonia, to be military commander there and enrich himself at their expense." Except for the reference to military authority, all of this sounds rather similar to Alexios I's grant to his brother Adrian.[107]

(ii) In some cases it is unclear whether a particular, important individual received a grant from the Komnenoi emperors. For example, M. Hendy suggested that the *kaisar* John Rogerios, son-in-law of John II and brother-in-law of Manuel I, was the recipient of such a grant. In a praktikon from 1152 for the monastery of the Eleousa outside Strumica, the official who drew up the document refers to himself as "the servant (*doulos*) of my holy despot and lord the *kaisar*," and the document bears the "Sign of Michael Tzagkitzakes, . . . servant of my holy despot and lord the *kaisar*." He notes that a copy of the praktikon would be placed "in our despot's treasury (*vestiarion*)." The praktikon includes two inserted documents from the same year, both of which refer to this Michael as the "man" (*anthropos*) of the emperor's brother-in-law. This *kaisar* has to be John Rogerios and these documents indicate that he exercised some kind of semi-autonomous governmental authority in the area of Strumica. However, while it may be reasonable to assume that John was given imperial grants commensurate with his administrative responsibilities, this is not proved by these documents.[108]

apanaža," 115. Choniates (ed. van Dieten, I, 101.67 = Bonn edn., 133) makes no mention of Kastoria and notes that he was made *doux* of Braničevo and Belgrade. Hendy, *Studies*, 88.

107 Kinnamos, 250.5: καὶ Κύπρον αὐτῷ φορολογεῖσθαι ἔδωκεν. Choniates, ed. van Dieten 138.95–1 = Bonn edn., 180: καὶ τὴν τῆς Κύπρου δασμολογίαν προσειληφώς, ὡς ἔχοι τὰς δαπάνας ἐκεῖθεν ἀντλεῖν. Eustathios, *The Capture of Thessaloniki*, ed. J. R. M. Jones (Canberra, 1988), §21, p. 28.8–10: καὶ δεδωκὼς τὴν τῶν Παφλαγόνων ἀνετεκληρώσατο γῆν, ὡς καὶ στρατοπεδαρχεῖν ἐκεῖσε καὶ τὰ ἐκεῖθεν εἰς κέρδος ἀπονοσφίζεσθαι. All references cited by Ahrweiler, *Byzance et la mer*, 218 note 4.

108 Hendy, *Studies*, 88. L. Petit, "Le monastère de Notre-Dame de Pitié en Macédoine," *IRAIK* 6 (1900), 34.7–8, 46.3–5, 44.29–30, 35.13–14, 36.24–26. B. Ferjančić, "Apanažni posed kesara Jovana Rogerija," *ZRVI* 12 (1970), 193–201. Weak evidence for another possible example of an imperial grant to a relative is found in a Greek inscription dated 1164 from a monastic church in Nerezi, near Skopje, in Macedonia which states that Alexios Komnenos, the son of Alexios I's youngest daughter Theodora, had helped beautify the church: N. Kondakov, *Makedonija. Arheologičeskoe putešestvie* (St. Petersburg, 1909), 174, cited by Hendy, *Studies*, 89. There is a drawing of the inscription, along with further notes, in *SnM*, I, 90–91, although the printed transcription has errors. This Alexios may have been connected to this church because he received an imperial grant (from John II, Manuel I, or, less likely for chronological reasons, Alexios I) or inherited a grant received by his mother in the area. Alexios III Angelos' 1198 chrysobull for Venice does mention an *episkepsis* in the area of Skopje (*Prouincia Scopie cum*

(iii) The two documents allegedly issued by the *doux* of Crete, Constantine Doukas, from the 1180s or 1190s *[2.6]* possibly refer to grants made to individuals on Crete at some earlier date, including members of the Skordiles family, but the mangled versions of the documents that have passed down to us make it difficult to be sure about this.

(iv) According to the chronicle of the monk Aubrey of Trois-Fontaines, Alexios Angelos, the brother of Isaac II Angelos, was given the Voukoleon palace in Constantinople and its adjacent port which, according to the chronicler, yielded a daily revenue of 4,000 pounds of silver. This would have occurred in 1187 or a little later. The figure Aubrey offers is absurd: at the traditional gold – silver ratio of 1:12 and the traditional equivalency of 72 nomismata to the pound, this would have amounted to 7 or 8 million nomismata per year (or some 24,000 per day).[109]

(v) Two Latin documents mention holdings by family members of Alexios III Angelos (1195–1203) and perhaps others, though their evidence is ambiguous. The *Partitio Romaniae*, a document from 1204 specifying the division of the Byzantine Empire between the new Latin emperor of Constantinople and the Republic of Venice, contains two such references. The first mentions properties in the western Morea: "The region of Patras and Methone, with everything belonging to it, namely the *pertinentia* of Vranas. The *pertinentia* of Kantakouzenos, along with the estates of *kyra* Irene, daughter of Emperor *kyr* Alexios [III Angelos], with the estates of Molinetes, of Pantokrator, and of other monasteries, or certain estates, that are in them, namely of *mikra* and *megale episkepseis*, i.e., of small and large *pertinentia*." Whether the *pertinentia* or *episkepsis* of Vranas and of Kantakouzenos and so on were granted by the emperor is unclear, but certainly we can assume that the estates of Irene were given to her by her father.[110]

The second reference in the *Partitio Romaniae* lists "The *pertinentia* of the empress, namely Vesene, Pharsala, Domokos, Revenikon, the two Almiroi with Demetrias" in Thessaly. The "empress" must be Euphrosyne Doukaina,

episkepsi Coriton): G. Tafel and G. Thomas, *Urkunden zu älteren Handels- und Staatsgeschichte der Republik Venedig* (Vienna, 1856–57), I, 261–62. But it is not difficult to think of other, equally reasonable explanations for his presence in the area.

109 *Monumenta Germaniae Historica, Scriptores*, vol. 23 (Berlin and Hanover, 1874), 870, cited by Hendy, *Studies*, 88. C. Brand, *Byzantium Confronts the West, 1180–1204* (Cambridge, Mass., 1968), 111, 345 note 83.

110 Tafel and Thomas, *Urkunden*, I, 469–70: *Orium Patron et Methonis, cum omnibus suis, scilicet pertinentiis Brana. Pertinentia de Cantacuzino, et cum uillis Kyreherinis, filie Imperatoris Kyrialexii, cum uillis de Molineti, de Pantocratora, et de ceteris monasteriorum, siue quibusdam uillis, que sunt in ipsis, scilicet de micra et megali episkepsi, i.e. de parua et magna pertinentia*. Hendy, *Studies*, 89.

Alexios III's wife; as the first reference shows, *pertinentia* was a synonym for *episkepsis* in the *Partitio*. But do we conclude that Euphrosyne had been granted the fiscal revenues or administrative rights over all these towns?[111]

And in the Latin translation of Alexios III Angelos' 1198 chrysobull for Venice there is a long list of imperial territories for which Venice received trade privileges. Among these areas was "The province of Nikopolis with the personal, ecclesiastic, and monastic *episkepseis* in it, and with these the *episkepseis* belonging to the close relatives of my majesty, the ever-most-happy [Gr. πανευτυχέστατος] *sevastokratores*, *kaisares*, and dear daughters of my majesty, and my most yearned-for *augusta*." This, the only mention of possessions held by specific people in the entire list, indicates that Alexios had chosen the area of Nikopolis to make numerous grants to his relatives, though their nature is a matter only for speculation. We note that the *Partitio* mentions the existence "of other [*pertinentia*] of archons and monasteries" (*et de ceteris archondorum et monasteriorum*) around Nikopolis, but omits any mention of Alexios' family, while the chrysobull says nothing of Irene's estates in the Morea or Euphrosyne's holdings in Thessaly.[112]

(vi) According to the terms of the accord concluded in 1204 between Venice and Boniface of Montferrat, leader of the Fourth Crusade, Boniface abdicated his rights over the island of Crete which "was given or promised" to him by Alexios IV (1203–04), 100,000 hyperpyra "promised" to him, and the city of Thessaloniki which Manuel I gave to his brother Renier as a "fief" *[3.4]*. Just as with Renier all we can say is that Boniface viewed his right to Crete and Thessaloniki as entitling him to some kind of governorship or mini-kingdom, with the corresponding power and economic benefits. From the Byzantine point of view these grants probably, if realized, would have paralleled Alexios I's grant of Thessaloniki to Nikephoros Melissenos and his grant of Crete to Nikephoros Diogenes.

All of these examples deal with grants or possible grants to "important" people, a close relative, and distinguished foreigners who married into the imperial family. This represents no innovation.

111 Tafel and Thomas, *Urkunden*, I, 487: *Pertinentia Imperatricis, scilicet Vesna, Fersala, Domocos, Ruenica, duo Almiri, cum Demetriadi*; and I, 487 note 5, and cf. I, 262 note 1, 468, 470. Hendy, *Studies*, 88–89.

112 Tafel and Thomas, *Urkunden*, I, 264: *Prouincia Nicopolon cum episkepsibus in ea existentibus personalibus, ecclesiasticis et monasterialibus, et cum ipsis episkepsibus subiacentibus intimis consanguineis Imperij mei, semper felicissimis seuastocratoribus Cesaribus et dilectis Imperij mei filiabus, ac desideratissime ipsi mee Auguste.* Hendy, *Studies*, 88. The adjective applied to the empress would indicate she was not living in the capital at the time. Tafel and Thomas, *Urkunden*, I, 471–72.

Let us sum up. Starting in the 1070s and continuing through the first half of Alexios I's reign there was an increase in the number of grants to laymen. By the time of Alexios I's accession, half of the empire's territory had been lost, the army weakened, and the treasury was nearly empty. There are two angles here: the fiscal and the military, a lack of cash and a lack of soldiers. What inspired Alexios I to make lifetime grants to soldiers of state property and the fiscal obligations of peasants? First, there was the need for cavalry soldiers. Second, there was a need to find a way to finance these cavalry soldiers without direct cash outlays.

So, using the tools and devices already in existence, Alexios I granted state land and *exkousseiai* of paroikoi, at first, only to important men and in hereditary tenure. Then, as the number of grants increased, these grants were made to men of lesser status, to soldiers, for whom it was understandable that the grant was to be held only so long as the man could serve the emperor, that is, for life. Inspired by grants to monasteries and powerful laymen, by the Byzantine institutions of *charistike* and other lifetime grants, and possibly even by western European and Muslim institutions, the pronoia grant was born.

5 | Pronoia during the period of exile (1204–1261)

In 1204 the Latins of the Fourth Crusade conquered Constantinople and much of the rest of the Byzantine Empire. Thrace, Macedonia, Thessaly, the Morea, Attica, Boeotia, and the Aegean islands were divided among the Crusaders and most were formed into feudal principalities, subordinate in principle to the Latin Empire of Constantinople. Byzantine resistance to the conquerors consolidated in two areas. Around Arta in western Greece and modern Albania, Michael Doukas (1204–15) organized the separatist state that modern historians call the Despotate of Epiros, soon extending from Naupaktos in the south to Dyrrachion in the north. In western Asia Minor a state which is referred to as the empire of Nicaea was organized by the despot Theodore Laskaris (1204–21), a son-in-law of Emperor Alexios III Angelos (1195–1203), who had fled to Asia Minor and organized local resistance from his base at Prousa.

The Latin Conquest has a bearing on the study of pronoia. In the twelfth century, all the references to the locations of pronoiai or properties held in pronoia were in Thrace *[2.2]* or Macedonia *[2.3–2.5]*. Since the Crusaders conquered these areas, reference to pronoiai in Thrace and Macedonia now disappear. Instead, during the thirteenth century pronoia makes its first appearance on the western coast of Asia Minor, in Thessaly, and in Epiros, that is, in those areas where Byzantine successor states were established.

The events of 1204 caused much confusion in regard to property relations. In areas conquered by the Latins many landowners and pronoia holders lost their property and peasants; others, to keep their holdings, cooperated with the new Latin rulers. Many changes occurred as well in areas which the Byzantines continued to hold. All of the religious foundations of Constantinople lost control of their properties outside Latin-controlled areas. In the areas around Smyrna and Miletos alone we read of numerous properties no longer in the possession of Constantinopolitan foundations such as the monasteries of the Virgin Panachrantos, of the Rouphinianai, of the Pantokrator, of Lips, and the Church of Hagia Sophia itself.[1]

[1] Ahrweiler, "Smyrne," 39, 99.

Such changes created opportunities for the leaders of the Byzantine successor states, an ability to start anew. Land that was now ownerless could be, and was, quickly distributed, often in full ownership to men of elevated status whose support the rulers sought. Sometimes these men did not wait for official sanction; they took such land and confirmation of their seizures followed later.

Byzantine leaders during the period of exile utilized this ownerless land to make new grants of pronoiai, especially as a means to create new armies. The extant documents that have come down to us from the first half of the thirteenth century, as few and as skewed a sample as they might be, present a rich picture of the exploitation of the institution of pronoia during this period. In fact, the examples that will be offered in this chapter provide a remarkable amount of detail involving the workings of pronoia, as if pronoia was something novel during this period, belying the fact that the institution had been in existence for over a century. In part, we can attribute this to the expansion of the institution due to military needs. But, even more importantly, I think, the institution was changing: it became regularized as bureaucratic processes were developed to more easily grant and regrant the components of a pronoia grant. Further, within at least some pronoia grants, we see for the first time the inclusion of the taxes on property that the state did not own. While this might appear to be a minor development, it is unknown in connection with pronoia grants prior to 1204, and from its initial occurrence it created a new type of property right in Byzantium.

Asia Minor

[5.1] Prostaxis of Theodore I Laskaris for the monastery of St. John on Patmos (1214)

The first reference to pronoia in the thirteenth century is found in an order (*prostaxis*) of Theodore I Laskaris from 1214. This reference is of great significance because it points to a new source of revenue to be exploited by the state and enjoyed by the pronoia holder. The purpose of the order was to free two ships belonging to the monastery of St. John Theologos on the island of Patmos from all taxes. In the course of this the emperor ordered that no one harass or demand any kind of tax or charge from these ships, "neither by those [. . .] in the theme of the Thrakesion and the theme of Mylasa and Melanoudion, nor by those having pronoiai [. . .] . . . and others." The first lacuna should be filled with a phrase denoting some kind of officials; the second contained either an indication of where the pronoiai were held or another category of people who should not harass the monastery.[2]

We learn from this document that "those having pronoiai" and officials of a theme were two groups of people who might improperly demand taxes from a monastery. Such documents commonly order government officials away from tax-exempt properties. Should a tax collector or other official mistakenly demand the taxes on the monastery's ships, the monks would present this document, and, in theory at least, the matter would be resolved. Yet this is the first evidence that the holders of pronoiai might be inclined to demand taxes from a specific monastic possession. How might this happen?

In Chapter 2 we viewed several conflicts between monasteries and holders of pronoiai. The Kontostephanos act from 1162 *[2.3]* refers to two separate conflicts: a pronoia holder refused to return a piece of land to Lavra which the monks had temporarily granted his predecessor, and a pronoia holder "took away" eight paroikoi of the monastery. The praktikon of Andronikos Vatatzes from 1181 *[2.4]* deals with a mistaken attribution to Cumans of sixty-two of Lavra's paroikoi. The *prostaxis* of Andronikos I Komnenos from 1184 *[2.5]* refers to several disputes. First, Cumans had built livestock enclosures on the monastery's property without paying the monks the charge for this privilege. Second, there is a suggestion that these Cumans were appropriating the paroikoi of the monastery. Third, the emperor ordered that the Vlachs belonging to the monastery should be permitted to pasture their animals freely without paying any fee and that neither tax collectors, soldiers, officials, nor the Cumans themselves should prevent them from this. Finally, the emperor acknowledged that two paroikoi belonging to Lavra had mistakenly been conferred in pronoia upon Cumans, and so he donated them to the monastery.

These three documents present or envision several conflicts or threats to a monastery's property. To summarize them, holders of pronoiai (i) were not abiding by a private arrangement involving the use of a monastery's land, (ii) appropriated eight paroikoi from a monastery, (iii) were mistakenly given sixty-two monastic paroikoi by state officials, (iv) built livestock enclosures on a monastery's land without paying a fee, (v) might appropriate the

[2] *Patmos*, I, no. 23.7: καὶ μήτε παρὰ τῶν [κατὰ καιροὺς ....]ούντων ἐν τῶ θέματι τῶν Θρακησίων καὶ τῶ θέματι Μυλάσης καὶ Μελανδουνίου, μήτε μὴν παρὰ τῶν ἐχόντων προνοίας [...ca.26 characters...] μέρεσι καὶ ἑτέρων, etc. The editor's completion of the first lacuna, τῶν κατὰ καιροὺς κρατούντων, is questionable because the substantive participle ὁ κρατῶν, usually reserved for the emperor, is rarely applied to officials (but cf. *Patmos*, I, no. 24). I would prefer to see perhaps ἐνεργούντων or δουκευόντων rather than κρατούντων. As for the second lacuna, the editor's restoration is too speculative even to present here.

paroikoi of a monastery, (vi) might illegally prevent monastic paroikoi from pasturing their flocks on certain lands, and (vii) improperly received two paroikoi from state officials. In these documents the holders of pronoiai were either improperly holding or utilizing a monastery's land, or improperly holding or harassing a monastery's paroikoi.

The closest parallel to the threat posed in the 1214 *prostaxis* is the clause in the act of 1184 that states that the Vlachs belonging to the monastery should be permitted to pasture their animals and should "not be hindered or kept away by anyone there, either from the tax collectors, or from the soldiers, or from the thematic [officials], or from the Cumans themselves." How might have tax collectors, soldiers, thematic officials, and the Cumans harassed the Vlachs? While, at first glance, the presence of tax collectors in the list might suggest that fees or taxes might be demanded of the Vlachs, the verbs employed, "hindered or kept away," have no fiscal connotation. This indicates that the Vlachs merely faced the threat of being deterred from pasturing their animals where they wished. If this was the case, this only shows that the holders of pronoiai were no less interested than any landholders in keeping trespassers off their property.

However, the passage from the 1214 *prostaxis* seems to have had a quite different intent. While there was a general threat of harassment, there was also a specific threat that pronoia holders, along with state officials, might demand taxes from a monastery's ships. Not only did the mere owning of property never confer a right to demand taxes from another property owner, but property owning was so far removed from tax collecting, that the sources never even mention disputes involving one property owner illegally trying to draw taxes from another property owner. Pronoia holders, evidently, were not quite like property owners. Because this document explicitly forbids pronoia holders from demanding taxes from the monastery's ships, there were some circumstances under which it would have been legal and proper for holders of pronoiai to claim taxes in such a way. Thus, this document tells us that, at least on occasion, pronoia holders had some legal claim to the taxes of other landholders and could have some rights that differed from those of other landholders.

[5.2] Orismos of John IV Laskaris for the monastery of St. John on Patmos (1258)

A similar passage is found in an order (*orismos*) issued by Michael VIII in October 1258 in the name of the child John IV Laskaris. The act confirmed the Patmos monastery's possession of its properties on Kos, on Leros, and at Pyrgos near Miletos, including its tax exemption on these properties and the paroikoi it held within them. Pertaining to this he added that "those [serving] successively as *doukes* in this region and the soldiers dwelling pronoiastically [around this place], as well as those sent successively to Kos [...] for some state service" should not trouble or demand any kind of tax or charge from the monastery.[3]

This is the earliest of only five or six known appearances of the adverb *pronoiastikōs* (προνοιαστικῶς). To dwell in an area "pronoiastically" should mean to live in an area "on account of holding a pronoia." That soldiers (*stratiotai*) should have been those referred to specifically in the act is no surprise. As in the twelfth century, a high percentage of thirteenth-century pronoia holders were soldiers. Further, this is the first evidence we have that suggests that pronoia holders lived near their grants.

Once again the categories of persons who were not to harass the monastery's property is interesting: *doukes* (provincial governors), soldiers "dwelling pronoiastically" in the area, and government officials sent to Kos (and perhaps elsewhere). If the threat envisioned to the monastery's property was that people might illegally appropriate land or paroikoi, why does the clause make no mention of "powerful landowners" or "other monasteries"? Indeed the potential threat seems not to come from people who might try to claim the monastery's property, but from those who might demand taxes from it. *Doukes* and other government officials clearly fit in the category of people who might "subject the monastery to tax demands," whether legally or accidentally. Once again, there is the implication that the holders of pronoiai might demand taxes from a private landholder.

[5.3] Orismos of John IV Laskaris for the monastery of the Kechionismene (1258)

In the same month as the above act Michael VIII issued another *orismos* in John Laskaris' name to safeguard the rights of the monastery of the Virgin Kechionismene near Miletos, a dependency of the Patmos monastery. As in the previous act this document concludes with a passage that similarly orders certain categories of people from harassing this monastery's property,

[3] *Patmos*, I, no. 26.20–22: καὶ οἱ κατὰ καιροὺς δουκικ[.......] ἐν τῇ τοιαύτῃ χώρα καὶ οἱ προνοιαστικῶς κατὰ [τὸν αὐτὸν τό]π[ον] οἰκοῦντες στρατιῶται, ἀλλὰ δὴ καὶ οἱ κατὰ καιροὺς ἀποστελλόμενοι ἐν τῇ Κῷ [............] διά τινας δημοσιακὰς δουλείας .... In place of the incomplete word δουκικ... one normally finds δουκευόντων (cf. *Patmos*, II, no. 73.3). The editor's restoration, κατὰ [τὸν αὐτὸν τό]π[ον], while far from certain, is reasonable. The final lacuna probably contained additional geographical locations.

though here the list of people forbidden to harass the monastery is much broader: "those serving successively as *doukes* [in this] region, *apographeis*, [reassessors,] and soldiers having pronoiai in this place, and even those of Miletos themselves, ought to keep the things belonging to such monastery without loss and unharmed."[4]

Not only does the passage use more abstract terms, "without loss and unharmed," that do not necessarily restrict themselves to the realm of taxation, but we find in the list of people "those of Miletos themselves" – which could certainly include any landholders – in addition to *doukes*, fiscal assessors (*apographeis*), and soldiers having pronoiai locally.

The *vestiarites* Basil Vlatteros

[5.4] Orismos of John III Vatatzes for the monastery of the Lemviotissa regarding the Gounaropouloi (1233)

The conferral upon pronoia holders of tax revenues from property that the state did not own led to complications that had to be resolved. Documents from the cartulary of the monastery of the Lemviotissa outside Smyrna deal with a number of quarrels over property that add greatly to our knowledge about pronoia during the first half of the thirteenth century. Compiled around 1310, this cartulary is an extraordinary collection of some 200 documents dating from the late twelfth through the late thirteenth century.[5] The cartulary's earliest mention of a pronoia involves a property transaction that took place in November 1207 when three brothers from the Gounaropoulos family sold portions of their hereditary property in the village of Vare near Smyrna to the *vestiarites* Basil Vlatteros. Between 1224 and 1228, after Vlatteros' death, Vare was granted by the emperor to the monastery of the Lemviotissa. Among other benefits, the monastery now received an *exkousseia* of the secondary taxes that were levied on the village's inhabitants.[6] Soon afterward a dispute arose over the ownership of the property sold by the Gounaropouloi which illuminates the evolving nature of pronoia grants.

[4] *Patmos*, I, no. 25.17–18: τῶν κατὰ καιροὺς δουκ[.]κευόντων ἐ[ν τῇ τ]οιαύτῃ χώρᾳ ἀπογρα[φέ]ων [τε καὶ ἐ]ξ[ισωτ]ῶν καὶ τῶν προνοίας ἐχόντων στρατιωτῶν ἐν τῷ αὐτῷ τόπῳ, ἀλλὰ δὴ καὶ αὐτῶν τῶν Παλατιανῶν. As in the previous document we should understand δουκευόντων for the document's misspelled δουκ[.]κευόντων. The rest of the editor's restorations are almost certain.

[5] Edited in MM, IV, 1–289.

[6] MM, IV, 185–87 (1207), and cf. 189–90 (1232). MM, IV, 3–4 (1228), and see Dölger, *Regesten*, III, no. 1710.

In 1230 Vlatteros' son-in-law John Ravdokanakes reported to the emperor John III Vatatzes that, in his opinion, the monks were unjustly laying claim to the property Vlatteros had purchased. He argued that the property should be his since Vlatteros had purchased it from the Gounaropouloi and then had given it to him in dowry. The emperor was persuaded to issue an order in 1230 confirming Ravdokanakes' rights to the property. Then in 1232, evidently now won over to the monastery's side, the emperor issued another order directing Ravdokanakes and Vlatteros' widow to give the monastery the disputed property and to cease harassing the monks over it. Again the son-in-law appealed to the emperor and in June 1233 again had his rights to the property confirmed.[7] But the emperor apparently decided that this dispute required a thorough investigation, and so he sent a very high official to the scene to make sense of the competing claims and resolve the matter once and for all.

The two sides presented their arguments. Ravdokanakes maintained that since his father-in-law had purchased the property from the Gounaropouloi, he had the right to hold the property in dowry. However, the monks argued that the sale of the property was illegal since the Gounaropouloi were paroikoi of Vlatteros, and so the property should be held by the monastery which had received the rest of the village from the emperor. The official's decision is found and confirmed in an imperial *orismos* from July 1233. The official ruled "that the Gounaropouloi ought not to have sold Vlatteros this land because it is subject to *paroikia*, and taxpayers ought not to sell the things held by them to those having these [same things] in the condition of pronoia since [these things] are arranged eternally under the hand of the fisc," and so the land should be held by the monastery.[8] In other words, the original sale was deemed illegal because the Gounaropouloi were paroikoi

[7] MM, IV, 218 (1230), 194–95 (1232), 219–20 (1233).

[8] MM, IV, 199.22–28: ὡς οὐκ ὤφειλον οἱ Γουναρόπουλοι διαπωλῆσαι πρὸς τὸν Βλαττερὸν τὴν τοιαύτην γῆν διὰ τὸ ὑπὸ παροικίαν τελεῖν ταύτην, καὶ μὴ ὀφείλειν τοὺς ὑποτελεῖν [sc. ὑποτελεῖς] πιπράσκειν τὰ παρ' αὐτῶν κατεχόμενα πρὸς τοὺς κατὰ λόγον προνοίας ἔχοντας αὐτά, ὡς ὑπὸ τὴν τοῦ δημοσίου χεῖρα ἀείποτε τελοῦντα. The literature on this case is extensive. See Uspenskij, "Značenie," 29; V. Vasil'evskij, "Materialy dlja vnutrennej istorii Vizantijskogo gosudarstva," *ŽMNP* 210 (1880), 149; B. Pančenko, "Krest'janskaja sobstvennost' v Vizantii," *IRAIK* 9 (1904), 94–98, 105; Charanis, "Monastic Properties," 89, 104–07; Charanis, "Social Structure," 125–26; Kazhdan, *Agrarnye otnošenija*, 216; A. Laiou-Thomadakis, *Peasant Society in the Late Byzantine Empire* (Princeton, 1977), 211; Ostrogorsky, *Féodalité*, 65–68; H. Glykatzi-Ahrweiler, "La politique agraire des empereurs de Nicée," repr. in Ahrweiler, *Études sur les structures administratives et sociales de Byzance* (London, 1971), no. IV, 61; idem, "La concession des droits incorporels," 111; C. Zuckerman, "The Dishonest Soldier Constantine Planites and His Neighbours," *Byz* 56 (1986), 324–25 (with numerous factual errors); and Dölger, *Regesten*, III, nos. 1676, 1718, 1723, 1724, 1728, 1732, 1733, 1734, 1799a.

of Vlatteros, and paroikoi were not permitted to sell their property to those who held this property in pronoia. Since the sale was invalid, the property now passed to the monastery. Nevertheless, the official added that if Ravdokanakes swore that his father-in-law had actually purchased the property, the monastery should reimburse the son-in-law for the original purchase price.[9]

The case finally was settled in 1236. Vlatteros' widow, daughter, and son-in-law, while still maintaining that they had done nothing improper, agreed to renounce all their rights to the property for both themselves and their descendants; the monastery compensated them with the curiously low sum of five hyperpyra. (In 1207 the Gounaropouloi had sold Vlatteros the disputed properties for forty hyperpyra.) In 1240 the widow of Michael Gounaropoulos sold the monastery at least some of the fields the family still possessed in the village, and ten years later their children sold at least some of the vineyards they still owned there.[10]

Meanwhile Michael Gounaropoulos, the son of one of the original brothers who had sold the disputed property to Vlatteros, tried to transfer his portion of the property to someone else. In 1249 the emperor ordered an official not to allow him to do this. Nevertheless, he was entitled to occupy the land as long as he rendered the property's taxes to the monastery and discharged the other obligations that he, as a paroikos, owed the monastery as holder of this land. If he was not able to take possession of it, it would devolve to the monastery and his relatives would lose any claim to it.[11]

The 1233 *orismos* does not provide any new terminology in regard to the use of the word *pronoia*. The construction ἔχειν τι κατὰ λόγον προνοίας "to have something by reason of pronoia" already appeared in the 1181 praktikon of Andronikos Vatatzes *[2.4]* under the form κατέχειν τι κατὰ λόγον προνοίας and where it was equivalent to κατέχειν τι κατὰ πρόνοιαν. Rather, the document provides useful information about the nature of such grants and the development of the institution. For instance, it provides us with an example of how the events of 1204 affected the pattern of landholding in Asia Minor. As we learn from other documents, the village of Vare, where the properties of the Gounaropouloi were located, had

[9] Zuckerman, "The Dishonest Soldier," 325, claims that the official ruled that the sale of land by the Gounaropouloi was invalid because they did not own what they sold and that "the fields which they held as paroikoi constituted an inalienable property of the state," but in fact the documents clearly state that the property in question was the hereditary property (*gonikon*) of the Gounaropouloi (MM, IV, 186.5).

[10] MM, IV, 192–94 (1236), 195–96 (1240), 200–01 (1250).

[11] MM, IV, 182–83. For the date, see Ahrweiler, "Smyrne," 145, and Dölger, *Regesten*, III, no. 1799a.

belonged to the Constantinopolitan monastery of the Pantokrator before 1204.[12]

In the disorder following the Latin Conquest, not only did the Pantokrator monastery lose its control over Vare, but even the Gounaropouloi suffered from these developments. In an *orismos* of Theodore I Laskaris from June 1207 we learn that Basil Vlatteros had reported to the emperor that "his kinsmen" (οἱ προσγενεῖς αὐτοῦ) Michael, John, and Nicholas Gounaropoulos had been holding certain fields as patrimony (*gonikothen*) for many years, but these were seized in 1204 by the inhabitants of Kyparissiou, a village subject to the church of Smyrna. The emperor decided that if this was true, the properties should be returned to the Gounaropouloi and the inhabitants of Kyparissiou should pay a rent (*morte*) for the time they improperly held the properties.[13]

Five months later these same three Gounaropouloi sold their shares of this property to Vlatteros, and this sale, which was at the root of the dispute of the 1230s, can explain Vlatteros' interest in the earlier plight of the Gounaropouloi. Sometime between the fall of Constantinople in April 1204 and November 1207 Vare was granted as a pronoia to Basil Vlatteros. Because it took Theodore I Laskaris some time to establish his authority, the grant to Vlatteros probably occurred closer to 1207 than 1204. What probably happened then was that, following the fall of the capital, Vare temporarily had no lord. Inhabitants from Kyparissiou seized some of its property from the paroikoi of the Pantokrator monastery which could no longer defend the interests of its paroikoi. Perhaps as late as early 1207 Vlatteros was granted Vare as a pronoia, and he sought to restore the territorial integrity of Vare. The document from June 1207 was part of this process. Even if he had not intended at the time, in June 1207, to purchase some of the Gounaropouloi's property, the recovery of these properties for his paroikoi increased the income of his pronoia because he would henceforth receive the *telos* of the properties.[14]

The Gounaropoulos family were paroikoi of Vlatteros who held them within his pronoia. This meant that they paid their taxes not to the fisc, but to Vlatteros. When Vlatteros purchased some of the property of his

[12] MM, IV, 194.18–19. Glykatzi-Ahrweiler, "Politique agraire," 57.

[13] MM, IV, 217–18. Dölger, *Regesten*, III, no. 1676.

[14] Since he calls the Gounaropouloi "his kinsmen," a familial relation could account for his interest as well. Yet none of the other documents dealing with this case suggest kinship, and in fact in the documents of the period there was a tendency to use familial terminology figuratively. In the same document in which Vlatteros calls the Gounaropouloi "his kinsmen," the emperor refers to an official named Alexios Komnenos as the "brother of my majesty" (MM, IV, 217.24), which seems to be counterfactual. On this phenomenon, see Ahrweiler, "Smyrne," 171.

paroikoi, he, in effect, now enjoyed a tax exemption on this property since he, as the owner of the property, now paid his taxes to himself, as the holder of the property in pronoia.[15] Before his death Vlatteros gave the property to his son-in-law in dowry, and after his death the rest of the village of Vare was granted by the emperor to the Lemviotissa monastery, which then claimed the properties held by Ravdokanakes as well.

Amid the land transfers, something had clearly gone wrong. Property taxes that had originally been assigned to Vlatteros through an imperial grant had been transferred to one of his relatives without imperial approval. In effect, tax revenues had passed from the control of the state. This was not supposed to happen. The official had to determine which of the property transactions was invalid so that the taxes of the property could be assigned by the state to the monastery. But which transaction was invalid? If Vlatteros legally owned the property and legally enjoyed a tax exemption on it, then it was legal for him to transmit it to his son-in-law in dowry. If Vlatteros legally received the taxes from the property within his pronoia, then it was legal for him to enjoy tax exemption for this property after he purchased it. If the Gounaropouloi legally owned the property, then it was legal to sell it to Vlatteros.

The official could have solved the dilemma in a number of ways. He might have declared that while the transfer of the property from Vlatteros to his son-in-law Ravdokanakes was legal, the transfer of tax exemption to Ravdokanakes was illegal since in origin the tax exemption he enjoyed on this property sprang, in part, from his status as a holder of a pronoia. Since his pronoia was not hereditary (being regranted, as a simple gift, by the emperor to the monastery after his death), the official might then have declared the property taxable and required that Ravdokanakes pay the monastery the taxes due on the property.

As it turned out the official based his decision on the monastery's argument. Perhaps he regarded the link between Vlatteros' tax exemption and his status as a holder of a pronoia as something too subtle on which to make his decision. Perhaps he had not thought of it. Or perhaps he simply wanted to resolve the problem in a way that would detach the Vlatteros family from any connection to the disputed property.

[15] In regard to Vlatteros' obligation to pay the *sitarkia* and *agape* on his pronoia, which some scholars have made much of (see Zuckerman, "The Dishonest Soldier," 328), these were *aggregate* charges levied on villages, not individual peasant properties. It is the *telos* burdening the Gounaropoulos family's own individual property that Vlatteros had received before he purchased the land, and which he more or less remitted to himself after the sale.

It is important to emphasize that there was nothing improper in the Gounaropouloi selling their property. Paroikoi regularly alienated their property through sale, donation, and dowry. Monastic paroikoi often sold or donated portions of their property to the monastery that held them. There were even cases, much rarer to be sure, in which paroikoi sold property to their secular lords. One such example involves the founding of the monastery of Nea Petra in Thessaly. During 1271–72 the founders, Nicholas Komnenos Maliasenos and his wife, purchased a series of properties from peasants in order to build and endow the monastery. At least some of these peasants were their paroikoi.[16] Nothing in the relevant documents indicates that Maliasenos held these paroikoi or any property specifically in pronoia. Indeed in one of the acts of sale the peasant notes that "the entire region . . . was bestowed on you [Maliasenos] by the . . . emperor, belonging to you in the manner of patrimony" (καὶ ἀπεχαρίσθη ὑμῖν παρὰ τοῦ . . . βασιλέως ἡ ἅπασα χώρα . . . , ὡς γονικόθεν σοι διαφέρουσα), which indicates that while an emperor granted the property to Maliasenos (or confirmed Maliasenos' existing possession of the property), Maliasenos was holding these paroikoi in a condition that went beyond a simple pronoia grant.[17] This could explain why it was permissible for Maliasenos' paroikoi to sell their property to Maliasenos, but improper for the Gounaropouloi to sell their property to Vlatteros.

Of what did Vlatteros' pronoia consist? The document specifies only that the property the Gounaropouloi sold Vlatteros was held by Vlatteros "in the condition of pronoia." But since this property was "subject to paroikia" (ὑπὸ παροικίαν), we may conclude that the Gounaropouloi themselves were paroikoi and were within his pronoia. Further, since other documents state that all of Vare passed from Vlatteros to the Lemviotissa monastery after Vlatteros' death, it is reasonable to conclude that the entire village was part of his pronoia.

Aside from paroikoi and the properties sold to Vlatteros we cannot be more specific about what exactly was in this pronoia. This makes it difficult to discuss what profit Vlatteros derived from his pronoia. At the very least he received the financial burdens and labor services that his paroikoi would normally have owed the state. The extent to which he could exploit the labor services of his paroikoi depended on whether state land was included

[16] E.g., MM, IV, 396–99 (esp. 397.32), 408.5.

[17] MM, IV, 397.32–35. Ostrogorsky, *Féodalité*, 69 note 1. Charanis, "Social Structure," 102 (and repeated in his "The Aristocracy of Byzantium in the Thirteenth Century," in *Studies in Roman Economic and Social History in Honor of A. C. Johnson* [Princeton, 1951], 347), wrote that Maliasenos literally received the region from his father, but the passage does not say that.

within his pronoia which these paroikoi could be asked to cultivate, as well as whether he owned other property that could take advantage of the labor services the paroikoi owed. Of course we know nothing of this.

The financial burdens of the paroikoi fell into two categories: fiscal charges levied on their village as a whole and for which each paroikos household was responsible for its share, and the property tax (the *telos*) levied on the specific properties (movable and immovable) owned by each paroikos household. The case of Vlatteros is connected only with the *telos*. The Gounaropouloi held their property as patrimony. They cultivated it, enjoyed its harvest, and paid the *telos* on it. This is why the document refers to them as "taxpayers." Vlatteros, on the other hand, held their property as a pronoia. He received the *telos* paid by the Gounaropouloi on their property. This is why both the Gounaropouloi and Vlatteros can be said to have "held" the property that was later sold to Vlatteros: "taxpayers ought not to sell the things held by them to those who have these [same] things in the condition of pronoia."

Constantine Zuckerman argued that during the first half of the thirteenth century pronoiai were not held tax exempt, that the paroikoi of a pronoia holder paid the fisc the *telos* on their properties.[18] The case of Vlatteros demonstrates that this view is incorrect. If, before they sold their property to Vlatteros, the Gounaropouloi had paid the fisc the *telos* levied on the property, what benefit, we may ask, did Vlatteros derive from holding the same property within his pronoia? Agricultural property can produce three kinds of return: taxes, a rent, and a harvest. Vlatteros, in order for there to be any purpose in his holding the property in pronoia, must have received at least one of these. If Vlatteros, as a pronoia holder, already had been receiving a rent or the harvest from the property, the property would have belonged to the fisc. This was not the case. The Gounaropouloi owned the property and so the only return that Vlatteros could have received from the property before he purchased it was the property tax burdening the property. (Vlatteros, as a holder of paroikoi, also received the secondary charges and corvées owed by his paroikoi, but these burdened the paroikoi themselves, not their properties.) Therefore, the state forswore the tax burden on the property owned by the paroikoi held by the recipient of a pronoia.

The only property within a pronoia grant that may have borne a tax burden was any state-owned property conferred on the pronoia holder. The pronoia holder received a rent or the harvest on such property and as such his tenure of the property would have yielded him a return even if he was

[18] Zuckerman, "The Dishonest Soldier," 325–29.

required to pay the *telos* on the property. The present case sheds no light on this phenomenon.

We learn a number of things from this story about the nature of pronoiai in the first half of the thirteenth century. First, the document tells us explicitly that it was improper for paroikoi to sell any of their property to the person who held their property within a grant of pronoia. Further, we learn indirectly that it was prohibited to alienate pronoiai. There is no clearer expression of this than the document's statement that property conferred in pronoia was "arranged eternally under the hand of the fisc" (ὑπὸ τὴν τοῦ δημοσίου χεῖρα ἀείποτε τελοῦντα). This accords with the passage in the 1262 *orismos* of Michael VIII Palaiologos discussed below *[5.6]* that property granted in pronoia belonged to the fisc (ἀνήκειν τὴν τοιαύτην γῆν . . . τῷ μέρει τοῦ δημοσίου). Nevertheless, it is not inconceivable that some holders of pronoiai were finding ways to alienate parts of their pronoia grants successfully. While the practice was prohibited, a less favored plaintiff than the Lemviotissa monastery might have declined to pursue his suit or have received a less favorable ruling.

We also learn that it was still not normal practice for wives, daughters, or sons-in-law to inherit pronoiai. If it had been, there would have been no case, for the Lemviotissa monastery would never have received the village of Vare. This is further confirmation of the evidence from the *Zavorda Treatise [2.1]* that the grant of a pronoia was a lifetime grant. Finally, the document confirms the evidence of earlier sources that the holder of a pronoia could receive the taxes from a property, and that the "taxpayers" who paid these taxes could be considered paroikoi (ὑπὸ παροικίαν).

The *metochion* of Pyrgos

[5.5] Act of Andronikos Mauropodos on the *metochion* of Pyrgos near Miletos (1216)

Evidence of pronoia holders in the area of Miletos and of the confusion caused by the events of 1204 is found in an act from 1216. In that year the monks of the monastery of St. John on Patmos asked the emperor for a *metochion* called Pyrgos in the area of Miletos (Palatia). Previously Pyrgos had been held by the Constantinopolitan monastery of the Virgin Panachrantos, but since the capital was now in Latin hands, Panachrantos was unable to assert its rights over the property, and so the emperor granted the monastery's request. An order to effect the transfer was received by the *doux* of the theme of Thrakesion who ordered the official Andronikos Mauropodos to carry it out.

Mauropodos examined numerous documents and determined that while paroikoi of the Panachrantos monastery held Pyrgos for a rent (χωροπακτικῶς) before 1204, after 1204, because the Panachrantos monastery could no longer assert its rights over the property, "certain of those in authority seized it" and cultivated it as their own land. Mauropodos concluded that these inhabitants of Miletos had no right to the property, and so he removed the paroikoi of the Panachrantos monastery who were cultivating it as well as those paroikoi of the people in authority in Miletos (τῶν ἐν τέλει) and he conferred the property upon the Patmos monastery. He added "from now on, someone of those 'pronoiarized' in Miletos shall not make a demand concerning Pyrgos at all, neither a Panachrantinos paroikos nor [a paroikos] of those in authority, nor make any trouble ever for the said monastery of Patmos, knowing that he has no right to the usufruct and possession of Pyrgos."[19]

This document contains the first of only two known appearances of the verb *pronoiazo* (προνοιάζω) in Byzantine sources. It derives directly from *pronoia*, and in this passage the passive form *pronoiazesthai* (προνοιάζεσθαι) means evidently "to be conferred as a pronoia," "to be held in pronoia," or "to be pronoia-ized" (or the more euphonic "to be pronoiarized," as the verb is usually rendered in English by modern scholars). The only other appearance of the verb is in Manuel II Palaiologos' 1408 *prostagma* for the monasteries of Mount Athos, referring to the "pronoiarization" of monastic property *[9.1]*.[20]

What was happening in this document? Why were two groups of paroikoi who were held in pronoia ordered to leave alone the property of the

[19] *Patmos*, II, no. 61.39–40: οὐ μεθέξει τις τῶν προνοιασθέντων εἰς τὰ Παλάτια ζήτησιν περὶ τοῦ Πύργου ὅλως ποιήσασθαι ἢ Πανάχραντινὸς πάροικος ἢ τῶν ἐν δημοσίῳ.... My interpretation of this passage differs from that of the editor of the document. In her summary of the document M. Nystazopoulou-Pelekidou writes that "no one of those holding a pronoia in Palatia, neither a Panachrantinos paroikos nor a public official" (οὐδεὶς τῶν ἐχόντων πρόνοιαν εἰς τὰ Παλάτια, οὔτε πάροικος Παναχραντηνός, οὔτε δημόσιος λειτουργός) were to bother the monastery: *Patmos*, II, p. 136. Since a paroikos obviously could not hold a pronoia, she has created three groups of people, which I think is incorrect. If the author of the act had wished to speak of "those holding pronoiai in Palatia," he could have written simply τις τῶν ἐχόντων προνοίας, as in the 1214 *prostaxis* of Theodore Laskaris *[5.1]*, rather than τις τῶν προνοιασθέντων.

[20] With no direct connection to the Byzantine institution, the verb appears a number of times in the *Chronicle of the Morea*, with the meaning "to enfief": ed. J. Schmitt (London, 1904), lines 1911, 1939, 1964, 1966, 1973, 2020, 2076, 2955, 7795. See *[7.2]* and the comments following *[7.13]* and *[7.14]* below.

Patmos monastery? After the fall of Constantinople in 1204, paroikoi of the Panachrantos monastery, who had been leasing the property, continued to cultivate the property. Local officials took advantage of the situation by appropriating some of the land for themselves and their paroikoi.

These local officials need not have necessarily been installed by either the former Byzantine administration or the government of Theodore Laskaris. The phrases used to describe them, "some of those in public authority" (line 31: τινὲς . . . τῶν ἐν τέλει δημοσίως), "those in authority" (line 35: τῶν ἐν τέλει), and "those in government" (line 40: τῶν ἐν δημοσίω), are vague enough to include even local magnates who, on their own authority, filled the power vacuum created by the collapse of 1204. Nevertheless, according to the document, both the Panachrantinoi paroikoi and the paroikoi of the local authorities were paroikoi held by pronoia holders. So the local authorities were pronoia holders. Whether they had first been granted their pronoia grants before or after 1204 is unknown.

But what of the Panachrantinoi paroikoi? Given that they no longer had any connection whatsoever with the Panachrantos monastery, they are referred to as Panachrantinoi only as a designation of origin, to distinguish them from the paroikoi of the local lords. Since they were paroikoi of pronoia holders, too, I imagine that when "those in authority" seized the property and cultivated it as their own, the lords effected two changes: the original Panachrantinoi paroikoi became their paroikoi, and they introduced their own paroikoi onto the property.

The story of Pyrgos explains why both "a paroikos of the monastery of the Panachrantos" and "(a paroikos of) those in public service" were specifically mentioned as two categories of people who should not make any claim to Pyrgos or harass its new owner, the Patmos monastery. The Panachrantinoi paroikoi were those who had been cultivating Pyrgos for Panachrantos; the paroikoi of "those in public service" (τῶν ἐν δημοσίω) were the paroikoi of the authorities of Miletos who had tried to appropriate some of Pyrgos for themselves.[21]

The document provides no hint as to who the men "in authority" were. However, it does mention some men who may well have been pronoia holders. These are found in a list of witnesses which begins the act. A few clergy are named, headed by the metropolitan of Miletos, followed by "from among the soldiers [*stratiotai*] and my comrades [καὶ ἀπὸ τῶν στρατιωτῶν καὶ συντρόφων μου], *kyr* Nikephoros Limniotes, *kyr* George

[21] Thirty-five years later, in 1251, there was another prohibition against inhabitants of Miletos interfering with Patmos monastery's rights to Pyrgos: *Patmos*, II, no. 64.

Magkaphas, *kyr* Theodore Gylielmos, *kyr* Alexios Teires: and from the landowners [*oikodespotai*], *kyr* Niketas Konstonetes, *kyr* Nicholas tes Lerias, [...] and others."

From their names, Theodore Gylielmos (sc. Guillaume) and Alexios Teires (sc. Thierry) were either Latins or recent descendants of Latins, and Theodore is known from an act of 1209 in which it is said that he held paroikoi, i.e., probably as a pronoia holder.[22] As for the appellation *syntrophos* ("comrade") it occurs several times, primarily during the early Nicaean period. We note that, while Andronikos Mauropodos (who has no title other than *megalodoxotatos*) refers to these soldiers as his *syntrophoi*, the *parakoimomenos* Alexios Krateros, Mauropodos' superior, refers to Mauropodos as his *syntrophos*.[23] While the known examples of the use of the word tend to reflect a subordinate's relation to his superior, the term does not consistently establish a hierarchy. In one case a local tax collector (*praktor*) and another man refer to a *logariastes* and a *protovestiarios* (a very high title) as "our *megalodoxotatoi syntrophoi*."[24] Rather it denotes men of the same class (parallel perhaps to the modern phrase "my esteemed colleague"), specifically members of the ruling and military class.

Gonia tou Petake and the Malachiotai

[5.6] Act of John Selagites, *doux* of Melanoudion, and John, bishop of Amazokorakia and Chalkolamnos on the field of Gonia tou Petake (1262), and *Orismos* of Michael VIII Palaiologos on the field of Gonia tou Petake (1262)

Another set of documents dealing with the Patmos monastery's property holdings in the area of Miletos illustrate the nature of pronoia during the middle of the thirteenth century. In May 1259 Michael VIII granted additional properties to those held by the Patmos monastery in the Meander valley. One of these was a field in the region of Miletos near Pyrgos called Gonia tou Petake which consisted of 4 *zeugaria* of land and which had been held recently by "the much-beloved son-in-law of my majesty, the

[22] MM, VI, 154.16–17, cited by H. Glykatzi-Ahrweiler, "Note additionnelle sur la politique agraire des empereurs de Nicée," repr. in Ahrweiler, *Études sur les structures administratives et sociales de Byzance* (London, 1971), no. IV, 135.

[23] *Patmos*, II, no. 61.18: Μεγαλοδοξότατε καὶ ἠγαπημένε μοι σύντροφε, κῦρ Ἀνδρόνικε Μαυρόποδε.

[24] MM, VI, 154.23–24 (1209). For other examples of the use of *syntrophos*, see MM, IV, 147.12 (1234); *Patmos*, II, no. 72.8 (1273); MM, IV, 230 (1293); and G. Smyrnakes, *Τὸ Ἅγιον Ὄρος* (Athens, 1903), 80.5–7 (a false chrysobull bearing the date 1294).

protosevastos kyr Manuel Komnenos Laskaris. For my majesty took it away from the deceased" and gave it to the monastery. Two months later the emperor ordered that the "men" (perhaps paroikoi, perhaps servants) of his "niece" the *protosevaste* Maria Komnene Laskarina (evidently the widow of Michael VIII's "son-in-law" Manuel) should not bother the monastery over this property. The adjective "much-beloved" and the fact that Laskaris was dead indicate that he had not lost his property because he had fallen from imperial favor but, most likely, because he had died and his wife was not permitted to keep Gonia tou Petake. In May 1262 Michael VIII issued another *orismos* about this property. He ordered that the inhabitants (*epoikoi*) of the nearby villages of Malachiou and Stomatou keep away from Gonia tou Petake and not trouble the monastery "since such land was taken away from Malachiou and given to the monastery by my majesty."[25]

Two months later, in July 1262, an act was issued by John Selagites, *doux* of Melanoudion, and John, bishop of Amazokorakia and Chalkolamnos. We read that the pair had been ordered by the emperor to determine whether the inhabitants of Malachiou held the land "by hereditary right and for state taxes" or if "they held it against a rent and pronoiastically and gave such rent sometimes to those having the said village of Malachiou *kata pronoian*, sometimes to those working for the fisc." They reported that since the inhabitants of Malachiou could not produce any documentation that they had paid taxes on the property, it was clear that "they held it [the land] for a rent and pronoiastically, giving the rent of such land to the [person] working for the fisc at the time." Since the peasants merely rented the property, the emperor's grant of the field to the monastery should stand.[26]

An *orismos* of Michael VIII from September 1262 confirmed this decision.[27] It states that the monastery had held the land for three years without the Malachiotai or others bothering it, but after the village of Malachiou "was granted for pronoia" to the emperor's uncle George Komnenos Angelos, this peace came to an end. At the instigation of Angelos, the inhabitants of Malachiou claimed the property as theirs "from hereditary right"

[25] *Patmos*, I, no. 14.48–49, and cf. no. 27.64–66. *Patmos*, I, no. 28.5–6 (July 1259), no. 29.6 (May 1262).

[26] *Patmos*, II, no. 67.4: ἐπὶ γονικῷ δικαίῳ καὶ τέλει δημοσιακῷ, lines 5–7: ἐπιμόρτως καὶ προνοιαστικῶς κατεῖχον αὐτὴν καὶ ἐδίδουν τὴν ταύτης μορτὴν ποτὲ μὲν τοῖς κατὰ πρόνοιαν ἔχοντες [sic] τῷ [sic] ῥηθὲν χωρίον Μαλαχίου ποτὲ δὲ τοῖς ἐνεργοῦσι τῷ μέρει τοῦ δημοσίου, and lines 13–14: ἐπιμόρτως καὶ προνοιαστικῶς κατεῖχον αὐτὴν ἀποδιδοῦντες τὴν μορτὴν τῆς ταύτης γῆς τῷ μέρει τοῦ δημοσίου τῷ κατὰ τὴν ἡμέραν ἐνεργοῦντι.

[27] *Patmos*, I, no. 30.3: εἰς πρόνοιαν δωρηθέντος, and lines 5–6: βάρη τελεσμάτων . . . δημοσιακῶν τε καὶ στρατιωτικῶν. On these documents, see Ostrogorsky, *Féodalité*, 69–71; Laiou, *Peasant Society*, 47–48; and Charanis, "Social Structure," 100.

(*gonikothen*). Angelos maintained the truth of this, that their tax lists (*viologioi*) included it, and that they had paid "state and military taxes" on behalf of the property.

In this *orismos* the emperor paraphrased his instructions to Selagites and the bishop of Amazokorakia to conduct an investigation: "if it should appear that such land . . . , while cultivated by the Malachiotai, belonged [to them] on account of a rent which was rendered toward the fisc or toward those successively having Malachiou for pronoia, then it should be held by the monastery." This inquiry had demonstrated, the emperor wrote, that "while this land was held and occupied by the Malachiotai, the Stomatianoi, and others, the appropriate rent was rendered by those who in succession worked [this land] either toward the fisc or toward those who held Malachiou for pronoia."[28] Since the peasants paid a rent to the fisc or to holders of pronoiai, "this land does not belong to the Malachiotai as patrimony, as the said uncle of my majesty, Angelos, maintained, but to the fisc." Therefore, as it was state property, the emperor had the right to grant it to the monastery. Since the property was not the patrimony of the Malachiotai, nor was it held by them for taxes, "it belonged completely to him who received its rent by right of ownership." The emperor concluded by adding that the property must not be bothered "by the present Malachiotai, nor by their descendants, nor by the uncle of my majesty, nor by those who shall hold such village of Malachiou in the future."[29]

We may reconstruct this affair as follows. The *protosevastos kyr* Manuel Komnenos Laskaris once held the village of Malachiou, of which the field Gonia tou Petake was a part. Laskaris leased Gonia tou Petake to inhabitants of Malachiou, Stomatou, and others, who, in return, rendered to Laskaris a rental payment. Early in 1259 Laskaris died and possession of Malachiou returned to the state (his widow was not permitted to keep it). The emperor

[28] *Patmos*, I, no. 30.8–9: πρὸς τὸ μέρος τοῦ δημοσίου ἢ πρὸς τοὺς κατὰ καιροὺς εἰς πρόνοιαν ἔχοντας τὰ Μαλαχίου, and lines 14–15: ἢ πρὸς τοὺς εἰς πρόνοιαν ἔχοντας τὰ Μαλαχίου. We note that the emperor, more logically, employs ἤ "or" (πρὸς τὸ μέρος τοῦ δημοσίου ἢ πρὸς τοὺς . . . εἰς πρόνοιαν ἔχοντας τὰ Μαλαχίου) while Selagites and the bishop employ καί "and" (ἐπιμόρτως καὶ προνοιαστικῶς), perhaps in some unusual disjunctive sense. G. Ostrogorsky, *Pronija* (Belgrade, 1951), 47, translated the key phrase as "*na osnovu zakupa ili pronije*" ("on the basis of a rent or a pronoia"). Cf. Ostrogorsky, *Féodalité*, 70–71. In the editor's summary of the act, the phrase is first rendered as εἴτε ἐπὶ ἐνοικίῳ εἴτε ὡς πρόνοιαν ("either for a rent or as pronoia"), and later as ἐπὶ ἐνοικίῳ καὶ ὡς πρόνοιαν ("for a rent and as pronoia"): *Patmos*, I, pp. 176–77.

[29] *Patmos*, I, no. 30.16: μὴ ἀνήκειν τὴν τοιαύτην γῆν τοῖς Μαλαχιώταις ὡς γονικήν . . . ἀλλὰ τῷ μέρει τοῦ δημοσίου, line 21: πάντως ἐκείνου ἦν, τοῦ λαμβάνοντος τὴν μορτὴν αὐτῆς δεσποτικῷ δικαίῳ, and lines 22–23.

now separated Gonia tou Petake from the rest of Malachiou, conferring it upon the Patmos monastery. In 1262 the rest of Malachiou was granted as a pronoia to George Komnenos Angelos.

At first the inhabitants of Malachiou, Stomatou, and the others renting the land appear to have accepted this situation, but in 1262 the inhabitants of Malachiou attempted to reassert their claims on the field. Since this dispute arose after Angelos was granted Malachiou in pronoia, it would seem that he was its motivating force. In order to attempt to regain possession of the field the Malachiotai argued that it was their hereditary property because they had been paying taxes on it. However, the officials who investigated the matter determined that they in fact had not been paying taxes on the field. Rather, whatever money they had been paying on the field was a rent, and so their claim was invalid.

The principle at work here is that one is the owner of property on which he pays taxes. Since the inhabitants of Malachiou and Stomatou did not hold the field "by hereditary right and for state taxes," but cultivated and possessed it "for a rent and pronoiastically," they were not its owners.

The Malachiotai had rendered this rent sometimes to whoever was holding Malachiou as a pronoia and sometimes to fiscal officials. This clearly implies that the property was state property which sometimes was granted as a pronoia to individuals. Who owned the property when it was held as a pronoia? In other words who owned a pronoia? Michael VIII's 1262 *orismos* plainly states that, before he granted it to the Patmos monastery, "the property did not belong to the Malachiotai as patrimony . . . but to the fisc." Yet a few lines later the emperor asserts that "Inasmuch as such land was found not to be the patrimony of the Malachiotai, nor held by them for taxes and charges, indeed it belonged to he who received its rent by the right of ownership" (*Patmos*, I, no. 30.16,21). On the one hand, it belonged to the state; on the other, it belonged to whoever received the rent, that is, sometimes the state, sometimes the person who held the property as a pronoia. Yet to receive a property as a pronoia was, in this case, the right to lease the property. In this example, then, the holder of a pronoia can be thought of as someone who received, perhaps only temporarily, certain aspects of the right of ownership over a property owned by the state, the right to act as the owner of a property and enjoy its fruits. But it could still be maintained that the property so granted remained the property of the state.

Who were the inhabitants (*epoikoi*) of Malachiou (the Malachiotai)? Were they peasants or larger landowners? And if they were peasants, were they paroikoi of the Patmos monastery or paroikoi of whoever held Gonia tou Petake before this monastery? Or were they paroikoi of George Angelos, that is, were they part of what he held as a pronoia in Malachiou? The documents provide no specific information on their identity or their status.[30] This in itself would suggest that they were not very distinguished people. Aside from this we note that the disputed property, Gonia tou Petake, was reckoned at four *zeugaria* in size, perhaps equivalent to as little as 400 modioi (100 acres) of quality land (on the *zeugarion*, see below, *[5.12]*). Since a passage from the 1262 *orismos* refers to "the Malachiotai, the Stomatianoi, and others," we are dealing with at least six people who had been renting this land, and probably dozens. The indications are that the Malachiotai were peasants who worked Gonia tou Petake themselves.

Were they paroikoi of the Patmos monastery? The answer to this is clearly no. An *orismos* of Michael VIII from May 1262 instructs an official to order the inhabitants of Malachiou and of Stomatou to stay away from Gonia tou Petake and not to trouble the monastery (*Patmos*, I, no. 29.5–6). Paroikoi of the monastery would not be ordered away from the monastery. From this we may also conclude that the inhabitants of Malachiou and of Stomatou were not paroikoi of whoever held Gonia tou Petake before the Patmos monastery.

But were they paroikoi of George Angelos? The inhabitants of Malachiou are known to us only as renters of land, and the mere fact that they rented Gonia tou Petake tells us nothing about whether or not they were anyone's paroikoi. However, George Angelos' interest in the affair suggests that the Malachiotai were his paroikoi. If, as it seems, he instigated the quarrel between the Malachiotai and the Patmos monastery, then he probably stood to gain from the Malachiotai reacquiring possession of Gonia tou Petake. The documents provide no direct information on this, but one might imagine that if the Malachiotai were paroikoi of Angelos, and if they had been successful in claiming that they had paid taxes on the property, then, once the property returned to their possession, they would render these taxes to Angelos himself. We recall that both Gonia tou Petake and Malachiou had once been a single unit held by Manuel Komnenos Laskaris.

Did Manuel Komnenos Laskaris hold Gonia tou Petake as a pronoia? This is almost certain. Since Laskaris held the property immediately before

[30] The editor of the *orismos* of September 1262 acknowledges that the restitution of an abbreviation, π(αροίκων), which would indicate that the Malachiotai were paroikoi, is unsure: *Patmos*, I, no. 30.2.

it was separated from Malachiou and granted to the Patmos monastery in 1259, he should have been one of those "who held Malachiou for pronoia" and who received the rent of the property from the Malachiotai and the others who worked the property. Since Gonia tou Petake was taken away from his family after his death, the situation accords with the evidence of the *Zavorda Treatise [2.1]* that a pronoia was granted by the emperor "for the life of a man." Nevertheless, it is quite possible that Manuel Laskaris' widow was permitted to keep the rest of Malachiou without Gonia tou Petake. We are not told who held the rest of Malachiou between the death of Laskaris and 1262 when it was granted to George Angelos. The fact that Michael VIII in July 1259 ordered the "men" of Maria Laskarina not to trouble the monastery over Gonia tou Petake indicates that Laskaris' widow maintained an economic interest in the area. In any event, even if she had been permitted to keep most of Malachiou, by 1262 she had lost it.

Who were Manuel Komnenos Laskaris and George Angelos? The *protosevastos* Manuel Komnenos Laskaris and his wife Maria Komnene Laskarina are known only from these documents. Michael VIII calls Manuel his *gamvros*, a word that means "in-law," usually son-in-law, and indicates that Laskaris was married to some relative of the emperor (see *ODB*, s.v. "gambros"). His title *protosevastos* was a rather exalted one. The emperor calls Maria his *anepsia*, which usually means "niece," but could be "cousin." Their specific relation to Michael VIII, or perhaps to his wife (a grandniece of John Vatatzes), is unknown. Since Manuel died before May 1259, he probably had received his grant prior to the death of Theodore II in August 1258. Thus, it seems that no later than the reign of Theodore II an individual with a relatively high title and with connections to the imperial family was granted a pronoia. As for George Komnenos Angelos, whom Michael VIII refers to as his "uncle," he too is unknown outside of these documents.

The two documents contribute to our understanding of the terminology used with regard to pronoia. The 1262 *orismos* of Michael VIII consistently uses the expression *eis pronoian*. Twice it states that the rent of Gonia tou Petake was rendered by the Malachiotai either to the fisc or to those "having Malachiou for pronoia" (τοὺς . . . εἰς πρόνοιαν ἔχοντας τὰ Μαλαχίου), and once it states that Malachiou "was granted for pronoia" (εἰς πρόνοιαν δωρηθέντος) to George Komnenos Angelos. The use of *doro*/*doroumai* (δωρῶ/δωροῦμαι) with *pronoia* is unique to this document, but certainly δωρεῖν τι εἰς πρόνοιαν parallels the expression παραδοῦναι τι εἰς πρόνοιαν as found in the 1184 *prostaxis* of Andronikos I Komnenos *[2.5]*.

The act of Selagites and the bishop John employs the expression "to have something *kata pronoian*" (ἔχειν τι κατὰ πρόνοιαν), which we have already encountered in the 1181 praktikon of Andronikos Vatatzes *[2.4]*. That this phrase is equivalent to "to have something for pronoia" (ἔχειν τι εἰς πρόνοιαν) is confirmed by the parallel passages in the 1262 *orismos* (τοῖς κατὰ πρόνοιαν ἔχοντες τῷ ῥηθὲν χωρίον Μαλαχίου compared to τοὺς . . . εἰς πρόνοιαν ἔχοντας τὰ Μαλαχίου).

Selagites and bishop John also employ the rare adverb *pronoiastikōs* twice, both times in the expression ἐπιμόρτως καὶ προνοιαστικῶς, yet there is something odd about the way the adverb "pronoiastically" (*pronoiastikōs*) is used. The pair determined that the Malachiotai held Gonia tou Petake "against a rent and pronoiastically, and gave such rent sometimes to those having the said village of Malachiou for pronoia, sometimes to those working for the fisc." Here the phrase "to hold a property pronoiastically" clearly did not mean "to hold a property as a pronoia." Rather it denoted a more general connection to a property that sometimes was held by another party as a pronoia: in this case it was connected to the leasing of such a property. This differs from the use of the word in the 1258 *orismos* of John IV Laskaris for the Patmos monastery *[5.2]* which mentions "the soldiers dwelling pronoiastically" in the area, a phrase which, by comparison with a parallel passage in the 1258 *orismos* of John IV Laskaris for the Kechionismene monastery *[5.3]*, appears to be equivalent to "soldiers having pronoiai in this place."

How could the people who held a property as a pronoia and the people who leased a property held by someone else as a pronoia both be said to hold property "pronoiastically"? The only way to make sense of this is to posit that Selagites and bishop John meant that the Malachiotai held Gonia tou Petake "because of a rental arrangement and because of a grant of a pronoia." The sense here is that both elements were essential for the present case to have arisen. If the property had not been held originally as a pronoia (that is, if it was private property), the emperor would not have had the right to grant it to the Patmos monastery, and only because the Malachiotai were leasing the property were their claims easy to dismiss.

The story of Gonia tou Petake confirms that, in the mid-thirteenth century, (i) property granted as a pronoia belonged to the state, (ii) it was not unusual for property held as a pronoia to return to the state after the death of the pronoia holder, and (iii) the benefit derived by those who were granted real property as a pronoia was the property's rent. Also, by the reign of Theodore II, individuals at the higher end of the social spectrum were receiving pronoiai.

The *vestiarites* Constantine Kalegopoulos

[5.7] Prostagma of John III Vatatzes for the monastery of the Lemviotissa (1234), and Act of the *vestiarites* Constantine Kalegopoulos and his son George (1234)

No less than in the twelfth century, pronoia holders came into conflict with monasteries over the contents of their grants. In 1227, at around the same time the Lemviotissa monastery received the village of Vare from the emperor, John Vatatzes also permitted the monastery to set up a fish pond on the gulf of Smyrna without fiscal charge. Seven years later, however, in February 1234, Vatatzes issued a *prostagma* dealing with a complaint of the monks. They said they were being forced to pay a charge on this pond to a certain *vestiarites* Constantine Kalegopoulos because "all the fish ponds there pay Kalegopoulos, since he holds for pronoia the rights of the river." They considered this unjust because the Hermos River had changed course and no longer fed their fish pond. The emperor ordered the *doux* of the theme of Thrakesion to investigate.[31]

The results of this investigation have not been preserved, but we do have an act issued by Kalegopoulos himself and his son George in April 1234. He begins by noting that the fish pond "was granted to me by reason of pronoia through a divine and imperial . . . *orismos*," and that the emperor had granted the monastery of the Lemviotissa an adjacent fish pond to which he had no claim. Kalegopoulos explains that a dispute developed over the fishing boats and the water channels that were within the property of the monastery's fish pond, Kalegopoulos claiming that charges on these were part of the rights he enjoyed from his fish pond on the Hermos River. Consequently, for some time the monastery "paid yearly for the sake of the boats some very small share to those having for a rent the fish pond of the river."[32] The *doux* of Thrakesion determined that this was unjust, evidently because the course of the Hermos had changed, as the 1234 *prostagma*

[31] MM, IV, 240 (1227), 239–40 (1234), esp. 239.28–30: τὰ ἐκεῖσε πάντα βιβάρια ἐτέλουν τῷ Καληγοπούλῳ, ὡς ἔχοντι εἰς πρόνοιαν τὰ δίκαια τοῦ ποταμοῦ. Dölger, *Regesten*, III, nos. 1714 and 1736, and cf. no. 1735. On the quarrel, P. Gounaridis, "La pêche dans le golfe de Smyrne," in *ΕΥΨΥΧΙΑ: mélanges offerts à Hélène Ahrweiler*, ed. M. Balard et al. (Paris, 1998), I, 265–71.

[32] MM, IV, 242.18–19: ἐδωρήθη μοι κατὰ λόγον προνοίας. MM, IV, 243.4–6: πρὸς τοὺς πακτικῶς ἔχοντας τὸ τοιοῦτου βιβάριον τοῦ ποταμοῦ. The documents refer to τὰ ἐξ ἀνέμου καὶ τὰ

explained, and so the boats were never intended to be part of Kalegopoulos' pronoia. Kalegopoulos abandoned any claim to the boats and promised that "those from time to time holding for a rent the fish pond under me of the river" would not trouble the monastery over the boats and the water channels. The next year the emperor, through a chrysobull, confirmed the monastery's possession of its fish pond, fishing boats, and the water channels (MM, IV, 21).

According to the *prostagma* Kalegopoulos received the tax or charge on fish ponds on a stretch of the Hermos River because he held "the rights of the river." Yet according to the act of Kalegopoulos he held a fish pond on the Hermos which he leased to others. The two documents are not describing the same arrangement. Either Kalegopoulos held, within his pronoia, both the river rights in that area *and* a fish pond on that river, or the information in one of the acts is faulty. If the latter, it is most likely that the monks misunderstood the situation when they made their initial complaint to the emperor, that Kalegopoulos merely held a fish pond which he leased and the monks confused the rental payment with a fishing charge that "all the fish ponds there pay." Thus, at the very least, a fish pond was contained within Kalegopoulos' pronoia grant. Because he leased the fish pond, he was acting as if he were the owner of this property. This means that this property was state property, and that Kalegopoulos was granted some of the rights that would appertain to a property owner.

These documents add a fish pond, and possibly river fishing rights, to the list of items that could be held within a pronoia, and the 1234 act of Kalegopoulos confirms that property held in pronoia was granted by the emperor and that the conferral was effected by the issuance of the type of document called an *orismos*. Finally, we see once again that those who were holding something "for pronoia" (*eis pronoian*) were granted this "by reason of pronoia" (*kata logon pronoias*). This is the last time the latter phrase appears.

αὐλάκια: MM, IV, 17, 21, 24, 31, 242–44. *Aulakia* would seem to be the network of channels used in fish ponds, but the phrase *ta ex anemou* ("the things from wind") is more problematic. Evidently it appears *only* in the documents dealing with this particular fish pond. At first glance, one might think of windmills (to regulate water height), but while windmills may have existed at the time in Byzantium, scholarly consensus is that they would not have been used for anything except grinding grain and crushing olives: see Ch. Bouras, "Aspects of the Byzantine City, Eighth–Fifteenth Centuries," *EHB*, II, 519. Tentatively, I have adopted the view of Gounaridis, "La pêche," 268, that "the things from wind" were simply sailboats used for fishing in the ponds, but I am not completely convinced.

The *kavallarios* Syrgares

Another example of property changes after 1204 is found in a series of documents dealing with a property dispute between the Lemviotissa monastery and the paroikoi of a pronoia holder named Syrgares. Aside from providing further evidence of pronoia holders in the area of Smyrna, these documents allow us to make some conclusions about the relationship between a pronoia holder and his paroikoi. The series of documents begins with an act from January 1234 by which the *vestiarites* George Kaloeidas and his wife donated to the Lemviotissa monastery a property of 10 modioi called ta Sphournou in the area near Smyrna. Kaloeidas notes that he had acquired the property from his wife's grandfather and that it had previously belonged to the Constantinopolitan monastery of the Rouphinianai. In April of the same year an imperial *prostagma* confirmed this donation and the tax-exempt status of the property.[33]

[5.8] Act of John Angelos, *doux* of Thrakesion, involving a dispute over ta Sphournou (1235)

However, an act of the *stratopedarches* Phokas, from March 1235, which contains a long, detailed list of all the properties held by the monastery reports that Phokas found, "settling without any right in . . . ta Sphournou, three paroikoi from the village of Potamou, subject to . . . Syrgares." The official ordered them to leave the property of the monastery and "go where they were installed previously."[34]

The paroikoi and the monastery then sent the issue to the emperor. An act of the *doux* of Thrakesion John Angelos from September 1235 describes the litigation. Angelos reports that the *hegoumenos* of the monastery presented him with an imperial *orismos*, addressed to Angelos, ordering him to investigate the dispute. This *orismos*, from June 1235, is inserted in Angelos' act and repeats the monastery's claim that "the paroikoi of Syrgares" had improperly settled on the monastery's property at ta Sphournou.[35]

[33] MM, IV, 32–33, 34. Dölger, *Regesten*, III, no. 1738. The property is later listed among the possessions of the monastery in a chrysobull from June 1235: MM, IV, 19.21–22, and Dölger, *Regesten*, III, no. 1749. On the case of ta Sphournou as a whole, see Ostrogorsky, *Féodalité*, 72–74, and Charanis, "Monastic Properties," 107–08, which is repeated nearly verbatim in Charanis, "Social Structure," 98–99.

[34] MM, IV, 7.8–13: τρεῖς πάροικοι . . . τελοῦντες ὑπὸ . . . τὸν Συργαρήν.

[35] MM, IV, 36.31–32, 37.3: τοὺς παροίκους τοῦ Συργαρῆ. Dölger, *Regesten*, III, no. 1750.

Angelos then states that "the Potamenoi from the pronoia of this same Syrgares" had presented to him a request they themselves had made to the emperor, along with the emperor's reply (another *orismos*). The texts of both of these are inserted in Angelos' act as well. According to the request, "the paroikoi of the *kavallarios* Syrgares," even though they originated from the village of Potamou, claimed that they and their parents had lived at ta Sphournou for a long time, that they had improved the property, that they had acquired several other parcels so that they would be able to pay state taxes, and that they had donated a water mill to the monastery. To drive them away from their patrimony (*gonikon*) would be an injustice. Responding to this request, the emperor issued an *orismos* in July 1235, which ordered Angelos to investigate.[36]

Angelos called witnesses from the villages of Rouzes and Drous to decide whether the claim of the Potamenoi was legitimate. Also present were some people "from the pronoia" (ἀπὸ τῆς προνοίας) of Syrgares, specifically, the priest and *nomikos* Nicholas Laodikenos, and five other men. Two others were "from the pronoia" of the *pansevastos prokathemenos* Alopos.[37]

Those from the villages of Rouzes and Drous affirmed that ta Sphournou was not the patrimony of the Potamenoi, but that at the time Henry of Flanders invaded the area (ca. 1211–12), the Potamenoi and other villagers were ordered to abandon their homes for more secure areas by the *sevastokrator* George Laskaris, Theodore I's brother. Some, including the Potamenoi, moved to ta Sphournou which had belonged to the Rouphinianai monastery. After the Latins left the area, the villagers returned to their previous homes, but those of Rouzes and Drous continued to cultivate ta Sphournou, paying a rent to its new owner, named Kastamonites, the grandfather of Kaloeidas' wife. After the property was donated to the Lemviotissa monastery by Kaloeidas, "the Potamenoi and Syrgares, the *lizios kavallarios* of our lord the holy emperor, who holds them in pronoia," persuaded the monastery's *hegoumenos* to receive them back anew on a temporary basis. Angelos ruled that since the Potamenoi held no patrimony at ta Sphournou, but settled as "strangers" (*xenoi*, according to the witness statement: MM, IV, 36.16), they should return to their previous homes.[38]

[36] MM, IV, 37.10–11: οἱ ἀπὸ τῆς προνοίας τοῦ αὐτοῦ Συργαρῆ Ποταμηνοί; 37.13–14: οἱ ἀπὸ τοῦ ἀγριδίου τὰ Ποταμοῦ ὁρμώμενοι πάροικοι τοῦ καβαλλαρίου τοῦ Συργαρῆ; 37–38. Dölger, *Regesten*, III, no. 1751.

[37] MM, IV, 38.14–19. On Laodikenos, see *[5.9]*.

[38] MM, IV, 39.10–11: οἱ Ποταμηνοὶ καὶ ὁ κατέχων αὐτοὺς εἰς πρόνοιαν λίζιος καβαλλάριος τοῦ αὐθέντου ἡμῶν τοῦ βασιλέως τοῦ ἁγίου ὁ Συργαρῆς. The original deposition of these witnesses, from July 1235, which adds further details that refute the testimony of the Potamenoi, is also extant: MM, IV, 34–36.

In January 1236 the emperor confirmed this decision, but then, in an act of the metropolitan of Smyrna, from May 1237, we learn that Syrgares' paroikoi had refused to leave ta Sphournou. The *hegoumenos* of the Lemviotissa complained to the emperor that Syrgares continued to maintain that the property belonged to his paroikoi and that the previous decisions had treated them unjustly. The metropolitan called the previous witnesses, and in the presence of "the said *kavallarios* and his Mantaianoi paroikoi . . . and his other Potamenoi paroikoi," it was decided that "the *kavallarios* and his paroikoi" should leave ta Sphournou, but be compensated for the vines and other trees near their huts at ta Sphournou. Further, "the Potamenoi and their lord [*authentes*]" sought from the monastery another place for the habitation of "the Potamenoi paroikoi of Syrgares." The metropolitan agreed, the monks accepted the decision, and the case was finally settled.[39]

Only one of the documents dealing with ta Sphournou employs the word *pronoia*. This is the act of Angelos, in which it appears four times. Indeed the act of Angelos itself contains three inserted documents, two *orismoi* and the request of the Potamenoi, but the word does not appear in any of these. Rather, it appears only in those parts of his act in which he wrote his own words. This means that there was nothing essential about the presence of the word *pronoia* in such documents, and it suggests that many other cases may exist involving similar relationships between men and their paroikoi which simply omit all reference to pronoia.

Angelos' act speaks of two pronoia holders, both of whom held paroikoi: the *kavallarios* Syrgares and the *prokathemenos* Alopos. Syrgares' status and identity, as well as the extent of his pronoia holdings, will be discussed with the next document dealt with in this chapter *[5.9]*.

As for the *prokathemenos* Alopos, he was certainly John Alopos, the *prokathemenos* of Smyrna, who issued a document in 1234, witnessed a land sale in 1236, and is referred to in a document from 1235 as having earlier performed an official transfer of property to the Lemviotissa monastery. Hélène Ahrweiler wrote that his pronoia was probably situated in the region south of Mantaia and that it was probably of modest extent, since Lemviotissa held property there as well. Michael Angold thought his pronoia consisted of the village of Pauchome, a weak guess based on parallel positions of witnesses in the July 1235 deposition, which does not mention Alopos, and in Angelos' act, which does (compare MM, IV, 35.2–9 with 38.12–19).[40]

39 MM, IV, 40–41. Dölger, *Regesten*, III, no. 1752. MM, IV, 42.11–13,21,26,28.

40 MM, IV, 146–50 (1234), 9.20–21 (1235), 193–94 (1236). Ahrweiler, "Smyrne," 157, and Glykatzi-Ahrweiler, "Politique agraire," 58. Ahrweiler notes that "*demosiarioi* paroikoi" lived in Mantaia,

Alopos is the first pronoia holder who was clearly not a soldier. Earlier documents dealing with Synadenos *[2.2]*, Pankratios Anemas *[2.3]*, and the *vestiarites* Vlatteros *[5.4]* have suggested that the holders of pronoiai need not have been soldiers, but this document confirms this. *Prokathemenoi* were civil officials who administered towns. They first appear in the twelfth century. No doubt in times of crisis the responsibilities of the *prokathemenos* would involve defense, but in times of peace, *prokathemenoi* handled civil matters.[41]

The relationship between Syrgares and his paroikoi is quite instructive. The Potamenoi were "the paroikoi of Syrgares," "from the pronoia of... Syrgares," and "subject to" or "arranged under" Syrgares. Syrgares "held them in pronoia" and was "their lord" (*authentes*).

It was certainly in Syrgares' interest for the paroikoi to acquire ta Sphournou, to have it recognized as their patrimonial property (*gonikon*). If their possessions increased, his revenues would increase proportionately. Yet, in some ways, he seems to be an equal partner with the Potamenoi in the litigation. The Potamenoi maintain a high degree of independence in the dispute. Michael Angold has noted that the paroikoi took their complaint directly to the emperor rather than pursuing the dispute through Syrgares, but, nevertheless, two years later Syrgares appeared in court on their behalf. What do we make of this? First, it would seem that in a simple property dispute with an outsider, the paroikoi of a pronoia holder did not have to pursue their case through their lord. He was not their legal spokesman, nor was he their judge. This is powerful evidence against the notion that the pronoia holder enjoyed administrative and judicial authority over his paroikoi.[42] Second, the fact that the paroikoi made a direct request for imperial intervention and received an imperial *orismos* puts them on a level, in regard to their legal status, parallel to the monastery which similarly made a request to the emperor and received an *orismos*. In the eyes of the law, the status of the

too (MM, ɪᴠ, 38.28), but I think this is a reference to the paroikoi held by pronoia holders. M. Angold, *A Byzantine Government in Exile* (London, 1975), 265.

41 Bartusis, *Late Byzantine Army*, 33–34.

42 Angold, *Byzantine Government*, 136. B. Gorjanov, *Pozdnevizantijskij feodalizm* (Moscow, 1962), 102, 181, in his eagerness to prove that pronoia holders held such rights, misread a couple of passages from these documents. He misinterpreted the clause πάροικοι τοῦ... Συργαρῆ προσεκάθισαν εἰς τόπον τῆς ὑπ' αὐτὸν μονῆς τὸν ἐπιλεγόμενον τὰ Σφούρνου (MM, ɪᴠ, 36.31–33) to mean that the "paroikoi of Syrgares must stand under his power in that which concerns Sphournou," when in fact ὑπ' αὐτόν modifies "monastery" not "paroikoi." Further, he wrote that ὁ... καβαλλάριος δικαίῳ τε οἰκείῳ καὶ δικαίῳ τῶν παροίκων αὐτοῦ (MM, ɪᴠ, 41.15–16) meant that Syrgares was invested "with the right of justice on his own possessions and also of justice over his paroikoi." The phrase actually means that Syrgares pursued the case "in his own right and in the right (i.e., name) of his paroikoi."

Potamenoi, as subjects of the emperor entitled to the normal legal protection an emperor owed his subjects, was not diminished once they became paroikoi of a pronoia holder. As for Syrgares appearing in court on their behalf, we might suggest that, after failing in their initial attempts to acquire ta Sphournou, the paroikoi asked for help from their lord Syrgares.[43]

[5.9] Act of the inhabitants of Panaretou involving a dispute over the olive trees of John Poleas (1251)

The pronoia of the *kavallarios* Syrgares appears once again in an act from 1251 dealing with a property transfer which occurred in 1209. In that year the priest John Poleas from the parish (*enoria*) of Mantaia and his son Thomas gave a relative, another priest named Leo Mouzethras, thirty olive saplings plus two old trees (MM, IV, 199–21). However, John later regretted this gift and a document from 1251 reports that Poleas, twenty-three years earlier, that is, in 1228, sent word "to his lord, the *lizios kavallarios* Syrgares," that he had given Mouzethras only twenty saplings and that the latter held the other ten illegally. "Syrgares sent this dispute to the *oikodespotai* of his pronoia," and an assembly was convened of "all the head men [*kreittones*] of his pronoia," including the priest and *nomikos* Nicholas Laodikenos.[44] These men, who, according to the document of 1251, were inhabitants of the village of Aureliou (MM, IV, 82.31), examined the relevant document and decided for Mouzethras. Poleas wished to take an oath as to his veracity, but Mouzethras, rather than let him swear falsely, renounced his rights to the ten disputed trees.

By 1251 Poleas, Mouzethras, and Syrgares had died. The son-in-law of Mouzethras, Constantine Volovontes, held twenty of the original trees, and

[43] I am unable to work out to my satisfaction some of the more subtle aspects of the relationship between Syrgares and his paroikoi because of chronological issues. Two documents explicitly state that the Potamenoi, paroikoi of Syrgares, settled on ta Sphournou while Gerasimos was *hegoumenos* of Lemviotissa and that the monastery was not able to remove them at that time (MM, IV, 36.5–14, 39.8–15). However, by the time Kaloeidas donated the ten modioi of ta Sphournou to Lemviotissa, Gerasimos was no longer *hegoumenos*. He held this position at least through November 1232 (IV, 260), but no later than April 1233 when a new *hegoumenos* first appears (IV, 198). Thus, the monastery seems to have had some presence at ta Sphournou before Kaloeidas donated ta Sphournou to them. Is it possible that the *proasteion* of ten modioi (a bit smaller than a baseball field) called ta Sphournou that Kaloeidas donated to the monastery was only part of a larger property owned by the monastery which also was called ta Sphournou?

[44] MM, IV, 81.13–14: πρὸς τὸν αὐθέντην αὐτοῦ, τὸν λίζιον καβαλλάριον τὸν Συργαρήν, 81.20–21: ὁ Συργαρὴς ἐπέπεμψε τὴν τοιαύτην κρίσιν πρὸς τοὺς οἰκοδεσπότας τῆς προνοίας αὐτοῦ, and 81.22–23.

the son of Poleas, Thomas, now a paroikos of a woman named Komnene Vranaina, held the other ten. Thomas, his brother George, and their mother now reopened the case by claiming "to their lady [τὴν κυρίαν αὐτῶν] the most well-born Komnene Vranaina" that Volovontes held his twenty trees illegally. Vranaina sent the case to the *oikodespotai* of the village of Panaretou, but before a decision was reached, Poleas harvested the disputed trees. As a result, Vranaina had Poleas tried by these *oikodespotai* who affirmed that the trees belonged to Volovontes and forbade Poleas and his family to reopen the case in any ecclesiastical or secular court.[45]

George Ostrogorsky thought that Poleas' status had changed between 1209 and 1228, that at the time of the original gift, Poleas and his son were free proprietors and not paroikoi. He based this conclusion on the fact that Poleas stipulated in his 1209 act granting the trees to Mouzethras that the latter had to pay Poleas $1\frac{1}{2}$ hyperpyra yearly "which the fisc demands." Because Poleas paid taxes directly to the state, Ostrogorsky reasoned, he was not a paroikos but a free proprietor; however, by 1228 he had become a paroikos of Syrgares. Thus, "as a result of the attribution of a territory in pronoia, the population of a village on this territory and which, up to then, was free, fell under the dependence of a pronoiarios, transforming themselves into his paroikoi."[46] There are a few problems here. First, there is the tone of the statement. To "fall under the dependence" of someone sounds onerous, and it indeed reflects Ostrogorsky's view that thirteenth-century (and later) paroikoi were dependent peasants closely paralleling the serfs of the medieval West. In fact, as the case involving ta Sphournou *[5.8]* shows, "falling under the dependence" of a pronoia holder could provide certain advantages. Specifically, it could provide the small property owner with a patron, in whose interest it was to protect the property rights of the small proprietor against the encroachments of powerful neighbors, such as monasteries or other lay landowners.[47]

Second, it is not clear that Poleas in fact was a "free proprietor" and not a paroikos in 1209. The fiscal device Poleas' 1209 act describes whereby Mouzethras was required to pay him an annual sum is known as an *epiteleia*. *Epiteleiai* first appear in the early thirteenth century in the documents

[45] On the case, Ostrogorsky, *Féodalité*, 75, 77, and Angold, *Byzantine Government*, 263.

[46] MM, IV, 121.17–18. Ostrogorsky, *Féodalité*, 76. Also noted by Angold, *Byzantine Government*, 134.

[47] If Syrgares' paroikoi paid all of their taxes to the fisc, as Zuckerman, "The Dishonest Soldier," 328–29, suggests as a possibility, there would be no economic incentive for him to care how much property his paroikoi owned.

of the Lemviotissa monastery, the earliest known case from 1208 (MM, IV, 183.29), and they continue to appear in other documents well into the fourteenth century. In the documents from the Lemviotissa cartulary, typically someone sold property, usually olive trees, to another and received, aside from the sale price, a relatively small annual quantity of money from the purchaser which is called an *epiteleia*. The function of the *epiteleia* was either to compensate the owner of property which enjoyed a fiscal exemption of taxes for the loss of this exemption when the owner sold or donated the property to another or to provide the seller with the property's *telos* which was owed to a pronoia holder or another privileged grant holder. Thus, an *epiteleia* was called for under two scenarios:

(i) When a landowner who owned a property which enjoyed an exemption of taxes sold or donated the property to another, he could either pass this exemption on to the new owner of the property or demand an annual *epiteleia* to compensate him for the loss.
(ii) When a landowner sold or donated the property, the *telos* of which was received by a pronoia holder or other grant holder (such as a monastery), the landowner was still obliged to render the *telos* to the pronoia holder or other grant holder. So the original landowner stipulated that the new owner of the property render to him an *epiteleia* corresponding to the *telos* the original owner was required to render to the third party. In this second case the original landowner was technically a paroikos, though he need not have been poor or even a peasant.

[5.10] Act of sale of Xenos Legas, his wife, and son (1231)

It must be admitted that while the first scenario above is reasonable, there is little evidence to support its existence.[48] The second scenario is of greater interest to this study because it was one method to finance pronoia grants. We have one secure example of this from the thirteenth century. The example involves Xenos Legas, a paroikos of the monastery of the Lemviotissa, who lived in the village of Vare. In 1231 he, his wife, and son, sold to the monastery eighteen olive trees located in the village of Panaretou which was held within the pronoia of the *kavallarios* Syrgares. Because Syrgares received from the emperor the tax revenue from all of the privately owned properties in Panaretou, henceforth "the monastery ought to pay each year

[48] As Zuckerman, "The Dishonest Soldier," 329–30, has noted.

for *epiteleia* 1 nomisma to . . . Syrgares."[49] Aside from illustrating one use for an *epiteleia*, this case proves that when a landowner's property tax was held by a pronoia holder, it did not necessarily mean that the landowner himself was held by the pronoia holder.

Scholars have long assumed that Syrgares had been granted the taxes from these olive trees and that the purpose of the *epiteleia* was to guarantee Syrgares' income after the transaction. However, Constantine Zuckerman suggested that Syrgares did not receive the taxes from these olive trees and that this *epiteleia* was not kept by Syrgares, but was passed on to the fisc.[50] Such a hypothesis is illogical. Neither Syrgares nor the state owned these olive trees; rather, they were owned by third-party private individuals. Therefore, what kind of benefit could Syrgares derive from them? Since he had no claim to the benefits that accrued to ownership, only the rights belonging to the fisc, that is, taxation, remain. Zuckerman's interpretation would make Syrgares merely a tax collector for this property.

Further, one cannot even suggest that Syrgares' connection to the olive trees somehow made the owners of the trees obligated toward him for labor services. Xenos Legas and his wife lived in the village of Vare, which was held by the Lemviotissa monastery, and were paroikoi of this monastery (MM, IV, 13.26). As such, Legas owed labor services to the monastery, not to Syrgares.

Ahrweiler summed up the case of Xenos Legas by writing that a peasant possessing lands in a domain parceled between several beneficiaries was not obliged to furnish labor services to each of them. He was not a paroikos of all of them, but only to the one beneficiary in whose praktikon he appeared. To the others he paid the charges burdening his property situated in the domain of each. Thus, while Legas was indebted to Syrgares, he was a paroikos of the monastery.[51]

The sale of these olive trees also raises the question of what it meant to be a paroikos, and, specifically, the paroikos of a pronoia holder. Was the essence of paroikos status the payment of taxes to a private individual or

[49] MM, IV, 61.20–22. H. Glykatzi(-Ahrweiler),"L'épiteleia dans le cartulaire de Lemviotissa," in Ahrweiler, *Études sur les structures administratives et sociales de Byzance* (London, 1971), no. V, 74 note 4. Charanis, "The Aristocracy of Byzantium in the Thirteenth Century," 342.

[50] Zuckerman, "The Dishonest Soldier," 325. Also see, generally, *ODB*, s.v. "epiteleia," and Angold, *Byzantine Government*, 137.

[51] Glykatzi-Ahrweiler, "Politique agraire," 60 note 6. Also, see Glykatzi(-Ahrweiler), "A propos de l'épitéleia," in Ahrweiler, *Études sur les structures administratives et sociales de Byzance* (London, 1971), no. VI, 371–72, and Glykatzi(-Ahrweiler), "L'épitéleia dans le cartulaire de Lemviotissa," 88–89, as well as Ostrogorsky, *Féodalité*, 78–79, and Charanis, "Social Structure," 98 = Charanis, "Monastic Properties," 88 = Charanis, "Aristocracy of Byzantium," 342.

corporation (such as a monastery), or was it the burden of labor services to a private individual or corporation? On the basis of the present case one might suggest the latter. However, the labor services we are speaking of were, no less than state taxes, originally burdens owed the state that devolved to private landholders.

How does Poleas' act fit into this? Poleas writes that "the fisc" demanded the $1\frac{1}{2}$ nomismata annually which is why Ostrogorsky concluded that Poleas was not a paroikos in 1209. But this would not be in accord with either scenario described above for the function of an *epiteleia*. Why would Poleas be required to pay what appears to be a tax on trees he no longer owned? Ostrogorsky, following Franz Dölger, assumed that the seller or donor, like Poleas, was required to pay the tax on the property until the next revision of the tax lists. However, there is no evidence to support this hypothesis. Further, *epiteleiai* are mentioned in many praktika which is inexplicable if *epiteleiai* were eliminated in the course of each fiscal revision. On the other hand, Zuckerman presented a convoluted theory to explain the situation. He argued that the people who received *epiteleiai* from those to whom they had sold or given property did so because they continued to own the property. Thus, the olive trees Poleas transferred to Mouzethras remained Poleas' property (or they remained part of Poleas' village unit) and so therefore the state continued to demand from Poleas the tax on the trees. Zuckerman's argument rests on the assumption that peasants were not permitted to alienate their property or even that their holdings which they inherited from their parents and passed to their children were not actually their property at all. A peculiar notion.[52]

I do not think we can conclude that Poleas paid the tax on his olives directly to the state prior to 1209. A simpler way to interpret the Poleas act is to posit that he was a paroikos in both 1209 and 1228, and that the $1\frac{1}{2}$ nomismata that he claims was demanded by the "fisc" actually was collected and kept by the recipient of an imperial grant, such as a pronoia holder or a privileged monastery. In 1209 the *epiteleia* was a new institution and the distinction between rendering the tax to the state and to a pronoia holder or another third party may have been moot to Poleas.

I would argue that the purpose of the *epiteleia* was to deal with the accounting problem caused when a paroikos alienated a property the taxes of which were assigned to a pronoia holder or other recipient of such an imperial privilege. This would explain why almost all the sellers or donors who were to be paid an *epiteleiai* by the buyer or recipient of the property

[52] Ostrogorsky, *Féodalité*, 78. Dölger, *Beiträge*, 55. Zuckerman, "The Dishonest Soldier," 320.

appear to be people at the lower end of the social spectrum; their taxes had been granted to some privileged individual or institution.

Ostrogorsky believed that Syrgares' pronoia included the villages of Aureliou and Potamou, and Angold claimed that the village of Panaretou was part of his pronoia. Somewhat more cautiously, Peter Charanis concluded that his pronoia included three villages – Potamou, Panaretou, and (incorrectly) Mantaia – or the greater part thereof. Similarly, Ahrweiler wrote merely that his pronoia was situated in the villages of Aureliou, Panaretou, and Potamou.[53]

Actually, all of these opinions go beyond the information the documents offer. Collating all the references to what the documents say Syrgares held in pronoia *[5.8][5.9]*, at the very least Syrgares held in his pronoia three unnamed paroikoi from Potamou, one paroikos from Aureliou (John Poleas), plus the *oikodespotai* of Aureliou (a minimum of two, plus the priest and *nomikos* Nicholas Laodikenos), and five other paroikoi of unspecified residence. Thus, all we can say with certainty is that his pronoia consisted of at least a dozen paroikoi, at least seven of whom lived in Aureliou or Potamou.

In addition, it is possible to go further and say that Syrgares held the entire village of Aureliou in pronoia. This conclusion is based on a comparison of several passages in the 1251 act. The document states that Syrgares sent the dispute "to the *oikodespotai* of his pronoia" and refers to "the headmen [*kreittones*] of his pronoia." Later the document mentions "the past decision by the inhabitants of the village of Aureliou" (MM, IV, 82.30–31). It is unlikely that the document would mention the earlier decision as one made by "the inhabitants of the village of Aureliou" if Syrgares held only a portion of the village.

At this point the word *oikodespotes* needs explication. Numerous definitions have been offered by scholars. While Nicolas Oikonomides rendered the word as "landowner" ("propriétaire terrien"), Angold treated both *oikodespotai* and *kreittones* as village representatives who constituted a kind of "peasant aristocracy." Ahrweiler, on the other hand, wrote that the word could be equivalent to paroikos. The present documents show that *oikodespotai* could easily fit all three of these definitions. Syrgares' *oikodespotai* were undeniably paroikoi, and yet, in the role they assumed in their village, they were the more eminent members of the community. In

53 Ostrogorsky, *Féodalité*, 78. Angold, *Byzantine Government*, 127, 263. Charanis, "Social Structure," 98. Glykatzi-Ahrweiler, "Politique agraire," 57–58.

addition, since it was not uncommon for paroikoi to own property, it would be these *oikodespotai* who were most likely to have been the larger property owners within the village.[54]

Aside from these paroikoi and probably the village of Aureliou, Syrgares held, under unspecified conditions, at least one other paroikos (one of the two "Mantaianoi paroikoi") of uncertain residence and fifty-four olive trees in Panaretou. The idea that he held the village of Panaretou within his pronoia is based on the 1231 act of sale of Xenos Legas discussed above and an act of sale of his son-in-law Niketas Kavoures. Legas sold eighteen olive trees in the village of Panaretou to the Lemviotissa monastery, and the next year Kavoures and his wife sold twenty-four olive trees in the same village to the same monastery. In each case the bill of sale stipulated that "the monastery ought to pay each year, for an *epiteleia*, 1 nomisma to the *kavallarios* Syrgares" (MM, IV, 135.6–7).

By 1251 lady Komnene Vranaina succeeded to Syrgares' role as the patron and lord of the Poleas family. Angold and, more tentatively, Ahrweiler identified her as Irene Komnene Vranaina, a woman known only for having donated a property in the village of Vare to the Lemviotissa monastery between 1232 and 1235. Both scholars wrote that after Syrgares' death the village of Panaretou passed to her.[55] Ahrweiler and Ostrogorsky, because they did not believe that a woman could hold a pronoia, state that she, unlike Syrgares, certainly did not hold the village in pronoia.[56]

Evidently the Poleas family were paroikoi of Komnene Vranaina (since they call her "their lady"), and evidently she held all or part of the village of Panaretou (since she sent Thomas Poleas to be judged by the *oikodespotai* of that village). But we do not know how she came into possession of Panaretou,

[54] N. Oikonomides, "Contribution à l'étude de la pronoia au XIIIe siècle," in Oikonomides, *Documents et études sur les institutions de Byzance* (London, 1976), no. VI, 166–67. Angold, *Byzantine Government*, 260–64. Ahrweiler, "Smyrne," 40 and note 78. That paroikoi of a pronoia holder could own property bothered Charanis and led him to hypothesize that the paroikoi of a pronoia should be distinguished from ordinary paroikoi, the former not necessarily being dependent peasants. "The ownership of their land and their social position was legally not affected by the fact that their village was granted as a pronoia to Syrgares. What was changed was their relationship to the government" (Charanis, "Social Structure," 142).

[55] Angold, *Byzantine Government*, 127, 263. Ahrweiler, "Smyrne," 169, and Glykatzi-Ahrweiler, "Politique agraire," 58–59. The terminus post quem for the donation of Irene Komnene Vranaina (MM, IV, 225) is March 1232, the last mention (MM, IV, 134.29) of the *hegoumenos* of the monastery preceding the *hegoumenos* Paul referred to in the document, and the terminus ante quem is March 1235, when a document (MM, IV, 14.15) first mentions this property as a possession of the monastery.

[56] Ostrogorsky, *Féodalité*, 77. Glykatzi-Ahrweiler, "Politique agraire," 58–59.

how she held the village and the Poleas family, and what her relationship to Syrgares was. That she did not hold her possessions in pronoia is merely an assumption.

Further, it is unclear why Komnene Vranaina, if she held only Panaretou, heard the complaint of Poleas, who lived in Aureliou. If she held Aureliou as well, why in 1251 did the *oikodespotai* of Panaretou hear the case involving Thomas Poleas? The 1251 act specifies that back in 1228 the case involving his father was heard by the *oikodespotai* of Aureliou. While we may hypothesize that she held the territories of both villages and that, with the passage of time, disputes involving the inhabitants of either locale were handled by the *oikodespotai* of Panaretou, this remains mere speculation.

Moreover, Ostrogorsky and Ahrweiler both suggested that the village of Aureliou was not given to Komnene Vranaina, but attributed to a certain *kavallarios* named *syr* Adam. Ostrogorsky in fact considered it probable that this village was attributed to Adam as a pronoia. *Syr* Adam is only known from a copyist's title to an unpreserved act in which he donated some olive trees in Aureliou to the Lemviotissa monastery, and in a later act confirming this donation from 1306 (or 1301), after his death.[57] Yet there is no indication that Adam held these olive trees within a pronoia (he might have owned them outright), and there is no real reason to think that Syrgares' pronoia included all of Aureliou. In 1260 a Nicholas Adam donated a church and property, at least some of which the emperor granted him on a tax-free basis, in the nearby village of Planou to the Lemviotissa monastery *[8.63]*. If Nicholas Adam was not *syr* Adam, then he was probably a relative. In any event, this family was already established in the Mantaia area at the same time as Syrgares.

Ahrweiler thought that the pronoiai of Vlatteros and Syrgares showed that Theodore I Laskaris was granting relatively large pronoiai, but that the alleged parceling of Syrgares' pronoia to several other persons after his death showed that John III Vatatzes tried to limit the size of pronoia grants. But even though Vlatteros' pronoia (the village of Vare) was certainly substantial, it is not at all clear how large Syrgares' pronoia was. Nor do we know for sure that it was first granted under Theodore I. In sum, we really cannot draw any firm conclusions regarding the extent of Syrgares' holdings in pronoia or the fate of his pronoia after his death. He may have been only one of a number of pronoia holders or other privileged persons who received grants of revenues or of imperial properties in these villages. Some of his holdings,

[57] Ostrogorsky, *Féodalité*, 79. Glykatzi-Ahrweiler, "Politique agraire," 58. MM, IV, 79, 103–04. On the date of the latter act, see Ahrweiler, "Smyrne," 152–54.

such as the olive trees in Panaretou, may not have been held within his pronoia at all.[58]

Some scholars have viewed Syrgares' involvement in settling a dispute between his paroikoi as evidence that pronoia holders enjoyed administrative and juridical rights over their paroikoi. For example, using the Poleas affair as evidence, Peter Charanis offered the generalization that lawsuits involving property disputes among the inhabitants of a pronoia were judged by the pronoia holder and the more distinguished inhabitants of the pronoia (*kreittones*). On the other hand, he wrote, lawsuits involving a pronoia holder or the paroikoi of a pronoia with another party were judged by the military governor of the region, as in the case involving the Potamenoi and ta Sphournou.[59]

This is not quite accurate. In the matter of Poleas' olive trees Syrgares did not judge the case; rather, the initial complaint was brought to him, and he convened the village assembly that decided the case. The resolution of the dispute was the business of the villagers. In other words, disputes between village members were solved by village members, with the pronoia holder acting, not as a state official, but as powerful member of the community who could persuade the other villagers to conduct an inquiry. Alternatively, disputes between a village member and an outsider required a court that had jurisdiction over both parties; it could be ecclesiastical or secular. A pronoia holder logically took the part of his paroikoi.

Then again, the Poleas case shows that lady Komnene Vranaina played a role no different from that of Syrgares, and indeed no scholar (rightly or wrongly) has ever considered her a pronoia holder. Perhaps, then, as Angold has written, should we conclude, more generally, "that the holders of privileged property were taking over some of the functions of the imperial administration"?[60] To answer this question, we really need to know the traditional manner in which litigation was conducted within the village community before the onset of the practice of granting rural property to

58 Glykatzi-Ahrweiler, "Politique agraire," 57–58. As for the village of Potamou, someone named Manuel Doukas held property there during the 1280s (MM, ɪᴠ, 104–05). Cf. Ahrweiler, "Smyrne," 168.

59 Charanis, "Social Structure," 97 note 12. For the latter type of dispute, he also cited the Kalegopoulos case *[5.7]* and another case discussed below *[8.65]*. Also, Gorjanov, *Pozdnevizantijskij feodalizm*, 181, interpreted the passage that Syrgares ἐπέπεμφε τὴν τοιαύτην κρίσιν πρὸς τοὺς οἰκοδεσπότας τῆς προνοίας αὐτοῦ (MM, ɪᴠ, 81.20–21) as evidence of Syrgares' judicial powers. However, because the *oikodespotai* themselves made the decision, κρίσις must mean, in this context, "dispute, issue," not, as Gorjanov thought, "decision, judgment."

60 Angold, *Byzantine Government*, 263.

privileged individuals; in other words, whether the resolution of local property disputes normally employed the services of state officials or whether such lawsuits were normally handled, at least in the early stages of litigation, entirely by the local inhabitants. If the latter alternative was the case, then the entry of a Syrgares or Vranaina into the village community and their involvement in its affairs need not have signaled any devolution of state judicial power into their hands. Rather, as eminent and, of course, wealthy personages, they may well have become simply the most important members of the village community. The lack of documents relating to disputes between village inhabitants supports this view.

Moreover, the documents involving Syrgares have been cited as evidence that the holders of pronoiai established administrative apparatuses. Ostrogorsky wrote that the priest and *nomikos* Nicholas Laodikenos, one of the paroikoi in Syrgares' pronoia in Aureliou, was "Syrgares' notary" and "notary of Syrgares' pronoia," and he concluded that "it is not at all surprising that pronoiarioi had on their possessions some special officials. The pronoiarios who had large domains with a large number of peasants from whom he collected taxes naturally felt the need to have on these lands a kind of administrative apparatus." Ostrogorsky's conclusion is reasonable, but his assumptions about Laodikenos are unwarranted.[61]

Neither document that mentions Laodikenos asserts that he was Syrgares' notary (*nomikos*), much less the "notary of Syrgares' pronoia." According to the 1235 act of Angelos *[5.8]*, among those present at the 1235 hearing were, "from the pronoia of Syrgares," the priest and *nomikos* Nicholas Laodikenos, and five other men. The 1251 act notes that, back in 1228, "all the headmen of his [Syrgares'] pronoia assembled, as well as the *nomikos* τοῦ αὐτοῦ χωρίου, the priest Nicholas Laodikenos" (MM, IV, 81.22–24). Ostrogorsky interpreted the phrase τοῦ αὐτοῦ χωρίου as "of his (Syrgares') village," but the usual way of expressing possession is to place the pronoun after the noun, as in τῆς προνοίας αὐτοῦ. I think it is more likely that the phrase means that Laodikenos was the *nomikos* "of the village itself," or "of this village."

Indeed it is misleading to translate *nomikos* as "notary," a functionary who, in the modern world, tends to operate within the secular sphere. A *nomikos* was an ecclesiastical official, and the documents dealing with the Lemviotissa monastery refer to many men who are described or who signed documents as "priest and *nomikos*." Evidently, Laodikenos was present at the 1228 hearing because of his function in the village of Aureliou, and he was singled out in the 1251 act because he was the only person there notable

[61] Ostrogorsky, *Féodalité*, 74–77.

in any way. He was a paroikos of Syrgares, but there is no evidence that he worked as an administrator of Syrgares' pronoia.

In the study of pronoia, Syrgares figures prominently. The reason for this goes beyond the fact that we know of him from three distinct and informative cases (two of which involve his pronoia). Unlike most pronoia holders before him, we also know something of his occupation and social status.

An examination of the full titulature accompanying Syrgares' name in the documents indicates that there was a strong desire to portray him as a distinguished person. There was, however, little consistency about how this was done. In the 1235 request of the Potamenoi he is simply "the *kavallarios* Syrgares" (MM, IV, 37.14). In both Niketas Kavoures' 1232 act of sale and the 1251 act of the inhabitants of Panaretou (the latter issued after his death), Syrgares is called "the liege [*lizios*] *kavallarios*" (IV, 135.7, 81.19). In Xenos Legas' 1231 act of sale he is "the all-most-noble liege *kavallarios.*" In three acts – the 1235 public affidavit, the September 1235 act of Angelos, and the 1237 act of the metropolitan of Smyrna – he is identified as "the liege *kavallarios* of the . . . emperor" (IV, 36.10–11, 39.10–11, 41.14–15). Similarly, in the two imperial documents – the June 1235 *orismos* and the January 1236 *prostagma* – he is, respectively, "the most brave *kavallarios* of my majesty" and "the most brave and most faithful liege *kavallarios* of my majesty" (MM, IV, 36.32–33; 40.5–6: ὁ ἀνδρικώτατος καὶ πιστότατος λίζιος τῆς βασιλείας μου καβαλλάριος).

Generally, as we should expect, the more formal the document, the more elaborate the identification. In every document he is, at least, "*kavallarios* Syrgares," and in all but one he is "liege *kavallarios.*" The epithet "most brave" (*andrikotatos*) in the two imperial documents underscores his military occupation.

Syrgares is, in fact, the first man known to have borne the word *kavallarios* as a title. *Kavallarios* (καβαλλάριος), or *kavallares* (καβαλλάρης), from the Latin *caballarius*, was one of several words employed in middle and late Byzantine demotic and semi-demotic written sources, and probably in the spoken Greek of the time, to designate the horse soldier generally. In the documentary sources of the thirteenth century the term does not mean "horse soldier" so much as "knight," a distinguished soldier usually of western origin.[62]

Including Syrgares, four *kavallarioi* are known from the thirteenth century, and they had a number of characteristics in common. All had the appellation of respect *syr* (the appropriation by the Byzantines of the

62 M. Bartusis, "The *Kavallarioi* of Byzantium," *Speculum* 63 (1988), 343, 345.

Western honorific "sir") attached to or accompanying their names (rather than the Greek *kyr*, or *kyrios*), at least three of them were (or most probably were) holders of pronoiai, and at least three of them had Western names. We may conclude that they were Latins (or recent descendants of Latins), and since a Latin "sir" with a "fief" is a knight, these four *kavallarioi* were horse soldiers. The status of the men is not difficult to determine. When the title *kavallarios* appears on Byzantine lists of precedence, it holds a very modest position. Further, other westerners are encountered in thirteenth-century sources, and some of these possess quite distinguished ranks. Therefore, *kavallarios* appears to have been the usual title for a Latin horse soldier.[63]

Syrgares was not only a *kavallarios*. He is referred to fairly consistently as a "liege" *kavallarios*. The Byzantine utilization of the concept of liege homage is well attested in the period prior to 1204, but this is the only example of the word itself attached directly to an individual's name in the period after 1204. However, the institution seems to have continued to exist even into Michael VIII's reign, because the historian Pachymeres notes that in order to ensure the fidelity of the Genoese of Galata in the 1270s, Michael "by kindnesses made them his own men – 'lieges' [*lizioi*] as one of them might say."[64]

The dossier on Syrgares confirms that paroikoi and probably entire villages could be held within a pronoia and provides us with new information about pronoia. We learn that a *kavallarios* and a *prokathemenos* could hold pronoiai. The paroikoi of a pronoia holder could own patrimonial property, which they sometimes sold, and the paroikoi considered the pronoia holder their "lord" (*authentes*). For his part, the pronoia holder took an interest in the property holdings of his paroikoi, which suggests that the more property a paroikos held, the greater the benefit was to the pronoia holder. Finally, the references to particular paroikoi "from someone's pronoia" gives the word *pronoia* a concrete quality.

Michael Petritzes

[5.11] Act of Michael Petritzes involving the olive trees of Nikodemos Planites (1257)

A good example of the complications caused by including tax revenues from private property within pronoia grants is provided by the case of the

[63] Bartusis, "*Kavallarioi*," 346–47.

[64] Pachymeres, ed. Failler, I, 471.8. Bartusis, "*Kavallarioi*," 346, and *ODB*, s.v. "lizios."

monk Nikodemos Planites. Nikodemos, perhaps before he became a monk, planted sixteen olive trees in the village of Mantaia in order to provide oil for illuminating a chapel that his family owned in the same village.[65] Prior to his death he willed these trees to this chapel. Then the Planites family donated the chapel to the Lemviotissa monastery. Michael Petritzes contested the monastery's possession of the trees because "the deceased monk Nikodemos was subject to paroikos status [*hypo paroikian*] of our pronoia." However, the *hegoumenos* of Lemviotissa proved to Petritzes that the trees were not inscribed the praktikon for his pronoia. And so, in June 1257, Petritzes composed a document conceding that he had no claim to the trees, inasmuch as they were "neither recorded in military praktika, nor kept in the fiscal survey of the deceased . . . *pinkernes* Komnenos, nor conferred in any military or state praktikon."[66]

The issue at stake in these documents was whether Nikodemos' olive trees were included within Petritzes' pronoia. If they were, then after Nikodemos donated them to the monastery, Petritzes would have been entitled to an *epiteleia* from the monastery for the trees, in order to compensate him for the tax on the trees that Nikodemos would no longer render to him. However, once the *hegoumenos* of the monastery proved that Petritzes' praktikon did not include the trees, Petritzes, at the monastery's insistence, renounced his claim to the trees. The controversy would be easiest to explain if Nikodemos had planted the trees after the creation of the praktikon, but we cannot determine how the confusion over the trees originated.

In any event, this case answers a number of questions raised by the new process of granting an individual property owner's taxes to a pronoia holder. If a paroikos of a pronoia holder improved his property, was the pronoia holder entitled to the additional taxes on these improvements? The answer is no, at least not until a fiscal assessor included the improvements in a new praktikon. Similarly, if a paroikos of a pronoia holder acquired additional property, the latter was not entitled to the taxes on this property unless and until the property was listed in his praktikon.

The information regarding the fiscal survey of the *pinkernes* Komnenos indicates that Petritzes had held his pronoia for some time. The *pinkernes* is John Komnenos Kantakouzenos, known from other documents as *doux* of the theme of Thrakesion at least from April 1244 to January 1247. His

[65] Although the Planites (Planetes) family is well-attested in the Lemviotissa cartulary, this is the only reference to a Planites with the monastic name "Nikodemos." No Planites with an alliterative given name (Nicholas, Nikephoros, Niketas, etc.) is known either.

[66] MM, IV, 71.6–7; 71.12–13; 70.19–22. A chrysobull from 1258 confirmed Lemviotissa's possession of the trees, along with its other properties: MM, IV, 24.33–34.

period as *doux* began no earlier than June 1241 and ended no later than August 1249 (both termini established by references to other *doukes* of that theme).[67] Thus Petritzes' pronoia was granted no later than August 1249, that is, during the reign of John Vatatzes. Because Komnenos' fiscal survey (and the resulting praktikon produced) do not necessarily reflect the original conferral of Petritzes' pronoia holdings (but perhaps only a periodic revision), Petritzes' pronoia may have been granted long before 1249, even before the *pinkernes*' tenure as *doux*. As for the identity and status of Michael Petritzes, while he refers to himself and signs this and another document as "the *doulos* [servant] of . . . the emperor Michael Petritzes" (MM, IV, 88.16–18), the references to "military praktika" strongly suggest he was a military man.[68]

In addition, the case of Nikodemos tells us something about the economic status of paroikoi. Nikodemos was "under the *paroikia*" of Michael Petritzes, yet Nikodemos' family owned a chapel which it donated to a monastery. Thus, they were far from being poor peasants. The new practice of granting tax revenues from private property to pronoia holders created a class of paroikoi much different from those of the twelfth and earlier centuries. A paroikos had been someone who was a tenant on another's property; in the thirteenth century a paroikos was someone, no matter how wealthy he was, who paid his taxes to a private party, in this case to a pronoia holder.

The process of conferring a pronoia in the mid-thirteenth century

The 1234 act of Constantine Kalegopoulos *[5.7]* showed that a pronoia was conferred by the emperor through a document called an *orismos* ("order"). The act of Michael Petritzes adds fiscal surveys (*apographai*) and praktika to the documents involved in conferring and managing pronoiai. An *apographe* was a periodic survey made by an official (in the thirteenth century, a *doux*; in the fourteenth century, usually an *apographeus*) of the current holdings

[67] *Patmos*, I, 234, and Ahrweiler, "Smyrne," 138, 144–45.

[68] The compiler of the cartulary, in the title appended to the act, calls him the "soldier Petritzes" (MM, IV, 69.25), but the opinion of the compiler of the cartulary is unreliable: see M. Bartusis, "On the Status of Stratiotai during the Late Byzantine Period," *ZRVI* 21 (1982), 56–57. Michael Petritzes or, rather, individuals who appear to be named "Michael Petritzes" are encountered in a few other documents. Acts from 1275 and 1276 most likely deal with a soldier named Michael Petritzes (MM, IV, 171.30, 172.4, 173.4,1–2), and an act from 1283 or 1288 (the dating passage is mangled) refers to another, different Michael Petritzes (MM, IV, 130.31). Neither of these is identifiable as the Michael Petritzes in the 1257 acts and the 1258 chrysobull, *pace* Ahrweiler, "Smyrne," 174, and Ostrogorsky, *Féodalité*, 80.

of private individuals and religious foundations. Following the *apographe*, the fiscal official might supply the individual landholder with a revised praktikon, reflecting changes since the landholdings were first granted or since the last *apographe*.[69] It seems that there was little difference in how this administrative procedure was applied to the holders of pronoiai and to other privileged landholders such as monasteries.

[5.12] A notarial form for the conferral of paroikoi (before 1259)

An unusual document found in a collection of notarial forms provides information about the initial steps in the process of administering a pronoia grant, the process of conferral itself. The collection, which was evidently to be used by officials when drawing up certain routine types of documents, is undated, and the only sure chronological sign is that the collection was copied in 1259, which establishes a terminus ante quem. Nicolas Oikonomides, who reedited the document of interest here, suggested that the collection was probably created and in use during the reign of John III Vatatzes (1222–54).[70] We may add that, inasmuch as the titles and practices described in the collection reflect practices known in the Nicaean state, the collection's general provenance was the eastern rather than the western (Epiros) part of the Byzantine world.

The form is entitled "Conferral of paroikoi by the *doux* of a region upon a soldier" (Παράδοσις παροίκων παρὰ τοῦ κατὰ χώραν δουκὸς πρὸς στρατιώτην), and, although it does not say this explicitly, it is in fact dealing with the granting of a pronoia. I present it here in translation (all the parenthetical phrases are found in the original text; words that I have added are in brackets):

In the present month of ______[71] of the current indiction __ of the year ____, a divine and worshipful imperial *prostagma* has been presented to us by the *megalodoxotatos* (or according to whatever honor, the ______) *kyr* ______, thus explaining verbatim (the *prostagma* needs to be inserted [here]).

According to the purport of such imperial *prostagma*, according to which we have authorization from our holy lord[72] and the *pansevastos sevastos* and *doux* (or

[69] See *ODB*, s.v. "praktikon," "apographeus," "cadaster."

[70] Oikonomides, "Contribution," 174–75, text on pp. 159–60.

[71] I have replaced each form of ὁ δεῖνα "such a one" as found in the document with a blank, which I think lends more clarity and is more in accord with modern usage than "In the village of so-and-so, so-and-so has so-and-so, a son so-and-so," etc.

[72] As Oikonomides, "Contribution," 161 note 34, noted, it is unclear from the Greek whether "our holy lord" refers to the *doux* or to the emperor, i.e., whether the "authorization" came from the emperor *and* from the *pansevastos sevastos doux*, or simply from the *doux*.

stratopedarches or even *paradotes*) of the theme of _____ to confer upon those who present to us divine and imperial *prostagmata*, we have conferred upon _____ however many *zeugaria* in the village of _____, that is, from the pronoia of _____.

In the village of _____:

_____ has [a wife] _____, a son _____, a daughter-in-law by him _____, a daughter _____, a son-in-law by her _____, two or however many *zeugaria*, __ cows, __ sheep, __ pigs.

_____ has [a wife] _____, a son _____, and in the same way this [person] and that [person], he has this and that (*zeugaria* or [he is] *voïdatos* or *aktemon* or *aporos*).

Such [soldier] is still lacking however many other *zeugaria*, and these will be conferred upon him when they are found.

Month _____ and indiction __.

And the official signs it.

Technically, the form is describing a *paradotikon gramma*, an act of conferral, in this case one transferring paroikoi to an individual. In some ways it is an odd document. It has almost a casual quality, suggesting that the author did not spend a great deal of time composing it. Nevertheless, the author had a real knowledge of fiscal practices. He knew that the elements of a grant often came from previous grants ("from the pronoia of _____"), and he knew the structure of a list of paroikoi. In terminology, phrasing, and format the form is quite similar to documents from around the middle of the thirteenth century.[73]

Much of the document parallels other *paradotika grammata* of the first half of the thirteenth century. The only element of interest in the first paragraph is the information that the soldier may bear the title *megalodoxotatos*, literally "great most glorious," an epithet of honor appearing in two dozen documents from the middle of the twelfth century through the end of the thirteenth century.[74] In the first half of the thirteenth century the epithet was indeed applied to pronoia holders, including Basil Vlatteros *[5.4]* and Constantine Tzirithnos *[5.15]*. And it was applied to at least one soldier (*stratiotes*): *kyr* George Manteianos, who is listed among the soldiers who

[73] Cf. the *paradotikon gramma* of the *prokathemenos* of Smyrna George Monomachos from November 1235: MM, IV, 44–45, or the lists of paroikoi found in *[6.3]*. Nevertheless, some of the terminology, phrasing, and format displayed in the form is rather dated: compare, e.g., *Patmos*, II, no. 54 (1089). From the mid-thirteenth century it becomes rare for any government document to begin with a dating passage.

[74] Oikonomides, "Contribution," 163–67. Unfortunately the *PLP* does not track holders of this epithet.

lived in the village of Mantaia and witnessed an act in 1280 (MM, IV, 128.14–19, 129.4–5). From this we may conclude that those *megalodoxotatoi* who were soldiers were among the more distinguished ranks of soldiers.

The structure of the second paragraph is entirely in accord with any *paradotikon gramma*. Of interest to us, first, is the authority, aside from the emperor, who ordered the official to make the conferral: a "*doux* (or *stratopedarches* or even *paradotes*)." In the first half of the thirteenth century, a *doux* was the governor of a theme. The *stratopedarches* and *paradotes* were the chief fiscal officials of a province. For example, the fiscal official Michael Phokas, who in March 1235 made a list of the properties held by the Lemviotissa monastery, was *stratopedarches* of the theme of Thrakesion and of Philadelphia.[75] Another official, named Theophanes, referred to as both *stratopedarches* and *paradotes* of Meander, performed a fiscal reassessment (*apokatastasis*) not long before 1251 (*Patmos*, II, no. 64.21–22).

The official who would have created such a document based on the form was not the *doux* himself, but a subordinate. It could have been the *stratopedarches* or a *paradotes*, or a relatively minor official subordinate to them.

Second, this official confers *zeugaria*, which, in the form, were from the pronoia of someone else (παραδεδώκαμεν τῷ δεῖνα ζευγάρια τόσα, ἐν τῷ χωρίῳ τῷ δεῖνα, ἤγουν ἀπὸ τῆς προνοίας τοῦ δεῖνα). In Byzantine fiscal terminology, *zeugarion* had two meanings: aside from its basic sense, literally a "yoke of oxen," the *zeugarion* was also a unit of account, presumably connected in some way to the quantity of land a yoke of oxen could cultivate each year.[76] While we are not told why the latter person lost his pronoia (whether through death, disfavor, or a neutral administrative act of exchange), the form indicates that the reassignment of pronoia holdings was a normal, regular process. The form then lists the paroikoi assigned to the soldier in the normal manner found in documents conferring paroikoi and adds that other *zeugaria* would be found and conferred at a later date.

The notarial form uses the word *zeugaria* four times. In the passage where it precedes the enumeration of a paroikos' cows, sheep, and pigs, it clearly means "yokes of oxen," its primitive sense. Similarly, in the passage where it precedes "*voïdatos* or *aktemon* or *aporos*," it would appear to have this sense as well, though, to improve the syntax of the passage, *zeugaratos*, meaning a peasant with two oxen, is the appropriate term to parallel *voïdatos*,

[75] MM, IV, 7. See Ahrweiler, "Smyrne," 141.

[76] See E. Schilbach, *Byzantinische Metrologie* (Munich, 1970), 67–70. Also, see *ODB*, s.v. "zeugarion." This entry, while attributed to me, was heavily rewritten. Cf. the entries for "zeugaratos" and "jugum."

aktemon, and *aporos*, the traditional designations for a peasant with a single ox, no oxen, and no property at all. On the other hand, in the first and last occurrences of *zeugaria*, the word cannot mean mere yokes of oxen but must refer to *zeugaria* in its more abstract sense.

In documents from the thirteenth through fifteenth centuries, land which was being donated, granted, bequeathed, or transferred in some other way (but not sold?) is occasionally quantified in terms of a certain number of *zeugaria*. To my knowledge, the earliest use of the word in the sense of a unit of account is found in a fragment of an act which dates between 1204 and 1227.[77] In the four known cases where the area of the land is provided in modioi as well (three of which are from the fifteenth century), the ratio between modioi and *zeugaria* ranges from 100 to almost 250 modioi (about 25 to 62 acres) per *zeugarion*.[78] Because of this wide variance, scholars have hypothesized that assessors took the quality of the land into consideration as well as its area. Thus, a field of 1,000 modioi of high-quality land might be assessed at ten *zeugaria*, while another field of the same area but of much lower quality might be assessed at five *zeugaria*. Thus, even if the *zeugarion* was based on some theoretical quantity of land that could be cultivated by a yoke of oxen, no particular area measurement corresponded to the *zeugarion*; it depended on the land involved.

The utility of the *zeugarion* was not as an area measurement; rather it was a tool that permitted comparisons of land of different values. For example, in 1234 John Vatatzes granted the Lemviotissa monastery "land of six *zeugaria*" from "state land" in the *zeugelateion* of Koukoulos (MM, IV, 146.25–27). According to the act of conferral three individual parcels in total were conferred, comprising five *zeugaria* of arable land and one *zeugarion* of pasture land. The official states that he conferred the one *zeugarion* of

[77] P. Gounaridis, "Σημείωμα γιά ένα (;) έγγραφο της Λεμβιώτισσας," *Σύμμεικτα* 11 (1997), 94. Glykatzi(-Ahrweiler), "L'épitéleia dans le cartulaire de Lemviotissa," 72. Schilbach, *Byzantinische Metrologie*, 70, assigns this reference to 1194, but this is the date of another document to which the later fragment is appended (see MM, IV, 185.22–23).

[78] *Zographou*, no. 10 (1286): 4 *zeugaria* corresponded to 400 modioi of land; and *Pantéléèmôn*, no. 17 (1407): 3 *zeugaria* of land corresponded to 723 or 748 modioi; *Pantéléèmôn*, no. 18 (1419): 4,039½ modioi corresponded to 30 *zeugaria*; and *Dionysiou*, no. 20 (1421): 2,135 modioi were 10 *zeugaria*. The example from 1106 discussed by Schilbach, *Byzantinische Metrologie*, 68–69, in which he calculates 83⅓ modioi to the *zeugarion* can be discounted. In this document Alexios I granted a monastery an *exkousseia* for 6 yokes of oxen (*zeugaria*) to work its 500 modioi of land. This tells us nothing about the size of the *zeugarion* because (i) in the document the word *zeugarion* means only a yoke of oxen, and (ii) the concession of an *exkousseia* for six yokes of oxen (and 150 sheep, 40 cows, and 10 mares as well according to the document) did not necessarily involve specific animals that the monastery already possessed. The concession was simply the right for the monastery to acquire that many tax-exempt animals.

pasture "since there is no other state land there" (MM, IV, 147–50, esp. 149.26). This indicates something about the usefulness of the *zeugarion* as a fiscal tool. Because only five *zeugaria* of normal arable land were available, the official conferred one *zeugarion* of pasture land, which, one assumes, was much larger in area than a single *zeugarion* of arable land. If, on the other hand, the emperor had granted, say, 500 modioi of land to the monastery, there would have been confusion over what quality of land was acceptable; if first-quality land was specified explicitly, the monastery would have been unhappy accepting any pasture land. The use of the *zeugarion* unit obviated these issues.

Fiscal officials in a particular area established the theoretical size of a *zeugarion* using criteria of which we know nothing. How did they determine the quantity of land a yoke of oxen could cultivate in that particular area? Perhaps they asked around, or consulted old records, or guessed. A simple way might have been to determine from their records what was the largest holding of first-quality land (in modioi of arable land) owned in the area by any property-owning peasant with a yoke of oxen. That became the *zeugarion* and the officials decided what its tax should be. From that point on, tax rates came into play. If land reckoned as second quality was taxed at, say, half the rate of first-quality land (because in theory it was half as productive), then a *zeugarion* of second-quality land was reckoned as twice as large in area as the *zeugarion* of first-quality land. Pasture land, taxed at a much lower rate than arable land, would accordingly have formed much larger *zeugaria*. Thus, the *zeugarion* was not a measure of land area, but a measure of the fiscal value of land; by expressing land in units of *zeugaria* it was possible to compare the relative fiscal value of land parcels. And for the Byzantine state, the type of value that mattered was not sale value, but *fiscal value*, the amount of revenue that the state could demand from the property. If the property was privately owned its fiscal value was its tax assessment (a real assessment if the property was taxed, and a theoretical assessment if the property was tax-exempt). If the property was owned by the state, the fiscal value would be its rental value. Thus, two properties assigned the same number of *zeugaria* were fiscally equivalent in the eyes of the state in that they were viewed as generating the same fiscal revenue. Thus, the *zeugarion* was a measurement of taxable property in terms of its fiscal value.

Returning to the notarial form, it would appear, on the face of things, that the official first conferred a quantity of land, then a number of paroikoi, and then noted that more land would be conferred later. While it is awkward to sandwich the conferral of paroikoi between references to conferrals of land, the process is in accord with Choniates' account that soldiers received "gifts of paroikoi" as well as "acres of land." But if the notarial form claims to be a conferral of *paroikoi*, why would it be conferring land at all? One way to make sense of this is to suppose that the paroikoi were tenants on the land being conferred.

Thus, the simplest interpretation of the form is that a soldier was granted by the emperor a certain quantity of land, expressed in *zeugaria*. The official who would have composed such a document sought a quantity of land corresponding to the number of *zeugaria* granted. In this case, the land he found, which had earlier been held in pronoia by someone else, constituted fewer *zeugaria* than the soldier had been assigned. Nevertheless, he conferred this land on the soldier and then in the act documenting the conferral (the form) he listed the paroikoi found on that land who worked it as tenant-farmers. Finally, acknowledging that the number of *zeugaria* conferred was less than the number of *zeugaria* granted by the emperor, the official noted that more *zeugaria* would be granted when they were found. In this interpretation the recipient of the grant benefitted from a grant of state land and from an (implied) *exkousseia* granted to the paroikoi. If the paroikoi were already working state land, there was no reason explicitly to mention the *exkousseia*.

This explanation assumes, as the author of the notarial form assumed, that the paroikoi had only personal property (oxen, cows, pigs) and no immovable property (arable land, vineyards, olives, etc.). In other words, the author of the notarial form created a scenario whereby the recipient of the pronoia was not receiving the taxes on any immovable property that someone else owned. This is not the situation encountered in numerous examples throughout this chapter *[5.1–5.2][5.4][5.9–5.11]*. Probably the author chose to deal with the simplest, least complicated scenario, which may well have been the most common case. Even though our documents give the impression that it was common to confer the taxes upon private property to pronoia holders, it may have been an innovation that was not particularly widespread. Obviously, the granting of taxes on private property to pronoia holders would have led to many more property disputes (and more documentation) than would the granting of state property and the tenant-paroikoi on that property.

Another interpretation of the notarial form was suggested by Oikonomides, though he later backed away from it.[79] Starting from the premise that the *zeugarion* was a unit of account that represented not the *amount*

[79] Oikonomides, "Contribution," 169, and cf. N. Oikonomides, "The Role of the Byzantine State in the Economy," in *EHB*, III, 1044.

of land that could be cultivated by a yoke of oxen, but the *fiscal revenue* that was produced by the quantity of land that could be cultivated by a yoke of oxen, then, hypothetically, the *zeugarion* could be used to quantify not only different types of land, but other taxable items as well. It could have been a common standard for reckoning the fiscal value of any kind of land. If arable and pasture land, why not vineyards and gardens? Indeed, why not individual trees, mills, and even *peasants*? Logically, if a peasant household was liable for the same taxes as a particular field, then both could be reckoned as equivalent to the same number of *zeugaria*. Perhaps, one *zeugaratos* peasant was considered equal to one *zeugarion*. The beauty of such a procedure is that it would have permitted the imperial administration, among other things, to create grants of equal size from a broad variety of components. Further, inasmuch as the *zeugarion* as a unit of account first appears at the same time as an expansion in the volume of grants given not only as pronoiai but as outright gifts to religious foundations and laymen, it is tempting to see a connection, to suggest that the *zeugarion* was developed to regularize the process of conferring imperial grants.

If the *zeugarion* can be viewed this way, then the passage in the notarial form which states that *zeugaria* were conferred on the soldier might not refer to *zeugaria* of land at all, but to *zeugaria* of peasant households. This would explain why the passage is followed by a list of peasants; these were the peasants conferred.

Nevertheless, as much as I am attracted to this alternative interpretation, there is little evidence to support it. While numerous passages in the documents refer to "*X zeugaria* of land," only one source appears to link *zeugaria* (in the sense of a unit of account) with peasants. This is a brief text intended to clarify another brief text, the *Apokope psomion*. The latter, written in 1231/2 and found in a collection of texts dealing with Cyprus, is regarded as a set of instructions for a tax official, which, among other things, provides figures for the values of the holdings of various categories of peasants, as well as the values of various categories of land, and stipulates the rates for calculating the taxes of these. The brief text added to the *Apokope*, which appears to be contemporary, provides a concrete example of the calculations to be followed when assessing taxes. What is remarkable is that the phrase "$11\frac{1}{2}$ *zeugaratoi*" is followed a few words later by "$11\frac{1}{2}$ *zeugaria*," suggesting that the words *zeugaratos* and *zeugarion* could be used interchangeably. Alas, the association occurs but once, and the text's recent editor simply replaces *zeugaratoi* with *zeugaria*, implying that the appearance of *zeugaratos* was due to an error on the part of either author or copyist. This is indeed a possibility. Therefore, at least for the moment, I have to regard the first interpretation, that the notarial form is dealing with the granting of land along with the paroikoi on that land, as the most likely interpretation of the form.[80]

Regardless of which of the two interpretations of *zeugarion* is appropriate for the form, the use of the word to denote a unit of account of some kind is noteworthy. It is a fact that the word appears with this sense for the first time in the thirteenth century, at the same time that Nicaean emperors were making grants of land on an unprecedented scale. Even if the *zeugarion* was only a measurement of the fiscal value of land (and not peasants), its appearance still may have been connected with the need more easily to compare and quantify the size of imperial grants.

Whatever was being conferred in the notarial form, this document helps us understand the process whereby pronoiai were granted, at least in the first half of the thirteenth century. One issue of interest is what documents were issued and how they were used. Aside from this form there are praktika *[8.11–8.17]* for grant holders and there are a handful of chrysobulls that vaguely speak of "service" (see *[8.27]* and Table 8.5). Choniates' "gifts of paroikoi" passage *[3.1]* mentions "imperial diplomas" (*vasilika grammata*) which conferred land. Of particular interest is whether these or any other document noted the specific obligations, military of otherwise, connected with the grant. The praktika do not, nor do the few chrysobulls which, in any event, were issued long after the original grant. The passage from Choniates also says nothing about this. The notarial form deals only with the conferral of the grant; if it were not for the word *stratiotes* in the title of the form, we would not even know that the recipient was a soldier. However, the form gives a hint. It states that the soldier presents a *prostagma* to the official and the *prostagma* is inserted in the official's act. Could this *prostagma* have mentioned the soldier's military obligations? There is a problem. No document exists that does this. We have praktika for laymen (see Chapter 8), but they contain no inserted *prostagma*, and we have documents that confer properties and contain the *prostagma* ordering the conferral, but the recipients are monasteries, and the inserted *prostagma* naturally mentions no obligations on the part of the recipient. Assuming that documents were created that were comparable to the notarial form,

[80] A. Beihammer, ed., *Griechische Briefe und Urkunden aus dem Zypern der Kreuzfahrerzeit* (Nicosia, 2007), 214, no. 84.11–15, cited by K. Smyrlis, "Taxation Reform and the Pronoia System in Thirteenth-Century Byzantium," in *On İkinci ve On Üçüncü Yüzyıllarda Bizans Dünyasinda Değişim = Change in the Byzantine World in the Twelfth and Thirteenth Centuries*, ed. A. Ödekan et al. (Istanbul, 2010), 215.

we ask two questions: First, did the inserted *prostagma* specify the obligations of the grant recipient, and, second, why are no such documents extant?

Certainly the *prostagma* mentioned in the form ordered a *doux* or other official to arrange for a soldier to receive a grant. Did it contain other information, such as an order to enroll the man in the army, or specific military obligations? We do not know the answer to this question, but we can speculate. First, we need to establish the conditions under which the emperor issued the *prostagma*. In other words, what prompted the emperor to issue the document? Assuming that the cases were relatively rare when the emperor, on his own initiative (perhaps having witnessed an act of bravery on the field), decided to give a particular soldier a grant, there had to be, in most cases, some sort of petition, either oral or written, by the soldier himself or through an intermediary. We know that high officials and acquaintances of the emperor did intercede for soldiers and others *[6.12] [8.3] [8.10]*, and sometimes men petitioned the emperor directly for a grant.[81] To receive a petition favorably, the emperor had to recognize the merits of the prospective grant holder and feel there was a need to make such a grant. While the petition, from the prospective recipient himself or from an intermediary, might have convinced the emperor of the worthiness of the applicant, it could not prove a need. For this the emperor first consulted his own knowledge of military needs or the knowledge provided by others around him. For grant holders who would serve in the capital or wherever the emperor was at the time, this may have sufficed. But most emperors spent most of their time in the capital. If the emperor was considering a petition to make a grant in the provinces to a soldier who would serve in the army in the provinces, he had to consult with provincial officials, the same ones under whom the soldier would serve. Further, it is difficult to imagine that a petition from a man in the provinces, who was unknown to the emperor and who had (as was likely the case) no important friends in the capital, would be received favorably. Yet most soldiers were precisely such men. The petition, then, could not have come directly from the soldier, but from someone in the provinces who could attest to the man's merits and attest to the military need, and that would be the *doux* or other high provincial official. It is necessary to conclude that, in most cases, the petition

[81] Bartusis, *Late Byzantine Army*, 209–10. *Theodori Ducae Lascaris Epistulae* CCXVII, ed. N. Festa (Florence, 1898), App. III, no. 8, p. 299. See R. Macrides, "The Ritual of Petition," in *Greek Ritual Poetics*, ed. D. Yatromanolakis and P. Roilos (Cambridge, Mass. and London, 2004), 356–70, which, however, says little of the role of intermediaries in the petition process.

to bestow a grant upon a soldier came from a provincial *doux* or similar official.

If this was the case, then the content of the *prostagma* is clear. It was addressed to the *doux* or other provincial official, and following the diplomatic form of a *prostagma*, it had to include reference to the request and its disposition. It must have said, at the very least, something along these lines: "Since you have found N. worthy of serving my majesty, enroll him in the military rolls and confer upon him the appropriate things." In other words, the *prostagma* must have made a link between military service and the grant, establishing the conditional element of the grant.

While thousands of these documents, and their inserted *prostagmata*, must have been produced (for soldiers alone, several hundred per generation for several generations), none has so far come to light. This is due to a combination of reasons:

(i) Only a minute fraction of documents have been preserved. For example, thousands of revised praktika were created for the grant holdings of soldiers, but only a handful have survived.

(ii) What documents we do have are not a representative sample. Most extant documents were preserved in monastic archives, and this was because, generally speaking, they safeguarded the privileges and properties of monasteries. When monasteries did preserve documents dealing with the property of a layman, most often that was because the property was later donated or sold to the monastery. But the kind of document we seek, which explicitly linked property and paroikoi to a military obligation, would, generally speaking, do little to serve the interests of a monastery. A document transforming a grant into a transferable property later donated to the monastery (of which examples are extant) was worth preserving; a document involving a property that was later donated to the monastery, which stated that the property was held on condition of military service, might not have been preserved, because its content could have been viewed as possibly damaging to the monastery's claim to the property.

(iii) Perhaps the grant holder never even received a copy of this initial *paradotikon gramma*. Indeed there was not much a man could do with such a document. It contained an incomplete listing of the component parts of his grant, but did not include the *telos* owed by each paroikos household. So it was useless for collecting revenue from his paroikoi. It contained the text of the *prostagma* linking the grant to a military

> obligation, but he knew he was a soldier. What he required was a praktikon stating the *telos* and other burdens on his paroikoi, and a list of the land he was given. These would come later.

According to the notarial form, the *prostagma*, once issued, was presented to the lower fiscal official by the recipient of the grant. At first glance, this suggests the unlikely scenario that the *prostagma* had been sent to the soldier, who now appeared unannounced and unexpected before the lower official. More likely, the *prostagma* was in the soldier's possession because he himself had carried the original petition from the *doux* to the emperor, he himself waited for the issuance of the *prostagma*, and he himself carried the *prostagma* back to the provinces, presenting it to the *doux*'s office.

Once the provincial official received the *prostagma*, according to the form, he created a *paradotikon gramma* conferring land and paroikoi upon the soldier. Initially, at least, the elements of the grant would have been sought in provincial tax records (*kodikes*). Some of these paroikoi and properties came from the previous holdings of other grant holders: as the form states, "from the pronoia of ______." These grant holders had lost their grants through their death or through loss of favor. Evidently, then, provincial officials had the ability to construct, from provincial records, a list of properties and paroikoi that were available for reassignment. But the author of the form presupposes that the entire amount of the grant would not be assembled at this time: "Such [soldier] is still lacking however many other *zeugaria*, and these will be conferred upon him when they are found." This is a reference to periodic revisions of the fiscal records (*exisoseis*), since, at any particular time, there were few spare state properties lying around; they had to be found. The process must have been quite dynamic. The soldier typically had to wait for more properties and paroikoi to become available from other grants or from a general *exisosis* in the province.

Figure 5.1 is an attempt to present, graphically, one possible reconstruction of the steps whereby a man might become a pronoia-holding soldier. It applies specifically to the first half of the thirteenth century, and by no means am I suggesting this was the only or primary way a man became a pronoia holder. But I do want to suggest that the process was a complex one (the arrows in the diagram represent the movement of documents). Thus,

(1) The *doux* provides the prospective grant holder with a petition.
(2) The grant holder travels to the emperor and presents the petition.

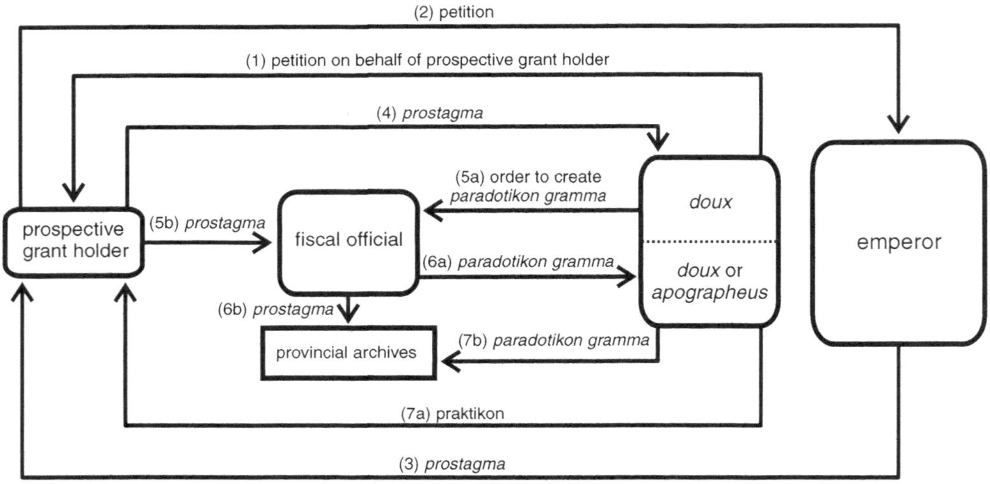

Figure 5.1 Schematic diagram of a possible procedure for the granting of a pronoia, mid-thirteenth century.

(3) If so inclined, the emperor grants the petition and issues a *prostagma* ordering the *doux* to bestow land and paroikoi.
(4) The prospective grant holder returns and presents the *prostagma* to the *doux*.
(5a) The *doux* orders a fiscal official to create a *paradotikon gramma*, and
(5b) the prospective grant holder presents the *prostagma* to the fiscal official.
(6a) The fiscal official consults provincial tax records, creates the *paradotikon gramma* (our notarial form), and presents it to the *doux* or another official and
(6b) the fiscal official files the *prostagma* in the provincial archives.
(7a) The *doux* or other official locates additional properties, confers them, and creates a praktikon, which is presented to the grant holder, and
(7b) the *doux* or other official files the *paradotikon gramma* in the provincial archives.

The literary sources

The historians who deal with the first half of the thirteenth century say very little about pronoia. George Akropolites, the main historian for the era, offers nothing about the institution of pronoia, either directly or indirectly. Yet there are a couple of references to the institution in other historians which tend to support the idea that the Nicaean emperors, particularly

John Vatatzes, dramatically increased the number of imperial grants, not only of pronoiai, but tax exemptions and simple grants of property as well.

[5.13] A passage from the history attributed to Theodore Skoutariotes (after 1261)

The earliest history to use the word *pronoia* in its technical sense is the work often attributed to Theodore Skoutariotes (born ca. 1230), composed sometime after Michael VIII's recovery of Constantinople in 1261, most likely not very long afterward. Much of this work is merely a paraphrase or exact reproduction of the histories of Niketas Choniates and George Akropolites, but in one passage the author elaborates upon the accomplishments of John III Vatatzes (1222–54). Because of his good governance, "all taxpayers became wealthy, and those of the military lists and the magnates had many times over the incomes from the pronoiai and the properties and the increases supplied to them for sustenance." As Angold pointed out, the author attributes an expansion of grants to both soldiers and aristocrats to Vatatzes. Indeed the documents provide very few references to pronoiai from early in the thirteenth century (only *[5.1]* and *[5.5]*), though certainly there could be other reasons for this.[82]

The author distinguishes two kinds of recipients of the emperor's benevolent policies: "those of the military lists" and "magnates," in other words, soldiers and aristocrats. Ostrogorsky wrote that the passage places pronoia holders on the same plane as representatives of the aristocracy. One could say it does just the opposite. Indeed, as with any conjunctive construction, the passage both associates and distinguishes. In fact, with a small stretch of the syntax, one could see a parallel construction through which Skoutariotes was differentiating one group from the other: soldiers received pronoiai and the aristocrats received properties (*ktemata*).

In any event, pronoiai as well as "properties" produced "incomes" for these men. "Properties" probably refers to properties not held as pronoia grants but outright gifts of property. The last phrase in the passage, "the

[82] *Georgii Acropolitae Opera*, ed. A. Heisenberg (Leipzig, 1903), I, 286.18–22 = K. Sathas, *Μεσαιωνικὴ Βιβλιοθήκη* (1872–94; repr. Athens, 1972), VII, 507: τοῖς τε ὑποστελέσιν ἐπεγένετο πᾶσι πλουτῆσαι, καὶ οἱ τῶν στρατιωτικῶν καταλόγων καὶ τῶν μεγιστάνων τὸ σύστημα πολλαπλασίους τὰς ἐκ τῶν προνοιῶν καὶ τῶν κτημάτων εἶχον εἰσόδους καὶ τὰ εἰς διατροφὰς κεχορηγημένα τούτοις πληθύνοντα. Ostrogorsky, *Féodalité*, 64. Angold, *Byzantine Government*, 124. Glykatzi-Ahrweiler, "Politique agraire," 60. On the authorship, see *ODB*, s.v. "Skoutariotes."

increases supplied to them for sustenance," or perhaps "multiplying the things supplied to them for sustenance," is obscure.

[5.14] George Pachymeres on the Anatolian highlanders (ca. 1307)

George Pachymeres, writing in the early fourteenth century, describes the expansion of pronoia and other imperial grants in connection with the measures Nicaean emperors took to minimize the depredations of marauding Turkoman and splinter Seljuk bands on the borders of the Nicaean empire. Foremost among them was the attempt to keep the civilian population inhabiting the mountainous frontiers from abandoning their homes. These highlanders performed a vital and quite hazardous function by acting as a buffer between the Turkish marauders and the valleys of the Nicaean empire. Pachymeres writes that the emperors, in order to maintain the eastern frontier, "turned to the mountains, securing [them] with many strong settlers from all over." Somewhat later, faced with increasing Turkish pressure, the emperors "did not leave those living on the mountains uncared for, who, not having an incentive to remain, were prepared to emigrate if anywhere enemies should attack." Rather, "they granted tax exemptions to all, pronoiai to the more illustrious among them, and imperial letters to those with a resolute spirit." Later in this same chapter, he adds, "those inhabiting the highlands held their heads high not only by the aforementioned tax exemptions and pronoiai, but even by daily imperial kindnesses."[83]

The policy of granting these men various benefits was designed to foster continued occupation of the border areas because the Nicaean emperors knew that continued occupation would include localized defense of their own lands and occasional sorties into Turkish territory for booty. In the sense that these duties were performed by the highlanders as a matter of personal survival even before they received special privileges, they did not technically become "soldiers," which is why the historian Pachymeres, our only source for these developments, does not in fact call them such. He simply writes that Nicaean policy affected "all" of those inhabiting the

[83] Pachymeres, ed. Failler, I, 29.24–26: ἀλλ᾽ἀτελείαις μὲν τοὺς πάντας, προνοίαις δ᾽ἐκ τούτων τοὺς ἐπιδοξοτέρους καὶ οἷς τολμῆεν τὸ φρόνημα γράμμασιν ἐδωροῦντο βασιλικοῖς, and 31.15–17: μὴ μόνον αἷς ἐρρέθη ἀτελείαις τε καὶ προνοίαις, ἀλλά γε καθημεριναῖς φιλοτησίαις βασιλικαῖς τῶν τὰς ἄκρας οἰκούντων βρενθυομένων (Bonn edn., I, 16, 17). Uspenskij, "Značenie," 13. Mutafčiev, "Vojniški zemi," 50/576, 595–96. Ostrogorsky, *Féodalité*, 63–64.

border areas, not a certain subset of the population who became "soldiers." After receiving their tax exemption and other benefits they performed no additional service and their only obligation to the state was to remain on their lands. The Nicaean highlanders were essentially a localized militia composed of the able inhabitants of the frontier zones who, without much organization or discipline, defended their lands and harassed their opposite numbers in Turkish territory as best they saw fit. In this they performed a function well worth the imperial attention lavished on them. As a result their economic condition improved and they were persuaded to remain, and their activities allowed Nicaean commanders to direct their military resources elsewhere.[84]

Pachymeres mentions four categories of benefaction granted to the highlanders: tax exemption, pronoiai, "imperial letters," and "daily imperial kindnesses." Tax exemption affected property they already held, and, he claims, everyone benefitted from it. More limited in number were grants of pronoiai and "imperial letters" (*grammata vasilika*). The former went to "the more illustrious among them," which means those of higher social status, and the latter, which appears to refer to imperial privileges granted through *orismos* or chrysobull, to "those with a resolute spirit," a poetic way to refer to those who especially distinguished themselves.

"Daily imperial kindnesses" is an unusual phrase.[85] If "daily" is taken literally, one might think of rations or a rations allowance. But that is unlikely. In the passage Pachymeres places these "daily kindnesses" on the same plane as the pronoiai and tax exemptions. It is difficult to imagine how either rations or a rations allowance would cause the men to "strut like peacocks" (an equally appropriate translation for the verb in the passage, *vrenthyomai*). Rather, Pachymeres must be speaking of either frequent cash rewards or gifts, or perhaps even a salary, depending on whether we render *kathemerinai* as "daily" in the sense of "frequent" or "regular." Supporting the idea of a salary for these men is a letter of Patriarch Gregory II *[8.3]*, which suggests that a grant of land could be accompanied by regular cash allotments. We will return to this in another passage in which Pachymeres uses a similar phrase *[6.11]*.

[84] Bartusis, "Smallholding Soldiers," 2–3.

[85] A similar phrase is found in the history of Michael Kritovoulos, *Critobuli Imbriotae historiae*, ed. D. Reinsch (Berlin and New York, 1983), bk. 2, ch. 1, sect. 4, line 7: ἐλεῶν τε αὐτοὺς καὶ καθημέραν φιλοτίμως εὐεργετῶν.

Epiros

[5.15] Act of John Apokaukos, metropolitan of Naupaktos, on the killing of a peasant by the steward of a pronoia holder (ca. 1225)

At this point we turn to the Byzantine successor state in western Greece, the so-called despotate of Epiros. From the period of exile there are three certain and three other possible references to the institution of pronoia. They represent the earliest evidence for the institution in the area. Three of these references are found in the writings of John Apokaukos, the metropolitan of Naupaktos (1199/1200–32). One is found in an act recording the circumstances and ecclesiastical penalties imposed for a killing. Written around 1225, the act is worth translating in its entirety:

Constantine Mela . . . os [the name was evidently illegible to the copyist], serving the *megalodoxotatos kyr* Constantine Tzirithnos, came to us today and related the following:

"I was left by my lord as steward of his pronoia in the region of [*vacat*], overseeing the paroikoi, the fields, and the acorn-bearing trees. And through prudent attention I looked after the tilling of the fields under the pronoia and the guarding of the acorns. For it was the season of both. The plowmen around Hermenea," he said, "attempted to work a property belonging to my lord. Thus with very harsh words and with contentious conversations I had already driven the plowmen away from the place personally. But neither word nor insult nor anything else biting to the ears was able to scare off their second attack upon the acorns. Therefore, out of necessity I seized a staff from one of those collecting the acorns, named Vratonas, and first tried to scare him from collecting, but I forgot to strike Vratonas on the fingers with the staff. Bearing down very severely on the entrails and belly, I hoped to halt his inclination toward the acorns. At that very moment, contrary to my expectations, he let out a gasp and was beheld among the dead, given neither an hour nor a half-hour by the wound. The blow of the staff burst his entrails at once, and at once it drove the soul of the man out from there."

Constantine related these things to his sorrow and was judged a willful murderer and received the appropriate penalties, which are these: [the remainder was omitted by the copyist].[86]

[86] S. Pétridès, "Jean Apokaukos, lettres et autres documents inédits," *IRAIK* 14 (1909), 19–20, no. 15: Οἰκονόμος κατελείφθην παρὰ τοῦ κυρίου μου τῆς ἐν τῇ χώρᾳ τοῦ [*vacat*] προνοίας αὐτοῦ, θεωρουμένης ἐν παροίκοις, ἐν χωραφίοις καὶ ἐν δένδροις βαλανηφόροις. Καὶ κατὰ τὴν προνοητικὴν ἐπιμέλειαν ἐφρόντιζον καὶ τῆς ἀροτριάσεως τῆς τῶν ὑπὸ τὴν πρόνοιαν χωραφίων καὶ τῆς φυλακῆς τῶν βαλάνων. The phrase "the fields under the pronoia" could almost be

Constantine Tzirithnos is otherwise unknown. His title *megalodoxotatos* was, during the thirteenth century, of middling status in the Byzantine hierarchy of titulature (see *[5.12]*).[87] The location of his pronoia cannot be determined.

We observe that this document does not indicate that Tzirithnos was receiving the taxes or even the rents on these properties (fields and oaks), or that he was receiving the taxes owed by the paroikoi. Rather, it implies that he was receiving the crops grown on the fields, the acorns from the oaks, and labor services from the paroikoi. In other words, he held a kind of domain land, which he did not rent to peasants (as the pronoia holders in *[5.6]*), but cultivated through corvée. The steward (*oikonomos*) was appointed to ensure that the paroikoi did their work and Tzirithnos received the full harvest.

Even though a steward managed the cultivation of the property, which we might wish to regard as evidence of a kind of rudimentary administrative apparatus for a pronoia, the entire operation seems to have been conducted on a small scale. The steward appears to have been in charge, yet there is no indication that he had subordinates. Indeed it was his personal duty to scare away trespassers. However, this does not necessarily mean that Tzirithnos' pronoia was small; this particular steward may have been overseeing only a portion of it.

[5.16] Act of John Apokaukos, metropolitan of Naupaktos, on the killing of a paroikos by his *pronoiarios* (1228)

Another act of Apokaukos describes another killing and the ecclesiastical penalties imposed by the metropolitan. It was composed in June 1228 and

rendered by *pronoia* in its simple sense "care," and in this context the phrase κατὰ τὴν προνοητικὴν ἐπιμέλειαν "through prudent attention" is noteworthy. As for the steward's surname, according to the *PLP*, nos. 17626–68, possible completions of the name are Μελαγχρηνός, Μελαχρηνός, Μελαχρινός, or Μελαχηλός. Other analyses of the letter: D. Angelov, "Prinos kŭm narodnostnite i pozemelni otnošenija v Makedonija (Epirskija despotat) prez pŭrvata četvurt na XIII vek," *Izvestija na Kamarata na narodnata kultura*, IV/3 (1947), 33; Ostrogorsky, *Féodalité*, 89; R. Macrides, "Killing, Asylum, and the Law in Byzantium," in *Kinship and Justice in Byzantium* (Aldershot, 1999), no. x, 524; and T. Maniati-Kokkini, "Μαρτυρία Ἰωάννου τοῦ Ἀποκαύκου γιὰ τὴν κοινωνία τοῦ ιγ′ αἰώνα. Δύο ὑποθέσεις φόνου," in *Πρακτικά του Α′ Αρχαιολογικού και Ιστορικού Συνεδρίου Αιτωλοακαρνανίας* (Agrinion, 1991), 297–306 (unavailable to me).

87 According to T. Maniati-Kokkini, "Μιὰ πρώτη προσέγγιση στὴ μελέτη τοῦ βυζαντινοῦ θεσμοῦ τῆς πρόνοιας: οἱ προνοιάριοι," in *Πρακτικὰ τοῦ Θ′ Πανελλήνιου Ἱστορικοῦ Συνεδρίου* (Thessaloniki, 1991), 54 and note 34, N. Oikonomides suggested that "Tzirithnos" is a copyist's error and that the name should be read "Tzirithon" (Τζιρίθων).

involves George Choniates, nephew of the historian Niketas Choniates. At the time George was *protovestiarites* of the despot Manuel Doukas, brother of the sovereign of Thessaloniki and of Epiros Theodore Doukas (1215–30). Manuel later succeeded his brother as ruler of Thessaloniki (1230–37).

So-and-so [ὁ δεῖνα][88] came to our church today and related the following:

"I was speaking," he said, "with *kyr* George Choniates the most eminent *protovestiarites* of the very-most-favored despot *kyr* Manuel Doukas in a certain village located in Vlachia. Since the said Choniates was intending to return from there, he called me by name and said, 'Today it is necessary to await me in your pronoia [ἐν τῇ προνοίᾳ σου δεῖ με μεῖναι] in the village [*vacat*]. Send word there that they prepare the things for hospitality to us.'

"And I did it," he said, "according to this command, and dispatching one of those under me [ἕνα τῶν ὑπ' ἐμέ] I instructed the head man [τῷ κρείττονι] of those there to prepare the things for the reception of the *protovestiarites*. Such villagers and especially the Vlach race, which is hard and stingy in regard to a leg of a sheep,[89] disregarded the message. They offered not one lamb for the meat of the *protovestiarites*. Nonetheless I was hoping that those attending me by reason of pronoia [οἱ κατὰ λόγον προνοίας ἐμοὶ προσανέχοντες] did not overlook my message. In any event, I myself and the said *protovestiarites* headed back toward my pronoia [πρὸς τὴν ἐμὴν . . . πρόνοιαν]. And as it was nearly evening and the day was closing and we found neither meat nor drink, I began to grieve and anguish about the probable reason, and I spoke quite sternly to him to whom I gave the message. Another one of those from that village, by name [*vacat*], came forward and assailed me who had said nothing to him. One of his words was shameless, something said privately by those speaking coarsely and rudely. This was, 'You prate on much. Take care!' Pierced by these words and for double the reason, that saying nothing to him I heard these things from him, and that a paroikos spoke with impudence, shooting forth bold words toward me his *pronoiarios* [πρὸς ἐμὲ τὸν αὑτοῦ προνοιάριον], I turned to him, seized his hair, and whirled his head and the rest of him against the ground, urging him not to behave impudently and belch forth rough things in front of me. After this the man lay on the ground, not speaking, not moving."

Indeed he was dead.

Having heard this story, the metropolitan judged the man "to be a murderer, not with forethought [οὐκ ἐκ προνοίας],[90] nor in a willful manner." Before assigning an appropriate ecclesiastical punishment, he offered his

[88] Replacing the man's name with this expression was a result of either Apokaukos' discretion or the copyist's inability to decipher the name.

[89] This sounds like an adage, but I have found no parallels. Cf. *Historia Alexandri Magni*, recensio γ (lib.2), 44.11–13, and recensio ε, 35.2.4–6, in the *TLG*.

[90] In legal language, "not with malice prepense."

thoughts on the matter: "Those who chastise children hold up the rod and rap them on the side of the head, and they pull out their hair by the roots. They do these things not in any way to kill, but to frighten. These are the things one should aim at. So-and-so ought to bridle his anger. . . ."[91]

This act, together with documents *[2.4] [5.4]* and *[5.7]*, comprise all of the appearances of the phrase *kata logon pronoias* (κατὰ λόγον προνοίας). Also, this is the first appearance of the rare word *pronoiarios*. *Pronoiarios* is derived from *pronoia* plus *-arios*, the Greek form of the Latin agent-noun suffix *-arius*. Medieval Greek had adopted this suffix through the importation of Latin words through simple transliteration: *notarios* from *notarius*, *chartoularios* from *chartularius*. It may have been Apokaukos' contact with Latin culture in Aitolia that facilitated the creation of *pronoiarios*. From this act it clearly means someone who holds a pronoia.

The act shows, like some of the documents discussed previously, that a pronoia could be a physical place. The extent of the pronoia in this act is unknown. Ostrogorsky felt that it included an entire village, which is likely. The pronoia was located in or quite near to an area called "Vlachia" and a large proportion of its inhabitants were Vlachs. Johannes Koder and Friedrich Hild place Vlachia between the Sperhios valley and the plain of Thessaly. This would be the area between modern Lamia and Pharsala.[92]

Aside from illustrating how little regard peasants sometimes had for representatives of the state, it also illuminates the negative side of relations between pronoia holders and the people associated with their pronoiai. A pronoia holder expected the people of his village to contribute food for the reception of a state official. Both this pronoia holder and John Apokaukos expected that a paroikos should be respectful toward his *pronoiarios*. Apokaukos likened the proper approach to handling disrespectful paroikoi to the way one should discipline children. Perhaps we should not read too much into this. In a hierarchical society such as Byzantium, it may have been accepted practice even for strangers to treat their inferiors in such manner.

So too we should probably not make too much of the social implications of these two acts of Apokaukos. In the first *[5.15]*, a steward kills a peasant and it is deemed willful murder; in the second, a pronoia holder kills a paroikos and it is deemed unwillful murder. Even though both killings were

[91] A. Papadopoulos-Kerameus, ed., "'Ιωάννης Ἀπόκαυκος καὶ Νικήτας Χωνιάτης," in *Τεσσαρακονταετηρὶς τῆς καθηγεσίας Κ. Σ. Κόντου* (Athens, 1909), 379–82. Ostrogorsky, *Féodalité*, 90. Other analyses of the letter: Macrides, "Killing, Asylum, and the Law," 521; and Maniati-Kokkini, "Μαρτυρία 'Ιωάννου τοῦ Ἀποκαύκου," 297–306.

[92] Ostrogorsky, *Féodalité*, 90. J. Koder and F. Hild, *Hellas und Thessalia* (Vienna, 1976), 40–41, and see *ODB*, s.v. "Vlachia."

not premeditated, the former case involved a weapon (a staff), the latter bare hands. This alone may have accounted for Apokaukos' distinctions.

Finally, we ask a basic question: did this pronoia holder live in the village where the killing took place, that is, did he live on his pronoia? The answer is no. The act mentions no home, and, more significantly, if this pronoia holder lived on his pronoia, he would have had something for George Choniates to eat. The act does not say that the food was insufficient or that it did not befit such an eminent guest; rather, "we found neither meat nor drink." This pronoia holder was far from home.

[5.17] Letter of John Apokaukos, metropolitan of Naupaktos, to Theodore Doukas (ca. 1226), and Letter of John Apokaukos to the imperial secretary Kamateros regarding olive trees (ca. 1226)

The last reference to pronoia in the writings of Apokaukos is in a letter he wrote to the ruler of Epiros Theodore Doukas in the mid-1220s. He complains about "the transfer to some landlord (*ergodotes*) by your order of the possession and use and usufruct of the olive trees granted to me for [my] old age and entire life."[93] These trees were in the *episkepsis* of Varesove, where there was substantial property belonging to his church.[94] Evidently referring to the new holder of the trees, he adds that "no Latin, even if he should serve for pay, and even if he professes the faithful things [swears faithfulness? adopts Orthodoxy?], is fit to hold for pronoia Roman men."[95] At about the same time he wrote to an official, an "imperial secretary" (*vasilikos grammatikos*) in Theodore's employ, seeking the latter's help in regaining the olive trees. "The mighty emperor granted [the trees] to me for life" (ἕως μέτρου ζωῆς), but "either willingly or mistakenly he gave these to a landlord, a Corinthian in the army" (ἐργοδότῃ Κορινθίῳ στρατευομένῳ).[96]

93 N. Bees, "Unedierte Schriftstücke aus der Kanzlei des Johannes Apokaukos des Metropoliten von Naupaktos (in Aetolien)," *Byzantinisch-Neugriechische Jahrbücher* 21 (1971–74), p. 131, no. 71.38–40.

94 Bees, "Unedierte Schriftstücke," p. 71, no. 11.32–34: τῆς ἐπισκέψεως Βαρεσόβης.

95 Bees, "Unedierte Schriftstücke," p. 132, no. 71.66–68: ὡς οὐδένα Λατῖνον, κἂν δουλεύῃ μισθοῦ, κἂν τὰ πιστὰ ἐπαγγέλληται, πρέπον εἶναι ἄνδρας Ῥωμαίους ἔχειν εἰς πρόνοιαν. Cf. the interpretation of the letter by A. Stavridou-Zafraka, "The Relations between Secular and Religious Authorities in the State of Epiros after 1204," in *Church and Society in Late Byzantium*, ed. D. Angelov (Kalamazoo, 2009), 19, which differs from mine.

96 Bees, "Unedierte Schriftstücke," p. 132, no. 72.14–16. On the date of both letters, E. Bee-Sepherle, "Προσθῆκαι καὶ παρατηρήσεις," *Byzantinisch-Neugriechische Jahrbücher* 21 (1971–74), 216; K. Lambropoulos, *Ιωάννης Απόκαυκος. Συμβολή στην έρευνα του βίου και του συγγραφικού έργου του* (Athens, 1988), 228–30; and A. Stavridou-Zafraka, "Η χρονολόγηση επιστολών και εγγράφων του Ιωάννη Αποκαύκου," *Egnatia* 4 (1993), 150.

It seems that the metropolitan had been given a lifetime grant of some olive trees from Theodore Doukas (Apokaukos writes that the trees were "few" but that may be an understatement). Later, Theodore ordered that the trees be transferred to a Latin military man from Corinth – a mercenary it seems – who held the trees along with the peasants who cultivated them. Apokaukos' precise use of the construction "to hold for pronoia" removes any doubt that the soldier held the trees and peasants as a pronoia grant. In fact, because Apokaukos held the same items as a lifetime grant, we could say that he was holding a pronoia as well.

[5.18] Ruling of Demetrios Chomatenos, archbishop of Ohrid, involving Theodore Demnites (ca. 1225–ca. 1236)

The only other source that links military service to holding pronoiai in Eprios is found in a ruling of Demetrios Chomatenos, archbishop of Ohrid (1216/7 to ca. 1236). Chomatenos' legal decisions make a number of references to soldiers, who may or may not have held pronoiai, but in one case it seems quite likely. This is the case of Theodore Demnites who "hailed from the eastern region but now resides in the theme of Acheloos" in Epiros. During an altercation he killed a tax collector who repeatedly had been harassing "certain men subject to him [Demnites] for service through life from a grant [*dorea*] of the despot." Demnites is not called a soldier directly, yet Chomatenos makes a couple of references to his "military labors." Ostensibly he was a soldier who was assigned men who had to "serve" him for life. Since tax collectors were bothering these men, it seems that they were not domestic servants but farmers, and that Demnites' original complaint was that the officials were unjustly demanding money or produce that they did not owe or else owed only to Demnites. Evidently Demnites was a pronoia soldier who had received a grant of paroikoi from either Theodore Komnenos Doukas, who took the title of emperor in the mid-1220s, or his successor and brother Despot Manuel Angelos, who ruled at Thessaloniki as emperor from around 1230 to around 1237. The connection between his pronoia and his military service is speculative but likely.[97]

97 Demetrios Chomatenos, *Demetrii Chomateni Ponemata diaphora*, ed. G. Prinzing (Berlin and New York, 2002), no. 118.2–3,19–20: παρενώχλουν ἀνδράσι τισίν, ἐκ δεσποτικῆς δωρεᾶς πρὸς ὑπηρεσίαν τὴν κατὰ βίον ὑποκειμένοις αὐτῷ, and pp. 234*–35*. Demnites could not have received his "grant of the despot" from Michael II Komnenos Doukas, the ruler of Epiros and Thessaly (ca. 1230 to between 1266 and 1268) who followed Theodore Komnenos Doukas, because Michael never claimed the imperial title and received the title of *despot* only after Chomatenos' death. For other soldiers in the writings of Chomatenos, see Bartusis, *Late Byzantine Army*, 370–71.

[5.19] Chrysobull of Michael II Doukas on pronoia holders (?) troubling Kerkyrans (1236)

To round out this very meager collection of references to pronoia in the Byzantine successor state of Epiros in the thirteenth century, one may cite two arcane and ambiguous references discussed by Paul Lemerle. In the first, the word *pronoiarios* may have been found in a chrysobull of Michael II Doukas of Epiros (ca. 1230–1267/8) issued in 1236. The text of the act exists only in an official Latin translation within an act of a notary of Brindisi from 1294. At that time emissaries from Kerkyra were seeking to obtain from Charles II, the Angevin king of Naples, a confirmation of old privileges granted by previous Byzantine rulers.

According to the Latin translation (made, the 1294 act notes, by three Greek priests from Brindisi), Michael II's chrysobull confirmed numerous privileges granted by earlier emperors to the inhabitants of the *kastron* of Kerkyra. Within the long list of privileges the document refers to certain peasants who had been pulled away or detached from the properties of these inhabitants by *feudatarii* and other people. Lemerle suggested that *feudatarii* may have been a translation of *pronoiarioi*.[98]

It is quite likely that Lemerle is correct. No other Greek word (other than the *Chronicle of the Morea*'s προνοιατόροι)[99] might reasonably be translated as *feudatarii*. Second, the appearance of the word *pronoiarios* in the 1228 act of John Apokaukos confirms that the word was in use in the despotate of Epiros at this time. If Michael II's original act did indeed mention *pronoiarioi*, then this is the first evidence that paroikoi of lay property owners were threatened by holders of pronoiai.

[5.20] Chrysobull of Michael II Doukas ordering pronoia holders (?) not to trouble Kerkyran priests (1246)

A similar appearance of a form of the word *pronoia* is quite likely encountered in another document issued by the same ruler of Epiros. A chrysobull of Michael II from 1246, translated into Latin and inserted in a Latin act from 1365 of Philip II of Taranto, prince of Achaia, states that in the territory of Kerkyra a group of thirty-three priests were to be regarded as "*extra*

[98] P. Lemerle, "Trois actes du despote d'Epire Michel II concernant Corfou connus en traduction latine," repr. in Lemerle, *Le monde de Byzance* (London, 1978), no. VI, 415–16. The edition of this (now lost) act is inaccessible to me (see Lemerle, "Trois actes," 406–07 and 407 note 6, for details of the very obscure brochure in which it appears).

[99] *Chronicle of the Morea*, ed. J. Schmitt (London, 1904), lines 1999, 2001, 2009, 2700, 2859.

omnem manum permasticam" and "*a manu promastica soluti.*" They were to be subject solely to the authority of the governor of the island and would pay only part of the taxes with which they would normally be burdened. Lemerle reasonably concluded that the words *permastica* and *promastica* were probably defective readings of *pronoiastike* (προνοιαστική).[100] The *Zavorda Treatise [2.1]* contains the adjective *pronoiatika*, but this, perhaps, is the earliest appearance of the adjective *pronoiastikos* (προνοιαστικός). If so, the key phrases might be translated, respectively, as "outside of every pronoiastic control" and "released from pronoiastic control."[101]

Observations

The sources of the first half of the thirteenth century, the so-called period of exile, tell us quite a lot about the development of the institution of pronoia. In fact, the information provided by these documents is often so detailed that it seems as if their authors were working out the parameters of what a pronoia was. After the accession of Michael VIII, many documents continue to deal with pronoia, but the amount of detail found in the acts declines noticeably.

So, what do we learn about pronoia during this period?

During the period of exile we find evidence of pronoiai in the empire of Nicaea on the coast of Asia Minor *[5.1–5.2]*, especially in the area of Miletos in the Meander valley *[5.3] [5.5–5.6]*, around Smyrna *[5.4] [5.7–5.11]*, and perhaps Appendix I, and on the eastern frontier *[5.14]*, and in the despotate of Epiros in the southern parts of Epiros and Thessaly *[5.15–5.18]*

100 I. Romanos, "Ἀνδηγαυϊκὸν δίπλωμα τοῦ Ταραντίνου ἡγεμόνος Φιλίππου τοῦ Β′, περιέχον μετάφρασιν χρυσοβούλλου Μιχαὴλ τοῦ Β′, Δεσπότου τῆς Ἠπείρου," *Δελτίον τῆς Ἱστορικῆς καὶ Ἐθνολογικῆς Ἑταιρείας τῆς Ἑλλάδος* 2 (1885), 594, 596. Lemerle, "Trois actes," 422 and note 54. D. Jacoby, *La féodalité en Grèce médiévale* (Paris, 1971), 255.

101 The first phrase can be rendered in Byzantine Greek as ἔξω πάσης προνοιαστικῆς ἐξουσίας or χειρός. Constructions similar to this appear in several Greek documents. In an act from 1216 we have ἐλεύθερον καὶ ἀκαταδούλωτον, ἔξω πάσης δημοσιακῆς ἐξουσίας, ἐκκλησιαστικῆς καὶ προσωπικῆς (*Patmos*, II, no. 61.10), and in one from 1259 we read ἔξω πάσης... χειρὸς καὶ ἐξουσίας καὶ ἀπαιτήσεως καὶ δόσεως καὶ δημοσιακῆς ὀχλήσεως (*Lavra*, II, 71.42–43). The second phrase, because of its simplicity, is more difficult to resolve. *Soluti* corresponds most closely to the Greek ἀπάλλασσω "to release" as found, for example, in an eleventh-century document: παροίκων... πάσης ἐνοχῆς ἀπηλλαγμένων "paroikoi released from all liability" (*Iviron*, II, no. 32.7). However, the use of that verb is rare after the eleventh century. The original Greek of the passage may not have involved a participle at all but a variant of a construction common to thirteenth-century documents such as ἐλεύθερον ἀπὸ προνοιαστικῆς ἐξουσίας or χειρός, such as appears in a document from 1295: ἐλεύθερον ὄντα καὶ ἀκαταδούλωτον πάσης τελεσματικῆς δόσεως (*Xéropotamou*, no. 12.4–5).

and on Kerkyra *[5.19–5.20]*. In Asia Minor the dramatic changes in the patterns of property holding brought about by the Latin Conquest freed up large quantities of church and monastic land that could now be granted to other religious foundations and to privileged laymen, especially as pronoiai *[5.4–5.5] [5.8]*.

All in all, there was much continuity with the institution of pronoia as found in the twelfth century. As in the twelfth century, it appears that pronoia holders could improperly appropriate the paroikoi of other property holders *[5.19]*, and generally could come into conflict with other landholders. As in the *Zavorda Treatise [2.1]*, pronoia remained a lifetime grant *[5.4] [5.6] [5.9] [5.17]* from the emperor *[5.4] [5.6–5.7] [5.12] [5.14] [5.18]* (or the ruler of Epiros *[5.17]*), which explains why the reassignment of pronoia holdings was a normal, regular process *[5.12]*. We do learn that a pronoia was conferred by the issuance of the kind of document called an *orismos [5.7]*, and, like other privileged landholders such as monasteries, pronoia holders received praktika, which itemized their holdings and were subject to periodic revision *[5.11]*. It was prohibited to alienate pronoiai. Nevertheless, it is possible that some holders of pronoiai found ways to alienate parts of their pronoia grants successfully *[5.4]*.

It seems that the first step in the process whereby pronoia grants lost their unique character occurred when they were granted to people at the highest level of society. In the twelfth century the recipients of pronoia grants tended to be soldiers and we know of none who held any kind of courtly rank or title. In the first half of the thirteenth century the situation changed somewhat. Soldiers remained a basic category of pronoia holders (*[5.2] [5.8–5.9] [5.18]*), but the first clear examples of non-soldiers holding pronoiai appear (a bishop, ca. 1226 *[5.17]* and a *prokathemenos*, fl. 1235 *[5.8]*), and the first pronoia holders appear with titles or titular epithets: two *vestiaritai*, fl.1207 *[5.4]* and fl. 1234 *[5.7]*, one *kavallarios*, fl. 1228–37 *[5.8–5.9]*, and one *megalodoxotatos*, ca.1225 *[5.15]*. These phenomena were due probably to two factors: pronoiai were being granted to a wider range of individuals, and more pronoiai were being granted (and hence the documents provide more cases for examination). But this does not seem to indicate a dramatic change in the institution. Except for the case of the metropolitan Apokaukos *[5.17]* all of the titles and epithets here were relatively modest,[102] and it is

[102] The epithet *megalodoxotatos* appears only in the thirteenth century, but the three other titles appear in the fourteenth-century lists of precedence where they are found at the very bottom of the lists of court ranks: see Pseudo-Kodinos, *Traité des offices*, ed. J. Verpeaux (Paris, 1966), esp. 301.

possible to view the development as a natural process. It is reasonable to think that some holders of pronoiai distinguished themselves and were given titles and other honors, thus broadening the social range of pronoia holders. Once pronoia grants were held by individuals with titles, it would have been easy for the emperor to grant pronoiai to others who held similar titles.

On the other hand, the appearance of pronoia grants to individuals with dramatically higher status represents a shift in policy. There is evidence that under John III Vatatzes aristocrats held pronoia *[5.13]*; by the later 1250s Manuel Komnenos Laskaris, whom Michael VIII calls his "son-in-law," is the first "important" individual known by name in the empire of Nicaea to hold a pronoia *[5.6]*. Since Laskaris died in early 1259, it is almost certain that he was granted his pronoia before the accession of Michael VIII, in other words from Theodore II Laskaris or John Vatatzes (and cf. *[8.1]* for another early example). Laskaris was followed in his tenure of his pronoia by the "uncle" of the emperor, George Komnenos Angelos, who was granted his pronoia early in the reign of Michael VIII. In the twelfth and early thirteenth century, there was no connection between such personages and pronoia grants. This shows a significant alteration in the application of the institution. Thus, expansion in the institution of pronoia took place along two directions: more recipients and a broader social range of recipients.

In regard to terminology, during the first half of the thirteenth century we encounter the first appearances of the verb *pronoiazo* (προνοιάζω: *[5.5]*), the adverb *pronoiastikōs* (προνοιαστικῶς: *[5.2]* and cf. *[5.6]*), the noun *pronoiarios* (προνοιάριος: *[5.16]* and perhaps *[5.19]*), and perhaps the adjective *pronoiastikos* (προνοιαστικός: *[5.20]*). As in the twelfth century *[2.2]*, *pronoia* could have a quite concrete sense, being used to designate a particular property or properties in a specific physical location *[5.8] [5.16–5.17]*, but, by the same token, we learn that a pronoia holder need not have lived on his pronoia *[5.16]*. Among the paroikoi and real property that could be held in pronoia *[5.6] [5.8–5.9] [5.16]*, the early thirteenth-century documents add the rights to a river, including a fish pond *[5.7]*. The sources discussed in this chapter also suggest that the word *pronoia* did not need to appear in documents dealing with the institution of pronoia, and that many other cases of pronoiai may exist in documents that simply omit any reference to pronoia *[5.8]*.

Perhaps most significant is that these documents expand our knowledge of the benefit a pronoia holder derived from his pronoia. Assembling all the evidence in this chapter we may conclude that a pronoia holder could derive at least three types of revenue from his pronoia:

(i) The rents from properties located within his pronoia that were owned by the state *[5.6–5.7]*.

(ii) The actual harvest produced by a kind of domain land, which he did not rent out to others, but cultivated through corvée of his paroikoi. A steward (*oikonomos*) might be appointed to ensure that the paroikoi did their work and the pronoia holder received the full harvest *[5.15]*.

(iii) At least in the Nicaean state (what little evidence there is for pronoia in the despotate of Epiros provides no evidence for this) the pronoia holder sometimes received the taxes from properties located within his pronoia that were owned by others *[5.1–5.2] [5.4] [5.7–5.9]*. The "taxpayers" who paid the taxes burdening the patrimonial property they owned *[5.8–5.9]* to a pronoia holder could be considered paroikoi (ὑπὸ παροικίαν) *[5.4]*. Even though paroikoi might refer to their pronoia holder as their "lord" (*authentes*) *[5.8]*, the assignment of a property owner's taxes to a pronoia did not alter a paroikos' legal status. As a subject of the emperor he remained entitled to the normal legal protection an emperor owed his subjects *[5.8]*. In simple property disputes with third parties, the paroikoi of a pronoia holder did not have to pursue their case through their lord. He was not their legal spokesman, nor was he their judge *[5.8]*. The paroikoi of a pronoia holder were permitted to sell their property *[5.8–5.9]*. The single qualification was that it was improper for paroikoi to sell any of their property to the person who held their property within a grant of pronoia *[5.4]*.

In the first two cases the holder of a pronoia could be thought of as someone who received certain aspects of the right of ownership over a property owned by the state, the right to act as the owner of a property and enjoy its fruits. But it could still be maintained that the property so granted remained the property of the state *[5.6]*.

The third case – whereby the pronoia holder received tax revenues from properties that were privately owned – is not attested as a characteristic of pronoia grants before the thirteenth century and represents an innovation. Nevertheless, there was precedent for this kind of arrangement. As discussed in the previous chapter Alexios I granted his brother Adrian the tax revenues of the Kassandra peninsula *[4.5]* and he granted another brother the *sevastokrator* Isaac the tax revenues from properties in the area near Thessaloniki (*Lavra*, I, no. 51). Yet, even if we put aside the gulf in status between Alexios' brothers and the thirteenth-century recipients of tax revenues in pronoia, there does not seem to be any institutional continuity between these late eleventh-century grants and the thirteenth-century phenomenon involving pronoiai.

What brought about this shift to granting taxes on private property? Was there a lack of state property to confer? At first thought, this would seem to be an unlikely explanation. After the conquests of Theodore I and especially of John Vatatzes there should have been plenty of land available. While some of the land reconquered by Nicaea might have been left in the hands of its current owner or restored to its pre-1204 owner, certainly some owners from before the Latin conquest would have disappeared. Further, there was opportunity for the Nicaean regime to confiscate land from Byzantines who had collaborated with the Latins. But while the conquests were extensive, they were not steady. There were many years during the period of exile in which Nicaea was on the defensive and quantities of state land may have been depleted. Further, the areas for which we happen to have evidence of pronoia grants during the period – around Smyrna and on the Meander – were those that did not witness great territorial expansion. State land would have disappeared quickly in those areas, while the areas of greatest expansion – to the north and of course in Europe – are poorly documented by the sources.[103]

Another possibility, that there were not enough tenant-paroikoi available to work state land, seems unlikely given the apparent economic health of the peasantry in the area around Smyrna.[104] The reason for the shift to granting the taxes of private property to pronoia holders may have been the natural result of running out of state property for such grants. Nevertheless, by doing this the Nicaean state was deviating from a hallowed Byzantine fiscal principle, to avoid losing control of fiscal revenues. For the moment at least, because the pronoia grant remained a lifetime grant, the alienation was not permanent. But that would come later.

[103] The documents mention some imperial property in the area of Smyrna in the thirteenth century, but one is struck more by how much land was imperial land before 1204 but was no longer. During the thirteenth century the state (as distinguished from pronoia holders) was not a significant landowner in the area of Smyrna: see Glykatzi-Ahrweiler, "Politique agraire."

[104] D. Kyritses and K. Smyrlis, "Les villages du littoral égéen de l'Asie Mineure au Moyen Âge," in *Les villages dans l'empire byzantin (IVe–XVe siècle)*, ed. J. Lefort et al. (Paris, 2005), 437–51.

Ultimately, perhaps the need for soldiers led to a significant increase in the number of pronoia grants, and this in turn led to the need to find new means to finance pronoia grants. This, I think, explains not only the decision to grant taxes from private property to pronoia holders but the use of the *zeugaria* more easily to quantify and regulate the size of grants as well. The thirteenth century was an age of improvisation. It would remain so through the reign of Michael VIII.

6 Pronoia during the era of Michael VIII Palaiologos

In August 1258 Theodore II Laskaris died. He had designated George Mouzalon as regent for his son and successor, the seven-year-old John IV Laskaris. Within little more than a week Mouzalon was murdered and the regency passed to Michael Palaiologos, a well-connected aristocrat and general who was probably complicit if not responsible for Mouzalon's murder. At the end of 1258 or the very beginning of 1259 he became co-emperor with John IV.

Half a year later, at the battle of Pelagonia in July 1259, Michael VIII's army defeated the combined forces of the ruler of Epiros Michael II Doukas, Manfred of Sicily, and William II Villehardouin, prince of Achaia. In July 1261 a Nicaean general captured Constantinople and drove out the Latins. After a triumphal entry into the city Michael VIII had himself recrowned as emperor with his toddler son Andronikos proclaimed as his heir. In December Michael had the young John IV blinded and removed from the scene, thus ending the Laskarid dynasty and establishing the Palaiologan dynasty.

Michael VIII directed most of his energies toward countering the threats from the West and toward extending his authority over the despotate of Epiros and the remaining Latin states in the Morea. Careful diplomacy was the means for attaining the first goal and force of arms the second. Michael's military policies centered on protecting Constantinople, amassing armies large enough to tackle the Latins in the Morea and the Greeks in Thessaly, and ensuring continued Byzantine control over the European provinces of Thrace and Macedonia.

Early in the reign of Michael VIII two significant developments occurred involving the institution of pronoia. First, pronoiai and other imperial grants were at long last systematically incorporated into the fiscal system. Second, hereditary rights were granted over some pronoia grants. When combined with other earlier developments, such as the granting of pronoiai to aristocrats, the effect was to blur the distinctions between pronoia grants and simple, hereditary grants of property and privileges to monasteries and laymen. What had been distinct types of grants were merged into a single type of concession called an *oikonomia* with a standardized quantification based on the fiscal value of the grant.

Posotes

The concept of the monetary *posotes* is one of the defining features of the late Byzantine fiscal system. It was probably Franz Dölger who first identified *posotes* as a fiscal term. Since then many scholars have connected the term with pronoiai or with imperial grants in general, each adding various nuances depending on his understanding of what a pronoia was.[1] Because their conceptions of what the term *posotes* meant are usually colored by their views on pronoia (which are often at odds with mine), there is little to be gained by tracing the historiography of the term. Rather, I will simply present my view of what the term *posotes* signified.

The words *posotes* and *poson* are themselves rather common. Both mean "quantity" or "amount," and both could be utilized in a variety of contexts. For example, in a document from 1176, *posotes* refers to a measurement of volume: "in exchange for such quantity [*posotes*] of grain." More often the words are applied to areas of land, as in a chrysobull from 1089 which makes reference to 1,500 modioi of land with the phrase "concerning such quantity [*posotes*] of land." Similarly, a document from the early twelfth century contains a repetitive list of witnesses to a land transaction, each of whom attests that he witnessed the measurement of 6,111 modioi "from the whole amount [*poson*]" of a particular property.[2]

The use of *posotes* to denote quantities of land continued into the thirteenth century. In a *prostagma* from 1234 John Vatatzes declared that "we confer all such land upon the holy monastery of the Lemviotissa, reckoned in the amount of 6 *zeugaria*." And in two documents from May

[1] Dölger, *Beiträge*, 126. Some other views on *posotes*: F. Dölger, "Die Frage des Grundeigentums in Byzanz" (1933), repr. in Dölger, *Byzanz und die europäische Staatenwelt* (Ettal, 1953; repr. Darmstadt, 1964), 227; Ostrogorsky, *Féodalité*, 105, 107, 122–23; Kazhdan, *Agrarnye otnošenija*, 214, 217; M. Sjuzjumov, "Vnutrennjaja politika Andronika Komnina i razgrom prigorodov Konstantinopolja v 1187 godu," *VizVrem* 12 (1957), 60; B. Gorjanov, *Pozdnevizantijskij feodalizm* (Moscow, 1962), 132–33; A. Hohlweg, *Beiträge zur Verwaltungsgeschichte des oströmischen Reiches unter den Komnenen* (Munich, 1965), 83; Ahrweiler, "La 'pronoia' à Byzance," 687; A. Laiou-Thomadakis, *Peasant Society in the Late Byzantine Empire* (Princeton, 1977), 47–48; Oikonomides, "A propos des armées," 354; Hvostova, *Osobennosti*, 207; J. Lefort, "Une grande fortune foncière aux xe–xiiie s.," *Structures féodales et féodalisme dans l'occident méditerranéen (x^e^–xiiie s.)* (Rome, 1980), 741; M. Kaplan, *Les hommes et la terre à Byzance du vi^e^ au xie siècle* (Paris, 1992), 181; N. Oikonomides, "The Role of the Byzantine State in the Economy," *EHB*, iii, 1043–47.

[2] *Patmos*, i, no. 22.6. *Xénophon*, no. 2.13–14. *Docheiariou*, no. 5.5–21.

1259 Michael VIII conferred a field "reckoned in the amount of 4 *zeugaria*" upon the monastery of St. John on Patmos. In July 1263 the *apographeus* of Rhodes and the Cyclades made a fiscal survey of the properties held on Kos by the monastery of St. John on Patmos. Among the properties were "all such land reaching the amount of 300 modioi" which were associated with a particular *metochion* on the island. The same document describes the component properties of a *proasteion* "reckoned in such amount of 150 modioi."[3]

An act of the *apographeus* Demetrios Apelmene from 1300 explains how the monastery of Xenophon held only a small portion of the land that it once had been granted in the area of Stomion in the Chalkidike, "the rest of such amount [*posotes*] was lost." Apelmene notes that the emperor ordered that it receive back "the amount [*posotes*] contained in" a *prostagma*. Because only measurements in modioi are found in this document, *posotes* refers to the area of the properties (*Xénophon*, no. 3.11,13).

Posotes is used just once to indicate a number of paroikoi. A *prostaxis* of Alexios II from 1181, found inserted within a praktikon of the same year, granted Lavra "a quantity [*posotes*] of another twenty paroikoi" in addition to what the monastery already held (*Lavra*, I, no. 65.11).

Frequently, *posotes* and *poson* refer to a quantity of money. In several of his letters, Patriarch Nicholas Mystikos in the early tenth century refers to "a *posotes* of gold."[4] In the penalty clauses of acts of sale, donation, or exchange from the late tenth through the middle of the eleventh century, *posotes* and *poson* are used, almost interchangeably, in reference to the purchase price or worth of a property. In an act from 982 the seller of a property swore that, if he violated the purchase agreement, he would "render the amount [*poson*] given by you [the buyer] . . . in double," and in an act of sale from 1001, we read that if the seller or his heirs renounced the agreement, they would pay the buyer "the price paid in double quantity [*posotes*]."[5]

[3] MM, IV, 149.23: τὴν καὶ πεποσωμένην εἰς ποσότητα ζευγαρίων ἕξ, and cf. 146.27, 147.16,19. *Patmos*, I, no. 14.47: καὶ συμποσούμενον εἰς ποσότητα ζευγαρίων τεσσάρων, and no. 27.64; II, no. 69.29–30: συμποσουμένης καὶ τῆς τοιαύτης ἁπάσης γῆς . . . εἰς ποσότητα μοδίων τριακοσίων, and lines 32–33: εἰς τὴν τοιαύτην δὲ ποσότητα τῶν ἑκατὸν πεντήκοντα μοδίων συγκατελογίσθη.

[4] *Nicholas I Patriarch of Constantinople*, Letters, ed. and trans. R. Jenkins and L. Westerink (Washington, D.C., 1973), no. 18.39,48, no. 19.26, no. 31.134, no. 92.12,23.

[5] *Iviron*, I, no. 3.22–23, no. 12.29. Similarly, *Iviron*, I, no. 11.26–27 (996), no. 13.29–30 (1007), no. 20.40 (1015), no. 21.29 (1015), no. 22.33 (1016 or 1017), no. 26.29 (1042). And cf. *Iviron*, I, no. 17B.36 (1012).

After the middle of the eleventh century *poson* and *posotes* no longer appear in such clauses,[6] but the use of the words to denote the value of a property continues. A document from 1237 refers to a "monetary quantity" (*nomismatikon poson*) as the compensation to be paid for a property granted to a monastery, and in 1384 the value of a dowry is "the *poson*."[7] And an act of the *protos* of Athos from 1316 explains how Esphigmenou and Vatopedi had disputed possession of a property on Athos. Ultimately it was decided to effect an exchange of properties, but first the property had to be given a value. A commission "established the value of this in a quantity [*posotes*] of 800 hyperpyra" (*Esphigménou*, no. 12.68).

None of the above uses of the words *posotes* and *poson* has anything to do with the institution of pronoia. I cite them to demonstrate how these words were rather ordinary and how their meaning was colored by the context in which they appeared. Nevertheless, another application of *posotes* and *poson* was connected to imperial grants of property, including pronoiai, and from the early 1260s it was the most common way the words were employed in documents. Indeed, as Constantine Zuckerman first observed, the use of a property's fiscal assessment rather than its size as the primary element of the property's description seems to have been introduced during the reign of Michael VIII.[8] Certainly it is first attested during Michael's reign. This is not to say that documents of earlier periods did not include fiscal assessments on properties or that the word *posotes* was not used from time to time throughout the Byzantine period to refer to a quantity of taxes. Indeed, tax documents (*kodikes* and the praktika) had always included fiscal assessments, and the word *posotes* simply meant "quantity." But beginning in the 1260s it became increasingly common for documents that had no direct connection to tax collection (e.g., imperial grants of properties to monasteries) to note only the fiscal assessment on the property (using the word *posotes*) rather than its size.

It is not difficult to illustrate how this application differs from the value or size of the property involved. For example, according to a *prostagma* from 1333 *[8.74]*, a monastery paid (*telei*) a man seven hyperpyra each year for a property it owned. The emperor granted the request that this tax be annulled and ordered that the man receive "another quantity [*posotes*] of seven hyperpyra in exchange [*anti*] for such land." The *posotes* of seven

[6] See, e.g., *Lavra*, I, no. 53.29–30 (1097); MM, VI, 163.23 (1213), 165.14 (1213); *Chilandar*, ed. Petit, no. 12.47–48 (1296), no. 25.52 (1309), no. 29.63–64 (1314).

[7] MM, IV, 42.23. *Docheiariou*, no. 49.14. And cf. *Patmos*, II, no. 57.4 (1197).

[8] C. Zuckerman, "The Dishonest Soldier Constantine Planites and His Neighbours," *Byz* 56 (1986), 326–28.

hyperpyra was the property tax assessed on the land. To cite another example, a chrysobull from 1325 confirmed the donation of the village of Prevista to Zographou by the tsar of Bulgaria. The emperor explains that Prevista, "being of a quantity [*posotes*] of 300 hyperpyra," had been purchased by the tsar from the *megale doukaina* Theodora Palaiologina "in a just price for a quantity [*posotes*] of 3,000 hyperpyra."[9] Here *posotes* is used to refer to both the "amount" of the purchase price and another less obvious "amount," ten times less than the purchase price. The latter is the fiscal assessment or ordinary tax burden assigned to the property.

In these contexts a *posotes* was an amount of money that represented the tax that was normally levied on a taxable item or collection of items if the items were not subject to any kind of tax exemption and if they did not form part of any kind of imperial grant to a private party. The items involved included real property, such as a field or the *stasis* of a paroikos, as well as intangible rights, such as the right to pasture animals or fishing rights in a particular area. For individual properties, including the *staseis* of paroikoi, the *posotes* was the *telos*, the basic property tax normally levied on such items; for rights, it was the tax or charge normally levied on these. For collections of properties such as villages and the holdings of large landowners such as monasteries, the *posotes* was the sum of all the individual taxes and charges that were normally levied on the individual items within the collection.

There were, in fact, three primary ways to quantify a property: (i) by its size (area, sometimes including number of trees and buildings, and number of paroikoi), (ii) by its purchase price, and (iii) by its fiscal assessment. In traditional societies, sales of land are relatively rare, and in large measure this explains why the documented sale prices per unit of land area display such variety in Byzantium. Further, sale prices were affected by non-economic factors such as the relative status of buyer and seller and, in the sale of property to religious foundations, the piety of the seller. Thus it was difficult for the Byzantines to estimate the sale price of a property, and thus sale price was an unreliable measure of the "worth" of a property. Size was a more accurate estimation of "worth," but to be more meaningful it had to take the quality of the property into consideration (as when documents specify the quality of a piece of land in addition to its area or employ the term *zeugarion*).

Fiscal assessment was by far the best way to gauge the "worth" of a property because it took into account the size and quality of the property.

[9] *Zographou*, no. 22.5,9–10.

Further, the fiscal assessment of a property, rather than the sale price, was a figure that the state had an interest in determining, and so it was much more likely for a property to have an established fiscal assessment. The fiscal assessment had another advantage over the size of a property, because it permitted properties of quite dissimilar contents to be compared (fields to vineyards or arable land to paroikos households). Two properties with quite different contents but the same fiscal assessment could be said to be of equal "worth," regardless of what they might be sold for or what was contained within them.

The granting of a tax exemption did not change the *posotes* of an item. Thus, fifty modioi of average arable land, as a rule, had a *posotes* of one hyperpyron (its normal tax assessment in the later thirteenth and fourteenth centuries) whether or not its owner enjoyed a tax exemption on the land. Similarly, granting these fifty modioi of arable land as a pronoia grant to a soldier or as an outright grant to a monastery or some aristocrat did not change its *posotes*.

In many cases the *posotes* of an individual property was the same as the property's "fiscal value," if by "fiscal value" we mean the actual amount of revenue the state could expect to draw from the property. Thus, if someone owned a field of fifty modioi and paid the normal *telos* of one hyperpyron to the state, both the *posotes* and the fiscal value of the property was one hyperpyron. Similarly, if that same fifty modioi were held tax exempt by someone, one could still say both its *posotes* and fiscal value were one hyperpyron. However, if the same field of fifty modioi was owned by the state and was leased to others, the fiscal value of the property would be greater than one hyperpyron (because the rent on a property was always higher than its tax), while its *posotes* would remain one hyperpyron. This is an important distinction because it applied as well if the state granted this property to a private party. The beneficiary could expect to derive an income from the fifty modioi in excess of the property's one-hyperpyron *posotes*, but the property's *posotes* nevertheless remained one hyperpyron.

Conversely, the *posotes* of a property, right, or collection of properties and rights that were conceded to a beneficiary as an imperial grant did not necessarily represent – and in fact rarely represented – the actual monetary value of that grant to the beneficiary. In other words, the *posotes* of a grant was usually significantly less than the income a beneficiary would ordinarily derive from the grant. This is because the *posotes* did not consider the rents a beneficiary would receive from the property he was granted, nor did it consider the value of the labor services owed by paroikoi included within the grant which were transferred from the state to the beneficiary.[10] The individual pronoia holder must have viewed the *posotes* as representing a collection of assets with more or less income-producing potential, a potential that could be exploited in various ways, requiring varying degrees of effort, and producing various levels of profit.

But if a *posotes* accurately represented neither the amount of resources the state was conceding to a beneficiary nor the value of the grant to the beneficiary, what was the utility of the concept of *posotes*? In truth, the posotes *did* accurately represent the *taxes* and *monetary charges* usually levied on an item or group of items, and if the emperor granted a tax exemption for those items to a third party, the *posotes* would indicate how much potential tax revenue the state was forsaking. But that was not the primary purpose of the *posotes*. Rather, its primary purpose was to simplify and regularize the quantification and administration of imperial grants. In fact, if emperors had not been making large numbers of grants, it is unlikely that the institution of the *posotes* would ever have emerged.

The concept of the *posotes* seems to have supplanted the *zeugarion*. If we consider a sample of twenty-one documents issued after 1262 that use the word *zeugarion* in its technical sense, we observe, first of all, that eleven of the documents date to the fifteenth century (1406 and later).[11] I suspect that the resurgence of the *zeugarion* in the fifteenth century was a direct result of the Turkish conquests in the Balkans in the later fourteenth century. The Ottomans appropriated Byzantine fiscal practices which they had encountered in Asia Minor in the later thirteenth century, either directly through the conquest of Byzantine territory or indirectly through their contact with the Seljuks of Ikonion who had appropriated some Byzantine fiscal practices of the twelfth and early thirteenth centuries, and brought them to the Balkans. After the Byzantines temporarily recovered some of

10 According to Hvostova, *Osobennosti*, 207, *posotes* refers not only to state taxes, but, when dealing with state land, the *posotes* was the rent paid by the paroikos on state land. In this context, she cites the documents dealing with the village of Malachiou *[5.6]*. However, neither the Malachiou documents, nor any other document, uses *posotes* or *poson* to denote a quantity of rent. These terms were used to denote only the area of a property, the price of a property, the tax on a property, or a number of paroikoi.

11 *Pantéléèmôn*, no. 16.5,8 (1406), no. 17.10 (1407), no. 18.2 (1419); Testament of Matthew for the monastery of Charsianeites (1407), in *Byzantine Monastic Foundation Documents*, ed. J. Thomas and A. Hero (Washington, D.C., 2000), IV, p. 1649; *Lavra*, III, no. 159.32,35,46,47 (1407), no. 161.28,33,47 (1409), no. 165.17,39,49 (1420); *Iviron*, IV, no. 99.4,7,8,11 (between 1430 and 1448); *Dionysiou*, no. 10.9,12,13,17,20 (1408), no. 18.7 (1420), no. 20.4,6,9,10 (1421).

these areas, they rediscovered the *zeugarion*, courtesy of the Turks.[12] Of the remaining ten documents from this sample of twenty-one, four are private acts, mostly donations of property to monasteries,[13] two simply confirm the Patmos monastery's possession of Gonia tou Petake, repeating phrases that date back to 1259,[14] and two use the term while confirming Hilandar's possession of a property donated to the monastery by Michael VIII.[15]

This leaves two documents from the sample of twenty-one. (i) A chrysobull inserted within an act of an official from 1286 orders the official to remit to a monastery four *zeugaria* in a village from the property a soldier possessed there. The official then gave the monastery 400 modioi of land *[8.73]*. (ii) In 1304 an official returned to a monastery in Melnik a property "amounting to land of two *zeugaria* for four hyperpyra," a unique example of both the number of *zeugaria* and a monetary *posotes* appearing together (*Vatopédi*, I, no. 36.9). Thus, from this sample of twenty-one documents, for nearly a century and half, from 1262 to 1406, only two of the documents are official acts using the word *zeugarion* in connection with property transfers that took place after the reign of Michael VIII. And when these documents do mention the *zeugarion*, they provide additional information – the area of the property or the *posotes* of the property – to make sure everyone understood what was meant.[16] The *zeugarion* had lost its currency.

And for good reason. With the adoption of the *posotes*, the *zeugarion* was no longer needed. However effective the *zeugarion* had been at creating units of land with a consistent fiscal value, it is not certain that it was ever used to create equivalencies between anything other than different types of land. Perhaps it is merely a reflection of how little we know about how the *zeugarion* was calculated, but the process seems cumbersome. First, officials would have to determine what quantity of land (first-quality land?) corresponded to one *zeugarion*. Then, they would need to determine what quantity of other types of land was equivalent to that quantity of land. If

[12] N. Oikonomides, "Ottoman Influence on Late Byzantine Fiscal Practice," *Südost-Forschungen*, 45 (1986), 2: "one sometimes has the feeling that Byzantine institutions which had disappeared in the Balkans before the XIVth century were re-introduced there by the Ottomans, who must have borrowed these institutions in Asia Minor well before the conquest of the Balkans." Although he discusses (pp. 14–16) the *zeugarion*, "which somehow becomes 'fashionable' during the first quarter of the XVth century," he does not make a connection with his earlier comments. See Chapter 10 below for more on this cross-cultural phenomenon.

[13] *Chilandar*, ed. Živojinović, I, no. 7.1,15 (1265); *Prodrome B*, no. 18.8 (1301); *Vatopédi*, I, no. 61.34 (1323); II, no. 107.17 (1356).

[14] *Patmos*, I, no. 15.5 (1292), no. 17.21 (1329).

[15] *Chilandar*, ed. Živojinović, I, no. 34.194 (1317), no. 35.76 (1317).

[16] It is interesting that in both documents, the equivalency seems to be 1 *zeugarion* = 100 modioi. (A *telos* or *posotes* of 4 hyperpyra normally corresponded to 200 modioi of land.)

the *zeugarion* was used not only to make imperial grants but to levy taxes, officials would need to determine as well what the tax should be on one *zeugarion*. In fact there is no real evidence that the *zeugarion* ever was used in the tax process.

The *posotes*, on the other hand, could compare any taxable item (land, paroikos *staseis*, mills, pasturing rights, and so on). Further, because the *posotes* of a property or of a right was the nominal tax burden on that item, something that fiscal officials were accustomed to calculating, the transition to the *posotes* required little retraining.

The *posotes* had numerous uses:

(i) It could now be determined, at a glance, how much tax revenue the state was forsaking for the benefit of a privileged beneficiary, and through simple addition it was possible to calculate the aggregate tax revenues so conceded either on a provincial level or throughout the empire. While there is no specific evidence to indicate that the fisc was making such calculations, one may assume such information was useful. It certainly would be of value to a modern state.

(ii) It was now possible to make ready comparisons between grants, regardless of the variety of individual elements (paroikos *staseis*, arable land, vineyards, mills, rights, etc.) within them. Questions such as, Was one grant larger than another? or Were all the grants of a similar size? could be answered by a glance at the total *posotes* of each. The army, as a hierarchical organization requiring multiple levels of grants, would benefit from the ability to create large numbers of several levels of grants, each with a uniform size. This may well have been what Athyvolos was up to in 1261 *[6.2]*.

(iii) The *posotes* made it much easier to effect state-ordered exchanges of properties and rights between grant holders *[6.4]*.

(iv) It also permitted logical and consistent incremental increases in grant size *[6.6]* as well as easy across-the-board reductions in grant sizes (attested during Andronikos II's reign: see *[8.34–8.36]*).

(v) Later, in the fourteenth century, the *posotes* permitted the granting of additional privileges, such as hereditary rights, by fractional increments (e.g., *[8.14] [8.44] [8.46]*).

The effect, if not the purpose, of the *posotes* was to render the component parts of any imperial grant fungible, whether composed of land, paroikoi, or the rights to other income-producing items.

Alexander Kazhdan suggested that the origins of the late Byzantine use of the word *posotes* can be found in the *Marcian Treatise*. In a passage from this work describing the *logisimon solemnion*, we read that an emperor could grant to a particular religious foundation "the *posotes* itself from the public tax of certain villages."[17] However, while this passage does deal with an imperial grant of a quantity of taxes on a beneficiary, the treatise uses *posotes* several other times in the context of simply calculating a village's tax burden: e.g., "the root [sum] of the village is the entire *posotes* of the figures found in the ledger of each village." Such passages have nothing to do with the *logisimon solemnion* or any other kind of conferral of taxes on a beneficiary. Moreover, the *Marcian Treatise* is concerned only with the *telos* of properties, and the *posotes* often included secondary and other charges as well as the *telos*. Further, no source until the reign of Michael VIII uses *posotes* in the late Byzantine sense, and since no one dates the *Marcian Treatise* later than the first half of the twelfth century, the element of continuity of application is lacking.[18]

If there is no Byzantine antecedent for the practice of quantifying properties by their fiscal revenue, whence came the inspiration for the *posotes*? One (and only one) of Byzantium's neighbors employed a fiscal practice nearly identical to the *posotes*. The Seljuk military *iqta* – a grant of tax revenues from the sultan in return for military service – had been quantified by its specific fiscal value (*ʿibra*, lit. "revenue") long before the concept of the *posotes* appeared in Byzantium.[19] Further, Michael VIII had the opportunity to learn firsthand about Seljuk institutions on at least three occasions. First, after suffering a defeat at the hands of the Mongols in 1256, Izz al-Din Kayka'us II, the Seljuk sultan of Rum, briefly sought refuge at the Nicaean court. Second, later that year Michael Palaiologos, before he became emperor, was forced to leave Nicaea because of court intrigues. He spent part of 1256 and early 1257 at the court of Izz al-Din who in the meantime had reestablished his authority in a part of his former domain. There Michael campaigned against the Mongols in the sultan's service. Third, seeking refuge from the Mongols yet again, Izz al-Din, his family, and retinue arrived at the Nicaean

[17] Kazhdan, *Agrarnye otnošenija*, 214, and *Derevnja i gorod*, 175. Cf. G. Litavrin, *Bolgarija i Vizantija v XI–XII vv.* (Moscow, 1960), 145, who concurred with, and overstated, Kazhdan's position. Dölger, *Beiträge*, 117.42: ἡ αὐτὴ ποσότης ἀπὸ δημοσίου κανόνος χωρίων τινῶν.

[18] Dölger, *Beiträge*, 114.22–23, and also 114.34–35 and 123.1. While the *ODB* entry "posotes" is attributed to me, the link between the late Byzantine term *posotes* and the *Marcian Treatise* was added by the editors.

[19] E.g., see H. Rabie, "The Size and Value of the *Iqtāʿ* in Egypt, 564–741 A.H. 1169–1341 A.D.," in *Studies in the Economic History of the Middle East*, ed. M. Cook (London and New York, 1970), 131–38, and C. Cahen, "L'évolution de l'iqtāʿ du IXe au XIIIe siècle," *Annales, économies-sociétés-civilisations* 8 (1953), 36, 46 and note, who suggests possible Roman antecedents. Indeed there was probably a great deal of mutual influence between Byzantine and Islamic civilizations in agrarian and fiscal institutions.

court in later 1260 or early 1261, just before Michael VIII's reconquest of Constantinople in July 1261. For the next few years, until he departed from the empire around the end of 1264, he lived in semi-captivity, a pawn in Michael's maneuverings with the Mongols. Further, ethnic Turks became a noticeable – in fact, significant – element within the post-1204 Byzantine army only after the accession of Michael VIII.[20] Such circumstantial evidence does fit the chronology: the first extant document to quantify a grant by a *posotes* dates to May 1261. Therefore, the possibility of Turkish influence on the transition to the administration of pronoiai and other grants via the *posotes* seems more than likely.

Oikonomia

When the *posotes* was used to quantify an entire grant in aggregate, this is often expressed as "the *posotes* of the oikonomia" of this or that person or monastery. In fact the reason we know so much about the concept of the *posotes* is because it affected more than pronoia grants to soldiers or to other laymen. The *posotes* was used to quantify the property holdings of monasteries as well. Before we look at some specific examples of the application of the *posotes*, we need to introduce another concept, the oikonomia.

From the beginning of the reign of Michael VIII a significant change occurred in official terminology involving imperial grants. Gradually the word *pronoia* fell from use, supplanted by a new word, *oikonomia*. This in itself would be a significant development, but the change was much greater than this. While the word *oikonomia* began to be applied to pronoia grants, it also was used to denote the total collection of property and rights held by *any* private party through a grant from the emperor. By the same token, the word *pronoia*, while it was falling from official use, was nevertheless occasionally used to refer, as well, to *any* imperial grant of property. Essentially there was a conflation of all varieties of imperial grants of property under the single rubric of "oikonomia," with an occasional use of "pronoia" to denote this rubric. Because this change, which is fundamental to the study of pronoia, is reflected in all of our sources, it is impossible to continue the story of the development of the institution without examining it.

The use of the word *oikonomia* as a synonym and ultimately, to a large degree, as a replacement for the word *pronoia* occurred gradually over half

[20] Bartusis, *Late Byzantine Army*, 51–54. I. Vásáry, *Cumans and Tatars: Oriental Military in the Pre-Ottoman Balkans, 1185–1365* (Cambridge and New York, 2005), 73–77.

a century. The area where this transformation was most complete and most rapid was in documents issued by the emperor, followed by those issued by imperial officials. Private acts were the slowest of documents to change and the literary sources (histories, letters, etc.) were the slowest of all. This is the expected course of development for technical terms created and imposed by the imperial chancery itself.

The word *oikonomia* is derived from *oikonomos* (οἰκονόμος) meaning "steward, manager," via the verb *oikonomo* (οἰκονομῶ), "to manage a household, to arrange," and ultimately from *oikos* (οἶκος), "house, household, family," and the verb *nemo* (νέμω), "to apportion, to manage." Hélène Ahrweiler wrote that inasmuch as the word *oikonomia*, in her dictionary, had forty-five meanings, "a semantic study through the word cannot help us sense the reality of the institution."[21] While it is true that a study of the use of the word alone will not permit us to understand the connection between oikonomia and pronoia, nevertheless one cannot ignore the original meanings of *oikonomia*. As in the case of *pronoia*, the technical sense of *oikonomia* was derived or evolved from its general senses.

Supervision, management. The most basic sense of *oikonomia* is "supervision" or "management." The sixth-century *Treatise on Strategy* refers to "the oikonomia of battle, of both personnel and materials." In the early tenth century Patriarch Nicholas I recommends the "prudent oikonomia" of metropolitans as they decide the level of contributions for their dioceses. Anna Komnene refers to the official charged with distributing the property of defeated Paulicians to Alexios I's soldiers as "the one undertaking this oikonomia." In 1198 Alexios III Angelos granted the monastery of Hilandar a property which would now be "under the authority and oikonomia" of the monks.[22]

Arrangement, accommodation, dispensation. Another sense of the word, encountered rarely in the Byzantine era, appears in a passage from the *Marcian Treatise* on taxation. The anonymous author describes two situations that could lead to the use of the fiscal tool called the *solemnion*. Other variations of the *solemnion* came into play, he writes, "when the oikonomia of such *solemnia* came about neither this way nor that."[23] Here *oikonomia*

21 Ahrweiler, "La 'pronoia' à Byzance," 681.

22 *Three Byzantine Military Treatises*, ed. G. Dennis (Washington, 1985), 44.7, and also, 94.2,4, 116.5. *Nicholas I*, ed. Jenkins and Westerink, no. 92.24. *Alexiad*, VI.2.4: ed. Reinsch, 171.1–2, and also VI.4.2: ed. Reinsch, 174.88–89 (= ed. Leib, II, 45.12–13, 49.7–8). *Chilandar*, ed. Živojinović, I, no. 4.26. Other examples: *Prôtaton*, no. 7.144; *Patmos*, I, no. 21.23; P. Gautier, "Le typikon du Christ Sauveur Pantokrator," *REB* 32 (1974), 1–145, lines 617, 689, 691, 1391, 1398, 1399, 1405, 1432, 1436, 1442; *Theodori Ducae Lascaris Epistulae CCXVII*, ed. N. Festa (Florence, 1898), no. 90.51.

23 Dölger, *Beiträge*, 118.8. Lemerle, *Agrarian History*, 84.

must mean something like "arrangement" in the specific sense of a creation or establishment, or "dispensing" from the meaning of the verb *nemo*.

Related to this sense is the most common non-technical meaning of the word *oikonomia* in the Byzantine era: "arrangement, accommodation, dispensation." The sense of a simple arrangement is seen in a letter of Patriarch Nicholas I. He asks another prelate to refrain from personal action against allegedly misbehaving bishops and, instead, to await their official "condemnation or some other oikonomia." In another example, in 1176 a yearly grant to the Patmos monastery of grain from imperial estates on Crete was terminated because these estates had been granted by the emperor to others *[3.5]*. A tax collector explained to the monks that henceforth a cash allowance would be given instead of wheat: "for concerning the wheat from Crete, there is some other oikonomia."[24]

In an extension of the sense of "arrangement," a settlement that resolved a problem was an oikonomia. This use of the word is found frequently in documents from the tenth through twelfth centuries. For example, in a document from 1153, the *protos* of Mount Athos, after deciding a property dispute, ordered penalties for anyone who wished "to upset our said oikonomia."[25]

General accommodation. Related to this is the sense of *oikonomia* as a general accommodation. An eleventh-century document refers to St. Paul's oikonomia regarding circumcision. In a property decision from 1153 the *protos* of Mount Athos notes that he transferred a seat in church and at a tribunal to someone "for the sake of an oikonomia." Patriarch Athanasios I complained once about high church officials (a metropolitan and a patriarch), whose actions had exceeded their authority: "Such seemingly good

[24] *Nicholas I*, ed. Jenkins and Westerink, no. 113.27. *Life* of Hosios Leontios: Makarios Chrysokephalos, archbishop of Philadelphia, *Λόγοι πανηγυρικοὶ ιδ′* (Vienna, 1793), 411. Passage quoted in *Patmos*, I, p. 62*. Another example: *Prôtaton*, no. 9.42.

[25] *Lavra*, I, no. 62.36 (1153). Other examples: *Iviron*, I, no. 4.33 (982), no. 24.17,19,20 (1020); *Actes de Kastamonitou*, ed. N. Oikonomides (Paris, 1978), no. 1.13,16 (1047); *Lavra*, I, no. 52.10 (1094); and *Pantéléèmôn*, no. 8.27 (1169). This is the most likely interpretation of *oikonomia* as found in an act of Paul, the *protos* of Mount Athos, issued during the reign of Alexios I Komnenos which transferred a long list of properties (movable and immovable) to the *hegoumenos* of Xenophon including "the oikonomia of the monastery of the Kekaumenoi and of Latzires being 200 hyperpyra." Alexander Kazhdan saw a pronoia here and the editor of the act, Denise Papachryssanthou, translated the act's *oikonomia* as "revenu fiscal": *Xénophon*, no. 1.150: ἡ οἰκονομία τῆς μονῆς τῶν Κεκαυμένων καὶ τοῦ Λατζίρη ὡσεὶ ὑπερπύρων σ′ (cf. App. I.83), and pp. 11, 17; Kazhdan, *Agrarnye otnošenija*, 210, 218; and Kazhdan, "Formen," 222. (But cf. Ostrogorsky, "Die Pronoia unter den Komnenen," 51, and Hohlweg, "Zur Frage der Pronoia," 298–99.) Whatever the story behind this "oikonomia," *protos* Paul did use *oikonomia* in the sense of an arrangement or agreement (*Actes de Philothée*, ed. W. Regel, E. Kurtz, and B. Korablev, *VizVrem* 20 [1913], suppl. 1, no. 1.36–37), and no source employs the word *oikonomia* to suggest a pronoia or a "fiscal revenue" for another century and a half.

oikonomiai have destroyed the edifice" of the Church.[26] And an act from 1087 reports that, at an earlier date, the *protos* Paul, at the request of the monks of the monastery of Chaldou on Mount Athos, "was asked for there to be an oikonomia for them for their sustenance and in order that they not be treated abusively by [their] neighbors." Paul attempted to resolve the problem by fixing the boundaries between Chaldou and its neighbors. Thus, the monks were asking the *protos* for an "accommodation," an "arrangement," or, simply, a "resolution" of their dispute.[27]

Dispensation. When religious figures or institutions exercise oikonomia in an official capacity, the word is usually rendered, with a more technical sense, as "dispensation." In his letter to the pope condemning the sanctioning of the fourth marriage of Leo VI, Patriarch Nicholas I repeatedly refers to the pope's action as an oikonomia, albeit a wrongful one. Similarly, while complaining that a bishop did not have the right to perform ordinations in a city not subject to him, Patriarch Athanasios I acknowledged that synods may have permitted this in the past "by way of an oikonomia" (κατ' οἰκονομίαν).[28]

Divine dispensation. The greatest of all dispensations were the work of God.[29] In the early tenth century Patriarch Nicholas I reflected on the death of a friend's sister: "I pondered the oikonomia of the Lord and Creator, knowing that he arranges [*oikonomei*] everything for the best and directs the affairs of his own creature better than we plan and devise for ourselves."[30]

[26] *Lavra*, I, no. 16.33; no. 62.29: οἰκονομίας χάριν. Athanasios, *The Correspondence of Athanasius I Patriarch of Constantinople*, ed. A.-M. Talbot (Washington, D.C., 1975), no. 69.101; and also, no. 25.21. Other examples: *Alexiad*, XIII.9.5: ed. Reinsch, 409.47 (= ed. Leib, III, 119.22): χάριν οἰκονομίας; *Lavra*, II, no. 72.39 (1263), and III, no. 133.9 (1353).

[27] *Actes de Philothée*, ed. Regel et al., no. 1.36–37: ᾐτεῖτο αὐτῷ οἰκονομίαν γενέσθαι αὐτοῖς τινὰ εἰς διατροφὴν αὐτῶν. A. Kazhdan, review of Ostrogorsky, *Féodalité*, in *VizVrem* 10 (1956), 226, wrote that this demonstrated that monasteries were holding pronoiai under the Komnenoi, an unwarranted conclusion. If *oikonomia* meant pronoia in the document, then the monks were asking for some new property or privileges "for their sustenance." But this was not the case; no *new* properties or privileges were conferred. Rather, the *protos* merely reestablished the monks in the possession of their property. In any event, the monks requested this oikonomia from the *protos*, and *protoi* did not grant pronoiai.

[28] *Nicholas I*, ed. Jenkins and Westerink, no. 32.215; also no. 32, lines 267, 356, 372–404 passim, 469, 504. Athanasios, *Correspondence*, no. 69.88.

[29] H. Hunger, *Prooimion: Elemente der byzantinischen Kaiseridee in der Arengen der Urkunden* (Vienna, 1964), 72, who also cites H. Thurn, *Οἰκονομία. Von der frühbyzantinischen Zeit bis zum Bilderstreite*, diss. Munich 1959–60, and J. Reumann, "Οἰκονομία as 'Ethical Accommodation' in the Fathers and its Pagan Backgrounds," *Studia Patristica* 3, fasc. 1 (1961), 370–79. Also, Ch. Kotsonis, *Προβλήματα τῆς ἐκκλησιαστικῆς οἰκονομίας* (Athens, 1957), and A. Failler, "Le principe de l'économie ecclésiastique vu par Pachymère," *JÖB* 32/4 (1982), 287–95.

[30] *Nicholas I*, ed. Jenkins and Westerink, no. 47 I.37–40, and also no. 34.24, no. 104.5. Also, Athanasios, *Correspondence*, no. 56.29: τῶν ἀπορρήτων Θεοῦ οἰκονομιῶν; and cf. no. 34.6; Akindynos, *Letters of Gregory Akindynos*, ed. A. Hero (Washington, 1983), no. 50.20; and *Lavra*, III, no. 146.13 (1375).

Moreover, divine oikonomia implies a special arrangement manifesting God's mercy. Thus, Patriarch Athanasios refers to the Incarnation as an "oikonomia of Christ." Particularly telling is a passage from a fourteenth-century letter of Gregory Akindynos implying that through the Incarnation the Old Law literally was "dispensed with": "the change concerning the oikonomia from the Law." On the one hand, we have Law, and on the other, there is Accommodation, authority tempered with mercy, together producing justice.[31]

Imperial dispensation. Oikonomia was closely associated with the imperial office, and there was little difference between the emperor granting a dispensation and arriving at an arrangement. Emperor Constantine VII Porphyrogennetos mentions an oikonomia made by Justinian regarding a bishopric, and in the 1091 *typikon* for the monastery of St. John on Patmos we read that, if necessary, the rules regulating the monastery could be modified "through imperial oikonomia." In both cases *oikonomia* may be translated as either "arrangement" or "dispensation."[32]

In a number of documents from the middle of the eleventh century until the early twelfth century the imperial gesture (usually the confirmation of a monastery's possession of a property or a decision granting a property to a monastery) documented by the chrysobull was frequently referred to as an oikonomia. For example, in a chrysobull from 1102, Alexios I Komnenos reports that the *hegoumenos* of Lavra "asked for an oikonomia to be issued by our most sereneness," and obligingly he "arranged and ordered the present oikonomia."[33] In these cases oikonomia is a mark of particularity, something out of the ordinary, a "special arrangement" made by the emperor. As Patriarch Nicholas I once wrote, "Oikonomia is an imitation of divine mercy."[34] When exercised by human agents, whether

[31] Athanasios, *Correspondence*, no. 34.34. Akindynos, *Letters of Gregory Akindynos*, ed. Hero, no. 37.160: ἡ ἐπὶ τὴν οἰκονομίαν ἀπὸ τοῦ νόμου μετάστασις. Other examples of divine oikonomia: (11th c.) P. Gautier, "Réquisitoire du patriarche Jean d'Antioche contre le charisticariat," *REB* 33 (1975), 105.214; (13th c.) *Theodori Ducae Lascaris Epistulae*, no. 95.25, and index s.v. oikonomia; (14th c.) Gregoras, *Nikephoros Gregoras, Antirrhetika I*, ed. H.-V. Beyer (Vienna, 1976), index s.v. oikonomia. (14th c. or later) Solovjev–Mošin, *Grčke povelje*, no. 45.53: in the Slavic translation (of unknown date), we find *s''motrenije* ("concern, attention, management"), the usual rendering of the Greek *oikonomia*; (15th c.) *Manuel II. Palaiologos, Dialoge mit einem "Perser,"* ed. E. Trapp (Vienna, 1966), index s.v. oikonomia. Cf. H. Ahrweiler, *L'idéologie politique de l'Empire byzantin* (Paris, 1975), 128–47.

[32] Constantine VII Porphyrogennetos, *De administrando imperio*, ed. Gy. Moravcsik (Washington, D.C., 1967), ch. 47.5. MM, VI, 67.18–19.

[33] *Lavra*, I, no. 55.9,13. Similarly, *Lavra*, I, no. 31.56 (1052), no. 56.67,95 (1104); Zepos, *JGR*, I, 350.17–18; *Patmos*, I, no. 47.12 (1087).

[34] *Nicholas I*, ed. Jenkins and Westerink, no. 32.379–80: οἰκονομία ἐστὶ μίμησις τῆς θείας φιλανθρωπίας. Cf. Athanasios, *Correspondence*, no. 73.21.

the emperor, the patriarch, the *protos* of Athos, or others, an oikonomia was an arrangement, accommodation, or dispensation made by those with authority, who, like God, had the ability, to the extent of their jurisdiction, to circumvent the letter of the law to arrive at just ends in accord with the spirit of the law.

Sustenance, maintenance. Finally, as the English word *accommodation* embraces the twin senses of "arrangement" and "lodgings," so *oikonomia* also had the sense of "sustenance" or "maintenance," as well as "arrangement." In novels of Constantine VII and Nikephoros II Phokas, the middle Byzantine military lands (*stratiotika ktemata*) are defined as "the places of the military service obligation, that is, the oikonomiai for serving in war." In 1386 Patriarch Neilos confirmed the arrangements of a will, most of which involved property donations to the monastery of Pantokrator: "Our mediocrity accepts all these things as being dear to God and meritorious and for oikonomia of the souls in the monastery." And in 1226 the emperor ordered an official to return certain properties to the monastery of Lemviotissa, so that the monks should "hold and enjoy these, collect and obtain each and every income from them for both the oikonomia of the church and their maintenance." Here there appears to be no other way to render *oikonomia* than with "maintenance or upkeep." The most concrete use of the word that I have found is in the *Chronicle of Morea* which employs the word once in the plural (τὲς οἰκονομίες) in the sense of supplies or provisions.[35]

At times it is difficult to determine which sense of *oikonomia* was intended, and sometimes it is tempting to link a passage to the institution of pronoia. Around 1200 Michael Choniates, metropolitan of Athens, wrote to a friend: "For hearing that you still do not have any kind of oikonomia, I was very much saddened." Because the letter provides no further information regarding the situation Choniates was referring to, we have no way to choose between "arrangement," that is, a solution to a problem, or "sustenance," provided by employment or a grant. If Choniates' friend's problem was penury, as it seems to be, then *oikonomia* could have included both of these senses. But we do not know.[36]

[35] Zachariä, *Jus*, III, 275.23: οἱ τόποι τῆς στρατείας ἤτοι αἱ ὑπὲρ τοῦ στρατεύειν οἰκονομίαι, and Zepos, *JGR*, I, 247–48 = Zachariä, *Jus*, III, 289–91. *Actes du Pantocrator*, ed. V. Kravari (Paris, 1991), no. 11.32: ὡς θεοφιλῆ καὶ θεάρεστα καὶ εἰς οἰκονομίαν ὄντα τῶν ἐν τῷ μοναστηρίῳ ψυχῶν. MM, IV, 146.12–13. *Chronicle of the Morea*, ed. J. Schmitt (London, 1904), line 6128, and cf. 5265: τὴν ρόγαν καὶ οἰκονομίαν of certain mercenaries. Also, *Docheiariou*, no. 47.8–9 (1381): ἔχων καὶ αὐτὸς τὴν σωματικὴν μου οἰκονομίαν.

[36] Michael Choniates, *Μιχαὴλ Ἀκομινάτου τοῦ Χωνιάτου τὰ σωζόμενα*, ed. S. Lampros (Athens, 1879–80), II, 17.20–22. Uspenskij, "Značenie," 21, and Ostrogorsky, *Féodalité*, 54, assumed he was alluding to the institution of pronoia.

In this cursory overview of the non-fiscal uses of the word *oikonomia*, I have not cited any example of the word used by any Palaiologan emperor. This is because, to my knowledge, no Palaiologan emperor, except Michael VIII, used the word in a non-fiscal sense in any imperial document. Michael VIII used the word in three documents in one of the above general senses. In a 1265 chrysobull he uses the word once in the sense of maintenance when he orders the *hegoumenos* of Vatopedi to be responsible for "the management and oikonomia" of another monastery. In a chrysobull from 1263 he uses the word six times with the sense of either sustenance or arrangement. For example, in one passage he points out how the poverty of Lavra had forced the solitary monks dwelling outside the monastery "into manual labor for the oikonomia customarily given to them" by the monastery. In another passage, he confirmed a property donation of his brother John to Lavra with the words: "my majesty confirm[s] such oikonomia." And last, in his chrysobull for the Great Church of Hagia Sophia, dated between 1267 and 1271, he employs the word four times: once in the sense of disposition ("we intended the best oikonomia of affairs") and three times in the sense of sustenance. Because of the Latin Conquest the property of the church "no longer belonged to the patriarch and the clergy for oikonomia [*eis oikonomian*]," but later the emperor added numerous properties "to those things my majesty found belonging for oikonomia [*eis oikonomian*] to the ministering corps of God." Further, referring to all the properties conferred by previous emperors and by himself, Michael VIII proclaimed that they were "for common oikonomia [*eis koinen oikonomian*]" for the patriarch and his successors and the whole clergy.[37]

To repeat, all of these non-fiscal senses of the word *oikonomia* disappear from imperial documents after the reign of Michael VIII. This is no coincidence. Back in 1883 Fedor Uspenskij was the first to suggest that the fiscal terms *pronoia* and *oikonomia* were equivalent. Since then, numerous scholars have written that the word *oikonomia* could be used to designate a pronoia.[38] Some have argued that there was an equivalence between

[37] *Vatopédi*, I, no. 16.37: τῆς διεξαγωγῆς καί οἰκονομίας. *Lavra*, II, no. 72.33,51–52, and also no. 72.7,12,15,39. Zepos, *JGR*, I, 665.27. Zepos, *JGR*, I, 661.1, 662.18, 663.37–38. The chrysobull for Hagia Sophia contains a reference to pronoia: see Appendix I.

[38] Uspenskij, "Značenie," 20, 22. Mutafčiev, "Vojniški zemi," 38/561. F. Dölger, "Die Frage des Grundeigentums in Byzanz," in Dölger, *Byzanz und die europäische Staatenwelt* (Ettal, 1953), 227. Kazhdan, *Agrarnye otnošenija*, 213. Charanis, "Monastic Properties," 89. Ahrweiler, *Byzance et la mer*, 213. Ahrweiler, "La concession des droits incorporels," 110.

the terms *pronoia* and *oikonomia*.[39] Others have gone further and claimed that the terms in their technical application were synonymous or often synonymous.[40] Indeed, one often encounters in the treatment of the institution of pronoia an implied equivalence between the two terms.[41]

All of these statements are true, at least in some measure. By the end of the reign of Michael VIII the term *oikonomia* did supplant the term *pronoia* in the vocabulary of the imperial chancery. But *oikonomia* from its inception at the beginning of Michael's reign had a much broader meaning than *pronoia* ever did. An oikonomia was *any* collection of properties and fiscal revenues granted by the emperor which the beneficiary was not permitted to transfer (alienate) outside of his family. That, of course, would include the pronoia grant as it was known in the early thirteenth century, for example, as well as the vast collections of tax-exempt properties and privileges enumerated in the praktika of monasteries.

Yet, at the same time that the concept of the oikonomia was being introduced, the term *pronoia* was acquiring a broader popular meaning and was being used to denote a wider range of grant varieties than previously: hereditary grants to soldiers and grants to men higher up the social ladder (the "magnates" that Skoutariotes wrote of *[5.13]*).

As a result, something very peculiar happened. While the emperor stopped using the word *pronoia* in his documents to refer to any type of grant, fiscal officials and private individuals in their documents continued to use the term to refer to any grant that could not be alienated by its holder, even those held by monasteries.

Applications of *posotes* and oikonomia

Until the reign of Michael VIII no document establishes a direct connection between the word *oikonomia* or the monetary *posotes* and any imperial

39 A. Kazhdan, "The Fate of the Intellectual in Byzantium A Propos of *Society and Intellectual Life in Late Byzantium* by Ihor Ševčenko," *The Greek Orthodox Theological Review* 27/1 (1982), 87. Hvostova, *Osobennosti*, 212. Charanis, "Social Structure," 133.

40 Gorjanov, *Pozdnevizantijskij feodalizm*, 99. Ahrweiler, "La 'pronoia' à Byzance," 681. Ostrogorsky, *Féodalité*, 9.

41 N. Svoronos, "Recherches sur le cadastre byzantin et la fiscalité aux XIe et XIIe siècles: le cadastre de Thèbes," in *Svoronos, Études sur l'organisation intérieure, la société et l'économie de l'empire byzantin* (London, 1973), no. III, 145. Lemerle, *Agrarian History*, 199. Kazhdan, "Formen," 222. Ks. Hvostova, "Pronija: social'no-ekonomičeskie i pravovye problemy," *VizVrem* 49 (1988), 20. Sjuzjumov, "Vnutrennjaja politika Andronika Komnina," 60. G. Ostrogorsky, "Drei Praktika weltlicher Grundbesitzer aus der ersten Hälfte des 14. Jahrhunderts," *ZRVI* 14–15 (1973), 98. Charanis, "Social Structure," 97.

grant. When *oikonomia* first appears it still has almost a general sense, but quickly evolves, in conjunction with *posotes*, into a technical fiscal term.

[6.1] Orismos of Michael VIII Palaiologos for the monastery of the Lemviotissa regarding the fish pond of the soldier Michael Angelos (1259)

The first document that links an imperial grant to the new use of the word *oikonomia* is an *orismos* from February 1259 involving two fish ponds near Smyrna, one held by the Lemviotissa monastery and one held by the soldier Michael Angelos. The document explains that while the monastery had earlier been granted the old bed of the Hermos River, where it had constructed a fish pond, "the flowing water of the present course of the Hermos was granted to the soldier Michael Angelos for his oikonomia." As a result of the proximity of the properties, the monks complained of harassment from "those leasing the fish pond of the soldier."[42] Michael VIII ordered that the monks hold their fish pond without disturbance. Ten years later, in a document from 1269, Anna, Michael Angelos' widow, and their three children note that they had recently given one-half of Angelos' fish pond to each of two monasteries (MM, IV, 245).

The rights that Michael Angelos had to the Hermos and the pond connected to it were the same rights that the *vestiarites* Constantine Kalegopoulos had held as a pronoia grant (*eis pronoian* and *kata logon pronoias*) back in 1234 *[5.7]*. Just like Kalegopoulos, Angelos rented out the pond. In fact, in the 1259 document the people renting the fish pond are still called "the party of Kalegopoulos." Thus, we can reconstruct the story of these rights as follows: sometime before 1234 the rights to the Hermos were granted as a pronoia to the *vestiarites* Kalegopoulos. Sometime before 1259 these rights were granted by the emperor to the soldier Michael Angelos. When Angelos died, his fish pond (at least) passed to his widow and children who, in 1269, donated it to two monasteries.

The story is noteworthy for two reasons. First, even though we know that Constantine Kalegopoulos had a son in 1234, the heirs of Constantine did

[42] MM, IV, 241.16: ἐδωρήθη πρὸς οἰκονομίαν αὐτοῦ, and 241.19–20: οἱ πακτωτικῶς ἐξωνούμενοι τὸ τοῦ στρατιώτου βιβάριον: literally, "those purchasing for a rent the pond of the soldier"). Dölger, *Regesten*, III, no. 1869. Ahrweiler, "Smyrne," 142. Ostrogorsky, *Féodalité*, 83–84. Mutafčiev, "Vojniški zemi," 38/561. Gorjanov, *Pozdnevizantijskij feodalizm*, 101. Dölger and Ostrogorsky suggested 1274 as an alternative date for the *orismos* of Michael VIII, but since Michael Angelos was dead by 1267 (MM, IV, 169), and since the *orismos* implies that Angelos was still alive at the time, the *orismos* can reasonably be dated to 1259.

not maintain possession of the rights to the Hermos. Rather, they eventually were granted to Michael Angelos. After Angelos' death, on the other hand, at least part of his grant passed to his wife and children. Since Angelos had two sons and a daughter, we cannot say whether the widow alone was permitted to hold the grant, whether it had legally passed to the children, or specifically to the sons.[43] Whether or not this is the first known example of the inheriting of a pronoia hinges on whether or not Michael Angelos was a pronoia holder. All the information is in accord with a pronoia grant: Angelos was a soldier who received an imperial grant of rights to a property which had previously been part of a pronoia grant. However, the word *pronoia* is not used in connection with Angelos' grant; rather, the emperor writes that Angelos was granted the property "for his oikonomia" (*pros oikonomian autou*). This is a simple but unusual construction. To my knowledge the preposition *pros* does not appear with *oikonomia* in any other document from the Byzantine era. In fact this modest document establishes the first link between pronoia in its technical sense and the word *oikonomia.*

Given the many meanings of the word *oikonomia*, how is it being used in this passage? The meaning of *oikonomia* which best fits the use of the word in the clause "the flowing water of the present course of the Hermos was granted to the soldier Michael Angelos for his oikonomia" is "sustenance" or "maintenance."[44] This is in accord with my hypothesis (in Chapter 2) that "for pronoia" (*eis pronoian*) originally indicated "for sustenance or maintenance." And if Angelos held the river rights as a pronoia grant, then "for his oikonomia" would be equivalent to "for pronoia." While we cannot be absolutely sure in this particular case that Angelos held the river rights as pronoia, this seems to be a reasonable conclusion. He was a soldier with no exalted title, and a predecessor held the same rights as a pronoia grant.

[6.2] Act of John Athyvolos regarding fifty-two *archontoupouloi* (1261)

The appearance of the word *oikonomia* in the 1259 *orismos* was not unique. It appears with a similar sense and in a similar context in a document issued

[43] Ostrogorsky, *Féodalité*, 82–84, 94–96. P. Charanis, "The Aristocracy of Byzantium in the Thirteenth Century," in *Studies in Roman Economic and Social History in Honor of Allan Chester Johnson*, ed. P. Coleman-Norton (Princeton, 1951), 344. M. Angold, *A Byzantine Government in Exile* (London, 1975), 140, incorrectly interposed the *vestiarites* Kadianos as an intermediate holder of this pronoia between Kalegopoulos and Angelos.

[44] I disagree with Kazhdan, *Agrarnye otnošenija*, 213, and Hvostova, *Osobennosti*, 221, who looked to *oikonomia* in its general sense of "lordship" (or, more accurately, "stewardship") as the original sense from which the fiscal sense developed.

two years later just before the recovery of Constantinople. An act of the fiscal official John Athyvolos from May 1261 is the first document which quantifies an imperial grant in terms of a monetary *posotes* and is also the first act that links the new use of the word *oikonomia* to such a monetary value. Athyvolos writes that he had been ordered by the emperor to go to Palatia (i.e., Miletos)

> and to examine all the *exaleimmata* in it and all else attached to this property for a monetary *posotes*, and to confer these [things] on the [party?] of the *oikeioi* of our mighty and holy lord and emperor, on *kyr* Constantine Peplatismenos [and?] on fifty-two *archontopouloi*, for the sake of their oikonomia, according to the monetary *posotes* appropriate to such men.

Athyvolos then explains that in the course of this work he encountered property owned by the monastery of Kechionismene, a dependency of the Patmos monastery. The remainder of the document enumerates twenty-seven paroikos households and one paroikos *stasis* belonging to this monastery (providing only the names of the household members without detailing the contents of each holding and without providing any *telos* figures) and is unimportant for our purposes.[45]

There are a number of peculiarities about this passage. The syntax of the passage dealing with the "fifty-two *archontopouloi*" is unsatisfying. Indeed, while the lacuna in πεντ[.....] δύο can be completed only as πεντ[ήκοντα] δύο, we would expect to find one or more words separating Peplatismenos' name from the reference to these fifty-two *archontopouloi*. The document appears to be an original, so there is no copyist error at work here.

Moreover, my translation "to examine all the *exaleimmata* in it and all else attached to this property for a monetary *posotes*" is weak and reflects the ambiguous syntax of the Greek. The phrase "for a monetary *posotes*" (*eis posoteta nomismatiken*) modifies either "to examine" (*peritereisasthai*) or "attached" (*prosarmosanta*). The verb *peritero* (περιτηρῶ) is quite rare but its meaning must be related closely to *tereo* (τηρέω), which in the

[45] *Patmos*, II, no. 66.1–4: καὶ περιτηρείσασθαι τὰ ἐν αὐτῷ ἅπαντα ὑπάρχοντα ἐξαλείματα [sic] καὶ τὰ ἄλλα πάντα τὰ προσαρμόσαντα τῷ τοιούτῳ κτήματι εἰς ποσότητα *ννομισματικήν*, καὶ παραδοῦναι ταῦτα τῷ [μέρει] τῶν οἰκείων τῷ κραταιῷ καὶ ἁγίῳ ἡμῶν αὐθέντῃ καὶ βασιλεῖ, κῦρ Κωνσταντίνῳ τῷ Πεπλατισμένῳ πεντ[ήκοντα] δύο ἀρχοντοπούλοις, χάριν οἰκονομίας αὐτῶν, κατὰ τὴν ἀναλογοῦσαν τοῖς τοιούτοις *ννομισματικὴν* ποσότητα. The editor of the act explains *ννομισματικήν* by pointing out that the double *nu* surmounted by a bar was an abbreviation for *nomismata*, here merged with the adjectival form of the word. The reading μέρει is questionable; ἀπό is equally possible, which would not alter the meaning of the passage substantially: "and to confer upon *kyr* Constantine Peplatismenos [from] the *oikeioi* of our mighty and holy lord and emperor, with fifty-two *archontopouloi*."

documentary sources means "to examine or investigate."[46] In the present act Athyvolos was ordered *peritereisasthai . . . kai paradounai* certain properties. What could it mean "to examine property for a monetary *posotes*"? The editor of the document suggests *kathorizo* (καθορίζω), "to determine, state precisely," as a modern equivalent for *peritereisasthai*. If this is correct, then the official meant that he had been ordered "to fix the values of the properties in terms of a monetary *posotes*," which is in accord with the context of the document. Because the alternative interpretation, "attached in/for a monetary *posotes*," makes much less sense, we may accept the editor's suggestion, while observing that it is merely a reasonable guess.

It should be noted that this document has been preserved because it detailed the possessions of a monastery, and so it is not surprising that the portion of the document of interest to us is somewhat vague. In any event, the official Athyvolos evidently had been given a specific charge to locate properties within the region of Miletos, including those that had been abandoned by their owners (*exaleimmata*), and to distribute these to Constantine Peplatismenos (otherwise unknown) and to fifty-two *archontopouloi* "for the sake of their oikonomia."[47]

In the thirteenth and fourteenth centuries *archontopouloi*, or *archontopoula*, literally "sons of archons," were a courtly group from which soldiers and other imperial servants were recruited. The word was applied to two groups of men. In documents where the word *archontopouloi* is found alongside "archons," it appears to be a kind of diminutive form denoting a gradation within the aristocracy, "lesser archons." On the other hand, the word *archontopouloi* was also applied to an informal group of young men who spent their early careers at the imperial court as aristocrats in training. Pseudo-Kodinos writes that *archontopouloi* "related to the emperor" appeared in court ceremony as attendants and took part in the ritual acclamation of the emperor. As adults these *archontopouloi* entered various types of imperial service and at least some retained the designation *archontopoulos*. Some appear in the sources performing the duties of fiscal officials or other imperial agents; others appear as landholders. It is impossible to know whether such men were called *archontopouloi* because they spent their youths at the palace or because they were merely lesser aristocrats. Possibly no such distinction even existed. The designation, while

[46] For example, in 1271 an official was ordered ἵνα τηρήσω καὶ ἐξισάσω certain properties, that is, to conduct a fiscal reassessment: *Patmos*, II, no. 70.9.

[47] On *exaleimmata*, M. Bartusis, "Ἐξάλειμμα: Escheat in Byzantium," *Dumbarton Oaks Papers* 40 (1986), 55–81.

imperially bestowed, was informal enough to adapt to the emperor's needs, and there was probably a great deal of overlap in the two "groups" of *archontopouloi*.[48]

Evidently this document is referring to a massive conferral of pronoiai on a group of lesser aristocrats. Indeed other documents from the thirteenth century, discussed in previous chapters, refer directly to pronoiai in the Meander valley around Miletos in 1216 *[5.5]*, in 1258 *[5.2] [5.3]*, and in 1262 *[5.6]*. Here the official was conferring *posotetes* from particular properties on a group of men. The purpose of these grants was "for the sake of their oikonomia" (χάριν οἰκονομίας αὐτῶν). Earlier in this chapter a document from 1153 issued by the *protos* of Mount Athos was mentioned which contains the phrase χάριν οἰκονομίας in the sense of "for the sake of an accommodation or arrangement." But the use of the possessive pronoun in the current phrase ("for the sake of their accommodation") makes this rendering unlikely. Rather, it seems necessary again (as in the 1259 *orismos*, involving Michael Angelos) to opt for the meaning "maintenance, sustenance"; thus, the revenues were granted to these men "for the sake of their maintenance," that is, for their livelihood. As in the 1259 *orismos*, *oikonomia* need not have a technical sense in this passage, but it seems that the passage is dealing with grants of pronoiai. An anonymous group of men received grants of property quantified by *posotetes* on the order of the emperor. The phrase "according to the monetary *posotes* appropriate to these" suggests that the grant these men each received was of some fixed standard size, appropriate to *archontopouloi*.[49]

[6.3] Praktikon of Nicholas Kampanos and Demetrios Spartenos for the monastery of Iviron (1262)

While the act of Athyvolos is the earliest document that refers to the new practice of quantifying imperial grants by their monetary *posotes*, the earliest document that actually attaches a specific monetary *posotes* to a property is a praktikon for the monastery of Iviron from March 1262. The fiscal officials Nicholas Kampanos and Demetrios Spartenos detail the monastery's possessions in six villages in Macedonia. After they list the paroikoi held by the monastery in the village of Hierissos the document reads, "*Exaleimmatikon* vineyard of Tlomatzes, four nomismata. Vineyard of Petraliphas for [*eis*]

[48] Bartusis, *Late Byzantine Army*, 205–06.

[49] Cf. Angold, *Byzantine Government*, 177, 219.

sixteen nomismata."[50] These are the only properties listed in the praktikon, and they are quantified not by their size, but by their fiscal assessment.

This is not the only element of interest in this document. The praktikon displays an innovation in its introductory sentence:

Making the fiscal survey [*apographe*] of the theme of Thessaloniki according to a worshipful *orismos* of the . . . emperor, reestablishing to each to maintain his own oikonomia, revising and reestablishing to the pious establishments each one of these to have its property, among the others we found the reverend monastery of Iviron . . . having these [things], and consequently we have conferred upon it the following.[51]

The initial phrase is common. For instance, an act of a *doux* from 1189 begins, "While we were performing, by divine and worshipful *orismos*, the fiscal survey of the theme of Mylasa and Melanoudion . . . ." (MM, IV, 319.6–7). But it is the second and third phrases that are novel: "reestablishing to each to maintain his own oikonomia, revising and reestablishing to the pious establishments each one of these to have its property [τὸ ἴδιον] . . . ." The awkward phrasing of the passage points to the novelty of the construction. On the face of things *oikonomia* in the passage could easily be translated as "livelihood." At the very least the use of the word *oikonomia* in this context implies that it was in the state's interest to ensure that a wide range of people, as well as institutions, "maintain" their "oikonomia."

[6.4] Acts of Despot John Palaiologos regarding the village of Kapraina (1268–70)

The earliest example of using the *posotes* to effect an exchange of property is found in a silver bull from 1268 or perhaps slightly earlier of the despot John Palaiologos, brother of Michael VIII. The despot granted possession of the village of Kapraina, near Demetrias in Thessaly, to the monastery of the Makrinitissa. The village is described as "reaching a *posotes* of fifty hyperpyra." In December 1268 Despot John instructed an official to return Kapraina to the monastery and to "give to the *tzakones* holding it [at that moment], that is, to Christopher and Papanikolopoulos, [something] of equal value to this elsewhere." A year and a half later, in May 1270, Despot John issued another act denying the request of Christopher that he maintain possession of Kapraina and again ordering the transfer to be made. Here it is

50 *Iviron*, III, no. 59.62. On Petraliphas, see *[8.1]*.

51 *Iviron*, III, no. 59.1–3: καὶ ἑκάστῳ ἀποκαθιστῶντες ἐμμένειν ἐν τῇ οἰκία [sc. οἰκεία] αὐτοῦ οἰκονομία.

noted that the village "amounted to fifty hyperpyra."[52] As terminology was evolving, we see that the phrases εἰς ποσότητα περιιστάμενον ὑπερπύρων πεντήκοντα and εἰς ὑπέρπυρα ποσούμενον πεντήκοντα were equivalent; in other words, the specific word *posotes* did not have to appear. Further, as we witness an administrative process at work, a substantial property had been given to a couple of *tzakones* (a type of urban guard soldier) in error, evidently as a pronoia; to correct the problem the pair were to get something from elsewhere with the same *posotes*. One should be suspicious of the *posotes* of Kapraina – fifty hyperpyra. Such a round number suggests that it was merely an approximation, not a true sum of all the taxes and charges burdening the village. The same observation can be made for the *posotes* of the village of Kastrion (Gradac) in a chrysobull of Michael VIII. The document confirmed Hilandar's possession of the village, "reaching a *posotes* of fifty hyperpyra," which the same Despot John had donated to the monastery.[53]

[6.5] Testament of the monk Theodosios Skaranos (ca. 1270–74)

One of the properties listed in the 1262 praktikon for Iviron discussed above consisted of eleven paroikos households and a couple of other properties at Hermeleia which had been held by the monk Theodosios Skaranos. Not long prior to the issuance of the praktikon, this collection of items had been taken away from Skaranos by the emperor and given to Iviron. Yet, by the time Skaranos composed his will, this property had been returned to him.[54]

In his will, which dates to ca. 1270–74, Skaranos adds some detail to this. He writes that, "Some malicious people reported to my lord the emperor that I had much and through his mercy he ordered Kerameas [a fiscal official] that what I had through praktikon I should have back." This allowed Skaranos to bequeath everything to the monastery of Xeropotamou: "my cell with what is shown of properties and things and the oikonomia consisting of paroikoi, which I have from the mercy of the emperor for the sake of his salvation, I leave in complete lordship and ownership" to the monastery of

52 MM, IV, 342.33: τὸ . . . χωρίον τὴν Κάπραινα τὸ εἰς ποσότητα περιιστάμενον ὑπερπύρων πεντήκοντα. On the date, B. Ferjančić, *Tesalija u XIII i XIV veku* (Belgrade, 1974), 63 note 94. MM, IV, 389.4–6: τοῖς δὲ γε κατέχουσι τοῦτο Τζέκωσιν ἐπίδος ἑτέρωθι ἰσόποσον τούτου, ἤγουν τῷ Χριστοφόρῳ καὶ τῷ Παπανικολοπούλῳ. On the date, see M. Bartusis, "Urban Guard Service in Late Byzantium," *Macedonian Studies* 5 (n.s. 2), fasc. 2 (1988), 74 note 62. MM, IV, 389.18–19: τὸ εἰς ὑπέρπυρα ποσούμενον πεντήκοντα. The grant held by these men is an early example of a jointly held pronoia: see *[8.1]* etc.

53 *Chilandar*, ed. Živojinović, I, no. 10.17: περιιστάμενον δὲ εἰς ποσότητα ὑπερπύρων πεντήκοντα.

54 *Iviron*, III, no. 58.82–83, and pp. 15, 94–95.

Xeropotamou.[55] Although my translation makes it appear ambiguous, the Greek is clear that the oikonomia alone was held "from the mercy of the emperor."

While the affair is somewhat vague, it seems that the monk Skaranos was accused of holding property in excess of what was inscribed in his praktikon. Some property, consisting of at least the paroikoi and properties listed in the 1262 praktikon, was confiscated and given to Iviron. Then, through the intercession of the emperor, the property was returned to him. This property was his "oikonomia consisting of paroikoi." Here the word *oikonomia* has an undeniably concrete sense, linked as it is with "properties" (*ktemata*) and "things" (*pragmata*). It is not simply his "livelihood" or his "means of subsistence" in the abstract. Rather, his oikonomia was something physical that he could point to, in this case a number of paroikos households from which he derived an income.

[6.6] *Prostagma* of Michael VIII Palaiologos for his son Andronikos (1272)

Up to this point none of these documents has offered any direct link between the new concepts of *posotes* and oikonomia and the institution of pronoia. The first document to do so is Michael VIII's 1272 *prostagma* for his thirteen-year-old son Andronikos, issued on the occasion of Andronikos' elevation as co-emperor. Among the contents is a section dealing with Andronikos' responsibilities while on campaign: "If a soldier should appear useful in his military service, he may be made a benefaction by you or may receive an addition to his oikonomia, up to twenty-four or even thirty-six hyperpyra." The emperor adds that those worthy of "a greater benefaction" were to be referred to Michael himself. Thus, there were two ways to reward soldiers: with a benefaction (*euergesia*), which would appear to be a simple gift, or by an addition to the soldier's oikonomia. The oikonomia is the soldier's pronoia, and since the potential increase is stated as a monetary amount, we are dealing with pronoia grants quantified by *posotetes*.

[55] *Xéropotamou*, no. 9A.31–32, and cf. 9B.47–49; no. 9B.91–94: τῆς διὰ παροίκων οἰκονομίας. Almost exactly the same passage is found in *Xéropotamou*, no. 9A.63–65, another version of this act employing curious orthography. On the use of *dia* in fiscal documents with the meaning "consisting of," see Svoronos, "Recherches sur le cadastre," 23 note 4. Other late Byzantine examples: *Lavra*, III, no. 122.6,30 (1334), and *Zographou*, no. 53.9–10 (1279). This usage dates back at least to the eleventh century: e.g., *Patmos*, II, no, 50.163. On the "mercy of the emperor," see Chapter 7.

Next, the emperor specified where such additional remuneration was to be found:

Neither from a pronoia vacant by accident, lest when [his] pronoia is diminished, some deficiency comes to a soldier in the corps [*allagion*], nor from some of the imperial taxes [*kephalaia*], because these must be guarded for distributions and salaries on behalf of Romania, but from some things which it is perhaps possible to find from a *perisseia* of fiscal assessors or from the seizure of things which someone holds by theft.[56]

While underscoring the fact that a pronoia provided a soldier's livelihood, the passage is an unequivocal statement of Michael VIII's policy regarding the further remuneration of pronoia soldiers. It prescribes where Andronikos may obtain the sums "up to twenty-four or even thirty-six hyperpyra" for the increase in their oikonomiai. Andronikos must take care not to deprive another soldier of his own pronoia, nor may he use imperial taxes. Instead, the only sources available to exploit were those resulting from a fiscal survey which found someone holding more land (*perisseia*, lit. "an excess") than allowed by his praktikon, or those resulting from the confiscation of illegally held property.[57]

The *prostagma* implies that ostensibly "vacant" pronoiai were often not really vacant. But what is a "pronoia vacant by accident" (*chereuouses kata tychen*)? I am not comfortable with this translation, but I do not see any other way to render the passage. The participle *chereuon* (χηρεύων) is not a fiscal term. It is most commonly used in regard to vacant episcopal sees or as a way of referring to widows ("bereaved"). Perhaps one should envision a situation whereby a fiscal official went to an estate, and asked the paroikoi who worked the land to whom they paid their rent. If they said their landlord had not collected the rent in some time, perhaps that would be considered a "vacant" pronoia.

In any event, the passage indicates that the sources for additional grants to soldiers were extremely limited, that there was no collection of state properties available for distribution to worthy soldiers at a moment's notice. As Ahrweiler once observed, the passage makes it appear as though all of

[56] A. Heisenberg, *Aus der Geschichte und Literatur der Palaiologenzeit, Sitzungsberichte der bayerischen Akademie der Wissenschaften, in Heisenberg, Quellen und Studien zur spätbyzantinischen Geschichte* (London, 1973), no. I, 40.78–92, esp. lines 84–86: πλὴν οὔτε ἀπὸ χηρευούσης κατὰ τύχην προνοίας, ἵνα μὴ τῆς προνοίας κολοβωθείσης λεῖψις τὶς στρατιώτου ἐν τῷ ἀλλαγίῳ γένηται. On the document, see M. Bartusis, "A Note on Michael VIII's 1272 Prostagma for His Son Andronikos," *BZ* 81 (1988), 268–71.

[57] On *perisseia*, see *Xéropotamou*, 167; Svoronos, "Recherches sur le cadastre," 38–39; Dölger, *Beiträge*, 153; Heisenberg, *Palaiologenzeit*, 78; *Vatopédi*, I, p. 181.

the sources of imperial grants that could be granted had been granted.[58] Indeed, if there was an expansion in the volume of pronoia grants under Vatatzes, this certainly appears to have continued under Michael VIII. The 1261 act of Athyvolos mentioning the grants to fifty-two *archontopouloi* "for their oikonomia" supports this idea.

Finally, in this section of the *prostagma* dealing with Andronikos' military responsibilities, the emperor adds one more point of interest to us: "If a soldier is not found conducting himself well in his military service, you should chasten him suitably and substitute for him another soldier who is deserving of the oikonomia of the one who erred."[59]

The relationship between pronoia and oikonomia in this document illustrates the evolving meaning of these words as well as the state of imperial grants during Michael VIII's reign.

In this *prostagma*, *pronoia* has a more concrete, specific sense, while *oikonomia* has a broader, more abstract sense. *Oikonomia* can be rendered in these passages as "livelihood," while *pronoia* cannot. The oikonomia appears to be the total collection of fiscal revenues conferred on the grantee, while the pronoia is the grant itself. Nevertheless, both words refer to the same thing: the imperial grant held by the soldier. This peculiarity is soon dealt with. For the next century and a half (that is, until 1415) no document issued by an emperor uses the word *pronoia* in its fiscal sense. *Oikonomia* becomes the term of choice when emperors refer to imperial grants.

In this *prostagma* the word *oikonomia* is evolving toward a concrete sense. We can discern two phases in the development of *oikonomia* as a fiscal term. In the first phase, *oikonomia* appears in prepositional phrases: a soldier holds property "for his oikonomia" (1259), and *archontopouloi* are granted *posotetes* "for their oikonomia" (1261). Then, in the second phase, fiscal officials desire to maintain private property holders "in their oikonomia" (1262), a monk "has an oikonomia" (ca. 1270–74), and soldiers have "oikonomiai" as well as "pronoiai" (1272).

[6.7] Chrysobull of Michael VIII Palaiologos for the monastery of Xeropotamou (1275), and Act of a fiscal official for the monastery of Xeropotamou (ca. 1315)

Another illustration of these two phases in the development of the term *oikonomia* is found in a pair of documents involving a property of the monastery of Xeropotamou. In the early 1270s the *apographeus* Demetrios

[58] Ahrweiler, "La concession des droits incorporels," 113.

[59] Heisenberg, *Palaiologenzeit*, 41.92–95.

Iatropoulos transferred to the monastery of Xeropotamou a collection of villages, *metochia*, fiscal charges, and land with a total *posotes* of 300 hyperpyra. A 1275 chrysobull of Michael VIII confirming the monastery's possessions describes this transfer in three ways:

(i) "the [things], being of a *posotes* of 300 hyperpyra, conferred by... Iatropoulos for oikonomia [*eis oikonomian*] upon the... monastery through his praktikon";
(ii) "the... 300 hyperpyra conferred by... (Iatropoulos) upon the... monastery... through his praktikon for the sake of oikonomia [*charin oikonomias*] of the... monastery"; and
(iii) "the [things] in a *posotes* of 300 hyperpyra conferred by... Iatropoulos upon the... monastery for its oikonomia [*eis oikonomian autes*]."[60]

A comparison of the first two phrases shows that *eis oikonomian* means *charin oikonomias*, that is, "for (the sake of) oikonomia." Further, only the properties within the 300-hyperpyra *posotes* are described by individual *posotetes*. All of the other properties listed in the document and held "from old" by the monastery are described in traditional terms, sometimes with the size of the property or the number of paroikoi supplied, but never with a monetary *posotes*. This would suggest that *posotes* information was added when needed, but no sooner than at the time of a new fiscal survey. The two ways of describing properties (by *posotes* and by areas or explicit contents) continued to exist side by side, and it appears that the practice was introduced as needed. When new grants were conferred, they were described by their fiscal assessment; older properties, evidently not having been reassessed yet according to the new procedure, were still described by areas or merely identified with neither fiscal assessment nor size.

Some forty years later, a fiscal official confirmed Xeropotamou's possession of this oikonomia: "holding... through an oikonomia a *posotes* of 300 hyperpyra: now... we conferred on it such oikonomia."[61] In the interval between these documents, usage had changed. From "conferring something

[60] *Xéropotamou*, no. 10.20–23,46–49,59–60. The authority for this transfer is not clear. It is known that Michael VIII's brother, the despot John Palaiologos, was responsible for the restoration of Xeropotamou, and the 1275 act itself mentions the properties granted to the monastery by John: *Xéropotamou*, p. 90, no. 10.7,58. However, the connection is not clear between (i) the properties John evidently donated to the monastery and (ii) those, comprising an oikonomia, that Iatropoulos conferred on the monastery. J. Bompaire hypothesized that both designations refer to the same collection of properties, that the oikonomia was identical to the properties donated by John. If so, then a collection of properties granted to a monastery "for its oikonomia" was donated by a despot.

[61] *Xéropotamou*, no. 18D, I.29–31 (ca. 1315–20). Hvostova, *Osobennosti*, 212. Kazhdan, "The Fate of the Intellectual," 88.

for (its) oikonomia" and "conferring something for the sake of oikonomia" to "holding an oikonomia" and "conferring an oikonomia." *Oikonomia* has acquired a more concrete sense.

Just as the word *pronoia* was first used in a simple sense ("for maintenance") to denote pronoia grants before becoming a technical term, so too was *oikonomia* first used in a similar simple sense before becoming likewise a technical term.

[6.8] Chrysobull of Michael VIII Palaiologos for the *protovestiarites* Demetrios Mourinos (1274–82)

A *posotes* could also be attached to properties that had been transformed from conditional grants to grants in full ownership. In a chrysobull for the *protovestiarites* Demetrios Mourinos from the later years of Michael VIII's reign, which the editor dates to the period from 1274 to 1282, and probably 1280/1, the emperor points out that he had granted requests before for Mourinos, who was always zealous in carrying out his duties, and would do so now (*Docheiariou*, no. 9.). Mourinos had asked for a chrysobull regarding the properties which he held "from a gift" (*dorea*) of the emperor in order to hold them "without vexation and unharassed and to improve and organize these and to do with them consequently whatever he wishes concerning their composition and improvement." The emperor granted this and added that the properties were freed of all tax burdens except for the *kastroktisia* and *katergoktisia* (respectively, for building fortifications and ships), "since these alone the properties hand over to the fisc, as other *prosopika* properties." *Prosopika* properties were those held by distinguished laymen, who, as Oikonomides suggested, enjoyed high status probably by virtue of their personal connections to the emperor, rather than through any office they held (*Docheiariou*, p. 106). Mourinos also received the right to improve the properties and to transmit them to his legitimate children and heirs, who would enjoy the same privileges over the properties, or to donate them or sell them if he wished. Mourinos' grant is not called an oikonomia (or a pronoia) because it had crossed the line: the emperor permitted Mourinos to alienate the properties within the grant.

Altogether the document lists seven properties. Two were held "through *prostagma*" or "*orismos*," and for four of the remaining five the name of the fiscal official who conferred the property is noted. Five of the properties were villages and for each its *posotes* is provided, totaling in all 830 hyperpyra. The other two properties were a piece of land (*topos*) and a winter pasturage. Two of the villages were in Asia Minor (or perhaps one was in Thrace near

Constantinople), while at least four of the other properties, including the village of Kravvata, were on the Chalkidike.

A *posotes* is supplied for each of the villages he was given, but for the *topos* and a winter pasturage he received as well, neither their fiscal value nor size is specified. The properties granted included the village of Gongyle, conferred on him "for a *posotes* of 200 hyperpyra" (εἰς ποσότητα ὑπερπύρων διακοσίων). Later in the document, this is restated in slightly different words: the village was conferred on Mourinos "for 200 hyperpyra" (εἰς ὑπέρπυρα διακόσια). Similarly, the 830 hyperpyra included the village of Antigoneia, conferred on him "for a *posotes* [*eis posoteta*] of 104 hyperpyra," and later, "for [*eis*] 104 hyperpyra" (*Docheiariou*, no. 9.20, 32, 25, 36). From this we conclude that the phrases εἰς ποσότητα ὑπερπύρων *X* and εἰς ὑπέρπυρα *X* were equivalent and that it was the appearance of a specific monetary figure, not the word *posotes* itself, which represents the innovation. Just as *nomismatike posotes* became simply *posotes*, so "for a *posotes* of *X* hyperpyra" became simply "for *X* hyperpyra."

[6.9] Praktikon of Constantine Tzimpeas and Alexios Amnon for the monastery of Zographou (1279)

A praktikon for the monastery of Zographou from 1279 is the first document that contains both the terms *pronoia* and *posotes*, and it is in fact one of the few such documents, given that *pronoia* fades from the documents just as *posotes* gains in currency. In the document the fiscal officials state that

> Since we have been ordered by the . . . emperor to make a fiscal survey and equalizing in the theme of Thessaloniki and revision of the pronoiai – ecclesiastic and monastic, and personal as well as military and all the rest – and to confer upon each the monetary *posotes* granted to him through . . . imperial *orismos*, along with others we reestablished the . . . monastery . . . of Zographou in what it owned of paroikoi, *metochia*, and other immovables . . .

The document then details the monastery's holdings in the eastern Chalkidike listing paroikoi and the *telos* they owed, as well as other properties with the *posotes* of each, for a total of nineteen hyperpyra.[62]

This occurrence of the word *pronoia* troubled George Ostrogorsky because it implies that monasteries and churches held pronoiai, something

[62] *Zographou*, no. 53.1–6: τῶν τε ἐκκλησιαστικῶν προνοιῶν καὶ μοναστηριακῶν, προσωπικῶν τε ἅμα, στρατιωτικῶν καὶ λοιπῶν ἁπάντων. Mutafčiev, "Vojniški zemi," 47/572. Kazhdan, *Agrarnye otnošenija*, 218. Hvostova, *Osobennosti*, 212. Solovjev–Mošin, *Grčke povelje*, 486. On the date of the document, *Esphigménou*, p. 78.

that Ostrogorsky thought was impossible. In his opinion "one can conclude only that the terminology of the praktikon . . . is not precise," by which he really meant that the terminology is incorrect.[63] Indeed, a similar locution, listing the specific types of properties surveyed, is found in the introductory formulas of numerous other praktika, but none of the others uses the word *pronoia*: one document, from 1189, reads "military, ecclesiastic, and monastic immovable possessions."[64] All of the others date to the period from around 1297 to 1333, and all but one of these refer to "properties" (*ktemata*) rather than "pronoiai."[65]

Do we conclude that monasteries and churches held pronoiai in 1279? Or do we conclude that the officials in the 1279 act were using imprecise terminology? The answer is that these questions are framed incorrectly. If we posit that monasteries and churches did not hold pronoiai in the twelfth century, we may then ask, was there a change in the manner in which monasteries and churches held property in the thirteenth century such that in 1279 they could be said to be holding pronoiai? The answer to this is no. There was no significant change in the various ways by which religious foundations held property from the twelfth to the thirteenth century. So were the fiscal officials simply using the wrong word? Again, the answer is no. In 1279, indeed from the 1260s until some time around the turn of the fourteenth century, there was no single "correct" word to use to designate the holdings of religious foundations.

But there is more. In the 1279 praktikon the fiscal officials state that they were ordered "to confer upon each the monetary [*nomismatike*] *posotes* granted to him through . . . imperial *orismos*." Aside from the 1261 act of John Athyvolos *[6.2]*, this is the only document that places the adjective *nomismatike* with *posotes* when the latter is used to indicate the fiscal value of a property. Evidently there was still something novel about this method of describing properties. We compare this to the parallel phrase in other fiscal documents. In the 1262 praktikon *[6.3]*: "reestablishing to each to maintain

[63] Ostrogorsky, *Féodalité*, 104 note 1. [64] MM, IV, 319.8–9: . . . ἀκινήτων κτήσεων.

[65] E.g., τῶν . . . προσωπικῶν, ἀρχοντικῶν, ἐκκλησιαστικῶν, μοναστηριακῶν, στρατιωτικῶν, χρυσοβουλλάτων καὶ λοιπῶν ἁπάντων κτήματων. Examples: L. Mavrommatis, "La pronoia d'Alexis Comnène Raoul à Prévista," *Σύμμεικτα* 13 (1999), 213, line 2 (ca. 1297); *Vatopédi*, I, no. 25.2–3 (1297); *Lavra*, II, no. 104.2–3 (1317), no. 105.2–3 (1317), App. VIII (1316); *Zographou*, no. 17.3–5 (1320); *Iviron*, III, no. 79.2–3 (1320); *Xénophon*, no. 13.3–4 (1320), no. 15.2–3 (1321), no. 16.2–3 (1321); *Esphigménou*, no. 15.2–4 (1321), no. 16.2–3 (1321); and P. Schreiner, "Zwei unedierte Praktika aus der zweiten Hälfte des 14. Jahrhunderts," *JÖB* 19 (1970), 37. (1323) The two exceptions, *Iviron*, III, no. 74.1–3 (1316) and *Xénophon*, no. 22 (1333), avoid the issue by omitting the substantive altogether: τὰ . . . ἐκκλησιατικά, μοναστηριακά, προσωπικά, ἀρχοντικά, στρατιωτικά, χρυσοβουλλάτα καὶ λοιπά.

his own oikonomia, revising and reestablishing to the pious establishments each one of these to have its property [*to idion*] . . . " In four documents, from 1284 and 1285, dealing with monastic holdings on Lemnos: "Since I was ordered by the . . . emperor to make an equalizing and reestablishment of the island of Lemnos and to reestablish to each of those on it [Lemnos] his own right [*to oikeion dikaion*] . . . ." The use of *dikaion* rather than *oikonomia* becomes a bit of a tradition, uniquely, on Lemnos: the phrase appears almost identically in praktika from 1355 and ca. 1400, and with some small variation in a 1430 praktikon.[66]

A few observations:

(i) the 1279 praktikon for Zographou employs *pronoiai* where it "ought" to employ *ktemata*;
(ii) the 1272 *prostagma* of Michael VIII employs *pronoia* and *oikonomia* almost interchangeably; and
(iii) the 1262 Iviron praktikon employs *oikonomia* where the 1279 praktikon for Zographou employs *posotes* and where the 1284–85 praktika made on Lemnos employ *dikaion*.

Pronoia, ktema, oikonomia, posotes, dikaion. Imprecise terminology it indeed may be, but it is more accurate to say that terminology was "fluid." Officials were trying to codify a new way of viewing property, one in which the officials saw no real distinction between the property held by religious institutions, soldiers, and other individuals. The fiscal officials in making a fiscal survey were doing two things: establishing the *posotetes* of individual properties and establishing private property holders in their oikonomiai. The purpose of all this was to administer imperial grants, not "ordinary" holdings of private property, but special holdings of privileged parties. Perhaps Tzimpeas and Amnon in 1279 were trying merely to fit all privileged holdings into a single mold and calling them "pronoiai."

It is not until the fourteenth century that some consistency comes to these introductory formulas. From 1300 to 1333, a series of praktika for both monasteries and laymen holding properties in the themes of Thessaloniki and of Serres begins with the statement of the *apographeus*, subject to only the slightest variation, that he had been ordered by the emperor to make a fiscal revision of the properties in a particular theme and "to confer on each

[66] *Lavra*, II, no. 73.2 (1284), no. 74.2 (1284), no. 76.1–2 (1285); *Patmos*, II, no. 74.2–3 (1285). *Lavra*, III, no. 136.2 (1355); V. Kravari, "Nouveaux documents du monastère de Philothéou," *TM* 10 (1987), 261–356, no. 7.2 (end 14th–beg. 15th c.); *Dionysiou*, no. 25.2 (1430).

[person or monastery] the *posotes* of his own oikonomia"[67] or "to confer on each his own *poson*."[68]

The hereditary transmission of pronoiai

If there was one thing that had distinguished the pronoia grants of the twelfth and early thirteenth centuries from the grants received by aristocrats and religious foundations, it was their lifetime tenure. The case of the soldier Michael Angelos changes that *[6.1]*. A policy of granting hereditary rights over the pronoia grants of some soldiers as well as to some aristocrats was yet another innovation of Michael VIII in regard to the institution of pronoia. This and the tendency to grant pronoiai to high personages blurred the distinction between pronoia grants and other imperial grants of property and fiscal rights.

The notion of a pronoia as a conditional, non-hereditary grant originated in Russian scholarship. On the basis of a single Slavic act from Bosnia, A. A. Majkov considered pronoia as analogous to the Muscovite *pomestie* and viewed it as a personal temporary allotment granted by the sovereign without the right of perpetual use. Vikentij Makušev, studying fifteenth-century Venetian acts from Dalmatia, also considered pronoia to be a lifetime grant that could neither be sold or otherwise alienated. Fedor Uspenskij, realizing that the character of Byzantine pronoia could not be deduced on the basis of Serbian or Venetian sources, examined the Byzantine sources and discovered that there was a tendency for Byzantine pronoia in the fourteenth century to be alienated and transferred by inheritance. He concluded that pronoia was a conditional estate which in the course of its development changed into patrimony.[69]

67 παραδοῦναι ἑκάστῳ τὴν τῆς ἰδίας οἰκονομίας αὐτοῦ ποσότητα: *Zographou*, no. 15 (1300); *Esphigménou*, nos. 8 (ca. 1300) and 14 (1318); *Iviron*, III, nos. 70 (1300) and 75 (1318); *Xéropotamou*, nos. 18A (ca. 1300) and 18D, I (ca. 1315–20); and *Xénophon*, no. 12 (1318), App. II.

68 παραδοῦναι ἑκάστῳ τὸ οἰκεῖον ποσόν: *Xénophon*, nos. 13 (1320), 15 (1321), 16 (1321), and 22 (1333); *Zographou*, no. 17 (1320); *Esphigménou*, nos. 15 (1321) and 16 (1321); *Lavra*, II, nos. 105 (1317), 112 (1321?), and App. VIII (1316); Schreiner, "Zwei unedierte Praktika," 37; and *Iviron*, IV, no. 88 (1344). Similarly, a 1323 praktikon from the area of Constantinople *[8.16]* uses the phrase "I should reestablish through praktikon the *posotes*" (καὶ περιστήσω διὰ πρακτικοῦ τὴν τούτων ποσότητα) of the properties in the area under his charge: *Chilandar*, ed. Petit, no. 92. And cf. *Lavra*, II, no. 104.8.

69 A. Majkov, "Čto takoe pronija v drevnej Serbii," *Čtenija v Imperatorskom obščestve istorii i drevnostej rossijskikh* (1868), kn. I, 231. V. Makušev, "O pronii v drevnej Serbii," *ŽMNP* (1874), 19–20. Uspenskij, "Značenie," 2–5, 15, 21–22, 28. Kazhdan, *Agrarnye otnošenija*, 202–04. Ostrogorsky, *Féodalité*, 2–3.

Since the late nineteenth century scholars have generally adopted Uspenskij's view, that according to its "original" nature, the pronoiai of the twelfth century were not hereditary but temporary, lifetime grants that could neither be bequeathed nor alienated.[70] For some scholars the non-hereditary nature of pronoia became one of the main distinctions between pronoia and the middle Byzantine military estates; the latter was hereditary and alienable, while, at first, the pronoia was granted for only a specific period, was not hereditary and, could not be alienated.[71] So deeply ingrained was this belief in Ostrogorsky's conception of the institution in the twelfth century that he excluded, as examples of pronoia, any grant that involved hereditary rights. This is why he wrote that the "fief" Manuel I granted to Boniface of Montferrat's brother *[3.4]* could not have been a true pronoia: it was hereditary.[72]

Evidence for or against the notion that pronoia grants were hereditary in the twelfth century is extremely scanty. We have the *Zavorda Treatise [2.1]*, which unequivocally states that pronoia grants were for life. On the other hand, there is the document relating to the Skordiles family which states that hereditary grants of land were made to people in Crete *[2.6]*. However, it is uncertain whether the original document referred to these grants as pronoiai. In sum, we must conclude that pronoia grants were not hereditary in the twelfth century.[73]

In the first half of the thirteenth century, what little evidence we have indicates that pronoia grants were not inherited. For whatever reason, the rights on the Hermos did not pass to Constantine Kalegopoulos' heirs *[6.1]*, and the property called Gonia tou Petake did not pass to Manuel Komnenos Laskaris' widow *[5.6]*.

[6.10] Pachymeres on the inheriting of soldiers' pronoiai (1) (ca. 1307)

With the reign of Michael VIII the situation changed. George Pachymeres addresses the matter directly in two passages from his history. In the first

[70] Among the many places one encounters this opinion: Ostrogorsky, *Féodalité*, 133; Charanis, "Social Structure," 97; Sjuzjumov, "Vnutrennjaja politika Andronika Komnina," 61; Ahrweiler, *Byzance et la mer*, 219; D. Jacoby, *La féodalité en Grèce médiévale* (Paris, 1971), 35; Hohlweg, *Beiträge zur Verwaltungsgeschichte*, 83; Hvostova, *Osobennosti*, 215.

[71] Charanis, "Social Structure," 132; Ostrogorsky, *Féodalité*, 15; F. Dölger, Review of Mutafčiev, "Vojniški zemi," *BZ* 26 (1926), 105.

[72] Ostrogorsky, *Féodalité*, 31.

[73] Hohlweg, "Zur Frage der Pronoia," 308 note 95, who was writing before seeing the *Zavorda Treatise* passage, suggested that the tradesmen, who, according to Choniates' "gifts of paroikoi" passage, gave up their trade might have received hereditary rights over their new incomes.

he explains that, after coming to the throne, Michael VIII allowed soldiers to transmit their pronoiai to their children, even if they were as yet unborn: "Loving the soldiery exceedingly, he established the pronoiai of these, should they fall in battle and die, as patrimonial property to the children, even if, for some, the women should have the fetus in the womb."[74] Even allowing for a measure of hyperbole, this is an important statement of policy. What can we discern about the status quo before this policy change? Conceivably, one could infer that the previous imperial policy was to grant hereditary rights solely to pronoia soldiers with adult or even minor children and that Michael's innovation was to extend such rights even to those soldiers with unborn children. But I think Pachymeres would have phrased such a minor change in policy differently. Evidently Pachymeres was impressed by the hereditary aspect in itself, and by its scale. Before Michael's policy change, it would seem, hereditary rights were not granted or were granted very infrequently.

What of widows who were neither mothers nor mothers-to-be? We can infer from the passage that neither before nor immediately after Michael's policy change were they normally permitted to inherit their husbands' pronoiai. Further, did Pachymeres' "children" (τοῖς παισί) imply only boys or both sexes? If we accept Pachymeres' statement that unborn children received such hereditary rights, we might conclude that there was no prejudice against daughters inheriting pronoiai. On the whole, however, one cannot imagine this specific case involving very many pronoia holders. Certainly, it is possible that the inheritance could have been conditional pending the delivery of the male child, but it is more likely that Pachymeres' reference to children in the womb inheriting pronoiai is simply hyperbole.

[6.11] Pachymeres on the inheriting of soldiers' pronoiai (2) (ca. 1307)

In the second passage Pachymeres writes that Michael VIII, again, early in his reign,

[74] Pachymeres, ed. Failler, I, 131.18–21 (Bonn edn., I, 92): τὸ δέ γε στρατιωτικὸν ὑπεραγαπᾶν καὶ τὰς ἐκείνων προνοίας, κἂν ἐν πολέμῳ πίπτοιεν, κἂν ἀποθνήσκοιεν, γονικὰς ἐγκαθιστᾶν τοῖς παισί, κἂν τισιν αἱ γυναῖκες κατὰ γαστρὸς ἔχοιεν τὸ κυοφορούμενον. Kazhdan, *Agrarnye otnošenija*, 219. Gorjanov, *Pozdnevizantijskij feodalizm*, 99–100, 113, incorrectly referred to these as *new* grants of pronoia accompanied by hereditary rights. Ostrogorsky, *Féodalité*, 93. Hohlweg, "Zur Frage der Pronoia," 305 note 84. M. V. Bibikov, "Svedenija o pronii v pis'mah Grigorija Kiprskogo i 'Istorii' Georgija Pahimera," *ZRVI* 17 (1976), 95.

provided for those of the senate simply magnificently, enlarging and adding to the pronoiai of these, allowing all to delight in all of the good things received as well as hoped for. And as for the soldiery . . . he increased the daily kindnesses and he fulfilled the things promised to them with chrysobulls and he made [them] better disposed for the future that they have forever the pronoiai of life and the granted *siteresia* for their children.[75]

Combining this information with the previous passage we may conclude that Michael granted hereditary rights to the children of pronoia soldiers who had distinguished themselves in some way, including through dying in battle. Perhaps this did not include the majority of soldiers, but it clearly was not restricted to a few isolated heroes.

Siteresion is a problematic word that had a number of meanings which fall into three main categories: (i) provisions in kind, especially to soldiers, but also at times to monasteries;[76] (ii) an allowance for provisions, again especially to soldiers, but also at times to monasteries;[77] (iii) salaries, especially to soldiers, but more generally to anyone in imperial service. It is this last sense of the word that is commonly found in thirteenth- and fourteenth-century literary sources. Choniates, in his passage dealing with the "gifts of paroikoi" *[3.1]*, claims that Manuel I "poured into the treasury, like water into a cistern, the *siteresia* given to the soldiers," clearly a reference to cash wages. In a letter to certain bishops Patriarch Athanasios compares the granting of monasteries to unworthy men to the emperor granting *siteresion* to unworthy soldiers:

Pitying and giving to every man is admirable, but to assign *siteresion* on the pretense of military service to some from those of the despot, to those hearkening not to the name of arms that soldiers bear, is not only a great mockery deserving punishment,

75 Pachymeres, ed. Failler, I, 139.3–8 (Bonn edn., I, 97): καὶ τοὺς μὲν τῆς γερουσίας οὕτω μεγαλοπρεπῶς ἐθεράπευε, προνοίας τούτοις ἐπαύξων καὶ προστιθείς, καὶ χαίρειν ἀφιεὶς τοῖς πᾶσι, τῶν ἀγαθῶν τὰ μὲν λαμβάνουσι, τὰ δ' ἐλπίζουσι. τὸ δὲ στρατιωτικόν . . . , τοὺς μὲν καθημεριναῖς φιλοτιμίαις ὤφελλε καὶ χρυσοβούλλοις τὰ ὑπεσχημένα τούτοις ἐπλήρου καὶ πρὸς τὸ μέλλον εὐθυμοτέρους καθίστα, ὡς ἀθανάτους τὰς τῆς ζωῆς προνοίας καὶ τὰ διδόμενα σιτηρέσια τοῖς παισὶν ἕξοντας. Mutafčiev, "Vojniški zemi," 45/570–71, 639. Kazhdan, *Agrarnye otnošenija*, 219. Hohlweg, "Zur Frage der Pronoia," 305 and note 84.

76 *ODB*, s.v. "opsonion." J. Haldon, *Recruitment and Conscription in the Byzantine Army c. 550–950* (Vienna, 1979), 45 and note 73; J. Thomas, *Private Religious Foundations in the Byzantine Empire* (Washington, D.C., 1987), 181, 183–84; Kazhdan, *Agrarnye otnošenija*, 215; Angold, *Byzantine Government*, 119, 193; Ahrweiler, "La concession des droits incorporels," 105. E.g., *Lavra*, I, no. 62.13–14 and *Patmos*, II, p. 242.15.

77 This is how the editor of a tenth-century treatise translates the word (though the meaning "in-kind allowances" fits the passage equally well): *Three Byzantine Military Treatises*, ed. G. Dennis (Washington, D.C., 1985), 214.29. *Lavra*, I, no. 7.39–40.

but is a ridiculous folly. And he who grants to indifferent men a place for the habitation of ascetics deserves punishment more than the above-mentioned.[78]

Here *siteresion* must be more than rations or a rations allowance; it is the remuneration of soldiers generally speaking.

In another example, when discussing the measures taken to finance the Catalan mercenaries, the historian Gregoras writes, "The expenditure of money, that which was spent for their attire, gifts, and the annual *siteresia*, amounted to so much greediness, that the imperial treasury was quickly emptied." It would be difficult to translate "annual *siteresia*" as anything but "yearly pay."[79] Gregory Palamas once asked rhetorically: "For a little *siteresion* is the soldier not prepared for deadly dangers and sacrifices?"[80] I doubt that Palamas believed that a soldier would risk life and limb for a "small rations allowance"; rather, to evoke a strongly affirmative answer to the question, *siteresion* has to mean "pay" generally.

In another passage Pachymeres (ed. Failler, IV, 459.10) himself uses the word *siteresion* to refer to the regular pay of the Catalans. Thus, it appears that in this passage involving "the pronoiai of life and the granted *siteresia*" *siteresion* means cash payments. Thus, Pachymeres seems to be indicating either that some soldiers received pay in addition to pronoiai, and that both at times became bequeathable, or that Michael made the pay of some mercenaries hereditary, distinguishing in the sentence two groups of soldiers: pronoia holders and mercenaries.[81]

It is interesting to compare what Pachymeres claims soldiers received to what he claims that the highlanders of the Nicaean era received *[5.14]*. Both received "daily kindnesses," that is, a salary or frequent cash payments; some of the soldiers and some of the highlanders held pronoiai. Some of the highlanders received "imperial letters" and this probably corresponds to the chrysobulls that some of the soldiers received. The only real difference comes in the tax exemption that the highlanders received.

Further, the passage indicates that not only soldiers, but "those of the senate," that is, aristocrats, held pronoiai. Inasmuch as George Ostrogorsky

78 Athanasios, *Correspondence*, no. 83.52–55: τὸ δὲ λόγῳ στρατείας σιτηρέσιον τάξαι τισὶν ἐκ τῶν τοῦ δεσπότου. The editor's suggestion (ibid., pp. 409–10) that the passage is connected to the granting of "the revenue from monastic lands... as pronoia" appears to me to be unfounded. I think the patriarch was making a simple analogy: some bishops were entrusting monasteries to unworthy men, and that is as bad as the emperor hiring unworthy soldiers.

79 Gregoras, I, 220.18–21. Mutafčiev, "Vojniški zemi," 598.

80 Migne, *PG*, 151, col. 293. Cited by O. Tafrali, *Thessalonique au quatorzième siècle* (Paris, 1913), 58 note 3.

81 Mutafčiev, "Vojniški zemi," 598, regarded *siteresion* as regular pay. Ostrogorsky, *Féodalité*, 94, ignored the word in this passage. Kazhdan, *Agrarnye otnošenija*, 215, linked it to a *solemnion*.

wished to maintain that, in general, only soldiers held pronoiai, he suggested, without citing any evidence, that these grants to "those of the senate" were perhaps not as widespread as Pachymeres indicates, and in any event, the practice remained isolated and was permitted only at the express favor of the emperor.[82] All this may be true, but nevertheless Pachymeres claims that "senators" held pronoiai. While this would seem to be further evidence to support the notion that Michael VIII was broadening the social class of recipients of pronoia grants, it may also reflect how broadly Pachymeres defined the pronoia (see Chapter 7).

[6.12] Letter of Patriarch Gregory II to Theodore Mouzalon regarding Chrysokompas (1283–89)

Further evidence for the possibility of the hereditary transmission of pronoiai is found in a letter of the patriarch of Constantinople, Gregory II Kyprios. Sometime during his tenure of office (1283–89) he wrote to the *megas logothetes* Theodore Mouzalon about the problems of a soldier named Chrysokompas, who was living in the area of Skamandros, in Asia Minor, with a wife and a son by a deceased previous wife. "Since the son was already sufficiently of age and more to take up arms and to be reckoned in the military ranks, [Chrysokompas] sent him to camp," while Chrysokompas stayed home either because of old age or because he wished to cultivate the civilian life. We are told that the son's relatives on his mother's side did not like the idea of the son serving while the father and stepmother remained at home, "since both pronoia and home, and whatever else there was for which one was obligated to be a soldier, belonged to the child from the mother."

While the son was on leave, his mother's relatives suggested that he throw his stepmother out of the house, but he refused out of regard for his father. A rumor began to circulate that he was having an affair with his stepmother, which stirred the interest, for some reason, of a local official, a *logariastes* entrusted with "the care of the fiscal matters [*demosia*] in Skamandros," who rushed to the "home of the soldiers" and did great damage "doing what barbarians might do." The patriarch asked Mouzalon to investigate the matter "lest torture and the gallows rob them of home and property."[83]

[82] Ostrogorsky, *Féodalité*, 94–95.

[83] Gregory II Kyprios, ed. S. Eustratiades, "Τοῦ σοφωτάτου καὶ λογιωτάτου καὶ οἰκουμενικοῦ πατριάρχου κύρου Γρηγορίου τοῦ Κυπρίου Ἐπιστολαί," *Ἐκκλησιαστικὸς Φάρος* 3 (1909), 295–96, no. 129: ἐπειδὴ ἥτε πρόνοια ἥτε οἰκία καὶ ὅ,τι ἕτερον ἐτύγχανεν ἐφ᾽ ᾧ στρατεύειν

It is particularly interesting that the patriarch asserts that both the family's estate and a military obligation encumbering the estate had come from the first wife's side of the family. Had she inherited the estate and obligation from her father, or had she been married previously to another soldier from whom the estate and obligation was transmitted? Was Chrysokompas' earlier military service based solely on the military obligation that had been transmitted through his first wife? Can we even be sure that this case involved the institution of pronoia? Were it not for the mention of pronoia, one might think the subject was a middle Byzantine military estate. The patriarch may have been using the word *pronoia* loosely, albeit in a technical sense, but perhaps not in the same sense the documents use the word. We know nothing of the socioeconomic status of these people (other than that their problems were being discussed at a very high level), nor any specifics regarding the estate and the military burden it bore.

The possible inheritance of a pronoia through a female is quite a tantalizing phenomenon, and since the son's mother was no longer alive in the 1280s, it would seem that the right to transmit this possible pronoia was granted during Michael VIII's reign. It is unfortunate that more definite conclusions cannot be made about the patriarch's letter.

The interrelation of developments during Michael VIII's reign

While Manuel I Komnenos seems to have institutionalized the pronoia grant, the thirteenth century was the era of its bureacratization, culminating in the policies of Michael VIII Palaiologos. During the period of exile up to Michael's reign the number of pronoia grants had grown steadily and the social range of recipients had broadened to include lower-level officials, then mid-level officials, and then aristocrats. Simultaneously the number of grants of privileges to monasteries increased, as did the number of simple unconditional grants of privileges to aristocrats.

Even the granting of hereditary rights over pronoiai may have been obliquely related to the increase in the number and range of grants. The more grants conferred, the more requests the emperor would receive for permission to transmit the grant to one's heirs. And if the supply of imperial properties and tax revenues to confer as grants had run out (see *[6.7]*), the

ὠφείλετο, μητρόθεν διέφερε τῷ παιδί. V. Laurent, *Les regestes des actes du patriarcat de Constantinople, I: Les actes des patriarches*, fasc. 4 (Paris, 1971), no. 1525. Bibikov, "Svedenija," 94.

granting of hereditary rights was a way to add additional privileges to the grant without increasing the size of the grant.

At the same time that we witness a tendency to grant pronoiai to aristocrats and the genesis of the hereditability of pronoiai, there were innovations in administrative terminology and procedures. While direct evidence is lacking, it is tempting to suppose that the first two developments led to the administrative innovations. The granting of hereditary rights over pronoia and the granting of pronoiai to a broader spectrum of recipients (particularly to those at the higher levels of society) blurred the distinction between pronoiai, simple grants to aristocrats, and even grants of property and fiscal privileges to monasteries. From an administrative point of view all of these grants were similar, and as their numbers increased it was necessary to find a better way to manage them. The solution was the *posotes* and the oikonomia.

The limitation and strict governance of the *posotes* was primarily an administrative device; *oikonomia* was simply a name that, unlike *pronoia*, could cover all categories of imperial grants, whether to soldiers, to aristocrats, to monasteries and churches, and even to individual monks. As well as embracing the pronoia of a soldier or aristocrat, it could cover the grant of paroikoi held by a monk, the village owned by a relative of the emperor, or the tax exemption on a piece of land owned by a monastery. For a short time, not lasting much longer than the reign of Michael VIII, everything was an oikonomia. I would argue that it was Michael VIII's intention to reduce all imperial grants to a common system of oikonomiai quantified by a *posotes*.

All of this makes it difficult to give a simple answer to what a pronoia was during Michael VIII's reign. In the twelfth century the elements that characterized the pronoia grant and made it different from other imperial grants were (i) it was not hereditary, (ii) it was granted to people of rather modest status who were often soldiers, and, as such, (iii) it was granted on condition of service. Further, (iv) it seems to have been composed exclusively of imperial land and the *exkousseiai* of paroikoi.

By the time of Michael VIII most of these elements were no longer applicable. On occasion the pronoia grant passed to heirs; it was frequently granted to people of elevated status; and its contents could be identical to the content of a grant to a monastery or a simple grant to an aristocrat. The single unique element which remained was the service requirement, and in this sense the pronoia grant remained a grant conditional on service. Nevertheless, that which was called a "pronoia" in the twelfth and first half of the thirteenth century temporarily becomes officially, during the reign of Michael VIII, just one variety of oikonomia and the term *pronoia* fades from official use.

Michael VIII was only partially successful in establishing a comprehensive new approach to dealing with imperial grants. His successors inherited an inconsistent vocabulary which required further clarification and which has led to a great deal of confusion among modern students of the institution of pronoia. At this point it is necessary to examine the terminology of pronoia and other grants during the later thirteenth and fourteenth centuries.

7 | Terminology, late thirteenth and fourteenth centuries

In regard to imperial grants, as in most other matters, Andronikos II continued the policies of his father. The shift in terminology from *pronoia* to *oikonomia*, the growth of the range of people who held pronoiai/oikonomiai, the use of the *posotes* to quantify grants, the existence of jointly held grants, and the granting of hereditary rights to imperial grants continued and expanded during Andronikos' long reign. Further, there were two innovations: the taxing of imperial grants and the granting of additional privileges on imperial grants in increments.

In the previous chapter I discussed how Michael VIII instituted a change in fiscal practices, ordering his fiscal assessors to begin assigning every property – or at least properties held in connection with an imperial grant – a *posotes*. Simultaneously, the word *oikonomia* appeared as a fiscal term and began to replace *pronoia* in references to imperial grants to laymen. Further, grants to monasteries began to be referred to as *oikonomiai* in official documents. At this point I would like to present, in a more or less orderly manner, what we know about the institution of pronoia from the later thirteenth through the second half of the fourteenth century. But before this can be done, it is necessary to deal with the complicated matter of terminology, and so that will be the subject of this chapter.

How do we identify pronoia grants in the sources? In my work on the Byzantine army, when I was looking for *soldiers* who held pronoiai, the question was easier to answer. Soldiers who held grants of property from the state held these as either pronoia holders or as smallholding property owners. The latter were relatively easy to distinguish because they were usually settled in groups based on their ethnicity or function (e.g., rowers or marines). Therefore, it was possible to conclude that the overwhelming majority of soldiers who held individual grants of property from the emperor held these grants as pronoiai. Certainly, this did not mean that every grant a soldier held from the emperor was a pronoia; it could have been a simple gift given as a reward. Nor did it mean that whenever a soldier held a property, it had to be held as part of a pronoia grant; like anyone else, a soldier might buy property, receive it in dowry, inherit it from relatives, or acquire it in other ways. Nevertheless, if there was a link between a soldier holding property and his service as a soldier, then that link was quite often a pronoia.

The situation becomes more difficult when the holder of property – whether or not we know that the property originated from an imperial grant – is not identified as a soldier, when he (and in some cases, she) held some other title or epithet or nothing but a name. Here, scholars have often been a bit casual in concluding the property was a pronoia or a simple gift from the emperor or patrimony, and so on. Thus, before I can lay out the characteristics of the mature pronoia grant, I will present my criteria for identifying a pronoia. It is all about terminology.

Pronoia

The easiest way to identify the institution of pronoia, naturally enough, is to look for the use of the word *pronoia* or any of its cognates in a document. In cases where we read, for example, that a soldier held a pronoia, we can be absolutely confident that the subject was the institution of pronoia. However, one of the reasons that it has been so difficult to establish the characteristics of the institution of pronoia is that the two primary terms used to refer to the institution – *pronoia* itself and *oikonomia* – not only had different meanings in different periods, but they were used to mean different things by different people, often at the same moment. Thus, the mere appearance of the term *pronoia* may not actually indicate that the property involved was a pronoia. (I address this in detail below when considering whether monasteries held pronoiai.)

In the literary sources there is even greater ambiguity. Histories, chronicles, correspondence, treatises, and the like, are slow to use the word *pronoia* in its technical sense and remain hesitant to include such terminology. In the documentary sources the word appears in its technical sense no later than 1136 *[2.2]* and perhaps earlier *[2.1]*, but it does not make its appearance in the literary sources until the 1220s. Not only do the major historians of the twelfth and thirteenth centuries (Anna Komnene, John Kinnamos, Niketas Choniates, George Akropolites) decline to use *pronoia* in this sense, but even the major historians of the fourteenth and fifteenth centuries use *pronoia* rarely (John Kantakouzenos) or not at all (Nikephoros Gregoras, George Sphrantzes, Leo Chalkokondyles, Doukas, Pseudo-Phrantzes). Only the historian George Pachymeres, who generally displays an openness to technical terminology, uses the word in a technical meaning rather frequently.

But the attitudes of the historians toward unusual vocabulary alone do not explain why some use *pronoia* in its technical sense and others do not. Certainly Choniates and Gregoras disapproved of "modern" and foreign terms, though they both occasionally deal with the agrarian and fiscal policies of the emperors. But others, such as Anna Komnene, include many foreign names in their works. In her case, she apologizes for how they detract from the beauty of her Greek, but she is nevertheless intrigued by the unusual. While there was nothing novel about the technical sense of the word *pronoia* when she wrote her history (ca. 1150), she displays little knowledge or interest in fiscal terminology generally.

Other explanations work for the other historians who eschew *pronoia*. Sphrantzes' history is brief, and the other fifteenth-century historians, Doukas and Chalkokondyles, whose works are filled with foreign and newfangled expressions, as well as the sixteenth-century compilation of Pseudo-Phrantzes (Makarios Melissourgos), were concerned with foreign relations, diplomacy, and wars, and not the internal history of Byzantium. In other words, the appearance or the absence of *pronoia* in its technical sense in the historians, or any other writers, has little relation to the prevalence or development of the institution of pronoia.

That being said, I have found the term *pronoia*, in its fiscal sense, in the works of nine Byzantine writers. In chronological order: a letter and two judicial rulings of John Apokaukos, metropolitan of Naupaktos (ca. 1226) *[5.15–5.17]*; one passage in the history attributed to Skoutariotes (after 1261) *[5.13]*; a marginal note to the history attributed to Skoutariotes (end of the thirteenth century or later) *[3.2]*; two letters of Patriarch Gregory II (1283–89) *[6.12] [8.3]*; a letter of Patriarch Athanasios (1289–93, 1303–09) *[7.1]*; numerous passages in the history of George Pachymeres (ca. 1307); a letter of Theodore Hyrtakenos (before 1328) *[8.10]*; one passage in a book of mathematical problems (early fourteenth century) *[8.8]*; and a pair of related passages in the history of John Kantakouzenos (ca. 1360) *[8.26]*. The term also appears in three Greek chronicles composed on the fringes of Byzantine civilization: the *Chronicle of the Morea* (numerous passages) *[7.2]*, the *Chronicle of the Tocco* (two passages) *[7.3]*, and the *Chronicle of Ioannina* (two passages) *[7.4]*.

I have already dealt with the first four of these writers (Apokaukos, Skoutariotes, the note in Skoutariotes, and Patriarch Gregory). Most of these passages make a link between a pronoia and Byzantine soldiers, allowing the conclusion that they most likely are dealing with the Byzantine institution of pronoia and can tell us something about that institution. Of the remaining eight works, three – Hyrtakenos, the book of math problems, and Kantakouzenos – clearly deal with the institution of pronoia because they either contain technical information, deal with soldiers, or both. These passages will be examined in the next chapter for the information they provide.

[7.1] Letter of Patriarch Athanasios I to Emperor Andronikos II Palaiologos (1303–09)

For the remaining five works, the situation is more ambiguous, often because there is not enough context to make an adequate determination of what the writer meant. A case in which it is impossible to know what the writer had in mind is found in a letter of Patriarch Athanasios I (1289–93, 1303–09). A number of the patriarch's letters condemn bishops for abandoning their sees and coming to live in Constantinople and urge the emperor to take action. In one such letter to Andronikos II Athanasios complains that "pronoiai and residences have been granted to any bishop who wishes as an allotment, and they make merry in the capital with impunity."[1] "As an allotment," the editor's translation, is as neutral a rendering of the phrase *eis kleron* (εἰς κλῆρον) as is possible. If Athanasios had this in mind, he might just as well have omitted it, so little does it add to the meaning of the passage. Elsewhere in his letters Athanasios uses *kleros* to mean either "clergy" or, less commonly, "heritage, patrimony." Assuming Athanasios did not intend the redundant "any bishop in the clergy," we are left to decide whether the expression *eis kleron* means simply "for an allotment" or whether it has the more specific sense of "as an inheritance," "in patrimony."[2]

Do we maintain the editor's translation or should we render the passage "pronoiai and residences have been granted as patrimony to any bishop wishing them"? Unfortunately, we do not know how the patriarch is using the word *pronoia* in the passage. He *is* using the word in a technical sense; that the word appears in its plural form makes that certain, as does the juxtaposition of "pronoiai" with "residences," giving the former a concrete sense. For the patriarch, pronoiai provided a livelihood. It would also seem that these "pronoiai" and residences were granted to the bishops by an

[1] *The Correspondence of Athanasius I Patriarch of Constantinople*, ed. and trans. A.-M. Talbot (Washington, D.C., 1975), no. 62.31: καὶ τῷ βουλομένῳ ἀρχιερεῖ εἰς κλῆρον προνοίας προσνενεμῆσθαι καὶ κατοικίας.

[2] A document from 1017 does use the expression in the latter sense: *Lavra*, I, no. 22.5. On the other hand, Patriarch Nicholas I (901–907) uses the expression to refer to those "in the clergy": *Nicholas I Patriarch of Constantinople, Letters*, ed. and trans. R. Jenkins and L. Westerink (Washington, D.C., 1973), no. 32.238.

authority higher than the bishops themselves, which would mean either the patriarch or the emperor. Certainly they were not granted by the patriarch, or he would have dealt with the matter himself. Since Athanasios was complaining to the emperor, it would appear that the emperor had granted these "pronoiai" and residences to certain bishops. But were they limited grants or simply gifts? We cannot say.

[7.2] The *Chronicle of the Morea* (early fourteenth century)

Ironically the one work which employs the word *pronoia* more than any other source tells us practically nothing about the Byzantine institution. The *Chronicle of the Morea* is the story of the Latin conquest of the Morea up through 1292. It exists in four versions – French, Italian, Aragonese, and Greek – the latter a narrative in over 9,000 lines of verse. The Greek version uses the term *pronoia* (or a word directly based on *pronoia* such as verbal forms) 33 or 35 times (depending on the manuscript).[3] In the Greek version (the word does not appear in the others) *pronoia* refers to any landholding conferred, usually by a Latin authority, upon an individual or a religious foundation. Even though we read that some Greeks held pronoiai in the chronicle, the work is not useful to learn about the Byzantine institution. This is because "*pronoia*" in the chronicle is simply the Greek author's (or translator's, depending on whether the Greek or French version of the chronicle was composed first) rendering of "fief." And in the thirteenth and fourteenth centuries in the medieval West "fief" was understood quite broadly to mean "holding, tenure, possession, property." The chronicle does use the word "fee" (φίε, φέη, φέον) 24 or 26 times (depending on the manuscript), but almost all of the occurrences appear in the brief section of the work (from around lines 1914 to 1987) which deals with the rather bureaucratic division of territories in 1209 on the order of William I of Champlitte. Each region parceled out was worth a certain number of "fees."[4]

[3] Ed. J. Schmitt (London, 1904; repr. Groningen, 1967), and ed. P. Kalonaros, *Τὸ Χρονικὸν τοῦ Μορέως* (Athens, 1940; repr. 1989). The content in line 2690 in the Copenhagen (H) and Turin (T) manuscripts is simply absent from the Paris (P) manuscript, and for προνοίαν in the H and T manuscripts (line 864), P reads φέον. All word-counts were calculated using the online *TLG*.

[4] The definitive analysis of this aspect of the chronicle is found in a series of articles by David Jacoby: "Les archontes grecs et la féodalité en Morée franque," in Jacoby, *Société et démographie à Byzance et en Romanie latine* (London, 1975), no. VI; "The Encounter of Two Societies," in Jacoby, *Recherches sur la Méditerranée orientale du XIIe au XVe siècle* (London, 1979), no. II; and "From Byzantium to Latin Romania," in *Byzantium, Latin Romania and the Mediterranean* (Aldershot, 2001), no. VIII. For the best effort to argue that the chronicle provides good evidence for the existence pronoia in the Morea before the Latin Conquest, see A. Carile, "Sulla pronoia nel

And so, while the *Chronicle of the Morea*, in and of itself, does not help us determine the essential characteristics of the Byzantine institution of pronoia, it illustrates how the word *pronoia* acquired a broader popular usage.

[7.3] The *Chronicle of the Tocco* (ca. 1430)

The idea that the word *pronoia* acquired the popular sense of any privileged property probably explains its appearance in the *Chronicle of the Tocco*. This chronicle, completed not long after 1425, details the rule of the Italian Carlo I Tocco (1376–1429) who, starting from Kephalenia and Zakynthos, eventually ruled most of Epiros. It contains a couple of minor references to pronoia: "properties, pronoiai of archons" (κρατήματα . . . προνοῖες τῶν ἀρχόντων), and "benefactions, property, and pronoiai" (εὐεργεσίες . . . , κράτημα καὶ προνοῖες). These were clearly privileged properties conferred by some ruler, but with no connection to the Byzantine institution.[5]

[7.4] The *Chronicle of Ioannina* (ca. 1440)

Similarly, *pronoia* appears in a vague sense in two passages in the *Chronicle of Ioannina*. This anonymous chronicle, written ca. 1440, describes the reign of the Serbian despot Thomas Preljubović who ruled Ioannina and northern Epiros from 1366/7 until his death in 1384. Recounting Thomas' alleged tyranny, the chronicle first notes his imposition of corvées (*angareiai*) and taxes: "about the wine, the grain and *angareiai* and burdens and taxes the whole time, and other kinds of sufferings, that is, *mitata* and pronoiai and monopolies, at one time on wine and grain, at another on meat, and then on cheese, always on fish and fruits, and sometimes for himself and sometimes for his archons."[6] The association of *mitata*, pronoiai, and *monopolia*, is puzzling. *Mitata* and monopolies were related: the former, in this case, were probably various rights of requisition of food and supplies in kind, and the latter, as they imply, were franchises granting the right to control the

Peloponneso bizantino anteriormente alla conquista latina," *ZRVI* 16 (1975), 55–61. T. Maniati-Kokkini, "Τὸ «Χρονικό τοῦ Μορέως» καὶ ἡ Βυζαντινή Πρόνοια," *Βυζαντιακά* 14 (1994), 483–508, adopts Jacoby's conclusions. For the chronicle in general, see *ODB*, s.v. "Chronicle of the Morea."

5 *Cronaca dei Tocco di Cefalonia di Anonimo*, ed. G. Schirò (Rome, 1975), lines 139–40, 935.

6 L. Vranouses, *Τὸ χρονικὸν τῶν Ἰωαννίνων κατ' ἀνέκδοτον δημώδη ἐπιτομήν* (Athens, 1965), reprint from *Ἀκαδημία Ἀθηνῶν. Ἐπετηρὶς τοῦ Μεσαιωνικοῦ Ἀρχείου* 12 (1962), par. 12, lines 21–30 (article pagination, p. 83): ἤγουν μιτᾶτα καὶ προνοίας καὶ μονοπώλια.

sale of commodities. It would be difficult to create any link between these and pronoiai except to say that they were all privileges that Thomas either created for himself or granted to certain of his favorites.

The chronicle describes further depredations of Thomas from 1380/1: "And as many of the paroikoi from the church who were left as a result of his misdeeds, while he cast them from the pronoia of the Serbs, he did not permit them in the church, but held them for himself."[7] At least this passage links "pronoia" to paroikoi and property: paroikoi were confiscated from the church and granted to Serbs as "pronoiai," and later taken from the Serbs. But the nature of this "pronoia" and its relation to the Byzantine institution cannot be determined.

Finally, we turn to the history of George Pachymeres, who refers to "pronoia" in connection with privileged property holding in eleven sections of his history. Three of these eleven sections have been discussed in earlier chapters, and these almost certainly are referring to pronoia in the technical sense I have been developing: the Nicaean emperors granted pronoiai to the "more illustrious" highlanders on the eastern frontier *[5.14]*; Michael VIII transferred the pronoiai of soldiers who fell in battle to their children *[6.10]*; Michael VIII increased the pronoia holdings of "those of the senate" and granted to some soldiers hereditary rights over their pronoiai *[6.11]*. In another passage, discussed in the next chapter *[8.25]*, he refers to soldiers abandoning their pronoiai.

The remaining seven references are more ambiguous: one deals with the possibility of monasteries and churches holding pronoiai and is discussed below *[7.12]*, and three deal with what appears to be the taxation of pronoiai *[8.34–8.36]* and these will be dealt with in the next chapter. Here I will discuss the three remaining passages which deal with the property holdings of distinguished individuals.

[7.5] Pachymeres on John Palaiologos (ca. 1307)

Pachymeres employs the word *pronoia* in connection with an "oikonomia" held by Michael VIII's brother, the despot John Palaiologos. Around 1272, evidently as part of the process whereby Michael's son Andronikos was elevated to the rank of co-emperor, Michael VIII "took away the great

[7] Vranouses, *Τὸ χρονικὸν τῶν Ἰωαννίνων*, par. 23, lines 31–37 (article p. 91): καὶ ὅσοι τῶν ἀπὸ τῆς ἐκκλησίας πάροικοι ἀπὸ τὴν κακοπραγίαν αὐτοῦ ἐναπελείφθησαν ἄνθρωποι, ἐξέβαλε μὲν αὐτοὺς ἀπὸ τῆς προνοίας τῶν Σερβῶν, οὐκ εἴασε δὲ αὐτοὺς ἐν τῇ ἐκκλησίᾳ, ἀλλὰ δι᾽ ἑαυτοῦ αὐτοὺς ἐπεκράτει. E. Naumov, "K istorii vizantijskoj i serbskoj pronii," *VizVrem* 34 (1973), 29–31.

part of [John's] oikonomia: all the islands [mentioned] earlier, I speak of Mytilene and Rhodes, and on land the most and greatest [things] that were for sufficient pronoia."[8]

George Ostrogorsky assumed that Pachymeres meant that John Palaiologos held Mytilene (Lesbos) and Rhodes as a pronoia grant. This conflicted with what he regarded as a pronoia, and so he concluded, "In such cases one should not, however, think of *pronoia* in the exact sense of the word," but rather, an "extended application of the concept of *pronoia*." Similarly, Hélène Ahrweiler referred to John's arrangement as an "appanage," which for her, whether or not it could be classified as a pronoia grant, was distinct from the "normal" kind of pronoia grant made to soldiers. Ljubomir Maksimović maintained that John did not hold a real pronoia because it was not what Maksimović regarded as a "feudal possession" – for him an essential characteristic of a pronoia grant. Rather, he too concluded that John held a large appanage with powers that extended far beyond those of a typical large landowner.[9]

The term "appanage," borrowed from the vocabulary of western European feudalism, appears in Byzantine historiography with two basic senses. In the narrower of the two, the word is used to designate a nearly independent territory granted by the emperor to a member of the imperial family, usually a younger son, for the purpose of securing the grantee a source of livelihood and of insuring a political and administrative connection between the provincial territory and the capital. The grantee characteristically derived his income from the exercise of administrative rights over the territory and from land he held within the territory, though the grant of the appanage itself did not implicitly include proprietary rights over any territory and certainly not the right of hereditary transmission. In effect an appanage, in this sense, was a kind of "mini-kingdom" granted by the emperor. Despite efforts to identify the practice earlier in Byzantine history, the granting of large parts of the empire to imperial relatives was a fourteenth- and fifteenth-century phenomenon, spurred by the civil wars

[8] Pachymeres, ed. Failler, I, 417.7–9 (Bonn edn., I, 321.8–10): καὶ γὰρ καὶ τὸ πολὺ τῆς οἰκονομίας ἀφῄρητο· νῆσοι γὰρ πᾶσαι τὸ πρότερον, Μιτυλήνη λέγω καὶ Ῥόδος, καὶ κατὰ γῆν πλεῖστά τε καὶ μέγιστά οἱ εἰς αὐτάρκη πρόνοιαν ἦσαν. Failler, p. 416, translates the key phrase as "une ample pronoia." Ostrogorsky, *Féodalité*, 100, 109. Mutafčiev, "Vojniški zemi," 46–47/572. Charanis, "Monastic Properties," 89, 152–53; and "Social Structure," 133 note 177. M. Bibikov, "Svedenija o pronii v pis'mah Grigorija Kiprskogo i 'Istorii' Georgija Pahimera," *ZRVI* 17 (1976), 96.

[9] G. Ostrogorsky, "Observations on the Aristocracy in Byzantium," *Dumbarton Oaks Papers* 25 (1971), 22. Ahrweiler, "La concession des droits incorporels," 112–13. Lj. Maksimović, "Geneza i karakter apanaža u Vizantiji," *ZRVI* 14/15 (1973), 119–22.

of the era. From the mid-fourteenth century almost every younger son of an emperor held an appanage at some time, and most of the areas remaining in the empire were held, on occasion, as appanages: Thrace, Thessaloniki with Macedonia, Thessaly, and most importantly, the Morea.

In a broader sense, the term *appanage* is sometimes applied to any imperial grant, revocable at the will of the emperor, of an important region or demesne in hereditary title to an individual or institution. Hélène Ahrweiler and Ljubomir Maksimović viewed John's oikonomia as an appanage in this broad sense.[10]

But is it even necessary to conclude that Pachymeres was claiming that John Palaiologos held Mytilene and Rhodes as a pronoia? The two islands as well as the properties on the mainland were, according to Pachymeres, within his "oikonomia." But the clause referring to a pronoia (οἳ εἰς αὐτάρκη πρόνοιαν ἦσαν) does not necessarily modify both the islands and the properties on the mainland. Pachymeres may have intended it to modify only the latter. Thus, we cannot conclude from this passage that entire islands were held in pronoia. Pachymeres may have been speaking of two different types of grants that John Palaiologos held: administrative rights over two important islands, and pronoiai in other areas.

The clause οἳ εἰς αὐτάρκη πρόνοιαν ἦσαν is interesting. The word *autarkes* can have several shades of meaning, including "independent." Fortunately, based on other uses of the word in Pachymeres' history, we can be confident that the word means "sufficient" or "ample." For example, elsewhere we have συνάμα μετὰ καὶ αὐτάρκους στρατοῦ, which clearly means "together with a sufficient force."[11] Nevertheless, my literal translation of the clause "that were in sufficient pronoia" is meaningless. How properly to render it?

In the discussion in Chapter 2 of the 1162 act of the *doux* of Thessaloniki John Kontostephanos *[2.3]* I concluded that the phrase should be rendered "for pronoia," and, based on the elementary senses of the word *pronoia*, I hypothesized that *eis pronoian* meant "for the purpose of (the recipient's personal) care or maintenance," rather than "for the purpose of administration (of the property and paroikoi)." This passage from Pachymeres' history supports this hypothesis. If we begin by translating *eis autarke pronoian* (εἰς αὐτάρκη πρόνοιαν) as "for an ample/sufficient pronoia," it is clear that *pronoia* must mean "maintenance" and not "administration."

[10] See J. Barker, "The Problem of Appanages in Byzantium during the Palaiologan Period," *Βυζαντινά* 3 (1971), 103–22; Maksimović, "Geneza i karakter apanaža," 103–54; Ahrweiler, "La concession des droits incorporels," 112–14.

[11] Pachymeres, ed. Failler, I, 451.17.

Thus, certain properties were held by John Palaiologos "for ample/sufficient maintenance," in the sense that these properties were "more than adequate for maintaining John." I think we must conclude that in Pachymeres' view a "pronoia" was a grant, the primary purpose of which was not to arrange the administration of something, but to provide someone with a livelihood.

But can we consider even the properties "on land" which John Palaiologos lost pronoiai at all? Here we run into the problem of idiosyncratic grants, that is, those issued to people very close to the emperor. It is unlikely that John received, orally or in writing, the information that he could hold these properties only so long as he lived. Rather, it must have been understood that he would hold the properties as well as the administrative rights over the islands as long as his brother the emperor wanted him to. In this sense the grant was conditional on the emperor's favor, but it was not really a pronoia.

[7.6] Pachymeres on John Asen III (ca. 1307)

A similar case in which Pachymeres seems to use the word *pronoia* in connection with an outright grant of property is found in a passage which describes how John Asen III had been living inside the empire. Through 1278, up until the time he proclaimed himself tsar of Bulgaria, he had been dwelling in the Troäd on the Skamandros River: "for there he lived, having things for pronoia sufficiently."[12] From an earlier passage in Pachymeres' history we learn that this arrangement had its origin sometime around 1262 or 1263 under Asen's father, Mytzes, lord of Trnovo: Michael VIII "providing for him sufficiently near the Skamandros, he [Mytzes] was established there somewhere with his children."[13] Here there can be no question that "having things for pronoia sufficiently" (αὐτάρκως τῶν εἰς πρόνοιαν ἔχων) really means "having things sufficiently for maintenance," or "having a sufficient livelihood." And, given that the grant to Mytzes was inherited by his son, we should probably not consider this a pronoia grant.

[12] Pachymeres, ed. Failler, I, 557.25–26 (Bonn edn., I, 438.18–19): ἐκεῖ γὰρ καὶ τὰς διατριβὰς ἐποιεῖτο, αὐτάρκως τῶν εἰς πρόνοιαν ἔχων. Bibikov, "Svedenija," 96. Ahrweiler, "La concession des droits incorporels," 113, speaks of this "pronoia" as an appanage as well.

[13] Pachymeres, ed. Failler, I, 451.19–21 (Bonn edn., I, 350): πρὸς τῷ Σκαμάνδρῳ ἀποχρώντως προμηθευσάμενος, ἐκεῖσέ που σὺν τοῖς τέκνοις κατασκηνοῖ. According to Gregoras (I, 60.24–61.2), Mytzes "receiving some villages around Troia and Skamandros from the emperor for a yearly income [εἰς ἐπέτειον πρόσοδον], he stayed there from then on with his wife and children."

[7.7] Pachymeres on Eltimir and Michael IX (ca. 1307)

Another passage in Pachymeres' history that uses *pronoia* in what appears to be a technical sense deals with two important men: a high-ranking foreigner and the heir to the throne. During a Bulgarian attack in 1304, Andronikos II started negotiations with Eltimir, son-in-law of Smilec and nephew of the Bulgarian tsar Svetoslav, who ruled at Krounos (Krn) in the Rhodope. In his unsuccessful effort to dissuade Eltimir from joining his uncle, Andronikos II "made arrangements to honor [him] with pronoiai from the [land] of the Romans." As with other passages in which Pachymeres uses the word *pronoia [7.5–7.6]*, Ahrweiler termed this proposed grant an "appanage."[14]

A few lines later Pachymeres writes that Michael IX (1294/5–1320), "having lost the things assigned to him of pronoiai throughout the East" because of Turkish advances, had received from Andronikos II the properties in the West of Despot Michael Angelos.[15]

Michael (born Demetrios) Angelos, son of the despot of Epiros Michael II Doukas (ca. 1230–1267/8), came to Byzantium after his father's death, and in 1277 or 1278 married Michael VIII's daughter Anna, receiving at that time the title of despot. In 1300 he left Anna and married the ex-wife of the Serbian king Milutin, the sister of the Bulgarian tsar Theodore Svetoslav (1300–22). In January 1304 Andronikos II, suspecting his former brother-in-law of treasonous dealings with the bellicose Svetoslav, convened an assembly of secular and ecclesiastical notables who, under the emperor's influence, decided in March of that year to deprive Michael of his possessions and to imprison him.[16]

In January 1304 Michael IX had returned to Europe from a long, unsuccessful expedition in Asia Minor against the Turks.[17] He was in fact one of countless refugees who had fled the East after having abandoned their possessions to the enemy. It was quite convenient, then, to transfer Michael Angelos' confiscated property to Michael IX. Michael IX's "pronoiai" were evidently located in one of the last areas of Anatolia held by the Byzantines,

[14] Pachymeres, ed. Failler, IV, 447.7–8 (Bonn edn., II, 407.4): καὶ προνοίαις ἐκ τῆς Ῥωμαίων ἀγάλλειν κατεπηγγέλλετο. Ahrweiler, "La concession des droits incorporels," 104, 113. A. Laiou, *Constantinople and the Latins* (Cambridge, Mass., 1972), 160. Dölger, *Regesten*, IV, no. 2264. Bibikov, "Svedenija," 96.

[15] Pachymeres, ed. Failler, IV, 447.14–17 (Bonn edn., II, 407.11–14): ἀποβαλόντι γὰρ τὰ ἀποτεταγμένα οἱ τῶν προνοιῶν κατ' ἀνατολὴν. Mentioned by Mutafčiev, "Vojniški zemi," 46–47/572; Ostrogorsky, *Féodalité*, 100; and Laiou, *Constantinople and the Latins*, 118.

[16] *Vizantijski izvori za istoriju naroda Jugoslavije*, ed. F. Barišić and B. Ferjančić, vol. 6 (Belgrade, 1986), 33 note 68, 61 note 132. *PLP*, no. 193.

[17] Laiou, *Constantinople and the Latins*, 160.

that is, the northeast corner of Asia Minor, west of the Sangarios River and no further south than Atramyttion. Michael Angelos' properties were somewhere in Thrace or Macedonia. In this and the other two passages *[7.5–7.6]* it is not clear at all that Pachymeres uses *pronoia* to mean anything more than property granted by the emperor.

Combining the information offered by Pachymeres in the various passages in his history, the following categories of recipients could hold pronoiai: (i) soldiers *[6.10–6.11] [8.25]*, (ii) the highlanders during the Nicaean period *[5.14]*, (iii) monasteries *[7.12]*, (iv) churches *[7.12]*, (v) the imperial entourage *[7.12]*, (vi) aristocrats *[6.11] [8.34]*, (vii) high-ranking foreigners *[7.6–7.7]*, (viii) the emperor's brother *[7.5]*, and (ix) a co-emperor *[7.7]*. Generally, these categories can be simplified: soldiers, religious institutions, and aristocrats. But should we conclude that a monastery or a church could hold a pronoia? To answer this, we first have to turn to the other major term that denoted pronoiai: *oikonomia*.

Oikonomia

[7.8] Two acts of Demetrios Apelmene for the monastery of Xenophon mentioning the pronoia/oikonomia of Peros Martinos (1300)

From the time of Michael VIII onward, the appearance of the term *oikonomia* is a fairly reliable indicator of the existence of pronoia, though it too, like *pronoia*, is sometimes applied in the documents and literary sources to other types of grants. Generally speaking, *pronoia* and *oikonomia* could be used synonymously. Two documents from the archives of Xenophon provide precisely the evidence one would like in order to support this assertion: two identical passages with the exception that one uses the word *pronoia* and the other, *oikonomia*. The two documents, which detail Xenophon's possessions, are from October 1300 and were issued by the fiscal assessor Demetrios Apelmene. Both are originals.

The first notes that, among the monastery's possessions, was a piece of land called Kanstamonitou in the region of the village of Psalis "taken from the oikonomia of the *kavallarios syr* Peros Martinos, amounting to 325 modioi." It then mentions another property of 300 modioi and adds that all 625 modioi had been received by the monastery in exchange for other land on the Kassandra peninsula. The second document, probably a revised version of the first, lists the same piece of land called Kanstamonitou "taken from the pronoia of *syr* Peros Martinos." This document notes similarly that

Kanstamonitou and another property, together comprising 625 modioi, had been given to the monastery by imperial *orismos* in exchange for land the monastery had held on the peninsula of Kassandra.[18]

Peros Martinos is otherwise unknown. His titles "*syr*" and "*kavallarios*," as well as his name (Peiro, or some other form of Peter), suggest he was a western European (cf. Syrgares) and a military man. The document offers no hint as to why Martinos lost this part of his pronoia/oikonomia. There is no indication that he was dead in 1300, nor can we assume that he was not compensated for the land he lost.

The equivalence between the two terms *pronoia* and *oikonomia* can be inferred from other documents as well. While in an act from 1304 George Doukas Troulenos refers to a "pronoia" given to him by the emperor *[8.50]*, in two imperial documents from 1317 and 1318 Andronikos II refers to this grant as an "oikonomia" *[8.37]*. *Pronoia* remained the informal way of referring to such holdings. Other times the equivalency is implicit. In his 1272 *prostagma* for his son Andronikos *[6.6]*, Michael VIII explains that a good soldier could be rewarded either with a lump-sum benefaction or with "an addition to his oikonomia" which, however, should not come "from a pronoia vacant by accident."

[7.9] Chrysobull of Andronikos III Palaiologos for Gervasios, *hegoumenos* of Hilandar (1334), *Prostagma* of Andronikos III Palaiologos for Gervasios (1334), Act of the *domestikos* of the themes Constantine Makrenos (1334), and Donation of Gervasios, *hegoumenos* of Hilandar (1335)

Another example of this equivalency is found in the series of documents involving the village of Choudena, which Andronikos III granted to Gervasios the *hegoumenos* of Hilandar. In a chrysobull from July 1334 Gervasios requested and was granted "the *posotes* of forty hyperpyra in Choudena on the Strymon which Kassandrenos previously held and was recently held by Lependrenos," along with the right "to transmit and donate it howsoever he should wish and will." At the same time the emperor issued another document ordering the *domestikos* of the themes Constantine Makrenos to confer upon Gervasios "the said *posotes*" inasmuch as the emperor wished that Gervasios receive "the oikonomia of 40 hyperpyra in the village of Choudena," and to compensate Lependrenos with something of equal value:

[18] *Xénophon*, no. 4.24: ἀποσπασθεῖσα ἀπὸ τῆς οἰκονομίας καβαλλαρίου τοῦ σῦρ Πέρου Μαρτίνου, and no. 5.17: ἀποσπασθεῖσα ἀπὸ τῆς προνοίας τοῦ σῦρ Πέρου Μαρτίνου.

"to the said Lependrenos, on the other hand, you will confer from your commission an equal amount [*isoposon*] and provide [that] he should hold his own amount [*poson*] without deficiency."

The next month Makrenos issued an act which begins by stating that he had been ordered by the emperor to confer upon Gervasios "the pronoia of Lependrenos . . . which Kassandrenos earlier held," and to give Lependrenos another pronoia. Accordingly, he writes, "I confer upon [Gervasios] such pronoia, and he ought to hold this and enjoy the income produced from it, as Lependrenos held this and Kassandrenos before him." The next year Gervasios transferred to his monastery "the oikonomia of forty hyperpyra . . . which Kassandrenos previously held, Lependrenos later."[19] In these documents there is clearly an equivalence between the words *pronoia* and *oikonomia.* "The pronoia of Lependrenos" and "the oikonomia of forty hyperpyra" both referred to something "in the village of Choudena."

Oikonomia is rarely encountered with this sense in the literary sources. While the word *pronoia* and its various forms appears many times in the *Chronicle of the Morea* the word *oikonomia* appears but twice in the entire work and has the sense of a payment in kind.[20] It appears with a technical sense in the works of only three authors. Theodore Hyrtakenos uses the word once in the same letter in which he mentions "pronoia" *[8.10]*, Kantakouzenos uses the word but once in his long memoirs *[7.19]*, and Pachymeres uses the word in a technical sense in three passages in his history: Michael VIII "took away the great part of [his brother John's] oikonomia" *[7.5]*; two distinguished Turks entered imperial service after Michael VIII granted them court titles and something "for oikonomia" *[8.28]*; and some soldiers in Asia illicitly increased their pronoiai while others abandoned their oikonomiai *[8.25]*.

There is a great deal of similarity between the fiscal senses of the words *pronoia* and *oikonomia.* Let us make a comparison of what the documents tell us about pronoia and oikonomia. No analysis here; we simply take the testimony of the sources at face value.

Pronoiai were granted by the emperor *[2.1] [5.7] [8.65]*, specifically through an *orismos [5.7] [8.65]*. Oikonomiai likewise were granted by the

[19] *Chilandar*, ed. Petit, no. 45.5–9, and no. 46.10–12: πρὸς δὲ τὸν διαληφθέντα Λεπενδρηνὸν παραδώσεις ἑτέρωθεν ἀπὸ τῆς δουλείας σου ἰσόποσον καὶ οἰκονομήσῃς καὶ κατέχῃ καὶ οὗτος ἀνελλιπῶς τὸ οἰκεῖον ποσόν, no. 47.3–12: παραδώσω . . . τὴν περὶ τὸν Στρυμμόνα εἰς τὸ χωρίον τὰ Χουδηνὰ πρόνοιαν τοῦ Λεπενδρηνοῦ, ἣν εἶχεν πρότερον ὁ Κασανδρηνός, and no. 126.11–12. Kazhdan, *Agrarnye otnošenija*, 213–14. Ostrogorsky, *Féodalité*, 150–52.

[20] *Chronicle of the Morea* (manuscript P) lines 5265 and 6600, and (manuscripts H and T), lines 5265 and 8184. In H and T line 6600 reads ψωμί "bread" rather than P's *oikonomia.*

emperor *[6.5–6.7] [7.9] [8.41]* through a *prostagma [8.41]*, which is the same as an *orismos*, as well as through chrysobull *[7.9]*. In one case an oikonomia was held (as opposed to granted) through a chrysobull *[7.17]*.

Pronoiai were held by soldiers *[2.3–2.5] [6.6] [6.9] [8.8]* and by *kavallarioi [5.8–5.10]*, as were oikonomiai (soldiers *[6.6] [8.4] [8.11–8.13] [8.27]*; *kavallarioi [7.8] [8.44]*). It is interesting that all the documents that refer to soldiers or *kavallarioi* holding pronoiai span the period from 1162 to 1279, while those speaking of soldiers or *kavallarioi* holding oikonomiai span the period from 1272 to 1343, with all but one in the period from 1300 to 1343.

Two or more men could share a pronoia in common *[2.3] [8.2–8.3] [8.8]*, and this is documented with oikonomiai as well *[8.4] [8.9]*. Pronoiai were also held by monasteries *[6.9] [7.12] [7.14]* and churches *[6.9]*. Oikonomiai, too, were held by monasteries *[6.3] [6.7] [8.11]*, a *hegoumenos [7.9]*, and a monk *[6.5]*.

Both pronoiai *[2.3–2.5] [7.9]* and oikonomiai *[6.2–6.3] [6.7]* were conferred by officials. Within pronoiai one found the usual kinds of productive agrarian resources that were commonly found within oikonomiai: fields *[5.15] [8.55]*, trees *[5.10–5.11] [5.15] [5.17]*, a vineyard *[8.54]*, patrimonial land of peasants *[5.4]*, *exaleimmata [8.54]*, other land *[8.69]*, and paroikoi *[2.3–2.5] [5.8] [5.11] [7.13]*, including a monk *[5.11]*, as well as larger agglomerations such as villages *[7.9] [8.56] [8.68]* and a *proasteion [2.3]*, the rights to a river *[5.7]*, and general property "rights" (δίκαια) *[8.18] [8.56] [8.68] [8.71]*. On the basis of the praktika providing in detail the contents of the oikonomiai of laymen *[8.11–8.15] [8.17]*, precisely the same things were found within oikonomiai.

What did the pronoia holder get from the pronoia? Sometimes this was in the form of rent *[5.6] [8.65]*, sometimes in the form of taxes *[9.3] [9.7]*. From the praktika for the oikonomiai of laymen we see that holders of oikonomiai received these same things, plus the labor services of paroikoi.

In regard to the transfer or alienation of pronoiai and oikonomiai, practices varied. There are only two statements of the principles involved for pronoia. The *Zavorda Treatise* specifies that pronoiai were held for life *[2.1]*, and in a document from 1233 we are told that paroikoi of a pronoia holder were not to sell their land to the pronoia holder *[5.4]*. In regard to oikonomiai, we have a statement from 1335 in which the emperor ordered that nothing should be sold or donated from an oikonomia *[8.51]*.

Nevertheless, both pronoiai and oikonomiai were alienated or transferred. Property held pronoiastically could be donated to a monastery with the stipulation that the donation was valid as long as the pronoia was held by the recipient *[8.54–8.55]*. Sometimes monasteries held property "from the pronoia" of laymen *[2.2] [7.8] [8.72]*, and in one case a pronoia was granted by the emperor to the *hegoumenos* of a monastery *[7.9]*. Similarly, an oikonomia could be bequeathed *[6.5]* or donated to a monastery *[8.21]*. Properties within someone's oikonomia often passed to monasteries *[8.75] [8.77]*, sometimes explicitly on imperial order *[7.18] [8.76]*, sometimes with the explicit information that the person was deceased *[7.18] [8.9]*, sometimes with the implication that a confiscation was involved *[7.8]*.

Both pronoiai and oikonomiai could pass to other people. Pronoia holdings were reassigned to other people *[5.12]*. Similarly, a deceased man's oikonomia, or property within his oikonomia, sometimes went to another man *[8.11] [8.17] [8.45]*, and in one case to his son *[7.17]*. Once paroikoi from a monastery's oikonomia went to a soldier's oikonomia *[8.11]*. In one case an oikonomia or property in a man's oikonomia was confiscated *[8.17]*. In another case, an oikonomia returned to the fisc after a man died *[8.75]*. Children inherited pronoiai *[8.54]* and oikonomiai *[7.17] [8.21]*.

This comparison of pronoiai and oikonomiai shows that the two were very similar. Both were granted by the emperor, both were held by soldiers and monasteries, both at times could be inherited, both at times could be burdened with a military obligation, both at times could be taxed, both evidently contained precisely the same diverse variety of income-producing elements. The few apparent differences between them can be attributed to the more extensive documentation that we have for oikonomiai in the first half of the fourteenth century. When we combine this with the documents and literary passages that suggest *pronoia* and *oikonomia* could be used interchangeably *[6.1] [7.5] [7.8–7.9]*, it seems difficult to escape the conclusion that *pronoia* and *oikonomia* were used synonymously to designate identical fiscal phenomena.

But what was the relationship between the two words such that both words would be employed to designate the same thing? I believe that the appearance of one of the words rather than the other reflects terminological fashion. Figures 7.1–7.3 illustrate this. The three graphs present by decade the number of documents that use the word *pronoia* (or its verbal, adjectival, and adverbial forms, or *pronoiarios*) and the number that use the word *oikonomia*. Only occurrences of the words that reflect their Byzantine fiscal usage are included. False documents are excluded (because of the difficulty in dating them), as are those few Greek documents referring to fiscal arrangements created by Serbs, Latins, or Turks, even when the institutions they reflect may have been appropriated from Byzantium.

A number of observations may be made. First of all, it is necessary to state that the results presented in these graphs reflect more than the use

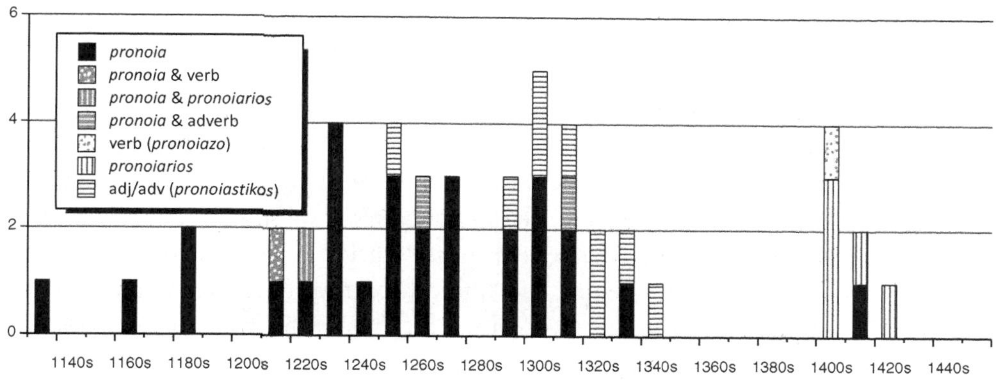

Figure 7.1 Documents containing the fiscal term *pronoia* and related forms.

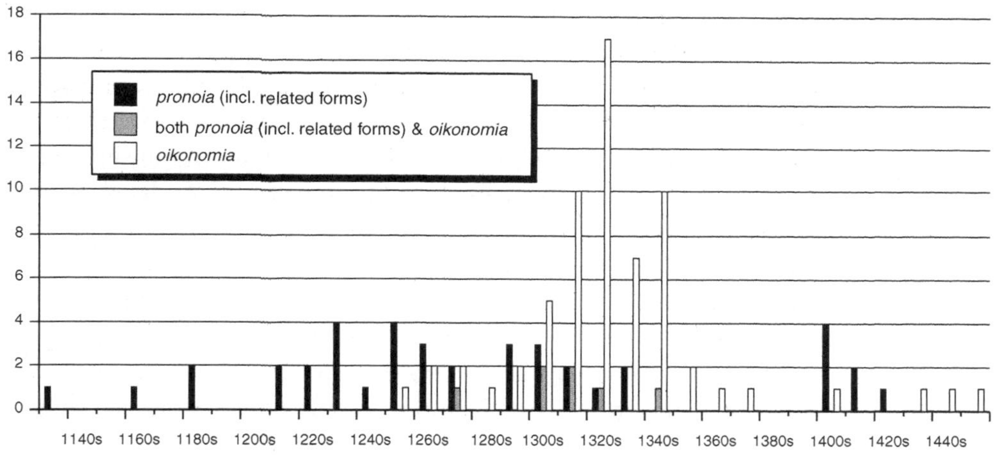

Figure 7.2 Documents containing the fiscal terms *pronoia* (and related forms) or *oikonomia*.

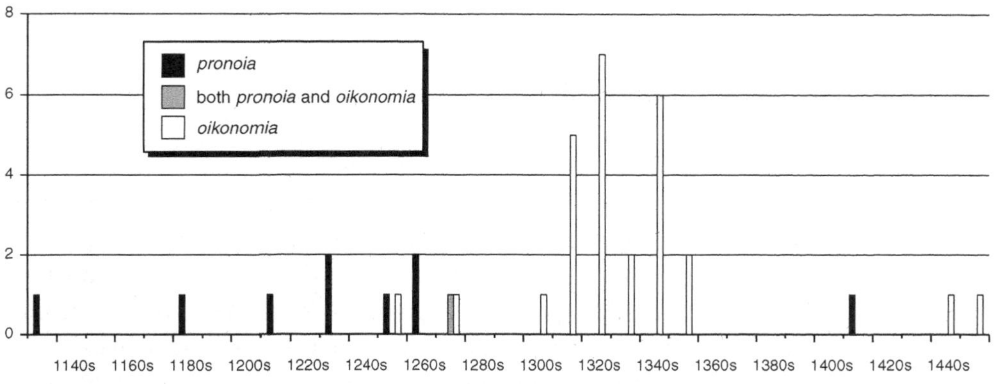

Figure 7.3 Imperial documents containing the fiscal terms *pronoia* or *oikonomia*.

and evolution of fiscal terminology. The scarcity of documents before 1200 reflects the general state of extant documentation during this period. Most of the thirteenth-century documents tallied reflect the preservation and publication of the archives of the monasteries of St. John on the island of Patmos and of the Virgin Lemviotissa outside Smyrna. By the same token most of the fourteenth- and fifteenth-century documents tallied in the graphs have been preserved in the archives of the monasteries of Mount Athos, and the majority of preserved Athonite documents date to the first half of the fourteenth century.

Further, some of the other characteristics of the graphs can be explained by specific political developments. The near absence of the word *pronoia* during the 1280s and 1290s can be explained by the Byzantine loss of Asia Minor, when the properties in that area held by the Patmos and Lemviotissa monasteries passed out of Byzantine fiscal control. The relative absence of the word *oikonomia* after the 1350s reflects the Byzantine loss of Macedonia. Similarly, the brief reestablishment of Byzantine authority in the area of Thessaloniki in the early decades of the fifteenth century explains the final brief reappearance of *pronoia* and its other forms.

All of this means that the change in frequency over time does not necessarily reflect the prevalence of the institutions connected with the words *pronoia* and *oikonomia*. For example, the graphs do not permit us to generalize that more documents including the word *pronoia* were issued in the thirteenth than in the fourteenth century. Nevertheless, the graphs do allow us to compare the relative frequency of the words *pronoia* and *oikonomia* at any particular moment. And what is most interesting is the decline of the word *pronoia* in the first quarter of the fourteenth century and the simultaneous increase in the frequency of the word *oikonomia*.

Monastic pronoiai/oikonomiai?

In order to interpret the graphs in Figures 7.1–7.3, and to explain why *oikonomia* appears to replace *pronoia* in the documents, it is necessary to turn to a subject I have deliberately sidestepped up to this point: the question of whether monasteries and other religious foundations held pronoiai or oikonomiai. Even though Fedor Uspenskij ("Značenie," 20) detected an equivalence between pronoia and oikonomia a century and a quarter ago, there has been much resistance to saying simply that the two were the same. In order to maintain his definition of pronoia as an imperial grant to laymen usually conditional on military service while acknowledging that pronoiai were often referred to as *oikonomiai*, Ostrogorsky needed to regard the institution of pronoia as a special subset of the institution of oikonomia, and he needed to dismiss all references to religious institutions and individuals holding pronoiai as imprecisions in terminology. Thus, in *Pour l'histoire de la féodalité* he regularly identified as a pronoia holder any layman who held an oikonomia, while denying that a monastery could hold a pronoia.[21]

The question of whether or not monasteries and other religious foundations held pronoiai and oikonomiai turns on how we define these institutions and on how we deal with the evidence of the sources. If we try to answer the question by a cursory examination of the terminology of the documents and of the literary sources, our initial conclusion would be that monasteries indeed held both pronoiai and oikonomiai. Chronologically, we need be concerned with the possible existence of the phenomenon no earlier than the reign of Michael VIII, because no source provides any evidence that religious foundations held pronoiai before that time. Similarly, no religious foundation could have held an oikonomia prior to the time of Michael VIII because the term "oikonomia" to denote a grant did not yet exist. But beginning with the period of Michael VIII's reign the sources do provide a number of instances in which religious institutions or clerics seem to be holding pronoiai and oikonomiai. Let us cite them, beginning with the evidence of religious foundations holding pronoiai:

[7.10] Greek praktikon for the Latin bishop of Kephalenia on Zakynthos (1264)

(i) The earliest such reference is found in the Greek praktikon of the properties of the Latin bishop of Kephalenia on Zakynthos from 1264, an island that had been in Latin hands since 1185. A list of properties is headed by the rubric "the [things] of Herakleion of the pronoia of St. George of the episcopate." Lists are also given of "the men of the pronoia of SS. Anargyroi," and of "those of the pronoia of St. George."[22]

[21] E.g., Ostrogorsky, *Féodalité*, 106–07, 126–27, 130–32, 139–40, 149, 175–76.

[22] Th. Tzannetatos, ed., *Τὸ Πρακτικὸν τῆς Λατινικῆς Ἐπισκοπῆς Κεφαλληνίας τοῦ 1264 καὶ ἡ ἐπιτομὴ αὐτοῦ, Κριτικὴ ἔκδοσις αὐτῶν* (Athens, 1965), line 916: καὶ τὰ τοῦ Ἡρακλείου τῆς προνειας [sic] τοῦ ἁγίου Γεωργίου τῆς ἐπισκοπῆς, line 1078: οἱ ἄνθρωποι τῆς προνοῖας τῶν ἁγίων Ἀναργύρων, and line 1082: οἱ τῆς προνοῖας τοῦ ἁγίου Γεωργίου. Kazhdan, *Agrarnye otnošenija*, 217. Hvostova, *Osobennosti*, 212. The *PLP*, no. 505, incorrectly claims that the priest Constantine Akridakes, one of "the men of the pronoia of SS. Anargyroi," was a pronoia holder. Moreover, other uses of the word *pronoia* in the praktikon do not necessarily imply that the bishopric held pronoiai. For instance, while the bishop held "those of the pronoia of Atres" (line 1086: οἱ τῆς προνοίας τῆς Ἄτρου), Atres was a toponym, and so the entire phrase could

(ii) In the 1279 praktikon for the monastery of Zographou discussed in the previous chapter *[6.9]* the fiscal official states, according to a variation of what would become a common formula, that the emperor had ordered him to make a fiscal revision "of the pronoiai – ecclesiastic, monastic, and personal as well as military and all the rest." In this case the official was applying the term *pronoia* to every grant of a *posotes* of fiscal revenue.

[7.11] Extract of a praktikon of Demetrios Apelmene for the monastery of Vatopedi (1300)

(iii) An extract of a praktikon, dated by its editors to 1300 and made by the fiscal official Demetrios Apelmene for the monastery of Vatopedi, begins with the phrase "Pronoia of the reverend imperial monastery of Vatopedi on the Holy Mountain." It proceeds with a list, in summary form, of the villages, *proasteia*, and other rights held by the monastery. For each village the document reports the total *telos* of the village's paroikoi, the global charges burdening the village, and the *telos* of the monastery's land in the village. For the properties within each *proasteia* and the other rights the monastery held, the document lists the *telos* in hyperpyra of each. The areas of land parcels are provided as well, but the emphasis of this document is the fiscal *posotes* of each monastic holding. Toward the end of the document Apelmene adds all of the *tele*, "the *posotes* of such oikonomia being 270 hyperpyra." Thus, a "pronoia" is referred to as an "oikonomia" which is quantified by a "*posotes*" of hyperpyra. A few months later, in January 1301, Apelmene produced a more elaborate praktikon for Vatopedi and these same holdings, and while the terms *oikonomia* and *posotes* are found in the formulaic introductory passage of the document, *pronoia* is absent.[23]

[7.12] Pachymeres on a plan for saving Asia Minor (ca. 1307)

(iv) Pachymeres suggests that monasteries and churches held pronoiai in a section of his history dealing with the failure of Andronikos II's efforts around the year 1303 to defend Asia Minor. He begins with a clear reference to pronoiai held by soldiers: "For the Roman forces were not only weakened, but abandoning pronoiai and homes, they fled the East and hastened toward the West, keeping only their lives. It was not feasible to install

be more a means of identifying a property (which had been held previously in pronoia), rather than indicating the bishopric held these people in pronoia in 1264. Cf., similarly, lines 1094 and 1098.

[23] *Vatopédi*, I, no. 29.1,15–16, and cf. *Vatopédi*, I, no. 30.

others with specified privileges."[24] And then continuing with this theme he writes that since neither military force nor negotiation seemed to offer much hope for success in countering Turkish advances in Anatolia, Andronikos II contemplated drastic action:

> Because of these things in the time of necessity [the following measure] was decreed by the impending situation: to release from [their] masters those still remaining, as many as were assigned in pronoiai to monasteries, churches, and the imperial entourage, [and] to assign [them] as soldiers, even cavalry, so that they themselves would stay and defend their own property.

But even though the patriarch was willing to acquiesce to this, "these things were wishes only" because of further Turkish inroads.[25]

[7.13] Praktikon of Tryphon Kedrenos for the monastery of Iviron mentioning the pronoia of a monastery (1316)

(v) A praktikon for Iviron from 1316 includes, among the possessions of the monastery, a paroikos named Nicholas Tzykalas "who was taken away from the pronoia of the monastery of St. George near Aigidomista." He had a wife and property and was assessed a *telos* of three hyperpyra.[26]

[24] Pachymeres, ed. Failler, ɪv, 425.15–18 (Bonn edn., ɪɪ, 389.10–13): αἱ μὲν γὰρ Ῥωμαϊκαὶ δυνάμεις οὐχ ὅπως ἐξησθένουν, ἀλλὰ καὶ, οἰκίας καὶ προνοίας ἀπολωλεκότες, ἀνατολὴν φεύγοντες ἐπὶ δύσεως ὥρμων, περιποιούμενοι ἑαυτοῖς μόνον τὸ ζῆν· ἑτέρους δ᾽ἐγκαθιστᾶν ἐπὶ ῥητοῖς γέρασιν ἀμήχανον ἦν. Cf. Charanis, "Monastic Properties," 110–11; Ostrogorsky, *Féodalité*, 100–01; Laiou, *Constantinople and the Latins*, 118; Bibikov, "Svedenija," 94; and Mutafčiev, "Vojniški zemi," 58/586, who interprets "pronoia" here as a reference to the old *stratiotika ktemata*. The elegant phrase *epi rhetois gerasin* appears in Thucydides (ɪ.13.1) with this meaning; it is used twice by Pachymeres in his history (cf. Pachymeres, ed. Failler, ɪɪ, 631.11).

[25] Pachymeres, ed. Failler, ɪv, 425.23–427.1 (Bonn edn., ɪɪ, 390.2–7): καὶ διὰ ταῦτα ἓν τῶν ἀναγκαίων ἔδοξε τῷ καιρῷ καὶ τοῖς ἐφεστῶσι πράγμασι· τὸ περιλειφθὲν τέως, ὅσον ἐν προνοίαις ἐτάττετο μοναῖς τε καὶ ἐκκλησίαις καὶ τοῖς βασιλεῖ παρασπίζουσιν, ἀφεικότας τῶν δεσποτῶν, τάττειν εἰς στρατιωτικόν, πλὴν καὶ μονοκελλικόν ξύμπαντας, ὡς ἐντεῦθεν αὐτοὺς ἐκείνους ὑπὲρ τῶν ἰδίων προσμένοντας μάχεσθαι. Except for one phrase, my translation of this often discussed passage follows A. Failler's interpretation: "Pachymeriana alia," *REB* 51 (1993), 248–59, with earlier interpretations and bibliography. I am persuaded by D. Kyritsis' argument that μο(υ)νοκελ(λ)ικόν is connected with horses: "Από χωρικοί, στρατιώτες: άλλο ένα σχόλιο σε γνωστό χωρίο του Παχυμέρη (xi.9)," in *Ψηφίδες. Μελέτες Ιστορίας, Αρχαιολογίας και Τέχνης. Στη μνήμη της Στέλλας Παπαδάκη-Oekland*, ed. O. Gratziou and H. Loukos (Herakleio, 2009), 87–94, esp. 90. In addition to his evidence, we may note that the ancient poet Poseidippos of Pella and the twelfth-century poet John Tzetzes both use μουνοκέλης and μονοκέλης, respectively, to modify horse: *Posidippi Pellaei quae supersunt omnia*, ed. C. Austin and G. Bastianini (Milan, 2002), ep. 71.1, 83.1, and *Ioannis Tzetzae historiae*, ed. P. Leone (Naples, 1968), 7.99.7, page 252 (both found in the online *TLG*).

[26] *Iviron*, ɪɪɪ, no. 74.100–01: ὃς ἀπεσπάσθη ἀπὸ τῆς προνοίας τῆς περὶ τὴν Ἀιγιδομίσταν μονῆς τοῦ ἁγίου Νικολάου.

(vi) The *Chronicle of Morea [7.2]* often mentions clergymen and religious foundations receiving and holding pronoiai. For example, when Geoffrey II Villehardouin met with the Latin clergy who refused the prince military help, Geoffrey in anger took away "the rights of all of the pronoiai of the churches" and held them himself for three years. He returned them to the clergy only when they promised to perform military service. Similarly, around 1270 Prince William "pronoia-ized four chaplains."[27]

[7.14] Chrysobull of Alexios III Komnenos, emperor of Trebizond, for the monastery of Soumela (1364)

(vii) In 1364 the emperor of Trebizond Alexios III Komnenos (1349–90) ordered that the monastery of Soumela should hold various properties as well as "the *allelengya* and the *pronoiastika* rights" as it held them previously. *Allelengyon*, evolving from its original sense as a fiscal burden on the neighbors of delinquent taxpayers, was probably the Trapezuntine equivalent of *exaleimmata*, escheated peasant properties that reverted to the monastery.[28] "Pronoiastic rights" would then be holdings specifically granted by the emperor.

Scholars have raised objections to connecting these passages with the institution of pronoia. Both the 1264 praktikon *[7.10]* and the passages from the *Chronicle of the Morea [7.2]* were influenced greatly by western European culture. David Jacoby has written that "pronoia" in the praktikon does not indicate the Byzantine institution but simply the general sense of "benefice" or even "property." Similarly, Ostrogorsky assumed that the terminology of the praktikon, because of western influence and because of the presumed poor understanding of Byzantine institutions in such a peripheral area as Zakynthos, lacked precision.[29]

To an even greater extent the same arguments can be made for the use of the word *pronoia* and its related verbal forms in the *Chronicle of the Morea.* There the verb *pronoiazo* (προνοιάζω) is used sometimes in regard

[27] *Chronicle of the Morea*, line 2651: τὰ δίκαια τῶν προνοίων ὁλῶν τῶν ἐκκλησίων, and lines 7795–96: ἐπρόνοιασεν τέσσαρους καπελλάνους. Kazhdan, *Agrarnye otnošenija*, 222. B. Gorjanov, *Pozdnevizantijskij feodalizm* (Moscow, 1962), 46. Other passages: lines 2639, 2667, 2690, 2696. Ostrogorsky, *Féodalité*, 60. Jacoby, "Archontes grecs," 434.

[28] MM, v, 279.5: τὰ ἀλληλέγγυα καὶ προνοιαστικὰ δίκαια. Kazhdan, *Agrarnye otnošenija*, 218. M. Bartusis, "Ἐξάλειμμα: Escheat in Byzantium," *Dumbarton Oaks Papers* 40 (1986), 61 note 38. *ODB*, s.v. "allelengyon." For another example of the term *allelengyon* in Trebizond: V. Laurent, "Deux chrysobulles inédits des empereurs de Trébizonde Alexis IV–Jean IV et David II," *Ἀρχεῖον Πόντου* 18 (1953), 262 lines 58–59, 265 line 103.

[29] Jacoby, "Archontes grecs," 436. Ostrogorsky, *Féodalité*, 104 note 1.

to Byzantines, as when Villehardouin "pronoia-ized" (ἐπρονοιασέ τους) three Greek archons from Monemvasia. But most commonly it is applied in regard to Latins where it can best be translated as "to enfief." For example, Geoffrey II Villehardouin once commanded his vassals to ready themselves for a campaign "to conquer the places which were pronoia-ized" but had not yet been divided. Similarly, Villehardouin "likewise pronoia-ized Sir Otto de Dourna to hold Kalavryta and twelve fiefs."[30] At one point Villehardouin "called for the book in which was written the share of each man and that which had been allotted to each to hold and to administer by [William of] Champlitte. Therein they found who were pronoia-ized." After enumerating the twelve baronies into which the principality was divided, the author adds, "We do not name the knights who each had a fief, as well as the sergeants who were pronoia-ized, because of the amount of writing it would require." Nevertheless, Villehardouin and Champlitte determined "which held the pronoiai, [and] who pronoia-ized them." The use of *pronoia* side by side with *fie* (φίε) in the lists of the number of fiefs attributed to Frankish knights, to Latin prelates and their chapters, and to religious orders led Jacoby to conclude that *pronoia* in the Greek version of the chronicle "is not a precise technical or juridical term."[31]

Similarly, we may question the significance of the document for the Soumela monastery of Trebizond *[7.14]*, since it originated on the fringes, or at least outside the mainstream of Byzantine civilization.

In the passage from Pachymeres' history *[7.12]*, it is clear that he was using the word *pronoia* in a technical sense; that the word appears in its plural form makes that certain. Nevertheless, as is often the case in his history, *pronoia* appears in the sense of property granted by the emperor under any circumstances and conditions. For Pachymeres, monasteries and churches could be said to hold "pronoiai." Thus, we should interpret the passage to mean that, since many soldiers had fled their pronoiai and it was not possible to install new pronoia soldiers, Andronikos was planning to turn the properties that had been held as "pronoiai," that is, any kind of imperial grants, by monasteries, churches, and laymen over to the paroikoi

[30] *Chronicle*, lines 2955, 2020: τοὺς τόπους ὅπου ἐπρονοιάστησαν νὰ τοὺς ἔχουν κερδίσει, and lines 1939–40: Τὸν μισὲρ Ὄτον ντὲ Ντουρνᾶ ἐπρόνοιασεν ὡσαύτως νὰ ἔχῃ τὰ Καλάβρυτα καὶ φίε δέκα καὶ δύο. Kazhdan, *Agrarnye otnošenija*, 222.

[31] *Chronicle*, line 1911: ἐν τούτῳ ηὑρέθησαν ἐκεῖ ὅπου ἦσαν προνοιασμένοι, lines 1965–67: Οἱ καβαλλάριοι, / ὅπου εἴχασιν πρὸς ἕνα φίε ὁ καθένας, / καὶ οἱ σιργέντες, ἀλλὰ δή, ὅπου ἦσαν προνοιασμένοι, / οὐδὲν τοὺς ὀνομάζομεν διὰ τὴν πολυγραφίαν, and line 1973: ὅπου εἶχαν τὲς προνοῖες, ὅπερ τοὺς ἐπρονοιάσαν. Uspenskij, "Značenie," 9–10. Jacoby, "Archontes grecs," 433–34, 436.

who had remained on the land. These paroikoi would then be enlisted as soldiers in the hope that they would stay and defend the area.

Pachymeres tells us little about the people and the properties involved. If the paroikoi were the kind of paroikoi we typically encounter at the time, they had been rendering to their lord, lay or monastic, their *telos*, secondary charges, and corvée labor, and very likely they rented land from their lord for which they paid a rent. If according to the plan they had been "released" from these burdens, then, in return for military service, they would have received freedom from taxation, and, effectively, the land of the lords that they had been working would have become theirs. (If the plan had materialized, a decision would have had to have been made about whether they would pay the normal taxes on this land). The plan would have created a body of smallholding soldiers, which appear from time to time in late Byzantium.[32]

Imprecision in terminology has been cited to explain the appearance of the word *pronoia* in the Zographou praktikon as well *[6.9]*. In passages paralleling the key phrase in other praktika one finds "properties" (*ktemata*) rather than "pronoiai." As already quoted in Chapter 6, Ostrogorsky thought that "one can only conclude that the terminology of the [1279] praktikon . . . is not precise." The same argument could be made for the passages from the praktika for Vatopedi *[7.11]* and Iviron *[7.13]*. Should we conclude that the use of the word *pronoia* in these documents is due to "imprecise" terminology also? It is not difficult to see that there is a problem with this line of reasoning. Scholars who consider pronoia "in its technical sense" as a grant on condition of service are forced to regard the term's association with monasteries and the clergy as the product of "imprecise terminology." Following Ostrogorsky, Ksenia Hvostova wrote, "As for pronoia and oikonomia in monastic documents, this signifies the administration of various economic objects, i.e., they [the words] are not used not in a technical sense, but in a broader sense, in accord with their etymology."[33]

The case for monasteries holding oikonomiai is much more compelling, at least at first glance. In the introductory formulas of praktika for monasteries from 1300 to 1341 we find many explicit references to monasteries "holding oikonomia." By "formulas," I mean the preambles of praktika (and sometimes including the concluding section as well) in which the fiscal official states that he was ordered to make a fiscal revision in a particular area. It was the fashion among fiscal assessors to begin their praktika

32 See Bartusis, *Late Byzantine Army*, 77, and Bartusis, "Smallholding Soldiers," 8, where I refer to this passage as an ambiguous example of smallholding soldiers.

33 Ostrogorsky, *Féodalité*, 104 note 1. Hvostova, *Osobennosti*, 215 note 39.

with some version of a statement along the following lines: "Since I have been ordered by the emperor to make a fiscal reassessment of the properties in theme A. and to confer on each the *posotes* of his own oikonomia, I have found monastery N. holding an oikonomia (*katechousan oikonomian*), and I confer this (or, this oikonomia) upon it." In twenty-three documents these formulas contain the word *oikonomia* one, two, or three times.[34]

If *pronoia* and *oikonomia* were synonymous, then, as Ihor Ševčenko once bluntly noted, there is monastic pronoia.[35] One could just as well speak of a monastery's "oikonomia" as a "pronoia." It would appear conclusive that monasteries held something called "oikonomiai." However, two facts complicate the matter: (a) aside from these documents in which the term *oikonomia* appears within the introductory formula, there are only four acts issued by state officials which refer to an oikonomia held by a religious institution.

(i) The extract from an earlier fiscal register entitled "Pronoia of the . . . monastery of Vatopedi." This document was cited above *[7.11]* as one of the few that refer to a pronoia held by a monastery. At the end of the document we read that the "*posotes* of this oikonomia" amounted to 270 hyperpyra.

(ii) A 1321 praktikon for the soldier Michael Saventzes *[8.11]* which lists a number of paroikoi in a certain village "from the oikonomia of the reverend monastery of Akapniou" (*Xénophon*, no. 15.12).

(iii) A *periorismos* from before 1337 which describes a property of 1,000 modioi held by the monastery of the Theotokos at Trilission (northeast of Serres). The official writes that the land was inscribed "inside the *posotes* of the oikonomia" of this monastery (*Prodrome B*, no. 121.21).

(iv) A praktikon of the *protokynegos* John Vatatzes from April 1341 that put Iviron in possession of a small, but substantial number of *metochia*, *ktemata*, and other properties in the vicinity of Serres which it had

[34] *Vatopédi*, I, no. 30 (1301), II, no. 70.3 (1322–26), no. 81.4 (1338); *Xéropotamou*, no. 18A.2–3 (ca. 1300), no. 18D, I.5–6 (ca. 1315–20), no. 18E, I.5–7 (ca. 1320–25); *Esphigménou*, no. 8.2–3 (ca. 1300), no. 14.2–6 (1318), no. 15.4–8 (1321), no. 16.3–5 (1321); *Iviron*, III, no. 59.2 (1262), no. 70.1–4 (1301), no. 74.4 (1316), no. 75.2–7 (1318), no. 79.5–6; IV, no. 85.5 (1341), no. 86.2 (1341), no. 87.1–2 (1341); *Zographou*, no. 15.2–6 (1315?), no. 17.5–10 (1320); *Xénophon*, no. 12.2–4 (1318); and *Lavra*, II, no. 111.1–2 (1321), no. 112.2 (1321?). In two cases at the end of such a praktikon there is another phrase noting that the monastery should hold the things belonging to it "concerning this oikonomia": *Iviron*, IV, no. 86.459 (1341), no. 87.245 (1341). And note *Xénophon*, no. 13.4–5 (1320), which, because it follows the pattern of *Xénophon*, no. 12, and because it replaces "the *posotes* of his own oikonomia" with "his own *poson*," loses any reference to the monastery having an oikonomia.

[35] I. Ševčenko, "An Important Contribution to the Social History of Late Byzantium," *The Annals of the Ukrainian Academy of Arts and Sciences in the U.S.*, 2, pt. 4 (1952), 458.

Table 7.1 Number of documents which mention a monastery or an individual holding an oikonomia (1259–1373)

	Oikonomia held by a monastery	Oikonomia held by an individual or a group of individuals
documents issued by an emperor	1 (1275)	25
documents issued by an official		
oikonomia appears only within a formula	23 (first appearance in 1262; all others 1300–41)	4 (first appearance ca. 1297)
oikonomia appears outside of a formula	4 (1300, 1321, before 1337, 1341)	8
private acts	0	5

held by virtue of chrysobulls, *prostagmata*, fiscal recensions, and other documents. Vatatzes states that these properties were free of all taxes (*eleuthera kai akatadoulota*) "and not reckoned in the *posotes* of the oikonomia of such reverend monastery."[36]

To put this number of references in perspective, we may note that while the extant documents contain far fewer references to the holdings of laymen than to those of monasteries, there are eight documents issued by officials and referring to the oikonomiai of individuals in which the reference is not part of a formula.

(b) The second fact that casts doubt on whether religious foundations held oikonomiai is derived from a comparison of acts issued by the emperor himself. While twenty-five acts issued by the emperor refer to oikonomiai held by individuals, only one act issued by the emperor uses the word *oikonomia* in reference to monastic landholdings. This one act was issued by Michael VIII in 1275 *[6.7]* which twice mentions a set of properties with a *posotes* of 300 hyperpyra conferred through a praktikon on a monastery "for its oikonomia" and once "for the sake of its oikonomia." In 1275 we are still in the early days of the institution of oikonomia, when the word did not necessarily have the concrete sense it would acquire.

These observations are summarized in Table 7.1. The documents issued by emperors are mostly scattered evenly throughout the period, except for a cluster of seven from 1342 to 1351, the era of the second civil wars. The documents issued by fiscal officials are evenly distributed around the

36 *Iviron*, IV, no. 85.4–5. The monastery acquired these properties before 1310, but the details are unknown: *Iviron*, III, p. 17. The editors (*Iviron*, IV, p. 20) interpret this as an exemption from all taxes, unusual in that only one property has a tax even listed, and that these properties would not even be considered in the fiscal books of the treasury.

Table 7.2 Number of documents which mention a monastery or an individual holding a pronoia (1262–1341)

	Pronoiai held by a monastery	Pronoiai held by an individual or a group of individuals
issued by an emperor	0	4 (all date to the period 1262–1300)
issued by an official		
pronoia appears only within a formula	1 (1279)	1 (same document as at left)
pronoia or a related term appears outside of a formula	2 (1300 and 1316)	15
private acts	0	4

three periods of fiscal activity: around 1300, around 1320, and around 1340.

From the evidence of documents issued by emperors, one would conclude that, as a rule, only individuals held oikonomiai; monasteries, churches, and any other corporate entity did not. What of the appearance of *oikonomia* in the documents of imperial officials? Why should emperors not speak of monasteries holding oikonomiai, but officials do so regularly? The answer, it seems, lies in the introductory formula for praktika. This preamble was established in the later thirteenth century, at a time when a grant of privileges to either individuals or corporate entities was called an *oikonomia*. This was connected to the introduction of the *posotes* to quantify imperial grants, regardless of the recipient. But after the reign of Michael VIII, perhaps even during the later years of his reign, the concept of monastic oikonomiai was abandoned. However, the phraseology of the introductory passages of praktika was maintained, and so the concept was kept as well as a kind of archaism. Henceforth, with only a few exceptions, emperors, officials, and private individuals restricted the use of the term *oikonomia* – at least in the documents – to the privileges granted to individuals.

A related phenomenon is observed in Table 7.2, a similar table made for the term *pronoia*. There we see that during the fourteenth century emperors did not use the word *pronoia* in their documents at all. Rather, it was imperial officials and the authors of private acts who kept the term alive. As for monasteries or any corporate entity holding pronoiai, there are but three documents that make the connection: the 1279 praktikon *[6.9]*, created during that period when terminology was still in flux, and two praktika from the early fourteenth century. One is the 1300 extract from a fiscal register *[7.11]* which also connects *oikonomia* to a monastery, and the other is the long praktikon from 1316 which makes a casual reference to a paroikos taken from the "pronoia" of a small monastery *[7.13]*.

In summary, with the exception of the introductory formulas of praktika, a mere *six* documents, one issued by the emperor in 1275 and the rest issued by imperial officials, refer to monasteries holding *either* pronoiai or oikonomiai, while scores of imperial acts, official acts, and private acts refer to individuals holding pronoiai or oikonomiai. This disparity is all the more dramatic given that the overwhelming majority of documents preserved from the thirteenth and fourteenth centuries deal with the property possessions of monasteries.

The only way to explain the data in the table is to suggest that *oikonomia* and *pronoia* were being used in a slightly broader sense by fiscal officials. To a fiscal official there was a fiscal and administrative equivalence between the holdings of monasteries and the imperial grants held by individuals. The elements of both were identical and fungible. But for the emperor there were important functional differences between the privileges granted to monasteries and the privileges granted to individuals. The former were more or less permanent while the latter were temporary, in theory if not also in practice. The former were not connected to any particular services to the state, while the latter usually were. And while hereditary rights were a matter that increasingly came up with grants to individuals, they were irrelevant in regard to grants to monasteries.

What did an official in, say, 1300, think of when he heard the word "pronoia"? I think he thought of an imperial grant consisting of the transfer of state fiscal resources to a privileged recipient. These resources were (i) the right to tax revenues collected by the grantee directly from a group of properties and taxpaying peasants, (ii) the right to collect rents or enjoy the harvest from state property, and/or (iii) the right to the labor services of peasants. Large or small, conditional on service to the crown or simply at the emperor's pleasure, temporary or permanent, for a single individual, a group, or an institution, the fiscal and economic aspects were similar.

But this does not explain Table 7.2, in which we see that fiscal officials continued to use the term *pronoia* long after imperial acts ceased employing it. My hypothesis to explain this phenomenon is that, despite the official shift to *oikonomia* to denote imperial grants to individuals, common speech maintained *pronoia* as a term to denote any kind of imperial grant to an individual and perhaps even extended its use to imperial grants to religious foundations.

The literary sources help illustrate this. Only two literary sources employ either *pronoia* or *oikonomia* in their fiscal sense more than once or twice.

These are the history of Pachymeres and the *Chronicle of the Morea*. Pachymeres uses *pronoia* in its technical sense in ten passages and *oikonomia* in three. Two of the passages using *oikonomia* also use *pronoia*. *Oikonomia* is used in connection with properties granted to two Turkish magnates who entered Byzantine service under Michael VIII *[8.28]*, to Michael VIII's brother John prior to 1272 *[7.5]*, and to soldiers toward the end of the thirteenth century *[8.25]*. As for pronoia, according to Pachymeres, soldiers, religious institutions, and aristocrats could be granted pronoiai.

Similarly, while the passages in the *Chronicle of the Morea [7.2]* referring to pronoiai have little to do with the Byzantine institution, the author uses *pronoia* (or a word directly based on *pronoia* such as verbal forms) thirty-three or thirty-five times (depending on the manuscript) to refer to any landholding conferred by an authority on anyone or any religious foundation;[37] *oikonomia* appears but twice in the entire work and has the sense of a payment in kind.[38] In the chronicle, "pronoia" appears to be a translation of "fief," which, in the thirteenth and fourteenth centuries, could mean just about any kind of landholding.

What do we make of these sources? I think Pachymeres and the *Chronicle of the Morea* provide some evidence of a third category of usage, aside from that found in imperial documents and in official documents: common speech. Pachymeres generally does not shy away from using the technical words of the day, particularly in fiscal matters. So rather than saying that he was using the word *pronoia* in an "imprecise" sense when he writes of monasteries or churches holding pronoiai, I would conclude that he was using the common term for referring to privileged properties in the early fourteenth century, regardless of who held them. And the chronicle uses the word *pronoia* as frequently as it does because that was a common way to refer to privileged properties in the fourteenth century, at the time it was composed or translated.

Thus, there are three types of usage for the fiscal terms *pronoia* and *oikonomia*: (i) the language used by the emperor in his documents, (ii) the language used by imperial officials in their documents and the language used in private acts, and (iii) the common speech of the day. According to imperial documents, only laymen ever held pronoiai and oikonomiai, and during the fourteenth century, laymen held only oikonomiai. From

[37] The content in *Chronicle of the Morea*, ed. Schmitt, line 2690, in the H and T manuscripts is simply absent from the P manuscript, and for προνοίαν in the H and T manuscripts (line 864), P reads φέον. Word-counts from the online *TLG*.

[38] Oikonomia: *Chronicle of the Morea*, ed. Schmitt (manuscript P), lines 5265 and 6600, and (manuscripts H and T), lines 5265 and 8184.

1259 to the later fourteenth century, emperors used the word *oikonomia* in their documents to designate grants to laymen which included a service obligation, and after 1272 through the beginning of the fifteenth century, with only a few exceptions, emperors did not use the word *pronoia* at all in their documents. According to the language of imperial officials, the assemblage of properties and privileges granted to a monastery could be called an oikonomia and, probably following common parlance, a pronoia. According to common parlance, the privileges and properties held through imperial grant by religious foundations could be called either pronoiai or oikonomiai.

I like to think that if you asked anyone in Byzantium during the fourteenth century whether monasteries held pronoiai or oikonomiai, the answer probably would have been, "Of course." But if you pursued the matter and asked whether monasteries held their "pronoiai" and "oikonomiai" in the same way as laymen, including soldiers, the answer probably would have been, "Well, of course not." And, further, if you pointed out that no act issued by a fourteenth-century emperor refers to any monastery holding a pronoia or an oikonomia, the response probably would have been, "Yes, technically, monasteries don't hold pronoiai or oikonomiai." If your conversation partner was an imperial *apographeus*, and if you asked why then did he write of monasteries holding oikonomiai in the preambles of praktika, he would probably have answered, "That's the formula we use."

My point is that it was no careless slip when an imperial official wrote of a monastery's pronoia or oikonomia. As I wrote in the previous chapter, if we posit that monasteries and churches did not hold pronoiai in the twelfth century, and if we posit that there was no change in the manner by which monasteries and churches held property in the thirteenth (and fourteenth) century, then one cannot say that they held pronoiai. There was no significant change in the various ways by which religious foundations held property from the twelfth to the fourteenth century. So when fiscal officials in the fourteenth century refer to monasteries as holding pronoiai or oikonomiai, they were using a terminology different from the emperor's. In everyday usage, probably any landholder who benefitted from an imperial concession over a property could be said to have held either a pronoia or an oikonomia.[39]

[39] And this is an answer to the rhetorical question posed by Carile, "Sulla pronoia nel Peloponneso bizantino," 60. As he attempted to prove that the word *pronoia* in the *Chronicle of the Morea* was a reference to the Byzantine institution of pronoia, he asked how the chronicle's author could possibly have confused hereditary landholdings with pronoiai.

So, did monasteries hold oikonomiai and pronoiai? The answer depends on whose terminology one wishes to adopt, that of the emperors, that of fiscal officials, or that of common parlance. Because acts issued by the emperor tend to pay more attention to terminology than do the acts of officials or private individuals, one's answer might have a bias toward the emperors and their terminology. As far as the emperors were concerned only individuals held oikonomiai or pronoiai. On the other hand, fiscal officials commonly applied the term *oikonomia* and sometimes *pronoia* to both. The point has been made by Jacques Lefort that the *posotes*, oikonomia, or fiscal income of a monastery, according to the documents, is of the same nature as what constitutes the pronoia of a soldier. The difference comes in the scale of the holding and the eternal character of monastic possession. "But the notion of oikonomia suffices henceforth to the fisc to guarantee and control the revenues that the state consigns to the monks, and to soldiers and their obligations."[40] Nevertheless, I must conclude that it is unproductive to suggest that monasteries held pronoiai or oikonomiai. These were ordinarily limited concessions which ordinarily could be revoked by the state. Imperial grants to monasteries were never so regarded. For our purposes, then, monasteries and other religious foundations did not hold pronoiai or oikonomiai.

Let us propose a chronology for the interrelation of the words *pronoia* and *oikonomia*:

(i) *Pronoia* first appears as a technical designation for a kind of imperial grant during the twelfth century. Until the reign of Michael VIII it is the only term used to designate pronoiai. *Oikonomia* does not appear as a fiscal term at all.

(ii) Under Michael VIII *oikonomia* was introduced as a replacement for *pronoia* and to designate grants to monasteries as well. This was a result of the process of introducing the *posotes* as a means of quantifying imperial grants. The first extant documents that clearly use *oikonomia* in a fiscal sense – from 1259 *[6.1]* and from 1261 *[6.2]* – deal with arrangements between the state and laymen. These two documents also illustrate the novelty of the use of the word *oikonomia* in a fiscal sense. They employ the word in uncommon phrases: "for oikonomia" and "for the sake of oikonomia." The former phrase does not appear in any other document, and the latter in only one other document, from 1275 *[6.7]*. The notion should be discarded that *oikonomia* appeared first in a context involving

[40] J. Lefort, "Une grande fortune foncière aux xᵉ–xɪɪɪᵉ s.: les biens du monastère d'Iviron," in *Structure féodales et féodalisme dans l'occident méditerranéen (xᵉ–xɪɪɪᵉ s.)* (Rome, 1980), 741.

religious foundations, and only later was it applied to arrangements involving laymen.

(iii) After the reign of Michael VIII, emperors, in their documents, tend to designate pronoia grants exclusively as *oikonomiai*. Of the sixteen documents containing a form of the word *pronoia* issued between 1214 and 1272, nine are either *prostagmata* or chrysobulls. But after 1272 and until the fifteenth century, there is only one extant imperial document that uses any form of the word *pronoia* (noun, adjective, verb, etc.) in its technical sense: a chrysobull of Michael IX from 1299–1300 *[8.68]*. *Oikonomia* became the official term for a conditional imperial grant of properties and privileges to an individual or a group of individuals during, at least, most of the fourteenth century. By "official term," I mean the word that emperors used in their official documents. Emperors used this word exclusively to denote this type of grant and they referred to this type of grant exclusively as an *oikonomia*. In imperial documents grants to monasteries had no specific name, and other types of grants to individuals were sometimes called gifts (*doreai*), or by no specific term.

(iv) After the reign of Michael VIII and through the middle of the fourteenth century, imperial officials continue to use the term *oikonomia* within the introductory clauses of praktika, to designate not only pronoia grants to laymen, but imperial grants to monasteries as well. Otherwise, imperial officials only rarely use *oikonomia* to designate a grant to a monastery. After 1301, only six fourteenth-century documents issued by imperial officials make any mention of the word *pronoia* or its other forms. Of these six, four documents are revisions of documents from 1301.

(v) In the fourteenth century, if not somewhat earlier, the documents of laymen refer to their imperial grants of pronoiai as pronoiai and oikonomiai interchangeably. In common speech, I suspect that *pronoia* was the normal term applied by everyone – emperors, officials, other laymen, and the clergy – to refer to imperial grants (or any property over which any imperial concession was granted) to laymen as well as to religious foundations and that *oikonomia* was used less frequently and more formally.

(vi) From 1360 to 1400 the near absence of *oikonomia* can be attributed to the loss of Macedonia, which, in turn, led to a dramatic decrease in the production of documents.

(vii) In the early fifteenth century, the term *pronoia*, in the form *pronoiarios*, makes a reappearance in documents issued by emperors. But this is getting ahead of our story, and this will be dealt with in detail in Chapter 9.

In brief, it seems that the word *oikonomia* gradually replaced *pronoia* and its various forms in the vocabulary of the chancery in the course of the second half of the thirteenth century and the early fourteenth century. It is reasonable to conclude that the words *pronoia* and *oikonomia*, when used to describe the particular kind of fiscal arrangement with which we are concerned, were synonymous, and that they represent an evolution in fiscal terminology. I conclude that, during the fourteenth century, in common parlance, among emperors, among officials, and among private individuals, these temporary imperial grants to laymen were generally called "pronoiai," as they had been in the thirteenth century. On the other hand, an "oikonomia," in common parlance, was any imperial grant, to an individual or to a monastery, a usage that began during the reign of Michael VIII and which continued to appear in the introductory formulas of praktika drawn up by imperial officials throughout the fourteenth century. Yet, in the fourteenth century, emperors, in their documents, restricted the use of the word *oikonomia* to limited imperial grants to individuals alone.

Posotes

Ostrogorsky felt that the connection between the word *posotes* and the institution of pronoia was so strong that whenever a document mentions a property's *posotes*, the subject was a pronoia grant. By the same token, he believed that when reference is made to a property without any mention of the words *posotes* or *oikonomia*, or *pronoia*, one should conclude that the property was held as a patrimonial property and not as part of a pronoia grant.[41] If Ostrogorsky's view is correct, we could greatly expand the number of known examples of pronoia, because many documents use the words *posotes* or *poson* with no mention of *oikonomia* or *pronoia*.

Unfortunately, the matter is not so simple. There are instances when a *posotes* is cited but the property holding was clearly not a pronoia. Such is the case of the *posotes* of forty hyperpyra granted to the *hegoumenos* Gervasios *[7.9]*. He was given the right to alienate the property and so we are not dealing with a pronoia. Similarly, the village of Prevista, with a *posotes* of 300 hyperpyra, was sold by the *megale doukaina* Theodora Palaiologina to the ruler of Bulgaria who then donated the village to a monastery (*Zographou*, no. 22). However she came into possession of Prevista, by the time she sold it, it could not be considered a pronoia. Nevertheless, it is easy to explain why both of these properties were quantified by a *posotes*. Gervasios' *posotes* had been taken from another individual who quite likely had held it as a

[41] Ostrogorsky, *Féodalité*, 107 note 1, 122–23.

pronoia. And Prevista, even though it had once been held by Alexios Raoul *[8.15]*, did not remain in Raoul's family, and thus was most likely held by Raoul as a pronoia. So, in both cases, the property with a *posotes* was not part of a pronoia at the time it is mentioned in the relevant document, but had been at an earlier time. But, still, properties quantified by a *posotes* were not necessarily part of an earlier pronoia grant; they may have been part of a simple gift to an individual or monastery, unconnected with the institution of pronoia at all. In other words, any property with a *posotes* had, at some point, entered the system of imperial grants, whether as a simple gift or as all or part of a pronoia. Thus, the quantification of a property by a *posotes* is a clue that the property might be or might have been all or part of a pronoia grant, but, in the absence of other information, a connection with pronoia, while quite possible, cannot be taken for granted.

Imperial grants of properties which had earlier been held by an individual or group of individuals

[7.15] Act of George Pharisaios for Demetrios Plytos (1322/3)

Another indication that we are dealing with a pronoia are references in which an individual or a religious foundation was granted property that was earlier held by now deceased individuals. For example, according to an act of George Pharisaios, around 1322 Demetrios Plytos was granted by the emperor "two *exaleimmatika stasia* of the deceased Trypanes and of Kekeris, [earlier] held by the deceased Tzainos." Trypanes and Kekeris were the original peasant proprietors of the *stasia*, Tzainos was the individual who received the *stasia* when the peasants died without heir. Because the properties did not remain in Tzainos' family, he most likely (though not certainly) held them as a pronoia grant. At the same time, Plytos was granted 900 modioi of land in the village of Chartophylakos which two soldiers of the Thessalonian *mega allagion*, "the deceased *sevastos* Euthymios Kardames and *kyr* Demetrios Isauros, held earlier."[42] A property taken from a soldier after his death and conferred on another individual strongly suggests (though does not prove) that the soldier held the property as a part of a pronoia grant.

[42] *Xénophon*, no. 19.1–4. Lefort, *Villages de Macédoine*, 52. On a Demetrios Isauros, see *Xéropotamou*, no. 22.9 (1317–34), where he holds a property on the Longos peninsula. Also, an Isauros (without first name) held land in Tylimne (location unknown) of 450 modioi, which in 1321 was attributed to Nicholas Maroules: *Xénophon*, no. 16.24. For the term *exaleimmatika stasia*, see below, pp. 377–79.

Property not held "in the manner of hereditary property"

The case of Demetrios Plytos introduces yet another phrase to (help) identify a pronoia grant. According to the act from 1322/3 Plytos received the 900 modioi of land and the two *exaleimmatika stasia* "as a benefaction [εὐηργέτηθη] through a divine and worshipful *prostagma kata logon gonikotetos*." The use of the verb *euergeto* (εὐεργετῶ, "to confer as a benefaction") strongly suggests that this was a new grant and not a pronoia grant. More importantly, the document introduces us to the phrase *kata logon gonikotetos* (κατὰ λόγον γονικότητος), which appears exclusively in documents from the fourteenth and fifteenth centuries.

The word *gonikotes* (γονικότης) is an abstract noun which, according to the online *TLG*, does not appear before the fourteenth century. It is formed from *gonikos* (γονικός) "belonging to one's parents, paternal, ancestral, patrimonial" (as, for example, νεότης "youth" is formed from νέος "young"). Therefore, the literal meaning of the phrase *kata logon gonikotetos* should be something like "by reason of patrimoniality" or, in clearer English, "by reason of hereditary transmission," or, simply, "by reason of inheritance." But such a literal rendering of the phrase does not work in our documents. In the most obvious case, monasteries often held property *kata logon gonikotetos*. For example, in what may be the earliest appearance of the phrase, a private act from 1307 or 1308 documenting the sale of a field to Hilandar, the sellers state that the monastery should hold the property henceforth "in full authority, absolutely, as its own, and *kata logon gonikotetos*."[43] Here, no literal rendering of the phrase will do. Obviously a monastery could not strictly hold a property "by inheritance." But even if we might say that a property held by a monastery for generations had passed "as patrimony" through the generations of the corporate body, Hilandar had *purchased* the property in the 1307–08 act. Therefore, the phrase *kata logon gonikotetos* denoted not how a property holder acquired the property, but the status of the property once it was held.

What was this status and from what other statuses did it differ? The use of the word *gonikon* preceded the use of *gonikotes* and is often encountered

[43] *Chilandar*, ed. Živojinović, I, no. 24.9: κυρίως, αὐθεντικῶς, ἰδικῶς καὶ κατὰ λόγον γονικότητος. (The world year of the Hilandar document corresponds to 1307, while the indiction corresponds to 1308. For some reason, the editors of the act assume "without doubt" that an incorrect world year is the source of the discordance.) The next extant document with the phrase is the chrysobull for Panaretos from 1313 *[8.41]*. Other examples of monasteries holding property *kata logon gonikotetos*: *Prodrome*, no. 25.12–13 (1329–41?) = *Prodrome B*, no. 218 (1338); *Xénophon*, no. 23.50 (1335); *Docheiariou*, no. 22.29 (1344); and *Lavra*, III, no. 141.22 (1362).

in connection with imperial grants beginning in the second half of the thirteenth century. Ordinarily the word means "patrimonial" or "hereditary." It can also be used as a noun meaning "patrimony" or "hereditary property." *Gonikon* could be owned by anyone, including peasants, and, generally speaking, it indicated the origin of the property: from one's parents. Beginning in the thirteenth century, even the property of monasteries was often referred to as *gonikon* in the sense of the property that a monastery had held for generations.[44] Thus, *gonikon* represented a type of ownership, more secure than property acquired, say, via purchase. Yet, when the word was connected to imperial grants, it took on a slightly different meaning. We have a very early example of this in a private act from November 1284. The *tzaousios* George Melissenos donated property to the Lemviotissa monastery including some houses "which the . . . emperor granted to me as my *gonika* [ὡς γονικά μου] in exchange for the houses which he took from me" *[8.62]*. Here *gonika* cannot be translated as "patrimony"; rather, it is property that the emperor granted the status of patrimony. And the most salient feature of patrimony is that one had the right to pass it on to one's heirs. And so in passages like this, *gonikon* can be best translated as "hereditary property," but only in the sense of property that could be bequeathed to one's heirs. The status of property as *gonikon* may have also included the right to improve the property.

The complex technical sense of both terms, *gonikon* and *gonikotes*, is demonstrated in an act of a fiscal official from 1337. The official put Docheiariou in possession of some property with these words: the monastery "ought to hold this [property] *kata logon gonikotetos* as it held [it] from the beginning, and to make and do with it all that [one can do] with the other *gonika* properties belonging to it, both from purchase and donation" (*Docheiariou*, no. 18.19–22). *Gonikon* here could mean neither property inherited from one's parents nor property that one may pass to one's heirs; indeed, the official suggests that two of the ways the monastery could acquire such property was through purchase or donation. There was only one other normal way for a monastery to acquire property and that was through imperial grant. It seems then that *gonika* property, property held "as *gonika*," and property held "by reason of *gonikotes*," all meant property acquired in a way other than through imperial grant, *even if it had been acquired through an imperial grant.* What makes the concept so peculiar is

[44] E.g., *Patmos*, II, no. 70.33 (1271): τὰ γονικὰ ἴδια χωράφια τῆς . . . μονῆς. Generally, see *ODB*, s.v. "gonikon," and E. Patlagean, "Γονικόν. Note sur la propriété allodiale à Byzance," in *Βυζάντιο. Κράτος και Κοινονία. Μνήμη Νίκου Οικονομίδη*, ed. A. Avramea et al. (Athens, 2003), 423–34.

that the emperor could *transform* property within an imperial grant *into gonikon* property. In one of the rare uses of a verbal form of the word, a man asked that the emperor "make *gonikon* for him" (γονικευθῇ αὐτῷ) 2,000 modioi of land *[8.40]*.[45]

So how should we translate this phrase *kata logon gonikotetos*? In one specific case Oikonomides suggested "as if it were his hereditary property."[46] But what of the cases in which the property holder actually *did* hold the property "by reason of patrimony"? I prefer to translate the phrase *kata logon gonikotetos* as "in the manner of hereditary property." Nevertheless, the phrase seems to be used for the most part in connection with properties benefitting from imperial benefaction.

[7.16] Chrysobull of Andronikos III Palaiologos for Theodotos Kalothetos (1328)

For example, in a chrysobull of Andronikos III from April 1328 the emperor granted the request of Theodotos Kalothetos to be given through chrysobull land of 900 modioi near the village of Tzangaroioannou "which the deceased Pantavenos Chadenos held." Kalothetos had asked to hold the land tax-free, as well as *kata logon gonikotetos*, with the right to improve it, transmit it to his heirs, and alienate it. The emperor permitted him to hold this land "without any *telos* and burden [line 11: ἐκτὸς τέλους καὶ βάρους παντός] *kata logon gonikotetos*," with the right to improve it, transmit it to his legitimate children and heirs, and, if he so chose, to alienate it through gift, sale, exchange, or donation to a religious foundation, "as owners [*despotai*] do with their property."[47] The right conferred comes as close to complete *dominium* as was possible in Byzantium.

[7.17] Chrysobull of John V Palaiologos for Xene Soultanina (1344)

The appearance of the phrase *kata logon gonikotetos* or *gonikon* indicates that the grant involved was not a pronoia/oikonomia. In one of the few cases

[45] Another example: *Lavra*, III, no. 139.95–96 (1361): ὑπόστασις . . . γονικευθείσης ἐκείνῳ διὰ προσκυνητοῦ προστάγματος.

[46] N. Oikonomides, "The Properties of the Deblitzenoi in the Fourteenth and Fifteenth Centuries," in *Charanis Studies*, ed. A. Laiou-Thomadakis (New Brunswick, NJ, 1980), 177.

[47] *Vatopédi*, I, no. 66. Prior to 1356, a Kalothetos (Theodotos or one of his heirs) donated this property to Vatopedi: *Vatopédi*, II, no. 108.24–25, and *Vatopédi*, I, p. 367, citing M. Goudas, "Βυζαντιακὰ ἔγγραφα τῆς ἐν Ἄθῳ ἱερᾶς μονῆς τοῦ Βατοπεδίου," *Ἐπετηρὶς Ἑταιρείας Βυζαντινῶν Σπουδῶν* 4 (1927), 239.

when the term *gonikon* appears with oikonomia, the object was to show that what was once an oikonomia was no longer. Thus, a chrysobull of John V from 1344 notes that the deceased Alexios Palaiologos Soultanos, husband of the nun Xene Soultanina, had possessed by chrysobull an oikonomia with a *posotes* of 380 hyperpyra which had been given to his son after his death. However, his widow was not considered one of his heirs and so she had no right to inherit the oikonomia (as in the case of John Orestes *[8.42]*), indicating that widows did not ordinarily inherit hereditary oikonomiai. In any event, Xene now asked that she receive a *posotes* of 100 hyperpyra from this oikonomia. The emperor acceded to her request, noting the zeal of Alexios and the piety of Xene, and ordered that she hold the *posotes* undisturbed "and outside of any burden, as the Thessalonians hold their *gonika* properties," and had the right to give it in dowry, sell it, exchange it, donate it, and improve it. After her death her children and heirs, or anyone else, had the right to receive it and any improvements and to hold both in the same way.[48] This phrase "as the Thessalonians hold their *gonika* property" is a reference to the "common" chrysobulls granted to the resident of certain towns in the European part of the empire by Nicaean emperors in the course of their conquests. There is some evidence that these chrysobulls permitted the inhabitants to alienate their *gonikon* property freely and perhaps to transfer any tax exemption on it to the new owner.[49]

Property held "by reason of a benefaction"

In 1337 the *megas domestikos* Alexios Raoul donated to the Prodromos monastery outside Serres some property "which recently our mighty and holy lord and emperor conferred upon me as a benefaction" (ὅπερ μοι ἀρτίως εὐηργέτησεν ὁ . . . βασιλεύς) *[8.61]*. When this terminology is compared to a document issued by a group of officials from 1407 which refers to

[48] *Vatopédi*, II, no. 89.12–13: καὶ ἐκτὸς βάρους τινός, καὶ ὡς κατέχουσι καὶ οἱ Θεσσαλονικεῖς τὰ γονικὰ αὐτῶν κτήματα. F. Dölger, *Aus den Schatzkammern des Heiligen Berges* (Munich, 1948), 48, 262. Ostrogorsky, *Féodalité*, 130–32, 134. Kazhdan, review of Ostrogorsky, *Féodalité*, in *VizVrem* 10 (1956), 224. Kazhdan, *Agrarnye otnošenija*, 218–19. Since nothing in the document suggests the son – referred to anonymously as merely "the son of the deceased" – was dead, it appears that the son now lost 100 hyperpyra from the inherited oikonomia as a result of this act. *Vatopédi*, II, pp. 163 and 425, identifies the son as Demetrios Palaiologos Soultanos, mentioned in an act from 1376 (*Vatopédi*, no. 152.14–15), but the connection between Demetrios and Xene is not unclear (e.g., mother or stepmother).

[49] See D. Kyritsis, "The 'Common Chrysobulls' of Cities and the Notion of Property in Late Byzantium," *Σύμμεικτα* 13 (1999), 229–45, esp. 232–33.

monks holding property "from imperial benefaction" (ἐξ εὐεργεσίας βασιλικῆς), we might conclude that the passages in the documents mentioning properties held through imperial "benefactions" (*euergesiai*) are dealing with simple gifts and not pronoiai (*Xéropotamou*, no. 29.9).

[7.18] Act of George Iagoupes and Antonios Kalothetos for the monastery of Panteleemon regarding its holdings on Lemnos (1407)

However, another document from 1407 casts doubt on this. Pursuant to an imperial order granting a certain quantity of property to the monastery of St. Panteleemon, a group of officials on Lemnos conferred upon the monastery "the holdings of the fields which the deceased Nicholas, son of Eudokimos, held by reason of a benefaction [*logo euergesias*] inside the *posotes* of his oikonomia, as shown in the great *apographike thesis*." The fact that the master tax record book on Lemnos showed that Nicholas' fields were "within the *posotes* of his oikonomia" "by reason of a benefaction" proves that we are dealing with a pronoia. Thus, cases in which someone held property "by reason of a benefaction" *may* involve pronoiai.[50]

Something from the "mercy" of the emperor

Another locution that could at times refer to a pronoia grant was the statement in a document that some property was held "from the mercy" of the emperor. For example, in 1303 a soldier leased some property to the monastery of Xenophon which he held "through a praktikon." He states that the monastery would hold the *stasia* "for as long as I am found holding such mercy of the . . . emperor," in other words, as long as he held his pronoia/oikonomia *[8.24]*. That holding property "through the mercy" of the emperor could indicate a pronoia is proved by a document from 1313 in which a man gave a monastery some properties, which were "held by me in the mercy of the . . . emperor." He notes that the donation was to be valid "as long as the pronoia is held by me and my children" *[8.54]*.

Most commonly, references to the "mercy of the emperor" are found in the introductory passages of praktika and have no direct connection to pronoia or any kind of grant at all. The *apographeus* states that having found a particular monastery or individual holding an "oikonomia,"

[50] *Pantéléèmôn*, no. 17.12–14.

he confers it upon that party "from the mercy of our holy and mighty emperor toward me." Such a passage is found in general praktika from 1318 to 1344, with all but one in the period 1318–23. The phrase was a particular favorite of the *apographeis* Constantine Pergamenos and George Pharisaios.[51] Other *apographeis*, such as Demetrios Apelmene and the *protokynegos* John Vatatzes, do not use the phrase at all.

Occasionally other officials use the phrase as well, such as an unknown official of Thessaloniki around 1344 who made a decision "from the mercy toward me of our . . . emperor."[52] And in one case a despot – Demetrios I Palaiologos, son of Andronikos II – uses the expression: "my majesty prescribes from the mercy and benefaction . . . of its holy majesty."[53]

In all of these cases in which officials utilize the phrase in connection with their administrative responsibilities the phrase indicates the authority through which an act was performed. "Mercy," therefore, corresponds roughly to "authority." However, the phrase seems to have its origin in private acts in which individuals use the expression to denote the authority by which they held property *[6.5] [8.60]*.

In a number of cases someone donates, bequeaths, or sells property and, on the one hand, notes that it was held "from the mercy of the emperor" and, on the other, notes explicitly that it was held within the family through generations *[8.57] [8.58]*. In all of these examples, the "mercy" phrase seems to indicate little more than that the property in question originated

51 ἀπὸ τῆς πρὸς ἡμᾶς ἐλεημοσύνης τοῦ κραταιοῦ καὶ ἁγίου ἡμῶν αὐθέντου καὶ βασιλέως. *Iviron*, III, no. 75.2–7 (1318: Kounales, Kontenos, Kalognomos) and no. 79.5–6 (1320: Pergamenos and Pharisaios); *Esphigménou*, no. 14.2–6 (1318: Kounales, Kontenos, Kalognomos); *Zographou*, no. 17.8 (1320: Perg. and Phar.); *Xéropotamou*, no. 18E, I.5–7 (unknown *apographeus*: ca. 1320–25); *Xénophon*, no. 15.1–6 (1321: Perg. and Phar.) and no. 16.1–5 (1321: Perg. and Phar.); *Esphigménou*, no. 15.4–8 (1321: Pharisaios?) and no. 16.3–5 (1321); *Lavra*, II, no. 111.1–2 (1321: Perg. and Phar.); P. Schreiner, "Zwei unedierte Praktika aus der zweiten Hälfte des 14. Jahrhunderts," *JÖB* 19 (1970), 37.4–6 (1323: Pharisaios?); *Vatopédi*, II, no. 81.6 and no. 82.30 (1338: Constantine Makrenos); *Iviron*, IV, no. 88 (1344: Edessenos). The phrase also appears in praktika (typically, a *sigilliodes gramma*) conveying specific properties to a monastery issued through the early fifteenth century: *Xéropotamou*, no. 18D, I.29–31 (ca. 1315–20: unknown *apographeus*); *Xénophon*, no. 14.6–7 (1320: Pergamenos and Pharisaios), no. 19.7 (1322/3: Pharisaios), and no. 21.6 (1325: Pharisaios); *Vatopédi*, II, no. 71.3 (ca.1330: Leo Panaretos); *Xénophon*, no. 22.8 (1333: Nicholas Tzeremogites), and no. 23 (1335: Constantine Makrenos); *Vatopédi*, II, no. 79.7 (ca. 1335–1338: Constantine Makrenos), no. 114.28 (1359: George Astras), and no. 147.4–5 (1375: Laskaris Metochites); *Xéropotamou*, no. 29.4 (1407: Paul Gazes, Michael Karianites, and George Prinkips); *Docheiariou*, no. 53 (1409: Gazes and Prinkips).

52 *Xénophon*, no. 27.13,45 (ca. 1344.), or in 1373 when three officials state that the emperor "ordered us from the mercy of his majesty" to conduct an investigation: *Docheiariou*, no. 41.9–10.

53 *Xéropotamou*, no. 23.11–12 (1324).

as some kind of imperial grant. Some could have been pronoiai; some almost certainly were not.[54]

Grants not made through chrysobull

[7.19] Kantakouzenos on a letter written by Andronikos II's brother-in-law Kokalas (ca. 1355)

In his memoirs, written around 1355, John Kantakouzenos uses the word *oikonomia* only five times, and in only one of these is it possible that he is referring to pronoiai. This one instance is special in its own right because it is found in a passage where he is quoting a letter written by someone else. He paraphrases a letter written to Andronikos II in October 1327 by the emperor's brother-in-law Kokalas. The letter mentions the privileges granted to the aristocrats who were enlisted in Andronikos II's struggle against his grandson Andronikos III. According to Kantakouzenos, Kokalas wrote that all the "archons and *archontopouloi*" who were with Andronikos III had secretly come over to Andronikos II's side. These men, who were prepared to hand the younger emperor over to his grandfather, held Andronikos II's "benefactions [*euergesiai*] through both oikonomiai and chrysobulls."[55] In quoting (or paraphrasing) the letter, Kantakouzenos distinguishes "benefactions" bestowed through oikonomiai from those bestowed through chrysobull, suggesting that there was a distinction between the two. Presumably he is implying that oikonomiai – that is, pronoiai – were bestowed through documents of lesser solemnity, and that chrysobulls were not used for ordinary pronoia grants.

The documents do provide some support for Kantakouzenos' distinction. Oikonomiai were normally initially granted, to laymen at least, through *orismoi* or *prostagmata*. In the cases in which someone held an oikonomia "through a chrysobull" the recipient had received additional privileges, usually the promise from the emperor that all or part of the oikonomia would pass to the recipient's heirs (e.g., see *[8.42]* and *[8.43]*). Conversely, there is an example of someone receiving what appears to be a grant under much more favorable conditions than the typical oikonomia. The 900 modioi of

[54] The phrase also appears in at least one Serbian document. In 1343 a man named Demetrios Čalapija, who held a village "by God and by the mercy [*po milosti*] of the lord kralj" donated it to the Htetovo monastery: *SnM*, III, 298 (84). See M. Bartusis, "Serbian Pronoia and Pronoia in Serbia," *ZRVI* 48 (2011), 191 note 47.

[55] Kantakouzenos, I, 236.7–11. Dölger, *Regesten*, IV, no. 2579. Kazhdan, *Agrarnye otnošenija*, 218.

land which Demetrios Plytos had "received as a benefaction" (εὐηργέτηθη) was granted "through a divine and worshipful *prostagma* in the manner of hereditary property" (*kata logon gonikotetos*) *[7.15]*. At best we can say that a grant held through a *prostagma* or *orismos* was probably an oikonomia.

"Incomes held from the emperor"

Even though John Kantakouzenos almost never uses the terms *pronoia* and *oikonomia* in his history, as he describes the wars of the fourteenth century he writes frequently about pronoiai and the soldiers and aristocrats who received them. Most commonly he refers to grants of revenues and properties from the emperor as "incomes" (*prosodoi*) with some kind of modifying phrase or adjective: "yearly incomes from villages," "incomes from villages," "yearly incomes," or "incomes from the emperor." Usually, but not always, such expressions refer to pronoia grants.

For Kantakouzenos there were two types of *prosodoi*: private, and public or state. Both were derived in large measure from the land. Thus, he quotes Andronikos III saying that, because of the civil wars between the Andronikoi, "the properties, from which [come] both the private and state incomes, are ruined."[56] Overall, he refers to "state incomes," or rather, "state revenues," infrequently, and sometimes omits the adjective. Thus, twice he mentions the "state revenues" (*demosiai prosodoi*) of the island of Chios, though once it is simply the "revenues" (*prosodoi*) of the island, and twice the revenues that the Genoese derived from Phokaia are simply "prosodoi."[57] Further, the phrase "yearly incomes" (*prosodoi etesioi*), which often refers to grants from the emperor, is used once to mean state tax revenues, and once to refer, not to an indirect grant of incomes from properties, but to an annual stipend to be granted to a distinguished individual. In 1329 Benedetto II Zaccaria, erstwhile co-ruler of Chios, was offered 20,000 gold pieces from the taxes of Chios "for the sake of a yearly income" in return for his support after Andronikos III took Chios.[58]

However, most frequently in Kantakouzenos' history *prosodoi* means a pronoia grant. The link between pronoia and "incomes" is made clear from the episode involving the *apographeus* Patrikiotes, who in 1341 agreed to restore from his own illicitly acquired wealth any of the pronoiai held by those of the senate, those otherwise wellborn, and soldiers that was

[56] Kantakouzenos, I, 158.17–18: καὶ τὰς κτήσεις, ἐξ ὧν αἵ τε ἰδιωτικαὶ καὶ αἱ δημόσιοι διαφθείρεσθαι πρόσοδοι.

[57] Kantakouzenos, I, 379.16, 380.2, 490.10–12; III, 82.8. Also, I, 538.21–22, and III, 80.19.

[58] Kantakouzenos, I, 181.14, 387.16–17.

lacking. In this one section of his history in which he uses the word *pronoia*, Kantakouzenos writes that he himself "ascertained the amount of pronoia given by the emperor to each" and then refers to these recipients of pronoiai as "those holding incomes from the emperor" *[8.26]*. While "incomes" or even "incomes from the emperor" by itself need not refer specifically to a grant of a pronoia, here the context is unambiguous. As an example of how ambiguous phrasing can hide a reference to pronoiai, Gregoras' brief account of this episode asserts that Kantakouzenos distributed "properties" (*ktemata*) to all the soldiers.[59]

A similar usage may be found in a passage involving the capture of the *megas stratopedarches* Andronikos Palaiologos, governor of the Rhodope area and a member of Andronikos II's faction, by the Vlach leader Syrbanos in 1322. Even though Syrbanos earlier had been treated badly as a prisoner of Andronikos Palaiologos, according to Kantakouzenos he graciously asked Andronikos III to free the man and to strip him "neither of his title, nor incomes nor imperial gifts," requests to which Andronikos III assented.[60] While it is clear that the *megas stratopedarches* held these "incomes" as a grant from the emperor (Andronikos II), it is not completely certain that the reference is to a pronoia. But it is likely.

"(Yearly) incomes from villages"

The most specific way that Kantakouzenos uses "incomes" to mean a pronoia grant is in the phrase "yearly incomes from villages." Shortly before the assassination of the rebel Syrgiannes in 1344 Kantakouzenos berated him for his ingratitude: "I helped [you] greatly . . . supplying yearly incomes from villages and appointing [you] a governor of cities." Even more clearly, he writes that after Sphrantzes Palaiologos assassinated Syrgiannes, Andronikos III honored him with the rank of *megas stratopedarches* and "proportionately granted [him] yearly incomes from villages."[61] This passage helps explain another passage in Kantakouzenos' history. At the time of Kantakouzenos' acclamation in Didymoteichon in 1341, "to some from the Latin army he bestowed the honor of *kavallarios*, doing all the customary things for them." "Doing all the customary things for them" is an odd

[59] Gregoras, II, 595.18–21. Mutafčiev, "Vojniški zemi," 527.

[60] Kantakouzenos, I, 148.20–21: μήτε τῆς ἀξίας ἀποστερηθῆναι μήτε τῶν προσόδων καὶ τῶν δωρεῶν τῶν βασιλικῶν. On this *megas stratopedarches*, see *PLP*, no. 21428.

[61] Kantakouzenos, I, 443.9–12: προσόδους τε παρέχων ἐτησίους ἐκ χωρίων, and I, 457.12–14: προσόδους τε παρέσχεν ἐτησίους ἐκ χωρίων ἀναλόγως.

phrase, but, by analogy with the cases of Sphrantzes Palaiologos, it is possible that it meant that Kantakouzenos granted them pronoiai or increased what they already held. In other words, it is possible that the conferral of a rank might have been linked to an appropriate grant of a pronoia.[62]

[7.20] Kantakouzenos on a fiscal reassessment of Andronikos II Palaiologos in 1322 (ca. 1355)

Even merely "incomes from villages" is sufficient to identify a pronoia grant if the incomes originated through an imperial act, especially if some of the recipients were soldiers. In 1322, after concluding the treaty of Epivatai which established a temporary peace between Andronikos II and his grandson Andronikos III, Andronikos II ordered a general fiscal reassessment (*exisosis*): "sending out *apographeis*, he equalized all the soldiery, as many as there were who had been assigned incomes from villages, as well as the senators, and through these things he governed the state."[63] Similarly, in 1341, while meeting with his military leaders, Kantakouzenos discussed his plans for a campaign in Thessaly and the Morea: "After spending a few days in Byzantion [Constantinople], I shall then take hold of the mercenaries of the army and the strongest of those holding incomes from villages."[64]

Later in 1341, after arranging for his "acclamation" as emperor in Didymoteichon, Kantakouzenos ordered that the pay of his mercenaries be brought up to date and additional quantities of gold be given to them. "To the others who held incomes from villages, distributing a fair amount of gold to them, he sent [them] home. They thanked him and promised to prove themselves worthy of the kindness [*euergesia*]."[65]

[62] Kantakouzenos, II, 166.20–22: πάντα ἐπ᾽ αὐτοῖς τὰ εἰθισμένα πράττων. M. Bartusis, "The *Kavallarioi* of Byzantium," *Speculum* 63 (1988), 344–45. Also, cf. Kantakouzenos, I, 517.21–22: in 1339 or 1340 in return for surrendering Rogo in Akarnania to Andronikos III, Alexios Kavasilas was given the title of *megas konostaulos* καὶ τοὺς ἄλλους ἀναλόγως.

[63] Kantakouzenos, I, 169.12–19: καὶ ἀπογραφέας δὲ ἀποστείλας, τὸ στρατιωτικὸν ἅπαν ὅσον ἦν ἐκ χωρίων ἀποτεταγμένον τὰς προσόδους ἔχειν, ἔτι δὲ καὶ τοὺς συγκλητικοὺς ἐξίσαζε καὶ διῴκει δι᾽ αὐτῶν τὴν ἡγεμονίαν.

[64] Kantakouzenos, II, 81.14–16: τὸ μισθοφορικὸν τῆς στρατιᾶς καὶ τῶν ἐκ χωρίων τὰς προσόδους ἐχόντων τοὺς δυνατωτέρους.

[65] Kantakouzenos, II, 175.5–9. The distinction between soldiers who received incomes and those who received pay is also found in the history of Doukas. In his only use of the word *prosodos*, he writes that in March 1453 Sultan Mehmed "sent messengers and heralds to all the provinces for everyone in the army to march out against the City. While the soldiers, as many as were registered through incomes and pay (διὰ προσόδων καὶ ῥόγας), streamed in, who can describe the countless unregistered?": Doukas, chap. 37, sect. 8, line 3. Naturally one wonders whether his knowledge of Byzantine military financing was coloring his portrayal of Ottoman affairs or whether he is displaying his familiarity with the Ottoman *timar*.

The historian Nikephoros Gregoras uses neither *pronoia* nor *oikonomia* in a technical sense. Instead, like Kantakouzenos, he tends to refer to imperial grants as "incomes," particularly those derived from villages. For example, he writes that Mytzes, lord of Trnovo, "migrated into the empire, spending time around Nicaea in Asia," and, around 1262 or 1263, because of activities on behalf of Michael VIII, "he received some villages around Troia and Skamandros from the emperor for a yearly income, henceforth settling down there with both wife and children."[66]

Examples of Gregoras linking "incomes" with "villages" are rather frequent. In return for aid against Andronikos II in 1320, Syrgiannes asked Andronikos III for "magnificent honors and many villages which could provide a great yearly income."[67] Gregoras reports that in 1329 Andronikos III created a new imperial tribunal of four judges. Evidently to make them less susceptible to bribes, the emperor gave them "villages well sufficient for a yearly income."[68] In 1337 the *vasilissa* Anna, the widow and murderer of John II Orsini, despot in Epiros (1323–36/7), submitted to Andronikos III and sought to place Epiros under Byzantine protection. She traveled to Thessaloniki, "and there receiving from the emperor sufficient villages for yearly incomes, decided to live there henceforth."[69] In 1347 John Asan, brother-in-law of Kantakouzenos, claimed that Anna of Savoy had earlier promised him and his brother Manuel Asan "incomes of properties as well as of money."[70] And according to the terms of the treaty of Rhegion in June 1321, Andronikos III was to hold Thrace from Christoupolis (Kavala) up to the suburbs of Constantinople around Rhegion, "along with the things of the villages of Macedonia which he distributed to those around him. For these things were many and in the many thousands comprising for each the yearly income."[71] This last passage is problematic. Andronikos III was to maintain control over the administration of the grants that he gave to his supporters in Macedonia, a reasonable demand on his part. But the final

66 Gregoras, I, 60.24–61.2: καὶ χωρία τινὰ περὶ Τροίαν καὶ Σκάμανδρον εἰληφὼς παρὰ βασιλέως εἰς ἐπέτειον πρόσοδον. Cf. Pachymeres' account of the same episode, which Gregoras certainly had before him: *[7.6]*.

67 Gregoras, I, 300.12–14: ἀξιωμάτων λαμπρότητες καὶ χωρία πολλὰ καὶ πολλὴν τὴν ἐπέτειον παρέχεσθαι δυνάμενα πρόσοδον.

68 Gregoras, I, 438.6–7: χωρία δοὺς ἀποχρῶντα καλῶς πρὸς ἐπέτειον πρόσοδον. Mutafčiev, "Vojniški zemi," 46. On the history, see P. Lemerle, "Le juge général des grecs et la réforme judiciaire d'Andronic III," in Lemerle, *Le monde de Byzance* (London, 1978), no. x, 295–96.

69 Gregoras, I, 546.7–10: κἀκεῖ πρὸς τοῦ βασιλέως ἱκανὰ χωρία λαβοῦσα προσόδων ἐτησίων ἕνεκα αὐτόθι κατοικεῖν ἔγνωκε τοῦ λοιποῦ.

70 Gregoras, II, 799.22: κτημάτων ὁμοῦ καὶ χρημάτων προσόδους.

71 Gregoras, I, 321.4–7: καὶ ἅμα τὰ παρ' αὐτοῦ τοῖς περὶ αὐτὸν διανεμηθέντα τῶν τῆς Μακεδονίας χωρίων· ἦσαν γὰρ ταῦτα πολλὰ καὶ ἐς πολλὰς χιλιάδας ἑκάστῳ τὴν ἐπέτειον ἀναφέροντα πρόσοδον.

phrase, referring to "many thousands," is far too high to mean the number of grants or the size (*posotes*) of each grant in hyperpyra. "Many thousands" must refer to the combined value of all the grants, but this interpretation does not fit the syntax very well.[72]

"Conferrals of villages"

Even the mere mention of "conferrals of villages" may be a reference to pronoiai. According to Gregoras, after the death of Andronikos III in 1341, the *megas doux* Alexios Apokaukos persuaded Patriarch John Kalekas to declare himself regent in the name of Andronikos' nine-year-old son with "further privileges and sources of incomes," specifically, by offering the many members of the patriarch's family "honors and making them wealthy with conferrals of villages."[73] By establishing a link between "incomes" and "conferrals of villages" the passage may be referring to proposed grants of pronoiai.

In all of these passages I have translated *chorion* as "village," following the way the word is used in the documents. Yet, another sense of the word *chorion* is "estate" or simply "landed property," both of which fit our passages equally well, and translators often use these words rather than "village."[74] Should we render these passages as "incomes from villages" or "incomes from estates"? In Kantakouzenos' history, very few of his ninety-five uses of the word *chorion* can easily be translated as "estate" or "landed property." The word tends to refer to larger units. Thus, his "unfortified *choria*" has to mean "unfortified villages," and "he encamped at a *chorion* called Pelekanon" has to be either "place" or "village." Once Kantakouzenos writes that among the inhabitants of a particular *chorion* were "123 women, children, and elderly."

[72] Dölger, *Regesten*, IV, no. 2660, renders it as "and the tax income belonging to it [that area from Christoupolis to Rhegion] in the amount of several thousand hyperpyra yearly."

[73] Gregoras, II, 696.20–21: προβιβασμοῖς γερῶν καὶ προσόδων πόροις, and 697.3–4: τιμαῖς ἄλλαις ἄλλους μετεωρίσας, καὶ χωρίων ἐπιδόσεσιν εὔπορον καταστήσας τὸν βίον αὐτοῖς. Mutafčiev, "Vojniški zemi," 46 note 1.

[74] E.g., J. L. van Dieten in his translation of Nikephoros Gregoras, *Rhomäische Geschichte*, Zweiter Teil, I. Halbband (Stuttgart, 1979), for Gregoras, I, 352.24: "Länderei"; and Magoulias in his translation of Niketas Choniates, for Choniates, ed. van Dieten, 369.62: "estate." Cf. in B. Leib's French translation of the *Alexiad*, "places" (VI.8.4, ed. Leib, II, 63.28) and "lieu" (VII.9.7, ed. Leib, II, 120.17), though elsewhere "village" (X.5.2, ed. Leib, II, 205.11). In T. Miller's translation of the beginning of Book 4 of Kantakouzenos' history (*The History of John Cantacuzenus (Book IV): Text, Translation and Commentary*, diss. Catholic Univ. (Ann Arbor, 1975), *chorion* is usually "piece of land" or "place," while in two passages, Kantakouzenos, III, 60.23 and 66.16, "village" and "villages" makes a much better translation than his "point" (in space) and "territories" (pp. 195, 201).

With a total population of a couple of hundred, this *chorion*, whether or not it was someone's "estate," would certainly have *appeared* to be a rather large village.[75]

Gregoras, in his history, uses *kome*, the more traditional word for village, twenty-three times, half as frequently as *chorion*, and in over half of these cases *kome* appears in conjunction with *polis*: *komai kai poleis*.[76] Oddly, *kome* does not appear in a large part of his history (books 9 through 23 of the twenty-four books, or precisely between pages 379 and 1131 of the continuously numbered volumes I and II of the Bonn edn.), while in that same chunk of his history *chorion* appears thirty-four times. When he writes of "*choria* and *poleis* [cities]" or "*choria* and *polichnia* [towns]," *chorion* is indeed best rendered as "village."[77] Yet there are occasional passages where "estate" or even "area" appears to be a more appropriate translation: "estate" seems to fit "the imperial *choria*" better than "village," and Turkish raiders pillaging and enslaving "throughout the vine-producing and grain-sown *choria*" up to the gates of Constantinople suggests "grain-sown lands" rather than "villages."[78]

Yet Kantakouzenos and Gregoras could not have been unaware that the normal word for village in fiscal documents was *chorion*. And so I have used the translation "incomes from villages." In fact the two translations – "incomes from villages" and "incomes from estates" – are rather compatible. Just as a medieval English village could be someone's manor, so a late Byzantine village, when held by a well-to-do layman or religious foundation, can be called an estate. Or perhaps we should simply avoid the problem altogether and translate "*prosodoi ek chorion*" as "incomes from the land."

[7.21] Gregoras on a distribution of property by John VI Kantakouzenos (ca. 1360)

The issue has some importance. Consider the situation in the spring of 1347 at the end of the civil war that followed Andronikos III's death in 1341. John

[75] Kantakouzenos, II, 228.2; I, 342.25; and I, 145.20–22.

[76] Gregoras, I, 14.13, 15.3–4, 16.11–12, 72.24, 128.10, 319.14–15, 355.23; II, 1131.22–23; III, 22.17, 41.1, 183.20–21, 190.8–9, 240.20. While Kantakouzenos employs the word *chorion* ninety-five times in his history, the traditional *kome* appears only thirty-five times.

[77] Gregoras, II, 642.11–12; III, 153.18; 249.2; I, 131.16; II, 728.1–2.

[78] Gregoras, II, 818.16–17; III, 178.2–3: διὰ τὰ... ἀμπελόφυτά τε καὶ σιτοσπόρα χωρία. The word *sitosporos* is uncommon, appearing in the online *TLG* only 14 times (including 3 times in Gregoras' works). Half of the occurrences are in astrological texts, which is probably where Gregoras picked up the word. Nevertheless, a scholium to the *Iliad* has the phrase χώραν σιτόσπορον: H. Erbse, *Scholia Graeca in Homeri Iliadem (scholia vetera)*, vols. 1–5, 7 (Berlin, 1969–88), book 9, verse 125a1 (cited from the *TLG*).

Kantakouzenos established himself as co-emperor with Andronikos' young son John V. Kantakouzenos' oldest son Matthew was given his own principality centered around Adrianople and Didymoteichon, but he nevertheless felt slighted that he had not been designated heir to the throne. In the fall of 1347 Matthew initiated a modest rebellion against his father and John V, and Kantakouzenos visited him to calm things down. Gregoras puts the following words in Kantakouzenos' mouth:

> Having in view the commands of the deceased emperor, [my] friend [Andronikos III], as is proper, I am forced to preserve the imperial succession for his son [John V]. Further, toward the things promised by oath, which I made by necessity to those who followed me and ventured into danger, . . . I am again forced to distribute to them the rest of the imperial *choria*, not at all with pleasure.[79]

Gregoras implies that Matthew was upset not only because he was denied imperial honors, but because he felt he had not received his proper share of the spoils resulting from his father's success. Being the ruler of an area in Thrace did not automatically provide him with vast landholdings or, evidently, substantial tax receipts from the territory under his authority.

According to Gregoras, Kantakouzenos had promised his supporters "the rest of the imperial *choria*." What does Gregoras mean here? "Imperial" must mean "belonging to the empire" (the crown or the fisc) rather than "belonging to the emperor personally" (in this case, Kantakouzenos himself), because Kantakouzenos would hardly have promised his supporters "the rest" of his property. And since there was not much difference between crown property and fisc property at this time, Gregoras is referring to a promise of all of the remaining state property. We still have a problem. Did this mean only the villages or, more properly, the "estates" that the state owned as a landowner (in other words, *episkepseis*), or all of the villages (agricultural property generally) which were neither privately owned nor granted previously to private individuals or religious foundations? By 1347, after a generation of civil war, and with the area of the empire shrinking relatively steadily since the 1280s, it is difficult to imagine that there were any agriculturally productive state *episkepseis* that had not been granted to someone for his support or as a reward. Perhaps in the middle of the fourteenth century, any village that was still paying its taxes to government tax collectors would have been considered an "imperial village." This would

[79] Gregoras, II, 818.9–17: αὖθις ἀναγκάζομαί σφισι διανέμειν τὰ λειπόμενα τῶν βασιλικῶν χωρίων, οὐ μάλα σὺν ἡδονῇ. In van Dieten's translation, III, p. 189, *choria* is translated as "Ländern." Futher, he notes that this distribution is not mentioned by Kantakouzenos himself in his own history.

suggest that by the middle of the fourteenth century all of the agricultural resources of the empire were in the hands of perhaps one or two hundred aristocrats, several hundred soldiers, and religious foundations.[80] This did not mean that the state no longer received any tax revenues from the land, for there is certainly evidence that these properties still paid some taxes.

I should emphasize that even though grants of incomes from agricultural property obviously refer to imperial grants, it is by no means certain that the grants were pronoiai, rather than simple gifts. For example, Petar Mutafčiev concluded that Gregoras used the word *chorion* to denote pronoiai and this may be true in the majority of cases, perhaps the overwhelming majority of cases.[81] But it might not be true in any particular case. This is a limitation of the literary sources. Unless there is some clear link between these grants and some other characteristic of pronoiai, such as military service, we can say only that it is likely that the grant is a pronoia.

"(Yearly) incomes"

Yet another phrase that can point to pronoiai is "yearly incomes." Here we are on even more shaky ground because "yearly incomes" can refer to an annual stipend or salary or even state revenues, and not necessarily any kind of grant involving rural property. For example, Gregoras writes that "the yearly income from these taxes came to nearly 200,000," and once he refers to the salaries of the Catalan Company as "yearly incomes."[82] And so other simple references to "yearly incomes" may have nothing to do with grants of land and fiscal revenues.[83] Along similar lines, Kantakouzenos writes that Andronikos III spent the summer of 1322 traveling around the cities under his authority, "providing the most illustrious of those around him with honors and gifts and the governance of provinces and cities, the others with money and yearly incomes." Similarly, he writes that in 1344, when the *protokynegos* John Vatatzes returned to Kantakouzenos' faction, along with some of his relatives, Kantakouzenos honored him with the rank of *megas stratopedarches*, and "to the rest of the relatives he granted honors

80 Cf. Ahrweiler, "La concession des droits incorporels," 113.

81 Mutafčiev, "Vojniški zemi," 46/571 note 4.

82 Gregoras, II, 842.2–4: τὴν μὲν ἐκείνων ἐκ τῶν φόρων ἐπέτειον γίνεσθαι πρόσοδον διακοσίων ἔγγιστα χιλιάδων. Similarly, Gregoras, II, 867.3–6. Gregoras, I, 223.28–9: τὴν ἀποτεταγμένην αὐτοῖς ἐτησίαν πρόσοδον.

83 E.g., Gregoras, I, 44.14–15; I, 180.10; I, 262.13.

and yearly incomes proportionately to each."[84] While it is quite likely that "yearly incomes" in both of these passages meant pronoia grants, it is by no means certain.

We can be more certain when the subject is hereditary yearly incomes. In 1341 just before the death of Andronikos III, Kantakouzenos reports that Alexios Apokaukos came to him and temporarily entertained the idea of entering a monastery. However, he asked that "his children be the heirs of the yearly incomes which the emperor furnished and which he enjoyed."[85] Since hereditary annual stipends were unknown in late Byzantium, the passage is certainly referring to a grant Apokaukos held from the emperor grounded in the land.

[7.22] Kantakouzenos on a fiscal revision (*exisosis*) in 1328 (ca. 1355)

When the context is grants to soldiers, we can be most secure in interpreting "yearly incomes" as pronoia grants. Kantakouzenos describes another *exisosis* that took place around May 1328. After Andronikos III heard that Theodore Synadenos had defeated a force from Constantinople under Constantine Asan, he

> added honors and other benefactions [*euergesiai*] to those with him from the senate and to the mercenary soldiers, and he strengthened the yearly incomes of the rest and he made them more eager for war by it. Setting *apographeis* in Thessaloniki, he managed and equalized [*exisaze*] the rest through them and he made other [military] lists in addition to the existing ones, so that the army should become larger.[86]

Because he distinguishes mercenaries from those soldiers who held "yearly incomes," it is clear that the latter refers to soldiers who held pronoia grants.

In another passage, Kantakouzenos quotes his own words to Alexios Apokaukos in the spring of 1343. During this period of civil war Apokaukos, loyal to the regency in Constantinople, had come to Thessaloniki with an army. Kantakouzenos pointed out to Apokaukos that this did not trouble him: "If you remain in Thessaloniki, no harm or difficulty shall come to me, other than the army around me will be delayed getting home and kept from

[84] Kantakouzenos, I, 119.13–16, and II, 476.6–7: τοῖς ἄλλοις δὲ τῶν συγγενῶν ἑκάστῳ ἀναλόγως καὶ τιμὰς παρείχετο καὶ προσόδους ἐτησίους.

[85] Kantakouzenos, I, 535.4–7. [86] Kantakouzenos, I, 287.18–288.2.

the incomes which they have yearly."[87] Here "yearly incomes" must again mean pronoia grants, since there would be no need for soldiers to return home to receive their mercenary pay.

One of the most interesting passages involving "yearly incomes" deals with the restoration of Byzantine rule to Epiros. In 1337, after she murdered her husband, the despot in Epiros John II Orsini, the *vasilissa* Anna Palaiologina decided to submit to Byzantine authority. Consequently, according to Kantakouzenos' account of the events, "the *vasilissa*... and [her] daughters were made appropriate pronoia, and she withdrew from government in order to live where it seemed best to him [Andronikos III]. They were provided with benefactions of honors and yearly incomes of which each was deemed worthy."[88] A page later Kantakouzenos writes that in 1338 Andronikos III arrived in Akarnania, ready for war, but since the area submitted peacefully, "the emperor, displaying toward them much gentleness and kindness, not only provided for the people of the cities with state benefactions [*koinais euergesiais*], but he rewarded the powerful in them with honors and yearly incomes and other benefactions." Without other matters pressing, "he went around all the cities of Akarnania not only to learn about them, for he had never seen them earlier, but to deem them worthy of proper pronoia."[89]

In these few lines we have much of Kantakouzenos' vocabulary for imperial acts of beneficence. Any concrete act of kindness on the emperor's part was a "benefaction" (*euergesia*); equally common is the verb *euergeto* (εὐεργετῶ), "to provide a benefaction." In these passages, the recipients are Anna and her daughters, the common people, and the powerful of Akarnania. More specifically, important people, such as Anna and the powerful, receive "honors" (*timai*), which included gifts and court titles, and "yearly incomes." In the case of the *vasilissa* Anna these "yearly incomes" were certainly a grant of incomes from property, for the parallel passage in Gregoras' history speaks of her "receiving from the emperor sufficient villages for yearly incomes."[90] One may assume that the powerful of the cities received the same.

87 Kantakouzenos, II, 367.19–20: καὶ τρεφομένης ἐν τῶν προσόδων, ἃς ἐτησίους ἔχουσιν.

88 Kantakouzenos, I, 501.23–502.2: βασιλίσσης τε τῆς... καὶ θυγατέρων πρόνοιαν τὴν προσήκουσαν ποιήσεσθαι, ἀποστάσης τῆς ἀρχῆς, ὥστε διάγειν ὅποι ἂν αὐτῷ βέλτιον δοκῇ. αὐτούς [including Anna's son] τε εὐεργετήσειν τιμαῖς τε καὶ προσόδοις ἐτησίοις ὧν ἂν ἕκαστος ἄξιος κριθῇ.

89 Kantakouzenos, I, 503.2–5: ἀλλὰ καὶ τοὺς δυναμένους παρ' αὐταῖς τιμαῖς τε καὶ προσόδοις ἐτησίοις καὶ ἄλλαις ἠμείψατο εὐεργεσίαις, and ἀλλὰ καὶ προνοίας ἀξιώσων τῆς δεούσης. For the history, D. Nicol, *The Despotate of Epiros, 1267–1479* (Cambridge, 1984), 113–14.

90 Gregoras, I, 546.8–9: πρὸς τοῦ βασιλέως ἱκανὰ χωρία λαβοῦσα προσόδων ἐτησίων ἕνεκα.

We are left with Kantakouzenos' use of the word *pronoia* in these passages. The *vasilissa* Anna and her daughters "were made appropriate pronoia" (πρόνοιαν τὴν προσήκουσαν ποιήσεσθαι), which, in context, is a play on words. Through this common idiomatic phrase (see Chapter 1), they were "taken care of properly," and yet, through the yearly incomes, they were "given fitting pronoiai." Thus, when Kantakouzenos writes that someone "was taken care of" by the emperor, this can indeed mean that an imperial grant of incomes was involved. But it is important to point out that this is not always the case, as seen in the second appearance of *pronoia* in these passages. When he writes that cities were "worthy of proper pronoia," there can be no question that he merely means proper care and attention in the simple sense of the word.

Even the mere reference to "incomes" (*prosodoi*) in Kantakouzenos and Gregoras can be a reference to pronoia. During negotiations with the anti-Zealot faction in Thessaloniki in 1345, Kantakouzenos reports that, in return for overthrowing the Zealots and turning the city over to Kantakouzenos, the faction demanded privately "greater honors and appropriate incomes" for their leaders and for the army and the others with them. And Gregoras writes that in 1327, in order to acquire support, Andronikos III promised "to the common people tax exemption and freedom from taxes, to those serving in the army resources of incomes [πόρους προσόδων] and increases of pay."[91]

A great deal of time can be spent looking through the sources for the occasional passage that "might" be dealing with the institution of pronoia.[92] There is no "silver bullet" which allows us to distinguish pronoiai/oikonomiai from outright gifts from the emperor. Even the words

[91] Kantakouzenos, II, 574.11–16: προσόδους τὰς προσηκούσας. Gregoras, I, 397.11–12. Mutafčiev, "Vojniški zemi," 526. Dölger, *Regesten*, IV, no. 2689.

[92] For example, K. Smyrlis, *La fortune des grands monastères byzantins* (Paris, 2006), 86 note 451, writes that a property located not far from the monastery of St. John Prodromos near Serres, named Keranitza, was taken from a pronoia holder and granted by the emperor to the monastery in 1302. This conclusion is based primarily on two documents: one from 1304 or 1319 which states that the Prodromos monastery had been holding Keranitza for seventeen years and that the deceased Megalonas had been holding some peasants for at least thirty years, and another document, from 1322, which states that Keranitza was taken from Megalonas and officially conferred upon Prodromos (*Prodrome B*, no. 127.34,53, no. 129.18–19). Thus, depending on the date of the first document, Megalonas' presence in the area may have dated back as far as the 1250s. But it is not possible to conclude that he was a pronoia holder. There is no suggestion of a pronoia or oikonomia or military service. He held paroikoi but so did laymen who were not pronoia holders. And nothing indicates why he lost the property. Certainly, the facts are consistent with the holding of a pronoia, but all we can say for sure is that the state took away a property from a man who had been holding paroikoi for at least thirty years, and that the state then granted the property to the Prodromos monastery.

pronoia and *oikonomia* were no certain indicators of the character of the grant. What all this means is that one needs more than one indicator to conclude with any confidence that the subject is a pronoia grant. We need to keep this in mind as we turn to the character of pronoia/oikonomia in the later thirteenth and fourteenth centuries.

8 | The nature of pronoia, ca. 1282–ca. 1371

A handbook in three parts

This chapter deals systematically with the characteristics of the pronoia grant in the later thirteenth and fourteenth centuries. My intention is to present in an orderly way everything that we know about the institution of pronoia as it existed during this period.

PART I. RECEIVING THE GRANT

The grantor and the grantee

As a rule, in territory under Byzantine control, it was the emperor who granted pronoiai. There were exceptions. In the thirteenth century, prior to the restoration of Constantinople to Byzantine authority, the rulers of Epiros granted pronoiai. Of course, this was in accord with their pretensions as the legitimate successors of the pre-1204 line of Byzantine emperors. Holding no such pretensions was the despot John Palaiologos, Michael VIII's brother, whose extensive authority in Macedonia and Thessaly may well have included the right to confer pronoiai. Manuel II Palaiologos, while he governed Thessaloniki as an appanage (1369–73 as despot, and 1382–87 as co-emperor), did make pronoia grants, and in the fifteenth century, the despots of the Morea had the power to make such grants (see Chapter 9). And foreign rulers conferred grants which they called pronoiai but, except for the case of the Serbs, these were only marginally related to the Byzantine institution (see Conclusion).

The typical recipient of a pronoia was a layman, and usually a soldier. Further, given the fact that each recipient was the beneficiary of an act from the emperor, it is quite likely that most, if not all, were among the higher ranks of the soldiery, that is, cavalrymen, if not officers. To get some idea of the predominance of soldiers among pronoia/oikonomia holders, Table 8.1 is a list of all of the holders of pronoiai/oikonomiai as found in the documents (i) who are connected with a specific court title or function and (ii) whom the documents explicitly refer to as holders of oikonomiai and/or pronoiai.

Table 8.1 Recipients of pronoiai/oikonomiai with known titles or functions, twelfth–fifteenth centuries

Date	Grantee	Title and/or function of grantee	Grant explicitly referred to as	Reference
1333–34	Vasilikos	*megas primmikerios*	oikonomia	*[8.20]*
1342	Arsenios Tzamplakon	*megas papias*	oikonomia	*[8.17]*
1333	Michael Monomachos	*eparchos*	oikonomia	*[8.14]*
1342	Vardales	*protasekretis*	oikonomia	*[8.17]*
1351 1373	George Katzaras	*megas adnoumiastes*	oikonomia	*[8.47]*
1307	Alexios Diplovatatzes	judge of the army	oikonomia	*[8.40]*
ca. 1300	Michael Elaiodorites Spanopoulos	*stratopedarches* of the *allagia*, *sevastos*	oikonomia	*[8.56]*
1207 1233	Basil Vlatteros	*vestiarites, megalodoxotatos*	pronoia	MM, IV, 217 MM, IV, 199
1234	Constantine Kalegopoulos	*vestiarites*	pronoia	*[5.7]*
1313	John Panaretos	*hetaireiarches*	oikonomia	*[8.41]*
1235	John Alopos	*prokathemenos, pansevastos*	pronoia	*[5.8]*
1277	Marmaras	*protonovelissimos*	oikonomia	*[8.65]*
ca. 1225	Constantine Tzirithnos	*megalodoxotatos*	pronoia	*[5.15]*
1261	52 men	*archontopouloi*	oikonomia	*[6.2]*
1235	Syrgares	*lizios kavallarios*	pronoia	MM, IV, 37, 39
1300 1300	Peros Martinos	*kavallarios, syr*	oikonomia pronoia	*[7.8]*
1321	Serpes	*kavallarios*	oikonomia	*[8.11]*
1343	Syrmanouel Mesopotamites	*kavallarios*	oikonomia	*[8.44]*
1335	Nicholas Doukas Sarantenos	*sevastos*	oikonomia	*[8.51]*
1328	Devlitzenos	*sevastos*	oikonomia	*[8.76]*
1292	Peter Doukopoulos	*sevastos*	pronoia	*[8.53]*
1317 1325 1325 1327	Nikephoros Martinos	soldier *sevastos* *sevastos* *pansevastos sevastos*	 oikonomia oikonomia oikonomia	*[8.75]*
1162	Theotimos and Leo Loukites, Andreas Romanos Rentinos	soldiers	pronoia	*[2.3]*

(*cont.*)

Table 8.1 (*cont.*)

Date	Grantee	Title and/or function of grantee	Grant explicitly referred to as	Reference
1181	16 Cumans	soldiers	pronoia	*[2.4]*
1259	Michael Angelos	soldier	oikonomia	*[6.1]*
1286	Gazes	from the Thessalonian *mega allagion*	oikonomia	*[8.73]*
1318, or forgery	Manuel Garianos	from the *Serriotikon mega allagion*	oikonomia	*[8.49]*
1321	Nicholas Maroules	from the Thessalonian *mega allagion*	oikonomia	*[8.12]*
1321	Michael Saventzes	from the Thessalonian *mega allagion*	oikonomia	*[8.11]*
1323	Basil Berilas	from the Thessalonian *mega allagion*	oikonomia	*[8.13]*
1342	Klazomenitai soldiers	soldiers	oikonomia	*[8.4]*

I have attempted to arrange the court titles in order of descending status based on the various fourteenth-century lists of precedence. The titles from *megas primmikerios* through *protasekretis* fall toward the lower half of the top third of courtly titles. The *megas adnoumiastes* and the judge of the army are in the lower half of the middle third. The reference to the *stratopedarches* of the *allagia* is found in a private act. This title is otherwise unattested, but by analogy with the *stratopedarches* of the *mourtatoi* and other similar *stratopedarchai*, this title would place the individual a few notches below the judge of the army.[1]

All of the rest of titles and functions in the table, from *sevastos* on down, are at the very bottom of the lists of precedence, when they appear at all. Consequently, the arrangement of the titles or functions in the table is meant only to approximate their relative status. "Soldier" (*stratiotes*) appears to be a function and never appears on any list of courtly titles.[2] Similarly, "from the Thessalonian/*Serriotikon mega allagion*" described a military function and appears on no list of titles. *Sevastos* appears on most fourteenth-century

[1] The lists of precedence on which these rankings are based are found in Pseudo-Kodinos, *Traité des offices*, ed. J. Verpeaux (Paris, 1966), e.g., 300–02, 319–23, and index. One might also add Alexios Komnenos Raoul who held an oikonomia around 1297 *[8.15]*. The relevant document gives him no title other than *gamvros* of the emperor, but he is almost certainly the Alexios Raoul who died in battle in 1303 and held at that time the title *megas domestikos*.

[2] See M. Bartusis, "On the Status of Stratiotai during the Late Byzantine Period," *ZRVI* 21 (1982), 57–59.

lists of precedence, occupying a position very near the bottom. We see that Nikephoros Martinos in later documents was no longer identified as a soldier, but as *sevastos* and then *pansevastos sevastos*, suggesting that the individuals referred to simply as "*sevastoi*" may have been soldiers of an elevated status. On the other hand, both *sevastos* and *pansevastos* (as well as *megalodoxotatos*) could appear with other titles, making them appear less court titles than honorifics, like *kyr* or the *syr* attached to the names of *kavallarioi*. There were men who bore the honorific *megalodoxotatos* who were soldiers *[5.12]*. *Kavallarios*, as well as *prokathemenos*, originated as functions but nevertheless appear as court titles near the bottom of some lists of precedence. *Archontopoulos* appears to designate a social category at the lower end of the aristocracy. The remaining titles – *vestiarites*, *hetaireiarches*, *protonovelissimos* – when they appear on lists of courtly titles, occupy a position near the bottom.[3]

As expected, quite a few of the recipients of pronoiai or oikonomiai were soldiers. Of the thirty-one cases in the table of individuals or groups of individuals who held oikonomiai or pronoiai and who had titles or functions attached to their names, fourteen cases involve soldiers (*stratiotai*, *kavallarioi*, or "from the *Serriotikon mega allagion*" or "from the Thessalonian *mega allagion*," that is, members of military units from the areas of Serres and Thessaloniki).[4]

[3] If one accepts as authentic a chrysobull attributed to John V, another *hetaireiarches* can be added to the list. In the document the emperor granted as a gift to the monastery of Philotheou, among other things, "the land in various places held through oikonomia [δι' οἰκονομίας] by the *hetaireiarches* Styleianos, and his paroikoi": *Actes de Philothée*, ed. W. Regel et al., *VizVrem* 20 (1913), suppl. 1, no. 10.125–28. The document then presents a list of six poor (*ptochoi*) paroikoi, a list of five *eleutheroi* paroikoi, a list of twenty parcels of land totaling 583 modioi, and finally a description of the property holdings and *telos* of five of the six poor paroikoi, which totaled 6 hyperpyra. W. Regel cast doubt on the authenticity of the document by pointing out in his edition that the indiction year of the document corresponds to 1354, while the world-year corresponds to 1355, and that the document's long preamble is "borrowed" from a chrysobull of Andronikos II (see Dölger, *Regesten*, IV, no. 2085). The editors of the acts of Lavra (*Lavra*, III, p. 60) wrote that the chrysobull was "manifestement fabriqué en partant de plusieurs documents." On the other hand, Dölger (*Regesten*, V, no. 3041) lists it without any hint that it could be a forgery, and V. Kravari, "Nouveaux documents du monastère de Philothéou," *TM* 10 (1987), 272, wrote that there was no reason to doubt its authenticity. She points out that the emperor's signature is identical to that found on *Lavra*, III, nos. 141 and 142. Nevertheless, the structure of the document is unusual and it strikes me as a composite: e.g., the beginning of the passage involving Styleianos (lines 124ff.) reads like the beginning of a new document. Fortunately, the document adds little to our subject.

[4] On the *megala allagia*, see M. Bartusis, "The Megala Allagia and the Tzaousios," *REB* 47 (1989), 183–207. Here I should mention an act from 1369 of the despot John Uglješa which addresses a quarrel between the bishop of Hierissos and the monastery of Zographou over a property in Hierissos "which the soldier called Saravares held in his pronoia" (ἣν εἶχεν εἰς πρόνοιαν αὐτῷ καὶ

What little the literary sources have to say about the holders of pronoiai suggests a broad range of recipients. However, as I argued in the previous chapter, the literary sources sometimes use the term *pronoia* in a much broader sense than the documents, applying it to almost any grant from the emperor. Nevertheless, there is at least one clear example of a high clergyman receiving a pronoia: John Apokaukos, metropolitan of Naupaktos, who received and lost a pronoia from the ruler of Epiros *[5.17]*.

The marginal note to the history often attributed to Skoutariotes has already been discussed *[3.2]*. Next to the passage where the chronicler paraphrased Choniates' "gifts of paroikoi" passage, an unknown copyist wrote "On military pronoiai" (Περὶ Στρατιωτικῶν προνοιῶν), a unique phrase ostensibly denoting pronoiai held by soldiers. While this shows that the copyist regarded Manuel Komnenos' grants to soldiers as pronoiai, it also suggests that the copyist regarded soldiers as only one category of recipients of pronoiai. If he felt that a pronoia grant was something only a soldier could hold, there would have been little reason to modify "pronoiai" by the adjective "military."

As discussed in Chapter 7, the recipients of pronoiai according to the history of George Pachymeres can be categorized as soldiers, aristocrats, and religious foundations. We can accept only his references to soldiers holding pronoiai or oikonomiai at face value. All other references may refer simply to gifts. Kantakouzenos and Gregoras too display the same ambiguity. Their "incomes from lands" may refer to pronoiai or simply to gifts, depending on the case. When the subject is soldiers, we may have confidence that the subject is pronoia, but when the subject is "those of the senate" or other references to elevated personages, the matter is unclear. At best the literary sources confirm the testimony of the documents: pronoiai/oikonomiai were granted to a wide range of individuals. But the literary sources add very little to our knowledge of this aspect of the institution.

As for the social status of pronoia holders, anyone who was the beneficiary of a grant issued through imperial order was, by definition, a privileged individual. Beyond this, the range of pronoia holders ran from groups of soldiers who jointly held an oikonomia through individual soldiers who held oikonomiai up to close relatives of the emperor. If there was an aristocracy in late Byzantium, I would say that any *individual* holder of an imperial

στρατιώτης Σαράβαρης ἐπικεκλημένος): Solovjev–Mošin, *Grčke povelje*, no. 36.75–77. However, there never was a soldier named Saravares. As the documents show, the dispute originated over property held by an old monastery on Athos called *tou Saravari*. See Bartusis, *Late Byzantine Army*, 376–77, and esp. M. Bartusis, "Serbian Pronoia and Pronoia in Serbia: The Diffusion of an Institution," *ZRVI* 48 (2011), 196.

privilege, whether an oikonomia or any other kind of privilege, was an aristocrat.

Jointly held grants

Occasionally two or more individuals shared a pronoia grant. This phenomenon was first recognized by Ostrogorsky, and soon afterward Lemerle similarly noted the existence of "une pronoia collective," though he thought it was rare.[5] Such joint grants of pronoiai may date back to the earliest appearance of pronoia. In the early twelfth century the soldiers Romanos Rentinos and the Loukites brothers may have possessed a joint pronoia consisting of a *proasteion [2.3]*. Later, during the reign of Isaac II Angelos, the Balkan brothers Peter and Asen asked the emperor for a "village producing a small income" in return for military service *[3.3]*. As Oikonomides observed, if the passage is taken literally, it is not impossible that it involved the request for the creation of a joint pronoia.[6]

[8.1] Chrysobull of Michael VIII Palaiologos for the monastery of Iviron (1259)

Whether or not jointly held pronoiai existed in the twelfth century, there is no evidence of the phenomenon in the thirteenth century until the 1250s. A possible example dates to January 1259 when Michael VIII granted Iviron most of the village of Hierissos "as the deceased Theodore Petraliphas and *kyr* Michael Laskaris enjoyed this." A praktikon from 1262 *[6.3]* repeats this information. Theodore Petraliphas was probably the brother-in-law of the despot of Epiros Michael II. In 1252 he delivered Kastoria to John Vatatzes and died in January 1259, right before Michael VIII issued the chrysobull. Michael Laskaris is probably the *megas doux* Michael Tzamantouros Laskaris, a great uncle of Theodore II.[7] It is likely that they were pronoia holders. If so, their grants originated under either John Vatatzes or Theodore II. It is also possible that they held a single pronoia jointly. The text does

[5] Ostrogorsky, *Féodalité*, 35, 146; *Pronija* (Belgrade, 1951), 22–23, 99. P. Lemerle, "Autour d'un prostagma inédit de Manuel II, L'aulé de Sire Guy à Thessalonique," in *Silloge Bizantina in onore di Silvio Giuseppe Mercati = Studi Bizantini e Neoellenici* 9 (1957), 271–86, repr. in Lemerle, *Le monde de Byzance* (London, 1978), no. xxiii, 274 note 3. Even though the phrase "collective pronoia" appears at times in English-language scholarship (including my *Late Byzantine Army*), here I have chosen to adopt a more common and clearer formulation, avoiding the misleading connotations of "collective."

[6] Oikonomides, "A propos des armées," 369 note 101.

[7] *Iviron*, iii, no. 58.86–87, no. 59.63–65, and p. 89. *PLP*, no. 14554.

accommodate such an interpretation. Yet, inasmuch as there is no obvious connection between the men to have warranted a joint grant, it is hard to fathom why Vatatzes or Theodore II would have granted them anything that they would have held in common. In later documents for Iviron that mention this property in Hierissos, the reference to Michael Laskaris disappears (only Petraliphas' name appears), and the property seems to have become smaller.[8] All in all, I think it most likely that the 1259 chrysobull was granting Iviron the properties of two pronoia holders (one of whom had just died) who held their grants individually.

During Michael VIII's reign we encounter the first certain example of a jointly held pronoia (or as certain as we can be about these things). In the late 1260s Christopher and Papanikolopoulos jointly held the village of Kapraina in Thessaly *[6.4]*. While the relevant documents refer neither to a pronoia nor to an oikonomia, merely to a village with a *posotes* of fifty hyperpyra, the easy transfer of the village from a monastery to these men and back again permits us to identify it as a pronoia. As for Christopher and Papanikolopoulos, they were urban guards (*tzakones*) of a relatively modest status, and this alone could explain their joint pronoia.

[8.2] Act of Theodosios, bishop of Hierissos, involving a pronoia (1290)

In the later thirteenth and fourteenth centuries joint pronoiai are encountered frequently. The recipients of such grants were often connected through family ties or they were members of the same military unit. Most common are examples of joint pronoiai shared by family members. A document from 1290 describes a quarrel between the monasteries of Hilandar and Zographou over gardens near Hierissos on the Chalkidike. A group of men intervened after an initial ruling against Hilandar. "When these Serbs [the monks of Hilandar] did not prevail, *kyr* Constantine Amnon, Isaac Amnon, George Ozianos, and Alexios Amnon arrived at their pronoia inside the diocese," which, for reasons undisclosed, led to a reopening of the case. While Oikonomides viewed this as an example of a pronoia held jointly by four men, Katia Tcheremissinoff has argued that the "pronoia" was not held by the Amnon family and Ozianos, but by Zographou itself, and that this is an example of a monastery holding a pronoia. To me, an interpretation involving a joint pronoia seems the most reasonable, but it must

[8] *Iviron*, III, no. 62.29–30 (1283), no. 72.107–08 (1310), pp. 13, 15, 89.

be admitted that there is something ambiguous about the phrasing of the passage.[9]

Another example of a joint pronoia grant is found in the Hilandar Slavic praktikon *[8.72]*. It lists among the monastery's possessions in the village of Kastrion (Gradac) nineteen paroikos households under the rubric "A [or "the"] pronoia from the children of Kiprijan" (od' detec' Kiprijanov'... pronija).[10] Because the praktikon elsewhere mentions numerous times paroikoi that had originated "from the pronoia" of various other individuals, the phrasing of the passage suggests that these nineteen paroikoi households constituted the entire grant of the children of Kyprianos who, evidently, inherited the grant and held it jointly until, for unknown reasons, it was transferred to the monastery.

In 1301 Germanos Kladon and his son-in-law Demetrios Rouphinos donated land of 3 *zeugaria* to the monastery of St. John Prodromos "belonging to us from a gift and mercy of our... emperor" *[8.59]*. And in 1314 two men donated some fields they held "pronoiastically" (προνοιαστικῶς) to the monastery of Docheiariou *[8.55]*. We observe that the latter donation is described as a part of a pronoia but in the case of Kladon and his son-in-law Rouphinos the donated field is a "gift" from the emperor. If it was truly a "gift," then we might conclude that it was not part of the men's oikonomia. Nevertheless, the fact that both were donated to monasteries shows that, in practice, there was little distinction between the two.

[8.3] Letter of Patriarch Gregory II to Theodore Mouzalon regarding Andronikos and his brother (1283–89)

A possible example of joint pronoia is found in a letter of Patriarch Gregory II Kyprios to the *megas logothetes* Theodore Mouzalon. The patriarch requested that Mouzalon intercede on behalf of Andronikos and his brother, the sons of Peter, a Turk who had been known as Fahr al-Din before he was baptized. The affair which prompted the sons to approach Gregory for help is not at all clear, but it seems they were in the process of being forcibly

[9] V. Mošin, "Akti iz svetogorskih arhiva," *Spomenik Srpske kraljevske akademije nauka* 91 (1939), 176 (Greek and Slavic trans.) = *Zographou*, no. 12.24 (Greek only): ἐλθόντες δὲ εἰς τὴν πρόνοιάν τους ὅ τε κῦρις Κωνσταντῖνος ὁ Ἀμνών... καὶ Ἀλέξιος ὁ Ἀμνὼν ἐντὸς τῆς ἐπισκοπῆς. K. Tcheremissinoff, "Un acte slave des archives de Zographou," *Byzantinoslavica* 42 (1981), 2–3. Cf. Oikonomides, "A propos des armées," 367. Tcheremissinoff tries to make much of the fact that the Slavic translation of the act translates the key phrase εἰς τὴν πρόνοιάν τους as "v sela svoja" ("in their own village"); but these Slavic translations are notorious for their creative rendering of Greek.

[10] Mošin, "Akti," 208.238–40.

transplanted. In the letter, the patriarch notes that he had explained the situation to the men with the words

> you shall be or you might already be deprived of the pronoia [τὴν μὲν πρόνοιαν . . . ἀφαιρεθήσεσθε, ἢ καὶ ἀφῄρησθε ἤδη], and you shall be moved to the region around Thrace and Macedonia, where you shall enroll yourself, by your wish, in the Persian [i.e., Turkish] military lists [μετὰ τῶν στρατιωτικῶν Περσικῶν καταλόγων], and *siteresia* shall be given and arable land as well.

Andronikos and his brother were Christianized and more or less Hellenized (for Gregory notes their eloquence in speaking). If we consider chronology, it would be appropriate for their father to have entered Byzantium with the Seljuk sultan Izz al-Din Kayka'us II, who, fleeing from the Mongols, had arrived with his retinue in 1260 or early 1261. His army followed, and within the next several years many of these Turks were baptized and enrolled themselves in the Byzantine army, participating in several of Michael VIII's campaigns.[11]

Ostensibly Gregory describes an exchange of something called "pronoia" for *siteresia* and arable land (γῆ ἀρόσιμος) somewhere in Thrace or Macedonia. For the meaning of *siteresion* (discussed in Chapter 6) we must choose between "provisions in kind," "an allowance for provisions," and "salary." The only internal clue is the link the patriarch creates between *siteresia* and "arable land," but this does not offer much help. A soldier who farmed his own land (a smallholding soldier) might need victuals less than cash with which to obtain equipment, but a pronoia soldier who leased his arable land to paroikoi might benefit from victuals. However, there is no evidence that either smallholding soldiers or pronoia soldiers received provisions during the late Byzantine period.[12] Moreover, there is the tendency of thirteenth- and fourteenth-century literary sources (Choniates, Pachymeres, Palamas, Gregoras) to employ the word in the sense of wage or salary. I conclude, with reservations, that the patriarch thought that Andronikos and his brother were going to receive land and some cash payments.

The nature of the "pronoia" that the brothers held is not specified by Gregory. It is something that had been granted to the sons – perhaps via their father – which provided them with a livelihood. If the patriarch was employing the word in the sense that we have encountered so far in the

[11] Gregory II Kyprios, ed. Eustratiades, in *Ἐκκλησιαστικὸς Φάρος* 4 (1909), 119, no. 159. V. Laurent, *Les regestes des actes du patriarcat de Constantinople*, I: *Les actes des patriarches*, fasc. 4 (Paris, 1971), no. 1536. M. Bibikov, "Svedenija o pronii v pis'mah Grigorija Kiprskogo i 'Istorii' Georgija Pahimera," *ZRVI* 17 (1976), 94. Bartusis, *Late Byzantine Army*, 52–54.

[12] Bartusis, *Late Byzantine Army*, 248.

documents, then he is speaking of a jointly held pronoia shared by the brothers. Yet it is possible that he was using the word *pronoia* more broadly to denote their previous means of livelihood, whatever it was. Whether they were Byzantine soldiers while they held this "pronoia" is unknown.

Indeed, we do not know why they lost this pronoia. Did the sons claim, but were not granted, their father's pronoia? Did they hold their own pronoia but somehow fell out of favor? Or did they lose their pronoia because of Turkish advances in Asia Minor? If they did in fact hold a pronoia grant, this last possibility seems the most likely. It would explain the patriarch's interest, as well as the patriarch's uncertainty regarding whether or not the pair had yet been "deprived" of their pronoia and why they were being permitted to enter (or re-enter) imperial service "by their wish." It would also explain Gregory's vagueness about where the two would be heading – to "Thrace and Macedonia" – if they had come from "the East."[13]

Regardless of how Andronikos and his brother lost their pronoia, the patriarch's letter tells us nothing about what it consisted of, nor can we be sure he was using the word in the same way as contemporary documents. The "arable land" that would replace the lost pronoia was of course a normal component of a pronoia grant, but the same words could have been used to describe the pair's enlistment as smallholding soldiers, those who lived in a colony, like a large group of Cumans settled by John Vatatzes, or the rowers called Prosalentai settled in various places by Michael VIII.[14]

In accord with the usage of the late thirteenth and fourteenth centuries, all of these examples of jointly held pronoiai are found in documents and sources not issued by emperors, who avoid the word *pronoia*. But there are also references to shared oikonomiai, which appear to be identical to joint pronoiai. For example, around 1315 the monk Ignatios Sarantenos and his brother Diomedes, with the consent of their other two brothers, the *sevastos* Nicholas Doukas Sarantenos and Alexander Doukas Sarantenos, donated a church with 700 modioi of land, a water mill, an orchard, a garden, and three vineyard parcels. All of this property is described as having come "from the oikonomia of the Sarantenoi" *[8.51]*.

Joint pronoiai were held as well by soldier companies (*syntrophiai*). One such were the Varvarenoi soldiers. From around 1327 to sometime before 1337 the Varvarenoi held land in Patrikona which had been confiscated from the monastery of Docheiariou in the early years of the fourteenth century.

13 In Bartusis, *Late Byzantine Army*, 375, I wrote that they "fell out of favor," without considering the possibility that it was the encroaching Turks, not the emperor, who deprived them of their pronoia.

14 On smallholding soldiers, see Bartusis, *Late Byzantine Army*, 157–61.

In 1337 the land was returned to the monastery.[15] And sometime after 1329 the village of Hagios Mamas was granted to the Varvarenoi soldiers. In 1346 Stefan Dušan returned it to its previous owner, the monastery of Vatopedi.[16]

[8.4] Chrysobull of John V Palaiologos for the Klazomenitai soldiers (1342)

Another soldier company were the Klazomenitai of Serres. A chrysobull from 1342 issued in the name of John V begins, "Since the Klazomenitai soldiers, found in and inhabiting the God-saved city of Serres, petitioned and requested that, from what *posotes* they hold through oikonomia, some of them should hold through chrysobull twelve hyperpyra each, others ten each," the emperor granted this request. He ordered that the soldiers hold these *posotetes* of ten and twelve hyperpyra undisturbed, with the right "to maintain and improve them" (συνιστᾶν καὶ βελτιοῦν αὐτάς). They were to hold these *posotetes* for life, and after their deaths, they were permitted to transmit them and the improvements made to them to their legitimate children and heirs who would hold them in the same way, "rendering the service owed in their behalf."[17]

Oikonomides hypothesized that the Klazomenitai hailed from Klazomenai (today Urla) near Smyrna in Asia Minor and, like many other soldiers, had come to Europe following the collapse of Byzantine authority in the east. He further hypothesized that they were the mercenary garrison of Serres who were granted, in addition to their mercenary pay, an oikonomia with a modest *posotes* for each.[18]

The entire *posotes* held "through oikonomia" was previously held by the Klazomenitai (but not necessarily for any length of time). But what we do not know is whether the Klazomenitai held a single oikonomia jointly or multiple oikonomiai individually, and whether the ten- and twelve-hyperpyra *posotetes* represented all of the oikonomia the group held in aggregate. The

15 *Docheiariou*, no. 18.12: "900 modioi in Rousaiou which the Varvarenoi soldiers held earlier" (1337); no. 21.6 (1343); no. 23.29 (1344); no. 41.24: "the *syntrophia* of Varvarenoi" (1373); and p. 140. Lefort, *Villages de Macédoine*, 92, 116, 139. Oikonomides, "A propos des armées," 360–63.

16 Solovjev–Mošin, *Grčke povelje*, no. 11.37; and confirmed in 1348: Solovjev–Mošin, *Grčke povelje*, no. 18.25,31. Lefort, *Villages de Macédoine*, 146.

17 *Kutlumus*, no. 20.1–3: ἵνα ἀφ' ἧς κατέχουσι δι' οἰκονομίας ποσότητος κατέχωσι δία χρυσοβούλλου, οἱ μὲν αὐτῶν ἀπὸ δώδεκα ὑπερπύρων, οἱ δὲ ἀπὸ δέκα, lines 8 and 18: ἀποδιδόντες τὴν ὀφειλομένην ὑπὲρ αὐτῶν δουλείαν. Ostrogorsky, *Féodalité*, 124–26. Kazhdan, *Agrarnye otnošenija*, 219. Evidently ἀπό is being used in the first phrase as a substitute for ἀνά: see G. W. H. Lampe, *A Patristic Greek Lexicon* (Oxford, 1961), s.v. ἀπό, IV.

18 Oikonomides, "A propos des armées," 368–69.

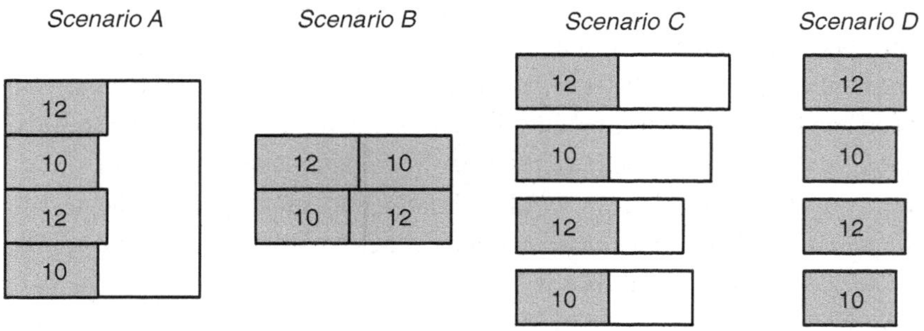

Figure 8.1 Four possible scenarios to illustrate the holdings of the Klazomenitai soldiers.

situation described in the chrysobull could fit one of four scenarios (illustrated in Figure 8.1, which, for simplicity, assumes that merely four soldiers – the minimum number implied by the document – were involved):

(A) The Klazomenitai held one oikonomia jointly. The emperor now permitted each of them to hold part of the oikonomia in hereditary tenure; some receiving ten- and others twelve-hyperpyra *posotetes* based on rank or merit or some other distinction. The sum of all these individual ten- and twelve-hyperpyra *posotetes* was less than the *posotes* of the entire oikonomia.

(B) The Klazomenitai held one oikonomia jointly. The emperor now permitted them to hold the entire oikonomia in hereditary tenure. Factoring in the size of the oikonomia, the number of soldiers, and their relative ranks, merit, and so on, their commander divided the entire oikonomia into ten- and twelve-hyperpyra parcels. The sum of all these individual ten- and twelve-hyperpyra *posotetes* equaled the *posotes* of the entire oikonomia.

(C) The Klazomenitai held individual oikonomiai, of either equal or varying *posotetes*, but which were each larger than twelve hyperpyra. According to rank, merit, etc., each now received hereditary rights over a *posotes* of ten or twelve hyperpyra from his own oikonomia.

(D) The Klazomenitai held individual oikonomiai with a *posotes* of either ten or twelve hyperpyra. Each now received hereditary rights over his entire *posotes*.

Scenario C is unlikely. This scenario is identical to the case of John Sgouros Orestes and his three brothers *[8.42]*. Each brother received a *posotes* of six hyperpyra "from what oikonomia each of them is found holding," clearly indicating that each of the brothers held a separate oikonomia. But the parallel phrase in the chrysobull for the Klazomenitai is "from what *posotes* they hold through oikonomia," suggesting a single total *posotes* from which the *posotetes* for the additional privileges were extracted. For the same reason Scenario D, while not impossible, is even less likely. Further, the chrysobull is vague about the division. If each soldier had already held a *posotes* of exactly ten or twelve hyperpyra, one would think the document would indicate this.

It is most likely that the Klazomenitai held a single oikonomia jointly as in Scenarios A and B, but it is not possible to decide between the two. Oikonomides favored Scenario B, hypothesizing that the reason why some of the men received ten and others twelve hyperpyra in hereditary tenure was that the total *posotes* of the group was not sufficient to grant each a *posotes* of twelve hyperpyra. However, I think it is perhaps a bit more likely that a partial transformation was occurring here. We have concrete examples of this and, from the point of view of practicality, partial transformations left room for the anticipation of further privileges.

Another reference to a group of joint pronoia holders, or perhaps another reference to the Klazomenitai soldiers themselves, is found in a document from 1348 in which the "*archontopouloi* of Serres," then under the rule of the Serbs, tried to appropriate at least eight paroikos families that belonged to the Athonite monastery of Alypiou.[19]

[8.5] Chrysobull of Stefan Dušan for sixteen *archontopouloi* (1344)

A similar reference to *archontopouloi* is found in a chrysobull from 1344 in which Stefan Dušan granted sixteen *archontopouloi* an untaxed estate (*eleutheron zeugelateion*). Each was granted hereditary rights over "his proper share" (lines 7–8: τὸ ἐπιβάλων αὐτὸ μερίδιον) along with the right to improve the property, install *eleutheroi* peasants and collect charges from them, to sell, donate, exchange, give in dowry, and to transmit the part he held to his legitimate children and heirs.[20] These are almost certainly the "*archontopouloi* of Zichna" who held a *zeugelateion* called Kraniare in hereditary tenure from Dušan which they sold to a man named John

[19] *Kutlumus*, no. 21. Oikonomides, "A propos des armées," 368.

[20] Kravari, "Nouveaux documents du monastère de Philothéou," no. 3. The recipients are named and all, to the extent their names can be read, have Greek names (lines 4–7): John Rezenos, Theodore My[. . .]os, John [. . .]es, John Kouvaras, John A[. . .], Andronikos Mesopotamites, John Manikaites, [. . .] Smoleanitzes, George M[. . .]ites, Manuel Antiochites, Leo Govenos, Niketas Archontitzes, Mamenos, [. . .] Kladon, John Katavolenos, and Aaron.

Masgidas prior to 1347.[21] The reference to shares of a single *zeugelateion* and the joint action of selling the property reflect the collective nature of the grant. As in other references to *archontopouloi* it is not possible to say whether these men were a soldier company, though they certainly were not relatives.

[8.6] Chrysobull of John VI Kantakouzenos for the monastery of Iviron mentioning the Digenatoi soldiers (1351)

Another example of joint grant holders involves soldiers who may have been related. These are the Digenatoi soldiers mentioned in a July 1351 chrysobull of John VI. In this document the emperor granted Iviron some land near the village of Melintzianis "which was earlier reckoned as *despoinike* [that is, as belonging to the empress Anne?] and was later given to the Digenatoi soldiers." He granted it with the *aleia* (right to fish) found in it.[22] The land in question had thus once been state land, was then transferred to these soldiers, clearly as a pronoia, and now was given to the monastery. If the word *despoinike* does indeed refer to Anna of Savoy, the property had to have been conferred upon the Digenatoi sometime after 1326 (when Anne married Andronikos III), and probably during the civil wars of the 1340s. The peculiar name "Digenatos" is otherwise unattested.[23] Whether "Digenatos" here is a family name, a descriptive term (from *dis* "twice" and *genea* "race," along the lines and meaning of "Gasmoulos"), or perhaps both, these Digenatoi soldiers were joint pronoia holders and possibly a soldier company.

[8.7] Prostagma of John V Palaiologos, and Act of Demetrios Phakrases mentioning the soldier company of Sgouros (1377)

And finally there was the company of the judge of the army Sgouros. A *prostagma* from June 1377 (or possibly 1362) deals with land located in a place called Raphalion which was confiscated from Vatopedi and given "years ago" "to the soldiers from the company [*syntrophia*] of the judge

[21] Kravari, "Nouveaux documents du monastère de Philothéou," no. 4.24–27, and p. 300.

[22] *Iviron*, IV, no. 91.86–87: ἥτις κατελογίζετο μὲν πρότερον ὡς δεσποινική, ἐδόθη δὲ ὕστερον τοῖς Διγενάτοις στρατιώταις, and lines 90–91, and repeated in an act of the patriarch: *Iviron*, IV, no. 92.47–48. Dölger, *Regesten*, V, no. 2980.

[23] The family name Digeneis/Digenes, however, does occur: K. Mertzios, *Μνημεῖα Μακεδονικῆς Ἱστορίας* (Thessaloniki, 1947), p. 51 (1425, in Thessaloniki), and M. Manoussacas, "Une Acte de donation a Sainte-Kyriake de Mouchli," *TM* 8 (1981), 319.21 (1457, in the Morea): *PLP*, no. 91789. Also, *PLP*, no. 91790.

of the army Sgouros." The *prostagma* returned the land to the monastery and ordered the soldiers not to trouble the monks (lines 4–5 and 12–13). That same month the official Demetrios Phakrases issued an act of conferral (*paradotikon gramma*) returning the land to the monastery. Here he notes that the land in Raphalion "was given years ago . . . to the soldiers under the charge [ὑπὸ τὴν ἐνοχήν] of the judge of the army Sgouros" (lines 1–2).[24]

There are also a few examples in which it appears that the holders of joint pronoiai were neither related nor members of soldier companies. For example, in a pair of rather idiosyncratic *periorismoi* created for Lavra in 1300 and 1321, there are two such examples (see Table 8.14). Further, in an act of the *apographeus* George Pharisaios from 1322/3, we read that Demetrios Plytos had received, through *prostagma*, land of 900 modioi in the village of Chartophylakos "which had earlier been held by Demetrios Isauros and the deceased *sevastos* Euthymios Kardames, both of the Thessalonian *mega allagion*" *[7.15]*. While these men were soldiers, there is nothing to suggest that they were part of a soldier company. Also, there is a possibility that Kardames and Isauros held the property serially.

[8.8] Book of mathematical problems (early fourteenth century)

Another case involving soldiers holding a pronoia jointly is found in an early fourteenth-century mathematical book. One problem involves the division of a joint pronoia grant:

Four soldiers have an imperial pronoia [πρόνοια βασιλική] of 600 hyperpyra, from which the first has $\frac{1}{3}$ or 200, the second $\frac{1}{4}$ or 150, the third $\frac{1}{5}$ or 120, and the fourth $\frac{1}{6}$ and $\frac{1}{20}$ or 130, altogether 600. With the pronoia of the soldiers thus divided, it occurs to the emperor after three years to add to them another soldier who would have a sixth part of the whole pronoia. One would like to know how the five soldiers should divide the 600 nomismata by proportion so that again the first receives $\frac{1}{3}$, the second $\frac{1}{4}$, the third $\frac{1}{5}$, the fourth $\frac{1}{6}$ and $\frac{1}{20}$, and the fifth $\frac{1}{6}$.

[24] Dölger, *Regesten*, v, no. 3084. I wish to thank the Centre d'histoire et civilisation du monde byzantin of the Collège de France for providing me with access to a photograph of the *prostagma* and its accompanying *paradotikon gramma*. Both of these documents will be published in the third volume of the *Actes de Vatopédi*. The exact location of Raphalion is not known, but it was not far from Thessaloniki to the northeast. In 1301 Vatopedi's property there measured 3,670 modioi. See *Vatopédi*, I, p. 35. Raphalion is listed among Vatopedi's property in 1348 and in 1356 (*Vatopédi*, II, no. 97.29 and no. 108.45), and so the confiscation must have taken place after the latter date.

The solution to the problem follows in which there is a passing mention of "he having the third part of the pronoia."[25] While the abstract phrasing of a mathematical problem does not necessarily reflect reality, the problem does suggest that conferring joint pronoiai and redividing such grants was not a particularly rare bureaucratic process. Further, the beneficiaries need not have been related.

[8.9] Prostagma of Andronikos III Palaiologos, Chrysobull of Andronikos II Palaiologos, and Chrysobull of Andronikos III Palaiologos, all for the monastery of Hilandar involving the oikonomia of the deceased Amnon and of Radenos (all 1321)

There is also one example of a jointly held oikonomia. According to a *prostagma* from June 1321, which was issued by Andronikos III as co-emperor, Andronikos II had given a monk of Hilandar 400 modioi of land near Hierissos. The monk had told Andronikos II that fifteen paroikoi "from the oikonomia of the deceased Amnon and of Radenos" were settled on this land, and so Andronikos II gave him these and their *staseis* as well. Chrysobulls of Andronikos II and Andronikos III from September of the same year confirmed Hilandar's possession of 500 modioi along with twenty paroikoi. The texts do not explain the reason for the increase from 400 to 500 modioi and from fifteen to twenty paroikoi. It is probably not an error, but a recalculation to the profit of the monastery. In any event, Ostrogorsky hypothesized that the reason that part of the oikonomia of these men was given to a monk (and then to Hilandar) was because part of the granted property was taken away after Amnon's death. This is reasonable, although the texts do not exclude the possibility that the entire oikonomia of the two men had been reassigned through these acts.[26]

This set of documents permits us to conclude that joint pronoiai and joint oikonomiai were identical. The reason why both terms are found in the sources is related to the way these words are used in the late thirteenth and fourteenth centuries: with rare exception imperial documents use *oikonomia*, while other documents and other sources have a preference for *pronoia*. The only reference to a joint *oikonomia* during Andronikos II's reign is this set of three documents, all issued by an emperor. None of the references to joint *pronoiai* comes from an imperial document.

[25] K. Vogel, ed., *Ein byzantinisches Rechenbuch des frühen 14. Jahrhunderts* (Vienna, 1968), 48–51, no. 32.1,4,5,13. Oikonomides, "A propos des armées," 367–68.

[26] *Chilandar*, ed. Petit, no. 66.5–6: ἀπὸ τῆς οἰκονομίας τοῦ Ἀμνὼν ἐκείνου καὶ τοῦ Ῥαδηνοῦ, and lines 12–13; no. 72.4–5; no. 73.4–5. Ostrogorsky, *Féodalité*, 144–46.

When the holders of joint pronoiai/oikonomiai were related or were members of a soldier company, we can at least speculate how the arrangement arose and why the emperor would accede to it. But the situation is much less clear when there is no indication that the recipients of the jointly held grant were related or part of a soldier company. In truth, I cannot see why the emperor would prefer to grant one pronoia to two men who were neither relatives nor members of a soldier company, rather than individual grants to each. One would think that, by their very nature, joint arrangements would have led to quarrels. This leads me to think that many of the joint holders of grants who appear to be unrelated were in fact related (e.g., father- and son-in-law).

The possibility of hybrid mercenaries–pronoia holders

During negotiations before the treaty of Epivatai in 1322, which temporarily quieted hostilities between Andronikos II and Andronikos III, Kantakouzenos writes that the younger emperor informed his grandfather about measures he had taken to benefit some of his soldiers:

> Increasing the pay of the mercenaries of the army, I provided measures of land to each of ten gold pieces. Concerning the increase in pay you yourself know it had to be done. At any rate I ask that the soldiers not be deprived of the land, partly because no loss has come to the public revenues from such a distribution, and partly because through its smallness the distribution seems a benefit affording no hindrance to the soldiers in regard to their activity on campaign.

Later, Kantakouzenos adds that the treaty, as concluded, stipulated that Andronikos III was to receive the money to pay his mercenaries and the mercenaries were permitted to keep the land they had been granted:

> Toward the emperor grandson alone the pay of the army was given, as it was written in the agreement by them, so that it could be furnished by him to the soldiers. Moreover, concerning the land distributed to the mercenaries themselves, it was not to be bothered by those managing the *demosia* [i.e., tax officials], but it was to be retained by them free of exactions.[27]

There are at least three distinct ways to interpret this episode depending on how one construes the phrase "measures of land of ten gold pieces." Petar Mutafčiev maintained that Andronikos III had granted his mercenaries parcels of arable land with a *value* of ten hyperpyra each. V. Parisot wrote

[27] Kantakouzenos, I, 164.23–165.7, 167.5–10.

that the mercenaries had received property with an *economic revenue* of ten hyperpyra. Oikonomides argued that the episode actually involved small grants of pronoiai, each with a *posotes* of ten hyperpyra.[28] The first two possibilities envision grants of land; the third, grants of pronoiai. To attempt to decide between them we need to consider the key elements of the passages: (i) Kantakouzenos refers to the grants three times as consisting of *ge*, the normal fiscal term for arable land; (ii) this "land" is quantified not by area but by a monetary description, "measures of ten gold pieces"; (iii) the grants caused no loss to public revenues; (iv) the grants were of a size sufficiently small so as not to interfere with the soldiers' military service; and (v) the land granted was exempt from taxation.

It is not difficult to construct a scenario that accords with each of these elements and involves simple grants of land, each with a value of ten hyperpyra. We might envision each mercenary being granted, on a tax-exempt basis and for his personal cultivation, a small quantity of land derived from state lands (or lands that had devolved to the state) not under cultivation at the time of the grant. Ten hyperpyra could purchase something on the order of ten or twenty modioi (1–2 hectares, or $2^1/_2$–5 acres) of average arable land.[29] Such a hypothetical arrangement fits each element of the scheme: "land" was involved; the grant, and its tax exemption, caused no loss to the fisc since it was not previously producing tax revenues anyway; and its small size (equivalent to about three soccer fields of arable land), suitable only for cultivation on a very modest scale, would not inordinately distract the mercenary from his military duties, should he choose to work the property directly. If the "ten gold pieces" referred to an economic revenue, either simple rent or the total agricultural yield of the property, the scenario is more or less the same, except that the size of the property becomes larger. For comparison, a rent of ten hyperpyra required a property consisting of about 100 modioi of arable land; a total economic yield of ten hyperpyra required about modioi.[30]

[28] Mutafčiev, "Vojniški zemi," 525 note 22 and 527. V. Parisot, *Cantacuzène, homme d'état et historien* (Paris, 1845), 59: "chaque militaire devenu . . . tenancier d'un immeuble lui donnant 10 pièces d'or de revenu." That Parisot had rents or harvest in mind when he spoke of "revenue" is clear from the clause immediately following that adds, incorrectly, "en restera nanti à la seule condition de payer l'impôt au fisc." Dölger, *Regesten*, IV, nos. 2479 and 2671, wrote of "Land mit einem Ertrag" of ten hyperpyra, an ambiguous phrase that similarly seems to imply an *economic* yield rather than a value or fiscal assessment. Oikonomides, "A propos des armées," 358. A. Laiou, *Constantinople and the Latins* (Cambridge, Mass., 1972), 290, in passing, also wrote of "pronoiai."

[29] C. Morrisson and J.-C. Cheynet, "Prices and Wages in the Byzantine World," in *EHB*, II, 818–21. For simplicity, I have used the equivalency 1 modios = 1,000 m^2.

[30] See *Lavra*, IV, 169 note 649.

For the grants to have involved pronoiai, the scenario would be something along the following lines. Each mercenary received a grant of a fiscal revenue (*posotes*) of ten hyperpyra drawn from the *telos* of certain properties held by the fisc that were not in production before the grant and for which the mercenary would find cultivators. Such a grant would not interfere seriously with the mercenary's service because he would not work the land himself, and, as Oikonomides has suggested, ten hyperpyra was such a small income that it would require the mercenary to continue to rely on his mercenary salary.

It is clear that there are a couple of difficulties in interpreting the process in terms of pronoia grants. First, we have to excuse Kantakouzenos' use of the word *ge*, which he never uses elsewhere in the context of soldiers or pronoiai, and assume that he really meant "revenues" (*prosodoi*), the term he commonly employs for pronoia grants. Second, the only way a grant of pronoia could cause no loss of revenues to the fisc is if the properties involved were not producing tax revenues prior to the grant (as my scenario suggests). However, this would mean (as I further suggest) that the mercenary would need to arrange the production of the property, a task that indeed might interfere with his military duties, at least initially. (If, on the other hand, the properties were in production prior to the grant, there would be a loss of income to the fisc of ten hyperpyra per grant.)

Nevertheless, the one obstacle to concluding that the grants were simply grants of land is the key phrase "measures of land of ten gold pieces," which appears to suggest a *posotes*, a quantity of fiscal revenues, not a valuation of land nor an economic return. The documentary sources ordinarily quantify land in only two ways: by its area and by its fiscal assessment (generally a function of its area). Land "prices" are encountered much less frequently (and economic returns not at all) because their inherent fluctuations were of little use to the fisc in establishing the tax liability of a property. It would not be adequate simply to say that the grants were of arable land with a *posotes* of ten hyperpyra because, in order to produce ten hyperpyra of *telos*, each grant, according to the usual fiscal assessment of one hyperpyron per fifty modioi of arable land of mixed quality, would need to amount to about 500 modioi (125 acres, or 50 hectares) of average arable land, which might well interfere with the soldiers' military duties.

From the standpoint of military financing, whatever was happening here is extremely important. Either mercenaries were receiving small quantities of land, making them hybrid mercenary–smallholding soldiers, or they were receiving small pronoiai, making them hybrid mercenary-pronoia soldiers. Both of these possibilities display creativity and subtlety in their approach to military financing. In my opinion, "simple grants of land with a value of ten hyperpyra" makes better sense in the passages than "grants of pronoiai yielding ten hyperpyra yearly." In any event, there is sufficient ambiguity to prevent us from using these passages as evidence of pronoia grants.

The process of conferring a pronoia and its documentation

Our knowledge of the process whereby pronoiai were conferred is limited. The best source is the mid-thirteenth-century notarial form for the conferral of paroikoi translated and discussed at length in Chapter 5 *[5.12]*. The procedure in the later thirteenth and fourteenth centuries seems to have been similar, at least from what we can glean from the documents of this later era. In fact, compared to those of the thirteenth century, fourteenth-century sources generally tell us little about the conferral of pronoiai. I attribute this to the firm establishment of the institution. The problems and complications encountered in the thirteenth century no longer arose.

As in the middle of the thirteenth century, a man petitioned the emperor for a pronoia, either directly or through an intermediary such as a high official. Alternatively, the emperor himself or an associate of the emperor, following some notable act on the part of the future grantee, may have proposed the granting of a pronoia without a petition. But we have no evidence of this.

The pronoia grant was conferred through a document called either a *prostagma* or an *orismos*, both of which designated nearly any kind of imperial order or command.[31] The two terms were used synonymously. For example, the *vestiarites* Kalegopoulos and the *protonovelissimos* Marmaras each received their pronoiai "through imperial *orismos*" *[5.7] [8.65]*, and George Doukas Troulenos was given a pronoia "through a divine and worshipful *prostagma*" *[8.50]*.

The *prostagma* or *orismos* was delivered to a provincial fiscal official who consulted the fiscal records of his province (called "the imperial book of the *thesis* of *apographeis*" or "the great *apographike thesis*") with the help of earlier surveys (*periorismoi*), and created a praktikon for the new pronoia holder.[32] Armed with the praktikon, the new pronoia holder could travel

[31] See *ODB*, s.v. "prostagma" and "horismos."

[32] According to one document τὸν βασιλικὸν βιβλίον τῆς τῶν ἀπογραφέων θέσεως: *Zographou*, no. 44.66–67 (1369); according to another, τῇ μεγάλῃ τῇ ἀπογραφικῇ θέσει: *Pantéléèmôn*, no. 17.13–14 (1407) *[7.18]*.

to the physical location of the paroikoi, properties, and rights, and assert his authority. As the thirteenth-century formula discussed in Chapter 5 indicates *[5.12]*, it was not unusual for the fiscal official to fail to find the entire *posotes* granted to the new pronoia holder. In this case, one supposes he simply waited impatiently.

[8.10] Letter of Theodore Hyrtakenos to Theodore Metochites (before 1328)

One of the few hints about the process is found in a letter written to the high official Theodore Metochites by the teacher Theodore Hyrtakenos. While complaining that he had not received a gift (*dosis*) promised to him by Andronikos II Palaiologos, Hyrtakenos alludes to the process of assembling and conferring pronoiai. "Now it is time for this [grant], when the great one among accountants . . . leads the sacred surveying with acreage and property lines, with outlays and incomes, with *episkepseis* of pronoiai, and with transfers and conferrals of archontic oikonomiai."[33]

The letter was written sometime during the dozen or so years prior to May 1328, that is, before Theodore Metochites fell from power at the time of Andronikos II's abdication.[34] It is impossible to say what Hyrtakenos had been promised, save that it was connected to a particular village called Nymphai (unknown to me). The passage of interest to us is a haphazard list of technical matters with which "the great one among accountants" dealt: measures and boundaries for farming, payments and revenues, *episkepseis* of pronoiai, grants and conferrals of archontic oikonomiai. The phrase "*episkepseis* of pronoiai" is unique. *Episkepsis* (literally, "inspection") had

33 Ed. F. La Porte-du Theil, "Notices et extraits d'un volume de la Bibliothèque Nationale, coté MCCIX parmi les manuscrits grecs, et contenant les opuscules et lettres anecdotes de Théodôre l'Hyrtacènien," *Notices et Extraits des Manuscrits de la Bibliothèque Nationale, et autres bibliothèques* 5 (1798), 738–39, no. 20: πλέθροις τὲ καὶ ὅροις γεωργικοῖς, ἐξόδοις τὲ καὶ προόδοις [read: προσόδοις], καὶ προνοῖων ἐπισκέψεσι, καὶ οἰκονομῖων ἀρχοντικῶν ἐπιδόσεσι τε καὶ παραδόσεσι, cited by C. Constantinides, *Higher Education in Byzantium in the Thirteenth and Early Fourteenth Centuries* (Nicosia, 1982), 94 and note 27. In my translation of the editor's ὁ τῆς ἱερεῦς γεωδαισίας, I have replaced ἱερεῦς with ἱερᾶς, as proposed by I. Ševčenko, "Theodore Metochites, the Chora, and the Intellectual Trends of His Time," in *The Kariye Djami, Vol. 4: Studies in the Art of the Kariye Djami and Its Intellectual Background*, ed. P. Underwood (Princeton, 1975), 28 note 66.

34 The letter bears the superscription "To the *megas logothetes* Metochites," reflecting the title Metochites evidently held from 1321, but since the manuscript is not an autograph, all of the superscriptions may have been supplied or altered by the copyist. Internally, the letter contains no chronological indications, but the datable information provided by the other letters in the collection falls into a period from the later 1310s through the mid-1320s.

three meanings: (i) Most commonly it referred to a particular property belonging to the imperial domain (*vasilike episkepsis*). It could refer also to (ii) a fiscal division of a theme (in documents up to the twelfth century), or (iii) the actual daily "administration of property," particularly of imperial property.[35] In this letter "*episkepseis* of pronoiai" presumably refers to the "overseeing" of imperial properties conferred as pronoiai. As for "archontic oikonomiai," this would have to be oikonomiai held by archons, that is, aristocrats of some sort. Hyrtakenos distinguishes pronoiai from oikonomiai but the distinction is not clear and, in his mind, the two are both clearly varieties of imperial grants.

Hyrtakenos implies that "the great one among accountants" (ὁ μέγας ἐν λογισταῖς), the literary form of the title *megas logariastes* (μέγας λογαριάστης),[36] was involved in the process of making these grants. There is little evidence to corroborate Hyrtakenos' view that this official had some connection to the granting of pronoiai. In the eleventh and twelfth centuries, *logariastai* were fiscal officials who headed the various financial offices of the government.[37] From the thirteenth century on, they appear only rarely: I know of six or seven.[38]

35 *ODB*, s.v. "episkepsis."

36 See Pseudo-Kodinos, ed. Verpeaux, 321.60–322.1: τῶν λογιστῶν ὁ μέγιστος, ὅ τε δεήσεις φέρων ("the greatest of the accountants, who carries requests"), and 336.74–75: τῶν λογιστῶν ὁ μέγας ("the great one of the accountants"); and compare Pseudo-Kodinos, 138.21, 301.1, 305.23–24, 307.28, 309.22, 345.8–9, 348.45. Ševčenko, "Theodore Metochites," 28 note 66, assumed that "the great one among accountants" referred to the *megas logothetes* Metochites. Metochites earlier was *logothetes* τῶν ἀγελῶν, *logothetes* τῶν οἰκειακῶν, and *logothetes* τοῦ γενικοῦ, but there is no evidence that he was ever a *logariastes* or *megas logariastes*: see J. Verpeaux, "Le cursus honorum de Théodore Métochite," *REB* 18 (1960), 195–98, and *ODB*, s.v. "Metochites, Theodore." If Hyrtakenos was referring to Metochites himself, then (i) he had a poor knowledge of titulature or deliberately chose to conflate *logothetes* with *logariastes*, (ii) he wished to imply that Metochites himself carried out such administrative procedures as surveying, and (iii) we would need to ignore or explain the fact that Hyrtakenos elsewhere refers to Metochites with the more expected paraphrases μεγίστε λογοθετῶν and λογοθέτην τὸν μέγιστον (La Porte-du Theil, "Notices," 736, no. 16; 739, no. 21).

37 See N. Oikonomides, "L'évolution de l'organisation administrative de l'Empire byzantin au XIe siècle (1025–1118)," in Oikonomides, *Byzantium from the Ninth Century to the Fourth Crusade* (London, 1992), no. X, 140, and R. Guilland, "Études sur l'histoire administrative de l'empire byzantin. Le logariaste, ὁ λογαριαστής; le grand logariaste, ὁ μέγας λογαριαστής," *JÖB* 18 (1969), 101–08. Regarding Guilland's list ("Études," 107–08) of thirteenth-century and later *logariastai*, it is doubtful that either of the seals of *logariastai* cited are from this period, and the *logariastes* he cites from *Zographou*, no. 35 (issued after 1261: see Dölger, *Regesten*, IV, no. 2612), lived before 1204.

38 MM, VI, 154 (from 1209 or 1224); MM, IV, 214 (1233); *Pantéléèmôn*, no. 9 (ca.1271); *[6.12]*; *PLP*, no. 215; and *PLP*, no. 11313.

The *megas logariastes*, attested frequently throughout the twelfth century, was the head of an office (*sekreton*) that dealt with fiscal matters. Very few *megaloi logariastai* are mentioned after 1204. Further, there is no evidence that any of these *megaloi logariastai* held their titles because of any particular function they performed. Indeed the Pseudo-Kodinos treatise states flatly that "the *megas logariastes* does not have a function now."[39]

As for what Hyrtakenos meant by "the great one among accountants," there are only two possibilities. (i) He may be referring to the official called the *megas logariastes*. Although there is no evidence that the *megas logariastes* performed the duties he describes in the period after 1204, fiscal duties were within the *megas logariastes*' ken prior to 1204, and so Hyrtakenos could have been using the title anachronistically, or poetically, to refer to the official who might perform such duties. Or (ii) he is referring, incorrectly, to the *megas logothetes* Theodore Metochites himself. The first possibility is the most likely, though neither tells us much about the administration of pronoia grants in the early fourteenth century.

The praktikon and its *posotes*

One of the difficulties in understanding the institution of pronoia is the fragmentary nature of source evidence. The narrative histories refer to pronoia in general and to major policies which illustrate the importance of pronoia, but say little of the way the institution worked. Moreover, the imprecise terminology of the historians, witnessed as well in the few references to pronoia in the epistolary sources, frequently creates nothing but ambiguity. The documentary sources, on the other hand, are more concerned with details, and while they employ a much more precise terminology, the fact that most deal with such narrow specific details, and in such variety, makes it difficult to transcend a myopic perspective. Fortunately, we possess a few documents which offer specific information, but as a group allow us to make some generalizations about pronoia holders. These are seven praktika which were created for individuals and which provide in detail the components of imperial grants. While many other documents indicate the variety of properties, people, and rights that were held within

[39] Oikonomides, "L'évolution," 140–41. Guilland, "Études," 108–13. *PLP*, nos. 2558, 10010, 14088, 16396, 30346, 91402. In 1239 there was a *megas logariastes* at the Nicaean court who was once identified as the historian George Akropolites (e.g., *PLP*, no. 518), but now see George Akropolites, *The History*, trans. R. Macrides (Oxford, 2007), 20. Pseudo-Kodinos, 182.26–27.

a pronoia grant, it is these documents which help us observe the "total package" the grantee held along with the value (*posotes*) of each individual item.

[8.11] Praktikon of Constantine Pergamenos and George Pharisaios for Michael Saventzes, soldier from the Thessalonian *mega allagion* (February 1321)

[8.12] Praktikon of Constantine Pergamenos and George Pharisaios for Nicholas Maroules, soldier from the Thessalonian *mega allagion* (February 1321)

The properties listed in the praktika for the soldiers Saventzes (translated in Appendix 2) and Maroules were located on the Longos peninsula of the Chalkidike and both praktika were both drawn up by the well-known team of *apographeis* Constantine Pergamenos and George Pharisaios.[40]

[8.13] Praktikon of George Pharisaios for Basil Berilas, soldier of the Thessalonian *mega allagion* (June 1323)

The praktikon for the soldier Basil Berilas was drawn up by George Pharisaios (his colleague Pergamenos having died in 1321) and his property was located in the *katepanikion* of Rentina, also on the Chalkidike.[41]

[8.14] Praktikon of the *protokynegos* John Vatatzes for the *eparchos* Michael Monomachos (1333)

Technically a *sigilliodes gramma*, Monomachos' praktikon (translated in Appendix 3) was issued pursuant to a chrysobull granting him hereditary

[40] *Xénophon*, nos. 15 and 16.

[41] P. Schreiner, "Zwei unedierte Praktika aus der zweiten Hälfte des 14. Jahrhunderts," *JÖB* 19 (1970), 33–49, with additional commentary and revised readings by N. Oikonomides, "Notes sur un praktikon de pronoiaire (juin 1323)," in Oikonomides, *Documents et études sur les institutions de Byzance* (London, 1976), no. XXIII, 336 note 4. Denise Papachryssanthou, *Xénophon*, p. 138, pointed out that Berilas' first name was Basil and not Manuel as found in Schreiner's text. To my knowledge, the new edition of Berilas' praktikon promised by Papachryssanthou never appeared.

rights "without service" over fifty hyperpyra from his *posotes* of approximately 100 hyperpyra.[42]

[8.15] Fragmentary praktikon for Alexios Komnenos Raoul involving the village of Prevista (ca. 1297)

This praktikon details the paroikoi, properties, and charges held in Prevista (today Paliokomi), a village to the east of the lower Strymon, by Alexios Komnenos Raoul. Unfortunately, the end of the praktikon is missing and so we have no idea of the total *posotes* of the grant held by Raoul, nor the date of the document. Nevertheless, the *posotes* was more than 250 hyperpyra, perhaps substantially greater, and the document was probably issued around 1297, based on the language of the document and the identity of Alexios Raoul, who died in 1303.[43]

[8.16] Praktikon for Kallinikos, a monk from the monastery of Hilandar (1323)

The praktikon of the monk Kallinikos documents the grant made by Andronikos II to Kallinikos of one-third of the *posotes* of the village of Mamitzona in Thrace outside Constantinople.[44]

[8.17] Praktikon of Michael Papylas for John Margarites (1342)

John Margarites was a partisan of the regency of John V during the civil wars of the 1340s. The praktikon issued for his benefit (technically a *sigilliodes gramma*) documents the initial grant to Margarites of a *posotes* of fifty-five hyperpyra tax-free and in hereditary title.[45]

The only praktikon in the list which beyond any doubt involves a pronoia grant is the praktikon for the *eparchos* Monomachos. We know this because Monomachos was receiving, as an additional right, the right to transmit part of his grant to his heirs. That means that originally he had no right to transmit any of his grant to his heirs and therefore the grant was a pronoia.

42 *Zographou*, no. 29.

43 L. Mavrommatis, "La pronoia d'Alexis Comnène Raoul à Prévista," *Σύμμεικτα* 13 (1999), 203–27. On Raoul, see *PLP*, no. 24109.

44 *Chilandar*, ed. Petit, no. 92. On Kallinikos: *PLP*, no. 10393.

45 P. Lemerle, "Un praktikon inédit des archives de Karakala (janvier 1342) et la situation en Macédoine orientale au moment de l'usurpation de Cantacuzène," in Lemerle, *Le monde de Byzance* (London, 1978), no. XVIII.

The fact that he still did not have the right to alienate any part of the grant to anyone aside from his heirs means that the entire grant was still a pronoia.

Most scholars have stated that the praktika for Saventzes, Maroules, and Berilas involve pronoia grants. In truth, that is merely an assumption. They *probably* involve pronoia grants. The uncertainty comes from the fact that these three praktika are revised praktika created in the course of a normal fiscal reassessment. As such, the praktika contain no information regarding how the men originally acquired the properties in their praktika. Nevertheless, the juxtaposition of two facts leads to the conclusion that they were probably pronoia holders. First, the beneficiaries were soldiers and, second, the total *posotetes* of their praktika are quite similar (between sixty and seventy hyperpyra) and, as it turns out, relatively modest. When we ask why soldiers should hold relatively modest assemblages of properties under privileged conditions, the first answer that comes to mind is that the properties constituted pronoia grants. However, we cannot say for a fact that the properties within their praktika were granted to them by the emperor – they may have been inherited – nor can we exclude the possibility, even if the properties were granted to them by the emperor, that the grants were simple gifts, perhaps for notable service. There is nothing in the praktika that indicates that the men could not alienate the properties within the praktika.

One could raise the objection that all three praktika refer to the assemblage of properties, paroikoi, and rights held by the three men as oikonomiai. Indeed they do, once, at the beginning of each praktikon in the introductory formula. The praktika for both Saventzes and Maroules begin with these words:

> Since we have been ordered by our mighty and holy lord and emperor to make a fiscal equalization and reestablishment in the theme of the God-saved city of Thessaloniki, that is, of the properties of archons related to our mighty and holy lord and emperor, and of other archons, ecclesiastic, monastic, military, *chrysovoullata*, and the rest, and to confer upon each his own quantity [*poson*], having found, among other things, the soldier from the Thessalonian *mega allagion kyr* Michael Saventzes [or Nicholas Maroules] holding an oikonomia, we confer this, from the mercy toward us of our mighty and holy lord and emperor, upon him, which has the following.[46]

This formula is paralleled by the introductory passages in dozens of praktika for monasteries. In fact the introductory formula for a praktikon for the

[46] *Xénophon*, no. 15.1–6, no. 16.1–5.

monastery of Esphigmenou from December 1321, issued by George Pharisaios, is nearly identical. The only difference (aside from those resulting from the number of fiscal officials involved) is in the name of the beneficiary of the praktikon: instead of "the soldier... Michael Saventzes," we read "the reverend imperial monastery... called Esphigmenou" (*Esphigménou*, no. 15.1–8). For that matter, there is nothing in the list of properties, paroikoi, fiscal charges, and taxes that follows in Saventzes', Maroules', and Berilas' praktika that distinguishes them from normal monastic praktika. In the previous chapter I argued that the appearance of the word *oikonomia* in the introductory formulas of fourteenth-century monastic praktika was merely an archaistic remnant from Michael VIII's reign and did not signify that monasteries held oikonomiai. My reasoning was that documents issued by the emperor, from the later thirteenth century through the end of the empire, never refer to the property holdings of any monastery as an oikonomia. Thus, if *oikonomia* in the introductory formula of a monastic praktikon does not mean that the monastery actually held an oikonomia, then *oikonomia* in such a passage in a praktikon for an individual cannot prove that the individual held the contents as an oikonomia.

As for the remaining three praktika, Raoul's praktikon states explicitly that his holdings were granted to him through a *prostagma*. It is quite likely that Raoul held a pronoia, especially since, after his death, the village of Prevista did not remain in his family. It next appears in documents from 1325 which deal with its sale by the *megale doukaina* Theodora Palaiologina to Michael Asen, tsar of Bulgaria. Asen then donated it, with the Byzantine emperor's permission, to the monastery of Zographou (*Zographou*, no. 22).

The praktikon for the monk Kallinikos is probably dealing with a simple gift and not a pronoia. There is little doubt that Kallinikos received the grant with the understanding that it would later pass to Hilandar. In other words, the grant parallels the grant to the *hegoumenos* Gervasios *[7.9]*.

The praktikon for Margarites is difficult to categorize. The praktikon notes that he had the right to pass the *posotes* to his children, but there is no mention of a right to alienate the properties in any other way. Thus, if the part of Monomachos' grant that became hereditary remained part of his pronoia, then one could say that Margarites held a hereditary pronoia.

As praktika, these documents were legal, official inventories of the properties and rights held by the men. The praktika for Saventzes, Maroules, Berilas, and Raoul were created subsequent to a fiscal reassessment (*apographike exisosis kai apokatastasis*) of a particular area by fiscal agents (*apographeis*) and represent revisions of earlier praktika. The purpose of these praktika was to record the results of the fiscal reassessment (*exisosis*) of the pronoiai (see Tables 8.2 and 8.3). The *exisosis* itself was made to ensure that each landholder was holding the proper *posotes* of property. Given that the first three of the men were soldiers, one could call their praktika "military praktika" (*stratiotika praktika*), but to my knowledge this expression appears only once.[47] Similarly, the properties within their praktika could be called *stratiotika ktemata*, but this too is a rare term after the eleventh century (when it referred to a quite different institution). From the end of the thirteenth through the fourteenth century it is occasionally found in the preambles of praktika, where the *apographeus* lists the types of properties he was reassessing: e.g., "*prosopika*, *archontika*, ecclesiastical, monastic, *stratiotika*, *chrysovoullata* and all the other *ktemata*."[48] In the case of Saventzes and Maroules the revision was of properties in the "theme of the city of Thessaloniki," and similarly Berilas' praktikon was part of a revision of the properties "in the area outside the God-saved city of Thessaloniki." The chronological and geographical differences between Saventzes', Berilas', and Maroules' praktika are slight enough that we can regard the praktika as three concrete manifestations of pronoia at about the same time and in more or less one area (precisely the same moment and area in the case of Saventzes' and Maroules' praktika). Thus, comparisons made between these praktika do not have to take into consideration the evolution of the pronoia institution or local variations in practices. In addition, and perhaps most importantly, the *posotetes* of the praktika, seventy, seventy-two, and eighty hyperpyra, are so similar as to suggest strongly that these are representative figures for pronoia holders who were *megaloallagitai* in the early 1320s.

Alexios Raoul's fragmentary praktikon was made during a revision of the properties in the "theme of Voleron and Mosynopolis, Serres and Strymon." The praktikon for Monomachos is also a revised praktikon, but it was not drawn up during a general fiscal revision, but rather after Monomachos received hereditary rights over one-half of the *posotes* of his grant. The praktikon for Margarites is the initial praktikon created following a new grant of paroikoi and property to Margarites.

The praktika of these men, when viewed in conjunction with other source evidence, illuminate quite a few of the major elements of the institution of

[47] MM, IV, 70.21–22 (1257). And see Mutafčiev, "Vojniški zemi," 535 note 66, and N. Oikonomides, "Contribution à l'étude de la pronoia au XIIIe siècle," in Oikonomides, *Documents et études sur les institutions de Byzance* (London, 1976), no. VI, 171.

[48] *Vatopédi*, I, no. 25.2–3 (1297), and II, no. 70.2–3 (1341).

Table 8.2 Components of the oikonomiai of Michael Saventzes, Nicholas Maroules, Basil Berilas, and Michael Monomachos

	soldier Michael Saventzes (1321)	soldier Nicholas Maroules (1321)	soldier Basil Berilas (1323)	*eparchos* Michael Monomachos (before January 1333)*
PART A (oikoumenon)				
paroikoi	8 households with 29 persons in four villages **12 hyperpyra**	17 households with 60 persons in two villages **29¼ hyp.**	13 households with 37 persons in one village **6⅙ hyp.**	27 households with 86 persons in two villages **28 hyp.**
ge	three parcels totaling 1700 modioi –34 hyp.	one parcel of 450 mod. –9 hyp.	one parcel of 2000 mod. –40 hyp.	several parcels –450 mod. of 1st quality; 100 mod. of 2nd and 3rd quality
garden				25 mod.
calculated *anti-oikoumenou*	**22⅔ hyp.**	**6 hyp.**	**26 hyp.**	**7 hyp.**
ennomion of acorns and *mandriatikion*			2 hyp.	
ampelopakton			2 hyp.	
exaleimmatika	vineyard of 1½ modioi	six *staseis* or parts of *staseis* –5⅓ hyp.	more than one vineyard parcel –1 hyp. total for above –5 hyp.	
calculated *anti-oikoumenou*	**⅓ hyp.**	**3⅓ hyp.**	**3⅓ hyp.**	

mill other rights & properties associated with mill calculated *anti-oikoumenou*			4 hyp. [4 hyp.][†] $\frac{1}{3}$ hyp. $\frac{2}{3}$ hyp. total for above –9 hyp. **[6 hyp.]**[†]	
fishing of Chantax & dock charge calculated *anti-oikoumenou*				50 hyp. **33$\frac{1}{2}$ hyp.**
Total *oikoumenon*	**35 hyp.**	**36 hyp.** **(by calculation, 38 $\frac{7}{12}$)**	**40 hyp.** **(by calculation, 41$\frac{1}{2}$)**	**(by calculation, 68$\frac{1}{2}$)**

PART B				
exaleimmatika			one *stasis* of 50 mod. of *ge* **1 hyp.**	dry vineyard of 4 mod. –$\frac{1}{2}$ hyp. 6 *staseis* –4 hyp.
zeugaratikion of his paroikoi				9$\frac{1}{2}$ hyp.
kaniskia, choirodekateia and *aer*				2 hyp. total "*exaleimmata*" **16 hyp.**

(*cont.*)

Table 8.2 (*cont.*)

	soldier Michael Saventzes (1321)	soldier Nicholas Maroules (1321)	soldier Basil Berilas (1323)	*eparchos* Michael Monomachos (before January 1333)*
fishing of Choudena and Nevoliani				**18 hyp.**
opheleia of the *empsychon*	**1 hyp.**	**2½ hyp.**		
choirodekateia and *melissoennomion*	**1 hyp.**	**2½ hyp.**	**1 hyp.**	
ennomion	of two villages **5 hyp.**		of his paroikoi's animals	
linovrocheion	of two villages **20 hyp.**			
epiteleia			for houses held by a monastery **1 hyp.**	
ge, held earlier, contiguous to *ge* in *oikoumenon*	one parcel of 400 mod. **8 hyp.**	one parcel of 1600 mod. **32 hyp.**	one parcel of 2500 mod. of 2nd and 3rd quality **37 hyp.**	
Total *Part B*	**35 hyp.**	**36 hyp. (by calculation, 37)**	**40 hyp.**	**(by calculation, 34 hyp.)**

TOTAL ***posotes*** (*PART A + PART B*)	**70 hyp.**	**72 hyp. (by calculation, 75 $^{7}/_{12}$)**	**80 hyp. (by calculation, 81$^{1}/_{2}$)**	**(by calculation, 102$^{1}/_{2}$ hyp.)**

PART C				
	oikomodion – 1 modios of wheat and barley per 3 hyperpyra		–	–
	oinometrion – 1 measure of local wine per hyperpyron			
	angareiai – 12 days per year per paroikos			
	3 *kaniskia*			
	oikoumenon to be received in two payments in September and March			

* I have rearranged the components of Monomachos' praktikon to reflect the structure of his oikonomia prior to January 1333: see the text.

† The information is incomplete due to a lacuna. Hypothetical restorations by Oikonomides, "Notes," 344–45.

Table 8.3 Components of the oikonomiai of Alexios Raoul, the monk Kallinikos, and John Margarites

	fragmentary praktikon for Alexios Raoul (ca. 1297)	praktikon for the monk Kallinikos (1323)	praktikon for John Margarites (1342)
paroikoi	62 households with 312 persons in one village **ca. 152 hyperpyra**	36 households with 127 persons in one village **65 7/12 hyp.**	19 households with 53 persons in four villages **19¼ hyp.**
exaleimmatikai staseis	8 *staseis* **30½ hyp.**		7 *staseis* **6 hyp.**
fair of St. Christopher	**figure missing**		
vineyards from various *exaleimmata*	16 modioi **4 hyp.**		
garden	2 mod.		
exaleimmatika	at least 6 walnut trees held earlier **no fiscal assessment provided**		
mandriatikon	**31 hyp., as earlier**		
ennomion		for a specific pasture **4 hyp.**	
aer of the inscribed paroikoi without the three state *kephalaia*	**13⅓ hyp.**	**3 hyp.**	
epiteleiai		for a vineyard of 1¼ mod. and its surrounding land (*esothyrion*) of 9 mod. **⅔ hyp.**	
		for a vineyard of 7 mod. **1½ hyp.**	
		for a field of 8 mod. **⅓ hyp.**	
		for a vineyard of 1⅓ mod. **⅓ hyp.**	
		for a field of 10 mod. **⅓ hyp.**	
		for a field of 6 mod. **¼ hyp.**	

pasture land			⅓ of two parcels	**4 hyp.**		
mill	held earlier	**2 hyp., as earlier**	⅓ of two water mills & ⅓ of half a windmill	**10 hyp.**	all-season mill	**3 hyp.**
vineyard	held earlier	**16 modioi**	–		8 mod., neglected	
ge	(data missing)	**unknown**	seven parcels of "best" land totaling 600 mod.	**24 hyp.**	1000 mod. of 3rd quality	**20 hyp.**
			1500 mod. of other land in several parcels	**30 hyp.**	two parcels of 550 mod.	
calculated *anti-oikoumenou*						**7 hyp.**
TOTAL *posotes*		**(greater than 250 hyp.)**		**145 hyp. (by calculation, 144)**		**55 hyp. (by calculation, 55¼)**

	(data missing)	customary *angareiai*	–
		3 *kaniskia*	

pronoia. Each praktikon gives a list of paroikoi, by village and by household, naming the members of each household, their movable (pigs, cows, asses, oxen, sheep, goats, beehives) and immovable property (arable land, vineyards, gardens, pear trees, a mill), sometimes indicating the legal status of the property (hereditary possession, *hypoteles*, from a dowry), and concluding with the *telos* on each paroikos household and its property. This is followed by a list of lands, their general location or name, usually their size, and a figure for each in hyperpyra representing the official tax liability on the land. Interspersed are other properties (in Berilas' case, the rights to a mill) and various fiscal charges, all with their yearly value in hyperpyra. After this the official value of the pronoia is given (the *posotes*). Finally, some of the praktika note how and when the payments are to be made to the grant holder, what corvée obligations (*angareiai*) burden the paroikoi, and the frequency of the customary "presents" in kind owed the pronoia holder (*kaniskia*). These praktika differ from the mid-thirteenth-century notarial formula *[5.12]* in that the latter transmits only paroikoi to a pronoia soldier, with no mention of land and rights, not even the holdings and *telos* of the paroikoi themselves.

Many of the limitations of the praktika as sources for the institution of pronoia spring from the same characteristics as those which make them useful. Their chronological and geographical affinities (a fifty-year period in Macedonia) in themselves contribute little to our knowledge of the evolution of the pronoia institution or its regional variations. The further one goes backward or forward in time to explain other references to pronoia through the use of these documents, the more likely the possibility of misinterpretation.

Further, the praktika only detail the holdings of one particular grant. The grant holders may have held other imperial grants or may have owned other allodial property which would not be recorded in their praktika. Indeed, Kallinikos had been granted other property by Andronikos II.[49] Other pronoia holders did in fact have possessions which were not part of their pronoiai. The soldier (*stratiotes*) Michael Petritzes sold a small orchard to the Lemviotissa monastery which he held as allodial property (MM, IV, 173). And the *megaloallagites* Manuel Garianos was apparently awarded hereditary tax-free status on his patrimonial *hypostasis* which also was "outside the value of his oikonomia," and therefore not part of his pronoia *[8.49]*. If one adds the element of hereditary pronoia and allodial

[49] *Chilandar*, ed. Petit, no. 74.3 (1321), and no. 90.11 (1323).

properties, the actual possessions and holdings of a soldier could be a rich mix of rights and properties, including those he inherited and could bequeath, partly pronoia, partly patrimony, as well as those he acquired during his lifetime, such as further grants of pronoia, part of which he possibly could bequeath, and properties he purchased or received as gifts. Moreover, the ownership or possession of such properties could be shared with other individuals or monasteries and be subject to complicated fiscal processes. But if these men owned properties that they did not receive from the emperor, the praktika say nothing of them.

Further, we cannot assume that all of the holdings listed in each of the revised praktika (those for Saventzes, Maroules, Berilas, Raoul) were part of the original grants of pronoiai, and that the stated *posotetes* of seventy, seventy-two and eighty hyperpyra as found in the praktika of Saventzes, Maroules, and Berilas, are not necessarily the *posotetes* of the original pronoia grants assigned to these men, but increases or perhaps decreases.

For each praktikon the total *posotes* was the sum of the constituent elements (see Tables 8.2 and 8.3). The fact that the sums by calculation are not always equal to the total stated *posotes* indicates that the *posotes* was set first and the task of the *apographeus* was to assemble a collection of income-producing instruments which together approximated the official *posotes* as closely as possible. If the exact *posotes* could not be constructed, the officials tended to confer a bit more revenue, going slightly beyond the official *posotes*. The praktika for Saventzes, Maroules, and Berilas are divided into two parts: a first part called the "*oikoumenon*" and a second part which is given no name (and so for simplicity I will refer to it as Part B). For these three soldiers, the sums of the *oikoumenon* and Part B are equal, and when totaled equal the *posotes*. For Monomachos, the *oikoumenon* was two-thirds of the total *posotes*. Since the stated subtotals do not always correspond to the sum by calculation, the subtotals of the *oikoumenon* and of Part B must have been established in advance, ostensibly on the basis of the preestablished total *posotes*.

Since we find, for example, arable land (*ge*) in both parts of the praktika, we may ask why the praktika were divided into two parts. The term *oikoumenon*, denoting the total tax on the paroikos *staseis* of a village (*paroikikon telos*), is first encountered in the later thirteenth century and is found exclusively in praktika and denotes the sum of the *telos* of the individual paroikos households in a village. The earliest securely dated documents to use *oikoumenon* to mean the total *paroikikon telos* of a village date from

1301, though a praktikon from either 1283–84 or 1298–89 is the earliest extant document to use the term.[50] Praktika from 1262 and 1284(?) do not employ the term.[51] Thus, while hardly indisputable, the term appears to have been introduced during the 1280s or 1290s. It is used most frequently from 1318 through the 1320s, and then becomes less common.[52] Originally the *oikoumenon* was intended to include nothing but the *telos* of the paroikoi held by a monastery, pronoia holder, or other landholder. In other words, a certain fraction of the *posotes* (in the four praktika in Table 8.2, either one-half or two-thirds) was supposed to be derived from the household *telos* of paroikoi, and the remainder from other taxes and charges. But for whatever reasons, the *apographeis* did not assign these four grant holders a *paroikikon* telos equal to one-half or two-thirds of the posotes. Rather, they made up for this by adding other income-producing lands (*ge*, garden plots, *exaleimmata*) and, in Berilas' case, charges (the *ampelopakton* and the *ennomion*) and a mill and its ancillary rights and properties. In every case the tax assessed on these items was calculated at a special rate, a rate *anti-oikoumenou*, that is, "in lieu of *oikoumenon*." In three of the praktika some if not all of the *ge* in the *oikoumenon* is contiguous with the *ge* in Part B of the praktikon, indicating the process the *apographeis* used to balance out the *oikoumenon* and Part B.[53]

Consider Maroules' *oikoumenon*. The *apographeis* assigned him the *telos* from seventeen paroikos households, but this amounted to only 29¼ hyperpyra. Since they wanted to create an *oikoumenon* of thirty-six hyperpyra, they added one piece of *ge* and six pieces of *exaleimmata*, and assessed these at a special rate. In nearly all praktika, when the quality of *ge* is not stated, the *ge* is assessed at one hyperpyron per fifty modioi, and in fact the tax for Maroules' 450 modioi of *ge* is first stated as nine hyperpyra. Then we read, "*anti-oikoumenou* six nomismata," which means that since Maroules was receiving this land "in lieu of *oikoumenon*," or "instead of the *telos* of additional paroikoi," the land, for the purposes of the praktikon, was assigned

50 *Iviron*, III, no. 70 (1301); *Vatopédi*, I, no. 30 (1301); and cf. *Lavra*, II, no. 91 (ca. 1300); *Xéropotamou*, no. 18A (ca. 1300); and *Esphigménou*, no. 8 (ca. 1300). *Esphigménou*, no. 7 (1283–84 or 1298–99).

51 *Iviron*, III, no. 59 (1262); *Lavra*, II, no. 77 (1284?).

52 A praktikon from 1338 does not use the term, but nevertheless presents the sum of all of the *paroikika tele* of a village before proceeding to the other charges and properties held by a monastery: *Vatopédi*, II, no. 81.12.

53 The only other appearance of the phrase, outside of the five praktika discussed here, is in a fragment of a praktikon for the Prodromos monastery near Serres, dated by the editor to sometime after 1342, which assesses one *exaleimmatike stasis* at 7 nomismata, *anti-oikoumenou* 4⅔ nomismata: *Prodrome B*, no. 186.12. Other *exaleimmatikai staseis* in the fragment are assessed normally.

a reduced fiscal value of six hyperpyra. In each case the normal fiscal value of the properties or charges was reduced by about one-third when assessed *anti-oikoumenou.*

Oikonomides hypothesized that the special *anti-oikoumenou* rate existed because it was somehow more profitable for the pronoia holder to receive a formal *telos* of *X* hyperpyra from paroikoi than a formal *telos* of *X* hyperpyra from other sources, and therefore it was necessary to adjust the *telos* of other lands and charges substituted for the *telos* of paroikoi in the *oikoumenon.*[54] Most likely the *telos* of paroikoi was preferred because it represented an income that required no further effort on the pronoia holder's part than to collect it, whereas the exploitation of property required more involvement on the part of the pronoia holder.

Further, the technique of the *telos anti-oikoumenou* permits us to make an observation about Monomachos' praktikon. Unlike the praktika for Saventzes, Maroules, and Berilas, the praktikon for Monomachos was a revised praktikon made for the specific purpose of setting aside fifty hyperpyra of *posotes* over which Monomachos was granted hereditary rights. This existing praktikon for Monomachos contains five basic parts:

(a) the telos of paroikoi in the villages of Chantax and Nesion – 27½ hyperpyra
(b) land with a *telos* calculated *anti-oikoumenou* – 7 hyperpyra

Together the praktikon notes that these formed an *oikoumenon* of 34½ hyperpyra.

(c) *exaleimmata* – 16 hyperpyra

The praktikon states that these first three elements together amounted to 50½ hyperpyra.
In addition, the praktikon contains

(d) the fishing of Choudena and Nevoliani – 18 hyperpyra, and
(e) the fishing of Chantax and a dock with a *telos* of 50 hyperpyra, which when calculated *anti-oikoumenou* was assessed at 33½ hyperpyra.

Unlike the praktika of Saventzes, Maroules, and Berilas, the *anti-oikoumenou* components appear in two distinct parts of the Monomachos' praktikon. I think the reason for this is that the *apographeus* Vatatzes rearranged the components of Monomachos' praktikon in order to create the fifty hyperpyra over which he was granted hereditary rights.

[54] Oikonomides, "Notes," 341–44.

It is possible that the earlier praktikon for Monomachos, before he received hereditary rights to fifty hyperpyra from his oikonomia, contained, in Part A (the *oikoumenon*), the components (a), (b), and (e), which totaled sixty-eight hyperpyra, and that Part B contained (c) and (d), amounting to thirty-four hyperpyra. The summary of Monomachos' praktikon as presented in Table 8.2 reflects this hypothetical restoration of the earlier praktikon for Monomachos. This earlier praktikon would have created a ratio between Part A and Part B of 2:1. However, it seems that the *apographeus*, in order to create a *posotes* of fifty hyperpyra over which Monomachos would hold hereditary rights, had to draw upon some items from Part A and some from Part B. As a result, the existing praktikon is divided into two parts which do not correspond to my Part A/Part B distinction: the first part of the existing praktikon has a *posotes* of $50\frac{1}{2}$ hyperpyra and contained one property calculated *anti-oikoumenou*, and the second part amounts to $51\frac{1}{2}$ hyperpyra and contains one *anti-oikoumenou* assessment. We observe that the ratio of *oikoumenon* to non-*oikoumenon* in both parts of the existing revised praktikon corresponds approximately to a 2:1 ratio.[55]

The contents of the grant and their sources

As a rule the emperor granted only those economic instruments in pronoia to which the state had or believed it had a right, quintessentially, as John Kantakouzenos put it, "revenues from villages." These fall into four categories: real property, taxes and charges in cash, taxes and charges in kind, and labor services. At this point we consider the contents of the praktika,

[55] L. Mavrommatis, "Η Πρόνοια του Μονομάχου και η Διαμάχη για τον Χάντακα (1333–1378)," *Σύμμεικτα* 14 (2001), 263, argued that Vatatzes conferred the $50\frac{1}{2}$ hyperpyra in hereditary tenure upon Monomachos and then conferred another $51\frac{1}{2}$ hyperpyra illegally. This is highly unlikely. If Vatatzes' action was illegal, the deception was so transparent that any Byzantine official, without recourse to any other information, could have seen that the action was illegal: Vatatzes wrote in the praktikon that Monomachos was granted hereditary rights over fifty hyperpyra, and then, according to Mavrommatis' interpretation, he conferred two sets of fifty hyperpyra with hereditary rights. The praktikon, then, would have been worthless for its intended purpose. Moreover, Mavrommatis seemed to assume that the 1333 praktikon reflected an initial grant of privileges to Monomachos, while it is clear, as the praktikon states, that the fifty hyperpyra were to be drawn "from his oikonomia, which he has on the Strymon." In my view Monomachos' total oikonomia amounted to around 100 hyperpyra. But if Monomachos did hold other properties within his oikonomia which are not listed in the praktikon at all, then it would be impossible not only to calculate the total *posotes* of Monomachos' oikonomia, but anyone else's as well. K. Pavlikjanov, *Istorija na bŭlgarskija svetogorski manastir Zograf ot 980 do 1804 g.* (Sofia, 2005), 52–53, with a detailed English summary: 211, adopts Mavrommatis' interpretation.

the holdings of pronoia holders, and how the seven praktika in Tables 8.2 and 8.3 relate to and illuminate references in other documents and other sources.

Real property

There were basically two types of real property which the emperor could exploit for pronoia grants, as well as any other kind of grant. These were properties owned by the emperor ex officio, or imperial properties, and properties owned by the treasury or fisc (*demosion*).

Imperial properties, called *vasilikai* (imperial) *episkepseis*, *vasilika proasteia*, *vasilika zeugelateia*, *vasilika ktemata*, or even simply *vasilike ge*, are encountered frequently in the sources of the tenth through thirteenth centuries. During the Nicaean era there are occasional references to imperial properties in Asia Minor,[56] but from the later thirteenth through the fifteenth century it is more difficult to find references to any imperial properties anywhere. Nevertheless, there are a handful of examples in which imperial land seems to have been granted to pronoia holders during this period. A document from 1285 lists among the properties which the monastery of St. John on Patmos held on Lemnos "from the imperial land in Vounaria of Exadaktyles the [part] cut from the *zeugelateion*, near the [part] given to the soldiers." These soldiers, about whom nothing else is known, received part of the imperial land either as a pronoia grant or as smallholdings.[57]

Around 1327 the imperial *zeugelateion* of Patrikona on the Chalkidike was given to George Katzaras and the Varvarenoi soldier company as part of their pronoia.[58] And a 1351 chrysobull of John VI *[8.6]* gave Iviron some land near the village of Melintzianis "which was earlier reckoned as *despoinike* and was later given to the Digenatoi soldiers." *Despoinike* means "belonging to an empress," here perhaps referring to Anna of Savoy, regent for John V during the civil wars of the 1340s. Thus, the land in question had once been imperial land, was then transferred to these soldiers, and now was given to the monastery. The apparent ease with which the property

56 MM, IV, 9 (1235), 142 (1231), and see Ahrweiler, "Smyrne," 63–64. *Patmos*, I, no. 36.11 (1269), and *Patmos*, II, no. 67.16 (1262).

57 *Patmos*, II, no. 74.16–17: ἀπὸ τῆς βασιλικῆς γῆς . . . τὸ ἀποκοπὲν ἀπὸ τοῦ ζευγηλατείου, πλησίον τὸ δοθὲν τοῖς στρατιῶταις.

58 *Docheiariou*, p. 140. References to Patrikona as imperial land: *Docheiariou*, no. 19.22 (1338), no. 20.38 (1341), no. 23.18 (1344); and *Iviron*, III, no. 70.345 (1301): τοῖς ἀπὸ τοῦ Πατρικωνᾶ βασιλικοῖς δικαίοις. Also see *[8.47]* below.

passed from one holder to another suggests that the Digenatoi held it as a pronoia, rather than as smallholdings.

Nikephoros Gregoras in his history refers to imperial property as well. He claims that John VI Kantakouzenos, amid the civil wars of the 1340s, had promised his supporters "the rest of the imperial estates" *[7.21]*. Whatever variety of grants Gregoras had in mind, the passage implies that soon there would be no imperial land at all.

Given that Macedonia is the best-documented area in the later thirteenth and fourteenth centuries, one would expect the majority of references to imperial properties to deal with imperial properties in that region. But aside from the two references cited above, there are only a handful of other references to imperial property in Macedonia.[59] Surprisingly more frequent, relative to its area and the percentage of documents that deal with the area, are references to imperial properties – *zeugelateion*, *ge*, *choraphion*, *dikaia*, and even a *kepos* (garden) – on the island of Lemnos.[60] This suggests that imperial properties remained more extensive on the islands, either because they were always more extensive or because emperors tended to make fewer grants of these properties to religious foundations, pronoia holders, and others.

Paralleling imperial properties were "fiscal" (*demosiaka*) properties, that is, properties that did not belong to the emperor, but to the fisc. It has been argued that there was not much of a distinction between "imperial" and "fiscal" property in late Byzantium. While there was certainly no absolute distinction between the two types of properties and while the emperor had control over the disposition of "fiscal" properties no less than "imperial" properties, it is possible to see a difference. For example, a 1347 chrysobull issued by John VI Kantakouzenos mentions "the land and the *ampelopakton* in the villages of Plagena and Therma, earlier belonging to the fisc [τῶν ὄντων μὲν πρότερον δημοσιακῶν], and after this given to the deceased *kyr*

[59] E.g., a general reference to imperial *zeugelateia* on the Chalkidike: *Esphigménou*, no. 7.5–6,15 (1283–84 or 1298–99); imperial *dikaia* on the lower Vardar: *Xéropotamou*, no. 19.14–16,22 (1319); an imperial *zeugelateion* consisting of the village tou Makrogenous near the Vardar river: *Zographou*, no. 17.80–84 (1320), and also, nos. 18 and 44, and *Lavra*, II, no. 110.4–5 (1321); an imperial *zeugelateion* called Vernares near the Strymon: *Prodrome*, no. 1.4 (1304) and no. 12.5 (1322); and τὰ βασιλικὰ τόπια on the Kassandra peninsula: *Dionysiou*, no. 20.17 (1421).

[60] *Lavra*, II, no. 73.20,25 (1284), no. 74.20,23 (1284), and no. 77.22,26 (1284?); *Patmos*, II, no. 74.16 (1285); *Lavra*, III, no. 127.13–14 (1346); *Vatopédi*, II, no. 128.8 (1368); *Actes du Pantocrator*, ed. V. Kravari (Paris, 1991), no. 12.2 (1388) and no. 20.12–13 (1394); *Pantéléèmôn*, no. 16.7 (1406); and *Dionysiou*, no. 22.17 (1425) and no. 25.47 (1430).

George Pharmakes."[61] Most likely Pharmakes received these items as part of a pronoia grant, but unlike "imperial" properties, one of the items granted was not a property but a rent, the *ampelopakton*, which in this case was due to the fisc. Another example of fiscal land passing to private individuals, perhaps as pronoia, perhaps as a simple grant, is found in a fragmentary *periorismos* from around 1335 for the holdings of an unknown monastery. One property, located in the delta region of the Vardar and Gallikos rivers, bordered on "the rights of the fiscal land [*demosiake ge*] held by Lykopoulos, Devlitzenos, [and] Servos."[62]

Similarly, an *orismos* from October 1342, probably issued by the regency for John V, which deals with some land and vines "from both *tzako*[*nikon*] and fiscal *hypostaseis*" in the villages of Kato Ouska and Rachova (both located around Zichna). The emperor exempted a man named Margarites (perhaps the Margarites of one of our praktika), who had been holding these properties previously, of the tax of nine hyperpyra on these properties and gave him the right to transmit this property to his children and heirs.[63] A *hypostasis* was usually a peasant holding, more commonly called simply a *stasis*. In this case the land and vines held by Margarites came from *hypostaseis* which had been held by *tzakones* (a category of urban guards) and by the state. No document ever refers to "imperial" *hypostaseis* or *staseis*. The reason why the fisc came into possession of these *hypostaseis* originally is probably because the property was *exaleimmata*.

All of the praktika except Kallinikos' include *exaleimmata* as part of the real property held by the grantee. *Exaleimmata*, or *exaleimmatika* properties, were properties which were temporarily "ownerless," either because they had been abandoned by their taxpaying owner or because their taxpaying owner had died without heir. Such properties were not necessarily vacant or unworked; some were fully cultivated, but not by their owners. *Exaleimma* was a fiscal and legal designation, not an agricultural description. An *exaleimma* was an individual property abandoned by its owner and an *exaleimmatikon stasion* or *exaleimmatike stasis* was an entire paroikos household holding which had been abandoned by its owner. In three of the praktika we find *exaleimmatika stasia* and in almost every instance the praktika supply a name with the property, the quantity of *ge*, *ampelion* (vineyard), *choraphion* (field), or combination of these, which it contained, and

[61] *Dionysiou*, no. 2.36–38. Both of these villages were located on the Chalkidike.

[62] Lefort, *Villages de Macédoine*, 185.4–5. And for another likely reference to the same property, see *Chilandar*, ed. Živojinović, I, no. 36.10,23 (1317), and pp. 62–63.

[63] *Prodrome*, no. 36.4–5: ἀπό τε Τζακω[νικῶν] ὑποστάσεων καὶ δημοσιακῶν.

a figure in hyperpyra representing its fiscal value, which corresponded to its *telos*. Five of the seven praktika contain individual *exaleimmatika* properties (fields, walnut trees, a dry vineyard) and when figures are provided, most of the fields were assessed at the normal assessment for *ge* (1 hyperpyron per 50 modioi).

Earlier in Byzantine history the taxes of such "deserted" properties were paid by the local community, that is, the village or neighboring landowners, until someone decided to cultivate them and accept their tax liability. After a certain amount of time, if the property's owner did not reclaim the land, such land could become *klasma*, that is, it was separated from the village community from the fiscal point of view and then either sold by the fisc at a reduced price or kept by the fisc and cultivated by the state. However, in the late period the intermediate stage disappeared and, paralleling escheat in the medieval West, such "abandoned" properties devolved to the state immediately. At that point the state could keep the property or dispose of it as it saw fit. If the property had been owned by a paroikos who was held by a pronoia holder or other landholder, it became increasingly common for the property simply to be added to the landholdings of that landholder, in which case its future cultivation was arranged by the landholder. Large pieces of *exaleimmatika* were often kept by the lord; smaller pieces were often reassigned to his paroikoi. While Kallinikos was granted no *exaleimmata* directly, one of his paroikoi received from the *apographeus* a house "from the *exaleimma* of Koukoudes" (*Chilandar*, ed. Petit, no. 92.59). Some *exaleimmata* were considered valuable enough for landowners to fight over their possession. On the whole, reassignment of the *exaleimmata* of paroikoi to the pronoia holder or other privileged landholder who had held the paroikoi was a practical means to compensate the landholder for the loss of income brought on by the death without heir or disappearance of the paroikoi.[64] Other sources confirm that *exaleimmata* were a major source of revenue for pronoia grants (e.g., *[6.2]* and *[8.75]*).

The administrative process whereby properties became *exaleimmata* can perhaps explain many of the references to "fiscal property" (*demosiaka*) in the documents. Because *exaleimmatika*, before being regranted, were

64 M. Bartusis, "'Εξάλειμμα: Escheat in Byzantium," *Dumbarton Oaks Papers* 40 (1986), 60–61. Many of Kallinikos' paroikoi held *ge* or fields through "conferral" (*paradosis*). It is possible that the practice here was to distribute *exaleimmata* among the other paroikoi, and whoever held the paroikoi would derive benefit from the *exaleimmata* indirectly through higher household *tele* on the paroikoi. On the other hand, no vines, a common component of *exaleimmata*, are found among the property the paroikoi held through conferral, so some other mechanism may have been in play.

technically the property of the fisc – as opposed to the emperor – references to "fiscal property" (*demosiaka*) may well be referring to *exaleimmata*. This is why the land and vines "from both *tzako*[*nikon*] and fiscal *hypostaseis*" for which Margarites received tax exemption and hereditary rights were derived from *exaleimmata*. Indeed only land and vineyards are mentioned within the contents of these *hypostaseis*, no paroikoi and no livestock. In another example, a 1285 praktikon for the monastery of St. John on Patmos lists, among the monastery's properties on Lemnos, a "fiscal vineyard [*ampelion demosiakon*] in Pterin, which Vrataina held" and the "fiscal vineyard" of a deceased man. These too appear to have been *exaleimmata*.[65]

Like imperial property, fiscal property is equally rare in Macedonia. Aside from the reference to "*tzakonikai* and fiscal *hypostaseis*" cited above, the only other example I know of is a reference in a Greek chrysobull of Stefan Dušan, issued in 1345 for the Prodromos monastery, which refers to "two fiscal mills." Another document, a 1359 chrysobull of Symeon Uroš, the independent Serb ruler at Trikkala, issued for the monastery of St. George at Zavlantia in Thessaly, refers to a "fiscal field."[66] And like imperial property, fiscal property appears inordinately frequently in documents involving Lemnos.[67]

The real property found within our praktika falls into several categories of agricultural land. *Ge* ("land") or *choraphia* ("fields") is arable farmland. It appears in all of our praktika except the fragmentary praktikon for Raoul where the data is simply missing. Because the large tracts of *ge* held by the men bear no names and are only identified by an approximate location, it seems that they were not privately owned, but imperial or fiscal land.

Vineyards were held by the grantee in five of the praktika. Raoul held one large vineyard and several smaller vineyards from *exaleimmata*; Margarites held a "neglected" vineyard as well as numerous vineyard parcels within the *exaleimmatikai staseis* assigned to him; Saventzes held a small vineyard from *exaleimmata*; Berilas held several vineyard parcels within his *exaleimmatika*; and Monomachos held a dry vineyard from *exaleimmata*. Kallinikos held no vineyards directly, but three of the *epiteleiai* he received (see below) were based on vineyards.

The remaining immovable property is found in only one or two of the praktika. Pasture land is found in Kallinikos' praktikon. A garden of 25 modioi is included in Monomachos praktikon and two modioi in Raoul's

65 *Patmos*, II, no. 74.14,21.

66 Solovjev–Mošin, *Grčke povelje*, no. 2.129 (1345), and no. 31.160–61 (1359) *[8.77]*.

67 *Lavra*, II, no. 74.9,37 (1284), no.76.5 (1284), no. 77.55 (1284?), no. 96.16 (1304); *Patmos*, II, no. 74.14,21 (1285); *Lavra*, III, no. 136.42,168 (1355); *Actes du Pantocrator*, no. 20.12–13 (1394).

praktikon. And there were walnut trees within the *exaleimmatika* held by Raoul. In other words, the collection of immovable property within these seven praktika was more or less the same as one would find in a praktikon for a monastery.

One unusual element in regard to the agricultural contents of these praktika is that the paroikoi in these seven praktika frequently held arable land (*ge* or *choraphia*). This presents a stark contrast to the praktika of monasteries in which the paroikoi listed usually hold neither *ge* nor *choraphia*.[68] One way to explain this difference, and it is a mere hypothesis, is that monasteries were accustomed to holding propertyless peasants and over the years had developed mechanisms to exploit large fields through corvée labor. And while monasteries had a much greater use for agricultural produce in kind, individual recipients of grants certainly would have preferred a cash *telos*. Also, organizing and managing the cultivation of domain lands required effort and personnel, and monasteries had the people to oversee their estates.

The only other type of real property held were mills. Berilas enjoyed the proceeds from a mill and the property associated with it, Raoul held a mill, and Kallinikos held a one-third share of two water mills and one-third share of half of a windmill.[69] These, too, are commonly found in monastic praktika. As in the case of land, the grant holder did not actually receive the *posotes* of the mill as stated in his praktikon. This was simply the normal state tax on the mill which was exempted for the grant holder. Rather, the grant holder's benefit from the mill was derived from his own use of it and, if it was used by others, from per-use charges.

Taxes and fiscal charges on property

The base property tax (*telos*) of a property was implicitly granted to the pronoia holder when the property was granted. Because the property bore no *telos* obligation when it was imperial or fiscal property, it bore no such obligation after it was conferred upon a pronoia holder. The *posotetes* attached to properties that were held directly by the pronoia holder represented the amount of tax revenue the fisc was forsaking for the benefit of the grant holder, not necessarily the economic benefit the recipient received from the property. The profit from land came from the harvest or the rental

[68] A. Laiou-Thomadakis, *Peasant Society in the Late Byzantine Empire* (Princeton, 1977), 161.
[69] On the tax on mills, see *Lavra*, IV, p. 164.

fees levied on the peasant cultivators of the land, and the profit from a mill came from the charges levied on those who used the mill.

The one exception to this involves the charge called the *ampelopakton* (literally, "vineyard rent"). Associated with his *exaleimmatika* vineyards Berilas received an *ampelopakton* of two hyperpyra (before being assessed *anti-oikoumenou*) from the *xenoparoikoi* and the paroikoi of Kerameus (another pronoia holder). *Xenoparoikoi* were paroikoi not held by the grantee (and therefore not listed in his praktikon). And generally speaking, the *ampelopakton* was a tax on vineyards leased by paroikoi not held by the person who held the vineyard, and that fits the context here.[70] In other words, the *ampelopakton* was a rent on a specific property which in this case was organized by the state for the benefit of Berilas. As such, it represented an approximation of the actual income Berilas derived from the vineyards he held, rather than merely the amount of revenue the state forsook by granting the vineyards to Berilas.

In rare cases a component of one's pronoia grant could be the taxes normally owed on one's own property, in which case the *posotes* held by a pronoia holder did correspond to the benefit received by him. There is only one known case of this. In 1349 Demetrios Devlitzenos' oikonomia consisted of a *posotes* of 400 hyperpyra. At least part of this *posotes* appears to have been formed from a tax exemption on properties he owned personally *[8.46]*.

A third source of taxes and charges for the pronoia grant arose when the emperor assigned the tax burdening a property owned by a private party to a grant holder for the latter's benefit. For example, an act of John V from 1351/2 or 1366/7 exempted Lavra from certain charges on its possessions including the *choirodekateia* (discussed below) which had been assigned to "Thessalonian soldiers."[71] In this case the monastery, not the soldiers, held the paroikoi who paid the charges. State revenues were, in effect, directed toward pronoia holders who had no hold on the economic instruments which produced the revenues.

In another case, Xenophon in 1325 received from a fiscal official two *exaleimmatikai staseis* in Hermeleia "to be leased for a tax [*kephalaion*]." The *apographeus* states that the monastery would hold these *staseis* forever, "and for these [*staseis*] I offer each year three nomismata hyperpyra to whomever I shall arrange."[72] In other words, the monastery would lease the

70 *ODB*, s.v. "pakton." *Lavra*, IV, p. 162. *Dionysiou*, p. 45. Solovjev–Mošin, *Grčke povelje*, 390.

71 *Lavra*, III, no. 131.5,9–10.

72 *Xénophon*, no. 21.3: ἐκλαβέσθαι ἐπὶ κεφαλαίῳ, and lines 46–47: πρὸς ὃν ἂν ἐγὼ τάξω.

staseis eternally (a kind of *emphyteusis*, or perpetual lease) in return for a tax of three hyperpyra which it would render yearly to someone (presumably a pronoia holder) designated by the *apographeus*. The document refers to the payment as a tax, yet technically the *staseis* remained the property of the state, and so the three hyperpyra paid annually by the monastery was a rent, as is implied by the verb "to be leased" (ἐκλαβέσθαι). This case is an excellent example of the blurring of the distinction between taxes and rent, and between ownership and possession.

Other documents note who was to receive such tax revenues. In 1333 Andronikos III freed a monastery of the seven hyperpyra it paid (τελεῖ) annually on land it owned to a man named Preakotzelos *[8.74]*. Similarly, a chrysobull of John VI Kantakouzenos from 1349 suppressed (ἐκκόπτει) the burden of eight hyperpyra a *metochion* had been required to pay (τελεῖν) yearly to a soldier named Katakalon *[8.66]*. Another example is found in a chrysobull of Stefan Dušan from January 1346 for the monastery of Iviron. The monastery had been paying for the properties of Radolivos and other nearby domains 400 hyperpyra annually – 200 hyperpyra for the *zeugaratikion* and 200 for the *kephalaion* – which "earlier [went] to the imperial *vestiarion* [i.e., the fisc] and later to soldiers."[73] This is a clear example of taxes bypassing the treasury and being redirected "at the source" from a taxpayer to the beneficiary of an imperial grant, in this case pronoia-holding soldiers. This arrangement was of limited duration. According to a praktikon from April 1341, the monastery for these same *metochia* of Radolivos, Ovelos, and Dovrovikeia paid as a *kephalaion* 200 hyperpyra to the fisc (*demosion*).[74] Thus, the 200 hyperpyra for the *kephalaion*, with the added 200 hyperpyra for the *zeugaratikion*, went to soldiers sometime between 1341 and 1346 when Dušan abolished the payment, a maximum of four and one-half years.

The common term for a charge redirected, on imperial order, from the treasury toward a grant holder was *epiteleia*. In Chapter 5 we encountered the earliest appearance of the term, in documents of the Lemviotissa monastery outside Smyrna from the early thirteenth century (see *[5.9]* and *[5.10]*). Individuals who sold or otherwise alienated property, usually olive trees, frequently demanded, aside from any purchase price, a small annual

[73] *Iviron*, IV, no. 89.12–13: προτερον μὲν εἰς τὸ βασιλικὸν βεστιάριον ὕστερον δὲ πρὸς τοὺς στρατιώτας. On these terms, see *ODB*, s.v. "zeugaratikion" and "kephalaion."

[74] *Iviron*, IV, no. 87A.241–42. From at least 1316 until at least 1341 Iviron was paying only 200 hyperpyra as *kephalaion* to the fisc, and cf. *Iviron*, III, no. 74.334–36. Ostrogorsky, *Féodalité*, 159. G. Ostrogorsky, "Radolivo, selo svetogorskog manastira Iviron," *ZRVI* 7 (1961), 72–73. Laiou, *Peasant Society*, 66 note 98. Hvostova, *Osobennosti*, 99.

payment from the buyer or recipient that was more or less equivalent to the normal tax on the property. The purpose of this was to maintain the income of the pronoia holder or other privileged party who had been granted the tax from the property by the emperor.

At first *epiteleiai* were private arrangements, but eventually the state involved itself in the process. To my knowledge no document issued by a state official mentions an *epiteleia* until the late thirteenth century. This is not surprising given that most references to *epiteleiai* (outside of thirteenth-century private acts) appear in praktika, and there are relatively few extant praktika that date before the fourteenth century. In any event, a praktikon for Lavra's property on Lemnos from 1284 lists one-half nomisma which the monastery received "from the *epiteleia* of the mill of Linardaina." Twenty years later another praktikon contains the same passage (*Lavra*, II, no. 74.64, no. 99.21).

In the fourteenth century the state took an active role in arranging *epiteleiai* for the benefit of privileged individuals and institutions. In fact, the *epiteleia* disappears entirely from private acts of sale. In a praktikon from 1301 for Iviron we read that the monastery held a field of one modios "which was sown by the deceased *kyr* Isaac Kokales . . . for which the party of the deceased [Kokales] pays [ἐπιτελεῖ] toward this monastery 2½ *kokkia*." In this case the monastery was receiving an *epiteleia* from the family of a deceased layman. The sum of 2½ *kokkia* (or 5/48 hyperpyra) was about five times higher than the normal *telos* on one modios of land. This fact, together with the information that Kokales had been cultivating the land, indicates that the *epiteleia* was essentially a rent. This arrangement was still in effect in 1341.[75]

Two similar examples are found in a fragmentary praktikon from around 1354 for the Prodromos monastery. The monastery held a small parcel (*topion*) on which were the houses of the *hetaireiarches* Katides and his sister, for which the two paid (τελοῦσι) the monastery yearly one nomisma. The same document notes that a man held (κρατεῖ) a vineyard, nine *stremmata* in area and belonging to the Prodromos monastery, "for which he pays [τελει]" the monastery three nomismata. Since a *stremma* was probably equal to a modios, three hyperpyra is more than 50 percent greater than the usual *telos* on such a quantity of vineyard. Therefore, it probably is referring to a rent.[76]

[75] *Iviron*, III, no. 70.444–46; IV, no. 86.448–50.

[76] *Prodrome B*, no. 166.61–63,67–68, and cf. no. 167.18–21,

What makes these cases unusual is that rental arrangements tended to be private affairs. It is difficult to understand why these should be recorded in a praktikon unless the arrangement was initiated by the state. Therefore, it would seem that the one modios leased by Kokales from Iviron had originally been fiscal or imperial property which Kokales leased from the state, and at some point the emperor granted the property to Iviron and the lease arrangement continued, but with the monastery as the beneficiary of the rent. Similarly, the land on which the *hetaireiarches*' houses stood and the vineyard of nine *stremmata* were probably state properties originally that were granted to the Prodromos monastery. The rental arrangements continued but with the monastery as the beneficiary rather than the state.[77]

[8.18] Praktika for the monastery of Iviron mentioning the *tzaousios* Manuel Devlitzenos (1301, 1318, 1320, 1341)

Laymen as well benefitted from these arrangements. The same praktikon of 1301 that mentioned the field of the deceased Kokales notes that Iviron held half interest in a mill in a place called Daphne (somewhere in the theme of Thessaloniki) for which it was required to pay (*epitelein*) one hyperpyron yearly to *kyr* Manuel Devlitzenos (or Doveltzenos), who was a military officer, *tzaousios* of the Thessalonian *mega allagion*. By 1317 Devlitzenos was dead, and from then until at least 1341, his children were entitled to receive this payment from Iviron.[78] Devlitzenos is known from other sources as a pronoia holder *[8.72]*. The receipt of such an *epiteleia* is consistent with the holding of a pronoia which, in this case, had become hereditary. As is often the case in this type of passage, we are not given enough information to determine how the *epiteleia* originated.[79]

[77] In one fifteenth-century document the arrangement is clearly created by the state. A man on Lemnos received an exemption of half of his *telos* of four hyperpyra, but paid (*epitelein*) the other two hyperpyra to a monastery (*Docheiariou*, no. 60.79). The reason for the partial tax exemption was explicitly connected to his *gasmoulike douleia*, that is, his service in the marine force called the Gasmouloi: see Bartusis, *Late Byzantine Army*, 44–45, 69–70. The rest of his *telos* was apparently granted as a gift to the monastery, but since the man was no ordinary paroikos of the monastery (i.e., he certainly would not have owed the monks labor services), the redirection of his taxes to the monastery is stated as an *epiteleia*.

[78] *Iviron*, III, no. 70.450–53 (1301), no. 75.594–96 (1318), no. 79.581–83 (1320), and *Iviron*, IV, no. 86.454–55 (1341).

[79] For another *epiteleia* involving a mill, see Table 8.14, note b. For an inscrutable example of an *epiteleia* involving a pronoia holder but where a monastery was the beneficiary, see *Lavra*, II, no. 111.28–29, and *Lavra*, II, App. X.29–30, and cf. *Lavra*, II, no. 111.20–22, and *Lavra*, II, App. X.17–18.

[8.19] Act of the *apographeus* Demetrios Kontenos (1315–16), and Act of the *apographeus* Edessenos involving soldiers (1344)

In a few cases we can see how an *epiteleia* came about. A number of "soldier archons" (*stratiotai archontes*) donated and sold 600 modioi of *exaleimmatike ge* in Hermeleia to Docheiariou, including four paroikos *staseis* donated by the soldier Euthymios Philommates. Evidently these transactions were improper because the properties were part of the oikonomiai of the soldiers involved. In 1315–16 the *apographeus* Kontenos permitted Docheiariou to maintain possession of 330 modioi of this property, in return for a *kephalaion* (ἔπι κεφαλαίω) of 10 hyperpyra. The monastery was made a gift of the remainder. As for the *kephalaion*, it was an *epiteleia* assigned to a man named Komnenoutzikos. A document from 1344 explains that Kontenos "took away" from the monastery 350 modioi (the increase in the figure is not explained) and subjected the property to a *telos kephalaion* (ἐπὶ τέλει κεφαλαίω), which the monks gave Komnenoutzikos as an *epiteleia*.[80] In fact, the actual possession of the land was never taken from the monks; the monks throughout continued to hold (*kateichen*) the land. But because the yearly *epiteleia* paid to Komnenoutzikos for the land had the appearance of a rent (a perpetual *emphyteusis*), the monks felt that the land had been taken from them and the owner had become either the state or Komnenoutzikos.[81]

Epiteleiai truly blurred the distinction between tax and rent, ownership and possession. A woman named Eudokia inherited an oikonomia from her father Komnenoutzikos (who may or may not be the same man as in the previous case). In 1364 she donated, along with the oikonomia she received from her father (see *[8.21]*), "the land in the place Psalis, being 150 imperial modioi, held by the reverend monastery of Xeropotamou, which pays [τελεῖ] me and my party yearly for it 3 hyperpyra, that is, 3 ounces of ducats." She stipulated that Xeropotamou should pay Xenophon this amount annually as long as Xeropotamou held the 150 modioi. Otherwise, Xenophon had the right to take the land as a donation.[82] The relationship between Eudokia and Xeropotamou would appear to be a lease, with Eudokia owning the 150 modioi and Xeropotamou possessing it. However, the three hyperpyra paid annually by Xeropotamou was precisely the normal *telos* on 150 modioi of *ge*, raising the question of who owned the 150 modioi. If the three hyperpyra

80 *Docheiariou*, no. 15.5–6, and p. 16; no. 22.9–11 (1344).

81 *Docheiariou*, no. 20.58–60 (1341), and p. 17; and cf. no. 18.14 (1337). *Docheiariou*, p. 129.

82 *Xénophon*, no. 30.21–24,45–47.

were a rent, then Eudokia owned the property, but if they were a *telos*, then Xeropotamou owned the property and the three hyperpyra represented an *epiteleia* which no doubt had originally been assigned to Eudokia's father as part of his pronoia grant.

Two of our praktika mention *epiteleiai* as elements producing part of the *posotes* for the grant holder. In the praktikon for Basil Berilas, there are two *epiteleiai*: (i) At the end of the list of paroikoi held by Berilas, there is an entry for a paroikos (name illegible) with wife, who owed a *telos* of "$\frac{1}{6}$ nomisma from *epiteleia* of Ntziles [i.e., Gilles] Iantritzos and Manuel Hioump[. . .]." A half line of illegible text follows which, to me, renders any attempt to interpret the meaning of this *epiteleia* futile. (ii) The second instance is found sandwiched between a group of fiscal charges Berilas held and the *telos* he held on an *exaleimmatike stasis*: "from an *epiteleia* of the reverend monastery of the Perivleptos for the sake of the Pantokratorena houses which [Berilas] holds from Indriomenos, 1 nomisma."[83] The origin of this *epiteleia* cannot be easily discerned. Ostensibly, Berilas received one hyperpyron annually from the monastery of the Perivleptos in Thessaloniki for some houses owned at an earlier time by a monastery named Pantokrator. It seems that Berilas held these houses in his pronoia and Indriomenos held them earlier. In any event the *telos* on the houses was now part of Berilas' *posotes*.

Kallinikos held six *epiteleiai* with values ranging from $\frac{1}{4}$ to $1\frac{1}{2}$ hyperpyra. They are as difficult to explain as Berilas'. The *epiteleia* with the most detailed description may be translated as follows: "for the *epiteleia* of the vineyard of the reverend monastery of the Great Martyr St. Demetrios the Myrovlytos in the God-glorified city, which [vineyard] [the monastery] has from donation of both George Galatenos and John [son] of the priest, at the place [called] Chandros, being 7 modioi, *telos* $1\frac{1}{2}$ hyperpyra" (*Chilandar*, ed. Petit, no. 92.129–33). Evidently two men George and John donated a vineyard to a monastery in Constantinople, and the tax levied on the vineyard was paid by the monastery (or by the donors?) and received by Kallinikos. We are not told why Kallinikos was receiving this *epiteleia*. Clearly the reason was connected to the transfer of property between the donors and the monastery. If the situation paralleled the case of Xenos Legas *[5.10]*, then perhaps the telos on the vineyard had earlier been assigned to whoever held the village of Mamitzona. Once the vineyard had been transferred to another party (the

[83] Schreiner, "Zwei Praktika," p. 38, line 15, and lines 25–26: ἀπὸ ἐπιτελείας τῆς σεβασμίας μονῆς τῆς Περιβλέπτου ἕνεκα τῶν παντοκρατωρηνῶν οἰκημάτων, ὧν ἔχει ἀπὸ τοῦ Ἰνδριωμένου, νόμισμα ἕν.

monastery), perhaps this party was required to assume the tax obligation on the vineyard. The other *epiteleiai* in Kallinikos' praktikon are even more inscrutable.[84]

In sum, when an *epiteleia* was received by a pronoia holder or other grant holder, it was a payment in specie, a redirection of taxes (or rent owed to the state) to the pronoia or other grant holder. As a rule it was organized by the state in order to form part of his *posotes*.

Taxes, fiscal charges, and other obligations on paroikoi

The benefits from the paroikoi held by a pronoia holder were perhaps the most important part of the grant. It is noteworthy that when Eudokia, the daughter of the deceased Komnenoutzikos, in 1364 donated to the monastery of Xenophon the oikonomia she inherited from her father, she describes it as "consisting of both men and the other things customarily given in the oikonomiai" *[8.21]*.

According to our seven praktika, the man with the fewest paroikoi was the soldier Michael Saventzes, who held eight households, and the man with the most was Alexios Raoul, who held sixty-two households. The other pronoia soldiers Berilas and Maroules, like Saventzes, held relatively small numbers of paroikos households, thirteen and seventeen. It would seem that a typical pronoia soldier held about a dozen paroikoi. A man of higher rank, the *eparchos* Monomachos, held twenty-seven households in his pronoia. The sixty-two households of Alexios Raoul are probably nearing the top of the range.

There is little other data with which to compare these figures. Eleven paroikoi evidently comprised the "oikonomia consisting of paroikoi" which the monk Theodosios Skaranos bequeathed to the monastery of Xeropotamou in the early 1270s *[6.5]*. In 1321 Andronikos II gave the monastery of Hilandar 400 modioi of land on which were found fifteen paroikoi

84 All five follow an identical pattern. For example, we have "for the *epiteleia* of the field of Theodore Regas, son-in-law of Tzitas, from Aphameia, being 6 modioi, *telos* ¼ hyperpyron" (lines 139–41). Aphameia is mentioned elsewhere in the praktikon as a place-name (line 163), and the syntax of the phrase suggests that Regas himself was "from Aphameia" (ὑπὲρ ἐπιτελείας τοῦ χωραφίου τοῦ ἀπὸ τῆς Ἀφαμείας Θεοδώρου τοῦ Ῥήγα . . .). And following exactly the same form, "for the *epiteleia* of the field of Theodore Chalkeus, son-in-law of Phrangos, from Pentalopoulos, being 10 modioi, *telos* ⅓ hyperpyron" (lines 133–35). While Pentalopoulos might appear to be a personal name, the parallel with "from Aphameia" would indicate that it is actually a toponym. None of the men mentioned in these five *epiteleiai* are listed elsewhere in the praktikon. Were they outsiders who owned fields within the geographical area of Mamitzona, and therefore owed the *telos* of their property to whoever held Mamitzona?

"from the oikonomia of the deceased Amnon and Radenos" *[8.9]*. A false chrysobull, bearing the date 1354, grants to the monastery of Philotheou as a gift "the land in various places and the paroikoi held through oikonomia [*di' oikonomias*] by the *hetaireiarches* Styleianos." The document then presents a list of eleven paroikoi and twenty parcels of land totaling 583 modioi.[85]

While it is possible that the oikonomiai of Skaranos, Amnon and Radenos, and Styleianos contained, respectively, exactly eleven, fifteen, and eleven paroikoi, all we can say for sure is that their oikonomiai contained at least those numbers of paroikos households. They may have contained a few more or even many more. Such references may be dealing with only part of an individual's oikonomia (and cf. *[8.72]*). The issue is an important one because we would like to know how small a pronoia could be. The answer would tell us something about how low a position a pronoia holder could occupy on the social and economic ladder. If the evidence is misread, a scholar might conclude that pronoia holders could occupy a rather low position. The fact remains that the oikonomia with the lowest known number of paroikoi was that of the soldier Michael Saventzes: eight households comprising a total of twenty-nine persons.

Despite the language of the documents which claim that a pronoia holder or a monastery or other privileged landholder "held" a paroikos, what these actually held was the right to the variety of obligations the paroikos hitherto owed the state. The pronoia holder no more owned paroikoi than the state did. Paroikoi were valuable for the taxes, charges, and labor services they owed, and these obligations were fixed by the state, ultimately in conjunction with custom and tradition. No doubt some pronoia holders tried to treat their paroikoi as property to be exploited as they wished, as if the paroikoi were pieces of land or livestock, but this was not in accord with the principles of the pronoia grant. And one wonders how successful such pronoia holders would have been at skirting the law, custom, and tradition.

The *telos* of paroikos households was the quintessential element of a grant of pronoia and all of our praktika begin with a listing of paroikos households held by the grantee. Using some procedure that is not very clear to us today, the fiscal assessor surveyed each household, and then, based on some combination of the number of household members, and the amount of each type of immovable and movable property, calculated a *telos* for each household. Even paroikoi with no property were assessed a *telos*, so that means there was some type of head tax applied. Beyond that, the quantity of arable land (*ge* and *choraphia*), vineyards, and oxen seem to have been

[85] *Actes de Philothée*, ed. Regel, no. 10.124–64, esp. lines 125–28. And see n. 3 above.

the most important determinants for the tax assessment. Nevertheless, it seems clear that assessment rates varied by assessor and by geographic area, and quite likely non-economic factors (such as the status of the household within the village) and custom came into play.[86] The praktika for Saventzes, Maroules, and Berilas specify that the *telos* was to be received twice per year by the grantee (September and March), and this parallels the practice found in monastic praktika.

Aside from the *telos* levied on each paroikos household, all of the praktika (except Margarites') contain a number of other taxes and charges. Some of these were paid to the grantee only by his paroikoi, and some were paid to the grantee by all of the residents of one or more of the villages in which the grantee's paroikoi lived. In earlier centuries most of these could be distinguished as surtaxes (a fixed percentage added to the base *telos* of the village) or collective charges connected to livestock which varied with the number of various types of animals owned by the peasants involved. However, by the late Byzantine period, the two categories blurred and some charges originally connected to livestock became simple surtaxes. For example, the *opheleia* of the *empsychon* (literally, "benefit of the living"), usually shortened to *opheleia*, was a charge the exact meaning and origin of which has not been satisfactorily established. Nevertheless, the rate of the *opheleia* was based on a percentage (generally 10 percent) of the *telos* of the grantee's paroikos households. It appears in three of our praktika. The figure of 10 percent works for Saventzes' and Maroules' praktika; in Berilas' case, the *telos* of his paroikoi was so small that three supplementary charges (the *opheleia*, the *choirodekateia* and the *melissoennomion*) were massed together.[87]

The *choirodekateia* ("pig-tithe") and *melissoennomion* ("bee pasturage charge") are two charges that are listed together in the praktika, forming a single *posotes*. And while there may have been a time when these charges were levied in proportion to the number of pigs and beehives owned by the paroikoi, the charges seems to have had no bearing on the number of pigs (*choiroi*) or beehives (*melissa*) held by the grantees' paroikoi. Saventzes' paroikoi held three beehives and no pigs, yet paid a *choirodekateia* and *melissoennomion* of one hyperpyron; Maroules' paroikoi held five pigs and

[86] J. Lefort, "Fiscalité médiévale et informatique: recherches sur les barèmes pour l'imposition des paysans byzantins du XIVe siècle," *Revue Historique* 252 [512] (1974), 315–56. Laiou, *Peasant Society*, esp. 176–80. Ks. Hvostova, "Sud'by parikii i osobennosti nalogooblozenija v Vizantii XIII–XIV vv.," *VizVrem* 39 (1978), 63–75.

[87] See *ODB*, s.v. "opheleia"; Laiou, *Peasant Society*, 181; and *Xéropotamou*, p. 146. At this point I invite the reader to look at Appendix 4, "A note on fiscal privileges."

fifty beehives, and paid $2^1/_2$ hyperpyra; Berilas' paroikoi owned five pigs and no beehives, and paid a combined charge of one hyperpyron for the *choirodekateia*, *melissoennomion*, *opheleia*, and *ennomion*. Rather, like the *opheleia*, this charge seems to have been a straight percentage (10 percent) of the *telos* of the grantee's paroikoi. In other words, these charges were levied strictly on the grantees' paroikoi and not on all of the paroikoi in the village or villages in which the grantees' paroikoi lived.

Berilas received a *posotes* of two hyperpyra "for the *ennomion* of the acorn and the *mandriatikon* of the district" of the village of Langivikeia.[88] The "*ennomion* of the acorn" (*valanion*) was another collective charge on the paroikoi of Berilas' village. Ostensibly it was connected with the pasturage of village pigs in local oak groves (his praktikon in fact notes the presence of walnut trees on his domain *ge*) and was probably equivalent to the rare charge called the *valanistron* (βαλάνιστρον), another variety of *ennomion*.[89] Only one of the thirteen paroikos households held by Berilas had any pigs (and then only five of them), but nothing in the praktikon indicates that there were not other peasants, who may have owned pigs, living in the village of Langivikeia. A close parallel to our text is found in the Slavic translation of the 1300 praktikon for Hilandar *[8.72]*. The monastery received six hyperpyra for the "*ennomion* and *valanistron*" within the borders of a particular village.[90]

The *mandriatikon* was another collective charge connected, at least originally, to animal pens (*mandrai*), particularly sheep-pens.[91] This charge appears in Raoul's as well as Berilas' praktikon. Raoul's paroikoi held hundreds of sheep, Berilas' held none, but, as already noted, there may have been other paroikoi in Berilas' village.

The *ennomion* was originally a charge for the use of state land as pasturage, or more generally a pasture charge on animals.[92] It appears in four of our praktika as one of a number of supplementary charges. We read that Saventzes received the *ennomion* "of the two villages of Psalis and Phournia

88 Schreiner, "Zwei Praktika," 38, line 21. The text should be read as ὑπὲρ ἐννομίου τοῦ βαλανίου καὶ μανδριατικοῦ τῆς ἐνορίας τοῦ αὐτοῦ χωρίου.

89 See *Iviron*, I, no. 9.51 (995): "the *valanistron* and the other *ennomia*"; *Chilandar*, ed. Petit, no. 61.41 (1321), no. 45.17 (1334), no. 138.24 (1351); and *Patmos*, II, no. 50.126 (1073): here the printed text reads βαλανιστηρίου, but a glance at the plate shows this is incorrect.

90 Mošin, "Akti," 214.530–34: *Za onomiju i valanistro v toižde meždei vsen u tomu selu* . . . . Solovjev–Mošin, *Grčke povelje*, 408–09, link the *valanistron* to the *choirodekateia*, but Berilas' praktikon and other documents include both charges. Also, see *ODB*, s.v. "swine."

91 See Oikonomides, *Fiscalité*, 75.

92 *ODB*, s.v. "ennomion." Solovjev–Mošin, *Grčke povelje*, p. 431. Dölger, *Beiträge*, 53–54. *Xéropotamou*, p. 151.

from the ingoing and outgoing animals," while Maroules who held paroikoi and property in the same villages received no *ennomion*. Raoul held the whole village of Prevista and in his praktikon the *ennomion* is combined with the *mandriatikon* and together they were assessed at the enormous sum of thirty-one hyperpyra, or about 20 percent of the *telos* of the paroikoi in the village. Here the *mandriatikon* is qualified as "of the sheep and pigs of the inscribed paroikoi," as well as "foreign animals" (*xena zoa*) which pastured in the district of Prevista. Thus, it seems that in these three praktika the *ennomion* was not based on the paroikoi held by the grantee, but on village-wide assessments.

In Kallinikos' praktikon it is unclear who paid the *ennomion*. What is unusual is that the *ennomion* appears to involve a single property: "for the *ennomion* in Livadion around the church of the Eliokallou each year, the garden being eight modioi, *telos* four hyperpyra." The phrase "in Livadion" (εἰς τὸ Λιβάδιον) may not refer to a toponym, but simply to a pasture (*livadion*), in which case the passage might read "for the *ennomion* for the pasture around the church . . . ." The reference to the garden is unclear syntactically and logistically; it was common to have a garden around a building, but not to have a garden near pasture land.

Monomachos also received 9½ hyperpyra for the *zeugaratikion* of the paroikoi listed in his praktikon. The *zeugaratikion* is a mysterious charge, evidently connected to yokes of oxen (*zeugaria*) or the peasants who owned them.[93] Here the charge appears to represent one-third of the combined *tele* of all the listed paroikos households (27½ hyperpyra, or actually 28 by calculation).

Thus, the secondary charges on paroikoi can be categorized as those burdening only the grantee's paroikoi, those burdening the paroikoi of one or more entire villages, and those burdening a specific property.

There were also specific charges for other specific agrarian activities. Saventzes received from the peasants of two villages the *linovrocheion*, the charge for the use of the place where flax was retted. The charge seems to be grouped with the *ennomion* of the same two villages and a charge for "ingoing and outgoing animals" (a kind of toll for passage through the villages?), with a total *posotes* of five hyperpyra. This would suggest Saventzes received a flat five hyperpyra paid collectively by the peasants of these villages for these three obligations, rather than a per-use charge for the flax-retting place.[94]

93 See *ODB*, s.v., "zeugaratikion."

94 On the *linovrocheion*, see *ODB*, s.v. "banality," and F. Dölger, *Sechs byzantinische Praktika des 14. Jahrhunderts für das Athoskloster Iberon* (Munich, 1949), 123. *Xénophon*, no. 15.24–26:

Saventzes also received "the lake Souda" for the very high posotes of twenty hyperpyra, fully $2/7$ of his entire *posotes.* Evidently this refers to fishing rights and presumably Saventzes did not actually receive this twenty hyperpyra, but exploited it directly or (more likely) leased it out to others for whatever rent he could get, like the pronoia holder Kalegopoulos in the thirteenth century *[5.7]*.[95] Similarly, the fishing and dock rights that Monomachos held were connected to real economic pursuits and they also represented a substantial portion – fully half – of his *posotes*, though, like Saventzes, he either exploited these directly or leased them to others. The charge for the fair (*panegyris*) of St. Christopher, found in Raoul's praktikon, was another specific levy, though we have no idea how it was assessed. In other words, was it a fixed, recurring charge paid jointly by the entire village, or was it a more expansive revenue source that varied with the amount of commerce conducted at the fair?[96]

Finally, a charge called the *aer* is found in the praktika for Raoul, Monomachos, and Kallinikos. In all three praktika it is expressly stated that the *aer* was paid by the paroikoi listed in the praktikon and was being granted "without the three state *kephalaia*, that is, *phonos*, *parthenophthoria*, and treasure trove."[97] The latter three items, which the fisc frequently, as in these cases, did not concede to privileged landholders, seem to have been fines for murder and rape, and the demand for any buried coins found (see *[8.37]* below). What was left of the *aer* seems to have been a fiscalized fine, that is, an annual charge that probably had little connection to any actual crime. It is not possible to determine how the rates of the *aer* that appear in our praktika were calculated.

ὑπὲρ τοῦ ἐννομίου καὶ τοῦ λινοβροχίου τῶν δύο χωρίων, τῆς Ψαλίδος καὶ τῶν Φουρνίων, ἀπὸ τῶν εἰσερχομένων καὶ ἐξερχομένων ζώων, νομίσματα πέντε, καθὼς προκατεῖχεν αὐτὰ ὁ Σμυρναῖος ἐκεῖνος, καὶ ἀπὸ τῆς λίμνης τῆς Σούδης νομίσματα εἴκοσιν. I am uncomfortable with the syntax of these lines. The literal translation: "For the *ennomion* and the *linovrocheion* of the two villages, Psalis and Phournia, from the incoming and outgoing animals, five nomismata, as Smyrnaios held these earlier, and from lake Souda, twenty nomismata." In her summary of the document (*Xénophon*, p. 138), D. Papachryssanthou saw four charges here: *ennomion*, *linovrocheion*, incoming–outgoing animals, and (the rights of) lake Souda. But I do not like how the preposition shifts from ὑπέρ to ἀπό. One could see a parallel construction: *ennomion* from the incoming–outgoing animals, and *linovrocheion* from lake Souda, but then only the *ennomion* could be "of the two villages" because lake Souda (if Papachryssanthou's identification is correct: see note 95, below) is far from these villages. The *linovrocheion* appears to be near Psalis and Phournia because there is an enigmatic marginal note next to the passage: ληνοβροχίου ἧς Κασάνδραν, which would suggest the eastern side of the Longos peninsula.

95 Papachryssanthou, *Xénophon*, p. 139, places lake Souda, now drained, southwest of lake Volve. See P. Bellier et al., *Paysages de Macédoine, leurs caractères, leur évolution à travers les documents et les récits des voyageurs* (Paris, 1986), carte 2, G8–9.

96 See *ODB*, s.v., "fishing" and "fair."

97 See *ODB*, s.v., "aerikon."

At the end of most of the praktika, after the total *posotes* is stated, a few additional demands on the paroikoi of the grantee are recorded. Saventzes' and Maroules' praktika include demands for the *oikomodion* and the *oinometrion*. The former gave them the right to demand a modios (by volume) of wheat and barley for every three hyperpyra of *telos* paid by his paroikoi (e.g., in Saventzes' case, four modioi). Analogously, the *oinometrion* provided them with one measure of local wine for every one hyperpyron of *telos* (again, for Saventzes, twelve measures).[98] Four of the praktika add that the paroikoi of the grantee were required to render the customary three *kaniskia* ("little baskets"), a charge in kind consisting of a small quantity of eggs, chicken, bread, and wine offered by each peasant household. The *kaniskion* was originally intended to feed the tax collector and his retinue, but when fiscal obligations of peasants were granted to privileged landholders (such as monasteries and later pronoia holders and other laymen), the charge was regularized and rendered to the landholder at fixed intervals.[99] Kallinikos' praktikon specifies the three times of year: Christmas, Shrove Tuesday, and Easter. The *kaniskion* could be paid in specie, and indeed Monomachos' praktikon includes it with the *choirodekateia* and *aer* for a fixed *posotes* of two hyperpyra.

It is quite possible that some of the other obligations of paroikoi to their lords were rendered in kind as well. Once the state transferred to privileged landholders all the various taxes and charges that paroikoi normally owed the state, landholders and paroikoi may have made their own arrangements. For example, it is not difficult to imagine circumstances in which it benefitted both a monastery and its paroikoi for the paroikoi to render their *telos* in kind to the monastery.

Finally, four of the praktika specify the labor services (*angareiai*) due to the grantee by the inscribed paroikoi. This labor obligation originated as a state demand which was transferred to the grantee. Saventzes', Maroules', and Berilas' praktika all obligate the paroikoi listed within to twelve days of labor per year. All three also add the qualification "according to the ability of the paroikos" (καθὼς ὁ πάροικος εὑρίσκεται ἔχων δυνάμεως), showing that there was some allowance for infirmity and perhaps other considerations. Kallinikos' praktikon states simply that the inscribed paroikoi were liable for the "customary *angareiai*," but still adds a phrase about the ability of each paroikos. It is not clear whether only one paroikos per household was responsible for these labor services or whether all able-bodied men (i.e.,

[98] On these demands, see *ODB*, s.v. "oikomodion," *Esphigménou*, p. 101, and *Xéropotamou*, p. 151.

[99] Oikonomides, *Fiscalité*, 78–79, 88–89. *ODB*, s.v. "kaniskion.".

including adult children and other adult household members) and even adult women were obligated.[100]

Similar phrases are found in monastic praktika as well. Nearly an identical passage to Saventzes' and Maroules' concluding demands appears in a praktikon for a monastery from 1318 (*Esphigménou*, no. 14.225–31). Another praktikon for a monastery, like Berilas' praktikon, contains the information about the days of work and the *kaniskia*, but lacks reference to the *oinometrion* and *oikomodion* (*Lavra*, II, no. 109 [1321]).

Replenishing grant resources: conquest, normal administrative procedures, confiscation

The resources available to the emperor for pronoia grants were regularly replenished in several ways: through conquest, through normal administrative procedures, and through extraordinary confiscations. A great deal of state land, especially during the middle of the thirteenth century, originated through conquest. As the armies of the rulers of Epiros and of Nicaea extended their authority through war, there were numerous options available for the disposition of conquered territory. It could be left in the hands of its current holder, added into the imperial domain, or immediately granted to religious institutions or to laymen. The story of the disposition and administration of conquered territory has been neglected in the scholarship. Essentially all of Thrace, Macedonia, and Thessaly was eventually brought back under Byzantine control. One wonders about the extent to which rulers such as John Vatatzes and Michael VIII permitted laymen to continue to hold their patrimonial property on condition of the property becoming an oikonomia.[101]

Normal administrative procedures included the redistribution of *exaleimmata* (which has already been discussed above), the redistribution of the grant contents of a deceased pronoia holder, and the redistribution of property reckoned as *perisseia* (see *[6.6]*). Pronoia holders died, and if they had not been granted hereditary rights over their grants, the contents reverted to the state. One of the paroikos families held by Michael Saventzes was "from the oikonomia of the deceased Smyrnaios." Two others were "from the oikonomia of the deceased *kavallarios* Serpes." Saventzes was also

100 *ODB*, s.v., "corvée," "angareia."

101 For some observations regarding the re-conquest, see D. Kyritsis, "The 'Common Chrysobulls' of Cities and the Notion of Property in Late Byzantium," *Σύμμεικτα* 13 (1999), 229–45, esp. 240–42.

the holder of the *ennomion* for the animals of Psalis and Phournia "which the deceased Smyrnaios had held earlier." Evidently, with the deaths of Smyrnaios and Serpes, at least some of the components of their oikonomiai were used to create a new pronoia grant. In the case of Saventzes, at least 22½ hyperpyra of his *posotes* of seventy hyperpyra consisted of paroikoi, property, and rights that had been held earlier by other people.

Sometimes it is not clear that the previous holder of a property was deceased. For instance, Maroules' 450 modioi of *ge* in the *oikoumenon* of his praktikon was land "from what Isauros earlier held." Possibly Isauros had died and his grant reverted to the state, or perhaps there was some other reason why he lost the property. One such possibility is mentioned in Saventzes' praktikon. Two of the three large parcels of arable land in the *oikoumenon* of his praktikon were 600 modioi "from that which was taken from Provatas by reason of *perisseia*" (*kata logon perisseias*) and 300 modioi "taken from Michael Keroulas by reason of *perisseia*" (*Xénophon*, no. 15.18–20). Apparently during an earlier *exisosis* the *apographeis* had found Provatas and Keroulas holding land *perisseia*, that is, in excess of the amount recorded in their own praktika; hence, "by reason of *perisseia*" this land was available for reassignment to Saventzes. This problem seems to have been common. Michael VIII's *prostagma* for his son Andronikos *[6.6]* states that one of the sources for increases of pronoia to deserving soldiers was property "found from a *perisseia* of the *apographeis*." Pachymeres complained that one of the problems with the army in Anatolia at the end of the thirteenth century was that "many of the soldiers, seizing frequent opportunities, increased their own pronoiai" *[8.25]*. And in 1319 an act of a surveyor mentions *perisseia ge* of the Vardariotai which had been taken from this group: 1,300 modioi were given to the monastery of Xeropotamou and the rest became imperial land, presumably awaiting its consignment to another pronoia holder like Saventzes. The identity of these Vardariotai (whether they had any relation to the palace guards of the same name) and the nature of their landholdings, whether part of an imperial grant or a private holding, is unknown.[102]

Even paroikoi could benefit from the redistribution of *perisseia*. In Kallinikos' praktikon, the property held by quite a few of his paroikoi was augmented by *ge* "through conferral." In only a few cases is the source or reason for the conferral noted. For example, one paroikos held through conferral fifteen modioi of *ge* "from what he cleared"; in other words, it

[102] *Xéropotamou*, no. 19. On the homonymous palace guards, see Bartusis, *Late Byzantine Army*, 279–81.

seems he was being rewarded for bringing land into production (*Chilandar*, ed. Petit, no. 90.104). Another household held eighty modioi of *ge* "through conferral from free [*ge*] taken from the inhabitants [*epoikoi*] of this village by reason of *perisseia*" (*Chilandar*, ed. Petit, no. 90.108–10). Evidently, some paroikoi of the village of Mamitzona had no claim to the *ge* they held and it was seized by the fisc and conferred on other paroikoi.

The technique of *perisseia* could be considered a form of confiscation, but because it was a normal administrative procedure, I prefer to distinguish it from the type of confiscation which was an extraordinary, irregular process. This latter type of confiscation was frequently used to replenish the state's supply of properties for grants, and its victims were both laymen and religious foundations.

It is important to emphasize that every new pronoia was not created out of whole cloth. Our praktika show that many of the properties, paroikoi, and rights held by these men had been held in pronoia previously by others. Men died or were stripped of their pronoiai for any number of reasons, and the pronoiai, with their component elements reshuffled, were dealt to other soldiers. There is the impression that once state property or state rights were "pronoiarized," they tended to remain so.

Most of the known confiscations of property from laymen which were used to create grants during the late Byzantine period center on the civil wars of the fourteenth century. For example, the *posotes* of fifty-five hyperpyra in John Margarites' praktikon came from the confiscated oikonomia of the *megas papias* Arsenios Tzamplakon, from a *zeugelateion* of John Kantakouzenos near Zichna, from land recently held by the *dioiketes* Manuel, and from the oikonomia of the *protasekretis* Vardales.[103]

Emperors could not resist appropriating monastic properties to fulfill their insatiable need for state property to confer as pronoiai. References to land "taken from" a monastery and given to laymen fall into three categories: first, those in which the monastery was compensated with another property; second, those in which the monastery was not compensated for its loss; and third, those in which we have no idea whether or not the monastery was compensated. The third category is a relatively large one, consisting of casual references to property taken from a monastery. For example, the praktikon for the soldier Michael Saventzes states that he held two paroikos households that previously had been held by a monastery.[104] This suggests a

[103] Lemerle, "Un praktikon inédit," lines 2, 8, 15, 23, 28. Other examples: *[8.39]* and *[8.78]*. Sometimes the reasons for a confiscation are not obvious: see *[9.2]*.

[104] *Xénophon*, no. 15.12. Other examples: *Docheiariou*, no. 21.4–7 (1343), and Solovjev–Mošin, *Grčke povelje*, no. 21.5–9. Cf. *Lavra*, II, no. 97.

confiscation, but it is possible that the monastery had been holding the two paroikos households improperly, and so one must be careful about drawing conclusions.

[8.20] Prostagma of Andronikos III Palaiologos for the monastery of St. John Prodromos near Serres involving the oikonomia of the *megas primmikerios* Vasilikos (1333 or 1334)

As for the other two categories, one could argue that both represented confiscations inasmuch as an involuntary deprivation of property is a case of state power trumping private property rights whether or not the state agreed to compensation. But this does raise the question of why the emperor would agree to compensation at all. Consider a likely example found in a *prostagma* of Andronikos III from January 1333 or 1334 for the monastery of St. John Prodromos. The document confirms the conferral upon the monks by Constantine Makrenos of a *posotes* from a number of villages, which was to compensate the monastery for "the oikonomia of the *megas primmikerios* Vasilikos of 100 nomismata, which was taken from them." The simplest reconstruction of this transaction is that the monastery held a *posotes* of 100 hyperpyra; this 100 hyperpyra was transferred to Vasilikos as an oikonomia; and then the monastery was compensated with another 100 hyperpyra from other properties. André Guillou suggested that Vasilikos was Nikephoros Vasilikos, governor of Melnik and faithful partisan of Andronikos II, who recognized Andronikos III as emperor only after Andronikos II's death in 1332. If Guillou is correct, that would link the grant of the oikonomia to Vasilikos to Nikephoros' submission to Andronikos III.[105]

The purpose of such a confiscation was not to acquire property with a *posotes* of 100 hyperpyra, but to acquire a *particular* property with a *posotes* of 100 hyperpyra. This means that, even though the components of an oikonomia were fungible with the holdings of any privileged landholder, the emperor or, more likely, the recipient himself desired a particular source

[105] *Prodrome*, no. 27.3–4 (with comments on Vasilikos) = *Prodrome B*, no. 205.3–5: τῆς ἀφαιρεθείσης ἐξ αὐτῶν οἰκονομίας τοῦ μεγάλου πριμμικηρίου τοῦ Βασιλικοῦ τῶν ρ' νομισμάτων. The reading "Vasilikos," while uncertain in Guillou's edition, is clear according to the edited text of Codex B. Cf. Dölger, *Regesten*, IV, no. 2790, which dates the document to ca. 1333. Kazhdan, *Agrarnye otnošenija*, 214. Ostrogorsky, *Féodalité*, 150. In Guillou's edition of the act (*Prodrome*, no. 27), the date passage at the end of the document has not been preserved. In another example of careless editing, L. Bénou assigns the act to "janvier, ind. 1" and "1333" (*Prodrome B*, p. 399 and note 384), while the text of her edition of Codex B reads μηνὶ Ἰαννουαρίω (ἰνδικτιῶνος) β(ας)' (!: *Prodrome B*, no. 205.12–13), which would correspond to 1334. For another example of a forced exchange, possibly to create pronoiai, see *[8.70]*.

of revenue. The state actually gained very little when compensation was involved.

From a practical point of view, it was easier of course to compensate minor confiscations than massive, large-scale confiscations. If the purpose of the confiscation was to provide land to pronoia holders, there was no compensation. The documents from the monastic archives make clear that there were quite a few non-compensated confiscations.[106]

A number of documents refer to confiscations of the monastery of Xenophon's land in the area of Psalis at the northern end of the Longos peninsula on the Chalkidike. A praktikon from 1300 lists, among the monastery's possessions in region of Psalis, 300 modioi of land called Neakitou, which were taken from the monastery by the *apographeis* Tzimpeas and Amnon and given through praktikon to the *kastrophylax* Demetrios Doukopoulos. However, Doukopoulos, who was dead in 1300, later donated the land back to Xenophon, an action evidently approved of by the emperor because an imperial *prostagma* was issued confirming the donation.[107] Constantine Tzimpeas was dead by 1283, and the team of *apographeis* Tzimpeas and Amnon are attested in 1279, so the grant to Doukopoulos probably occurred around that date.[108]

Xenophon seems to have lost other property in this area as well. A praktikon from 1338 explains that *exaleimmatika stasia* among the monastery's land in Psalidophourna were "taken away not a few years earlier and assigned to Prosalentai [a military division of rowers], then given to Thessalonian soldiers who gave these [*stasia*] through donation to this reverend monastery."[109] The phrase "not a few years earlier" means that the confiscation had occurred many years earlier, perhaps as early as 1279.

[8.21] Donation of Eudokia, daughter of Komnenoutzikos (1364)

Yet another document mentions a confiscation from Xenophon in the same area. In 1364 Eudokia, the daughter of the deceased Komnenoutzikos,

[106] See the table in K. Smyrlis, *La fortune des grands monastères byzantins* (Paris, 2006), 172–74.

[107] *Xénophon*, no. 5.8–9, and cf. no. 4.8. Originally this property had probably belonged to the Athonite monastery of Neakitou: see *Actes de Kastamonitou*, ed. N. Oikonomides (Paris, 1978), p. 12. Also, the property called Kanstamonitou which the pronoia holder Peros Martinos had held in the same area *[7.8]* suggests that the property had once belonged to the monastery of Kastamonitou on Mount Athos: *Actes de Kastamonitou*, p. 2 note 8.

[108] *Esphigménou*, p. 78.

[109] *Xénophon*, no. 25.109–11: ἀποκατέστη εἰς προσαλέντας, εἶτα ἐδόθη πρὸς στρατιώτας θεσσαλονικεῖς. On the Prosalentai, see Bartusis, *Late Byzantine Army*, 47–48, 158–59, and Bartusis, "Smallholding Soldiers,"17–19.

donated to the monastery of Xenophon "the oikonomia belonging to me in absolute ownership, having come to my deceased father from the mercy of the . . . emperor and from him to me, everything [all the rights and privileges], consisting of both men and the other things customarily given in the oikonomiai."[110] She states that this land, located in Psalidophourna on the Longos peninsula of the Chalkidike, had been held by the monastery as patrimonial property (line 27: γονικῶς) through acts of earlier emperors (going as far back as Basil II), but "when much later matters turned," this land had been taken away from the monastery and "given to some people" (line 29: ἐδόθησαν δὲ πρὸς πρόσωπα τινά), evidently as oikonomiai. She writes that after they learned that their properties had belonged to Xenophon, they donated them back to the monastery. One of these people was her father, and now, having inherited the property, she returned it to Xenophon.

Thus, a series of emperors had confirmed Xenophon's possession of a property, but at some point the property was among those confiscated and given to "some people," one of whom was Komnenoutzikos, who received the property as an oikonomia. Later he received hereditary rights to his oikonomia, which passed to his daughter after his death. The daughter, now holding her father's oikonomia, donated it back to the monastery. On the face of things, we have a confiscation of property from a monastery and, after the passage of many years, the return of this land to the monastery through donations. But is it possible that Eudokia is referring to the confiscation that occurred around 1279? From a chronological standpoint, Eudokia's father could not have been one of the original beneficiaries of the confiscation that benefitted Demetrios Doukopoulos, but he could well have been a descendant of one. Further, the phrase in Eudokia's act, "given to some people," may well parallel the passage in the 1338 praktikon, "assigned to Prosalentai, then given to Thessalonian soldiers." It is possible that all three documents refer to a single confiscation at Psalidophourna which occurred in the 1270s. First the property was assigned to Prosalentai (who held their land as hereditary smallholdings and not as pronoiai), and then at least some of it was later given to pronoia soldiers, of whom Eudokia's father was one or a descendant of one. But if this scenario is valid, it is unlikely that Doukopoulos would have been one of the initial recipients of the confiscated property; it is improbable that he rose from rower to *kastrophylax* with his own praktikon. Rather, it is possible that the phrase

110 *Xénophon*, no. 30.19–21: τὴν . . . δεσποτικῶς μοι προσοῦσαν οἰκονομίαν, ἀπὸ ἐλεημοσύνης τοῦ . . . βασιλέως περιελθοῦσαν τῶ πατρί μου ἐκείνω καὶ ἐκ τούτου κἀμοί, ἅπασαν, διά τε ἀνθρώπων καὶ τῶν ἄλλων τῶν ἐν ταῖς οἰκονομίαις συνήθως διδομένων. This passage is found, in nearly identical form, in the notarial summary that prefaces the act (lines 3–6).

"assigned to Prosalentai, then given to Thessalonian soldiers" in the 1338 praktikon should not be taken literally. Doukopoulos may have received his property as a pronoia at the same time that property was being confiscated for the benefit of rowers. A Serbian document indicates also that Michael VIII was confiscating monastic property for the military.[111]

Further, the editor of the act, D. Papachryssanthou, added one last wrinkle to the story of these confiscations. She hypothesized that there were a number of lay landholdings – some pronoiai, some not; some earlier held by Xenophon, some not – scattered among Xenophon's large holdings at Psalis. During the fourteenth century, she wrote, Xenophon devoted itself to acquiring these properties, whether or not it had originally held them. Therefore, while the documents indicate a substantial confiscation of Xenophon's property in the area, this may be an exaggeration.[112] Nevertheless, the case of Doukopoulos shows that there had been some secularization of property in the area. As for Eudokia, in 1364 the Chalkidike was in the hands of the Serbs and so it may have been little sacrifice on her part to return the properties to Xenophon.

In the fourteenth century similar confiscations occurred, and, as in the above case, the property confiscated was often returned to the monastery. In 1321 the soldier Neokastrites held 600 modioi of land in the Chalkidike which had been "taken from the monastery of Docheiariou" in the early years of the fourteenth century. In 1337 this land was returned to the monastery.[113] At the same time 900 modioi of land, called "tou Gaze," which around 1327 were taken from Docheiariou and given to the Varvarenoi soldier company, were returned to Docheiariou. These 900 modioi are perhaps the same as a property that had been taken away from the monastery sometime between 1321 and 1325 and given to someone named Adrian. If so, after a rather short time the property returned to the monastery before being again taken away and granted to the Varvarenoi.[114] The Varvarenoi also held the village of Hagios Mamas which had been taken from the monastery of Vatopedi sometime after 1338. In 1346 Stefan Dušan gave the monastery of Vatopedi the village of Hagios Mamas with all the rights and privileges "as the Varvarenoi soldiers and those holding this village before them earlier held it."[115]

[111] See Bartusis, "Serbian Pronoia," 182–83. [112] *Xénophon*, p. 40.

[113] *Lavra*, II, no. 108.349–50. *Docheiariou*, pp. 140–41. Lefort, *Villages de Macédoine*, 139, 172.

[114] *Docheiariou*, no. 16.14 (1325–32), and pp. 16, 116, and 140, and no. 18.12–13 (1337), no. 21.4–7 (1343), no. 23.27–29 (1344), and no. 41 (1373). Lefort, *Villages de Macédoine*, 116, 139. *PLP*, no. 91066.

[115] *Vatopédi*, II, no. 81.54 (1338), no. 93.16 (1346), no. 97.8,10 (1348). Lefort, *Villages de Macédoine*, 92, 146.

The monastery of Esphigmenou lost a number of its properties between 1334 and 1346, most likely during the era of the civil wars of the early 1340s. "Half of the village of Portarea" near Hagios Mamas on the Chalkidike was "seized and taken away" from the monastery "and given to the deceased Anatavlas." In 1346 Stefan Dušan restored this portion of the village to the monastery and confirmed its possession of the other half.[116] Similarly, two-thirds of the village of Krousovo (near the mouth of the Strymon) had been "taken away through a fiscal recension, and the one part was given to the deceased Gavrielopoulos, while the other [third] to Pharmakes . . . , so as to leave to the monastery only the third part of this village." In 1347 Dušan returned these properties to Esphigmenou (*Esphigménou*, no. 23.15–17).

[8.22] Chrysobull of Stefan Dušan for the monastery of St. George near Zavlantia (1348)

These examples show that Dušan courted the support of monasteries and frequently returned properties that had been confiscated. Another such instance occurred in 1348 when Dušan issued a chrysobull returning the village of Zavlantia in Thessaly and its paroikoi to the nearby monastery of St. George. Sometime between 1342 and 1348 the now deceased governor of Thessaly, the *sevastokrator* John Angelos, had taken the village from the monastery. The monastery held the village before the *sevastokrator* John took it away, "that is, the paroikoi from those found in it were set in the order of soldiers." The document lists ten paroikoi and six *exaleimmatika stasia*. Earlier scholars tended to think that Angelos had transformed peasants into soldiers, and years ago when I first examined the document I was hesitant to conclude that this view was incorrect. Now I am certain that, even though the passage is phrased poorly, the purpose of the document was to return to a monastery paroikoi which had been confiscated by Byzantine authorities and granted to pronoia soldiers.[117]

[8.23] Act of the universal judges of Thessaloniki involving the Serbian conquests (1375)

Nevertheless, there is evidence that Dušan confiscated property from a monastery for the purpose of creating pronoia grants. We read that when the Serbs invaded the area of Verrhoia around 1344, they took a *metochion*

116 *Esphigménou*, no. 22.13,27–28. Lefort, *Villages de Macédoine*, 130 (the date "1347" should be corrected to "1346").

117 Solovjev–Mošin, *Grčke povelje*, no. 20.18–21: καὶ εἰς τάξιν στρατιωτῶν ἀποκαθισταμένους. See Bartusis, "Smallholding Soldiers," 7–8.

from the monastery of Prodromos tes Petras and "the Serbs gave this in a pronoiastic way to various persons." When Byzantine control was restored over the area in 1356, the monks received the property back from the emperor. At the very least we can say that it appeared to the monks that some of the Serb conquerors had been granted the monastery's property as pronoia grants.[118]

Another round of confiscations from monasteries in order to fund pronoia grants seems to have taken place in 1350 in the area around Thessaloniki. Since the anti-aristocratic uprising in 1342 known as the Zealot revolt, the city had been effectively independent of either faction during the Byzantine civil wars of the 1340s. By 1350 the revolt had run its course, and John Kantakouzenos and his son-in-law and co-emperor John V Palaiologos entered the city. A number of documents point to confiscations of monastic property at this time. In a *prostagma* probably from December 1350 John V (whom Kantakouzenos officially appointed as the governor of the Thessaloniki) confirmed Demetrios Kokalas' possession of numerous properties that he had been given recently through an official act, including half of the property that two monasteries had held in the village of Hagios Mamas *[8.38]*. In an act from May 1355 the *megas dioiketes* John Doukas Valsamon explains that he had received a *prostagma* ordering him to confer on Docheiariou the village to the southeast of Revenikeia called Atouvla "which the monastery held earlier" and which later "was taken away from it and conferred on the deceased *kyr* Michael Pitzikopoulos from the western *archontopouloi* [ἀπὸ τῶν δυσικῶν ἀρχοντοπούλων], who met his fate some time ago." Similarly, he was ordered to confer upon the monastery land of 1000 around Rousaiou which it held earlier and was taken from it "for some reasons" and conferred upon the deceased Theodore Mouzalon from the Thessalonian *mega allagion*. Mouzalon was "killed by the enemy Turks some time ago," probably in 1352 or 1353, and after his death the monastery received the property back through "a *prostagma* of our mighty and holy lady and *despoina*," i.e., Anna of Savoy.[119]

A similar process is described in more general terms in a chrysobull of John V from September 1355. The monks of Docheiariou reported that they had held land called Diavolokampos, land in Hermeleia, and land in Amygdaleai. But "the half of the inscribed [properties] were taken away and given to various people some time ago, by *orismos* of the father of my

[118] *Vatopédi*, II, no. 144.19–20: τῶν Σέρβων καὶ τοῦτο διδόντων προνοιαστικῷ τρόπῳ πρὸς διάφορα πρόσωπα. Bartusis, "Serbian Pronoia," 189–90.

[119] *Docheiariou*, no. 29.4–9. Lefort, *Villages de Macédoine*, 140. *PLP*, no. 19438.

majesty the emperor Kantakouzenos." With this chrysobull John V reestablished their rights to these properties.[120] Oikonomides concluded that these confiscations occurred in the fall of 1350 as part of John Kantakouzenos' anti-Serb military efforts and may have affected other monasteries as well. The latter conclusion is based on a poorly preserved act of John V from 1351/2 which granted Lavra's request that the monastery no longer pay certain taxes or charges to "Thessalonian soldiers." Further, he wrote that the transformation of this monastic land into pronoia holdings was gradually reversed by John V and Anna of Savoy as the pronoia holders died.[121]

Yet another confiscation for the benefit of pronoia holders occurred in the later 1350s or 1360s when a piece of land was taken from the monastery of Vatopedi and given to soldiers from a soldier company. In 1377, on imperial order, the property was returned to Vatopedi *[8.7]*.

From this series of examples one might get the impression that these confiscations from monasteries tended to be temporary, that eventually the monasteries got their properties back. Indeed monasteries displayed great tenacity in their attempts to regain their rights, but this should not obscure the fact that most of our extant documents come from monastic archives. These archives probably over-represent those instances when a monastery succeeded in regaining and maintaining its property holdings. When a property was confiscated from a monastery and never recovered, the property simply disappeared from the preserved documentation. This is illustrated by the case of Radoslav Sampias who in 1378 received from the emperor the right to transmit the village of Neochorion to his children and who in 1405 donated the property to the monastery of Saint Paul *[8.48]*. Neochorion had been a possession of Lavra, last mentioned as a possession of the monastery in a document from around 1344.[122] While it is always possible that Lavra was compensated with another property, there is no evidence for this. Thus, it would seem that the property was confiscated from Lavra, conferred as part of a pronoia grant on a layman, and never recovered.

Following the battle of Marica in 1371, in which the despot John Uglješa and his brother Vukašin were defeated by the Ottoman Turks, Manuel Palaiologos, then governing Thessaloniki, undertook a massive confiscation of monastic property for military ends by distributing monastic property as pronoia grants. This episode had long-lasting repercussions, setting the

[120] *Docheiariou*, no. 33.22–23: καὶ ἀπεσπάσθησαν καὶ ἐδόθησαν πρὸς διάφορα πρόσωπα τὰ ἡμίση τῶν ἀναγεγραμμένων πρὸ καιροῦ τινός.

[121] *Docheiariou*, pp. 192, 203. *Lavra*, III, no. 131.5.

[122] Lefort, *Villages de Macédoine*, 108–09. *Xénophon*, no. 27.

course for the evolution of the institution of pronoia through the fifteenth century. As such, discussion of this episode will be reserved for the following chapter where the confiscation and its aftermath will be treated at length.

A few Byzantine writers protested over the confiscation of monastic property. In the second half of the fourteenth century Nicholas Kavasilas, in his *Discourse Concerning Illegal Acts of Officials against Things Sacred*, addressed the issue of the confiscation of monastic land for military ends. He wrote that his opponents would argue, among other things, that such confiscations were justifiable because "we arm soldiers from these things."[123] Similarly, in 1383 Isidore, the metropolitan of Thessaloniki, complained that church property which belonged to his see in Thessaloniki was threatened with confiscation for military ends.[124]

The legal status of the pronoia grant

There is little evidence that Byzantine jurists pondered the implications and underpinnings of the institution of pronoia. Statements regarding the legal status of pronoia grants are quite rare. One is found in the *orismos* from September 1262 in which Michael VIII renders his decision involving the property called Gonia tou Petake *[5.6]*. Because the peasants who had been cultivating the property paid a rent, either to the state or to those who held the property in pronoia, the property did not belong to them "but to the fisc [*demosion*]." From this we can infer that whether or not a piece of real property was exploited directly by the fisc or held by a pronoiar, it belonged to the state. Yet a few lines later the emperor states that the property belonged to whoever received the rent "by right of ownership." There is a certain ambiguity here, which characterizes the nature of pronoia.

A related view is found in an act of an official contained within an *orismos* of John III Vatatzes from 1233 *[5.4]*. At issue was the sale of property by the Gounaropouloi to the pronoia holder Basil Vlatteros. In the course of

[123] I. Ševčenko, "Nicolas Cabasilas' 'Anti-Zealot' Discourse: A Reinterpretation," in Ševčenko, *Society and Intellectual Life in Late Byzantium* (London, 1981), no. IV, 93, ch. 6, lines 20–21. Also, see G. Dennis, "Nicholas Cabasilas Chamaëtos and His Discourse on Abuses Committed by Authorities against Sacred Things," in Dennis, *Byzantium and the Franks, 1350–1420* (London, 1982), no. XI, esp. p. 85, and recently, K. Smyrlis, "The State, the Land, and Private Property: Confiscating Monastic and Church Properties in the Palaiologan Period," in *Church and Society in Late Byzantium*, ed. D. Angelov (Kalamazoo, 2009), 69–71.

[124] G. Dennis, *The Reign of Manuel II Palaeologus in Thessalonica, 1382–1387* (Rome, 1960), 89–91. I. Ševčenko, "A Postscript to Nicolas Cabasilas' 'Anti-Zealot' Discourse," in Ševčenko, *Society and Intellectual Life in Late Byzantium*, no. VI, 405–06.

explaining that the paroikoi of a pronoia holder were not permitted to sell their property holding to the pronoia holder, the official made the quasi-formal statement that things held "in the condition of pronoia" (*kata logon pronoias*) "are arranged eternally under the hand of the fisc." In other words, they were subject to the state. Unlike the *orismos* dealing with Gonia tou Petake, the official did not write that the elements of the pronoia grant were the *property* of the state. In fact, that was not always true. The praktika show that a pronoia grant was a bundle of properties, rights, and privileges. Some of these elements – paroikoi and state taxes – were not property of the state at all. Yet they, no less than real property which *was* owned by the state, were under the *control* of the state.

Thus, in order to consider the legal status of the pronoia grant, it is necessary to consider separately each of the categories of components of the grant, whether immovable property, state taxes and charges, or paroikoi.

Immovable property within the grant (arable land, vineyards, gardens, pasture land, and the various bundles of escheated property that constituted *exaleimmatika*) is the simplest to deal with. The emperor, while maintaining state ownership (*dominium*) over the property, transferred possession and usufruct of the property to the grant holder. Further, by not charging a property tax on the property conferred, the state was indirectly conferring a tax exemption on the pronoia holder.

A case could be made that merely an incorporeal right was transferred – the right to enjoy the income from the property – and not possession of the property itself. Peasants, under any circumstances, would be the ones working the land, and the grant holder's benefit from the property could be viewed as merely the rent or fruits of the property that these peasants rendered to him. The state, by quantifying the value of the property conceded to the grant holder as a *posotes* representing the *telos* of the property, certainly viewed things in these terms. However, if we combine Choniates' statement that land was actually conferred on grant holders in the twelfth century with the fact that there is evidence (see below) that grant holders did indeed play an active role in organizing the production of the property they held, it appears that real possession both preceded and superceded the mere right to an income.

The concession by the state to the pronoia holder of the numerous taxes and charges listed in the praktika involved no concession of any property right. This was the case whether these taxes and charges were owed by particular individuals (as in the case of *epiteleiai*), by the peasants the pronoia holder held (as in the case of the *zeugaratikion* in Monomachos' praktikon), or by all the inhabitants of a specific area (as in the case of the *ennomion* in Saventzes' praktikon). The pronoia holder simply received the *posotes* for the tax or charge as stated in his praktikon.

The transfer of taxes owed by one party to the pronoia holder can be considered a temporary *logisimon*, that is, through a special act of the state, the taxes owed to the state were temporarily "reckoned" to a private party. But *logisima* by nature were intended to be permanent, whereas the transfer of taxes to a pronoia holder need not have been permanent. In any event, the term *logisimon* and its related verb do not appear in the sources after the twelfth century, and so there is little point in appealing to that institution. Legally the grant of the right of one party's taxes to another could be considered a franchise. In this way a pronoia holder could be thought of as a kind of tax farmer.

In the late eleventh century the monastery of Lavra had feared that rendering its property taxes to a third party would call into question its ownership of its property, that the taxes so rendered would be regarded as a rent, that the monks of Lavra had become paroikoi, and, thus, that the arrangement would be used as evidence that the monastery did not own its property *[4.5]*. By the thirteenth century, property owners no longer had this fear. It had become a common practice to render one's taxes to a third party.

For some items within the praktika it is not clear whether the pronoia holder received a flat tax (represented by the *posotes* of the item) or whether the income from the item was based on rents or per-use charges. This is the case, for example, with mills, fish ponds, and flax-retting ponds (*linovrocheia*).

The granting of paroikoi to a grant holder is a complicated matter. While the sources routinely state that a monastery or a layman "held" (*katechei*) paroikoi, this was a fictitious possession which involved no transfer of any property right to the grant holder. Rather, a grant of paroikoi conferred the right to collect the household taxes of one or more peasants (the *telos*), the right to demand secondary taxes and charges from these peasants, and the right to demand labor services from them. In the eleventh and twelfth centuries the grant of paroikoi to laymen or to religious foundations was interpreted as an *exkousseia* whereby the peasants, from the point of view of the fisc, were "exempted" of their personal taxes, secondary taxes and charges, and labor services normally owed to the state. A religious foundation or layman was then granted the license to collect these taxes, charges, and labor services from the peasants. In the eleventh century the peasants involved in this process were all landless and essentially propertyless so that the basic property tax did not come into play. At the same time, most likely because of their lack of property, they were usually peasants who had never been enrolled in the tax lists, which meant that the concession of their fiscal obligations to a third party was less of a loss to the fisc than the concession of the taxes, charges, and labor services of peasants who were currently fulfilling an obligation toward the fisc.

In the twelfth century the theoretical underpinnings of this process had to be modified as privileged religious foundations and laymen were granted peasants who were not propertyless but owned, at the very least, livestock, which ordinarily was taxable. The documents still maintain that these peasants received an *exkousseia*, but this was an *exkousseia* that now included a property tax – something that heretofore the state had been reluctant to concede – as well as the personal tax, secondary taxes and charges, and labor services. The moment that the state decided not to collect a property tax on the property holdings, whether movable or immovable, of such peasants and to grant these peasants to a third party, it was in effect granting a *logisimon* to the third-party beneficiary. Whether or not the third party – religious foundation or layman – actually demanded the tax on the property of these peasants was irrelevant.

Even though the term *exkousseia* was still used on rare occasions in the early thirteenth century to refer to a grant of paroikoi, the term became increasingly inappropriate as the *telos* of property-owning peasants was conferred on laymen and on religious foundations. In sum, the pronoia holder was entitled to a bundle of benefits from his paroikoi: their *telos*, which was now the combined hearth, personal, and real property taxes on each household; surtaxes and secondary taxes levied collectively on the paroikoi as a group; a few demands in kind; and labor services.

Many scholars have attempted to place the institution of pronoia within a legal context, defining it in terms of the extent to which it conformed or did not conform to Roman or western European medieval forms of possession or ownership.[125] Their lack of success is due, in part, to our limited understanding of the mechanics of the institution, but also to a conceptual problem. By attempting to place pronoia within a legal context, they were trying to do something the Byzantines never did. In my view the institution of pronoia stood apart from Byzantine law. Rather, in its essence pronoia was an "arrangement" as one of the senses of the word *oikonomia* implies, a special arrangement that transcended the law. Whatever revenues and

125 E.g., M. Mladenovič, "Zur Frage der Pronoia und des Feudalismus im byzantinischen Reiche," *Südost-Forschungen* 15 (1956), 138; Hvostova, *Osobennosti*, 214–15; and Kazhdan, *Agrarnye otnošenija*, 216.

properties were granted to the pronoia holder were granted on a conditional, temporary, and limited basis, the limited element following from the temporary element. The limitations on the grant which made it conditional could involve service, lifetime tenure, and restrictions on the right to alienate or bequeath the privileges. Pronoia was based on a quasi-personal relationship between emperor and beneficiary.

PART II. HOLDING THE GRANT

Residence

After receiving his complete praktikon the new pronoia holder presumably visited his pronoia, made his presence known to his paroikoi and the others who worked his lands, and cleared up any confusion about financial arrangements. After this, unless his services were immediately needed, he set up house somewhere. Was this near his pronoia? The question is worth asking, not only because it is so straightforward and really unavoidable, but because the geographic proximity between a man and the economic instruments which provide his livelihood is relevant for defining the nature of the man's control over these instruments and, in turn, his social status in an agrarian society. Yet no easy answer is forthcoming. At the very least we can say that someone holding a pronoia in the theme, say, of Thessaloniki, lived in that theme, if for no other reason than that he had periodically to collect his income, in cash or in kind, from his pronoia. Beyond this, in favor of the thesis that landholders lived on rural estates and, as Ostrogorsky wrote, "were masters of the paroikoi who tilled their lands," a thesis grounded in the western European feudal model, there is little evidence.[126] Occasionally a document notes the presence of pronoia holders in a village (MM, IV, 128.14–19) or the residence of pronoia holders near agricultural land *[5.2]*. In 1321 there was a dwelling place (*kathedra*) within the land that a man named Angelos held within his pronoia.[127] This might serve as evidence that a pronoia holder might have a residence on a property he held as a pronoia, though it might have been nothing more than a place to stay while visiting his holding or a residence for a steward.[128] But such

[126] G. Ostrogorsky, "Observations on the Aristocracy in Byzantium," *Dumbarton Oaks Papers* 25 (1971), 11.

[127] *Lavra*, II, no. 108.431: τῆς καθέδρας τοῦ Ἀγγέλου. Lefort, *Villages de Macédoine*, 113 and map 7.

[128] J. Lefort, "The Rural Economy, Seventh–Twelfth Centuries," *EHB*, I, 240. Cf. the lodgings of judges: *Vatopédi*, I, no. 11.26–29.

references are quite rare and usually inconclusive. Nor of course do our six praktika mention that the soldiers received any habitation in pronoia. The act of John Apokaukos which describes how a pronoia holder traveled to a village he held in pronoia only to find that his paroikoi prepared nothing for his arrival is an example of a pronoia holder who did not live on or near his pronoia and provides evidence that the Byzantine landholder was less the lord of a manor than an absentee landlord *[5.16]*.

The Byzantine tradition of civic life would militate against the idea of the pronoia holder isolating himself out in the countryside. Rather than looking for comparison to the French or German model, it might be better to consider medieval northern Italy, where civic life endured the early medieval crises. The Italian seigneur lived an urban life, the life of an absentee landlord, no less than his ancient Roman counterpart. We should expect the pronoia holder, fundamentally a landlord as well, to have preferred the community of population centers.

Tending the grant: exploiting, improving, and increasing the domain land

The pronoia holder's direct involvement in the organization, management, and exploitation of his grant was restricted to the agricultural property within the grant that was owned by the state. This "domain land" included *ge*, vineyards, gardens, pasture land, and the property contained within *exaleimmata*. Excluded were the property holdings (*staseis*) of the pronoia holder's paroikoi, and the various fiscal charges, including *epiteleiai*, held by the pronoia holder because these were fixed and could not be altered.

In the seven praktika studied above, the amount of arable land (*ge*) within the domain land varied from a low of 550 modioi (about 138 acres) in Monomachos' praktikon to a high of 4,550 modioi (about 1,125 acres) in Berilas' praktikon (Table 8.4). Excluding Monomachos, the range is 1,550 to 4,550 modioi. The small quantity of *ge* held by Monomachos can be explained by the fact that while a substantial portion of most of the other men's grants was derived from *ge*, the bulk of Monomachos' grant was composed of fishing rights and dock charges. Four of the praktika distinguish *ge* by its quality, usually assessing normal *ge* at the rate of one hyperpyron per fifty modioi. The 600 modioi of "best" *ge* in Kallinikos' praktikon were assessed at a much higher rate of one hyperpyron for twenty-five modioi, and the 2,500 modioi of second- and third-quality *ge* in Berilas' praktikon was assessed at one hyperpyra per 67.6 modioi. However, the 1,000 modioi of third-quality *ge* held by Margarites was assessed at the

Table 8.4 Arable land (*ge* and *choraphia*) within seven praktika

	Arable land owned by paroikoi (in modioi)	Arable land outside *exaleimmata* (in modioi)	Arable land within *exaleimmata* (in modioi)	Total arable land (in modioi)	Domain land as percentage of total arable land
Michael Saventzes	170	2100	0	2270	93%
Nicholas Maroules	428	2050	$>197\frac{2}{3}$	$>2675\frac{2}{3}$	$\approx$84%
Basil Berilas	30	4500	50	4580	99%
Michael Monomachos	734	550	not specified	>1284	$\approx$43%
Alexios Raoul	2387	unknown	at least 153	unknown	–
Kallinikos	1772	2100	0	3872	54%
John Margarites	230	1550	>154	>1934	$\approx$88%

standard rate of one hyperpyron per fifty modioi. Compared to the arable land held by the paroikoi of each of the men, the domain land comprised around half to nearly all of the arable land listed within each praktikon.

The evidence suggests that pronoia holders managed the properties they held from the emperor much like any landholder would. In some cases, they were forced to take an active interest. Among the properties received by John Margarites was a "neglected vineyard," which would have been of little value at all unless he arranged for someone to work it.[129]

There were several methods by which the pronoia holder could exploit his domain land. Two of them are noted in the praktikon for the monk Kallinikos. The document specifies that the "best" land (600 modioi) that he was granted within the village of Mamitzona would be cultivated through the labor services (*angareia*) which the paroikoi he was granted owed him. The other land he was granted (1,500 modioi) would be leased (*hypomortou*) to others.[130]

There were two ways to lease land. The pronoia holder could lease part of his domain land to peasants, either his own paroikoi or other peasants living locally, who, in turn, paid him a rent (*morte* or *dekateia*) on the land, representing a share of the produce.[131] A document from 1262 notes that the peasants of the village of Malachiou had paid a rent (*morte*), sometimes to the fisc, sometimes to pronoia holders, on land they worked but did not own in that village *[5.6]*. And in the mid-1270s the *protonovelissimos* Marmaras collected a rent for what seems to have been a large quantity of arable land called Vrasta. An imperial official ruled that Vrasta was not part of Marmaras' pronoia, but that it belonged to the monastery of

129 Lemerle, "Un praktikon inédit," 285, lines 37–38: ἀμπέλιον ἠμελημένον.

130 *Chilandar*, ed. Petit, no. 92.149–50,162.

131 *ODB*, s.v. "rent," "morte," "tithe," "pakton."

Nea Petra *[8.65]*. Clearly, this land was under cultivation by peasants who paid a rent to whoever held the property, and nothing in the documentation indicates that these peasants were paroikoi of either Marmaras or the monastery.

Such cases where peasants leased land from a landowner were subject to private arrangements, the details of which are not recorded in praktika or other documents. The assumption is that peasants paid a rent in kind, in a sharecropping arrangement, whereby the landlord received one-third or perhaps even one-half of the harvest. There is also some evidence that peasants might lease land for a fixed rent in specie, and that the peasants of a particular area acted collectively when arranging their leases. All of this would vary by locality and time period.[132]

[8.24] Act of lease of the soldier Demetrios Armenopoulos (1303)

Alternatively, the pronoia holder could lease part of his grant to another party who would arrange the exploitation of the land. In 1299/1300 the "imperial soldier" (*vasilikos stratiotes*) Demetrios Armenopoulos leased seven *exaleimmatika stasia* to the monastery of Lavra which he was holding "through a praktikon" (*dia praktikou*) in the village of Tripotamos on the Longos peninsula. However, for unspecified reasons, Armenopoulos cancelled the agreement, and in August 1303 he leased the *stasia* to the monastery of Xenophon for a rental payment of three hyperpyra yearly "for the sake of the *morte*." Armenopoulos states that Xenophon should hold the *stasia* "for as long as I am found holding such mercy of the . . . emperor," in other words, as long as he held his oikonomia.[133] Armenopoulos implicitly acknowledged that he had no right to the permanent alienation of these properties. At his death, or at the pleasure of the emperor, the lease would be dissolved. Such an arrangement was rather complicated. The emperor granted land as pronoia to Armenopoulos; Armenopoulos leased it to a monastery for a cash rent; and then the monastery exploited the land presumably through peasant labor, either through the corvée obligation burdening the monastery's own paroikoi or through lease to other peasants.

There is no direct evidence that pronoia holders worked their domain lands through hired labor, but because it was not uncommon for other

132 A. Laiou, "The Agrarian Economy, Thirteenth–Fifteenth Centuries," *EHB*, I, 337–39, 345–46. Laiou, *Peasant Society*, 61, 216–21.

133 *Xénophon*, no. 6.17: ἵνα κατέχῃ μέχρης [sic] ἂν τὴν τοιαύτην ἐλεημοσύνην τοῦ . . . βασιλέως εὑρίσκομαι κατέχων.

landholders – both lay and monastic – to employ day laborers and other hired men, it is reasonable to conclude that pronoia holders did likewise.[134] Almost certainly the steward (*oikonomos*) of the pronoia holder Constantine Tzirithnos in the 1220s was a hired man *[5.15]*.

Even though we can speak of this land that the pronoia holder received as a kind of domain land, we should not think of it as a quantity of land that the pronoia holder could exploit in any way he saw fit. Most of the land that a pronoia holder received, if it had any agricultural value, was probably already under cultivation at the moment he received it. In some combination, parts were leased and worked by paroikoi held by the previous pronoia holder who held the land or by the fisc itself, parts were worked through corvée obligations that were due to the previous holder or to the state, and, yes, perhaps some of the land was temporarily not under cultivation because the paroikoi leasing the land had moved away or died. Only the land previously worked by corvée labor or that was temporarily vacant was available for the implementation of creative arrangements by the new pronoia holder. Otherwise, the peasants who were leasing any of this land were generally long-term lessees whose parents and grandparents may well have leased the same land.

The proportions of this arable land leased by the pronoia holder's own paroikoi, leased by other paroikoi, and cultivated through corvée are impossible to determine, but one may hypothesize: Saventzes' praktikon included a total of 2,100 modioi of *ge* and eight paroikos households. If Saventzes' paroikoi were leasing all of his *ge*, each paroikos household would have been cultivating an average of 262 modioi, which is quite unlikely – impossible in fact – given that these eight households owned in all a total of three oxen. Corvée labor could not have accounted for much of the production: eight men working twelve days per year, even with the use of oxen by Saventzes, would hardly have put a dent into the 2,100 modioi of *ge* Saventzes held. We are left with the possibility that outside peasants leased much of these 2,100 modioi, but the matter is far from settled.[135]

In any event, we should not think that most pronoia holders, newly assigned quantities of land, were at liberty to exploit these properties however they pleased. Custom and tradition constrained them, and this was not necessarily a bad thing. Why disturb lease arrangements among stable peasant households that had existed perhaps for generations? One could

134 Laiou, "The Agrarian Economy," 336–37.
135 These issues and others are discussed in detail in Laiou, "The Agrarian Economy," 328–46.

argue that such peasants had more claim to the land they were leasing than the new pronoia holder.

Another option was to improve the property so that it would become more productive. One might clear land, or plant olives or vines on a parcel. The *sevastos* Peter Doukopoulos built a water mill on land within his pronoia *[8.53]*.

Improving the property within one's pronoia grant could lead to problems. Consider a piece of pasture land within a man's oikonomia which through his own efforts he had brought into cultivation, increasing its productivity. At the next revision of his praktikon, if he wished to keep this land, he would have to convince the fiscal official not to change the parcel's *posotes* or, alternatively, he would have to ask the emperor to grant him an increase in the *posotes* of his oikonomia to account for the increased tax value of the parcel. Otherwise the parcel could be declared *perisseia* ("excess") and he could lose some of the property within his oikonomia. Thus pronoia holders normally had little incentive to improve their properties, and we should not look to the institution of pronoia for any positive contribution to agricultural productivity.

To avoid problems with the fisc, grant holders might seek imperial approval to make improvements without this affecting the fiscal status of their properties, and this was not a phenomenon unique to pronoia grants or to the late Byzantine period. For example, in the eleventh century Gregory Pakourianos *[4.2]* received from the emperor a "chrysobull concerning the improvements on my properties, the construction of *kastra*, of villages, and of monasteries."[136]

The right to improve property normally accompanied the granting of hereditary rights to a grant of property. Thus, it was assumed that over the course of time the grant holder would make improvements to his properties that would increase their value. In fact, in the thirteenth and fourteenth centuries explicit permission to improve the property within a grant is found exclusively in documents granting the right of hereditary transmission of the grant (e.g., *[6.8] [8.4] [8.46]*).

The right to improve one's properties was, of course, not simply the right to better manage one's resources. It was the right to have these improvements not affect the *posotes* of one's grant in future fiscal reassessments. It was a fiscal concession. A document issued by the official Manglavites from

[136] P. Gautier, "Le typikon du sébaste Grégoire Pakourianos," *REB* 42 (1984), 127.1796–97. S. Dmitriev, "Melioration (*Beltiosis*) in Byzantine Documents (10th–15th Centuries)," *JÖB* 49 (1999), 61–88, treats at length improvement clauses in documents involving sales, donations, and leases, but does not address these clauses in the context of imperial grants.

1319 or 1320 for John Orestes makes this clear *[8.42]*. Pursuant to imperial order Manglavites conferred a *posotes* of six hyperpyra drawn from the oikonomia Orestes held from the emperor. The official states, as many other documents do, that Orestes had the right to improve the properties within this *posotes*, but unlike other documents he adds explicitly that no *apographeus* was permitted to raise or lower the *posotes*, even if the *posotes* increased. The *posotes* of six hyperpyra was to remain unchanged regardless of improvements to the properties.[137]

And last, another option was to acquire more property, whether near to one's pronoia holdings or not. Naturally, such property was not part of one's oikonomia, unless the emperor specifically made it so.

The grant holder's relations with the fisc (*exisoseis*)

Periodic inspections of properties followed by revisions (*exisoseis*, literally "equalizings") of the tax lists were a basic feature of late Byzantine fiscal policy in the thirteenth and fourteenth centuries. They had a number of purposes: to increase state revenues by reevaluating the values of property; to ensure that everyone was holding his property lawfully, and especially to ensure that imperial grants, including pronoiai, were still in the possession of those to whom they had been granted; and to locate available properties to confer as pronoia grants. This is when *perisseia* would be found. A fiscal assessor (*apographeus*) traveled through a particular region reevaluating the *posotetes* of properties, rights, and paroikos households, and then creating new, revised praktika. The praktika of Saventzes, Maroules, Berilas, and Raoul, are examples of periodic revisions of pronoiai. We might assume that the *apographeus* evaluated all of the property within his geographical jurisdiction, but there is no direct evidence for this. Aside from a few references to *exisoseis* in the literary sources which are all concerned with the institution of pronoia, the bulk of the evidence is found in the documentary evidence which deals with *exisoseis* conducted on the property holdings of either monasteries or privileged individuals. All of the extant praktika were issued for landholders – monasteries and individuals – who benefitted from imperial privileges. Whether praktika were issued for landowners who held unprivileged property is unknown. These landowners would have held rather modest holdings, because every indication is that large landowners and landholders all received privileges over their properties.

[137] *Vatopédi*, I, no. 52.28–30.

[8.25] Pachymeres on the weakness of the army in Asia Minor (ca. 1307)

From the end of the thirteenth through the middle of the fourteenth century there were at least four *exisoseis* carried out specifically to strengthen the army. In 1298 Andronikos II sent John Tarchaneiotes to Anatolia with money and troops to make one last effort to set in order the fiscal affairs of the region. According to Pachymeres,

Many of the soldiers, seizing frequent opportunities, increased their own pronoiai and lived idly through bribing their leaders with gifts and offerings; others, often more worthy, fell into poverty since they abandoned their own oikonomiai, producing for them an obstacle to military service. Both of these were a loss to the state, and this inequality required an *exisosis.*[138]

In 1322 Andronikos II ordered an empire-wide *exisosis [7.20]*, and in 1328 another *exisosis* was conducted in the western provinces "so that the army should become larger" *[7.22]*.

[8.26] Kantakouzenos on Patrikiotes (ca. 1355)

The most detailed account of an *exisosis* appears in the history of John Kantakouzenos. In 1341, shortly after the death of Andronikos III, Kantakouzenos was directing the military affairs of the empire in the name of Andronikos' nine-year-old son, John V Palaiologos. When war with Bulgaria loomed on the horizon, he ordered the soldiers throughout the empire to ready themselves for service. However,

seeing not only many of the military list, but not a few others, by reason of the wealth assigned to each by the emperor not being intact, entirely neglecting military service and depriving the state of the benefit from them, he [Kantakouzenos] decided to deliver them from pressing indigence, replacing that which each lacked of the

[138] Pachymeres, ed. Failler, III, 285.22–28 (Bonn edn., II, 258.13ff). Kazhdan, *Agrarnye otnošenija*, 219. Ostrogorsky, *Féodalité*, 101. Laiou, *Constantinople and the Latins*, 87–88, 118. Laiou, "The Byzantine Aristocracy in the Palaeologan Period," 141–42. Oikonomides, "A propos des armées," 355. Bibikov, "Svedenija," 94. In their analysis of this passage Mutafčiev, "Vojniški zemi," 58/586, and B. Gorjanov, *Pozdnevizantijskij feodalizm* (Moscow, 1962), 223–24, distinguished the soldiers that held pronoiai from those that held oikonomiai, which they interpreted as referring to the old *stratiotika ktemata*. This is untenable. Not only is there no evidence for the existence of the middle Byzantine *stratiotika ktemata* in the late thirteenth century, but it is self-evident that Pachymeres is distinguishing soldiers who illicitly increased their pronoiai from those who abandoned their pronoiai. In fact he is creating an equivalence between pronoia and oikonomia.

pronoia from the emperor, and he should treat each according to his need, ordaining that all contribute something to benefit the state.[139]

He learned that a certain Patrikiotes, who had served for some time as an *apographeus*, had abused his position, as was common, and had become a rich man. But because Patrikiotes came forward without being summoned, Kantakouzenos decided not to lay charges against him, and in fact Patrikiotes was willing "to equalize [*epanisoun*] again the means of living of the soldiers" from the wealth he had obtained illicitly.[140] This was not a typical *exisosis* for Kantakouzenos himself was directly involved in the process:

After this the *megas domestikos* [i.e., Kantakouzenos] summoned one by one those of the senate, those otherwise distinguished by birth, and then the soldiers [*stratiotai*], and he ascertained the amount of pronoia given by the emperor to each and whether he now held more or less than that which was assigned. According to the answers of each in regard to what he held, he ordered Patrikiotes to restore the necessary amounts for those deprived, and to add over and above as much as seemed good to him, proportionately adding to each the beneficence [*euergesia*]. To those holding incomes from the emperor which were not deficient, he ordered similarly that other incomes be added to what they were holding.

And indeed in sixty days the redistribution took place: for those holding less he added that which was lacking along with a [further] addition, and for those lacking nothing the addition was added. And everyone considered that he was in command of sufficient revenues and professed great gratitude toward the *megas domestikos*, and they were eager to fight the enemies of the Romans of whatever land. And cleansing their arms, they reequipped themselves, and they procured horses, more and better ones than before. And in short they appeared vexed that they were not led right away for defense against enemies.[141]

We observe that while this *exisosis* arose out of a desire to strengthen the army, not only pronoia soldiers were affected by it, but "those of the senate" and "others distinguished by birth" as well. Also, there is no concern expressed over pronoia holders who held rights and properties beyond the value assigned to them. In fact, additional grants of pronoia were given to those who had not lost any part of their grants.

139 Kantakouzenos, II, 58.13–23. Mutafčiev, "Vojniški zemi," 546–47. A. Heisenberg, *Aus der Geschichte und Literatur der Palaiologenzeit*, in Heisenberg, *Quellen und Studien zur spätbyzantinischen Geschichte* (London, 1973), no. I, 71 note 2.

140 Kantakouzenos, II, 58 and 61. Ostrogorsky, *Féodalité*, 101–03. Heisenberg, *Palaiologenzeit*, 74–75.

141 Kantakouzenos, II, 63.12–22. Bartusis, *Late Byzantine Army*, 177–78.

The grant holder's relations with the emperor

Obligations of the grant holder: service

From the earliest modern historiography on the subject, a pronoia has been considered a grant conditional on the recipient being alive (that is, a lifetime grant), conditional on the recipient performing service, or both. Certainly in the sources of the twelfth and first half of the thirteenth centuries there is much evidence implicitly linking the holding of pronoiai to military service. The evidence of Choniates links the grant of pronoiai by Manuel I to an obligation to perform military service. The documents of the twelfth century involving the Cumans of Moglena, and the documents of the first half of the thirteenth century dealing with soldiers who held pronoiai imply that soldiers who held pronoiai were obligated to perform military service by virtue of holding the grant.

With the shift to oikonomiai and the broader range of recipients of such grants, the link between military service and the holding of an imperial grant becomes more tenuous. Why did emperors grant oikonomiai? To what extent were these grants conferred as rewards and to what extent were they given in consideration of future services?

Direct testimony tying the holding of oikonomiai to military service is not uncommon. Michael VIII's 1272 *prostagma [6.6]* makes this connection directly, as does the testimony of the historians Pachymeres and Kantakouzenos. A handful of other sources do so too, such as the letter written by the patriarch of Constantinople, Gregory II Kyprianos (1283–89), dealing with the problems of the soldier Chrysokompas *[6.12]*. Regarding Chrysokompas' son the patriarch wrote that "both pronoia and home, and whatever else there was for which one was obligated to be a soldier, had passed to the child from the mother's side."

[8.27] Chrysobull of Andronikos II Palaiologos for the inhabitants of Ioannina (1319)

The link between holding the imperial grant and military service is also found in the 1319 chrysobull of Andronikos II for the town of Ioannina. Andronikos asserted that the *kastrenoi* of Ioannina, evidently the better off inhabitants of the *kastron*, "should neither be forced nor constrained to serve militarily outside of this city, since only those assigned soldiers, reckoned among the units of the military divisions [τὰς συντάξεις τῶν ἀλλαγίων] and having an oikonomia ought to serve."[142] There can be no question that this document links military service to the holding of an oikonomia. The principle seems to be that the only inhabitants of Ioannina liable for military service outside the city were registered soldiers who held oikonomiai. On the other hand, we can infer that all inhabitants were liable for local defense.

[8.28] Pachymeres on the Vasilikoi (ca. 1307)

Pachymeres writes of two Turkish magnates, Basil Vasilikos and a relative, who had become friends of Michael VIII while he was at the court of the Seljuk sultan. When they later sought refuge in Byzantium around 1259, Michael honored them with high-ranking court titles, and "they received not a little from the emperor for oikonomia [*eis oikonomian*]; quite faithfully and good-naturedly, transforming themselves into Romans, they served the emperor." Ostrogorsky concluded that the pair received oikonomiai.[143] The passage is rather vague but certainly the subject could be a pronoia. While the service of these men is not specified as military service, the passage implies that the grant of something "for oikonomia" would be accompanied by some kind of service toward the emperor.

Aside from these specific references linking service to the holding of a pronoia or oikonomia, documents dealing with imperial grants to individuals or groups of individuals occasionally refer to the beneficiary's "service" toward the empire and emperor. Sometimes this is clearly a reference to military service, sometimes it is more vague. Such references to "service" (*douleia*, or less commonly *doulosyne*) in a number of documents have often been interpreted by scholars as referring to personal service which, depending on the terms stated in the particular document, was or was not owed by the beneficiary of the grant.[144]

The word *douleia* is a very general word. In the late Byzantine era it generally means "service" in the sense of tasks or employment or duties

[142] MM, v, 81.17–20, 83.14–21.

[143] Pachymeres, ed. Failler, I, 183.15–18. *PLP*, nos. 2452, 2458. Ostrogorsky, *Féodalité*, 99–100. Cf. Ahrweiler, "Smyrne," 27 and note 142, where she relates the case to pronoia, while in Ahrweiler, "La concession des droits incorporels," 113, she places it in her "appanage" category (large, revocable, hereditary grant).

[144] Ostrogorsky, *Féodalité*, 124–25, 127, 128, 181–83; G. Ostrogorsky, "Drei Praktika weltlicher Grundbesitzer aus der ersten Hälfte des 14. Jahrhunderts," *ZRVI* 14–15 (1973), 98; Kazhdan, *Agrarnye otnošenija*, 220–21; D. Zakythinos, *Le despotat grec de Morée*, rev. ed. (London, 1975), II, 119; F. Dölger, "Ein Chrysobull des Kaisers Andronikos II. für Theodoros Nomikopulos aus dem Jahre 1288," in *Παρασπορά* (Ettal, 1961), 191; Hvostova, *Osobennosti*, 222; Laiou, "The Byzantine Aristocracy in the Palaeologan Period," 142, 145.

undertaken more or less voluntarily. Among various forms of service, one could serve another individual, a monastery or other religious foundation, or one could serve the emperor. Service toward the state or emperor took many forms. Predominant among them was military service. In 1266 the *sevastos* George Petritzes donated some land to the monastery of the Lemviotissa near Smyrna. In the act of donation, he swore to uphold the agreement, and, if not, "I shall no longer be worthy to serve militarily our mighty and holy lord and emperor."[145] In other cases the reference to military service is implicit. In a chrysobull from 1318 of questionable authenticity Andronikos II notes that the soldier Manuel Garianos of the *Serriotikon mega allagion* had been active "in the services of my majesty" *[8.49]*. And in a chrysobull from 1351 John V notes that the *megas adnoumiastes* George Katzaras, known elsewhere as the head or administrator of the Varvarenoi soldier company, had been "faithful to our majesty and attentive . . . in its service," a reference either to administrative duties or to actual military service *[8.47]*.

But aside from military service, *douleia* could refer to other varieties of imperial service as well. The responsibilities of fiscal officials and *kephalai* (the governors of towns or provinces) was called *demosiake douleia*.[146] For example, in 1427 George Gemistos Plethon was granted the right to hold a *kastron* and govern it as a *kephale* (κρατῶν καὶ κεφαλιτικεύων), "being under an obligation to serve" (ἐκδουλεύειν ὀφείλων) the despot of the Morea Theodore II Palaiologos. Gemistos at the time was in his late sixties and so we can conclude with some certainty that "to serve" here did not mean personal *military* service.[147]

[8.29] Chrysobull for the *parakoimomenos* of the *megale sphendone* Manuel Sergopoulos (later fourteenth century)

An example of an administrative appointment which has similarities to a pronoia grant is found in a chrysobull *orismos* from the later fourteenth

145 MM, IV, 160.9–11. A year and a half later he was dead and the monastery was claiming another parcel of land which it said Petritzes had intended to transfer to the monastery in return for ten hyperpyra the monastery had given Petritzes "to outfit himself for military service": MM, IV, 161.23–24. According to a source from 1205, the equipment of a cavalryman, including horse, cost some 80 hyperpyra: Morrisson and Cheynet, "Prices and Wages in the Byzantine World," 862 note 116. Ostrogorsky, *Féodalité*, 81, wrote that Petritzes was a military pronoia holder, but, while it is quite likely, nothing in these documents proves this. Petritzes' lack of cash does not exclude him from being a pronoia holder, since one of the disadvantages of receiving income from the land is a tendency to be cash-poor.

146 MM, IV, 261.3–5; *Patmos*, I, no. 26.22.

147 S. Lampros, *Παλαιολόγεια καὶ Πελοποννησιακά* (Athens, 1912–30; repr. Athens, 1972), IV, 104.12–14 = MM, III, 173–74. And see *[9.8]*.

century. The emperor conferred the island of Marmara at the western end of the sea of Marmara on a man named Manuel Sergopoulos for life (ἐφ' ὅρῳ τῆς ζωῆς αὐτοῦ). Sergopoulos "served and yet serves my majesty faithfully, rightly, and in good repute in the services in which he is ordered and assigned by it." The emperor ordered that Sergopoulos improve the island howsoever he could and "tend to both the watch and the rest of the fortification and buildings and its security." In other words he was being appointed the island's governor, or *kephale*. In return for this, Sergopoulos was granted all the state revenue (*panta demosiaka dikaia*) of the island which, surprisingly, consisted explicitly only of the *ennomion* of the island's sheep, the *kommerkion*, and a limited right of first purchase of the island's produce. The fact that there is no mention whatsoever of property taxes on land suggests depopulation and an island in economic crisis. Indeed a chronicle reports that the island suffered a devastating earthquake in 1344. In light of this, Sergopoulos' appointment probably should be viewed as an attempt to restore the health of the island. Whether this was a pronoia grant, or whether it was an administrative appointment accompanied by a pronoia grant, or whether it was a pragmatic and idiosyncratic arrangement from which we ought not make any generalizations, depends on one's point of view. I favor the latter interpretation.[148]

In other cases the service involved could be informal. For example, the Serbian monk Kallinikos, known for his diplomatic work between Byzantium and Serbia, was the recipient of a number of property grants in the early 1320s. In the praktikon for Kallinikos discussed at length in this chapter the emperor rewarded him "because of the exertion, diligence, and zeal which he displayed in the services of our majesty."[149] And then there is the case of the monk Jacob, a loyal partisan of Andronikos III. He was rewarded with an imperial grant for his faithfulness and "having given service for my majesty."[150] What specific actions were being rewarded is anyone's guess, but certainly not military service.

In an even broader sense "service" can also refer to a much wider collection of obligations, including the corvée services (*angareiai*) of paroikoi. In a letter to Theodore II Laskaris, Nikephoros Vlemmydes describes a quarrel

148 P. Magdalino, "An Unpublished Pronoia Grant of the Second Half of the Fourteenth Century," *ZRVI* 18 (1978), 155–63. On the *kephalai* of islands, see Lj. Maksimović, *The Byzantine Provincial Administration under the Palaiologoi* (Amsterdam, 1988), 85–88.

149 *Chilandar*, ed. Petit, no. 90.11 (1323), and also, no. 74.3 (1321). *PLP*, no. 10393.

150 *Prodrome*, no. 28.15 (1333) = *Prodrome B*, no. 154.16–17 (1328). The dates do not coincide because the indiction years differ in the two existing transcriptions of the document. *PLP*, no. 7921.

he had over some paroikoi with a soldier named Skordyllios who held a pronoia near Ephesus. Vlemmydes asked the emperor to grant him these paroikoi (whom he calls "Samians," a classical reference to the inhabitants of the area). Otherwise, he proposed a division of the paroikoi's obligations: "if your majesty deems it proper, let them [the peasants] give a share of their taxes and burdens to . . . Skordyllios, except the service of the Samians."[151]

Thus, when we encounter documents involving imperial grants that specify that an individual or group of individuals owes or does not owe "service," it is not an easy matter to determine what kind of service was implied. References to "service" appear occasionally in documents, usually chrysobulls, in the context of the privileges and conditions under which an individual received privileges, usually hereditary rights, over, usually, a specific immovable property (as opposed to a *posotes*). Such references are found in about half of the extant documents that deal with hereditary rights to individuals. The questions we need to ask are, What is meant by "service" in these documents? Specifically, is the service directly connected to an imperial grant? And why do some documents refer to service and others do not? Is there any thread that connects all the documents that speak of continued service? And is there any thread connecting those that say "no service"?

Table 8.5 displays all of the known cases of imperial grants of property or of *posotetes* in which there is any mention of "service" within the conditions under which the grant was to be held. Of the twelve cases, seven make some demand for "service," while five involve documents which state that the property granted to the recipient was granted "without service" or a similar phrase. Let us consider the latter first. In all five of these cases hereditary rights were granted over the property involved. In four of the five cases, the property involved is designated as *eleutheros* (i.e., tax-exempt) and the recipient was granted the right to alienate the property. These four cases are unique in that they are the *only* known cases involving the granting of hereditary rights in which the property is designated as *eleutheros* and they represent four of the five Byzantine documents which link the explicit right to alienate a property to the right of hereditary transmittal.[152] Further, the

[151] *Theodori Ducae Lascaris Epistulae* CCXVII, ed. N. Festa (Florence, 1898), App. III, no. 8, p. 299.33–36: τὰ τέλη δὲ αὐτῶν καὶ ζητήματα, εἴπερ εὐδοεῖ ἡ Βασιλεία σου, ἀποχαρισάσθω . . . τῷ σκορδυλλίῳ, πλήν τῆς τῶν Σαμίων δουλείας. This pronoia holder was probably a member of the Skordiles family of Crete *[2.6]*.

[152] The other document is a chrysobull for Theodotos Kalothetos *[7.16]*. The chrysobull for Xene Soultanina *[7.17]* granted the right to alienate a *posotes*, but without specifically mentioning hereditary rights. And Stefan Dušan's grant to a group of *archontopouloi* mentions both hereditary rights and the right to alienate, and refers to the property granted as *eleutheros [8.5]*.

Table 8.5 References to "service" in the privilege clauses of documents

Beneficiary	Date	Hereditary?	Right to alienate?	Service?	Tax free?	Property
monk/priest Modenos and son *[8.30]*	ca. 1278	yes	yes		yes (*eleutheros*)	*hypostasis*
	1320			no		
	1321			no		
	1321					
Nomikopoulos *[8.33]*	1288	yes		yes		village
Koteanitzes *[8.31]*	1293 or forgery	yes	yes	no	yes (*eleutheros*)	land
Manuel Angelos Patrikios *[App. 5]*	forgery	yes	yes	no	yes (*eleutheros*)	*zeugelateion* with *proskathemenoi*
Dragon *[App. 5]*	forgery	yes	yes	no	yes (*eleutheros*)	*zeugelateion*
Michael Monomachos *[8.14]*	1333	yes		no		50 hyp.
Klazomenitai soldiers *[8.4]*	1342	yes		yes		10/12 hyp. *posotetes*
megas adnoumiastes George Katzaras and son *[8.47]*	1351	yes		yes		48 hyp./2400 mod.
	1373			yes		
Sergopoulos *[8.29]*	later 14th c.	no	(no)	yes	yes	island
Radoslav Sampias and son *[8.48]*	1378	yes		yes		2 villages
	1405	yes		yes	yes	2 villages
Manuel Tarchaneiotes *[8.32]*	1378	yes		yes		village
George Gemistos Plethon and sons *[9.8]*	1427	yes		yes	limited	*kastron*
	1428	yes		yes	limited	village
	1428	yes		yes	limited	village
	1433	yes		yes	limited	*kastron* and village
	1449	yes		yes	yes	"
	1450			yes	yes	"

documents for all four of the cases are found in the archives of Hilandar and the documents for three of the four are of questionable authenticity, two almost certainly being forgeries. Of these four cases, the only one that involves clearly authentic documents concerns a priest named Modenos, and the "service" connected to his property grant had nothing to do with personal service at all.

[8.30] Chrysobull of Michael VIII Palaiologos for the priest Modenos (ca. 1278), *Prostagma* of Andronikos II for Basil, son of Modenos (January 1320), Chrysobull of Andronikos II Palaiologos for the monastery of Hilandar (February 1321), and Chrysobull of Andronikos II Palaiologos for the monastery of Hilandar (June 1321)

Sometime during the last years of Michael VIII's reign Modenos received a *stasis* in the village of Zdravikion from the emperor. After Modenos' death, a *prostagma* of Andronikos II from January 1320 granted one of his sons, Basil, who had inherited a third of his father's property and was childless, permission to sell his estate to Hilandar. The document notes that Basil's father held land, through a chrysobull, "completely free and beyond all service," and that Basil now held this land "completely free of all service." Basil sold the property to the monastery and died soon thereafter. According to a chrysobull from February 1321 the monks requested confirmation of their rights to Basil's land. The emperor confirmed their possession of the property sold by Modenos, "held by him through chrysobull, being free and without all service."[153]

That the word "service" in these passages had nothing to do with any kind of personal service is seen from a much earlier document, a chrysobull of Michael VIII that was probably issued a few years prior to 1281. The emperor explains that the *stasis* in Zdravikion which the priest Modenos held through imperial grant was "completely free and *akatadouloton*." Modenos had asked the emperor for a chrysobull permitting him to hold the *stasis* "free and without every *paroikikon* burden" and to pass it to his legitimate children, that they may hold it in the same way. The emperor agreed to the request and ordered that Modenos hold his *stasis* "without every burden and state *telos*," as he had held it up to then, and to do with it what he wished as its legitimate "lord" (*despotes*), transferring it to his children and heirs, and that these ought to hold it the same way as their father had.[154]

153 *Chilandar*, ed. Petit, no. 52.5–6: γῆν ἐλευθέραν παντελῶς καὶ ἀνωτέραν πάσης δουλείας, and lines 18–19: ἐλευθέρα παντελῶς πάσης δουλείας, and no. 58.26,42: ἐλευθέρα ὄντα καὶ πάσης δουλείας ἐκτός.

154 *Chilandar*, ed. Živojinović, I, no. 26.3: ἐλευθέραν πάντη καὶ ἀκαταδούλωτον, line 7: ἐλευθέραν καὶ βάρους ἐκτὸς παροικικοῦ παντός, and lines 13–14: ἐκτὸς βάρους καὶ τέλους δημοσιακοῦ παντός. Further, he requested that his son-in-law the priest Michael Vorkinos, "who up to now was kept free, without every *paroikia* and every state *telos*," enjoy the same exemption (*exkousseia*) (lines 10–11, 19). In November 1281, at Modenos' request, Andronikos II, as co-emperor, confirmed this arrangement and exempted John Porianites, another son-in-law of Modenos, of all charges: *Chilandar*, ed. Živojinović, I, no. 27.

In other words, the phrases "beyond all service,""free of all service," and "without all service" in the documents from the 1320s correspond to *akatadouloton* and "without every *paroikikon* burden" in the chrysobull of Michael VIII. *Akatadouloton* is a fiscal term meaning "unsubjected to fiscal charges," usually connected to the secondary charges and corvées burdening peasants, particularly the latter which were called *leitourgiai* or *leitourgemata* (both literally "public service"), or most commonly *angareiai*. *Akatadoulotos*, then, meant not subject to these secondary services.[155] In context the phrases meant that Modenos' property enjoyed a fiscal exemption from the secondary labor services to the state that ordinarily burdened the paroikoi on private land. In other words, at issue was not Modenos' personal "service" to the emperor or empire, but the "public service" of the paroikoi working Modenos' land, that is, the corvées and secondary charges for which peasants were liable. Thus, when the *stasis* of the priest Modenos was freed from "service," it was merely a fiscal exemption, with no connection whatsoever to personal service. This interpretation is confirmed by a chrysobull of Andronikos II from June 1321 which notes "that years ago a certain priest called Modenos held through chrysobull land . . . free and not subject to any burden and tax."[156]

We observe that here, as in all of the other documents relating to Modenos, the expressions "free," "not subject," and "without service" modify the property itself, not Modenos. This probably is the case in regard to the documents for Patrikios and Dragon which both use the phrase *ektos douleias* as found in one of the documents involving Modenos. It is certainly the case with the document involving Koteanitzes.

[8.31] Chrysobull of Andronikos II Palaiologos for Leo Koteanitzes (1293, or forgery)

The grant for Leo Koteanitzes is found in a document bearing the date 1293 and allegedly issued by Andronikos II. The document is at best a medieval facsimile of an original chrysobull and at worst a forgery. But even in the latter case, the content is worth presenting because someone thought the

155 On the term *akatadoulotos*, see I. Karagiannopoulos, *Λεξικό βυζαντινής ορολογίας. Οικονομικοί όροι*, vol. 1 (Thessaloniki, 2000), 85–86, and Solovjev–Mošin, *Grčke povelje*, 386. Kyritsis, "The 'Common Chrysobulls' of Cities," 233, wrote that *ektos douleias* in such documents was equivalent to *eleutheron*, that is, a general tax-exempt status, but I prefer to see a distinction between the two expressions.

156 *Chilandar*, ed. Petit, no. 62.5: ἐλευθέραν καὶ μὴ ὑποκειμένην βάρει καὶ τέλει τινί. The same phrase is repeated in a chrysobull of Andronikos III issued at around the same time: *Chilandar*, ed. Petit, no. 63.7.

situation described by the document plausible. According to the document, Koteanitzes, because of his faithfulness and usefulness to the emperor which he displayed "in the face of enemy attacks," was granted land in Preasnitza [Breznica] near Strumica with its mills and walnut trees, "which had been taken away from various Vlachs" (line 5). While the document does not state explicitly that Koteanitzes had the right to transmit the property to his heirs, this is clearly implied. The emperor granted Koteanitzes and his "legitimate children and heirs" (lines 22–23) the right to alienate the property through sale, gift, donation, exchange, or dowry (lines 15–16) and to deal with the property in whatever way the law permits "owners of property" (lines 16–17: τοῖς τῶν πρ[αγ]μάτων . . . [δεσ]πότ[αις]). Further, the property was to be "completely free and without any service" (lines 14–15: ἐλευθέραν πάντη καὶ χωρὶς [τῆς τυ]χούσης δουλείας), which parallels the more common phrase "completely free and *akatadouloton*." There is no mention of an oikonomia or pronoia, and nothing indicates that Koteanitzes held this property before the issuance of the document. Of course, Koteanitzes, like all the men in this category, may have held an oikonomia in addition to these particular properties.[157]

The only case we are left with in which there was an explicit statement that the grant was to be held without service is that of Michael Monomachos. Unlike all of the other documents listed in Table 8.5 the document for Monomachos was not issued by an emperor (or a despot in the Morea). It is a praktikon issued by an official. In the key phrase the official states that Monomachos was to hold a *posotes* of 55 hyperpyra "as his *gonikon* and without service" (ὡς γονικὴν αὐτοῦ καὶ ἄνευ δουλείας). To my knowledge the phrase *aneu douleias* appears only in this one document. It could well mean merely an exemption of fiscal obligations on the *posotes*.

[8.32] Chrysobull of Andronikos IV Palaiologos for Manuel Tarchaneiotes (1378)

The remaining cases in Table 8.5 all demand continued "service" by the heirs of the beneficiary. For example, in May 1378 Andronikos IV (1376–79) granted *kyr* Manuel Tarchaneiotes the village of Loroton in the region of Kalamaria on the Chalkidike peninsula. Previously Loroton had been held

[157] *Chilandar*, ed. Živojinović, I, no. 12 = *Chilandar*, ed. Petit, no. 11. Gorjanov, *Pozdnevizantijskij feodalizm*, 133, considered Koteanitzes' grant a pronoia. Dölger, *Regesten*, IV, no. 2155, considered this a false act, but the recent editors have concluded tentatively that the document is a medieval facsimile. The Koteanitzes family later donated this property to a monastery, and this would explain why someone might fabricate a document that allowed Koteanitzes to alienate the property. See Bartusis, "Serbian Pronoia," 197–98.

by George Tzamplakon and by his deceased brother, another Tzamplakon. The part of Loroton held by the latter had recently been given through a *prostagma* to Manuel Raoul Koustougiannis, probably by John V, and now Andronikos IV ordered that Tarchaneiotes hold the entire village "for the course of his life, giving the service owed for and pertaining to it." After his death he was permitted to transmit it, along with any improvements, to his son John (and to him alone, line 15: πρὸς μόνον τὸν . . . υἱόν) on condition that he similarly perform the service owed.[158] What did this mean? In five cases (*[8.4] [8.32–8.33] [8.47] [9.8]*) we have some variation of this phrase "rendering the service belonging to and owed by them." Such a phrase is ambiguous in that it could refer to personal service of the beneficiaries or to fiscal burdens on the properties involved.

Fortunately, the documentation for one of the cases provides further details. In a document from 1373 three officials state that George Katzaras' son John claimed that his father was given the right to transmit the property to his children "and they serve as their father" (ἐκδουλεύουσι). Later in the document the officials paraphrase the 1351 chrysobull received by Katzaras, repeating that the emperor originally granted the land to Katzaras so that he could hold it as his *gonikon* and transmit it to his legitimate children and heirs and "that . . . they serve my majesty for the sake of this [land]" (ἵνα . . . ἐκδουλεύωσιν ἕνεκεν ταύτης τῇ βασιλείᾳ μου) *[8.47]*. Clearly, the service here was some type of personal service. The 1378 chrysobull for Radoslav Sampias contain a similar, though fragmentary, phrase, "service of our majesty as the father himself" (δουλοσ[ύνη]ς τῆς βασιλείας ἡμῶν καθὼς καὶ αὐτὸς ὁ πατήρ) which, inasmuch as it parallels the phrase in the Katazaras document, would seem to indicate personal service toward the emperor as well.[159]

Thus, it appears that phrases "without service" and "rendering the service owed by them" are referring to completely different types of "service." The

[158] *Lavra*, III, no. 149.5–6: ἐφ' ὅρῳ τῆς ζωῆς αὐτοῦ, ἀποδιδοὺς τὴν ἀνήκουσαν καὶ ὀφειλομένην ὑπὲρ αὐτοῦ δουλείαν. Ostrogorsky, *Féodalité*, 127–28; Hvostova, *Osobennosti*, 222; and Dölger, *Regesten*, V, no. 3158.

[159] A chrysobull from 1405 refers to this property *[8.48]*. In a key passage, Binon's edition reads ὑπὸ τὴν δουλωσύνην εὑρισκόμενα τῆς βασιλείας τῶν Ῥωμαίων, καὶ ἐκδουλεύοντα, which would have to refer to the properties and mean that they were fiscally under the purview of the Byzantine state: S. Binon, *Les origines légendaires et l'histoire de Xéropotamou et de Saint-Paul de l'Athos* (Louvain, 1942), 284.3–4. On the other hand, in his edition of the document, A. Kazhdan, "Dva pozdnevizantijskih akta iz sobranija P. I. Sevastjanova," *VizVrem*, n.s. 2 (1949), 314, who was unaware of Binon's edition, read εὑρισκομένους and ἐκδουλεύοντας, which would have to refer to Sampias and his children and indicate that the service was owed by them. In his analysis of the document, Ostrogorsky, *Féodalité*, 129–30, shifts from speaking of the properties' "service" to the empire, to Sampias' service to the empire. F. Dölger, *Facsimiles byzantinischer Kaiserurkunden* (Munich, 1931), col. 41, reads ἐκδουλεύονται.

former phrase is rendering a tax exemption; the latter phrase is demanding continued personal service. And so there is no document which explicitly states that a particular individual was not obligated to render personal service.

If this is so, then what distinguishes the seven cases which explicitly demand continued personal service from other cases dealing with similar grants? In other words, of the scores of imperial grants known from the documents, why do only these seven cases demand continued personal service?

Of these seven cases, the document for Sergopoulos is an imperial appointment as a governor. It is a special and unique case and the reference to service is expected. Therefore, it may be excluded from further discussion. So we are left with six cases in which service is demanded. What do they all have in common? They all deal with hereditary property – in one case, property that was already hereditary (Nomikopoulos), and in the other cases, property that the emperor made hereditary.

[8.33] Chrysobull of Andronikos II Palaiologos for Theodore Nomikopoulos (1288)

The chrysobull from April 1288 for the *pansevastos sevastos* Theodore Nomikopoulos is another unique document. At Nomikopoulos' request, the emperor confirmed his possession of "his hereditary village" called Kranidion in the region of Damala (today, Kranidi, about twenty-four miles southeast of Nafplio in the Argolid peninsula in the Morea). Andronikos II permitted Nomikopoulos to hold the village "as long as he is reckoned among the living with nevertheless the corresponding service [lines 20–21: τῆς ἀνηκούσης δουλείας], then to pass this to his legitimate children and be held by them the same way as by their father, rendering the service owed [line 23: τὴν ὀφειλομένην δουλείαν] for it." The emperor adds that Nomikopoulos and his children may hold a vineyard of twenty modioi in the same manner.[160]

Technically, the area of Kranidion was under continuous Frankish rule since early in the thirteenth century. However, a decade of confusion following the death of William II Villehardouin in 1278 may have permitted a temporary restoration of Byzantine authority in this part of the Argolid. This might explain why Nomikopoulos sought such a confirmation of his rights

160 Dölger, "Ein Chrysobull des Kaisers Andronikos II. für Theodoros Nomikopulos," 191–93. Hvostova, *Osobennosti*, 221–22.

to his property. Alternatively, even though the document makes no mention of a "pronoia" or "oikonomia" or a "*posotes*," we cannot exclude the possibility that Nomikopoulos originally had received Kranidion as an imperial grant with only temporary rights of tenure, and that after time hereditary (*gonikon*) status was conferred. This could be true even if Nomikopoulos' possession of Kranidion was fictive, an imperial grant in anticipation of a restoration of Byzantine authority.

None of the documents dealing with these six cases mention that the recipient had the right to alienate the property or properties involved. This makes sense. If the property was sold, donated, or otherwise alienated, the link between holding the property and personal service would disappear. And all of the cases involve the grant of hereditary rights over what may be the entirety of the grant to the recipients. In the cases of Nomikopoulos, Tarchaneiotes, and Gemistos, the mentioned properties seem to constitute the entire grant held by the recipient, and in the other three cases, for the Klazomenitai, Katzaras, and Sampias, the mentioned properties or *posotetes* might have constituted the entire grant held by the recipient. If this was the entire grant, then it is understandable why the continued service clause should appear. A man who received hereditary rights over his entire grant (whether he had held it previously or not) might think that he now held the grant free of all obligation. The service clause made sure he did not feel this way.

This would explain why grants of hereditary rights over part of one's grant never include such a service clause. If only part of one's oikonomia became hereditary, the other part did not. This other part continued to demand service, and since personal service is not divisible, acquiring hereditary rights to only part of a grant did not change the standing service obligation. And so there was no need to state the obvious. But the problem with concluding that the service obligation appears whenever the entirety of a grant was made hereditary is that there are many similar grants of hereditary rights over the entirety of a grant where the clause does not appear (Table 8.7).

In the end we may have to conclude that the appearance of the service clause is idiosyncratic; as in the case of Nomikopoulos' grant, it depends on the circumstances of the grant. The Klazomenitai were a soldier company and the emperor may have wanted to emphasize that, despite the granting of hereditary rights, military service was still demanded of the men and their heirs. George Katzaras was head of the Varvarenoi soldier company and the emperor may have wanted to ensure that Katzaras maintained this responsibility even after his grant acquired hereditary status. Radoslav

Sampias was a Serb, and, as George Ostrogorsky suggested, the emperor, Andronikos IV, may have thought it necessary to be quite explicit about why he was making the grant and what obligations were still attached to it.[161] Then again, Manuel Tarchaneiotes received his hereditary grant with its service clause from Andronikos IV as well. Andronikos came to the throne through a coup d'état in 1376, and both Tarchaneiotes and Sampias received their grants the following year. The presence of the service clause may well be connected to Andronikos' desire to establish loyal servants during a troubled time. And finally, we have Gemistos Plethon. One of the two properties over which he received hereditary rights was a *kastron* over which he held the administrative appointment as governor (*kephale*). And this might explain the service clause.

Everything in the above paragraph is mere speculation. All we can say for sure is that the demand for continued service only appears in documents granting hereditary rights over a grant, and then, only in a handful of these. I cannot say why the clause appears in a few such documents and not in many others. Most grant documents say nothing about service, but that does not mean there was no personal service obligation. As for what kind of "personal service" was implied in any particular case, the only clues we have come from the function or status of the recipient. Soldiers presumably fought, administrators presumably administered, and so on.

There are cases in which it is absolutely certain that the holder of a pronoia grant was not a military man and could not have been expected to perform any kind of military service in return for his grant. For such men (and a few women), pronoiai were granted as a reward or in consideration of future, non-military services. Such was the case of bishop John Apokaukos who had received a pronoia from Theodore Doukas of Epiros in the 1220s *[5.17]*, as well as the case of the teacher Theodore Hyrtakenos who claimed he was promised a village, evidently as a pronoia, from Andronikos II *[8.10]*. It would seem that, no later than the early thirteenth century, a pronoia could be a grant in consideration of future services or a reward. These services were usually military, but they could be other services to the emperor, or perhaps even mere loyalty.

My conclusions about "service" are as follows. Documents which grant properties to someone "without service" are referring to the exemption of fiscal obligation on such properties. Properties that demand further service to the grantee and his heirs are referring to some kind of personal service, sometimes military, sometimes not. All imperial grants to individuals – even

161 Ostrogorsky, *Féodalité*, 130.

those granting hereditary rights with the right to alienate the grant – required personal service, at least in the broad sense of loyalty toward the emperor.

Pronoia holders who were soldiers formed one of the three basic types of soldier in the later Byzantine period: mercenaries, smallholding soldiers, and pronoia holders. Each bore a service obligation based on a different source of income. Mercenaries received cash. Smallholding soldiers received outright grants of land and were often settled in colonies based on their ethnicity (e.g., Serbs) or on their military function (rowers). Pronoia holders had their grants.

Each type of soldiers had its own particular strengths and weaknesses. Mercenaries were the most versatile troops. At least theoretically, they could be hired and fired at will, and they could serve on extended campaigns as long as they could obtain rations and as long as they could be convinced that they would be paid their salaries. However, mercenaries were also the most expensive troops and their pay was a direct and immediate drain on the treasury.

Smallholding soldiers were a bargain requiring merely a one-time outlay of land. Further, their direct attachment to the land made them particularly suited to frontier defense. But, as far as we can tell, smallholding soldiers were at best light cavalry, and since they were often clannish foreigners, they were not the most reliable or disciplined troops.

Pronoia soldiers were usually heavy cavalry and because they were paid "at the source," thus saving some of the expenses of administration, they were less expensive than mercenaries. Further, the grants they received gave them an attachment to the land which gave them a stake in the fortunes of the empire. Yet pronoia soldiers often held their properties and paroikoi in out-of-the-way places. Even if they did not live on their pronoia grants, practicality would dictate that they live reasonably nearby. This made them difficult to muster, and their dependence on the revenues they collected locally hindered their participation in prolonged or distant campaigns.

Some pronoia soldiers, such as the Klazomenitai of Serres *[8.4]*, were garrison troops, but most seem to have been campaign soldiers. While there is no evidence that pronoia soldiers were obligated for anything but personal service, pronoia holders with court titles campaigned with servants and military retainers. It is possible that pronoia holders with smaller grants were accompanied by domestic servants whom they financed out of their own pockets. The normal campaign season began in March and ran through December, though campaigns were usually not begun in the fall. Presumably when not campaigning, pronoia soldiers honed their military skills, acquired animals and weapons, and managed their grants.

On the whole, there is no evidence that pronoia soldiers at any time made any particularly significant contribution – either positively or negatively – to the Byzantine military effort. Some scholars have suggested that pronoia grants created an effective military force under the Komnenian emperors and the Laskarids of Nicaea, that is, in the twelfth and first half of the thirteenth centuries, but that the effectiveness of this group of soldiers declined in the later thirteenth century with the loss of land in Asia Minor and the increasing tendency to grant hereditary rights over pronoiai. However, all we can really say is that the army did a good job through the twelfth and much of the thirteenth century, and that it did not from the later thirteenth century on. To lay the blame at the feet of pronoia soldiers is an overstatement. One could just as well say that the empire's mercenary units were effective in the twelfth century, but ineffective in the fourteenth. Such arguments ignore the matter of leadership as well as external circumstances. If the Komnenoi had faced the same panoply of enemies with the same paucity of economic resources that the fourteenth-century emperors faced, their successes may have been limited as well.[162]

The taxation of pronoiai

There is very little evidence to suggest that pronoia grants were ever subject to taxation. Because the grant by its nature was a redirection of fiscal revenues to a beneficiary, any taxation of the grant was in effect a de facto reduction in the magnitude of the grant. How a pronoia grant might be taxed depended on its constituent components, and these varied over time. In the twelfth century, the only known components were grants of state immovable property and *exkousseiai* of paroikoi. Theoretically, the state land granted could have been taxed; the pronoia holder would still have received income from renting out the land, and his net benefit would have been the rent minus any taxes. But such an arrangement, I think, would have made little sense. If the purpose of the pronoia grant was to finance a soldier, any significant tax burden on the property would have lessened the grant's value to the soldier and necessitated a larger grant than one that was not taxed. Further, taxing the property in a grant might have raised ownership issues (according to the Byzantine principle of he who pays the tax is, usually, considered the owner). As for the paroikoi within the pronoia

[162] Bartusis, *Late Byzantine Army*, 227–35, 343–45.

grant, while it would have been possible to tax them by demanding some of their labor services (corvées) or by demanding the meager taxes that could be levied on the livestock they owned, the loss of labor services to the pronoia holder would have similarly necessitated larger grants.[163]

When we turn to the thirteenth century, the situation becomes a bit more complicated. In the first half of the century the pronoia grant consisted of state property and taxes. The state property was leased out by the pronoia holder or cultivated directly through corvée of his paroikoi. In this category one could perhaps include the river rights held by Kalegopoulos in the sense that the state owned the river and anyone who wanted to exploit the river's resources (by setting up a fish pond) paid a rent to the pronoia holder *[5.7]*. The taxes received by the pronoia holder came from immovable property (e.g., a field, the *stasis* of a paroikos, a mill) located within his pronoia which neither the state nor the pronoia holder owned. The owners of the properties were considered his paroikoi and they could owe personal taxes (labor services) to the pronoia holder as well.

It was possible to demand from the pronoia holder a tax on any of these elements, though, as in the twelfth century, every nomisma demanded from the pronoia holder reduced the value of the grant as a means of financing imperial servants. In regard to the taxes received by the pronoia holder, these could not have been taxed in full (otherwise the pronoia holder would have gotten no benefit from holding them), but they could have been taxed partially, I suppose. But I do not think these were taxed. With Michael VIII the pronoia becomes an oikonomia quantified by a *posotes* and the possibility of taxation becomes even more unlikely. The *posotes* as conferred is a nominal collection of taxes conceded to the grantee. In effect, to tax these with the initial grant would be to reduce the *posotes*.

[8.34] Pachymeres on the taxing of "pronoiai" in 1283 (ca. 1307)

There is only one circumstance under which it would make sense to tax oikonomiai: if all the state property and state taxes that could be conferred as oikonomiai had been so conferred, expenses had been cut to the bone, the currency debased, and still there was not enough cash for pressing exigencies. That situation is the one Andronikos II found himself in at the beginning of his reign. According to George Pachymeres, in order to

[163] There is a possible case of the taxing of pronoia grants in the twelfth century: the people who received land granted from *episkepseis* on Crete from Manuel I did pay a tax or a charge on this land *[3.5]*. If these were pronoia grants (as N. Oikonomides believed, but I do not), then these pronoiai were taxed.

finance a military campaign to Thessaly in 1283, Andronikos II accepted the recommendation of his advisors to gather the necessary funds from a "common collection" (ἐκ κοινῆς συγκροτήσεως), that is, a tax: "This was the tenth of the pronoia of those having pronoiai. While it was collected ostensibly from the rights of the lords, the paroikoi of the powerful paid everything."[164]

[8.35] Pachymeres on the taxing of "pronoiai" in 1296 (ca. 1307)

Pachymeres notes that, because of a chronic lack of money, this tax was used in 1296 to settle Cretan mercenaries in Anatolia: "This was, as said earlier, the tenth of the pronoia of each." And once again "the burden was on the paroikoi."[165]

What did Pachymeres mean by the word *pronoia*? Since *pronoia* no longer existed as an official term at the time Pachymeres' wrote, he was using the word in the common, broader sense to refer to any collection of fiscal privileges conferred on an individual, a group of individuals, or a religious foundation. As he writes elsewhere, "pronoiai" were held by soldiers, aristocrats, and monasteries. So this 10 percent tax was not levied strictly on pronoia holders, but on the many holders of imperial privileges, that is, anyone or any foundation that held paroikoi or any other imperial grant of fiscal revenues.[166] We can see how the Byzantine state had backed itself into a corner with these grants. The only way for the emperor to raise cash was to rescind some of the tax exemptions given to the beneficiaries of imperial grants.

Pachymeres provides no further information about this new policy of Andronikos and so its details are elusive. Yet, given that the only ready

[164] Pachymeres, ed. Failler, III, 81.13–16 (Bonn edn., II, 69.2–5): ἡ δ' ἦν τὸ τῆς προνοίας τῶν ἐχόντων προνοίας δέκατον. ὃ δὴ καὶ συνήγετο μὲν ὡς δῆθεν ἐκ τῶν δικαίων τῶν δεσποτῶν, τὸ πᾶν δ' οἱ παροικοῦντες ἀπετίννυον δυναστευόντων ἐκείνων. A. Laiou, "Le débat sur les droits du fisc et les droits régaliens au début du 14e siècle," *REB* 58 (2000), 102; Laiou, *Constantinople and the Latins*, 38–39, 116; Gorjanov, *Pozdnevizantijskij feodalizm*, 103; Bibikov, "Svedenija," 97.

[165] Pachymeres, ed. Failler, III, 237.3–5 (Bonn ed., II, 209.11–13): τὸ δ' ἦν, ὡς ἐρρέθη τὰ πρότερα, τὸ τῆς ἐφ' ἑκάστῳ προνοίας δέκατον. Laiou, *Constantinople and the Latins*, 117, 123. I. Ševčenko, "An Important Contribution to the Social History of Late Byzantium," *The Annals of the Ukrainian Academy of Arts and Sciences in the U.S.*, 2, pt. 4 (1952), 457–58. Mutafčiev, "Vojniški zemi," 65/593–94.

[166] D. Angelov, "Byzantine Imperial Panegyric as Advice Literature (1204–c.1350)," in *Rhetoric in Byzantium*, ed. E. Jeffreys (Aldershot, 2003), 71, interprets a letter from 1285 of Patriarch Gregory II Kyprios to Andronikos II as a complaint against the practice of tax-farming.

quantification of imperial grants that was available to the imperial government was its *posotes*, we may assume that the 10 percent tax was calculated from this. So, if the official *posotes* of one's grant was 100 hyperpyra, the holder now rendered ten hyperpyra to the fisc. But from where did these ten hyperpyra come?

Pachymeres writes that the burden was collected from the "rights of the lords" but it was their paroikoi who actually paid the tax. Does this mean that, rather than suffering any diminution of their annual incomes, the grant holders made up for the money they had to turn over to the treasury by passing the additional charge on to their paroikoi? Two questions arise: Could the grant holder have forced his paroikoi to pay additional charges, and were his paroikoi able to pay the additional charges? While we cannot be certain about this, I doubt that the grant holder, arriving at his villages at tax collection time, waving an imperial order, and demanding additional money, would have had much success. According to the 1323 praktikon for the soldier Basil Berilas, from a slightly later time, his paroikoi were assessed at a little over six hyperpyra for their *telos* and perhaps six hyperpyra for other taxes. The *posotes* of Berilas' oikonomia was nominally hyperpyra. Thus, if Berilas' paroikoi were required to pay the 10 percent tax on his *posotes*, their tax burden would have increased by two-thirds, from around twelve hyperpyra to twenty hyperpyra. Even if the paroikoi were willing to accede to Andronikos II's novel demand, there would have been some grant holders, like Berilas, whose paroikoi would have found it difficult to assume the additional burden. Moreover, the true income that Berilas derived from his pronoia was much larger than eighty hyperpyra, probably over 200 hyperpyra (see Table 8.13). Rather, I think it most likely that the holders of oikonomiai paid the tax themselves, being more diligent about collecting the *telos* of their paroikoi. In this light, Pachymeres' statement that "the burden was on the paroikoi" is perhaps nothing more than an acknowledgment that the origin of all agrarian tax revenues lay in the labor of peasants. After all, the emperor was in a better position to demand 10 percent of the *posotes* of each imperial grant than grant holders to demand additional taxes from their paroikoi.

[8.36] Pachymeres on the taxing of "pronoiai" in 1304 (ca. 1307)

Was this 10-percent tax levied only under dire circumstances (as it was in 1283 and 1296), or was it levied continuously from 1283 to 1296 and beyond? Given the example of earlier Byzantine taxes (as well as the example of modern governments), it would seem the latter was the case; a temporary measure took on a nearly permanent character. In fact it seems that Andronikos increased this tax. In another passage, Pachymeres writes about the measures Andronikos II took around late 1304 in order to raise money to pay the Catalan Grand Company of mercenaries: "He fastened onto the pronoiai of the West, and he took away a third from these, for years earlier he cut back the pay of those serving in the palace and out of necessity debased the nomisma."[167] Unlike the other passages, the verb used by Pachymeres is *aphaireo* (ἀφαιρῶ), which means "to take away," usually in the sense of an appropriation. For example, using the same verb, Patriarch Gregory told Andronikos and his brother *[8.3]*, "you shall be or you might already be deprived of the pronoia," and Pachymeres himself used the verb in this sense when he wrote of how Michael VIII "took away most of the oikonomia" of his brother John *[7.5]*. In these passages there is the sense, not of a tax levy, but of a permanent confiscation.

However, if Andronikos II really did confiscate one-third of the oikonomiai of those in the western (i.e., European) part of the Byzantine Empire, there is no evidence of this. A comparison of the properties held "pronoiastically" as found in the 1300 and 1321 *periorismoi* for the Lavra monastery *[8.71]* shows that numerous pronoia holders held what appears to be the same quantity of property in both years. Therefore, Pachymeres would have to be referring to another tax on imperial grants, albeit at a higher rate than in the two previous passages.[168] Yet, outside of Pachymeres, no document or any other source provides any evidence to corroborate this policy. The handful of cases in which the holders of privileged properties were required to pay substantial taxes seem idiosyncratic and not part of a general policy affecting all holders of such privileges.[169] It is possible, as Angeliki Laiou suggested, that the policy was always considered temporary and so it maintained an informal character. Indeed, it is the kind of policy that, for different reasons, neither emperor (assuring landholders of its temporary nature) nor landholder (hoping it would be temporary) might have wished to see codified in chrysobulls or praktika. Still, this is an argument from silence, and it demonstrates how we still have much to learn.

167 Pachymeres, ed. Failler, IV, 541.2–3 (Bonn edn., II, 493.14–15): καὶ τῶν κατὰ δύσιν προνοιῶν ἥπτετο καὶ τὸ τρίτον ἐκ τούτων ἀφῄρει.

168 Cf. Laiou, "Le débat sur les droits du fisc," 103; Laiou, *Constantinople and the Latins*, 141, 188; and Bibikov, "Svedenija," 97.

169 For examples, see Laiou, "Le débat sur les droits du fisc," 103 note 19, and *Lavra*, IV, p. 158 note 599.

Another case in which pronoia holders may have been subject to taxation is described by Gregoras (I, 205.11–19). According to him, in 1301 more than 10,000 Alans entered the empire and enlisted in the army:

Since it was necessary to give them money and horses and arms, some of these were given from the imperial administration, the rest from the soldiery, and from the common people, and from private people. Thus, those levying taxes in the countryside were sent out in groups and individually. The tax collectors raised the taxes. Every weapon and every horse was collected. Villages, cities, the homes of the best, the homes of those enrolled in military service, hermitages, the countryside, theaters, markets, were searched and all surrendered horses and money, involuntarily and with lamentation.

"Those enrolled in military service" could well be a reference to military pronoia holders. In any event, the passage is both vague and overblown, and the measures were temporary.

[8.37] Chrysobull of Andronikos II Palaiologos for George Troulenos (1318)

Despite these extraordinary cases, as a general rule, pronoiai were not taxed. However, once hereditary rights were granted over oikonomiai or portions of oikonomiai, the situation changed. In 1318 George Troulenos was granted hereditary rights over two properties totaling 1,600 modioi "within the amount" of his oikonomia near Serres. He asked the emperor for a chrysobull that he might "hold this land as hereditary property [*gonikon*]." Also, he asked that if any *xenoi* and *eleutheroi* (peasants with no property of their own) were settled on the property, they would not be bothered by the fisc. The emperor granted Troulenos the right to transmit the two properties to his "legitimate children and heirs" and included the right to enjoy any improvements Troulenos made to the properties in the same way. In regard to the peasants which Troulenos might put on these lands, Andronikos II granted Troulenos' request with one limitation. The emperor freed them

of each and every state *epereia* and contribution except the tax [*kephalaion*] of the *sitarkia*, the *kastroktisia*, the *orike*, the *phonos*, and treasure trove. These alone ought to be demanded from them, as it is the custom to demand these for all properties, even from *chrysovoullata* [properties benefitting from privileges conferred via chrysobull], for the common services and the common need.[170]

[170] *Prodrome*, no. 8.2,7, and lines 15–20: πάσης καὶ παντοίας δημοσιακῆς ἐπηρείας καὶ συζητήσεως, ἄνευ μέντοι τοῦ κεφαλαίου τῆς σιταρκίας, τῆς καστροκτισίας, τῆς ὀρικῆς, τοῦ

Thus, the peasants Troulenos might settle on this property were to be exempt of all secondary fiscal burdens except for five specific burdens (because the peasants had no property of their own, the issue of the *telos* was irrelevant for them). The nature of these particular burdens remains unclear. While we know what each of them was connected to – respectively, grain (*sitos*), the building of fortifications (*kastra*), wood-cutting in mountain (*oros*) forests, murder (*phonos*), and finding treasure – it is unclear how each was levied. Treasure trove and *phonos* were probably regalian rights entitling the state to confiscate treasure caches and the property of a murderer. The others were probably annual charges levied in specie, but this is only a hypothesis.[171] What *is* clear is that these items, like all secondary charges, were demanded from peasants and not the land *per se*, and further, these peasants that Troulenos might settle were not part of his oikonomia. Therefore, Troulenos was asking for an additional privilege not connected to his oikonomia, and the emperor granted the request, but only in part. In no other chrysobull granting hereditary rights does the beneficiary ask for such an additional privilege unconnected to his oikonomia, and that is, most likely, why these other chrysobulls granting hereditary rights do not mention the burdens levied on these peasants. In any event, the fact that the emperor felt it important to explain the reason for demanding these burdens suggests that the "custom" of which he wrote might not have been particularly well established.

Overall, the explicit denial of specific taxes or rights in the documents is quite rare. Table 8.6 shows most of the known examples from the reign of Michael VIII through the early fifteenth century. The table includes the properties of both laymen and monasteries, and in some cases the properties of the monasteries is specifically referred to as an oikonomia (e.g., the entry under "1316" for Iviron). Aside from *phonikon* (or *phonos*), treasure trove, *sitarkia*, and *orike*, a few other burdens are often included within the exceptions to a complete exemption of secondary charges. One is the

φόνου καὶ τῆς εὑρέσεως τοῦ θησαυροῦ· ταῦτα γὰρ καὶ μόνα ὀφείλουσιν ἀπαιτεῖσθαι ἐξ αὐτῶν, καθὼς καὶ ἐν πᾶσι κτήμασι καὶ αὐτοῖς τοῖς χρυσοβουλλάτοις ἐστὶ συνήθεια ἀπαιτεῖσθαι ταῦτα ὑπὲρ τῶν κοινῶν δουλειῶν καὶ τῆς κοινῆς χρήσεως. On the document: Uspenskij, "Značenie," 22; G. Ostrogorsky, "Pour l'histoire de l'immunité à Byzance," *Byz* 28 (1958), 211–12; Ostrogorsky, *Féodalité*, 108–10; and Gorjanov, *Pozdnevizantijskij feodalizm*, 99–100, 181.

171 On *sitarkia*, N. Oikonomides, "The Role of the Byzantine State in the Economy," *EHB*, III, 1036–37; Oikonomides, *Fiscalité*, 104; and *ODB*, s.v. "sitarkia." On *kastroktisia*, Oikonomides, *Fiscalité*, 110–11, and M. Bartusis, "State Demands for the Building and Repairing of Fortifications in Late Byzantium and Medieval Serbia," *Byzantinoslavica* 49 (1988), 205–12. On *orike*, Lefort, "Rural Economy," 262, 270; Oikonomides, "The Role of the Byzantine State," 1034; Oikonomides, *Fiscalité*, 84; and *ODB*, s.v. "orike." On *phonos*, *ODB*, s.v. "phonikon." On the finding of treasure, *ODB*, s.v. "treasure trove."

Table 8.6 Documents in which a beneficiary of imperial privileges is specifically not granted a particular tax or right

		kastroktisia	*katergoktisia*	*sitarkia*	*orike*	*parthenophthoria*	*phonos/phonikon*	treasure trove	local theme of property
						"the three *kephalaia*"			
1272	monasteries of Makrinitissa and Nea Petra	×	×						(Thessaly)
1274	monasteries of Makrinitissa and Nea Petra	×							(Thessaly)
1274–82	Demetrios Mourinos *[6.8]*	×	×						(multiple areas)
1283/4 or 1298/9	monastery of Esphigmenou					×	×	×	Thessaloniki
ca. 1297	Alexios Komnenos Raoul *[8.15]*					×	×	×	Serres–Strymon
1316	monastery of Iviron						×	×	Serres–Strymon
1317	monastery of Lavra					×	×	×	Serres–Strymon
1318	George Troulenos *[8.37]*	×		×	×		×	×	Serres–Strymon
1333	Michael Monomachos *[8.14]*					×	×	×	Serres–Strymon
1334	monastery of Esphigmenou			×		×	×	×	Serres–Strymon
1341	monastery of Iviron					×	×	×	Serres–Strymon
1344	John Choumnos *[8.78]*					×	×	×	Serres–Strymon
1409?	monastery of Esphigmenou					×	×	×	Thessaloniki

References to monastic beneficiaries: MM, IV, 332.15–16 (1272), 335.17–18 (1274); *Esphigménou*, no. 7.7–8 (1283/4 or 1298/9), no. 20.11–13,21–23 (1334), no. 31.8–9 (1409?); *Iviron*, III, no. 74.332 (1316), IV, no. 87.A237–38,B265–66 (1341); and *Lavra*, II, no. 104.165–67 (1317).

parthenophthoria ("virgin corruption"), probably a judicial fine like the *phonikon*, and another is the *katergoktisia* ("ship-building," which paralleled *kastroktisia*).[172] It should be pointed out that when the holder of an oikonomia was explicitly *not* granted one of these taxes or rights, it did not mean that he had to pay them out of his own pocket. In the case of rights like treasure trove, it meant merely that the holder of the oikonomia did not receive that particular right. Even when the item involved was a tax (such as *kastroktisia*), one ought not to think of this as a "tax" on the oikonomia; it was only a benefit the holder of the oikonomia did not receive. It represented no loss to the holder of the oikonomia.

Naturally the situation was different when the beneficiary had initially received these taxes and rights, and then they were rescinded at a later date. This seems to be the case involving a village named Doxompous which Lavra was granted in 1259. At that time a chrysobull of Michael VIII exempted all of Lavra's properties, specifically including the newly granted village of Doxompous, of the *phonikon* and *parthenophthoria*, as well as numerous other charges. Yet a praktikon from 1317 (the entry under "1317" for Lavra in Table 8.6) detailing Lavra's possession of Doxompous specifies that Lavra was given "the *aer* of these paroikoi without the three state taxes, that is, *phonos*, *parthenophthoria*, and treasure trove."[173] In Troulenos' case we do not know whether he ever had received any of the charges and rights he was denied in 1318.

All in all, I wonder how much significance we should attach to the appearance of these charges and rights in our documents. In particular one may observe that of the ten cases in Table 8.6 in which a property holder was specifically *not* exempted from one or more of the so-called "three *kephalaia*" (*phonos*, treasure trove, *parthenophthoria*), eight date to the first half of the fourteenth century, and these eight all deal with properties in the theme of Serres-Strymon. Given the vast number of imperial documents and official praktika (for properties both in and outside of this area) which do *not* mention any of these burdens, one wonders whether their appearance was idiosyncratic to that region.[174] If we really wish to

172 See *ODB*, s.v. "parthenophthoria," and for the *katergoktisia*, Oikonomides, *Fiscalité*, 111.

173 *Lavra*, II, no. 71.79–80 and no. 104.165–67.

174 The *phonikon*, in some cases, was specifically not demanded from some landholders: in a chrysobull for the episcopal see of Kanina and in two chrysobulls for Lavra, it is specified that the *phonikon* was only to be levied on those responsible for the murder: P. Alexander, "A Chrysobull of the Emperor Andronicus II Palaeologus in Favor of the See of Kanina in Albania," *Byz* 15 (1940–41), 180–82 (1307); *Lavra*, II, no. 89.179–88 (1298); and *Lavra*, III, no. 118.202–09 (1329).

establish that emperors were attempting to hold onto some revenues or some rights, we should look to cases where the holder of imperial privileges was required to pay money to the fisc. There are rare cases in which monasteries found themselves in this position, but none involving pronoia holders.[175]

There is one final aspect to the story of George Troulenos' hereditary rights that makes the case interesting – and humbles us as we try to reconstruct the individual stories behind these property arrangements. In August 1317, a little over a year prior to the chrysobull granting Troulenos hereditary rights over part of his oikonomia, Andronikos II issued an *orismos* dealing with Troulenos. In the document we learn that an earlier dispute between the monks of the Prodromos monastery and Troulenos over a piece of land had been decided in favor of the monastery. However, the emperor writes, "recently, employing trickery and deceiving us the said Troulenos sought to have this land inscribed in the praktikon which was made for him concerning his oikonomia, and grasping a pretext from this he simply seized this land" and drove the monks off the property. The emperor ruled for the monastery and ordered Troulenos to leave the monks and their property alone.[176] Thus, after Troulenos "deceived" the emperor by having a property added illicitly to his oikonomia (holding something "by theft" in the language of the 1272 *prostagma* of Michael VIII), rather than confiscating the oikonomia or otherwise chastising Troulenos, the emperor granted him, albeit a year later, hereditary rights over a significant portion of his oikonomia. (At the standard rate of 1 hyperpyron per 50 modioi, the *posotes* of the 1,600 modioi of land would have been 32 hyperpyra.) One wonders what happened during that year to make Andronikos II feel differently about Troulenos.

[175] E.g., see *Iviron*, III, pp. 21–22.

[176] *Prodrome B*, no. 161.13–17: τὸ πρακτικὸν ὅπερ ἐποιήσατο πρὸς αὐτὸν ἐπὶ τῇ οἰκονομίᾳ αὐτοῦ; cf. *Prodrome*, no. 5.14. A. Guillou dated the *orismos* to 1312 based on the indiction ("10") found in the edition of the act published by Miklosich and Müller. However, the codex edited by L. Bénou, offers a different indiction, "15," corresponding to 1317, which is much more likely since the act refers to an *orismos* of a deceased *augusta*, who would have to be Irene of Montferrat who died in 1317. The property in Livadia is probably the three *zeugaria* that Germanos Kladon and his son-in-law donated to Prodromos in 1301 *[8.59]*. The act of donation (*Prodrome B*, no. 18.18–19) notes that the land was adjacent to a field of "Amyras," and the pronoia of someone named "Ameras" passed to Troulenos *[8.50]*. Elsewhere in the published acts of Prodromos, the size of this property varies from 200 to 600 modioi: *Prodrome B*, no. 166.38–39 and no. 167.31 (200 modioi), no. 187.39 (300), 190.38–39 (600); cf. *Prodrome*, no. 9.33, no. 10.35, no. 35.28, and no. 39.51, where A. Guillou changed all the numbers to "300." If he is correct, then the *zeugarion* would measure 100 modioi.

Additional rights – increases in *posotes*

On two occasions Kantakouzenos writes of a general increase in the holdings of pronoia soldiers. The first occurred in 1328. Andronikos III granted honors and gifts to those of the "senate" (aristocrats) and to the mercenary soldiers "and he strengthened the yearly incomes of the rest and he made them more eager for war by it" *[7.22]*. In the other instance, during the *exisosis* conducted in 1341, the dishonest *apographeus* Patrikiotes restored from his own ill-gotten resources the amounts of pronoia necessary for those who were in need and "to add over and above as much as seemed good" to Kantakouzenos. For those holding pronoiai intact, Kantakouzenos ordered "that other incomes be added to what they were holding" *[8.26]*. Further, Gregoras reports that in 1327 Andronikos III promised mercenaries and pronoia soldiers, respectively, pay raises and further grants of revenues" (Gregoras, I, 397.8–12: πόρους προσόδων). All of this emphasizes the link between holding a pronoia and military service, and aristocrats were expected to perform military service in return for their pronoiai no less than ordinary soldiers.

[8.38] Prostagma of John V Palaiologos for Demetrios Kokalas (1350, or perhaps 1365)

Despite these passages, it is very difficult to find evidence in the documents of anyone having the *posotes* of his pronoia enlarged through an additional imperial grant. The only possible example of this that I know of is from a *prostagma* of John V, which tentatively has been dated by its editors to December 1350 (or possibly 1365). The emperor ordered his officials to confer on Demetrios Kokalas "in the amount of his oikonomia" a number of properties, including paroikoi. Among the properties were half of the property held by the monastery of Hypomimneskontos and by the monastery of Panteleemon in the village of Hagios Mamas.[177] The phrase "in the amount of his oikonomia" is nearly meaningless. The question is whether the preposition *eis* should be translated as "into" or "for." Were the properties and paroikoi transferred *into* Kokalas' oikonomia (making this a further grant) or were they transferred *for* his oikonomia (which would imply that this was an initial grant)?

This question is answered by a 1321 praktikon for Lavra in which the *apographeis* state that they conferred upon Lavra "in the amount of its

[177] *Lavra*, III, no. 129.3: ἵνα παραδώσουσι . . . εἰς τὸ ποσὸν τῆς οἰκονομίας αὐτοῦ, and lines 6–8.

oikonomia" (εἰς τὸ ποσὸν τῆς οἰκονομίας αὐτῆς) a collection of fields at Hermeleia.[178] The privileged property holdings of Lavra were, of course, dramatically larger than this, so *eis* must mean merely "into," and so there is really no difference between saying "we confer these properties into the amount of Lavra's oikonomia" and "we confer these properties into Lavra's oikonomia." This means that references to monetary amounts "in" someone's or a monastery's property holdings tell us little about the *total* amount of fiscal revenue someone held. It also means that Kokalas probably was receiving an increase in the size of his oikonomia.

Additional rights – the right of hereditary transmission and of amelioration

After the reign of Michael VIII the practice of granting hereditary rights to imperial grants continued and accelerated. While the historians of the fourteenth century, aside from Pachymeres, say nothing of hereditary grants, the documentary sources provide numerous examples of the granting of hereditary rights over oikonomiai, and just as importantly, occasional examples of the denial of these rights.

There is no doubt that emperors were under pressure to confer hereditary rights on any new grant and to convert temporary grants into hereditary grants. Aside from grantees themselves, who understandably experienced the urge to pass their estates on to their children, polemicists as well who had the emperor's ear advocated this practice. In his encomium to Andronikos II, composed between 1296 and 1303, Nicholas Lampenos praised the emperor for permitting the rewards, gifts, and properties that he had granted to soldiers to pass, not only to the legitimate children of those who fell in combat, but to illegitimate children and even to strangers. Thomas Magistros, in his essay *On Kingship*, composed in the early years of the fourteenth century, similarly advocated that the children of those who died in state service be provided for as if they were the emperor's own and that they be granted "the father's position" (τὴν πατρῴαν τάξιν ἀποδιδούς), which may be a reference to the hereditary transmission of pronoia. In fact neither of these authors specifically mentions pronoiai or oikonomiai, but because they both criticize the use of mercenaries, the passages cited almost certainly have to be dealing with pronoia soldiers. Dimiter Angelov suggests that

[178] *Lavra*, II, no. 111.1–2: εἰς τὸ ποσὸν τῆς οἰκονομίας αὐτῆς. Also found in a falsified version of this praktikon, *Lavra*, II, App. X.

the policy mentioned by Lampenos may have been rescinded by the time Thomas wrote his treatise, but it is possible that Lampenos was referring to a more limited privilege, that is, allowing the children of fallen soldiers (and perhaps anyone whom the soldier desired) to keep the extraordinary gifts and kindnesses granted by the emperor.[179]

Late Byzantine emperors conferred hereditary rights over property held by laymen according to two scenarios. Either hereditary rights were conferred over the components of a new grant or hereditary rights were conferred over the components of a previously held grant. From the 1280s through the 1370s there are sufficient examples of the concession of hereditary rights to allow us to make some generalizations. In the case of new grants (Table 8.7), the emperor usually granted a specific property rather than a *posotes*. The *posotes* of the property was usually not listed. In the known cases, neither the term *oikonomia* nor *pronoia* appears. The grant was often described as a reward for faithful service, and it was usually fully tax exempt (both *telos* and secondary charges) and included the right to improve the property (e.g., convert pasture to arable without incurring a tax for the value added). Fundamentally, such grants can be thought of as gifts, not pronoiai, and are therefore of concern to us only for purposes of comparison.

[8.39] Chrysobull of John V Palaiologos for George Margarites (1342)

It is possible that one of the grants in the table is not a new grant, but one previously held. In a chrysobull from November 1342, issued in the name of John V, we read that *kyr* George Margarites requested "that he be issued a chrysobull . . . for the *posotes* of fifty hyperpyra that he possessed outside the *poson* of his oikonomia," located near Kalamaria. This *posotes* included paroikoi and land which had been held by a number of "unfaithful" men: Demetrios Pharmakes, the "rebel" John VI Kantakouzenos, one of his cousins Nikephoros Kantakouzenos, and the *dioiketes* Manuel. The emperor granted Margarites hereditary rights (*kata logon gonikotetos*), the

179 Lampenos, *῾Ο λόγιος Νικόλαος Λαμπηνὸς καὶ τὸ ἐγκώμιον αὐτοῦ εἰς τὸν Ἀνδρόνικον Β΄ Παλαιολόγον*, ed. I. Polemes (Athens, 1992), ch. 65, p. 68, lines 2–14. Thomas Magistros, *On Kingship*, ch. 10: Migne, *PG*, 145, col. 461. D. Angelov, *Imperial Ideology and Political Thought in Byzantium, 1204–1330* (Cambridge and New York, 2007), 136–37, 303. Laiou, "Le débat sur les droits du fisc," 99–100.

Table 8.7 Hereditary rights granted over a new grant

		What was granted?	Drawn from an oikonomia?	Any tax exemption noted?	"Service" required?	Right to improve noted?	Referred to as a reward?	Right to alienate noted?
1293 or forgery	Leo Koteanitzes *[8.31]*	property		full (no "service")			yes	yes
1322/3	Demetrios Plytos *[7.15]*	property						
1328	Theodotos Kalothetos *[7.16]*	property		full		yes		yes
1342	John Margarites *[8.17]*	*posotes*		full		yes		
1342	George Margarites *[8.39]*	*posotes*				yes		
1344	John Choumnos *[8.78]*	property w/*posotes*		limited exemption of secondary burdens		yes	yes	
1344	*archontopouloi [8.5]*	property		full		yes		yes
1344	Xene Soultanina *[7.17]*	*posotes*	yes (her husband's)	full		yes	yes	yes
forgery	Dragon *[App. 5]*	property		full (no "service")		yes	yes	yes
1378	Manuel Tarchaneiotes *[8.32]*	property			yes	yes		

right to improve the property, and the right to transfer it to his children and heirs.[180]

Given that the properties conferred upon Margarites had been taken from these "unfaithful" men no earlier than October 1341, when John Kantakouzenos had himself crowned emperor, there are two ways to view this grant. (i) Paralleling the case of John Sgouros Orestes (as in Table 8.8), the *posotes* of fifty hyperpyra was extracted from Margarites' existing oikonomia, which he had been holding for no more than one year.[181] (ii) Alternatively, this *posotes* was a new grant, created with newly granted properties, distinct from an oikonomia that Margarites already held previously. Even though the chrysobull states that Margarites already "held" (κέκτηται) the *posotes* over which he desired hereditary rights, this merely means that the usual procedure had been followed: Margarites first received a *prostagma* granting him the *posotes*, followed by a chrysobull granting the additional hereditary rights.

I tend to favor the second interpretation because the period of time between the original confiscations from the "unfaithful" men and the conferral of hereditary rights over this *posotes* was so short. Nevertheless, it is certainly possible that Margarites received an oikonomia, perhaps quite larger than fifty hyperpyra sometime after October 1341 and then, perhaps only a few months later, received hereditary rights over a *posotes* of fifty hyperpyra.

In the case of the concession of hereditary rights over previously held property (Table 8.8), the grant is usually a *posotes*. Usually the right to improve the property was granted and usually the grant of hereditary rights was over only part of the recipient's oikonomia. In fact there is no known case in which it is clear that hereditary rights were granted over an entire oikonomia. In four cases (Table 8.9) this is a possibility.

Further, there are a number of cases in which further rights were granted over property that was already held in hereditary tenure (Table 8.10). In these cases, either the origin of the property is unclear (i.e., whether it was an imperial grant), or, if it appears to have been an imperial grant, whether hereditary rights were granted initially (i.e., whether it was a gift or an oikonomia). Nevertheless, I present these here as a comparison as well.

180 Kravari, "Nouveaux documents du monastère de Philothéou," 297, no. 2.4–5: [ἐπὶ τῇ] τῶ[ν πεν]τήκοντα ὑπερπύρων ποσ[ότη]τι ἣν κέκτηται ἐκτὸ[ς] τοῦ πο[σοῦ τῆς] ο[ἰκο]νομίας αὐτοῦ. Kravari discusses the problems involving this man's identity. Further, since she indicates that the *kappa* in ἐκτός is only partially visible, there is a possibility, albeit small, that the phrase should be read "within (ἐντός) the *poson* of his oikonomia." On the document: Ostrogorsky, *Féodalité*, 123, and Kazhdan, *Agrarnye otnošenija*, 219.

181 Cf. *Vatopédi*, I, no. 52.7–8: κατέχειν ἐκτὸς τοῦ ποσοῦ τῆς οἰκονομίας αὐτοῦ τὴν ποσότητα τοῦ εἰρημένου γονικοῦ τῶν ἓξ ὑπερπύρων.

Table 8.8 Hereditary rights granted over part of a previously held grant

		What was granted?	Drawn from an oikonomia?	Any tax exemption noted?	Right to improve noted?	Referred to as a reward?	Right to alienate noted?
1307	judge of the army Alexios Diplovatatzes *[8.40]*	property	yes	secondary charges and corvées	yes		
1313	*hetaireiarches* John Panaretos *[8.41]*	*posotes*	yes				
1318	George Troulenos *[8.37]*	property	yes	limited exemption of secondary burdens for peasants to be settled	yes		
1319/20	John Orestes and each of his brothers *[8.42]*	*posotes*	yes		yes		
1333	Michael Monomachos *[8.14]*	*posotes*	yes	full (no "service")			
1343	Syrmanouel Mesopotamites *[8.44]*	*posotes*	yes		yes		
1347	Demetrios Kavasilas *[8.45]*	*posotes*			yes	yes	
1349	Demetrios Devlitzenos *[8.46]*	*posotes*	yes		yes		
forgery	Manuel Angelos Patrikios *[App. 5]*	property		full (no "service")	yes	yes	yes

The right to improve one's property is not unexpected in property over which hereditary rights are granted, and indeed such a clause appears in most of the cases dealt with here. But since it does not always appear, should we conclude that its absence meant that this privilege was not conceded? One might explain its absence from the acts for Modenos *[8.30]*, Koteanitzes *[8.31]*, and Nomikopoulos *[8.33]* by noting that these are three of the earliest extant grants of hereditary rights. I would think the content of the clause was implicit in the grant, but that the clause only became firmly established in the 1320s.

The examples cited below include very few men who are actually called "soldiers." Many of the men who were granted this privilege were titled aristocrats (judge of the army, *megas adnoumiastes*, *hetaireiarches*), men whom we should regard as military leaders (if they had any military competence). It stands to reason that the list of men who received special privileges from the emperor would be biased toward the higher social levels.

Hereditary rights granted over part of a previously held grant

Sometimes hereditary rights were granted over a portion of a grant previously held. In these cases (Table 8.8) the object of the grant is usually described as a *posotes* and usually the right to improve the associated property is explicitly granted. It should be noted that for only four of these cases (Orestes, Monomachos, Devlitzenos, Patrikios) do the texts assert that the *posotes* or property referred to constituted only part of the recipient's holdings. In the other five cases we are told only that the *posotes* or property was "inside" or "from" a *posotes*, an oikonomia, or a collection of properties received earlier from the emperor. There is a slight possibility that one or more of these may have involved the *entire* oikonomia of the recipient.

[8.40] Chrysobull of Andronikos II Palaiologos for the judge of the army Alexios Diplovatatzes (1307)

In 1307 Andronikos II granted the request of the judge of the army Alexios Diplovatatzes that the emperor "make *gonikon* for him land of one thousand modioi called Pelorhygion from his oikonomia around Serres."[182]

[182] *Prodrome*, no. 2.2–3: ἵνα διορίσηται ἡ βασιλεία μου καὶ γονικευθῆ αὐτῷ γῆ μοδίων χιλίων ἀπὸ τῆς . . . οἰκονομίας αὐτοῦ. On the document: Laiou, "The Byzantine Aristocracy in the Palaeologan Period," 145, and Uspenskij, "Značenie," 15, 21–22. Inexplicably, Gorjanov, *Pozdnevizantijskij feodalizm*, 100, referred to this as a *new* grant of a pronoia. Pelorhygion was located somewhere south of Zichna, to the east of the Strymon. It is mentioned also in a document from 1330 in which the daughters of the deceased *protokynegos* Sarantenos Indanes sold a property in Pelorhegion to the monastery of Zographou for 500 hyperpyra (*Zographou*, no. 28). Indanes is

Henceforth, Diplovatatzes held this property "as his *gonikon*" (line 10: ὡς γονικὴν αὐτοῦ) with the right to improve it, and after his death the land and any improvements could be transmitted to his legitimate children and heirs and be held by them "in the same way as *gonikon*" (lines 6–7: κατὰ τὸν ὅμοιον τρόπον ὡς γονική). It is likely that the 1,000 modioi (which at the standard rate at the time would have had a *posotes* of hyperpyra) represented but a fraction of his oikonomia. As for the tax status of the property, the document states only that it was to be "above all vexation" (line 7: ἀνωτέρα πάσης ἐνοχλήσεως) and "above all imposition and vexation" (line 18: ἀνωτέραν πάσης ἐπιθέσεως καὶ ὀχλήσεως), phrases that generally are connected to exemption of secondary charges and corvées, not the base *telos*.[183]

What about the *telos*? Certainly Diplovatatzes, like every other holder of an oikonomia, was not ordinarily liable for the *telos* of his oikonomia, because the *telos* formed the *posotes* which was the essence of the state's concession to the holder of the oikonomia. However, once he was granted the right to transfer the property to his heirs, did he now owe the property's *telos*, which was its *posotes*? Even though the document says nothing about exemption of the *telos*, I conclude that he was not required to pay the *telos* after he received hereditary rights. First there is the practical argument: what would be the benefit of having hereditary rights if one now had to pay the *telos*? As the case of John Orestes below shows, it was assumed, if not in Diplovatatzes' day then certainly a dozen years later, that an oikonomia would pass to one's children. If Diplovatatzes could expect his son to receive his oikonomia, why would he seek hereditary rights to part of the oikonomia if that meant burdening himself and his son with the *telos* of the property? Certainly, by receiving the hereditary rights he now had the *guaranteed* right to transmit the property to his son, but did this outweigh the yearly *telos*? The only other additional benefit Diplovatatzes and his heirs received from

known as a pronoia holder from other sources *[8.71]*. The daughters claimed that the emperor had granted their father the property in full ownership, and that their father had granted it to a deceased third daughter, Anna, for her dowry. Curiously, Anna was married to a man named Manuel Diplovatatzes, deceased in 1330 as well. Given that 500 hyperpyra was a reasonable price for arable land of 1,000 modioi at this time and in this area (see *Vatopédi*, ii, p. 99), it is possible there was some duplicity here. The property that the women were selling may not have come from their father, but from their brother-in-law. If so, as in-laws, they may have had no right to the property. In any event, by 1330 Pelorhegion may have denoted a much larger area than in 1307: Zographou had a *metochion* there in 1325 (*Zographou*, no. 23.20), and the monastery of Philotheou had a presence there at the same time as well (*Actes de Philothée*, ed. Regel, no. 6.41).

183 Cf. *Esphigménou*, no. 6.69 (a chrysobull from 1258/9): ἀνωτέρα πάσης δημοσιακῆς ἐνοχλήσεως, ἤγουν ἀγγαρείας, παραγγαρίας, ζημίας, ψωμοζημίας, πλωίμων, etc. The specific items are all corvées or demands in kind.

the grant was the right to improve the property. At the very least this meant that no additional burden would ever be placed on the property even if the value of the property increased through the efforts of Diplovatatzes or his heirs. This was not a negligible benefit, but it was hypothetical. All in all, if he was required to pay the *telos* on the newly hereditary property, the benefits were years down the road, while the additional burden of the *telos* was immediate. I do not think holders of oikonomiai were required to pay the *telos* on portions of their oikonomiai over which they received hereditary rights.

But if the *telos* was exempted, why does the document for Diplovatatzes not say so? In this respect the case of Diplovatatzes is not unique. If we compare Table 8.7 to Table 8.8, it appears that grants of hereditary rights over newly granted properties tend to specify a complete tax exemption while grants of hereditary rights over parts of a previously held grants, like Diplovatatzes', tend to mention either an exemption of secondary charges or no tax exemptions at all. It would seem, then, that a tax exemption of the *telos* was only mentioned when the property or *posotes* involved was not part of an oikonomia. When it *was* part of an oikonomia, no tax exemption of the *telos* is mentioned. Why? My hypothesis is that while holders of oikonomiai did not pay the *telos* on the properties within their oikonomia, this was not due to a tax exemption (technically, a *logisimon*, by which the *telos* would have been "reckoned to their account"). A tax exemption was permanent; the holding of an oikonomia with its privileges was not. Therefore, what they received was a special arrangement (literally, an "oikonomia") which temporarily conceded to them that which belonged to the state. The property within the oikonomia remained state property and the recipient held it and its *telos* temporarily. Thus, while holding an oikonomia, a beneficiary was not actually holding any tax exemption. Thus, when hereditary rights were granted over part of an oikonomia, the previous status of the taxes was maintained. This situation is found in documents involving monastic property as well. Often the emperor, when confirming a monastery's possession of its property, says nothing about taxes. The current status continued and so there was no need to mention it.[184]

[8.41] Chrysobull of Andronikos II Palaiologos for the *hetaireiarches* John Panaretos (1313)

More common than a grant of hereditary rights over property within an oikonomia was a grant of hereditary rights over a part of the total *posotes*. In

[184] E.g., one of many such examples: *Vatopédi*, I, no. 31.

a chrysobull of March 1313, the *hetaireiarches* John Panaretos, known from other sources as an *apographeus*, asked that he be granted "a *posotes* of thirty hyperpyra in the village of Kato Ouska from the oikonomia given to him through *prostagma*," so that he might hold it undisturbed and in hereditary title (*kata logon gonikotetos*). The emperor ordered that Panaretos be permitted to transfer the *posotes* to his legitimate children, heirs, and successors who may hold it "in the same and similar way as their father." Further, no governors (*kephalai*) or fiscal officials were to bother the property. There is no other mention of taxation.[185]

As is frequently the case when additional rights were granted over part of a *posotes*, the documents in question do not specify the original, total *posotes* from which the additional concession was made. Panaretos received additional rights over a *posotes* of thirty hyperpyra, but what was the *posotes* of his entire oikonomia? To provide a rough answer to the question, I propose a "20–50 percent rule." This rule is based on the logic that (i) grants of additional privileges on anything less than 20 percent of a pronoia holder's oikonomia would be so inconsequential as to mock the concept of an imperial reward, not warrant a personal imperial act, and perhaps even be viewed as an insult, and (ii) a grant of additional privileges on more than half, but less than all of a pronoia holder's oikonomia would not provide much incentive for future loyal service, and would drastically lessen the symbolic value of the imperial grant by making the emperor appear unnecessarily niggardly. These numbers are in accord with the only two complete figures we have: Michael Monomachos was granted hereditary rights over 50 hyperpyra of his oikonomia of 100 hyperpyra *[8.14]*, and Demetrios Devlitzenos was granted hereditary rights over 100 hyperpyra of his oikonomia of 400 hyperpyra *[8.46]*. If we apply the rule to Panaretos' case, we may estimate that the total size of Panaretos' oikonomia was between 150 and 60 hyperpyra.

[185] *Prodrome*, no. 6.3–5: ἀπὸ τῆς... δοθείσης πρὸς αὐτὸν διὰ προστάγματος... οἰκονομίας... ποσότητα ὑπερπύρων τριάκοντα, and line 19. The passages confirming Panaretos' undisturbed possession of the *posotes* are paralleled in other documents for monastic property: e.g., *Vatopédi*, I, no. 31.107–08 and no. 53.10. On Panaretos, *PLP*, no. 21641. A fragmentary praktikon, dated by the editor to ca. 1342, mentions someone named Panaretos holding land in Kato Ouska: *Prodrome B*, no. 142.2. In a chrysobull from 1345 Stefan Dušan confirmed the monastery of St. John Prodromos' possession of an "oikonomia of 100 hyperpyra" in the same village: Solovjev–Mošin, *Grčk povelje*, no. 2.91–92 = *Prodrome*, no. 39.60. If the passage in the 1345 act is a reference to Panaretos' oikonomia, it would explain why the 1313 act was found in the archives of the Prodromos monastery. On these two documents, Ostrogorsky, *Féodalité*, 106–07; Uspenskij, "Značenie," 15, 22; Gorjanov, *Pozdnevizantijskij feodalizm*, 99–100, 107; and Kazhdan in *VizVrem* 10 (1956), 223.

[8.42] Act of the *apographeus* Manuel Manglavites for John Sgouros Orestes (1319/20, or perhaps 1304/5)

A more elaborate case, and one that provides us with a rare look at the inner workings of the process of granting hereditary rights over pronoiai, is found in two documents for the benefit of John Sgouros Orestes. The first of these is an act of the *apographeus* of the theme of Melnik, Manuel Manglavites. The document bears only the indiction year "3" and its editors tentatively dated it to 1319/20. In the act Manglavites writes that each of four brothers, Theodore, Constantine, Nicholas, and John Sgouros Orestes, who were "from the western *archontopouloi*" (οἱ ἀπὸ τῶν δυσικῶν ἀρχοντοπούλων), had petitioned the emperor and received a chrysobull ordering "that from the oikonomia which each of them was found holding, a *posotes* of six hyperpyra be pulled out and assigned as his *gonikon*, and such *posotes* be held and enjoyed by both him and his party from now on untroubled and unharassed."[186]

Specifically, in regard to John Orestes, Manglavites established that he "hold outside the *poson* of his oikonomia the *posotes* of said *gonikon* of six hyperpyra" (lines 7–8). The official then lists ten properties (houses, fields, vineyards, etc.) which constituted this *posotes* of six hyperpyra. In all, there were 110 modioi of arable land, 14 modioi of vineyards, a garden of $1\frac{1}{2}$ modioi, and various buildings. At normal assessment rates, the arable and vineyards alone would have had a *posotes* of about five hyperpyra. The properties were strewn throughout a relatively large area in and around Melnik, southward to the village of Krousovos (today Achladochorion, about seventeen miles south-southeast of Melnik as the crow flies, easily double that by foot), and around Radoviš to the east (about fifteen miles southeast of Štip). He notes that John should hold and enjoy this *posotes* of six hyperpyra (lines 25–26) with the right to keep whatever improvements he should make to the properties even if they increased the value of the properties (lines 26–27), and that no *apographeus* had the right to increase or decrease the *posotes* of six hyperpyra (lines 28–30).

At this point the physical condition of the document deteriorates substantially, requiring numerous conjectural restorations by the editors. While these seem quite reasonable, it is unfortunate, because here the content becomes rather interesting. Manglavites writes that John had the right to transmit the *posotes* of six hyperpyra to his child "toward whom namely his oikonomia ought to pass, and be held in completely the same and equal

186 *Vatopédi*, I, no. 52.1,4–6. According to my "20–50 percent rule," the total grant for each of the four brothers would have been between 30 and 12 hyperpyra.

way, and [. . .] for the future and always, and for the rest of the descendants successively in his function." However, if John were to die "childless, his oikonomia ought to be seized by the fisc and given to whomever our mighty and holy lord and emperor ordains." Nevertheless, in this event, the *posotes* of six hyperpyra should be held by his wife, and then, after her "death, it be seized in like manner by the fisc."[187]

Thus, John Orestes received six hyperpyra from his oikonomia in hereditary tenure. He was permitted to transmit both this *posotes* of six hyperpyra and the rest of his oikonomia to a child who would hold both in the same way. But if John died childless, the oikonomia would be returned to the fisc; his widow could hold the *posotes* of six hyperpyra until her death, after which it too would return to the fisc.

The new "*gonikon*" with a *posotes* of six hyperpyra was no longer considered part of Orestes' oikonomia: it was "outside the *poson* of his oikonomia" and Manglavites clearly distinguishes one from the other (lines 36–38). And yet, in the anticipated normal scheme of things, Orestes would have a son, and this son would receive both the oikonomia and the *gonikon*, and both were expected to pass to later heirs, should these heirs exist and follow in the footsteps of Orestes and his son. So what was the difference between Orestes' oikonomia and his *gonikon* with a *posotes* of six hyperpyra? Orestes clearly had no right to alienate either (because Manglavites assumes he would still have possession of both at the time of his death), and it was expected that both would pass to his son. One difference is that Orestes now had a legal right to transfer the *gonikon* to his son, while the fate of the oikonomia remained in the hands of the emperor. In practice, this might not have meant a great deal; if the emperor decided to withdraw Orestes' oikonomia, it seems likely that the *gonikon* would have followed. Another difference is that, if Orestes had no son, the *gonikon* represented a kind of "survivor's benefit" that would provide a livelihood for his wife as long as she lived. This stipulation may have addressed a significant or perhaps even a crucial concern for men like Orestes. But the purpose of Manglavites' act was to do more than account for the disposition of Orestes' oikonomia should he

[187] *Vatopédi*, I, no. 52.33–36: [πρὸς τὸν] γνησιον [π]α[ῖ]δα αὐτοῦ πρὸς ὃν [δη]λονότ[ι ὀφείλ]ει π[ερι]έρχεσθαι καὶ ἡ οἰκ[ονομ]ία αὐτοῦ, καὶ κατέχεσθαι κατα πάντα τὸν ἶσον καὶ ὃμοιον τρόπον καὶ [...ca. 12 characters...εἰς τὸ] εξῆς μέχρι παντὸς καὶ εἰς τοὺς λοιποὺς ἀπογόν[ους κατὰ δι]αδοχὴν τῆς αὐτ[οῦ] τάξεως. For my translation of the last five words I have followed the rendering of the editors of the act ("qui lui succéderont dans sa fonction"), although I am uncomfortable with it. *Vatopédi*, I, no. 52.36–37: ἄπαι[ς,....ἡ οἰκο]νομία αὐτοῦ ὀφείλει κρατεῖσθαι παρὰ [τοῦ μέρους τοῦ δημο]σίου καὶ δίδοσθαι πρὸς ὃν ἂν διορίσηται ὁ κραταιὸς καὶ ἅγιος ἡμῶν αὐθέντης καὶ βασιλεύς, lines 39: [τε]λευτὴν κρατεῖσθαι καὶ ταύτην ὁμοί[ως] π[αρὰ τοῦ δη]μ[οσίου].

die childless. Rather, the main difference between the oikonomia and the *gonikon* is that Orestes now had the right to enjoy the benefit of improving the properties within the *gonikon*, something that was not the case in regard to the properties within his oikonomia.

Three times the document mentions either Orestes' right to improve (line 27: βελτιοῦν) the *gonikon* or the improvements (lines 33 and 43: βελτιωθησόμενα) he may make. And as the document states, no *apographeus* had the right to add or take anything away from this *posotes* even if its value should increase (lines 28–31). As a matter of state policy, an oikonomia holder was not entitled to keep the improvements he made to his oikonomia without state approval because these improvements would increase the *posotes* of his oikonomia. However, any property extracted from the oikonomia and transformed into *gonikon* was not subject to this limitation. That was the true value to Orestes of the procedure.

Moreover, we can conclude that, at the time of this document, it was presumed that a son would succeed to his father's oikonomia. And yet, we can also conclude that, at the same time, a son had no right to inherit his father's oikonomia. We have to create this distinction in order to explain this document. Even the terminology of the document suggests this distinction. Manglavites writes that a *gonikon* – here a kind of conditional property – may be transmitted (line 32: παραπέμπεσθαι) to a son, but an oikonomia – not a type of property but a privilege – may "come round" (line 34: περιέρχεσθαι) to a son.

[8.43] Chrysobull of Andronikos II Palaiologos for John Sgouros Orestes (1323)

A few years later, in August 1323, a chrysobull of Andronikos II confirmed John Orestes' rights over a collection of sixteen properties.[188] At least nine of them can be identified with the properties mentioned in the 1319/20

188 *Vatopédi*, I, no. 60. Among the properties mentioned in the document are two peasant households which were held "through chrysobull" by Orestes' father-in-law and given to Orestes as a dowry (lines 7–9). Because the father-in-law held these households "through chrysobull," the editors of the act (p. 323) suggest that the father-in-law held them as part of an oikonomia and, further, that their transfer to Orestes in dowry indicates that "an *oikonomia* became transferable" through an imperial concession. However, this interpretation is unwarranted. As a rule, any reference to someone holding property "through chrysobull" means simply that the emperor had confirmed his rights to the property. Nothing can be inferred about the property's origin. Indeed, in the 1323 chrysobull for Orestes the emperor confirmed Orestes' possession of property he had received through dowry. Orestes could now assert that he held these properties "through chrysobull." A chrysobull was the most secure deed of ownership.

act, despite the fact that of the seven for which areas are provided in both documents, three had grown in size and three had shrunk.[189] The emperor explains that Orestes, who is here referred to by the epithet *pansevastos sevastos*, asked for a chrysobull regarding his properties. The emperor confirmed the fact that Orestes held these properties "as *gonika*" (line 35) and could do with them as he pleased. Further, the emperor additionally granted that these properties were to be held and enjoyed by Orestes "above each and every public *epereia* and every other vexation" (lines 39–40), which means that, at the very least, the properties were not subject to secondary charges and corvées. The emperor notes that after Orestes' death these properties "shall be held in the same way by the legitimate children from his loins and his heirs and by others toward whom he proposes to leave some of them."[190] We observe that Orestes received only an unlimited right of bequest (perhaps his wife was one of the "others" to whom he might leave the property), but no explicit right to alienate the properties through sale or donation.

In this document there is no mention of the "*posotes* of six hyperpyra," no mention of Orestes' oikonomia, and no explicit limitation on how Orestes could dispose of the properties, including those that had been part of the *posotes* of six hyperpyra. Evidently Orestes had received additional privileges between the time of the two documents (further evidence that the first document dates to 1304/5).

Thus, four brothers each held an oikonomia from the emperor. One of the brothers, John Orestes, held in addition to his oikonomia other property, some of which he received through dowry. In 1319/20 (or perhaps 1304/5) they each received the right to transmit a *posotes* of six hyperpyra extracted from their oikonomiai to their children. The terms of the concession to John Orestes, which were probably identical for all four brothers, were that the six-hyperpyra *posotes* was now to be considered "outside the *poson* of his oikonomia" and to be regarded "as *gonikon*." The *posotes* of six hyperpyra, as well as his oikonomia, was to pass to John's son who would hold them

[189] Some of the small changes in areas might be explained by simple recalculation of their areas: e.g., one field decreased in size from 13 to 10 modioi, another from 11 to 7. In some instances, the document implicitly explains the increase: a field of 10 modioi grew to 100 evidently because of additional purchases from several men (see *Vatopédi*, I, p. 324). Evidently the addition of contiguous parcels to these properties through sale or exchange was regarded as legitimate (was this an element of the right to "improve" one's property?). One wonders how these additions would have been disposed of if Orestes and then his wife had died childless. In any event, the number of changes in the property sizes does raise the question whether the gap between the documents could have been less than four years (from Sept. 1319–August 1320 to August 1323). It is certainly possible that the act of Manglavites dates to 1304/5.

[190] *Vatopédi*, I, no. 60.44–47: πρὸς οὓς μέλλει καταλεῖψαι τινὰ ἐξ αὐτῶν.

in the same way as his father. If John had no children, the six-hyperpyra *posotes* would pass to John's widow after he died, but only as a lifetime grant that she had no right to alienate. At her death, the property representing this *posotes* would return to the fisc. As for John's oikonomia, if John died childless, that would return to the fisc immediately.

The document from 1319/20 makes it clear that the designation of a property as "*gonikon*" did not by any means imply the right of full ownership. The designation signified a limited right to transfer a property under certain conditions (in this case to a son), as opposed to property within an oikonomia which one could not transfer at all (though it was expected to "pass" to a son). Neither the oikonomia nor the *posotes* of 6 hyperpyra could be alienated through sale or gift.

Further, the document from 1319/20 implies that, at that time, it was not rare for children, but not including wives, to receive the oikonomiai of their fathers. From the document itself, it is not clear whether this meant *male* children exclusively. The oikonomia was to pass to John's "son," but in truth *pais* in the phrase [πρὸς τὸν] γνησιον [π]α[ῖ]δα αὐτοῦ can be rendered as either "son" or "child." Moreover, the conditional phrase, "If perhaps the said Orestes dies childless" (ἄπαι[ς]), is no formulaic construction. I have not encountered it in any other document dealing with an imperial grant. This suggests that in John's case there were no adult children at the time, and perhaps no children at all. If the emperor had wished to specify male children as the sole permissible heirs, this would have been the place to note "without male child," rather than the general "childless." Further, we do have Pachymeres' statement that Michael VIII permitted the unborn children of pronoia holders to receive their father's grants, which suggests that the beneficiary need not have been male *[6.10]*. Nevertheless, cases of women holding oikonomiai are very rare, and this fact should probably trump all other evidence. We should probably conclude that, when the right to transmit an oikonomia was granted, sons were the presumptive beneficiaries.

This pair of documents for John Orestes is of great value because they prove that documents which confirm someone's possession of "*gonikon*" property, even if the document says that such "*gonikon*" was acquired through purchase or exchange, may have originated through an imperial grant. If only the 1323 chrysobull was known to us, we might conclude simply that John Orestes was a man who owned a number of properties in full ownership which he obtained through patrimony, purchase, exchange, and dowry, and over which he desired the emperor to confirm his ownership rights. Taken by itself, there is nothing in the 1323 chrysobull which indicates that any of the properties mentioned within the document originated as an imperial grant. To cite merely one example, the 1323 chrysobull lists, as one of John Orestes' properties, "another field from purchase from the same Kokkos of ten modioi, which [Kokkos] held from patrimony [*apo gonikotetos*]." The phrase makes it appear as though Orestes purchased the field from Kokkos. But according to the act of Manglavites, this field was one of the ten properties within Orestes' oikonomia that were set apart to form the *posotes* of six hyperpyra. Its "genealogy" is rather complicated. Manglavites lists it ("another [field] from the same *stasis* of Kokkos . . . of ten modioi") together with two other fields and prefaces the enumeration of all three with the following words: "And from an exchange of certain fields of *kyr* Tauros tou Chrysou [which were] given to Valdouvinos, these [three] fields, that is, [those] from the *stasis* of Kokkos held earlier by this Valdouvinos."[191] In other words, while the 1323 chrysobull notes that the field of ten modioi (as well as the other two fields) was sold by Kokkos, it was not sold to Orestes (but evidently to Tauros). Then, according to Manglavites' act, some kind of exchange was effected and all three fields passed to Valdouvinos (or Baldwin), without doubt as part of an oikonomia. Then, for whatever reason, Valdouvinos lost the fields and they were reassigned to Orestes. And so, without the act of Manglavites, we would conclude that the field of ten modioi was purchased by Orestes, when in fact it was part of his oikonomia granted by the emperor. The designation of the field as "from purchase" was merely a way of identifying the field ("the field of ten modioi purchased from Kokkos"), unusual from our perspective, but apparently one that did not cause confusion for the principals.

The two documents involving John Orestes force us to conclude that even if property is called *gonikon* and even if we read that the property was "from purchase" or "exchange," with no reference to an oikonomia or a *posotes* or a pronoia or a gift from the emperor, or any other terminology that suggests an imperial grant, the property may nevertheless have originated as part of an oikonomia.

[8.44] Chrysobull of John V Palaiologos for the *kavallarios* Syrmanouel Mesopotamites (1343)

The grants in Table 8.8 are of particular importance to our study because they almost all involve pronoia grants. The recipients are frequently military men. Thus, in 1343 the "most brave and most faithful" *kavallarios*

[191] *Vatopédi*, I, no. 60.15–17, no. 52.22–23,17–19.

Syrmanouel Mesopotamites requested and received from John V hereditary rights over a *posotes* of twenty hyperpyra "from his oikonomia" at a place called Drachova, with the right to improve it "and to transmit this to the legitimate children and heirs." There is no specific mention of any tax exemption, only the standard phrase that he should hold the *posotes* unharassed.[192] According to my "20–50 percent rule" (see *[8.41]*), Syrmanouel's pronoia probably had a *posotes* somewhere between 40 and 100 hyperpyra yearly, well in the range of typical pronoia soldiers.

[8.45] Chrysobull of John VI Kantakouzenos for the *megas papias* Demetrios Kavasilas (1347)

In 1347 John VI Kantakouzenos granted the *megas papias* Demetrios Kavasilas a *posotes* of 250 hyperpyra in hereditary title (*kata logon gonikotetos*) in the region of Kalamaria because he fought and suffered for the side of Kantakouzenos during the civil war. The *posotes* was to be drawn "from what he holds through *prostagma* of my majesty": from the village of Katakale, from the oikonomia of the deceased Gavras at Kalamaria, and from another piece of land and the *ampelopakton* of two villages that had once belonged to the state and which were then given to the deceased George Pharmakes. His legitimate heirs would hold this *posotes* in the same way.[193] Even though this document does not refer to Kavasilas' holdings as an oikonomia, the fact that this *posotes* was to be drawn from what Kavasilas held through *prostagma* almost certainly indicates one. Because the emperor notes that all of Kavasilas' property had been confiscated during the civil wars, there is a slight possibility that this *posotes* of 250 hyperpyra represented Kavasilas' entire *posotes*. Aside from the forged chrysobull for Patrikios *[App. 5]*, the case of Demetrios Kavasilas is the only example of a grant of hereditary rights over a previously held property which does not mention an oikonomia at all. In any event, he held one of the largest known oikonomiai.

[8.46] Chrysobull of John VI Kantakouzenos for Demetrios Devlitzenos (1349)

Another military man was Demetrios Devlitzenos. In 1349 John VI Kantakouzenos granted him hereditary rights (*kata logon gonikotetos*) over a

[192] *Chilandar*, ed. Petit, no. 132.12–14,9–10,18,20–21. On the document, Gorjanov, *Pozdnevizantijskij feodalizm*, 134, and Kazhdan, *Agrarnye otnošenija*, 219. The village of Drachova might be the same as the village of Rachova near Zichna.

[193] *Dionysiou*, no. 2.33,46,51,53–54,57,34. Hvostova, *Osobennosti*, 213.

Table 8.9 Hereditary rights granted, but unclear whether over part or all of a previously held grant

		What was granted?	Drawn from an oikonomia?	Any tax exemption noted?	"Service" required?	Right to improve noted?	Referred to as a reward?	Right to alienate noted?
1323	John Sgouros Orestes *[8.43]*	property	probably			maybe		yes
1342	Klazomenitai soldiers *[8.4]*	*posotes*			yes	yes		
1351	George Katzaras *[8.47]*	property with a *posotes*			yes	yes	yes	
1378	Radoslav Sampias *[8.48]*	property			yes	yes		

posotes of 100 hyperpyra from his oikonomia of 400 hyperpyra. Devlitzenos asked that this 100 hyperpera be ascribed from his *posotes* in Hermeleia to the extent possible. The emperor granted his request, permitting him to hold the *posotes* undisturbed, in hereditary title, and with the right to improve it, and pass the *posotes* and any improvements to his legitimate children and heirs who would hold the *posotes* in the same way. Oikonomides argued that Devlitzenos may have owned much of the actual property that made up the oikonomia. If so, the concession here is like an hereditary tax exemption. Demetrios Devlitzenos is mentioned as an "imperial soldier" (*vasilikos stratiotes*) in a document from 1311, which means that he had to have been at least in his late fifties when he received the hereditary rights.[194]

Hereditary rights granted over all of a previously granted property

I am aware of only one example of an emperor granting hereditary rights over all of a property previously granted. This is the case of the priest Modenos who received hereditary rights over a tax-exempt *stasis* Michael VIII had earlier granted him *[8.30]*. However, in a few cases, while it is clear that the recipient of a concession of hereditary rights held the property or *posotes* involved previously, it is not clear whether the emperor was granting hereditary rights over all or only part of the previously held grant (Table 8.9).

194 *Docheiariou*, no. 26. N. Oikonomides, "The Properties of the Deblitzenoi in the Fourteenth and Fifteenth Centuries," in *Charanis Studies*, ed. A. Laiov-Thomadakis (New Brunswick, N. J., 1980) 177–79. Ostrogorsky, *Féodalité*, 126–27. *PLP*, no. 91756.

What makes these cases interesting is that most of them state that "service" was required by the recipient and his heirs.

[8.47] Chrysobull of John V Palaiologos for the *megas adnoumiastes* George Katzaras (1351), and Act of three officials regarding John Katzaras' claim to Patrikona (1373)

Around 1327 George Katzaras and the Varvarenoi soldier company, of which he was head, received as a pronoia, among other properties, the imperial *zeugelateion* called Patrikona on the Chalkidike.[195] In 1351 John V issued a chrysobull for Katzaras, addressing him as the *megas adnoumiastes* and *oikeios* of the emperor, "faithful to our majesty and attentive . . . to its services," a reference either to administrative duties or to actual military service. According to the chrysobull Katzaras explained "that he held for twenty-four years through assessors' conferrals [*apographikai paradoseis*] in Kalamaria . . . , in the amount [*eis to poson*] of his oikonomia, land called Patrikona with the *kathedra* in it, being 2,400 modioi for [*eis*] 48 hyperpyra and he holds and enjoys this undisturbed up to now and requested that he be issued a chrysobull of our majesty and hold this henceforth *kata logon gonikotetos*." The emperor permitted him to hold the land undisturbed and *kata logon gonikotetos*, with the right to improve it and transmit it to his legitimate children and heirs who would hold it in the same way, "rendering the service belonging to and owed by them."[196]

It is unclear whether the amount of hyperpyra "in the amount of his oikonomia" represented the entire amount of Katzaras' oikonomia or only one amount "inside" his oikonomia. As pointed out above *[8.38]*, references to monetary amounts "in" someone's or a monastery's oikonomia tell us little about the *total* amount of fiscal revenue held. These references only provide us with the *minimum* amount of fiscal revenue held within an oikonomia. Thus, we know only that the size of the *megas adnoumiastes* Katzaras' oikonomia was at least 48 hyperpyra.

If Katzaras had been able to transmit this *posotes* to any of his heirs, they would not have enjoyed it for long, for Patrikona, along with most of the Chalkidike, was conquered by the Serbs at the end of 1355 or the beginning of 1356. It remained in Serbian hands until 1371 when, following the battle

[195] *Docheiariou*, p. 140. Lefort, *Villages de Macédoine*, 116.

[196] *Docheiariou*, no. 27.2–3: ἐπιμελὴς [...........] εἰς τὰς δουλείας αὐτῆς, and lines 7 and 32: ἀποδιδόντες καὶ αὐτοὶ τὴν ἀνήκουσαν καὶ ὀφειλομένην ὑπὲρ αὐτῶν δουλείαν. Ostrogorsky, *Féodalité*, 127.

of the Marica, Serbian authority disintegrated in Macedonia.[197] At the end of 1372 or in early 1373 Katzaras' son John attempted to reclaim the property, but by then the monastery of Docheiariou had acquired Patrikona. At John Katzaras' request Manuel II Palaiologos, then governor of Thessaloniki, ordered three officials – George Doukas Tzykandyles, Laskaris Metochites, and Laskaris Kephalas – to investigate the matter and in February 1373 the three issued their ruling.

In their decision they explained that John Katzaras presented to them the chrysobull of 1351 for his father. However, the monks of Docheiariou argued that it was not George Katzaras but the Varvarenoi soldier company that held Patrikona, and they produced acts of Andronikos III that returned certain properties to the monastery that had been given to the Varvarenoi. This was a bit disingenuous on their part because, while a property adjacent to Patrikona had indeed been confiscated from Docheiariou and given to the Varvarenoi as a pronoia, Patrikona itself, despite the claims of the monks, had never belonged to Docheiariou.[198] Nevertheless, the officials asked John Katzaras "if he had an assessor's conferral giving him and his father unilaterally and personally such 2,400 modioi of land of Patrikona in the *posotes* of his oikonomia and not jointly with his company, the Varvarenoi."[199] He replied that this document was lost "due to the anomalies of the times," a reference to the Serbian occupation of the area. The officials asked if he could produce witnesses to confirm that his father had received Patrikona personally or if, through a visit to the spot, he could mark out the boundaries of the land which he claimed his father had received separately from the Varvarenoi. Evidently owing to the Serbian occupation, John had little familiarity with the property, and he answered negatively to both questions. Therefore, the officials ruled that unless John could produce evidence to support the 1351 chrysobull, Patrikona should remain the property of Docheiariou.

A comparison of the terminology in the two documents allows us to make a few observations. The act from February 1373 notes that the 48 hyperpyra had been "in the *posotes* of his oikonomia," demonstrating that *poson* (which appears in the 1351 chrysobull) and *posotes* were equivalent terms. Also, the 1373 notes that John Katzaras claimed that his father was permitted to hold the land "as his *gonikon*" (ὡς γονικὴν αὐτοῦ), demonstrating that

[197] N. Oikonomides, "Οἱ δύο Σερβικὲς κατακτήσεις τῆς Χαλκιδικῆς τὸν ΙΔ' αἰῶνα," *Δίπτυχα* 2 (1980–81), 294–300.

[198] *Docheiariou*, p. 233.

[199] *Docheiariou*, no. 41.29–32: μονομερῶς καὶ ἰδίως . . . καὶ οὐκ ἡνωμένως, μετὰ τῆς συντροφίας αὐτοῦ, ἤγουν τῶν Βαρβαρηνῶν.

this phrase was equivalent to *kata logon gonikotetos* which appears in the chrysobull (*Docheiariou*, no. 41.31,20).

[8.48] Chrysobull of Andronikos IV Palaiologos for Radoslav Sampias (1378), and Chrysobull of John VII Palaiologos for Radoslav Sampias (1405)

Merely receiving hereditary rights over a pronoia did not automatically grant the beneficiary the right to alienate the property. In November 1378 Radoslav Sampias asked Andronikos IV to confirm his rights on the abandoned villages of Avramitai and Neochorion in the area of Kalamaria which he previously held, to allow him to build a tower there with his own resources, and to transmit these to his legitimate children and heirs. He received a chrysobull granting him the right to improve the properties plus hereditary rights (*kata logon gonikotetos*) over the villages. A poorly preserved passage in the document notes that the heirs would hold the property rendering the "service of our majesty as the father himself."[200] According to a chrysobull from 1405 Sampias asked and received from John VII permission to bequeath half of his property, which he held "as his *gonikon* property" to the monastery of St. Paul, and to transmit the other half to his son, so that on his death, this half as well would pass to the monastery, which would hold it *kata logon gonikotetos*.[201]

Additional rights granted over hereditary property previously held

It is necessary to distinguish cases in which hereditary rights were conceded from those in which further rights were conceded over a grant that was already held in hereditary tenure. While there are only three instances of this (Table 8.10), in each a property rather than a mere *posotes* was involved and each was characterized as a reward. Further, in each case it is not clear that the property involved was ever considered an oikonomia or a pronoia.

[200] F. Dölger, *Aus den Schatzkammern des Heiligen Berges* (Munich, 1948), no. 11.9,16,12: δουλοσ[ύνη]ς τῆς βασιλείας ἡμῶν καθὼς καὶ αὐτὸς ὁ πατὴρ. Line 12 almost certainly parallels ἀποδιδόντα . . . τὴν . . . ὑπὲρ αὐτοῦ δουλείαν καθὼς καὶ ὁ πατὴρ αὐτοῦ κατέχων αὐτό in lines 15–17 of the act for Tarchaneiotes *[8.32]*. Ostrogorsky, *Féodalité*, 128. On the original Slavic form of the name "Sampias," see D. Bubalo, "Ραδοσθλάβος Σάμπιας – Radoslav Sablja," *ZRVI* 44 (2007), 459–63.

[201] Binon, *Les origines légendaires*, 284.2,13. A *prostagma* of 1406 of John VII confirmed St. Paul's rights over these villages: Dölger, *Schatzkammern*, no. 42.

Table 8.10 Additional rights granted over hereditary property previously held

		What was granted?	Drawn from an oikonomia?	Recipient requested	Any tax exemption noted?	"Service" required?	Right to improve noted?	Referred to as a reward?	Right to alienate noted?
1274–82	Demetrios Mourinos *[6.8]*	properties, some with *posotetes*		right to hold property undisturbed and to improve	limited exemption of secondary burdens		yes	yes	yes
1288	Theodore Nomikopoulos *[8.33]*	property		a chrysobull confirming his possession		yes		yes	
1318 or forgery	Manuel Garianos *[8.49]*	property		tax-free status for him and his heirs	full		yes	yes	

[8.49] Chrysobull of Andronikos II Palaiologos for Manuel Garianos, a soldier of the *Serriotikon mega allagion* (1318, or forgery)

An example of this is the grant for the soldier Manuel Garianos found in a document bearing the date 1318 and allegedly issued by Andronikos II. Like the act for Leo Koteanitzes *[8.31]*, the document is either a medieval facsimile of an authentic chrysobull or a forgery. But even in the latter case, the content is worth presenting because someone thought the situation described by the document plausible. According to the document, Andronikos II granted the monk Kallinikos' request on behalf of the king of Serbia Milutin to issue a chrysobull for the sake of Manuel Garianos, a soldier from the *Serriotikon mega allagion*, so that his hereditary property (*gonike hypostasis*) in the village of Evniane (τὴν Hὔνιανην, i.e., Chouniane) would have tax-free status for him and his heirs. The emperor notes that Garianos had been active "in the services of my majesty," and thus permitted him to hold "his hereditary property . . . [tax-]free and unsubjected outside the *poson* of his oikonomia and above all *telos* and charge."[202]

On the face of things, the chrysobull granted a complete tax exemption (*telos* and secondary charges) on hereditary property which the soldier Garianos held outside of his oikonomia (and thus no connection to any imperial grant). It is likely that this property was the same one that Garianos would sell to Hilandar prior to 1321.[203] The purpose of Kallinikos' request, then, would have been to prepare the way for the sale of the *hypostasis* to the Serbian monastery by having the emperor certify that the property was outside Garianos' oikonomia and grant a tax exemption on the property. This would explain Milutin's involvement.

Hereditary rights not granted

Often we read in the documents that a particular property held by a monastery or by a layman was "from the oikonomia of the deceased N." or "earlier held by the deceased N." or simply "earlier held by N." For example, in 1321 Lavra received four *exaleimmatikai staseis* "from the oikonomia of the deceased Hagiotriadites earlier held by the beloved nephew of our

[202] *Chilandar*, ed. Živojinović, I, no. 37.3–7,15–16: τὴν . . . γονικὴν αὐτοῦ ὑπόστασιν . . . ἐλευθέραν καὶ ἀκαταδούλωτον ἐκτὸς τοῦ ποσοῦ τῆς οἰκονομίας αὐτοῦ καὶ ἀνωτέραν παντὸς τέλους καὶ βάρους = Dölger, *Schatzkammern*, no. 50. L. Petit (*Chilandar*, ed. Petit, no. 35) and F. Dölger, *Regesten*, IV, no. 2399, doubted the authenticity of the document, but the recent editors, with reservations, conclude that its content is authentic.

[203] *Chilandar*, ed. Živojinović, I, p. 245.

mighty and holy lord and emperor, *kyr* Constantine Palaiologos," the latter probably being the son of Andronikos II's sister Anna. In the same document Lavra received an *epiteleia* of $3^1/_2$ hyperpyra "which the deceased Hagiotriadites held."[204] In the majority of cases like this, we may assume that the previous holder of the property had not been granted hereditary rights to that particular property. It is reasonable to think that properties that acquired hereditary status would have lost their fungible character as far as pronoiai were concerned. When a pronoia holder died, any properties over which he had received hereditary rights obviously would not be among those returning to the state to be re-dealt to other grant recipients, and when fiscal officials sought properties in a particular area to grant to another beneficiary, they certainly (I think) would turn to properties within oikonomiai which had not received hereditary status before turning to these. Nevertheless, there is always the small possibility that some of these properties that were transferred from one recipient to another had received hereditary status, but they had been confiscated from their holders for some type of disloyalty, poor service, or other offence. It is also a possibility that, even if hereditary rights to the property had been granted to the previous holder, he died without legitimate heir and so the property returned to the state.

However, what we do not know in most of these cases is what caused the previous holder to lose the property. If the previous holder is not designated as deceased (*ekeinos*, as the documents refer to the dead), the transfer may have involved merely an exchange of properties and compensation for the previous holder. Thus, we may assume that Constantine Palaiologos, "the beloved nephew" of Andronikos II in the example above, was compensated with something else because we know he was alive in 1321. Alternatively, other living previous holders may have simply lost their properties due to any number of reasons: disloyalty, poor service, illegally acquiring land, illegally alienating property, and so on. When the previous holder is designated as deceased, we might tend to assume the loss occurred because of his death, but it is also possible that he died after the transfer took place and the transfer occurred for other reasons. Indeed, when the previous holder is not specifically designated as deceased, this does not necessarily mean he was still alive.

Even in cases for which we have more information, it is difficult to conclude that hereditary rights were not granted over a particular property. The praktikon for Alexios Komnenos Raoul from ca. 1297 is a case in point

[204] *Lavra*, II, no. 111.20–22,28–29. On Constantine, see *Lavra*, II, p. 281, and *PLP*, no. 21495. Other examples: *[7.8] [8.9] [8.45]* and *Xénophon*, no. 15.9,12,14–15,26.

[8.15]. Raoul's oikonomia consisted at least of the village of Prevista and other properties on the lower Strymon. The *megas domestikos* Alexios Raoul died in 1303. Prevista eventually passed to the *megale doukaina* Theodora Palaiologina who sold it to the ruler of Bulgaria, Michael Asen, in 1325. Asen in turn donated it to Zographou. Since Theodora Palaiologina was no direct relation of Raoul, it would appear that Raoul did not receive hereditary rights over his oikonomia prior to his death.[205] And yet, while Raoul's family (and he did appear to have children) did not hold Prevista in 1325, we cannot say for certain that hereditary rights to Prevista were not granted to Raoul. Raoul died in battle, and we may assume his family would have requested continued possession of Prevista. What happened to Prevista between 1303 and 1325 is anyone's guess.[206]

[8.50] Act of George Doukas Troulenos involving his pronoia (1304)

Nevertheless, there are two cases during Andronikos II's reign where we can safely say that hereditary rights were not granted over someone's oikonomia. One involves the oikonomia of George Doukas Troulenos. We recall that in 1318 Troulenos was granted hereditary rights over two properties totaling 1,600 modioi "within the amount" of his oikonomia near Serres *[8.37]*. An act from 1304 explains where this oikonomia had come from: "through a . . . *prostagma* of our . . . emperor the pronoia of the deceased Ameras was granted to me." At that time Troulenos found himself in a property dispute with a man named Vatatzes, the son-in-law of Ameras through a stepdaughter of the deceased. Vatatzes had appropriated some fields which Troulenos believed were within the pronoia. Even though he had given Troulenos some *exaleimmatika* fields in exchange, Troulenos took the matter to the court of the empress Irene, which decided the matter in Vatatzes' favor. In his act, Troulenos agreed to abide by its decision.[207]

[205] Mavrommatis, "La pronoia d'Alexis Comnène Raoul," 213–19, line 3, and pp. 204–07. On Raoul, see S. Fassoulakis, *The Byzantine Family of Raoul-Ral(l)es* (Athens, 1973), 28–29, no. 13, and *PLP*, no. 24109.

[206] Mavrommatis, "La pronoia d'Alexis Comnène Raoul," 211, suggested that, after a period of vacancy, Prevista was granted to Theodora Palaiologina and her husband, the Catalan Ferran Ximenes de Arenos, at the time of their wedding around 1308, when Ferran was granted the title *megas doux*, but actually we have no idea when, prior to 1325, Theodora acquired Prevista.

[207] *Prodrome B*, no. 160.1–2. The name Ameras is otherwise unattested in late Byzantium, but a document from 1301 mentions a field τοῦ Ἀμυρᾶ in the same area: *Prodrome B*, no. 18.9. For a Demetrios Amoiras, see *PLP*, no. 796: landholder on the Chalkidike, 1312–21.

Thus, the property contained within Troulenos' pronoia had not passed to Ameras' son-in-law or any other heir of Ameras. Nevertheless, the fact that a (somewhat distant) relative of Ameras successfully disputed the content of Troulenos' pronoia indicates that Ameras held some property that should not have passed to Troulenos as part of his pronoia grant. After the litigation, this property passed to Ameras' son-in-law. Ameras may have simply purchased these fields or acquired them some other way, but there is the possibility that they were originally part of Ameras' pronoia before being transformed into a hereditary possession through an imperial concession.

One can imagine how easily these disputes might arise. An emperor grants a pronoia holder hereditary rights to part of his pronoia. This part is expressed as a monetary quantity, a *posotes*. The pronoia holder equates that *posotes* with a particular group of his properties, presumably the choicest parcels, and fiscal officials document the transformation. Yet, with the passage of time, the grant holder or his heirs might prefer that a different collection of properties receive the hereditary privilege. The death of the grant holder and the reassignment of his pronoia without the change being documented could easily give rise to a dispute between the heirs and the new pronoia holder.

Another clear example of hereditary rights not being granted over an oikonomia is found in a series of documents which deal with the transfer of a small village (*agridion*) from the soldier Nikephoros Martinos to the monastery of St. John Prodromos. A pair of *prostagmata* from 1325 explicitly note that Martinos was to be compensated with another *posotes* equal to that of the agridion (thirty hyperpyra) and describe how he should be compensated *[8.75]*. One of these *prostagmata*, from April 1325, explains,

> Since the oikonomia . . . which the husband of the daughter of the deceased Rhomaios, called Sarakenos, held, being of a *posotes* . . . of eighty hyperpyra, [and] which the wife of the deceased [Rhomaios] held recently contrary to *orismos* of my majesty [παρ' ὁρισμὸν τῆς βασιλείας μου], receiving [it] by marriage unlawfully into her hands,

the emperor ordered that a *posotes* of thirty hyperpyra from the eighty be conferred upon Martinos and the rest returned to the fisc until the emperor decided what to do with it.[208]

The other *prostagma*, from October or November 1325, states that Martinos should receive his thirty hyperpyra "from the oikonomia which the daughter of the deceased Rhomaios held around Serres," but then, in later

[208] *Prodrome*, no. 16.28–36 = *Prodrome B*, no. 207.30–38. Both Guillou, in his summary of the act, and Dölger, *Regesten*, IV, no. 2526, interpret ἡ γυνὴ ἐκείνου as "the daughter of the deceased Rhomaios."

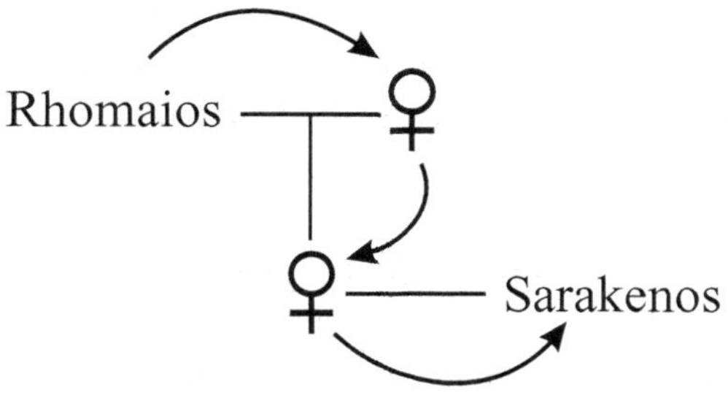

Figure 8.2 Path of the illegal transmission of an oikonomia.

passages, it mentions "the said oikonomia of the deceased Rhomaios" and "the oikonomia of Rhomaios."[209] These phrases make it clear that the oikonomia, originally held by the deceased Rhomaios, improperly passed to his widow, and then to his daughter and son-in-law Sarakenos (Figure 8.2).

Alexander Kazhdan wrote that these documents show that women could hold pronoiai.[210] Actually, this depends, in part, on the content of the order which the transmission violated ("contrary to *orismos* of my majesty"). This order, which is not preserved, forbade the transmission of Rhomaios' oikonomia to his widow, or, perhaps, to anyone. Yet the mere fact that Rhomaios' widow had held her dead husband's oikonomia for a time and passed it on to her daughter suggests, whether or not it was an illegal act, that it was not an unheard-of scenario. In any event, for whatever reason, the emperors did not permit Rhomaios' oikonomia of eighty hyperpyra to pass to his wife, his daughter, or to his son-in-law Sarakenos. Rather, part of it went to compensate another holder of an oikonomia and the rest was ordered returned to the fisc.

Observations

A few observations may be made. First, the examples cited of pronoia holders who received hereditary rights over their oikonomiai include very few men who are actually called "soldiers." Many of the men who were granted this privilege were titled aristocrats (judge of the army, *megas adnoumiastes*, *hetaireiarches*, *eparchos*), men whom I regard as military leaders (if they had any military competence), and whom I would exclude from a definition

[209] *Prodrome*, no. 17.10–11,15–16,25–26,29–30 = *Prodrome B*, no. 208.11–12,16–17,27,31.

[210] Kazhdan, review of Ostrogorsky, *Féodalité*, in *VizVrem* 10 (1956), 224. Also, see Ostrogorsky, *Féodalité*, 131, 147–49, and Laiou, "The Byzantine Aristocracy in the Palaeologan Period," 145.

of "soldier." It stands to reason that the list of men who received special privileges from the emperor would be biased toward the higher social levels. Nevertheless, since the Klazomenitai soldiers received hereditary rights over rather small *posotetes [8.4]*, we may assume that it was not uncommon for soldiers to hold hereditary pronoiai.

As Ostrogorsky noted long ago, the civil wars of the 1340s contributed to this tendency to transform pronoiai into hereditary possessions.[211] From the reign of Michael VIII through 1378 there are twenty-four more or less authentic documents issued by Byzantine authorities that deal with the granting of hereditary rights over an imperial grant held by an individual or group of individuals. Of these twenty-four documents, eight were issued during the six-year period from 1342 to 1347, the era of the civil war between John VI Kantakouzenos and the regency for John V Palaiologos.

Further, there is no evidence that an emperor ever granted someone hereditary rights to a grant without a continuing service obligation. Those few documents that refer to someone holding a property "without service" are referring to a fiscal exemption, not to personal service.[212] On the other hand, it seems that hereditary grants "with service," while never automatic, became common, particularly since they cost the state little.

Also, we note that the *posotes* or land granted in hereditary tenure is described as "from the oikonomia" of the pronoia holder, or more specifically, "inside the value of his oikonomia," which, in my view, means that the custom was to grant hereditary rights over fractions of the oikonomia. Indeed in the cases of Demetrios Devlitzenos and Michael Monomachos, hereditary rights were granted over 25 and 50 percent, respectively, of their oikonomiai.

On the whole, Ostrogorsky was correct when he wrote that pronoiai that became hereditary did not cease being pronoiai, that the only rights the pronoia holder received "in the manner of patrimony" (*kata logon gonikotetos*) were the right of amelioration and the right to transmit the grant to his legitimate heirs. Service of some sort (though not necessarily military service as Ostrogorsky wrote) remained. And the explicit demand for continued service generally appears only when a whole grant became hereditary.[213] Thus, in the fourteenth century the conditional character of pronoiai was not based on the absence of hereditary rights but on a continuing service obligation.

211 Ostrogorsky, *Féodalité*, 123.

212 Cf. Oikonomides, "Notes," 339, who wrote that the oikonomiai of John Margarites and Michael Monomachos ceased to be pronoiai because service was no longer demanded.

213 Ostrogorsky, *Féodalité*, 133–35.

There is some evidence to the contrary. Eudokia, the daughter of the deceased Komnenoutzikos, wrote that the oikonomia which the emperor had granted to her father and then had passed "from him to me" was held by her "in absolute ownership" *[8.21]*. Eudokia's claim that her oikonomia was private property is understandable in light of the fact that she was donating the property and paroikoi involved to a monastery. The state always wanted to think that it was in control of the things it granted to private parties, and these private parties always wanted to believe that they had control over these same things. The handful of documents linking continued personal service to the holding of a hereditary grant suggests that Eudokia was incorrect, that oikonomiai which became hereditary were not the property of the beneficiary (or, at least, not "full" property). And in this case, when there is a discrepancy in principles espoused by a private act and official acts, one ought to rely on the testimony of the official documents.

Yet there is also the 1319/20 document issued by the fiscal official Manglavites for John Orestes which distinguishes between Orestes' oikonomia and the *posotes* of six hyperpyra extracted from his oikonomia over which he received hereditary rights *[8.42]*. The *posotes* of six hyperpyra was "outside the amount [*poson*] of his oikonomia," which might indicate that the portion of an oikonomia that became hereditary was no longer part of an oikonomia. But because the document envisions not only these six hyperpyra but all of Orestes' oikonomia passing to a son of Orestes, there was little difference in fact between the two. From a legal point of view, the six-hyperpyra *posotes*, as *gonikon*, was now the property of Orestes and, should he have a son, it would be the property of the son, while the oikonomia from which it was drawn was not Orestes' property nor, under the conditions of Manglavites' act, would it be the property of the son to whom it was expected to pass. But service would be owed from the son as from the father. Was Eudokia's situation unique, or was Orestes'?

In any event, the real test of whether property granted by the emperor belonged to the recipient was whether the recipient had the right to alienate the property through sale, donation, or gift. What one may dispose of, one owns. And now we turn to the ultimate additional right conferred on pronoiai – the right to alienate the grant.

Additional rights – the right to alienate

Restrictions on the alienation of oikonomiai

The documents provide many relatively mundane examples of people buying and selling and donating property. Generally, individuals had the right to donate (or sell) property they had inherited or purchased legitimately.[214] This was not the case with pronoiai. There was a basic principle against the alienation of state property in Byzantium, and this included pronoiai/oikonomiai. Thus, it was generally forbidden to alienate one's oikonomia in whole or in part.[215] Because the emperor had granted the oikonomia, he wished to maintain control over it, to have it directed toward the goal to which he intended.

Even without corroborating evidence, logic would dictate that if the emperor permitted, as a matter of course, the beneficiaries of imperial grants to sell or otherwise alienate the properties within these grants, the grants would lose their utility as a means of financing imperial service, especially military service. Since we know that a large percentage, probably the majority, of oikonomia holders were soldiers, it is inconceivable that such men, as a rule, could have been permitted to alienate any part of their grants. As Kantakouzenos wrote, those soldiers who had not kept their pronoia grants intact neglected military service thus "depriving the state of the benefit from them" *[8.26]*.

[8.51] Act of Constantine Makrenos for the monastery of Xenophon involving the oikonomia of the Sarantenoi (1335)

There are a couple of explicit statements from the documents that confirm that, as a rule, it was improper to alienate oikonomiai and several other passages that imply this. In a document from July 1335 the fiscal official Constantine Makrenos, in the course of conducting a fiscal survey in the area from Christoupolis (Kavala) and westward, writes, "According to the *orismos*

[214] Nevertheless, under the name *plesiasmos*, the rules of preemption (protimesis) in acquiring and alienating property persisted into the late period: e.g., *Iviron*, III, no. 73; *Vatopédi*, I, no. 54; *Docheiariou*, nos. 42–44; and see *ODB*, s.v. "protimesis."

[215] The lone dissenting voice on this matter was that of Alexander Kazhdan. In his *Agrarnye otnošenija*, 219, he argued that it was not prohibited to alienate pronoiai by citing three examples: (i) The 1325 sale of the village of Prevista by the *megale doukaina* Theodora Palaiologina to Michael Asen of Bulgaria who then donated the village to Zographou. Prevista had a *posotes* of 300 hyperpyra, but it is not referred to as an oikonomia or pronoia. Theodora, or perhaps her husband, was granted Prevista by the emperor, but we do not know under what terms – oikonomia or a simple gift. But even if it was an oikonomia, the transaction was explicitly sanctioned by the emperor: *Zographou*, no. 22.5. (ii) The case of the *hegoumenos* Gervasios who received an oikonomia of forty hyperpyra. However, the emperor granted Gervasios the right to alienate the oikonomia to whomever he desired *[7.9]*. (iii) A case in which Kazhdan claimed that the Prodromos monastery received an oikonomia of 100 hyperpyra as a donation from a private person: Solovjev–Mošin, *Grčke povelje*, no. 2.91–94 (1345) = *Prodrome*, no. 39. However, the references to the oikonomia and to the donation are in two different clauses and unrelated save that all the properties involved were located in the same village.

to me of the . . . emperor ordering me that if I find from some oikonomiai something sold or donated from them, I should seize it and confiscate it at once [καὶ δημοσιεύσω αὐτὸ παρευθύς]." On the basis of this he had planned to take several properties away from the monastery of Xenophon because they had passed to the monastery from the oikonomia of the Sarantenoi brothers who had held them through a chrysobull. However, when he learned that the monastery had received these properties through a donation of the Sarantenoi more than twenty years earlier, that the monastery's possession of these properties had been confirmed by a chrysobull, and that the monks had effected ameliorations on the properties, he decided to confirm the monks' "hereditary" possession of the properties. And so, while in this case the donation of properties from an imperial grant seems to have been sanctioned, albeit grudgingly, the operative principle was that such alienations were illegal by their nature.[216]

It is noteworthy that a donation confirmed by a chrysobull could be declared invalid years later. Aside from illustrating the weak nature of property rights in Byzantium, it shows us that the existence of a chrysobull confirming a transaction was not necessarily proof of the legality of the transaction, at least in the eyes of a later emperor. While Andronikos II might not have confirmed the donation if he had known the origin of the property, clearly Andronikos III had adopted a new policy, or at least a more stringent enforcement of traditional policy. It would seem that, from a technical point of view, it was improper to donate property from one's oikonomia, though the cases at our disposal suggest that this policy was not consistently enforced.

There is one example that appears to illustrate the problems such donations created. After a number of soldier-archons donated 600 modioi of *exaleimmatike ge* to Docheiariou, the *apographeus* Kontenos made an arrangement with the monks of Docheiariou whereby they were permitted to keep the land, but agreed to pay an *epiteleia* of 10 hyperpyra to a man for 330 modioi of the land *[8.19]*. The principal at work here is fairly clear. The original donations of the soldiers were improper, evidently because the properties involved were part of the soldiers' oikonomiai. Nevertheless, rather than confiscating the properties from the monastery, the *apographeus*

216 *Xénophon*, no. 23, esp. lines 7–9, and see pp. 45 and 175 where it is pointed out that since these properties are not mentioned in Xenophon's praktikon of 1338 (*Xénophon*, no. 25), it is possible that Makrenos' decision was overruled. Ostrogorsky, *Féodalité*, 152–54. This original donation was confirmed by Andronikos II in February 1322 in a chrysobull confirming all of the possessions of Xenophon: *Xénophon*, no. 17.53–54. The restriction on alienating pronoiai is found in Serbia as well: see Bartusis, "Serbian Pronoia," 183–84, 190–91, 207, 210–11.

opted for a compromise. The monks would pay a charge (*epiteleia*) on part of the property, which would at least partially make up for the loss of revenues to the state. This *epiteleia*, rather than being paid to the fisc, was paid to an individual and constituted part of his oikonomia.

[8.52] Act of sale of Demetrios Doukas Souloumpertes and his wife, residents of Melnik (1344)

The other document which refers to a general prohibition to alienate parts of oikonomiai is an act of sale from April 1344. Demetrios Doukas Souloumpertes and his wife, residents of the town of Melnik, sold a piece of arable land "from our oikonomia" to a monastery located in Melnik. In the act of sale they explain that while "in other places and towns the selling of *hypostaseis* from any oikonomiai is normally completely forbidden, in our town of Melnik by imperial *orismos* for a long time it was conceded and agreed to." Consequently, according to the arrangement established by the emperor, the natives of Melnik "daily" sold *hypostaseis* "from oikonomiai [which were] perhaps *stratiotikai*."[217] *Stratiotikai* ("military") oikonomiai were obviously those held by soldiers in return for military service.

The privileges enjoyed by the inhabitants of Melnik date back to 1246 when John III Vatatzes issued a chrysobull on their behalf prior to the town submitting to him.[218] Similar privileges are found in other "common chrysobulls" (as the sources call them) known to have been issued for the inhabitants of a number of towns: Thessaloniki, Verrhoia, Phanarion in Thessaly, Kroai in Albania, Monemvasia, Ioannina, and Rentina. Generally, these chrysobulls granted tax exemption to the properties held by the inhabitants of the privileged town and further granted the inhabitants the right to transmit the properties and the tax exemption to their heirs. The praktikon for John Margarites discussed earlier in this chapter *[8.17]* refers to such a privilege. Margarites was to enjoy his *posotes* of fifty-five hyperpyra "as the other inhabitants of the God-saved city of Thessaloniki hold their *gonika* properties." Evidently, they had received complete tax exemption and the right to alienate not only their *gonika* to whomever they wished, but

[217] *Vatopédi*, II, no. 88.2–3: ἐν ἄλλοις μὲν τόποις καὶ πόλεσι τὸ ἐξ οἰκονομιῶν τινῶν ὑποστασεις πιπράσκεσθαι πάντη κατο εἰκὸς ἀπηγόρευται· ἐν τῇ καθ᾽ ἡμᾶς δε τοῦ Μελενίκου πόλει ἐκ βασιλικοῦ ὁρισμοῦ ἀνέκαθεν ὡς λόγος ἐξεδόθη καὶ συγκεχώρηται, and lines 4–5: ἐκ στρατιωτικ[ῶν] δήπου οἰκονομιῶν.

[218] Akropolites, *Georgii Acropolitae Opera*, ed. A. Heisenberg (Leipzig, 1903; repr. Stuttgart, 1978), 77.

the tax exemption as well.[219] Otherwise, mere *gonikon* status seems to have included only the right to improve the properties and to transmit them to legitimate heirs.

Nevertheless, none of the other grants of privileges to towns suggests that their inhabitants had the right to alienate parts of their oikonomiai. In fact the specific privilege mentioned in the 1344 act of sale – the right to sell part of one's oikonomia – could not have been granted in a chrysobull issued by John Vatatzes, because in Vatatzes' day there was no such thing as an "oikonomia." It had to have been a later emperor – Michael VIII or Andronikos II – who, by *orismos* as the document notes, added oikonomiai to the sources of property which the inhabitants could sell. The fact that this was the policy "for a long time" combined with Andronikos III's hard-line position about oikonomiai probably excludes him as the author of such an *orismos*.

Demetrios Kyritsis suggested in his overview of these common chrysobulls that it is difficult to imagine that most of the empire's European towns enjoyed the privileges conferred by these common chrysobulls.[220] But it would be harder still to imagine that many towns enjoyed this specific privilege held by the inhabitants of Melnik, the right to sell properties within oikonomiai. Permitting soldiers to alienate parts of their oikonomiai would have led to the situation Kantakouzenos describes. What were the consequences for a soldier who liquidated his oikonomia and then did not have the resources to fulfill his military obligation? One wonders what the inhabitants of Melnik had done to merit such a concession. The history of the city during the Palaiologan era is poorly known, but we can note that the town remained loyal to Andronikos II during the civil wars of the 1320s. The residents recognized Andronikos III as emperor only in 1332, when Andronikos II died, four years after the latter's abdication.[221]

The information provided by the 1344 act of sale raises questions about the legal status of oikonomiai. Normally, when an oikonomia included real property, as it usually did, it could be said that the emperor conferred merely the right of usufruct and possession, as distinct from ownership, and that is why it was not permissible to alienate it. Mere possession, usufruct, or use never included the right to alienate the property, at least not in traditional Roman law. But if the inhabitants of Melnik had been granted the right to sell property within their oikonomiai, this situation would no longer have

219 Lemerle, "Un praktikon inédit," 281–86, line 44. Hvostova, *Osobennosti*, 213. See Kyritsis, "The 'Common Chrysobulls' of Cities," 232–33.

220 Kyritsis, "The 'Common Chrysobulls' of Cities," 241 note 52.

221 T. Vlachos, *Die Geschichte der byzantinischen Stadt Melenikon* (Thessaloniki, 1969), 52.

applied. Once part or all of an oikonomia was sold, it was no longer the property of the state but of the buyer. And according to the principle that one cannot transfer a right that one does not have, it would appear that the owner of the oikonomia was the holder of the oikonomia, not the state. The conferral of the right to alienate a grant implied the conferral of the right of ownership.

Given the legal complications caused by granting the right to alienate oikonomiai to these residents of Melnik, I wonder whether the properties and privileges they – and the residents of other towns that perhaps received similar concessions – held in their oikonomiai had not been held by them before becoming oikonomiai. It would make a great deal of sense for the Nicaean emperors and Michael VIII, as they conquered Thrace and Macedonia, to make special arrangements with the residents of towns that capitulated to them. Allow most of them to keep their property – whatever the original source – but demand, as a sign of loyalty to the new ruler, that the property be held henceforth as an oikonomia (a "fief de reprise" in the terminology of the medieval West). This hypothesis would complicate further the theoretical underpinnings of the ownership of oikonomiai (creating a kind of dual *dominium*), but in practice it would explain how the residents of Melnik could be permitted to alienate their oikonomiai.

If all of the property held by a resident of Melnik was part of the resident's oikonomia, the alienation of part of this property would not affect the resident's obligations, military or otherwise, toward the emperor. As long as the resident continued to hold any part of his property holdings, the emperor could continue to demand service.

Conditional donations

[8.53] Donation of Peter Doukopoulos to the monastery of Iviron (1292)

In a few cases, a donor indicates that the property he was donating was part of his oikonomia, and he acknowledges that he did not have the right to make a complete alienation. In 1292 the *sevastos* Peter Doukopoulos donated a mill he had built himself, along with its neighboring garden and trees, to the monastery of Iviron. However, the transfer was complicated by the fact that the mill was "in the area of the village named Daphne belonging to me in pronoia of the . . . emperor," and "the ground of the said water mill and its rights are subject yearly to a tax of two hyperpyra," as recorded in the act of conferral by which Doukopoulos received the village. In other words, the land on which the mill stood was part of Doukopoulos' pronoia. This land had been assessed a tax (*telos*) of two hyperpyra which formed part of Doukopoulos' *posotes.* Clearly the monks were concerned that Doukopoulos might demand these two hyperpyra from them. To put them at ease, he explains, "I allowed the monastery henceforth these [hyperpyra], so that it not be taxed, not forever, but as long as I myself am numbered among the living and this village . . . is held by me."[222] Doukopoulos was aware of the temporary nature of his tenure of his pronoia. Any arrangement he made with the monastery regarding the tax for the land on which the mill stood was valid only as long as he lived and as long as he held his pronoia.

[8.54] Donation to the monastery of Docheiariou by an unknown individual (1313)

While it is possible that Doukopoulos envisioned merely that the monastery might be required to pay the two hyperpyra annually after his death or he lost his oikonomia, other donors indicate that the donation itself was of limited duration. In 1313 a man (the portion of the document that furnished his name is lost) gave the monastery of Docheiariou some *exaleimmatika* fields and a vineyard at Hermeleia on the Chalkidike, which were "held by me in the mercy of the . . . emperor." The donation was to be valid "as long as the pronoia is held by me and my children."[223] Nicolas Oikonomides, who edited the document, suggested that the mere reference to "children" and not something more general, such as "heirs," implies that hereditary rights to pronoiai were at first granted only to the first generation of the pronoia holder's heirs. In practice, this certainly meant little, for the next generation, twenty or thirty years hence, would demand the same concession for *its* children, on the basis of precedent. Nevertheless, the legal fiction could be maintained that the rights granted in pronoia forever belonged to the state and remained under the state's control.

The conditional nature of this donation, that it was to be valid as long as the donor and his children held the oikonomia, confirms the fact that oikonomiai were not transferable, and that, in order to satisfy the pious desires of some oikonomia holders, a legal means had to be found to alienate portions of an oikonomia without it technically appearing as such. How does

222 *Iviron*, III, no. 66.8–9,23–26.

223 *Docheiariou*, no. 13.3–4,6–7: μέχρις ἂν δηλαδὴ παρ' ἐμοῦ καὶ τῶν παίδων μου ἡ πρόνοια κατέχηται. Ks. Hvostova, "Pronija: social'no-ekonomičeskie i pravovye problemy," *VizVrem* 49 (1988), 20.

this document accord with the process described in the documents for John Sgouros Orestes *[8.42–8.43]*? The property donated by the individual in 1313 complied with one of three scenarios:

(i) The property was part of the individual's oikonomia and had not been privileged with hereditary rights (paralleling all of the properties within John Orestes' grant before a *posotes* of six hyperpyra was separated by Manglavites).

(ii) The property was part of his oikonomia and had been privileged with limited hereditary rights (paralleling the properties within the *posotes* separated from Orestes' oikonomia at the time of Manglavites' act).

(iii) The property had been separated from his oikonomia and privileged with rights to transmit as he pleased (paralleling the situation of the properties within the *posotes* of six hyperpyra after the issuance of the 1323 chrysobull).

Scenario (iii) can be dismissed because, if the individual had an unlimited right to transfer the property, the donation would not have been conditional on whether he and his children continued to hold the pronoia. As for scenarios (i) and (ii), we do not have sufficient data to choose between them. Under scenario (i) the donation was technically illegal; certainly if the individual or his children lost the pronoia, the donation would have been invalidated. Yet this scenario assumes that the individual anticipated that his children would continue to hold his pronoia. Scenario (ii) may be more likely, positing that the individual had been given the right to transfer this particular property to his children. Nevertheless, the donation of the property to a monastery, based on the restrictions imposed upon Orestes in the act of Manglavites, would still have been illegitimate. In either case there was an anticipation of the granting of hereditary rights to imperial grants.

[8.55] Donation to the monastery of Docheiariou by two men (1314)

A similar document was issued the following year. Again the names of the donors are lost, but the use of the dual form throughout the document indicates that two men were involved, who were evidently joint oikonomia holders and, according to Oikonomides, quite likely brothers. In 1314 the pair donated some fields they held "pronoiastically" (προνοιαστικῶς), also at Hermeleia, to the monastery of Docheiariou. They state that the donation was to be valid "as long as our pronoia is held by us both," thereby maintaining the fiction that the alienation was not absolute.[224]

Implied restrictions

[8.56] Donation of Michael Elaiodorites Spanopoulos, *stratopedarches* of the *allagia*, to the monastery of the Spelaiotissa at Melnik (ca.1300)

There are also occasional passages in the documents in which the donors or sellers themselves imply that there were restrictions to alienating property held within an oikonomia. One manifestation of this are the details the donor or seller provides about the property's origin or the manner by which he held the property. For example, in an act of donation, dated by its editors only to the end of the thirteenth or early fourteenth century, the *sevastos* Michael Elaiodorites Spanopoulos, *stratopedarches* of the *allagia* (i.e., most likely a military officer), points out that the mill in the market (*emporion*) of Melnik that he was donating to the monastery of the Spelaiotissa at Melnik was not part of his oikonomia. He writes that the monks ought to hold the mill "without harassment and inviolate, as I myself held this in the manner of *gonikon* outside the *poson* of my oikonomia."[225] According to the act of sale of Demetrios Doukas Souloumpertes and his wife *[8.52]* residents of Melnik had the right to sell parts of their oikonomiai in 1344. On the face of things, the residents of Melnik probably received permission to alienate parts of their oikonomiai *after* the time of Spanopoulos' act or else Spanopoulos need not have specified that the property was not part of his oikonomia.

[8.57] Contract of sale between Symeon Madarites and his family and the monastery of St. John Prodromos near Serres (1310)

In a number of examples the seller or donor of a property notes that the property originated as an imperial grant, but emphasizes that he inherited the property, which apparently was evidence that he had the right to alienate it. Often the donors or sellers employ the "mercy of the emperor" phrase

[224] *Docheiariou*, no. 14.1,6: μέχρις ἂν παρ' ἡμῶν ἀμφοτέρων ἡ ἡμῶν κατέχηται πρόνοια. Oikonomides, "A propos des armées," 367. Hvostova, "Pronija," 20.

[225] *Vatopédi*, I, no. 21.3,4–5: καθῶς εἶχον καγῶ τοῦτο γονικῶθεν ἐκτὸς τοῦ ποσοῦ τῆς οἰκονομίας μου.

that was introduced in the previous chapter (above, pp. 321–23). Thus, in 1310 when Symeon Madarites, along with his wife and children, sold a field of thirty modioi to the monastery of St. John Prodromos for 200 hyperpyra, he stated, "I confer upon the said divine monastery our *gonikon* field which is [tax-]free and unsubjected [to the fisc], not liable for any burden, ours from ancestors from the mercy toward us of our mighty and holy lords and emperors."[226] Evidently, this field originated as an imperial grant to one of Madarites' ancestors and Madarites inherited it.

[8.58] Donation of Arsenios Tzamplakon to the monastery of Vatopedi (1355)

In another case the monk Arsenios Tzamplakon describes the property along with paroikoi he was donating to the monastery of Vatopedi in 1355 as "from my ancestral properties" (ἀπὸ τῶν γονικῶν μου κτημάτων). He writes that the monastery should hold it "as [tax-]free and from patrimony, as I myself held these things from the mercy toward me of the . . . emperor." He explains that he inherited the property from his father, who acquired it from *his* father, a *domestikos* of the *scholai*, who received it originally from John III Vatatzes through a chrysobull.[227]

[8.59] Donation of Germanos Kladon and Demetrios Rouphinos to the monastery of St. John Prodromos near Serres (1301)

In one case a donor specifically notes that the property donated had been a "gift." In 1301 the monk Germanos Kladon and his son-in-law Demetrios Rouphinos donated a field of three *zeugaria* to the monastery of St. John Prodromos "belonging to us from a gift [*apo doreas*] and mercy of our . . . emperor."[228] The field clearly originated as an imperial grant but, in this case, the use of the word "gift" suggests that the field was not part of an oikonomia. While these donors may have added the phrase to legitimize their donation, the appearance of the word *dorea* ("gift," but also "grant") or a related word does not prove that we are not dealing with a pronoia. In an act composed by George Doukas Troulenos in 1304 he writes that a pronoia "was granted to me" using the verb *doroumai* (δωροῦμαι) *[8.50]*. Even an emperor employed this usage *[5.6] [6.1]*.

[226] *Prodrome B*, no. 19.32–36.

[227] *Vatopédi*, II, no. 105.8,22–23: ὡς ελεύθερα καὶ ἐκ γονικόθεν, καθὼς κατεῖχον καὶ αὐτὸς ταῦτα ἀπὸ τῆς πρὸς ἐμὲ ἐλεημοσύνης τοῦ . . . βασιλέως.

[228] *Prodrome B*, no. 18.6–7.

[8.60] Donation of the nun Eugenia to the monastery of the Lemviotissa (1261)

Here and in other cases (e.g., *[8.21]*), the "mercy" phrase seems to indicate little more than that the property being donated originated as some kind of imperial grant. The phrase by itself could hardly justify the alienation of the property and so other information is provided. However, in a number of cases, people donate to monasteries property that was clearly part of an imperial grant without giving any indication of what right they had to do this. Such was the case of the *protovestiaritissa* Irene, widow of George Zagarommates and now a nun named Eugenia who donated a paroikos to the Lemviotissa monastery in 1261 "along with all the rights I hold through my praktikon from the mercy of our mighty and holy lords and emperors for the sake of their spiritual salvation and ours." She and her husband had received this paroikos and other property from John III Vatatzes but the circumstances are unknown. Perhaps the statement that the donation was partly for the "spiritual salvation" of the emperors was an attempt to legitimize the transfer. This document provides the earliest extant example of the use of the "mercy" phrase.[229]

[8.61] Donation of the *megas domestikos* Alexios Raoul to the monastery of St. John Prodromos near Serres (1337)

A couple of documents use the "mercy" phrase in a slightly different way, suggesting that it indicated permission to alienate property. For example, the phrase takes on a more powerful sense, indicating the legitimate authority by which a donation was being made, in a 1337 act of donation in which the *megas domestikos* Alexios Raoul donated property to the monastery of St. John Prodromos. He writes, "I confer . . . from the mercy toward me of the . . . emperor" two properties, one of which, a field with *exaleimmata* "which recently the . . . emperor granted to me as a benefaction."[230] While

[229] MM, IV, 236.18–20, and for two other examples, see *Vatopédi*, II, no. 75.1–2, and *[6.5]*. A praktikon from 1235 mentions fields in the plain of Memaniomenos which John III Vatatzes granted to the *protovestiarites* Zagarommates: MM, IV, 11. In 1253 Irene donated one of these fields – not entirely voluntarily – to Lemviotissa: MM, IV, 232–33. The closest example I can find to the "mercy" phrase prior to 1261 is a request of the monks of Patmos from 1145 (*Patmos*, I, no. 19.3): "along with all the other mercies of which he [Alexios I Komnenos] showed to us, he granted to us an *exkousseia* of twelve paroikoi" (καὶ μετὰ τῶν ἄλλων δὲ πασῶν ἐλεημοσυνῶν, ὧν πρὸς ἡμᾶς ἐνδείξατο . . .).

[230] *Prodrome B*, no. 123.4–6,9–10: ὅπερ μοι ἀρτίως εὐηργέτησεν ὁ . . . βασιλεύς. On this Alexios Raoul, who is to be distinguished from the recipient of the praktikon from around 1297 *[8.15]*, *see PLP*, no. 24111. There is a possibility that this act was issued in 1352, in which case the "emperor" referred to would have been Stefan Dušan.

the use of the verb *euergeto* ("to confer as a benefaction") can be used in connection with normal oikonomiai, in this case "mercy" could well be translated as "permission." The donor was making it clear that the property was not part of his oikonomia.

Similarly, in an act of donation from May 1331 Demetrios Kavasilas gave Vatopedi two *staseis* near Hermeleia: "I confer from the mercy I have of our mighty and holy lord and emperor upon the . . . monastery [of Vatopedi] . . . the *stasia* which I have in Hermeleia" (*Vatopédi*, II, no. 72.1–3). He identifies these as the *stasia* of Tripanes (or Trypanes) and Kekeris, which have interesting histories. From other documents we know that Demetrios Plytos had been granted these *stasia* in 1322/3 *[7.15]*. In 1325 Plytos was dead and a fiscal official granted the monastery of Xenophon's request to lease these *stasia* in return for an annual payment (ἐκλαβέσθαι ἐπὶ κεφαλαίω) which the monastery would make to a person designated by the official. The official conferred the *stasia* on the monastery and granted it eternal possession of them.[231] Nevertheless, for unknown reasons, the properties passed to Kavasilas who donated them to Vatopedi. Kavasilas' statement of transfer, as quoted above, reads like an act of a fiscal official conferring land on a monastery. Were it not for his assertion that he held these *stasia* (and that he was donating them for the sake of his salvation), we might confuse this with an official act. In any event, the "mercy of the emperor" in this document indicates that Kavasilas had permission to make the transfer.

[8.62] Donation of the *tzaousios* George Melissenos to the monastery of the Lemviotissa (1284)

Often it is quite difficult to distinguish oikonomiai from actual patrimony when dealing with donations and other alienations of property. One can easily fall into the trap of assuming that alienated property must not have been part of an oikonomia because it was alienated or assuming that evidence of an alienation necessarily implies a lawful alienation. For the latter, even the implicit approval suggested by the listing of a donation in the praktikon of a monastery cannot be assumed. In 1284 the *tzaousios* George Melissenos donated to the Lemviotissa monastery "our patrimonial [*gonike*] estate, which our God and the . . . emperor granted to us." This estate consisted of movable and immovable property including 12 modioi of vineyards,

[231] *Xénophon*, no. 21.3,5,46–47. Even though the transaction was framed as a lease, it was more of a transfer of possession in return for payment of the *stasia*'s tax. As a kind of *epiteleia*, the tax was now directed toward a third party, forming part of his oikonomia.

300 modioi of arable land, and "the houses which are in Magnesia, which the . . . emperor granted to me as my *gonika* in exchange for the houses which he took from me."[232] It would appear that this estate originated as an imperial grant and had become Melissenos' hereditary property by the time of the donation. In a similar case the *protostrator* Theodore Palaiologos Synadenos, an uncle of Andronikos III, "received as a benefaction" (εὐεργετηθέντος) through a chrysobull of Andronikos III the property (*ktema*) of Ezova in hereditary tenure (*kata logon gonikoteteos*). Prior to 1338 he donated some property within it to the monastery of Xenophon (*Xénophon*, no. 25.140–43). But, in either case, were the properties donated ever part of oikonomiai?

[8.63] Donation of Nicholas Adam to the monastery of the Lemviotissa (1260)

A case illustrating the difficulty in determining the origin of properties involves a donation of Nicholas Adam. In 1260 he donated to the Lemviotissa monastery a property (*topion*) in Planou consisting of a church, the land on which the church stood, and three olive trees growing around the church. In regard to the trees, Adam explains that they "belong to me by inheritance [γονικόθεν] from Lestes, now deceased, and Planetes, which the . . . emperor granted to me completely without tax and without burden [ἀτελῶς πάντη καὶ ἀβαρῶς], as the . . . emperor granted my completely exempt [properties] [πανεξκουσσάτα]."[233]

Adam claims that he held the trees by inheritance, that they came from two men, only one of whom was dead, and that the emperor granted him a tax exemption on these trees and other properties. *Gonikothen* does not mean that Adam necessarily inherited the trees from anyone; he may have been granted hereditary rights over a grant by the emperor. Lestes and Planetes may have been simply previous holders – jointly or successively – of a pronoia which included the trees. The emperor (probably Michael VIII) certainly granted tax exemption on the trees, and may well have granted the trees themselves. But none of this is certain. The only thing we know for sure is that, because Adam held the trees "by hereditary right," he had the

[232] MM, IV, 266.25–27: τὴν γονικὴν ἡμῶν κλήραν, ἥνπερ ὁ θεὸς ἡμῖν ἐδωρήσατο καὶ ὁ . . . βασιλεύς, and 267.6–7: ἅπερ μοι ἐδωρήσατο . . . ὁ βασιλεὺς . . . ὡς γονικά μου ἀντὶ τῶν ὀσπητίων, ὧν μοι ἀπῆρε.

[233] MM, IV, 91–92. The *PLP*, no. 287, identifies Nicholas Adam with the "*kavallarios syr* Adam" who donated olive trees in Aurelios to Lemviotissa and who was dead by 1306 (MM, IV, 79, 104).

right to bequeath them. Evidently he also felt that this gave him the right to donate them to the monastery.

[8.64] Chrysobull of Andronikos II Palaiologos for Theodore Sarantenos (1324), and Testament of Theodore Sarantenos (1325)

The safest course was to seek imperial approval of a donation made from an imperial grant. This is what the *skouterios* Theodore Sarantenos did in 1324 when he wished to donate some properties to the monastery he founded in Verrhoia. These properties had been given to him by the emperor on account of his services. One of these properties was pasture land in the village of Kritzista with a *posotes* of five hyperpyra "taken away from the deceased Bogdan" which Sarantenos "received as a benefaction from the great mercy of the . . . emperor . . . through a divine and august chrysobull to me, by the mercy and favor of old of his mighty and holy majesty." In 1324 Andronikos II issued a chrysobull which, among other things, granted Sarantenos' request that the monastery be permitted to own this land tax free (*eleuthera*).[234]

While it is clear that Sarantenos was requesting tax-free status for the property as well as seeking official acknowledgment of the donation, it is less clear whether he also was requesting permission to make the donation. In other words, was the donation of this property that Sarantenos originally received from the emperor valid without a chrysobull reflecting imperial approval of the transfer? Part of the answer can be found in the document itself. The chrysobull briefly mentions (without enumeration) other properties that Sarantenos donated to the monastery which he had acquired through dowry and which the monastery was to hold tax free because of common chrysobulls granted to the inhabitants of Verrhoia, as well as properties he had acquired through purchase which similarly were to be held tax free (*Vatopédi*, I, no. 62.69–77). The dowry property was already tax free and, by its nature, alienable; therefore, the reference to it in the chrysobull must have been merely an additional safeguard, an imperial document specifically noting its status. This would suggest that the chrysobull may have merely been officially recognizing the donation of the pasture land. Yet, the fact that the chrysobull provides complete details of the origin of the pasture land suggests that Sarantenos wanted proof that the emperor was

[234] *Vatopédi*, I, no. 62.52–53, and no. 64.80–82: Εὐηργετήθην ἀπὸ τῆς μεγάλης ἐλεημοσύνης τοῦ . . . βασιλέως, etc.

aware that property originating as an imperial grant was being alienated to a monastery.

The right to alienate granted over property given by the emperor

There are few examples of emperors granting the right to alienate properties, and when such examples do exist, they do not seem to have been part of oikonomiai (or pronoiai). There are eleven cases in which an individual received the explicit right to alienate property which originated as an imperial grant (Table 8.11).[235] The cases may best be distinguished according to whether the right of alienation was full or limited.

In the four "limited" cases, the emperor granted the beneficiary only the right to transmit the property to a monastery. One of these "limited" cases involves the monk Kallinikos, whom we have already encountered as the recipient of a praktikon for the village of Mamitzona in 1323 *[8.16]*. In 1321 Andronikos II granted him a small monastery (*monydrion*), because the emperor regarded him as "a good man and having goodwill toward my majesty and caring for its services." Kallinikos was given the right to improve the property which was not to be bothered by any treasury official "for the sake of any demand or offering." After his death the monastery was to pass into the possession of Hilandar, as Kallinikos desired.[236]

The case of Gervasios is similar; while he was granted the right to "transmit and donate" his *posotes* to whomever he wished, it is clear that his monastery, Hilandar, was to be the ultimate beneficiary of the grant.[237] The right to donate property from an imperial grant to a religious institution, specifically a monastery, could be bestowed either at the time of the initial creation of the grant or at a later time as a further reward. The case of these "limited" rights to alienate is not of as much interest to us because, by

[235] There are two other similar cases involving granting authorities other than a Byzantine emperor: in one case Stefan Dušan *[8.5]* and in the other the despot Thomas Palaiologos in 1454 (Lampros, *Παλαιολόγεια καὶ Πελοποννησιακά*, IV, 236–37). In both the object of the grant was a property and both cases follow the pattern of Kalothetos in the table.

[236] *Chilandar*, ed. Petit, no. 74.3,21–22: χάριν ἀπαιτήσεως καὶ δόσεως τινος. Also, in July 1323, "because of the exertion, diligence and zeal which he [Kallinikos] displayed in the services of our majesty" (*Chilandar*, ed. Petit, no. 90.11), Andronikos II and Andronikos III confirmed the donation of a monastery in Thessaloniki by the metropolitan of Thessaloniki to Kallinikos. Dölger, *Regesten*, IV, no. 2673. Kallinikos was given the right to improve the monastery, but there is no mention about the disposition of the monastery after Kallinikos' death.

[237] In this category we might also add the sale of the village of Prevista to the tsar of Bulgaria in 1325 by Theodora Palaiologina. The tsar then donated the village to Zographou and Andronikos II confirmed the grant: *Zographou*, no. 22.

Table 8.11 Cases in which permission to alienate an imperial grant was given explicitly

	Date	Hereditary?	Right to alienate?	Referred to as an oikonomia?	Original or later privilege?	Any tax exemption noted?	Property
Demetrios Mourinos *[6.8]*	1274–82	yes	full		later	limited exemption of secondary burdens	villages with a total *posotes* of 830 hyperpyra plus other properties
Leo Koteanitzes *[8.31]*	1293, or forgery	yes	full		original	full	*ge*
Manuel Angelos Patrikios *[App. 5]*	forgery	yes	full		later	full	a *zeugelateion* and *proskathemenoi*
Basil Modenos *[8.30]*	1320	yes	limited		later	full	1000 modioi
monk Kallinikos (*Chilandar*, ed. Petit, no. 74)	1321		limited		original	full	a small monastery
John Orestes *[8.43]*	1323	yes	full		later		multiple properties
Dragon *[App. 5]*	forgery	yes	full		original	full	a *zeugelateion*
Theodotos Kalothetos *[7.16]*	1328	yes	full		original	full	900 mod.
hegoumenos Gervasios *[7.9]*	1334		limited	yes	original	at least secondary burdens	a *posotes* of 40 hyp. consisting of a village; later both emperor and Gervasios each call it an oikonomia in other documents
Xene Soultanina *[7.17]*	1344	yes	full	yes (her husband's)	original?	full	100 hyp.
son of Sampias *[8.48]*	1405	yes	limited		later		2 villages

keeping watch and approving into whose hand the property was passing, the emperor was maintaining his control over the property.

The seven "full" cases granted the recipient the unlimited right to sell or donate the property involved. In five of these cases the emperor explicitly noted that the grant was a reward for past actions. When the emperor granted property to an individual with an unlimited right to alienate the property, this was usually accompanied by the right to bequeath the property.

Of these seven cases the relevant documents for two of them are probably forgeries (Patrikios and Dragon) and for one at least questionable (Koteanitzes). The four remaining cases (Mourinos, Orestes, Kalothetos, Soultanina) are genuine. In all eleven cases only once is the grant referred to as either an oikonomia or a pronoia. The act of Xene Soultanina refers to the grant as an oikonomia, though it is only her father's oikonomia which is so designated.

Given that an imperial chrysobull permitting someone to donate property to a monastery would have been a desirable document for a monastery to preserve, the fact that so few such documents are extant suggests that few were issued. Rather, most of our knowledge of donations of property originating from imperial grants is derived from the private acts of donation themselves and, to a lesser extent, from the praktika of monastic possessions created by fiscal officials as they made their rounds of the provinces.

Observations

In regard to the transfer or alienation of pronoiai, practices varied. The sources provide us with four statements of the principles involved. The *Zavorda Treatise* states that pronoiai were held for life *[2.1]*, and in a document from 1233 we are told that paroikoi of a pronoia holder were not to sell their land to the pronoia holder *[5.4]*. We have a statement from 1335 in which the emperor ordered that nothing should be sold or donated from an oikonomia *[8.51]*, and the 1344 act of sale by the couple from Melnik which states that normally it was forbidden to sell property from one's oikonomia *[8.52]*. The prohibition on alienating property that originated through an imperial grant is certainly connected to the fear that any such alienation would lead to a corresponding loss of service to the crown. But perhaps the hesitancy to confer the right to alienate property from an imperial grant was connected as well to the hesitancy to allow the transmission of tax exemption and other privileges to another.

Nevertheless, both pronoiai and oikonomiai were alienated or transferred. Pronoiai were donated to monasteries with the stipulation that the donation was valid as long as the pronoia was held by the recipient *[8.53–8.55]*. I conclude that throughout the late Byzantine period it was generally forbidden to sell or donate parts of oikonomiai, but that the policy may not have been applied and enforced consistently. Consequently, we cannot assume that every property acquired by a monastery through donation or purchase as listed in the praktika was legitimate, that is, the property was not part of an oikonomia or if it was, its alienation was permitted by the emperor. Further, it appears that hereditary rights granted over oikonomiai did not include the right to alienate properties within the oikonomia.[238] It was rare for the emperor to grant the right to alienate property from an imperial grant. When such rights were granted with the initial grant of property, I would consider the grant not to be an oikonomia but a gift. When such rights were granted subsequent to the initial bestowal of the grant, I conclude that the grant was no longer an oikonomia.

Over time, as it became more common for individuals to receive hereditary rights over their oikonomiai, it probably also became more common for individuals to make donations of all or part of their oikonomiai to monasteries, even if, technically, such transfers were invalid. (Sales may have always been much less common.) Perhaps this was a gray area. Perhaps individuals made such donations without imperial approval if they thought it was permissible. On the other hand, perhaps some emperors (such as Andronikos III) thought the practice was getting out of hand and consequently ordered that it be stopped.

The pronoia holder's relations with his paroikoi

When we speak of the relationship between a pronoia holder and paroikoi, we must include not only the paroikoi he held directly but other paroikoi who had less direct relationships with the pronoia holder. Generally speaking, there were four basic types of relationships that a privileged landholder (a pronoia holder, a monastery, another variety of privileged layman) could have with peasants:

(i) Some peasants simply leased land from a landholder with no other social, fiscal, or economic relation between them. In this case, the peasants

[238] On the other hand, Dölger, *Schatzkammern*, p. 48 and p. 262, thought a hereditary pronoia could be alienated to anyone.

were not paroikoi of this particular landholder (though they could have been paroikoi of another landholder) and the relationship between the two parties was a private arrangement. A thirteenth-century lease formula stipulates rent payments to be paid in cash every six months. In other cases, the rent was a fraction of the harvest, usually one-third.[239] The monk Kallinikos' praktikon *[8.16]* specifically notes that part of his domain land would be cultivated "by lease." The lessees need not have been paroikoi of Kallinikos.

(ii) Peasants who were paroikoi of a landholder had an obligation to cultivate the domain land of the landholder and render his personal taxes and other charges to the landholder. These are the paroikoi explicitly listed by household and by village in landholders' praktika. Both corvées and taxes originated as burdens owed to the state, but when the peasants were assigned to the landholder, the landholder became the beneficiary of these burdens. In regard to labor services, paroikoi typically owed twelve days or twenty-four of service per year, depending on the area, and in one case fifty-two days of service is encountered.[240]

(iii) A peasant might be required to pay the tax on a property he owned to a pronoia holder (or to another landholder). In this case the emperor had granted the pronoia holder (or other privileged person or institution) the tax on the property. The peasant need not have been a paroikos of the pronoia holder or other landholder. For example, Xenos Legas, who lived in the first half of the thirteenth century, was a paroikos of the Lemviotissa monastery but he owned olive trees which were part of the pronoia of Syrgares. Legas paid a yearly tax to Syrgares for the trees *[5.10]*.

(iv) Peasants might merely live near the property of a wealthy landholder. This created a social connection, not directly related to economic concerns, which reflected the influence of powerful local landholders. A dramatic example of this involves Theodora Kantakouzene, a large landholder around Serres (though we know nothing of how she held this property), who acquired 110 parcels of land mostly through purchase (and a few through exchange or gift) between November 1337 and March 1338. Theodora was the mother of the *megas domestikos* John Kantakouzenos, the future John VI, who at the time was the closest friend and right-hand man of the emperor Andronikos III. These 110 parcels, located in the area of Serres, totaled around 1,400 modioi. Most were small, less than five modioi each. The fact

[239] K. Sathas, *Μεσαιωνική Βιβλιοθήκη* (1872–94; repr. Athens, 1972), vi, 622–23. See *ODB*, s.v. "rent."

[240] The economic side of the relationship between landholders and their paroikoi is treated in detail by Laiou, "The Agrarian Economy," 328–46.

that Theodora Kantakouzene was able to acquire 110 parcels of land over a five-month period shows that she exercised great authority and influence in the area. In fact, the transaction acts tend to refer to her as "the holy aunt of the emperor," though she was not related at all to the emperor at the time, Andronikos III (*Vatopédi*, II, no. 80).

Most peasants fit into more than one of these categories; many fit into all four. For example, a paroikos of a monastery who paid his personal taxes to the monastery, leased some of the monastery's land, performed corvées for the monastery, and was subject to the social influence of the monastery, can be placed within all four categories of relationships.

The manner by which these four basic relationships played themselves out depended on a number of variables:

(a) The number of paroikoi a landholder held. No less than slave owners and their slaves or employers and their employees, anyone or any institution (pronoia holder or other lay landholder, monastery or other religious foundation) who held large numbers of paroikoi would have a different relationship with his paroikoi than a person or institution that held a small number of paroikoi.

Of course size is a relative concept. From our three lay praktika for pronoia soldiers, we see that on average each of these pronoia soldiers held 42 paroikoi (Berilas: 37, Saventzes: 29, and Maroules: 60). If we add to this five people for the soldier's own family, a few servants (military and domestic) plus their families, plus perhaps a few households of *eleutheroi*, it appears likely that the typical pronoia soldier – at the low end of the pronoia spectrum – headed an economic unit consisting of well over three score people. These people devoted nearly all their efforts to supporting the soldier or were supported by the soldier.

(b) The percentage of peasants a landholder held in a particular locality. A landholder who held an entire village (such as the pronoia holder Alexios Raoul who held the entire village of Prevista) would have a different relationship with the residents of the village than one who held only a fraction of the peasants in a particular village (such as Michael Saventzes who held one paroikos household in the village of Phournia).

(c) The landholder's personal fortune and status within society, regardless of the particular size of his imperial grant.

(d) Perhaps even the length of time the landholder held property in a particular locale. It is a fact that pronoia holders often held their grants for rather short periods of time, while peasant tenures were usually long. A landholder who recently received his grant and his paroikoi would have a different relationship with the local community than one who held a grant for decades, creating good and bad relations with his neighbors and perhaps acquiring more property in the area.

On the whole, the relations between the pronoia holder and his paroikoi mirrored the relations that other landholders had with their paroikoi, with some differences. One is the matter of scale. The landholders we know the most about are monasteries – large monasteries – with wealthy laymen a distant second. Most pronoia holders were probably smaller landholders like the soldiers Saventzes, Maroules, and Berilas. Smaller landholders could have closer and more frequent relationships with their paroikoi. But the entire gamut of human relations that can exist between lord and peasant undoubtedly existed for any category or class of landholders and peasants.

As an example of what appears to be harmonious relations between a landholder and his paroikoi, we have the case of Nicholas Maliasenos and his wife, large landholders in Thessaly. In 1271 they decided to build a monastery for women in a particular village. For the site they chose a spot which had been occupied for years by a peasant named Michael Archontitzes and his family. Maliasenos bought the land, but in the act of sale the purchase is framed more as an act of generosity, rather than a necessity. Archontitzes acknowledged that as his master and lord Maliasenos could have taken the land without any compensation, but Maliasenos and his wife chose to pay for it:

> you did not wish to seize this [land] as our lords and masters, since the entire area . . . was granted to you by our most mighty and holy lord and emperor, belonging to you . . . as hereditary property, but being most just and Christ-loving by nature, you, like outsiders, desired to purchase it from us.

According to another document issued by the inhabitants of Archontitzes' village, the tax that Archontitzes used to pay ($2\frac{1}{3}$ hyperpyra) would now be paid jointly by all the peasants of his village: "we submit to the said yearly tax and add this to our annual tax burdens, so that this [tax] is paid by us proportionately according to the ability of each."[241]

Despite the fact that the first document claims that Maliasenos was granted the area by the emperor (at that time Michael VIII), this was probably not true. Maliasenos' father Constantine was well established as a wealthy landholder in the area long before Nicholas was born.[242] This is probably an example of a large landholder being allowed to keep his property following the conquests of Michael VIII. Constantine Maliasenos held his property under the rulers of Epiros (whether as a pronoia grant we

[241] MM, IV, 397.31–398.1, 392.23–26. [242] See *PLP*, no. 16523.

do not know), Nicholas inherited it, and once the area was conquered by Michael VIII he was permitted to keep it under the new ruler's terms. Only in this sense was he "granted" the area by the emperor. I would not consider it a pronoia.

But what do we make of the land sale? The peasant Archontitzes states that Maliasenos could have simply taken the land because the entire area was granted to Maliasenos by the emperor as hereditary property. Either Maliasenos had a right to take the land from Archontitzes or he did not. Now, the only way he could have had the *right* to take away Archontitzes' land was if Archontitzes was merely leasing the land from Maliasenos. If the proper formalities were followed, a landlord *could* dispossess even a long-time leaseholder from his property. But if Archontitzes was merely renting the land, then why was there any need to purchase the land at all? Archontitzes claims that Maliasenos and his wife acted like "outsiders and strangers," in other words, they purchased the property as if they had no prior connection to Archontitzes at all.

I have to conclude that Maliasenos had no legal or customary right to take Archontitzes' land because Archontitzes actually *owned* the land he sold to Maliasenos. If this was the case, then the only way to make sense of the act of the sale is to stipulate that Maliasenos, if he wanted Archontitzes' land, was *supposed* to acquire it through purchase, but, being the powerful man he was, Archontitzes acknowledged that he could have taken it without paying for it. The act of the peasants of Archontitzes' village in which they agreed to pay the tax on the land can also be explained by viewing Maliasenos as a powerful man. For that matter, the sale itself may not have been entirely voluntary, but a product of non-economic coercion.

Whether Archontitzes' sale is an example of harmonious relations between landholder and paroikos or an example of the submissiveness of peasants in the face of a powerful landholder, a counter-example is found in an act of John Apokaukos, metropolitan of Naupaktos. This is the story of the pronoia holder who ordered his paroikoi to make preparations for his arrival in a particular village. But when he and a government official arrived and no food was to be found, an argument ensued, and the pronoia holder, enraged at the comments of one of his paroikoi, threw him to the ground and killed him *[5.16]*.

It is much easier to dismiss the notion that landholders, as a rule, were "masters" of their paroikoi. Consider Michael Saventzes *[8.11]*. He held eight families of paroikoi in his pronoia: three in the village of Psalis, one in the neighboring village of Phournia, two in the village of Ourliakon, and two in the village of Adam. If the idea was to make Michael the master of a group of paroikoi, then the *apographeis* Pergamenos and Pharisaios could not have dealt him a more challenging hand. It is clear that aside from the traditional corvées (up to twelve days per year per paroikos) and *kaniskia* they gave Saventzes, the paroikoi, from Saventzes' point of view, were essentially income-producing units representing, according to his praktikon, one-half, or one, or two, hyperpyra per year for his support.

Whether or not the pronoia holder or other landholder lived near his properties, he would have hired men to manage his domain lands. The more property he held, the more servants he would have to manage his properties. The role of such stewards is not well documented, but it is quite likely that peasants had much greater dealings with stewards than with actual landholders. In Chapter 5 the case was discussed of Constantine Melachrenos, steward on the pronoia of Constantine Tzirithnos. When local peasants attempted to harvest acorns from Tzirithnos' property, Melachrenos struck and killed one of them *[5.15]*.

While steward Melachrenos' problem was with peasants from outside his master's pronoia, pronoia holders often found themselves in disputes with their own paroikoi which arose with increasing frequency in the thirteenth century because of two developments. First, there was the new practice of granting real property not owned by the state to pronoia holders. And second, as more and more individuals became paroikoi – that is, as the taxes of more and more individuals were conferred as an imperial privilege on pronoia holders, other favored laymen, and monasteries – it is natural that disputes over property would increase.

Sometimes these disputes could be resolved easily. For example, sometime prior to 1257 a monk who was a paroikos of Michael Petritzes bequeathed sixteen olive trees to a monastery. Petritzes initially disputed the transfer of the trees, but after it was demonstrated that the olives were not listed in any praktikon, he conceded that the trees had never been transmitted into his possession, that is, that the trees were not part of his pronoia *[5.11]*.

Pronoia holders also were involved in the disputes between their paroikoi. A paroikos of the *kavallarios* Syrgares appealed to Syrgares in a quarrel involving olive trees between villagers within his pronoia. An assembly was convened of villagers who decided the matter. The woman Komnene Vranaina, who held these paroikoi after Syrgares' death, similarly sent the case to villagers when the quarrel was reopened. In both instances, Syrgares and Komnene Vranaina acted as patrons of their paroikoi and referees in disputes between them. Significantly, they did not judge the cases themselves, but allowed the peasants to deal their own justice *[5.9]*. There is no evidence that pronoia holders, any more than other privileged landholders such as monasteries and lay holders of paroikoi, had the right to judge their paroikoi.[243]

In disputes with outsiders, the pronoia holder, like any landholder, tended to take the side of his paroikoi. The pronoia holder took an interest in the property holdings of his paroikoi, which suggests that the more property a paroikos held, the greater the benefit was to the pronoia holder. There are a number of examples of paroikoi and their lords working together for a common end, usually the acquisition of more property. For example, in Chapter 5 the case of Gonia tou Petake was discussed in which the inhabitants of the village of Malachiou, at the instigation of their lord George Komnenos Angelos who held them in pronoia, claimed the property as theirs *[5.6]*. And in the early years of the fourteenth century, Constantine Doukas Nestongos – described as an uncle of Michael VIII and *parakoimomenos* of the *megale sphendone* – held the village of Prinovare (under unknown circumstances) not far from Vare which belonged to Lemviotissa. His paroikoi trespassed on the property of the monastery, harassed the monks, and illegally cultivated their property. The monks complained to Michael VIII who ordered an investigation. The peasants were found guilty, but the investigation showed that Nestongos did nothing to stop them, and perhaps was behind the attacks on the monastery.[244]

Generally speaking, the property owned by a paroikos was his to dispose of. The one exception in which the holder of a paroikos had some control over the disposition of the property of a paroikos was when the head of a paroikos household died without children. In this case his or her property (*stasis*) became an *exaleimma*, and ownership of the *stasis* passed to the holder of the paroikos. This practice was sanctioned not by positive law, but by custom. In 1081 Alexios I granted a monastery permission to hold some *exaleimmatikai staseis* of its paroikoi; in 1175 an *anagrapheus* attributed four *exaleimmatikai staseis* to a monastery; and in 1280 a monastery simply appropriated the *exaleimma* of one of its paroikoi. Over two centuries a privilege became a normal practice. For lay landholders the practice may have started at a later date. In 1196 an *anagrapheus* ordered a woman to surrender the *exaleimmatikai staseis* she was holding, but by the early fourteenth century it was common practice for lords to appropriate the *exaleimmatikai staseis* of their paroikoi. The attempts of imperial legislation

243 Ostrogorsky's notion (*Féodalité*, 116–17, 362–64) that the holders of paroikoi had the right (at least) of "low" justice over their paroikoi is unfounded. See *ODB*, s.v. "aerikon."

244 MM, IV, 257, 260. On Nestongos, *PLP*, no. 20201.

and the pleadings of at least one patriarch to limit the practice to a fraction of the deceased's *stasis* were of little avail.[245]

Examples of landholders acquiring peasant holdings in this way are fairly common. In 1311 two paroikoi who were brothers and a man named Doukopoulos who held the two paroikoi in hereditary tenure donated half of a mill to the monastery of Docheiariou. Each of the three men owned one-sixth of the mill (and the monastery of Lavra owned the other half). Doukopoulos acquired his share in the mill when a brother of the two paroikoi died without children. The deceased brother's *stasis* became an *exaleimma* and passed to Doukopoulos.[246]

In another case Markos Doukas Glavas *syr* Mourinos inherited property and paroikoi on the Chalkidike, probably from his grandfather Demetrios Mourinos who received hereditary rights over this property *[6.8]*. Mourinos and one of his paroikoi each owned half of a mill at Hermeleia. The paroikos had promised the monastery that was leasing the mill that it would receive his share of the mill after his death. However, when the paroikos died childless around 1343 (and the entire *stasis* of the paroikos then became an *exaleimma*), Mourinos acquired ownership of the entire *stasis* of the paroikos, including the paroikos' half-share in the mill. He then sold the entire mill to a different monastery (*Docheiariou*, no. 40).

In 1301 two paroikoi of Alexios Amnon, along with a "man" (i.e., servant) of Amnon, sold a field that they jointly owned to a monastery. Because the act of sale – with its atrocious orthography, grammar, and syntax – specifies that the sale took place "with the will and permission" of Amnon, evidently it was in Amnon's power to block the sale. A reference to *exaleimma* led Angeliki Laiou to conclude that the land in question did not really belong to the paroikoi and the "man" of Amnon, but had devolved to the estate holder (Amnon) like all *exaleimmata*. If Laiou's interpretation is correct, then we have an example of an estate holder *not* exercising his right to keep the holding of one of his paroikoi who died without children.[247]

While the appropriation of the property of one's deceased paroikos may seem to be a harsh practice, it addressed practical issues. When a paroikos died childless, his holder (whether a monastery, pronoia holder, or other

245 *Docheiariou*, pp. 117–18. *ODB*, s.v. "abiotikion." Bartusis, "'Ἐξάλειμμα: Escheat in Byzantium," 60–61.

246 *Docheiariou*, no. 11. The interpretation of this act by A. Kazhdan in *ODB*, s.v. "abiotikion," is at variance with mine.

247 *Esphigménou*, no. 10.4–5: μετὰ βουλῆς καὶ καταδωχίς [sic]. Laiou, *Peasant Society*, 144–45. Cf. Kazhdan, *Agrarnye otnošenija*, 217.

variety of lay landholder) lost the labor services owed by the paroikos. This would be the case even if the property of the paroikos was distributed to other relatives and their taxes were correspondingly increased. Appropriating the property of the paroikos was a way to compensate the lord for the loss of the labor services of the paroikos.

Alienations of paroikos property also caused complications. While it must have been very unusual for a paroikos to liquidate his entire *stasis*, partial alienations through sale and donation were not uncommon. Because the *telos* of the paroikos was related to the property he owned, any diminution of his property theoretically reduced the *telos* he was obligated to render to his lord. If the property was alienated toward another paroikos of the lord or to the lord himself, the lord would not incur a loss (this being a closed system). But any alienation directed toward someone or an institution outside the holdings of the paroikos' lord would produce a financial loss to the lord.

In the case of pronoia holders the matter was even more pressing. The paroikoi of pronoia holders tended to hold more property than the paroikoi of monasteries. And pronoia holders tended to hold far fewer paroikoi than the typical monastery. Thus, any loss of labor services or any loss of tax revenues was a significant concern. To compensate for the loss of labor services, the pronoia holder was permitted to appropriate the property of the paroikos. To compensate for the loss of tax income should the paroikos alienate property to a third party, the pronoia holder demanded an *epiteleia*. It was in the state's interest to maintain the income of the pronoia holder.

The bonds between rural inhabitants took varied forms. The picture that emerges is not one of constant exploitation of the weak at the hands of the powerful, but a more nuanced situation in which peasants had opportunities to assert their autonomy.

The pronoia holder's relations with other property holders

Like all landholders, pronoia holders fought their share of squabbles with other landholders. Among many examples, the *vestiarites* Kalegopoulos and the monks of Lemviotissa quarreled over a fish pond *[5.7]*, and George Troulenos and the son-in-law of the previous holder of his pronoia argued over who had the right to some *exaleimmatika* fields *[8.50]*.

These disputes could become quite complicated as they played out before the backdrop of the turbulent events of late Byzantine history. Within the village of Kontogrikou, held by the monastery of Xeropotamou, was a "state" iron forge or foundry (*demosiakon siderokauseion*) for which the monastery paid the fisc twenty hyperpyra annually, as either a rent or a tax, depending on whether the monastery actually owned the foundry. At some point this twenty hyperpyra was redirected to the *skouterios* Andreas Indanes, evidently as all or part of a pronoia grant. However, once the area of Kontogrikou was occupied by the Serbs in 1345, the monks of Xeropotamou stopped paying the annual charge to Indanes and in fact received a chrysobull from Stefan Dušan in 1346 confirming their possession of the foundry (*Xéropotamou*, no. 25.29). Once the Serb occupation had ended Indanes appealed to the emperor to require Xeropotamou to render to him back payment of the annual twenty hyperpyra which had lapsed with the Serb occupation. John V ordered the monks to comply or else come to Thessaloniki to present their counter-case. The monks opted for the latter course and two officials were selected to decide the matter. A *prostagma* of John V from March 1351 confirmed their decision, evidently that in return for a lump-sum payment from the monks of thirty-seven hyperpyra, the monastery would maintain full ownership of the foundry (*Xéropotamou*, no. 27).

[8.65] Act of the *pinkernes* Raoul involving the *protonovelissimos* Marmaras (1277)

Typical of the disputes that arose between pronoia holders and other landholders was a quarrel between the monastery of Nea Petra in Thessaly and a pronoia holder named Marmaras. In September 1274, Michael VIII issued a chrysobull confirming, among other things, the monastery's possession of a *zeugelateion* called Vrasta.[248] However, a document issued in July 1277 by the *pinkernes* Raoul describes a conflict between the monastery and the *protonovelissimos* Marmaras, who held "through pronoia the separately demarcated village of Trinovon." According to the monks, Marmaras was improperly collecting the rent (once called the *morte*, later the *dekateia*) from nearby Vrasta (called "Vrastos" in this document). But Marmaras argued that Vrasta was within the district of Trinovon and since "I hold

[248] MM, IV, 334.1–2, 335.11–13. The following month the patriarch likewise confirmed the monastery's possession of Vrasta: MM, IV, 374.22–23.

Trinovon [as] pronoia through imperial *orismos* along with the district belonging to it," he should receive the rent from Vrasta as well. An examination of the relevant documents and the testimony of witnesses who knew the area determined that Vrasta was outside of the district of Trinovon, and the *pinkernes* Raoul ordered Marmaras to return the rent he had collected unjustly.[249]

Trinovon is probably modern Tirnavos, ten miles northwest of Larissa. The history of this area is poorly known. Prior to 1259 it was held by the despot of Epiros, but following the battle of Pelagonia in the summer of that year, it came under the control of the Palaiologoi. Evidently Michael VIII established some kind of imperial control over part of Thessaly as early as September 1259, for in that year John Palaiologos, the emperor's brother, issued a document on behalf of a monastery in the area of Demetrias (MM, IV, 384–85). Throughout the 1260s and 1270s the emperor, the patriarch, and officials of the restored Byzantine Empire continued to produce documents involving monasteries and their properties in the area. Thus, Marmaras could not have been granted his pronoia until after the battle of Pelagonia. Nothing else is known of Marmaras. His title "*protonovelissimos*" was quite exalted in the twelfth century, but declined thereafter; it is found near the bottom in one fifteenth-century list of precedence.[250]

The issue turned on who was entitled to the rent on the property. The monastery maintained that since it owned the property outright, and since

[249] MM, IV, 419.22–23: ἔχει διὰ προνοίας καὶ ὁ Μαρμαρᾶς χωρίον τὸν Τρίνοβον ἰδιοπεριόριστον, 419.25–26, and 419.27–28: δι᾽ ὁρισμοῦ βασιλικοῦ κατέχω τὸν Τρίνοβον πρόνοιαν μετὰ τῆς ἐνούσης αὐτῷ περιοχῆς. The relatively common term ἰδιοπεριόριστον, "separately demarcated," simply means that Trinovon was not part of any other fiscal unit. On the *morte* and *dekateia*, see *ODB*, s.v. "morte." The document introduces the very rare expression ἔχειν διὰ προνοίας, "to hold through pronoia." The phrase διὰ προνοίας appears in only one other document, of questionable authenticity: see Bartusis, "Serbian Pronoia," 199–201. Nevertheless, the document itself shows that it is equivalent to κατέχειν πρόνοιαν. Among the numerous works that have commented on this document: Dölger, *Regesten*, *III*, no. 2030 (which, without grounds, indicates that the pronoia was granted immediately prior to Raoul's act); Ostrogorsky, *Féodalité*, 98–99 (his assertion that the *morte*/*dekateia* was "une rente seigniorial," rather than a simple rent, is unwarranted); Laiou, *Peasant Society*, 216 (the date stated therein is to be corrected); P. Charanis, "The Aristocracy of Byzantium in the Thirteenth Century," in *Studies in Roman Economic and Social History in Honor of Allan Chester Johnson*, ed. P. R. Coleman-Norton (Princeton, 1951), 348 = "Town and Country in the Byzantine Possessions of the Balkan Peninsula During the Later Period of the Empire," in *Aspects of the Balkans, Continuity and Change*, ed. H. Birnbaum and S. Vryonis, Jr. (The Hague and Paris, 1972), 121 = "Social Structure," 103; B. Ferjančić, *Tesalija u XIII i XIV veku* (Belgrade, 1974), 67, 87; and also *PLP*, no. 17098. On the *pinkernes* Raoul Komnenos, see Ferjančić, *Tesalija*, 67 note 114, and Fassoulakis, *The Byzantine Family of Raoul-Ral(l)es*, 19–21.

[250] *ODB*, s.v. "nobellisimos." Pseudo-Kodinos, 308.18–19.

the emperor had confirmed this ownership, it had the right to the rent from the property. Marmaras, on the other hand, claimed that Vrasta was included within his pronoia, which, in this case, meant he was claiming possession of the property, and therefore the rent should go to him. It was not a question of the taxes on the property. His claim was that he had been granted the property itself.

Estimating the economic value of a pronoia grant

The *posotetes* of the seven praktika discussed earlier in this chapter ranged from fifty-five hyperpyra (for the hereditary grant given to John Margarites) through more than 250 hyperpyra (for the pronoia granted to Alexios Raoul). Between these extremes were the *posotetes* of the pronoiai of the soldiers Saventzes, Maroules, and Berilas, respectively, seventy, seventy-two, and eighty hyperpyra, the *posotes* of the pronoia of the *eparchos* Michael Monomachos at just over 100 hyperpyra, and the *posotes* of the (non-pronoia) grant to the monk Kallinikos at around 145 hyperpyra. In order to place these figure in context we can compare them to the *posotetes* of other grants. After this we consider the true economic value of a pronoia and compare that to the known figures for mercenary pay.

The sources provide us with quite a few figures for properties and rights held in pronoia. Table 8.12 presents a list of men and the incomes (in hyperpyra) the sources say they held. The list is fairly complete down to *posotetes* of about twenty hyperpyra. After that I have included only a sampling of the numerous references to small (and some very small) *posotetes*. Certainly the monk Kallinikos' *posotes* was not a pronoia, given that the grant was initiated for the purpose of transferring the properties involved to his monastery. And Demetrios Mourinos' *posotes* was not a pronoia from the moment he received the right to alienate it, though it probably was a pronoia earlier. Even John Margarites' and George Margarites' *posotetes* would not be considered pronoiai if one excludes hereditary property from the discussion. But I am not sure that the Byzantines themselves knew how to categorize consistently hereditary oikonomiai.

In some cases only a figure in modioi is provided. These I have converted to hyperpyra (and listed in brackets), using the standard ratio of one hyperpyron per fifty modioi of *ge*. And when a single property passed from one holder to another, I have made only one entry in the list for its *posotes*.

The first question we should ask of this list is whether each *posotes* figure represents the entire grant the individual received from the emperor. In

Table 8.12 A list of *posotetes* held by individuals or groups of individuals

Holder (and reference)	*Posotes* in hyperpyra	*Ge* in modioi
1. Demetrios Mourinos *[6.8]* p	830, plus a *topos* and a winter pasturage	
2. Demetrios Devlitzenos *[8.46]* p	400	
3. Alexios Palaiologos Soultanos *[7.17]* p	380	
4. Alexios Komnenos Raoul *[8.15]* p	more than 250	
5. *megas papias* Demetrios Kavasilas *[8.45]* p	250	
6. monk Kallinikos *[8.16]*	145	
7. Manuel Angelos Patrikios *[App. 5]*	[132]	6600
8. *eparchos* Michael Monomachos *[8.14]* p	102½, by calculation	
9. *megas primmikerios* Vasilikos *[8.20]* p	100	
10. Sarakenos (*Prodrome*, no. 16) p	80	
11. Basil Berilas *[8.13]* p	80	
12. Nicholas Maroules *[8.12]* p	72	
13. Michael Saventzes *[8.11]* p	70	
14. John Margarites *[8.17]*	55	
15. George Margarites *[8.39]*	50	
16. *megas adnoumiastes* George Katzaras *[8.47]* p	48	2400
17. anonymous *[9.6]* p	48	
18. Maurophoros, then *stratopedarches* of the *monokavalloi* John Choumnos *[8.78]* p	40	
19. *logariastes* of the court Kassandrenos *[7.9]* p	40	
20. *sevastos* Devlitzenos *[8.76]* p	33	
21. George Troulenos *[8.37]* p	[32]	1600
22. *hetaireiarches* John Panaretos *[8.41]* p	30	
23. Nikephoros Martinos *[8.75]* p	30	
24. Syrmanouel Mesopotamites *[8.44]* p	20	
25. judge of the army Alexios Diplovatatzes *[8.40]* p	[20]	1000
26. Neokastrites (*Docheiariou*, no. 18)	[12]	600
27. Klazomenitai soldiers *[8.4]* p	10 or 12 each	
28. Katakalon *[8.66]* p	8	
29. Komnenoutzikos *[8.19]* p	[7]	350
30. *kastrophylax* Demetrios Doukopoulos (*Xénophon*, no. 5)	[ca. 7]	300, including 7 mod. of vineyard
31. Preakotzelos *[8.74]* p	7	
32. Peros Martinos *[7.8]* p	[6½]	325
33. *tzaousios* of the Thessalonian *mega allagion* Manuel Devlitzenos *[8.18]* p	1	

p = was or had been (or almost certainly was or had been) a pronoia grant or part of a pronoia grant some cases we can conclude that the figure does represent, or probably represents, the total oikonomia of the individual, either because a praktikon exists (nos. 4, 8, 11, 12, 13, 14), because the holdings are being reassigned at the death of the holder (nos. 3 and 10), because the *posotes* is spoken of as the oikonomia of the individual (nos. 2, 9, and 20), because the grant is an initial, new grant (nos. 14, 18), or because the context of the relevant document makes it clear that the figure represents the entire grant (no. 1). On the other hand, in a number of cases we can be fairly certain that the *posotes* offered represents only a part of the total holdings of the individual, most commonly because the *posotes* (or the land spoken of) represents something "from the individual's oikonomia" (ἀπὸ τῆς οἰκονομίας αὐτοῦ, nos. 22, 24, and 25), "inside the value of his oikonomia" (εἰς τὸ ποσὸν or ἐντὸς τοῦ ποσοῦ τῆς οἰκονομίας αὐτοῦ, nos. 16, 21, and 23), or even "outside the value of his oikonomia" (ἐκτὸς τοῦ ποσοῦ τῆς οἰκονομίας αὐτοῦ, no. 15) over which part the individual was being granted hereditary rights, and once because the holding was something the individual had lost from his oikonomia (ἀποσπασθεῖσαν ἀπὸ τῆς οἰκονομίας, no. 32). The case of Kallinikos is again special because we know that he held other properties from the emperor in addition to the village for which he held his praktikon.

The point that must be made is that since the praktika for Saventzes, Maroules, Berilas, Kallinikos, Monomachos, and Raoul show that imperial grants were composed of a rich mixture of diverse income-producing elements, many of which had at one time or another been held by other grant holders, and since these praktika, and other documents, depict a relatively vigorous traffic in regard to bestowing, transferring, exchanging and expropriating the elements of imperial grants, it is not possible to conclude that any *posotes* encountered in the sources, no matter how large, represented the total *posotes* of a pronoia holder, unless the document offers a clear indication that the *posotes* is the total *posotes*. Both Preakotzelos' *epiteleia* of seven hyperpyra which he received yearly from a monastery (no. 31) and the forty-eight hyperpyra assigned to the pronoia holder who held the village of Lantzon (no. 17), could represent either the total oikonomia of a pronoia holder or a mere fraction of his total oikonomia. The praktika indicate, if anything, that we should regard *epiteleiai*, the *telos* of paroikoi, extraordinary charges, rights to state land, *exaleimmata*, and all the other elements held in pronoia, as building blocks.

This does not leave us in a very comfortable position. From the list of thirty-four *posotetes*, we are left with only nine which reasonably seem to represent a total *posotes* of a pronoia:

1. *protovestiarites* Demetrios Mourinos	830+ hyperpyra
2. imperial *stratiotes* Demetrios Devlitzenos (1311)	400
3. Alexios Palaiologos Soultanos (died before 1344)	380
8. *eparchos* Michael Monomachos (1333)	102½
9. *megas primmikerios* Vasilikos (1333 or 1334)	100
10. Sarakenos (died before 1325)	80
11. *megaloallagites kyr* Basil Berilas (1323)	80
12. *megaloallagites kyr* Nicholas Maroules (1321)	72
13. *megaloallagites kyr* Michael Saventzes (1321)	70

And while ten of the thirty-four were held by pronoia soldiers (*megaloallagitai*: nos. 11, 12, 13; *stratiotai*: nos. 2, 23, 26, 27, 28; *kavallarioi*: nos. 24, 32), we know the total *posotes* of only four (nos. 2, 11, 12, and 13).

As expected, the *posotetes* of the pronoia soldiers tend to fall at the lower end of the scale. The apparently anomalous case of the pronoia soldier Demetrios Devlitzenos is interesting. His oikonomia seems to be five times as large as those of the *megaloallagitai*. But if one considers the true value of the oikonomiai involved, the difference is not so striking. We recall that Devlitzenos' pronoia amounted to an *exkousseia* of 400 hyperpyra for the taxes burdening his patrimonial property in Hermeleia. The pronoia did not make him a landlord; he already was one. The value of Devlitzenos' "oikonomia," that is, that part of his holdings which he held as pronoia, was 400 hyperpyra, the same as its official *posotes*.

This was not the case with the other oikonomiai in the list. Their official *posotetes* differed substantially from the actual value of the oikonomiai. The reason for this is that most grants contained a quantity of *ge* which was state-owned and which was leased or cultivated through corvée labor. If leased, the lessees, whether the grant holder's own paroikoi or others peasants, paid a rent on this *ge* amounting to a part of the land's produce, generally considered to be one-third of the produce. This has been calculated to be the equivalent of one hyperpyron for every ten modioi of land under normal production, or five times the normal *telos* on the land.[251] Thus, the actual economic value of a pronoia grant was substantially greater than its official *posotes*.

We can attempt to estimate the "true" value of the grants itemized in the six complete praktika by focusing on the *ge* within each praktikon. Assuming that the pronoia holder or other grant holder could hope to

[251] *Lavra*, IV, p. 169 note 649.

Table 8.13 Estimated income of six grants as compared to the official *posotes*

	Saventzes	Maroules	Berilas	Monomachos	Margarites	Kallinikos
A official total *posotes*	70 hyperpyra	72 hyp.	80 hyp.	100 hyp.[a]	55 hyp.	145 hyp.
B *posotes* of *ge*	$30\frac{2}{3}$ hyp.	38 hyp.	63 hyp.	7 hyp.	27 hyp.	54 hyp.
C full *telos* of *ge*[b]	42 hyp.	41 hyp.	78 hyp.	10 hyp.	31 hyp.	54 hyp.
D possible rent on *ge* (C×5)	210 hyp.	205 hyp.	390 hyp.	50 hyp.	155 hyp.	210 hyp.
E estimated rent on *ge* (D/2)	105 hyp.	$102\frac{1}{2}$ hyp.	195 hyp.	25 hyp.	$77\frac{1}{2}$ hyp.	105 hyp.
F total *posotes* less *posotes* of *ge* (A–B)	$39\frac{1}{3}$ hyp.	34 hyp.	16 hyp.	94 hyp.	28 hyp.	91 hyp.
G estimated rent on *ge* plus total *posotes* less *posotes* of *ge* (E+F)	$144\frac{1}{3}$ hyp.	$136\frac{1}{2}$ hyp.	211 hyp.	119 hyp.	$105\frac{1}{2}$ hyp.	196 hyp.
ratio of estimated income of grant to official *posotes* (G/A)	2.1	1.9	2.6	1.2	1.9	1.4

[a] By calculation, Monomachos' *posotes* was $102\frac{1}{2}$ hyperpyra, but it is clear the *apographeus* was trying to reach 100.

[b] The "full *telos*" is the *telos* of the *ge* without considering any *anti-oikoumenou* reduction.

realize only about half of the maximum rent on his land,[252] we can estimate the rent on the *ge* in each praktikon by multiplying the stated or calculated tax on the land by five, and then taking half of the product. By adding the result to the rest of the taxes and charges in each praktikon that were unconnected to the *ge*, we arrive at a rough estimate of the true value of a grant (Table 8.13).

So, according to Table 8.13, the rent on the *ge* alone in each praktikon increased the value of each pronoia by a factor of 1.2 to 2.6 over the official *posotes*. If one added to these figures the value of the *kaniskia*, the *oikomodion*, and the *oinometrion*, plus possible rents obtained from any of the other properties in the praktika (such as mill fees, dock fees, and perhaps rents on *exaleimmata*), the difference between the official *posotetes* and the true value of the pronoiai would be even more dramatic.[253]

252 This is the estimate used by Svoronos when calculating the yearly income of Lavra in the early fourteenth century: *Lavra*, IV, pp. 169–70.

253 Laiou's calculation of the rental income from Lavra's land in 1321 uses assumptions that, if applied to these six praktika, would produce much higher figures: see Laiou, "The Agrarian Economy," 349, and Lefort, "Rural Economy," 301. For example, if her formula was applied to the *ge* of Saventzes and Maroules, the resulting rental income for each would be in the 164–189 hyperpyra range. One of the reasons for the disparity is that her formula is based on all of the *ge*

The range of 105 to 211 hyperpyra for the value of the six grants in the table renders Devlitzenos' straight 400 hyperpyra, which was the true value of his pronoia, a bit less towering. This is not to say that every pronoia holder actually collected 1.2 to 2.6 times the official *posotes* of his oikonomia, but it does represent the income he could attain, if diligent and fortunate. The goal was, after all, a rate of return on one's holdings equivalent to that of a private landlord.

Three of the grants in the table were held by soldiers of the Thessalonian *mega allagion*: Saventzes, Maroules, and Berilas. How do my estimates of the true value of their pronoiai compare to mercenary pay? Mercenary pay is generally cited in the sources as a monthly rate of pay. There are only a handful of figures for mercenaries fighting for Byzantium in the late period: the 1261 treaty of Nymphaion gives the pay rate for the soldiers on the Genoese galleys in the service of Byzantium as $2\frac{1}{2}$ hyperpyra per month plus a rations allotment; according to Ramon Muntaner, the Catalan Company, hired by Andronikos II in 1303, received 4 gold ounces per month for cavalry and one for infantry; Pachymeres notes that the Alans accompanying the Catalans were paid 3 hyperpyra per month plus horses. Because there are so few figures for mercenaries in the service of Byzantium, it is useful to add to these the pay rates for mercenaries in Venetian service in the Aegean area. In order to produce remotely comparable figures, we need to annualize the rates of mercenary pay, while acknowledging that this is a bit unrealistic because mercenaries were often hired for short periods. We also need to convert all the pay rates to a common currency. The Venetian ducat is best for this, because Venetian pay rates are usually cited in this currency, and it remained relatively stable from the time it was first struck in 1284 through the fourteenth century.

Thus, according to the testimony of Venetian sources the mercenary pay-scale was 23 to 62 ducats per year for crossbowmen, archers, marines, and sergeants in Venice's employ in the Aegean area. Most of what few Byzantine figures we have for rates of mercenary pay tend to fall within this range: the Genoese marines' rate of pay would be around 20 ducats per year; the pay of the Catalans, if calculated on a yearly basis, would have been 68 ducats for infantry and 276 for cavalry; and the Alans' 3 hyperpyra per month would have been about 24 ducats per year. The one outlier was the pay rate for

being leased (which is more plausible for a large monastery than for a pronoia holder, though still unlikely).

Similar figures to those in my table for the value of the pronoiai of Saventzes, Maroules, and Berilas are found in Bartusis, *Late Byzantine Army*, 173. Oikonomides, "The Role of the Byzantine State," 1046, regarded those estimates as "excessively optimistic."

the Catalan cavalry.[254] Since the soldiers of the *megala allagia* would have been cavalry, how did the pay of a Catalan horse soldier compare to the true value of a Byzantine *megaloallagites*' pronoia?

The Catalan horseman received the equivalent of 276 ducats if calculated on a yearly basis. The 136½ to 211 hyperpyra range of pronoia values calculated above corresponds to 91–141 ducats per year. When compared to the estimated pronoia values of other horsemen, the Catalan cavalry pay rate is no longer so outrageous.[255]

In fact, the calculated incomes of our pronoia grants may have been preferable to the pay of the Catalan cavalry. Many mercenaries, and certainly the Catalans, were not employed year round. A six-month campaign season would cut any of these annual rates in half, and that assumes that the pay was forthcoming as promised, often not the case. It is quite likely that a man would have preferred the vagaries of agricultural production and the inconvenience of collecting taxes from peasants to accepting a nominally higher sum that would place him at the mercy of stingy paymasters for his monthly sustenance. A grant of property was real; a salary was a promise.[256]

Geographical distribution of pronoiai

By region

There is little information for the geographical distribution of pronoiai during the twelfth century. The few pronoiai that can be localized were in the lake area to the east of Thessaloniki *[2.3]*, at the northern end of the Gallipoli peninsula in Thrace *[2.2]*, and in the theme of Moglena north of Vodena in Macedonia *[2.4–2.5]*. There is nothing unusual about these locations. Otherwise, it would be reasonable to think that the emperors of the twelfth century created pronoiai near the main military camps. During the reigns of John II and Manuel I Komnenos these were in Asia Minor near Lopadion on the Rhyndakos plain, and in Europe at Pelagonia in Macedonia, at Serdica (mod. Sofia) in Bulgaria, and at the mouth of the Marica river in Thrace. It would also be reasonable to think that pronoiai would have been created in areas that had been newly reconquered, that is, in parts of Asia

254 Bartusis, *Late Byzantine Army*, 151–53.

255 For the equivalency, T. Bertelé, "Moneta veneziana e moneta bizantina," *Venezi e il Levante fino ad secolo xv* (Florence, 1973), 41–42.

256 Bartusis, *Late Byzantine Army*, 173–74.

Minor and the Balkans. But we know nothing of this.[257] The real growth of pronoia as an institution does not occur until the thirteenth century. We can summarize what is known of the geographical distribution of pronoiai from that point on:

Pronoiai first appear in Asia Minor during the early thirteenth century in the areas of Smyrna and Miletos *[5.1] [5.4–5.5] [5.7–5.8]*. Patriarch Gregory II makes one comment about the existence of a pronoia in the Skamandros region *[6.12]*. Pachymeres writes in general terms about pronoiai in Asia Minor, some held by soldiers and some held by the highlanders of the Sangarios frontier, the latter receiving their pronoiai from John Vatatzes *[5.14]*. His comments about monasteries and churches holding pronoiai there indicate he was using the word to indicate any grant from the emperor*[7.12]*.

The accession of Michael VIII Palaiologos in 1259 and the Byzantine recovery of Constantinople two years later signaled important changes in the orientation of Byzantine politics during the thirteenth century. Evidently there were still pronoia holders around the area of Smyrna during Michael's reign (see Appendix 3), but Michael VIII's interest in re-extending Byzantine authority over all of Greece strained the resources of the restored empire and led to the relatively rapid loss of Asia Minor. By the year 1300 everything except for the northwest corner of Asia Minor was lost, and within the next couple of decades this too fell outside Byzantine control. This in itself explains why there are no more references to pronoiai in Asia Minor after 1271.

Very little is known about the existence of pronoia in Thrace and the vicinity of Constantinople. After the one twelfth-century reference *[2.2]*, only a couple of sources indicate pronoiai existed in Thrace. One is a decision of a patriarchal synod from 1330. In it we read that Theodore Padyates had squandered the dowry given to his son when the latter married the daughter of George Strategos, *domestikos* of the western themes. In order to rectify this, Padyates had pledged a property (*ktema*) called Hagia Irene located near Vera (mod. Feres) in partial recompense for the lost dowry. After Padyates' death "the imperial property was seized" (ἐκρατήθη τὸ κτῆμα βασιλικόν), evidently a reference to Hagia Irene, but when Strategos asserted his claim to it, the emperor granted the property to him through a *prostagma*. Another of Padyates' sons then undertook a long and ultimately fruitless quest to acquire possession of the property. The most recent editors of the document refer to Hagia Irene as a "*Pronoiagrundstück*," that is, a property contained within a pronoia which ostensibly was held by Padyates. Indeed, there is no

[257] M. Angold, *The Byzantine Empire 1025–1204*, 2nd ed. (London and New York: 1997), 258–59.

other way to explain why Hagia Irene is called an "imperial property" than to conclude that it was held in pronoia. If so, this would explain why it was "seized" after Padyates' death. Nevertheless, it was improper for Padyates to pledge such a property to Strategos, and this would explain why an imperial concession was required to permit Strategos to keep the property.[258]

[8.66] Chrysobull of John VI Kantakouzenos for the monastery of Psychosostria (1349)

The other reference is found in a chrysobull John VI Kantakouzenos issued in 1349 for the monastery of Psychosostria in Constantinople. A *metochion* of the monastery called St. Elias was freed from a burden which, the act notes, dated back to the time of Andronikos II. The monastery had been required "to pay yearly eight hyperpyra to Katakalon, from the Thelematarioi soldiers." John VI now "suppresses" (*ekkoptei*) the *telos* of 8 hyperpyra and orders that neither Katakalon nor anyone else should trouble the monastery about it. Even though the words *pronoia* and *oikonomia* are absent, the assigning of state revenue owed by a property owned by the *metochion* to Katakalon leaves no doubt that Katakalon was a pronoia holder. One may imagine that initially – that is, more than twenty years earlier, during the reign of Andronikos II – Katakalon had been assigned a property as part of his pronoia; later he sold or donated the property to the *metochion*; and then to maintain the value of his *posotes*, the *metochion* was required to pay an *epiteleia* of 8 hyperpyra to Katakalon. Whether Katakalon was otherwise compensated for his loss is unknown, though it is clear that he was still alive in 1349.[259]

In numerous other cases involving Thrace we do not know the terms under which someone held property, even if that property was granted by the emperor. For example, the arrangement whereby John VI Kantakouzenos gave his oldest son Matthew Kantakouzenos western Thrace as an appanage must have included property grants and tax exemption to him and to his followers.[260] Yet there may not have been anything conditional about these grants; they may have been outright gifts that do not fit my definition of

[258] H. Hunger and O. Kresten, *Das Register des Patriarchats von Konstantinopel*, I (Vienna, 1981), no. 101, esp. line 25–26, and p. 569. *PLP*, nos. 21291–92, 26902.

[259] *Vatopédi*, II, no. 102.85: τελεῖν κατ᾽ ἔτος πρὸς τὸν ἀπὸ τῶν θεληματαρίων στρατιωτῶν τὸν Κατακαλών, and lines 91–94. On Katakalon, *PLP*, no. 11423.

[260] D. Nicol, *The Last Centuries of Byzantium, 1261–1453*, 2nd edn. (Cambridge, Eng., 1993), 215–16.

pronoia.[261] Similarly, much further down the social scale, it is impossible to say whether the two soldiers (*stratiotai*), Makros and Jacob, who appear as landowners in the region of Parapolia near Constantinople in 1334 were pronoia holders, smallholding soldiers, or even mercenaries that held some property.[262]

A possible example of a plan to create pronoia soldiers in Thrace is found in a synodal decision from 1367. John V's uncle, the monk Antonios Glavas Tarchaneiotes, had informed the patriarch that same year that the emperor was planning "to establish soldiers in the villages outside of Constantinople up to Selymbria and to give them the fields in them and all the land in them." But two villages in this area, named Oikonomeiou and Paspara, were held by the Church itself. Antonios proposed that the emperor "will hold these for a year, and if he accomplishes what he intends, he shall continue to hold them and give the Church another income equal to that of these properties; but if he does not accomplish what he wishes, these [properties] will be returned to it [i.e., the Church]." Nevertheless, the patriarch refused to agree to the plan, forcing the monk Antonios to offer another suggestion on behalf of John V: "Since you [i.e., the synod] will not give up these [villages] to him [i.e., the emperor], lease them so that he may hold [them] as others hold [them], and sow in them and render the *morte* to the Church."[263] The patriarch and an assembled synod still refused to acquiesce to this action and there is no evidence that John V actually carried out any aspect of the scheme. Seventeen years later, one of the villages in question was still in the possession of the Church, although it was nearly deserted.[264]

The conclusion in the scholarship is more or less unanimous that John V was planning to settle smallholding soldiers in the villages between Constantinople and Selymbria. While this is possible, it is equally possible that the soldiers were to be pronoia holders. Nothing in the document suggests

[261] According to Lj. Maksimović, "Geneza i karakter apanaža u Vizantiji," *ZRVI* 14/15 (1973), 120, 134, Kantakouzenos refers to the appanage of Matthew Kantakouzenos in Thrace as a pronoia. However, I interpret the text differently. In the relevant section of his history, Kantakouzenos explains that if John V's plans to take over the empire for himself succeeded, Matthew Kantakouzenos felt that he and his supporters would be in danger. Thus, Matthew thought it was necessary to act in order "to take some care of himself and them" (ἀλλὰ πρόνοιάν τινα αὑτοῦ ποιεῖσθαι καὶ αὑτῶν): Kantakouzenos, III, 47.19–20. Cf. Miller's translation, *The History of John Cantacuzenus (Book IV): Text, Translation and Commentary*, ed. T. Miller, diss., Catholic Univ. (Ann Arbor, Mich., 1975), p. 183: "to take some thought for himself and the others."

[262] *Lavra*, III, no. 122, lines 10–11 and 13. *PLP*, no. 7938.

[263] MM, I, 507.15–18, 22–25, 508.13–17.

[264] MM, II, 62, cited by Laiou, *Peasant Society*, 218. Oikonomeiou, modern Kumburgaz, is on the coast about eleven miles east of Selymbria.

unequivocally that the soldiers were to inhabit the area mentioned; rather, they were to be "established" there (using the vague verb καθίστημι) and "given" the land (using the equally vague δίδωμι). Moreover, the most troublesome aspect of seeing this as a proposal to settle smallholding soldiers is the reference to a one-year trial period in the first plan. If soldiers were settled and matters did not work out, were they then to be uprooted, and either discharged or sent elsewhere? Assuming the area involved was more or less uncultivated at the time of the proposal (since there would be no point in driving out productive peasants), would it not be unreasonable to expect new settlers, whether or not they were soldiers, to break even, much less show a profit, in one-year's time? Such a short trial period would better accommodate a paper transaction, that is, the shift of revenues (*prosodoi*) from one group to another, from the Church to pronoia holders. Nevertheless, we simply do not know enough about the conditions of the soldiers' anticipated tenure of these lands in order to use the case as an example of a plan to create smallholding soldiers.[265]

All in all, it is not surprising that there is so little known of pronoia in Thrace and the area of Constantinople. Our best sources, the monastic archives, simply do not deal much with this area. We should not conclude that Thrace was not full of pronoia holders from the reign of John Vatatzes on.

[8.67] Chrysobull of Stefan Uroš II Milutin for the monastery of St. George near Skopje (1299/1300)

Most of the references to pronoiai/oikonomiai in this chapter – indeed in this book – are localized to the area of Macedonia. Generally speaking, this is the area bounded by the area of Skopje to the north, the Chalkidike peninsula to the south, the upper Vardar valley to the west, and the lower Strymon valley to the east. The northernmost location of a property definitely granted as a pronoia by a Byzantine ruler is a small parcel in the village of Rečice, just southwest of modern Tetovo, about twenty-six miles due west of Skopje. This parcel is mentioned in a Slavic chrysobull from 1299/1300 of King Stefan Milutin. It had been confiscated from the monastery of St. George near Skopje during the reign of Michael VIII and granted as a pronoia to a man named Dragota, who later transferred the property to his son-in-law Manota as a dowry. Milutin explains that the property was not the *baština* – that is, allodial or patrimonial property – of Dragota, but an

[265] Bartusis, "Smallholding Soldiers," 9.

"imperial pronoia" (*carska pronija*), i.e., one conferred by the Byzantine emperor. Consequently, Milutin returned the property to the monastery while nevertheless stipulating that Manota, as well as his heirs, was permitted to continue to hold the property on condition that he and his heirs serve the monastery as soldiers. While the principle that a pronoia remained the property of the state accords with the Byzantine institution, the practice of "delivering oneself to the church" is unknown in Byzantium and reflects Serbian practices.[266]

[8.68] Chrysobull of Michael IX Palaiologos for the monastery of Hilandar, and Chrysobull of Andronikos II Palaiologos for the monastery of Hilandar, mentioning the village of Banjane (both 1299–1300)

Slightly further north, about eight miles north-northwest of Skopje, is the village of Banjane. In early 1299 Stefan Milutin granted a Serbian monastery to Hilandar, and by the end of 1300 Michael IX issued a chrysobull confirming the gift which included "the pronoiastic village called Banianis with all its rights" belonging to the Serbian monastery.[267] The parallel chrysobull of the senior emperor, Andronikos II, which was probably issued at the same time, has not been preserved, but it does exist in a Slavic translation. While this Slavic translation bears the date May 1308, it was produced in the middle of the fourteenth century and contains a number of fabricated interpolations. Nevertheless, it too speaks of "the village of Banjane, a pronoia, with all its rights."[268] A composite act, with falsified interpolations, of Milutin from around 1303 mentions Milutin's earlier donation of St. Niketas and its properties, including the village of Banjane, to a dependency of Hilandar. Here Banjane is called simply a "village" (*selo*), not a pronoia.[269]

Banjane came under Serbian control following Milutin's conquest of the region of Skopje in 1282. We do not know why Banjane was called a

[266] *SnM*, I, 225–26 (33) = S. Novaković, *Zakonski spomenici srpskih država srednjega veka* (Belgrade, 1912), 614–15 xxxiii. See Bartusis, "Serbian Pronoia," 180–86. T. Taranovski, *Istoria srpskog prava u Nemanjićkoj državi*, I (Belgrade, 1931), 39.

[267] *Chilandar*, ed. Živojinović, I, no. 18.14–15 = *SnM*, I, 289 (3) = *Chilandar*, ed. Petit, no. 51.12–13: ἔτι δὲ καὶ χωρίον προνοιαστικὸν καλούμενον Μπάνιανιν μετὰ πάντων τῶν δικαίων αὐτοῦ. On the village, with other references, see V. Kravari, *Villes et villages de Macédoine occidentale* (Paris, 1989), 94, map 3. On the date, see *SnM*, I, 286–87, but cf. Dölger, *Regesten*, IV, no. 2624 ("1308").

[268] *SnM*, I, 319: *selo Banjane pronija s' vsêmi pravinami jego*; and see 317.

[269] *SnM*, I, 313.137 (and see 297–99) = Novaković, *Zakonski spomenici*, 477 iii = *Actes de Chilandar, II. Actes slaves*, ed. B. Korablev, *VizVrem* 19 (1915), suppl. 1, no. 16.13.

"pronoiastic village." If it was so called because it had recently been held by a pronoia holder, it would have been originally granted by Milutin after 1282, or more likely by a Byzantine emperor during one of three periods: before 1203, between ca. 1218 and 1230 (by a despot of Epiros), or between 1246 and 1282 (by a Nicaean emperor or Michael VIII).[270] But there are other possibilities, among which is the possibility that, following Serbian practice, the village passed to the church as a pronoia.[271]

The northernmost possible location of a property granted by a Byzantine emperor as a pronoia is slighty further to the north, in a village southwest of Prizren described in a Slavic act from 1326 as a village "that pronoiars held." The area around Prizren was likewise conquered by Stefan Milutin in 1282–83, and so it had been outside of Byzantine control for more than forty years. Nevertheless, we cannot say whether these pronoia holders were Greeks or Serbs, or whether they, or even their fathers, had received their initial grant before or after Milutin's conquest.[272]

The preponderance of references to pronoiai in Macedonia, rather than indicating any particular concentration of pronoiai in this region, can be explained merely on the basis of the provenance of most of the documents referring to Macedonian pronoiai: the archives of the monasteries of Mount Athos. Just as the dossiers of the Patmos and Lemviotissa monasteries show a concentration of pronoiai in the regions of Smyrna and Miletos in the first half of the thirteenth century, the dossiers of Athonite monasteries overemphasize Macedonia, particularly the Chalkidike, as the location of pronoiai during the later thirteenth and fourteenth centuries. In truth, there is no reason to think that Byzantine Thrace, no less securely in Byzantine hands than Macedonia during this era, or even the areas of northwest Anatolia through the early fourteenth century, had any less a density of pronoia holdings than Byzantine Macedonia. The concentration of pronoiai in these areas may in fact have been greater than in Macedonia.

After 1204 the first reference to pronoia in Macedonia comes quite late. It is found in the 1279 praktikon in which the *apographeus* Alexios Amnon writes that he was ordered to make a fiscal revision in the theme of Thessaloniki of "the pronoiai – ecclesiastical and monastic, *prosopika* and *stratiotika*, and all the rest" *[6.9]*. As I argued earlier, this document was produced at a time when terminology was fluid, and here "pronoia" meant any kind of privilege granted over agricultural property. After this, the next reference

[270] On this chronology, Kravari, *Villes et villages*, 161.

[271] See Ostrogorsky, *Féodalité*, 191–92. Ostrogorsky misidentifies some of the relevant documents.

[272] *SnM*, III, 265 ii = Novaković, *Zakonski spomenici*, 638 ii: *što su dr'žali pronijarije*. Ostrogorsky, *Féodalité*, 203. See Bartusis, "Serbian Pronoia," 187.

to pronoia in Macedonia is found in a document from 1286 which contains an imperial *prostagma* ordering an official to compensate a man for the loss of a property with another property to maintain the size of the man's oikonomia *[8.73]*.

During the first half of the fourteenth century there are numerous references to pronoiai in Macedonia, notably in the lower Strymon valley, the valley east of Strumica, and above all on the Chalkidike peninsula. After the 1360s, with the Turkish conquest of the area, all mention of the institution disappears until the fifteenth century, when documents refer to the transformation of much of the monastic property in Macedonia into pronoiai by Manuel II soon after 1371. The last reference to pronoia in Macedonia is found in a document from 1420 *[9.4]*.

The rulings and letters of John Apokaukos, metropolitan of Naupaktos, testify to the existence of pronoia in the despotate of Epiros during the 1220s *[5.15–5.17]*. Apokaukos himself was the beneficiary of a pronoia grant that was later granted to a soldier. Documents from the 1270s refer to a pronoia grant in Thessaly which seems to have been granted by Michael VIII *[8.65]*. When the area of Akarnania submitted to Andronikos III in 1338, "the emperor . . . not only provided for the people of the cities with state benefactions, but he rewarded the powerful in them with honors and yearly incomes [*prosodoi*] and other benefactions."[273]

[8.69] Falsified act involving the monastery of Lavra's property on Lemnos (mid-fifteenth century)

The only evidence for the existence of pronoia on the islands of the Aegean is found in a falsified act dealing with the properties of a *metochion* of Lavra on the island. The act bears the date 1415, but it was probably composed after 1447. It contains the following passage:

Ἐδόθη τῆ τοιαύτη μονῆ ἀντὶ τῆς διὰ πρακτικοῦ γῆς Φιλανθρωπηνοῦ [*vacat*] ὑποστάσεως τοῦ Σταυρηνοῦ καὶ δοθείσης πρὸς στρατιώτην Δαυὶδ εἰς τὸ χωρίον τοῦ Πολυφύλλου καὶ πρὸς [*vacat*] παροίκους, μοδίων οὔσης ἑκατόν, ἀπὸ τῆς προνοιαστικῆς γῆς τοῦ Ἀπλημελὲ εἰς τὸ Λειβάδι μοδίων κδ΄.[274]

Earlier documents help make the meaning of this obscure passage clearer. George Doukas Philanthropenos was governor (*kephale*) of Lemnos in 1346,

[273] Kantakouzenos, I, 503.2–5. For the history, D. Nicol, *The Despotate of Epiros, 1267–1479* (Cambridge, Eng., 1984), 113.

[274] *Lavra*, III, app. XVIII.32–35.

and probably it is he who issued the praktikon mentioned in the passage.[275] Praktika from 1355 and 1361 note that among the possessions of a *metochion* that Lavra held on Lemnos was "in Polyphyllon an *exaleimma* of Staurenos," which included a vineyard of five modioi and fields of 50 modioi, plus another fifty modioi (the 1355 praktikon reads "thirty modioi" here) of land and a dry vineyard of 4 modioi taken from his brother-in-law and given to him.[276] Thus, we can account for the 100 modioi mentioned in the passage. As for Aplemele (a variant of Apelmene), these two praktika mention an *epistemonarches* (an official who maintained order in church) named Aplemele, who donated a vineyard of four modioi in a place called Petzea to the *metochion*.[277] He was probably a relative.

This information allows us to offer a paraphrase of the passage:

> Twenty-four modioi from the pronoiastic land of Aplemele in Leivadi were given to the monastery in exchange for the (*exaleimmatike*) *hypostasis* of Staurenos, being 100 modioi, (which much earlier had been granted to the monastery) through Philanthropenos' praktikon. (The *hypostasis* of Staurenos) was given to the soldier David and to . . . paroikoi.

Assuming this transfer had some basis in fact, it occurred sometime after 1361. The soldier David is otherwise unknown. The name itself, while a common religious name, is quite rare as a given name in late Byzantium. In any event, this is the only technical appearance of any form of the word *pronoia* in regard to Lemnos.

There is no concrete evidence that pronoiai ever existed in the Morea, at least not until the fifteenth century when George Gemistos Plethon received such a grant *[9.8]*. Michael Angold has suggested that the absence of pronoiai in the Morea was due to the fact that prior to the Latin conquest the area was untouched by war and invasion and "came under the supervision of the Grand Duke, who was responsible for the naval administration of the Empire."[278]

[8.70] Chrysobull of Andronikos II Palaiologos for the monastery of Vrontochiou at Mistra (February 1320)

Even in the fourteenth century, evidence for pronoiai in the Morea is quite weak. It is possible that an inscription from Mistra refers to pronoia. At

[275] See *Lavra*, III, nos. 125, 126, 127. [276] *Lavra*, III, no. 136.95–97, no. 139.104–06.
[277] *Lavra*, III, no. 136.98, no. 139.170.
[278] Angold, *The Byzantine Empire*, 2nd edn., 151, 258–59.

some time between 1312 and 1320, 600 modioi of land were given to the monastery of Vrontochiou in exchange for an unspecified quantity of land in the neighboring mountain range that had been "given to soldiers." But it is just as possible that this same quantity of land had been granted to a small number of smallholding soldiers who personally were settled on the land.[279]

Ljubomir Maksimović wrote that Kantakouzenos regarded the Morea as "a great pronoia" and sent his son, the despot Manuel, there in 1349. Maksimović translates the passage as "the emperor decided to create a pronoia from [Peloponnesian] cities and villages. Not having the older son with him, he sent the [second] son, despot Manuel, with ships to administer the Peloponnesians and make a powerful pronoia." Maksimović regarded this "powerful pronoia" as an "appanage" conferred upon Manuel by his father, but I think the passage means less than this.[280] If we translate the passage by viewing the construction *poieisthai pronoian* (ποιεῖσθαι πρόνοιαν) as the idiom common in Kantakouzenos' history "to take care of something," the passage becomes "the emperor thought to show a certain care for these [cities and villages]. Not having the older son [available (for Matthew Kantakouzenos was governing Thrace at the time)], he sent the despot Manuel with ships to rule and to take strong care of the Peloponnesians."[281]

It is not impossible that the institution of pronoia existed around Trebizond during the twelfth century, when the area was still under direct Byzantine control. But there is no evidence for it. Moreover, it is possible that the institution existed and flourished during the thirteenth and later centuries, as it did in Byzantium proper, but we know almost nothing of such matters.

Maksimović wrote an article about pronoia holders in the empire of Trebizond.[282] Without citing any source that uses the words *pronoia* or *oikonomia*, or any of the other terms or phrases that designate a pronoia

279 G. Millet, "Inscriptions byzantines de Mistra," *Bulletin de Correspondence Hellénique* 23 (1899), pp. 112–15, no. 4.6–9: καὶ δοθείσης [later: παραδοθείσης] πρὸς στρατιώτας, and line 17. Bartusis, "Smallholding Soldiers," 8.

280 Maksimović, "Geneza i karakter apanaža," 120, 135.

281 Kantakouzenos, III, 85.11–14: πρόνοιάν τινα αὐτῶν (i.e., cities and villages) ποιήσασθαι ἐσκέψατο ὁ βασιλεύς. μείζω δὲ οὐκ ἔχων τὸν υἱὸν ἔπεμψε δεσπότην τὸν Μανουὴλ τριήρεσιν, ἄρξοντα Πελοποννησίων καὶ πρόνοιαν ποιησόμενον τὴν δυνατήν. In his edition, Miller, *The History of John Cantacuzenus (Book IV)*, p. 124, line 12, removes the comma after ἔχων as found in the Bonn edition. Miller's translation of the passage, pp. 218–19, appropriately, I think, renders *pronoia* in a non-technical sense, though he incorrectly treats μείζω as an adverb ("being unable to do anything more") when it is a masculine adjective.

282 Lj. Maksimović, "Pronijari u Trapezuntskom carstvu," *Zbornik Filozofskog fakulteta* 12–1 (Belgrade, 1974) (= *Mélanges Georges Ostrogorsky*), 393–404.

in Byzantium proper, he concluded that pronoia was a common institution in fourteenth-century Trebizond. He approached the question from the point of view of what is known of the class structure of the empire of Trebizond. Just as in the empire of Nicaea, the despotate of Epiros, and then the restored empire of the Palaiologoi, men whom the documentary sources of Trebizond refer to as *stratiotai* (literally, "soldiers") occupy a rather distinguished position among the residents of Trebizond. Further, the military organization of Trebizond displays some similarities with that of the empire proper, and this led Maksimović to conclude that the majority of pronoia holders in Trebizond were soldiers of an elevated station.

All this is true and indeed it is quite possible that conditional grants of state revenues were conceded by the emperors of Trebizond to people including soldiers. Yet, oddly, Maksimović does not mention the single source from the empire of Trebizond that *does* use a form of the word *pronoia* in the fiscal sense: the chrysobull of the emperor of Trebizond Alexios III Komnenos from 1364 which confirmed the monastery of Soumela's possessions of its properties including its "*allelengya* and pronoiastic rights" *[7.14]*. As discussed earlier, *allelengya* is perhaps the Trapezuntine equivalent of *exaleimmata*, and "pronoiastic rights" would then be holdings specifically granted by the emperor. But with no other evidence with which to work, it is impossible to say whether this means that, in the empire of Trebizond, a pronoia was something a monastery could hold or whether this usage was idiosyncratic.

Nevertheless, grants of property were made to laymen in Trebizond. In a chrysobull from 1371, Alexios III Komnenos confirmed George Doranites' possession of the village of Chorove which had been granted to Doranites' father by the Trapezuntine emperor Basil I Komnenos (1332–40) almost forty years earlier. Doranites was a high official and the grant to his father is framed as a gift (*dorea*) which the son inherited.[283]

In summary it seems that after 1204 the two Byzantine successor states in Asia Minor and in Epiros utilized pronoia for military and other purposes. As these states expanded, they created new pronoiai in conquered territory: Thessaly and the Morea for the despotate of Epiros; Thrace, Macedonia, then Thessaly and the Morea for the empire of Nicaea and the restored empire under Michael VIII. Reconquest provided a wonderful opportunity

283 Edited independently by Sp. Lampros, *Νέος Ἑλληνομνήμων* 2 (1905), 196–98, and by E. L(obel), "A Chrysobull of Alexios III Grand Komnenos," *Bodleian Quarterly Record* 3 (1921), 141–43. A. Bryer, "Rural Society in Matzouka," in *Continuity and Change in Late Byzantine and Early Ottoman Society*, ed. A. Bryer and H. Lowry (Birmingham and Washington, D.C., 1986), 64, refers to this as a pronoia.

to create additional pronoiai that served the rulers well. Conquered land could be granted to soldiers and others as pronoiai, or the existing owner of the land could be allowed to keep it, but only as a pronoia.

Within a region

The one area of the empire where we can get some idea of how pronoiai were distributed across the landscape is in Macedonia, specifically the western Chalkidike.

[8.71] Periorismoi of Demetrios Apelmene for the monastery of Lavra (1300), and *Periorismoi* of Constantine Pergamenos and George Pharisaios for the monastery of Lavra (1321)

We are fortunate to have two major property descriptions (*periorismoi*) for the property within the theme of Thessaloniki of the monastery of the Great Lavra. The first of these was created in 1300 by the *apographeus* Demetrios Apelmene, and the other is from 1321, created by Constantine Pergamenos and George Pharisaios. Because Lavra was the largest private landowner within the western Chalkidike (part of the theme of Thessaloniki), because the *periorismoi* are so detailed, and because part of the information contained within the *periorismoi* is a listing of the properties that bordered each of Lavra's properties, it is possible not only to map out the boundaries of Lavra's properties, but to localize the properties of other landholders, including pronoia holders. Further, because these documents for the most part deal with the same properties, it is possible to view changes over time in the possession of properties. The following discussion is greatly indebted to Jacques Lefort's *Villages de Macédoine*, which in many respects is an extended analysis of these two documents.[284]

The documents employ two constructions when referring to pronoiai. One is "the pronoiastic rights of N." (τὰ προνοιαστικὰ δίκαιά τινος) and the other is "the rights held pronoiastically by N." (τὰ δίκαια προνοιαστικῶς κατεχόμενα παρά τινος). While the authors of the acts show a certain care in their use of these forms of the word *pronoia*, it is by no means absolute. At times the designation is omitted entirely. For example, at the same point in the property demarcations of both *periorismoi* we read "the pronoiastic

[284] *Lavra*, II, nos. 90 and 108. In addition to Lefort's volume, also see, regarding these documents, R. Radić, "Novi podaci o pronijarima iz prvih decenija XIV veka," *ZRVI* 21 (1982), 85–93.

rights of Glavas," but a few lines later, while the document from 1300 refers to "the said pronoiastic rights of Glavas," the *periorismoi* from 1321 note simply "the rights of Glavas." In another example, "the said pronoiastic rights of Drougoumanos and of Radenos" in 1300 becomes simply "the rights of Dragoumanos and Radenos" in 1321.[285] By the same token, one cannot conclude that the absence of the designation "pronoiastic" meant that the "rights" involved were *not* held "pronoiastically."

Moreover, the phrasing found in the documents sometimes makes it unclear whether or not a particular landowner held a certain property as pronoia. In both documents we find the phrases, at the same respective locations, "the pronoiastic rights of Radenos, of Drougoumanos, of Hagia Maria, and of the demarcated [i.e., the monastery of Lavra]," "the pronoiastic rights of Drougoumanos and of Radenos," and "the said pronoiastika rights." Also, both documents refer to "the pronoiastic rights of Drougoumanos, of Radenos, of the monastery of Chortaïtes, and of the demarcated."[286] Were it not for the simple reference to "the pronoiastic rights of Drougoumanos and of Radenos," we might conclude, on the basis of syntax, that the village of Hagia Maria and the monasteries of Lavra and Chortaïtes held pronoiastic rights.

At times the descriptions are identical, or nearly identical, in both *periorismoi*, indicating that the same person (or family) held the particular property at the time each document was drawn up. Thus, "the pronoiastic rights of Mammenos [sc. Mamenos]," as well as "the pronoiastic rights of Chrysaphes," appear in both documents in the same location. Similarly, in both documents we find "the pronoiastic rights from [the village of] Krene." (In 1300 these rights were held by the pronoia holder Petomenos.) "The pronoiastic rights of the *protokynegos* Sarantenos Indanes" becomes "the pronoiastic rights of Indanes."[287]

But the documents also show changes in property holdings over the twenty-one years separating them. Thus, "the pronoiastic rights of Cheimones and of Andronikopoulos" in 1300 becomes "the pronoiastic rights of *sevastos* Andronikopoulos and of Michael Keroulas" in 1321. "The

285 *Lavra*, II, no. 90.139,142; no. 108.213,216. *Lavra*, II, no. 90.229, no. 108.294.

286 *Lavra*, II, no. 90.196: τὰ προνοιαστικὰ δίκαια τοῦ ῾Ραδηνοῦ, τοῦ Δρουγουμάνου, τῆς Ἁγίας Μαρίας καὶ τοῦ περιοριζομένου, and lines 197 and 203; no. 108.257–58,258–59 (in these two passages: τοῦ Δραγουμάνου), 265–66. *Lavra*, II, no. 90.208–09: τὰ προνοιαστικὰ δίκαια τοῦ Δρουγουμάνου, τοῦ ῾Ραδηνοῦ, τῆς μονῆς τοῦ Χορταΐτου καὶ τοῦ περιοριζομένου, and no. 108.272 (here: τοῦ Δραγομάνου).

287 *Lavra*, II, no. 90.159–60, no. 108.863 (here: τοῦ Μαμηνοῦ); no. 90.184, no. 108.239. *Lavra*, II, no. 90.221, no. 108.286. *Lavra*, II, no. 90.144, no. 108.218–19.

pronoiastic rights of Vlachernites" becomes "the pronoiastic rights of *kyr* John Tarchaneiotes held earlier by *kyr* Michael Vlachernites." "The pronoiastic rights of Vlachernites" becomes "the pronoiastic rights of Phouskes."[288]

In one case pronoiastic rights disappear entirely. "The pronoiastic rights of Petomenos called Pantokratorena" in the village of Krene becomes "the said rights of Krene."[289] This property had been held by a monastery named Pantokrator before coming into Petomenos' possession. By 1321 either Petomenos passed from the scene or the officials simply omitted his name.

The adverb "pronoiastically" (προνοιαστικῶς) is encountered in these documents much less frequently than the phrase "pronoiastic rights." It appears only once in the *periorismoi* from 1300. "The rights of Hagios Andreas held pronoiastically by the *pansevastos* Skouterios" appear in both *periorismoi*.[290] Aside from this reference it appears five other times in the *periorismoi* of 1321. "The [rights] held pronoiastically by *kyr* Theodore Kounales from the [village of] Mystakones" replaces "the rights of the village of Panagia," a neighboring village.[291] "The rights of Kounales held pronoiastically from Mystakones" appears two other times in the 1321 *periorismoi*, dealing with properties not described in the 1300 document, as does "the rights held pronoiastically by Angelos from the [village of] Ptelea."[292]

That the phrase "the pronoiastic rights of N." is equivalent to "the rights held pronoiastically by N." is seen by a comparison of two parallel passages dealing with a change of property holders. In 1300 "the rights of Isauros, of Hagia Maria [sc. Hagia Marina], and of the demarcated [i.e., Lavra]" and "the pronoiastic rights of John Isauros from the [village of] Chliaropotamou" become in 1321 "the rights held pronoiastically by *kyr* Theodore Lampenos, of Hagia Maria [sc. Hagia Marina], and of the demarcated" and "the said rights of Lampenos."[293] Since the officials in 1321 had to indicate that Isauros was replaced by Lampenos, they rewrote the passage using the adverbial construction they favored. Also, we observe once again the ambiguous syntax of the *periorismoi* regarding the actual holders of pronoiastic rights.

288 *Lavra*, II, no. 90.142, no. 108.216–17. *Lavra*, II, no. 90.245–46, no. 108.369–70. *Lavra*, II, no. 90.283, no. 108.419.

289 *Lavra*, II, no. 90.233: τοῖς προνοιαστικοῖς δικάιοις τοῦ Πετωμένου τοῖς καὶ παντοκρατορηνοῖς λεγομένοις, and no. 108.300.

290 *Lavra*, II, no. 90.8–9: τὰ τοῦ Ἁγίου Ἀνδρέου δίκαια τὰ προνοιαστικῶς παρὰ τοῦ πανσεβάστου Σκουτερίου κατεχόμενα, and no. 108.110–11.

291 *Lavra*, II, no. 108.379, no. 90.254. 292 *Lavra*, II, no. 108.422–23,476–77,429–30.

293 *Lavra*, II, no. 90.241–42, no. 108.364–66.

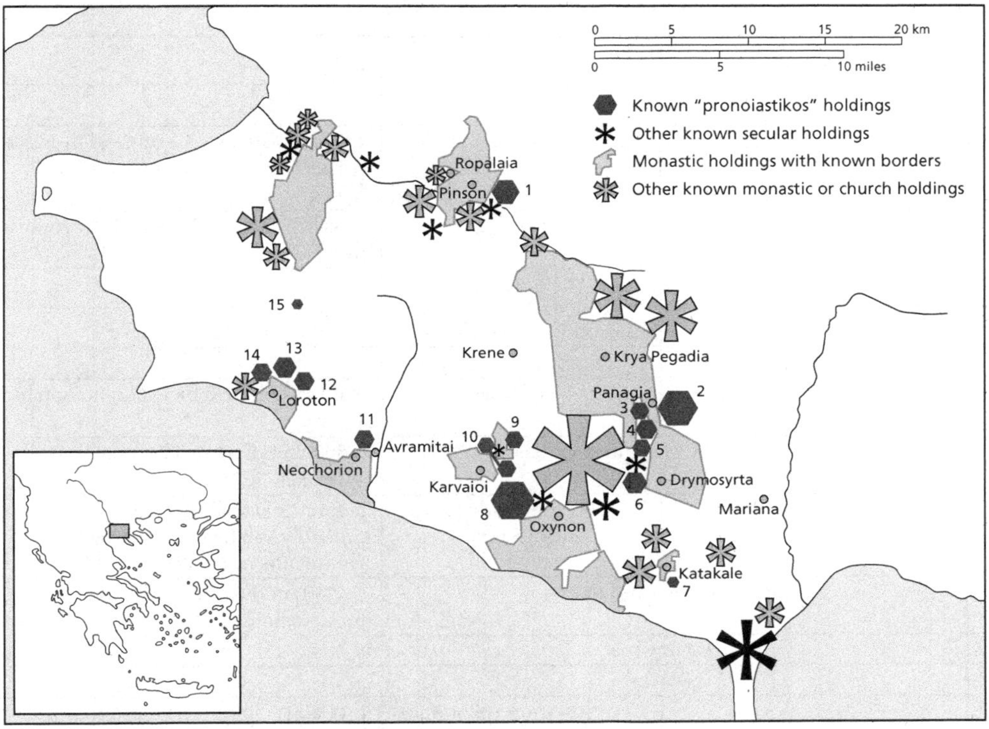

Figure 8.3 The western Chalkidike, ca. 1320.

These "pronoiastic" holdings are fairly evenly distributed through the regions containing most of the good agricultural land of the western Chalkidike. Figure 8.3 provides a representation of where these and other known holdings were located and Table 8.14 lists the pronoia holders involved. Because the only documents which define actual borders of properties deal with the properties of monasteries, on the map the only holdings with defined borders are those of monasteries. The borders of the holdings of other monasteries, pronoia holders, and other laymen which lay adjacent to these defined borders are unknown, but the size of the symbol representing the holding gives a rough approximation of the size of the property. While the map distinguishes known "pronoiastic" holdings from other secular holdings, it is possible that many of these secular holdings were pronoia holdings as well, but we have no evidence indicating that. The empty areas on the map were, of course, held by someone (monastery, church, pronoia holder, other layman, or the state), but we have no data for these areas.

Table 8.14 List of pronoiai in Figure 8.3

No	1300	1321	notes
1	*pansevastos* Skouterios[a]		
2	"the rights of Mystakones"	Theodore Kounales	not associated with Kounales in 1300; perhaps the same Kounales as no. 7 below[b]
3		Angelos	possibly part of Vlachernites' pronoia in 1300[c]
4	Michael Vlachernites	Phouskes	
5		John Tarchaneiotes	ca. 1000 modioi[d]
6	John Isauros	Theodore Lampenos[e]	
7		Kounales	300 modioi; held by Esphigmenou in 1346[f]
8	Theodore Chrysaphes Vranas		>6000 modioi; held by Vranas until at least ca. 1335[g]
9	Petomenos	"the pronoiastic rights from Krene"	before 1300 held by a monastery; probably still held in pronoia by Petomenos in 1321[h]
10	Dragoumanos and Radenos		>1700 modioi; probably joint pronoia holders[i]
11	Mamenos[j]		
12	Glavas[k]		
13	Cheimones and Andronikopoulos	*sevastos* Andronikopoulos and Michael Keroulas	probably a jointly-held pronoia[l]
14	*protokynegos* Sarantenos Indanes[m]		
15		Michael Saventzes	300 modioi; location approximate; taken from Michael Keroulas (above no. 13) by reason of *perisseia*[n]

[a] Lefort, *Villages de Macédoine*, 123–24, 142, map 5.

[b] Lefort, *Villages de Macédoine*, 89, 105, 113, maps 6, 7. *PLP*, no. 13476. Laiou, *Peasant Society*, 50f, 301. *Lavra*, ii, no. 90.286. A praktikon from 1321 (*Lavra*, ii, no. 109.966–67, and iv, p. 91 and note 189) notes that Theodore Kounales had been receiving from Lavra an *epiteleia* of 2 hyperpyra for a mill at Drymosyrta, and adds that by virtue of a chrysobull the monastery no longer had to pay this sum. The mill, which had been purchased by Lavra before 1298 from someone named Iovlachas (*Lavra*, ii, no, 89.120), stands at what was probably the southern border of the property Kounales held in pronoia. The ruins of this mill still exist just west of the ancient ruins on the twin hills called Spartovounon (40°21.6′ N, 23°16.5′ E) in the two *periorismoi*. A local farmer who gave me a tour of the area in 2004 referred to the ancient site as "Skartelo" (Σκαρτέλο). In 1300 and 1321 a Kounales (with no first name) held the property between nos. 5 and 6 in Figure 8.3: Lefort, *Villages de Macédoine*, 47, 53, map 7. Although this is likely the same Kounales, the documents do not say specifically that he held this property in pronoia.

Table 8.14 (*cont.*)

[c] Lefort, *Villages de Macédoine*, 89, 113, map 7. Angelos and the property are not mentioned in the 1300 document and the property (in 1321) was adjacent to Phouskes' property. On the other hand, the 1300 document omits describing one of the borders of the property Angelos later held, and both the 1300 and 1321 documents mention a field of a paroikos of Angelos named Manuel that bordered the village of Drymosyrta: *Lavra*, II, nos. 90.259, 108.386, and Lefort, *Villages de Macédoine*, 47, map 7, 133 and note 1. This was located about 1.25 miles to the east of the property Angelos held in pronoia. This indicates that Angelos had a presence in the area in 1300 and held, if not the property he held in 1321, then some other property in pronoia in 1300.

[d] Lefort, *Villages de Macédoine*, 47, 53, 54 note 1, 89, 113, map 7. *PLP*, no. 2830.

[e] Lefort, *Villages de Macédoine*, 47, 53, map 7. *PLP*, nos. 8289, 14427.

[f] *Esphigménou*, no. 22.15–16, and Lefort, *Villages de Macédoine*, 118, map 8.

[g] Lefort, *Villages de Macédoine*, 66, 67 note 3, 78, 111, 185 line 21, map 10.

[h] Lefort, *Villages de Macédoine*, 59, 86, map 10. Cf. *Lavra*, II, nos. 90.221 and 108.286. A paroikos of Petomenos possessed a vineyard south of the domain of Lavra at Genna: *Lavra*, II, no. 90.214, and Lefort, *Villages de Macédoine*, 87 note 1.

[i] Lefort, *Villages de Macédoine*, 59, 66, 67 note 2, 778, 163, map 10. *PLP*, nos. 5871, 91829 (both referring to the same Dragoumanos). Oikonomides, "A propos des armées," 367. Radenos may be the Radenos mentioned in a praktikon from 1321. Among the paroikoi held by Lavra in the village of Karvaioi was one paroikos, who held within his *stasis* "a vineyard of one modios, taxable to Radenos" (ἀμπέλιον ὑποτελὲς τῷ ῾Ραδηνῷ), and another paroikos, who held within his stasis "another [vineyard] . . . of ½ modios, taxable to Radenos" (ἕτερον . . . ὑποτελὲς τῷ ῾Ραδηνῷ μοδίου ἡμίσεος): *Lavra*, II, no. 109.299,301. The designation "taxable to Radenos" meant, in all likelihood, that all or part of the taxes burdening these vineyards was received by this Radenos. If this is the same Radenos, then the tax on the vineyards probably was part of his pronoia. On the term *hypoteles*, *Lavra*, IV, 161. For the *vasilikos stratiotes kyr* John Radenos, who witnessed an act in 1324, see *Chilandar*, ed. Petit, no. 97.10–11. Dragoumanos may be the John Dragoumanos (d. bef. 1328) found in several acts who, along with his wife, donated a *metochion* called Hagios Elias located between the village of Ropalaia and a place called Phouskoulou to the monastery of Hilandar before 1316: *Chilandar*, ed. Živojinović, I, nos. 33.20, 34.140, 35.31; *Chilandar*, ed. Petit, no. 117.24; Lefort, *Villages de Macédoine*, 136–37; and *PLP*, no. 5788. This is some eleven miles north of the area where Dragoumanos and Radenos held their property in pronoia.

[j] Lefort, *Villages de Macédoine*, 25, 108, map 11. *PLP*, no. 16568.

[k] Lefort, *Villages de Macédoine*, 94, 102 note 2, map 11. *PLP*, no. 4213.

[l] Lefort, *Villages de Macédoine*, 33, 94, 102 note 2, 103 note 2, map 11. *PLP*, nos. 11700, 91203, 30772. Oikonomides, "A propos des armées," 367.

[m] Lefort, *Villages de Macédoine*, 87, 88 notes 1 and 4, 94, map 11. The *PLP*, no. 8207, suggests an identification of this Indanes with another (no. 8206), but the latter was a paroikos as stated in *Xénophon*, no. 14.5: *Xénophon*, no. 14.53 (1320), and also nos. 25.92 (1338) and App. II.120. Also, see *[8.40]*.

[n] *Xénophon*, no. 15.19–20. Lefort, *Villages de Macédoine*, 33, map 11.

All of the properties which the *periorismoi* of 1300 and 1321 note were held in pronoia are located in the western part of the Chalkidike peninsula. The two documents also list the properties Lavra held in the eastern part of the Chalkidike, as well as on the Longos and Kassandra peninsulas attached to the Chalkidike, but there is no mention of anyone holding "pronoiastic" rights in these areas. There are several possible reasons of this. First, the properties of the Lavra monastery in the eastern Chalkidike (outside of the territory of Mount Athos) and on the Longos and Kassandra peninsulas were not as extensive as in the western Chalkidike. Therefore, there was less chance there for its properties to border on the holdings of pronoia holders. Also, the eastern Chalkidike has a much lower percentage of arable land than the western Chalkidike, which would account for fewer properties held in pronoia.

Further, it is quite likely that the 1300 and 1321 *periorismoi* are a pastiche of the work of several officials, and the officials who drew up the original descriptions for the western Chalkidike may have chosen to refer to pronoia holdings, while those producing the descriptions for the other areas did not. For the purposes of these *periorismoi*, there was no real reason to include this information at all; as we have seen, it is omitted at times.

These reasons alone could explain the absence of references to pronoia holdings in other sections of these documents. Therefore, one cannot conclude that these other areas did not have pronoia holders (and in fact they did). And yet the documents do show that the area adjacent to the Athos peninsula was dominated by landholdings of monasteries including Lavra. We can at least say that the area around, say, Hierissos, did not have many properties held in pronoia.

Finally, we must ask why these documents contain so many references to "pronoiastic rights" or "rights held pronoiastically." Both the adjectival and adverbial form of *pronoia* are quite rare. These *periorismoi* aside, the adjective *pronoiastikos* appears only eight times in no more than eight documents dealing with no more than four specific cases of Byzantine pronoia. For example, a praktikon for Iviron from 1301 refers to "the pronoiastic rights earlier held by Adrian" (τὰ προνοιαστικά [sic] δίκαια τὰ προκατεχόμενα παρὰ τοῦ Ἀδριανοῦ) as bordering a field of the monastery on the Gallikos river (west of Thessaloniki). With minor orthographic variations, this is repeated in later revisions of this praktikon from 1318, 1320, and 1341. The use of the verb προκατέχω suggests that Adrian (otherwise unknown) no longer held the land bordering the monastery's field. It would have made more sense to indicate who the present holder of the property was, if not in 1301, then certainly by 1341. It seems that the *apographeus* in 1301 was satisfied with indicating who the previous holder of the property was and that later *apographeis* did not think it necessary to revise the passage.[294]

The adverb "pronoiastically" (προνοιαστικῶς) is equally rare, appearing but five times in four documents.[295] Neither word appears in any non-documentary (literary) source. Yet in these two *periorismoi* either the adjective or adverb appear eighteen times in each of the documents.

Granted these *periorismoi* are lengthy documents, but that hardly explains the matter. Rather, we must ask other questions. First, were these documents, by their nature, unique? Evidently both documents were drawn up, not on the basis of an imperial order, but at the request of Lavra. To this extent they are unusual. Nevertheless, many documents, from the same period and by the same fiscal officials, contain *periorismoi* that utilize the same format, and the praktika for Iviron mentioned above even mentions borders formed by neighboring "pronoiastic rights." It was not a peculiarity of the authors of these *periorismoi* to specify this information.

But were the authors of the *periorismoi* using the terms idiosyncratically or carelessly? This would be the case if they referred to all rights held by laymen as "pronoiastic rights." However, in both *periorismoi* there are some "rights" held by laymen that consistently are not prefixed by the adjective or modified by the adverb. For example, in the 1300 and 1321 *periorismoi* for the village of Pinson, where we find mention of "the rights of [the village of] Hagios Andreas held pronoiastically by the *pansevastos* Skouterios (Fig. 8.3, no. 1)," we also encounter "the rights of Plexeidas" and just south of Ropalaia (only in the 1300 *periorismoi*) "the rights of Kassandrenos."[296]

Once these possibilities are excluded, it is difficult to avoid the simple conclusion that the western Chalkidike contained a significant number of pronoia holders. Of all the monasteries for which property archives have been preserved, Lavra was far and away the largest landholder in this area. Either the *periorismoi* of the possessions of other monasteries which might have mentioned neighboring pronoia holdings in the area have not been

294 *Iviron*, III, nos. 70.441–44 (1301), 75.586 (1318), 79.573 (1320); IV, 86.446–47 (1341). The other documents containing the adjective: *[8.68] [8.69]* and perhaps in *[5.20]*. The adjective appears in a few more documents referring to grants made by an authority other than the Byzantine emperor: *[8.23] [10.1]*.

295 *[5.2] [5.6] [8.55]* and probably in Lefort, *Villages de Macédoine*, 185.

296 *Lavra*, II, no. 90.9,11–13,37–38, no. 108.110,112–14. The secular property further to the south of Ropalaia (about four miles southwest of no. 1 in Figure 8.3) was held by someone named Kassandrenos in 1301 and in documents from 1318, 1320, and 1341 by an anonymous *logariastes* of the court: *Iviron*, III, no. 70.398, no. 75.530, no. 79.520; *Iviron*, IV, no. 86.407. There was a *logariastes* of the court named Kassandrenos, who was in fact a pronoia holder at this time *[7.9]*, so all of these references probably are dealing with the same man: see *PLP*, no. 11313.

preserved, or the more limited possessions of these other monasteries, by chance, did not border on any pronoia holdings.[297]

A number of additional conclusions can be drawn from this discussion of the geographical distribution of pronoia holdings in the western Chalkidike:

(i) They appear to be rather evenly distributed among the properties held by other privileged landholders, specifically monasteries. It is not surprising that there would be many quarrels between pronoia holders and monasteries over property rights.

(ii) On average the properties held in pronoia tend to be smaller than the properties held by monasteries.

(iii) My map suggests that for every acre held by monasteries, pronoia holders held perhaps one quarter of an acre. This is significant in terms of estimating the density of pronoia holdings throughout the empire, that is, the percentage of arable land devoted to pronoiai. If an area of the empire where the great monasteries of Mount Athos had a substantial portion of their landholdings nevertheless contains a significant proportion of landholdings held in pronoia, then we should expect that other areas of the empire would have no less a percentage of pronoia properties. A conservative estimate would be that a quarter of the empire's arable land was held by pronoia holders.

(iv) The number of properties held in pronoia by the same individual in both 1300 and 1321 show that it was not uncommon for a man's tenure of a particular property in pronoia to span decades.

Within a village

[8.72] Slavic translation of a praktikon for the monastery of Hilandar (1300)

Simply looking at a map with properties held in pronoia gives a misleading impression of how pronoia grants were distributed. These properties constituted the domain land of the pronoia holder. But pronoiai included not only real property but paroikoi and other rights and taxes as well. The villages containing paroikoi that pronoia holders held can be laid out on a map, but often that would not indicate the complexity of the arrangements. At the village level, some pronoia holders held an entire village, as Alexios Raoul held the village of Prevista. Others, like the soldiers Saventzes, Maroules, and Berilas, held paroikoi and property in parts of one or more villages.

[297] See, e.g., *Docheiariou*, no. 19, and *Xénophon*, no. 3.

This was probably the most common situation. The best example of how a single village could be shared by several pronoia holders is found in the praktikon for the monastery of Hilandar from November 1300 and involves the village of Kastrion. The praktikon lists the paroikoi and property held by Hilandar in the theme of Thessaloniki. The original is lost, but we possess a Slavic translation of the original which appears to be a more or less reliable translation. The praktikon lists Hilandar's possessions in seven villages which together had a *posotes* totaling 580 hyperpyra. Of interest to us is one village in particular in which the monastery held numerous paroikoi that had come "from the pronoiai" of laymen. The village is Gradec (or Gradac), the Slavic translation of the Greek Kastrion or Kastrin. Kastrion (today Kastri) is located in the lower Strymon valley, about two and a half miles west of the Strymon and about four miles from the Aegean.[298]

The largest group of paroikoi held by a layman in Kastrion was twenty-six paroikoi "previously held by Vardan." Vladimir Mošin assumed that Vardan (in Greek, Vardanes, a relatively uncommon surname) had held these paroikoi in pronoia, while Ostrogorsky thought he held them as an allodial holding.[299] In truth we do not know how Vardanes held these paroikoi. Following the twenty-six paroikoi once held by Vardanes, the praktikon lists a series of paroikos households in Kastrion once held by six pronoia holders. The document explains that Hilandar held seven paroikos households "from the pronoia of Manoil Develcin" (*od' pronije Devel'cina Manoila*), nine paroikos households "from the pronoia of Gazi Sirijan" (*od' pronije Gazija Sirijanova*), one paroikos household "from the pronoia of Nikifor Hris" (*od' pronije Nikifora Hrisova*), another "from the pronoia

[298] According to the editors of the recent edition of the acts of Hilandar, Kastrion was donated to the monastery by Michael VIII's brother John in the early 1270s, was taken from the monastery sometime after 1277, and then was regranted to the monastery in June 1300: *Chilandar*, ed. Živojinović, I, pp. 36–37, 44, as well as Mošin, "Akti," 197, 217. However, it is not clear, at least to me, whether the despot John was donating his own property or state property. Further, it is quite possible that only part of Kastrion was granted to Hilandar in the 1270s: (i) the 1277 chrysobull confirming the monastery's possession of Kastrion refers to it, not as a village, but as a *ktema* (a property); (ii) the fiscal value of the *ktema* in 1277 was a mere 50 hyperpyra, while in 1300 the total *posotes* of the village of Kastrion exceeded 300 hyperpyra; and (iii) the chrysobull of 1277 confirms also the monastery's possession of a church within the village of Kastrion, an unnecessary clause if Hilandar was holding the entire village: *Chilandar*, ed. Živojinović, I, no. 10.17,21–22, App. II, pp. 293 and 295. If Hilandar was granted only part of Kastrion during the 1270s, then the pronoia holders in Kastrion, dispossessed when the entire village was transferred to Hilandar, may have been holding their pronoiai in the village long before 1277.

[299] Mošin, "Akti," 205.12–13: *prêžde dr'žav'šomu je Var'danu*, and note 3. Ostrogorsky, *Féodalité*, 141. *Chilandar*, ed. Živojinović, I, App. II, provides a detailed French paraphrase of the act. On the name Vardanes, *PLP*, nos. 2188–92.

of Georgije Kapsokavada" (*od' pronije Geor'gija Kap'sokavade*), another "from the pronoia of Nikola Filomat" (*od' pronije Filomata Nikole*), and nineteen paroikos households comprising the "pronoia from the children of Kiprijan" (*od' detec' Kiprijanov' . . . pronija*). The section of the praktikon on the paroikoi of Kastrion concludes with a list of seven *eleutheroi* paroikoi not associated with any previous holder. Evidently they were recently attached to the village.[300]

The people who once held part of Kastrion as pronoia grants all seem to have been Greeks. Manoil Develcin is the Slavic form of Manuel Devlitzenos. From a series of praktika for Iviron we know of a *kyr* Manuel Devlitzenos (or Doveltzenos), *tzaousios* of the Thessalonian *mega allagion* in 1301, and dead by 1317. Iviron was paying him, and later his children, one hyperpyron yearly as an *epiteleia* for half interest in a mill it held *[8.18]*.[301] The receipt of such an *epiteleia* is consistent with the holding of a pronoia.

Gazi Sirijan would be, in its Greek form, Gazes Syrgiannes or Syrianos. Both Gazes and Syrianos are not uncommon family names.[302] Syrgiannes is a famous name, but with a known connection to only three people. The Cuman chieftain Sytzigan took the name Syrgiannes upon entering Byzantine service and becoming a Christian in the mid thirteenth century. It is evidently derived from "*syr* Ioannes" (Sir John).[303] His son, an associate of Andronikos III Palaiologos, was Syrgiannes Philanthropenos Palaiologos. Because his wife was known as Maria Doukaina Palaiologina Syrgiannina, the name, which originated as a given name, became a family name.[304] However, in 1300 the name probably would still have to be only a first name. Therefore, it would seem that our pronoia holder was named either Syrgiannes Gazes with Syrgiannes as a given name (transposed by the Slavic translator of the praktikon due to unfamiliarity) or N. Gazes Syrianos (a double surname). I think the former case is the most likely.

Hilandar held only one paroikos family in Kastrion from each of the pronoiai of three other men. Nikifor Hris is certainly the Slavic form of Nikephoros Chrysos. He is otherwise unknown.[305] Georgije Kapsokavada is George Kapsokavades. This surname is attested on the Chalkidike in the early

300 Mošin, "Akti," 207–10, lines 136–37, 171–72, 217–18, 228–29, 233–34, 239–40, and 295–311.

301 For other members of the family, see Oikonomides, "The Properties of the Deblitzenoi," 176–98, and also F. Barišić, "Prvi popis grčkih akata na starosrpskom s kraja XIII veka u Hilandaru," *Hilandarski Zbornik* 7 (1989), 35–36.

302 See *PLP*, nos. 3443–52 and nos. 27169–78.

303 See *PLP*, nos. 27233 and 24401.

304 *PLP*, nos. 27167–68.

305 Chrysos appears as both a given name and surname: *PLP*, nos. 2985, 31177–91. Chryses appears a couple of times as a surname as well: *PLP*, nos. 31086–87.

fourteenth century.[306] Nikola Filomat is Nicholas Philommates or Philomates. A fourteenth-century list of (now lost) acts in Hilandar's archives mentions "Porphyrogennetos' writ for Philommates" (*Por'firogenitova kniga za Filomata*). This refers to an act of Constantine, the younger son of Michael VIII, and, possibly, this same Philommates, issued perhaps in 1280.[307] Although no Nicholas is otherwise attested, other members of the family of Philommates appear in fourteenth-century documents.[308]

The reference to a "pronoia from the children of Kiprijan" consisting of nineteen paroikos households in Kastrion is interesting because of its form. In each of the six other instances in which the document uses the word *pronija* it is found in the expression "od' pronije" (of someone), which is equivalent to the Greek ἀπὸ τῆς προνοίας τινός. In these six cases we cannot determine whether the paroikoi "from someone's pronoia" represented all or only part of the person's pronoia grant (the implication is, of course, the latter). However, the passage dealing with a "pronoia from the children of Kiprijan" suggests that these nineteen paroikoi households constituted their entire pronoia grant. Further, that the children of Kiprijan should have held a pronoia suggests the transmittal of a pronoia as an inheritance, as well as a joint pronoia held by more than one person. The name Kiprijan corresponds to the Greek name Kyprianos, which is an uncommon surname.[309]

Figure 8.4 shows the relative distribution of the paroikoi who were held by this group of men before Kastrion was granted to Hilandar. There was also a large quantity of land in Kastrion, 8,000 modioi, which, according to the praktikon, was rented out. This land was assessed at 160 hyperpyra, reflecting the normal rate at the time.[310] Presumably this land had been held by some of the pronoia holders who had held Kastrion. The evidence of Figure 8.4 could be misread to suggest that some pronoia holders occupied a rather low social position as they held merely one paroikos family, but indeed we do not know whether these were the *only* possessions held within

306 *PLP*, nos. 10852, 11589–90, and cf. no. 11565. See Lefort, *Villages de Macédoine*, 132 note 4, 146.

307 A. Solovjev, "Un inventaire des documents byzantins de Chilandar," *Seminarium Kondakovianum* 10 (1938), 37, and Barišić, "Prvi popis," 37–38, no. 47 and cf. no. 40. F. Barišić, "Konstantin Porfirogenit Paleolog," *ZRVI* 22 (1983), 55–56.

308 See Lefort, *Villages de Macédoine*, 88 note 4, 94, 176–77; *Chilandar*, ed. Petit, no. 117.160; *Lavra*, II, no. 90.147, no. 102.6, no. 108.582, and App. X.26; *Docheiariou*, no. 15.15, no. 22.7; and *PLP*, nos. 29914–33.

309 *PLP*, nos. 13938–45, 92473–74. It is quite common as a religious name (*PLP*, nos. 13908ff) leaving open the small possibility that Kyprianos was the monastic name taken by the man.

310 Mošin, "Akti," 214.519–22.

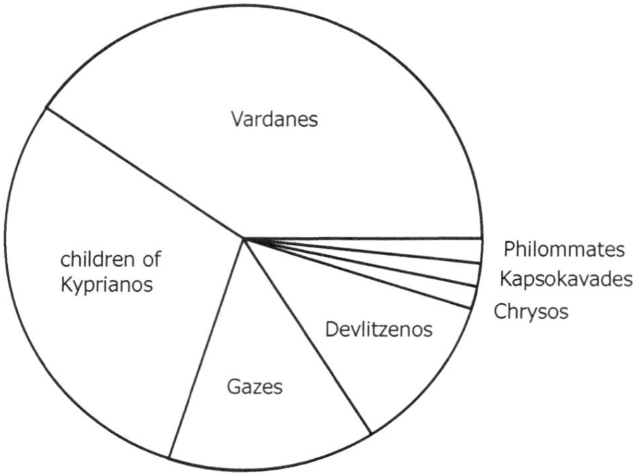

Figure 8.4 Distribution by holder of paroikoi in Kastrion, late thirteenth century.

the pronoiai of these men.[311] Only in the case of the "pronoia from the children of Kyprianos" (which contained nineteen paroikos households) is it likely, though not certain, that these paroikoi comprised the entire quantity of paroikos households held in pronoia. On the other hand, it is very likely that the Manuel Devlitzenos of the praktikon held an *epiteleia* from the monastery of Iviron at this same time *[8.18]*, suggesting that his possessions in Kastrion did not represent the full extent of his pronoia.

Proportion of property held as grants: how many pronoiai were there?

It is extremely difficult to make even a rough estimate of the proportion of property and paroikoi within the empire that was held by pronoia holders or of the number of pronoia grants that existed at any one time. What documentary evidence we have is fragmentary, generally deals with pronoia only incidentally, and since most of it comes from monasteries (those of Mount

[311] Without citing any sources, Gorjanov, *Pozdnevizantijskij feodalizm*, 105–06, 123, wrote, "Chrysobulls show that a significant part of the lands of the monastery of Vatopedi was composed of the earlier possessions of small pronoiars. The sizes of these possessions are seen from the number of peasants ascribed to them, which fluctuates from one to twenty-six." Even though the Hilandar praktikon is neither a chrysobull nor deals with the possessions of Vatopedi, it is obvious that Gorjanov had it in mind. Gorjanov's assertion was cited uncritically by A. Laiou, "The Byzantine Aristocracy in the Palaeologan Period," *Viator* 4 (1973), 142.

Athos, the Lemviotissa monastery outside Smyrna, and the monastery of St. John on Patmos), it probably does not deal with geographic areas that are representative of the empire as a whole. The literary sources are even less useful for any kind of quantification.

Nevertheless, the questions are quite important because their answers would tell us how important the class of pronoia holders was to the social structure of the society as well as to the army and how the granting of pronoiai affected the economy and fiscal structure of the empire. Despite the weakness of our sources to address these issues it is possible to make a few observations that point in the direction of answers to these questions. Readers with little tolerance for numeric speculation should pass over this section quickly. I will be the first to admit that most of my quantitative conclusions, while not quite in the realm of utter fantasy, are at least on the frontiers. But for those who want my best guess about the prevalence of pronoia, read on.

First, it is a given that the percentage of the empire's territory that was granted as pronoiai was inversely related to the tax revenues received by the imperial treasury. In other words, the more property, paroikoi, and taxes that were granted as pronoiai, the less revenue the treasury received. If taxes from the countryside were still a significant source of revenue, however small, that would mean that a certain portion of the revenues from the countryside had not been granted to privileged landholders. Here we are not so much interested in how much tax revenue was collected from the provinces but whether the provinces were still considered a productive source for the tax revenues. In the early fourteenth century, it appears they were. Pachymeres writes that in the early fourteenth century Andronikos II had tried to be more diligent about "collecting the usual taxes from property so that these might be used as pay for the army." And according to Gregoras, by 1321 through increased taxation and the greater diligence of tax collectors, the fisc amassed nearly 1 million hyperpyra. Andronikos II's plan was "to establish twenty permanent triremes against sea and coastal enemies, and a land army in Bithynia of one thousand permanent cavalry and in Thrace and Macedonia, two thousand of the same," and to spend the remainder on embassies and other expenses. Oikonomides thought Gregoras was writing about pronoia soldiers, but the connection between cash and soldiers suggests mercenaries.[312]

[312] Pachymeres, Bonn edn., II, 618. Gregoras, I, 317–18. Oikonomides, "The Role of the Byzantine State," 1058.

These plans came to nothing because of the civil war that began that same year. The first periods of civil war of the fourteenth century, between Andronikos II and Andronikos III (1321, 1321–22, and 1327–28), were rather minor affairs compared to what would follow. Whatever taxes had been flowing into the treasury for the most part continued to do so. And the numbers were not negligible. According to Kantakouzenos (I, 387.16–17), in 1329 the taxes from the island of Chios amounted to more than 20,000 hyperpyra.

The next phase of civil war (1341–47), between John Kantakouzenos and the regency for John V Palaiologos, was much more disastrous from a fiscal point of view. There was more fighting and it was accompanied by foreign invasion, mainly by Serbs and Turks. Gregoras claims that by the late 1340s the treasury was empty, but this may be mere hyperbole.[313] This was a period characterized by recourse to extraordinary means to finance the government: confiscations of monastic land and church treasure, pawning the crown jewels to Venice (1343), appeals to the empire's subjects for voluntary contributions, Kantakouzenos funding state expenses out of his own wealth. Even after the civil wars of the first half of the fourteenth century, tax revenues were still coming in. Kantakouzenos (III, 291) writes about the financial terms of the 1354 agreement ending hostilities between John V and Kantakouzenos: "Concerning the money collected yearly from the public taxes, whatever should be needed for the mercenaries of the army and the preparation of the triremes and the other needs of the public administration, is to be spent by the government as usual."

The civil wars of the fourteenth century increased the number of property grants, including pronoiai. The reason is quite simple: each side wished to gain and maintain supporters. Of the two historians who write in detail about the era of the civil wars, John Kantakouzenos and Nikephoros Gregoras, it is only Gregoras who emphasizes the role of property grants. This is understandable in light of the fact that Kantakouzenos wished to present the civil wars as a struggle for justice, while for Gregoras they were a struggle for power. Because Gregoras was a partisan for Andronikos II and later (moderately so) for the regency for John V Palaiologos, he often presents the supporters of Andronikos III and Kantakouzenos as motivated by greed. Thus, according to Gregoras (I, 300.12–14), in 1320 Syrgiannes claimed that Andronikos II offered him "magnificent honors and many villages [χωρία, or estates] which could bring great yearly incomes" for his support. By the terms of the treaty of Rhegion concluded between

[313] Gregoras, II, 790, cited by Nicol, *The Last Centuries of Byzantium*, 2nd edn., 219 note 20.

Andronikos II and Andronikos III in 1321, the younger emperor was to hold Thrace from Christoupolis (Kavala) up to the suburbs of Constantinople, "along with the things distributed by him to those around him of the villages [or estates, χωρίων] of Macedonia" (Gregoras, I, 321.4–5). In 1327, to win supporters Andronikos III promised "to those serving in the army resources of incomes [πόρους προσόδων] and increases of pay" (Gregoras, I, 397.11–12).

According to Gregoras the struggle between John Kantakouzenos and the regency for John V Palaiologos renewed the pressure to grant property to supporters to the point where there was no state land left *[7.21]*. He reports that at a time in 1344 when morale was low in Didymoteichon, Kantakouzenos' base – soldiers, generals, and relatives – pressured him with individual requests: "For amid the impending dangers, each approached him privately: some demanded Lesbos, others Lemnos, others Chios. Others [demanded] other lands and resources of incomes" (Gregoras, II, 709.6–8: ἄλλα τε χωρία καὶ προσόδων εὐπορίας). In 1347 John Asan, brother-in-law of Kantakouzenos, claimed that Anna of Savoy had earlier promised him and his brother Manuel Asan "incomes of properties as well as of money" (Gregoras, II, 799.22: κτημάτων ὁμοῦ καὶ χρημάτων προσόδους).

The second half of the fourteenth century continues the story of war, invasion, and infighting which did, finally, destroy the fiscal base of the empire. By the end of the century Byzantium was a petty vassal state of the Ottomans. But even during the first half of the fourteenth century, state revenues were not particularly impressive. It was noted above that Andronikos II once was able to raise a million hyperpyra. Normal revenues were much less. According to the terms of the treaty of Epivatai in 1322 Andronikos III, as co-emperor, was to receive a pension and money for the support of his army. Four years and four months later Kantakouzenos reports (I, 237) that this money had not been delivered as promised and that Andronikos II owed his grandson 350,000 hyperpyra. Dividing 350,000 by $4\frac{1}{3}$ we arrive at an annual income for Andronikos III of around 81,000 hyperpyra. Assuming Andronikos II's budget would have been at least as large as this, we can conclude that in the early 1320s Kantakouzenos thought it reasonable to expect that the imperial treasury could take in about 200,000 or 300,000 hyperpyra per year. This is not a very large sum. Nicolas Svoronos estimated that the annual revenue of the monastery of Lavra in the early fourteenth century was more than 12,000 hyperpyra (*Lavra*, IV, p. 171). If all these estimates have any basis in fact (always a big assumption), this would mean that the state was pulling in revenues equal to merely twenty times or so of those of a large monastery.

Unfortunately, a budget of 200,000 or 300,000 hyperpyra does not tell us how much revenue actually came from the land. For there were commercial taxes which were not negligible, at least compared to revenues from land. Gregoras writes (II, 842) that by 1348 the annual revenue from customs at Constantinople was "barely" 30,000 hyperpyra, while the Geneose of Galata were receiving 200,000 per year. If 30,000 hyperpyra were being produced by trade during a difficult period, the amount of revenue produced by trade in better days may have represented quite a sizable chunk of state revenues.

In the end, no matter how modest the sums were that the state could harvest from agrarian taxation, these taxes were still worth the trouble to collect. Tax assessors still wandered the countryside itemizing property holdings, making sure that no one had more than he was entitled to.

What can we say about the patterns of agrarian property holding in late Byzantium as they relate to pronoia? We can begin with the Byzantines' own categorization of property holdings as found in the introductory formulas of some praktika: *ekklesiastika*, *monasteriaka*, *prosopika*, *archontika*, *stratiotika*, *chrysovoullata*. The formulas always contain the final phrase "and the rest," indicating the list was not all-inclusive.[314] Indeed, in addition to these, there was state-owned property and the property of paroikoi. And so we can draw up the categories as follows:

State-owned real property

A. Property owned and managed directly by the state. Such properties could be called *vasilika* if they belonged to the emperor *ex officio*; otherwise, they could be called *demosiaka*. It is difficult to find any of this in the late Byzantine period. Most of it was granted out to pronoia holders or to others. (By "agrarian property" I am grouping together arable land, including vineyards and gardens, as well as pastures, trees, fish ponds, docks, and any other immovable agricultural asset.)

B. State property held by pronoia holders. This is what I have been calling the "domain land" of the pronoia holder (the land held by his paroikoi is found below). In some of the documents this property is called *pronoiastika*. Because of the tendency for pronoia holders to be soldiers, this might be what the introductory formulas of praktika mean when they refer to *stratiotika*, literally "military (properties)." Yet there is always the possibly that the appearance of *stratiotika* in these formulas is an anachronism, referring to the old "military lands" of the middle

[314] E.g., *Xéropotamou*, no. 18; *Zographou*, no. 17; *Iviron*, III, no. 74.

Byzantine period, that is, properties on which there was a military service burden (*strateia*) or, later, a special category of tax.

Privately owned real property

C. *Chrysovoullata.* These are properties owned by an individual as a result of an imperial grant confirmed by a chrysobull. The actual grant may have included the property itself (with or without tax exemption) or only some variety of tax exemption over property previously owned by the individual. Because monasteries and churches often received chrysobulls that granted them ownership of properties or privileges over previously acquired properties, we might specify that the owners of *chrysovoullata* were individuals and not corporate entities.

D. *Monasteriaka* and *ekklesiastika*, respectively, properties owned by monasteries and by churches. The manner by which the properties were acquired was irrelevant; thus, many of such properties were owned through imperial grants or enjoyed privileges granted by the emperor.

E. *Archontika.* These properties, which appear only in lists of types of properties, were literally the properties of "archons," which meant "leaders" in the most general of senses. The meaning of the word "archon" was quite fluid in the late period. High officials, civil and military, were certainly considered archons; minor officials were certainly not. But the dividing line between the two was not fixed and varied with who was using the term. If we wish to distinguish *archontika* from *chrysovoullata* and pronoiai, we might stipulate that *archontika* were properties that did not benefit from any imperial privilege, that their owners acquired them through their own means (patrimony, purchase, dowry, and so on) and paid the normal taxes levied on such properties. Because the owners of such properties would do everything they could to get tax exemption on these properties (making them *chrysovoullata*), the percentage of the empire's arable land in this category would be quite small.

F. *Prosopika.* Literally, the properties owned by "persons" (*prosopa*). It is likely that *prosopika* was another category of non-privileged property occupying a place between *archontika* and the holdings of paroikoi. Consider a merchant or a common pronoia soldier or a minor official who purchased a piece of land. Such men were neither archons nor paroikoi, nor, for that matter, did the hypothetical piece of land that they owned benefit from any imperial privilege. *Prosopika* would be the logical category for such properties. These properties were small, but there were many of them.

G. *Paroikikai staseis*, "paroikos holdings." These properties can be further distinguished according to the recipients of the taxes, charges, and labor services paid by their owners. Paroikoi were held by several categories of individuals and corporate entities:

1. the state. If paroikoi rendered their fiscal obligations to a government official, their property would fit in this category. After the middle of the thirteenth century or so, it is quite difficult to find paroikoi who actually paid their taxes to the state. So their percentage is quite small.
2. pronoia holders. Through imperial grant, the emperor conferred households of paroikoi upon the pronoia holder and these, from the evidence of the praktika, often owned land of their own.
3. the holders of chrysobulls. Individuals, who held paroikoi but did not hold them as part of a pronoia grant, held them through the power of a chrysobull. They might have inherited the paroikoi, but nevertheless one of their ancestors had received the original imperial privilege granting the family the paroikoi.
4. monasteries and churches. These held paroikoi exclusively through imperial grant. According to the documents, monastic paroikoi tended to own very little land of their own, so the estimate should be small.

The state derived its revenues from its own land directly (A) and from taxes levied on *archontika*, *prosopika*, and paroikoi who paid their taxes directly to the state (E, F, G1). The state also got some tax revenue from *chrysovoullata* (C) and a bit from the properties of monasteries and churches (D).

On the other hand, the state normally received no tax revenue from pronoia holders (B) or from the paroikos holdings of private landholders (G2, G3, G4). Add to this the lion's share of property in categories C and D, and the percentage of arable land that was exempted of taxation by the state was substantial, unquestionably the overwhelming majority of arable land.

One way to get an idea of how extensive (and expensive) pronoia grants were is to make a calculation based on the total income of the monastery of Lavra on Mount Athos. After the state itself, Lavra was probably the largest landowner in Macedonia. In the theme of Thessaloniki, Lavra and its paroikoi owned about 4 percent of the arable land in the early fourteenth century.[315] N. Svoronos has estimated that in the early fourteenth century

[315] Lavra owned 54,000 modioi and its paroikoi about 2,000; 56,000 modioi is equivalent to about 56 km^2 (using the normal equivalence, 1 modios = 1,000 m^2): *Lavra*, IV, pp. 170–71. In 1961 there were 1388 km^2 of arable land in the modern Greek *nomoi* of Thessaloniki and the Chalkidike, which approximately correspond to the Byzantine theme of Thessaloniki: Laiou, *Peasant Society*, 42.

Table 8.15 *Posotes* of the holdings of six Athonite monasteries in the theme of Thessaloniki, 1300–21

Hilandar (1300)	580 hyp.
Vatopedi (1301)	270 hyp.
Esphigmenou (1318)	500 hyp.
Zographou (1320)	138 hyp.
Iviron (1320)	677 hyp.
Lavra (1321)	ca. 3000 hyp.
total	ca. 5165 hyp.

Sources: Chilandar, ed. Živojinović, I, App. II, p. 296; *Vatopédi*, I, no. 30.46; *Esphigménou*, no. 14.225; *Zographou*, no. 17.86–87; *Iviron*, III, no. 79.586–87; *Lavra*, II, no. 109 (p. 222).

the total annual income for all of Lavra's possessions (in the theme of Thessaloniki, the theme of Serres and the Strymon, and on Lemnos) totaled something more than 12,000 hyperpyra (*Lavra*, IV, p. 171). If (according to Table 8.13) the total annual income produced by the pronoiai of the three soldiers Saventzes, Maroules, and Berilas was around 150 hyperpyra, how many pronoiai grants could be created by confiscating all of Lavra's property? Dividing 12,000 hyperpyra by 150 hyperpyra per pronoia soldier we get 80 pronoia soldiers. In other words, liquidating all of the property of the largest private landowner in Macedonia could finance pronoiai for eighty soldiers.

A similar calculation can be made using not the estimated annual income of property, but the official posotes. For this we look to the theme of Thessaloniki, the best-documented area in late Byzantium, and consider the *posotetes* of the property of large landowners. The only large landowners for whom we have figures for the total *posotes* of their holdings are six of the monasteries of Mount Athos. For this calculation we will assume a typical pronoia grant for a soldier had a *posotes* of seventy-five hyperpyra (roughly averaging the official *posotetes* of the soldiers Saventzes, Maroules, and Berilas). Table 8.15 provides the total *posotetes* of the possessions of six of the larger monasteries of Mount Athos in the theme of Thessaloniki in the early fourteenth century. If all of the property of these monasteries located in the theme of Thessaloniki was confiscated and distributed to soldiers in pronoiai, each with a *posotes* of 75 hyperpyra, this property would be sufficient to fund only 69 soldiers ($\approx 5165 \div 75$). The *posotes* of Lavra itself, the largest monastery, could fund 40 soldiers. There is some internal consistency in these numbers, for if we consider Svoronos' estimate of the annual revenue of Lavra only in the theme of Thessaloniki (about 7,500 hyperpyra: *Lavra*, IV, p. 171) and divide this by my estimate of the typical income of a military pronoia (150 hyperpyra), the quotient is 50, the number of pronoia soldiers that could be financed by confiscating Lavra's property in the theme of Thessaloniki.

The evidence suggests that, at any one time in the thirteenth and fourteenth centuries, there could not have been more than several hundred pronoia holders. The overwhelming majority of these would have been soldiers with smaller holdings, typically in the 70–80 hyperpyra range as indicated by the praktika of Saventzes, Maroules, and Berilas. A hundred or two officers and other privileged individuals held pronoiai with higher *posotetes*, and a handful held much higher *posotetes* in the hundreds of hyperpyra. We can make a rough (perhaps fanciful) estimate of the total tax revenues devoted to pronoia grants as follows:

400 pronoia soldiers × 75 hyperpyra =	30,000 hyperpyra
150 officers, officials, and other individuals × 150 hyp. =	22,500 hyperpyra
50 military commanders, high officials, and other close associates of the emperor × 400 hyp. =	20,000 hyperpyra
total	72,500 hyperpyra

This total figure offers simply an order of magnitude based on the range of *posotetes* we know of and an estimate of the number of pronoia soldiers and other varieties of pronoia holders in the empire. It is difficult to think that the total tax revenue devoted to pronoia grants could have been less than 50,000 hyperpyra, and it is hard to imagine it could have been more than 200,000 hyperpyra.[316] The figure obviously excludes all of the other categories of privileged landholders in late Byzantium. If we added the tax revenues granted to monasteries and churches, and to the holders of *chrysovoullata* properties, one could easily triple the figure.

PART III. RELINQUISHING THE GRANT

A pronoia holder could be separated from all or part of his grant for a number of reasons. The principal way to distinguish these is whether the separation was voluntary or involuntary.

[316] For another set of estimates, see M. Bartusis, "The Cost of Late Byzantine Warfare and Defense," *Byzantinische Forschungen* 16 (1990), 84–85.

Voluntary transfers – donation, sale, exchange, hereditary transmission

There is certainly sufficient evidence to prove that when hereditary rights were granted over an oikonomia, the oikonomia passed to the pronoia holder's heirs. Less well documented is the phenomenon of a pronoia holder who had been granted the right to donate, sell, bequeath, exchange, or otherwise alienate his oikonomia actually doing so. This is not surprising because, as previously discussed, it does not appear that emperors often granted the right to alienate oikonomiai. We recall the couple from Melnik who sold part of their oikonomia in 1344, a special privilege granted to the residents of that town *[8.52]*.

One possible example of a voluntary exchange between landholders involving a pronoia is found in a praktikon for Iviron from 1316. The document lists, among the possessions of the monastery in the village of Ovelos, a paroikos named John *tou Gianoulas* who, along with his family, had been "exchanged for a paroikos of the monastery [Vatopedi] called Kyprianos in [the village of] Saniane from the pronoia of Slotas Skopiotes." Iviron and Skopiotes (evidently a Slav from the town of Skopje) had exchanged paroikos households, though we do not know who initiated the transfer or why. But we can assume that the transfer was authorized by the state and effected by fiscal officials.[317]

Some pronoia holders who did not have the right to alienate or bequeath their oikonomiai did so anyway. When Kantakouzenos writes that some soldiers did not have their pronoia intact, he quite likely meant that they sold portions of their oikonomiai for cash *[8.26]*. It is easy to imagine a man misrepresenting a parcel of land he was selling. These invalid transactions could be rectified in several ways. In the case described by Kantakouzenos, new pronoia components were granted to the soldiers involved. In the case of the 1335 act of Constantine Makrenos, Andronikos III ordered that such properties alienated should be confiscated from their new possessors *[8.51]*.

Involuntary transfers

With the passage of time many pronoia holders lost all or part of the component parts of their pronoia grants against their will. If they were compensated for the loss, the transfer was an involuntary exchange; if not,

[317] *Iviron*, III, no. 74.293–94.

it was either a loss through death or disfavor, in which case the pronoia returned to the emperor, or a loss through enemy invasion, in which case it did not.

Forced exchanges

The components of a pronoia grant were fungible and because these components were, in aggregate, identical to the components of properties held by monasteries and other privileged landowners, the fisc could easily make exchanges, exchanging one property held by a pronoia holder for another with the same *posotes*. The documented cases of such exchanges usually came about when the emperor decided to grant a monastery a property held within someone's pronoia. In order not to diminish the total *posotes* of the pronoia, the emperor ordered that the fiscal official making the transfer find an equivalent *posotes* from other property to compensate the pronoia holder (e.g., *[7.9]* and possibly *[8.69]*). From a *prostagma* inserted in a 1304 act of Theodore Tzimpeas, the monks of the Great Lavra had asked the emperor to be granted a *posotes* of 260 hyperpyra in the village of Longos consisting of paroikoi and land. The emperor granted this request and ordered an *apographeus* to "confer upon the soldiers [*stratiotai*] from whom you intend to take away this *posotes* another equal *posotes* from elsewhere from your commission, that these [soldiers] not be deprived of anything."[318] The monks probably had a specific set of properties in mind, the combined *posotes* of which was a substantial sum. This *posotes* would have had to have come from a number of pronoia holders, and this explains why we are told only that the pronoia holders were soldiers. However, usually the information provided is much more specific.

[8.73] Act of the *apographeus* Nikephoros Choumnos for the monastery of Zographou involving Gazes, a soldier from the Thessalonian *mega allagion* (1286)

An act of the fiscal official Nikephoros Choumnos from September 1286 includes a *prostagma* of Andronikos II. The emperor ordered Choumnos to remit to the monastery of Zographou 4 *zeugaria* in the village of Lozikin from what a soldier from the Thessalonian *mega allagion* named Gazes

[318] *Lavra*, II, no. 97.6–7: πρὸς δὲ τοὺς στρατιώτας ἐξ ὧν μέλλεις ἀποσπᾶσαι τὴν τοιαύτην ποσότητα παραδώσεις ὁμοίως ἀλλαχόθεν ἀπὸ τῆς δουλείας σου ἑτέραν ἴσην ποσότητα, καὶ οὐδὲν στερηθῶσιν οἱ τοιοῦτοι τοῦ τυχόντος ἐξ αὐτῶν.

possessed, and that Gazes be compensated "from free properties . . . so that he should have the sufficient [amount] of his own oikonomia." So, according to the act of September 1286, Choumnos gave Zographou 400 modioi of land at Lozikin, "which we found that the deceased Gazes held beyond the amount of his praktikon."[319]

We know nothing of Gazes except for what this document reports. He was a soldier from the Thessalonian *mega allagion* who evidently died during the short interval between the time the emperor ordered the transfer and the time the transfer was effected. The transfer itself was a simple one, demonstrating once again the fungibility of the component parts of an oikonomia and the interchangeability of recipients – soldier or monastery. Gazes was to be compensated with other "free" (*eleuthera*) properties. Usually, the term *eleutheuros* signifies "properties free of all fiscal burdens," or simply "tax-free" properties. Properties could have this status either through imperial order or through having never been assessed. Here, the former sense was probably intended, though the real meaning of the phrase is "not in anyone else's oikonomia."

Nevertheless, it seems there was a complication. Choumnos claims that the 400 modioi of land identified (evidently equivalent to the "four *zeugaria*" stipulated by the emperor) were "beyond the amount of [Gazes'] praktikon." We can compare the usage of the relatively uncommon preposition *epekeina* (ἐπέκεινα, "beyond") in a document from 1234 in which the emperor ordered an official to confer upon the monastery of the Lemviotissa some state land in a place called Koukoulos "beyond [*epekeina*] the land it has in Koukoulos."[320] In other words, the monastery evidently already held land there. Therefore, it would seem that the 400 modioi that Choumnos identified was not contained in Gazes' praktikon and thus not in his oikonomia.

Was Gazes compensated for the loss of this 400 modioi? Ostrogorsky thought the answer to this was no, that since the 400 modioi was not part of Gazes' oikonomia, he received nothing in exchange.[321] Indeed there appears to be no other reason why Choumnos would mention that the 400 modioi were not listed in Gazes' praktikon except as a preemptive justification for why Gazes should receive nothing in return. The most common explanation for such a confiscation is that Gazes held the 400

[319] *Zographou*, no. 10.20–22: ἀπὸ ἐλευθέρων τινῶν . . . ὅπως εἴη καὶ οὗτος ἔχων τὸ ἱκανὸν τῆς οἰκείας οἰκονομίας, and lines 28–29: ἣν εὕρομεν ὅτι κατεῖχεν ὁ Γαζῆς ἐκεῖνος ἐπέκεινα τῆς ποσότητος τοῦ πρακτικοῦ αὐτοῦ.

[320] MM, iv, 146.29–30. Dölger, *Regesten*, iii, no. 1737. Cf. MM, iv, 142 (from 1231).

[321] Ostrogorsky, *Féodalité*, 139–40.

modioi improperly, either through an earlier error of a fiscal official or simply illegally, and Choumnos used this opportunity to set matters right (cf. *[6.6]*). The only other possibility is that the 400 modioi were private property that Gazes had obtained unconnected to his pronoia. But this possibility can probably be dismissed, for the emperor clearly indicates that the four *zeugaria* were to come from Gazes' oikonomia.

The fact that Gazes was now dead adds another wrinkle to the case. If Gazes' heirs had no claim to his oikonomia, regardless of when Gazes died – before or after Choumnos' investigation – the issue of compensation, as well as the precise source of the 400 modioi, would have been mooted, because the entire oikonomia, including improperly held properties, would have reverted to the state. On the other hand, if Gazes held hereditary rights, there would have been much more reason to specify that neither Gazes nor his heirs had any right to claim compensation for the loss of the improperly held 400 modioi. While not the strongest evidence for the hereditability of such imperial grants, the case of the soldier Gazes points in this direction.

Because emperors granted the request of monasteries to exchange one property for another, it is reasonable to think that pronoia holders themselves sometimes asked to exchange one component of their grant for another component, such as a property in one location for another. This would be a voluntary transfer. However, there is no example of this.

[8.74] Prostagma of Andronikos III for the benefit of the monastery of Asomatoi near Zichna involving an *epiteleia* paid to Preakotzelos (1333)

A pronoia holder could receive compensation for the loss of an *epiteleia*. In 1333 Andronikos III issued a *prostagma* on behalf of the monastery of the Asomatoi near Zichna. The metropolitan of Zichna had explained to the emperor "that for the land it owns the monastery of the Asomatoi pays [*telei*] to . . . [a man named] Preakotzelos 7 hyperpyra each year, and he requested that this tax be annulled" (ἵνα γένηται ἐκκοπὴ τοῦ τοιούτου τέλους). The emperor granted the metropolitan's request and ordered that Preakotzelos receive "another *posotes* of 7 hyperpyra in exchange [ἀντί] for such land." The effect of this was to give the monastery a tax exemption.[322]

[322] *Prodrome*, no. 29.2–5,7 = *Prodrome B*, no. 214.2–4,6–7. *Prodrome*, no. 29, dates the document to "juillet" but the Greek text (line 11) reads "June"; *Prodrome B*, no. 214, assigns the act to "juin" (p. 415), but the Greek text (line 11) reads "July" (!). Dölger, *Regesten*, IV, no. 2794, assigned the document to July. Hvostova, *Osobennosti*, 210.

A similar case in which we do not know for sure whether the property taken from a man was part of a pronoia or simply personal property involves the father of the soldier Alexander Euripiotes. In August 1321 Irene-Adelaide, as co-empress, issued an *orismos* at the request of the children of the deceased Alexander Euripiotes, a soldier in the Thessalonian *mega allagion*, which confirmed their rights to a *gonikon palaiochorion* ("patrimonial abandoned village") called Poungion.[323] The empress notes that their grandfather, Alexander's father, donated some houses to a monastery in Thessaloniki, in return for which the despot John Palaiologos (a stepbrother of Michael IX and the son of the empress Irene-Yolande) gave him Poungion. This exchange must have taken place before the despot John Palaiologos' death in 1307 (at the age of twenty-one), most probably during the period 1304–07 when he governed Thessaloniki under the aegis of his mother.[324] According to the *orismos* of 1321, the children of Alexander Euripiotes received *prostagmata* from Andronikos II and Michael IX (who had died in October 1320) confirming their possession of Poungion, as well as a *sigilliodes gramma* (i.e., a praktikon) from a team of *apographeis* active during the period 1315–18. However, "recently" the *apographeus* George Pharisaios had wanted to seize the *palaiochorion* and confer it upon the *panhypersevastos* John Palaiologos (a nephew of Andronikos II).[325] The 1321 *orismos* confirmed their right to Poungion without disturbance. There is no mention of any kind of tax exemption.

The abandoned village Poungion was a property held by three generations of the Euripiotes family. Two elements suggest that it was originally part of an imperial grant: first, the grandfather Euripiotes was given Poungion by the despot John Palaiologos. This appears to have been an administrative act compensating the grandfather for his donation of the houses in Thessaloniki to the monastery, a "donation" that may not have been the grandfather's idea. Such a scenario would be consistent with the grandfather holding the original houses within an oikonomia. Second, the *apographeus* Pharisaios' attempt to confiscate Poungion from Alexander Euripiotes' children suggests that their right to Poungion was disputable. This would have been the case if Poungion had passed to Alexander as part of his oikonomia and the *apographeus* was unaware that Alexander's children had the right to inherit the village. It is likely that Pharisaios, searching for properties to confer on the *panhypersevastos* Palaiologos, found Poungion with its

[323] *Chilandar*, ed. Petit, no. 67. On the identity of the issuer of the document, see F. Barišić, "Povelje vizantijskih carica," *ZRVI* 13 (1971), 175–79, 198.

[324] *PLP*, no. 21475. [325] *PLP*, no. 21479.

previous holder Alexander deceased, and sought to reassign it to another grant holder. Since the document states that Pharisaios merely "wanted" to take the property from the children, the documents that they were able to produce may well have ultimately satisfied Pharisaios. In any case, to stop the seizure or to avoid future inconvenience, they sought a new confirmation of their rights.[326] While it is possible that the grandfather had wanted to donate the houses in Thessaloniki to a monastery and the despot had been willing to compensate him with another property, it seems most likely that the house had been part of the father's pronoia grant and after a "forced" donation he obtained Poungion as compensation.

[8.75] Chrysobull of Andronikos II Palaiologos for the monastery of St. John Prodromos (September 1317), *Prostagma* of Andronikos II Palaiologos to a fiscal official (April 1325), *Prostagma* of Andronikos II Palaiologos to a fiscal official (November 1325), and *Orismos* of Andronikos III Palaiologos to a fiscal official (1327), regarding the *agridion* of Monospeton

As one would expect, these exchanges were frequently unwelcome to the pronoia holder, and sometimes the pronoia holder tried to resist the exchange (e.g., *[6.4]*). In another case, shortly before September 1317 Andronikos II granted the monastery of St. John Prodromos possession of an *agridion* (small village) with a *posotes* of 24 hyperpyra named Monospeton "which the soldier Martinos held." The official transfer was made and in September 1317 the emperor issued a chrysobull confirming the monastery's possession of the *agridion.*[327] Andronikos II and Andronikos III both issued chrysobulls in 1321 confirming the monastery's possession of the property,[328] but by 1325 the monastery still had not acquired possession of the property. In a *prostagma* of Andronikos II from April 1325 we read that Nikephoros Martinos had "held through praktikon in the *posotes* of his oikonomia" this *agridion* with a *posotes* of 30 hyperpyra, and that after the property was granted to the Prodromos monastery the emperor had ordered fiscal officials to give Martinos an equal *posotes* in compensation. Now the emperor again ordered a fiscal official to make the transfer of Monospeton to the monastery and to compensate Martinos with an equal *posotes.* In this

[326] By 1351 this property seems to have passed to Hilandar: *Chilandar*, ed. Petit. no. 138.33, which would explain the presence of the 1321 *orismos* in the monastery's archives.

[327] *Prodrome*, no. 7 = *Prodrome B*, no. 189.21.

[328] *Prodrome*, no. 9.10 = *Prodrome B*, no. 187; *Prodrome*, no. 10.12 = *Prodrome B*, no. 190.13.

document the emperor specifies that the compensation was to come from the oikonomia of the deceased Rhomaios.[329]

Still, the transfer did not take place. In November (or perhaps October) 1325 Andronikos II issued yet another *prostagma* which refers to the *agridion* that "was held earlier through praktikon for oikonomia" by Martinos. Martinos refused to accept the compensation offered and held on to Monospeton. The emperor again ordered that Monospeton be transferred to the monastery and that Martinos receive compensation from the other oikonomia of the deceased Rhomaios. A clearly annoyed Andronikos adds that "if the said *sevastos* Martinos does not wish to accept such *posotes* [in compensation], he shall be deprived of it."[330]

The last document to deal with the transfer is an *orismos* issued by Andronikos III as co-emperor in 1327. It refers to the *agridion* "which was taken away years ago . . . from the oikonomia of . . . Martinos," but which still had not been transferred to the monastery. This shows that there was a distinction between taking away a *posotes* from an oikonomia and actually transferring possession of the property constituting that *posotes* to another party, the former fiscal and legal, the latter physical. In the document Andronikos III explains that Martinos had taken advantage of the civil war between Andronikos II and Andronikos III in 1321–22 by persuading Andronikos III's uncle, the governor of Thessaloniki Constantine Palaiologos, to return Monospeton to Martinos, an act that Andronikos II inadvertently confirmed through a *prostagma*. With the *orismos* of 1327 Andronikos III ordered that Monospeton be transferred to the monastery and Martinos be compensated with an equal *posotes* from *exaleimmatika* and "free" (*eleuthera*) properties. The oikonomia of Rhomaios is not mentioned.[331]

Evidently the monastery of St. John Prodromos did eventually acquire possession of Monospeton, for a praktikon from 1339 lists it among the monastery's properties. Yet, oddly, the document notes that the metropolitan of Zichna (the founder of the monastery) acquired it "through purchase" (*ex agorasias*) "from the soldier Martinos."[332]

329 *Prodrome*, no. 16.8–15 = *Prodrome B*, no. 207.9–16.

330 *Prodrome*, no. 17.6–7: ὅπερ κατείχετο πρότερον διὰ πρακτικοῦ εἰς οἰκονομίαν παρὰ τοῦ . . . Μαρτίνου, and lines 32–33 = *Prodrome B*, no. 208.6–7,33–34. In another example of L. Bénou's careless editing, she dates this *prostagma* of 1325 (no. 208 in her edition of Codex B) to the month of October (p. 404 and note 394), writing that Guillou's edition of the text indicates a different month (November). However, her edition of the Codex B text inexplicably reads μηνὶ Νοεμβρίω (!: line 38).

331 *Prodrome*, no. 22.6–8: ὃ δὴ ἀπεσπάσθη πρὸ χρόνων . . . ἀπὸ τῆς οἰκονομίας τοῦ . . . Μαρτίνου, and line 26 = *Prodrome B*, no. 209.7–9,28.

332 *Prodrome B*, no. 179.9. Cf. no. 181.7–9.

The case of the soldier Nikephoros Martinos and the *agridion* of Monospeton shows that, even though the components of a pronoia grant were *fiscally* fungible, an individual pronoia holder might resist the exchange of one property for another. Indeed Martinos was prepared to use devious means to maintain possession of Monospeton within his pronoia.

Forced exchange or return to the state?

In quite a few cases the reason why a pronoia holder lost a property within his pronoia is not provided. For example, two acts from 1300 note that the monastery of Xenophon held 325 modioi of land "taken from the oikonomia of the *kavallarios syr* Peros Martinos" (and the other act substitutes *pronoia* for *oikonomia*) *[7.8]*. The documents offer no hint as to why Martinos lost this part of his pronoia/oikonomia. There is no indication that he was dead in 1300, nor can we assume that he was not compensated for the land he lost.

In another example from a chrysobull from July 1294 Andronikos II gave the monastery of Karakallou "the village of Dekalista with its region and rights with the land around the [rights] there of 600 modioi held up to now by the *oikeios* to my majesty *kyr* Constantine Komnenos Laskaris, now taken away from him by an *orismos* of [my majesty] and given to such monastery."[333] In this brief passage there is no indication that Laskaris was dead nor any hint that he had fallen into any kind of disfavor.

In a chrysobull from December 1324 Andronikos II confirmed his grant to the monk Matthew of Hilandar of "land of 300 modioi in Lozikion from the land that Peter Doukopoulos held there."[334] In September 1327 Andronikos II granted the monk Matthew's request to receive the remaining portion of Doukopoulos' land, which Matthew could now transmit to Hilandar in addition to the 300 modioi of "land held by Peter Doukopoulos, from the *paidopouloi* of my majesty."[335] The emperor's manner of describing

333 P. Lemerle, "Un chrysobulle d'Andronic II Paléologue pour le monastère de Karakala," in Lemerle, *Le monde de Byzance* (London, 1978), no. xvii, 432.23–25 = Dölger, *Schatzkammern*, no. 38. *PLP*, no. 14542. On Dekalista, *Iviron*, iii, p. 62 and p. 193 (fig. 4): to the east of the Strymon, northwest of Prevista.

334 *Chilandar*, ed. Petit, no. 100.2–3. In another chrysobull from the same month Andronikos III granted Hilandar, in addition to the 300 modioi, all the rest of what Doukopoulos held: *Chilandar*, ed. Petit, no. 102.6. This document is probably a falsification (see Dölger, *Regesten*, iv, no. 2676) for a number of reasons: unlike all of the other references to Doukopoulos from the 1320s, in one passage this act suggests that he was dead (*ekeinos*) in 1324; further, Andronikos II did not grant the rest of Doukopoulos' land to Matthew until 1327.

335 *Chilandar*, ed. Petit, no. 114.5–6: γῆ κατείχετο παρὰ τοῦ ἀπὸ τῶν παιδοπούλων τῆς βασιλείας μου Πέτρου τοῦ Δουκοπούλου. Other documents dealing with this transfer: *Chilandar*, ed. Petit,

Doukopoulos indicates that he was alive at the time and had not fallen from favor.

[8.76] Chrysobull of Andronikos III Palaiologos for the monastery of Zographou regarding the oikonomia of the *sevastos* Devlitzenos (1328)

In a chrysobull from 1328 the monks of Zographou requested confirmation of their possession of "the oikonomia of the *sevastos* Devlitzenos at Hierissos, given through *prostagma*... being of a *posotes* of 33 hyperpyra." With a similar phrase the emperor granted this request.[336] The use of the word *oikonomia* in this passage seems to be as a means of identifying the property, not an indication of its status in 1328.

Similarly, in a praktikon for Lavra from 1321 we read that an *epiteleia* of two hyperpyra for a mill in Drymosyrta was "taken away from the *epiteleia* of Theodore Kounales, as shown by documents of the monastery as well as an... imperial chrysobull." Thus, the two hyperpyra which the monastery had been paying Kounales were now kept by the monastery.[337]

According to the Hilandar Slavic praktikon from November 1300 nearly all of the paroikoi that Hilandar received in the village of Kastrion had been taken from pronoia holders *[8.72]*. With an even more explicit phrasing the praktikon also mentions five paroikos households "in the village of Kontogrikou, from the pronoia of Skorev, taken away by order of the emperor."[338] These five paroikos households were all that Hilandar held in

no. 110.29–30 (1326, probably a falsification); no. 116.5–6,24,69–70 (1327); no. 120 (1330); no. 130.84–86 (1339); no. 138.46–47 (1351). Also, see the false chrysobull bearing the date 1342 which describes Doukopoulos' holding as an "oikonomia" with a *posotes* of 20 hyperpyra: *Zographou*, no. 34.24; cf. no. 27.14 (1328). Dölger, *Regesten*, v, no. 2875.

336 *Zographou*, no. 27.29–31: ἥ τε δοθεῖσα διὰ προστάγματος... εἰς τὸν Ἐρισὸν οἰκονομία τοῦ σεβαστοῦ τοῦ Δεβλιτζενοῦ, ποσότητος οὖσα ὑπερπύρων τριάκοντα τριῶν, and lines 50–51. This is repeated in two falsified chrysobulls: *Zographou*, no. 33.38–40, no. 34.45–46. Ostrogorsky, *Féodalité*, 149–50. Kazhdan, *Agrarnye otnošenija*, 214, 218.

337 *Lavra*, II, no. 109.966–67, and *Lavra*, IV, p. 91 and note 189. *PLP*, no. 13476.

338 Mošin, "Akti," 212.443–44: *od' pronije Skorêv' povêle od' cara od'r'vati se*. The Slavic verb *ot'r'vati*, literally "to tear away," is the precise equivalent of the Greek *apospo* (ἀποσπῶ), a verb often found in passages in the documents dealing with property transferred from one holder to another. Thus, in the original Greek, the phrase would have been something like ἀπὸ τῆς ἀποσπασθείσης δι' ὁρισμοῦ βασιλικοῦ προνοίας τοῦ Σκόρη. The location of Kontogrikou is known only approximately. It was situated on the Chalkidike, not far from the gulf of Hierissos, some seven miles northwest of Hierissos: see the map, *Chilandar*, ed. Živojinović, I, p. 60, which revises the earlier placement found in *Lavra*, IV, p. 74. At first glance, the Slavic form "Skorev" should be the patronymic of the Greek "Skores" or even "Skoures" (Σκόρης, Σκούρης), a name attested in various locations on the Chalkidike in the fourteenth century: see Lefort,

the village. Unlike the case of Kastrion, the monks held no land or fiscal charges aside from what was contained in the *staseis* of the paroikoi. We do not know when these paroikoi were granted to Hilandar, but since the praktikon states they were "taken away by order of the emperor," this probably means they were granted to the monastery by the emperor reigning in 1300, Andronikos II, that is, between 1282 and 1300. There are no other explicit references, before or after the time of this praktikon, to possessions of Hilandar in this village. However, the monastery had held, for some time prior to 1300, a *metochion* in nearby Roudava, and Mirjana Živojinović wrote that it is likely that these five paroikos households were associated with it.[339]

[8.77] Greek chrysobull of Symeon Uroš for the monastery of St. George in Zavlantia (1359)

A Greek chrysobull, issued in 1359, for the monastery of St. George in Zavlantia confirmed the monastery's possession of and rights over a number of properties. One was the *metochion* of St. George in a place called Kotzekovo with its "men, vineyards, fields, and water mills, as well as the share of the deceased Eudokia [. . .] around Voxista, which Vodeses held for his oikonomia."[340] From the syntax it is not clear whether Vodeses held the entire complex or merely the "share" (*meridion*, i.e., the *stasis*) of the deceased Eudokia. Vodeses appears to have been a pronoia holder, but

Villages de Macédoine, 81, map 8 note 6; *Dionysiou*, no. 43.4,33; *Lavra*, II, no. 108.556–86, app. x.26; *Xénophon*, no. 21.14; *Xéropotamou*, p. 71.4,6; and *Docheiariou*, p. 111. *PLP*, nos. 26142–43, 26175, 94518. On the other hand, around the year 1300 there were paroikoi in villages neighboring Kontogrikou with the patronym or family name Σκορίβα(ς). It is possible that Skorev is the Slavic rendering of the Greek Skoriva, which itself probably derived from the Greek Skores via the Slavic Skorev: Σκούρης → Σκόρης → Skorev → Σκορίβα(ς). Thus, the pronoia holder Skorev, in the original Greek act, was called either Skores or Skorivas. K. Pavlikjanov, *Istorija na bŭlgarskija svetogorski manastir Zograf ot 980 do 1804 g.* (Sofia, 2005),74, who comes to a similar conclusion regarding this "Skorev," writes that M. Živojinović, *Istorija Hilandara I: Od osnivanja manastira 1198. do 1335. godine* (Belgrade, 1998), 149, claimed that he was a well-known person. But while Živojinović's *izvestan* means "famous" in Bulgarian, it means merely "(a) certain (person)" in Serbian.

339 M. Živojinović, "Le monastère de Chilandar et ses métoques dans la région de l'Athos," *ZRVI* 26 (1987), 65.

340 Solovjev–Mošin, *Grčke povelje*, no. 31.42–46: ὅπερ κατεῖχεν ὁ Βοδέσης εἰς οἰκονομίαν αὐτοῦ. The dependency of St. George is again listed as a possession of the Zavlantia monastery in a chrysobull from 1366 of the same ruler. Here it is simply "St. George near Kotzekovo": Solovjev–Mošin, *Grčke povelje*, no. 34.77–79. For another act of Symeon Uroš which appears to involve a pronoia but is of questionable authenticity, see Bartusis, "Serbian Pronoia," 200–01.

nothing can be said about when or from whom he received his oikonomia, whether from a Byzantine emperor, from Stefan Dušan, from Symeon himself, or even from Nikephoros II. Even his ethnicity is unknown. Nevertheless, this particular property he held within his oikonomia did not pass to his heirs, but to a monastery.

Return to the state: death and disfavor

The components of a pronoia grant returned to the state when the holder died without having been granted hereditary rights over the pronoia, or when the holder lost imperial favor, usually through gross disloyalty. I do not place the concept of *perisseia* in this category, for the usual circumstance under which property of a pronoia holder was deemed *perisseia* and confiscated was property that was never part of one's oikonomia, and therefore its loss was not a diminution of one's pronoia (see *[6.6]*). Similarly, properties seized because they had been improperly alienated from one's oikonomia do not fit this category either, because they had already been relinquished by the pronoia holder before seizure. Overall, the word "confiscation" should be avoided. First, it is laden with onerous connotations, and the most common case – the normal return of a pronoia to the fisc after the death of its owner – was an ordinary, anticipated event. But more to the point, confiscation implies the appropriation of private property by the state, and a pronoia was never the property of its holder to begin with.

Probably the overwhelming majority of pronoiai that returned to the state did so because of their holders' death. Perhaps the earliest examples of a pronoia holder losing a pronoia because of his death are found in the twelfth century. Among the properties that John II Komnenos had donated to the monastery of the Pantokrator in Constantinople was "the pronoia of the deceased Synadenos" *[2.2]*. And then there is the act of the *doux* of Thessaloniki John Kontostephanos from 1162 which tells its convoluted story of the village or *proasteion* of Archontochorion. During the course of Kontostephanos' inquiry, Pankratios Anemas claimed that some paroikos houses were built during the time of "the deceased Loukites" who was holding Archontochorion before Anemas *[2.3]*. In neither of these cases is it certain that the death of the men preceded the loss of their pronoiai, but it seems likely.

In fact, it is difficult to find a single case where it is indisputably clear that the reason for the loss of a pronoia was death. Rather, it is the sheer number of these cases that makes it clear that we are dealing with the death of the pronoia holder and the return of his pronoia to the emperor. Let us cite some:

(i) Basil Vlatteros held the village of Vare near Smyrna as a pronoia until John III Vatatzes granted it to the monastery of the Lemviotissa sometime between 1224 and August 1228. A *prostagma* from 1232 states that the village was taken away "from the hand of the deceased Vlatteros."[341] While it is possible that Vlatteros died in the interval between the donation and 1232, it is most likely that his death was the catalyst for the donation.

(ii) Pasture land with a *posotes* of 5 hyperpyra had come to Theodore Sarantenos "from the land taken away from the deceased Bogdan" *[8.64]*.

(iii) And in 1346 Stefan Dušan confirmed the monastery of Esphigmenou's possession of 300 modioi of land at a place called Pephlegmenou which "had been taken away from the oikonomia of the deceased Kounales" and given to the monastery.[342] As we saw in the case of the pronoia of Rhomaios (discussed following *[8.50]* above), there is some evidence of resistance on the part of the holder's relatives to the return of a pronoia after the holder's death.

Pronoiai were also lost when the recipient lost the favor of the emperor. In particular, the grants given to those close to the emperor were held particularly precariously. Whether or not we should consider it a pronoia, such was the case of the substantial grant held by John Palaiologos, Michael VIII's brother, lost around 1272 when John lost his brother's confidence *[7.5]*. Similarly, Michael Angelos, son of the despot of Epiros Michael II Doukas, lost his property in 1304 when Andronikos II suspected him of treason *[7.7]*. Rather than being examples of pronoia grants lost through disfavor, both cases show the fragility of property rights for those in the highest ranks of society.

The earliest example of men being deprived of their pronoia grants is found in Pachymeres' history. He writes of the measures the Laskarid emperors of the early and mid-thirteenth century implemented to support the highlanders who inhabited the mountainous frontiers at the fringes of the Nicaean state. In order to persuade them to remain despite the incursions

[341] MM, IV, 194.15–18. Dölger, *Regesten*, III, no. 1710. And see *[5.4]*.

[342] *Esphigménou*, no. 22.15–16: ἀποσπασθεῖσαν ἀπὸ τῆς οἰκονομίας τοῦ Κουνάλη ἐκείνου. *PLP*, no. 13473. Since this property is not mentioned in the praktika for Esphigmenou from December 1321 (*Esphigménou*, nos. 15 and 16), the land was taken from Kounales after this time.

of irregular Turkish bands, the emperors granted "tax exemptions to all, pronoiai to the more illustrious among them, and imperial letters to those with a resolute spirit" *[5.14]*.

Policy toward the highlanders changed under Michael VIII. According to Pachymeres, shortly after and as a result of the blinding of John IV Laskaris in December 1261, a popular revolt erupted in the mountainous area called Trikokkia, the frontier region to the east of Nicaea. After quite some time, the episode ended through negotiations which divided the rebels. Most, through various threats and promises, were eventually persuaded to lay down their arms; others fled to the Turks. At some point after or in the midst of the Trikokkia revolt, Michael sent an official named Chadenos to Asia Minor to initiate a new agrarian program. "And as quickly as possible," Pachymeres writes,

> stopping at the places and finding exceedingly rich men, heavy with property and animals, he [Chadenos] marches them away [as soldiers] from their properties from which they derived their livelihood. And reckoning out [as pay] forty nomismata to each, and most of these [nomismata coming] from each man's own property, he [Chadenos] ordered that the rest of the tax established [i.e., the state's profit through the program], being not a little, be sent to the imperial treasury.

Pachymeres adds that they served well as long as their pay was forthcoming, but once payments became chronically unreliable, they fled the area.[343]

Thus, evidently with the triple purpose of reestablishing control over the frontier regions in the east, of forcing some well-off malingerers to give their share of military service, and of raising more imperial revenues, Michael VIII sent Chadenos to one or more regions in Asia Minor, where the latter found men who were benefitting from tax exemption, pronoiai, and other imperial favors, but were, perhaps, not contributing sufficiently to the defense of the area. In what can be characterized only as a draconian measure, Chadenos confiscated their property, including their pronoiai, and enrolled them as soldiers serving for pay. When, after some time, the pay became increasingly infrequent, the frontiers became increasingly porous.[344]

The first documentary evidence of men being deprived of their pronoia grants because they had lost the emperor's favor appears in connection with the civil wars of the 1340s which set John VI and later his son Matthew against the regency for John and then John V himself. The few documented

343 Pachymeres, ed. Failler, I, 33.3–8 (Bonn edn., I, 18.10–17), and I, 293.

344 M. Bartusis, "The Chadenos Affair (Pachymeres, Book I, Chapters 5–6)," *ZRVI* 45 (2008), 157–69. The interpretation I presented in Bartusis, *Late Byzantine Army*, 55–56, is, I now believe, incorrect.

cases of the partisan of one emperor being deprived of his pronoia by the other emperor suggest that quite a few properties changed hands during this period.

The grants to John Margarites *[8.17]* and to George Margarites *[8.39]* were composed of properties, including pronoiai, held by the rival emperor John Kantakouzenos and his supporters. Kantakouzenos (II, 256) mentions the losses of Arsenios Tzamplakon in Thessaloniki, though it is unclear whether a pronoia was involved. Similarly, a 1347 chrysobull of John VI mentions that all of Demetrios Kavasilas' property was confiscated, but it is unknown whether pronoia was involved *[8.45]*.

[8.78] Chrysobull of John V Palaiologos for the *stratopedarches* of the *monokavalloi* John Choumnos (1344)

In 1344 John V granted the *pansevastos sevastos stratopedarches* of the *monokavalloi* John Choumnos, for his fidelity, hereditary rights over the village of Loktista, near Zichna, a mountain pasturage, and 300 modioi of land in the village of Nevolianis, which together comprised a *posotes* of 40 hyperpyra and "which the unfaithful Maurophoros earlier held." He was to hold this *posotes*, as well as two other properties which he had purchased, *kata logon gonikotetos*, with the right to transmit them to his legitimate heirs and to improve them. The properties were exempted of all (secondary) taxes except for the regalian rights called *phonos*, *parthenophthoria*, and treasure trove (on these, see *[8.37]*).[345]

Loss through conquest

Pronoia holders also lost their grants through enemy conquest, just like any property holder. No doubt a great number of men lost their pronoia grants following the Latin Conquest, but the sources tell us nothing of this. Nor do they tell us much about the men granted pronoiai by the rulers of Epiros who lost these as Nicaean armies moved through Macedonia and into Thessaly. Other pronoia holders certainly lost their grants with Serbian and Bulgarian conquests in the thirteenth century.

The prolonged Turkish conquest of the empire, beginning toward the end of Michael VIII's reign, resulted in the loss of pronoiai *[7.7]* *[7.12]* *[8.3]*, as

345 *Actes de Philothée*, ed. Regel, no. 8.23,36–37. Ostrogorsky, *Féodalité*, 122–23, and Kazhdan, *Agrarnye otnošenija*, 219. *PLP*, no. 17504. Later Maurophoros entered the service of Stefan Dušan: see A. Solovjev, "Grečeskie arhonty v serbskom carstve XIV v.," *Byzantinoslavica* 2 (1930), 282–83.

did Serbian advances in the fourteenth century. In particular the policies of Stefan Dušan in conquered Byzantine territory acted to the detriment of pronoia holders. There are several cases in which Dušan took away pronoiai from laymen and bestowed them upon monasteries.[346] In 1346 he returned the village of Hagios Mamas to Vatopedi. This village had been taken away from the monastery years earlier and granted to pronoia holders, including the soldier company known as the Varvarenoi. Dušan ordered that Vatopedi was to hold it "as the Varvarenoi soldiers earlier held this and those before them held this same village."[347] In 1347 Dušan granted Lavra half of the "refuge" of Siderokauseia (τὸ εἰς τὰ Σιδηροκαυσεῖα καταφύγιον), "as much as is *demosiakon* and *pronoiastikon*" (ὅσον εὑρίσκεται δημοσιακὸν καὶ προνοιαστικόν), that is, as much as was state land or land held as pronoia. Since Lavra held the other half of Siderokauseia, it is almost certain that this property earlier had been confiscated from Lavra (*Lavra*, III, no. 128.29). And sometime between 1342 and 1348 paroikoi and *exaleimmatika stasia* in the village of Zavlantia in Thessaly were granted to pronoia soldiers. Once Stefan Dušan conquered the area he returned the paroikoi and property to the monastery of St. George *[8.22]*.

Regranting the components of a pronoia grant

Elements of the pronoia grant – property, paroikoi, and rights to state revenues – which returned to the state for any of the reasons described above were rarely kept to be exploited directly by the state. Rather, they were regranted to pronoia holders or to other privileged landholders. The process was dynamic. There were probably always men waiting to receive the full *posotes* granted to them by the emperor. And, having come full circle, this handbook on pronoia concludes.

[346] Ostrogorsky, *Féodalité*, 206–07.

[347] *Vatopédi*, II, no. 93.16. Bartusis, *Late Byzantine Army*, 204.

9 Pronoia in the later fourteenth and fifteenth centuries

During the last twenty-five years of the fourteenth century there are no Byzantine documents that refer to a pronoia or oikonomia conferred by the Byzantine emperor. Until the fifteenth century, the last document to mention an oikonomia conferred by the emperor is a decision from 1373 by a group of officials dealing with the oikonomia of the *megas adnoumiastes* George Katzaras *[8.47]*. The last fourteenth-century document to use the term *pronoia* or any of its related forms in a technical sense is a praktikon for Iviron from 1341, where the reference was copied from much earlier praktika (*Iviron*, IV, no. 86).

The reasons for this are not difficult to discern. Almost all of the documents discussed in Chapter 8 dealt with properties in Macedonia. In the 1340s most of Macedonia was conquered by the Serbian ruler Stefan Dušan. From the late 1350s the Ottoman Turks began their conquest of the Balkan peninsula. By around 1365 Byzantium as a political unit was reduced to Constantinople and its suburbs for some twenty or thirty miles; Thessaloniki and its environs, now isolated and in tenuous contact with the capital; the Byzantine Morea, entirely on its own; a number of Aegean islands such as Lemnos, Thasos, and Tenedos; a few coastal cities on the Sea of Marmara and the Black Sea such as Selymbria, Rhaidestos, and Anchialos; and a few odds and ends such as distant Philadelphia in Asia Minor which had long since lost all contact with the capital. The once proud empire was now but a minor state dependent on the Ottoman Empire. With the Turkish capture of Thessaloniki in 1387, Byzantium by 1400 was little more than Constantinople and a few islands ruled by Manuel II Palaiologos, and a principality run by the emperor's brother Theodore in a corner of the Morea.

Once the era covered by the histories of Kantakouzenos and Gregoras comes to an end, the non-documentary sources fall silent as well. The historians who deal with the last century of Byzantium (Doukas, Chalkokondyles, Sphrantzes) were not interested in the internal history of the decrepit Greek state but rather the interplay between the decline of Byzantium and the rise of the Ottoman Empire. As a result, what little the documentary sources tell us about pronoia in the later fourteenth century is connected with the appropriation of the institution of pronoia by the Serbs and even by the Turks. These will be dealt with in due course.

That the Byzantine Empire lasted past the turn of the fifteenth century was due only to civil war and the other crises that racked the Ottoman state. It was the battle of Ankara in 1402 that delayed the end for another half century. The Mongols under Timur destroyed the Ottoman army and captured Sultan Bayezid himself. The Ottoman state fragmented: the emirs of southwestern Asia Minor reasserted their authority, and the sons of Bayezid each grabbed what they could of what remained of their father's domain. All of this was good news for Byzantium. Süleyman Çelebi, the eldest son of Bayezid, established himself in Adrianople as the new sultan (1402–11) and concluded a treaty in 1403 which permitted the Byzantines to regain Thessaloniki and the Chalkidike, several Aegean islands, and territory in Thrace along the Black Sea. With the restoration of Byzantine rule over part of Macedonia we hear once again about the institution of pronoia in a series of documents that shed light not only on developments during the fifteenth century but on the last decades of the fourteenth century as well.

The area around Thessaloniki

[9.1] Prostagma of Manuel II Palaiologos for the monasteries of Mount Athos (1408)

The document central to the discussion is a *prostagma* of Manuel II from December 1408 for the monks of Mount Athos. The emperor writes:

> A long time ago, soon after the death of the despot of Serbia, the deceased Uglješa, because the incursions which had taken place then by the Turks were burdensome and constant, it seemed appropriate, thinking of the public good, that half of the *metochia* of the [monasteries] of Mount Athos and of Thessaloniki, simply everything, should be pronoiarized [ἵνα προνοιασθῶσι τὰ ἡμίση τῶν μετοχίων τε Ἁγιοριτῶν καὶ τῶν Θεσσαλονικέων καὶ ἁπλῶς πάντα], in order that they not be swallowed up completely. For clearly the times then threatened things. We had and we have the intention, if God should deliver better times, to restore the things concerning those [*metochia*] to them, as it was from the beginning, and that they have their things completely. May God grant this. For this shall gladden us more than those who shall be receiving.

However, circumstances had not improved, and so it was necessary

to add other burdens to these. I do not refer to the time during which the Turks seized and held these things completely, but before this and afterward. Now since my majesty has come to the God-saved city of Thessaloniki, those present there of the Holy Mountain asked that, for the half of the villages and properties they hold, they gain benefactions from the things added to their properties, as was said. And my majesty, receiving their request favorably, grants [the following] to them.

Here the emperor exempts them from the tax on wine the monks produce and addresses regulations concerning the selling of wine. He continues,

And since some [things] were earlier taken away from half their properties in whole or in part, we order that they have the half of these, as this is in accord with the previous intention, and they should hold the half of these. Since we granted a benefaction toward these from their *haradj*, which the great emir personally granted to us, that they should have two-thirds, [and since] it happened for some that they gave half the *haradj* from the part which they hold, we order that they give from this one-third, as from the beginning we declared and ordered.[1]

For the first time in over a century a document issued by the Byzantine emperor contains a form of the term *pronoia*. This document presents the second and only other appearance in the Byzantine sources of the rare verb *pronoiazo* (προνοιάζω), in the passive form *pronoiazesthai* (προνοιάζεσθαι). In the first appearance of this verb, in the 1216 act of Andronikos Mauropodos *[5.5]*, it was found in the phrase τις τῶν προνοιασθέντων, which I translated as "someone of those pronoiarized," giving the passive form of the verb the meaning "to be granted a pronoia" or "to be made a pronoia holder." In the 1408 act the meaning of the verb is slightly different. Here the *metochia* themselves were the things pronoiarized, so that the passive form of the verb acquires the meaning "to transform into the constituent elements of a pronoia grant," or, more simply, "to confer as a pronoia."

To begin the discussion of this document and Manuel's policy toward these monasteries, it is useful to recount briefly the history of the area of Thessaloniki. From the mid-1350s until 1371 most of Macedonia, including the Chalkidike, was in Serbian hands. Only Thessaloniki and its immediate environs remained under Byzantine control. This situation came to an end

[1] V. Mošin, "Akti iz svetogorskih arhiva," *Spomenik Srpske kraljevske akademije nauka* 91 (1939), 165–67. Ostrogorsky, *Féodalité*, 161–62. *Lavra*, IV, 56–57. As in Chapter 5, I transliterate the Greek προνοιάζω as "pronoiarize" because the more accurate "pronoia-ize" is unattractive and difficult to pronounce.

in September 1371, when the despot John Uglješa and his brother King Vukašin were killed battling the Turks at Černomen on the Marica River in Thrace. Since the fragmentation of Stefan Dušan's empire upon his death in 1355, Vukašin had been ruling the district between Prilep and Ohrid, while Uglješa had been ruling the area north of Serres. In 1366 Uglješa added to his domain a large area around Serres, which up to that time had been controlled by Dušan's widow Helen. The deaths of Vukašin and Uglješa, which marked the end of Serbian power in the Middle Ages, presented the Byzantines with the opportunity to restore Byzantine authority to Macedonia. Quickly Manuel II, then governing Thessaloniki, recaptured Serres in November 1371 and restored the Chalkidike, including Mount Athos, to Byzantine authority. Although Serres may have been taken soon afterward by the Ottomans, the Chalkidike, more important for the developments dealt with here, remained under nominally effective Byzantine authority until 1384, when the Ottoman general Hayreddin Paşa began his three-year siege of Thessaloniki.

In April 1387 Thessaloniki surrendered to Hayreddin, and for the next sixteen years the second city of the empire was in Turkish hands. With the recovery of Thessaloniki following the battle of Ankara, Manuel II's nephew, John VII, was sent to govern the city in late 1403 or early 1404 and he lived there until his death in 1408. From late 1408 through early 1409 Manuel II visited Thessaloniki to install his minor son Andronikos as the new governor. It was during this visit that he issued our *prostagma.*

Manuel refers to a policy decision he made shortly after the battle of the Marica in September 1371. "For the common good" and in order that the monastic dependencies (*metochia*) in the area of Mount Athos and Thessaloniki "not be swallowed up completely" by the Turks, he decided to "pronoiarize" half of all the *metochia.* As a result of this action, the monks ended up with only "half of [their] villages and properties" (τὰ ἡμίση τῶν χωρίων καὶ τῶν κτημάτων). What had happened?

In order to explain what Manuel II had done in the months after September 1371 we need to consult other documents for traces of this policy. In some documents the results of Manuel's policy are stated more or less explicitly. In August 1404 John VII restored to Lavra at its request all of the village of Drymosyrta and the income derived from those paroikoi installed there. The monastery had possessed the village "from time immemorial," but "half had become fiscal by the trouble and storm of matters."[2] In a *prostagma* of

[2] *Lavra,* III, no. 155.18: γενόμενον δὲ τούτου τὸ ἥμισυ τοῦ δημοσίου ὑπὸ τῆς τῶν πραγμάτων ζάλης καὶ τρυκιμίας, and IV, p. 52.

Manuel II for Docheiariou from 1409, we read that the village of Mariana had been purchased from a laywoman, but the monastery lost it in abnormal conditions. The monks' request to get it back was granted, but in regard to the village of Hermeleia, the monks "should have half, the [other] half is the state's, like the other properties of monasteries." The editor of the document suggested that the seemingly extraneous mention of Hermeleia might best be explained by hypothesizing that their petition included a request, not only for the return of Mariana, but for all of Hermeleia as well.[3]

Other references to this policy are less explicit, mentioning only that a particular monastery held half of a particular village. In 1409 a document refers to the monks of Lavra holding "half of the village [of Karvaioi]," "half of the paroikoi, land, and water there [in Sykea]," and "half of this village [of Gomatou] and the paroikoi in it." Another document from the same year notes that Docheiariou held "the whole of the tower of Perigardikeia, half of their tower of Hermeleia, the whole of the village of Mariana, and the half of Kalokampos."[4]

In fact, any reference in documents issued after 1371 to "half" of a village deserves attention in this context, though all such references may not necessarily refer to Manuel II's policy.[5] Documents that refer to confiscations of monastic property, even if they fit into the required chronology to be part of Manuel's policy, must be viewed with caution. Monasteries lost their properties under many different circumstances, nor was Manuel II unique in appropriating them for the benefit of pronoia holders. For example, the village of Neochorion in the western Chalkidike was held by Lavra ca. 1344 (*Xénophon*, no. 27), but in 1378 was held by Radoslav Sampias as an imperial grant *[8.48]*. Even though the chronology can accommodate Manuel II's pronoiarization, we are not permitted to link the example to this particular policy because Sampias appears to have received *all* of Neochorion, rather than one-half, and because we have absolutely no information regarding

[3] *Docheiariou*, no. 52.12–13: ἵνα ἔχωσι τὸ ἥμισυ μέρος, τὸ δὲ ἥμισυ ἵνα ἔνι τοῦ δημοσίου, ὡς καὶ τὰ ἄλλα κτήματα τῶν μοναστηρίων. Ostrogorsky, *Féodalité*, 163; *Lavra*, IV, p. 52.

[4] *Lavra*, III, no. 161.17,49,56,60. *Docheiariou*, no. 53.2–3. Also, Lefort, *Villages de Macédoine*, 147, refers to an unpublished praktikon from 1409 in which Vatopedi received half of the families of Hagios Mamas.

[5] For example, there is an act of two officials from 1409 which confirms Manuel Kavasilas' possession of the village of Katakale that he inherited from his father and "the half of Aloupochorion" (τὸ ἥμισυ τοῦ Ἀλουποχωρίου): *Dionysiou*, no. 11. K. Smyrlis, "The State, the Land, and Private Property," in *Church and Society in Late Byzantium*, ed. D. Angelov (Kalamazoo, 2009), 67, links the confiscation of Raphalion from Vatopedi *[8.7]* to Manuel's pronoiarization, but the relevant documents (probably from 1377) mention nothing about "half" of anything, and, to me, the phrase "years ago" suggests more than the passing of six years.

why Lavra no longer held this property (it may have exchanged it for another property).

Another set of documents that may refer to the pronoiarization of Manuel II deals with a property called Stylarion, located near the village of Hagios Mamas in the south-central Chalkidike. Three documents are involved: (i) An act of donation of the *megas domestikos* Alexios Laskaris Metochites from June 1369 in which he donates Stylarion, consisting of 13,000 modioi of land, and its paroikoi to Vatopedi.[6] (ii) An act of conferral of the *megas chartoularios* Laskaris Metochites from December 1375. Pursuant to an imperial order, he conferred on Vatopedi two-thirds of the land and paroikoi of Stylarion, the other third going to the fisc. According to this document, the entire size of Stylarion was now only 6,361½ modioi.[7] (iii) A third document involving Stylarion is an imperial *prostagma*, known only through a medieval copy that bears no date. The emperor explains that the deceased *protostrator* Chrysos took away an unspecified quantity of land at Stylarion from Vatopedi, and the emperor ordered the return of this land to the monastery. Further, he ordered that the complaint of a certain George Philommates, who claimed the property as his, should be investigated.[8]

A number of elements within these documents may refer back to the pronoiarization of Manuel II. The most likely is the reduction in the size of Vatopedi's property at Stylarion from 13,000 modioi in 1369 to 6,361½ modioi in 1375, a remarkable coincidence if unrelated to the pronoiarization. Another is the fact that the *protostrator* Chrysos, an otherwise unknown figure, "took away" part of Stylarion from Vatopedi. The use of the verb *apospo* (ἀποσπῶ) suggests that he was performing an official act when he "took away" part of Vatopedi's property. And George Philommates, who laid claim to the part of Stylarion that Chrysos "took away" (which could have been the other 6,500 or so modioi lost between

[6] *Vatopédi*, II, no. 130. Lefort, *Villages de Macédoine*, 176.

[7] *Vatopédi*, II, no. 147. Cf. the conclusions of N. Oikonomides, "Le Haradj dans l'empire byzantin du XVe siècle," in Oikonomides, *Documents et études sur les institutions de Byzance* (London, 1976), no. XIX, 683–64, based on a different dating (Dec. 1405).

[8] *Vatopédi*, II, no. 142. Dölger suggested a date of around 1380 for the *prostagma*; Lefort proposed 1369–75 (i.e., the period between the first two documents): F. Dölger, "Neues zu Alexios Metochites und zu Theodoros Meliteniotes," in Dölger, *Byzantinische Diplomatik* (Ettal, 1956), 326–30; Dölger, *Regesten*, V, no. 3119; and Lefort, *Villages de Macédoine*, 21, who also, for reasons unclear to me, specifies that the act was issued in the month of April. In truth we can say only that the *prostagma* was issued after the original donation in 1369. In structure and wording this document is not very different from *prostagmata* issued in the early fifteenth century: e.g., *Docheiariou*, no. 52 (1409); *Lavra*, III, no. 157 (1405); and especially, *Lavra*, III, no. 166 (1428 or 1443 or 1353), which illustrates well the difficulties in determining dates.

1369 and 1375), may have been one of the people who benefitted from the pronoiarization.[9]

Moreover, it is difficult to confirm Manuel II's claim that the properties of the monasteries of Thessaloniki (in addition to those of Mount Athos) were pronoiarized. The only evidence that has ever been cited in this regard is an act from 1393 concerning the village of Achinos, on the Strymon, south of Serres *[10.1]*. Lemerle wrote that "the history of the village of Achinos, held half by the Thessalonian monastery of Akapniou and half by a pronoiarios," demonstrates that the pronoiarization "was not limited to the monasteries of Athos."[10] However, the matter is not as simple as this. First of all, the document refers to "half of the village of Achinos, which the . . . monastery of Akapniou held from time immemorial" (*Esphigménou*, no. 30.2–3: ἐξ ἀμνημονεύτων χρόνων). All that this means is that Akapniou held half of Achinos a very long time before 1393, certainly before 1371. Although the passage does not exclude the possibility that *all* of Achinos had been held "from time immemorial" (and that the monastery had lost one half in 1371), one cannot assume this. Ultimately, we do not know whether Akapniou ever held all of Achinos or why the monastery held only half of the village in 1393. Further, the "*pronoiarios*" who held the other half of Achinos in 1393 was one Demetrios Vryennios Laskaris who received his half of Achinos from the Ottoman sultan after the Turkish capture of Thessaloniki in 1387 *[10.1]*. It is possible that Laskaris originally had received the half of the village from the Byzantine emperor, but the documents say nothing about this. We simply do not know who held the other half of Achinos in the years immediately after 1371, and consequently, this document provides at best weak evidence with which to corroborate Manuel's assertion that half of the *metochia* of Thessalonian monasteries were pronoiarized.

[9.2] Prostagma of Manuel II Palaiologos for two Thessalonian monasteries (1415)

There is one document that suggests that Manuel's pronoiarization policy was not limited to monastic property. According to a *prostagma* of Manuel II from 1415, Anna of Savoy, the wife of Andronikos III, had donated years earlier to the convent of the Saints Anargyroi in Thessaloniki a courtyard

[9] As for why the official in 1375 conferred upon Vatopedi only two-thirds of the property (that is, some 4,241 modioi) and two-thirds of the paroikoi, is unclear. No other document from this period mentions any policy to deprive monasteries of an additional one-third of their property, but the appearance of such an arbitrary fraction suggests it was a policy, perhaps relating to the further demands Manuel II notes that he was forced to place upon monasteries.

[10] *Lavra*, IV, 53 note 248.

(*aule*) with houses and shops in the same city, which had once belonged to someone named "Syrge" (Guy of Lusignan, or his son Michael). Later, during the winter of 1370–71, Manuel, while passing through the Morea on his way to Venice, granted this property to a certain *vasilissa* Kantakouzene, perhaps Isabelle of Lusignan, the daughter of Guy of Lusignan and the wife of the despot of the Morea Manuel Kantakouzenos. "After this, when matters took a different turn, this courtyard was confiscated by my majesty and granted to some [people] for their pronoia."[11] At the time Manuel was unaware the courtyard had been granted earlier to the Saints Anargyroi.

The *prostagma* explains that later, in 1384, he granted the courtyard to the monastery of Nea Mone in Thessaloniki, which had been holding it up to 1415, when Manuel visited the city. At the request of the nuns of the Saints Anargyroi, an investigation was conducted, and because it was determined that the convent had been unjustly deprived of the property, the decision was made to set things right. Because of the improvements made to the property by the monks of Nea Mone during their tenure and for other reasons, Manuel's present *prostagma* ordered that Nea Mone and the Saints Anargyroi should each henceforth own one half of the courtyard.

Thus, the confiscation of the courtyard in Thessaloniki, and its subsequent conferral in pronoia, occurred between the summer or fall of 1371 (after Manuel returned from Venice) and 1384. It is possible that it was connected with events following the battle of Marica (September 1371), though the fact that the entire property was appropriated (rather than one half) and the fact that the property was taken from a laywoman rather than a monastery, does not permit us to connect it with the specific *monastic* "pronoiarization" program of Manuel II. Nevertheless, it would be difficult to distinguish the meaning of the construction "to be confiscated by my majesty and to be granted to people for their pronoia" from that of "to be pronoiarized" (*pronoiazesthai*).[12] Common sense would dictate that any other available properties that Manuel could confer on pronoia holders would be included in his attempts to protect the region he was governing. In the simplest scenario, the *vasilissa* Kantakouzene died and the absence of

[11] *Lavra*, III, no. 163.15–16: δημοσιεύθη ἡ τοιαύτη αὐλὴ παρὰ τῆς βασιλείας μου, καὶ εὐηργετήθη πρός τινας εἰς πρόνοιαν αὐτῶν.

[12] The phrase "for their pronoia" (εἰς πρόνοιαν αὐτῶν) harkens back to the meaning of *pronoia* as "maintenance," so that the entire clause could be translated "granted to some people for their maintenance." Further, P. Lemerle, "Autour d'un prostagma inédit de Manuel II, L'aulé de Sire Guy à Thessalonique," in Lemerle, *Le monde de Byzance* (London, 1978), no. XXIII, 274 note 3, pointed out that the phrase "to people for their pronoia" does not necessarily mean that more than one person held the entire property as a pronoia at the same time (a joint pronoia). Rather, alternative interpretations, either that two or more persons held it successively or the property was divided between two or more pronoiars, easily accommodate the text.

an heir who could pursue ownership of the property prompted Manuel to confer the property as a pronoia.

While we may conclude that at least a large percentage of the possessions in the theme of Thessaloniki of the monasteries of Mount Athos were affected by Manuel's policy (and perhaps the properties of some laymen as well), we still must consider what precisely happened in the period following the battle of Marica. What did it mean when a monastery held "half" of a village and the other "half" was held by the state? What was being divided?

Mošin, Ostrogorsky, Charanis, and others viewed the process as a "secularization" of monastic property.[13] More recently, based on his own analysis of the documents, Oikonomides was "led to think that the transformation of monastic properties into pronoiai had not affected the monasteries' property rights to the land at all; it concerned only the possession, the revenues – fiscal revenues as well as revenues of the landowner." And Lemerle, dealing with how the pronoiarization affected the properties of one particular monastery, wrote,

> the monastery was not dispossessed of the properties thus cited, but it lost temporarily the normal basic income for the benefit of those to whom it was attributed in pronoia. This is the reason why one should not speak of a "confiscation" or even of "secularization" of the half of the Athonite properties after Marica: at the most of a partial "fiscalization" for the purpose of pronoia.[14]

The question, then, is whether half of all the properties were secularized, that is, confiscated and reassigned, as if they were state property, to pronoia holders, or whether the monasteries involved maintained property title to their properties but lost only half of the revenues of their properties, either half of the fiscal revenues (taxes) or half of the total revenues (taxes plus rents). Manuel II's *prostagma* itself supports the "secularization" interpretation; it refers only to *metochia*, villages, and properties, and explains that the monks ended up with only "half of [their] villages and properties." If only "revenues" were involved, one might think that the 1408 *prostagma* would have said that the monks lost half of their *prosodoi* ("incomes, revenues"), not half of their properties (*ktemata*), villages (*choria*), and *metochia*.

[13] E.g., Mošin, "Akti," 164; G. Ostrogorsky, *History of the Byzantine State*, rev. ed. (New Brunswick, N.J., 1969), 541 note 3; Ostrogorsky, *Féodalité*, 161–62; Charanis, "Monastic Properties," 116–17; I. Ševčenko, "A Postscript to Nicolas Cabasilas' 'Anti-Zealot' Discourse," in Ševčenko, *Society and Intellectual Life in Late Byzantium* (London, 1981), VI, 406, and recently, Smyrlis, "The State, the Land, and Private Property," 71.

[14] Oikonomides, in *Docheiariou*, p. 273. Lemerle, in *Lavra*, IV, p. 53. In Bartusis, *Late Byzantine Army*, 169, I adopted Lemerle's interpretation.

[9.3] Act of Paul Gazes and George Prinkips for the monastery of Docheiariou (1409)

Lemerle's interpretation of Manuel II's policy is based chiefly on an act of two fiscal officials, Paul Gazes and George Prinkips, from May 1409. By virtue of a decision of Manuel II, the monastery of Docheiariou received confirmation of its possessions on the Chalkidike. Most prominent among these properties were "the whole of the tower of Perigardikeia, half of their tower of Hermeleia, the whole of the village of Mariana, and half of Kalokampos." The document lists the paroikoi in each of these properties, as well as the taxes burdening each. Most of this section is straightforward, except that the document states that, for the "*monasteriakoi* men" of Kalokampos (evidently the paroikoi held by the monastery), of their combined *telos* of 22 hyperpyra, only $7^5/_{14}$ hyperpyra, or approximately one-third, should go to the state. Also at Kalokampos, 5 hyperpyra were assessed on a place or a person called Vrizas, of which $2^1/_2$ went to the emperor, so that the total for Kalokampos was rounded upward to 13 hyperpyra. In all, for these four properties, the monks bore a fiscal burden of $17^1/_2$ hyperpyra,

> which those inscribed [paroikoi] of the named villages ought to give annually and prudently in two payments to those *pronoiarioi* who should be assigned them [πρὸς οὓς ἂν προσταχθῶσι προνοιαρίους]. Moreover, toward the said most esteemed monks [the paroikoi should] have the appropriate respect and obedience, and render each year the customary and assigned corvées, when they should be assigned by them, as well as the tithe [*dekateia*] of the fruits of their *zeugaria* and all that [the monks] have the right to receive customarily from such villages, that is, the *melissoennomion*, the *aer*, and in short all to which they have, as was said, a right.

The document adds a few other minor properties that the monastery possessed and notes that the oxen (*doulika zeugaria*) held by the monastery in these villages were to be tax exempt. A standard clause is included: "all of which the said . . . monks ought to hold undisturbed and unshaken by both successive *pronoiarioi* and every other state [tax] exacter."[15] This information is gathered in Table 9.1, where the symbol "–" signifies that the tax or charge is not mentioned, and "NA" means that it is mentioned but no quantity is provided.

Lemerle concluded that this document shows that there was no confiscation of monastic property, but rather a "fiscalization"; the revenues from property and paroikoi, not the property itself, had been assigned to

[15] *Docheiariou*, no. 53.20–24,30: ἀνενοχλήτως καὶ ἀδιασείστως παρά τε τῶν κατὰ καιροὺς προνοιαρίων καὶ παντὸς ἑτέρου δημοσιακοῦ ἀπαιτητοῦ.

Table 9.1 The monastery of Docheiariou's major holdings on the Chalkidike in 1409

	Perigardikeia	half of Hermeleia	Mariana	half of Kalokampos
inhabitants:				
number of families	7	15	23	2
number of widows	4	2	1	1
telos	36 hyperpyra	50 hyp.	$58\frac{1}{2}$ hyp.	(22 hyp.→) $7\frac{5}{14}$ hyp.
other *telos*	–	–	–	(5 hyp. →) $2\frac{1}{2}$ hyp.
kephalatikion	–	15 hyp.	–	3 hyp.
dekaton of their *zeugaria*	NA (to monastery)			
melissoennomion				
aer				
other charges				
total (to state)	36 hyp.	65 hyp.	$58\frac{1}{2}$ hyp.	13 hyp.

pronoia holders. Ostrogorsky interpreted this act to mean that the taxes of the peasants in Perigardikeia, Hermeleia, and Mariana went to pronoia holders, and in Kalokampos slightly more than a third, so that pronoia holders received most of the paroikoi's *telos*, while the monks received the traditional corvée obligations and the secondary charges. He concluded that not only did the monasteries lose half of their possessions to pronoia holders, but the major part of the tax revenues of the remaining half had been attributed to pronoia holders as well. Base taxes and *kephalatikion* (evidently the Byzantine appropriation of the early Ottoman head tax) went to pronoia holders.[16]

Neither of these interpretations is quite accurate. Lemerle's interpretation assumes that the fiscal arrangements described in this act constituted the pronoiarization, and the entire extent of the pronoiarization, of these properties. But it is not certain that the detailed fiscal arrangements described in the document have any connection to Manuel II's pronoiarization policy at all. The document explains that taxes were levied on monastic properties and these taxes were to be received by *pronoiarioi*, in other words, an example of tax revenues as a benefit of holding something in pronoia. Yet in the details of the taxes levied there is no trace of "half" of anything that was pronoiarized. Rather, the only reference to "half" of anything is to the half of Hermeleia and half of Kalokampos that Docheiariou held. This, I think, is where we should look for Manuel's pronoiarization.

Docheiariou's possession of its property at Kalokampos (called Diavolokampos before the fifteenth century) and Hermeleia had been

[16] *Lavra*, IV, 53. Ostrogorsky, *Féodalité*, 164–72, 291 note 1.

confirmed by chrysobull as late as 1355 (*Docheiariou*, no. 33), and neither this or any other document before the act of 1409 makes any reference to "half" of either of these properties. Nevertheless, references to the region of Diavolokampos in fourteenth-century documents often include more than the domain of Docheiariou. At times it included the villages of Rousaiou and Patrikona, also held by Docheiariou, as well as the land of Hagia Trias, held by Iviron, and the village of Oxynon, held by Lavra.[17] Similarly, Docheiariou never held all of Hermeleia. In the early fifteenth century the monasteries of Xeropotamou and Vatopedi held property there as well, as did Zographou in the first half of the fourteenth century.[18] Earlier documents referring to Docheiariou's possessions in the village refer to the "land" the monastery owned in Hermeleia. Thus, it would seem that when the 1409 act mentions "half of their tower of Hermeleia" and "half of Kalokampos," this means half of what Docheiariou held previously in Hermeleia and in Kalokampos. Since there is no evidence that the monastery lost half of its holdings in Hermeleia or Kalokampos for any other reason, it is likely that the loss was a result of Manuel II's policy.

The important point is that neither the 1409 act nor any other late fourteenth- or fifteenth-century source tells us anything at all about the *other* halves of Hermeleia and Kalokampos. I think that it was these other halves that reflect the effects of the pronoiarization policy of Manuel II. And since they were no longer under the monastery's control, documents dealing with the possessions of the monasteries say nothing about them.

Here it should be noted that the situation with Perigardikeia and Mariana was different, for the 1409 act states that Docheiariou held these properties in their entirety. Why did the monastery not hold only half of these? The village of Mariana, located in the central Chalkidike about four miles north of Hagios Mamas, was purchased by Docheiariou in August 1373.[19] Since none of the several documents that mention Docheiariou's possession of Mariana suggest that the monastery ever held only one-half of the village, it is quite possible that this property was unaffected by Manuel's policy. The simplest explanation of this is that Docheiariou acquired the property after Manuel had implemented his pronoiarization policy and thus it was exempt from the procedure.

17 Lefort, *Villages de Macédoine*, 57–58, 116–17, 138–41.

18 *Xéropotamou*, 24, 211. *Zographou*, no. 27.15.

19 Lefort, *Villages de Macédoine*, 97–98. *Docheiariou*, nos. 42 (1373), 43 (1375), 44 (1375). A *prostagma* from January 1409 confirmed the monastery's possession of all of Mariana, and it suggests that Docheiariou had temporarily lost the village in the recent past, perhaps in 1403–04, a development with no direct connection to Manuel II's pronoiarization policy: *Docheiariou*, no. 52 and notes.

Such a hypothesis will not work for Perigardikeia. Located in the eastern Chalkidike on the gulf of Athos, Perigardikeia (today Pyrgadikia) was a large holding, surpassing 20,000 modioi (*Docheiariou*, pp. 51–52). And, as in the case of Mariana, there is no evidence of any other monastery holding property in the village of Perigardikeia. However, unlike Mariana, Docheiariou had been holding Perigardikeia since the eleventh century. Further, Perigardikeia's location cannot be a factor in its ostensible exemption from Manuel's policy, for there is clear evidence that Lavra's nearby *metochion* at Gomatou was affected by the pronoiarization (see *[9.4]* below). Docheiariou may have lost half of Perigardikeia and then regained it at a later date through an imperial benefaction, or, through a special exception, it may never have lost half of Perigardikeia. Nothing more can be said.

It seems, therefore, that Ostrogorsky and the other scholars who write of a secularization or even a confiscation of monastic property were nearer the truth than Lemerle, who described a mere "fiscalization." Yet Ostrogorsky assumed that the taxation arrangements of the 1409 act were related to the pronoiarization. I do not think that this was the case.

Ostrogorsky thought that the combined figure of 17½ hyperpyra included the total *telos* of the paroikoi that Docheiariou held in Perigardikeia, Hermeleia, and Mariana, and one-third of the *telos* of the paroikoi of Kalokampos, and this is why he concluded that not only did the state secularize half of the properties of the monasteries (or in this case, at least two of the four), but for the benefit of *pronoiarioi* the state received the majority of the fiscal revenue produced by these properties. Yet he also observed that the taxes levied upon the inscribed paroikoi were several times higher than we might expect, based on usual fourteenth-century figures. He hypothesized that perhaps this was due to the devaluation of the hyperpyron or to increased burdens placed on the peasantry. Oikonomides thought the former suggestion unlikely because in the fifteenth century the hyperpyron was merely a money of account (most monetary transactions involved exchanges of Venetian currency). As for the latter, Oikonomides wrote that "naturally such an augmentation of the tax was possible only if it was accompanied by a reduction of other charges the paroikoi rendered to their lord (notably of land rent)." He considered that such alterations in the Byzantine fiscal system "ought to be attributed to the old Ottoman administration, the fiscal system of which had been conserved without modification by the Byzantines."[20]

[20] Ostrogorsky, *Féodalité*, 164–65, 169. *Docheiariou*, p. 274.

Further, through a comparison of the inscribed *telos* for each paroikos household of each property in this act and for each paroikos household of Drymosyrta and Gomatou (see *[9.4]*), Oikonomides observed that the *telos* levied on the paroikoi in Mariana, Hermeleia, and Perigardikeia, was one-half to one-third the *telos* levied on the paroikoi of Kalokampos, Drymosyrta, and Gomatou. He concluded that the reason for this was that the paroikoi of Mariana, Hermeleia, and Perigardikeia "rendered their taxes directly to the fisc, and consequently, only paid a third of their normal tax. In contrast, the inhabitants of Kalokampos (as well as those of the villages of Lavra) paid the totality of their taxes to their monastery, which in turn rendered a third to the fisc or to a *pronoiarios*" (*Docheiariou*, pp. 274–75). This explains why the document notes that of the 22 hyperpyra owed by the paroikoi of Kalokampos, only $7\frac{5}{14}$ hyperpyra (approximately one-third) went to the state, and it also would explain why no parallel phrase is found regarding the other properties.

As for why the properties were paying only one-third of the *telos*, we refer back to the 1408 *prostagma*: "we granted a benefaction toward these [monasteries] from their *haradj*, which the great emir personally granted to us, that they should have two-thirds . . . as from the beginning we declared and ordered." The *haradj* was the main tax that the Ottomans levied on non-Muslims.[21] A *prostagma* of Manuel II from 1404 to the official Demetrios Vouliotes explained how the taxes for Mount Athos were to be organized now that the region of Thessaloniki had once again become Byzantine. Manuel chose to retain the taxation framework in effect during the Ottoman occupation. He tells Vouliotes: "demand the entire third of their *haradj* [χαράτζιν] goodly and wholly according to the earlier usage and custom, as it was demanded in the time of the deceased emir Bayezid bey, so that neither we nor the monasteries have a loss from this." The emperor explained that he granted the state's third of the *haradj* to John VII, who now governed Thessaloniki. All other taxes would be similarly divided (one-third to the fisc and two-thirds to the monastic landholders), except for the otherwise unknown tax called the *phosatiakon* (φοσατιακόν or φοσατακόν), which was remitted entirely.[22]

In the 1409 act this division of the other taxes (one-third to the fisc and two-thirds to the monastic landholders) was not performed quite like

[21] See Oikonomides, "Haradj," 681–88. Mošin's edition of the 1408 *prostagma* misread τοῦ χαρατζίου as τοῦ χορηγεῖον in this passage: on this correction, see *Lavra*, IV, 58 note 265.

[22] Arkadios Vatopedinos, "Ἁγιορειτικὰ ἀνάλεκτα ἐκ τοῦ ἀρχείου τῆς μονῆς Βατοπεδίου," *Γρηγόριος ὁ Παλαμᾶς* 2 (1918), 449–52, no. 15. Dölger, *Regesten*, V, nos. 3300–01. Oikonomides, "Haradj," 682–83.

this. The *kephalatikion* was paid for Hermeleia and Kalokampos, but not mentioned at all in regard to Perigardikeia and Mariana. Oikonomides suggested that this may have been due to some kind of arrangement between the monastery and the fisc (*Docheiariou*, p. 275).

In conclusion, pronoia holders derived, or may have derived, benefit from the monastic properties described in the 1409 act in two distinct ways. First, in regard to the portions of these properties that the monastery still held, they received, explicitly, one-third of the *telos* (*haradj*) of the paroikoi settled on these properties, and they received the *kephalatikion* of two of the properties (which may have represented a fiscal accommodation by which, instead of levying one-third the *kephalatikion* for all four properties, the *kephalatikion* of two properties was exempted and the full *kephalatikion* was rendered for two properties, resulting in a comparable levy). These arrangements may have had their origin during the Turkish occupation and did not necessarily have any connection to the pronoiarization policy of Manuel II. Second, the other halves of Hermeleia and Kalokampos, which Docheiariou once held, but no longer held, reflect Manuel's pronoiarization. If *pronoiarioi* held these properties in 1409 (there is no evidence for or against this), they derived the same benefit that any pronoia holder derived from holding paroikoi and land in pronoia. In other words, Manuel II took away one-half of the monasteries' properties. Despite the fact that the Turks evidently reintroduced taxation on these properties, the monks continued to enjoy substantial fiscal privileges over the remaining half of their properties.

[9.4] Act of Paul Gazes and George Prinkips for the monastery of Lavra (1409)

Our understanding of Manuel's pronoiarization is further increased by an act of Paul Gazes and George Prinkips from April 1409. The monks of Lavra had asked Manuel II for an exchange of properties. They desired to give up their holdings in the village of Siderokauseia "which is considered as imperial in its entirety because they find much vexation by the successive *pronoiarioi* found here," and to receive instead "the imperial rights" of the villages of Drymosyrta and Pinson, plus their abandoned village of Loroton, "that the monks should have these wholly in their entirety."[23] The emperor agreed to their request, and the order was given to effect the exchange.

[23] *Lavra*, III, no. 161.4–5: μονομερῶς βασιλικόν, διὰ τὸ εὑρίσκειν αὐτοὺς πολλὴν ἐπήρειαν παρὰ τῶν ἐκεῖ εὑρισκομένων κατὰ καιροὺς προνοιαρίων, and lines 6–7: ἐξ ὁλοκλήρου μονομερῶς.

Table 9.2 The monastery of the Lavra's holdings in two villages in 1409

<table>
<tr><th></th><th>Drymosyrta</th><th>Pinson</th></tr>
<tr><td>inhabitants:</td><td></td><td></td></tr>
<tr><td>number of families</td><td>35</td><td>16 [18]</td></tr>
<tr><td>number of widows</td><td></td><td>3 [2]</td></tr>
<tr><td>telos of paroikoi</td><td>244 hyperpyra</td><td>142 [149] hyp.</td></tr>
<tr><td>dekaton of their zeugaria</td><td>160 hyp.</td><td>30 hyp.</td></tr>
<tr><td>dekaton of wine</td><td rowspan="2">20 hyp.</td><td>10 hyp.</td></tr>
<tr><td>oinopoleion</td><td>8 hyp.</td></tr>
<tr><td>melissoennomion</td><td>10 hyp.</td><td>–</td></tr>
<tr><td>kephalatikion</td><td>29 hyp.</td><td>16 hyp.</td></tr>
<tr><td>kokkiatikon of the zeugaria of paroikoi</td><td colspan="2">NA (to state)</td></tr>
<tr><td>total (without kokkiatikon)</td><td>464 [463] hyp.</td><td>206 [213] hyp.</td></tr>
</table>

The officials Gazes and Prinkips investigated the matter and found that the taxes and other rights of Siderokauseia amounted to 812 hyperpyra, and that the taxes and other rights of Drymosyrta, Pinson, and Loroton also equaled 812 hyperpyra. For unclear reasons (perhaps to create an even exchange) the exchange also involved the village of Karvaioi, for the officials note that "the half of such village was conferred by the monks upon the imperial side." And so, in exchange for Siderokauseia and Karvaioi, the officials conferred on the monastery the villages of Drymosyrta, Pinson, and Loroton, together, of course, with the paroikoi living there.[24]

The officials then list the paroikos families in Drymosyrta and Pinson with the *telos* assessed upon each, along with the secondary charges burdening the village. The sums of the numbers of paroikoi and the taxes as provided by the officials are not always accurate; the figures in brackets in Table 9.2 represent the totals by modern calculation.[25] The officials add that no one

[24] It is peculiar that in August 1404 John VII issued a chrysobull restoring all of Drymosyrta to Lavra. The document explicitly states that half of this village had been taken away and held by the fisc, and that henceforth Lavra should hold all of it, free of all taxes and other charges (*Lavra*, III, no. 155). It mentions 37 households of paroikoi owing a *telos* of 208 hyperpyra, figures which correspond closely to the data found in the 1409 act (35 households and 244 hyperpyra). If Lavra received back all of Drymosyrta in 1404, why did it agree in 1409 to give up what it held in Siderokauseia and Karvaioi in order to hold all of Drymosyrta and Pinson? And why does the 1409 act not mention the 1404 chrysobull? The scholars who have written about both the 1404 and 1409 acts have not noted this problem: see *Lavra*, IV, 127–28, and Lefort, *Villages de Macédoine*, 47. Evidently Lavra did not recover Drymosyrta in 1404.

[25] The total of 812 was arrived at by adding 670 hyperpyra (464 hyperpyra + 206 hyp.) to 128 hyperpyra for the *triteuma* of the villages (one-third of the *telos* or *haradj*: [244 hyperpyra +

should demand the *kephalatikion*, the *telos*, the *dekaton*, the *oinopoleion*, or anything else, except the *kokkiatikon* owed by the *zeugaria* of the paroikoi. Further, the oxen of the monastery (*doulika zeugaria*) would not owe even this.

After this, the officials conferred upon the monastery a number of abandoned villages (*palaiochoria*). Within Drymosyrta were the abandoned villages of Panagia, Krya Pegadia, Mystakones, Hagia Maria (acquired by exchange from two men), and Oxynon, and within Pinson, the deserted village of Hagia Euphemia. In the early fourteenth century Lavra had held all of these properties, and the officials indeed state that the monks "ought to have [these abandoned villages] as they earlier held and enjoyed [them], along with the above-mentioned villages as contained in their old charters." They add that the monks turned over to the state the abandoned villages associated with Siderokauseia and with Karvaioi, the latter being Genna, Elaia, and Linovrocheion, except for a few minor properties in the region. Further, Lavra turned over to the fisc the abandoned village of Sarantarea and its property at Gournai. Finally, half of the paroikoi, land, and water of the village of Sykea was given to the monks.

There are only a few passages in the document indicating that the exchange involved halves of properties. We read that the monks gave the state half of Karvaioi, that they received half of Sykea, and that the reason they gave up Siderokauseia was because it was considered "imperial in its entirety," clearly implying that they had been holding only a part of this property. A praktikon from 1420 in fact confirms that Lavra had been holding half of both Karvaioi and Siderokauseia (*Lavra*, III, no. 165.45 = *[9.6]* below). But only in the case of Siderokauseia do we get a clear idea of who was holding each half of the village before (the state and Lavra) and after (the state) the exchange. This and the particular properties involved make it clear that the exchange was connected to Manuel II's pronoiarization policy.[26]

Table 9.3 presents the list of properties involved in the exchange. In aggregate, this is nearly a complete listing of all the locations where Lavra is known to have held property during the first half of the fourteenth

142 hyp.]/3 ≈ 128 hyp.), giving the total of 812 hyperpyra (actually, 797, 798, 804, or 805, depending on how one chooses to add the figures). This created a fictional fiscal value for the villages because it counted part of the paroikos *telos* twice.

[26] Loroton is last attested as one of Lavra's possessions in 1329. Between 1329 and 1378 it was confiscated in its entirety (and therefore is evidently not connected to Manuel II's pronoiarization) and attributed to laymen. As late as 1378 the entire village was in the hands of a layman. See Lefort, *Villages de Macédoine*, 94.

Table 9.3 Exchange between the monastery of the Lavra and the fisc in 1409

To the state:	To Lavra:
half of Siderokauseia	(half of?) Drymosyrta
half of Karvaioi	including Panagia
including Genna	Krya Pegadia
Elaia	Mystakones
Linovrocheion	Hagia Maria
(half of?) Sarantarea	Oxynon
(half of?) Gournai	(half of?) Pinson
	including Hagia Euphemia
	(all of?) Loroton
	half of Sykea

century in the *katepanikia* of Kalamaria, Hermeleia, and Hierissos, that is, the Chalkidike excluding the Kassandra, Longos, and Athos peninsulas. The only major property omitted is the village of Gomatou, which is in fact mentioned later in the document. And the village of Mystakones, adjacent to Panagia and Drymosyrta, is the only property listed here for which there is no evidence of its possession by Lavra prior to 1409.[27]

The 1409 act deals with yet another matter connected to Manuel's pronoiarization: "Since the said monks asked that there be a division in the village of Gomatou, so that they might have undisturbed the half of such village and the paroikoi in it," the officials made the division. Gomatou was divided into two equal parts, half was now Lavra's and the other half the state's, "so that no one had the right to seize the other part or to take away anything from the other." The officials then list the paroikoi in "the half part of such village" that now went to Lavra. They conclude the document by stating that the monks were to pay the imperial treasury 38 hyperpyra annually for the "third of the *haradj*" (τοῦ . . . τριτου χαρατζίου) of Gomatou, while the other two-thirds were remitted to the monks as the emperor ordered generally for monasteries. An *orismos* of Andronikos Palaiologos, despot of Thessaloniki, issued the same month confirmed everything contained in this document.[28]

27 For the majority of these toponyms and their history, see Lefort, *Villages de Macédoine*. Siderokauseia was the name applied to a village somewhere in the vicinity of the modern town of Stratonike in the eastern Chalkidike. In our document this name probably denoted all of Lavra's holdings in the area, which, according to documents from the early fourteenth century, included a property called Stratonion and paroikoi found in the villages of Selas, Gradista, Metallin, and Arsenikeia. On these toponyms, see *Lavra*, IV, index.

28 *Lavra*, III, no. 161.55–67, no. 162.

It seems to me that the point of the division in 1409 was to make the original division of Lavra's property, dating back to around 1372, permanent. It was the transformation of a property division from *de facto* into *de jure*. From 1372 through 1383 (when the area around Thessaloniki was captured by the Ottomans), the monasteries did not ask for this change because the pronoiarization could still have been viewed as temporary. But the restoration of Byzantine authority to the area in 1403 did not bring about the annulment of the pronoiarization measures, and Manuel II's December 1408 *prostagma* confirmed that they were still in effect. Evidently, the monks of Lavra reconciled themselves to this state of affairs by asking for a permanent division of Gomatou four months later. This was a way to make the best of an unsatisfactory situation. They no longer had any hope of having all of Gomatou restored to them and so they asked for a permanent division of Gomatou.

In fact, the entire 1409 act for Lavra reflects this attitude on the part of the monks. The exchange of Siderokauseia, Karvaioi, and the other properties, for Drymosyrta, Pinson, etc., is another form this consolidation could take. The monks were in effect acknowledging that they were never going to regain possession of the other halves of their *metochia*, and so, rather than continuing to endure the encroachment of state officials and *pronoiarioi*, they ceded their ownership rights to some of their *metochia* so that they could own and possess other *metochia* completely and undivided (*monomeros*).

The original temporary nature of the pronoiarization can also explain why Manuel pronoiarized half of *each* monastic *metochion*, rather than pronoiarizing some *metochia* completely and leaving others (of the same aggregate value) entirely to the monks. Efficiency would have dictated that the state take properties A, C, and E, and leave the monasteries properties B, D, and F. This way the state would have had larger properties to work with and not have the monks on the scene to make trouble. The monasteries themselves too would have profited more from this type of division. Why would they choose to have a state presence adjacent to every one of their remaining properties? Because the pronoiarization was originally conceived as a temporary measure, as Manuel himself indicates in the 1408 *prostagma*, the monasteries did not immediately ask for exchanges of halves of *metochia* so that they would hold entire *metochia*, free from the presence of state officials. Initially the monasteries preferred a division of each of their *metochia* because this allowed them to maintain a presence in each, the better to ensure the properties remained productive and to confirm their claim to the entire *metochion*. It is not difficult to imagine that the monks felt that if they abandoned a *metochion* entirely to the state, this would have become permanent. As Oikonomides suggested, it is quite possible that the monasteries kept the property titles to both halves of their properties. This is why the documents speak of "half" of this or that property. Further, Oikonomides observed that in these documents the fiscal assessors were interested nearly exclusively in the paroikoi (as taxpayers), and that they omit mentioning the large domain lands that once were associated with each of the properties. He hypothesized that "the transformation of monastic properties into pronoiai had not affected the monasteries' property rights to the land at all; it concerned only the possession [and] the revenues" of these properties and paroikoi (*Docheiariou*, pp. 273–74).

Technically, this interpretation is correct. The monasteries continued to "own" all the property in their *metochia*; no new property titles were drawn up after the pronoiarization. What was lost was the possession of half of their property. But this does not explain why the documents do not mention the land associated with these *metochia.* The simplest explanation for this is that the domain land still held by the monasteries was untaxed and so there was no need to refer to the land in our documents. This would imply that the restored Byzantine authority appropriated Ottoman fiscal practices wholesale. Land in itself, technically all belonging to the sultan, was not taxed. Those who actually worked the land were taxed. This would explain the higher tax rates on paroikoi in the fifteenth century than in the fourteenth century. The new tax rates partially took into account the fact that land was not taxed. Oikonomides has argued that the overall tax burden that paroikoi owed their lords under Ottoman domination was lower than when the area of Thessaloniki was under Byzantine control and it dared not return to fourteenth-century fiscal practices.[29] But beyond this, under the Ottomans monasteries had effectively lost the more or less complete tax exemption they enjoyed under Byzantine auspices. The tax levied on their paroikoi, which hitherto had been kept entirely by the monasteries themselves, was, under the Ottomans, shared with the state. When the Byzantines adopted the Ottoman system, it was a windfall for the state. The losers in all this were the monasteries which, aside from losing half of their property through the pronoiarization of Manuel II, lost much of the revenue they had derived from their paroikoi once the Ottomans imposed their fiscal practices on the area.

According to the 1409 act of Gazes and Prinkips the monastery of Lavra received half of Sykea as part of the exchange, implying that they had been holding half of Sykea up to that time. But the matter is not so clear.

[29] N. Oikonomides, "The Role of the Byzantine State in the Economy," *EHB*, III, 1039.

The earliest reference to Sykea (or Sykai as it was also called) is found in a *prostagma* of John V, a document from December 1350 (or just possibly from 1365). The emperor ordered his officials to confer upon Demetrios Kokalas "in the amount [*poson*] of his oikonomia" the *agridion* of Sykea, plus other properties *[8.38]*. Then, at a later time (the relevant document is difficult to date) a man named Kalavaris donated a property near Sykea to Lavra. He notes that one of his motivations was that "the emperor" had donated "the place [*topos*] of Kokalas" to the Lavra monastery. Kalavaris is probably the same person as the Kalavar known from a 1347 Serbian document as an official of Stefan Dušan, and so the "emperor" to whom Kalavaris refers was probably Dušan himself.[30] This would suggest that Dušan had confiscated Kokalas' holding. Given that both of these documents are found in the archives of Lavra, and given the fact that Lavra would later hold Sykea, it is reasonable to assume that "the place of Kokalas" is related to the *agridion* of Sykea. Indeed, in the early 1360s, the *agridion* of Sykea was counted among Lavra's properties.[31]

[9.5] Act of Paul Gazes and Michael Karianites for the monastery of Vatopedi (1406)

Sykea is next mentioned in May 1406, when the officials Paul Gazes and Michael Karianites returned the village of Lantzon to the monastery of Vatopedi and ordered that Lantzon not be bothered "by successive *pronoiarioi* from the villages on either side of it, that is, Sykea and Akroterion."[32] So, assuming that *agridion* of Sykea had now become the village of Sykea, sometime between the 1360s and 1406, Sykea (or part of Sykea) was taken from Lavra and conferred on pronoia holders.

30 *Lavra*, III, no. 130.2–3 and notes (where the date 1350/1 is proposed for the donation); IV, p. 119. A. Solovjev, *Odabrani spomenici srpskog prava* (Belgrade, 1926), 144 = S. Novaković, *Zakonski spomenici srpskih država srednjega veka* (Belgrade, 1912), 433 iii, and cf. P. Lemerle and A. Solovjev, "Trois chartes des souverains serbes conservées au monastère de Kutlumus," in Lemerle, *Le monde de Byzance* (London, 1978), no. XIX, 135.14–15.

31 This reference to Sykea appears in an interpolated version of a 1329 chrysobull of Andronikos III. This falsified document includes all the properties Lavra had acquired up to 1355 or 1361, but does not mention acquisitions from 1367 on, and so it was probably created during the early 1360s: *Lavra*, III, app. XI.49, based on *Lavra*, III, no. 118.

32 Arkadios Vatopedinos, "Ἁγιορειτικὰ ἀνάλεκτα," *Γρηγόριος ὁ Παλαμᾶς* 3 (1919), 337, no. 36.19–21: ἀπὸ τῶν κατὰ καιροὺς προνοιαρίων τῶν ἑκατέρωθεν τούτου χωρίων, ἤγουν τῶν Συκεῶν καὶ τοῦ Ἀκροτηρίου. This is the first appearance of the term *pronoiarios* since its earliest appearance in 1228 *[5.16]*; altogether it appears in five fifteenth-century documents, all issued by officials. For the reading "Karianites," see *Docheiariou*, p. 281. A *prostagma* of John VII from September 1404 had confirmed Vatopedi's possession of all of Lantzon: F. Dölger, *Facsimiles byzantinischer Kaiserurkunden* (Munich, 1931), no. 55. Dölger, *Regesten*, v, no. 3204.

Three years later, in 1409, the officials Paul Gazes and George Prinkips gave Lavra part of the village of Sykea *[9.3]*: "the monks were given from the *palaiochorion* of Sykea around Rentina the part they prove through blessed documents to have owned, that is, the half of the paroikoi, the land, and the water there, so that they should hold this as they held and enjoyed it before with everything inscribed" (*Lavra*, III, no. 161.48–50). Evidently then, immediately prior to 1409, Lavra did not hold any part of Sykea (now called a *palaiochorion* or "ruined" village), but according to the 1409 act, Lavra received the half of Sykea for which it could prove ownership. It is possible, then, that Lavra lost half of Sykea through Manuel II's pronoiarization, and, at a later date, it lost the other half. The 1409 act seems to have restored to Lavra the half it lost at the later date.[33]

[9.6] Praktikon of Stephen Doukas Radenos, Constantine Palaiologos Oinaiotes, and John Radenos for the monastery of Lavra (1420)

Oddly, despite what the 1409 act tells us, it seems that Lavra did not get any of Sykea back in 1409. According to a praktikon for Lavra from January 1420 the monks had asked "that they receive a benefaction of their *metochion* near Rentina called Sykai, taken away years ago and dependent completely to the side of the fisc." The fiscal officials, on the order of Manuel II and his son, returned this property in full ownership to Lavra, freeing it of all impositions. The *metochion* was to be held without harassment "by either a *pronoiarios* or anyone else."[34]

According to my translation of the passage, which is based on the punctuation of the edited text, it would seem that at some time in the past ("years ago" suggests a substantial expanse of time, and at any event before 1409) all of Sykea was appropriated by the state. According to the act of 1409, half of the village was restored to Lavra at that time, and from 1420 Lavra held all of Sykea. What is not clear, as the editors of the act have pointed out, is whether all of Sykea was restored to Lavra in 1420 (that is, Lavra never received back even half of Sykea in 1409, for whatever reason) or Lavra received the other half of Sykea in 1420 (the first half restored in 1409).[35]

[33] On the other hand, the editors of the 1409 act thought it more likely that the confiscation of Sykea after the 1360s was most likely connected to Lavra's irregular acquisition of Sykea during the Serbian occupation under Dušan: *Lavra*, IV, pp. 52 and 128 note 433.

[34] *Lavra*, III, no. 165.2–3,12–13: ἀπό τε προνοιαρίου καὶ ἑτέρου παντός. Ostrogorsky, *Féodalité*, 170–71, 291 note 1.

[35] *Lavra*, IV, 130 note 446.

In any event, it would seem that, at the time of the 1406 act of Paul Gazes and Michael Karianites *[9.5]*, Sykea, having been confiscated from Lavra, was held by one or more *pronoiarioi*. In 1409, part of Sykea was to be returned to Lavra (if they could prove they owned it); evidently, the remainder was still to be held by one or more *pronoiarioi*. From 1420 all of Sykea was again in Lavra's possession, and the relevant document explicitly states that *pronoiarioi* were not to bother the property.

The purpose of the 1406 act of Gazes and Karianites was to return to Vatopedi the village of Lantzon, a village bordered on one side by Sykea and on the other by Akroterion, both of which were held, at least in part, by pronoiars. Lantzon was south of lake Volve, and north of Lozikion (mod. Melissourgos).[36] Akroterion must have been to the north of Lantzon and received its name, as the word implies, from a promontory on lake Volve. Sykea was between Lantzon and Lozikion (see the map of the Chalkidike), probably in the area of modern Kokkalou (about two miles north-northeast of Melissourgos). Inasmuch as the village of Sykea was once held by someone named Kokalas, it is curious that there is a modern village called Kokkalou. Oddly enough, in a Slavic chrysobull from 1347 Stefan Dušan granted the monastery of Hilandar "the village of Kokalas Ljutovoj near Lozikion" (*selište Kokalino Ljutovês prêma Lužcu*).[37] The relation between Ljutovoj Kokalas and Demetrios Kokalas is unknown. Nor can we say what connection there was between the village of Ljutovoj Kokalas (the modern Kokkalou?), which was given to Hilandar (but which no other document attributes to this monastery), and Sykea, which was held by Demetrios Kokalas and given to Lavra.

Two other acts deal with Lantzon, and one of them includes another technical reference to pronoia. An act of Demetrios Leontares from February 1415 reports that, although Vatopedi had been enjoying tax-exempt status for many years ever since the emperor granted it, it had come to the emperor's attention that the monks "encounter harassment by those serving successively in the finding of Gasmouloi [marines] and in other vexations." Leontares affirmed that by imperial order their *zeugelateion* at Lantzon was free of all charges, except for their *haradj*, which as in

[36] A "Landža" (mod. Limni) is found on numerous maps to the north of lake Volve. However, a "Landža ciftlik" is found just to the south of lake Volve (a half mile northwest of mod. Apollonia) on an Austrian military topographical map: Österreichisch-Ungarischen Monarchie, die dritte militärische Aufnahme, 1:200,000 (ca. 1910), sheet "Saloniki": ⟨http://lazarus.elte.hu/hun/digkonyv/topo/200e/41–41.jpg⟩.

[37] Solovjev, *Odabrani spomenici*, 144 = Novaković, *Zakonski spomenici*, 433 iii.

the other acts discussed in this chapter corresponds to the *telos* of their paroikoi.[38]

[9.7] Act of Michael Tzamplakon, John Radenos, and Stephen Doukas Radenos for the monastery of Vatopedi (1415)

The next month the *apographeis* Michael Tzamplakon, John Radenos, and Stephen Doukas Radenos issued a document on behalf of the monastery of Vatopedi. They reasserted that by the emperor's order the properties there belonging to Vatopedi "should be inviolate and unchanged by the fisc and by us and by successive *pronoiarioi*." Further, the monastery should "give to the assigned *pronoiarios* from now on for the families found there forty-eight hyperpyra in two payments and no more."[39] This charge of forty-eight hyperpyra must be a reference to the *haradj* mentioned in the previous act, and, if two-thirds of the *telos* was still remitted to the monastery (as in 1409), then the total *telos* on the paroikoi of Lantzon was 144 hyperpyra.

From the document from May 1406 *[9.5]* we learn that pronoia holders associated with the villages neighboring Lantzon were harassing this village. Although the document does not explain what this association was, it would be most likely that these *pronoiarioi* held property in pronoia in these neighboring villages. They may have lived there as well. What is least likely, indeed highly improbable, is that they lived in Sykea and Akroterion but held their pronoiai in an entirely different location. Thus, we should conclude that in 1406 at least part of the villages of Sykea and Akroterion was held by *pronoiarioi*.

The two acts from 1415 dealing with Lantzon describe a much different situation. In them the pronoia holder had a claim to a certain tax (the *haradj*) from Lantzon itself. His claim to this tax had absolutely no connection to the possession of property; he merely received revenues owed the state from paroikoi held by a third party (the monastery). As such, we cannot assume that this *pronoiarios* had any connection to the *pronoiarioi* in the 1406 act or that he lived anywhere near Lantzon. Thus, in 1415, a *pronoiarios* derived at least part of his income from the taxes owed by the village of Lantzon. Since the *pronoiarios* received money for the paroikos families held by a monastery, we are dealing with another example of the redirection of state taxes toward

[38] Arkadios Vatopedinos, "Ἁγιορειτικὰ ἀνάλεκτα," *Γρηγόριος ὁ Παλαμᾶς* 3 (1919), 335, no. 34: ἀπὸ τῶν κατὰ καιροὺς ὑπηρετῶν εἰς βασμούλων εὕρεσιν καὶ εἰς ἄλλας ἐπηρείας.

[39] Arkadios Vatopedinos, 336, no. 35: ἀπὸ τῶν κατὰ καιροὺς προνοιαρίων, and δίδωσε δὲ πρὸς τὸν ἀποταχθέντα προνοιάριον κατὰ τὸ παρὸν ὑπὲρ τῶν εὑρισκομένων ἐκεῖ φαμιλιῶν διὰ δύο καταβολῶν ὑπέρπυρα 48 καὶ οὐ πλέον.

a pronoia holder. It must be emphasized that neither the references in the 1406 act nor those in the 1415 act have any direct connection to Manuel II's pronoiarization.

Manuel II's policy, of course, had precedents. In the previous chapter numerous examples were given of confiscations of monastic property for the benefit of pronoia holders earlier in the fourteenth century (see the discussions of *[8.20]*,*[8.21]*, and *[8.22]*). Some of those confiscations even involved fractions of a monastery's property in a particular village. Between 1334 and 1346, probably in the early 1340s, Esphigmenou lost half of the village of Portarea and two-thirds of the village of Krousovo. In the *prostagma* from 1350 (or perhaps 1365) *[8.38]* (also discussed above under *[9.4]*), half of the property of the monastery of Hypomimneskontos and half of the property of the Athonite monastery of Panteleemon in the village of Hagios Mamas were given to Demetrios Kokalas. Also around 1350 half of the properties of the monastery of Docheiariou in Diavolokampos, Hermeleia, and Amygdaleai were confiscated and "given to various people" by John VI Kantakouzenos. And even though most of these confiscations were later rescinded, they provide a very close parallel that makes Manuel II's policy not seem quite so extraordinary. Nevertheless, it is true that Manuel II's policy remained in effect for a long time (helped of course by the temporary Ottoman conquest of the area). Monasteries were extremely patient and persistent in their efforts to reacquire lost properties. The 1409 act involving the exchange of properties and the division of Gomatou show that the patience of Lavra had been exhausted.

Let us summarize what we learn from these documents. After the battle of the Marica, half of the properties of the monasteries of Athos and Thessaloniki were "pronoiarized," and the purpose of the policy was defensive *[9.1]*. It is possible that the pronoiarization affected non-monastic properties as well *[9.2]*. This policy continued to be in effect into the fifteenth century, surviving the Turkish occupation of the region of Thessaloniki, and there is no evidence that it was ever abandoned.

The pronoiai referred to in these documents were held in the region of Thessaloniki *[9.1]*, specifically on the Chalkidike *[9.3–9.7]* and in Thessaloniki *[9.2]*. This certainly reflects the diminution of the empire's size and the lack of archival material from the area of Constantinople. There is no evidence that the pronoiarization affected holdings inside the territory of Mount Athos (*Lavra*, IV, p. 124).

The economic resources that made up pronoia grants remain similar to those found in earlier documents: properties (*ktemata*) and villages (*choria*) *[9.1]* and paroikoi *[9.3]* *[9.7]*. Only the one document that speaks of the conferral in pronoia of a courtyard with houses and shops *[9.2]* broadens our list. The only benefits of holding pronoiai that are stated explicitly relate to *pronoiarioi* receiving the taxes paid by monastic paroikoi *[9.3] [9.7]*. For the portions of the monastic *metochia* held by the *pronoiarioi*, their benefits would be the usual collection of taxes, fiscal charges, rents, corvées, and harvest that the monasteries had earlier derived from their properties.

The increased proximity between properties held by monasteries and those held by *pronoiarioi* pursuant to the enactment of Manuel's pronoiarization resulted in the neighboring *pronoiarioi* infringing on the properties still held by the monasteries *[9.3] [9.5]*. The monasteries' answer to this was to seek consolidation of their properties or permanent division between their properties and those held by the *pronoiarioi [9.3]*, in addition to specific clauses in their documents protecting them from such harassment *[9.4] [9.6]*.

In dramatic contrast to earlier terminology, the word *pronoiarios* appears in five of these documents *[9.3–9.7]*. The word *pronoia* itself appears in a technical sense only once, in the construction "to be granted to some people for their pronoia" (εὐηργετεῖσθαι πρός τινας εἰς πρόνοιαν αὐτῶν) *[9.2]*, which seems to be synonymous with the verb *pronoiazesthai* (προνοιάζεσθαι, "to be conferred as pronoia") *[9.1]*. And finally, as in earlier documents, property held by *pronoiarioi* is considered "imperial" (*vasilikon*) *[9.4]*, reflecting the origin of the grant.

The case of George Gemistos and sons

[9.8] The George Gemistos dossier (1427–50)

Outside Macedonia, the only area where there is even a hint of the existence of pronoia is the Morea. A series of six documents from 1427 through 1450 deal with two grants made to the scholar George Gemistos Plethon:

(i) In a silver bull from 1427 Despot Theodore II Palaiologos (1408–43) granted Gemistos the *kastron* and region of Phanarion. Gemistos would receive "each year into his income all the rights of the *kephalatikion* of this region, the *myzai* [unknown taxes or charges]" except for the *phloriatikon* (a tax ostensibly for the building of the Hexamilion, a wall across the isthmus of Corinth) which went to the fisc. Gemistos was to be governor (*kephale*) of Phanarion and was "obliged to serve for all his life." After his death his sons Demetrios and Andronikos were permitted to hold and govern the *kastron*, and they would receive "the above-inscribed charges [*doseis*]" as long as "they would render to our majesty the appertaining service for these" (τὴν ἀνήκουσαν ὑπὲρ τούτων δουλείαν).[40]

(ii) A chrysobull of Emperor John VIII (1425–48), Despot Theodore's brother, from October 1428 contains another silver bull of Theodore which further grants Gemistos the village of Vrysis near Kastrion. Gemistos was to receive an income from it consisting of "the [charge] for the *kephalatikion*... and the two *meizai* [sic], the *exaleimmatika stasia* in it, and every other state right, except the taxes [*kephalaia*] assigned or to be assigned for the Hexamilion [i.e., the *phloriatikon*]." After his death his sons ought to hold the village "eternally rendering for it the appertaining service."

(iii) John VIII's chrysobull of 1428 confirmed this arrangement.[41]

(iv) A silver bull from 1433 of Theodore II granted the sons of Gemistos, Demetrios and Andronikos, respectively, the *kastron* of Phanarion and the village of Vrysis (near Kastrion). Both would hold these as *kephale* under essentially the same conditions as their father, receiving the charges for the *kephalatikion*, both *myzai*, and the *exaleimmatika*, but not the *phloriatikon*. In addition Andronikos received the *vigliatikon*. Both brothers were to hold these properties for life, "giving the appropriate service for these," "receiving all such lordly *doseis* for their incomes and oikonomiai without any kind of deduction" and

40 MM, III, 173–74 = S. Lampros, *Παλαιολόγεια καὶ Πελοποννησιακά* (Athens, 1912–30; repr. Athens, 1972), IV, 104–05. The *myzai* or "two *meizai*" have not yet been explained satisfactorily. S. Kougeas, "Χρυσόβουλλον Κωνσταντίνου τοῦ Παλαιολόγου πρωτόγραφον καὶ ἀνέκδοτον," *Ἑλληνικά* 1 (1928), 382, argued it was a tax on fresh and dried fruit. E. Vranoussi, "Notes sur quelques institutions de Péloponnèse byzantine," *Études balkaniques* 14 (1978), 81–88, claims it was an inheritance tax. I might offer yet another unlikely hypothesis: the *myzai* may have been a type of *kommerkion*, or tax on trade, especially in silk, which *kephalai* were often granted. There was an Ottoman commercial tax called *mizan* (lit. "scales, balance" in Arabic and Turkish), often connected with the silk trade: see H. Inalcik with D. Quataert, *An Economic and Social History of the Ottoman Empire, 1300–1914* (Cambridge, 1994), 226, and S. Shaw, *History of the Ottoman Empire and Modern Turkey*, vol. 1 (Cambridge, 1976), 160. On the scales, M. Bulut, *Ottoman-Dutch Economic Relations in the Early Modern Period, 1571–1699* (Hilversum, 2001), 51 and note 84. The Morea was a well-known center for silk production. A *mizan* tax is attested in the Morea in 1769: F. Zarinebaf et al., *A Historical and Economic Geography of Ottoman Greece* (Princeton, 2005), 38. On the other hand, the Florentine merchant Pegolotti, writing around the year 1340, mentions a tax called *missa* levied on shipping on Cyprus: K. Fleet, *European and Islamic Trade in the Early Ottoman State* (Cambridge and New York, 1999), 82 and note 18. Vranoussi, "Notes," 85, observes that the medieval Latin *misa* meant a levy. *Myzai* probably was derived from that directly or through the French *mise*. In any event, we still do not know the nature of the levy.

41 MM, III, 174–76 = Lampros, *Παλαιολόγεια καὶ Πελοποννησιακά*, III, 331–33. Ostrogorsky, *Féodalité*, 181–83.

"if they are deemed worthy of greater incomes, receiving these within the *posotes* of their incomes." The properties would pass to the male descendants (ἐξ ἀρρενογονίας) of each.[42]

(v) The 1433 silver bull of Theodore II was confirmed by a chrysobull of Emperor Constantine XI (1449–53) in 1449. As an added benefit, the emperor granted each of them the *phloriatikon* of their respective property.[43]

(vi) A silver bull of Despot Demetrios Palaiologos (1449–60) from 1450 reaffirmed the grant to each.[44]

The phrasing of these documents is unlike that found in fourteenth-century documents, and only in the last three of these documents is there a mention of the terms *oikonomia* and *posotes*. Nevertheless, the appearance of these terms, the conferral of a village and tax revenues for life, with hereditary rights added, strongly suggests a pronoia grant.

But what makes these documents peculiar and what truly distinguishes the grants received by George Gemistos and his sons from most of the grants dealt with in the preceding chapter is the conferral of administrative authority. The only parallel we have is the document from the mid-fourteenth century that appointed Manuel Sergopoulos *kephale* of the island of Marmara with the right to collect state revenues which, I think, was an idiosyncratic arrangement *[8.29]*.

Nevertheless, we might wonder whether in the very last days of the empire it became common to grant administrative rights with pronoia grants. The problem, of course, is that we have very little with which to compare the grants to the Gemistoi. One exception is found in a silver bull issued by Constantine Palaiologos, the future emperor, in 1444 for the benefit of Demetrios Mamonas Gregoras. At the time Constantine was despot of the Morea, sharing the title with his brother Thomas. Because of his services Constantine granted Gregoras, a man otherwise unknown, a house in Elos with its tower and the village of Prinikon and its region. Constantine notes that Gregoras would "receive each year for its management the *dekata* [εἰς κυβέρνησίν του τὰ δέκατα]" and what was due "through lordship

[42] Lampros, *Παλαιολόγεια καὶ Πελοποννησιακά*, IV, 106–09; 108.10–11: ἀποδιδόντες καὶ τὴν ἀνήκουσαν ὑπὲρ τουτῶν δουλείαν, 108.11–15: δεχόμενοί τε πάσας τὰς τοιαύτας δόσεις αὐθεντικὰς εἰς προσόδια καὶ οἰκονομίας αὐτῶν ἄνευ τῆς οἱασοῦν ἀφαιρέσεως, and 108.13–15: ἐντὸς τῆς ποσότητος τῶν προσοδίων αὐτῶν.

[43] Kougeas, "Χρυσόβουλλον Κωνσταντίνου τοῦ Παλαιολόγου," 373–75 = Lampros, *Παλαιολόγεια καὶ Πελοποννησιακά*, IV, 19–22. Ostrogorsky, *Féodalité*, 184.

[44] MM, III, 225–27= Lampros, *Παλαιολόγεια καὶ Πελοποννησιακά*, IV, 192–95. Hvostova, *Osobennosti*, 222. Kazhdan, *Agrarnye otnošenija*, 221. Ostrogorsky, *Féodalité*, 186.

[*authentia*] or through service [i.e., corvées] or through charges."[45] There is a strong sense of Gregoras being master of this village, but unlike the Gemistos documents, there is no use of the word *kephale* here, or any of its verbal forms. In the end, I think it is likely that in the waning days of the empire, it became more usual to grant governmental powers to grant holders, in a spirit of desperation. By the late 1430s Byzantium was merely Constantinople and part of the Morea, owing its pathetic existence solely to the sultan's pleasure.

45 MM, III, 258–59 = Lampros, *Παλαιολόγεια καὶ Πελοποννησιακά*, IV, 17–18.

10 | Pronoia and *timar*

The Ottoman institution of the *timar* – a grant of state revenues and property in return for military and other service – had a great deal in common with the Byzantine pronoia. Here we are concerned with the degree to which pronoia and *timar* were related, what influence, if any, one had upon the other. To do this we must first present how Ottomanists currently understand the institution of the *timar*.

As with the Byzantine pronoia, much has been written about the *timar*, often by those who, like myself, do not read Turkish and must rely on secondary authorities. Here I think it is best to ignore the secondary literature by scholars who cannot evaluate the primary sources and base my observations on the relatively small group of scholars who have actually looked at the Ottoman sources.

Like the pronoia grant, the *timar* evolved over time. Thus, if we are trying to compare the two institutions, it is best to limit the examination of the *timar*, if possible, to its earliest manifestations, if not in the fourteenth century, then at least no later than the middle of the fifteenth century. Further, in different parts of the Ottoman Empire the *timar* had different characteristics. For our purposes the focus will be on the Balkans (Rumeli in the Turkish sources), although comparisons between the *timar* as it appeared there and its appearance in areas of Anatolia can be illuminating.

The *timar*

Recipients and their obligations

Both military and non-military men, plus a few monasteries and a very few women, held *timars*, although, as with pronoiai, the vast majority of *timars* were held by soldiers. In almost all cases the recipients owed some type of service in return for the grant, and usually the service was military service.[1] Military *timar* holders (*sipahis*) were primarily light horsemen,

[1] N. Beldiceanu, *Le timar dans l'État ottoman (début* XIVe*–début* XVIe *siècle)* (Wiesbaden, 1980), 38–45. V. Mutafchieva, *Agrarian Relations in the Ottoman Empire in the 15th and 16th Centuries* (Boulder, Co., 1988), 20.

but officers and some soldiers assigned to fortress service and those with duties connected to the sea held *timars* as well.[2] Very significant for our purposes is the fact that many *sipahis* in the early years of the Ottoman Empire were Christian. This suggests a policy that numerous Ottomanists have tried to prove, that many *pronoiarioi* became *sipahis* and that many pronoiai became *timars*.[3] Nevertheless, one of the most dramatic differences between pronoia and *timar* is that the latter was at times granted not by the central government but by provincial governors (*beylerbeys*, *sancakbeys*).[4]

As with the pronoia, it was not uncommon for a single *timar* to be shared by more than one *sipahi*. However, contrary to Byzantine practices, it was much less common to find that the joint *timar* holders were related.[5]

Almost every *timar* was held on condition of service and usually this meant military service. Unlike military pronoia holders, *sipahis* whose grants reached a certain level were required to render not merely personal service, but to campaign with one or more armed retainers (*cebelü*). According to the Code of Customary Law of Mehmed II, a timariot (*timar* holder) holding a revenue of less than 2,000 akçe was expected to serve by himself; a timariot holding 2,000–3,000 akçe presented himself with a military servant (*gulam*); those holding 4,000–5,000 akçe served with an armed retainer (*cebelü*) and a servant; those holding 5,500–8,000 akçe served with two armed retainers; those holding 9,000 akçe served with three armed retainers; those holding 10,000–11,000 akçe served with three armed retainers and a servant; those holding 12,000 and 15,000 akçe served, respectively, with four and five armed retainers, and so on up to 20,000. Those with an income of at least 4,000 akçe were also expected to bring along one or more tents.[6] *Subaşis*, the district commanders of *sipahis*, who held revenues from around 20,000 akçe to a bit over 100,000 akçe, provided an armed retainer for every 4,000 akçe of revenue, while *sancakbeys*, district governors, held revenues in the hundreds of thousands of akçe and provided armed retainers at the rate of one per 5,000 akçe of revenue. Both *subaşis* and *sancakbeys*

2 Beldiceanu, *Le timar*, 46–47.

3 H. Inalcik, "Timariotes chrétiens en Albanie au xve siècle," *Mitteilungen des österreichischen Staatsarchiv* 4 (1952), 118–38. B. Cvetkova, "Novye dannye o hristianah-spahijah na balkanskom poluostrove v period tureckogo gospodstva," *VizVrem* 13 (1958), 184–97.

4 Mutafchieva, *Agrarian Relations*, 19, 39–40. Beldiceanu, *Le timar*, 71–72.

5 H. Inalcik with D. Quataert, *An Economic and Social History of the Ottoman Empire, 1300–1914* (Cambridge, 1994), 114–15. Mutafchieva, *Agrarian Relations*, 28–30. In Beldiceanu, *Le timar*, the phenomenon of joint *timars* is not mentioned at all (though it is frequently encountered in his articles).

6 Beldiceanu, *Le timar*, 80, 85. B. McGowan, *Economic Life in Ottoman Europe* (Cambridge, 1981), 47, appears to misinterpret the requirements at each level.

were obliged to provide various types of tents and sets of armor as well.[7] There is evidence that even some non-military timariots, such as judges (*qadi*) and monasteries, were required to provide soldiers for campaigns.[8]

Contents of the grant

While there were cases in which timariots collected revenues from urban populations, in most cases the timariot was entitled to part of the taxes, charges, and labor services owed by a defined set of peasants (*reaya*).[9] Prospective *timar* holders "were given certificates for a timar of a certain size," although the eventual size of the grant was based on what was available.[10] The emphasis was always on the total amount of revenue granted.[11] According to Halil Inalcik, the average *timar* was around 1,000 akçe in the fifteenth century, and the minimum subsistence level for a timariot was established by legislation as 500–750 akçe, while Vera Mutafchieva estimates that the average *timar* in the first half of the fifteenth century had a revenue of from 1,000 to 3,000 akçe.[12]

As with the pronoia, a *timar* could be formed from a single village or parts of several villages, and a single village could be divided among several timariots.[13] Stanford Shaw wrote that "[t]he *Sipahi* lived in the village where the lands of his timar were located," while Mutafchieva wondered how this notion arose and concludes that the *timar* holder need not have lived on his *timar*.[14] It seems that the timariots enjoyed no rights of justice over his peasants independent of the local government.[15]

Most Ottomanists are careful to point out that the timariot did not receive many of the taxes levied on the peasants within his *timar*.[16] While practices

[7] Beldiceanu, *Le timar*, 74–80.

[8] Beldiceanu, *Le timar*, 41–45. Beldiceanu notes that the Serbian monastery of Ravanica was required to furnish soldiers, while the Greek Prodromos monastery near Serres was not: was this a reflection of the pre-conquest Serbian custom of having soldiers assigned to the service of monasteries? See M. Bartusis, "Serbian Pronoia and Pronoia in Serbia: The Diffusion of an Institution," *ZRVI* 48 (2011), 184–86.

[9] Beldiceanu, *Le timar*, 34–36.

[10] Inalcik, *Economic and Social History*, 73.

[11] Beldiceanu, *Le timar*, 15, 71.

[12] Inalcik, *Economic and Social History*, 141. Mutafchieva, *Agrarian Relations*, 32, 50, 52.

[13] Mutafchieva, *Agrarian Relations*, 34–36, 39. Inalcik, *Economic and Social History*, 114.

[14] S. Shaw, *History of the Ottoman Empire and Modern Turkey*, vol. 1 (Cambridge, 1976), 16. Mutafchieva, *Agrarian Relations*, 54–55. Inalcik, *Economic and Social History*, 71, agrees with Shaw.

[15] Inalcik, *Economic and Social History*, 114. Mutafchieva, *Agrarian Relations*, 45.

[16] The exception is Shaw, *History of the Ottoman Empire*, I, 121: the timariot "kept all the revenues in the holding."

varied greatly from region to region, from time to time, and from *timar* to *timar*, a list of the more common charges extracted from the peasantry and their typical division between the state and the *timar* holder might look like this:

Charges retained by the state:

cizye (or *baş harac*) – often called a capitation or poll tax, the *cizye* was actually a hearth tax, levied only on non-Muslims usually at a flat rate per household. Almost always it went to the state, though there are a few cases in which it was granted to a *timar* holder.[17]

levies on livestock – the most important of these was the tax on sheep (*adet-i agnam*). In the fiscal survey of the village of Radolivos, a *timar* with a value of 10,758 akçe in the period not long after 1453, the sheep tax is not listed, presumably indicating that it was received by the state. In other cases, the sheep tax was held by the timariot or shared between timariot and *sancakbey*. There was a tax on horses, though its details are unclear, and Ottomanists assume there was a tax on cattle, although the sources never mention it.[18]

extraordinary levies and customary charges (*avariz-i divaniye ve tekalif-i örfiye*), including state corvées (*angarya*) – this category included miscellaneous charges varying by region and occasional taxes for special purposes (such as a campaign). Over time these charges became the largest single source of state revenue.[19]

Charges received by the *timar* holder:

ispence – a tax levied usually only on non-Muslim households. Sometimes the *ispence* was levied as a flat charge for all households, but usually households headed by widows were taxed at a lower rate. Alternatively, the tax usually paid by Muslim peasants (and some non-Muslims as well) was the *resm-i çift* or *resm-i kulluk*, calculated proportionately, based on the household's ability to pay. Peasants who owed the *resm-i çift* were divided into several categories: those with a full holding

[17] Mutafchieva, *Agrarian Relations*, 186–87. Beldiceanu, *Le timar*, 32–34, 62. Inalcik, *Economic and Social History*, 68.

[18] Mutafchieva, *Agrarian Relations*, 177–78. H. Lowry, "Changes in Fifteenth-Century Ottoman Peasant Taxation: The Case Study of Radolifo (Radolibos)," in *Continuity and Change in Late Byzantine and Early Ottoman Society*, ed. A. Bryer and H. Lowry (Birmingham and Washington, 1986), 26. Beldiceanu, *Le timar*, 60. On the date of the *defter* containing the fiscal survey, see M. Ursinus, "An Ottoman Census Register for the Area of Serres of 859 H. (1454–1455)? A Reconsideration of the Date of Composition of Tahrir Defteri TT 3," *Südost-Forschungen* 45 (1986), 25–36.

[19] Mutafchieva, *Agrarian Relations*, 182–89. Beldiceanu, *Le timar*, 32.

(*çift*), those with a half-holding, families with less than a half-holding, widows and bachelors with less than a half-holding, and those with no property.[20]

tithes (*ösür*) on produce – these were individual charges levied on each and every variety of agricultural produce (cereals, grapes, fodder, lentils, chickpeas, flax, etc.). Ostensibly the rate was one-tenth, but the rates as attested in the sources range from one-eighth to three-tenths.[21]

Together, the *ispence* and tithes formed the heart of the revenues of the *timar*. But there were many other charges levied on his peasants as well which varied from *timar* to *timar*:

bad-i hava – occasional levies consisting of marriage charges, fines, registration fees, etc.[22]

a tax on pigs[23]

taxes on fishing, docks, etc.[24]

corvées (*angarya*), if the *timar* was granted domain land

The revenues from the *timar* were received directly by the *timar* holder or leased to tax farmers.[25]

In addition to the revenues from peasants, some *timar* holders, like *pronoiarioi*, held domain land (*hassa*) as part of their *timar* grants. However, there is some disagreement over the significance of this element of the grant. In large measure this disagreement stems from whether one places more importance on legislation or on the evidence of the *timar* registers, whether one regards the particular *timar* registers of this or that region as characteristic of the system, and whether one considers only smaller grants as true *timar*s or includes great holdings as well. The Law Code (*kanunname*) of Mehmed II defines the *hassa* as a farm such as a peasant might own (i.e., a *çift*), with arable land, vineyards, pasture land, and water mills, and specifies that the main method of exploiting such property was through the corvées of the peasants who were listed in the *timar*. Thus, Inalcik states that each *sipahi* was given direct possession of a *çift*, although, according to Mutafchieva, only one *timar* register describes *hassa*s that correspond to this legislation.[26] Mutafchieva writes that while *hassa*s contained in aggregate a great variety

20 Beldiceanu, *Le timar*, 31, 59–60. Mutafchieva, *Agrarian Relations*, 176–77. Inalcik, *Economic and Social History*, 69, 149–50.

21 Mutafchieva, *Agrarian Relations*, 174–75. Beldiceanu, *Le timar*, 32, 61–62.

22 Mutafchieva, *Agrarian Relations*, 179–80. Beldiceanu, *Le timar*, 31, 60.

23 Mutafchieva, *Agrarian Relations*, 178.

24 Beldiceanu, *Le timar*, 60.

25 Beldiceanu, *Le timar*, 64. Inalcik, *Economic and Social History*, 74.

26 Inalcik, *Economic and Social History*, 117. Mutafchieva, *Agrarian Relations*, 56.

of elements (vineyards, fruit trees, pasturage, marshland, mills, plus fishing rights, dock charges, and fair taxes, all found as well within pronoiai), very few of them contained the basic element of the domain land within a pronoia: arable land. However, Beldiceanu wrote, "Most often [the timarial reserve consists] of one or more tenures (čift, čiftlik)," that is, farms, though the examples he cites tend to support Mutafchieva's view.[27]

In most cases, *timar* holders who held *hassa*s leased them to their peasants or temporarily transferred them to their peasants through a deed of registration. Because a number of decrees forbid transferring *hassa* land to others for nothing more than the deed registration charge (*tapu*), it would seem that the *hassa* was desirable neither to the timariot nor to his peasants. There is some agreement among Ottomanists over whether the *timar* holder was at all efficient in exploiting this land.[28]

Hereditability

Ottomanists have varying views regarding the hereditability of *timar*s. Inalcik wrote that the granting of hereditary rights was against the principle of the *timar*. When timariots were permitted to bequeath their grants, as in Albania in the first half of the fifteenth century, this was a transitory measure reflecting the early stages of administration in border areas. Beldiceanu wrote that "every Ottomanist knows that in the early period of the empire the timar was not, in principle, hereditary," but that there were exceptions to this as early as the reign of Murad I (1362–89). According to Mutafchieva nearly the opposite was true. Fifteenth- and sixteenth-century legislation "devoted a lot of space to the 'inheritance' of the *timar*, that is, its transfer, with the obligations involved, to the son of a deceased or aged *timar* holder" and "unconditionally expressed a preference for transfer from father to son." However, she wrote, in practice relatively few *timar*s passed to the sons of *sipahi*s; rather, the sons of *sipahi*s often received a different *timar*, not the one their fathers held.[29]

One point that Ottomanists agree on was the practice of rotating *timar*s into the hands of new holders. It seems that many *timar* holders held their grant for short periods, perhaps as little as a year. Some scholars speculate

[27] Mutafchieva, *Agrarian Relations*, 56–59. Beldiceanu, *Le timar*, 52–54.

[28] Mutafchieva, *Agrarian Relations*, 58. Beldiceanu, *Le timar*, 56–58. Inalcik, *Economic and Social History*, 117–18.

[29] Inalcik, *Economic and Social History*, 115. Beldiceanu, *Le timar*, 65, 68–69. Mutafchieva, *Agrarian Relations*, 22–23, 37–38.

that this was because there were more potential *sipahi*s than there were *timar*s available; others think this was a deliberate policy to prevent *sipahi*s from becoming too attached to their *timar*s.[30]

Whether there was "fierce competition for the limited number of *timar*s" (Inalcik) or "sometimes the Porte experienced difficulties in the recruitment of new timariots" (Beldiceanu), there is no question that the *timar* was a fundamental and significant part of both the agrarian and military systems of the Ottoman Empire. In 1473, according to Ö. Barkan, there were some 64,000 *sipahi*s in Europe and Anatolia, which represented 62 percent of the Ottoman army, and in 1527, also according to Barkan, *timar* holders received 46 percent of the total land tax revenues in the European territory of the empire.[31]

Comparisons with pronoiai

The similarities: both were granted to a similar range of recipients, and most of the recipients of either were soldiers; both emphasized service to the state; both could be shared by more than one person; the essence of the grant in each case was a defined quantity of revenues drawn from a defined set of peasants; both pronoiai and *timar*s could be formed from a single village or parts of several villages, and a single village could be divided among several grant holders; neither *pronoiarios* nor timariot appears to have enjoyed rights of justice over his peasants independent of the local government; practices involving the hereditary transmission of both grants varied; the *timar* was part of a fiscal system similar to that found in Byzantium (but more on that below).

The differences: unlike pronoiai, *timar*s were often granted by provincial officials; depending on their revenue level *sipahi*s were required to furnish additional warriors aside from themselves; domain land (and hence the corvée labor of the peasants assigned to the *timar*) was not as central to the *timar* as it was with the pronoia; the paroikoi of *pronoiarioi* generally paid all their taxes to the *pronoiarios*, while the timariot's peasants paid significant taxes to the state; there is no evidence of *pronoiarioi* leasing their revenues to

30 Inalcik, *Economic and Social History*, 115–16. Mutafchieva, *Agrarian Relations*, 38–39. Beldiceanu, *Le timar*, 66–67.

31 Inalcik, *Economic and Social History*, 116, also 72–73. Beldiceanu, *Le timar*, 70. Barkan cited by Inalcik, *Economic and Social History*, 88, and Shaw, *History of the Ottoman Empire*, I, 127 and 167 note 3, respectively.

tax farmers; there was more frequent reassignment of *timars*; *sipahis* were a more important part of the Ottoman army than pronoia soldiers were to the late Byzantine army (though the percentage of agrarian revenues tied up in pronoiai was perhaps comparable). We note that most of the differences are merely of degree.

What of the social level of *pronoiarios* and timariot? One way to make a comparison is to compare the value of a typical pronoia to a typical *timar*. As noted above Inalcik and Mutafchieva wrote that the official revenue of the average *timar* in the first half of the fifteenth century was in the 1,000–3,000 akçe range.[32] Both were basing their figures on the earliest extant register of *timars*, the register created in 1431 for the Arvanid *sancak* (the area of central and southern modern Albania and part of northern Greece and western Macedonia). In this document 61 percent of the *timars* have official revenues of from 1,000 to 2,000 akçe, and 82 percent from 500 to 4,000 akçe (no *timar* has a revenue below 500 akçe). So let us use 2,000 akçe as the revenue of a "typical" *timar* in the first half of the fifteenth century in Rumeli. Mutafchieva points out that estimating the "typical" income of the "typical" timariot is difficult because not a few *timars* were shared between several timariots, and during the period between fiscal surveys the timariot had the opportunity to enlarge his *timar* by the appropriation of abandoned land within the geographical area of his *timar*.[33] Nonetheless, 2,000 akçe will provide us with an order of magnitude.

For the "typical" value of a pronoia, we use the figures from the three praktika for soldiers from the Thessalonian *mega allagion* from 1321 to 1323. As noted in Chapter 8, we have very few figures for the total *posotes* of a pronoia, and while these figures (seventy, seventy-two, and eighty hyperpyra) are the lowest figures we have, they represent the best guess we have for the revenues of a typical cavalry soldier. So let us use seventy-five hyperpyra as the typical *posotes*.

Obviously we need to convert akçe to hyperpyra, and we can do this via Venetian ducats, a relatively stable currency during the fourteenth and fifteenth centuries. In the 1320s seventy-five hyperpyra was equal to about fifty ducats, and in the first half of the fifteenth century 2,000 akçe was equivalent to around fifty-seven ducats.[34] Even if we double the pronoia's

[32] Inalcik, *Economic and Social History*, 141. Mutafchieva, *Agrarian Relations*, 32, 50, 52.

[33] Mutafchieva, *Agrarian Relations*, 28–30.

[34] For the equivalency of hyperpyra to ducats: T. Bertelé, "Moneta veneziana e moneta bizantina," *Venezi e il Levante fino ad secolo xv* (Florence, 1973), 41–42. In the first half of the fifteenth century there were about thirty-five akçe to the ducat: Ş. Pamuk in Inalcik, *Economic and Social History*, 454.

posotes to approximate the "true" value of the pronoia, and increase the *timar*'s value to account for a small quantity of domain land, the figures are comparable. This suggests that the social level of the typical *pronoiarios* and *sipahi* was similar.

At the higher end of *posotetes*, we can use the figure of 400 hyperpyra, equivalent to around 270 ducats. In the first half of the fifteenth century, this would be equivalent to some 9,500 akçe. In the Arvanid register, only 9 percent of timariots held a revenue of more than 7,000 akçe. And so the high end of pronoia revenues appears to be similar to the high end of *timar* revenues.

But what of the obligation on *sipahi*s to provide additional men for campaigns, a burden for which there is no evidence in regard to the pronoia? In fact a *sipahi* with an official revenue of 2,000 akçe was required to appear on campaign with only one military servant and perhaps a tent. It is quite likely that the pronoia soldiers of the *megala allagia* did the same, though there is no evidence for such an obligation. Even *timar* holders of 10,000 to 20,000 akçe, equivalent to the high end of known pronoia revenues, were required to serve with a mere handful of armed retainers and a few servants, and, again, it is quite likely that Byzantine aristocrats would have had their armed retainers by their side on campaign. In sum, it seems that the social status of timariots and *pronoiarioi* was similar.[35]

The relationship between pronoia and *timar*

The relationship between pronoia and *timar* is poorly understood. In order to consider whether the pronoia influenced the development of the *timar* (or vice versa), it would be desirable to know when the *timar* first appeared and under whose auspices (the Persian Buyids, the Mongol Il-Khanids, the Seljuks of Rum, one of the Seljuk successor emirates, or the Ottomans), and, assuming it evolved over time like most institutions, what characteristics the *timar* had at any particular point in its development. Unfortunately, there is little consensus among Ottomanists for any of these questions.

Some scholars connect the *timar* to the Islamic institution of *iqta*, whereby state land was leased to officials in return for service. *Iqta*, in the form of a grant of state revenues to civil and military officials, was fully articulated in the tenth century under the Buyids and passed to the Seljuk Turks when they conquered Baghdad in 1055. The *iqta* system was adopted by the Seljuks of

[35] Beldiceanu, *Le timar*, 80, 88. Bartusis, *Late Byzantine Army*, 225–34.

Ikonion in Anatolia, though the extent of its use as a means of financing soldiers is unclear.[36]

Stanford Shaw wrote that the *timar* was simply the old Seljuk *iqta* with a new name. Other scholars distinguish the *timar* from the *iqta*, but nonetheless see its origin in the Seljuk state. Thus, Nicoara Beldiceanu concluded that the *timar* existed in the Ottoman state from its beginning. Further, the significant regional variations of the *timar* in the fifteenth-century Ottoman Empire, along with hints that grants of state revenues existed in the Seljuk state and its non-Ottoman successors (the emirates of Aydin, Mentesche, and Qaraman), show that its origins, however indecipherable, are found in pre-Ottoman Anatolia.[37]

And other scholars think the *timar* was a purely Ottoman institution. For Vera Mutafchieva the *timar* was the result of mixing the Ottomans with the agrarian systems they conquered. When the Ottoman Turks invaded Europe they did not bring the *timar* but the agrarian and military system they knew from northwest Asia Minor. According to the *uc* system imposed on the tribal Turkomans by the Seljuk government, large hereditary military estates were conferred upon tribal leaders at the frontier. From these estates they raised their armies. With the conquests in Europe the Ottomans made the move to a regular army by first creating bodies of smallholding soldiers (*yaya* and *müsellem*) and then the *timar*. She concludes that one can speak of the *timar* in its "classical" form only after the middle of the fourteenth century.[38]

The one opinion that is rare to find among modern Ottomanists is that the *timar* developed from the pronoia. This used to be a rather common view among Ottomanists. However, in recent decades, as Ottoman and Turkish scholarship has grown more sophisticated and learned to stand on its own feet, the notion that Ottoman civilization owes anything significant to Byzantium has come to be eschewed.[39]

[36] See, e.g., J. Barnes, *An Introduction to Religious Foundations in the Ottoman Empire* (Leiden and New York, 1987), 27. Also, C. Cahen, "L'évolution de l'iqtâʿ du ɪxᵉ au xɪɪɪᵉ siècle," *Annales* 8 (1953), 25–52; C. Cahen, *La féodalité et les institutions politiques de l'Orient latin* (Rome, 1956); and A. Bombaci, "The Army of the Saljuqs of Rūm," *Istituto orientale di Napoli, Annali*, n.s. 38 (1978), 350–52.

[37] Shaw, *History of the Ottoman Empire*, ɪ, 26, and cf. M. Köprülü, *Some Observations on the Influence of Byzantine Institutions on Ottoman Institutions*, trans. G. Leiser (Ankara, 1999), 76–99, esp. 96 (this is a translation of Köprülü's 1931 Turkish study). Beldiceanu, *Le timar*, 21–30, 94.

[38] Mutafchieva, *Agrarian Relations*, 8–13.

[39] The traditional view of *timar* developing from pronoia is best illustrated by Jean Deny's article "Timar" in *The Encyclopaedia of Islam*, 1st edn. (Leiden, 1913–38), ɪᴠ, 767–76.

Of course, the problem is a lack of sources which makes it difficult to determine the lines of institutional continuity, if in fact there was such continuity. The word *timar* first appears in an institutional sense in the fiscal registers produced under Murad II (1421–51).[40] Fifteenth-century and later Turkish sources (both histories and documents) may be interpreting as *timars* earlier fiscal and agrarian relationships that had nothing to do with the institution. And fundamentally, we still do not know that much about Seljuk institutions, let alone those of the Mongol Il-Khanids. Specifically in regard to the former, Joel Shinder noted, "It is hardly proper, then, to fill in early Ottoman unknowns with Seljuk vaguely knowns."[41]

The word *timar* is Persian. Among other meanings it could connote "care, solicitude, maintenance"; in other words, it was a fair synonym for *pronoia*.[42] But, like all the other similarities between pronoia and *timar*, it may be coincidental. Indeed, if the essence of both is the grant of some kind of state revenue, property, or both, in return for (mostly) military service, then many medieval civilizations from western Europe to Russia and India and on to the Orient had institutions similar to pronoia and *timar*. And both Byzantine and Muslim civilizations had similar institutions in their earlier histories. In the end the evidence for a Byzantine influence on the *timar* is essentially circumstantial, as is the evidence that the *timar* was the direct descendant of any other institution. Unless one can find good evidence of the establishment of *timars* as a significant military institution during the pre-Ottoman era in an area that had been outside of Byzantine control since the twelfth century, the question will continue to be open.

But let us step away from the direct question of the relation between pronoia and *timar* and instead observe two aspects of the fiscal policy of the Turks as they conquered Byzantine Macedonia. Here we return to a few of the documents that were discussed in Chapter 9 in the course of dealing with Manuel II's "pronoiarization" program in the area of Thessaloniki. The three extant fifteenth-century acts which provide detailed lists of paroikoi in the area of Thessaloniki display an interesting development *[9.3–9.4] [9.6]*. The first aspect to note is how the fiscal policy of the Turks transformed the structure of these documents. As described in Chapter 9, once Byzantine authority was restored to the area around Thessaloniki after 1402, the authorities maintained the fiscal system the Ottomans had

40 Beldiceanu, *Le timar*, 21–22.

41 J. Shinder, "Early Ottoman Administration in the Wilderness: Some Limits on Comparison," *International Journal of Middle East Studies* 9 (1978), 509.

42 Beldiceanu, *Le timar*, 20.

imposed. Among the innovations were the appearance of taxes that did not appear in the fourteenth century, the division of paroikoi into two rubrics (families and widows), and the absence of any mention of a tax on the domain land of monasteries. The manner in which these three documents enumerate the paroikoi held by each monastery is quite unlike fourteenth-century Byzantine practices. Rather than listing the members of each paroikos household and itemizing the immovable and movable property of each (arable land, vineyards, gardens, oxen, pigs, sheep, etc.), the entry for each paroikos household is quite brief, noting simply the name of the head of the household, whether the household held a yoke of oxen (*zeugarion*), an ox (*vodin*), or a cow (*argon*), and the *telos* of the household in nomismata. Some households, including those headed by widows, have no animals listed.[43] The list of paroikoi in each village in the two praktika from 1409 ends with a total number given for "families" (*phamiliai*) and "widows."

It is important to point out that these changes are found only in documents issued in the area around Thessaloniki. The only other fifteenth-century listings of paroikoi that we have are praktika from Lemnos, and because Lemnos remained in Byzantine hands continuously into the fifteenth century, these documents follow the customary fourteenth-century Byzantine form.

It is clear that the Ottoman Turks did not simply appropriate the Byzantine fiscal system they encountered once they conquered Thessaloniki. Nor did they appropriate the fiscal system they encountered as they conquered Bithynia during the 1280s and 1290s, for this was essentially the same fiscal system that existed in the later fourteenth century. So where did the fiscal system imposed on the area around Thessaloniki come from? One possibility is that it came from Byzantium, but not the Byzantium of the fourteenth century, but rather of the eleventh through early thirteenth centuries. It was during that period that Byzantine praktika routinely characterized peasants according to whether they held a team of oxen (and thus were *zeugaratoi*), a single ox (and were therefore *voïdatoi*), or no oxen (and were classified as *pezoi, aktemones, kapnikarioi,* or other names). And the taxes of the peasants were based on this classification (e.g., *Patmos,* II, no. 50). This was the fiscal system that the Seljuks encountered when they invaded Asia Minor

[43] The entries for a few households with no animals listed note that the head of household was living with his mother (e.g., "Michael Slanainas with his mother") which probably means the son was a minor or at least unmarried.

in the second half of the eleventh century. This classification disappears in Byzantium not long after the middle of the thirteenth century.[44]

Thus, the Seljuks may have borrowed a few elements from the Byzantine taxation system which they encountered at the time of their conquest of Anatolia, and these elements passed to the Ottomans and then were faintly reflected in fifteenth-century Byzantine documents from areas that had been under Ottoman control. Nevertheless, many elements of these fifteenth-century documents do not reflect earlier Byzantine fiscal practices (such as the division between "families" and "widows"). These have their roots elsewhere, in Turkish or earlier Islamic practices.[45]

But what of pronoia? While the Seljuk Turks first encountered the Byzantine fiscal and agrarian system when they conquered a large part of Asia Minor in the second half of the eleventh century, they did not encounter pronoia at this time because pronoia did not yet exist. The Seljuks could not have encountered pronoia firsthand until they moved into the southwestern part of Asia Minor following the Latin Conquest of Byzantium in 1204. If pronoia existed in this area (to the south of the Meander River), they may have appropriated the institution of pronoia at this time for this area, adapting it to their own agrarian system as needed. It is not necessary to think that they would have applied the system to any area outside of these recently conquered areas. However, while the institution of pronoia certainly existed in Byzantium prior to 1204, there is no evidence that it existed specifically in the southwestern corner of Anatolia. Thus, the Seljuk Turks may not have encountered pronoia directly in the years immediately following the Latin Conquest.

The first time for certain that the Turks encountered pronoia is when they conquered the Meander valley beginning around 1280. But it was not the Seljuk Turks of Rum that did the conquering; rather, it was the Turks of the emirate of Mentesche. Tralles fell to these Turks around 1280, Miletos around 1285. Because we know that pronoia existed in the area of Miletos during the thirteenth century, we can date the Turkish encounter with pronoia to no later than the 1280s. This would answer the question of why the Ottomans would adopt an inefficient agrarian and fiscal institution of a crumbling state, especially when they supposedly had the institution

44 The last documents to classify peasants this way: MM, IV, 182–83 (1249); *Iviron*, III, no. 59 (1262); *Pantéléèmôn*, no. 9 (dated to 1271 with great uncertainty).

45 The origin of the Ottoman *çift-hane* system is debated, particularly whether tithe and *resm-i çift* are continuations of the classical Islamic taxes *haradj mukasama* and *haradj muwazzafa*: see N. K. Singh, ed., *International Encyclopaedia of Islamic Dynasties* (New Delhi, 2002), 689–90, and H. Gerber, *The Social Origins of the Modern Middle East* (Boulder, Co., 1987), 12.

of *iqta* to draw upon instead.[46] In the 1280s the Byzantine Empire may not have appeared to be crumbling and the institution of pronoia may have not appeared to be inefficient.

But the second aspect that needs to be considered is what happened during the Turkish occupation of the area around Thessaloniki to the half of the monasteries' properties that had been confiscated after 1371 and granted to *pronoiarioi*. Given that the Byzantine documents indicate that no small number was state land after 1403, one wonders whether they were state land under the Ottomans. If so, it is likely that they were transformed into *timar*s and granted either to new, presumably Turkish, holders or to previous Byzantine holders on condition of serving the sultan.[47] What is interesting about this possibility is that the taxation system that applied to monastic land during the Turkish occupation must have been applied to these erstwhile pronoia holdings as well. Because it appears certain that the Byzantine government maintained this taxation system after it recovered the region of Thessaloniki, this would suggest that the properties that were Byzantine pronoiai before the 1380s and were Ottoman *timar*s during the Turkish occupation became pronoiai again after 1402, but following Ottoman taxation practices. Thus, it is possible that what the fifteenth-century documents from the area of Thessaloniki refer to as *pronoiai* and *pronoiarioi* were actually Byzantine *timar*s and Byzantine *sipahi*s.

[10.1] Act of the tribunal of the metropolitan of Serres for the monastery of Esphigmenou involving Demetrios Vryennios Laskaris (1393)

This is more than speculation. A document from 1393 – an act of the tribunal of the metropolitan of Serres (firmly under Turkish control by that time) – suggests how this might have happened (*Esphigménou*, no. 30). The document deals with a complaint made by the monks of Esphigmenou against a man named Demetrios Vryennios Laskaris in regard to half of the village of Achinos, located on the right bank of the Strymon. According to the document the monastery of Akapniou had possessed half of the village for a long time, but it had lost it during the siege of Thessaloniki

[46] Barnes, *An Introduction to Religious Foundations*, 28, asks this question.

[47] On the integration of Byzantine landholders into Ottoman society, see, for example, S. Vryonis, "Byzantine and Turkish Societies and their Sources of Manpower," in *War, Technology and Society in the Middle East*, ed. V. J. Parry and M. E. Yapp (London, 1975), 147, and B. Cvetkova, "Influence exercée par certaines institutions de Byzance et des Balkans du moyen âge sur le système féodal ottoman," *Byzantinobulgarica* 1 (1962), 240–41.

(1383–87). Sometime during the siege the grand vizir Hayreddin Paşa (d. 1387) granted (line 4: εὐεργετηθείς) it to a certain Makarios Vryennios, and then sometime after the city surrendered to the Turks (April 9, 1387), Makarios returned the half of the village to the monastery. Afterwards the monastery decided to sell the property, evidently to pay its taxes (one of the few reasons for which church property could be alienated). The monks of Koutloumousiou wanted to buy the property, but because they owned no property near the village (to qualify to purchase by right of preemption), they conspired with Demetrios Vryennios Laskaris who, sometime after the surrender of Thessaloniki, had received the other half of Achinos as a "pronoia" from the sultan, either Murad I (1362–89) or Bayezid I (1389–1402). Koutloumousiou furnished the purchase price to Demetrios who bought Akapniou's half of the village (exercising his right of preemption) and then turned it over to Koutloumousiou under the pretext of a donation.

In 1392 the monastery of Hilandar, which had fields neighboring the village, complained to the metropolitan of Serres that Demetrios had no right of precedence to purchase the property, "not holding the other half of the village of Achinos in the manner of patrimony nor by other legal authority, but by pronoiastic right."[48] An investigation was conducted and the ruse was discovered. Demetrios admitted his part, the donation and the sale were effectively annulled, and in the end the metropolitan's tribunal ruled that the monks of Esphigmenou, whose property in the area were intermingled with those of Akapniou, had the best claim to purchase Akapniou's half of the village.

There are a number of ways to reconstruct the story to fill in a few of the gaps. The editor of the document, Jacques Lefort, suggested that Makarios and Demetrios were probably father and son, and that perhaps Akapniou had been dispossessed of the entire village during the siege, and that Makarios had received *all* of Achinos from Hayreddin, returning only half of the village to the monastery in 1387. In this case, after Makarios' death Demetrios received the sultan's permission to hold, in his own name, the half of Achinos that Makarios kept. Demetrios did not hold his half of Achinos as a hereditary possession, and this explains why he had no right of preemption.[49]

[48] *Esphigménou*, no. 30.18–19: οὔτε κατὰ γονικότητος λόγον οὔτε κατὰ νομικὴν ἄλλην αὐθεντίαν, τὴν ἑτέραν ἡμίσην τοῦ Ἀχιανοῦ χώραν, ἀλλὰ κατὰ προνοιαστικὴν ἐσχηκότι ἀξίαν.

[49] *Esphigménou*, p. 172. On Demetrios Vryennios Laskaris, see *PLP*, no. 14529, and K. Smyrlis, "The First Ottoman Occupation of Macedonia (ca. 1383–ca. 1403): Some Remarks on Land Ownership, Property Transaction and Justice," in *Diplomatics in the Eastern Mediterranean 1000–1500*, ed. A. Beihammer et al. (Leiden and Boston, 2008), 332–33.

Yet it is also possible that the division of Achinos was connected to Manuel II's "pronoiarization" program following the battle on the Marica. Perhaps half of Achinos had been taken from the monastery of Akapniou in or soon after 1371 and granted to Makarios Vryennios. During the siege of Thessaloniki Hayreddin granted him Akapniou's remaining half (evidently as full property), which he returned to the monastery after 1387. Makarios then died and his son Demetrios was granted the original half of the village that Makarios held as a pronoia.

Either scenario is consistent with the most important element in the story for our purposes, that Demetrios was granted half of the village as a "pronoia" by the sultan. As the document notes, Demetrios was holding it "by reason of the ruler's pronoia" (line 10: ἐσχηκότι λόγω προνοίας αὐθεντικῆς), distinguishing this pronoia conferred by the sultan from that conferred by the emperor ("imperial pronoia").

But in fact ought not a grant from the sultan which did not confer upon its recipient full property rights be more properly called a *timar*? And what fiscal system was applied within Demetrios "pronoia"? If, as the fifteenth-century Byzantine documents show, the Ottomans rearranged and restructured the taxes on monastic properties, requiring the monasteries to render taxes to the state, it is hardly likely that the holdings of new "*pronoiarioi*" like Demetrios (or old *pronoiarioi*, for that matter) would have been permitted to keep the pre-Ottoman tax system in which the grant was held tax free. What I am suggesting is that the pronoiai that appear in fifteenth-century Macedonia were more or less *timar*s under Byzantine control.

This rather odd development would explain the change in vocabulary of the fifteenth-century documents from Macedonia. Gone is *oikonomia*, and *pronoia* and its various derivative forms reappear in what must be described as a new context. We recall that the official way to refer to a pronoia in the fourteenth century was by the word *oikonomia*. The emperor used this word exclusively. *Pronoia*, in my view, had a more informal tone in the fourteenth century. It appears less frequently than *oikonomia* and is found only in acts issued by officials and by private individuals. In the fifteenth century all of this changes. The word *oikonomia*, as a fiscal term, disappears almost entirely from the Byzantine sources. It appears only in a document from Lemnos from 1407 *[7.18]*, and in the set of documents dealing with Gemistos Plethon and sons in the Morea *[9.8]*, that is, in areas that had not yet experienced a Turkish occupation and where fourteenth-century Byzantine practices remained in effect. But as for Macedonia, the very last appearance of *oikonomia* in its fiscal sense is in a document from 1373, referring to the oikonomia of George Katzaras *[8.47]*.

The manner in which the term *pronoia* and its other forms is used in fifteenth-century documents mirrors the dramatic changes that Macedonia had gone through:

(a) In one document the emperor uses the word *pronoia* in its fiscal sense. From extant documents, the last time an emperor used the word *pronoia* before this was in 1272, in Michael VIII's *prostagma* for Andronikos II *[6.6]*.
(b) In one document the emperor uses the verb *pronoiazo*, referring to the *metochia* of the monasteries of Athos and Thessaloniki that were "pronoiarized." From extant documents, the last time (and the only other time) this verb appeared was in 1216, when an official used it to refer to individuals who had received pronoiai *[5.5]*. The meaning of the word had changed.
(c) In five fifteenth-century documents from Macedonia an official uses the word *pronoiarios*. The only other appearance of this word in a Byzantine source is found in a letter of John Apokaukos from 1228 *[5.16]*.

What seems to have happened is that when the Ottomans conquered areas of Macedonia (and presumably this occurred earlier in Bithynia and then in Thrace as well), they dispossessed some Byzantine pronoia holders and replaced them with Turks, while other Byzantine pronoia holders kept their pronoiai in return for loyalty toward the sultan. The same process was employed with monastic possession as well: some were transferred to Turks, others were permitted to be kept by their monasteries. At some point following the conquests the Ottoman government introduced changes in the fiscal obligations of all of these properties. Probably some continued to resist, but given the relatively lenient terms of submission, and especially when the petty rulers of the Balkans, as well as the monasteries of Athos, were making their own peace with the Turks in return for power and privileges, it must have been rare.

The evidence for Christian *sipahis* certainly suggests there was no difficulty in exchanging pronoia for *timar*. From the beginning of Osman's conquest of Bithynia, conquered Byzantine subjects joined the Turks.[50]

[50] S. Vryonis, *The Decline of Medieval Hellenism in Asia Minor and the Process of Islamization from the Eleventh through the Fifteenth Century* (Berkeley, 1971), 468. A curious Turkish document asserts that a Sampias (perhaps Radoslav *[8.48]*) was granted two villages on the Chalkidike by the sultan Orhan (1326–1362) as a *timar*. V. Boškov, "Jedan originalan nišan Murata I iz 1386. godine u manastiru Svetog Pavla na Svetoj Gori," *Prilozi za orijentalnu filologiju* (Sarajevo) 27 (1977), 225–47. See N. Beldiceanu and I. Beldiceanu-Steinherr, "Un faux document ottoman concernant Radoslav Sampias," *Turcica* 12 (1980), 161–68, who regard the document as a fake,

When Byzantine authority returned to these areas after 1403, there appears to have been little attempt to restore traditional Byzantine fiscal practices to these properties. Rather, Ottoman fiscal practices were maintained. The terms *pronoia* and *timar* became more or less interchangeable. The Greek translation of the terms of surrender that Sinan, *beylerlbey* of Rumeli, delivered to the besieged town of Ioannina in 1430 contains an interesting reference to *timars*. Sinan promised that Ioannina would be treated like Thessaloniki, which had capitulated to him six months earlier, and "the archons, as many as have *timars*, shall again have their patrimony [*gonika*], their estates [*hypostatika*], and their goods."[51] In several passages the fifteenth-century historian Doukas refers to *timars* as "pronoiai."[52] And in one version of the sixteenth-century history attributed to Dorotheos of Monemvasia the author refers to erstwhile Latin holdings in the Morea as "fiefs called pronoiai, or *feuda*, that is, *spelikia*" (φύαις λέγονται πρόνοιαις, ἢ φέουδα, ἤγουν σπελίκια), thereby employing the more common term in his time "*spelikion*," that is, *spahilik*, the *timar* of a *sipahi*, to denote fief and pronoia.[53]

while H.-G. Majer, "Some Remarks on the Document of Murad I from the Monastery of St. Paul on Mount Athos (1386)," in *Ὁ Ἄθως στοὺς 14ο–16ο αἰῶνες* (Athens, 1997), 33–39, argues for its authenticity. In my view, the idea that Radoslav Sampias had been granted two villages as a *timar* by Orhan (two villages different from those over which he received hereditary rights from the Byzantine emperor in 1378) is far-fetched. The Turks had no firm presence in the Chalkidike during Orhan's reign. It is much more likely that the arrangement was concluded under his successor Murad I.

51 Ed. A. Rigo, "Lo *Horismòs* di Sinân Pascià, la Presa di Ioannina (1430) e la 'Lettera' del Sultano Murâd II," *Θησαυρίσματα* 28 (1998), 62.24–25 (older ed. MM, III, 283.6–8): οἱ ἄρχοντες ὅσοι ἔχουσι τιμάρια, πάλιν νὰ τὰ ἔχωσιν, τὰ γονικά τους, τὰ ὑποστατικά τους, καὶ τὰ πράγματά τους.

52 *Ducas. Istoria Turco-Bizantină (1341–1462)*, ed. V. Grecu (Bucharest, 1958), 149.8,24, 179.12, 215.24, and perhaps 115.3.

53 *Chroniques étrangères relatives aux expéditions françaises pendant le XIII*[e] *siècle*, ed. J.-A. Buchon (Paris, 1875), Notice, p. xxi. Uspenskij, "Značenie," 10.

Conclusion

The study of the institution scholars call pronoia is complicated by a number of factors. First, the sources do not always refer to the institution by the word *pronoia*. The literary sources at times employ alternate language, such as Choniates' "gifts of paroikoi" or Kantakouzenos' "incomes from land," and the documentary sources display an evolution in terminology, so that, for example, in the fourteenth century, Byzantine officials, and particularly the emperor, were wont to use the term *pronoia* at all, preferring *oikonomia* instead. Yet private individuals continued to use the word *pronoia*. Second, so many varieties of arrangements could fit under the umbrella of the word *pronoia* that it is not clear that the sources, even contemporaneous sources, are employing the term, or its alternate manifestations, to describe the same institution. The term *pronoia*, as well as *oikonomia*, was employed by different people to mean different things. For example, a contemporary Byzantine historian might have had something different in mind when writing about pronoiai than an imperial official composing an official act or a private individual composing a private act. It is one thing for Byzantine historians, chroniclers, churchmen, and private individuals to employ terminology loosely, but when it appears that the terminology employed by imperial fiscal officials such as *apographeis* "is not precise," we need to ask whether there was such a "precise" sense to the term. Third, like most institutions, the institution of pronoia evolved over the centuries. This work has tried to show that the institution underwent a continuous evolution from its genesis in the early twelfth century through its final appearance in the fifteenth. Changes occurred through changes in circumstances, changes in governmental needs, and through pressure from the recipients of the grants. Pronoia would never have become hereditary were it not for the latter. Consequently, one must anticipate that the characteristics pronoia bore at a nascent stage may no longer have existed by the time it was institutionalized, and, in turn, further changes may have occurred by the time it reached a more mature stage. It is unprofitable to seek the origins of the pronoia based on the fundamental characteristics of the fourteenth-century grant.

Any attempt to determine the origins of the institution of pronoia depends upon how one wishes to define the institution, or which characteristics of the institution one wishes to emphasize, and at what point it become distinct from its institutional antecedents. The matter, in this sense, is not unlike the problems faced when studying the origin of other institutions: think of monasticism, democracy, or capitalism. In their early stages, these looked only vaguely like their institutionalized or mature forms, and the sources pertaining to them did not necessarily employ the terminology that later became common.

Pronoiai almost certainly existed by the end of the reign of Alexios I Komnenos, but it is difficult to say when it first acquired its earliest form. If one views the institution as essentially a means of providing people with benefactions, with the presumption of continued loyalty to the crown, then we should look to the later eleventh century for its institutional antecedents, focusing on the various grants of state property made by emperors in lieu of cash disbursements. On the other hand, it is not until around the middle of the twelfth century that the term *pronoia* begins to appear in the sources, by which time it had become institutionalized. Certainly if pronoiai are viewed fundamentally as a means of raising an army, we should look to what Choniates considered the innovations of Manuel I Komnenos (1143–80) as the genesis of the "institution."

What was the defining element of what we call a pronoia? Was it (as the twelfth-century *Zavorda Treatise* states) the grant to a man for life from the emperor? Was it the cession of fiscal revenues drawn at the source? Is it to be found in the relationships it created between the cultivators of the soil, the pronoia holder, and the state (its social and economic character), or might it be sought in the legal status of the grant (its juridical character)? I have concluded the defining element was service to the state.

Summary of the evolution of the institution of pronoia

Here we may summarize the evolution of the pronoia grant as it relates to other grants of agrarian property and revenues:

(i) From the tenth century through the early eleventh century, monasteries received numerous *exkousseiai* for their properties and *exkousseiai* were frequently granted to their paroikoi for the benefit of the monasteries. Monasteries also received *solemnia* of various kinds and taxes from *excusati*. They rarely received grants of land and never exemptions (*logisima*) of the basic property tax (the *telos*) on their property. The usual way to reward laymen was through court titles providing an annual cash stipend (*roga*). Only rarely were grants of land made to laymen (ethnic groups of soldiers, distinguished people).

(ii) During the middle of the eleventh century, the means of rewarding monasteries and laymen took more varied forms. For monasteries, *solemnia* became less frequent and grants of land become more common, and grants of *exkousseiai* for their peasants continued. Laymen of high status frequently received *charistikai* and sometimes *sekreta*, and sometimes property, often in compensation for properties lost in Asia Minor through Turkish advances or as a reward.

(iii) In the later eleventh century Alexios I Komnenos increasingly granted revenues and property to relatives and people of high status, naturally with no formal strings attached, and then to persons of slightly lower status. *Rogai* to title holders end; grants of *sekreta* are uncommon. Monasteries continued to receive numerous *exkousseiai* for their properties and paroikoi; *solemnia* almost disappear. They received some land, but only rarely *logisima* or gifts of villages.

(iv) In the twelfth century the first pronoia grants are mentioned. They consist of grants of state land and *exkousseiai* for the peasants who work that land. These seem to be granted only to soldiers. The grants have obvious conditions attached: they are for life and they demand military service. Like grants to monasteries at the time, these pronoia grants were probably quantified by a fixed number of paroikoi assigned to them.

Aside from pronoia grants, two other kinds of grant were common in the twelfth century: grants to monasteries and churches and grants to laymen of high status. While canon law maintained that grants to religious foundations were inalienable and irrevocable, they nevertheless were subject to imperial control. Such grants included fiscal exemptions (sometimes *logisima*), grants of the services of paroikoi, and sometimes land. Cash *solemnia* disappear, and there is a decline in *parechomena solemnia*. Grants to persons of high status, frequently relatives of the emperor, which originated as simple rewards or gifts, were held on condition of the emperor's favor, and no doubt at times included the presumption of the recipient's administrative or military service toward the emperor.

Generally speaking, the evolution of grants from the eleventh through the twelfth century was an expansion from monasteries and persons of high status to persons of lower status. As the grants were thus institutionalized, they became explicitly conditional.

(v) Following the Latin Conquest of 1204, the practice of granting pronoiai to soldiers continued and became common. During the early to mid-thirteenth century most pronoia holders were soldiers, including those called *kavallarioi*. Innovations took the form of granting taxes (the *telos*) on properties owned by private parties to pronoia holders, and grants of pronoiai to lower-level officials. Further, the *zeugarion* was introduced as a means of quantifying the value of properties conferred as grants. During this period monasteries received with increasing frequency fiscal privileges: land, exemption (*logisima*) from the property tax (*telos*), and gifts of villages which included paroikoi. *Exkousseiai* for their property and paroikoi were universal. Laymen of high status, such as relatives of the emperor, continued to receive outright grants of properties with exemption of the *telos*, along with *exkousseiai* for the peasants who worked them.

(vi) Beginning with the reign of Michael VIII the concepts of the oikonomia (first attested in 1259) and the *posotes* (first attested in 1261) were introduced, both in regard to grants held by soldiers. This was part of an attempt to merge the administration of all imperial grants (to religious foundations, to laymen of high status, to lesser officials, and to soldiers) into a single system, characterized by a specific quantity of fiscal revenue. Paralleling the manner by which the term *pronoia* was introduced into the fiscal vocabulary (the phrases *eis pronoian* and *kata pronoian* yielding to simply "pronoia"), the earliest appearances of *oikonomia* are in the phrases *pros oikonomian* ("for oikonomia") and then *charin oikonomias* ("for the sake of oikonomia"), before acquiring a concrete sense (e.g., "holding an oikonomia").

By the second half of the thirteenth century, the pronoia grant had lost some of its original character: occasionally the emperor permitted children to receive their fathers' pronoiai, blurring the distinction between pronoia grants and grants to monasteries, which were fundamentally enduring, and grants to laymen of high status, which were presumed to be hereditary even if the statement was never explicit. This blurring can be seen in the terminology used. During the twelfth and early thirteenth centuries, every holder of what was termed a *pronoia* was either a soldier (*stratiotes* or *kavallarios*) or a man with an unknown vocation. No officials or relatives of the emperor were among those who held pronoiai. However, beginning during the reign of John III Vatatzes, the first pronoia holder appears who was a high functionary and not a soldier (John Alopos, *prokathemenos* of Smyrna, mentioned in a document from 1235 *[5.8]*). The first relative of the emperor to have held something explicitly called a *pronoia* was George Komnenos Angelos, one of Michael VIII's uncles, who shortly before May 1262 "was granted in pronoia" the village of Malachiou *[5.6]*.

(vii) By the beginning of the fourteenth century, if not a bit earlier, the attempt to regard all imperial grants as oikonomiai was abandoned by the emperor, specifically Andronikos II Palaiologos. With surprising consistency imperial documents refer to pronoia grants exclusively as oikonomiai. These documents never refer to a grant to a monastery or an outright grant of property to a layman as an *oikonomia*, and they cease to use the term *pronoia* in a technical sense entirely. The emperor granted "gifts" (*doreai*) to monasteries but "livelihoods" (*oikonomiai*) to laymen. On the other hand, documents issued by officials and by private individuals refer to pronoia grants as both *pronoiai* and *oikonomiai*, while official documents in formulaic passages refer to grants to monasteries as *oikonomiai*. Occasionally, official documents even refer to monastic grants as *pronoiai*. This suggests that *pronoia* was the common way of referring to any grant. From the economic and fiscal point of view, all of these grants, whether the gifts granted to laymen and monasteries or the pronoiai granted to soldiers and other laymen (those of high status and lesser officials), were essentially identical, containing the same elements (land, the taxes and labor services of paroikoi, tax revenues) and varying only by their magnitude. Nonetheless, the difference in vocabulary between the emperor and his fiscal officials in regard to these grant is probably attributable to the fact that the various types of grants were politically and juridically different. Grants to monasteries were subject to canon law and were motivated by piety and by the desire to acquire the loyalty of the monastic community. Grants of alienable property to laymen were the closest thing to private property that existed in late Byzantium (an imperial document safeguarding possession more securely than mere rights of patrimony) and were made to reward service and assure future loyalty. Pronoia grants, even if transferable to heirs, remained conditional in that they were not otherwise alienable and required some type of service. While it would never become a general right, during the fourteenth century an expectation developed that pronoia grants would pass to the sons of pronoia holders. Occasionally a pronoia grant was transferred to a female descendant of a pronoia holder.

(viii) In the later fourteenth century, as Thrace and Macedonia were conquered by the Ottoman Turks, the pronoiai of these areas were either lost or converted into *timar*s, an Ottoman institution with many similarities to the contemporary pronoia. Many Byzantine pronoia holders thereby became *timar* holders.

(ix) In the early fifteenth century, the fiscal arrangements imposed on pronoiai in Macedonia by the Ottomans during their temporary occupation were probably maintained by Byzantine authorities when these areas came once again under Byzantine control. We know nothing of the terms of service or the recipients of pronoiai in fifteenth-century Macedonia, and little about the recipients of pronoiai anywhere else in the empire. Nevertheless, there is a strong possibility that, at least in Macedonia, most of the *timars* that existed during Turkish rule which had been held by erstwhile Byzantine subjects continued to exist unchanged, but were now referred to as "pronoiai." New pronoiai seem to have been created in the image of the *timar*. The pronoia, in fact, became a *timar*.

Throughout this evolution, what remained constant was the conditional nature of the pronoia grant. At first it was a temporary (lifetime) grant held on condition of personal service (military or otherwise). But even when permission was secured by some grant holders for the pronoia to pass to their heirs, the grant of a pronoia/oikonomia remained conditional in that it still bore an obligation that the holder perform service. In the rare cases in which a pronoia became alienable, it was no longer a pronoia and no longer referred to as a pronoia or oikonomia.

The diffusion of the institution and the term to Byzantium's neighbors

By the fifteenth century the fiscal term *pronoia* appears here and there in most areas of the Balkans south of the Danube. What it means is another matter. It appears a couple of times in the *Chronicle of the Tocco* which deals with the situation in Epiros in the late fourteenth and early fifteenth centuries. Further north, a contract from Kerkyra (Corfu) from 1472 mentions a "sir Stephen Phiomachos *pronoiarios*" (σὲρ Στεφανῆ Φιομάχον προνιάριον) as one of the parties. While George Ostrogorsky saw the survival of the Byzantine institution of pronoia, Michel Lascaris thought that the term *pronoiarios* was employed to designate the holder of one of the baronies instituted since the occupation of Kerkyra by the Angevins of Naples in 1272, and that the reference is actually to a fief that remained in the hands of the Fiomaco family up through the seventeenth century.[1]

The term *pronoia* is found as well in fifteenth-century Venetian documents dealing with their possessions in the Aegean, specifically on Tinos

[1] *Cronaca dei Tocco di Cefalonia di Anonimo*, ed. G. Schirò (Rome, 1975), lines 139–40, 935. M. Lascaris, "Cinq notes à la Πρόνοια de M. Ostrogorsky," *Byz.* 21 (1951), 270–71. D. Jacoby, "Les archontes grecs et la féodalité en Morée franque," in D. Jacoby, *Société et démographie à Byzance et en Romanie latine* (London, 1975), no. VI, 437. D. Jacoby, "Les états latins en Romanie," in Jacoby, *Recherches sur la Méditerranée orientale du XIIe au XVe siècle* (London, 1979), no. I, 9 note 28. Ostrogorsky, *Féodalité*, 252 note 1. On the situation on the island, see also C. Asdracha and S. Asdrachas, "Quelques remarques sur la rente féodale," *TM* 8 (1981), 7–14; and C. Asdracha, "From the Byzantine Paroikoi to the Vassalli Angarii," *Études balkaniques* 22, 1 (1986), 114–22.

and Mykonos. For example, in 1442 the *rector* of Tinos granted a man named Michael Aspergi a pronoia and other properties that had belonged to the widow Paraschi who was childless. In return Aspergi and his descendants were required to do homage to the *rector* and serve as crossbowmen aboard ship. David Jacoby has pointed out that in these cases the grants did not involve fiscal revenues, but agricultural land and even houses exploited directly by the recipients for which they paid taxes. The men seem to be of a relatively modest social level, and the only difference between these men and the rest of the population was found in the service they owed. Jacoby hypothesized that the use of the term *pronoia* can be explained by the fact that with rare exception the recipients of these grants were Greeks.[2]

References to pronoia are also found in the area of Zeta, the Adriatic littoral roughly from Kotor to Skadar. The earliest evidence that the institution of pronoia existed there dates to the very end of the fourteenth century, to the period of Venetian control over the area of Skadar which began in 1396. This suggests that it was the Venetians who introduced pronoia into Zeta. Throughout the fifteenth century numerous Venetian documents and a few from other archives illuminate the adaptation of pronoia to the tribal culture of Zeta, as well as the manner in which the Venetians accommodated that adaptation of pronoia. Most notable is the so-called Cadaster of Skadar from 1416–17 which lists, among the villages owing taxes to Venice, a number of villages held by pronoiars. Altogether sixteen pronoia holders appear in the document. This document, combined with the other fifteenth-century documents dealing with the area of Skadar, dwarfs the Byzantine sources available for the study of pronoia. The subject deserves a monograph in its own right.[3]

[2] F. Thiriet, *Régestes des délibérations du Senat de Venice concernant la Romanie* (Paris, 1958–61), III, no. 2575 (text note 1). Jacoby, "Les archontes grecs," 437. D. Jacoby, *La féodalité en Grèce médiévale* (Paris, 1971), 243–44, 247–49. Also, on Tinos, from 1432: C. Sathas, *Μνημεῖα Ἑλληνικῆς Ἱστορίας. Documents inédits relatifs à l'histoire de la Grèce au moyen âge* (Paris, 1880–90), III, 412.36–38, and also 413.12 (Thiriet, *Régestes*, III, no. 2273). Jacoby, "Les archontes grecs," 437. And for Mykonos, see Jacoby, *La féodalité*, 237–42, 245–52.

[3] The Cadaster is found under entries 2045, 2107, and 2158 in *Acta Albaniae Veneta saeculorum XIV et XV*, ed. G. Valentini, part 2, vol. 8 (Milan, 1970); vol. 9 in the series is the valuable index to vol. 8. Ostrogorsky's chapter on pronoia in Zeta (Ostrogorsky, *Féodalité*, 222–57) remains the best introduction to the subject, though it only scratched the surface and it is colored by his own understanding of Byzantine pronoia. For further bibliography, see M. Bartusis, "Serbian Pronoia and Pronoia in Serbia: The Diffusion of an Institution," *ZRVI* 48 (2011), 206 note 92. It is surprising that O. Schmitt's hefty 700-page book, *Das venezianische Albanien (1392–1479)* (Munich, 2001), devotes a mere seven pages (pp. 167–73) to pronoia (and most of his analysis is based on scholarship dealing with pronoia in Byzantium).

In most cases such as this, it would be misleading to say that the *institution* of pronoia had passed to Byzantium's neighbors. Rather, it is more accurate to say that the *term pronoia*, signifying some kind of property grant from a governmental authority, had been appropriated. Indeed there appears to have been something almost magical about the word *pronoia* that it would be incorporated into the land-tenure jargon of areas that in some cases had not known a Byzantine presence for centuries. The abundant Venetian sources dealing with the appearance of the term *pronoia* on the Adriatic coast and the islands of the Aegean tell us about how the Venetians accommodated the indigenous institutions they encountered in their conquests but nothing about any Byzantine institution. Consequently, any conclusions regarding how Byzantium's neighbors appropriated the institution of pronoia can be no more reliable than our understanding of the native institutions of these peoples. George Ostrogorsky concluded that the institution as imported into these areas confirmed his understanding of Byzantine pronoia. Indeed, if one posits that any difference between, say, Albanian "pronoia" and Byzantine pronoia is due to the influence of native institutions, *any* conception of Byzantine pronoia will be confirmed.[4]

Oddly enough, there is no evidence that the term *oikonomia* in its fiscal sense was ever imported by any of Byzantium's neighbors including Serbia. This is yet another indication that most of Byzantium's neighbors who began to use the term *pronoia* were not in fact appropriating the Byzantine institution of pronoia at all. Rather, they appear to have appropriated the term *pronoia* to designate any grant of property or privileges from the government with only a vague connection with the Byzantine institution. If this is true, then the appearance of the term *pronoia* in non-Byzantine sources to describe non-Byzantine agrarian and fiscal relationships throws little light on our understanding of the Byzantine institution.

I tend to regard many of these appearances of "pronoia" outside of a Byzantine context as curiosities which in the end may tell us as little about the societies in which they appeared as they do about Byzantium. On the whole, the study of "pronoia" as it appears in these non-Byzantine areas is best left to specialists interested in those areas.

The one exception to this is Serbia, whose rulers first encountered pronoia in the later decades of the thirteenth century and, through the conquest of Byzantine territory, actively administered Byzantine pronoiai. But more than this, we have many documents that deal not only with the Serb administration of pronoiai within conquered Byzantine territory, but also with

[4] Ostrogorsky, *Féodalité*, 191, 224–25.

pronoiai as the institution eventually manifested itself in traditional Serbian territories. Thus, we are on much firmer ground when dealing with Serbian pronoia. It bore a certain resemblance to Byzantine pronoia, and the circumstances of Serbian contact with Byzantium and information provided by the documentary evidence permit us to make some generalizations about Serbian pronoia and do in fact illuminate some aspects of the Byzantine institution.

Another exception should be Bulgaria, which similarly conquered Byzantine territories in the thirteenth and fourteenth centuries and certainly must have encountered pronoiai in its administration of conquered Byzantine territories. Even though the scholarship occasionally states the existence of pronoiai in Bulgaria as a fact,[5] not a single Bulgarian source makes any mention of the institution of pronoia, nor does any other source refer to pronoia in Bulgaria. This is probably due to nothing more than the fact that we have so few extant documents dealing with the area of later medieval Bulgaria. The area where Bulgaria came into contact with Byzantium – Thrace – did not have the good fortune to be an area where the monasteries of Mount Athos had substantial holdings. I would certainly bet on the existence, even on the extensive existence, of pronoiai in fourteenth-century Bulgaria, but I cannot prove it.

For the Serbs the genesis of the institution probably dates to the conquests in 1282–83 of King Stefan Uroš II Milutin (1282–1321) in the area of Skopje, where there was a significant presence of Byzantine pronoiai. The appropriation of the institution of pronoia by the Serbs was a two-step process. First, Serbian rulers had to figure out what to do with Byzantine pronoiai in territories that they had conquered, fitting it into their fiscal, economic, agrarian, and military systems. And second, they began to create their own pronoiai, indicating that the institution was evidently of some utility. One example of how the Serbs accommodated the institution within their practices is found in a chrysobull issued by Milutin in 1299/1300 *[8.67]*. A small parcel of land in the village of Rečice which had been confiscated from the monastery of St. George near Skopje and granted as a pronoia by Michael VIII to a man was returned to the monastery by Milutin. However,

[5] E.g., J. Sedlar, *East Central Europe in the Middle Ages, 1000–1500* (Seattle, 1994), 73: "When Bulgaria reverted to Byzantine rule in 1018, its territories were organized on the Byzantine model into military fiefs called pronoias"; D. Nicolle and A. McBride, *Hungary and the Fall of Eastern Europe, 1000–1568* (London, 1988), 24: the Second Bulgarian Empire "controlled large areas held by *pronoia* cavalry and other troops"; and J. Fine, *The Early Medieval Balkans* (Ann Arbor, 1991), 303. On the other hand, the comprehensive work of I. Biliarski, *Instituciite na srednovekovna Bŭlgarija: Vtoro bŭlgarsko carstvo, XII–XIV vek* (Sofia, 1998), does not mention pronoia at all.

Milutin permitted the current holder of the property, the son-in-law of the original recipient, to continue to hold the property on condition that he and his heirs serve the monastery as soldiers.

A few lines later the document specifies that no pronoia holder (*pronijar*) was to enter Rečice "except [the monastery of] St. George." The only way this statement can be literally true is if the son-in-law was not considered a pronoia holder and if the church was considered the *pronoiarios* of their properties. Supporting the latter view is the final section dealing with Rečice which concludes with a passage referring to "church pronoia" (*cr'kvna pronija*), distinguishing it from the *baština* of others. This raises the question of the status of the parcel after it was granted to the monastery. If the parcel was considered a pronoia, was it held by Manota or by the monastery? If it was the monastery that held the pronoia, then Manota was simply part of the traditional Serbian practice of assigning men, including lesser nobles, to serve monasteries as soldiers. The Serbian innovation would be that a monastery could hold a pronoia. If Manota was the *pronoiarios*, then the traditional Serbian practice of assigning military men to monasteries was modified to account for the introduction of pronoia into Serbia.[6]

With the conquests of Stefan Dušan (1331–55) the Serbs came into even greater contact with Byzantine pronoia. Chapter 8 dealt with a number of Greek documents issued by Dušan involving property in Macedonia and Thessaly (esp. *[8.5]* and *[8.22]*). That these documents help us to understand Byzantine pronoia shows that Dušan did little to inject Serbian practices into the Greek-speaking areas that he conquered and that he simply continued Byzantine administrative practices. Thus, while it does appear that Dušan granted pronoiai to Serbs in the Byzantine territories he conquered *[8.23]*, it is often difficult to know whether pronoiai in areas taken by Dušan had been created by Dušan, by his successors, or by Byzantine rulers. For example, Dušan's 1345 Slavic act for a church at Ohrid forbids government officials as well as pronoiars from entering church property.[7] Dušan acquired the town of Ohrid in 1334 by treaty with Byzantium, and Dušan's act indicates there were pronoia holders in the area of Ohrid in 1345, but what we do not know is whether these pronoia holders were Greeks or

6 *SnM*, I, 226–27 (35), 227 (35). See Bartusis, "Serbian Pronoia," 180–86. This is the first Slavic document to contain either of the terms *pronija* or *pronijar*. *Pronija* obviously is derived from the Greek *pronoia*. As for *pronijar*, it derived either from the Greek *pronoiarios* (see *[5.16]*) or independently by adding the common Slavic agent-noun suffix *-ar* (e.g., *pisar* "writer," *ulijar* "beekeeper") to *pronija*.

7 S. Novaković, *Zakonski spomenici, srpskih država srednjega veka* (Belgrade, 1912), 673 xvi = A. Solovjev, *Odabrani spomenici srpskog prava* (Belgrade, 1926), 129.

Serbs, or whether they received their pronoiai from a Byzantine or Serb ruler. On the other hand, other documents testify to the earlier presence of pronoiai held by Greeks in the valley east of Strumica, captured by Dušan around 1332. According to Slavic acts two men – Tutko Asan and Laskar Siderofag – who are explicitly identified as Greeks held pronoiai there, and a number of documents refer to a "pronoiar's pear tree" in the area.[8] The fact that we do not know whether a Byzantine or Serbian ruler granted numerous pronoiai shows that the Serbian appropriation of the institution often did not disrupt landholding patterns. It is when the conquering Serbs acted in a heavy-handed fashion, dispossessing local landholders (as in Verrhoia *[8.23]* and Ioannina *[7.4]*), that we learn clearly who was granting the pronoiai.

While it is possible, perhaps even likely, that pronoiai were conferred by Milutin or his successor Stefan Dečanski, the earliest clear evidence that Serbian rulers were granting pronoiai in areas that were *not* under Byzantine control at any time during the thirteenth or fourteenth centuries is found in a chrysobull from 1346. Dušan granted a monastery near Novi Pazar two villages "as pronoiars held them earlier" (*kako jesu dr'žali pr'vo pronijarije*). One of these was Ulotino, northwest of the town of Plav in Montenegro, near the Albanian border, in an area that had not been under Byzantine authority since before the Latin Conquest of 1204. Therefore, it is quite unlikely that the document is referring to men (be they Serb or Greek) who received grants of pronoiai from a Byzantine emperor.[9]

One of the most important sources for the history of medieval Serbia is the *Zakonik*, or Law Code, of Stefan Dušan. This collection of laws contains three passages referring to pronoia, all of which date to the initial issuance of the code in 1349. Article 59, entitled "Concerning pronoia," forbids the buying, selling, or pious donation of pronoiai. Confirming the information from the 1299/1300 chrysobull of Milutin, *baština* could be alienated or acquired privately; pronoia could not. Article 68, entitled "On the law," deals perhaps with the integration of the Byzantine institution of pronoia into the medieval Serbian agrarian and fiscal system. The article specifies the financial and labor obligations of *meropsi* (the Serbian equivalent of

[8] Novaković, *Zakonski spomenici*, 400 vii, 401 viii. *Actes de Chilandar, II. Actes slaves*, no. 27.54–56,67–68. S. Ćirković, "Hreljin poklon Hilandaru," *ZRVI* 21 (1982), 116–17: *na pronijarêvo krušije*, which is rendered in a Greek act as εἰς τὴν προνοιαρικὴν ἀπιδέαν: V. Mošin and A. Sovre, *Supplementa ad acta graeca Chilandarii* (Ljubljana, 1948), no. 8.53. This is the only appearance of the adjective *pronoiarikos* (προνοιαρικός), which clearly derives from the Serbian *pronijarevo*. See Bartusis, "Serbian Pronoia," 198–99.

[9] Novaković, *Zakonski spomenici*, 631 i, iv = L. Slaveva and V. Mošin, *Srpski gramoti od Dušanovo vreme* (Prilep, 1988), 219. See Bartusis, "Serbian Pronoia," 190.

paroikoi) toward their *pronijar*. As in Byzantium these included corvées and money payments, though in Serbia corvée obligations were much more onerous: two days per week according to the Law Code, while in Byzantium twelve or twenty-four days per year was the obligation most commonly attested. Finally yet another article in the Law Code points to the higher status of pronoia holders, distinguishing *pronijarevići* – literally "sons of pronoiars" – from commoners (*sebri*).[10]

In the political fragmentation that followed Dušan's death in 1355, relatives, governors, and military leaders took control over the various provinces of his territory. Here and there the documents make mention of pronoia.[11] The Serbian despot John Uglješa (1366–71), who ruled a substantial portion of Byzantine Macedonia from his base at Serres, issued a pair of Slavic documents in 1369 which mention pronoiai: in one a village, some twelve miles east of Strumica, which he donated to a monastery had been held by pronoiars, and in the other he confirmed a gift of property to a church near Strumica with a clause forbidding courtiers, government officials, and pronoiars from troubling the church over the property. Ostrogorsky, noting that two of the eight or nine extant documents issued by John Uglješa mention the institution of pronoia, thought this indicated something of the widespread frequency of pronoia grants in the part of Macedonia ruled by Uglješa. On the other hand, the fact that neither Dušan's son and heir, Stefan Uroš V (1355–71), nor his successor Prince Lazar (1371–89), both based in Skopje, issued any extant documents mentioning pronoia might suggest the limited establishment of the institution of pronoia in Serbian lands.[12]

Nevertheless, pronoia reappears in Serbia under Lazar's son Stefan Lazarević (1389–1427) in three documents: one explains that he granted a number of properties, located northeast of Novi Pazar, which he had confiscated from another man "because of his unfaithfulness," to one of his nobles in pronoia (*vlastelinu momu u proniju*); another gave his mother a

[10] *Zakonik cara Stefana Dušana: 1349 i 1354*, ed. N. Radojčić (Belgrade, 1960), art. 59, pp. 54, 106; art. 68, pp. 56, 108; art. 106, pp. 63, 119. A reference to "pronoiaric corvées" (*pronoiarski rabot*) in one document (*SnM*, III, 270 x = Novaković, *Zakonski spomenici*, 640 x) is more a reflection of a Serbian than Byzantine practice. In Serbia there was a much greater emphasis on corvées, whereas Byzantium was more monetized.

[11] See *[8.77]*, and Solovjev–Mošin, *Grčke povelje*, no. 32.41–42, discussed in Bartusis, "Serbian Pronoia," 200–01.

[12] P. Lemerle and A. Solovjev, "Trois chartes des souverains serbes conservées au monastère de Kutlumus," in Lemerle, *Le monde de Byzance* (London, 1978), no. XIX, p. 135.14–15. Novaković, *Zakonski spomenici*, 751 ii. *Pantéléèmôn*, actes serbes, no. 5 (summary). Ostrogorsky, *Féodalité*, 212.

village in the area south of Kragujevac, which a man "held in pronoia" (*što je dr'žal' u proniju*) from Lazarević's father. She was to hold it as *baština* or *kupljenica* (purchased property), which would permit her to donate it to a monastery. As in Byzantium, something described as a pronoia might be transferred by a ruler to another party as an alienable grant.[13]

A document from Dubrovnik issued during the reign of Lazarević's successor George Branković (1427–56) shows that Serbian rulers maintained control over the pronoiai of Serbs residing in Dubrovnik. Another act, involving a businessman from Dubrovnik who held villages "in pronoia" in Serbia in 1453, shows that by the middle of the fifteenth century there was no necessary connection between pronoiai and military service in Serbia.[14]

Until the very end of the medieval Serbian kingdom, there is evidence of the institution of pronoia. For example, George Branković's son, Despot Lazar (1456–58), granted his treasurer Radoslav additional privileges over some villages and other properties in the area of Smederevo and of Golubac (near Braničevo) that Lazar had granted him as a pronoia. If Radoslav died or became a monk, these properties were to pass to his nephews, "to hold these in pronoia and to work and fight as the other pronoiars." This is the one clear example where a pronoia in Serbia was hereditary. As in Byzantium it seems that it could not be otherwise alienated and the heirs were to hold it under the same conditions as the initial recipient. Despite the fomulaic reference to military service, Radoslav was no military man, and so, as in the Dubrovnik document, we may infer that military service was no longer an essential component of holding a pronoia in Serbia.[15]

While our knowledge of pronoia in Serbia is rather limited, it is possible to make a few observations. As in Byzantium, in Serbia pronoiai were granted exclusively by rulers. As in Byzantium it was forbidden to alienate property held as pronoia, though the granting of hereditary rights as a special privilege, as in Byzantium, meant that the property could be transmitted to heirs. Following the Byzantine model, and given the nature of the ruling class in both Serbia and Byzantium, we might think that most of the recipients of such privileges were military men, despite the examples cited above.

Nevertheless, the most important question – how significant the institution was to medieval Serbia – still cannot be answered with any confidence.

13 Novaković, *Zakonski spomenici*, 458 i. Solovjev, *Odabrani spomenici*, 190–91.

14 Ostrogorsky, *Féodalité*, 215, 216 note 1. B. Krekić, "Contribution to the Study of the Pronoia in Medieval Serbia," in Krekić, *Dubrovnik, Italy and the Balkans in the Late Middle Ages* (London, 1980), no. XVIII, 1, 4, 6–8.

15 M. Lascaris, "Actes serbes de Vatopédi," *Byzantinoslavica* 6 (1935), 183–84, no. 9.2–3,6–7: *da ih dr'že u proniju a da od nih rabotaju i vojuju kako i ini proniarie*, and cf. line 11.

And most certainly we cannot assume that the pronoiai that Serbian rulers granted to their nobles and soldiers were granted under the same terms and were regarded as the same kind of grant as pronoiai in Byzantium. Yet the appearance of pronoiai throughout the territory of Serbia for well over a century, and particularly the several references to pronoia in Dušan's *Zakonik*, suggests that it did play an appreciable role in medieval Serbia.

Significance of the institution to Byzantium

The institution of pronoia is the institution that characterizes later Byzantium. To understand the institution of pronoia, and how the institution differed from other ways to reward individuals (including soldiers) and corporate bodies (preeminently monasteries), is to understand the fiscal, agrarian, and military systems, and, to a more limited extent, the social system of later Byzantium. There is no other institution that illuminates so much about Byzantium from the twelfth century onward.

Alan Harvey, in the course of explaining how Byzantium can be thought of as a "feudal society," downplayed the importance of the institution of pronoia. The pronoia, he wrote, "was a much more marginal phenomenon in Byzantium than the fief in western Europe" because leading aristocrats did not hold their property as pronoiai, Byzantium did not know subinfeudation, and pronoia grants did not include jurisdictional rights over the paroikoi contained within them.[16] There is much truth in this: big pronoia holders did not grant pronoiai to smaller pronoia holders; *pronoiarioi*, as far as I can tell, did not judge their peasants. And yet, as for how aristocrats held their property, much of what any aristocrat held after 1204 originated as an imperial grant. And even if a great landowner considered his property patrimony, such as Demetrios Devlitzenos with his *posotes* of 400 hyperpyra *[8.46]* which probably consisted of a tax exemption on his hereditary property, the privileges attached to the property were of imperial origin. In any event there were large landholders, such as Demetrios Mourinos with his *posotes* of 830 hyperpyra *[6.8]*, whose property did indeed originate as a pronoia grant.

Further, an institution need not be the most common of its type or have had the greatest direct impact to be the defining one for its society. Pronoia soldiers were never the most numerous soldiers, nor is there much evidence that they formed the most effective units within late Byzantine

[16] A. Harvey, *Economic Expansion in the Byzantine Empire, 900–1200* (Cambridge, 1989), 6–7.

armies. Nevertheless, it is the military *pronoiarios* who characterizes the late Byzantine military and gives it its distinctive quality.[17]

In fairness, for the period that Harvey was studying (the tenth through twelfth centuries), the institution of pronoia does not seem to have played a particularly great role in Byzantine society. But the twelfth century was pronoia's first century, and in fact one could argue that if all of our sources after, say, 1100 disappeared, the fief itself would appear to have been a "marginal phenomenon" in the medieval West. Moreover, to say that because a pronoia did not have the characteristics historians have traditionally ascribed to the fief, obviously does not make the pronoia *a priori* less significant.

From a purely economic point of view, the institution of pronoia was quite important. By the early fourteenth century the Byzantine state received no tax revenue from the overwhelming majority of agrarian properties. This property was in the hands of monasteries and the Church, it was in the hands of privileged laymen who had received tax exemption from the emperor, and it was in the hands of pronoia holders. It was also in the hands of the paroikoi held by all of these categories of privileged landholders. Consequently, the basic property tax (the *telos*) along with all the many other taxes, charges, and labor obligations was received, in large measure, by these privileged landholders, of which pronoia holders were a part. Whether the quantity of property and paroikoi held as pronoiai was greater than that held by religious foundations and the most elite laymen who held their properties through outright grant of the emperor is impossible to say. But, beyond any doubt, the number of pronoia holding laymen dwarfed the combined number of religious foundations and all other privileged landholding individuals. In other words, one can say with certainty that the majority of landlords in late Byzantium were pronoia holders.

Moreover, pronoia was a sign of a transformation in Byzantine society that affected more than economic, fiscal, or even military affairs. Until the second half of the eleventh century grants of land and grants of fiscal exemption to anyone or any institution were rare. But starting in the middle of the eleventh century, accelerating during the reign of Michael VII Doukas, and exploding under Alexios I Komnenos, privileges that were once reserved for a handful of laymen were granted to an ever-widening circle of imperial subjects. Gone were the salaries for any but the lowest palace staff, replaced by grants of property and fiscal concessions, particularly to the emperor's relatives. Scholars have long noted that under the Komnenoi the empire became a

[17] See Bartusis, *Late Byzantine Army*, 188.

family business. Privileges become less special. It was a gradual process culminating in Manuel I Komnenos' large-scale conferral of pronoiai upon soldiers. There was a "banalisation du privilège" and a "drift to government by concession."[18]

This gradual shift can be seen in other areas as well. During the twelfth century the tax register of an area (the *kodix*) gave way to the tax register of a specific individual or corporate body (the *praktikon*). Paul Magdalino points out that there was a widening gap between the inherited corpus of written law and the emperor as the source of legal enactments, a confusion over the emperor's role as a source of law and as a source of exceptions to the law, that is, a source of gifts. The Komnenoi issued both general and special laws, but both were usually issued in the form of chrysobulls and *prostagmata* rather than the traditional novel and edict.[19]

By the time Michael VIII Palaiologos came to the throne, the process was nearly complete. Whereas Manuel I Komnenos institutionalized privilege, Michael VIII oversaw its bureaucratization. A single system was created to quantify the privileges granted not only to pronoia holders but to religious foundations and to other privileged laymen. The majority of the state's fiscal revenues had been granted to individuals and to corporations. Most peasants rendered their fiscal burdens not to the state but to private parties. Even here one can observe the element of accommodation. As early as the eleventh century, Oikonomides concluded, it was common for the monastic beneficiary of a grant of paroikoi to demand a lower rate of taxation from its paroikoi than that to which it was entitled.[20]

As Magdalino points out, while Alexios I and Manuel I Komnenos issued many grants of land and fiscal concessions, these were frequently directed toward groups of beneficiaries and their intention was often to solve general problems. In this sense the era of the Komnenoi was a transitional period from the age of normative law to the age of the Palaiologoi who responded to problems with "specific political favors, i.e. with grants of privilege."[21]

Indeed historians rarely speak of the "legislation" of the Palaiologan emperors. Michael VIII and his successors certainly implemented "policies" and issued "orders," but they made few "laws." In fact from 1204 until the end of the empire, a total of two laws were issued involving civil matters, one by Michael VIII and one by Patriarch Athanasios and his synod in 1304.

[18] Oikonomides, *Fiscalité*, 219, and cf. Oikonomides, "The Role of the Byzantine State in the Economy," *EHB*, III, 1042. P. Magdalino, *The Empire of Manuel I Komnenos, 1143–1180* (Cambridge, 1993), 265.

[19] Magdalino, *The Empire of Manuel I Komnenos*, 265.

[20] Oikonomides, *Fiscalité*, 215.

[21] Magdalino, *The Empire of Manuel I Komnenos*, 263–64.

Dimiter Angelov writes, "Instead of general laws, the Byzantine emperors after 1204 preferred to issue privileges addressing a specific individual, city, monastery, bishopric, foreign dignitary, or urban community."[22]

Venality and favoritism were not new to later Byzantium, but from the late eleventh to the fourteenth century they were transformed from vices to necessities, and then to virtues. The Komnenoi through the Palaiologoi ran their governments by handing out privileges. Every office had to be accompanied by a grant of property. Monasteries and lay landowners received their fiscal privileges through chrysobull, soldiers and other received their pronoiai, even foreign merchants received their concessions. We end up, as Angeliki Laiou wrote, with "government by friendship, by connection," that is, "government, justice, and even legislation by privilege which had been developing since the 12th century and was fully developed by the 14th century."[23]

The old dynamic of order (*taxis*) vs. accommodation (*oikonomia*) was at play. And in the end accommodation won out. We see this is the vocabulary of imperial acts: "gift" (*dorea*), "benefaction" (*euergesia*), "mercy" (*eleemosyne*), and of course *oikonomia* and *pronoia*. *Oikonomia* as livelihood merges with *oikonomia* as accommodation in the sense of an "arrangement." A just act was a merciful act. A grant might have been considered better than private property because its holding was secured through an imperial act. And while an imperial act was better than an act of sale, connections at court trumped all.

This is why, in my view, it has been so difficult to fit the institution of pronoia into the framework of Roman law. The pronoia holder, through an extralegal act shrouded in the fiction of an act of imperial mercy, was given a limited privilege to share in state power, a license to collect state taxes, to demand labor services owed to the state, and to manage state property. No more than the administrator of an imperial estate did he "possess" or have "usufruct" of the estate. The institution of pronoia was the most obvious sign that Byzantium had severed its ties to the ancient world, that in its dispensation and arrangements of land and of privileges it had become a society remarkably medieval.

22 D. Angelov, *Imperial Ideology and Political Thought in Byzantium, 1204–1330* (Cambridge and New York, 2007), 5. Magdalino, *The Empire of Manuel I Komnenos*, 264–65.

23 A. Laiou, "The Correspondence of Gregorios Kyprios as a Source for the History of Social and Political Behavior in Byzantium or, On Government by Rhetoric," in *Geschichte und Kultur der Palaiologenzeit*, ed. W. Seibt (Vienna, 1996), 99, 107–08.

Appendix 1: Chrysobull of Michael VIII Palaiologos for the church of Hagia Sophia (1267–71)

A book which purports to be a definitive study of the institution of pronoia must deal with all of the various passages that mention pronoia and attempt to explain their meaning, even if the result is only a hypothetical interpretation. Such is the case in regard to a reference to pronoiai found in a chrysobull of Michael VIII, issued sometime between 1267 and 1271, on behalf of the Great Church of Hagia Sophia. The document reestablished Constantinople as the patriarchal see, confirmed properties and privileges granted to the patriarchate during the Nicaean era, and bestowed additional privileges. In one passage in the long document the emperor formally restored to the church of Hagia Sophia properties it held in the area around Smyrna before 1204. In addition, he granted the church "the *poros*, the *kommerkion*, the *ennomion*, the *topiatikon*, and the *kephalaia* given ἀπὸ τῶν ἐκτὸς προνοιῶν, [that is,] the [charge] of the *ploïmoi*, of the *agape*, and of the *sitarkia*."[1] This was not a grant of taxes paid by other taxpayers, but an *exkousseia* of the taxes that ordinarily had to be paid on the properties listed. Thus, for these properties, the emperor confirmed that the church did not have to pay the *poros* (a charge for transporting goods), the *kommerkion* (the basic tax on trade), the *ennomion* (a charge on pasturage), and something called the *topiatikon* (which is otherwise unknown and may represent a scribal error).[2]

Similarly, the emperor granted the three *kephalaia* called the *ploïmoi*, the *agape*, and the *sitarkia*. *Kephalaia* means taxes (literally, "chapters" in the sense of tax headings or categories), and other documents confirm that the *agape* and *sitarkia* were occasionally included within the *kephalaia*.[3]

[1] Zepos, *JGR*, I, 663.2–5: πρὸς τούτοις, τὸν πόρον, τὸ κομμέρκιον, τὸ εὐνοιῶν [sc. ἐννόμιον], τὸ τοπιατικόν, καὶ τὰ ἀπὸ τῶν ἐκτὸς προνοιῶν διδόμενα κεφάλαια, τὸ τῶν πλωΐμων, τὸ τῆς ἀγάπης, καὶ τὸ τῆς σιταρκίας. After 1204 possession of these properties remained in the hands of the exiled patriarchs of Constantinople. With the return of the capital to Byzantine authority in 1261, the patriarch reclaimed his church and see. As such, the formal restoration of these properties to Hagia Sophia was primarily of symbolic value. On the date of the document, see Dölger, *Regesten*, III, no. 1941a.

[2] On the *poros*, or *poriatikon*, see Solovjev–Mošin, *Grčke povelje*, 483. *ODB*, s.v. "kommerkia," "ennomion."

[3] E.g., MM, IV, 4.8–9, 249.10–11.

None of these three specific taxes has been studied adequately. The *ploïmoi* (from the adjective *ploïmos*, "fit for sailing") had something to do with building, manning, outfitting, or maintaining the navy. As for the *agape*, literally "brotherly love," Hélène Ahrweiler hypothesized that, inasmuch as a treaty of friendship with a foreign state was sometimes called an *agape*, the tax was connected with diplomatic expenses. The *sitarkia*, literally "provisions," was some kind of tax or levy on grain (*sitos*).[4]

In any event, the difficulty in understanding this passage, and its interest to this study, comes from the phrase τὰ ἀπὸ τῶν ἐκτὸς προνοιῶν διδόμενα κεφάλαια. Numerous scholars have attempted to explain the meaning of the phrase. Should τῶν go with προνοιῶν, and should the adverb ἐκτός modify the latter like an attributive adjective, we might translate the phrase as "the taxes given from the outside pronoiai." Evidently, this is how Constantine Zuckerman read the passage. As part of his attempt to show that pronoiai, up through the early part of Michael VIII's reign, were subject to taxation, he wrote that the passage means that "the pronoiai situated in the vicinity remained outside the territory donated, yet the church was entitled to exact in its favour the taxes due from these pronoiai, namely *ton ploïmon*, *agape* and *sitarkia*."[5] This would have created an odd situation whereby taxes on properties held by pronoia holders were redirected to the church.

If, on the other hand, we rearrange the words into a modern Greek construction (τὰ ἐκτὸς ἀπὸ τῶν προνοιῶν διδόμενα κεφάλαια), we can partially explain Franz Dölger's and Peter Wirth's loose translation of the phrase as "the charges due aside from the pronoia" (or, more accurately, "the *kephalaia* given apart from [or except for] the pronoiai"). However, they offer no suggestion as to what their translation means.[6]

In a brief reference to this passage Ahrweiler seemed to adopt a similar reading by suggesting that the passage meant that the state would keep to itself certain taxes and charges, which she calls τὰ ἐκτὸς τῶν προνοιῶν, "the things outside of the pronoiai," a reading which takes some liberty with the text. It is not clear whether she thought the *ploïmoi*, *agape*, and *sitarkia*, were among the taxes the Great Church was *not* to receive.[7]

4 *ODB*, s.v. "kephalaion," "sitarkia." On the *ploïmoi* and the *agape*, see M. Angold, *A Byzantine Government in Exile* (London, 1975), 199–200, 223–25. I disagree with Angold's hypothesis that the *agape* and *ploïmoi* were the main taxes of the Nicaean era. Ahrweiler, "La concession des droits incorporels," 109 note 35.

5 C. Zuckerman, "The Dishonest Soldier Constantine Planites and His Neighbours," *Byz* 56 (1986), 328.

6 Dölger, *Regesten*, III, no. 1941a: "den außer der pronoia gebührenden Abgaben."

7 Ahrweiler, "La concession des droits incorporels," 109.

Another way to explain the phrase is to conclude that τῶν and προνοιῶν refer to different things. Apparently this is what Michael Angold did. He interpreted the passage to mean that the Great Church was granted special exemption of the *ploïmoi*, *sitarkia*, and *agape*, and that, under normal circumstances, these charges were paid on all property except that which was granted out in pronoia. Even though he provided no translation of the passage, it seems he was rendering the passage as "the *kephalaia* [ordinarily] given from the [properties] with the exception of pronoiai."[8]

The reluctance of previous scholars to offer a formal translation of the passage is understandable. The passage is ambiguous. Nevertheless, it is possible to exclude the interpretations of Dölger–Wirth and of Ahrweiler by comparing the phrase in question to a phrase that immediately follows the section of the document quoted above. After referring to the *ploïmoi*, *agape*, and *sitarkia*, the emperor grants further privileges: "In addition, the [things] given on behalf of a rental payment from various regions and persons" (τὰ ὑπὲρ πακτωτικοῦ διδόμενα ἀπὸ διαφόρων χωρῶν καὶ προσώπων).[9] The word-order of our passage can now be rearranged to reflect a parallel construction: τὰ κεφάλαια διδόμενα ἀπὸ τῶν ἐκτὸς προνοιῶν. There can be no doubt that ἀπό in both phrases means "from" or "by." Thus, the interpretations of Dölger–Wirth and of Ahrweiler may be discounted.

We are left to decide whether the phrase ἀπὸ τῶν ἐκτὸς προνοιῶν means "from the outside pronoiai" (Zuckerman), "from the [properties] except for pronoiai" (Angold), or some other interpretation. Zuckerman's interpretation, that pronoia holders in the area paid taxes to the Great Church, is dubious because it is based on the notion that pronoia holders did not receive the taxes of the properties they held in pronoia. There is very little evidence that pronoia holders paid taxes on any of the properties or people within their pronoiai. On the contrary, the sources discussed in Chapter 5 indicate clearly that one of the basic elements of a pronoia at the time was that it gave its recipient a claim to the taxes owed by others *[5.1–5.2] [5.4] [5.7–5.9]*. The interest that some pronoia holders took in the property acquisitions of their paroikoi can best be explained by positing that the more property a paroikos owned, the more taxes the pronoia holder would receive *[5.6][5.8]*.

Angold's interpretation is a possibility. It would make sense whether or not there were pronoiai in the area of the Church's property. The Church's

8 Angold, *Byzantine Government*, 223–24.

9 Zepos, *JGR*, I, 663.5–6. The term *paktotikon*, from *pakton*, is quite rare. I have found it otherwise only in *Lavra*, I, no. 35.7–8 (from 1071), in an adverbial form.

property was exempted from the *kephalaia* levied on ordinary property but not levied on pronoiai. My only reservation is that I would find this interpretation more palatable if the passage read "(the emperor grants the Church) the *kephalaia* owed from the (properties) except for pronoiai *and other privileged properties.*" Pronoiai, indeed, were not the only properties whose holders enjoyed tax exemption. Yet Angold's interpretation is reasonable.

Nevertheless, it is possible to construct an explanation of our passage that takes into account the fact that there *were* pronoiai in the area of Smyrna, and that, in fact, explains why the passage refers to pronoiai at all. Because the document notes that the Great Church held villages, it unquestionably held at least two types of possessions: properties it owned outright, from which it received the rents or the harvests, depending on how it chose to exploit them, and the properties and persons of paroikoi, from which it received taxes and corvée services.

But let us suppose that, because of the disruptions in property possession caused by the Latin Conquest, or for other reasons, some of the Church's private property had been conferred in pronoia. The Church still owned such property but the taxes (*kephalaia*) due on such property had been granted to pronoia holders (or the Church still technically owned the propery but the property was held by pronoia holders). The emperor decided against dispossessing any of the pronoia holders in the area of Smyrna of their claims to these taxes, so he stipulated in this document that the Church no longer had to pay the *kephalaia* on all of its properties in the area, *except the* kephalaia *that had been granted to pronoia holders.* Thus, we can translate the key passage as "(the Church is granted) the *kephalaia* given from (or by) the (properties) outside of pronoiai." In other words, it was granted the *kephalaia* on those properties it owned, except for those that had been granted as pronoiai.

Such an interpretation, while hardly certain, does take into account both the text and the situation in the Smyrna area. If it is valid, it is an interesting example of the emperor's attempt to accommodate the interests of two kinds of privileged property holders: the Great Church and local pronoia holders.

Appendix 2: A translation of the praktikon of Pergamenos and Pharisaios for Michael Saventzes (1321)

The following is an English translation of a revised praktikon for the soldier Michael Saventzes *[8.11]*. While the translation itself is quite literal, paragraph breaks have been added for clarity.

Since we have been ordered by our mighty and holy lord and emperor to make an assessor's equalization and reestablishment [*apographiken exisosin kai apokatastasin*] in the theme of the God-saved city of Thessaloniki, that is, of the properties of the archons of the kin of our mighty and holy lord and emperor and of the other archons – ecclesiastic, monastic, military, of archons, *chrysovoullata* – and the rest, and to confer upon each his proper quantity, finding among other [things] the oikonomia held by *kyr* Michael Saventzes of the Thessalonian *mega allagion*, we confer this upon him from the mercy of our mighty and holy lord and emperor toward us, which has the following:

In the *katepanikion* of Akros [i.e., Longos] in the village of Psalis:

Nicholas Photenos has a wife Anna, sons Demetrios, Athanasios, and Lampetes, a daughter [*vacat*], a brother John, 1 ass, 100 goats, a vineyard in two parcels by purchase from Philippopolites of $1\frac{2}{3}$ modioi, and 30 modioi of land. 3 nomismata.

Michael, the son of Stamates Vardas, has a wife [*vacat*], a vineyard of $1\frac{2}{3}$ modioi, and 50 modioi of land. $1\frac{1}{3}$ nomismata.

In the same village from the oikonomia of Smyrnaios:

Gregory, the son of Michael Vechas, has a brother Nicholas, a sister-in-law by him Argyre, a son John, 30 goats, a vineyard of 1 modios, and 40 modioi of land. $1\frac{1}{2}$ nomismata.

In the village of Phournia:

Demetrios, the son of Modestos Tzykalas, has a wife Kale, sons Stamates and George, a daughter [*vacat*], 1 ox, 2 cows, 3 beehives, a vineyard of 1 modios. 1 nomisma.

In the village of Ourliakon from the oikonomia of the reverend monastery of Akapniou:

Demetrios, the son-in-law of George Pissyris, that is, Kometzianos, has a wife Kale, a son Michael, 1 ox, 2 cows, a garden of 2 modioi in which there are 2 pear trees. 1 nomisma.

Nicholas Nephaïtis, his son-in-law by a daughter, has a wife Anna, 1 cow, a vineyard from a dowry of 1½ modioi. ½ nomisma.

In the village of Adam from the oikonomia of the deceased *kavallarios* Serpes:

The widow Irene, wife of Niketas Diakonos, has a son Theodore, daughters Maria and [*vacat*], 1 ox, 1 cow, 1 ass, a vineyard of 5 modioi, and 50 modioi of land. 3 nomismata.

The widow Martinia has a daughter Kale, 1 cow, a vineyard of 1½ modioi. ⅔ nomismata.

Land [*ge*] in the region of Tzykandyles, which he held previously, of 800 modioi, at 16 nomismata, in lieu of *oikoumenon* 10⅔ nomismata. Another land in Ourliakon from that which was taken away from Provatas by reason of *perisseia*, of 600 modioi at 12 nomismata, in lieu of *oikoumenon* at 8 nomismata. Another land in Apostolitai in the place of Kamara from that which was taken away from Michael Keroulas by reason of *perisseia*, of 300 modioi at 6 nomismata, in lieu of *oikoumenon* at 4 nomismata. Given to him in Ourliakon is the *exaleimmatikon* vineyard of Vranas which has a vineyard of 1½ modioi, in lieu of *oikoumenon* at ⅓ nomisma.

In all, the *oikoumenon* [is] 35 nomismata.

For the *opheleia* of the livestock 1 nomisma, for the *choirodekateia* and *melissoennomion* 1 nomisma. Another land, which he held previously, adjacent to that which was given in lieu of *oikoumenon*, of 400 modioi, in Tzykandyles, at 8 nomismata. For the *ennomion* and the *linovrocheion* of the two villages, Psalis and Phournia, from entering and departing animals, 5 nomismata, as the deceased Smyrnaios previously held these, and from the lake of Souda, 20 nomismata.

Altogether, these [are] 35 nomismata, so as to make the whole 70 nomismata, which [Saventzes] ought to hold and enjoy and to take for himself the income from them, and to demand the *oikoumenon* through two payments yearly, that is, half in September and the other half in March, and to receive for the *oikomodion* 1 modios of grain for each 3 hyperpyra [of *telos*], for the *oinometrion* 1 measure of local wine per 1 hyperpyron [of *telos*], corvées for 12 days per year, as the paroikos is able, and the customary three *kaniskia* per year. For this our present praktikon is signed as customary and guaranteed by a lead seal, which is given to the distinguished *kyr* Michael Saventzes in surety in the month of February, indiction 4.

[signed] + The servants of our mighty and holy lord and emperor, the assessors of the theme of Thessaloniki, *sevastoi* Constantine Pergamenos and George Pharisaios +

Appendix 3: A translation of the praktikon of the *protokynegos* John Vatatzes for the *eparchos* Michael Monomachos (1333)

This is an English translation of a revised praktikon for the *eparchos* Michael Monomachos, issued after the emperor Andronikos III Palaiologos had granted him hereditary rights over a *posotes* of 50 hyperpyra from his oikonomia *[8.14]*. As in Appendix 2, while the translation itself is quite literal, paragraph breaks have been added for clarity.

Since our mighty and holy lord and emperor ordered through a divine and august chrysobull that the *pansevastos eparchos kyr* Michael Monomachos, *oikeios* to his mighty and holy majesty, should have from his oikonomia, which he has on the Strymon, a *posotes* of 50 hyperpyra as his hereditary property and without service, according to the directive of such divine and august chrysobull such quantity of 50 hyperpyra was conferred upon him through the present document with a seal [*sigilliodes gramma*], which [*posotes*] has the following:

Village of Chantax:

George Theophylaktos has Eudokia, a daughter Anna, *oikoumenon*, 1 yoke of oxen, 1 cow, a *monoxylon* [a type of boat], a vineyard of 2 modioi, and land of 32 modioi. Tax: 1 hyperpyron.

His brother John has Eudokia, sons Michael and Theodore, *oikoumenon*, 1 ox, 1 cow, a *monoxylon*, a vineyard of 1 $^1/_2$ modioi, and land of 24 modioi. Tax: 1 hyperpyron.

His other brother Nikephoros has Paraskeue, son Leo, *oikoumenon*, 1 yoke of oxen, 1 cow, 3 pigs, a *monoxylon*, a vineyard of 1 modios, and land of 23 modioi. Tax: 1 hyperpyron.

His other brother Theophylaktos has Eudokia, son Michael, daughter-in-law by him Anna, *oikoumenon*, 1 yoke of oxen, 1 cow, 3 pigs, a *monoxylon*, a vineyard of 1 modios, and land of 25 modioi. Tax: $^1/_2$ hyperpyron.

George Italiotes has Anna, son John, 1 ox, 2 pigs, *oikoumenon*, a *monoxylon*, a vineyard of 1 modios, and land of 11 modioi. Tax: $^1/_2$ hyperpyron.

Nicholas Kontevos has Synadene, son Therianos, 1 ox, 1 cow, a *monoxylon*, *oikoumenon*, a vineyard of 1 modios, and land of 15 modioi. Tax: $^1/_2$ hyperpyron.

The widow Eudokia Kontovia has a son John, *oikoumenon*, 1 ox, 2 pigs, a *monoxylon*, a vineyard of 2 modioi, and land of 25 modioi. Tax: 1 hyperpyron.

Theodore Podaritzes has Euphemia, 1 ox, 1 cow, *oikoumenon*, 3 pigs, a *monoxylon*, a vineyard of 1 modios, and land of 15 modioi. Tax: $\frac{1}{2}$ hyperpyron.

Michael Saveres has Eudokia, daughters Kale and Maria, 1 yoke of oxen, 1 cow, 2 pigs, *oikoumenon*, a *monoxylon*, a vineyard of 2 modioi, and land of 36 modioi. Tax: 1 hyperpyron.

George Tzyvinis has Kale, a son, *oikoumenon*, a yoke of oxen, 1 cow, 2 pigs, a *monoxylon*, a vineyard of 3 modioi, and land of 25 modioi. Tax: $1\frac{1}{2}$ hyperpyra.

Constantine Saveres has Eudokia, *oikoumenon*, 1 ox, 3 pigs, a *monoxylon*, a vineyard of 4 modioi, and land of 22 modioi. Tax: $1\frac{1}{2}$ hyperpyra.

Theodore Tzytzymas has a mother Kale, *oikoumenon*, a *monoxylon*, a vineyard of 2 modioi, and land of 26 modioi. Tax: 1 hyperpyron.

Peter Tzytzymas has Maria, sons Theodore and [vacat], *oikoumenon*, 1 ox, 1 cow, a *monoxylon*, a vineyard of 2 modioi, and land of 25 modioi. Tax: $\frac{1}{2}$ hyperpyron.

Irene, the widow of Nikephoros has a son Thomas, *oikoumenon*, 3 pigs, a *monoxylon*, a vineyard of 3 modioi, and land of 25 modioi. Tax: 1 hyperpyron.

The widow Kale Photeine has a grandson John, *oikoumenon*, 2 oxen, a cow, 3 pigs, a *monoxylon*, a vineyard of 4 modioi, and land of 30 modioi. Tax: $1\frac{1}{2}$ hyperpyra.

John Vlachos has Maria, a son Constantine, a daughter [vacat], 1 ox, 1 cow, 2 pigs, *oikoumenon*, a *monoxylon*, a vineyard of 4 modioi, and land of 30 modioi. Tax: $1\frac{1}{2}$ hyperpyra.

Nicholas Tempeliakos has Irene, a daughter Kale, a son-in-law by her John, *oikoumenon*, a *monoxylon*, a vineyard of 3 modioi, and land of 25 modioi. Tax: $1\frac{1}{2}$ hyperpyra.

George Pangkalos has a mother Chryse, a brother Nicholas, *oikoumenon*, 1 ox, 1 cow, 3 pigs, a *monoxylon*, a vineyard of 4 modioi, and land of 16 modioi. Tax: $1\frac{1}{2}$ hyperpyra.

John Maroulas has Euphrosyne, a brother Xenos, a sister-in-law by him Eudokia, a nephew Pepisomenos, *oikoumenon*, 2 pigs, a *monoxylon*, a vineyard of 2 modioi, and land of 25 modioi. Tax: 1 hyperpyra.

Michael, the brother-in-law [or son-in-law] of Father George, has Maria, *oikoumenon*, 2 pigs, a *monoxylon*, a vineyard of 1 modios, and land of 24 modioi. Tax: $\frac{1}{2}$ hyperpyron.

The village of Nesion:

Photeinos has Maria, a daughter Tycha, a son-in-law by her Chrysos, 1 ox, 1 cow, an ass, a *monoxylon*, an *hypoteles* [literally, "beyond the tax"] vineyard of 2 modioi, and land of 3 modioi. Tax: 1 hyperpyron.

Alieus Linardos has Theodora, a son Constantine, a daughter Constantia, 1 cow, 2 pigs, a *monoxylon*, and land of 3 modioi. Tax: 1 hyperpyron.

Constantine Vagianos has Kale, sons Vagianos and Michael, 1 ox, 1 cow, a *monoxylon*, a *hypoteles* vineyard of 5 modioi, and land of 70 modioi. Tax: $1\frac{1}{2}$ hyperpyra.

George Ortholaginos has Kale, sons Constantine and John, 1 ox, 1 cow, 2 pigs, a *monoxylon*, land of 70 modioi. Tax: $1\frac{1}{2}$ hyperpyra.

The widow Andronikia has sons John and Karvonos, and land of 3 modioi. Tax: 1 hyperpyron.

The widow Kyriako has sons Athanasios and Kyriakos, 1 cow, a *monoxylon*, a *hypoteles* vineyard of 2 modioi, and land of 70 modioi. Tax: $1\frac{1}{2}$ hyperpyra.

Servos has Chymeutes, sons George and John, a vineyard in Chantax of 1 modios, a *monoxylon*, and land of 36 modioi. Tax: $\frac{1}{2}$ hyperpyron.

In all, the line tax [*stoichikon telos*, i.e., tax on the *stichoi*, "lines"] of the inscribed is $27\frac{1}{2}$ hyperpyra [actually, 28 hyperpera].

Given to him is the land of Chantax called Karyanitissa, being 400 modioi in several parcels, and the [land] of Nesion, it being 150 modioi, of which 50 is arable and 100 is unplowed and marshy; and on the far side of the river near the public road, a garden plot of 25 modioi; the whole being 575 modioi, in lieu of *oikoumenon* at 7 hyperpyra. And the whole *oikoumenon* [is] $34\frac{1}{2}$ hyperpyra.

The *exaleimmata* are these: in Chantax, a dry vineyard, that is, of Varangka and of Stamatikos, 4 modioi, at $\frac{1}{2}$ hyperpyron. Similarly, the [*exaleimmata*] of Nesion, that is, of Skyloïoannes, of Goulitzas, of Ormisas, of Savvas, of Father Constantine, and of Provoneangkos, at 4 hyperpyra. For the *zeugaratikion* of the inscribed paroikoi, $9\frac{1}{2}$ hyperpyra. For their *kaniskia*, *choirodekateia* and *aer*, without the three charges of the *phonos*, the *parthenophthoria*, and treasure trove, 2 hyperpyra. In all, the [things] of the *exaleimmata* [are] 16 hyperpyra, so that the whole becomes $50\frac{1}{2}$ hyperpyra.

Similarly, I confer upon him the entire fishing of Choudena and of Nevoliani, which earlier Chantax enjoyed and Kassandrenos owned and possessed as property for a time, at 18 hyperpyra. For the fishing on such property of Chantax worked by *monoxyla* from outside, and for the shipping dock, 50 hyperpyra, in lieu of *oikoumenon* $33^1/_2$ hyperpyra. Which ought to be held and enjoyed, and to be paid the whole, entire income from them according to the order of the holy, divine, and august chrysobull furnished to him, as hereditary and without service. For the sake of this our present document with a seal is signed as customary and guaranteed by a lead seal, [and] is given to the distinguished *pansevastos eparchos* Monomachos in surety in the month of January, indiction 1.–These things are had by signature

[signed] + The servant of our mighty and holy lord and emperor, John Vatatzes, the *protokynegos*.

The present copy also examined and found in everything identical to the prototype, and signed by me in surety.
[signed] + The humble bishop of Skopelos and Skiathos, Theodoulos +

Appendix 4: A note on fiscal privileges

In this book my discussion of secondary taxes and charges paid in specie is based on the traditional view among scholars that when privileged landholders such as monasteries and pronoia holders were exempted of particular secondary taxes and charges (*opheleia*, *aer*, the various *ennomia*, etc.), these taxes and charges were paid to the privileged landholder by whomever owed them. If the landholder's paroikoi owed these charges, they paid them to the privileged landholder; if other peasants or other landowners owed these charges, they paid them to the privileged landholder; and if the tax or charge was levied on something that was owned by or granted to the privileged landholder (such as domain land), in this case alone the *posotes* of the item in the landholder's praktikon simply represented the amount of tax exempted and not any actual payment to the landholder. In other words, the landholder replaced the state in the collection of these taxes and charges, just as the landholder replaced the state in the collection of the *telos* of the paroikoi which the landholder held.[1]

This understanding has always made the analysis of praktika a messy business. Some of the *posotetes* listed in a praktikon represented a real income for the landholder and were paid to him by his paroikoi, or some other group of peasants, or by another landholder, while other *posotetes* in the praktikon represented only the amount of fiscal revenue (tax) that the fisc was forsaking for the benefit of the privileged landholder, and the actual income derived from the item associated with the *posotes* depended on how the landholder organized the exploitation of the item.

However, in recent years this view has been challenged. In 1994 the editors of the third volume of the *Actes d'Iviron* argued that it was the landholders themselves who theoretically owed these secondary taxes and charges in the first place – not their paroikoi or anyone else. Consequently, when the landholder was "granted" any of these taxes and charges, it was merely a tax exemption, something that produced no real revenue for the landholder.

[1] E.g., *Lavra*, IV, 171; *Esphigménou*, p. 101; A. Laiou-Thomadakis, *Peasant Society in the Late Byzantine Empire* (Princeton, 1977), 149, 181; and Oikonomides, *Fiscalité*, 76 (in regard to the *ennomion*).

These exempted secondary taxes and charges were simply taxes and charges that the landholder did not have to pay. The editors' reasoning for this conclusion is as follows:

(i) In one set of praktika (*Iviron*, nos. 70, 75, 79) all of the taxes and charges listed in the praktika are grouped into two categories: the *oikoumenon*, which is the combined *tele* of all the paroikos households, and the "*exaleimmata*," which is everything else: taxes on the monastery's property (land and items such as mills), rights (such as dock or fishing rights), and all the secondary taxes and charges such as the *opheleia*, the *aer*, and the *melissoennomion*. The editors argued that the monastery received the *oikoumenon* and was exempted of the "*exaleimmata*." Because the exemption of the tax on the monastery's land was not real revenue for the monastery, they concluded that the secondary taxes and charges were simply an exemption as well and not a real revenue for the monastery.

(ii) The only payments which the praktika specify that paroikoi were to make in specie was the *oikoumenon* (their individual household *telos*). Therefore, paroikoi were not liable for secondary taxes and charges paid in specie such as the *opheleia* and the various *ennomia*.

(iii) Whenever the *aer* is mentioned in the praktika for monasteries, it is the monastery that is exempted from the charge.[2]

I disagree with their view.

(i) The three praktika cited by the editors all deal with the same set of properties held by Iviron. Much of their wording is identical. Thus it is really only the first of the three – issued in 1301 by Demetrios Apelmene – that is of importance. The other two praktika simply copy the structure, principles, and phrasing of his praktikon. In any event, this clear-cut division of taxes and charges into the *oikoumenon* and the "*exaleimmata*" is found only in these praktika. As for why Apelmene used the term *exaleimma* in such an unusual way, I would point out two things: First, Apelmene does tend to use technical terms in "expansive" senses: the monastery of Vatopedi has a "pronoia" in one document *[7.11]*; and in one draft of a document a man holds an oikonomia, while in a second draft he holds a "pronoia" *[7.8]*. Second, perhaps Apelmene was thinking of one of the original senses of the verb from which the term *exaleimma* is derived, *exaleipho* "to strike off a tax list." Possibly, "*exaleimmata*" in his 1301 praktikon are taxes, charges, and properties "struck off the tax list," that is, exempted. In any event, nothing

[2] *Iviron*, III, p. 26 and note 145. Their view was adopted by A. Laiou, "The Agrarian Economy, Thirteenth–Fifteenth Centuries," *EHB*, I, 349, and implicitly by K. Smyrlis, *La fortune des grands monastères byzantins* (Paris, 2006), 209–11.

about the use of the term "*exaleimma*" in this praktikon tells us upon whom the burden of the secondary taxes and charges normally fell.

Yet two other documents use *exaleimma* in an odd context: two of the seven praktika I discussed extensively in chapter 8 *[8.13] [8.14]*. In one section of the 1323 praktikon for Basil Berilas (see Table 8.2), 2 hyperpyra for the *ennomion* of acorns and the *mandriatikon* are added to 2 hyperpyra for the *ampelopakton* and to 1 hyperpyron for several *exaleimmatika* vineyard parcels to produce a total of 5 hyperpyra, which is then assessed *anti-oikoumenou* at 3⅓ hyperpyra. Why are these three taxes linked together? The answer may be very simple. The praktikon states that he held these three items earlier (προκατεῖχεν), and so the *apographeus* may have grouped them together for no other reason than this.[3]

In the 1333 praktikon for Michael Monomachos an even stranger passage appears:

> The *exaleimmata* are these: in Chantax, a dry vineyard [*chersampelon*], that is, of Varangka and of Stamatikos, 4 modioi, at ½ hyperpyron. Similarly, the [*exaleimmata*] of Nesion, that is, of Skyloïoannes, of Goulitzas, of Ormisas, of Savvas, of Father Constantine and of Provoneangkos, at 4 hyperpyra. For the *zeugaratikion* of the inscribed paroikoi, 9½ hyperpyra. For their *kaniskion*, the *choirodekateia*, and the *aer*, without the three charges of the *phonos*, the *parthenophthoria*, and treasure trove, 2 hyperpyra. In all, the [things] of the *exaleimmata* [are] 16 hyperpyra . . . .[4]

The passage begins normally. Monomachos holds an *exaleimmatikon* dry vineyard and what appears to be the *exaleimmatikai staseis* of a number of peasants from the village of Nesion. But then the *apographeus* adds a number of taxes: *zeugaratikion*, *kaniskion*, *choirodekateia*, and *aer*. And then totals all of this up as the "*exaleimmata*."

Was this perhaps the collection of items on which Monomachos was exempted of paying taxes? Clearly not, because immediately following this passage the *apographeus* confers on Monomachos "the entire fishing of Choudena and of Nevoliani." Was the *apographeus* simply trying to fill up a category called "*exaleimmata*" with whatever he could find? This is truly perplexing, whether one accepts the Iviron editors' thesis or the traditional interpretation of these charges that I favor.

3 P. Schreiner, "Zwei unedierte Praktika aus der zweiten Hälfte des 14. Jahrhunderts," *JÖB* 19 (1970), 38, lines 20–22: "for the *exaleimmatika* vineyards there, 1 nomisma; for the *ampelopakton* from his *xenoparoikoi* and the paroikoi of Kerameus, 2 nomismata; for *ennomion* of acorns and *mandriatikon* of the area of the village itself, 2 hyperpyra; as he held earlier the things of the *exaleimmatika* vineyards, of the *ampelopakton*, and of the *ennomion*, 5 nomismata, *anti-oikoumenou* 3⅓ hyperpyra."

4 *Zographou*, no. 29.84–92.

(ii) It is a fact, as the Iviron editors point out, that those praktika which specify that the paroikoi are to make their payments in specie to the privileged landholder twice a year mention only the *oikoumenon*, and not the other charges that appear in the praktika such as the *opheleia* and the various *ennomia*. This is a good argument. The only problem with it is that only a few *apographeis* in a relatively narrow time frame include this clause about paying the *oikoumenon* twice a year in their praktika. It is used by Demetrios Apelmene, by Constantine Pergamenos and George Pharisaios (as in the praktika for Saventzes and Maroules *[8.11] [8.12]*), and by Pharisaios alone (as in the praktikon for Basil Berilas *[8.13]*). It is also used by Nicholas Kampanos and Demetrios Spartenos, though they leave out the word *oikoumenon*.[5] On the other hand, it is not used by the unknown *apographeus* of the praktikon for Kallinikos, by the *protokynegos* John Vatatzes (as in the praktikon for Michael Monomachos), or by Michael Papylas (as in the praktikon for John Margarites). Nor is it used by Alexios Amnon, by Tryphon Kedrenos, by George Strategos and Nicholas Theologites, by John Oinaiotes and Theodore Aaron, by Constantine Makrenos, or by John Kryvitziotes.[6] Nor is it used by the team of *apographeis*, Kounales, Kontenos, and Kalognomos, unless they were revising an earlier praktikon which uses the clause.[7] In fact the clause seems to appear in early praktika, when monasteries were holding simply paroikoi and property, without any of the secondary charges like the *ennomia*, then continued to appear when monasteries started to receive these secondary charges, and then disappears, perhaps because *apographeis* realized the phrase was too restrictive. Unfortunately, the lack of many praktika from before 1300 makes this only a hypothesis.

(iii) I do not understand why the Iviron editors mention the charge called the *aer*, but it appears that they are arguing that the *aer*, if it was not exempted, would have been levied on the privileged landholders themselves and not their paroikoi. This is demonstrably untrue. A number of fifteenth-century acts state clearly that privileged monasteries received the *aer* and various *ennomia* from their paroikoi. For example, an act from 1409 specifies

[5] Apelmene: *Vatopédi*, I, no. 30 (1301). Kampanos and Spartenos: *Iviron*, III, no. 59 (1262). Also used by an unknown *apographeus*: *Esphigménou*, no. 7 (1283–84 or 1298–89).

[6] Amnon: *Zographou*, no. 53 (1279); Kedrenos: *Iviron*, III, no. 74 (1316); Strategos and Theologites: *Lavra*, II, nos. 104 and 105 (both from 1317); Oinaiotes and Aaron: *Lavra*, II, no. 112 (from 1321?); Makrenos: *Vatopédi*, II, no. 81 (1338) and *Xénophon*, no. 25 (1338); Kryvitziotes: *Vatopédi*, II, no. 98 (1348).

[7] Kounales, Kontenos, and Kalognomos: *Xénophon*, no. 12 (1318), but *Esphigménou*, no. 14 (1318), and cf. *Esphigménou*, no. 7 (1283–84 or 1298–89 composed by an unknown *apographeus*; *Iviron*, III, no. 75 (1318), and cf. *Iviron*, III, no. 70 (1301).

explicitly that the inscribed paroikoi were to render their *telos* to pronoiars and the customary corvées and a number of specific charges uncluding the *melissoennomion* and *aer* to the monastery of Docheiariou *[9.3]*.[8]

One could respond that fifteenth-century documents cannot shed much light on earlier practices, and to some extent this is true. So I will cite an eleventh-century document. In the will of the nun Maria from 1098 she ordered that "at the time of my death, the paroikoi of all my properties be kept uncharged and untaxed from all the taxes [*telesmata*] which they pay to me today, I speak of the *oikomodion*, *zeugologion*, *dekata* [i.e., *ennomia*] of their animals, and all their other annual taxes."[9]

In my view, when a document states that a monastery or other privileged landholder was exempted from the *aer* or any other charge that was not connected to a specific property (such as a mill), this generally means that it was not required to render to the fisc a charge that it collected from someone else, usually its paroikoi but others as well.[10]

It is certain to me that the editors of the third volume of the *Actes d'Iviron* are incorrect about the meaning of the *posotetes* attached to the secondary taxes and charges found in the praktika. Compare two passages involving the *ennomion*, the charge for allowing animals to wander on pasturage. In his praktikon Basil Berilas received the *ennomion* of the animals of his paroikoi. According to the Iviron editors this meant that if Berilas was an ordinary landowner who enjoyed no tax exemption, he would have had to pay this pasturage charge for animals his paroikoi, not he, owned. It is difficult to imagine that a landholder would not have tried his best to pass this charge on to his paroikoi.

But let us go a step further and consider a passage from the praktikon for Michael Saventzes: "For the *ennomion* and the *linovrocheion* of the two villages, Psalis and Phournia, from the incoming and outgoing animals, 5 nomismata" (*Xénophon*, no. 15.24–25). For the thesis of the Iviron

[8] *Dionysiou*, nos. 17 and 18, make the same point.

[9] *Iviron*, II, no. 47.49–50. The document the Iviron editors cite as evidence, a chrysobull of Michael VIII from 1259 (*Iviron*, III, nos. 58.45), does free a monastery of *aer*, as well as of nearly two dozen other charges, including corvées (*angareia*). Given that nowhere else in the document are the monastery's paroikoi freed of corvées toward the state, I would think the passage is more likely related to demands that fiscal officials might impose on the monastery's paroikoi rather than on the monks themselves. The other document cited by the editors simply copied the same long list of exemptions verbatim: *Iviron*, no. 72.64.

[10] Indeed, an act from 1418 (*Docheiariou*, no. 56.3–4) notes that the monks of Docheiariou held one of the villages included in the act from 1409 free from a number of charges including the *melissoennomion*, yet from the 1409 act we know that the paroikoi of the monastery paid these charges to the monastery.

editors to be correct, Saventzes had to be given something for which he was exempted of the tax. In the case of the *linovrocheion*, it is possible that is exactly what happened. But what about the *ennomion* and those animals? Was he given all the livestock in the two villages? Of course not. Was he given all the peasants in the two villages as paroikoi and owed the *ennomion* on their animals? No, he held three paroikos households in Psalis and one in Phournia (and their total telos was $7\frac{1}{6}$ hyperpyra). Was he given all the pasture land in the two villages? No, his praktikon lists *ge* and a small vineyard, but no pasture land. The thesis of the Iviron editors must be discarded. The *ennomion* was a charge that burdened, in Saventzes' case, all of the peasants of Psalis and Phournia, and it was paid collectively for the right to pasture their animals on state land in the vicinity of their villages. And since the charge for the *ennomion* was simply lumped together with the charge for the ingoing and outgoing animals and the *linovrocheion*, these charges must have provided Saventzes with a real income as well. In this case, then, the *linovrocheion*, as listed in Saventzes' praktikon, was not a piece of property like a vineyard but rather a charge, a fixed charge that the peasants of the two villages paid to the state, and now to Saventzes, for the right to use a local flax-retting area. Combining the three charges, Saventzes received a real income of five nomismata. Similarly, Berilas' paroikoi owed an *ennomion* for their animals. Instead of paying it to the state, they paid it to Berilas.

But let me beat a dead horse. In the praktika for Saventzes, Maroules, Berilas, and Kallinikos, their paroikoi were obligated to give them, in kind, three *kaniskia* per year (little payments of foodstuffs). However, in the praktikon for Monomachos the *kaniskion* is a monetized charge and included with the *choirodekateia* (another kind of *ennomion*) and the *aer*, for a combined posotes of 2 hyperpyra. Certainly the Iviron editors and I would agree that the *kaniskion*, when it was levied *in kind*, was paid by each paroikos household to state officials, unless the lord of these paroikoi was granted the right to keep the *kaniskia* for himself. Privileged monasteries and pronoia holders, among others, were granted this right. But according to the thesis of the Iviron editors, when the *kaniskion* was levied *in specie*, it was not a charge that a privileged landholder received from his paroikoi. Rather, it was a charge that the landholder himself owed the state, unless the charge was exempted. And so, while Saventzes, Maroules, Berilas, and Kallinikos received the *kaniskia* three times a year from their paroikoi, Monomachos received nothing from his paroikoi. No *kaniskia* in kind and no two hyperpyra. This interpretation is illogical. *Kaniskia* were paid to the state, whether in kind or in specie, by peasants. If the peasants were paroikoi, their lord received the *kaniskia*, whether in kind or in specie. Monomachos received the two hyperpyra directly from his peasants, and this was not just for the *kaniskion*, but for the *choirodekateia* and *aer* (other secondary charges) as well. (John Margarites' praktikon does not mention these *kaniskia* at all. Indeed, it was up to him to try to collect it from his peasants.)

Appendix 5: The chrysobulls for Dragon and for Manuel Angelos Patrikios

Because there are so few explicit statements regarding the characteristics of the pronoia grant, comparisons between different types of imperial grants are very useful when attempting to reconstruct the characteristics of the pronoia grant. Two important documents in this regard are found in the archives of the Hilandar monastery. They are among the very few documents that (a) specifically exempt property granted from "service," (b) refer to a property grant as a reward, and (c) grant someone the right to alienate his property grant. One is a chrysobull issued for a man named Dragon and the other a chrysobull issued for a man named Manuel Angelos Patrikios, neither of whom are known from any other source.

The document for Dragon bears the date 1324 and was ostensibly issued by Andronikos II. Because of the zeal "which he had displayed in the services" of the empire, the emperor granted Dragon and his heirs the *zeugelateion* of Melintzianis in hereditary tenure (*kata logon gonikotetos*). He had the right to improve, sell, give as dowry, donate to a religious foundation, and transmit the property to his legitimate children, heirs, and successors, who would hold it in the same way and without service (*ektos douleias*).[1]

This chrysobull is nearly identical, in form and wording, to the chrysobull of Andronikos II for the benefit of Manuel Angelos Patrikios. While Dragon was given the *zeugelateion* of Melintzianis, Patrikios was given the *zeugelateion* of Ptelea on the Strymon consisting of nine *proskathemenoi* and 6,600 modioi of land. The terms of the concession to Patrikios are identical to those for Dragon. One of the few significant differences in the grants is that the chrysobull for Patrikios suggests that his father had held the *zeugelateion* and so, unlike Dragon's grant, this was a grant of additional rights over a previously held property.[2]

1 *Chilandar*, ed. Petit, no. 96. Kazhdan, *Agrarnye otnošenija*, 220, and B. Gorjanov, *Pozdnevizantijskij feodalizm* (Moscow, 1962), 133, both wrote that Dragon held this property prior to the 1324 concession (i.e., the grant of hereditary rights was an additional concession), but nothing in the text of the act supports this. Gorjanov also claimed this grant was a pronoia. By 1351 this property may have ended up in the hands of the monastery of Iviron: see *Iviron*, IV, p. 15 note 107.

2 *Chilandar*, ed. Petit, no. 23.

Some scholars have questioned the authenticity of the Patrikios act.[3] Among other irregularities, the world year (6814 = 1305/6) and indiction year of the document (11, which corresponds, for example, with 1312/13) do not agree. Further, the document implies that Ptelea was one of the properties that Patrikios held previously and his father had held before him (the emperor calls it "his" *zeugelateion*). If Ptelea had already passed from father to son, why would Patrikios ask to hold it *kata logon gonikotetos*? As for a motive for the forgery, in 1361 Tsar Stefan Uroš confirmed the donation of a village on the Strymon called Patrikijevo or the "patrimony of Patrikios" (*baština Patrikijeva*) to Hilandar. If Patrikijevo is Ptelea, then it seems likely that someone in Hilandar created this document to replace a lost document in order to ensure that Hilandar could hold the property tax-free.[4]

The act for Dragon is equally problematic. The first few lines of the chrysobull do not make sense. Here is an attempt at a translation, of the first few lines of the two chrysobulls:

Chrysobull for Dragon	Chrysobull for Patrikios
Since the *oikeios* to my majesty *kyr* Dragon along with his kin	Since the *oikeios* to my majesty *kyr* Manuel Angelos Patrikios
reported and asked	owns through chrysobulls and other ancient documents
the village around the theme of Serres as well as of the God-saved city of Thessaloniki, which in particular is mentioned in these, along with the service appropriate to him,	villages around both the theme of Serres as well as the God-saved city of Thessaloniki, which in particular are mentioned in these, along with the service appropriate to him, as his father held these, such Patrikios sought and asked my majesty,
that my majesty should grant the *zeugelateion* on the Strymon Melintzianis with what *proskathemenoi* it has	that my majesty should grant his *zeugelateion* on the Strymon Ptelea with its surrounding land and with what *proskathemenoi* it has [here the document lists the peasants by name]

(*cont.*)

[3] *Chilandar*, ed. Petit, no. 23 notes, and Dölger, *Regesten*, IV, no. 2294.

[4] S. Novaković, *Zakonski spomenici srpskih država srednjega veka* (Belgrade, 1912), 439. See M. Živojinović, "Od Ptelee do Patrika, prilog vizantijskoj i srpskoj diplomatici," *ZRVI* 34 (1995), 63–68, esp. 65, where the author argues that the chrysobull for Patrikios was created by the same scribe who produced the extant copy of the chrysobull granting hereditary possession of Melintzianis to Dragon which, in my view, is a forgery as well. The Patrikios family and/or Ptelea appear in quite a few documents from *Prodrome B* (nos. 27–31, 36, 142, 145, 146, 148) according to which Ptelea (or Ptelaia) is in the plain of Zichna near Kato Ouska: *Prodrome B*, no. 148.30.

Chrysobull for Dragon	Chrysobull for Patrikios
and make this *eleutheron*, and he should hold [it] along with all his heirs and successors without service and, further, in the manner of patrimony...	and make this *eleutheron*, and he should hold [it] along with all his heirs and successors without service and, further, in the manner of patrimony...

If the section with the underscoring is removed from the chrysobull for Dragon, the passage is comprehensible. Dölger (*Regesten*, IV, no. 2505) tried to make sense of the passage by suggesting that Melintzianis lay between the two themes, but it does not; it is on the Strymon. Further, it is suspicious that Melintzianis is called a "village" in the underscored section and a *zeugelateion* everywhere else in the document. And to what does "in these" in the underscored section refer?

We might conclude simply that the Dragon document is an inaccurate copy of an authentic document. However, a comparison of these first few lines with the first few lines of the chrysobull for Patrikios suggests that the initial passage from the Dragon document is difficult to understand for a reason. The parallel section of the Patrikios document is completely clear. Patrikios owned villages in both themes and owed "service," that is, fiscal obligations, for them. The ostensible purpose of Patrikios' request was to acquire tax exemption (*eleutheros*) for the *zeugelateion* Ptelea which he already held (hence, "his *zeugelateion*"), having received it from his father. In Dragon's case, however, there is no indication that Melintzianis was a prior possession. Evidently Dragon had no chrysobulls, so whoever composed the act had to remove the reference to "chrysobulls and other ancient documents" and change "villages" from the plural to the singular. Further, the chrysobull for Patrikios, because it claims that Patrikios held properties in both the themes of Thessaloniki and of Serres, notes that Patrikios should hold Ptelea "as the Thessalonians hold their *gonika* property" (line 34: ὡς οἱ Θεσσαλονικεῖς κατέχωσι τὰ γονικὰ αὐτῶν κτήματα). In an otherwise identical passage, this phrase does not appear in Dragon's chrysobull.

Thus, it would seem that the chrysobull for Dragon is a medieval forgery based on the Patrikios chrysobull, which itself is a forgery. While either document may well be an attempt to "fill a gap" in missing, legitimate documentation, neither is of much use to us as we seek to determine the characteristics of imperial grants.

Bibliography of works cited

This list does not include works listed in the Abbreviations, pp. xxvii–xxxiv.

Greek documents

Actes de Kastamonitou, ed. Nicolas Oikonomides. Archives de l'Athos IX. Paris: P. Lethielleux, 1978.

Actes de Philothée, ed. W. Regel, E. Kurtz, and B. Korablev. *VizVrem* 20 (1913), suppl. 1.

Actes du Pantocrator, ed. Vassiliki Kravari. Archives de l'Athos XVII. Paris: Centre National de la Recherche Scientifique and P. Lethielleux, 1991.

Alexander, Paul. "A Chrysobull of the Emperor Andronicus II Palaeologus in Favor of the See of Kanina in Albania." *Byz* 15 (1940–41), 167–207.

Arkadios Vatopedinos. "Ἁγιορειτικὰ ἀνάλεκτα ἐκ τοῦ ἀρχείου τῆς μονῆς Βατοπεδίου." *Γρηγόριος ὁ Παλαμᾶς* 2 (1918), 449–52; 3 (1919), 209–23, 326–39, 429–41.

Attaleiates, Michael and Paul Gautier, ed. *La diataxis de Michel Attaleiate*. Paris, 1981. Repr. from P. Gautier. "La diataxis de Michel Attaleiate." *REB* 39 (1981), 1–143. Also in K. Sathas, *Μεσαιωνικὴ Βιβλιοθήκη* (repr. Athens: Gregoriades, 1972), vol. 1.

Beihammer, Alexander, ed. *Griechische Briefe und Urkunden aus dem Zypern der Kreuzfahrerzeit: die Formularsammlung eines königlichen Sekretärs im Vaticanus palatinus graecus 367*. Nicosia: Kentro Epistemonikon Ereunon Kyprou, 2007.

Binon, S. *Les origines légendaires et l'histoire de Xéropotamou et de Saint-Paul de l'Athos*. Louvain: Bureaux du Muséon, 1942.

Brand, Charles, trans. "Two Byzantine Treatises on Taxation." *Traditio* 25 (1969), 35–60.

Byzantine Monastic Foundation Documents: A Complete Translation of the Surviving Founders' Typika *and Testaments*. Ed. John Thomas and Angela Constantinides Hero, with the assistance of Giles Constable. 5 vols. Washington, D.C.: Dumbarton Oaks Research Library and Collection, 2000.

Dölger, Franz. *Aus den Schatzkammern des Heiligen Berges. 115 Urkunden und 50 Urkundensiegel aus 10 Jahrhunderten*. 2 vols.: Textband, Tafelband. Munich: Münchener Verlag, 1948.

"Ein Chrysobull des Kaisers Andronikos II. für Theodoros Nomikopulos aus dem Jahre 1288." *Orientalia Christiana Perdiodica* 21 (1955), 58–62. Repr. in F. Dölger, *Παρασπορά*, 189–93. Ettal: Buch-Kunstverlag, 1961.

Facsimiles byzantinischer Kaiserurkunden. Munich, 1931.

"Neues zu Alexios Metochites und zu Theodoros Meliteniotes," 238–51. In *Miscellanea Giovanni Mercati III (Letterature e storia Bizantina)*. Studi e testi 123 (1946). Repr. in Dölger, *Byzantinische Diplomatik: 20 Aufsätze zum Urkundenwesen der Byzantiner*, 325–37. Ettal: Buch-Kunstverlag, 1956.

Sechs byzantinische Praktika des 14. Jahrhunderts für das Athoskloster Iberon. Abhandlungen der bayerischen Akademie der Wissenschaften, Phil.-hist. Kl., N.F. 28. Munich, 1949.

Eustratiades, S. "Τυπικὸν τῆς ἐν Κωνσταντινουπόλει Μονῆς τοῦ Ἁγίου μεγαλομάρτυρος Μάμαντος." *Ἑλληνικά* 1 (1928), 256–314.

Gautier, Paul. "Réquisitoire du patriarche Jean d'Antioche contre le charisticariat." *REB* 33 (1975), 77–132.

"Le typikon de la Théotokos Evergétis," *REB* 40 (1982), 5–101.

"Le typikon de la Théotokos Kécharitoménè." *REB* 43 (1985), 1–165.

"Le typikon du Christ Sauveur Pantokrator." *REB* 32 (1974), 1–145.

"Le typikon du sébaste Grégoire Pakourianos." *REB* 42 (1984), 5–145.

Gelzer, H. "Ungedruckte und wenig bekannte Bistümsverzeichnisse der orientalischen Kirche II." *BZ* 2 (1893), 22–72.

Gerland, E. *Histoire de la noblesse crétoise au moyen âge*. Paris, 1907. Extract from *Revue de l'Orient latin* 10 (1903–04), 172–247; 11 (1905–08), 7–115.

Goudas, Michael. "Βυζαντιακὰ ἔγγραφα τῆς ἐν Ἄθῳ ἱερᾶς μονῆς τοῦ Βατοπεδίου." *Ἐπετηρὶς Ἑταιρείας Βυζαντινῶν Σπουδῶν* 3 (1926), 113–34; 4 (1927), 211–48.

Gounaridis, Paris. "Σημείωμα γιά ένα (;) έγγραφο της Λεμβιώτισσας." *Σύμμεικτα* 11 (1997), 83–96.

Grégoire, Henri. "Un édit de l'empereur Justinien II." *Byz* 17 (1944–45), 119–25.

Heisenberg, August. *Aus der Geschichte und Literatur der Palaiologenzeit, Sitzungsberichte der bayerischen Akademie der Wissenschaften*, Philos.-philol. und hist. Kl., Abh. 10. Munich, 1920. Repr. in A. Heisenberg, *Quellen und Studien zur spätbyzantinischen Geschichte*, no. I. London: Variorum Reprints, 1973.

Hunger, H. and O. Kresten. *Das Register des Patriarchats von Konstantinopel, 1. Teil: Edition und Übersetzung der Urkunden aus den Jahren 1315–1331*. CFHB 19/1. Vienna: Verlag der Österreichischen Akademie der Wissenschaften, 1981.

Jalabert, Louis and René Mourtede. *Inscriptions grecques et latines de la Syrie*, II. Paris, 1939.

Kazhdan, A. P. "Dva pozdnevizantijskih akta iz sobranija P. I. Sevastjanova." *VizVrem*, n.s. 2 (1949), 313–21.

Kosmas Magistros and Günter Weiss, "Die Entscheidung des Kosmas Magistros über das Parökenrecht: Ein Beitrag zur Rechtsgrundlage bäuerlicher Ansiedlungen in Byzanz." *Byz* 48 (1978), 477–500.

Kougeas, S. "Χρυσόβουλλον Κωνσταντίνου τοῦ Παλαιολόγου πρωτόγραφον καὶ ἀνέκδοτον, δι' οὗ ἐπικυροῦντα δωρεαὶ εἰς τοὺς υἱοὺς τοῦ Γεμιστοῦ (1449)." *Ἑλληνικά* 1 (1928), 371–400.

Kravari, Vassiliki. "Nouveaux documents du monastère de Philothéou." *TM* 10 (1987), 261–356.

Lampros, Spyridon. "Ἀνέκδοτον χρυσόβουλλον Ἀλεξίου Γ' τοῦ Μεγάλου Κομνηνοῦ Αὐτοκράτορος Τραπεζοῦντος." *Νέος Ἑλληνομνήμων* 2 (1905), 187–98.

Παλαιολόγεια καὶ Πελοποννησιακά, 4 vols. Athens, 1912–30; repr. Athens: V. Gregoriades, 1972.

Laurent, Vitalien. "Deux chrysobulles inédits des empereurs de Trébizonde Alexis IV–Jean IV et David II." *Ἀρχεῖον Πόντου* 18 (1953), 241–78.

Lemerle, Paul. "Autour d'un prostagma inédit de Manuel II, L'aulé de Sire Guy à Thessalonique." *Silloge Bizantina in onore di Silvio Giuseppe Mercati = Studi Bizantini e Neoellenici* 9 (1957), 271–86. Repr. in Lemerle, *Le monde de Byzance*, no. XXIII.

"Un chrysobulle d'Andronic II Paléologue pour le monastère de Karakala." *Bulletin de Correspondence Hellénique* 60 (1936), 428–46. Repr. in Lemerle, *Le monde de Byzance*, no. XVII.

"Un praktikon inédit des archives de Karakala (janvier 1342) et la situation en Macédoine orientale au moment de l'usurpation de Cantacuzène." *Χαριστήριον εἰς Α. Κ. 'Ορλάνδον*, I, 278–98. Athens, 1965. Repr. in Lemerle, *Le monde de Byzance*, no. XVIII.

"Trois actes du despote d'Epire Michel II concernant Corfou connus en traduction latine." *Προσφορὰ εἰς Στ. Π. Κυριακίδην*, 405–26. Thessaloniki, 1953. Repr. in Lemerle, *Le monde de Byzance*, no. VI.

and Alexander Solovjev. "Trois chartes des souverains serbes conservées au monastère de Kutlumus." *Seminarium Kondakovianum* 11 (1940), 129–46. Repr. in Lemerle, *Le monde de Byzance*, no. XIX.

L(obel), E. "A Chrysobull of Alexios III Grand Komnenos." *Bodleian Quarterly Record* 3 (1921), 140–43.

McGeer, Eric, trans. *The Land Legislation of the Macedonian Emperors*. Mediaeval Sources in Translation 38. Toronto: Pontifical Institute of Mediaeval Studies, 2000.

Magdalino, Paul. "An Unpublished Pronoia Grant of the Second Half of the Fourteenth Century." *ZRVI* 18 (1978), 155–63

Manoussacas, M. "Une acte de donation à Sainte-Kyriakè de Mouchli (1457)." *TM* 8 (1981), 315–19.

Mavrommatis, Lenos. "La pronoia d'Alexis Comnène Raoul à Prévista." *Σύμμεικτα* 13 (1999), 203–27.

Mertzios, K. *Μνημεῖα Μακεδονικῆς Ἱστορίας*. Thessaloniki: Hetaireia Makedonikon Spoudon, 1947.

Meyer, P. *Die Haupturkunden für die Geschichte der Athosklöster*. Leipzig, 1894.

Millet, Gabriel. "Inscriptions byzantines de Mistra." *Bulletin de Correspondence Hellénique* 23 (1899), 97–156.

Mošin, Vladimir. "Akti iz svetogorskih arhiva." *Spomenik Srpske kraljevske akademije* 91 (1939), 153–260.

Mošin, Vladimir and A. Sovre. *Supplementa ad acta graeca Chilandarii.* Razred za zgodovinske in zemljepisne vede, za filozofijo in filologijo. Akademija znanosti in umetnosti v Ljubljani. Ljubljana: 1948.

Papazoglou, G. *Τυπικὸν Ἰσαακίου Ἀλεξίου Κομνηνοῦ τῆς Μονῆς Θεοτόκου τῆς Κοσμοσωτείρας (1151/52).* Komotini: Demokriteio Panepistemio Thrakes, 1994.

Peira. In Zepos, *JGR,* IV, 11–260.

Petit, Louis. "Le monastère de Notre-Dame de Pitié en Macédoine." *IRAIK* 6 (1900), 1–153.

"Typikon du monastère de la Kosmosotira près d'Aenos." *IRAIK* 13 (1908), 17–77.

Rhalles, G. and M. Potles. *Σύνταγμα τῶν θείων καὶ ἱερῶν κανόνων*, 6 vols. Athens, 1852–59.

Rigo, Antonio. "Lo *Horismòs* di Sinân Pascià, la Presa di Ioannina (1430) e la 'Lettera' del Sultano Murâd II." *Θησαυρίσματα* 28 (1998), 57–78.

Sathas, Constantine N. *Μνημεῖα Ἑλληνικῆς Ἱστορίας. Documents inédits relatifs à l'histoire de la Grèce au moyen âge.* 9 vols. Paris, 1880–90.

Schlumberger, Gustave. *Sigillographie de l'empire byzantine.* Paris, 1884.

Schreiner, Peter. "Zwei unedierte Praktika aus der zweiten Hälfte des 14. Jahrhunderts." *JÖB* 19 (1970), 33–49.

Smyrnakes, Gerasimos. *Τὸ Ἅγιον Ὄρος.* Athens, 1903.

Svoronos, Nicolas. *Les Novelles des empereurs Macédoniens concernant la terre et les stratiotes. Introduction, édition, commentaires.* Édition posthume et index établis par P. Gounaridis. Athens: Centre de Recherches Byzantines, F.N.R.S. and Fondation Culturelle de la Banque Nationale, 1994.

Synaxarium ecclesiae Constantinopolitane, Propylaeum ad Acta Sanctorum Novembris, ed. Hippolyte Delehaye. Brussels, 1902.

Trinchera, Francesco. *Syllabus graecarum membranarum.* Naples, 1865.

Tsiknopoullos, Ioannis. *Κυπριακὰ Τυπικά.* Πηγαὶ καὶ μελέται τῆς Κυπριακῆς Ἱστορίας, no. 2. Leukosia: Kentron Epistemonikon Ereunon, 1969.

Tzannetatos, Theseus, ed. *Τὸ πρακτικὸν τῆς Λατινικῆς Ἐπισκοπῆς Κεφαλληνίας τοῦ 1264 καὶ ἡ ἐπιτομὴ αὐτοῦ, Κριτικὴ ἔκδοσις αὐτῶν.* Athens, 1965.

Vatopedi no. III, 8; E.-A.-N. 30 (Dölger, *Regesten,* V, no. 3084): *prostagma* of John V Palaiologos and *paradotikon gramma* of Demetrios Phakrases (June 1377).

Vogel, K., ed. *Ein byzantinisches Rechenbuch des frühen 14. Jahrhunderts. Text, Übersetzung und Kommentar.* Wiener Byzantinistische Studien VI. Vienna: Österreichische Akademie der Wissenschaften, 1968.

Voïlas, Eustathios. S. Vryonis, trans. "The Will of a Provincial Magnate, Eustathios Boïlas (1059)." *Dumbarton Oaks Papers* 11 (1957), 263–77.

Xanthoudides, S. "Τὸ δίπλωμα (προβελέγιον) τῶν Σκορδιλῶν Κρήτης." *Ἐπετηρὶς Ἑταιρείας Κρητικῶν Σπουδῶν* 2 (1939), 299–312.

Zavorda Treatise. J. Karayannopulos, ed. "Fragmente aus dem Vademecum eines byzantinischen Finanzbeamten," 318–34. In *Polychronion: Festschrift Franz Dölger zum 75. Geburtstag.* Heidelberg: Winter, 1966.

Greek literary sources

Akindynos, Gregory. *Letters of Gregory Akindynos*, Greek text and English translation by Angela Constantinides Hero. Dumbarton Oaks Texts 7. CFHB 21. Washington, D.C.: Dumbarton Oaks Center for Byzantine Studies, 1983.

Akropolites, George. *Georgii Acropolitae Opera*, ed. A. Heisenberg. 2 vols. Leipzig: Teubner, 1903; repr. Stuttgart: Teubner, 1978.

The History, trans. Ruth Macrides. Oxford University Press, 2007.

Apokaukos, John, metropolitan of Naupaktos. A. Papadopoulos-Kerameus, ed. "Ἰωάννης Ἀπόκαυκος καὶ Νικήτας Χωνιάτης," 373–82. In *Τεσσαρακονταετηρὶς τῆς καθηγεσίας Κ. Σ. Κόντου*. Athens, 1909.

Nikos Bees, ed. "Unedierte Schriftstücke aus der Kanzlei des Johannes Apokaukos des Metropoliten von Naupaktos (in Aetolien)." *Byzantinisch-Neugriechische Jahrbücher* 21 (1971–74), 55–160. And E. Bee-Sepherle."Προσθῆκαι καὶ παρατηρήσεις." *Byzantinisch-Neugriechische Jahrbücher* 21 (1971–74), 161–243.

Sophrone Pétridès, ed. "Jean Apokaukos, lettres et autres documents inédits." *IRAIK* 14 (1909), 1–32.

Athanasios. *The Correspondence of Athanasius I Patriarch of Constantinople*, ed. and trans. Alice-Mary Talbot, Dumbarton Oaks Texts 3. CFHB 7. Washington, D.C.: Dumbarton Oaks Center for Byzantine Studies, 1975.

Attaleiates, Michael. *Michaelis Attaliotae Historia*, ed. W. Brunet de Presle. CSHB. Bonn, 1853.

Miguel Ataliates, Historia, ed. and trans. Immaculada Pérez Martín. Nueva Roma, 15. Madrid: Consejo Superior de Investigaciones Científicias, 2002.

Bessarion. Spyridon Lampros, ed. "Τρεῖς ἐπιστολαὶ τοῦ καρδιναλίου Βησσαρίωνος ἐν τῇ δημώδει γλώσσῃ." *Νέος Ἑλληνομνήμων* 5 (1908), 19–39.

Chomatenos, Demetrios. *Demetrii Chomateni Ponemata diaphora*, ed. Günter Prinzing. CFHB 38. Berlin and New York: W. de Gruyter, 2002.

Choniates, Michael, metropolitan of Athens. *Μιχαὴλ Ἀκομινάτου τοῦ Χωνιάτου τὰ σωζόμενα*, ed. Spyridion Lampros. 2 vols. Athens, 1879–80.

Choniates, Niketas. English trans. Harry J. Magoulias, *O City of Byzantium, Annals of Niketas Choniatēs*. Detroit: Wayne State University Press, 1984.

Chronicle of the Morea. John Schmitt, ed., London: Methuen, 1904; repr. Groningen: Bouma's Bockhuis, 1967.

Τὸ Χρονικὸν τοῦ Μορέως. Τὸ ἑλληνικὸν κείμενον κατὰ τὸν Κώδικα τῆς Κοπεγχάγης μετὰ συμπληρώσεων καὶ παραλλαγῶν ἐκ τοῦ Παρισινοῦ. Introduction, notes, and edition by Petros Kalonaros. Athens, 1940; repr. Hekate, 1989.

Chroniques étrangères relatives aux expéditions françaises pendant le XIIIe siècle, ed. J.-A. Buchon. Paris, 1875.

Constantine VII Porphyrogennetos. *Constantine Porphyrogenitus. De administrando imperio*, ed. Gy. Moravcsik, English trans. by R. J. H. Jenkins. New rev. edn. Dumbarton Oaks Texts 1. Washington, D.C., 1967.

Cronaca dei Tocco di Cefalonia di Anonimo, ed. and trans. Giuseppe Schirò. CFHB 10. Rome: Accademia nazionale dei Lincei, 1975.

Delehaye, Hippolyte. "Vita S. Pauli iunioris in monte Latro." *Analecta Bollandiana* 11 (1892), 5–74 and 136–82.

Doukas. *Ducas. Istoria Turco-Bizantină (1341–1462)*, ed. Vasile Grecu. Scriptores Byzantini I. Bucharest: Editura Academiei Republicii Populare Romîne, 1958.

Erbse, H. *Scholia Graeca in Homeri Iliadem (scholia vetera)*. 7 vols. Berlin: W. de Gruyter, 1969–88.

Eustathios, archbishop of Thessaloniki. *Eustathios of Thessaloniki, The Capture of Thessaloniki*, ed. and trans. John R. Melville Jones. Australian Association for Byzantine Studies, Byzantina Australiensia 8. Canberra, 1988.

Georgii monachi chronicon. Ed. C. de Boor. 2 vols. Leipzig: Teubner, 1904; repr. Stuttgart: Teubner, 1978 (with corrections by P. Wirth).

Glykas, Michael. *Michaelis Glycae Annales*, ed. I. Bekker. CSHB. Bonn, 1886.

Gregoras, Nikephoros. *Nikephoros Gregoras, Antirrhetika I*, ed. Hans-Veit Beyer. Wiener Byzantinistische Studien XII. Vienna Österreichische Akademie der Wissenschaften, 1976.

Nikephorus Gregoras, Rhomäische Geschichte, Historia Rhomaïke, German trans. by Jan Louis van Dieten. Stuttgart: Anton Hiersemann, 1973, 1979, 1988, 1994, 2003, 2007.

Gregory II Kyprios, patriarch of Constantinople. Ed. Sophronios Eustratiades, "Τοῦ σοφωτάτου καὶ λογιωτάτου καὶ οἰκουμενικοῦ πατριάρχου κύρου Γρηγορίου τοῦ Κυπρίου Ἐπιστολαί." *Ἐκκλησιαστικὸς Φάρος* 1 (1908), 77–108, 409–39; 2 (1908), 195–211; 3 (1909), 5–48, 281–96; 4 (1909), 5–29, 97–128; 5 (1910), 213–26, 339–52, 444–52, 489–500. Repr. in *Γρηγορίου τοῦ Κυπρίου οἰκουμενικοῦ πατριάρχου Ἐπιστολαὶ καὶ Μῦθοι*, ed. S. Eustratiades. Alexandria, 1910.

Hyrtakenos, Theodore. F. J. G. La Porte-du Theil, ed. "Notices et extraits d'un volume de la Bibliothèque Nationale, coté MCCIX parmi les manuscrits grecs, et contenant les opuscules et lettres anecdotes de Théodôre l'Hyrtacènien." *Notices et Extraits des Manuscrits de la Bibliothèque Nationale, et autres bibliothèques* 5 (1798), 709–44; 6 (1800), 1–48.

Kantakouzenos, John. *The History of John Cantacuzenus (Book IV): Text, Translation and Commentary*, ed. Timothy Miller. Diss., Catholic Univ. Ann Arbor, Mich.: University Microfilms, 1975.

Kekaumenos. *Sovety i rasskazy Kekavmena, sočinenie vizantijskogo polkovodca XI veka*, ed. G. G. Litavrin. Moscow: Nauka, 1972.

Kinnamos, John. *Ioannis Cinnami epitome*, ed. A. Meineke. CSHB. Bonn, 1836.

Komnene, Anna. *The Alexiad of Anna Comnena.* Trans. E. R. A. Sewter. Baltimore, MD: Penguin, 1969.

The Alexiad of the Princess Anna Comnena. Trans. Elizabeth A. S. Dawes. London: Kegan, Paul, Trench, Trubner, 1928.

Kritovoulos. *Critobuli Imbriotae historiae*, ed. Diether Reinsch. CFHB 22. Berlin and New York: W. de Gruyter, 1983.

Lampenos, Nicholas. *Ὁ λόγιος Νικόλαος Λαμπηνὸς καὶ τὸ ἐγκώμιον αὐτοῦ εἰς τὸν Ἀνδρόνικον Β΄ Παλαιολόγον*, ed. I. D. Polemes. Diptychon Paraphylla, 4. Athens: Hetaireia Vyzantinon kai Metavyzantinon Meleton, 1992.

Magoulias. *See* Choniates.

Makarios Chrysokephalos, archbishop of Philadelphia. *Λόγοι πανηγυρικοὶ ιδ΄.* Vienna, 1793.

Manuel II Palaiologos. *The Letters of Manuel II Palaeologus*, ed. and trans. George T. Dennis. Dumbarton Oaks Texts 4. CFHB 8. Washington, D.C., 1977.

Manuel II. Palaiologos, Dialoge mit einem "Perser," ed. Erich Trapp. Wiener Byzantinistische Studien II. Vienna: Österreichische Akademie der Wissenschaften, 1966.

Maurikios. *Das Strategikon des Maurikios*, ed. George T. Dennis, German trans. Ernst Gamillscheg. CFHB 17. Vienna: Österreichische Akademie der Wissenschaften, 1981.

Nicholas I, patriarch of Constantinople. *Nicholas I Patriarch of Constantinople, Letters*, ed. and trans. R. Jenkins and L. Westerink. Dumbarton Oaks Texts 2, CFHB 6. Washington, D.C., 1973.

Nikephoros II Phokas. *Le traité sur la guérilla (De velitatione) de l'empereur Nicéphore Phocas*, ed. G. Dagron and H. Mihaescu. Paris: Éditions du Centre National de la Recherche Scientifique, 1986.

Planoudes, Maximos. *Maximi monachi Planudis epistulae*, ed. Maximilian Treu. Breslau, 1886–90; repr. Amsterdam: Hakkert, 1960.

Poseidippos of Pella. *Posidippi Pellaei quae supersunt omnia*, ed. C. Austin and G. Bastianini. Milan: LED, 2002.

Psellos, Michael. *Chronographie ou Histoire d'un siècle de Byzance (976–1077)*, ed. and trans. Émile Renauld. 2 vols. Paris: Les Belles Lettres, 1926–28.

Pseudo-Kodinos. *Traité des offices*, ed. and French trans. Jean Verpeaux. Paris: Éditions du Centre National de la Recherche Scientifique, 1966.

Regel, Wilhelm V. E., and N. Novasadskij. *Fontes rerum byzantinarum.* 2 pts. St. Petersburg, 1892; repr. Leipzig: Zentralantiquariat der Deutschen Demokratishchen Republik, 1982.

Sathas, K. *Μεσαιωνικὴ Βιβλιοθήκη*, 7 vols. 1872–94; repr. Athens: Gregoriades, 1972.

Skylitzes, John. *Ioannis Scylitzae synopsis historiarum*, ed. J. Thurn. CFHB. Berlin and New York: W. de Gruyter, 1973.

Skylitzes Continuatus. *Ἡ συνέχεια τῆς Χρονογραφίας τοῦ Ἰωάννου Σκυλίτση (Ioannes Skylitzes Continuatus)*, ed. Eudoxos Tsolakes. Thessaloniki Hetaireia Makedonikon Spoudon, 1968.

Strabo, Geographica. S. L. Radt, ed. and tr. *Strabons Geographika*. 10 vols. Göttingen: Vandenhoeck and Ruprecht, 2002–.

Theodori Ducae Lascaris Epistulae CCXVII, ed. N. Festa. Pubblicazioni del Reale Istituto di studi superiori pratici e di perfezionamento in Firenze, Sezione di filosofia e lettere, no. 29. Florence, 1898.

Theophanes Continuatus. *Theophanes Continuatus, Ioannes Cameniata, Symeon Magister, Georgius Monachus*, ed. I. Bekker. CSHB. Bonn, 1838.

Thomas Magistros. *On Kingship (Λόγος περὶ βασιλείας)*. In Migne, *PG*, 145, cols. 447–496.

Three Byzantine Military Treatises, text, trans., and notes by George T. Dennis, Dumbarton Oaks Texts 9. CFHB 25. Washington, D.C.: Dumbarton Oaks Research Library and Collection, 1985.

Tzetzes, John. *Ioannis Tzetzae historiae*, ed. P. L. M. Leone. Naples: Libreria Scientifica Editrice, 1968.

Vlemmydes, Nikephoros. *Nicephori Blemmydae Curriculum Vitae et Carmina*, ed. August Heisenberg. Leipzig: Teubner, 1896.

Vranouses, L. "Τὸ χρονικὸν τῶν Ἰωαννίνων κατ' ἀνέκδοτον δημώδη ἐπιτομήν." *Ἀκαδημία Ἀθηνῶν. Ἐπετηρὶς τοῦ Μεσαιωνικοῦ Ἀρχείου* 12 (1962), 57–115. And printed separately, Athens, 1965.

Zonaras, John. *Ioannis Zonarae Epitomae Historiarum libri* XVIII, ed. M. Pinder, 3 vols. Bonn, 1841–97.

Western, Slavic, and Turkish sources

Acta Albaniae Veneta saeculorum XIV *et* XV. Ed. Giuseppe Valentini. 25 vols. Milan, 1967–79.

Actes de Chilandar, II. *Actes slaves*, ed. B. Korablev. *VizVrem* 19 (1915), suppl. 1. Repr. Amsterdam: Hakkert, 1975.

Aubrey of Trois-Fontaines. *Chronicle. In Monumenta Germaniae Historica, Scriptores*. Vol. 23. Berlin and Hanover, 1874.

Barišić, Franjo. "Prvi popis grčkih akata na starosrpskom s kraja XIII veka u Hilandaru." *Hilandarski Zbornik* 7 (1989), 27–56.

Boškov, V. "Jedan originalan nišan Murata I. iz 1386. godine u manastiru Svetog Pavla na Svetoj Gori." *Prilozi za orijentalnu filologiju* (Sarajevo) 27 (1977), 225–47.

Ćorović, Vladimir. *Spisi sv. Save*. Belgrade, 1928.

Lascaris, Michel. "Actes serbes de Vatopédi." *Byzantinoslavica* 6 (1935), 166–85.

Novaković, Stojan. *Zakonski spomenici srpskih država srednjega veka*. Belgrade: Srpska Kraljevska Akademija, 1912.

Ricotti, Ercole. *Liber iurium rei publicae Genuensis.* 2 vols. Vol. 7 and 9 of *Historiae patriae monumenta.* Turin, 1854, 1857.

Romanos, I. A. "Ἀνδηγαυϊκὸν δίπλωμα τοῦ Ταραντίνου ἡγεμόνος Φιλίππου τοῦ Β', περιέχον μετάφρασιν χρυσοβούλλου Μιχαὴλ τοῦ Β', Δεσπότου τῆς Ἠπείρου." *Δελτίον τῆς Ἱστορικῆς καὶ Ἐθνολογικῆς Ἑταιρείας τῆς Ἑλλάδος* 2 (1885), 587–608.

Sanguineti, Angelo and Gerolamo Bertolotto. *Nuova serie di documenti sulle relazioni di Genova coll'Impero bizantino.* Società ligure di storia patria, Atti, vol. 28, fasc. 2, pp. 337–573. Genoa, 1898.

Slaveva, Lidija and Vladimir Mošin. *Srpski gramoti od Dušanovo vreme,* Institut za Istražuvanje na Staroslovenskata Kultura, posebna izdanija, knjiga IV. Prilep, 1988.

Solovjev, Aleksandar. "Un inventaire des documents byzantins de Chilandar." *Seminarium Kondakovianum* 10 (1938), 31–47.

Odabrani spomenici srpskog prava (od XII do kraja XV veka). Belgrade: Gece Kona, 1926.

Tafel, G. L., and G. Thomas. *Urkunden zu älteren Handels- und Staatsgeschichte der Republik Venedig.* 2 vols. Vienna, 1856–57; repr. Amsterdam: Hakkert, 1967.

Yahya ibn Said. "Histoire de Yahya-ibn-Said d'Antioche," ed. and trans. I. Kratchkovsky and A. Vasiliev. In *Patrologia Orientalis,* vol. 18, fasc. 5 (Paris, 1924), 699–833; vol. 23, fasc. 3 (Paris, 1932), 347–520.

Zakonik cara Stefana Dušana: 1349 i 1354, ed. N. Radojčić. Belgrade: SANU, 1960. English trans. M. Burr, "The Code of Stephan Dušan." *Slavonic and East European Review* 28 (1949–50), 198–217, 516–39.

Secondary works

Ahrweiler, Hélène. See also Glykatzi-Ahrweiler.

"Charisticariat et autres formes d'attribution de donations pieuses aux Xe–XIe siècles." *ZRVI* 10 (1967), 1–27.

Études sur les structures administratives et sociales de Byzance. London: Variorum Reprints, 1971.

L'idéologie politique de l'empire byzantin. Paris: Presses Universitaires de France, 1975.

Anastasijević, D. and G. Ostrogorsky. "Les Koumanes pronoïaires." *Annuaire de l'Institut de philologie et d'histoire orientale et slave* 11 (1951) = *Mélanges H. Grégoire III,* 19–29.

Angelov, Dimiter G. "Byzantine Imperial Panegyric as Advice Literature (1204–c.1350)," 55–72. In *Rhetoric in Byzantium: Papers from the Thirty-fifth Spring Symposium of Byzantine Studies, Exeter College, University of Oxford, March 2001.* Ed. Elizabeth Jeffreys. Aldershot: Ashgate/Variorum, 2003.

Imperial Ideology and Political Thought in Byzantium, 1204–1330. Cambridge University Press, 2007.

Angelov, D. *Agrarnite otnošenija v severna i sredna Makedonija prez XIV vek.* Sofia, 1958.

"Prinos kŭm narodnostnite i pozemelni otnošenija v Makedonija (Epirskija despotat) prez pŭrvata četvurt na XIII vek (glavno spored dokumenti na Ohridskata arhiepiskopija)." *Izvestija na Kamarata na narodnata kultura* (Serija: Humanitarni nauki), IV/3 (1947), 1–46.

Angold, Michael. *The Byzantine Empire 1025–1204: A Political History.* London and New York: Longman, 1984; 2nd ed. 1997.

A Byzantine Government in Exile: Government and Society Under the Laskarids of Nicaea (1204-1261). Oxford University Press, 1975.

Asdracha, Catherine. "From the Byzantine Paroikoi to the Vassalli Angarii: The Case of the Fiefs of Corfou." *Études balkaniques* 22, 1 (1986) 114–22.

La région des Rhodopes aux XIIIe et XIVe siècles, Étude de géographie historique. Texte und Forschungen zur Byzantinisch-Neugriechischen Philologie 49. Athens: Byzantinisch-Neugriechische Jahrbücher, 1976.

and Spyros Asdrachas, "Quelques remarques sur la rente féodale: les baronnies (pronoiai) de Corfou." *TM* 8 (1981), 7–14.

Banescu, Nicolae. "La signification des titres de Πραίτωρ et de Προνοητής à Byzance aux XIe et XIIe siècles," 387–98. *Miscellanea Giovanni Mercati, III = Studi e Testi* 123. Vatican: Biblioteca Apostolica Vaticana, 1946.

Barišić, Franjo. "Konstantin Porfirogenit Paleolog." *ZRVI* 22 (1983), 43–58.

"Povelje vizantijskih carica." *ZRVI* 13 (1971), 143–202 (Fr. summary, 194–202).

Barker, John W. "The Problem of Appanages in Byzantium during the Palaiologan Period." *Βυζαντινά* 3 (1971), 103–22.

Barnes, John Robert. *An Introduction to Religious Foundations in the Ottoman Empire.* Leiden and New York: E. J. Brill, 1987.

Bartusis, Mark. "The Chadenos Affair (Pachymeres, Book I, Chapters 5–6)." *ZRVI* 45 (2008), 157–69.

"The Cost of Late Byzantine Warfare and Defense." *Byzantinische Forschungen* 16 (1990), 75–89.

"'Εξάλειμμα: Escheat in Byzantium." *Dumbarton Oaks Papers* 40 (1986), 55–81.

"The *Kavallarioi* of Byzantium." *Speculum* 63 (1988), 343–50.

"The Megala Allagia and the Tzaousios: Aspects of Provincial Military Organization in Late Byzantium." *REB* 47 (1989), 183–207.

"A Note on Michael VIII's 1272 Prostagma for His Son Andronikos." *BZ* 81 (1988), 268–71.

"On the Status of Stratiotai during the Late Byzantine Period." *ZRVI* 21 (1982), 53–59.

"Serbian Pronoia and Pronoia in Serbia: The Diffusion of an Institution." *ZRVI* 48 (2011), 177–216.

"State Demands for the Building and Repairing of Fortifications in Late Byzantium and Medieval Serbia." *Byzantinoslavica* 49 (1988), 205–12.

"Urban Guard Service in Late Byzantium: The Terminology and the Institution." *Macedonian Studies* 5 (n.s. 2), fasc. 2 (1988), 52–77.

Beldiceanu, Nicoară. *Le timar dans l'État ottoman (début XIV*[e]*-début XVI*[e] *siècle).* Wiesbaden: O. Harrassowitz, 1980.

and Irène Beldiceanu-Steinherr. "Un faux document ottoman concernant Radoslav Sampias." *Turcica* 12 (1980), 161–68.

Bellier, P., R. Bondoux, J.-C. Cheynet, B. Geyer, J. P. Grélois, V. Kravari. *Paysages de Macédoine, leurs caractères, leur évolution à travers les documents et les récits des voyageurs.* Paris: De Boccard, 1986.

Bertelé, T. "Moneta veneziana e moneta bizantina." *Venezi e il Levante fino ad secolo XV*, Convegno internazionale di storia della civiltà veneziana, no. 1, Venice, 1968, I, pt. 1, 3–146. Florence: L. S. Olschki, 1973.

Bibikov, M. V. "Svedenija o pronii v pis'mah Grigorija Kiprskogo i 'Istorii' Georgija Pahimera." *ZRVI* 17 (1976), 93–99.

Biliarski, Ivan. *Instituciite na srednovekovna Bŭlgarija: Vtoro bŭlgarsko carstvo, XII–XIV vek.* Sofia: Presses universitaires "St. Clément Ochridski," 1998.

Bloch, Marc. *Feudal Society.* 2 vols. University of Chicago Press: 1961.

Bombaci, Alessio. "The Army of the Saljuqs of Rūm." *Istituto orientale di Napoli, Annali*, n.s. 38 (1978), 343–69.

Bouras, Charalambos. "Aspects of the Byzantine City, Eighth–Fifteenth Centuries." In *EHB*, II, 497–528.

Boutruche, Robert. *Seigneurie et féodalité, II: L'apogée (XI*[e]*–XIII*[e] *siècles).* Paris: Aubier, 1970.

Brand, Charles. *Byzantium Confronts the West, 1180–1204.* Cambridge, Mass.: Harvard University Press, 1968.

Bryer, Anthony. "Rural Society in Matzouka," 53–95. In *Continuity and Change in Late Byzantine and Early Ottoman Society*, ed. A. Bryer and H. Lowry. Birmingham, Eng. and Washington, D.C., 1986.

Bubalo, Djordje. "Ραδοσθλάβος Σάμπιας – Radoslav Sablja." *ZRVI* 44 (2007), 459–63 (with English summary).

Bulut, Mehmet. *Ottoman–Dutch Economic Relations in the Early Modern Period, 1571–1699.* Hilversum: Verloren, 2001.

Cahen, Claude. "L'évolution de l'iqtâ' du IXe au XIIIe siècle: contribution à une histoire comparée des sociétés médiévales." *Annales, économies – sociétés – civilisations* 8 (1953), 25–52.

La féodalité et les institutions politiques de l'Orient latin. Rome: Accademia nazionale dei Lincei, 1956. 26 pp.

Carile, Antonio. "Sulla pronoia nel Peloponneso bizantino anteriormente alla conquista latina." *ZRVI* 16 (1975), 55–61.

Chalandon, F. *Les Comnènes. Études sur l'empire byzantin au XI*[e] *et au XII*[e] *siècles.* 2 vols. Paris, 1900–12; repr. New York: B. Franklin, 1971.

Charanis, Peter. "The Aristocracy of Byzantium in the Thirteenth Century," 336–55. In *Studies in Roman Economic and Social History in Honor of Allan Chester Johnson*, ed. P. R. Coleman-Norton. Princeton University Press, 1951.

Social, Economic and Political Life in the Byzantine Empire: Collected Studies. London: Variorum Reprints, 1973.

"Town and Country in the Byzantine Possessions of the Balkan Peninsula During the Later Period of the Empire," 117–37. In *Aspects of the Balkans, Continuity and Change*, ed. H. Birnbaum and S. Vryonis, Jr. The Hague and Paris: Mouton, 1972.

Cheynet, Jean-Claude. *Pouvoir et contestations à Byzance (963–1210).* Paris: Publications de la Sorbonne, 1990

Ćirković, Sima. "Hreljin poklon Hilandaru." *ZRVI* 21 (1982), 103–17.

Constantelos, Demetrios J. *Byzantine Philanthropy and Social Welfare.* Rutgers Byzantine Series. New Brunswick, N.J.: Rutgers University Press, 1968.

Constantinides, C. N. *Higher Education in Byzantium in the Thirteenth and Early Fourteenth Centuries (1204–ca.1310).* Cyprus Research Centre, Texts and Studies of the History of Cyprus XI. Nicosia, 1982.

Cvetkova, Bistra. "Influence exercée par certaines institutions de Byzance et des Balkans du moyen âge sur le système féodal ottoman." *Byzantinobulgarica* 1 (1962), 237–57.

"Novye dannye o hristianah-spahijah na balkanskom poluostrove v period tureckogo gospodstva." *VizVrem* 13 (1958), 184–97.

Daničić, Djura. *Rječnik iz književnih starina srpskih*, 3 vols. 1863–64; repr. Belgrade: Vuk Karadžić, 1975.

Darkó, E. "La militarizzazione dell'Impero Bizantino." *Atti del V Congresso internazionale bizantini*, Rome 1936, I = *Studi bizantini e neoellenici* 5 (1939), 88–99.

Day, Gerald, W. *Genoa's Response to Byzantium, 1155–1204: Commercial Expansion and Factionalism in a Medieval City.* Urbana and Chicago: University of Illinois Press, 1988.

Dennis, George T. "Nicholas Cabasilas Chamaëtos and His Discourse on Abuses Committed by Authorities against Sacred Things." *Byzantine Studies/Études byzantines* 5 (1978), 80–87. Repr. in G. Dennis, *Byzantium and the Franks, 1350–1420*, no. XI. London: Variorum Reprints, 1982.

The Reign of Manuel II Palaeologus in Thessalonica, 1382–1387. Orientalia Christiana Analecta 159. Rome: Pontificium institutum orientalium studiorum, 1960.

Deny, Jean. "Timar." In *The Encyclopædia of Islam*, 1st edn., IV, 767–76. Leiden: Brill, 1913–38.

Dmitriev, Sviatoslav. "Melioration (*Beltiosis*) in Byzantine Documents (10th–15th Centuries)." *JÖB* 49 (1999), 61–88.

Dölger, Franz. "Der Feudalismus in Byzanz." *Studien zum mittelalterlichen Lehenswesen, Vorträge und Forschungen*, v, 185–92. Lindau and Constance: Thorbecke, 1960.

"Die Frage des Grundeigentums in Byzanz." *Bulletin of the International Committee of Historical Sciencess* 5 (1933), 5–15. Repr. in Dölger, *Byzanz und die europäische Staatenwelt*, 217–31. Ettal, 1953; repr. Darmstadt: Wissenschaftliche Buchgesellschaft, 1964.

"Die mittelalterliche Kultur auf dem Balkan als byzantinisches Erbes." *Revue international des études balkaniques* 2 (1935), 108–24. Repr. in Dölger, *Byzanz und die europäische Staatenwelt*, 261–81. Ettal, 1953; repr. Darmstadt: Wissenschaftliche Buchgesellschaft, 1964.

Review of P. Mutafčiev, *Vojniški zemi i vojnici v Vizantija prez XIII–XIV v. BZ* 26 (1926), 102–13.

"Zur Textgestaltung der Lavra-Urkunden und zu ihrer geschichtlichen Auswertung." *BZ* 39 (1939), 23–66.

Du Cange, Charles du Fresne. *Glossarium ad scriptores mediae et infimae graecitatis*, 2 vols. Paris, 1688; repr. Graz, 1958.

Failler, Albert. "Pachymeriana alia." *REB* 51 (1993), 238–60.

"Le principe de l'économie ecclésiastique vu par Pachymère." *XVI. Internationaler Byzantinistenkongress*, Vienna 1981, *Akten*, II/4 = *JÖB* 32/4 (1982), 287–95.

Fassoulakis, Sterios. *The Byzantine Family of Raoul-Ral(l)es*. Athens: S. Fassoulakis, 1973.

Ferjančić, Božidar. "Apanažni posed kesara Jovana Rogerija." *ZRVI* 12 (1970), 193–201.

Tesalija u XIII i XIV veku. Vizantološki institut SANU, posebna izdanja, knjiga 15. Belgrade, 1974.

Fine, John V. A. *The Early Medieval Balkans: A Critical Survey from the Sixth to the Late Twelfth Century*. Ann Arbor: University of Michigan Press, 1991.

Fleet, Kate. *European and Islamic Trade in the Early Ottoman State: The Merchants of Genoa and Turkey*. Cambridge Studies in Islamic Civilization. Cambridge University Press, 1999.

Geanakoplos, Deno. *Byzantium: Church, Society, and Civilization Seen Through Contemporary Eyes*. University of Chicago Press, 1984.

Gerber, Haim. *The Social Origins of the Modern Middle East*. Boulder, Co.: Rienner, 1987.

Glykatzi. See also Ahrweiler.

Glykatzi (-Ahrweiler), Hélène. "L'épitéleia dans le cartulaire de Lemviotissa." *Byz* 24 (1954), 71–93, repr. in Ahrweiler, *Études sur les structures*, no. v.

"A propos de l'épitéleia." *Byz* 27 (1957), 369–72, repr. in Ahrweiler, *Études sur les structures*, no. VI.

Glykatzi-Ahrweiler, Hélène. "La politique agraire des empereurs de Nicée." *Byz* 28 (1958), 51–66. Repr. in Ahrweiler, *Études sur les structures*, no. IV.

"Note additionnelle sur la politique agraire des empereurs de Nicée." *Byz* 28 (1959), 135–36. Repr. in Ahrweiler, *Études sur les structures*, no. IV.

"Recherches sur l'administration de l'empire byzantin aux IXe–XIe siècles." *Bulletin de Correspondance Hellénique* 84 (1960), 1–109. Repr. in Ahrweiler, *Études sur les structures*, no. VIII.

Gorjanov, B. T. *Pozdnevizantijskij feodalizm*. Moscow: Akademija nauk SSSR, 1962.

Gounaridis, Paris. "La pêche dans le golfe de Smyrne," I, 265–71. In *ΕΥΨΥΧΙΑ: mélanges offerts à Hélène Ahrweiler*. 2 vols. Ed. Michel Balard et al. Série Byzantina Sorbonensia 16. Paris: Publications de la Sorbonne, 1998.

Guilland, Rodolphe. "Études sur l'histoire administrative de l'empire byzantin. Le logariaste, ὁ λογαριαστής; le grand logariaste, ὁ μέγας λογαριαστής." *JÖB* 18 (1969), 101–13.

Haldon, John. "Approaches to an Alternative Military History of the Period ca. 1025–1071," 45–74. In *Η Αυτοκρατορία σε Κρίση (;) Το βυζάντιο τον 11ο αιώνα (1025–1081)*. National Hellenic Research Foundation, Institute for Byzantine Research, International Symposium 11. Athens, 2003.

"Military Service, Military Lands, and the Status of Soldiers: Current Problems and Interpretations." *Dumbarton Oaks Papers* 47 (1993), 1–68. Repr. in J. Haldon, *State, Army and Society in Byzantium: Approaches to Military, Social and Administrative History, 6th–12th Centuries*. Aldershot: Variorum, 1995, no. VII.

Recruitment and Conscription in the Byzantine Army c. 550–950. A Study of the Origins of the Stratiotika Ktemata, Sitzungsberichte der österreichischen Akademie der Wissenschaften, Philos.-hist. Kl., vol. 357. Vienna, 1979.

Harvey, Alan. *Economic Expansion in the Byzantine Empire, 900–1200*. Cambridge University Press, 1989.

Hendy, Michael. *Studies in the Byzantine Monetary Economy c. 300–1450*. Cambridge University Press, 1985.

Herrin, Judith. "The Collapse of the Byzantine Empire in the Twelfth Century: A Study of a Medieval Economy." *University of Birmingham Historical Journal* 12 (1970), 188–203.

Hohlweg, Armin. *Beiträge zur Verwaltungsgeschichte des oströmischen Reiches unter den Komnenen*, Miscellanea Byzantina Monacensia, Heft 1. Munich: Institut für Byzantinistik und neugriechische Philologie der Universität, 1965.

Howard-Johnston, James D. "Crown Lands and the Defence of Imperial Authority in the Tenth and Eleventh Centuries," 75–100. In *Bosphorus: Essays in Honour of Cyril Mango (= Byzantinische Forschungen* 21 [1995]), ed. Stephanos Efthymiadis, Claudia Rapp, and Dimitris Tsougarakis. Amsterdam: Adolf M. Hakkert, 1995.

Hunger, Herbert. *Prooimion: Elemente der byzantinischen Kaiseridee in der Arengen der Urkunden*, Wiener Byzantinistische Studien 1. Vienna Österreichischen Akademie der Wissenschaften, 1964.

Hvostova, Ksenia V. "Pronija: social'no-ekonomičeskie i pravovye problemy." *VizVrem* 49 (1988), 13–23.

"Sud'by parikii i osobennosti nalogooblozenija v Vizantii XIII–XIV vv." *VizVrem* 39 (1978), 63–75.

Inalcik, Halil. "Timariotes chrétiens en Albanie au XVe siècle." *Mitteilungen des österreichischen Staatsarchiv* 4 (1952), 118–38.

with Donald Quataert. *An Economic and Social History of the Ottoman Empire, 1300–1914.* Cambridge University Press, 1994.

Jacoby, David. "From Byzantium to Latin Romania: Continuity and Change." *Mediterranean Historical Review* 4, no. 1 (1989), 1–44. Also in *Latins and Greeks in the Eastern Mediterranean After 1204*, ed. Benjamin Arbel, Bernard Hamilton, and David Jacoby, 1–44. London: Frank Cass, 1989. Repr. in Jacoby, *Byzantium, Latin Romania and the Mediterranean*, no. VIII. Aldershot: Ashgate/Variorum, 2001.

"Les archontes grecs et la féodalité en Morée franque." *TM* 2 (1967), 421–81. Repr. in D. Jacoby, *Société et démographie à Byzance et en Romanie latine*, no. VI. London: Variorum Reprints, 1975.

"The Encounter of Two Societies: Western Conquerors and Byzantines in the Peloponnesus after the Fourth Crusade." *American Historical Review* 78 (1973), 873–906. Repr. in Jacoby, *Recherches sur la Méditerranée orientale*, no. II.

"Les états latins en Romanie: phénomènes sociaux et économiques (1204–1350 environ)." *XVe Congrès international d'études byzantines, Athens 1976, Rapports et co-rapports, I. Histoire: 3. La symbiose dans les Etats latins formés sur les territoires byzantins*, 1–51. Athens, 1976. Repr. in Jacoby, *Recherches sur la Méditerranée orientale*, no. I.

La féodalité en Grèce médiévale: les "Assises de Romanie." Sources, application et diffusion. Paris: Mouton, 1971.

Recherches sur la Méditerranée orientale du XIIe au XVe siècle: Peuples, sociétés, économies. London: Variorum Reprints, 1979.

Juzbašjan, K. N. "'Varjagi' i 'pronija' v sočinenii Aristakesa Lastivertci." *VizVrem* 16 (1959), 14–28.

Kaplan, Michel. *Les hommes et la terre à Byzance du VIe au XIe siècle. Propriété et exploitation du sol.* Série Byzantina Sorbonensia 10. Paris: Publications de la Sorbonne, 1992.

Karayannopoulos (Karagiannopoulos), Ioannes E. "Ein Beitrag zur Militärpronoia der Palaiologenzeit," 71–89. In *Geschichte und Kultur der Palaiologenzeit*, ed. W. Seibt. Vienna Österreichische Akademie der Wissenschaften, 1996.

Λεξικό βυζαντινής ορολογίας. Οικονομικοί όροι. Vol. 1. Thessaloniki: Aristoteleio Panepistimio Thessalonikis, Kentro Vyzantinon Ereunon, 2000.

Kazhdan, Alexander P. "The Fate of the Intellectual in Byzantium A Propos of *Society and Intellectual Life in Late Byzantium* by Ihor Ševčenko." *The Greek Orthodox Theological Review* 27/1 (1982), 83–97.

"*Pronoia*: The History of a Scholarly Discussion," 133–63. In *Intercultural Contacts in the Medieval Mediterranean*. Ed. Benjamin Arbel. London and Portland, Or.: Cass, 1996. Orig. published in *Mediterranean Historical Review* 10, nos. 1–2 (1995), 133–63.

Review of G. Ostrogorskij, *Pour l'histoire de la féodalité byzantine*. *VizVrem* 10 (1956), 218–28.

Review of H. Glykatzi-Ahrweiler, "La concession des droits incorporels." *VizVrem* 27 (1967), 344–46.

Review of Nicolas Oikonomides, *Fiscalité et exemption à Byzance (IXe–XIe s.)*. *BZ* 91 (1998), 174–78.

Koder, Johannes, and Friedrich Hild. *Hellas und Thessalia*, Tabula imperii byzantini 1. Vienna: Österreichischen Akademie der Wissenschaften, 1976.

Kolias, Taxiarchis G. *Byzantinische Waffen: ein Beitrag zur byzantinischen Waffenkunde von den Anfängen bis zur lateinischen Eroberung*. Byzantina Vindobonensia 17. Vienna: Österreichischen Akademie der Wissenschaften, 1988.

Kondakov, Nikodim Pavlovich. *Makedonija. Arheologičeskoe putešestvie*. Izdanie Otdelenija russkago jazyka i slovesnosti Imperatorskoj Akademii Nauk. St. Petersburg, 1909.

Köprülü, Mehmed Fuad. *Some Observations on the Influence of Byzantine Institutions on Ottoman Institutions*. Trans. Gary Leiser. Ankara: Türk Tarih Kurumu, 1999.

Kotsonis, Ch. *Προβλήματα τῆς ἐκκλησιαστικῆς οἰκονομίας*. Athens: Damaskos, 1957.

Kourouses, Stauros I. "Ὁ λόγιος οἰκουμενικὸς πατριάρχης Ἰωάννης ΙΓ΄ ὁ Γλυκύς." *Ἐπετηρὶς Ἑταιρείας Βυζαντινῶν Σπουδῶν* 41 (1974), 297–405.

Kravari, Vassiliki. *Villes et villages de Macédoine occidentale*. Réalités Byzantines. Paris: P. Lethielleux, 1989.

Krekić, Bariša. "Contribution to the Study of the Pronoia in Medieval Serbia." *Dubrovnik, Italy and the Balkans in the Late Middle Ages*, no. XVIII, pp. 1–9. London: Variorum Reprints, 1980. Translation of "Prilog proučavanju pronije u srednjovekovoj Srbiji." *ZRVI* 8/2 (1964), 227–33.

Kucharski, Andrzej. *Najdawniejsze pomniki prawodawstwa słowiańskiego (Drevnejšija pamjatniki slovjanskago zakonodatel'stva)*. Warsaw, 1838. Latin title: *Antiquissima monumenta juris slovenici*.

Kyritses (Kyritsis), Demetrios (Dimitris). "Από χωρικοί, στρατιώτες: άλλο ένα σχόλιο σε γνωστό χωρίο του Παχυμέρη (xi.9)," 87–94. In *Ψηφίδες. Μελέτες Ιστορίας, Αρχαιολογίας και Τέχνης. Στη μνήμη της Στέλλας Παπαδάκη-Oekland*. Ed. Olga Gratziou and Hristos Loukos. Herakleio: Panepistemiakes Ekdoseis Kretes & Hetaira Kretikon Historikon Meleton, 2009.

"The 'Common Chrysobulls' of Cities and the Notion of Property in Late Byzantium." *Σύμμεικτα* 13 (1999), 229–45.

and Kostis Smyrlis. "Les villages du littoral égéen de l'Asie Mineure au Moyen Âge," 437–51. In *Les villages dans l'empire byzantin (IVe–XVe siècle)*. Ed. J. Lefort, C. Morrisson, and J.-P. Sodini. Paris: Lethielleux, 2005.

Laiou, Angeliki E. "The Agrarian Economy, Thirteenth–Fifteenth Centuries." In *EHB*, I, 311–75.

"The Byzantine Aristocracy in the Palaeologan Period: A Story of Arrested Development." *Viator* 4 (1973), 131–51.

"A Byzantine Prince Latinized: Theodore Palaeologus, Marquis of Montferrat." *Byz* 38 (1968) 386–410.

Constantinople and the Latins: The Foreign Policy of Andronicus II, 1282–1328. Cambridge, Mass.: Harvard University Press, 1972.

"The Correspondence of Gregorios Kyprios as a Source for the History of Social and Political Behavior in Byzantium or, On Government by Rhetoric," 91–108. In *Geschichte und Kultur der Palaiologenzeit. Referate des Internationalen Symposions zu Ehren von Herbert Hunger, Wien, 30. November bis 3. Dezember 1994*, ed. Werner Seibt. Österreichische Akademie der Wissenschaften, philosophisch-historische Klasse, Denkschriften, 241. Band. Vienna, 1996.

"Le débat sur les droits du fisc et les droits régaliens au début du 14e siècle." *REB* 58 (2000), 97–122.

Laiou-Thomadakis, Angeliki E. *Peasant Society in the Late Byzantine Empire: A Social and Demographic Study.* Princeton University Press, 1977.

Lambropoulos, Kosmas. *Ιωάννης Απόκαυκος. Συμβολή στην έρευνα του βίου και του συγγραφικού έργου του.* Ιστορκές Μονογραφίες, 6. Athens: Historikes Ekdoseis St. D. Basilopoulos, 1988.

Lampe, G. W. H. *A Patristic Greek Lexicon.* Oxford University Press, 1961–68.

Lascaris, Michel. "Cinq notes à la Πρόνοια de M. Ostrogorski." *Byz* 21 (1951), 265–74.

Laurent, Vitalien. *Les regestes des actes du patriarcat de Constantinople, I: Les actes des patriarches, fasc. 4: Les regestes de 1208 à 1309.* Paris: Institut français d'études byzantines, 1971.

Lefort, Jacques. "Fiscalité médiévale et informatique: recherches sur les barèmes pour l'imposition des paysans byzantins du XIVe siècle." *Revue Historique* 512 (1974), 315–56.

"Une grande fortune foncière aux Xe–XIIIe s.: les biens du monastère d'Iviron." *Structures féodales et féodalisme dans l'occident méditerranéen (X^e–XIIIe s.).* Collection de l'école française de Rome 44, 727–42. Rome, 1980.

"The Rural Economy, Seventh–Twelfth Centuries." In *EHB*, I, 231–310.

Lemerle, Paul. "Un aspect du rôle des monastères à Byzance: les monastères donnés à des laïcs, les charisticaires." *Académie des Inscriptions et Belles-Lettres, Comptes rendus des séances de l'anné 1967*, 9–28. Paris, 1967. Repr. in Lemerle, *Le monde de Byzance*, no. XV.

Lemerle, Paul. "Le juge général des grecs et la réforme judiciaire d'Andronic III," 292–316. In *Mémorial Louis Petit.* Bucharest, 1948. Repr. in Lemerle, *Le monde de Byzance*, no. X.

Le monde de Byzance: Histoire et Institutions. London: Variorum Reprints, 1978.

Litavrin, G. G. *Bolgarija i Vizantija v XI–XII vv.* Moscow: Akademija Nauk SSSR, 1960.

Vizantijskoe obščestvo i gosudarstvo v X–XI vv. Moscow: Nauka, 1977.

Lowry, Heath. "Changes in Fifteenth-Century Ottoman Peasant Taxation: The Case Study of Radolifo (Radolibos)," 23–37. In *Continuity and Change in Late Byzantine and Early Ottoman Society*, ed. A. Bryer and H. Lowry. Birmingham and Washington, D.C., 1986.

Macrides, Ruth J. "Killing, Asylum, and the Law in Byzantium." *Speculum* 63 (1988), 509–38. Repr. in *Kinship and Justice in Byzantium, 11th–15th Centuries*, no. x. Aldershot: Ashgate-Variorum, 1999.

"The Ritual of Petition," 356–70. In *Greek Ritual Poetics*, ed. Dimitrios Yatromanolakis and Panagiotis Roilos. Cambridge, Mass. and London: Harvard University Press, 2004.

Magdalino, Paul. "The Byzantine Army and the Land: From Stratiotikon Ktema to Military Pronoia," 15–36. In *Τὸ Ἐμπόλεμο Βυζάντιο (9ος-12ος αι.) [Byzantium at War (9th–12th c.)]*. National Hellenic Research Foundation, Institute for Byzantine Research, International Symposium 4 (1996, Athens). Athens: Idryma Goulandri-Hori, 1997.

The Empire of Manuel I Komnenos, 1143–1180. Cambridge University Press, 1993.

Majer, Hans-Georg. "Some Remarks on the Document of Murad I from the Monastery of St. Paul on Mount Athos (1386)," 33–39. In *Ὁ Ἄθως στοὺς 14ο–16ο αἰῶνες (Mount Athos in the 14th–16th Centuries). National Hellenic Research Foundation, Institute for Byzantine Research. Ἀθωνικὰ Σύμμεικτα*, 4. Athens, 1997.

Majkov, A. A. "Čto takoe pronija v drevnej Serbii?" *Čtenija v Imperatorskom obščestve istorii i drevnostej rossijskih* (1868), kniga 1, 227–32.

"O zemel'noj sobstvennosti v drevnej Serbii." *Čtenija v Imperatorskom obščestve istorii i drevnostej rossijskih* (1860), kniga 1, 1–30.

Maksimović, Ljubomir. *The Byzantine Provincial Administration under the Palaiologoi.* Amsterdam: Hakkert, 1988.

"Geneza i karakter apanaža u Vizantiji." *ZRVI* 14/15 (1973), 103–54.

"Pronijari u Trapezuntskom carstvu." *Zbornik Filozofskog fakulteta* 12/1 (Belgrade, 1974) (=*Mélanges Georges Ostrogorsky*), 393–404.

Makušev, Vikentij. "O pronii v drevnej Serbii." *ŽMNP* 175 (Sept. 1874), 1–20.

Maniati-Kokkini, Triantafyllitsa. *Ο Βυζαντινός θεσμός της πρόνοιας: συμβολή στή μελέτη του χαρακτήρα του.* Diss. University of Thessaloniki, 1990. 444 pp. Available online at <http://www.phdtheses.ekt.gr>.

"Μαρτυρία Ἰωάννου τοῦ Ἀποκαύκου γιὰ τὴν κοινωνία τοῦ ιγ' αἰώνα. Δύο ὑποθέσεις φόνου" (with French summary), 297–306. In Πρακτικά του Α' Αρχαιολογικού και Ιστορικού Συνεδρίου Αιτωλοακαρνανίας. Αγρίνιο, 21–22–23 Οκτωβρίου 1988. Μνημειακή κληρονομιά και ιστορία της Αιτωλοακαρνανίας. Agrinion: Nomarchia Aitoloakarnanias ST Ephoreia Proïstorikon kai Klassikon Archaioteton, 1991. Inaccessible to me.

"Μιὰ πρώτη προσέγγιση στὴ μελέτη τοῦ βυζαντινοῦ θεσμοῦ τῆς πρόνοιας: οἱ προνοιάριοι," 47–60. In Πρακτικὰ τοῦ Θ' Πανελλήνιου Ἱστορικοῦ Συνεδρίου (Thessaloniki, May 1988). Thessaloniki: Hellenike Historike Hetaireia, 1991.

"Τὸ «Χρονικό τοῦ Μορέως» καὶ ἡ Βυζαντινὴ Πρόνοια." *Βυζαντιακά* 14 (1994), 483–508.

Mavrommatis, Lenos. "Η Πρόνοια του Μονομάχου και η Διαμάχη για τον Χάντακα (1333–1378)." *Σύμμεικτα* 14 (2001), 257–72.

McGowan, Bruce. *Economic Life in Ottoman Europe: Taxation, Trade and the Struggle for Land, 1600–1800.* Cambridge University Press, 1981.

Mladenović, Miloš. "Zur Frage der Pronoia und des Feudalismus im byzantinischen Reiche." *Südost-Forschungen* 15 (1956), 123–40.

Morris, Rosemary. "Monastic Exemptions in Tenth- and Eleventh-Century Byzantium," 200–20. In *Property and Power in the Early Middle Ages*, ed. Wendy Davies and Paul Fouracre. Cambridge University Press, 1995.

Monks and Laymen in Byzantium, 843–1118. Cambridge University Press, 1995.

Morrisson, Cécile. "Byzantine Money: Its Production and Circulation." In *EHB*, III, 909–66.

and Jean-Claude Cheynet. "Prices and Wages in the Byzantine World." In *EHB*, II, 815–78.

Moustoxydes, Andreas. *Ἑλληνομνήμων ἢ Συμμικτὰ ἑλληνικά*, φυλλάδια [parts] 1–12. 1843–53; repr. Athens: Karavia, 1965.

Mutafčiev, Petar. *Istorija na bŭlgarskija narod*, II. Sofia: Chemus, 1944.

Izbrani proizvedenija. 2 vols. Sofia: Nauka i izkustvo, 1973.

"Pronijata v Vizantija i otnošenieto u kjum voennata služba." *Izvestija na istoričeskoto družestvo v Sofija* 6 (1924), 1–30. A separate printing of his chapter on pronoia in "Vojniški zemi," 37–61; repr. in *Izbrani proizvedenija*, I, 561–89.

Mutafchieva, Vera P. *Agrarian Relations in the Ottoman Empire in the 15th and 16th Centuries.* Boulder, Co.: East European Monographs, 1988. A translation of Mutafchieva, *Agrarnite otnošenija v Osmanskata imperija prez XV–XVI v.* Sofia: Bŭlgarska akademija na naukite, 1962.

Naumov, E. P. "K istorii vizantijskoj i serbskoj pronii." *VizVrem* 34 (1973), 22–31.

Neville, Leonora. *Authority in Byzantine Provincial Society, 950–1100.* Cambridge University Press, 2004.

"The Marcian Treatise on Taxation and the Nature of Bureaucracy in Byzantium." *Byzantinische Forschungen* 26 (2000), 47–62.

Nicol, Donald M. *The Despotate of Epiros, 1267–1479: A Contribution to the History of Greece in the Middle Ages.* Cambridge University Press, 1984.

The Last Centuries of Byzantium, 1261–1453. 2nd edn. Cambridge University Press, 1993.

Nicolle, D. and A. McBride. *Hungary and the Fall of Eastern Europe, 1000–1568.* London: Osprey, 1988.

Nissen, Waldemar. *Die Diataxis des Michael Attaleiates von 1077.* Jena, 1894.

Novaković, Stojan. "Pronijari i baštinici (spahije i čitluk sahibije). Prilog k istoriji nepokretne imovine u Srbiji XIII do XIX v." *Glas* 1 (1887), 1–102.

Stara Srpska vojska: istorijske skice iz dela "Narod i zemlja u staroj srpskoj državi". Belgrade, 1893.

Oikonomides, Nicolas. *Byzantium from the Ninth Century to the Fourth Crusade.* London: Variorum Reprints, 1992.

"Contribution à l'étude de la pronoia au XIIIe siècle." *REB* 22 (1964), 158–75. Repr. in Oikonomides, *Documents et études*, no. VI.

"Ἡ διανομὴ τῶν βασιλικῶν «ἐπισκέψεων» τῆς Κρήτης (1170–1171) καὶ ἡ δημοσιονομικὴ πολιτικὴ τοῦ Μανουὴλ Α' Κομνηνοῦ." *Πεπραγμένα τοῦ Β' Διεθνοῦς Κρητολογικοῦ Συνεδρίου*, Khania 1966, 3 vols., III, 195–201. Athens, 1968. Repr. in Oikonomides, *Documents et études*, no. XVII.

Documents et études sur les institutions de Byzance (VIIe–XVe s.). London: Variorum Reprints, 1976.

"The Donation of Castles in the Last Quarter of the 11th Century (Dölger, *Regesten*, no. 1012)," 413–17. In *Polychronion, Festschrift Franz Dölger zum 75. Geburtstag.* Heidelberg: Winter, 1966. Repr. in Oikonomides, *Documents et études*, no. XIV.

"Οἱ δύο Σερβικὲς κατακτήσεις τῆς Χαλκιδικῆς τὸν ΙΔ' αἰῶνα." *Δίπτυχα* 2 (1980–81), 294–300.

"L'évolution de l'organisation administrative de l'Empire byzantin au XIe siècle (1025–1118)." *TM* 6 (1976), 125–52. Repr. in Oikonomides, *Byzantium from the Ninth Century to the Fourth Crusade*, no. X.

"La fiscalité byzantine et la communauté villageoise au XIe s.," 89–102. In *Septième Congrès International d'Études du Sud-Est Européen (Thessalonique, 29 août–4 septembre 1994). Rapports.* Association International d'Études du Sud-Est Européen. Comité National Grec des Études du Sud-Est Européen. Athens, 1994.

"Le Haradj dans l'empire byzantin du XVe siècle." *Actes du premier Congrès international des études balkaniques*, III, 681–88. Sofia: Bŭlgarska akademija na naukite, 1969. Repr. in Oikonomides, *Documents et études*, no. XIX.

"Notes sur un praktikon de pronoiaire (juin 1323)." *TM* 5 (1973), 335–46. Repr. in Oikonomides, *Documents et études*, no. XXIII.

"Ottoman Influence on Late Byzantine Fiscal Practice." *Südost-Forschungen* 45 (1986), 1–24.

"The Properties of the Deblitzenoi in the Fourteenth and Fifteenth Centuries." *Charanis Studies*, ed. A. Laiou-Thomadakis, 176–98. New Brunswick, N.J.: Rutgers University Press, 1980.

"The Role of the Byzantine State in the Economy." In *EHB*, III, 973–1058.

Society, Culture and Politics in Byzantium. Ed. E. Zachariadou. Aldershot: Ashgate/Variorum, 2005.

"St. George of Mangana, Maria Skleraina, and the 'Maly Sion' of Novgorod." *Dumbarton Oaks Papers* 34–35 (1980–81), 239–46. Repr. in Oikonomides, *Byzantium from the Ninth Century to the Fourth Crusade*, no. XVI.

Osipova, K. A. "K voprosu o roli gosudarstva v utverždenii feodalizma v Vizantii." *XVI. Internationaler Byzantinistenkongress, Résumés des Kurzbeiträge*, section 4.1. Vienna: Österreichische Akademie der Wissenschaften, 1981. 2 pp.

Österreichisch-Ungarischen Monarchie. Die dritte militärische Aufnahme. *Topographical maps.* 1:200000 (ca. 1910). <http://lazarus.elte.hu/hun/digkonyv/topo/3felmeres.htm>.

Ostrogorsky (Ostrogorski, Ostrogorskij), George (Georges, Georgije). "Agrarian Conditions in the Byzantine Empire in the Middle Ages," I, 205–34. *The Cambridge Economic History of Europe*, 2nd edn., ed. M. M. Postan. Cambridge, 1966.

"Die ländliche Steuergemeinde des byzantinischen Reiches im x. Jahrhundert." *Vierteljahreschrift für Sozial- und Wirtschaftsgeschichte* 20 (Stuttgart, 1927), 1–108. Reprinted separately: Amsterdam: Hakkert, 1969.

"Drei Praktika weltlicher Grundbesitzer aus der ersten Hälfte des 14. Jahrhunderts." *ZRVI* 14–15 (1973), 81–101.

"Još jednom o proniarima Kumanima," 63–74. *Zbornik Vladimira Mošina*, ed. Dimitrije Dogdanović, B. Jovanović-Štipčević, Dj. Trifunović. Belgrade: Savez bibliotečkih radnika Srbije, 1977.

"Le grand domaine dans l'Empire byzantin," 35–50. In *Recueils de la Société Jean Bodin, IV. Le Domaine.* Wetteren: Scaldis, 1949.

History of the Byzantine State. Rev. ed. New Brunswick, N.J.: Rutgers University Press, 1969.

"Observations on the Aristocracy in Byzantium." *Dumbarton Oaks Papers* 25 (1971), 1–32.

"Pour l'histoire de l'immunité à Byzance." *Byz* 28 (1958), 165–254.

Pronija, prilog istoriji feudalizma u Vizantiji i u južnoslovenskim zemljama. SAN, Posebna izdanja, Knjiga 171. Vizantološki institut, Knjiga 1. Belgrade, 1951.

"Radolivo, selo svetogorskog manastira Ivirona." *ZRVI* 7 (1961), 67–84.

"Le système de la pronoia à Byzance et en Serbie médiévale." *Actes du VIe Congrès international d'études byzantines, Paris 1948*, 2 vols., I, 181–89. Paris, 1950–51. Summary of his *Pronija.*

"Vizantijskie piscovye knigi." *Byzantinoslavica* 9 (1948), 203–306.

Pančenko, B. A. "Krest'janskaja sobstvennost' v Vizantii. Zemledel'českij zakon i monastyrskie dokumenty." *IRAIK* 9 (1904), 1–234.

Parisot, V. *Cantacuzène, homme d'état et historien.* Paris, 1845.

Patlagean, Évelyne. "Γονικόν. Note sur la propriété allodiale à Byzance," 423–34. In *Βυζάντιο. Κράτος και Κοινονία. Μνήμη Νίκου Οικονομίδη.* Ed. Anna Avramea, Angeliki Laiou, and E. Chrysos. Athens: Institouto Vyzantinon Ereunon, 2003.

Pavlikjanov, Kiril. *Istorija na bŭlgarskija svetogorski manastir Zograf ot 980 do 1804 g. Svidetelstvata na dvadeset i sedem neizvestni dokumenta.* Sofia: Universitetsko izdatelstvo "Sv. Kliment Ohridski", 2005.

Polemis, Demetrios I. *The Doukai: A Contribution to Byzantine Prosopography.* London: Athlone, 1968.

Rabie, Hassanein. "The Size and Value of the *Iqṭāʿ* in Egypt, 564–741 A.H. 1169–1341 A.D.," 129–38. In *Studies in the Economic History of the Middle East: From the Rise of Islam to the Present Day*, ed. M. A. Cook. University of London, School of Oriental and African Studies. London and New York: Oxford University Press, 1970.

Radić, Radovan. "Novi podaci o pronijarima iz prvih decenija XIV veka." *ZRVI* 21 (1982), 85–93.

Reumann, J. "Οἰκονομία as 'Ethical Accommodation' in the Fathers, and its Pagan Background," 370–79. In *Studia Patristica*, vol. 3, fasc. 1 = *Texte und Untersuchungen zur Geschichte der altchristlichen Literatur*, vol. 78. Berlin: Akademie–Verlag, 1961.

Reynolds, Susan. *Fiefs and Vassals. The Medieval Evidence Reinterpreted.* Oxford University Press, 1994.

Ross, G. R. "A Survey of Pronoia in the Historiography of Byzantium." *The New Review: A Journal of East-European History* 10 (1970), 1–29.

Rouillard, G. "Un grand bénéficiaire sous Alexis Comnène: Léon Képhalas." *BZ* 30 (1930), 444–50.

Šafařík, Paul J. *Geschichte der südslawischen Literatur*, 3 vols. Prague, 1864–65.

Schilbach, Ernst. *Byzantinische Metrologie.* Munich: C. H. Beck, 1970.

Schmitt, Oliver Jens. *Das venezianische Albanien (1392–1479).* Südosteuropäische Arbeiten 110. Munich: R. Oldenbourg, 2001.

Sedlar, J. *East Central Europe in the Middle Ages, 1000–1500.* Seattle: University of Washington Press, 1994.

Seibt, Werner. "War Gagik II. von Grossarmenien ca. 1072–1073 Megas Doux Charsianou?," II, 159–68. In *Τὸ Ἑλληνικόν. Studies in Honor of Speros Vryonis, Jr.*, ed. J. S. Langdon, S. W. Reinert, J. S. Allen, and C. P. Ioannides. 2 vols. New Rochelle, N.Y.: Caratzas, 1993.

Ševčenko, Ihor. "An Important Contribution to the Social History of Late Byzantium." *The Annals of the Ukrainian Academy of Arts and Sciences in the U.S.*, 2, pt. 4 (1952), 448–59.

"Nicolas Cabasilas' 'Anti-Zealot' Discourse: A Reinterpretation." *Dumbarton Oaks Papers* 11 (1957), 79–171. Repr. in Ševčenko, *Society and Intellectual Life in Late Byzantium*, no. IV.

"A Postscript to Nicolas Cabasilas' 'Anti-Zealot' Discourse." *Dumbarton Oaks Papers* 16 (1962 [1963]), 403–08. Repr. in Ševčenko, *Society and Intellectual Life in Late Byzantium*, no. VI.

Society and Intellectual Life in Late Byzantium. London: Variorum Reprints, 1981.

"Theodore Metochites, the Chora, and the Intellectual Trends of His Time," 17–91. In *The Kariye Djami, Vol. 4: Studies in the Art of the Kariye Djami and Its Intellectual Background*, ed. Paul Underwood. Bollingen Series 70. Princeton University Press, 1975.

Shaw, Stanford. *History of the Ottoman Empire and Modern Turkey*. Vol. 1: *Empire of the Gazis: The Rise and Decline of the Ottoman Empire, 1280–1808*. Cambridge University Press, 1976.

Shinder, Joel. "Early Ottoman Administration in the Wilderness: Some Limits on Comparison." *International Journal of Middle East Studies* 9 (1978), 497–517.

Singh, N. K., ed. *International Encyclopaedia of Islamic Dynasties*. New Delhi: Anmol, 2002.

Sjuzjumov, Michail Ja. "Suvernitet, nalog i zemelnaja renta v Vizantii." *Antičnaja drevnost' i srednie veka*, 9 (1973), 57–65.

"Problemy ikonoborčestva v Vizantii." *Učenye zapiski Sverdlovskogo pedagogičeskogo instituta* 4 (1948), 48–109.

"Vnutrennjaja politika Andronika Komnina i razgrom prigorodov Konstantinopolja v 1187 godu." *VizVrem* 12 (1957), 58–74.

Skabalanovič, Nikolaj. *Vizantijskoe gosudarstvo i cerkov v XI v.* Saint Petersburg, 1884.

Smyrlis, Kostis. "The First Ottoman Occupation of Macedonia (ca. 1383–ca. 1403): Some Remarks on Land Ownership, Property Transaction and Justice," 327–48. In *Diplomatics in the Eastern Mediterranean 1000–1500: Aspects of Cross-cultural Communication*. Ed. A. Beihammer, M. Parani, and C. Schabel. The Medieval Mediterranean, v. 74. Leiden and Boston: Brill, 2008.

La fortune des grands monastères byzantins (fin du Xᵉ–milieu du XIVᵉ siècle). Monographies 21. Paris: Association des amis du Centre d'histoire et civilisation de Byzance, 2006.

"The State, the Land, and Private Property: Confiscating Monastic and Church Properties in the Palaiologan Period," 58–87. In *Church and Society in Late Byzantium*, ed. Dimiter G. Angelov. Studies in Medieval Culture XLIX. Kalamazoo: Medieval Institute Publications, 2009.

"Taxation Reform and the Pronoia System in Thirteenth-Century Byzantium," 211–17. In *On İkinci ve On Üçüncü Yüzyıllarda Bizans Dünyasinda Değişim = Change in the Byzantine World in the Twelfth and Thirteenth Centuries*. Ed. Ayla Ödekan et al. Proceedings of the First International Sevgi Gönül Byzantine Studies Symposium, 2007 Istanbul. Istanbul: Vehbi Koç Vafki, 2010.

Sokolov, I. I. "Materialy po zemel'no-hozjajstvennomu bytu Vizantii." *Izvestija Akademii nauk SSSR, Otdelenie obščestvennyh nauk* (1931), no. 6, pp. 683–712.

Solovjev, Aleksandar V. "Grečeskie arhonty v serbskom carstve XIV v." *Byzantinoslavica* 2 (1930), 275–87.

Stadtmüller, G. *Michael Choniates, Metropolit von Athen (ca.1138–ca.1222)*. Orientalia Christiana 33, no. 2. Rome: Pontificium institutum orientalium studiorum, 1934.

Stanescu, Eugen. "Les 'stratiotès': diffusion et survivance d'une institution byzantine dans le sud-est de l'Europe." *Actes du premier Congrès international des études balkaniques et sud-est européennes*, III, 227–34. Sofia, 1969.

Stavridou-Zafraka, Alkmini. "The Relations between Secular and Religious Authorities in the State of Epiros after 1204," 11–24. In *Church and Society in Late Byzantium*, ed. Dimiter G. Angelov. Studies in Medieval Culture XLIX. Kalamazoo: Medieval Institute Publications, 2009.

"Η χρονολόγηση επιστολών και εγγράφων του Ιωάννη Αποκαύκου." *Egnatia* 4 (1993), 143–68.

Svoronos, Nicolas G. "'Η «χαριστική δωρεά»," 69–70. In *Βυζαντινὸς Ἑλληνισμός. Μεσοβυζαντινοὶ χρόνοι (1071–1204). Ὑστεροβυζαντινὸ χρόνοι (1204–1453).* Ἱστορία τοῦ Ἑλληνικοῦ Ἔθνους, vol. 9. Athens: Ekdotike Athenon, 1980.

Études sur l'organisation intérieure, la société et l'économie de l'empire byzantin. London: Variorum Reprints, 1973

"Les privilèges de l'église à l'époque des Comnènes: un rescrit inédit de Manuel Ier Comnène." *TM* 1 (1965), 325–91. Repr. in Svoronos, *Études sur l'organisation intérieure, la société et l'économie de l'empire byzantin*, no. VII.

"Recherches sur le cadastre byzantin et la fiscalité aux XIe et XIIe siècles: le cadastre de Thèbes." *Bulletin de Correspondance Hellénique* 83 (1959), 1–166. Also published separately, and in Svoronos, *Études sur l'organisation intérieure, la société et l'économie de l'empire byzantin*, no. III.

Tafrali, O. *Thessalonique au quatorzième siècle.* Paris, 1913.

Taranovski, Teodor. *Istoria srpskog prava u Nemanjićkoj državi*, 3 vols. Belgrade: Gece Kona, 1931–35.

Tcheremissinoff, Katia. "Un acte slave des archives de Zographou." *Byzantinoslavica* 42 (1981), 1–9.

Thiriet, Freddy. *Régestes des délibérations du Senat de Venice concernant la Romanie.* 3 vols. Documents et recherches sur l'économie de pays byzantins, islamiques et slaves et leurs relations commerciales au moyen-âge, I, II, IV. Paris: Mouton, 1958–61.

Thomas, John P. *Private Religious Foundations in the Byzantine Empire.* Dumbarton Oaks Studies 24. Washington, D.C., 1987.

Thurn, H. *Οἰκονομία. Von der frühbyzantinischen Zeit bis zum Bilderstreite.* Diss. Munich 1959–60.

Treadgold, Warren. *A History of the Byzantine State and Society.* Stanford University Press, 1997.

Byzantium and Its Army, 284–1081. Stanford, Calif.: Stanford University Press, 1995.

Tsougarakis, Dimitris. *Byzantine Crete: From the 5th Century to the Venetian Conquest.* Athens: Historical Publications St. D. Basilopoulos, 1988.

Ursinus, Michael. "An Ottoman Census Register for the Area of Serres of 859 H. (1454–1455)? A Reconsideration of the Date of Composition of Tahrir Defteri TT 3." *Südost-Forschungen* 45 (1986), 25–36.

Uspenskij, Fedor I. "Mnenija i postanovlenija." *IRAIK* 5 (1900), 1–46.

Očerki po istorii Vizantijskoj obrazovannosti. St. Petersburg, 1892.

"Sledy piscovyh knig v Vizantii." *ŽMNP* 231 (Jan. 1884), 1–43; (Feb. 1884), 289–335.

Varnalides (Barnalides), Soterios A. *Ὁ θεσμὸς τῆς Χαριστικῆς (Δωρεᾶς) τῶν μοναστηρίων εἰς τοὺς Βυζαντινούς.* Βυζαντινὰ Κείμενα καὶ Μελέται 21. Thessaloniki: Kentro Vyzantinon Ereunon, 1985.

Varzos (Barzos), Konstantinos. *Ἡ γενεαλογία τῶν Κομνηνῶν.* 2 vols. Βυζαντινὰ Κείμενα καὶ Μελέται 20. Thessaloniki: Kentro Vyzantinon Ereunon, 1984.

Vásáry, István. *Cumans and Tatars: Oriental Military in the Pre-Ottoman Balkans, 1185–1365.* Cambridge University Press, 2005.

Vasiliev, A. A. "On the Question of Byzantine Feudalism." *Byz* 8 (1933), 584–604. Essentially reprinted in his *History of the Byzantine Empire*, 2nd English edn., revised, 2 vols., 563–79. Madison: University of Wisconsin Press, 1952.

Vasil'evskij, V. G. "Materialy dlja vnutrennej istorii Vizantijskogo gosudarstva." *ŽMNP* 202 (March 1879), 160–232; (April 1879), 386–438; 210 (1880), 98–170; 355–440.

Trudy. 4 vols. Leningrad, 1908–1930; repr. The Hague, 1968.

"Zakonodatel'stvo ikonoborcev." *ŽMNP* 199 (October 1878), 258–309; 200 (November 1878), 95–129.

Verpeaux, Jean. "Le cursus honorum de Théodore Métochite." *REB* 18 (1960), 195–98.

Vizantijski izvori za istoriju naroda Jugoslavije. 1966. Vol. 6, ed. F. Barišić and B. Ferjančić. Vizantološki institut SANU, posebna izdanja, knjiga 18. Belgrade, 1986.

Vlachos, Theodoros N. *Die Geschichte der byzantinischen Stadt Melenikon.* Institute for Balkan Studies, 112. Thessaloniki, 1969.

Vojnogeografski institut (Belgrade). *Topographical maps.* 1:200000. Sheet 62, "Voden" (1963), and sheet 63, "Solun" (1966).

Vranoussi, Era. "Notes sur quelques institutions de Péloponnèse byzantine (l'ἀβιωτίκιον, le φλωριατικὸν et les δύο μεῖζαι ου μύζαι)." *Études balkaniques* 14 (1978), 81–88.

Vryonis, Speros, Jr. "Byzantine and Turkish Societies and their Sources of Manpower." *War, Technology and Society in the Middle East*, ed. V. J. Parry and M. E. Yapp, 125–52. Oxford University Press, 1975.

The Decline of Medieval Hellenism in Asia Minor and the Process of Islamization from the Eleventh through the Fifteenth Century. Berkeley: University of California Press, 1971.

Wasilewski, Tadeusz. "Les titres de duc, de catépan et de pronoétès dans l'empire byzantin du IXe jusqu'au XIIe siècle." *Actes du XIIe Congrès international d'études byzantines, Ohrid 1961*, II, 233–39. Belgrade, 1964.

Xanalatos, Diogenes. *Beiträge zur Wirtschafts- und Sozialgeschichte Makedoniens im Mittelalter, hauptsächlich auf Grund der Briefe des Erzbischofs Theophylaktos von Achrida*. Speyer: Pilger-Druckerei, 1937.

Zakythinos, Dionysios A. *Le despotat grec de Morée*, 2 vols. Paris: Les Belles Lettres, 1932; Athens: L'hellénisme contemporain, 1953. Rev. ed. by Chryssa Maltezou. London: Variorum Reprints, 1975.

Zarinebaf, Fariba, John Bennet and Jack L. Davis. *A Historical and Economic Geography of Ottoman Greece: The Southwestern Morea in the 18th Century*. Princeton, NJ: American School of Classical Studies at Athens, 2005.

Zekos, N. "Εζεβαί· ένας βυζαντινός οικισμός στο κάτω τμήμα της κοιλάδας του Στρυμόνα," 77–104. In *Μνήμη Μανόλη Ἀνδρόνικου*. Thessaloniki: Hetaireia Makedonikon Spoudon, 1997.

Živojinović, Mirjana. *Istoria Hilandara I: Od osnivanja monastira 1198. do 1335. godine*. Belgrade: Prosveta, 1998.

"Le monastère de Chilandar et ses métoques dans la région de l'Athos." *ZRVI* 26 (1987), 35–67.

"Od Ptelee do Patrika, prilog vizantijskoj i srpskoj diplomatici." *ZRVI* 34 (1995), 63–68.

Zlatarski, V. *Istorija na bŭlgarskata dŭržava prez srednite vekove*, II. Sofia: Nauka i izkustvo, 1934; repr. 1972.

Zuckerman, Constantine. "The Dishonest Soldier Constantine Planites and His Neighbours." *Byz* 56 (1986), 314–31.

Index